SELF, COSMOS, GOD

SELF, COSMOS, GOD

Composed and Arranged by

DANIEL KOLAK and RAYMOND MARTIN

Harcourt Brace Jovanovich College Publishers

Fort Worth Philadelphia San Diego New York Orlando Austin San Antonio
Toronto Montreal London Sydney Tokyo

Cover illustration: The great pyramid of Uxmál against the setting sun. On the right side is a steep stairway leading to the uppermost temple. Photo by Horst Ungerer.

Editor in Chief	Ted Buchholz
Acquisitions Editor	Jo-Anne Weaver/David Tatom
Developmental Editor	Tracy R. Napper
Project Editor	Angela Williams
Production Manager	J. Montgomery Shaw
Senior Book Designer	John Ritland

Address for Editorial Correspondence
Harcourt Brace Jovanovich, 301 Commerce Street, Suite 3700, Forth Worth, TX 76102

Address for Orders
Harcourt Brace Jovanovich, 6277 Sea Harbor Drive, Orlando, FL 32887
1-800-782-4479, or 1-800-433-0001 (in Florida)

ISBN: 0–03–054197–2

Library of Congress Catalogue Number: 92–70307

Printed in the United States of America

3 4 5 6 7 8 9 0 1 2   016   9 8 7 6 5 4 3 2 1

PREFACE

Philosophy arises from the attempt to understand and answer questions of ultimate concern: Who am I? Where do I—and everything else—ultimately come from? What, if anything, is the meaning of my life? What will be my fate? The ultimate fate of everything? How, if at all, can I find out what is true? How should I live?

Initial answers to such questions tend to be handed down from religious and cultural authorities. They may tell you, for instance, that God created the cosmos and you; that you have an immortal soul which will be the vehicle for your personal survival of bodily death; and that to go to heaven you must belong to one church and live by its dictates, or subscribe to certain religious beliefs, rather than, say, belong to another church or suspend belief until you can discover for yourself what is true. Soon enough, though, each of us arrives at what must be one of life's most momentous insights—the realization that what we have been taught to believe by our authorities differs dramatically from what others have been taught to believe by their authorities and also, perhaps, from what humans have learned scientifically about the world and its origins.

How you respond individually to this insight can make a great difference to how you lead your life. How we respond collectively can make a great difference to our collective fate as well—perhaps even to whether there will be a future for human life on this planet. Will we dig in our heels and assume that the answers conveyed to us by our authorities are superior to the answers conveyed to others by their authorities—a response that historically has been the typical one and has led to narrowness, intolerance, and war—or will we use our awareness of our differences to rethink our most fundamental commitments? That is the decisive question. This book is for those who choose the philosophical path, the path of rethinking.

When we examine questions of ultimate concern, we soon discover that it is not possible to divide them neatly into separate compartments. What we should think, for instance, about our ultimate fates is tied to what we should think about God and about the ultimate fate of the cosmos. The philosophical questions we most want answered about self, cosmos, and God are so profoundly interrelated that it is scarcely possible to discuss any one of them without considering the others as well. This interconnectedness is reflected in the ways these questions have been discussed by people past and present, and it is largely what makes the attempt to understand issues of ultimate concern both difficult and profound. *Self, Cosmos, God* has been designed both to reflect this interconnectedness and also to provide you with the easiest possible deep access to the issues.

To provide access to the interconnectedness of the ideas of self, cosmos, and God, and also to give a historical perspective, Part I, "Seminal Masterworks," includes perhaps the two most important contributions to these issues in the modern history of Western philosophy: René Descartes' *Meditations* (I–III), published in 1640, and David Hume's *Dialogues Concerning Natural Religion,* published in 1779. These texts are historical classics that set the agenda for much subsequent discussion in the philosophy of religion and have influenced nearly every area of philosophy. Mastering them will provide you with one of the best possible introductions to the study of philosophy.

Second, we have placed throughout the book short, uncomplicated mini essays, called *boxes,* that provide key insights on important issues and make connections among the readings. These boxes are not summaries. They are designed to capture important ideas vividly, thereby stimulating your curiosity about central issues that are discussed at greater length in the main selections.

Third, we have buttressed the longer selections and boxes with numerous short selections and quotations from a wide and rich variety of sources. These *vignettes* enhance the multicultural dimension of the text without diffusing or watering down the treatment of traditional Western issues. In most cases the vignettes introduce or express profound and influential ideas, but some of them are included as examples of points of view which, although quite prevalent in our culture, are stupid, sexist, or simply outdated. Thus we have used these vignettes to introduce ideas dramatically that we believe, for a variety of reasons, deserve to be discussed in a classroom setting.

In composing and arranging this work, we have had the benefit of much expert advice. We would especially like to thank: Marshall Missner, University of Wisconsin, Oshkosh; Kate Wheeler, writer, Boston; Robert M. Adams, University of California, Los Angeles; Bart Gruzalski, Northeastern University; Frederick Ferré, University of Georgia; Allen Stairs, University of Maryland; Richard Taylor, formerly of the University of Rochester; Robert McKim, University of Illinois at Urbana-Champaign; Edward Henderson, Louisiana State University; Stephen T. Davis, Claremont McKenna College; James Muyskens, University of Kansas; Paul Edwards, formerly of Brooklyn College; Philip Quinn, University of Notre Dame; Wallace Matson, University of California, Berkeley; John Fischer, University of California, Riverside; James Woelful, University of Kansas; Heidi Storl, Augustana College; Elliot Deutsch, University of Hawaii at Manoa; David F. Haight, Plymouth State College; Dallas M. High, University of Kentucky; Alvin Plantinga, University of Notre Dame; Stephen M. Cahn, City University of New York; Marie Friquenon, William Paterson College; Telegore Satish, St. John's College of Santa Fe; Keith Campbell, University of Maryland; and Kwasi Wiredu, University of South Florida.

We have also profited greatly from the criticisms and advice of William F. Nietmann, Northern Arizona University; Judith Barad, Indiana State University; Leah Shelleda, College of Marin; Scott Davis, University of Southern California; Anthony Adams, Tennessee State University; and Robert Boyd, Texas Christian University, each of whom expertly reviewed the penultimate version of this anthology at the request of our publisher.

We owe a special debt of gratitude to Horst Ungerer of Bethesda, Maryland, for allowing us to select most of the illustrations for this book from his extraordinary and extensive collection of original slides of religious sites and artifacts.

Finally, we would like to thank Tracy Rogers Napper, the developmental editor for this anthology, for her extremely able and generous help, our copyeditor, Anne Lesser, for a truly outstanding job, our project editor, Angela Williams, for being so extraordinarily competent and helpful, our designer, John Ritland, for a cover design that is a pleasure to look at, our production manager, Monty Shaw, for overseeing the production process and keeping all of us on schedule, and our acquisitions editor, Jo-Anne Weaver, for her vision, encouragement, and continuing support.

To n

CONTENTS

VIII. The Scientific Challenge

X. Morality and Values

PART I

Seminal Masterworks

Natural formation in Monument Valley, Utah.

René Descartes

MEDITATIONS ON FIRST PHILOSOPHY,

IN WHICH THE EXISTENCE OF GOD, AND THE REAL DISTINCTION OF MIND AND BODY, ARE DEMONSTRATED.

RENÉ DESCARTES (1596–1650), the founder of modern philosophy, was one of the most original and influential philosophers and mathematicians of all time. At the age of eight he entered the celebrated Jesuit college La Flèche, where for ten years he studied literature, science, and philosophy. He took a degree in law but instead of practicing it took to fencing, horsemanship, and gambling. Descartes once even fought a duel over a love affair. In 1618 he became a soldier and served eventually

John Veitch trans. *Open Court*, 1901, with emendations by the editors.

in three armies—in the Netherlands, in Bavaria, and in Hungary. At thirty-three, disillusioned by "the book of the world," he moved to Holland and began developing his iconoclastic philosophy, along the way making significant contributions to science and mathematics, including inventing analytic geometry and the Cartesian coordinate system, which was named after him.

Descartes' transition from basing knowledge on accepted authority to basing it on one's own rational intuitions signaled the beginning of the modern age in philosophy. His *Meditations on First Philosophy* was quickly acknowledged as a deep criticism of all established philosophy and as a radical new beginning. It provoked many responses at the time of its publication in 1640 and has continued to do so down to the present day. Its primary impact was to raise the question of how—whether through rational intuition or sense experience—we can know the things we claim to know about the external world. This question was a major preoccupation not only of Locke, Berkeley, and Hume, but even of twentieth-century philosophers. Among its other important influences, Descartes' thought was a forerunner of Kant's critique of dogmatic metaphysics and influenced the idealist movement with his arguments that we know our own minds more immediately than the material world. On the topic of God, Descartes accepted some of the arguments of the scholastics, for whom generally he had contempt, and claimed that the existence of God can be logically demonstrated; Lamettrie and other atheistic philosophers were convinced that Descartes' "proof" was tongue-in-cheek, but most historians today believe that he was sincere.

Among Descartes' great works are *The Discourse on Method* (1637), *The Principles of Philosophy* (1644), and the *Passions of the Soul* (1650). He also wrote *Le Monde*, a scientific treatise that he did not publish in his lifetime because of its heretical views about the movement of the earth and the infinity of the cosmos.

MEDITATION I

Of the Things of Which We May Doubt

Several years have now elapsed since I first became aware that I had accepted, even from my youth, many false opinions for true, and that consequently what I afterwards based on such principles was highly doubtful; and from that time I was convinced of the necessity of undertaking once in my life to rid myself of all the opinions I had adopted, and of commencing anew the work of building from the foundation, if I desired to establish a firm and abiding superstructure in the sciences. But as this enterprise appeared to me to be one of great magnitude, I waited until I had attained an age so mature as to leave me no hope that at any stage of life more advanced I should be better able to execute my design. On this account, I have delayed so long that I should henceforth consider I was doing wrong were I still to consume in deliberation any of the time that now remains for action. To-day, then, since I have opportunely freed my mind from all cares, and am happily disturbed by no passions, and since I am in the secure possession of leisure in a peaceable retirement, I will at length apply myself earnestly and freely to the general overthrow of all my former opinions. But, to this end, it will not be necessary for me to show that the whole of these are false—a point, perhaps, which I shall never reach; but as even now my reason convinces me that I ought not the less carefully to withhold belief from what is not entirely certain and indubitable, than from what is manifestly false, it will be sufficient to justify the rejection of the whole if I shall find in each some ground for doubt. Nor for this purpose will it be necessary even to deal with each belief individually, which would be truly an endless labour; but, as the removal from below of the foundation necessarily involves the downfall of the whole edifice, I will at once approach the criticism of the principles on which all my former beliefs rested.

All that I have, up to this moment, accepted as possessed of the highest truth and certainty, I received either from or through the senses. I observed, however, that these sometimes misled us; and it is the part of prudence not to place absolute confidence in that by which we have even once been deceived.

But it may be said, perhaps, that, although the senses occasionally mislead us respecting minute objects, and such as are so far removed from us as to be beyond the reach of close observation, there are yet many other of their informations (presentations), of the truth of which it is manifestly impossible to doubt; as for example, that I am in this place, seated by the fire, clothed in a winter dressing-gown, that I hold in my hands this piece of paper, with other intimations of the same nature. But how could I deny that I possess these hands and this body, and withal escape being classed with persons in a state of insanity, whose brains are so disordered and clouded by dark bilious vapours as to cause them pertinaciously to assert that they are monarchs when they are in the greatest poverty; or clothed in gold and purple when destitute of any covering; or that their head is made of clay, their body of glass, or that they are gourds? I should certainly be not less insane then they, were I to regulate my procedure according to examples so extravagant.

Though this be true, I must nevertheless here consider that I am a man, and that, consequently, I am in the habit of sleeping, and representing to myself in dreams those same things, or even sometimes other less probable, which the insane think are presented to them in their waking moments. How often have I dreamt that I was in these familiar circumstances,—that I was dressed, and occupied this place by the fire, when I was lying undressed in bed? At the present moment, however, I certainly look upon this paper with eyes wide awake; the head which I now move is not asleep; I extend this hand consciously and with express purpose, and I perceive it; the occurrences in sleep are not so distinct as all this. But I cannot forget that, at other times, I have been deceived in sleep by similar illusions; and, attentively considering those cases, I perceive so clearly that there exist no certain marks by which the state of waking can ever be distinguished from sleep, that I feel greatly astonished; and in amazement I almost persuade myself that I am now dreaming.

Let us suppose, then, that we are dreaming, and that all these particulars—namely, the opening of the eyes, the motion of the head, the forth-putting of the hands—are merely illusions; and even that we really possess neither an entire body nor hands such as we see. Nevertheless, it must be admitted at least that the objects which appear to us in sleep are, as it were, painted representations which could not have been formed unless in the likeness of realities; and, therefore, that those general objects, at all events,—namely, eyes, a head, hands, and an entire body—are not simply imaginary, but really existent. For, in truth, painters themselves, even when they study to represent sirens and satyrs by forms the most fantastic and extraordinary, cannot bestow upon them natures absolutely new, but can only make a certain medley of the members of different animals; or if they chance to imagine something so novel that nothing at all similar has ever been seen before, and such as is, therefore, purely fictitious and absolutely false, it is at least certain that the colours of which this is composed are real.

And on the same principle, although these general objects, viz., a body, eyes, a head, hands, and the like, be imaginary, we are nevertheless absolutely necessitated to admit the reality at least of some other objects still more simple and universal than these, of which, just as of certain real colours, all those images of things, whether true and real, or false and fantastic, that are found in our consciousness, are formed.

To this class of objects seem to belong corporeal nature in general and its extension; the figure of extended things, their quantity or magnitude, and their number, as also the place in, and the time during, which they exist, and other things of the same sort. We will not, therefore, perhaps reason illegitimately if we conclude from this that Physics, Astronomy, Medicine, and all the other sciences that have for their end the consideration of composite objects, are indeed of a doubtful character; but that Arithmetic, Geometry, and the other sciences of the same class, which regard merely the simplest and most general objects, and scarcely inquire whether or not these are really existent, contain something that is certain and indubitable: for whether I am awake or dreaming, it remains true that two and three make five, and that a square has but four sides; nor does it seem possible that truths so apparent can ever fall under a suspicion of falsity or incertitude.

Nevertheless, the belief that there is a God who is all-powerful, and who created me, such as I am, has, for a long time, obtained steady possession of my mind. How, then, do I know that he has not arranged that there should be neither earth, nor sky, nor any extended thing, nor figure, nor magnitude, nor place, providing at the same time, however, for the rise in me of the perceptions of all these objects, and the persuasion that these do not exist otherwise than as I perceive them? And further, as I sometimes think that others are in error respecting matters of which they believe themselves to possess a perfect knowledge, how do I know that I am not also deceived each time I add together two and three, or number the sides of a square, or form some judgment still more simple, if more simple indeed can be imagined? But perhaps Deity has not been willing that I should be thus deceived, for He is said to be supremely good. If, however, it were repugnant to the goodness of Deity to have created me subject to constant deception, it would seem likewise to be contrary to his goodness to allow me to be occasionally deceived; and yet it is clear that this is permitted. Some, indeed, might perhaps be found who would be disposed rather to deny the existence of a Being so powerful than to believe that there is nothing certain. But let us for the present refrain from opposing this opinion, and grant that all which is here said of a Deity is false: nevertheless in whatever way it be supposed that I reached the state in which I exist, whether by fate, or chance, or by an endless series of antecedents and consequents, or by any other means, it is clear (since to be deceived and to err is a certain defect) that the probability of my being so imperfect as to be the constant victim of deception, will be increased exactly in proportion as the power possessed by the cause, to which they assign my origin, is lessened. To these reasonings I have assuredly nothing to reply, but am constrained at last to avow that there is nothing of all that I formerly believed to be true of which it is impossible to doubt, and that not through thoughtlessness or levity, but from cogent and maturely considered reasons; so that henceforward, if I desire to discover anything certain, I ought not the less carefully to refrain from assenting to those same opinions than to what might be shown to be manifestly false.

But it is not sufficient to have made these observations; care must be taken likewise to keep them in remembrance. For those old and customary opinions perpetually recur—long and familiar usage giving them the right of occupying my mind, even almost against my will, and subduing my belief; nor will I lose the habit of deferring to them and confiding in them so long as I shall consider them to be what in truth they are, viz., opinions to some extent doubtful, as I have already shown, but still highly probable, and such as it is much more reasonable to believe than deny. It is for this reason I am persuaded that I shall not be doing wrong, if, taking an opposite judgement of deliberate design, I become my own deceiver, by supposing, for a time, that all those opinions are entirely false and imaginary, until at length, having thus balanced my old by my new prejudices, my judgment shall no longer be turned aside by perverted usage from the path that may conduct to the perception of truth. For I am assured that, meanwhile, there will arise neither peril nor error from this course, and that I cannot for the present yield too much to distrust, since the end I now seek is not action but knowledge.

I will suppose, then, not that Deity, who is sovereignly good and the fountain of truth, but that some malignant demon, who is at once exceedingly potent and deceitful, has employed all his artifice to deceive me; I will suppose that the sky, the air, the earth, colours, figures, sounds, and all external things, are nothing better than the illusions of dreams, by means of which this being has laid snares for my credulity; I will consider myself as without hands, eyes, flesh, blood, or any of the senses, and as falsely believing that I am possessed of these; I will continue resolutely fixed in this belief, and if indeed by this means it be not in my power to arrive at the knowledge of truth, I shall at least do what is in my power, viz., suspend my judgment, and guard with settled purpose against giving my assent to what is false, and being imposed upon by this deceiver, whatever be his power and artifice.

But this undertaking is arduous, and a certain indolence insensibly leads me back to my ordinary course of life; and just as the captive, who, perchance, was enjoying in his dreams an imaginary liberty, when he begins to suspect that it is but a vision, dreads awakening, and conspires with the agreeable illusions that the deception may be prolonged; so I, of my own accord, fall back into the train of my former beliefs, and fear to arouse myself from my slumber, lest the time of laborious wakefulness that would succeed this quiet rest, in place of bringing any light of day, should prove inadequate to dispel the darkness that will arise from the difficulties that have now been raised.

MEDITATION II

Of the Nature of the Human Mind; and That It Is More Easily Known Than the Body

The Meditation of yesterday has filled my mind with so many doubts, that it is no longer in my power to forget them. Nor do I see, meanwhile, any principle on which they can be resolved; and, just as if I had fallen all of a sudden into very deep water, I am so greatly disconcerted as to be unable either to plant my feet firmly on the bottom or sustain myself by swimming on the surface. I will, nevertheless, make an effort, and try anew the same path on which I had entered yesterday, that is, proceed by casting aside all that admits of the slightest doubt, not less than if I had discovered it to be absolutely false; and I will continue always in this track until I shall find something that is certain, or at least, if I can do nothing more, until I shall know with certainty that there is nothing certain. Archimedes, that he might transport the entire globe from the place it occupied to another, demanded only a point that was firm and immoveable; so also, I shall be entitled to entertain the highest expectations, if I am fortunate enough to discover only one thing that is certain and indubitable.

I suppose, accordingly, that all the things which I see are false; I believe that none of those objects which my fallacious memory represents ever existed; I suppose that I possess no senses; I believe that body, figure, extension, motion, and place are merely fictions of my mind. What is there, then, that can be esteemed true? Perhaps this only, that there is absolutely nothing certain.

But how do I know that there is not something different altogether from the objects I have now enumerated, of which it is impossible to entertain the slightest doubt? Is there not a God, or some being, by whatever name I may designate him, who causes these thoughts to arise in my mind? But why suppose such a being, for it may be I myself am capable of producing them? Am I, then, at least not something? But I before denied that I possessed senses or a body; I hesitate, however, for what follows from that? Am I so dependent on the body and the senses that without these I cannot exist? But I had the persuasion that there was absolutely nothing in the world, that there was no sky and no earth, neither minds nor bodies; was I not, therefore, at the same time, persuaded that I did not exist? Far from it; I assuredly existed, since I was persuaded. But there is I know not what being, who is possessed at once of the highest power and the deepest cunning, who is constantly employing all his ingenuity in deceiving me. Doubtless, then, I exist, since I am deceived; and, let him deceive me as he may, he can never bring it about that I am nothing, so long as I shall be conscious that I am something. So that it must, in fine, be maintained, all things being maturely and carefully considered, that this proposition I am, I exist, is necessarily true each time it is expressed by me, or conceived in my mind.

But I do not yet know with sufficient clearness what I am, though assured that I am; and hence, in the next place, I must take care, lest perchance I inconsiderately substitute some other object in room of what is properly myself, and thus wander from truth, even in that knowledge which I hold to be of all others the most certain and evident. For this reason, I will now consider anew what I formerly believed myself to be, before I entered on the present train of thought; and of my previous opinion I will retrench all that can in the least be invalidated by the grounds of doubt I have adduced, in order that there may at length remain nothing but what is certain and indubitable. What then did I formerly think I was? Undoubtedly I judged that I was a man. But what is a man? Shall I say a rational animal? Assuredly not; for it would be necessary forthwith to inquire into what is meant by animal, and what by rational, and thus, from a single question, I should insensibly glide into others, and these more difficult than the first; nor do I now possess enough of leisure to warrant me in wasting my time amid subtleties of this sort. I prefer here to attend to the thoughts that sprung up of themselves in my mind, and were inspired by my own nature alone, when I applied myself to the consideration of what I was. In the first place, then, I thought that I possessed a countenance, hands, arms, and all the fabric of members that appears in a corpse, and which I called by the name of body. It further occurred to me that I was nourished, that I walked, perceived, and thought, and all those actions I referred to the soul; but what the soul itself was I either did not stay to consider, or, if I did, I imagined that it was something extremely rare and subtle, like wind, or flame, or ether, spread through my grosser parts. As regarded the body, I did not even doubt of its nature, but thought I distinctly knew it, and if I had wished to describe it according to the notions I then entertained, I should have explained myself in this manner: By body I understand all that can be terminated by a certain figure; that can be comprised in a certain place, and so fill a certain space as therefrom to exclude every other body; that can be perceived either by touch, sight, hearing, taste, or smell; that can be moved in different ways, not indeed of itself, but by something foreign to it by which it is touched and from which it receives the impression; for the power of self-motion, as likewise that of perceiving and thinking, I held as by no means pertaining to the nature of body; on the contrary, I was somewhat astonished to find such faculties existing in some bodies.

But as to myself, what can I now say that I am, since I suppose there exists an extremely powerful, and, if I may so speak, malignant being, whose whole endeavours are directed towards deceiving me? Can I affirm that I possess any one of all those attributes of which I have lately spoken as belonging to the nature of body? After attentively considering them in my own mind, I find none of them that can properly be said to belong to myself. To recount them were idle and tedious. Let us pass, then, to the attributes of the soul. The first mentioned were the powers of nutrition and walking; but, if it be true that I have no body, it is true likewise that I am capable neither of walking nor of being nourished. Perception is another attribute of the soul; but perception too is impossible without the body: besides, I have frequently, during sleep, believed that I perceived objects which I afterwards observed I did not in reality perceive. Thinking is another attribute of the soul; and here I discover what properly belongs to myself. This alone is inseparable from me. I am—I exist: this is certain; but how often? As often as I think; for perhaps it would even happen, if I should wholly cease to think, that I should at the same time altogether cease to be. I now admit nothing that is not necessarily true: I am therefore, precisely speaking, only a thinking thing, that is, a mind, understanding, or reason,—terms whose signification was before unknown to me. I am, however, a real thing, and really existent; but what thing? The answer was, a thinking thing. The question now arises, am I aught besides? I will stimulate my imagination with a view to discover whether I am not still something more than a thinking being. Now it is plain I am not the assemblage of members called the human body; I am not a thin and penetrating air diffused through all these members, or wind, or flame, or vapour, or breath, or any of all the things I can imagine; for I supposed that all these were not, and, without changing the supposition, I find that I still feel assured of my existence.

But it is true, perhaps, that those very things which I suppose to be non-existent, because they are unknown to me, are not in truth different from myself whom I know. This is a point I cannot determine, and do not now enter into any dispute regarding it. I can only judge of things that are known to me: I am conscious that I exist, and I who know that I exist inquire into what I am. It is, however, perfectly certain that the knowledge of my existence, thus precisely taken, is not dependent on things, the existence of which is as yet unknown to me: and consequently it is not dependent on any of the things I can feign in imagination. Moreover, the phrase itself, I frame an image, reminds me of my error; for I should in truth frame one if I were to imagine myself to be anything, since to imagine is nothing more than to contemplate the figure or image of a corporeal thing; but I already know that I exist, and that it is possible at the same time that all those images, and in general all that relates to the nature of body, are merely dreams. From this I discover that it is not more reasonable to say, 'I will excite my imagination that I may know more distinctly what I am,' than to express myself as follows: 'I am now awake, and perceive something real; but because my perception is not sufficiently clear, I will of express purpose go to sleep that my dreams may represent to me the object of my perception with more truth and clearness.' And, therefore, I know that nothing of all that I can embrace in imagination belongs to the knowledge which I have of myself, and that there is need to recall with the utmost care the mind from this mode of thinking, that it may be able to know its own nature with perfect distinctness.

But what, then, am I? A thinking thing, it has been said. But what is a thinking thing? It is a thing that doubts, understands, conceives, affirms, denies, wills, refuses, that imagines also, and perceives. Assuredly it is not little, if all these properties belong to my nature. But why should they not belong to it? Am I not that very being who now doubts of almost everything; who, for all that, understands and conceives certain things; who affirms one alone as true, and denies the others; who desires to know more of them, and does not wish to be deceived; who imagines many things, sometimes even despite his will; and is likewise percipient of many, as if through the medium of the senses. Is there nothing of all this as true as that I am, even although I should be always dreaming, and although he who gave me being employed all his ingenuity to deceive me? Is there also any one of these attributes that can be properly distinguished from my thought, or that can be said to be separate from myself? For it is of itself so evident that it is I who doubt, I who understand, and I who desire, that it is here unnecessary to add anything by way of rendering it more clear. And I am as certainly the same being who imagines; for, although it may be (as I before supposed) that nothing I imagine is true, still the power of imagination does not cease really to exist in me and to form part of my thought. In fine, I am the same being who perceives, that is, who apprehends certain objects as by the organs of sense, since, in truth, I see light, hear a noise, and feel heat. But it will be said that these presentations are false, and that I am dreaming. Let it be so. At all events it is certain that I seem to see light, hear a noise, and feel heat; this cannot be false, and this is what in me is properly called perceiving, which is nothing else than thinking. From this I begin to know what I am with somewhat greater clearness and distinctness than heretofore.

But, nevertheless, it still seems to me, and I cannot help believing, that corporeal things, whose images are formed by thought, which fall under the senses, and are examined by the same, are known with much greater distinctness than that I know not what part of myself which is not imaginable; although, in truth, it may seem strange to say that I know and comprehend with greater distinctness things whose existence appears to me doubtful, that are unknown, and do not belong to me, than others of whose reality I am persuaded, that are known to me, and appertain to my proper nature; in a word, than myself. But I see clearly what is the state of the case. My mind is apt to wander, and will not yet submit to be restrained within the limits of truth. Let us therefore leave the mind to itself once more, and, according to it every kind of liberty, permit it to consider the objects that appear to it from without, in order that, having afterwards withdrawn it from these gently and opportunely, and fixed it on the consideration of its being and the properties it finds in itself, it may then be the more easily controlled.

Let us now accordingly consider the objects that are commonly thought to be the most easily, and likewise the most distinctly known, viz., the bodies we touch and see; not, indeed, bodies in general, for these general notions are usually somewhat more confused, but one body in particular. Take, for example, this piece of wax; it is quite fresh, having been but recently taken from the bee-hive; it has not yet lost the sweetness of the honey it contained; it still retains somewhat of the odour of the flowers from which it was gathered; its colour, figure, size, are apparent (to the sight); it is hard, cold, easily handled; and sounds when struck upon with the finger. In fine, all that contributes to make a body as distinctly known as possible, is found in the one before us. But, while I am speaking, let it be placed near the fire—what remained of the taste exhales, the smell evaporates, the colour changes, its figure is destroyed, its size increases, it becomes liquid, it grows hot, it can hardly be handled, and, although struck upon, it emits no sound. Does the same wax still remain after this change? I must be admitted that it does remain; no one doubts it, or judges otherwise. What, then, did I know so distinctly in this piece of wax? Assuredly, it could be nothing of all that I observed by means of the senses, since all the things that fell under taste, smell, sight, touch, and hearing are changed, and yet the same wax remains. It was perhaps what I now think, viz., that this wax was neither the sweetness of honey, the pleasant odour of flowers, the whiteness, the figure, nor the sound, but only a body that a little before appeared to me conspicuous under these forms, and which is now perceived under others. But, to speak precisely, what is it that I imagine when I think of it in this way? Let it be attentively considered, and, abstracting from all that does not belong to the wax, let us see what remains. There certainly remains nothing, except something extended, flexible, and movable. But what is meant by flexible and movable? Is it not that I imagine that the piece of wax, being round, is capable of becoming square, or of passing from a square into a triangular figure? Assuredly such is not the case, because I conceive that it admits of an infinity of similar changes; and I am, moreover, unable to compass this infinity by imagination, and consequently this conception which I have of the wax is not the product of the faculty of imagination. But what now is this extension? Is it not also unknown? for it becomes greater when the wax is melted, greater when it is boiled, and greater still when the heat increases; and I should not conceive clearly and according to truth, the wax as it is, if I did not suppose that the piece we are considering admitted even of a wider variety of extension than I ever imagined. I must, therefore, admit that I cannot even comprehend by imagination what the piece of wax is, and that it is the mind alone which perceives it. I speak

Descartes' Journey: Inner Space

The rift between the subjective and objective points of view began when philosophers first tried to form views that took modern science into account (see box on p. 22). The first philosopher to do this—and who, for that reason, is called the founder of modern philosophy—was René Descartes.

A contemporary of Galileo, Descartes was the first true epistemologist, the first to attempt to completely subordinate his account of *what* we know to an account of *how* we know it. He tried to build his entire view of self, cosmos, and God around his method of inquiry. While the first modern scientists (see box on p. 22) provided the new knowledge, Descartes tried to explain how knowledge was possible—not what specific methods the scientists used but, rather, what underlies those methods and guarantees their validity.

Unlike almost all the medieval philosophers he was reacting against, Descartes rejected from the onset all dependence on revelation and traditional authority in determining what we know. But in repudiating traditional and indirect paths to knowledge, he discovered, he thought, a direct path. Surprisingly, since Descartes was the first philosopher to try to accommodate the new science, he argued that the validity of science depends, in the first instance, on knowledge of self and, in the second, on knowledge of God. Only when these are secure is knowledge of the cosmos secure.

In other words, Descartes looked for the ultimate foundations on which the entire edifice of our knowledge of self, cosmos, and God could be based. In an effort to distance himself from the tyranny of tradition, he suspended everything he had been taught by various religious and secular authorities. Inside a completely darkened room, removed from the world, he meditated inwardly into an abyss of unknowing. There, at the center of an invisible labyrinth of outwardly increasing levels of uncertainty and doubt, he slowly discovered, he thought, the undoubtable *I* of consciousness—a thinking self. He

of one piece in particular; for, as to wax in general, this is still more evident. But what is the piece of wax that can be perceived only by the understanding or mind? It is certainly the same which I see, touch, imagine; and, in fine, it is the same which, from the beginning, I believed it to be. But (and this it is of moment to observe) the perception of it is neither an act of sight, of touch, nor of imagination, and never was either of these, though it might formerly seem so, but is simply an intuition of the mind, which may be imperfect and confused, as it formerly was, or very clear and distinct, as it is at present, according as the attention is more or less directed to the elements which it contains, and of which it is composed.

But, meanwhile, I feel greatly astonished when I observe the weakness of my mind, and its proneness to error. For although, without at all giving expression to what I think, I consider all this in my own mind, words yet occasionally impede my progress, and I am almost led into

---

found certainty inside himself and in the link self-knowledge provides to God. Ironically, objective and absolute certainty lay hidden at the center of subjectivity: the self.

Seeking to find what, if anything, he could know independently of any outward authority and with absolute certainty, Descartes discovered that all of his beliefs about the external world of space, matter, and motion could be mistaken. But why, then, was Descartes so certain that the self existed? The answer is that although he, a thinking, conscious subject, could doubt the existence of all objects—could doubt, even, the existence of the entire cosmos—he *could not,* in any act of doubting, doubt his own existence: The act of doubting is, itself, the demonstration that a doubter exists.

"I think, therefore I am," Descartes wrote, certain that even if he thought false thoughts, the fact that he thought *any* thoughts, false or true, established the absolute certainty that he, a thinker, existed. Descartes thus places the *I* at the heart of philosophy and takes it as the starting point—the fundamental bedrock—of all inquiry.

By using his own existence as the ultimate basis of all knowledge, Descartes had to find a way back to the external, "objective," world, including a way back to the knowledge that was being discovered by the new science. He needed a bridge from the subjective self to the objective cosmos, and he found one.

According to Descartes, God gives us a natural inclination to believe in an external, objective world. But if that belief were false, there would be no way for us to know that it was false, and hence God would be a deceiver. But God, Descartes reasoned, is not a deceiver. By having a rational intuition of one's own existence and a demonstrative knowledge of a nondeceiving God, we can then attain probable knowledge of the cosmos. Descartes' bridge between self and cosmos is God.

error by the terms of ordinary language. We say, for example, that we see the same wax when it is before us, and not that we judge it to be the same from its retaining the same colour and figure: whence I should forthwith be disposed to conclude that the wax is known by the act of sight, and not by the intuition of the mind alone, were it not for the analogous instance of human beings passing on in the street below, as observed from a window. In this case I do not fail to say that I see the men themselves, just as I say that I see the wax; and yet what do I see from the window beyond hats and cloaks that might cover artificial machines, whose motions might be determined by springs? But I judge that there are human beings from these appearances, and thus I comprehend, by the faculty of judgment alone which is in the mind, what I believed I saw with my eyes.

The man who makes it his aim to rise to knowledge superior to the common, ought to be ashamed to seek occasions of doubting from the vulgar forms of speech: instead, therefore, of doing this, I shall proceed with the matter in hand, and inquire whether I had a clearer and more perfect perception of the piece of wax when I first saw it, and when I thought I knew it by means of the external sense itself, or, at all events, by the common sense, as it is called, that is, by the imaginative faculty; or whether I rather apprehend it more clearly at present, after having examined with greater care, both what it is, and in what way it can be known. It would certainly be ridiculous to entertain any doubt on this point. For what, in that first perception, was there distinct? What did I perceive which any animal might not have perceived? But when I distinguish the wax from its exterior forms, and when, as if I had stripped it of its vestments, I consider it quite naked, it is certain, although some error may still be found in my judgment, that I cannot, nevertheless, thus apprehend it without possessing a human mind.

But, finally, what shall I say of the mind itself, that is, of myself? for as yet I do not admit that I am anything but mind. What, then! I who seem to possess so distinct an apprehension of the piece of wax,—do I not know myself, both with greater truth and certitude, and also much more distinctly and clearly? For if I judge that the wax exists because I see it, it assuredly follows, much more evidently, that I myself am or exist, for the same reason: for it is possible that what I see may not in truth be wax, and that I do not even possess eyes with which to see anything; but it cannot be that when I see, or, which comes to the same thing, when I think I see, I myself who think am nothing. So likewise, if I judge that the wax exists because I touch it, it will still also follow that I am; and if I determine that my imagination, or any other cause, whatever it be, persuades me of the existence of the wax, I will still draw the same conclusion. And what is here remarked of the piece of wax, is applicable to all the other things that are external to me. And further, if the notion or perception of wax appeared to me more precise and distinct, after not only sight and touch, but many other causes besides, rendered it manifest to my apprehension, with how much greater distinctness must I now know myself, since all the reasons that contribute to the knowledge of the nature of wax, or of any body whatever, manifest still better the nature of the mind? And there are besides so many other things in the mind itself that contribute to the illustration of its nature, that those dependent on the body, to which I have here referred, scarcely merit to be taken into account.

But, in conclusion, I find I have insensibly reverted to the point I desired; for, since it is now manifest to me that bodies themselves are not properly perceived by the senses nor by the faculty of imagination, but by the intellect alone; and since they are not perceived because they are seen and touched, but only because they are understood or rightly comprehended by thought, I readily discover that there is nothing more easily or clearly apprehended than my own mind. But because it is difficult to rid one's self so promptly of an opinion to which one has been long accustomed, it will be desirable to tarry for some time at this stage, that, by long continued meditation, I may more deeply impress upon my memory this new knowledge.

MEDITATION III

Of God: That He Exists

I will now close my eyes, I will stop my ears, I will turn away my senses from their objects, I will even efface from my consciousness all the images of corporeal things; or at least, because this can hardly be accomplished, I will consider them as empty and false; and thus, holding converse only with myself, and closely examining my nature, I will endeavour to obtain by degrees a more intimate and familiar knowledge of myself. I am a thinking (conscious) thing, that is, a being who doubts, affirms, denies, knows a few objects, and is ignorant of many,—who loves, hates, wills, refuses,—who imagines likewise, and perceives; for, as I before remarked, although the things which I perceive or imagine are perhaps nothing at all apart from me and in themselves, I am nevertheless assured that those modes of consciousness which I call perceptions and imaginations, in as far only as they are modes of consciousness, exist in me. And in the little I have said I think I have summed up all that I really know, or at least all that up to this time I was aware I knew. Now, as I am endeavouring to extend my knowledge more widely, I will use circumspection, and consider with care whether I can still discover in myself anything further which I have not yet hitherto observed. I am certain that I am a thinking thing; but do I not therefore likewise know what is required to render me certain of a truth? In this first knowledge, doubtless, there is nothing that gives me assurance of its truth except the clear and distinct perception of what I affirm, which would not indeed be sufficient to give me the assurance that what I say is true, if it could ever happen that anything I thus clearly and distinctly perceived should prove false; and accordingly it seems to me that I may now take as a general rule, that all things which I perceive very clearly and very distinctly are true.

Nevertheless I before received and admitted many things as wholly certain and manifest, which yet I afterwards found to be doubtful. What, then, were those? They were the earth, the sky, the stars, and all the other objects which I was in the habit of perceiving by the senses. But what was it that I clearly and distinctly perceived in them? Nothing more than that the ideas and the thoughts of those objects were presented to my mind. And even now I do not deny that these ideas are found in my mind. But there was yet another thing which I affirmed, and which, from having been accustomed to believe it, I thought I clearly perceived, although, in truth, I did not perceive it at all; I mean the existence of objects external to me, from which those ideas proceeded, and to which they had a perfect resemblance; and it was here I was mistaken, or if I judged correctly, this assuredly was not to be traced to any knowledge I possessed arising from my perception.

But when I considered any matter in arithmetic and geometry, that was very simple and easy, as, for example, that two and three added together make five, and things of this sort, did I not view them with at least sufficient clearness to warrant me in affirming their truth? Indeed, if I afterwards judged that we ought to doubt of these things, it was for no other reason than because it occurred to me that a God might perhaps have given me such a nature as that I should be deceived, even respecting the matters that appeared to me the most evidently true. But as often as this preconceived opinion of the sovereign power of a God presents itself to my mind, I am constrained to admit that it is easy for him, if he wishes it, to cause me to err, even in matters where I think I possess the highest evidence; and, on the other hand, as often as I direct my attention to things which I think I apprehend with great clearness, I am so persuaded of their truth that I naturally break out into expressions such as these: Deceive me who may, no one will yet ever be able to bring it about that I am not, so long as I shall be conscious that I am, or at any future time cause it to be true that I have never been, it being now true that I am, or make two and three more or less than five, in supposing which, and other like absurdities, I discover a manifest contradiction.

And in truth, as I have no ground for believing that Deity is deceitful, and as, indeed, I have not even considered the reasons by which the existence of a Deity of any kind is established, the ground of doubt that rests only on this supposition is very slight, and, so to speak, metaphysical. But, that I may be able wholly to remove it, I must inquire whether there is a God, as soon as an opportunity of doing so shall present itself; and if I find that there is a God, I must examine likewise whether he can be a deceiver; for, without the knowledge of these two truths, I do not see that I can ever be certain of anything. And that I may be enabled to examine this without interrupting the order of meditation I have proposed to myself, and which is little by little to pass from the notions that I shall find first in my mind to those I shall afterwards discover in it, it is necessary at this stage to divide all my thoughts into certain classes, and to consider in which of these classes truth and error are, strictly speaking, to be found.

Of my thoughts some are, as it were, images of things, and to these alone properly belongs the name *idea;* as when I think [represent to my mind] a man, a chimera, the sky, an angel, or God. Others, again, have certain other forms; as when I will, fear, affirm, or deny, I always, indeed, apprehend something as the object of my thought, but I also embrace in thought something more than the representation of the object; and of this class of thoughts some are called volitions or affections, and others judgments.

Now, with respect to ideas, if these are considered only in themselves, and are not referred to any object beyond them, they cannot, properly speaking, be false; for, whether I imagine a goat or a chimera, it is not less true that I imagine the one than the other. Nor need we fear that falsity may exist in the will or affections; for, although I may desire objects that are wrong, and even that never existed, it is still true that I desire them. There thus only remain our judgments, in which we must take diligent heed that we be not deceived. But the chief and most ordinary error that arises in them consists in judging that the ideas which are in us are like or conformed to the things that are external to us; for assuredly, if we but considered the ideas themselves as certain modes of our thought (consciousness), without referring them to anything beyond, they would hardly afford any occasion of error.

But, among these ideas, some appear to me to be innate, others to come to me (adventitious), and others to be made by myself (factitious); for, as I have the power of conceiving what is called a thing, or a truth, or a thought, it seems to me that I hold this power from no other source than my own nature; but if I now hear a noise, if I see the sun, or if I feel heat, I have all along judged that these sensations proceeded from certain objects existing out of myself; and, in fine, it appears to me that sirens, hippogryphs, and the like, are inventions of my own mind. But I may even perhaps come to be of opinion that all my ideas are of the class which I call adventitious, or that they are all innate, or that they are all factitious, for I have not yet clearly discovered their true origin; and what I have here principally to do is to consider, with reference to those that appear to come from certain objects without me, what grounds there are for thinking them like these objects.

The first of these grounds is that it seems to me I am so taught by nature; and the second that I am conscious that those ideas are not dependent on my will, and therefore not on myself, for they are frequently presented to me against my will,—as at present, whether I will or not, I feel heat; and I am thus persuaded that this sensation or idea of heat is produced in me by something different from myself, viz., by the heat of the fire by which I sit. And it is very reasonable to suppose that this object impresses me with its own likeness rather than any other thing.

But I must consider whether these reasons are sufficiently strong and convincing. When I speak of being taught by nature in this matter, I understand by the word nature only a certain spontaneous impetus that impels me to believe in a resemblance between ideas and their objects, and not a natural light that affords a knowledge of its truth. But these two things are widely different; for what the natural light shows to be true can be in no degree doubtful, as, for example, that I am because I doubt, and other truths of the like kind: inasmuch as I possess no other faculty whereby to distinguish truth from error, which can teach me the falsity of what the natural light declares to be true, and which is equally trustworthy; but with respect to seemingly natural impulses, I have observed, when the question related to the choice of right or wrong in action, that they frequently led me to take the worse part; nor do I see that I have any better ground for following them in what relates to truth and error. Then, with respect to the other reason, which is that because these ideas do not depend on my will, they must arise from objects existing without me, I do not find it more convincing than the former; for, just as those natural impulses, of which I have lately spoken, are found in me, notwithstanding that they are not always in harmony with my will, so likewise it may be that I possess some power not sufficiently known to myself capable of pro-

Cartesian Knowledge

How, in Descartes' view, do we attain knowledge of the world? Contemplating a piece of wax, Descartes reasoned that it is intuition, not experience, that gives us access to its true nature. When you hold the wax near the fire and it begins to melt, all of its sensible properties change. Yet it does not become something different; it remains the same piece of wax with the same essential nature. If knowledge of the wax is based solely on experience, then you would have to conclude that there is not one piece of wax in your hand, but an ever-changing series of different collections of ephemeral properties.

So too with the self. Descartes claimed that you know that you exist and what your essential nature is—a thinking thing—through rational intuition. For instance, you know you have a self because you cannot consistently doubt your own existence. What we experience of our selves, however, like what we experience of a piece of wax, is constantly changing. But the self is known, via rational intuition, to persist through the changes, just as we know by rational intuition that the wax remains the same piece of wax in spite of its undergoing a complete change in its perceptible properties. So too the persisting self beneath ever-changing experience, like the persisting wax, is not something that ever shows up in experience. Rather, it is something that lies behind experience and is the owner of the ever-changing psychological states.

ducing ideas without the aid of external objects, and, indeed, it has always hitherto appeared to me that they are formed during sleep, by some power of this nature, without the aid of anything external. And, in fine, although I should grant that they proceeded from those objects, it is not a necessary consequence that they must be like them. On the contrary, I have observed, in a number of instances, that there was a great difference between the object and its idea. Thus, for example, I find in my mind two wholly diverse ideas of the sun; the one, by which it appears to me extremely small, draws its origin from the senses, and should be placed in the class of adventitious ideas; the other, by which it seems to be many times larger than the whole earth, is taken up on astronomical grounds, that is, elicited from certain notions born with me, or is framed by myself in some other manner. These two ideas cannot certainly both resemble the same sun; and reason teaches me that the one which seems to have immediately emanated from it is the most unlike. And these things sufficiently prove that hitherto it has not been from a certain and deliberate judgment, but only from a sort of blind impulse, that I believed in the existence of certain things different from myself, which, by the organs of sense, or by whatever other means it might be, conveyed their ideas or images into my mind and impressed it with their likenesses.

But there is still another way of inquiring whether, of the objects whose ideas are in my mind, there are any that exist out of me. If ideas are taken in so far only as they are certain modes of consciousness, I do not remark any difference or inequality among them, and all seem, in the same manner, to proceed from myself; but, considering them as images, of which one represents one thing and another a different, it is evident that a great diversity obtains among them. For, without doubt, those that represent substances are something more, and contain in themselves, so to speak, more objective reality [that is, participate by representation in higher degrees of being or perfection], than those that represent only modes or accidents; and again, the idea by which I conceive a God, eternal, infinite, immutable, all-knowing, all-powerful, and the creator of all things that are out of himself,—this, I say, has certainly in it more objective reality than those ideas by which finite substances are represented.

Now, it is manifest by the natural light that there must at least be as much reality in the efficient and total cause as in its effect; for whence can the effect draw its reality if not from its cause? and how could the cause communicate to it this reality unless it possessed it in itself? And hence it follows, not only that what is cannot be produced by what is not, but likewise that the more perfect—in other words, that which contains in itself more reality—cannot be the effect of the less perfect: and this is not only evidently true of those effects, whose reality is actual or formal, but likewise of ideas, whose reality is only considered as objective. Thus, for example, the stone that is not yet in existence, not only cannot now commence to be, unless it be produced by that which possesses in itself, formally or eminently, all that enters into its composition, in other words, by that which contains in itself the same properties that are in the stone, or others superior to them; and heat can only be produced in a subject that was before devoid of it, by a cause that is of an order [degree or kind], at least as perfect as heat; and so of the others. But further, even the idea of the heat, or of the stone, cannot exist in me unless it be put there by a cause that contains, at least, as much reality as I conceive existent in the heat or in the stone: for, although that cause may not transmit into my idea anything of its actual or formal reality, we ought not on this account to imagine that it is less real; but we ought to consider that, as every idea is a work of the mind, its nature is such as of itself to demand no other formal reality than that which it borrows from our consciousness, of which it is but a mode, that is, a manner or way of thinking. But in order that an idea may contain this objective reality rather than that, it must doubtless derive it from some cause in which is found at least as much formal reality as the idea contains of objective; for, if we suppose that there is found in an idea anything which was not in its cause, it must of course derive this from nothing. But, however imperfect may be the mode of existence by which a thing is objectively or by representation in the understanding by its idea, we certainly cannot, for all that, allege that this mode of existence is nothing, nor, consequently, that the idea owes its origin to nothing. Nor must it be imagined that, since the reality which is considered in these ideas is only objective, the same reality need not be formally (actually) in the causes of these ideas, but only objectively: for, just as the mode of existing objectively belongs to ideas by their peculiar nature, so likewise the mode of existing formally appertains to the causes of these ideas (at least to the first and principal), by their peculiar nature. And although an idea may give rise to another idea, this regress cannot, nevertheless, be infinite; we must in the end reach a first idea, the cause of which is, as it were, the archetype in which all the reality or perfection that is found objectively or by representation in these ideas is contained formally and really. I am thus clearly taught by the natural light that ideas exist in me as pictures or images, which may in truth readily fall short of the perfection of the objects from which they are taken, but can never contain anything greater or more perfect.

And in proportion to the time and care with which I examine all those matters, the conviction of their truth brightens and becomes distinct. But, to sum up, what conclusion shall I draw from it all? It is this;—if the objective reality or perfection of any one of my ideas be such as clearly to convince me, that this same reality exists in me neither formally nor eminently, and if, as follows from this, I myself cannot be the cause of it, it is a necessary consequence that I am not alone in the world, but that there is besides myself some other being who exists as the cause of that idea; while, on the contrary, if no such idea be found in my mind, I shall have no sufficient ground of assurance of the existence of any other being besides myself; for, after a most careful search, I have, up to this moment, been unable to discover any other ground.

But, among these my ideas, besides that which represents myself, respecting which there can be here no difficulty, there is one that represents a God; others that represent corporeal and inanimate things; others angels; others animals; and, finally, there are some that represent men like myself. But with respect to the ideas that represent other men, or animals, or angels, I can easily suppose that they were formed by the mingling and composition of the other ideas which I have of myself, of corporeal things, and of God, although there were, apart from myself, neither men, animals, nor angels. And with regard to the ideas of corporeal objects, I never discovered in them anything so great or excellent which I myself did not appear capable of originating; for, by considering these ideas closely and scrutinising them individually, in the same way that I yesterday examined the idea of wax, I find that there is but little in them that is clearly and distinctly perceived. As belonging to the class of things that are clearly apprehended, I recognise the following, viz., magnitude or extension in length, breadth, and depth; figure, which results from the termination of extension; situation, which bodies of diverse figures preserve with reference to each other; and motion or the change of situation; to which may be added substance, duration, and number. But with regard to light, colours, sounds, odours, tastes, heat, cold, and the other tactile qualities, they are thought with so much obscurity and confusion, that I cannot determine even whether they are true or false; in other words, whether or not the ideas I have of these qualities are in truth the ideas of real objects. For although I before remarked that it is only in judgments that formal falsity, or falsity properly so called, can be met with, there may nevertheless be found in ideas a certain material falsity, which arises when they represent what is nothing as if it were something. Thus, for example, the ideas I have of cold and heat are so far from being clear and distinct, that I am unable from them to discover whether cold is only the privation of heat, or heat the privation of cold; or whether they are not real qualities: and since, ideas being as it were images, there can be none that does not seem to us to represent some object, the idea which represents cold as something real and positive will not improperly be called false, if it be correct to say that cold is nothing but a privation of heat; and so in other cases. To ideas of this kind, indeed, it is not necessary that I should assign any author besides myself: for if they are false, that is, represent objects that are unreal, the natural light teaches me that they proceed from nothing; in other words, that they are in me only because something is wanting to the perfection of my nature; but if these ideas are true, yet because they exhibit to me so little reality that I cannot even distinguish the object represented from non-being, I do not see why I should not be the author of them.

With reference to those ideas of corporeal things that are clear and distinct, there are some which, as appears to me, might have been taken from the idea I have of myself, as those of substance, duration, number, and the like. For when I think that a stone is a substance, or a thing capable of existing of itself, and that I am likewise a substance, although I conceive that I am a thinking and non-extended thing, and that the stone, on the contrary, is extended and unconscious, there being thus the greatest diversity between the two concepts,—yet these two ideas seem to have this in common that they both represent substances. In the same way, when I think of myself as now existing, and recollect besides that I existed some time ago, and when I am conscious of various thoughts whose number I know, I then acquire the ideas of duration and number, which I can afterwards transfer to as many objects as I please. With respect to the other qualities that go to make up the ideas of corporeal objects, viz., extension, figure, situation, and motion, it is true that they are not formally in me, since I am merely a thinking being; but because they are only certain modes of substance, and because I myself am a substance, it seems possible that they may be contained in me eminently.

There only remains, therefore, the idea of God, in which I must consider whether there is anything that cannot be supposed to originate with myself. By the name God, I understand a substance infinite, eternal, immutable, independent, all-knowing, all-powerful, and by which I myself, and every other thing that exists, if any such there be, were created. But these properties are so great and excellent, that the more attentively I consider them the less I feel persuaded that the idea I have of them owes its origin to myself alone. And thus it is absolutely necessary to conclude, from all that I have before said, that God exists: for though the idea of substance be in my mind owing to this, that I myself am a substance, I should not, however, have the idea of an infinite substance, seeing I am a finite being, unless it were given me by some substance in reality infinite.

And I must not imagine that I do not apprehend the infinite by a true idea, but only by the negation of the finite, in the same way that I comprehend repose and darkness by the negation of motion and light: since, on the contrary, I clearly perceive that there is more reality in the infinite substance than in the finite, and therefore that in some way I possess the perception (notion) of the infinite before that of the finite, that is, the perception of God before that of myself, for how could I know that I doubt, desire, or that something is wanting to me, and that I am not wholly perfect, if I possessed no idea of a being more perfect than myself, by comparison of which I knew the deficiencies of my nature?

And it cannot be said that this idea of God is perhaps materially false, and consequently that it may have arisen from nothing, in other words, that it may exist in me from my imperfection, as I before said of the ideas of heat and cold, and the like: for, on the contrary, as this idea is very clear and distinct, and contains in itself more objective reality than any other, there can be no one of itself more true, or less open to the suspicion of falsity.

The idea, I say, of a being supremely perfect, and infinite, is in the highest degree true; for although, perhaps, we may imagine that such a being does not exist, we cannot, nevertheless, suppose that his idea represents nothing real, as I have already said of the idea of cold. It is likewise clear and distinct in the highest degree, since whatever the mind clearly and distinctly conceives as real or true, and as implying any perfection, is contained entire in this idea. And this is true, nevertheless, although I do not comprehend the infinite, and although there may be in God an infinity of things that I cannot comprehend, nor perhaps even compass by thought in any way; for it is of the nature of the infinite that it should not be comprehended by the finite; and it is enough that I rightly understand this, and judge that all which I clearly perceive, and in which I know there is some perfection, and perhaps also an infinity of properties of which I am ignorant, are formally or eminently in God, in order that the idea I have of him may become the most true, clear, and distinct of all the ideas in my mind.

But perhaps I am something more than I suppose myself to be, and it may be that all those perfections which I attribute to God, in some way exist potentially in me, although they do not yet show themselves, and are not reduced to act. Indeed, I am already conscious that my knowledge is being increased and perfected by degrees; and I see nothing to prevent it from thus gradually increasing to infinity, nor any reason why, after such increase and perfection, I should not be able thereby to acquire all the other perfections of the Divine nature; nor, in fine, why the power I possess of acquiring those perfections, if it really now exist in me, should not be sufficient to produce the ideas of them. Yet, on looking more closely into the matter, I discover that this cannot be; for, in the first place, although it were true that my knowledge daily acquired new degrees of perfection, and although there were potentially in my nature much that was not as yet actually in it, still all these excellences make not the slightest approach to the idea I have of the Deity, in whom there is no perfection merely potentially but in whom all is actual; for it is an infallible token of imperfection in my knowledge, that it is augmented by degrees. Further, although my knowledge increase more and more, nevertheless I am not, therefore, induced to think that it will ever be actually infinite, since it can never reach that point beyond which it shall be incapable of further increase. But I conceive God as actually infinite, so that nothing can be added to his perfection. And, in fine, I readily perceive that the objective being of an idea cannot be produced by a being that is merely potentially existent, which, properly speaking, is nothing, but only by a being existing formally or actually.

And, truly, I see nothing in all that I have now said which it is not easy for any one, who shall carefully consider it, to discern by the natural light; but when I allow my attention in some degree to relax, the vision of my mind being obscured, and, as it were, blinded by the images of sensible objects, I do not readily remember the reason why the idea of a being more perfect than myself, must of necessity have proceeded from a being in reality more perfect. On this account I am here desirous to inquire further, whether I, who possess this idea of God, could exist supposing there were no God. And I ask, from whom could I, in that case, derive my existence? Perhaps from myself, or from my parents, or from some other causes less perfect than God; for anything more perfect, or even equal to God, cannot be thought or imagined. But if I were independent of every other existence, and were myself the author of my being, I should doubt of nothing, I should desire nothing, and, in fine, no perfection would be lacking to me; for I should have bestowed upon myself every perfection of which I possess the idea, and I should thus be God. And it must not be imagined that what is now wanting to me is perhaps of more difficult acquisition than that of which I am already possessed; for, on the contrary, it is quite manifest that it was a matter of much higher difficulty that I, a thinking being, should arise from nothing, than it would be for me to acquire the knowledge of many things of which I am ignorant, and which are merely the accidents of a thinking substance; and certainly, if I possessed of myself the greater perfection of which I have now spoken, in other words, if I were the author of my own existence, I would not at least have denied to myself things that may be more easily obtained, as that infinite variety of knowledge of which I am at present destitute. I could not, indeed, have denied to myself any property which I perceive is contained in the idea of God, because there is none of these that seems to me to be more difficult to make or acquire; and if there were any that should happen to be more difficult to acquire, they would certainly appear so to me (supposing that I myself were the source of the other things I possess), because I should discover in them a limit to my power. And though I were to suppose that I always was as I now am, I should not, on this ground, escape the force of these reasonings, since it would not follow, even on this supposition, that no author of my existence needed to be sought after. For the whole time of my life may be divided into an infinity of parts, each of which is in no way dependent on any other; and, accordingly, because I was in existence a short time ago, it does not follow that I must now exist, unless in this moment some cause create me anew as it were,—that is, conserve me. In truth, it is perfectly clear and evident to all who will attentively consider the nature of duration, that the conservation of a substance, in each moment of its duration, requires the same power and act that would be necessary to create it, supposing it were not yet in existence; so that it is manifestly a dictate of the natural light that conservation and creation differ merely in respect of our mode of thinking and not in reality. All that is here required, therefore, is that I interrogate myself to discover whether I possess any power by means of which I can bring it about that I, who now am, shall exist a moment afterwards; for, since I am merely a thinking thing (or since, at least, the precise question, in the meantime, is only of that part of myself), if such a power resided in me, I should, without doubt, be conscious of it; but I am conscious of no such power, and thereby I manifestly know that I am dependent upon some being different from myself.

But perhaps the being upon whom I am dependent, is not God, and I have been produced either by my parents, or by some causes less perfect than Deity. This cannot be: for, as I before said, it is perfectly evident that there must at least be as much reality in the cause as in its effect; and accordingly, since I am a thinking thing, and possess in myself an idea of God, whatever in the end be the cause of my existence, it must of necessity be admitted that it is likewise a thinking being, and that it possesses in itself the idea and all the perfections I attribute to Deity. Then it may again be inquired whether this cause owes its origin and existence to itself, or to some other cause. For if it be self-existent, it follows, from what I have before laid down, that this cause is God; for, since it possesses the perfection of self-existence, it must likewise, without doubt, have the power of actually possessing every perfection of which it has the idea,—in other words, all the perfections I conceive to belong to God. But if it owe its existence to another cause than itself, we demand again, for a similar reason, whether this second cause exists of itself or through some other, until, from stage to stage, we at length arrive at an ultimate cause, which will be God. And it is quite manifest that in this matter there can be no infinite regress of causes, seeing that the question raised respects not so much the cause which once produced me, as that by which I am at this present moment conserved.

Nor can it be supposed that several causes concurred in my production, and that from one I received the idea of one of the perfections I attribute to Deity, and from another the idea of some other, and thus that all those perfections are indeed found somewhere in the universe, but do not all exist together in a single being who is God; for, on the contrary, the unity, the simplicity or inseparability of all the properties of Deity, is one of the chief perfections I conceive him to possess; and the idea of this unity of all the perfections of Deity could certainly not be put into my mind by any cause from which I did not likewise receive the ideas of all the other perfections; for no power could enable me to embrace them in an inseparable unity, without at the same time giving me the knowledge of what they were and of their existence in a particular mode.

Finally, with regard to my parents from whom it appears I sprung, although all that I believed respecting them be true, it does not, nevertheless, follow that I am conserved by them, or even that I was produced by them, in so far as I am a thinking being. All that, at the most, they contributed to my origin was the giving of certain dispositions (modifications) to the matter in which I have hitherto judged that I or my mind, which is what alone I now consider to be myself, is enclosed; and thus there can here be no difficulty with respect to them, and it is absolutely necessary to conclude from this alone that I am, and possess the idea of a being absolutely perfect, that is, of God, that his existence is most clearly demonstrated.

There remains only the inquiry as to the way in which I received this idea from God; for I have not drawn it from the senses, nor is it even presented to me unexpectedly, as is usual with the ideas of sensible objects, when these are presented or appear to be presented to the external organs of the senses; it is not even a pure production or fiction of my mind, for it is not in my power to take from or add to it; and consequently there but remains the alternative that it is innate, in the same way as is the idea of myself. And, in truth, it is not to be wondered at that God, at my creation, implanted this idea in me, that it might serve, as it were, for the mark of the workman impressed on his work; and it is not also necessary that the mark should be something different from the work itself; but considering only that God is my creator, it is highly probable that he in some way fashioned me after his own image and likeness, and that I perceive this likeness, in which is contained the idea of God, by the same faculty by which I apprehend myself,—in other words, when I make myself the object of reflection, I not only find that I am an incomplete, imperfect, and dependent being, and one who unceasingly aspires after something better and greater than he is; but, at the same time, I am assured likewise that he upon whom I am dependent possesses in himself all the goods after which I aspire, and the ideas of which I find in my mind, and that not merely indefinitely and potentially, but infinitely and actually, and that he is thus God. And the whole force of the argument of which I have here availed myself to establish the existence of God, consists in this, that I perceive I could not possibly be of such a nature as I am, and yet have in my mind the idea of a God, if God did not in reality exist,—this same God, I say, whose idea is in my mind—that is, a being who possesses all those lofty perfections, of which the mind may have some slight conception, without, however, being able fully to comprehend them—and who is wholly superior to all defect, and has nothing that marks imperfection: whence it is sufficiently manifest that he cannot be a deceiver, since it is a dictate of the natural light that all fraud and deception spring from some defect.

But before I examine this with more attention, and pass on to the consideration of other truths that may be evolved out of it, I think it proper to remain here for some time in the contemplation of God himself—that I may ponder at leisure his marvellous attributes—and behold, admire, and adore the beauty of this light so unspeakably great, as far, at least, as the strength of my mind, which is to some degree dazzled by the sight, will permit. For just as we learn by faith that the supreme felicity of another life consists in the contemplation of the Divine majesty alone, so even now we learn from experience that a like meditation, though incomparably less perfect, is the source of the highest satisfaction of which we are susceptible in this life.

Self vs. Science: The Rift between Subject and Object

In addition to the rift between science and religion, the science of the eighteenth century produced a rift between the objective world of nonconscious matter and the subjective world of conscious experience. Progress in the sciences inevitably focused attention on a new question: Where, in this vast cosmic machine of science, does the self fit in? Philosophers have answered either by placing the self at the center of our understanding of the cosmos or by placing it at the periphery (or even excluding it from the cosmos altogether).

The issue is not just theoretical. For some, perhaps for most of us, the rift between the objective world of cosmos (space, time, and matter) and the subjective world of self (experience, and thought) may occasion uneasiness, even fear or dread. Where, in a world of atoms pushing atoms, in the complex blur of neural activity and chemical changes that is the human brain, is the self? Surely the self cannot be identified with any part of that biological machine, for instance, with some particular neurons. If the self fits in anywhere at all, it must somehow be embodied in the whole brain. But once we have the brain, what need do we have for self at all?

Self, like God, becomes an explanatory hypothesis that, however useful it may have been in prescientific times, has been superseded by more potent scientific models. In other words, the self is like a God within, and so far as science is concerned, when you claim to experience yourself as a self—claim to *know* directly that the self exists—you are much like a mystic claiming to have direct knowledge of God.

The mysterious circle of Stonehenge, England: Sun temple? Sepulchral monument? Device to predict astronomical occurrences? All we are sure of is that it was built between 1850 B.C. and 1500 B.C.

David Hume

DIALOGUES CONCERNING NATURAL RELIGION

DAVID HUME (1711–1776), the third and last of the three great British empiricists (the other two were John Locke and George Berkeley) has had an enormous influence on twentieth-century philosophy, particularly in English-speaking countries. In two of his most important works, *Treatise of Human Nature* (1739) and *An Inquiry Concerning Human Understanding* (1748), Hume developed the empiricism of Locke and Berkeley—whose central idea is that our knowledge of the world is derived from experience—to its logical conclusion. He pushed it far beyond the limits of common sense, denying even the existence of self (see box "Hume's Solution: Dissolution of the Self" in Part II) and providing influential empirical analyses of many difficult concepts, such as causation, morality, space, time, and freedom. Hume also formulated skeptical objections to all inferences that go beyond immediate experience; Kant said that Hume's skepticism "awoke him from his dogmatic slumbers." Hume was a severe critic of popular religious belief, claiming not only that it was logically indefensible but, in addition, that it was morally harmful. His *Dialogues Concerning Natural Religion,* part of which follows, regarded by many as the greatest treatise ever written in the philosophy of religion, was published in 1779, after his death.

PART II

I must own, Cleanthes, said Demea, that nothing can more surprise me than the light in which you have all along put this argument. By the whole tenor of your discourse, one would imagine that you were maintaining the Being of a God against the cavils of atheists and infidels, and were necessitated to become a champion for that fundamental principle of all religion. But this, I hope, is not by any means a question among us. No man, no man at least of common sense, I am persuaded, ever entertained a serious doubt with regard to a truth so certain and self-evident. The question is not concerning the *being* but the *nature* of God. This I affirm, from the infirmities of human understanding, to be altogether incomprehensible and unknown to us. The essence of that supreme Mind, his attributes, the manner of his existence, the very nature of his duration—these and every particular which regards so divine a Being are mysterious to men. Finite, weak, and blind creatures, we ought to humble ourselves in his august presence, and, conscious of our frailties, adore in silence his infinite perfections which eye hath not seen, ear hath not heard, neither hath it entered into the heart of man to conceive. They are covered in a deep cloud from human curiosity; it is profaneness to attempt penetrating through these sacred obscurities, and, next to the impiety of denying his existence, is the temerity of prying into his nature and essence, decrees and attributes.

But lest you should think that my *piety* has here got the better of my *philosophy,* I shall support my opinion, if it needs any support, by a very great authority. I might cite all the divines, almost from the foundation of Christianity, who have ever treated of this or any other theological subject; but I shall confine myself, at present, to one equally celebrated for piety and philosophy. It is Father Malebranche who, I remember, thus expresses himself.[1] "One ought not so much," says he, "to call God a spirit in order to express positively what he is, as in order to signify that he is not matter. He is a Being infinitely perfect—of this we cannot doubt. But in the same manner as we ought not to imagine, even supposing him corporeal, that he is clothed with a human body, as the anthropomorphites asserted, under colour that that figure was the most perfect of any, so neither ought we to imagine that the spirit of God has human ideas or bears any resemblance to our spirit, under colour that we know nothing more perfect than a human mind. We ought rather to believe that as he comprehends the perfections of matter without being material . . . he comprehends also the perfections of created spirits without being spirit, in the manner we conceive spirit: that his true name is *He that is,* or, in other words, Being without restriction, All Being, the Being infinite and universal."

After so great an authority, Demea, replied Philo, as that which you have produced, and a thousand more which you might produce, it would appear ridiculous in me to add my sentiment or express my approbation of your doctrine. But surely, where reasonable men treat these subjects, the question can never be concerning the *being* but only the *nature* of the Deity. The former truth, as you well observe, is unquestionable

1. *Recherche de la Vérité,* liv. 3, cap. 9.

and self-evident. Nothing exists without a cause; and the original cause of this universe (whatever it be) we call God, and piously ascribe to him every species of perfection. Whoever scruples this fundamental truth deserves every punishment which can be inflicted among philosophers, to wit, the greatest ridicule, contempt, and disapprobation. But as all perfection is entirely relative, we ought never to imagine that we comprehend the attributes of this divine Being, or to suppose that his perfections have any analogy or likeness to the perfections of a human creature. Wisdom, thought, design, knowledge—these we justly ascribe to him because these words are honourable among men, and we have no other language or other conceptions by which we can express our adoration of him. But let us beware lest we think that our ideas anywise correspond to his perfections, or that his attributes have any resemblance to these qualities among men. He is infinitely superior to our limited view and comprehension, and is more the object of worship in the temple than of disputation in the schools.

In reality, Cleanthes, continued he, there is no need of having recourse to that affected scepticism so displeasing to you in order to come at this determination. Our ideas reach no further than our experience. We have no experience of divine attributes and operations. I need not conclude my syllogism, you can draw the inference yourself. And it is a pleasure to me (and I hope to you, too) that just reasoning and sound piety here concur in the same conclusion, and both of them establish the adorably mysterious and incomprehensible nature of the Supreme Being.

Not to lose any time in circumlocutions, said Cleanthes, addressing himself to Demea, much less in replying to the pious declamations of Philo, I shall briefly explain how I conceive this matter. Look round the world, contemplate the whole and every part of it: you will find it to be nothing but one great machine, subdivided into an infinite number of lesser machines, which again admit of subdivisions to a degree beyond what human senses and faculties can trace and explain. All these various machines, and even their most minute parts, are adjusted to each other with an accuracy which ravishes into admiration all men who have ever contemplated them. The curious adapting of means to ends, throughout all nature, resembles exactly, though it much exceeds, the productions of human contrivance—of human design, thought, wisdom, and intelligence. Since therefore the effects resemble each other, we are led to infer, by all the rules of analogy, that the causes also resemble, and that the Author of nature is somewhat similar to the mind of man, though possessed of much larger faculties, proportioned to the grandeur of the work which he has executed. By this argument *a posteriori,* and by this argument alone, do we prove at once the existence of a Deity and his similarity to human mind and intelligence.

I shall be so free, Cleanthes, said Demea, as to tell you that from the beginning I could not approve of your conclusion concerning the similarity of the Deity to men, still less can I approve of the mediums by which you endeavour to establish it. What! No demonstration of the Being of God! No abstract arguments! No proofs *a priori!* Are these which have hitherto been so much insisted on by philosophers all fallacy, all sophism? Can we reach no farther in this subject than experience and probability? I will not say that this is betraying the cause of a Deity; but surely, by this affected candour, you give advantages to atheists which they never could obtain by the mere dint of argument and reasoning.

What I chiefly scruple in this subject, said Philo, is not so much that all religious arguments are by Cleanthes reduced to experience, as that they appear not to be even the most certain and irrefragable of that inferior kind. That a stone will fall, that fire will burn, that the earth has solidity, we have observed a thousand and a thousand times; and when any new instance of this nature is presented, we draw without hesitation the accustomed inference. The exact similarity of the cases gives us a perfect assurance of a similar event, and a stronger evidence is never desired nor sought after. But wherever you depart, in the least, from the similarity of the cases, you diminish proportionably the evidence, and may at last bring it to a very weak *analogy,* which is confessedly liable to error and uncertainty. After having experienced the circulation of the blood in human creatures, we make no doubt that it takes place in Titius and Maevius; but from its circulation in frogs and fishes it is only a presumption, though a strong one, from analogy that it takes place in men and other animals. The analogical reasoning is much weaker when we infer the circulation of the sap in vegetables from our experience that the blood circulates in animals; and those who hastily followed that imperfect analogy are found, by more accurate experiments, to have been mistaken.

If we see a house, Cleanthes, we conclude, with the greatest certainty, that it had an architect or builder because this is precisely that species of effect which we have experienced to proceed from that species of cause. But surely you will not affirm that the universe bears such a resemblance to a house that we can with the same certainty infer a similar cause, or that the analogy is here entire and perfect. The dissimilitude is so striking that the utmost you can here pretend to is a guess, conjecture, a presumption concerning a similar cause; and how that pretension will be received in the world, I leave you to consider.

It would surely be very ill received, replied Cleanthes; and I should be deservedly blamed and detested did I allow that the proofs of Deity amounted to no more than a guess or conjecture. But is the whole adjustment of means to ends in a house and in the universe so slight a resemblance? the economy of final causes? the order, proportion, and arrangement of every part? Steps of a stair are plainly contrived that human legs may use them in mounting; and this inference is certain and infallible. Human legs are also contrived for walking and mounting; and this inference, I allow, is not altogether so certain because of the dissimilarity which you re-

"The Absurdity of Religion"

Arthur Schopenhauer

. . . [R]eligions admittedly appeal, not to conviction as the result of argument, but to belief as demanded by revelation. And as the capacity for believing is strongest in childhood, special care is taken to make sure of this tender age. This has much more to do with the doctrines of belief taking root than threats and reports of miracles. If, in early childhood, certain fundamental views and doctrines are paraded with unusual solemnity, and an air of the greatest earnestness never before visible in anything else; if, at the same time, the possibility of a doubt about them be completely passed over, or touched upon only to indicate that doubt is the first step to eternal perdition, the resulting impression will be so deep that, as a rule, that is, in almost every case, doubt about them will be almost as impossible in ten thousand will have the strength of mind to ask himself seriously and earnestly is that true? To call such as can do it strong minds, *esprits forts,* is a description apter than is generally supposed. But for the ordinary mind there is nothing so absurd or revolting but what, if inculcated in that way, the strongest belief in it will strike root. If, for example, the killing of a heretic or infidel were essential to the future salvation of his soul, almost every one would make it the chief event of his life, and in dying would draw consolation and strength from the remembrance that he had succeeded. As a matter of fact, almost every Spaniard in days gone by used to look upon an *auto da fe* as the most pious of all acts and one most

mark; but does it, therefore, deserve the name only of presumption or conjecture?

Good God! cried Demea, interrupting him, where are we? Zealous defenders of religion allow that the proofs of a Deity fall short of perfect evidence! And you, Philo, on whose assistance I depended in proving the adorable mysteriousness of the Divine Nature, do you assent to all these extravagant opinions of Cleanthes? For what other name can I give them? or, why spare my censure when such principles are advanced, supported by such an authority, before so young a man as Pamphilus?

You seem not to apprehend, replied Philo, that I argue with Cleanthes in his own way, and, by showing him the dangerous consequences of his tenets, hope at last to reduce him to our opinion. But what sticks most with you, I observe, is the representation which Cleanthes has made of the argument *a posteriori;* and, finding that the argument is likely to escape your hold and vanish into air, you think it so disguised that you can scarcely believe it to be set in its true light. How, however much I may dissent, in other respects, from the dangerous principle of Cleanthes, I must allow that he has fairly represented that argument, and I shall endeavour so to state the matter to you that you will entertain no further scruples with regard to it.

Were a man to abstract from everything which he knows or has seen, he would be altogether incapable, merely from his own ideas, to determine what kind of scene the universe must be, or to give the preference to one state or situation of things above another. For as nothing which he clearly conceives could be esteemed impossible or implying a contradiction, every chimera of his fancy would be upon an equal footing; nor could he assign any just reason why he adheres to one idea or system, and rejects the others which are equally possible.

Again, after he opens his eyes and contemplates the world as it really is, it would be impossible for him at first to assign the cause of any one event, much less of the whole of things, or of the universe. He might set his fancy a

agreeable to God. A parallel to this may be found in the way in which the Thugs (a religious sect in India, suppressed a short time ago by the English, who executed numbers of them) express their sense of religion and their veneration for the goddess Kali; they take every opportunity of murdering their friends and traveling companions, with the object of getting possession of their goods, and in the serious conviction that they are thereby doing a praiseworthy action, conducive to their eternal welfare. The power of religious dogma, when inculcated early, is such as to stifle conscience, compassion and finally every feeling of humanity. But if you want to see with your own eyes and close at hand what timely inoculation of belief will accomplish, look at the English. Here is a nation favored before all others by nature; endowed, more than all others, with discernment, intelligence, power of judgment, strength of character; look at them, abased and made ridiculous, beyond all others, by their stupid ecclesiastical superstition, which appears among their other abilities like a fixed idea or monomania. For this they have to thank the circumstance that education is in the hands of the clergy, whose endeavor it is to impress all the articles of belief, at the earliest age, in a way that amounts to a kind of paralysis of the brain; this in its turn express itself all their life in an idiotic bigotry, which makes otherwise most sensible and intelligent people among them degrade themselves so that one can't make head or tail of them. If you consider how essential to such a masterpiece is inoculation in the tender age of childhood, the missionary system appears no longer only as the acme of human importunity, arrogance and impertinence, but also as an absurdity. . . .

rambling, and she might bring him in an infinite variety of reports and representations. These would all be possible, but, being all equally possible, he would never of himself give a satisfactory account for his preferring one of them to the rest. Experience alone can point out to him the true cause of any phenomenon.

Now, according to this method of reasoning, Demea, it follows (and is, indeed, tacitly allowed by Cleanthes himself) that order, arrangement, or the adjustment of final causes, is not of itself any proof of design, but only so far as it has been experienced to proceed from that principle. For aught we can know *a priori,* matter may contain the source or spring of order originally within itself, as well as mind does; and there is no more difficulty in conceiving that the several elements, from an internal unknown cause, may fall into the most exquisite arrangement, than to conceive that their ideas, in the great universal mind, from a like internal unknown cause, fall into that arrangement. The equal possibility of both these suppositions is allowed. But, by experience, we find (according to Cleanthes) that there is a difference between them. Throw several pieces of steel together, without shape or form, they will never arrange themselves so as to compose a watch. Stone and mortar and wood, without an architect, never erect a house. But the ideas in a human mind, we see, by an unknown, inexplicable economy, arrange themselves so as to form the plan of a watch or house. Experience, therefore, proves that there is an original principle of order in mind, not in matter. From similar effects we infer similar causes. The adjustment of means to ends is alike in the universe, as in a machine of human contrivance. The causes, therefore, must be resembling.

I was from the beginning scandalized, I must own, with this resemblance which is asserted between the Deity and human creatures, and must conceive it to imply such a degradation of the Supreme Being as no sound theist could endure. With your assistance, therefore, Demea, I shall endeavour to defend what you justly call the adorable mysteriousness of the Divine Nature, and shall refute this reasoning of Cleanthes, provided he allows that I have made a fair representation of it.

When Cleanthes had assented, Philo, after a short pause, proceeded in the following manner.

That all inferences, Cleanthes, concerning fact are founded on experience, and that all experimental reasonings are founded on the supposition that similar causes prove similar effects, and similar effects similar causes, I shall not at present much dispute with you. But observe, I entreat you, with what extreme caution all just reasoners proceed in the transferring of experiments to similar cases. Unless the cases be exactly similar, they repose no perfect confidence in applying their past observation to any particular phenomenon. Every alteration of circumstances occasions a doubt concerning the event; and it requires new experiments to prove certainly that the new circumstances are of no moment or importance. A change in bulk, situation, arrangement, age, disposition of the air, or surrounding bodies—any of these particulars may be attended with the most unexpected consequences. And unless the objects be quite familiar to us, it is the highest temerity to expect with assurance, after any of these changes, an event similar to that which before fell under our observation. The slow and deliberate steps of philosophers here, if anywhere, are distinguished from the precipitate march of the vulgar, who, hurried on by the smallest similitude, are incapable of all discernment or consideration.

But you can think, Cleanthes, that your usual phlegm and philosophy have been preserved in so wide a step as you have taken when you compared to the universe houses, ships, furniture, machines, and, from their similarity in some circumstances, inferred a similarity in their causes? Thought, design, intelligence, such as we discover in men and other animals, is no more than one of the springs and principles of the universe, as well as heat or cold, attraction or repulsion, and a hundred others which fall under daily observation. It is an active cause by which some particular parts of nature, we find, produce alterations on other parts. But can a conclusion, with any propriety, be transferred from parts to the whole? Does not the great disproportion bar all comparison and inference? From observing the growth of a hair, can we learn anything concerning the generation of a man? Would the manner of a leaf's blowing, even though perfectly known, afford us any instruction concerning the vegetation of a tree?

But allowing that we were to take the *operations* of one part of nature upon another for the foundation of our judgment concerning the *origin* of the whole (which never can be admitted), yet why select so minute, so weak, so bounded a principle as the reason and design of animals is found to be upon this planet? What peculiar privilege has this little agitation of the brain which we call *thought,* that we must thus make it the model of the whole universe? Our partiality in our own favour does indeed present it on all occasions, but sound philosophy ought carefully to guard against so natural an illusion.

So far from admitting, continued Philo, that the operations of a part can afford us any just conclusion concerning the origin of the whole, I will not allow any one part to form a rule for another part if the latter be very remote from the former. Is there any reasonable ground to conclude that the inhabitants of other planets possess thought, intelligence, reason, or anything similar to these faculties in men? When nature has so extremely diversified her manner of operation in this small globe, can we imagine that she incessantly copies herself throughout so immense a universe? And if thought, as we may well suppose, be confined merely to this narrow corner and has even there so limited a sphere of action, with what propriety can we assign it for the original cause of all things? The narrow views of a peasant who makes his domestic economy the rule for the government of kingdoms is in comparison a pardonable sophism.

But were we ever so much assured that a thought and reason resembling the human were to be found throughout the whole universe, and were its activity elsewhere vastly greater and more commanding than it appears in this globe, yet I cannot see why the operations of a world constituted, arranged, adjusted, can with any propriety be extended to a world which is in its embryo state, and is advancing towards that constitution and arrangement. By observation we know somewhat of the economy, action, and nourishment of a finished animal, but we must transfer with great caution that observation to the growth of a foetus in the womb, and still more to the formation of an animalcule in the loins of its male parent. Nature, we find, even from our limited experience, possesses an infinite number of springs and principles which incessantly discover themselves on every change of her position and situation. And what new and unknown principles would actuate her in so new and unknown a situation as that of the formation of a universe, we cannot, without the utmost temerity, pretend to determine.

A very small part of this great system, during a very short time, is very imperfectly discovered to us; and do we thence pronounce decisively concerning the origin of the whole?

Admirable conclusion! Stone, wood, brick, iron, brass, have not, at this time, in this minute globe of earth, an order or arrangement without human art and contrivance; therefore, the universe could not originally attain its order and arrangement without something similar to human art. But is a part of nature a rule for another part very wide of the former? Is it a rule for the whole? Is a very small part a rule for the universe? Is nature in one situation a certain rule for nature in another situation vastly different from the former?

And can you blame me, Cleanthes, if I here imitate the prudent reserve of Simonides, who, according to the noted story, being asked by Hiero, *What God was?* desired a day to think of it, and then two days more; and after that manner continually prolonged the term, without ever bringing in his definition or description? Could you even blame me if I had answered, at first, *that I did not know,* and was sensible that this subject lay vastly beyond the reach of my faculties? You might cry out sceptic and rallier, as much as you pleased; but, having found in so many other subjects much more familiar the imperfections and even contradictions of human reason, I never should expect any success from its feeble conjectures in a subject so sublime and so remote from the sphere of our observation. When two *species* of objects have always been observed to be conjoined together, I can *infer,* by custom, the existence of one wherever I *see* the existence of the other; and this I call an argument from experience. But how this argument can have place where the objects, as in the present case, are single, individual, without parallel or specific resemblance, may be difficult to explain. And will any man tell me with a serious countenance that an orderly universe must arise from some thought and art like the human because we have experience of it? To ascertain this reasoning it were requisite that we had experience of the origin of worlds; and it is not sufficient, surely, that we have seen ships and cities arise from human art and contrivance.

Philo was proceeding in this vehement manner, somewhat between jest and earnest, as it appeared to me, when he observed some signs of impatience in Cleanthes, and then immediately stopped short. What I had to suggest, said Cleanthes, is only that you would not abuse terms, or make use of popular expressions to subvert philosophical reasonings. You know that the vulgar often distinguish reason from experience, even where the question relates only to matter of fact and existence, though it is found, where that *reason* is properly analyzed, that it is nothing but a species of experience. To prove by experience the origin of the universe from mind is not more contrary to common speech than to prove the motion of the earth from the same principle. And a caviller might raise all the same objections to the Copernican system which you have urged against my reasonings. Have you other earths, might he say, which you have seen to move? Have . . .

Yes! cried Philo, interrupting him, we have other earths. Is not the moon another earth, which we see to turn around its centre? Is not Venus another earth, where we observe the same phenomenon? Are not the revolutions of the sun also a confirmation, from analogy, of the same theory? All the planets, are they not earths which revolve about the sun? Are not the satellites moons which move round Jupiter and Saturn, and along with these primary planets round the sun? These analogies and resemblances, with others which I have not mentioned, are the sole proofs of the Copernican system; and to you it belongs to consider whether you have any analogies of the same kind to support your theory.

In reality, Cleanthes, continued he, the modern system of astronomy is now so much received by all inquirers, and has become so essential a part even of our earliest education, that we are not commonly very scrupulous in examining the reasons upon which it is founded. It is now become a matter of mere curiosity to study the first writers of that subject who had the full force of prejudice to encounter, and were obliged to turn their arguments on every side in order to render them popular and convincing. But if we peruse Galileo's famous *Dialogues* concerning the system of the world, we shall find that the great genius, one of the sublimest that ever existed, first bent all his endeavours to prove that there was no foundation for the distinction commonly made between elementary and celestial substances. The schools, proceeding from the illusions of sense, had carried this distinction very far; and had established the latter substances to be ingenerable, incorruptible, unalterable, impassible; and had assigned all the opposite qualities to the former. But Galileo, beginning with the moon, proved its similarity in every particular to the earth: its convex figure, its natural darkness when not illuminated, its density, its distinction into solid and liquid, the variations of its phases, the mutual illuminations of the earth and moon, their mutual eclipses, the inequalities of the lunar surface, etc. After many instances of this kind, with regard to all the planets, men plainly saw that these bodies became proper objects of experience, and that the similarity of their nature enabled us to extend the same arguments and phenomena from one to the other.

In this cautious proceeding of the astronomers you may read your own condemnation, Cleanthes, or rather may see that the subject in which you are engaged exceeds all human reason and inquiry. Can you pretend to show any such similarity between the fabric of a house and the generation of a universe? Have you ever seen nature in any such situation as resembles the first arrangement of the elements? Have worlds ever been formed under your eye, and have you had leisure to observe the whole progress of the phenomenon, from the first appearance of order to its final consummation? If you have, then cite your experience and deliver your theory.

PART III

How the most absurd argument, replied Cleanthes, in the hands of a man of ingenuity and invention, may acquire an air of probability! Are you not aware, Philo, that it became necessary for Copernicus and his first disciples to prove the similarity of the terrestrial and celestial matter because several philosophers, blinded by old systems and supported by some sensible appearances, had denied this similarity? But that it is by no means necessary that theists should prove the similarity of the works of *nature* to those of *art* because this similarity is self-evident and undeniable? The same matter, a like form; what more is requisite to show an analogy between their causes, and to ascertain the origin of all things from a divine purpose and intention? Your objections, I must freely tell you, are no better than the abstruse cavils of those philosophers who denied motion, and ought to be refuted in the same manner—by illustrations, examples, and instances rather than by serious argument and philosophy.

Suppose, therefore, that an articulate voice were heard in the clouds, much louder and more melodious than any which human art could ever reach; suppose that this voice were extended in the same instant over all nations and spoke to each nation in its own language and dialect; suppose that the words delivered not only contain a just sense and meaning, but convey some instruction altogether worthy of a benevolent Being superior to mankind—could you possibly hesitate a moment concerning the cause of this voice, and must you not instantly ascribe it to some design or purpose? Yet I cannot see but all the same objections (if they merit that appellation) which lie against the system of theism may also be produced against this inference.

Might you not say that all conclusions concerning fact were founded on experience; that, when we hear an articulate voice in the dark and thence infer a man, it is only the resemblance of the effects which leads us to conclude that there is a like resemblance in the cause; but that this extraordinary voice, by its loudness, extent, and flexibility to all languages, bears so little analogy to any human voice that we have no reason to suppose any analogy in their causes; and, consequently, that a rational, wise, coherent speech proceeded, you know not whence, from some accidental whistling of the winds, not from any divine reason or intelligence? You see clearly your own objections in these cavils, and I hope too you see clearly that they cannot possibly have more force in the one case than in the other.

But to bring the case still nearer the present one of the universe, I shall make two suppositions which imply not any absurdity or impossibility. Suppose that there is a natural, universal, invariable language, common to every individual of human race, and that books are natural productions which perpetuate themselves in the same manner with animals and vegetables, by descent and propagation. Several expressions of our passions contain a universal language: all brute animals have a natural speech, which, however limited, is very intelligible to their own species.

And as there are infinitely fewer parts and less contrivance in the finest composition of eloquence than in the coarsest organized body, the propagation of an *Iliad* or *Aeneid* is an easier supposition than that of any plant or animal.

Suppose, therefore, that you enter into your library thus peopled by natural volumes containing the most refined reason and most exquisite beauty; could you possibly open one of them and doubt that its original cause bore the strongest analogy to mind and intelligence? When it reasons and discourses; when it expostulates, argues, and enforces its views and topics; when it applies sometimes to the pure intellect, sometimes to the affections; when it collects, disposes, and adorns every consideration suited to the subject; could you persist in asserting that all this, at the bottom, had really no meaning, and that the first formation of this volume in the loins of its original parent proceeded not from thought and design? Your obstinacy, I know, reaches not that degree of firmness; even your sceptical play and wantonness would be abashed at so glaring an absurdity.

But if there be any difference, Philo, between this supposed case and the real one of the universe, it is all to the advantage of the latter. The anatomy of an animal affords many stronger instances of design than the perusal of Livy or Tacitus; and any objection which you start in the former case, by carrying me back to so unusual and extraordinary a scene as the first formation of worlds, the same objection has place on the supposition of our vegetating library. Choose, then, your party, Philo, without ambiguity or evasion; assert either that a rational volume is no proof of a rational cause or admit of a similar cause to all the works of nature.

Let me here observe, too, continued Cleanthes, that this religious argument, instead of being weakened by that scepticism so much affected by you, rather acquires force from it and becomes more firm and undisputed. To exclude all argument or reasoning of every kind is either affectation or madness. The declared profession of every reasonable sceptic is only to reject abstruse, remote, and refined arguments; to adhere to common sense and the plain instincts of nature; and to assent, wherever any reasons strike him with so full a force that he cannot, without the greatest violence, prevent it. Now the arguments for natural religion are plainly of this kind; and nothing but the most perverse, obstinate metaphysics can reject them. Consider, anatomize the eye, survey its structure and contrivance, and tell me, from your own feeling, if the idea of a contriver does not immediately flow in upon you with a force like that of sensation. The most obvious conclusion, surely, is in favour of design; and it requires time, reflection, and study, to summon up those frivolous though abstruse objections which can support infidelity. Who can behold the male and female of each species, the correspondence of their parts and instincts, their passions and whole course of life before and after generation, but must be sensible that the propagation of the species is intended by nature? Millions and millions of such instances present themselves through every part of the universe, and no language can convey a more intelligible irresistible meaning than the curious adjustment of final causes. To what degree, therefore, of blind dogmatism must one have attained to reject such natural and such convincing arguments?

Some beauties in writing we may meet with which seem contrary to rules, and which gain the affections and animate the imagination in opposition to all the precepts of criticism and to the authority of the established masters of art. And if the argument for theism be, as you pretend, contradictory to the principles of logic, its universal, its irresistible influence proves clearly that there may be arguments of a like irregular nature. Whatever cavils may be urged, an orderly world, as well as a coherent, articulate speech, will still be received as an incontestable proof of design and intention.

It sometimes happens, I own, that the religious arguments have not their due influence on an ignorant savage and barbarian, not because they are obscure and difficult, but because he never asks himself any question with regard to them. Whence arises the curious structure of an animal? From the copulation of its parents. And these whence? From *their* parents? A few removes set the objects at such a distance that to him they are lost in darkness and confusion; nor is he actuated by any curiosity to trace them farther. But this is neither dogmatism nor scepticism, but stupidity: a state of mind very different from your sifting, inquisitive disposition, my ingenious friend. You can trace causes from effects; you can compare the most distant and remote objects; and your greatest errors proceed not from barrenness of thought and invention, but from too luxuriant a fertility which suppresses your natural good sense by a profusion of unnecessary scruples and objections.

Here I could observe, Hermippus, that Philo was a little embarrassed and confounded; but, while he hesitated in delivering an answer, luckily for him, Demea broke in upon the discourse and saved his countenance.

Your instance, Cleanthes, said he, drawn from books and language, being familiar, has, I confess, so much more force on that account; but is there not some danger, too, in this very circumstance, and may it not render us presumptuous, by making us imagine we comprehend the Deity and have some adequate idea of his nature and attributes? When I read a volume, I enter into the mind and intention of the author; I become him, in a manner, for the instant, and have an immediate feeling and conception of those ideas which revolved in his imagination while employed in that composition. But so near an approach we never surely can make to the Deity. His ways are not our ways, his attributes are perfect but incomprehensible. And this volume of nature contains a great and inexplicable riddle, more than any intelligible discourse or reasoning.

The ancient Platonists, you know, were the most religious and devout of all the pagan philosophers, yet many of them, particularly Plotinus, expressly declare that intellect or understanding is not to be ascribed to the Deity, and that our most perfect worship of him consists, not in acts of veneration, reverence, gratitude, or love, but in a certain mysterious self-annihilation or total extinction of all our faculties. These ideas are, perhaps, too far stretched, but still it must be acknowledged that, by representing the Deity as so intelligible and comprehensible, and so similar to a human mind, we are guilty of the grossest and most narrow partiality, and make ourselves the model of the whole universe.

All the *sentiments* of the human mind, gratitude, resentment, love, friendship, approbation, blame, pity, emulation, envy, have a plain reference to the state and situation of man, and are calculated for preserving the existence and promoting the activity of such a being in such circumstances. It seems, therefore, unreasonable to transfer such sentiments to a supreme existence or to suppose him actuated by them; and the phenomena, besides, of the universe will not support us in such a theory. All our *ideas* derived from the senses are confessedly false and illusive, and cannot therefore be supposed to have place in a supreme intelligence. And as the ideas of internal sentiment, added to those of the external senses, composed the whole furniture of human understanding, we may conclude that none of the *materials* of thought are in any respect similar in the human and in the divine intelligence. Now, as to the *manner* of thinking, how can we make any comparison between them or suppose them anywise resembling? Our thought is fluctuating, uncertain, fleeting, successive, and compounded; and were we to remove these circumstances, we absolutely annihilate its essence, and it would in such a case be an abuse of terms to apply to it the name of thought or reason. At least, if it appear more pious and respectful (as it really is) still to retain these terms when we mention the Supreme Being, we ought to acknowledge that their meaning, in that case, is totally incomprehensible, and that the infirmities of our nature do not permit us to reach any ideas which in the least correspond to the ineffable sublimity of the Divine attributes.

PART IV

It seems strange to me, said Cleanthes, that you, Demea, who are so sincere in the cause of religion, should still maintain the mysterious, incomprehensible nature of the Deity, and should insist so strenuously that he has no manner of likeness or resemblance to human creatures. The Deity, I can readily allow, possesses many powers and attributes of which we can have no comprehension; but, if our ideas, so far as they go, be not just and adequate and correspondent to his real nature, I know not what there is in this subject worth insisting on. Is the name, without any meaning, of such mighty importance? Or how do you mystics, who maintain the absolute incomprehensibility of the Deity, differ from sceptics or atheists, who assert that the first cause of all is unknown and unintelligible? Their temerity must be very great if, after rejecting the production by a mind—I mean a mind resembling the human (for I know of no other)—they pretend to assign, with certainty, any other specific intelligible cause; and their conscience must be very scrupulous, indeed, if they refuse to call the universal unknown cause a God or Deity, and to bestow on him as many sublime eulogies and unmeaning epithets as you shall please to require of them.

Who could imagine, replied Demea, that Cleanthes, the calm philosophical Cleanthes, would attempt to refute his antagonists by affixing a nickname to them, and, like the common bigots and inquisitors of the age, have recourse to invective and declamation instead of reasoning? Or does he not perceive that these topics are easily retorted, and that *anthropomorphite* is an appellation as invidious, and implies as dangerous consequences, as the epithet of *mystic* with which he has honoured us? In reality, Cleanthes, consider what it is you assert when you represent the Deity as similar to the human mind and understanding. What is the soul of man? A composition of various faculties, passions, sentiments, ideas—united, indeed, into one self or person, but still distinct from each other. When it reasons, the ideas which are the parts of its discourse arrange themselves in a certain form or order which is not preserved entire for a moment, immediately gives place to another arrangement. New opinions, new passions, new affections, new feelings arise which continually diversify the mental scene and produce in it the greatest variety and most rapid succession imaginable. How is this compatible with that perfect immutability and simplicity which all true theists ascribe to the Deity? By the same act, say they, he sees past, present, and future; his love and hatred, his mercy and justice, are one individual operation; he is entire in every point of space, and complete in every instant of duration. No succession, no change, no acquisition, no diminution. What he is implies not in it any shadow of distinction or diversity. And what he is this moment he ever has been and ever will be, without any new judgment, sentiment, or operation. He stands fixed in one simple, perfect state; nor can you ever say, with any propriety, that this act of his is different from that other, or that this judgment or idea has been lately formed and will give place, by succession, to any different judgment or idea.

I can readily allow, said Cleanthes, that those who maintain the perfect simplicity of the Supreme Being, to the extent in which you have explained it, are complete mystics, and chargeable with all the consequences which I have drawn from their opinion. They are, in a word, atheists, without knowing it. For though it be allowed that the Deity possesses attributes of which we have no comprehension, yet ought we never to ascribe to him any attributes which are absolutely incompatible with that intelligent nature essential to him. A mind whose acts and sentiments and ideas are not distinct and successive, one that is wholly simple and totally immutable, is a mind which has no thought, no reason, no will, no sentiment, no love, no hatred; or, in a word, is no mind at all. It is an abuse of terms to give it that appellation, and we may as well speak of limited extension without figure, or of number without composition.

Pray consider, said Philo, whom you are at present inveighing against. You are honouring with the appellation of *atheist* all the sound, orthodox divines, almost, who have treated of this subject; and you will at last be, yourself, found, according to your reckoning, the only sound theist in the world. But if idolaters be atheists, as, I think, may justly be asserted, and Christian theologians the same, what becomes of the argument, so much celebrated, derived from the universal consent of mankind?

But, because I know you are not much swayed by names and authorities, I shall endeavor to show you, a little more distinctly, the inconveniences of that anthropomorphism which you have embraced, and shall prove that there is no ground to suppose a plan of the world to be formed in the Divine mind, consisting of distinct ideas, differently arranged, in the same manner as an architect forms in his head the plan of a house which he intends to execute.

It is not easy, I own, to see what is gained by this supposition, whether we judge of the matter by *reason* or by *experience*. We are still obliged to mount higher in order to find the cause of this cause which you had assigned as satisfactory and conclusive.

If *reason* (I mean abstract reason derived from inquiries *a priori*) be not alike mute with regard to all questions concerning cause and effect, this sentence at least it will venture to pronounce: that a mental world or universe of ideas requires a cause as much as does a material world or universe of objects, and, if similar in its arrangement, must require a similar cause. For what is there in this subject which should occasion a different conclusion or inference? In an abstract view, they are entirely alike; and no difficulty attends the one supposition which is not common to both of them.

Again, when we will needs force *experience* to pronounce some sentence, even on these subjects which lie beyond her sphere, neither can she perceive any material difference in this particular between those two kinds of worlds, but finds them to be governed by similar principles, and to depend upon an equal variety of causes in their operations. We have specimens in miniature of both of them. Our own mind resembles the one; a vegetable or animal body the other. Let experience, therefore, judge from these samples. Nothing seems more delicate, with regard to its causes, than thought; and as these causes never operate in two persons after the same manner, so we never find two persons who think exactly alike. Nor indeed does the same person think exactly alike at any two different periods of time. A difference of age, of the disposition of his body, a weather, of food, of company, of books, of passions—any of these particulars, or others more minute, are sufficient to alter the curious machinery of thought and communicate to it very different movements and operations. As far as we can judge, vegetables and animal bodies are not more delicate in their motions, nor depend upon a greater variety or more curious adjustment of springs and principles.

How, therefore, shall we satisfy ourselves concerning the cause of that Being whom you suppose the Author of nature, or, according to your system of anthropomorphism, the ideal world into which you trace the material? Have we not the same reason to trace that ideal world into another ideal world or new intelligent principle? But if we stop and go no farther, why go so far? Why not stop at the material world? How can we satisfy ourselves without going on *in infinitum?* And, after all, what satisfaction is there in that infinite progression? Let us remember the story of the Indian philosopher and his elephant. It was never more applicable than to the present subject. If the material world rests upon a similar ideal world, this ideal world must rest upon some other, and so on without end. It were better, therefore, never to look beyond the present material world. By supposing it to contain the principle of its order within itself, we really assert it to be God: and the sooner we arrive at that Divine Being, so much the better. When you go one step beyond the mundane system, you only excite an inquisitive humour which it is impossible ever to satisfy.

To say that the different ideas which compose the reason of the Supreme Being fall into order of themselves and by their own nature is really to talk without any precise meaning. If it has a meaning, I would fain know why it is not as good sense to say that the parts of the material world fall into order of themselves and by their own nature. Can the one opinion be intelligible, while the other is not so?

We have, indeed, experience of ideas which fall into order of themselves and without any *known* cause. But, I am sure, we have a much larger experience of matter which does the same, as in all instances of generation and vegetation where the accurate analysis of the cause exceeds all human comprehension. We have also experience of particular systems of thought and of matter which have no order; of the first in madness, of the second in corruption. Why, then, should we think that order is more essential to one than the other? And if it requires a cause in both, what do we gain by your system, in tracing the universe of objects into a similar universe of ideas? The first step which we make leads us on for ever. It were, therefore, wise in us to limit all our inquiries to the present world, without looking farther. No satisfaction can ever be attained by these speculations which so far exceed the narrow bounds of human understanding.

It was usual with the Peripatetics, you know, Cleanthes, when the cause of any phenomenon was demanded, to have recourse to their *faculties* or *occult qualities,* and to say, for instance, that bread nourished by its nutritive faculty, and senna purged by its purgative. But it has been discovered that this subterfuge was nothing but the disguise of ignorance, and that these philosophers, though less ingenuous, really said the same thing with the sceptics or the vulgar who fairly confessed that they knew not the cause of these phenomena. In like manner, when it is asked, what cause produced order in the ideas of the Supreme Being, can any other reason be assigned by you, anthropomorphites, than that it is a *rational* faculty, and that such is the nature of the Deity? But why a similar answer will not be equally satisfactory in accounting for the order of the world, without having recourse to any such intelligent creator as you insist on, may be difficult to determine. It is only to say that *such* is the nature of material objects, and that they are all originally possessed of a *faculty* of order and proportion. These are only more learned and elaborate ways of confessing our ignorance; nor has the one hypothesis any real advantage above the other, except in its greater conformity to vulgar prejudices.

You have displayed this argument with great emphasis, replied Cleanthes: You seem not sensible how easy it is to answer it. Even in common life, if I assign a cause for any event, is it any objection, Philo, that I cannot assign the cause of that cause, and answer every new question which may incessantly be started? And what philosophers could possibly submit to so rigid a rule?—philosophers who confess ultimate causes to be totally unknown, and are sensible that the most refined principles into which they trace the phenomena are still to them as inexplicable as these phenomena themselves are to the vulgar. The order and arrangement of nature, the curious adjustment of final causes, the plain use and intention of every part and organ—all these bespeak in the clearest language an intelligent cause or author. The heavens and the earth join in the same testimony: The whole chorus of nature raises one hymn to the praises of its Creator. You alone, or almost alone, disturb this general harmony. You start abstruse doubts, cavils, and objections; you ask me what is the cause of this cause? I know not; I care not; that concerns not me. I have found a Deity; and here I stop my inquiry. Let those go farther who are wiser or more enterprising.

I pretend to be neither, replied Philo; and for that very reason I should never, perhaps, have attempted to go so far, especially when I am sensible that I must at last be contented to sit down with the same answer which, without further trouble, might have satisfied me from the beginning. If I am still to remain in utter ignorance of causes and can absolutely give an explication of nothing, I shall never esteem it any advantage to shove off for a moment a difficulty which you acknowledge must immediately, in its full force, recur upon me. Naturalists indeed very justly explain particular effects by more general causes, though these general causes themselves should remain in the totally inexplicable, but they never surely thought it satisfactory to explain a particular effect by a particular cause which was no more to be accounted for than the effect itself. An ideal system, arranged of itself, without a precedent design, is not a whit more explicable than a material one which attains its order in a like manner; nor is there any more difficulty in the latter supposition than in the former.

PART V

But to show you still more inconveniences, continued Philo, in your anthropomorphism, please to take a new survey of your principles. *Like effects prove like causes.* This is the experimental argument; and this, you say too, is the sole theological argument. Now it is certain that the liker the effects are which are seen and the liker the causes which are inferred, the stronger is the argument. Every departure on either side diminishes the probability and renders the experiment less conclusive. You cannot doubt of the principle; neither ought you to reject its consequences.

All the new discoveries in astronomy which prove the immense grandeur and magnificence of the works of nature are so many additional arguments for a Deity, according to the true system of theism; but, according to your hypothesis of experimental theism, they become so many objections, by removing the effect still farther from all resemblance to the effects of human art and contrivance. For if Lucretius, even following the old system of the world, could exclaim:

> Quis regere immensi summam, quis habere profundi
> Indu manu validas potis est moderanter habenas?
> Quis pariter coelos omnes convertere? et omnes
> Ignibus aetheriis terras suffire feraces?
> Omnibus inque locis esse omni tempore praesto?[2]

If Tully [Cicero] esteemed this reasoning so natural as to put it into the mouth of his Epicurean:

> Quibus enim oculis animi intueri potuit vester Plato fabricam illam tanti operis, qua construi a Deo atque aedificari mundum facit? quae molitio? quae ferramenta? qui vectes? quae machinae? qui ministri tanti muneris fuerunt? quemadmodum autem obedire et parere voluntati architecti aer, ignis, aqua, terra potuerunt?[3]

If this argument, I say, had any force in former ages, how much greater must it have at present when the bounds of Nature are so infinitely enlarged and such a magnificent scene is opened to us? It is still more unreasonable to form our idea of so unlimited a cause from our experience of the narrow productions of human design and invention.

2. *De Rerum Natura,* lib. XI [II], 1094. (Who can rule the sum, who hold in his hand with controlling force the strong reins, of the immeasurable deep? Who can at once make all the different heavens to roll and warm with ethereal fires all the fruitful earths, or be present in all places at all times?)—(Translation by H. A. J. Munro, G. Bell & Sons, 1920.)

3. *De Natura Deorum,* lib. I [cap. VIII]. (For with what eyes could your Plato see the construction of so vast a work which, according to him, God was putting together and building? What materials, what tools, what bars, what machines, what servants were employed in such gigantic work? How could the air, fire, water, and earth pay obedience and submit to the will of the architect?)

The discoveries by microscopes, as they open a new universe in miniature, are still objections, according to you, arguments, according to me. The further we push our researcher of this kind, we are still led to infer the universal cause of all to be vastly different from mankind, or from any object of human experience and observation.

And what say you to the discoveries in anatomy, chemistry, botany? . . . These surely are no objections, replied Cleanthes; they only discover new instances of art and contrivance, it is still the image of mind reflected on us from innumerable objects. Add a mind *like the human,* said Philo. I know of no other, replied Cleanthes. And the liker, the better, insisted Philo. To be sure, said Cleanthes.

Now, Cleanthes, said Philo, with an air of alacrity and triumph, mark the consequences. *First,* by this method of reasoning you renounce all claim to infinity in any of the attributes of the Deity. For, as the cause ought only to be proportioned to the effect, and the effect, so far as it falls under our cognizance, is not infinite, what pretensions have we, upon your suppositions, to ascribe that attribute to the Divine Being? You will still insist that, by removing him so much from similarity to human creatures, we give in to the most arbitrary hypothesis, and at the same time weaken all proofs of his existence.

Secondly, you have no reason, on your theory, for ascribing perfection to the Deity, even in his finite capacity, or for supposing him free from every error, mistake, or incoherence, in his undertakings. There are many inexplicable difficulties in the works of nature which, if we allow a perfect author to be proved *a priori,* are easily solved, and become only seeming difficulties from the narrow capacity of man, who cannot trace infinite relations. But according to your method of reasoning, these difficulties become all real, and, perhaps, will be insisted on as new instances of likeness to human art and contrivance. At least, you must acknowledge that it is impossible for us to tell, from our limited views, whether this system contains any great faults or deserves any considerable praise if compared to other possible and even real systems. Could a peasant, if the *Aeneid* were read to him, pronounce that poem to be absolutely faultless, or even assign to it its proper rank among the productions of human wit, he who had never seen any other production?

But were this world ever so perfect a production, it must still remain uncertain whether all the excellences of the work can justly be ascribed to the workman. If we survey a ship, what an exalted idea must we form of the ingenuity of the carpenter who framed so complicated, useful, and beautiful a machine? And what surprise must we feel when we find him a stupid mechanic who imitated others, and copied an art which, through a long succession of ages, after multiplied trials, mistakes, corrections, deliberations, and controversies, had been gradually improving? Many worlds might have been botched and bungled, throughout an eternity, ere this system was struck out; much labour lost, many fruitless trials made, and a slow but continued improvement carried on during infinite ages in the art of world-making. In such subjects, who can determine where the truth, nay, who can conjecture where the probability lies, amidst a great number of hypotheses which may be proposed, and a still greater which may be imagined?

And what shadow of an argument, continued Philo, can you produce from your hypothesis to prove the unity of the Deity? A great number of men join in building a house or ship, in rearing a city, in framing a commonwealth; why may not several deities combine in contriving and framing a world? This is only so much greater similarity to human affairs. By sharing the work among several, we may so much further limit the attributes of each, and get rid of that extensive power and knowledge which must be supposed in one deity, and which, according to you, can only serve to weaken the proof of its existence. And if such foolish, such vicious creatures as man can yet often unite the framing and executing one plan, how much more those deities or demons, whom we may suppose several degrees more perfect!

To multiply causes without necessity is indeed contrary to true philosophy, but this principle applies not to the present case. Were one deity antecedently proved by your theory who were possessed of every attribute requisite to the production of the universe, it would be needless, I own (though not absurd) to suppose any other deity existent. But while it is still a question whether all these attributes are united in one subject or dispersed among several independent beings, by what phenomena in nature can we pretend to decide the controversy? Where we see a body raised in a scale, we are sure that there is in the opposite scale, however concealed from sight, some counterposing weight equal to it; but it is still allowed to doubt whether that weight be an aggregate of several distinct bodies or one uniform united mass. And if the weight requisite very much exceeds anything which we have ever seen conjoined in any single body, the former supposition becomes still more probable and natural. An intelligent being of such vast power and capacity as is necessary to produce the universe, or, to speak in the language of ancient philosophy, so prodigious an animal exceeds all analogy and even comprehension.

But further, Cleanthes: Men are mortal, and renew their species by generation; and this is common to all living creatures. The two great sexes of male and female, says Milton, animate the world. Why must this circumstance, so universal, so essential, be excluded from those numerous and limited deities? Behold, then, the theogeny of ancient times brought back upon us.

And why not become a perfect anthropomorphite? Why not assert the deity or deities to be corporeal, and to have eyes, a nose, mouth, ears, etc.? Epicurus maintained that no man had ever seen reason but in a human figure; therefore, the gods must have a human figure. And this argument, which is deservedly so much ridiculed by Cicero, becomes, according to you, solid and philosophical.

In a word, Cleanthes, a man who follows your hypothesis is able, perhaps, to assert or conjecture that the universe sometime arose from something like design; but beyond that position he cannot ascertain one single circumstance, and is left afterwards to fix every point of his theology by the utmost license of fancy and hypothesis. This world, for aught he knows, is very faulty and imperfect, compared to a superior standard, and was only the first rude essay of some infant deity who afterwards abandoned it, ashamed of his lame performance; it is the work only of some dependent, inferior deity, and is the object of derision to his superiors; it is the production of old age and dotage in some superannuated deity, and ever since his death has run on at adventures, from the first impulse and active force which it received from him. You justly give signs of horror, Demea, at these strange suppositions; but these, and a thousand more of the same kind, are Cleanthes' suppositions, not mine. From the moment the attributes of the Deity are supposed finite, all these have place. And I cannot, for my part, think that so wild and unsettled a system of theology is, in any respect, preferable to none at all.

These suppositions I absolutely disown, cried Cleanthes: they strike me, however, with no horror, especially when proposed in that rambling way in which they drop from you. On the contrary, they give me pleasure when I see that, by the utmost indulgence of your imagination, you never get rid of the hypothesis of design in the universe, but are obliged at every turn to have recourse to it. To this concession I adhere steadily; and this I regard as a sufficient foundation for religion.

PART VI

It must be a slight fabric, indeed, said Demea, which can be erected on so tottering a foundation. While we are uncertain whether there is one deity or many, whether the deity or deities, to whom we owe our existence, be perfect or imperfect, subordinate or supreme, dead or alive, what trust or confidence can we repose in them? What devotion or worship address to them? What veneration or obedience pay them? To all the purposes of life the theory of religion becomes altogether useless; and even with regard to speculative consequences its uncertainty, according to you, must render it totally precarious and unsatisfactory.

To render it still more unsatisfactory, said Philo, there occurs to me another hypothesis which must acquire an air of probability from the method of reasoning so much insisted on by Cleanthes. That like effects arise from like causes—this principle he supposes the foundation of all religion. But there is another principle of the same kind, no less certain and derived from the same source of experience, that, where several known circumstances are observed to be similar, the unknown will also be found similar. Thus, if we see the limbs of a human body, we conclude that it is also attended with a human head, though hid from us. Thus, if we see, through a chink in a wall, a small part of the sun, we conclude that were the wall removed we should see the whole body. In short, this method of reasoning is so obvious and familiar that no scruple can ever be made with regard to its solidity.

Now, if we survey the universe, so far as it falls under our knowledge, it bears a great resemblance to an animal or organized body, and seems actuated with a like principle of life and motion. A continual circulation of matter in it produces no disorder; a continual waste in every part is incessantly repaired; the closest sympathy is perceived throughout the entire system; and each part or member, in performing its proper offices, operates both to its own preservation and to that of the whole. The world, therefore, I infer, is an animal; and the Deity is the *soul* of the world, actuating it, and actuated by it.

You have too much learning, Cleanthes, to be at all surprised at this opinion which, you know, was maintained by almost all the theists of antiquity, and chiefly prevails in their discourses and reasonings. For though, sometimes, the ancient philosophers reason from final causes, as if they thought the world the workmanship of God, yet it appears rather their favourite notion to consider it as his body whose organization renders it subservient to him. And it must be confessed that, as the universe resembles more a human body than it does the works of human art and contrivance, if our limited analogy could ever, with any propriety, be extended to the whole of nature, the inference seems juster in favour of the ancient than the modern theory.

There are many other advantages, too, in the former theory which recommended it to the ancient theologians. Nothing more repugnant to all their notions because nothing more repugnant to common experience than mind without body, a mere spiritual substance which fell not under their senses nor comprehension, and of which they had not observed one single instance throughout all nature. Mind and body they knew because they felt both; an order, arrangement, organization, or internal machinery, in both they likewise knew, after the same manner; and it could not but seem reasonable to transfer this experience to the universe, and to suppose the divine mind and body to be also coeval and to have, both of them, order and arrangement naturally inherent in them and inseparable from them.

Here, therefore, is a new species of *anthropomorphism,* Cleanthes, on which you may deliberate, and a theory which seems not liable to any considerable difficulties. You are too much superior, surely, to *systematical prejudices* to find any more difficulty in supposing an animal body to be, originally, of itself or from unknown causes, possessed of order and organization, than in supposing a similar order to belong to mind. But the *vulgar prejudice* that body and mind ought always to accompany each other ought not, one should think, to be entirely neglected; since it is founded on *vulgar experience,* the only guide which you profess to follow in all these theological inquiries. And if you assert that our limited experience is an unequal standard by which to judge of the unlimited extent of nature, you entirely abandon your own hypothesis, and must thenceforward adopt our mysticism, as you call it, and admit of the absolute incomprehensibility of the Divine Nature.

This theory, I own, replied Cleanthes, has never before occurred to me, though a pretty natural one; and I cannot readily, upon so short an examination and reflection, deliver any opinion with regard to it. You are very scrupulous, indeed, said Philo. Were I to examine any system of yours, I should not have acted with half that caution and reserve in stating objections and difficulties to it. However, if anything occur to you, you will oblige us by proposing it.

Why then, replied Cleanthes, it seems to me that, though the world does, in many circumstances, resemble an animal body, yet is the analogy also defective in many circumstances the most material: no organs of sense; no seat of thought or reason; no one precise origin of motion and action. In short, it seems to bear a stronger resemblance to a vegetable than to an animal, and your inference would be so far inconclusive in favour of the soul of the world.

But, in the next place, your theory seems to imply the eternity of the world; and that is a principle which, I think, can be refuted by the strongest reasons and probabilities. I shall suggest an argument to this purpose which, I believe, has not been insisted on by any writer. Those who reason from the late origin of arts and sciences, though their inference wants not force, may perhaps be refuted by considerations derived from the nature of human society, which is in continual revolution between ignorance and knowledge, liberty and slavery, riches and poverty; so that it is impossible for us, from our limited experience, to foretell with assurance what events may or may not be expected. Ancient learning and history seem to have been in great danger of entirely perishing after the inundation of the barbarous nations; and had these convulsions continued a little longer or been a little more violent, we should not probably have now known what passed in the world a few centuries before us. Nay, were it not for the superstition of the popes, who preserved a little jargon of Latin in order to support the appearance of an ancient and universal church, that tongue must have been utterly lost; in which case the Western world, being totally barbarous, would not have been in a fit disposition for receiving the Greek language and learning, which was conveyed to them after the sacking of Constantinople. When learning and books had been extinguished, even the mechanical arts would have fallen considerably to decay; and it is easily imagined that fable or tradition might ascribe to them a much later origin than the true one. This vulgar argument, therefore, against the eternity of the world seems a little precarious.

But here appears to be the foundation of a better argument. Lucullus was the first that brought cherry-trees from Asia to Europe, though that tree thrives so well in many European climates that it grows in the woods without any culture. Is it possible that, throughout a whole eternity, no European had ever passed into Asia and thought of transplanting so delicious a fruit into his own country? Or if the tree was once transplanted and propagated, how could it ever afterwards perish? Empires may rise and fall, liberty and slavery succeed alternately, ignorance and knowledge give place to each other; but the cherry-tree will still remain in the woods of Greece, Spain, and Italy, and will never be affected by the revolutions of human society.

It is not two thousand years since vines were transplanted into France, though there is no climate in the world more favourable to them. It is not three centuries since horses, cows, sheep, swine, dogs, corn, were known in America. Is it possible that during the revolutions of a whole eternity there never arose a Columbus who might open the communication between Europe and that continent? We may as well imagine that all men would wear stockings for ten thousand years, and never have the sense to think of garters to tie them. All these seem convincing proofs of the youth or rather infancy of the world, as being founded on the operation of principles more constant and steady than those by which human society is governed and directed. Nothing less than a total convulsion of the elements will ever destroy all the European animals and vegetables which are now to be found in the Western world.

And what argument have you against such convulsions? replied Philo. Strong and almost incontestable proofs may be traced over the whole earth that every part of this globe has continued for many ages entirely covered with water. And though order were supposed inseparable from matter, and inherent in it, yet may matter be susceptible of many and great revolutions, through the endless periods of eternal duration. The incessant changes to which every part of it is subject seem to intimate some such general transformations; though, at the same time, it is observable that all the changes and corruptions of which we have ever had experience are but passages from one state of order to another; nor can matter ever rest in total deformity and confusion. What we see in the parts, we may infer in the whole; at least, that is the method of reasoning on which you rest your whole theory. And were I obliged to defend any particular system of this nature, which I never willingly should do, I esteem none more plausible than that which ascribes an eternal inherent principle of order to the world, though attended with great and continual revolutions and alterations. This at once solves all difficulties; and if the solution, by being so general, is not entirely complete and satisfactory, it is at least a theory that we must sooner or later have recourse to, whatever system we embrace. How could things have been as they are, were there not an original inherent principle of order somewhere, in thought or in matter? And it is very indifferent to which of these we give the preference. Chance has no place, on any hypothesis, sceptical or religious. Everything is surely governed by steady, inviolable laws. And were the inmost essence of things laid open to us, we should then discover a scene of which, at present, we can have no idea. Instead of admiring the order of natural beings, we should clearly see that it was absolutely impossible for them, in the smallest article, ever to admit of any other disposition.

Were anyone inclined to revive the ancient pagan theology which maintained, as we learned from Hesiod, that this globe was governed by 30,000 dieties, who arose from the unknown powers of nature, you would naturally object, Cleanthes, that nothing is gained by this hypothesis; and that it is as easy to suppose all men animals, beings more numerous but less perfect, to have sprung immediately from a like origin. Push the same inference a step further, and you will find a numerous society of deities as explicable as one universal deity who possesses within himself the powers and perfections of the whole society. All these systems, then, of Scepticism, Polytheism, and Theism, you must allow, on your principles, to be on a like footing, and that no one of them has any advantage over the others. You may thence learn the fallacy of your principles.

PART VII

But here, continued Philo, in examining the ancient system of the soul of the world there strikes me, all of a sudden, a new idea which, if just, must go near to subvert all your reasoning, and destroy even your first inferences on which you repose such confidence. If the universe bears a greater likeness to animal bodies and to vegetables than to the works of human art, it is more probable that its cause resembles the cause of the former than that of the latter, and its origin ought rather to be ascribed to generation or vegetation than to reason or design. Your conclusion, even according to your own principles, is therefore lame and defective.

Pray open up this argument a little further, said Demea, for I do not rightly apprehend it in that concise manner in which you have expressed it.

Our friend Cleanthes, replied Philo, as you have heard, asserts that, since no question of fact can be proved otherwise than by experience, the existence of a Deity admits not of proof from any other medium. The world, says he, resembles the works of human contrivance; therefore its cause must also resemble that of the other. Here we may remark that the operation of one very small part of nature, to wit, man, upon another very small part, to wit, that inanimate matter lying within his reach, is the rule by which Cleanthes judges of the origin of the whole; and he measures objects, so widely disproportioned, by the same individual standard. But to waive all objections drawn from this topic, I affirm that there are other parts of the universe (besides the machines of human invention) which bear still a greater resemblance to the fabric of the world, and which, therefore, afford a better conjecture concerning the universal origin of this system. These parts are animals and vegetables. The world plainly resembles more an animal or a vegetable than it does a watch or a knitting-loom. Its cause, therefore, it is more probable, resembles the cause of the former. The cause of the former is generation or vegetation. The cause, therefore, of the world we may infer to be something similar or analogous to generation or vegetation.

But how is it conceivable, said Demea, that the world can arise from anything similar to vegetation or generation?

Very easily, replied Philo. In like manner as a tree sheds its seed into the neighboring fields and produces other trees, so the great vegetable, the world, or this planetary system, produces within itself certain seeds which, being scattered into the surrounding chaos, vegetate into new worlds. A comet, for instance, is the seed of a world; and after it has been fully ripened, by passing from sun to sun, and star to star, it is, at last, tossed into the unformed elements which everywhere surround this universe, and immediately sprouts up into a new system.

Or if, for the sake of variety (for I see no other advantage), we should suppose this world to be an animal: a comet is the egg of this animal; and in like manner as an ostrich lays its egg in the sand, which, without any further care, hatches the egg and produces a new animal, so . . . I understand you, says Demea. But what wild, arbitrary suppositions are these! What *data* have you for such extraordinary conclusions? And is the slight, imaginary resemblance of the world to a vegetable or an animal sufficient to establish the same inference with regard to both? Objects which are in general so widely different, ought they to be a standard for each other?

Right, cries Philo: This is the topic on which I have all along insisted. I have still asserted that we have no *data* to establish any system of cosmogony. Our experience, so imperfect in itself and so limited both in extent and duration, can afford us no probable conjecture concerning the whole of things. But if we must needs fix on some hypothesis, by what rule, pray, ought we to determine our choice? Is there any other rule than the greater similarity of the objects compared? And does not a plant or an animal, which springs from vegetation or generation, bear a stronger resemblance to the world than does any artificial machine, which arises from reason and design?

But what is this vegetation and generation of which you talk? said Demea. Can you explain their operations, and anatomize that fine internal structure on which they depend?

As much, at least, replied Philo, as Cleanthes can explain the operations of reason, or anatomize that internal structure on which it depends. But without any such elaborate disquisitions, when I see an animal, I infer that it sprang from generation; and that with as great certainty as you conclude a house to have been reared by design. These words *generation, reason* mark only certain powers and energies in nature whose effects are known, but whose essence is incomprehensible; and one of these principles, more than the other, has no privilege for being made, a standard to the whole of nature.

In reality, Demea, it may reasonably be expected that the larger the views are which we take of things, the better will they conduct us in our conclusions concerning such extraordinary and such magnificent subjects. In this little corner of the world alone, there are four principles, *reason, instinct, generation, vegetation,* which are similar to each other, and are the causes of similar effects. What a number of other principles may we naturally suppose in the immense extent and variety of the universe could we travel from planet to planet, and from system to system, in order to examine each part of this mighty fabric? Any one of these four principles above mentioned (and a hundred others which lie open to our conjecture) may afford us a theory by which to judge of the origin of the world; and it is a palpable and egregious partiality to confine our view entirely to that principle by which our own minds operate. Were this principle more intelligible on that account, such a partiality might be somewhat excusable; but reason, in its internal fabric and structure, is really as little known to us as instinct or vegetation; and, perhaps, even that vague, undeterminate word *nature,* to which the vulgar refer everything is not at the bottom more inexplicable. The effects of these principles are all known to us from experience; but the principles themselves and their manner of operation are totally unknown; nor is it less intelligible or less conformable to experience to say that the world arose by vegetation, from seed shed by another world, than to say that it arose from a divine reason or contrivance, according to the sense in which Cleanthes understands it.

But methinks, said Demea, if the world had a vegetative quality and could sow the seeds of new worlds into the infinite chaos, this power would be still an additional argument for design in its author. For whence could arise so wonderful a faculty but from design? Or how can order spring from anything which perceives not that order which it bestows?

You need only look around you, replied Philo, to satisfy yourself with regard to this question. A tree bestows order and organization on that tree which springs from it, without knowing the order; an animal in the same manner on its offspring; a bird on its nest; and instances of this kind are even more frequent in the world than those of order which arise from reason and contrivance. To say that all this order in animals and vegetables proceeds ultimately from design is begging the question; nor can that great point be ascertained otherwise than by proving, *a priori,* both that order is, from its nature, inseparably attached to thought and that it can never of itself or from original unknown principles belong to matter.

But further, Demea, this objection which you urge can never be made use of by Cleanthes, without renouncing a defense which he has already made against one of my objections. When I inquired concerning the cause of that supreme reason and intelligence into which he resolves everything, he told me that the impossibility of satisfying such inquiries could never be admitted as an objection in any species of philosophy. *We must stop somewhere,* says he; *nor is it ever within the reach of human capacity to explain ultimate causes or show the last connections of any objects. It is sufficient if any steps, as far as we go, are supported by experience and observation.* Now that vegetation and generation, as well as reason, are experienced to be principles of order in nature is undeniable. If I rest my system of cosmogony on the former, preferably to the latter, it is at my choice. The matter seems entirely arbitrary. And when Cleanthes asks me what is the cause of my great vegetative or generative faculty, I am equally entitled to ask him the cause of his great reasoning principle. These questions we have agreed to forbear on both sides; and it is chiefly his interest on the present occasion to stick to this agreement. Judging by our limited and imperfect experience, generation has some privileges above reason; for we see every day the latter arise from the former, never the former from the latter.

Compare, I beseech you, the consequences on both sides. The world, say I, resembles an animal; therefore it is an animal, therefore it arose from generation. The steps, I confess, are wide, yet there is some small appearance of analogy in each step. The world, says Cleanthes, resembles a machine; therefore it is a machine, therefore it arose from design. The steps are here equally wide, and the analogy less striking. And if he pretends to carry on *my* hypothesis a step further, and to infer design or reason from the great principle of generation on which I insist, I may, with better authority, use the same freedom to push further *his* hypothesis, and infer a divine generation or theogony from his principle of reason. I have at least some faint shadow of experience, which is the utmost that can ever be attained in the present subject. Reason, in innumerable instances, is observed to arise from the principle of generation, and never to arise from any other principle.

Hesiod and all the ancient mythologists were so struck with this analogy that they universally explained the origin of nature from an animal birth, and copulation. Plato, too, so far as he is intelligible, seems to have adopted some such notion in his *Timaeus*.

The Brahmins assert that the world arose from an infinite spider, who spun this whole complicated mass from his bowels, and annihilates afterwards the whole or any part of it, by absorbing it again and resolving it into his own essence. Here is a species of cosmogony which appears to us ridiculous because a spider is a little contemptible animal whose operations we are never likely to take for a model of the whole universe. But still here is a new species of analogy, even in our globe. And were there a planet wholly inhabited by spiders (which is very possible), this inference would there appear as natural and irrefragable as that which in our planet ascribes the origin of all things to design and intelligence, as explained by Cleanthes. Why an orderly system may not be spun from the belly as well as from the brain, it will be difficult for him to give a satisfactory reason.

I must confess, Philo, replied Cleanthes, that, of all men living, the task which you have undertaken, of raising doubts and objections, suits you best and seems, in a manner, natural and unavoidable to you. So great is your fertility of invention that I am not ashamed to acknowledge myself unable, on a sudden, to solve regularly such out-of-the-way difficulties as you incessantly start upon me, though I clearly see, in general, their fallacy and error. And I question not, but you are yourself, at present, in the same case, and have not the solution so ready as the objection, while you must be sensible that common sense and reason are entirely against you, and that such whimsies as you have delivered may puzzle but never can convince us.

PART VIII

What you ascribe to the fertility of my invention, replied Philo, is entirely owing to the nature of the subject. In subjects adapted to the narrow compass of human reason there is commonly but one determination which carries probability or conviction with it; and to a man of sound judgment all other suppositions but that one appear entirely absurd and chimerical. But in such questions as the present, a hundred contradictory views may preserve a kind of imperfect analogy, and invention has here full scope to exert itself. Without any great effort of thought, I believe that I could, in an instant, propose other systems of cosmogony which would have some faint appearance of truth, though it is a thousand, a million to one if either yours or any one of mine be the true system.

For instance, what if I should revive the old Epicurean hypothesis? This is commonly, and I believe justly, esteemed the most absurd system that has yet been proposed; yet I know not whether, with a few alterations, it might not be brought to bear a faint appearance of probability. Instead of supposing matter infinite, as Epicurus did, let us suppose it finite. A finite number of particles is only susceptible of finite transpositions; and it must happen, in an eternal duration, that every possible order or position must be tried an infinite number of times. This world, therefore, with all its events, even the most minute, has before been produced and destroyed, and will again be produced and destroyed, without any bounds and limitations. No one who has a conception of the powers of infinite, in comparison of finite, will ever scruple this determination.

But this supposes, said Demea, that matter can acquire motion without any voluntary agent or first mover.

And where is the difficulty, replied Philo, of that supposition? Every event, before experience, is equally difficult and incomprehensible; and every event, after experience, is equally easy and intelligible. Motion, in many instances, from gravity, from elasticity, from electricity, begins in matter, without any known voluntary agent; and to suppose always, in these cases, an unknown voluntary agent is mere hypothesis and hypothesis attended with no advantages. The beginning of motion in matter itself is as conceivable *a priori* as its communication from mind and intelligence.

Besides, why may not motion have been propagated by impulse through all eternity, and the same stock of it, or nearly the same, be still upheld in the universe? As much is lost by the composition of motion, as much is gained by its resolution. And whatever the causes are, the fact is certain that matter is and always has been in continual agitation, as far as human experience or tradition reaches. There is not probably, at present, in the whole universe, one particle of matter at absolute rest.

And this very consideration, too, continued Philo, which we have stumbled on in the course of the argument, suggests a new hypothesis of cosmogony that is not absolutely absurd and improbable. Is there a system, an order, an economy of things, by which matter can preserve that perpetual agitation which seems essential to it, and yet maintain a constancy in the forms which it produces? There certainly is such an economy, for this is actually the case with the present world. The continual motion of matter, therefore, in less than infinite transpositions, must produce this economy or order, and by its very nature, that order, when once established, supports itself for many ages if not to eternity. But wherever matter is so poised, arranged, and adjusted, as to continue in perpetual motion, and yet preserve a constancy in the forms, its situation must, of necessity, have all the same appearance of art and contrivance which we observe at present. All the parts of each form must have a relation to each other and to the whole; and the whole itself must have a relation to the other parts of the universe, to the element in which the form subsists, to the materials with which it repairs its waste and decay, and to every other form which is hostile or friendly. A defect in any of these particulars destroys the form, and the matter of which it is composed is again set loose, and is thrown into irregular motions and fermentations till it unite itself to some other regular form. If no such form be prepared to receive it, and if there be a great quantity of this corrupted matter in the universe, the universe itself is entirely disordered, whether it be the feeble embryo of a world in its first beginnings that is thus destroyed or the rotten carcase of one languishing in old age and infirmity. In either case, a chaos ensues till finite though innumerable revolutions produce, at last, some forms whose parts and organs are so adjusted as to support the forms amidst a continued succession of matter.

Suppose (for we shall endeavour to vary the expression) that matter were thrown into any position by a blind, unguided force; it is evident that this first position must, in all probability, be the most confused and most disorderly imaginable, without any resemblance to those works of human contrivance which, along with a symmetry of parts, discover an adjustment of means to ends and a tendency to self-preservation. If the actuating force cease after this operation, matter must remain for ever in disorder and continue an immense chaos, without any proportion or activity. But suppose that the actuating force, whatever it be, still continues in matter, this first position will immediately give place to a second which will likewise, in all probability, be as disorderly as the first, and so on through many successions of changes and revolutions. No particular order or position ever continues a moment unaltered. The original force, still remaining in activity, gives a perpetual restlessness to matter. Every possible situation is produced and instantly destroyed. If a glimpse or dawn of order appears for a moment, it is instantly hurried away and confounded by that never-ceasing force which actuates every part of matter.

Thus the universe goes on for many ages in a continued succession of chaos and disorder. But is it not possible that it may settle at last, so as not to lose its motion and active force (for that we have supposed inherent in it), yet so as to preserve an uniformity of appearance, amidst the continual motion and fluctuation of its parts? This we find to be the case with the universe at present. Every individual is perpetually changing, and every part of every individual; and yet the whole remains, in appearance, the same. May we not hope for such a position or rather be assured of it from the eternal revolutions of unguided matter; and may not this account for all the appearing wisdom and contrivance which is in the universe? Let us contemplate the subject a little, and we shall find that this adjustment if attained by matter of a seeming stability in the forms, with a real and perpetual revolution or motion of parts, affords a plausible, if not a true, solution of the difficulty.

It is in vain, therefore, to insist upon the uses of the parts in animals or vegetables, and their curious adjustment to each other. I would fain know how an animal could subsist unless its parts were so adjusted? Do we not find that it immediately perishes whenever this adjustment ceases, and that its matter, corrupting, tries some new form? It happens indeed that the parts of the world are so well adjusted that some regular form immediately lays claim to this corrupted matter; and if it were not so, could the world subsist? Must it not dissolve, as well as the animal, and pass through new positions and situations till in great but finite succession it fall, at last, into the present or some such order?

It is well, replied Cleanthes, you told us that this hypothesis was suggested on a sudden, in the course of the argument. Had you had leisure to examine it, you would soon have perceived the insuperable objections to which it is exposed. No form, you say, can subsist unless it possess those powers and organs requisite for its subsistence; some new order of economy must be tried, and so on, without intermission, till at last some order which can support and maintain itself is fallen upon. But according to this hypothesis, whence arise the many conveniences and advantages which men and all animals possess? Two eyes, two ears are not absolutely necessary for the subsistence of the species. The human race might have been propagated and preserved without horses, dogs, cows, sheep, and those innumerable fruits and products which serve to our satisfaction and enjoyment. If no camels had been created for the use of man in the sandy deserts of Africa and Arabia, would the world have been dissolved? If no loadstone had been framed to give that wonderful and useful direction to the needle, would human society and the human kind have been immediately extinguished? Though the maxims of nature be in general very frugal, yet instances of this kind are far from being rare; and any one of them is a sufficient proof of design—and of a benevolent design—which gave rise to the order and arrangement of the universe.

At least, you may safely infer, said Philo, that the foregoing hypothesis is so far incomplete and imperfect, which I shall not scruple to allow. But can we ever reasonably expect greater success in any attempts of this nature? Or can we ever hope to erect a system of cosmogony that will be liable to no exceptions, and will contain no circumstance repugnant to our limited and imperfect experience of the analogy of nature? Your theory itself cannot surely pretend to any such advantage, even though you have run into *anthropomorphism,* the better to preserve a conformity to common experience. Let us once more put it to trial. In all instances which we have ever seen, ideas are copied from real objects, and are ectypal, not archetypal, to express myself in learned terms. You reverse this order and give thought the precedence. In all instances which we have ever seen, thought has no influence upon matter except where that matter is so conjoined with it as to have an equal reciprocal influence upon it. No animal can move immediately anything but the members of its own body; and, indeed, the equality of action and reaction seems to be an universal law of nature; but your theory implies a contradiction to this experience. These instances, with many more which it were easy to collect (particularly the supposition of a mind or system of thought that is eternal or, in other words, an animal ingenerable and immortal)—these instances, I say, may teach all of us sobriety in condemning each other, and let us see that as no system of this kind ought ever to be received from a slight analogy, so neither ought any to be rejected on account of a small incongruity. For that is an inconvenience from which we can justly pronounce no one to be exempted.

All religious systems, it is confessed, are subject to great and insuperable difficulties. Each disputant triumphs in his turn, while he carries on an offensive war, and exposes the absurdities, barbarities, and pernicious tenets of his antagonist. But all of them, on the whole, prepare a complete triumph for the *sceptic,* who tells them that no system ought ever to be embraced with regard to such subjects: for this plain reason that no absurdity ought ever to be assented to with regard to any subject. A total suspense of judgment is here our only reasonable resource. And if every attack, as is commonly observed, and no defence among theologians is successful, how complete must be *his* victory who remains always, with all mankind, on the offensive, and has himself no fixed station or abiding city which he is ever, on any occasion, obliged to defend?

PART IX

But if so many difficulties attend the argument *a posteriori,* said Demea, had we not better adhere to that simple and sublime argument *a priori* which, by offering to us infallible demonstration, cuts off at once all doubt and difficulty? By this argument, too, we may prove the *infinity* of the Divine attributes, which, I am afraid, can never be ascertained with certainty from any other topic. For how can an effect which either is finite or, for aught we know, may be so—how can such an effect, I say, prove an infinite cause? The unity, too, of the Divine Nature it is very difficult, if not absolutely impossible, to deduce merely from contemplating the works of nature; nor will the uniformity alone of the plan, even were it allowed, give us any assurance of that attribute. Whereas the argument *a priori* . . .

You seem to reason, Demea, interposed Cleanthes, as if those advantages and conveniences in the abstract argument were full proofs of its solidity. But it is first proper, in my opinion, to determine what argument of this nature you choose to insist on; and we shall afterwards, from itself, better than from its *useful* consequences, endeavour to determine what value we ought to put upon it.

The argument, replied Demea, which I would insist on is the common one. Whatever exists must have a cause or reason of its existence, it being absolutely impossible for anything to produce itself or be the cause of its own existence. In mounting up, therefore, from effect to causes, we must either go on in tracing an infinite succession, without any ultimate cause at all, or must at least have recourse to some ultimate cause that is *necessarily* existent. Now that the first supposition is absurd may be thus proved. In the infinite chain or succession of causes and effects, each single effect is determined to exist by the power and efficacy of that cause which immediately preceded; but the whole eternal chain or succession, taken together, is not determined or caused by anything, and yet it is evident that it requires a cause or reason, as much as any particular object which begins to exist in time. The question is still reasonable why this particular succession of causes existed from eternity, and not any other succession or no succession at all. If there be no necessarily existent being, any supposition which can be formed is equally possible; nor is there any more absurdity in *nothing's* having existed from eternity than there is in that succession of causes which constitutes the universe. What was it, then, which determined *something* to exist rather than *nothing*, and bestowed being on a particular possibility, exclusive of the rest? *External causes*, there are supposed to be none. *Chance* is a word without a meaning. Was is *nothing?* But that can never produce anything. We must, therefore, have recourse to a necessarily existent Being who carries the *reason* of his existence in himself, and who cannot be supposed not to exist, without an express contradiction. There is, consequently, such a Being—that is, there is a Deity.

I shall not leave it to Philo, said Cleanthes, though I know that starting objections is his chief delight, to point out the weakness of this metaphysical reasoning. It seems to me so obviously ill-grounded, and at the same time of so little consequence to the cause of true piety and religion, that I shall myself venture to show the fallacy of it.

I shall begin with observing that there is an evident absurdity in pretending to demonstrate a matter of fact, or to prove it by arguments *a priori*. Nothing is demonstrable unless the contrary implies a contradiction. Nothing that is distinctly conceivable implies a contradiction. Whatever we conceive as existent, we can also conceive as non-existent. There is no being, therefore, whose non-existence implies a contradiction. Consequently there is no being whose existence is demonstrable. I propose this argument as entirely decisive, and am willing to rest the whole controversy upon it.

It is pretended that the Deity is a necessarily existent being; and this necessity of his existence is attempted to be explained by asserting that, if we knew his whole essence or nature, we should perceive it to be as impossible for him not to exist, as for twice two not to be four. But it is evident that this can never happen, while our faculties remain the same as at present. It will still be possible for us, at any time, to conceive the non-existence of what was formerly conceived to exist; nor can the mind ever lie under a necessity of supposing any object to remain always in being; in the same manner as we lie under a necessity of always conceiving twice two to be four. The words, therefore, *necessary existence* have no meaning or, which is the same thing, none that is consistent.

But further, why may not the material universe be the necessarily existent Being, according to this pretended explication of necessity? We dare not affirm that we know all the qualities of matter; and, for aught we can determine, it may contain some qualities which, were they known, would make its non-existence appear as great a contradiction as that twice two is five. I find only one argument employed to prove that the material world is not the necessarily existent Being; and this argument is derived from the contingency both of the matter and the form of the world. "Any particle of matter," it is said, "may be *conceived* to be annihilated, and any form may be *conceived* to be altered. Such an annihilation or alteration, therefore, is not impossible."[4] But it seems a great partiality not to perceive that the same argument extends equally to the Deity, so far as we have any conception of him, and that the mind can at least imagine him to be non-existent or his attributes to be altered. It must be some unknown, inconceivable qualities which can make his non-existence appear impossible or his attributes unalterable; and no reason can be assigned why these qualities may not belong to matter. As they are altogether unknown and inconceivable, they can never be proved incompatible with it.

Add to this that in tracing an eternal succession of objects it seems absurd to inquire for a general cause or first author. How can anything that exists from eternity have a cause, since that relation implies a priority in time and a beginning of existence?

In such a chain, too, or succession of objects, each part is caused by that which preceded

4. Dr. Clarke [Samuel Clarke, the rationalist theologian (1675–1729)].

it, and causes that which succeeds it. Where then is the difficulty? But the *whole,* you say, wants a cause. I answer that the uniting of several distinct countries into one kingdom, or several distinct members into one body is performed merely by an arbitrary act of the mind, and has no influence on the nature of things. Did I show you the particular causes of each individual in a collection of twenty particles of matter, I should think it very unreasonable should you afterwards ask me what was the cause of the whole twenty. This is sufficiently explained in explaining the cause of the parts.

Though the reasonings which you have urged, Cleanthes, may well excuse me, said Philo, from starting any further difficulties, yet I cannot forbear insisting still upon another topic. It is observed by arithmeticians that the products of 9 compose always either 9 or some lesser product of 9 if you add together all the characters of which any of the former products is composed. Thus, of 18, 27, 36, which are products of 9, you make 9 by adding 1 to 8, 2 to 7, 3 to 6. Thus 369 is a product also of 9; and if you add 3, 6, and 9, you make 18, a lesser product of 9.[5] To a superficial observer so wonderful a regularity may be admired as the effect either of chance or design; but a skillful algebraist immediately concludes it to be the work of necessity, and demonstrates that it must for ever result from the nature of these numbers. Is it not probable, I ask, that the whole economy of the universe is conducted by a like necessity, though no human algebra can furnish a key which solves the difficulty? And instead of admiring the order of natural beings, may it not happen that, could we penetrate into the intimate nature of bodies, we should clearly see why it was absolutely impossible they could ever admit of any other disposition? So dangerous is it to introduce this idea of necessity into the present question! and so naturally does it afford an inference directly opposite to the religious hypothesis!

5. *Republique des Lettres,* Aut 1685.

But dropping all these abstractions, continued Philo, and confining ourselves to more familiar topics, I shall venture to add an observation that the argument *a priori* has seldom been found very convincing, except to people of a metaphysical head who have accustomed themselves to abstract reasoning, and who, finding from mathematics that the understanding frequently leads to truth through obscurity, and contrary to first appearances, have transferred the same habit of thinking to subjects where it ought not to have place. Other people, even of good sense and the best inclined to religion, feel always some deficiency in such arguments, though they are not perhaps able to explain distinctly where it lies—a certain proof that men ever did and ever will derive their religion from other sources than from this species of reasoning.

PART X

It is my opinion, I own, replied Demea, that each man feels, in a manner, the truth of religion within his own breast, and, from a consciousness of his imbecility and misery rather than from any reasoning, is led to seek protection from that Being on whom he and all nature is dependent. So anxious or so tedious are even the best scenes of life that futurity is still the object of all our hopes and fears. We incessantly look forward and endeavor, by prayers, adoration, and sacrifice, to appease those unknown powers whom we find, by experience, so able to afflict and oppress us. Wretched creatures that we are! What resource for us amidst the innumerable ills of life did not religion suggest some methods of atonement, and appease those terrors with which we are incessantly agitated and tormented?

I am indeed persuaded, said Philo, that the best and indeed the only method of bringing everyone to a due sense of religion is by just representations of the misery and wickedness of men. And for that purpose a talent of eloquence and strong imagery is more requisite than that of reasoning and argument. For is it necessary to prove what everyone feels within himself? It is only necessary to make us feel it, if possible, more intimately and sensibly.

The people, indeed, replied Demea, are sufficiently convinced of this great and melancholy truth. The miseries of life, the unhappiness of man, the general corruptions of our nature, the unsatisfactory enjoyment of pleasures, riches, honours—these phrases have become almost proverbial in all languages. And who can doubt of what all men declare from their own immediate feeling and experience?

In this point, said Philo, the learned are perfectly agreed with the vulgar; and in all letters, *sacred* and *profane,* the topic of human misery has been insisted on with the most pathetic eloquence that sorrow and melancholy could inspire. The poets, who speak from sentiment, without a system, and whose testimony has therefore the more authority, abound in images of this nature. From Homer down to Dr. Young, the whole inspired tribe have ever been sensible that no other representation of things would suit the feeling and observation of each individual.

As to authorities, replied Demea, you need not seek them. Look round this library of Cleanthes. I shall venture to affirm that, except authors of particular sciences, such as chemistry or botany, who have no occasion to treat of human life, there is scarce one of those innumerable writers from whom the sense of human misery has not, in some passage or other, extorted a complaint and confession of it. At least, the chance is entirely on that side; and no one author has ever, so far as I can recollect, been so extravagant as to deny it.

There you must excuse me, said Philo: Leibniz has denied it, and is perhaps the first[6] who ventured upon so bold and paradoxical an opinion; at least, the first who made it essential to his philosophical system.

And by being the first, replied Demea, might he not have been sensible of his error? For is this a subject in which philosophers can propose to make discoveries especially in so late an age? And can any man hope by a simple denial (for the subject scarcely admits of reasoning) to bear down the united testimony of mankind, founded on sense and consciousness?

And why should man, added he, pretend to an exemption from the lot of all other animals? The whole earth, believe me, Philo, is cursed and polluted. A perpetual war is kindled amongst all living creatures. Necessity, hunger, want stimulate the strong and courageous; fear, anxiety, terror agitate the weak and infirm. The first entrance into life gives anguish to the new-born infant and to its wretched parent; weakness, impotence, distress attend each stage of that life, and it is, at last finished in agony and horror.

Observe, too, says Philo, the curious artifices of nature in order to embitter the life of every living being. The stronger prey upon the weaker and keep them in perpetual terror and anxiety. The weaker, too, in their turn, often prey upon the stronger, and vex and molest them without relaxation. Consider that innumerable race of insects, which either are bred on the body of each animal or, flying about, infix their stings in him. These insects have others still less than themselves which torment them. And thus on each hand, before and behind, above and below, every animal is surrounded with enemies which incessantly seek his misery and destruction.

Man alone, said Demea, seems to be, in part, an exception to this rule. For by combination in society he can easily master lions, tigers, and bears, whose greater strength and agility naturally enable them to prey upon him.

On the contrary, it is here chiefly, cried Philo, that the uniform and equal maxims of nature are most apparent. Man, it is true, can, by combination, surmount all his *real* enemies and become master of the whole animal creation; but does he not immediately raise up to himself *imaginary* enemies, the demons of his fancy, who haunt him with superstitious terrors

6. That sentiment had been maintained by Dr. King and some few others before Leibniz, though by none of so great fame as that German philosopher.

and blast every enjoyment of life? His pleasure, as he imagines, becomes in their eyes a crime; his food and repose give them umbrage and offence; his very sleep and dreams furnish new materials to anxious fear; and even death, his refuge from every other ill, presents only the dread of endless and innumerable woes. Nor does the wolf molest more the timid flock than superstition does the anxious breast of wretched mortals.

Besides, consider, Demea: This very society by which we surmount those wild beasts, our natural enemies, what new enemies does it not raise to us? What woe and misery does it not occasion? Man is the greatest enemy of man. Oppression, injustice, contempt, contumely, violence, sedition, war, calumny, treachery, fraud—by these they mutually torment each other, and they would soon dissolve that society which they had formed were it not for the dread of still greater ills which must attend their separation.

But though these external insults, said Demea, from animals, from men, from all the elements, which assault us from a frightful catalogue of woes, they are nothing in comparison of those which arise within ourselves, from the distempered condition of our mind and body. How many lie under the lingering torment of disease? Here the pathetic enumeration of the great poet.

> Intestine stone and ulcer, colic-pangs,
> Demoniac frenzy, moping melancholy,
> And moon-struck madness, pining atrophy
> Marasmus, and wide-wasting pestilence.
> Dire was the tossing, deep the groans: *Despair*
> Tended the sick, busiest from couch to couch
> And over them triumphant *Death* his dart
> Shook: but delay'd to strike, though oft invok'd
> With vows, as their chief good and final hope.[7]

The disorders of the mind, continued Demea, though more secret, are not perhaps less dismal and vexatious. Remorse, shame, anguish, rage, disappointment, anxiety, fear, dejection, despair—who has ever passed through life without cruel inroads from these tormentors? How many have scarcely ever felt any better sensations? Labour and poverty, so abhorred by everyone, are the certain lot of the far greater number; and those few privileged persons who enjoy ease and opulence never reach contentment or true felicity. All the goods of life united would not make a very happy man, but all the ills united would make a wretch indeed; and any one of them almost (and who can be free from every one?), nay, often the absence of one good (and who can possess all?) is sufficient to render life ineligible.

Were a stranger to drop on a sudden into this world, I would show him, as a specimen of its ills, an hospital full of diseases, a prison crowded with malefactors and debtors, a field of battle strewed with carcases, a fleet floundering in the ocean, a nation languishing under tyranny, famine, or pestilence. To turn the gay side of life to him and give him a notion of its pleasures—whither should I conduct him? To a ball, to an opera, to court? He might justly think that I was only showing him a diversity of distress and sorrow.

There is no evading such striking instances, said Philo, but by apologies which still further aggravate the charge. Why have all men, I ask, in all ages, complained incessantly of the miseries of life? . . . They have no just reason, says one: these complaints proceed only from their discontented, repining, anxious disposition. . . . And can there possibly, I reply, be a more certain foundation of misery than such a wretched temper?

But if they were really as unhappy as they pretend, says my antagonist, why do they remain in life? . . .

> Not satisfied with life, afraid of death—

This is the secret chain, say I, that holds us. We are terrified, not bribed to the continuance of our existence.

It is only a false delicacy, he may insist, which a few refined spirits indulge, and which

7. Milton: *Paradise Lost,* Bk. XI.

has spread these complaints among the whole race of mankind. . . . And what is this delicacy, I ask, which you blame? Is it anything but a greater sensibility to all the pleasures and pains of life? And if the man of a delicate, refined temper, by being so much more alive than the rest of the world, is only so much more unhappy, what judgment must we form in general of human life?

Let me remain at rest, says our adversary, and they will be easy. They are willing artificers of their own misery. . . . No! reply I: an anxious languor follows their repose; disappointment, vexation, trouble, their activity and ambition.

I can observe something like what you mention in some others, replied Cleanthes, but I confess I feel little or nothing of it in myself, and hope that it is not so common as you represent it.

If you feel not human misery yourself, cried Demea, I congratulate you on so happy a singularity. Others, seemingly the most prosperous, have not been ashamed to vent their complaints in the most melancholy strains. Let us attend to the great, the fortunate emperor, Charles V, when tired with human grandeur, he resigned all his extensive dominions into the hands of his son. In the last harangue which he made on that memorable occasion, he publicly avowed *that the greatest prosperities which he had ever enjoyed had been mixed with so many adversities that he might truly say he had never enjoyed any satisfaction or contentment.* But did the retired life in which he sought for shelter afford him any greater happiness? If we may credit his son's account, his repentance commenced the very day of his resignation.

Cicero's fortune, from small beginnings, rose to the greatest lustre and renown; yet what pathetic complaints of the ills of life do his familiar letters, as well as philosophical discourses, contain? And suitably to his own experience, he introduces Cato, the great, the fortunate Cato protesting in his old age that had he a new life in his offer he would reject the present.

Ask yourself, ask any of your acquaintance, whether they would live over again the last ten or twenty years of their life. No! but the next twenty, they say, will be better:

> And from the dregs of life, hope to receive
> What the first sprightly running could not give.[8]

Thus, at last, they find (such is the greatness of human misery, it reconciles even contradictions) that they complain at once of the shortness of life and of its vanity and sorrow.

And it is possible, Cleanthes, said Philo, that after all these reflections, and infinitely more which might be suggested, you can still persevere in your anthropomorphism, and assert the moral attributes of the Deity, his justice, benevolence, mercy, and rectitude, to be of the same nature with these virtues in human creatures? His power, we allow, is infinite; whatever he wills is executed; but neither man nor any other animal is happy; therefore, he does not will their happiness. His wisdom is infinite; he is never mistaken in choosing the means to any end; but the course of nature tends not to human or animal felicity; therefore, it is not established for that purpose. Through the whole compass of human knowledge there are no inferences more certain and infallible than these. In what respect, then, do his benevolence and mercy resemble the benevolence and mercy of men?

Epicurus' old questions are yet unanswered.

"Is he willing to prevent evil, but not able? then is he impotent. Is he able, but not willing? then is he malevolent. Is he both able and willing? whence then is evil?"

You ascribe, Cleanthes (and I believe justly), a purpose and intention to nature. But what, I beseech you, is the object of that curious artifice and machinery which she has displayed in all animals—the preservation alone of individuals, and propagation of the species? It seems enough for her purpose, if such a rank be barely upheld in the universe, without any care or concern for

8. John Dryden, *Aureng-Zebe,* Act IV, sc. 1.

the happiness of the members that compose it. No resource for this purpose: no machinery in order merely to give pleasure or ease; no fund of pure joy and contentment; no indulgence without some want or necessity accompanying it. At least, the few phenomena of this nature are overbalanced by opposite phenomena of still greater importance.

Our sense of music, harmony, and indeed beauty of all kinds, gives satisfaction, without being absolutely necessary to the preservation and propagation of the species. But what racking pains, on the other hand, arise from gouts, gravels, megrims, toothaches, rheumatisms, where the injury to the animal machinery is either small or incurable? Mirth, laughter, play, frolic seem gratuitous satisfactions which have no further tendency; spleen, melancholy, discontent, superstition are pains of the same nature. How then does the Divine benevolence display itself, in the sense of you anthropomorphites? None but we mystics, as you were pleased to call us, can account for this strange mixture of phenomena, by deriving it from attributes infinitely perfect but incomprehensible.

And have you, at last, said Cleanthes smiling, betrayed your intentions, Philo? Your long agreement with Demea did indeed a little surprise me, but I find you were all the while erecting a concealed battery against me. And I must confess that you have now fallen upon a subject worthy of your noble spirit of opposition and controversy. If you can make out the present point, and prove mankind to be unhappy or corrupted, there is an end at once of all religion. For to what purpose establish the natural attributes of the Deity, while the moral are still doubtful and uncertain?

You take umbrage very easily, replied Demea, at opinions the most innocent and the most generally received, even amongst the religious and devout themselves; and nothing can be more

"The Endemic Evil of Theological Utterance"

Antony Flew

Once upon a time two explorers came upon a clearing in the jungle. In the clearing were growing many flowers and many weeds. One explorer says, 'Some gardener must tend this plot.' The other disagrees, 'There is no gardener.' So they pitch their tents and set a watch. No gardener is ever seen. 'But perhaps he is an invisible gardener.' So they set up a barbed-wire fence. They electrify it. They patrol with bloodhounds. (For they remember how H. G. Wells's *The Invisible Man* could be both smelt and touched though he could not be seen.) But no shrieks ever suggest that some intruder has received a shock. No movements of the wire ever betray an invisible climber. The bloodhounds never give cry. Yet still the Believer is not convinced. 'But there is a gardener, invisible, intangible, insensible to electric shock, a gardener who has no scent and makes no sound, a gardener who comes secretly to look after the garden which he loves.' At last the Sceptic despairs, 'But what remains of your original assertion? Just how does what you call an invisible, intangible, eternally elusive gardener differ from an imaginary gardener or even from no gardener at all?'

In this parable we can see how what starts as an assertion, that something exists or that there is some analogy between certain complexes of phenomena, may be reduced step by step to an altogether different status. . . . Someone may dissipate his assertion completely without noticing that he has done so. A fine brash hypothesis may thus be killed by inches, the death by a thousand qualifications.

And in this, it seems to me, lies the peculiar danger, the endemic evil, of theological utterance.

From Antony Flew, "Theology and Falsification," *University*, 1950–51.

surprising than to find a topic like this—concerning the wickedness and misery of man—charged with no less than atheism and profaneness. Have not all pious divines and preachers who have indulged their rhetoric on so fertile a subject, have they not easily, I say, given a solution of any difficulties which may attend it? This world is but a point in comparison of the universe; this life but a moment in comparison of eternity. The present evil phenomena, therefore, are rectified in other regions, and in some future period of existence. And the eyes of men, being then opened to larger views of things, see the whole connection of general laws, and trace, with adoration, and benevolence and rectitude of the Deity through all the mazes and intricacies of his providence.

No! replied Cleanthes, no! These arbitrary suppositions can never be admitted, contrary to matter of fact, visible and uncontroverted. Whence can any cause be known but from its known effects? Whence can any hypothesis be proved but from the apparent phenomena? To establish one hypothesis upon another is building entirely in the air; and the utmost we ever attain by these conjectures and fictions is to ascertain the bare possibility of our opinion, but never can we, upon such terms, establish its reality.

The only method of supporting Divine benevolence—and it is what I willingly embrace—is to deny absolutely the misery and wickedness of man. Your representations are exaggerated; your melancholy views mostly fictitious; your inferences contrary to fact and experience. Health is more common than sickness; pleasure than pain; happiness than misery. And for one vexation which we meet with, we attain, upon computation, a hundred enjoyments.

Admitting your position, replied Philo, which yet is extremely doubtful, you must at the same time allow that, if pain be less frequent than pleasure, it is infinitely more violent and durable. One hour of it is often able to outweigh a day, a week, a month of our common insipid enjoyments; and how many days, weeks, and months are passed by several in the most acute torments? Pleasure, scarcely in one instance, is ever able to reach ecstasy and rapture; and in no one instance can it continue for any time at its highest pitch and altitude. The spirits evaporate, the nerves relax, the fabric is disordered, and the enjoyment quickly degenerates into fatigue and uneasiness. But pain often, good God, how often! rises to torture and agony; and the longer it continues, it becomes still more genuine agony and torture. Patience is exhausted, courage languishes, melancholy seizes us, and nothing terminates our misery but the removal of its cause or another event which is the sole cure of all evil, but which, from our natural folly, we regard with still greater horror and consternation.

But not to insist upon these topics, continued Philo, though most obvious, certain, and important, I must use the freedom to admonish you, Cleanthes, that you have put the controversy upon a most dangerous issue, and are unawares introducing a total scepticism into the most essential articles of natural and revealed theology. What! no method of fixing a just foundation for religion unless we allow the happiness of human life, and maintain a continued existence even in this world, with all our present pains, infirmities, vexations, and follies, to be eligible and desirable! But this is contrary to everyone's feeling and experience; it is contrary to an authority so established as nothing can subvert. No decisive proofs can ever be produced against this authority; nor is it possible for you to compute, estimate, and compare all the pains and all the pleasures in the lives of all men and of all animals; and thus, by your resting the whole system of religion on a point which, from its very nature, must for ever be uncertain, you tacitly confess that that system is equally uncertain.

But allowing you what never will be believed, at least, what you never possibly can prove, that animal or, at least, human happiness in this life exceeds its misery, you have yet done nothing; for this is not, by any means, what we expect from infinite power, infinite wisdom, and infinite goodness. Why is there any misery at all in the world? Not by chance, surely. From some cause then. Is it from the intention of the Deity? But he is perfectly benevolent. Is it contrary to his intention? But he is almighty. Nothing can shake the solidity of this reasoning, so short, so clear, so decisive, except we assert that these subjects exceed all human capacity, and that our common measures of truth and falsehood are not applicable to them—a topic which I have all along insisted on, but which you have, from the beginning, rejected with scorn and indignation.

But I will be contented to retire still from this intrenchment, for I deny that you can ever force me in it. I will allow that pain or misery in man is *compatible* with infinite power and goodness in the Deity, even in your sense of these attributes: what are you advanced by all these concessions? A mere possible compatibility is not sufficient. You must *prove* these pure, unmixt, and uncontrollable attributes from the present mixt and confused phenomena, and from these alone. A hopeful undertaking! Were the phenomena ever so pure and unmixt, yet, being finite, they would be insufficient for that purpose. How much more, where they are also so jarring and discordant!

Here, Cleanthes, I find myself at ease in my argument. Here I triumph. Formerly, when we argued concerning the natural attributes of intelligence and design, I needed all my sceptical and metaphysical subtilty to elude your grasp. In many views of the universe and of its parts, particularly the matter, the beauty and fitness of final causes strike us with such irresistible force that all objections appear (what I believe they really are) mere cavils and sophisms; nor can we then imagine how it was ever possible for us to repose any weight on them. But there is no view of human life or the condition of mankind from which, without the greatest violence, we can infer the moral attributes or learn that infinite benevolence, conjoined with infinite power and infinite wisdom, which we must discover by the eyes of faith alone. It is your turn now to tug the labouring oar, and to support your philosophical subtilties against the dictates of plain reason and experience.

PART XI

I scruple not to allow, said Cleanthes, that I have been apt to suspect the frequent repetition of the word *infinite,* which we meet with in all theological writers, to savour more of panegyric than of philosophy, and that any purposes of reasoning, and even of religion, would be better served were we to rest contented with more accurate and more moderate expressions. The terms *admirable, excellent, superlatively great, wise,* and *holy*—these sufficiently fill the imaginations of men, and anything beyond, besides that it leads into absurdities, has no influence on the affections or sentiments. Thus, in thy present subject, if we abandon all human analogy, as seems your intention, Demea, I am afraid we abandon all religion and retain no conception of the great object of our adoration. If we preserve human analogy, we must forever find it impossible to reconcile any mixture of evil in the universe with infinite attributes; much less can we ever prove the latter from the former. But supposing the Author of nature to be finitely perfect, though far exceeding mankind, a satisfactory account may then be given of natural and moral evil, and every untoward phenomenon be explained and adjusted. A less evil may then be chosen in order to avoid a greater; inconveniences be submitted to in order to reach a desirable end; and, in a word, benevolence, regulated by wisdom and limited by necessity, may produce just such a world as the present. You, Philo, who are so prompt at starting views and reflections and analogies, I would gladly hear, at length, without interruption, your opinion of this new theory; and if it deserve our attention, we may afterwards, at more leisure, reduce it into form.

My sentiments, replied Philo, are not worth being made a mystery of; and, therefore, without any ceremony, I shall deliver what occurs to me with regard to the present subject. I must, I think, be allowed that, if a very limited intelligence whom we shall suppose utterly unacquainted with the universe were assured that it were the production of a very good, wise, and powerful Being, however finite, he would, from his conjectures, form *beforehand* a different notion of it from what we find it to be by experience; nor would he ever imagine, merely from these attributes of the cause of which he is informed, that the effect could be so full of vice and misery and disorder, as it appears in this life. Supposing now that this person were brought into the world, still assured that it was the workmanship of such a sublime and benevolent Being, he might, perhaps, be surprised at the disappointment, but would never retract his former belief if founded on any very solid argument, since such a limited intelligence must be sensible of his own blindness and ignorance, and must allow that there may be many solutions of those phenomena which will for ever escape his comprehension. But supposing, which is the real case with regard to man, that this creature is not antecedently convinced of a supreme intelligence, benevolent, and powerful, but is left to gather such a belief from the appearances of things—this entirely alters the case, nor will he ever find any reason for such a conclusion. He may be fully convinced of the narrow limits of his understanding, but this will not help him in forming an inference concerning the goodness of superior powers, since he must form that inference from what he knows, not from what he is ignorant of. The more you exaggerate his weakness and ignorance, the more diffident you render him, and give him the greater suspicion that such subjects are beyond the reach of his faculties. You are obliged, therefore, to reason with him merely from the known phenomena, and to drop every arbitrary supposition or conjecture.

Did I show you a house or palace where there was not one apartment convenient or agreeable, where the windows, doors, fires, passages, stairs, and the whole economy of the building were the source of noise, confusion, fatigue, darkness, and the extremes of heat and cold, you would certainly blame the contrivance, without any further examination. The architect would in vain display his subtilty, and prove to you that, if this door or that window were altered, greater ills would ensue. What he says may be strictly true: the alteration of one particular, while the other parts of the building remain, may only augment the inconveniences. But still you would assert in general that, if the architect had had skill and good intentions, he might have formed such a plan of the whole, and might have adjusted the parts in such a manner as would have remedied all or most of these inconveniences. His ignorance, or even your own ignorance of such a plan, will never convince you of the impossibility of it. If you find any inconveniences and deformities in the building, you will always, without entering into any detail, condemn the architect.

In short, I repeat the question: Is the world, considered in general and as it appears to us in this life, different from what a man or such a limited being would, *beforehand,* expect from a very powerful, wise, and benevolent Deity? It must be strange prejudice to assert the contrary. And from thence I conclude that, however consistent the world may be, allowing certain suppositions and conjectures with the idea of such a Deity, it can never afford us an inference concerning his existence. The consistency is not absolutely denied, only the inference. Conjectures, especially where infinity is excluded from the Divine attributes, may perhaps be sufficient to prove a consistency, but can never be foundations from any inference.

There seem to be *four* circumstances on which depend all or the greatest part of the ills that molest sensible creatures; and it is not impossible but all these circumstances may be necessary and unavoidable. We know so little beyond common life, or even of common life, that, with regard to the economy of a universe, there is no conjecture, however wild, which may not be just, nor any one, however plausible, which may not be erroneous. All that belongs to human understanding, in this deep ignorance and obscurity, is to be sceptical or at least cautious, and not to admit of any hypothesis whatever, much less of any which is supported by no appearance of probability. Now this I assert to be the case with regard to all the causes of evil and the circumstances on which it depends. None of them appear to human reason in the least degree necessary or unavoidable, nor can we suppose them such, without the utmost license of imagination.

The *first* circumstance which introduces evil is that contrivance or economy of the animal creation by which pains, as well as pleasures, are employed to excite all creatures to action, and make them vigilant in the great work of self-preservation. Now pleasure alone, in its various degrees, seems to human understanding sufficient for this purpose. All animals might be constantly in a state of enjoyment; but when urged by any of the necessities of nature, such as thirst, hunger, weariness, instead of pain, they might feel a diminution of pleasure by which they might be prompted to seek that object which is necessary to their subsistence. Men pursue pleasure as eagerly as they avoid pain; at least, they might have been so constituted. It seems, therefore, plainly possible to carry on the business of life without any pain. Why then is any animal ever rendered susceptible of such a sensation? If animals can be free from it an hour, they might enjoy a perpetual exemption from it, and it required as particular a contrivance of their organs to produce that feeling as to endow them with sight, hearing, or any of the senses. Shall we conjecture that such a contrivance was necessary, without any appearance of reason, and shall we build on that conjecture as on the most certain truth?

But a capacity of pain would not alone produce pain were it not for the *second* circumstance, viz., the conducting of the world by general laws; and this seems nowise necessary to a very perfect Being. It is true, if everything were conducted by particular volitions, the course of nature would be perpetually broken, and no man could employ his reason in the conduct of life. But might not other particular volitions remedy this inconvenience? In short, might not the Deity exterminate all ill, wherever it were to be found, and produce all good, without any preparation or long progress of causes and effects?

Besides, we must consider that, according to the present economy of the world, the course of nature, though supposed exactly regular, yet to us appears not so, and many events are uncertain, and many disappoint our expectations. Health and sickness, calm and tempest, with an infinite number of other accidents whose causes are unknown and variable, have a great influence both on the fortunes of particular persons and on the prosperity of public societies; and indeed all human life, in a manner, depends on such accidents. A being, therefore, who knows the secret springs of the universe might easily, by particular volitions, turn all these accidents to the good of mankind and render the whole world happy, without discovering himself in any operation. A fleet whose purposes were salutary to society might always meet with a fair wind. Good princes enjoy sound health and long life. Persons born to power and authority be framed with good tempers and virtuous dispositions. A few such events as these, regularly and wisely conducted, would change the face of the world, and yet would no more seem to disturb the course of nature or confound human conduct than the present economy of things where the causes are secret and variable and compounded. Some small touches given to Caligula's brain in his infancy might have converted him into a Trajan. One wave, a little higher than the rest, by burying Caesar and his fortune in the bottom of the ocean, might have restored liberty to a considerable part of mankind. There may, for aught we know, be good reasons why Providence interposes not in this manner, but they are unknown to us; and, though the mere supposition that such reasons exist may be sufficient to *save* the conclusion concerning the Divine attributes, yet surely it can never be sufficient to *establish* that conclusion.

If everything in the universe be conducted by general laws, and if animals be rendered susceptible of pain, it scarcely seems possible but some ill must arise in the various shocks of matter and the various concurrence and opposition of general laws; but this ill would be very rare were it not for the *third* circumstance which I proposed to mention, viz., the great frugality with which all powers and faculties are distributed to every particular being. So well adjusted are the organs and capacities of all animals, and so well fitted to their preservation, that, as far as history or tradition reaches, there appears not to be any single species which has yet been extinguished in the universe. Every animal has the requisite endowments, but these endowments are bestowed with so scrupulous an economy that any considerable diminution must entirely destroy the creature. Wherever one power is increased, there is a proportional abatement in the others. Animals which excel in swiftness are commonly defective in force. Those which possess both are either imperfect in some of their senses or are oppressed with the most craving wants. The human species, whose chief excellence is reason and sagacity, is of all others the most necessitous, and the most deficient in bodily advantages, without clothes, without arms, without food, without lodging, without any convenience of life, except what they owe to their own skill and industry. In short, nature seems to have formed an exact calculation of the necessities of her creatures, and, like a *rigid master,* has afforded them little more powers or endowments than what are strictly sufficient to supply those necessities. An *indulgent parent* would have bestowed a large stock in order to guard against accidents, and secure the happiness and welfare of the creature in the most unfortunate concurrence of circumstances. Every course of life would not have been so surrounded with precipices that the least departure from the true path, by mistake or necessity, must involve us in misery and ruin. Some reserve, some fund, would have been provided to ensure happiness, nor would the powers and the necessities have been adjusted with so rigid an economy. The Author of nature is inconceivably powerful; his force is supposed great, if not altogether inexhaustible, nor is there any reason, as far as we can judge, to make him observe this strict frugality in his dealings with his creatures. It would have been better, were his power extremely limited, to have created fewer animals, and to have endowed these with more faculties for their happiness and preservation. A builder is never esteemed prudent who undertakes a plan beyond what his stock will enable him to finish.

In order to cure most of the ills of human life, I require not that man should have the wings of the eagle, the swiftness of the stag, the force of the ox, the arms of the lion, the scales of the crocodile or rhinoceros; much less do I demand the sagacity of an angel or cherubim. I am contented to take an increase in one single power or faculty of his soul. Let him be endowed with a greater propensity to industry and labour, a more vigorous spring and activity of mind, a more constant bent to business and application. Let the whole species possess naturally an equal diligence, with that which many individuals are able to attain by habit and reflection, and the most beneficial consequences, without any allay of ill, is the immediate and necessary result of this endowment. Almost all the moral as well as natural evils of human life arise from idleness; and were our species, by the original constitution of their frame, exempt from this vice or infirmity, the perfect cultivation of land, the improvement of arts and manufactures, the exact execution of every office and duty, immediately follow; and men at once may fully reach that state of society which is so imperfectly attained by the best regulated government. But as industry is a power, and the most valuable of any, nature seems determined, suitably to her usual maxims, to bestow it on man with a very sparing hand, and rather to punish him severely for his deficiency in it than to reward him for his attainments. She has so contrived his frame that nothing but the most violent necessity can oblige him to labour; and she employs all his other wants to overcome, at least in part, the want of diligence, and to endow him with some share of a faculty of which she has thought fit naturally to bereave him. Here our demands may be allowed very humble, and therefore the more reasonable. If we required the endowments of superior penetration and judgment, of a more delicate taste of beauty, of a nicer sensibility to benevolence and friendship, we might be told that we impiously pretend to break the order of nature, that we want to exalt ourselves into a higher rank of being, that the presents which we require, not being suitable to our state and condition, would only be pernicious to us. But it is hard, I dare to repeat it, it is hard that, being placed in a world so full of wants and necessities, where almost every being and element is either our foe or refuses its assistance . . . we should also have our own temper to struggle with, and should be deprived of that faculty which can alone fence against these multiplied evils.

The *fourth* circumstance whence arises the misery and ill of the universe is the inaccurate workmanship of all the springs and principles of the great machine of nature. It must be acknowledged that there are few parts of the universe which seem not to serve some purpose, and whose removal would not produce a visible defect and disorder in the whole. The parts hang all together, nor can one be touched without affecting the rest, in a greater or less degree. But at the same time, it must be observed that none of these parts or principles, however useful, are so accurately adjusted as to keep precisely within those bounds in which their utility consists; but they are, all of them, apt, on every occasion, to run into the one extreme or the other. One would imagine that this grand production had not received the last hand of the maker—so little finished is every part, and so coarse are the strokes with which it is executed. Thus the winds are requisite to convey the vapours along the surface of the globe, and to assist men in navigation; but how often, rising up to tempests and hurricanes, do they become pernicious? Rains are necessary to nourish all the plants and animals of the earth; but how often are they defective? how often excessive? Heat is requisite to all life and vegetation, but is not always found in the due proportion. On the mixture and secretion of the humours and juices of the body depend the health and prosperity of the animal; but the parts perform not regularly their proper function. What more useful than all the passions of the mind, ambition, vanity, love, anger? But how often do they break their bounds and cause the greatest convulsions in society? There is nothing so advantageous in the universe but what frequently becomes pernicious, by its excess or defect; nor has nature guarded, with the requisite accuracy, against all disorder or confusion. The irregularity is never perhaps so great as to destroy any species, but is often sufficient to involve the individuals in ruin and misery.

On the concurrence, then, of these *four* circumstances does all or the greatest part of natural evil depend. Were all living creatures incapable of pain, or were the world administered by particular volitions, evil never could have found access into the universe; and were animals endowed with a large stock of powers and faculties, beyond what strict necessity requires, or were the several springs and principles of the universe so accurately framed as to preserve always the just temperament and medium, there must have been very little ill in comparison of what we feel at present. What then shall we pronounce on this occasion? Shall we say that these circumstances are not necessary, and that they might easily have been altered in the contrivance of the universe? This decision seems too presumptuous for creatures so blind and ignorant. Let us be more modest in our conclusions. Let us allow that, if the goodness of the Deity (I mean a goodness like the human) could be established on any tolerable reasons *a priori,* these phenomena, however untoward, would not be sufficient to subvert that principle, but might easily, in some unknown manner, be reconcilable to it. But let us still assert that, as this goodness is not antecedently established but must be inferred from the phenomena, there can be no grounds for such an inference while there are so many ills in the universe, and while these ills might so easily have been remedied, as far as human understanding can be allowed to judge on such a subject, I am sceptic enough to allow that the bad appearances, notwithstanding all my reasonings, may be compatible with such attributes as you suppose, but surely they can never prove these attributes. Such a conclusion cannot result from scepticism, but must arise from the phenomena, and from our confidence in the reasonings which we deduce from these phenomena.

Look round this universe. What an immense profusion of beings, animated and organized, sensible and active! You admire this prodigious variety and fecundity. But inspect a little more narrowly these living existences, the only beings worth regarding. How hostile and destructive to each other! How insufficient all of them for their own happiness! How contemptible or odious to the spectator! The whole presents nothing but the idea of a blind nature, impregnated by a great vivifying principle, and pouring forth from her lap, without discernment or parental care, her maimed and abortive children!

Here the Manichaean system occurs as a proper hypothesis to solve the difficulty; and, no doubt, in some respects it is very specious and has more probability than the common hypothesis, by giving a plausible account of the strange mixture of good and ill which appears in life. But if we consider, on the other hand, the perfect uniformity and agreement of the parts of the universe, we shall not discover in it any marks of the combat of a malevolent with a benevolent being. There is indeed an opposition of pains and pleasures in the feelings of sensible creatures; but are not all the operations of nature carried on by an opposition of principles, of hot and cold, moist and dry, light and heavy? The true conclusion is that the original Source of all things is entirely indifferent to all these principles, and has no more regard to good above ill than to heat above cold, or to drought above moisture, or to light above heavy.

There may *four* hypotheses be framed concerning the first causes of the universe: that they are endowed with perfect goodness; that they have perfect malice; that they are opposite and have both goodness and malice; that they have neither goodness nor malice. Mixed phenomena can never prove the two former unmixed principles; and the uniformity and steadiness of general laws seem to oppose the third. The fourth, therefore, seems by far the most probable.

What I have said concerning natural evil will apply to moral with little or no variation; and we have no more reason to infer that the rectitude of the Supreme Being resembles human rectitude than that his benevolence resembles the human. Nay, it will be thought that we have still greater cause to exclude from him moral sentiments, such as we feel them, since moral evil, in the opinion of many, is much more predominant above moral good than natural evil above natural good.

But even though this should not be allowed, and though the virtue which is in mankind should be acknowledged much superior to the vice, yet, so long as there is any vice at all in the universe, it will very much puzzle you anthropomorphites how to account for it. You must assign a cause for it, without having recourse to the first cause. But as every effect must have a cause, and that cause another, you must either carry on the progression *in infinitum* or rest on that original principle, who is the ultimate cause of all things . . .

Hold! hold! cried Demea: Whither does your imagination hurry you? I joined in alliance with you in order to prove the incomprehensible nature of the Divine Being, and refute the principles of Cleanthes, who would measure everything by human rule and standard. But I now find you running into all the topics of the greatest libertines and infidels, and betraying that holy cause which you seemingly espoused. Are you secretly, then, a more dangerous enemy than Cleanthes himself?

And are you so late in perceiving it? replied Cleanthes. Believe me, Demea, your friend Philo, from the beginning, has been amusing himself at both our expense; and it must be confessed that the injudicious reasoning of our vulgar theology has given him but too just a handle of ridicule. The total infirmity of human reason, the absolute incomprehensibility of the Divine Nature, the great and universal misery, and still greater wickedness of men—these are strange topics, surely, to be so fondly cherished by orthodox divines and doctors. In ages of stupidity and ignorance, indeed, these principles may safely be espoused; and perhaps no views of things are more proper to promote superstition than such as encourage the blind amazement, the diffidence, and melancholy of mankind. But at present . . .

Blame not so much, interposed Philo, the ignorance of these reverend gentlemen. They know how to change their style with the times. Formerly, it was a most popular theological topic to maintain that human life was vanity and misery, and to exaggerate all the ills and pains which are incident to men. But of late years, divines, we find, begin to retract this position and maintain, though still with some hesitation, that there are more goods than evils, more pleasures than pains, even in this life. When religion stood entirely upon temper and education, it was thought proper to encourage melancholy, as, indeed, mankind never have recourse to superior powers so readily as in that disposition. But as men have now learned to form principles and to draw consequences, it is necessary to change the batteries, and to make use of such arguments as will endure at least some scrutiny and examination. This variation is the same (and from the same causes) with that which I formerly remarked with regard to scepticism.

Thus Philo continued to the last his spirit of opposition, and his censure of established opinions. But I could observe that Demea did not at all relish the latter part of the discourse; and he took occasion soon after, on some pretence or other, to leave the company.

PART II

Self, Freedom, and Immortality

Cemetery in Stuttgart, Germany.

Plato

"IMMORTALITY"

PLATO (427–347 B.C.), born to a prominent Athenian family, was Socrates' pupil and one of the most influential thinkers of all time. In addition to writing philosophy, poetry, and drama, Plato worked as a politician and was even a champion wrestler. After 399 B.C., when the democratic leaders of Athens sentenced Socrates to death, Plato left Athens and began writing his famous dialogues in which the protagonist is his beloved mentor; his *Apology*, *Crito*, and *Phaedo*, for instance, poignantly recount the trial, imprisonment, and death of Socrates. Twelve years later, in 387 B.C., Plato returned to Athens and founded the first university, which he named after the hero, Academus. It lasted more than a thousand years. Plato's other famous works include *Protagoras*, *Gorgias*, *Symposium*, *Republic*, *Phaedrus*, *Theaetetus*, *Parmenides*, *Sophist*, and *Timaeus*. Such was Plato's influence that philosopher Alfred North Whitehead has called the entire subsequent two thousand years of Western philosophy merely "a series of footnotes to Plato."

From *The Dialogues of Plato,* Benjamin Jowett trans., (London: The Clarendon Press, 1892), 64–68, 245–249, 614–15.

PHAEDO

And now, O my judges, I desire to prove to you that the real philosopher has reason to be of good cheer when he is about to die, and that after death he may hope to obtain the greatest good in the other world. And how this may be, Simmias and Cebes, I will endeavor to explain. For I deem that the true votary of philosophy is likely to be misunderstood by other men; they do not perceive that he is always pursuing death and dying; and if this be so, and he has had the desire of death all his life long, why when his time comes should he repine at that which he has been always pursuing and desiring?

'Have we not found,' they will say, 'a path of thought which seems to bring us and our argument to the conclusion, that while we are in the body, and while the soul is infected with the evils of the body, our desire will not be satisfied? and our desire is of the truth. For the body is a source of endless trouble to us by reason of the mere requirement of food; and is liable also to diseases which overtake and impede us in the search after true being: it fills us full of loves, and lusts, and fears, and fancies of all kinds, and endless foolery, and in fact, as men say, takes away from us the power of thinking at all. Whence come wars, and fightings, and factions? Whence but from the body and the lusts of the body? Wars are occasioned by the love of money, and money has to be acquired for the sake and in the service of the body; and by reason of all these impediments we have no time to give to philosophy; and, last and worst of all, even if we are at leisure and betake ourselves to some speculation, the body is always breaking in upon us, causing turmoil and confusion in our enquiries, and so amazing us that we are prevented from seeing the truth. It has been proved to us by experience that if we would have pure knowledge of anything we must be quit of the body—the soul in herself must behold things in themselves: and then we shall attain the wisdom which we desire, and of which we say that we are lovers; not while we live, but after death; for if while in company with the body, the soul cannot have pure knowledge, one of two things follows—either knowledge is not to be attained at all, or, if at all, after death. For then, and not till then, the soul will be parted from the body and exist in herself alone. In this present life, I reckon that we make the nearest approach to knowledge when we have the least possible intercourse or communion with the body, and are not surfeited with the bodily nature, but keep ourselves pure until the hour when God himself is pleased to release us. And thus having got rid of the foolishness of the body we shall be pure and hold converse with the pure, and know of ourselves the clear light everywhere, which is no other than the light of truth.' For the impure are not permitted to approach the pure. These are the sort of words, Simmias, which the true lovers of knowledge cannot help saying to one another, and thinking. You would agree, would you not?

Undoubtedly, Socrates.

But, O my friend, if this be true, there is great reason to hope that, going whither I go, when I have come to the end of my journey, I shall attain that which has been the pursuit of my life. And therefore I go on my way rejoicing, and not I only, but every other man who believes that his mind has been made ready and that he is in a manner purified.

Certainly, replied Simmias.

And what is purification but the separation of the soul from the body, as I was saying before; the habit of the soul gathering and collecting herself into herself from all sides out of the body; the dwelling in her own place alone, as in another life, so also in this, as far as she can;—the release of the soul from the chains of the body?

Very true, he said.

And this separation and release of the soul from the body is termed death?

To be sure, he said.

And the true philosophers, and they only are ever seeking to release the soul. Is not the separation and release of the soul from the body their especial study?

That is true.

And, as I was saying at first, there would be a ridiculous contradiction in men studying to live as nearly as they can in a state of death, and yet repining when it comes upon them.

Clearly.

And the true philosophers, Simmias, are always occupied in the practice of dying, wherefore also to them least of all men is death terrible. Look at the matter thus:—if they have been in every way the enemies of the body, and are wanting to be alone with the soul, when this desire of their is granted, how inconsistent would they be if they trembled and repined, instead of rejoicing at their departure to that place where, when they arrive, they hope to gain that which in life they desired—and this was wisdom—and at the same time to be rid of the company of their enemy. Many a man has been willing to go to the world below animated by the hope of seeing there an earthly love, or wife, or son, and conversing with them. And will he who is a true lover of wisdom, and is strongly persuaded in like manner that only in the world below he can worthily enjoy her, still repine at death? Will he not depart with joy? Surely he will, O my friend, if he be a true philosopher. For he will have a firm conviction that there, and there only, he can find wisdom in her purity. And if this be true, he would be very absurd, as I was saying, if he were afraid of death.

PHAEDRUS

The soul through all her being is immortal, for that which is ever in motion is immortal; but that which moves another and is moved by an-

The Origin of the Soul

According to many contemporary Christians, your self consists of a nonphysical, spiritual substance—an immaterial *soul*. Selves, by being *ensouled*, thus differ from mere physical matter, which is not thought to be the sort of thing that by itself—without a soul—can think, react intentionally to the surrounding environment, have desires, emotions, and so on. Souls, which are nonphysical and come directly from God, can. Thus, souls are not of this world but something placed into the body sometime between conception and birth. This spiritual self, or soul, shares the life of a body until the body dies. At death, a person's soul is liberated from bondage to this world and enters the hereafter, a heaven where it lives as a spiritual being for eternity.

Where did this curious view of souls come from? One major influence was ancient Greek philosophy. The earliest discussion of souls in Western philosophy occurs in Plato's *Phaedo*, a dialogue in which Socrates, on the day of his death, argues for the immortality of the soul partly on the grounds that it is not divisible and therefore not destructible. Only extended, bodily things, Socrates maintains, are divisible. The soul, he claims, is an indestructible, spiritual thing that is housed in the body throughout a lifetime and then released from the body upon death.

other, in ceasing to move ceases also to live. Only the self-moving, never leaving self, never ceases to move, and is the fountain and beginning of motion to all that moves besides. . . . all things must have a beginning. And therefore the self-moving is the beginning of motion; and this can neither be destroyed nor begotten, else the whole heavens and all creation would collapse and stand still, and never again have motion or birth. But if the self-moving is proved to be immortal, he who affirms that self-motion is the very idea and essence of the soul will not be put to confusion. For the body which is moved from without is soulless; but that which is moved from within has a soul, for such is the nature of the soul. . . .

Of the nature of the soul, though her true form be ever a theme of large and more than mortal discourse, let me speak briefly, and in a figure. And let the figure be composite—a pair of winged horses and a charioteer. Now the winged horses and the charioteers of the gods are all of them noble and of noble descent, but those of other races are mixed; the human charioteer drives his in a pair; and one of them is noble and of noble breed, and the other is ignoble and of ignoble breed; and the driving of them of necessity gives a great deal of trouble to him. I will endeavor to explain to you in what way the mortal differs from the immortal creature. The soul in her totality has the care of inanimate being everywhere, and traverses the whole heaven

---

Zoroastrians were another ancient influence on contemporary Christian thought, first by influencing the Jews and, through them, the Christians. Zoroastrians, who believed that the souls of the dead survive disembodied from the time of their deaths until sometime in the future when there will be a general bodily resurrection of the dead, began to influence Judaism around 538 B.C., when the neo-Babylonian Empire was annexed to the first Persian Empire. The Zoroastrian influence then spread through Judaism to Christianity and even to Islam.

There are, of course, alternative religious traditions that have a different view of the soul and its fate. Perhaps the most interesting contrast is with those religious traditions, like Hinduism, that subscribe to reincarnation. Whereas according to the Christian view, your soul simply goes to heaven (or hell) upon bodily death, the Hindu view states that the essential you—your soul, or *atman*—once released from the body typically enters a new body here on earth and is reborn for another lifetime. The Christian view contends that your soul always retains its individuality; the Hindu view maintains that after many rebirths, your soul may eventually lose its individuality and become one with Being itself, *Brahman*.

---

in divers forms appearing:—when perfect and fully winged she soars upward, and orders the whole world; whereas the imperfect soul, losing her wings and drooping in her flight at last settles on the solid ground—there, finding a home, she receives an earthly frame which appears to be self-moved, but is really moved by her power; and this composition of soul and body is called a living and mortal creature.

"The Inner Self"

Bhagavad Gita

He who sees me everywhere
and sees everything in me
will not be lost to me,
and I will not be lost to him.

I exist in all creatures,
so the disciplined man devoted to me
grasps the oneness of life;
wherever he is, he is in me.

When he sees identity in everything,
whether joy or suffering,
through analogy with the self,
he is deemed a man of pure discipline. . . .

I am the source of all the universe,
just as I am its dissolution.

Nothing is higher than I am . . .
all that exists
is woven on me,
like a web of pearls on thread.

I am the taste in water . . .
the light in the moon and sun,
OM resonant in all sacred lore,
the sound in space, valor in men.

I am the pure fragrance
in earth, the brilliance in fire,
the life in all living creatures, . . .

every creature's timeless seed,
the understanding of intelligent men,
the brilliance of fiery heroes. . . .

Know that nature's qualities
come from me—lucidity,
passion, and dark inertia;
I am not in them, they are in me.

All this universe, deluded
by the qualities inherent in nature,
fails to know that I am
beyond them and unchanging.

Composed of nature's qualities,
my divine magic is hard to escape;
but those who seek refuge in me
cross over this magic. . . .

Trusting me, men strive
for freedom from old age and death;
they know the infinite spirit,
its inner self and all its action.

Men who know me as its inner being,
inner divinity, and inner sacrifice
have disciplined their reason;
they know me at the time of death. . . .

Neither the multitude of gods
nor great sages know my origin,
for I am the source of all
the gods and great sages.

A mortal who knows me
as the unborn, beginningless
great lord of the worlds
is freed from delusion and all evils.

Understanding, knowledge, nondelusion,
patience, truth, control, tranquility,
joy, suffering, being, nonbeing,
fear, and fearlessness. . . .

I am the source of everything,
and everything proceeds from me . . .

I am the self abiding
in the heart of all creatures;
I am their beginning, their middle, and their end. . . .

Barbara Stoler Miller, trans., 1986.

John Locke

"CONSCIOUSNESS, SELF, AND IDENTITY"

JOHN LOCKE (1632–1706), the first of the British empiricists, was educated at Oxford University while it was still under the influence of medieval scholasticism. A student of classics, philosophy, and medicine, Locke was most interested in the views recently formulated by Descartes, particularly the idea of working out a theory of knowledge that could accommodate the progress being made in the newly emerging sciences. But whereas Descartes was a rationalist who believed that our primary source of knowledge is reason, Locke was an empiricist who argued that our knowledge of the world comes almost exclusively through sense experiences. In his *Essay Concerning Human Understanding* (1690), he argued that we experience only our own "ideas"—or sense-contents—directly and that physical objects are known only indirectly. His *Letters on Toleration* (1689), in which he argued for complete religious freedom for all groups *except Roman Catholics and atheists*, was a major influence on Jefferson (see vignette, "An Act for Establishing Religious Freedom" in Part XI) and the founders of the U.S. Constitution.

PERSONAL IDENTITY

To find wherein personal identity consists, we must consider what "person" stands for; which I think, is a thinking intelligent being, that has reason and reflection, and can consider itself as itself, the same thinking thing, in different times and places; which it does only by that consciousness which is inseparable from thinking, and it seems to me essential to it: it being impossible for any one to perceive, without perceiving that he does perceive. When we see, hear, smell, taste, feel, meditate, or will any thing, we know that we do so. Thus it is always as to our present sensations and perceptions: and by this every one is to himself that which he calls "self"; it not being considered, in this case, whether the same self be continued in the same or diverse substances. For since consciousness always accompanies thinking, and it is that that makes every one to be what he calls "self," and thereby distinguishes himself from all other thinking things; in this alone consists personal identity, *i.e.,* the sameness of rational being: and as far as this consciousness can be extended backwards to any past action or thought, so far reaches the identity of that person; it is the same self now it was then; and it is by the same self with this present one that now reflects on it, that that action was done.

CONSCIOUSNESS MAKES PERSONAL IDENTITY

. . . For it being the same consciousness that makes a man be himself to himself, personal

From *An Essay Concerning Human Understanding,* Book II, Chapter 27. First published in 1690.

identity depends on that only, whether it be annexed solely to one individual substance, or can be continued in a succession of several substances. For as far as any intelligent being can repeat the idea of any past action with the same consciousness it had of it at first, and with the same consciousness it has of any present action; so far it is the same personal self. For it is by the consciousness it has of its present thoughts and actions that it is self to itself now, and so will be the same self, as far as the same consciousness can extend to actions past or to come; and would be by distance of time, or change of substance, no more two persons than a man be two men, by wearing other clothes to-day than he did yesterday, with a long or short sleep between: the same consciousness uniting those distant actions into the same person, whatever substance contributed to their production.

PERSONAL IDENTITY IN CHANGE OF SUBSTANCES

. . . Suppose a Christian, Platonist, or a Pythagorean, should, upon God's having ended all his works of creation the seventh day, think his soul hath existed ever since; and should imagine it has revolved in several human bodies, as I once met with one who was persuaded his had been the soul of Socrates: (how reasonably I will not dispute: this I know, that in the post he filled, which was no inconsiderable one, he passed for a very rational man; and the press has shown that he wanted not parts or learning:) would any one say, that he, being not conscious of any of Socrates's actions or thoughts, could be the same person with Socrates? Let any one reflect upon himself, and conclude, that he has in himself an immaterial spirit, which is that which thinks in him, and in the constant change of his body keeps him the same; and is that which he calls himself: let him also suppose it to be the same soul that was in Nestor or Thersites, at the siege of Troy, (for souls being, as far as we know any thing of them, in their nature indifferent to any parcel of matter, the supposition has no apparent absurdity in it), which it may have been as well as it is now the soul of any other man: but he now having no consciousness of any of the actions either of Nestor or Thersites, does or can he conceive himself the same person with either of them? Can he be concerned in either of their actions? attribute them to himself, or think them his own, more than the actions of any other man that ever existed? So that this consciousness not reaching to any of the actions of either of those men, he is no more one self with either of them, than if the soul or immaterial spirit that now informs him had been created and began to exist when it began to inform his present body, though it were never so true that the same spirit that informed Nestor's or Thersite's body were numerically the same that now informs his. For this would no more make him the same person with Nestor, than if some of the particles of matter that were once a part of Nestor were now a part of this man; the same immaterial substance, without the same consciousness, no more making the same person by being united to any body, than the same particle of matter, without consciousness, united to any body, makes the same person. But let him once find himself conscious of any of the actions of Nestor, he then finds himself the same person with Nestor.

And thus we may be able, without any difficulty, to conceive the same person at the resurrection, though in a body not exactly in make or parts the same which he had here, the same consciousness going along with the soul that inhabits it. But yet the soul alone, in the change of bodies, would scarce to any one, but to him that makes the soul the man, be enough to make the same man. For, should the soul of a prince, carrying with it the consciousness of the prince's past life, enter and inform the body of a cobbler, as soon as deserted by his own soul, every one sees he would be the same person with the prince, accountable only for the prince's actions: but who would say it was the same man? The body too goes to the making of the man, and would, I guess, to every body determine the man in this case, wherein the soul, with all its princely thoughts about it, would not make another man; but he would be the same cobbler to every one besides himself. I know that, in the ordinary way of speaking, the same person and the same man stand for one and the same thing. And, indeed, every one will always have a liberty to speak as he pleases, and to apply what articulate sounds to what ideas he thinks fit, and change them as often as he pleases. But yet, when we will inquire what makes the same spirit, man, or person, we must fix the ideas of spirit, man, or person in our minds; and having resolved with ourselves what we mean by them, it will not be hard to determine in either of them, or the like, when it is the same and when not.

CONSCIOUSNESS MAKES THE SAME PERSON

But though the same immaterial substance or soul does not alone, wherever it be, and in whatsoever state, make the same man; yet it is plain, consciousness, as far as ever it can be extended, should it be to ages past, unites existences and actions, very remote in time, into the same person, as well as it does the existences and actions of the immediately preceding moment: so that whatever has the consciousness of present and past actions is the same person to whom they both belong. Had I the same consciousness that I saw the ark and Noah's flood, as that I saw an overflowing of the Thames last winter, or as that I write now, I could no more doubt that I who write this now, that saw the Thames overflowed last winter, and that viewed the flood at the general deluge, was the same self, place that self in what substance you please, than that I who write this am the same myself now whilst I write (whether I consist of all the same substance, material or immaterial, or no) that I was yesterday. For, as to this point of being the same self, it matters not whether this present self be made up of the same or other substances, I being as much concerned and as justly accountable for any action that was done a thousand years since, appropriated to me now by this self-consciousness, as I am for what I did the last moment.

SELF DEPENDS ON CONSCIOUSNESS

Self is that conscious thinking thing (whatever substance made up of, whether spiritual or material, simple or compounded, it matters not) which is sensible or conscious of pleasure and pain, capable of happiness or misery, and so is concerned for itself, as far as that consciousness extends. Thus every one finds, that whilst comprehended under that consciousness, the little finger is as much a part of himself as what is most so. Upon separation of this little finger, should this consciousness go along with the little finger, and leave the rest of the body, it is evident the little finger would be the person, the same person; and self then would have nothing to do with the rest of the body. As in this case it is the consciousness that goes along with the substance, when one part is separate from another, which makes the same person, and con-

"The Truth about the Soul"

The Catholic Encyclopaedia

The notion that God has a supply of souls that are not any body's in particular until He infuses them into human embryos is entirely unwarranted by any evidence . . . The soul is created by God at the time it is infused into matter.

stitutes this inseparable self, so it is in reference to substances remote in time. That with which the consciousness of this present thinking thing can join itself makes the same person, and is one self with it, and with nothing else; and so attributes to itself and owns all the actions of that thing as its own, as far as that consciousness reaches, and no farther; as every one who reflects will perceive. . . .

This may show us wherein personal identity consists, not in the identity of substance, but, as I have said, in the identity of consciousness; wherein if Socrates and the present mayor of Queenborough agree, they are the same person. If the same Socrates waking and sleeping do not partake of the same consciousness, Socrates waking and sleeping is not the same person; and to punish Socrates waking for what sleeping Socrates thought, and waking Socrates was never conscious of, would be no more of right than to punish one twin for what his brother-twin did, whereof he knew nothing, because their outsides were so like that they could not be distinguished. . . .

Speaking of Souls

When we survey different religions we tend to focus on their differing views of God and cosmos. It is startling to realize that although we are all human beings, and the world's religions are the religions of one single species of animal, different religions also presuppose many radically different views of the self, views that differ just as greatly, sometimes even more so, than their views of God. Surprisingly, people do not just look inwardly and see themselves in the same way, regardless of the cultures they live in. But why? Don't we have direct access to our inner lives—to ourselves?

The surprising answer is that we do not. The problem is not just one of looking and then seeing ourselves clearly. We would do that if we could. The problem is that the reports people give about what they see when they do look inwardly suggest that there is nothing clear and unambiguous there to be seen: What we see when we look depends in part on what we expect to find, which is itself influenced by our beliefs and by the social setting in which we look.

Thus the self—or what we take to be ourselves—may not be a fixed, objective entity but rather a complex theoretical construction. Or the self may be fixed and objective but hidden behind illusory appearances. Either way, our experience of ourselves is not a solid foundation on which to build different views about God and the cosmos, but is itself in part determined by those views.

George Berkeley

"THE NOTIONS OF SELF AND GOD"

GEORGE BERKELEY (1685–1753) was born in Kilkenny, Ireland, and at the age of fifteen entered Trinity College, Dublin, where seven years later he was lecturing on Greek, Hebrew, and divinity. He remained at Trinity College for thirteen years, during which time he wrote his most important works: *Essays towards a New Theory of Vision* (1709), *Three Dialogues between Hylas and Philonous* (1713), and *A Treatise Concerning the Principles of Human Knowledge* (1710), from which the following selection is taken. He lived for a while in Rhode Island and visited and gave much encouragement to Yale and Harvard; Berkeley, California, is named after him. He wanted to open a college in Bermuda for Indians and young American colonists but was forced to drop the project.

Bishop Berkeley is best known for his idealist or immaterialist doctrine that the existence of so-called material objects—rocks, plants, tables, and so on—consists solely in their being perceived. His view was importantly motivated by his dissatisfaction with Locke's theory of knowledge and by his desire to find a new justification for belief in God. He claimed that color exists only when seen, sound only when heard, shape only when seen or touched, and that it is impossible to imagine any of these existing unperceived. God enters the picture to ensure the stable existence of the public world; on those occasions when no finite sentient being is perceiving it, God is.

138. . . . [B]y the word 'spirit' we mean only that which thinks, wills, and perceives; this, and this alone, constitutes the signification of that term. If therefore it is impossible that any degree of those powers should be represented in an idea, it is evident there can be no idea of a spirit.

139. But it will be objected that, if there is no idea signified by the terms 'soul,' 'spirit,' and substance,' they are wholly insignificant, or have no meaning in them. I answer, those words do mean or signify a real thing, which is neither an idea nor like an idea, but that which perceives ideas, and wills, and reasons about them. What I am myself, that which I denote by the term 'I,' is the same with what is meant by 'soul' or 'spiritual substances.' If it be said that this is only quarreling at a word, and that, since the immediate significations of other names are by common consent called 'ideas' no reason can be assigned why that which is signified by the name 'spirit' or 'soul' may not partake in the same appellation: I answer, all the unthinking objects of the mind agree in that they are entirely passive, and their existence consists only in being perceived; whereas a soul or spirit is an active being, whose existence consists, not in being perceived, but in perceiving ideas and thinking.

From *A Treatise Concerning the Principles of Human Knowledge*. First published in 1710.

It is therefore necessary, in order to prevent equivocation and confounding natures perfectly disagreeing and unlike, that we distinguish between *spirit* and *idea.*

140. In a large sense, indeed, we may be said to have an idea or rather a notion of *spirit,* that is, we understand the meaning of the word, otherwise we could not affirm or deny anything of it. Moreover, as we conceive the ideas that are in the minds of other spirits by means of our own, which we suppose to be resemblances of them; so we know other spirits by means of our own soul; which in that sense is the image or idea of them; it having a like respect to other spirits that blueness or heat by me perceived has to those ideas perceived by another.

141. It must not be supposed that they who assert the natural immortality of the soul are of opinion that it is absolutely incapable of annihilation even by the infinite power of the Creator who first gave it being, but only that it is not liable to be broken or dissolved by the ordinary laws of nature or motion. They indeed who hold the soul of man to be only a thin vital flame, or system of animal spirits, make it perishing and corruptible as the body; since there is nothing more easily dissipated than such a being, which it is naturally impossible should survive the ruin of the tabernacle wherein it is enclosed. And this notion hath been greedily embraced and cherished by the worst part of mankind, as the most effectual antidote against all impressions of virtue and religion. But it hath been made evident that bodies of what frame or texture soever, are barely passive ideas in the mind, which is more distant and heterogeneous from them than light is from darkness. We have shown that the soul is indivisible, incorporeal, unextended, and it is consequently incorruptible. Nothing can be plainer than that the motions, changes, decays, and dissolutions which we hourly see befall natural bodies (and which is what we mean by the *course of nature*) cannot possibly affect an active, simple, uncompounded substance; such a being

"The Self as Community"

Richard Thomas

A good case can be made for our nonexistence as entities. We are not made up, as we had always supposed, of successively enriched packets of our own parts. We are shared, rented, occupied. At the interior of our cells, driving them, providing the oxidative energy that sends us out for the improvement of each shining day, are the mitochondria, and in a strict sense they are not ours. They turn out to be little separate creatures, the colonial posterity of migrant prokaryocytes, probably primitive bacteria that swam into ancestral precursors of our eukaryotic cells and stayed there. Ever since, they have maintained themselves and their ways, replicating in their own fashion, privately, with their own DNA and RNA quite different from ours. They are as much symbionts as the rhizobial bacteria in the roots of beans. Without them, we would not move a muscle, drum a finger, think a thought.

Mitochondria are stable and responsible lodgers, and I choose to trust them. But what of the other little animals, similarly established in my cells, sorting and balancing me, clustering me together? My centrioles, basal bodies, and probably a good many other more obscure tiny beings at work inside my cells, each with its own special genome, are as foreign, and as essential, as aphids in anthills. My cells are no longer the pure line entities I was raised with; they are ecosystems more complex than Jamaica Bay. . . .

As for me, I am grateful for differentiation and speciation, but I cannot feel as separate an entity as I did a few years ago, before I was told these things, nor, I should think, can anyone else. . . .

From "The Lives of a Cell" (1973).

therefore is indissoluble by the force of nature; that is to say, *the soul of man is naturally immortal.*

142. After what hath been said, it is, I suppose, plain that our souls are not to be known in the same manner as senseless, inactive objects, or by way of *idea. Spirits* and *ideas* are things so wholly different, that when we say 'they exist,' 'they are known,' or the like, these words must not be thought to signify anything common to both natures. There is nothing alike or common in them: and to expect that by any multiplication or enlargement of our faculties we may be enabled to know a spirit as we do a triangle, seems as absurd as if we should hope to see a sound. This is inculcated because I imagine it may be of moment towards clearing several important questions, and preventing some very dangerous errors concerning the nature of the soul. We may not, I think, strictly be said to have an *idea* of an active being, or of an action, although we may be said to have a *notion* of them. I have some knowledge or notion of my mind, and its acts about ideas, inasmuch as I know or understand what is meant by these words. What I know, that I have some notion of. I will not say that the terms 'idea' and 'notion' may not be used convertibly, if the world will have it so; but yet it conduceth to clearness and propriety that we distinguish things very different by different names. It is also to be remarked that, all relations including an act of the mind, we cannot so properly be said to have an idea, but rather a notion of the relations and habitudes between things. But if, in the modern way, the word 'idea' is extended to spirits, and relations, and acts, this is, after all, an affair of verbal concern. . . .

144. . . . [N]othing seems more to have contributed towards engaging men in controversies and mistakes with regard to the nature and operations of the mind, than the being used to speak of those things in terms borrowed from sensible ideas. For example, the will is termed the *motion* of the soul: this infuses a belief that the mind of man is as a ball in motion, impelled and determined by the objects of sense, as necessarily as that is by the stroke of a racket. Hence

Berkeley's God

What, according to Berkeley, would happen to objects in the external world were no one perceiving them? Would they simply vanish? They would, answers Berkeley, were it not for the fact that someone is always experiencing them. And that someone is God. In other words, to ensure that there is more to the cosmos than just self and ephemeral experience, Berkeley, like Descartes, relies on God, but in a different way.

In Descartes' view, God ensures our knowledge of the external world not primarily by doing something, but inactively, by not being a deceiver. Whereas for Berkeley, God ensures the existence of the external world by doing something: by perceiving it. Ironically, it seems, when empiricism—the view that our knowledge of the world is derived from experience—is pushed to the limits, as it almost was in Berkeley's analysis, it leads to idealism, the view that only the mind and its contents are real.

arise endless scruples and errors of dangerous consequence in morality. All which, I doubt not, may be cleared, and truth appear plain, uniform, and consistent, could but philosophers be prevailed on to retire into themselves, and attentively consider their own meaning.

145. From what hath been said, it is plain that we cannot know the existence of other spirits otherwise than by their operations, or the ideas by them excited in us. I perceive several motions, changes, and combinations of ideas, that inform me there are certain particular agents, like myself, which accompany them and concur in their production. Hence, the knowledge I have of other spirits is not immediate, as is the knowledge of my ideas; but depending on the intervention of ideas, by me referred to agents or spirits distinct from myself, as effects or concomitant signs.

146. But though there be some things which convince us human agents are concerned in producing them; yet it is evident to everyone that those things which are called the works of nature, that is, the far greater part of the ideas or sensations perceived by us, are not produced by, or dependent on, the wills of men. There is therefore some other Spirit that causes them; since it is repugnant that they should subsist by themselves. But if we attentively consider the constant regularity, order, and concatenation of natural things, the surprising magnificence, beauty, and perfection of the larger, and the exquisite contrivance of the smaller parts of creation, together with the exact harmony and correspondence of the whole, but above all the never enough admired laws of pain and pleasure, and the instincts or natural inclinations, appetites, and passions of animals; I say if we consider all these things, and at the same time attend to the meaning and import of the attributes. One, Eternal, Infinitely Wise, Good, and Perfect, we shall clearly perceive that they belong to the aforesaid Spirit, "who works all in all," and "by whom all things consist."

147. Hence, it is evident that God is known as certainly and immediately as any other mind or spirit whatsoever distinct from ourselves. We may even assert that the existence of God is far

Locke and Berkeley's Inconsistency

Locke and Berkeley, like Descartes, claimed that we intuit the self. Hence neither of them was a consistent empiricist. The self, according to Locke and Berkeley, is an active, causal agent. Ideas—our experiences—are passive.

Consider, for instance, your visual image of this page. If you pay close attention you will see that it is static. It may be succeeded by other static images with a rapidity that suggests motion and causation, much as the frames of a motion picture, although individually static, suggest active causality among the scenes depicted on the frames when the frames are succeeding each other rapidly. But individual ideas—the immediate data of our experience—do not do anything. Yet it may seem that they, and they alone, are capable of being perceived. The self, on the other hand, would be an active agent, not a passive perception. That is why Locke and Berkeley claimed you cannot perceive the self.

more evidently perceived than the existence of men; because the effects of nature are infinitely more numerous and considerable than those ascribed to human agents. There is not any one mark that denotes a man, or effect produced by him, which does not more strongly evince the being of that Spirit who is the Author of Nature. For it is evident that in affecting other persons the will of man hath no other object than barely the motion of the limbs of his body; but that such a motion should be attended by, or excite any idea in the mind of another, depends wholly on the will of the Creator. He alone it is who, "upholding all things by the word of His power," maintains that intercourse between spirits whereby they are able to perceive the existence of each other. And yet this pure and clear light which enlightens everyone is itself invisible.

148. . . . A human spirit or person is not perceived by sense, as not being an idea; when therefore we see the color, size, figure, and motions of a man, we perceive only certain sensations or ideas excited in our own minds; and these being exhibited to our view in sundry distinct collections, serve to mark out unto us the existence of finite and created spirits like ourselves. Hence it is plain we do not see a man—if by *man* is meant that which lives, moves, perceives, and thinks as we do—but only such a certain collection of ideas as directs us to think there is a distinct principle of thought and motion, like to ourselves, accompanying and represented by it. And after the same manner we see God; all the difference is that, whereas some one finite and narrow assemblage of ideas denotes a particular human mind, whithersoever we direct our view, we do at all times and in all places perceive manifest tokens of the Divinity: everything we see, hear, feel, or anywise perceive by sense being a sign or effect of the power of God; as is our perception of those very motions which are produced by men.

David Hume

"THE SELF AND PERSONAL IDENTITY"

The following selection, one of the most famous in Western philosophy, is from Hume's *A Treatise of Human Nature*, first published in 1738, when Hume was twenty-seven years old.

There are some philosophers, who imagine we are every moment intimately conscious of what we call our *Self;* that we feel its existence and its continuance in existence; and are certain, beyond the evidence of a demonstration, both of its perfect identity and simplicity. . . . For my part, when I enter most intimately into what I call *myself,* I always stumble on some particular perception or other, of heat or cold, light or shade, love or hatred, pain or pleasure. I never can catch *myself* at any time without a perception, and never can observe any thing but the

From *A Treatise of Human Nature.* First published in 1738.

perception. When my perceptions are remov'd for any time, as by sound sleep; so long am I insensible of *myself,* and may truly be said not to exist. And were all my perceptions remov'd by death, and cou'd I neither think, nor feel, nor see, nor love, nor hate after the dissolution of my body, I shou'd be entirely annihilated, nor do I conceive what is farther requisite to make me a perfect non-entity. If any one upon serious and unprejudic'd reflexion, thinks he has a different notion of *himself,* I must confess I can reason no longer with him. All I can allow him is, that he may be in the right as well as I, and that we are essentially different in this particular. He may, perhaps, perceive something simple and continu'd, which he calls *himself;* tho' I am certain there is no such principle in me.

But setting aside some metaphysicians of this kind, I may venture to affirm of the rest of mankind, that they are nothing but a bundle or collection of different perceptions, which succeed each other with an inconceivable rapidity,

Hume's Solution: Dissolution of the Self

Hume pushed the empiricist analysis even further than Locke and Berkeley. There is, claims Hume, *no self!* Locke had accepted a rift between what we can experience directly (ideas in the mind of a perceiver) and what actually exists (both self and cosmos). Berkeley's outwardly turned empiricism, by reducing the cosmos to ideas in the mind of a perceiver, eliminated one-half of this rift. Hume did away with the rest. Under the force of his inwardly turned empiricism, Hume reduced the self, too, to ideas. Only this time, the reduction could not be to ideas in the mind of a perceiver, since perceivers themselves had been reduced to bundles of passive ideas!

Just as Newtonian science reduces objects to *physical* atoms, Hume reduces both objects and the self—everything—to *experiential* atoms: elements of conscious experience, what Hume calls "impressions and ideas." In other words, according to Hume, reality is nothing but a succession of individual, discrete sense impressions unconnected even by causality. Whereas Descartes, Locke, and Berkeley thought that we could know the self—an active, causal agent, a perceiver—intuitively, Hume does not think so. According to Hume, we cannot know either the self or anything that is an active, causal agent.

Ordinarily, when we think of the self, we tend to think of something active. Ancient ideas about the soul conceive of it as an active, animating force—a life force—that moves the body. Hume is suggesting the opposite: In reality there is no active, conscious perceiver, no observer; there are just the individual "experiential atoms," and these are passive. That is, there is experience but no experiencer. Unlike physical atoms, however, which were conceived of by Newton as persisting, the elements of experience, Hume argued, are all impermanent.

and are in a perpetual flux and movement. Our eyes cannot turn in their sockets without varying our perceptions. Our thought is still more variable than our sight; and all our other senses and faculties contribute to this change; nor is there any single power of the soul, which remains unalterably the same, perhaps for one moment. The mind is a kind of theatre, where several perceptions successively make their appearance; pass, re-pass, glide away, and mingle in an infinite variety of postures and situations. There is properly no *simplicity* in it at one time, nor *identity* in different; whatever natural propension we may have to imagine that simplicity and identity. The comparison of the theatre must not mislead us. They are the successive perceptions only, that constitute the mind; nor have we the most distant notion of the place, where these scenes are represented, or of the materials, of which it is compos'd.

What then gives us so great a propension to ascribe an identity to these successive perceptions, and to suppose ourselves possest of an invariable and uninterrupted existence thro' the whole course of our lives? . . .

. . . every distinct perception, which enters into the composition of the mind, is a distinct existence, and is different, and distinguishable, and separable from every other perception, either contemporary or successive. But, as, notwithstanding this distinction and separability, we suppose the whole train of perceptions to be united by identity, a question naturally arises concerning this relation of identity; whether it be something that really binds our several perceptions together, or only associates their ideas in the imagination. That is, in other words, whether in pronouncing concerning the identity of a person, we observe some real bond among his perceptions, or only feel one among the ideas we form of them. This question we might easily decide, if we wou'd recollect what has been already prov'd at large, that the understanding never observes any real connexion among objects, and that even the union of cause and effect, when strictly examin'd, resolves itself into a customary association of ideas. For from thence it evidently follows, that identity is nothing really belonging to these different perceptions, and uniting them together; but is merely a quality, which we attribute to them, because of the union of their ideas in the imagination, when we reflect upon them. Now the only qualities, which can give ideas an union in the imagination, are these three relations above-mention'd. These are the uniting principles in the ideal world, and without them every distinct object is separable by the mind, and may be separately consider'd, and appears not to have any more connexion with any other object, than if disjoin'd by the greatest difference and remoteness. 'Tis, therefore, on some of these three relations of resemblance, contiguity and causation, that identity depends; and as the very essence of these relations consists in their producing an easy transition of ideas; it follows, that our notions of personal identity, proceed entirely from the smooth and uninterrupted progress of the thought along a train of connected ideas, according to the principles above-explain'd.

The only question, therefore, which remains, is, by what relations this uninterrupted progress of our thought is produc'd, when we consider the successive existence of a mind or thinking person. And here 'tis evident we must confine ourselves to resemblance and causation, and must drop contiguity, which has little or no influence in the present case.

To begin with *resemblance;* suppose we cou'd see clearly into the breast of another, and observe that succession of perceptions, which constitutes his mind or thinking principle, and suppose that he always preserves the memory of a considerable part of past perceptions; 'tis evident that nothing cou'd more contribute to the bestowing a relation on this succession amidst all its variations. For what is the memory but a faculty, by which we raise up the images of past perceptions? And as an image necessarily resembles its object, must not for the frequent placing of these resembling perceptions in the chain of thought, convey the imagination more easily from one link to another, and make the whole seem like the continuance of one object? In this particular, then, the memory not only discovers the identity, but also contributes to its production, by producing the relation of resemblance among the perceptions. The case is the same whether we consider ourselves or others.

As to *causation;* we may observe, that the true idea of the human mind, is to consider it as a system of different perceptions or different existences, which are link'd together by the relation of cause and effect, and mutually produce, destroy, influence, and modify each other. Our impressions give rise to their correspondent ideas; and these ideas in their turn produce other impressions. One thought chases another, and draws after it a third, by which it is expell'd in its turn. In this respect, I cannot compare the soul more properly to any thing than to a republic or commonwealth, in which the several members are united by the reciprocal ties of government and subordination, and give rise to other persons, who propagate the same republic in the incessant changes of its parts. And as the same individual republic may not only change its members, but also its laws and constitutions; in like manner the same person may vary his character and disposition, as well as his impressions and ideas, without losing his identity. Whatever changes he endures, his several parts are still connected by the relation of causation. And in this view our identity with regard to the

The No-Soul of Buddhism

According to many Buddhists you have no self at all, neither after life nor *during* life! That is, not only will you not survive your bodily death, you won't even survive reading this page, since there is no one to do the surviving. And yet, Buddhists tend to believe in rebirth (reincarnation, but without the soul) and even karma, the process by which (your) circumstances in this life are affected by (your) actions in past lives, and (your) actions in this life affect (your) circumstances in future lives. This appears to be an outright contradiction.

People, or selves, in the Buddhist view, are like fictional entities—for instance, like the constellation the "Big Dipper." There is no real entity that is the Big Dipper. There are just the individual stars, in various relationships with each other, connected into a pattern by the mind of the observer. That pattern is not an objective fact about the world, but rather just the way the stars may appear when they are viewed from a certain limited perspective. But, if there are no selves, then who perceives these patterns that are but configurations of imaginary pattern people? No one. There is the perception—perceptions are one of the psychological elements in the mix—but no perceivers. In other words, you are not right now reading this line, but there is the reading of this line. You didn't just have a thought, but there was the thinking of a thought. You aren't right now wondering about the self, but there is wondering about the self.

passions serves to corroborate that with regard to the imagination, by the making our distant perceptions influence each other, and by giving us a present concern for our past or future pains or pleasures.

As memory alone acquaints us with the continuance and extent of this succession of perceptions, 'tis to be consider'd, upon that account chiefly, as the source of personal identity. Had we no memory, we never shou'd have any notion of causation, nor consequently of that chain of causes and effects, which constitute our self or person. But having once acquir'd this notion of causation from the memory, we can extend the same chain of causes, and consequently the identity of our persons beyond our memory, and can comprehend times, and circumstances, and actions, which we have entirely forgot, but suppose in general to have existed. For how few of our past actions are there, of which we have any memory? Who can tell me, for instance, what were his thoughts and actions on the first of *January* 1715, the 11th of *March* 1719, and the 3d of *August* 1733? Or will he affirm, because he has entirely forgot the incidents of these days, that the present self is not the same person with the self of that time; and by that means overturn all the most establish'd notions of personal identity? In this view, therefore, memory does not so much *produce as discover* personal identity, by shewing us the relation of cause and effect among our different perceptions. 'Twill be incumbent on those, who affirm that memory produces entirely our personal identity, to give a reason why we can thus extend our identity beyond our memory.

The whole of this doctrine leads us to a conclusion, which is of great importance in the present affair, *viz.* that all the nice and subtle questions concerning personal identity can never possibly be decided, and are to be regarded rather as grammatical than as philosophical difficulties. Identity depends on the relations of ideas; and these relations produce identity, by means of that easy transition they occasion. But as the relations, and the easiness of the transition may diminish by insensible degrees, we have no just standard, by which we can decide any dispute concerning the time, when they acquire or lose a title to the name of identity. All the disputes concerning the identity of connected objects are merely verbal, except so far as the relation of parts gives rise to some fiction or imaginary principle of union, as we have already observ'd.

Everything and Nothing

If we were shocked at Berkeley's claim that the cosmos itself does not exist unless it is being perceived, then how much more shocked should we be at Hume's claim that there is no perceiver, no self? Nor for Hume is there a God to come to the rescue, for the idea of God as active, causal agent is just as unintelligible for Hume as the idea of self as active, causal agent.

Hume is *not* denying the obvious fact that there *seems* to be a self. He is claiming, rather, that this perception is, in reality, a misperception. The self is an illusion. You are a bundle of perceptions and misperceptions. If Hume is right that there are no perceivers and Berkeley is right that without a perceiver there is no cosmos, then there is just nothing!

Thomas Reid

"CRITIQUE OF LOCKE AND HUME ON BEHALF OF COMMON SENSE"

THOMAS REID (1710–1796) was the son of a minister who also became a minister. A severe critic of the "theory of ideas" promulgated by Descartes, Locke, Berkeley, and Hume, according to which it is *ideas*, not *real objects*, that are immediately given in perception, Reid founded the Scottish School of Common Sense. In his view, certain fundamental commonsense beliefs need no proof because they cannot seriously be doubted; there is nothing more certain to which one might appeal in doubting them.

. . . It is proper to consider what is meant by identity in general, what by our own personal identity, and how we are led into that invincible belief and conviction which every man has of his own personal identity, as far as his memory reaches.

Identity in general I take to be a relation between a thing which is known to exist at one time, and a thing which is known to have existed at another time. If you ask whether they are one and the same, or two different things, every man of common sense understands the meaning of your question perfectly. Whence we may infer with certainty, that every man of common sense has a clear and distinct notion of identity.

If you ask a definition of identity, I confess I can give none; it is too simple a notion to admit of logical definition. . . .

I see evidently that identity supposes *an uninterrupted continuance of existence.* That which has ceased to exist cannot be the same with that which afterwards begins to exist; for this would be to suppose a being to exist after it ceased to exist, and to have had existence before it was produced, which are manifest contradictions. Continued uninterrupted existence is therefore necessarily implied in identity. Hence we may infer, that identity cannot, in its proper sense, be applied to our pains, our pleasures, our thoughts, or any operation of our minds. The pain felt this day is not the same individual pain which I felt yesterday, though they may be *similar* in kind and degree, and have the same cause. The same may be said of every feeling, and of every operation of mind. They are all successive in their nature, like time itself, no two moments of which can be the same moment. It is otherwise with the parts of absolute space. They always are, and were, and will be the same. So far, I think, we proceed upon clear ground in fixing the notion of identity in general.

NATURE AND ORIGIN OF OUR IDEA OF PERSONAL IDENTITY

It is perhaps more difficult to ascertain with precision the meaning of *personality;* but it is

From *Essays on the Intellectual Powers of Man,* first published in England in 1785, and *An Inquiry into the Human Mind on the Principles of Common Sense*, first published in 1764. Edited by Tom L. Beauchamp and reprinted with his permission.

not necessary in the present subject: it is sufficient for our purpose to observe, that all mankind place their personality in something that *cannot be divided, or consist of parts.* A part of a person is a manifest absurdity. When a man loses his estate, his health, his strength, he is still the same person, and has lost nothing of his personality. If he has a leg or an arm cut off, he is the same person he was before. The amputated member is no part of his person, otherwise it would have a right to a part of his estate, and be liable for a part of his engagements. It would be entitled to a share of his merit and demerit, which is manifestly absurd. A person is something indivisible, and is what Leibniz calls a *monad.*

My personal identity, therefore, implies the continued existence of that indivisible thing which I call *myself.* Whatever this self may be, it is something which thinks, and deliberates, and resolves, and acts, and suffers. I am not thought, I am not action, I am not feeling; I am something that thinks, and acts, and suffers. My thoughts, and actions, and feelings, change every moment; they have no continued, but a successive, existence; but that *self,* or *I,* to which they belong, is permanent, and has the same relation to all the succeeding thoughts, actions, and feelings which I call mine.

Such are the notions that I have of my personal identity. But perhaps it may be said, this may all be fancy without reality. How do you know,—what evidence have you,—that there is such a permanent self which has a claim to all the thoughts, actions, and feelings which you call yours?

To this I answer, that the proper evidence I have of all this is *remembrance.* I remember that twenty years ago I conversed with such a person; I remember several things that passed in that conversation: my memory testifies, not only that this was done, but that it was done by me who now remember it. If it was done by me, I must have existed at that time, and continued to exist from that time to the present: if the identical person whom I call myself had not a part in that conversation, my memory is fallacious; it gives a distinct and positive testimony of what is not true. Every man in his senses believes what he distinctly remembers, and everything he remembers convinces him that he existed at the same time remembered.

Although memory gives the most irresistible evidence of my being the identical person that did such a thing, at such a time, I may have other good evidence of things which befell me, and which I do not remember: I know who bore me, and suckled me, but I do not remember these events.

It may here be observed, (though the observation would have been unnecessary, if some great philosophers had not contradicted it), that it is not my remembering any action of mine that *makes* me to be the person who did it. This remembrance makes me to *know* assuredly that I did it; *but I might have done it, though I did not remember it.* That relation to me, which is expressed by saying that *I did it,* would be the same, though I had not the least remembrance of it. . . .

When we pass judgment on the identity of other persons than ourselves, we proceed upon other grounds, and determine from a variety of circumstances, which sometimes produce the firmest assurance, and sometimes leave room for doubt. The identity of persons has often furnished matter of serious litigation before tribunals of justice. But no man of a sound mind ever doubted of his own identity, as far as he distinctly remembered. . . .

Thus it appears, that the evidence we have of our own identity, as far back as we remember, is totally of a different kind from the evidence we have of the identity of other persons, or of objects of sense. The first is grounded on *memory,* and gives undoubted certainty. The last is grounded on *similarity,* and on other circumstances, which in many cases are not so decisive as to leave no room for doubt.

It may likewise be observed, that the identity of *objects of sense* is never perfect. All bodies, as they consist of innumerable parts that may be disjoined from them by a great variety of causes, are subject to continual changes of their substance, increasing, diminishing, changing insensibly. When such alterations are gradual, because languages could not afford a different name for every different state of such a changeable being, it retains the same name, and is considered as the same thing. Thus we say of an old regiment, that it did such a thing a century ago, though there now is not a man alive who then belonged to it. We say a tree is the same in the seed-bed and in the forest. A ship of war, which has successively changed her anchors, her tackle, her sails, her masts, her planks, and her timbers, while she keeps the same name, is the same.

The identity, therefore, which we ascribe to bodies, whether natural or artificial, is not perfect identity; it is rather something which, for the conveniency of speech, we call identity. It admits of a great change of the subject, providing the change be *gradual;* sometimes, even of a total change. And the changes which in common language are made consistent with identity differ from those that are thought to destroy it, not in *kind,* but in *number* and *degree.* It has no fixed nature when applied to bodies; and questions about the identity of a body are very often questions about words. But identity, when applied to persons, has no ambiguity, and admits not of degrees, or of more and less. It is the foundation of all rights and obligations, and of all accountableness; and the notion of it is fixed and precise.

STRICTURES ON LOCKE'S ACCOUNT OF PERSONAL IDENTITY

In a long chapter, *Of Identity and Diversity,* Mr. Locke has made many ingenious and just observations, and some which I think cannot be defended. . . .

This doctrine has some strange consequences, which the author was aware of. (1) Such as, that if the same consciousness can be transferred from one intelligent being to another, which he thinks we cannot show to be impossible, *then two or twenty intelligent beings may be the same person.* (2) And if the intelligent being may lose the consciousness of the actions done by him, which surely is possible, then he is not the person that did those actions; so that *one intelligent being may be two or twenty different persons,* if he shall so often lose the consciousness of his former actions.

(3) There is another consequence of this doctrine, which follows no less necessarily, though Mr. Locke probably did not see it. It is, *that a man may be, and at the same time not be, the person that did a particular action.* Suppose a brave officer to have been flogged when a boy at school for robbing an orchard, to have taken a standard from the enemy in his first campaign, and to have been made a general in advanced life; suppose, also, which must be admitted to be possible, that, when he took the standard, he was conscious of having been flogged at school, and that, when made a general, he was conscious of his taking the standard, but had absolutely lost the consciousness of his flogging. These things being supposed, it follows, from Mr. Locke's doctrine, that he who was flogged at school is the same person who took the standard, and that he who took the standard is the same person who was made a general. Whence it follows, if there be any truth in logic, that the general is the same person with him who was flogged at school. But the general's consciousness does not reach so far back as his flogging; therefore, according to Mr. Locke's doctrine, he is not the person who was flogged. Therefore the general is, and at the same time is not, the same person with him who was flogged at school.

Leaving the consequences of this doctrine to those who have leisure to trace them, we may observe, with regard to the doctrine itself,—

First, that Mr. Locke attributes to consciousness the conviction we have of our past actions, as if a man may now be conscious of what he did twenty years ago. It is impossible to understand the meaning of this, unless by *consciousness* he meant *memory,* the only faculty by which we have an immediate knowledge of our past actions. . . .

When, therefore, Mr. Locke's notion of personal identity is properly expressed, it is, that personal identity *consists in distinct remembrance;* for, even in the popular sense, to say that I am conscious of a past action means nothing else than that I distinctly remember that I did it.

Secondly, it may be observed, that, in this doctrine, not only is consciousness confounded with memory, but, which is still more strange, *personal identity* is confounded with *the evidence which we have of our personal identity.*

It is very true, that my remembrance that I did such a thing is the evidence I have that I am the identical person who did it. And this, I am apt to think, Mr. Locke meant. But to say that my remembrance that I did such a thing, or my consciousness, *makes* me the person who did it, is, in my apprehension, an absurdity too gross to be entertained by any man who attends to the meaning of it; for it is to attribute to memory or consciousness a strange magical power of producing its object, though that object must have existed before the memory or consciousness which produced it. Consciousness is the testimony of one faculty; memory is the testimony of another faculty; and to say that the testimony is the cause of the thing testified, this surely is absurd, if any thing be, and could not have been said by Mr. Locke, if he had not confounded the testimony with the thing testified.

When a horse that was stolen is found and claimed by the owner, the only evidence he can have, or that a judge or witnesses can have, that this is the very identical horse which was his property, is similitude. But would it not be ridiculous from this to infer that the identity of a horse *consists* in similitude only? The only *evidence* I have that I am the identical person who did such actions is, that I remember distinctly I did them; or, as Mr. Locke expresses it, I am conscious I did them. To infer from this, that personal identity consists in consciousness, is an argument which, if it had any force, would prove the identity of a stolen horse to consist solely in similitude.

Thirdly, is it not strange that the sameness or identity of a person should consist in a thing *which is continually changing,* and is not any two minutes the same?

Our consciousness, our memory, and every operation of the mind, are still flowing like the water of a river, or like time itself. The consciousness I have this moment can no more be the same consciousness I had last moment, than this moment can be the last moment. Identity can only be affirmed of things which have a continued existence. Consciousness, and every kind of thought, are transient and momentary, and have no continued existence; and, therefore, if personal identity consisted in consciousness, it would certainly follow, that *no man is the same person any two moments of his life;* and as the right and justice of reward and punishment are founded on personal identity, no man could be responsible for his actions. . . .

Fourthly, there are many expressions used by Mr. Locke, in speaking of personal identity, which to me are altogether unintelligible, unless we suppose that he confounded that sameness or identity which we ascribe to an individual with the identity which, in common discourse, is often ascribed to many individuals of the same species.

When we say that pain and pleasure, consciousness and memory, are the same in all men, this sameness can only mean similarity, or sameness *of kind.* That the pain of one man can be the same individual pain with that of another man is no less impossible, than that one man should be another man: the pain felt by me yesterday can no more be the pain I feel today, than yesterday can be this day; and the same thing may be said of every passion and of every operation of the mind. The same kind or species of operation may be in different men, or in the same man at different times; but it is impossible that the same individual operation should be in different men, or in the same man at different times.

When Mr. Locke, therefore, speaks of "the same consciousness being continued through a succession of different substances"; when he speaks of "repeating the idea of a past action, with the same consciousness we had of it at the first," and of "the same consciousness extending to actions past and to come"; these expressions are to me unintelligible, unless he means not the same individual consciousness, but a consciousness that is similar, or of the same kind. If our personal identity consists in consciousness, as this consciousness cannot be the same individually any two moments, but only of the *same kind,* it would follow, that we are not for any two moments the same individual persons, but the same *kind* of persons. As our consciousness sometimes ceases to exist, as in sound sleep, our personal identity must cease with it. Mr. Locke allows, that the same thing cannot have two beginnings of existence, so that our identity would be irrecoverably gone every time we cease to think, if it was but for a moment. . . .

STRICTURES ON HUME'S ACCOUNT OF PERSONAL IDENTITY

Locke's principle must be, that identity consists in remembrance; and consequently a man must lose his personal identity with regard to every thing he forgets.

Nor are these the only instances whereby our philosophy concerning the mind appears to

"Narration and Personal Identity"

Alasdair MacIntyre

A central thesis then begins to emerge: man is in his actions and practice, as well as in his fictions, essentially a story-telling animal. He is not essentially, but becomes through his history, a teller of stories that aspire to truth. But the key question for men is not about their own authorship; I can only answer the question 'What am I to do?' if I can answer the prior question 'Of what story or stories do I find myself a part?' We enter human society, that is, with one or more imputed characters—roles into which we have been drafted—and we have to learn what they are in order to be able to understand how others respond to us and how our responses to them are apt to be construed. It is through hearing stories about wicked stepmothers, lost children, good but misguided kings, wolves that suckle twin boys, youngest sons who receive no inheritance but must make their own way in the world and eldest sons who waste their inheritance on riotous living and go into exile to live with the swine, that children learn or mislearn both what a child and what a parent is, what the cast of characters may be in the drama into which they have been born and what the ways of the world are. Deprive children of stories and you leave them unscripted, anxious stutterers in their actions as in their words. Hence there is no way to give us an understanding of any society, including our own, except through the stock of stories which constitute its initial dramatic resources. Mythology, in its original sense, is at the heart of things. . . .

What the narrative concept of selfhood requires is thus twofold. On the one hand, I am what I may justifiably be taken by others to be in the course of living out a story that runs from my birth to my death; I am the *subject* of a history that is my own and no one else's, that has its own peculiar meaning. When someone complains—as do some of those who attempt or commit suicide—that his or her life is meaningless, he or she is often and perhaps characteristically complaining that the narrative of their life has become unintelligible to them, that it lacks any point, any movement towards a climax or a *telos.* Hence the point of doing any one thing rather than another at crucial junctures in their lives seems to such a person to have been lost.

. . . [P]ersonal identity is just that identity presupposed by the unity of the character which the unity of a narrative requires. Without such unity there would not be subjects of whom stories could be told.

From *After Virtue* (1981).

The entrance to the neolithic temple of Hagar Quim, Malta, erected about 5,500 years ago.

be very fruitful in creating doubts, but very unhappy in resolving them.

Descartes, Malebranche, and Locke, have all employed their genius and skill, to prove the existence of a material world; and with very bad success. . . .

The present age, I apprehend, has not produced two more acute or more practised in this part of philosophy than [George Berkeley] the Bishop of Cloyne, and the author of the Treatise of Human Nature [David Hume, who] . . . undoes the world of spirits, and leaves nothing in nature but ideas and impressions, without any subject on which they may be impressed.

It seems to be a peculiar strain of humor in this author, to set out in his introduction, by promising with a grave face, no less than a complete system of the sciences, upon a foundation entirely new, to wit, that of human nature; when the intention of the whole work is to show, that there is neither human nature nor science in the world. It may perhaps be unreasonable to complain of this conduct in an author, who neither believes his own existence, nor that of his reader; and therefore could not mean to disappoint him, or to laugh at his credulity. Yet I cannot imagine, that the author of the Treatise of Human Nature is so skeptical as to plead this apology. He believed, against his principles, that he should be read, and that he should retain his personal identity, till he reaped the honor and reputation justly due to his metaphysical *acumen*. Indeed he ingenuously acknowledges, that it was only in solitude and retirement that he could yield any assent to his own philosophy; society, like daylight, dispelled the darkness and fogs of skepticism, and made him yield to the dominion of common sense. Nor did I ever hear him charged with doing any thing, even in solitude, that argued such a degree of skepticism, as his principles maintain. . . .

That the natural issue of this system is skepticism with regard to every thing except the existence of our ideas, and of their necessary relations which appear upon comparing them, is evident: for ideas being the only objects of thought, and having no existence but when we are conscious of them, it necessarily follows, that there is no object of our thought, which can have a continued and permanent existence. Body and spirit, cause and effect, time and space, to which we were wont to ascribe an existence independent of our thought, are all turned out of existence by this short dilemma: Either these things are ideas of sensation or reflection, or they are not: if they are ideas of sensation or reflection, they can have no existence but when we are conscious of them; if they are not ideas of sensation or reflection, they are words without any meaning.

Neither Descartes nor Locke perceived this consequence of their system concerning ideas. Bishop Berkeley was the first who discovered it. . . . But with regard to the existence of spirits or minds, he does not admit the consequence; and if he had admitted it, he must have been an absolute skeptic. . . .

Thus we see, that Descartes and Locke take the road that leads to skepticism, without knowing the end of it; but they stop short for want of light to carry them farther. Berkeley, frighted at the appearance of the dreadful abyss, starts aside, and avoids it. But the author of the Treatise of Human Nature, more daring and intrepid, without turning aside to the right hand or to the left, like Virgil's Alecto, shoots directly into the gulf. . . .

We ought, however, to do this justice both to the Bishop of Cloyne and to the author of the Treatise of Human Nature, to acknowledge, that their conclusions are justly drawn from the doctrine of ideas, which has been so universally received. On the other hand, from the character of Bishop Berkeley, and of his predecessors Descartes, Locke, and Malebranche, we may venture to say, that if they had seen all the consequences of this doctrine, as clearly as the author before mentioned did, they would have suspected it vehemently, and examined it more carefully than they appear to have done.

The theory of ideas, like the Trojan horse, had a specious appearance both of innocence and beauty; but if those philosophers had known that it carried in its belly death and destruction to all science and common sense, they would not have broken down their walls to give it admittance. . . .

It is certain, no man can conceive or believe smelling to exist of itself, without a mind, or something that has the power of smelling, of which it is called a sensation, an operation or feeling. Yet if any man should demand a proof, that sensation cannot be without a mind or sentient being, I confess that I can give none; and that to pretend to prove it, seems to me almost as absurd as to deny it.

This might have been said without any apology before the Treatise of Human Nature appeared in the world. For till that time, no man, as far as I know, ever thought either of calling in question that principle, or of giving a reason for his belief of it. Whether thinking beings were of an ethereal or igneous nature, whether material or immaterial, was variously disputed; but that thinking is an operation of some kind of being or other, was always taken for granted, as a principle that could not possibly admit of doubt. . . .

If there are certain principles, as I think there are, which the constitution of our nature leads us to believe, and which we are under a necessity to take for granted in the common concerns of life, without being able to give a reason for them; these are what we call the principles of common sense; and what is manifestly contrary to them, is what we call absurd. . . .

It is a fundamental principle of [Hume's] ideal system, that every object of thought must be an impression, or an idea, that is, a faint copy of some preceding impression. This is a principle so commonly received, that the author above mentioned, although his whole system is built upon it, never offers the least proof of it. It is upon this principle, as a fixed point, that he erects his metaphysical engines, to overturn heaven and earth, body and spirit. And indeed, in my apprehension, it is altogether sufficient for the purpose. For if impressions and ideas are the only objects of thought, then heaven and earth, and body and spirit, and every thing you please, must signify only impressions and ideas, or they must be words without any meaning. It seems, therefore, that this notion, however strange, is closely connected with the received doctrine of ideas, and we must either admit the conclusion, or call in question the premises. . . .

The triumph of ideas was completed by the Treatise of Human Nature, which discards spirits also, and leaves ideas and impressions as the sole existences in the universe. What if at last, having nothing else to contend with, they should fall foul of one another, and leave no existence in nature at all? This would surely bring philosophy into danger; for what should we have left to talk or to dispute about? However, hitherto these philosophers acknowledge the existence of impressions and ideas; they acknowledge certain laws of attraction, or rules of precedence, according to which ideas and impressions range themselves in various forms, and succeed one another: but that they should belong to a mind, as its proper goods and chattels, this they have found to be a vulgar error. These ideas are as free and independent as the birds of the air. . . . They make the whole furniture of the universe; starting into existence, or out of it, without any cause; combining into parcels which the vulgar call *minds;* and succeeding one another by fixed laws, without time, place, or author of those laws. . . .

The Treatise of Human Nature . . . seems to have made but a bad return, by bestowing upon them this independent existence; since thereby they are turned out of house and home, and set adrift in the world, without friend or connection, without a rag to cover their nakedness; and who knows but the whole system of ideas may perish by the indiscreet zeal of their friends to exalt them?

However this may be, it is certainly a most amazing discovery that thought and ideas may be without any thinking being: a discovery big with consequences which cannot easily be traced by those deluded mortals who think and reason in the common track. We were always apt to imagine, that thought supposed a thinker, and love a lover, and treason a traitor; but this, it seems, was all a mistake; and it is found out, that there may be treason without a traitor, and love without a lover, laws without a legislator, and punishment without a sufferer, succession without time, and motion without any thing moved, or space in which it may move; or if, in these cases, ideas are the lover, the sufferer, the traitor, it were to be wished that the author of this discovery had farther condescended to acquaint us, whether ideas can converse together, and be under obligations of duty or gratitude to each other; whether they can make promises, and enter into leagues and covenants, and fulfil or break them, and be punished for the breach? If one set of ideas makes a covenant, another breaks it, and a third is punished for it, there is reason to think that justice is no natural virtue in this system.

It seemed very natural to think, that the Treatise of Human Nature required an author, and a very ingenious one too; but now we learn, that it is only a set of ideas which came together, and arranged themselves by certain associations and attractions.

After all, this curious system appears not to be fitted to the present state of human nature. How far it may suit some choice spirits, who are refined from the dregs of common sense, I cannot say. It is acknowledged, I think, that even these can enter into this system only in their most speculative hours, when they soar so high in pursuit of those self-existent ideas, as to lose sight of all other things. But when they condescend to mingle again with the human race, and to converse with a friend, a companion, or a fellow citizen, the ideal system[1] vanishes; common sense, like an irresistible torrent, carries them along; and, in spite of all their reasoning and philosophy, they believe their own existence, and the existence of other things. . . .

1. [Berkeley's idealism.]

This philosophy is like a hobby-horse, which a man in bad health may ride in his closet, without hurting his reputation; but if he should take him abroad with him to church, or to the exchange, or to the play house, his heir would immediately call a jury, and seize his estate.

John Perry

A DIALOGUE ON PERSONAL IDENTITY AND IMMORTALITY

JOHN PERRY, professor of philosophy at Stanford University, has written extensively on the philosophy of language, the philosophy of mind, and personal identity. In the following dialogue, a dying philosophy professor and two of her friends discuss the nature of personal identity and its relevance to the question of survival of bodily death.

The main philosophical problem of personal identity is that of specifying what makes a person the *same* person over time. Three different answers are discussed in Perry's dialogue: first, the metaphysical view according to which you are your soul (Miller's first view); second, the psychological view according to which your identity is sustained by certain psychological links—such as beliefs, intentions, memories, and preferences—between your earlier and later states (Miller's second view); and, finally, the physical view according to which you are your body (Weirob's view).

This is a record of conversations of Gretchen Weirob, a teacher of philosophy at a small midwestern college, and two of her friends. The conversations took place in her hospital room on the three nights before she died from injuries sustained in a motorcycle accident. Sam Miller is a chaplain and a longtime friend of Weirob's; Dave Cohen is a former student of hers.

From John Perry, *A Dialogue on Personal Identity and Immortality*, 1978, Hackett Publishing Co., Inc. Indianapolis, IN and Cambridge, MA. With permission of the publisher.

THE FIRST NIGHT

COHEN: I can hardly believe what you say, Gretchen. You are lucid and do not appear to be in great pain. And yet you say things are hopeless?

WEIROB: These devices can keep me alive for another day or two at most. Some of my vital organs have been injured beyond anything the doctors know how to repair, apart from certain rather radical measures I have rejected. I am not in much pain. But as I understand it that is not a particularly good sign. My brain was uninjured and I guess that's why I am as lucid as I ever am. The whole situation is a bit depressing, I fear.

But here's Sam Miller. Perhaps he will know how to cheer me up.

MILLER: Good evening, Gretchen. Hello, Dave. I guess there's not much point in beating around the bush, Gretchen; the medics tell me you're a goner. Is there anything I can do to help?

WEIROB: Crimenetley, Sam! You deal with the dying every day. Don't you have anything more comforting to say than "Sorry to hear you're a goner"?

MILLER: Well, to tell you the truth, I'm a little at a loss for what to say to you. Most people I deal with are believers like I am. We talk of the prospects for survival. I give assurance that God, who is just and merciful, would not permit such a travesty as that our short life on this earth should be the end of things. But you and I have talked about religious and philosophical issues for years. I have never been able to find in you the least inclination to believe in God; indeed, it's a rare day when you are sure that your friends have minds, or that you can see your own hand in front of your face, or that there is any reason to believe that the sun will rise tomorrow. How can I hope to comfort you with the prospect of life after death, when I know you will regard it as having no probability whatsoever?

WEIROB: I would not require so much to be comforted, Sam. Even the possibility of something quite improbable can be comforting, in certain situations. When we used to play tennis, I beat you no more than one time in twenty. But this was enough to establish the possibility of beating you on any given occasion, and by focusing merely on the possibility I remained eager to play. Entombed in a secure prison, thinking our situation quite hopeless, we may find unutterable joy in the information that there is, after all, the slimmest possibility of escape. Hope provides comfort; and hope does not always require probability. But we must believe that what we hope for is at least possible. So I will set an easier task for you. Simply persuade me that my survival after the death of this body is *possible* and I promise to be comforted. Whether you succeed or not, your attempts will be a diversion, for you know I like to talk philosophy more than anything else.

MILLER: But what is possibility, if not reasonable probability?

WEIROB: I do not mean possible in the sense of likely, or even in the sense of conforming to the known laws of physics or biology. I mean possible only in the weakest sense—of being conceivable, given the unavoidable facts. Within the next couple of days, this body will die. It will be buried and it will rot away. I ask that, given these facts, you explain to me how it even makes *sense* to talk of me continuing to exist. Just explain to me what it is I am to *imagine,* when I imagine surviving, that is consistent with these facts, and I shall be comforted.

MILLER: But then what is there to do? There are many conceptions of immortality, of survival past the grave, which all seem to make good sense. Surely not the possibility, but only the probability, can be doubted. Take your choice! Christians believe in life, with a body, in some Hereafter—the details vary, of course, from sect to sect. There is the Greek idea of the body as a prison, from which we escape at death—so that we have continued life without a body. Then there are conceptions in which, so to speak, we merge with the flow of being—

WEIROB: I must cut short your lesson in comparative religion. Survival means surviving, no more, no less. I have no doubts that I shall merge with being; plants will take root in my remains, and the chemicals that I am will continue to make their contribution to life. I am enough of an ecologist to be comforted. But survival, if it is anything, must offer comforts of a different sort, the comforts of *anticipation.* Survival means that tomorrow, or sometime in the future, there will be someone who will experience, who will see and touch and smell—or at the very least, think and reason and remember. And this person will be *me.* This person will be related to me in such a way that it is correct for me to anticipate, to look forward to, those future experiences. And I am related to her in such a way that it will be right for her to remember what I have thought and done, to feel remorse for what I have done wrong, and pride in what I have done right. And the only relation that supports anticipation and memory in this way, is simply *identity.* For it is never correct to anticipate, as happening to oneself, what will happen to someone else, is it? Or to remember, as one's own thoughts and deeds, what someone else did? So don't give me merger with being, or some such nonsense. Give me identity, or let's talk about baseball or fishing—but I'm sorry to get so emotional. I react strongly when words which mean one thing are used for another—when one talks about survival, but does not mean to say that the same person will continue to exist. It's such a sham!

MILLER: I'm sorry. I was just trying to stay in touch with the times, if you want to know the truth, for when I read modern theology or talk to my students who have studied Eastern religions, the notion of survival simply as continued existence of the same person seems out of date. Merger with Being! Merger with Being! That's all I hear. My own beliefs are quite simple, if somewhat vague. I think you will live again—with or without a body, I don't know—*I* draw comfort from my belief that you and I will be together again, after I also die. We will communicate, somehow. We will continue to grow spiritually. That's what I believe, as surely as I believe that I am sitting here. For I don't know how God could be excused, if this small sample of life is all that we are allotted: I don't know why He should have created us, if these few years of toil and torment are the end of it—

WEIROB: Remember our deal, Sam. You don't have to convince me that survival is probable, for we both agree you would not get to first base. You have only to convince me that it is possible. The only condition is that it be real survival we are talking about, not some up-to-date ersatz survival, which simply amounts to what any ordinary person would call totally ceasing to exist.

MILLER: I guess I just miss the problem, then. Of course, it's possible. You just continue to exist, after your body dies. What's to be defended or explained? You want details? Okay. Two people meet a thousand years from now, in a place that may or may not be part of this physical universe. I am one and you are the other. So you must have survived. Surely you can imagine that. What else is there to say?

WEIROB: But in a few days *I* will quit breathing, *I* will be put into a coffin, *I* will be buried. And in a few months or a few years *I* will be reduced to so much humus. That, I take it, is obvious, is given. How then can you say that I am one of these persons a thousand years from now?

Suppose I took this box of Kleenex and lit fire to it. It is reduced to ashes and I smash the ashes and flush them down the john. Then I say to you, go home and on the shelf will be *that very box of Kleenex.* It has survived! Wouldn't that be absurd? What sense could you make of it? And yet that is just what you say to me. I will rot away. And then, a thousand years later, there I will be. What sense does that make?

MILLER: There could be an *identical* box of Kleenex at your home, one just like it in every respect. And, in this sense, there is no difficulty in there being someone identical to you in the Hereafter, though your body has rotted away.

WEIROB: You are playing with words again. There could be an *exactly similar* box of Kleenex on my shelf. We sometimes use "identical" to mean "exactly similar," as when we speak of "identical twins." But I am using "identical" in a way in which *identity* is the condition of memory and correct anticipation. If I am told that tomorrow, though I will be dead, someone else that looks and sounds and thinks just like me will be alive—would that be comforting? Could I correctly *anticipate* having her experiences? Would it make sense for me to fear her pains and look forward to her pleasures? Would it be right for her to feel remorse at the harsh way I am treating you? Of course not. Similarity, however exact, is not identity. I use identity to mean there is but one thing. If I am to survive, there must be one person who lies in this bed now, and who talks to someone in your Hereafter ten or a thousand years from now. After all, what comfort could there be in the notion of a heavenly imposter, walking around getting credit for the few good things I have done?

MILLER: I'm sorry. I see that I was simply confused. Here is what I should have said. If you were merely a live human body—as the Kleenex box is merely cardboard and glue in a certain arrangement—then the death of your body would be the end of you. But surely you are more than that, fundamentally more than that. What is fundamentally you is not your body, but your soul or self or mind.

WEIROB: Do you mean these words, "soul," "self," or "mind" to come to the same thing?

MILLER: Perhaps distinctions could be made, but I shall not pursue them now. I mean the nonphysical and nonmaterial aspects of you, your consciousness. It is this that I get at with these words, and I don't think any further distinction is relevant.

WEIROB: Consciousness? I am conscious, for a while yet. I see, I hear, I think, I remember. But "to be conscious"—that is a verb. What is the subject of the verb, the thing which is conscious? Isn't it just this body, the same object that is overweight, injured, and lying in bed?—and which will be buried and not be conscious in a day or a week at the most?

MILLER: As you are a philosopher, I would expect you to be less muddled about these issues. Did Descartes not draw a clear distinction between the body and the mind, between that which is overweight, and that which is conscious? Your mind or soul is immaterial, lodged in your body while you are on earth. The two are intimately related but not identical. Now clearly, what concerns us in survival is your mind or soul. It is this which must be identical to the person before me now, and to the one I expect to see in a thousand years in heaven.

WEIROB: So I am not really this body, but a soul or mind or spirit? And this soul cannot be seen or felt or touched or smelt? That is implied, I take it, by the fact that it is immaterial?

MILLER: That's right. Your soul sees and smells, but cannot be seen or smelt.

WEIROB: Let me see if I understand you. You would admit that I am the very same person with whom you had lunch last week at Dorsey's?

MILLER: Of course you are.

WEIROB: Now when you say I am the same person, if I understand you, that is not a remark about this body you see and could touch and I fear can smell. Rather it is a remark about a soul, which you cannot see or touch or smell. The fact that the same body that now lies in front of you on the bed was across the table from you at Dorsey's—that would not mean that the same *person* was present on both occasions, if the same soul were not. And if, through some strange turn of events, the same soul were present on both occasions, but lodged in different bodies, then it *would* be the same person. Is that right?

MILLER: You have understood me perfectly. But surely, you understood all of this before!

WEIROB: But wait. I can repeat it, but I'm not sure I understand it. If you cannot see or touch or in any way perceive my soul, what makes you think the one you are confronted with now *is* the very same soul you were confronted with at Dorsey's?

MILLER: But I just explained. To say it is the same soul and to say it is the same person, are the same. And, of course, you are the same person you were before. Who else would you be if not yourself? You *were* Gretchen Weirob, and you *are* Gretchen Weirob.

WEIROB: But how do you know you are talking to Gretchen Weirob at all, and not someone else, say Barbara Walters or even Mark Spitz!

MILLER: Well, it's just obvious. I can see who I am talking to.

WEIROB: But all you can see is my body. You can see, perhaps, that the same body is before you now that was before you last week at Dorsey's. But you have just said that Gretchen Weirob is not a body but a soul. In judging that the same person is before you now as was before you then, you must be making a judgment about souls—which, you said, cannot be seen or touched or smelt or tasted. And so, I repeat, how do you know?

MILLER: Well, I *can* see that it is the same body before me now that was across the table at Dorsey's. And I know that the same soul is connected with the body now that was connected with it before. That's how I know it's you. I see no difficulty in the matter.

WEIROB: You reason on the principle, "Same body, same self."

MILLER: Yes.

WEIROB: And would you reason conversely also? If there were in this bed Barbara Walters' body—that is, the body you see every night on the news—would you infer that it was not me, Gretchen Weirob, in the bed?

MILLER: Of course I would. How would you have come by Barbara Walters' body?

WEIROB: But then merely extend this principle to Heaven, and you will see that your conception of survival is without sense. Surely this very body, which will be buried and as I must so often repeat, *rot away,* will not be in your Hereafter. Different body, different person. Or do you claim that a body can rot away on earth, and then still wind up somewhere else? Must I bring up the Kleenex box again?

MILLER: No, I do not claim that. But I also do not extend a principle, found reliable on earth, to such a different situation as is represented by the Hereafter. That a correlation between bodies and souls has been found on earth does not make it inconceivable or impossible that they should separate. Principles found to work in one circumstance may not be assumed to work in vastly altered circumstances. January and snow go together here, and one would be a fool to expect otherwise. But the principle does not apply in southern California.

WEIROB: So the principle, "same body, same soul," is a well-confirmed regularity, not something you know "a priori."

MILLER: By "a priori" you philosophers mean something which can be known without observing what actually goes on in the world—as I can know that two plus two equals four just by thinking about numbers, and that no bachelors are married, just by thinking about the meaning of "bachelor"?

WEIROB: Yes.

MILLER: Then you are right. If it was part of the meaning of "same body" that wherever we have the same body we have the same soul, it would have to obtain universally, in Heaven as well as on earth. But I just claim it is a generalization we know by observation on earth, and it need not automatically extend to Heaven.

WEIROB: But where do you get this principle? It simply amounts to a correlation between being confronted with the same body and being confronted with the same soul. To establish such a correlation in the first place, surely one must have some *other* means of judging sameness of soul. You do not have such a means; your principle is without foundation; either you really do not know the person before you now is Gretchen Weirob, the very same person you lunched with at Dorsey's, or what you do know has nothing to do with sameness of some immaterial soul.

MILLER: Hold on, hold on. You know I can't follow you when you start spitting out arguments like that. Now what is this terrible fallacy I'm supposed to have committed?

WEIROB: I'm sorry. I get carried away. Here—by way of a peace offering—have one of the chocolates Dave brought.

MILLER: Very tasty. Thank you.

WEIROB: Now why did you choose that one?

MILLER: Because it had a certain swirl on the top which shows that it is a caramel.

WEIROB: That is, a certain sort of swirl is correlated with a certain type of filling—the swirls with caramel, the rosettes with orange, and so forth.

MILLER: Yes. When you put it that way, I see an analogy. Just as I judged that the filling would be the same in this piece as in the last piece that I ate with such a swirl, so I judge that the soul with which I am conversing is the same as the last soul with which I conversed when sitting across from that body. We *see* the outer wrapping and infer what is inside.

WEIROB: But how did you come to realize that swirls of that sort and caramel insides were so associated?

MILLER: Why, from eating a great many of them over the years. Whenever I bit into a candy with that sort of swirl, it was filled with caramel.

WEIROB: Could you have established the correlation had you never been allowed to bite into a candy and never seen what happened when someone else bit into one? You could have formed the hypothesis, "same swirl, same filling." But could you have ever established it?

MILLER: It seems not.

WEIROB: So your inference, in a particular case, to the identity of filling from the identity of swirl would be groundless?

MILLER: Yes, it would. I think I see what is coming.

WEIROB: I'm sure you do. Since you can never, so to speak, bite into my soul, can never see or touch it, you have no way of testing your hypothesis that sameness of body means sameness of self.

MILLER: I daresay you are right. But now I'm a bit lost. What is supposed to follow from all of this?

WEIROB: If, as you claim, identity of persons consisted in identity of immaterial unobservable souls, then judgments of personal identity of the sort we make every day whenever we greet a friend or avoid a pest are really judgments about such souls.

MILLER: Right.

WEIROB: But if such judgments were really about souls, they would all be groundless and without foundation. For we have no direct method of observing sameness of soul, and so—and this is the point made by the candy example—we can have no indirect method either.

MILLER: That seems fair.

WEIROB: But our judgments, about persons are not all simply groundless and silly, so we must not be judging of immaterial souls after all.

MILLER: Your reasoning has some force. But I suspect the problem lies in my defense of my position, and not the position itself. Look here—there *is* a way to test the hypothesis of a correlation after all. When I entered the room, I expected you to react just as you did—argumentatively and skeptically. Had the person with this body reacted completely differently perhaps I would have been forced to conclude it was not you. For example, had she complained about not being able to appear on the six o'clock news, and missing Harry Reasoner, and so forth, I might eventually have been persuaded it *was* Barbara Walters and not you. Similarity of psychological characteristics—a person's attitudes, beliefs, memories, prejudices, and the like—is observable. These are correlated with identity of body on the one side, and of course with sameness of soul on the other. So the correlation between body and soul can be established after all by this intermediate link.

WEIROB: And how do you know that?

MILLER: Know what?

WEIROB: That where we have sameness of psychological characteristics, we have sameness of soul.

MILLER: Well, now you are really being just silly. The soul or mind is just that which is responsible for one's character, memory, belief. These are aspects of the mind, just as one's height, weight, and appearance are aspects of the body.

WEIROB: Let me grant for the sake of argument that belief, character, memory, and so forth are states of mind. That is, I suppose, I grant that what one thinks and feels is due to the states one's mind is in at that time. And I shall even grant that a mind is an immaterial thing—though I harbor the gravest doubts that this is so. I do not see how it follows that similarity of such traits requires, or is evidence to the slightest degree, for identity of the mind or soul.

Let me explain my point with an analogy. If we were to walk out of this room, down past the mill and out towards Wilbur, what would we see?

MILLER: We would come to the Blue River, among other things.

WEIROB: And how would you recognize the Blue River? I mean, of course if you left from here, you would scarcely expect to hit the Platte or Niobrara. But suppose you were actually lost, and came across the Blue River in your wandering, just at that point where an old dam partly blocks the flow. Couldn't you recognize it?

MILLER: Yes, I'm sure as soon as I saw that part of the river I would again know where I was.

WEIROB: And how would you recognize it?

MILLER: Well, the turgid brownness of the water, the sluggish flow, the filth washed up on the banks, and such.

WEIROB: In a word, the states of the water which makes up the river at the time you see it.

MILLER: Right.

WEIROB: If you saw blue clean water, with bass jumping, you would know it wasn't the Blue River.

MILLER: Of course.

WEIROB: So you expect, each time you see the Blue, to see the water, which makes it up, in similar states—not always exactly the same, for sometimes it's a little dirtier, but by and large similar.

MILLER: Yes, but what do you intend to make of this?

WEIROB: Each time you see the Blue, it consists of *different* water. The water that was in it a month ago may be in Tuttle Creek Reservoir or in the Mississippi or in the Gulf of Mexico by now. So the *similarity* of states of water, by which you judge the sameness of river, does not require *identity* of the water which is in those states at these various times.

MILLER: And?

WEIROB: And so just because you judge as to personal identity by reference to similarity of states of mind, it does not follow that the mind, or soul, is the same in each case. My point is this. For all you know, the immaterial soul which you think is lodged in my body might change from day to day, from hour to hour, from minute to minute, replaced each time by another soul psychologically similar. You cannot see it or touch it, so how would you know?

MILLER: Are you saying I don't really know who you are?

WEIROB: Not at all. *You* are the one who says personal identity consists in sameness of this immaterial, unobservable, invisible, untouchable soul. I merely point out that *if* it did consist in that, you *would* have no idea who I am. Sameness of body would not necessarily mean sameness of person. Sameness of psychological characteristics would not necessarily mean sameness of person. I am saying that if you do know who I am then you are wrong that personal identity consists in sameness of immaterial soul.

MILLER: I see. But wait. I believe my problem

is that I simply forgot a main tenet of my theory. The correlation can be established in my own case. I know that *my* soul and my body are intimately and consistently found together. From this one case I can generalize, at least as concerns life in this world, that sameness of body is a reliable sign of sameness of soul. This leaves me free to regard it as intelligible, in the case of death, that the link between the particular soul and the particular body it has been joined with is broken.

WEIROB: This would be quite an extrapolation, wouldn't it, from one case directly observed, to a couple of billion in which only the body is observed? For I take it that we are in the habit of assuming, for every person now on earth, as well as those who have already come and gone, that the principle "one body, one soul" is in effect.

MILLER: This does not seem an insurmountable obstacle. Since there is nothing special about my case, I assume the arrangement I find in it applies universally until given some reason to believe otherwise. And I never have been.

WEIROB: Let's let that pass. I have another problem that is more serious. How is it that you know in your own case that there is a single soul which has been so consistently connected with your body?

MILLER: Now you really cannot be serious, Gretchen. How can I doubt that I am the same person I was? Is there anything more clear and distinct, less susceptible to doubt? How do you expect me to prove anything to you, when you are capable of denying my own continued existence from second to second? Without knowledge of our own identity, everything we think and do would be senseless. How could I think if I did not suppose that the person who begins my thought is the one who completes it? When I act, do I not assume that the person who forms the intention is the very one who performs the action?

WEIROB: But I grant you that a single *person* has been associated with your body since you were born. The question is whether one immaterial soul has been so associated—or more precisely, whether you are in a position to know it. You believe that a judgment that one and the same person has had your body all these many years is a judgment that one and the same immaterial soul has been lodged in it. I say that such judgments concerning the soul are totally mysterious, and that if our knowledge of sameness of persons consisted in knowledge of sameness of immaterial soul, it too would be totally mysterious. To point out, as you do, that it is not mysterious, but perhaps the most secure knowledge we have, the foundation of all reason and action, is simply to make the point that it cannot consist of knowledge of identity of an immaterial soul.

MILLER: You have simply asserted, and not established, that my judgment that a single soul has been lodged in my body these many years is mysterious.

WEIROB: Well, consider these possibilities. One is that a single soul, one and the same, has been with this body I call mine since it was born. The other is that one soul was associated with it until five years ago and then another, psychologically similar, inheriting all the old memories and beliefs, took over. A third hypothesis is that every five years a new soul takes over. A fourth is that every five minutes a new soul takes over. The most radical is that there is a constant flow of souls through this body, each psychologically similar to the preceding, as there is a constant flow of water molecules down the Blue. What evidence do I have that the first hypothesis, the "single soul hypothesis" is true, and not one of the others? Because I am the same person I was five minutes or five years ago? But the issue in question is simply whether from sameness of person, which isn't in doubt, we can infer sameness of soul. Sameness of body? But how do I establish a stable relationship between soul and body? Sameness of thoughts and sensations? But they are in constant flux. By the nature of the case, if the soul cannot be observed, it cannot be observed to be the same. Indeed, no sense has ever been assigned to the phrase "same soul." Nor could any sense be attached to it! One would have to say what a single soul looked like or felt like, how an encounter with a single soul at different times differed from encounters with different souls. But this can hardly be done, since a soul according to your conception doesn't look or feel like *anything* at all. And so of course "souls" can afford no principle of identity. And so they cannot be used to bridge the gulf between my existence now and my existence in the hereafter.

MILLER: Do you doubt the existence of your own soul?

WEIROB: I haven't based my argument on there being no immaterial souls of the sort you describe, but merely on their total irrelevance to questions of personal identity, and so to questions of personal survival. I do indeed harbor grave doubts whether there are any immaterial souls of the sort to which you appeal. Can we have a notion of a soul unless we have a notion of the *same* soul? But I hope you do not think that means I doubt my own existence. I think I lie here, overweight and conscious. I think you can see me, not just some outer wrapping, for I think I am just a live human body. But that is not the basis of my argument. I give you these souls. I merely observe that they can by their nature provide no principle of personal identity.

MILLER: I admit I have no answer.

I'm afraid I do not comfort you, though I have perhaps provided you with some entertainment. Emerson said that a little philosophy turns one away from religion, but that deeper understanding brings one back. I know no one who has thought so long and hard about philosophy as you have. Will it ever lead you back to a religious frame of mind?

WEIROB: My former husband used to say that a little philosophy turns one away from religion, and more philosophy makes one a pain in the neck. Perhaps he was closer to the truth than Emerson.

MILLER: Perhaps he was. But perhaps by tomorrow night I will have come up with a better argument.

WEIROB: I hope I live to hear it.

THE SECOND NIGHT

WEIROB: Well, Sam, have you figured out a way to make sense of the identity of immaterial souls?

MILLER: No, I have decided it was a mistake to build my argument on such a dubious notion.

WEIROB: Have you then given up on survival? I think such a position would be a hard one for a clergyman to live with, and would feel bad about having pushed you so far.

MILLER: Don't worry. I'm more convinced than ever. I stayed up late last night thinking and reading, and I'm sure I can convince you now.

WEIROB: Get with it, time is running out.

MILLER: First, let me explain why, independently of my desire to defend survival after death, I am dissatisfied with your view that personal identity is just bodily identity. My argument will be very similar to the one you used to convince me that personal identity could not be identified with identity of an immaterial soul.

Consider a person waking up tomorrow morning, conscious, but not yet ready to open her eyes and look around and, so to speak, let the new day officially begin.

WEIROB: Such a state is familiar enough, I admit.

MILLER: Now couldn't such a person tell who she was? That is, even before opening her eyes and looking around, and in particular before looking at her body or making any

The temple of Mnajdra, Malta, circa 3500 B.C.

judgments about it, wouldn't she be able to say who she was? Surely most of us, in the morning, know who we are before opening our eyes and recognizing our own bodies, do we not?

WEIROB: You seem to be right about that.

MILLER: But such a judgment as this person makes—we shall suppose she judges "I am Gretchen Weirob"—*is* a judgment of personal identity. Suppose she says to herself, "I am the very person who was arguing with Sam Miller last night." This is clearly a statement about her identity with someone who was alive the night before. And she could make this judgment without examining her body at all. You could have made just this judgment this morning, before opening your eyes.

WEIROB: Well, in fact I did so. I remembered our conversation of last night and said to myself: "Could I be the rude person who was so hard on Sam Miller's attempts to comfort me?" And, of course, my answer was that I not only could be but was that very rude person.

MILLER: But then by the same principle you used last night personal identity cannot be bodily identity. For you said that it could not be identity of immaterial soul because we were not judging as to identity of immaterial soul when we judge as to personal identity. But by the same token, as my example shows, we are not judging as to bodily identity when we judge as to personal identity. For we can judge who we are, and that we are the very person who did such and such and so and so, without having to make any judgments at all about the body. So, personal identity, while it may not consist of identity of an immaterial soul, does not consist in identity of material body either.

WEIROB: I did argue as you remember. But I also said that the notion of the identity of an immaterial unobservable unextended soul seemed to make no sense at all. This is one reason that cannot be what we are judging about, when we judge as to personal identity. Bodily identity at least makes sense. Perhaps we are assuming sameness of body, without looking.

MILLER: Granted. But you do admit that we do not in our own cases actually need to make a judgment of bodily identity in order to make a judgment of personal identity?

WEIROB: I don't think I will admit it. I will let it pass, so that we may proceed.

MILLER: Okay. Now it seems to me we are even able to imagine awakening and finding ourselves to have a *different* body than the one we had before. Suppose yourself just as I have described you. And now suppose you finally open your eyes and see, not the body you have grown so familiar with over the years, but one of a fundamentally different shape and size.

WEIROB: Well, I should suppose I had been asleep for a very long time and lost a lot of weight—perhaps I was in a coma for a year or so.

MILLER: But isn't it at least conceivable that it should not be your old body at all? I seem to be able to imagine awakening with a totally new body.

WEIROB: And how would you suppose that this came about?

MILLER: That's beside the point. I'm not saying I can imagine a procedure that would bring this about. I'm saying I can imagine it happening to me. In Kafka's *Metamorphosis,* someone awakens as a cockroach. I can't imagine what would make this happen to me or anyone else, but I can imagine awakening with the body of a cockroach. It is incredible that it should happen—that I do not deny. I simply mean I can imagine experiencing it. It doesn't seem contradictory or incoherent, simply unlikely and inexplicable.

WEIROB: So, if I admit this can be imagined, what follows then?

MILLER: Well, I think it follows that personal identity does not just amount to bodily identity? For I would not, finding that I had a new body, conclude that I was not the very same person I was before. I would be the same *person,* though I did not have the same *body.* So we would have identity of person but not identity of body. So personal identity cannot just amount to bodily identity.

WEIROB: Well suppose—and I emphasize *suppose*—I grant you all of this. Where does it leave you? What do you claim I have recognized as the same, if not my body and not my immaterial soul?

MILLER: I don't claim that you have recognized anything as the same, except the person involved, that is, you yourself.

WEIROB: I'm not sure what you mean.

MILLER: Let me appeal as you did to the Blue River. Suppose I take a visitor to the stretch of river by the old Mill, and then drive him toward Manhattan. After an hour-or-so drive we see another stretch of river, and I say, "That's the same river we saw this morning." As you pointed out yesterday, I don't thereby imply that the very same molecules of water are seen both times. And the places are different, perhaps a hundred miles apart. And the shape and color and level of pollution might all be different. What do I see later in the day that is identical with what I saw earlier in the day?

WEIROB: Nothing except the river itself.

MILLER: Exactly. But now notice that what I see, strictly speaking, is not the whole river but only a part of it. I see different parts of the same river at the two different times. So really, if we restrict ourselves to what I literally see, I do not judge identity at all, but something else.

WEIROB: And what might that be?

MILLER: In saying that the river seen earlier, and the river seen later, are one and the same river, do I mean any more than that the stretch of water seen later and that stretch of water seen earlier are connected by other stretches of water?

WEIROB: That's about right. If the stretches of

water are so connected there is but one river of which they are both parts.

MILLER: Yes, that's what I mean. The statement of identity, "This river is the same one we saw this morning," is in a sense about rivers. But in a way it is also about stretches of water or river parts.

WEIROB: So is all of this something special about rivers?

MILLER: Not at all. It is a recurring pattern. After all, we constantly deal with objects extended in space and time. But we are seldom aware of the objects wholes, but only of their parts or stretches of their histories. When a statement of identity is not just something trivial, like "This bed is this bed," it is usually because we are really judging that different parts fit together, in some appropriate pattern, into a certain kind of whole.

WEIROB: I'm not sure I see just what you mean yet.

MILLER: Let me give you another example. Suppose we are sitting together watching the first game of a doubleheader. You ask me, "Is this game identical with this game?" This is a perfectly stupid question, though, of course, strictly speaking it makes sense and the answer is "yes."

But now suppose you leave in the sixth inning to go for hot dogs. You are delayed, and return after about forty-five minutes or so. You ask, "Is this the same game I was watching?" Now your question is not stupid, but perfectly appropriate.

WEIROB: Because the first game might still be going on or it might have ended, and the second game begun, by the time I return.

MILLER: Exactly. Which is to say somehow different parts of the game—different innings, or at least different plays—were somehow involved in your question. That's why it wasn't stupid or trivial but significant.

WEIROB: So, you think that judgments as to the identity of an object of a certain kind—rivers or baseball games or whatever—involve judgments as to the *parts* of those things being connected in a certain way, and are significant only when different parts are involved. Is that your point?

MILLER: Yes, and I think it is an important one. How foolish it would be, when we ask a question about the identity of baseball games, to look for something *else,* other than the game as a whole, which had to be the same. It could be the same game, even if different players were involved. It could be the same game, even if it had been moved to a different field. These other things, the innings, the plays, the players, the field, don't have to be the same at the different times for the game to be the same, they just have to be related in certain ways so as to make that complex whole we call a single game.

WEIROB: You think we were going off on a kind of a wild-goose chase when we asked whether it was the identity of soul or body that was involved in the identity of persons?

MILLER: Yes. The answer I should now give is neither. We are wondering about the identity of the person. Of course, if by "soul" we just mean "person," there is no problem. But if we mean, as I did yesterday, some other thing whose identity is already understood, which has to be the same when persons are the same, we are just fooling ourselves with words.

WEIROB: With rivers and baseball games, I can see that they are made up of parts connected in a certain way. The connection is, of course, different in the two cases, as is the sort of "part" involved. River parts must be connected physically with other river parts to form a continuous whole. Baseball innings must be connected so that the score, batting order, and the like are carried over from the earlier inning to the later one according to the rules. Is there something analogous we are to say about persons?

MILLER: Writers who concern themselves with this speak of "person-stages." That is just a stretch of consciousness, such as you and I are aware of now. I am aware of a flow of thoughts and feelings that are mine, you are aware of yours. A person is just a whole composed of such stretches as parts, not some substance that underlies them, as I thought yesterday, and not the body in which they occur, as you seem to think. That is the conception of a person I wish to defend today.

WEIROB: So when I awoke and said to myself, "I am the one who was so rude to Sam Miller last night," I was judging that a certain stretch of consciousness I was then aware of, and an earlier one I remembered having been aware of, from a single whole of the appropriate sort—a single stream of consciousness, we might say.

MILLER: Yes, that's it exactly. You need not worry about whether the same immaterial soul is involved, or even whether that makes sense. Nor need you worry about whether the same body is involved, as indeed you do not since you don't even have to open your eyes and look. Identity is not, so to speak, something under the person-stages, nor in something they are attached to, but something you build from them.

Now survival, you can plainly see, is no problem at all once we have this conception of personal identity. All you need suppose is that there is, in Heaven, a conscious being, and that the person-stages that make her up are in the appropriate relation to those that now make you up, so that they are parts of the same whole—namely, you. If so, you have survived. So will you admit now that survival is at least possible?

WEIROB: Hold on, hold on. Comforting me is not that easy. You will have to show that it is possible that these person-stages or stretches of consciousness be related in the appropriate way. And to do that, won't you have to tell me what that way is?

MILLER: Yes, of course. I was getting ahead of myself. It is right at this point that my reading was particularly helpful. In a chapter of his *Essay On Human Understanding* Locke discusses this very question. He suggests that the relation between two person-stages or stretches of consciousness that makes them stages of a single person is just that the later one contains memories of the earlier one. He doesn't say this in so many words—he talks of "extending our consciousness back in time." But he seems to be thinking of memory.

WEIROB: So, any past thought or feeling or intention or desire that I can remember having is mine?

MILLER: That's right. I can remember only my own past thoughts and feelings, and you only yours. Of course, everyone would readily admit that. Locke's insight is to take this relation as the source of identity and not just its consequence. To remember—or more plausibly, to be able to remember—the thoughts and feelings of a person who was conscious in the past is just what it is to be that person.

Now you can easily see that this solves the problem of the possibility of survival. As I was saying, all you need to do is imagine someone at some future time, not on this earth and not with your present thoughts and feelings, remembering the very conversation we are having now. This does not require sameness of anything else, but it amounts to sameness of person. So, now will you admit it?

WEIROB: No, I don't.

MILLER: Well, what's the problem now?

WEIROB: I admit that if I remember having a certain thought or feeling had by some person in the past, then I must indeed be that person. Though I can remember watching others think, I cannot remember their thinking, any more than I can experience it at the time it occurs if it is theirs and not mine. This is the kernel of Locke's idea, and I don't see that I could deny it.

But we must distinguish—as I'm sure you will agree—between *actually* remembering and merely *seeming* to remember. Many men who think that they are Napoleon claim to remember losing the battle of Waterloo. We may suppose them to be sincere, and to really seem to remember it. But they do not actually remember because they were not at the battle and are not Napoleon.

MILLER: Of course I admit that we must distinguish between actually remembering and only seeming to.

WEIROB: And you will admit too, I trust, that the thought of some person at some far place and some distant time seeming to remember this conversation I am having with you would not give me the sort of comfort that the prospect of survival is supposed to provide. I would have no reason to anticipate future experiences of this person, simply because she is to *seem* to remember my experiences. The experiences of such a deluded imposter are not ones I can look forward to having.

MILLER: I agree.

WEIROB: So the mere possibility of someone in the future seeming to remember this conversation does not show the possibility of my surviving. Only the possibility of someone actually remembering this conversation—or, to be precise, the experiences I am having—would show that.

MILLER: Of course. But what are you driving at? Where is the problem? I can imagine someone being deluded, but also someone actually being you and remembering your present thoughts.

WEIROB: But, what's the difference? How do you know *which* of the two you are imagining, and *what* you have shown possible?

MILLER: Well, I just imagine the one and not the other. I don't see the force of your argument.

WEIROB: Let me try to make it clear with another example. Imagine two persons. One is talking to you, saying certain words, having certain thoughts, and so forth. The other is not talking to you at all, but is in the next room being hypnotized. The hypnotist gives to this person a post-hypnotic suggestion that upon awakening he will remember having had certain thoughts and having uttered certain words to you. The thoughts and words he mentions happen to be just the thoughts and words which the first person actually thinks and says. Do you understand the situation?

MILLER: Yes, continue.

WEIROB: Now, in a while, both of the people are saying sentences which begin, "I remember saying to Sam Miller—" and "I remember thinking as I talked to Sam Miller." And they both report remembering just the same thoughts and utterances. One of these will be remembering and the other only seeming to remember, right?

MILLER: Of course.

WEIROB: Now which one is *actually* remembering?

MILLER: Why, the very one who was in the room talking to me, of course. The other one is just under the influence of the suggestion made by the hypnotist and not remembering talking to me at all.

WEIROB: Now you agree that the difference between them does not consist in the content of what they are now thinking or saying.

MILLER: Agreed. The difference is in the relation to the past thinking and speaking. In the one case the relation of memory obtains. In the other, it does not.

WEIROB: But they both satisfy part of the conditions of remembering, for they both *seem to remember*. So there must be some further condition that the one satisfies and the other does not. I am trying to get you to say what that further condition is.

MILLER: Well, I said that the one who had been in this room talking would be remembering.

WEIROB: In other words, given two putative rememberers of some past thought or action, the real rememberer is the one who, in addition to seeming to remember the past thought or action, actually thought it or did it.

MILLER: Yes.

WEIROB: That is to say, the one who is identical with the person who did the past thinking and uttering.

MILLER: Yes, I admit it.

WEIROB: So, your argument just amounts to this. Survival is possible, because imaginable. It is imaginable, because my identity with some Heavenly person is imaginable. To imagine it, we imagine a person in Heaven who, First, seems to remember my thoughts and actions, and Second, is me.

Surely, there could hardly be a tighter circle. If I have doubts that the Heavenly person is me, I will have doubts as to whether she is really remembering or only seeming to. No one could doubt the possibility of some future person who, after death, seemed to remember the things he thought and did. But that possibility does not resolve the issue about the possibility of survival. Only the possibility of someone *actually* remembering could do that—for that, as we agree, is sufficient for identity. But doubts about survival and identity simply go over without remainder into doubts about whether the memories would be actual or merely apparent. You guarantee me no more than the possibility of a deluded Heavenly imposter.

COHEN: But wait, Gretchen. I think Sam was less than fair to his own idea just now.

WEIROB: You think you can break out of the circle of using real memory to explain identity, and identity to mark the difference between real and apparent memory? Feel free to try.

COHEN: Let us return to your case of the hypnotist. You point out that we have two putative rememberers. You ask what marks the difference, and claim the answer must be the circular one—that the real rememberer is the person who actually had the experiences both seem to remember.

But that is not the only possible answer. The experiences themselves cause the later apparent memories in the one case, while the hypnotist causes them in the other. We can say that the rememberer is the one of the two whose memories were *caused in the right way* by the earlier experiences. We thus distinguish between the rememberer and the hypnotic subject, without appeal to identity.

The idea that real memory amounts to apparent memory plus identity is misleading anyway. I seem to remember, as a small child, knocking over the Menorah so the candles fell into and spoiled a tureen of soup. And I did actually perform such a feat. So we have apparent memory and identity. But I do *not* actually remember; I was much too young when I did this to remember it now. I have simply been told the story so often I seem to remember.

Here the suggestion that real memory is apparent memory that was caused in the appropriate way by the past events fares better. Not my experience of pulling over the Menorah, but hearing my parents talk about it later, caused my memory-like impressions.

WEIROB: You analyze personal identity into memory, and memory into apparent memory which is caused in the right way. A person is a certain sort of causal process.

COHEN: Right.

WEIROB: Suppose now for the sake of argument I accept this. How does it help Sam in his defense of the possibility of survival? In ordinary memory, the causal chain from remembered event to memory of it never leads us outside the confines of a single body. Indeed, the normal process of which you speak surely involves storage of information somehow in the brain. How can the states of my brain, when I die, influence in the appropriate way the apparent memories of the Heavenly person Sam takes to be me?

COHEN: Well, I didn't intend to be defending the possibility of survival. That is Sam's problem. I just like the idea that personal identity can be explained in terms of memory, and not just in terms of identity of the body.

MILLER: But surely, this does provide me with the basis for further defense. Your challenge, Gretchen, was to explain the difference between two persons in Heaven, one who actually remembers your experience—and so is you—and one who simply seems to remember it. But can I not just say that the one who is you is the one whose states were caused in the appropriate way? I do not mean the way they would be in a normal case of earthly memory. But in the case of the Heavenly being who is you, God would have created her with the brain states (or whatever) she has *because* you had the ones you had at death. Surely it is not the exact form of the dependence of my later memories on my earlier perceptions that makes them really memories, but the fact that the process involved has preserved information.

WEIROB: So if God creates a Heavenly person, designing her brain to duplicate the brain I have upon death, that person is me. If, on the other hand, a Heavenly being should come to be with those very same memory-like states by accident (if there are accidents in Heaven) it would not be me.

MILLER: Exactly. Are you satisfied now that survival makes perfectly good sense?

WEIROB: No. I'm still quite unconvinced.

The problem I see is this. If God could create one person in Heaven, and by designing her after me, make her me, why could he not make two such bodies, and cause this transfer of information into both of them? Would both of these Heavenly persons then be me? It seems as clear as anything in philosophy that from

A is B

and

C is B

where by "is" we mean identity, we can infer,

A is C.

So, if each of these Heavenly persons is me, they must be each other. But then they are not two but one. But my assumption was that God creates two, not one. He could create them physically distinct, capable of independent movement, perhaps in widely separated Heavenly locations, each with her own duties to perform, her own circle of Heavenly friends, and the like.

So either God, by creating a Heavenly person with a brain modeled after mine, does not really create someone identical with me but merely someone similar to me, or God is somehow limited to making only one such being. I can see no reason why, if there were a God, He should be so limited. So I take the first option. He could create someone similar to me, but not someone who would *be* me. Either your analysis of memory is wrong, and such a being does not, after all, remember what I am doing or saying, or memory is not sufficient for personal identity. Your theory has gone wrong somewhere, for it leads to absurdity.

COHEN: But wait. Why can't Sam simply say that if God makes one such creature, she is you, while if he makes more, none of them is you? It's possible that he makes only one. So it's possible that you survive. Sam always meant to allow that it's *possible* that you won't survive. He had in mind the case in which there is no God to make the appropriate Heavenly persons, or God exists, but doesn't make even one. You have simply shown that there is another way of not surviving. Instead of making too few Heavenly rememberers, He makes too many. So what? He might make the right number, and then you would survive.

WEIROB: Your remarks really amount to a change in your position. Now you are not claiming that memory alone is enough for personal identity. Now, it is memory *plus* lack of competition, the absence of other rememberers, that is needed for personal identity.

COHEN: It does amount to a change of position. But what of it? Is there anything untenable about the position as changed?

WEIROB: Let's look at this from the point of view of the Heavenly person. She says to herself, "Oh, I must be Gretchen Weirob, for I remember doing what she did and saying what she said." But now that's a pretty tenuous conclusion, isn't it? She is really only entitled to say, "Oh, either I'm Gretchen Weirob, or God has created more than one being like me, and none of us is." Identity has become something dependent on things wholly extrinsic to her. Who she is now turns on not just her states of mind and their relation to my states of mind, but on the existence or nonexistence of other people. Is this really what you want to maintain?

Or look at it from my point of view. God creates one of me in Heaven. Surely I should be glad if convinced this was to happen. Now he creates another, and I should despair again, for this means I won't survive after all. How can doubling a good deed make it worthless?

COHEN: Are you saying that this is some contradiction in my suggestion that only creation of a unique Heavenly Gretchen counts as your survival?

WEIROB: No, it's not contradictory, as far as I can see. But it seems odd in a way that shows that something somewhere is wrong with your theory. Here is a certain relationship I have with a Heavenly person. There being such a person, to whom I am related in this way, is something that is of great importance to me, a source of comfort. It makes it appropriate for me to anticipate having her experiences, since she is just me. Why should my having that relation to another being destroy my relation to this one? You say because then I will not be identical with either of them. But since you have provided a theory about what that identity consists in, we can look and see what it amounts to for me to be or not to be identical. If she is to remember my experience, I can rightly anticipate hers. But then it seems the doubling makes no difference. And yet it must, for one cannot be identical with two. So you add, in a purely *ad hoc* manner, that her memory of me isn't enough to make my anticipation of her experiences appropriate, if there are two rather than one so linked. Isn't it more reasonable to conclude, since memory does not secure identity when there are two Heavenly Gretchens, it also doesn't when there is only one?

COHEN: There is something *ad hoc* about it, I admit. But perhaps that's just the way our concept works. You have not elicited a contradiction—

WEIROB: An infinite pile of absurdities has the same weight as a contradiction. And absurdities can be generated without limit from your account. Suppose God created this Heavenly person before I died. Then He in effect kills me; if He has already created her, then you really are not talking to whom you think, but someone new, created by Gretchen Weirob's strange death moments ago. Or suppose He first creates one being in Heaven, who is me. Then He creates another. Does the first cease to be me? If God can create such beings in Heaven, surely He can do so in Albuquerque. And there is nothing on your theory to favor this body before you as Gretchen Weirob's, over the one belonging to the person created in Albuquerque. So I am to suppose that if God were to do this, I would suddenly cease to be. I'm tempted to say I would cease to be Gretchen Weirob. But that would be a confused way of putting it. There would be here, in my place, a new person with false memories of having been Gretchen Weirob, who has just died of competition—a strange death if ever there was one. She would have no right to my name, my bank account, or the services of my doctor, who is paid from insurance premiums paid for by deductions from Gretchen Weirob's past salary. Surely this is nonsense; however carefully God should choose to duplicate me, in Heaven or in Albuquerque, I would not cease to be, or cease to be who I am. You may reply that God, being benevolent, would never create an extra Gretchen Weirob. But I do not say that he would, but only that if he did this would not, as your theory implies, mean that I cease to exist. Your theory gives the wrong answer in this possible circumstance, so it must be wrong. I think I have been given no motivation to abandon the most obvious and straightforward view on these matters, I am a live body, and when that body dies, my existence will be at an end.

THE THIRD NIGHT

WEIROB: Well, Sam, are you here for a third attempt to convince me of the possibility of survival?

MILLER: No, I have given up. I suggest we talk about fishing or football or something unrelated to your imminent demise. You will outwit any straightforward attempts to comfort you, but perhaps I can at least divert your mind.

COHEN: But before we start on fishing—although I don't have any particular brief for survival—there is one point in our discussion of the last two evenings that still bothers me. Would you mind discussing for a while the notion of personal identity itself, without worrying about the more difficult case of survival after death?

WEIROB: I would enjoy it. What point bothers you?

COHEN: Your position seems to be that personal identity amounts to identity of a human body, nothing more, nothing less. A person is just a live human body, or more precisely, I suppose, a human body that is alive and has certain capacities—consciousness and perhaps rationality. Is that right?

WEIROB: Yes, it seems that simple to me.

COHEN: But I think there has actually been an episode which disproves that. I am thinking of the strange case of Julia North, which occurred in California a few months ago. Surely you remember it.

WEIROB: Yes, only too well. But you had better explain it to Sam, for I'll wager he has not heard of it.

COHEN: Not heard of Julia North? But the case was all over the headlines.

MILLER: Well, Gretchen is right. I know nothing of it. She knows that I only read the sports page.

COHEN: You only read the sports page!

WEIROB: It's an expression of his unconcern with earthly matters.

MILLER: Well, that's not quite fair, Gretchen. It's a matter of preference. I much prefer to spend what time I have for reading in reading about the eighteenth century, rather than the drab and miserable century into which I had the misfortune to be born. It was really a much more civilized century, you know. But let's not dwell on my peculiar habits. Tell me about Julia North.

COHEN: Very well. Julia North was a young woman who was run over by a streetcar while saving the life of a young child who wandered onto the tracks. The child's mother, one Mary Frances Beaudine, had a stroke while watching the horrible scene. Julia's healthy brain and wasted body, and Mary Frances' healthy body and wasted brain, were transported to a hospital where a brilliant neurosurgeon, Dr. Matthews, was in residence. He had worked out a procedure for what he called a "body transplant." He removed the brain from Julia's head and placed it in Mary Frances', splicing the nerves, and so forth, using techniques not available until quite recently. The survivor of all of this was obviously Julia, as everyone agreed—except, unfortunately, Mary Frances' husband. His shortsightedness and lack of imagination led to great complications and drama, and made the case more famous in the history of crime than in the history of medicine. I shall not go into the details of this sorry aspect of the case—they are well reported in a book by Barbara Harris called *Who is Julia?,* in case you are interested.

MILLER: Fascinating!

COHEN: Well, the relevance of this case is obvious. Julia North had one body up until the time of the accident, and another body after the operation. So one person had two bodies. So a person cannot be simply *identified* with a human body. So something must be wrong with your view, Gretchen. What do you say to this?

WEIROB: I'll say to you just what I said to Dr. Matthews—

COHEN: You have spoken with Dr. Matthews?

WEIROB: Yes. He contacted me shortly after my accident. My physician had phoned him up about my case. Matthews said he could perform the same operation for me he did for Julia North. I refused.

COHEN: You refused? But Gretchen, why—?

MILLER: Gretchen, I *am* shocked. Your decision practically amounts to suicide! You passed up an opportunity to continue living? Why on earth—

WEIROB: Hold on, hold on. You are both making an assumption I reject. If the case of Julia North amounts to a counterexample to my view that a person is just a live human body, and if my refusal to submit to this procedure amounts to suicide, then the survivor of such an operation must be reckoned as the same person as the brain donor. That is, the survivor of Julia North's operation must have been Julia, and the survivor of the operation on me would have to be me. This is the assumption you both make in criticizing me. But I reject it. I think Jack Beaudine was right. The survivor of the operation involving Julia North's brain was Mary Frances Beaudine, and the survivor of the operation using my brain would not have been me.

MILLER: Gretchen, how on earth can you say that? Will you not give up your view that personal identity is just bodily identity, no matter how clear the counterexample? I really think you simply have an irrational attachment to the lump of material that is your body.

COHEN: Yes, Gretchen, I agree with Sam. You are being preposterous! The survivor of Julia North's operation had no idea who Mary Frances Beaudine was. She remembered being Julia—

WEIROB: She *seemed* to remember being Julia. Have you forgotten so quickly the importance of this distinction? In my opinion, the effect of the operation was that Mary Frances Beaudine survived deluded, thinking she was someone else.

COHEN: But as you know, the case was litigated. It went to the Supreme Court. They said that the survivor was Julia.

WEIROB: That argument is unworthy of you, Dave. Is the Supreme Court infallible?

COHEN: No, it isn't. But I don't think it's such a stupid point.

Look at it this way, Gretchen. This is a case in which two criteria we use to make judgments of identity conflict. Usually we expect personal identity to involve both bodily identity and psychological continuity. That is, we expect that if we have the same body, then the beliefs, memories, character traits, and the like also will be enormously similar. In this case, these two criteria which usually coincide do not. If we choose one criterion, we say that the survivor is Mary Frances Beaudine and she has undergone drastic psychological changes. If we choose the other, we say that Julia has survived with a new body. We have to choose which criterion is more important. It's a matter of choice of how to use our language, how to extend the concept "same person" to a new situation. The overwhelming majority of people involved in the case took the survivor to be Julia. That is, society chose to use the concept one way rather than the other. The Supreme Court is *not* beside the point. One of their functions is to settle just how old concepts shall be applied to new circumstances—how "freedom of the press" is to be understood when applied to movies or television, whose existence was not forseen when the concept was shaped, or to say whether "murder" is to include the abortion of a fetus. They are fallible on points of fact, but they are the final authority on the development of certain important concepts used in law. The notion of *person* is such a concept.

WEIROB: You think that *who* the survivor was, was a matter of convention, of how we choose to use language?

COHEN: Yes.

WEIROB: I can show the preposterousness of all that with an example.

Let us suppose that I agree to the operation. I lie in bed, expecting my continued existence, anticipating the feelings and thoughts I shall have upon awakening after the operation. Dr. Matthews enters and asks me to take several aspirin, so as not to have a headache when I awake. I protest that aspirin upsets my stomach; he asks whether I would rather have a terrible headache tomorrow or a mild stomachache now, and I agree that it would be reasonable to take them.

Let us suppose that you enter at this point, with bad news. The Supreme Court has changed its mind! So the survivor will not be me. So, I say, "Oh, then I will not take the aspirin, for it's not me that will have a headache, but someone else. Why should I endure a stomachache, however mild, for the comfort of someone else? After all, I am already donating my brain to that person."

Now this is clearly absurd. If I were correct, in the first place, to anticipate having the sensations and thoughts that the survivor is to have the next day, the decision of nine old men a thousand or so miles away wouldn't make me wrong. And if I was wrong to so anticipate, their decision couldn't make me right. How can the correctness of my anticipation of survival be a matter of the way we use our words? If it is not such a matter, then my identity is not either. My identity with the survivor, my survival, is a question of fact, not of convention.

COHEN: Your example is persuasive. I admit I am befuddled. On the one hand, I cannot see how the matter can be other than I have described. When we know all the facts what can remain to be decided but how we are to describe them, how we are to use our language? And yet I can see that it seems absurd to suppose that the correctness or incorrectness of anticipation of future experience is a matter of convention to decide.

MILLER: Well, I didn't think the business about convention was very plausible anyway. But I should like to return you to the main question, Gretchen. Fact or convention, it still remains. Why will you not admit that the survivor of this operation would be you?

WEIROB: Well, *you* tell *me,* why you think she would be me?

MILLER: I can appeal to the theory I developed last night. You argued that the idea that personal identity consists in memory would not guarantee the possibility of survival after death. But you said nothing to shake its plausibility as an account of personal identity. It has the enormous advantage, remember, of making sense of our ability to judge our own identity, without examination of our bodies. I should argue that it is the correctness of this theory that explains the *almost* universal willingness to say that the survivor of Julia's operation was Julia. We need not deliberate over how to extend our concept, we need only apply the concept we already have. Memory is sufficient for identity and bodily identity is *not* necessary for it. The survivor remembered Julia's thoughts and actions, and so was Julia. Would you but submit to the operation, the survivor would remember your thoughts and actions, would remember this very conversation we are now having, and would be you.

COHEN: Yes, I now agree completely with Sam.

The theory that personal identity is to be analyzed in terms of memory is correct, and according to it you will survive if you submit to the operation.

Let me add another argument against your view and in favor of the memory theory. You have emphasized that identity is the condition of *anticipation*. That means, among other things, that we have a particular concern for that person in the future whom we take to be ourselves. If I were told that any of the three of us were to suffer pain tomorrow, I should be sad. But if it were you or Sam that were to be hurt, my concern would be altruistic or unselfish. That is because I would not anticipate having the painful experience myself. Here I do no more than repeat points you have made earlier in our conversations.

Now what is there about mere sameness of body that makes sense of this asymmetry, between the way we look at our own futures, and the way we look at the futures of others? In other words, why is the identity of your body—that mere lump of matter, as Sam put it—of such great importance? Why care so much about it?

WEIROB: You say, and I surely agree, that identity of person is a very special relationship—so special as perhaps not even happily called a relationship at all. And you say that since my theory is that identity of person is identity of body, I should be able to explain the importance of the one in terms of the importance of the other.

I'm not sure I can do that. But does the theory that personal identity consists in memory fare better on this score?

COHEN: Well, I think it does. Those properties of persons which make persons of such great value, and mark their individuality, and make one person so special to his friends and loved ones, are ultimately psychological or mental. One's character, personality, beliefs, attitudes, convictions—they are what makes every person so unique and special. A skinny Gretchen would be a shock to us all, but not a Gretchen diminished in any important way. But a Gretchen who was not witty, or not gruff, or not as honest to the path an argument takes as is humanly possible—those would be fundamental changes. Is it any wonder that the survivor of that California fiasco was reckoned as Julia North? Would it make sense to take her to be Mary Frances Beaudine, when she had none of her beliefs or attitudes or memories?

Now if such properties are what is of importance about a person to others, is it not reasonable that they are the basis of one's importance to oneself? And these are just the properties that personal identity preserves when it is taken to consist in links of memory. Do we not have, in this idea, at least the beginning of an explanation of the importance of identity?

WEIROB: So on two counts you two favor the memory theory. First, you say it explains how it is possible to judge as to one's own identity, without having to examine one's body. Second, you say it explains the importance of personal identity.

COHEN: Now surely you must agree the memory theory is correct. Do you agree? There may be still time to contact Dr. Matthews—

WEIROB: Hold on, hold on. Try to relax and enjoy the argument. I am. Quit trying to save my life and worry about saving your theory—for I'm still not persuaded. Granted the survivor will *think* she is me, will *seem* to remember thinking my thoughts. But recall the importance of distinguishing between real and merely apparent memory—

COHEN: But *you* recall that this distinction is to be made on the basis of whether the apparent memories were or were not caused by the prior experiences in the appropriate way. The survivor will not seem to remember your thoughts because of hypnosis or by coincidence or overweening imagination. She will seem to remember them because the traces those experiences left on your brain now activate her mind in the usual way. She will seem to remember them because she does remember them, and will be you.

WEIROB: You are very emphatic, and I'm feeling rather weak. I'm not sure there is time left to untangle all of this. But there is never an advantage to hurrying when doing philosophy. So let's go over this slowly.

We all agree that the fact that the survivor of this strange operation Dr. Matthews proposes would *seem* to remember doing what I have done. Let us even suppose she would take herself to be me, claim to be Gretchen Weirob—and have no idea who else she might be. (We are then assuming that she differs from me in one aspect—her theory of personal identity. But that does not show her not to be me, for I could change my mind by then.) We all first agree that this much does not make her me. For this could all be true of someone suffering a delusion, or a subject of hypnosis.

COHEN: Yes, this is all agreed.

WEIROB: But now you think that some *future* condition is satisfied, which makes her apparent memories *real* memories. Now what exactly is this future condition?

COHEN: Well, that the same brain was involved in the perception of the events, and their later *memory*. Thus we have here a causal chain of just the same sort as when only a single body is involved. That is, perceptions when the event occurs leave a trace in the brain, which is later responsible for the content of the memory. And we agreed, did we not, that apparent memory, caused in the right way, is real memory?

WEIROB: Now is it absolutely crucial that the same brain is involved?

COHEN: What do you mean?

WEIROB: Let me explain again by reference to Dr. Matthews. In our conversation he explained a new procedure on which he was working, called a *brain rejuvenation*. By this process, which is not yet available—only the feasibility of developing it is being studied—a new brain could be made which is an exact duplicate of my brain—that is, an exact duplicate in terms of psychologically relevant states. It might not duplicate all the properties of my brain—for example, the blood vessels in the new brain might be stronger than in the old brain.

MILLER: What is the point of developing such a macabre technique?

WEIROB: Dr. Matthews' idea is that when weaknesses which might lead to stroke or other brain injury are noted, a healthy duplicate could be made to replace the original, forestalling the problem.

Now Dave, suppose my problem were not with my liver and kidneys and such, but with my brain. Would you recommend such an operation as to my benefit?

COHEN: You mean, do I think the survivor of such an operation would be you?

WEIROB: Exactly. You may assume that Dr. Matthews' technique works perfectly so the causal process involved is no less reliable than that involved in ordinary memory.

COHEN: Then I would say it was you—No! Wait! No, it wouldn't be you—absolutely not.

MILLER: But why the sudden reversal? It seems to me it would be her. Indeed, I should try such an operation myself, if it would clear up my dizzy spells and leave me otherwise unaffected.

COHEN: No, don't you see, she is leading us into a false trap. If we say it *is* her, then she will say, "then what if he makes two duplicates, or three or ten? They can't all be me, they all have an equal claim, so none will be me." It would be the argument of last night, reapplied on earth. So the answer is no, absolutely not, it wouldn't be you. Duplication of brain does not preserve identity. Identity of the person requires identity of the brain.

MILLER: Quite right.

WEIROB: Now let me see if I have managed to understand your theory, for my powers of concentration seem to be fading. Suppose we have two bodies, A and B. My brain is put into A, a duplicate into B. The survivor of this, call them "A-Gretchen" and "B-Gretchen," both seem to remember giving this very speech. Both are in this state of seeming to remember, as the last stage in an information-preserving causal chain, initiated by my giving this speech. Both have my character, personality, beliefs, and the like. But one is *really* remembering, the other is not. A-Gretchen is really me, B-Gretchen is not.

COHEN: Precisely. Is this incoherent?

WEIROB: No, I guess there is nothing incoherent about it. But look what has happened to the advantages you claimed for the memory theory.

First, you said, it explains how I can know who I am without opening my eyes and recognizing my body. But on your theory Gretchen-A and Gretchen-B cannot know who they are even if they do open their eyes and examine their bodies. How is Gretchen-A to know whether she has the original brain and is who she seems to be, or has the duplicate and is a new person, only a few minutes old, and with no memories but mere delusions? If the hospital kept careless records, or the surgeon thought it was of no great importance to keep track of who got the original and who got the duplicate, she might never know who she was. By making identity of person turn into identity of brain, your theory makes the ease with which I can determine who I am not less but more mysterious than my theory.

Second, you said, your theory explains why my concern for Gretchen-A, who is me whether she knows it or not, would be selfish, and my anticipation of her experience correct while my concern for Gretchen-B with her duplicated brain would be unselfish, and my anticipation of having her experiences incorrect. And it explains this, you said, because by insisting on the links of memory, we preserve in personal identity more psychological characteristics which are the most important features of a person.

But Gretchen-A and Gretchen-B are psychologically indiscernible. Though they will go their separate ways, at the moment of awakening they could well be exactly similar in every psychological respect. In terms of character and belief and the contents of their minds, Gretchen-A is no more like me than Gretchen-B. So there is nothing in your theory after all to explain why anticipation is appropriate when we have identity and not otherwise.

You said, Sam, that I had an irrational attachment for this unworthy material object, my body. But you too are as irrationally attached to your brain. I have never seen my brain. I should have easily given it up for a rejuvenated version, had that been the choice with which I was faced. I have never seen it, never felt it, and have no attachment to it. But my body? That seems to me all that I am. I see no point in trying to evade its fate, even if there were still time.

But perhaps I miss the merit of your arguments. I am tired, and perhaps my poor brain, feeling slighted, has begun to desert me—

COHEN: Oh, don't worry, Gretchen, you are still clever. Again you have left me befuddled. I don't know what to say. But answer me this. Suppose you are right and we are wrong. But suppose these arguments had not occurred to you, and, sharing in our error, you had agreed to the operation. You anticipate the operation until it happens, thinking you will survive. You are happy. The survivor takes herself to be you, and thinks she made a decision before the operation which has now turned out to be right. She is happy. Your friends are happy. Who would be worse off, either before or after the operation?

Suppose even that you realize identity would not be preserved by such an operation, but have it done anyway, and as the time for the operation approaches, you go ahead and anticipate the experiences of the survivor. Where exactly is the mistake? Do you really have any less reason to care for the survivor than for yourself? Can mere identity of body, the lack of which alone keeps you from being her, mean that much? Perhaps we were wrong, after all, in focusing on identity as the necessary condition of anticipation—

MILLER: Dave, it's too late.

Curt J. Ducasse

"IS LIFE AFTER DEATH POSSIBLE?"

CURT J. DUCASSE, born in 1881 in France, and for most of his career professor of philosophy at Brown University, wrote extensively on metaphysics and philosophy of mind. He is perhaps best known for his defense of mind-body dualism. And, though he was an atheist, he defended the real possibility of survival of bodily death. He died in 1969.

The question whether human personality survives death is sometimes asserted to be one upon which reflection is futile. Only empirical evidence, it is said, can be relevant, since the question is purely one of fact.

But no question is purely one of fact until it is clearly understood; and this one is, on the contrary, ambiguous and replete with tacit assumptions. Until the ambiguities have been removed and the assumptions critically examined, we do not really know just what it is we want to know when we ask whether a life after death is possible. Nor, therefore, can we tell until then what bearing on this question various facts empirically known to us may have.

To clarify its meaning is chiefly what I now propose to attempt. I shall ask first why a future life is so generally desired and believed in. Then I shall state, as convincingly as I can in the time available, the arguments commonly advanced to prove that such a life is impossible. After that, I shall consider the logic of these arguments, and show that they quite fail to establish the impossibility. Next, the tacit but arbitrary assumption, which makes them nevertheless appear convincing, will be pointed out. And finally, I shall consider briefly a number of specific forms which a life after death might take, if there is one.

Let us turn to the first of these tasks.

WHY MAN DESIRES LIFE AFTER DEATH

To begin with, let us note that each of us here has been alive and conscious at all times in the past which he can remember. It is true that sometimes our bodies are in deep sleep, or made inert by anesthetics or injuries. But even at such times we do not experience unconsciousness in ourselves, for to experience it would mean being conscious of being unconscious, and this is a contradiction. The only experience of unconsciousness in ourselves we ever have is, not experience of total unconsciousness, but of unconsciousness of *this or that;* as when we report: "I am not conscious of any pain," or "of any bell-sound," or "of any difference between those two colors," etc. Nor do we ever experience unconsciousness in another person, but only the fact that, sometimes, some or all of the ordinary activities of his body cease to occur. That consciousness itself is extinguished at such times is thus only a hypothesis which we construct to account for certain changes in the behavior of another person's body or to explain in him or in ourselves the eventual lack of memories relating to the given period.

Being alive and conscious is thus, with all men, a lifelong experience and habit; and conscious life is therefore something they naturally—even if tacitly—expect to continue. As J. B. Pratt has pointed out, the child takes the continuity of life for granted. It is the fact of death that has to be taught him. But when he has learned it, and the idea of a future life is then put explicitly before his mind, it seems to him the most natural thing in the world.[1]

The witnessing of death, however, is a rare experience for most of us, and, because it breaks so sharply into our habits, it forces on us the question whether the mind, which until then was manifested by the body now dead, continues somehow to live on, or, on the contrary, has become totally extinct. This question is commonly phrased as concerning "the immortality of the soul," and immortality, strictly speaking, means survival forever. But assurance of survival for some considerable period—say a thousand, or even a hundred, years—would probably have almost as much present psychological value as would assurance of survival strictly forever. Most men would be troubled very little by the idea of extinction at so distant a time—even less trouble than is now a healthy and happy youth by the idea that he will die in fifty or sixty years. Therefore, it is survival for some time, rather than survival specifically forever, that I shall alone consider.

The craving for continued existence is very widespread. Even persons who believe that death means complete extinction of the individual's consciousness often find comfort in various substitute conceptions of survival. They may, for instance, dwell on the continuity of the individual's germ plasm in his descendants. Or they find solace in the thought that, the past being indestructible, their individual life remains eternally an intrinsic part of the history of the world. Also—and more satisfying to one's craving for personal importance—there is the fact that since the acts of one's life have effects, and these in turn further effects, and so on, therefore what one has done goes on forever influencing remotely, and sometimes greatly, the course of future events.

Gratifying to one's vanity, too, is the prospect that, if the achievements of one's life have been great or even only conspicuous, or one's benefactions or evil deeds have been notable, one's name may not only be remembered by acquaintances and relatives for a little while, but may live on in recorded history. But evidently survival in any of these senses is but a consolation prize—but a thin substitute for the continuation of conscious individual life, which may not be a fact, but which most men crave nonetheless.

The roots of this craving are certain desires which death appears to frustrate. For some, the chief of these is for reunion with persons dearly loved. For others, whose lives have been wretched, it is the desire for another chance at the happiness they have missed. For others yet, it is desire for further opportunity to grow in ability, knowledge or character. Often, there is also the desire, already mentioned, to go on counting for something in the affairs of men. And again, a

1. J. B. Pratt, *The Religious Consciousness,* p. 225.

future life for oneself and others is often desired in order that the redressing of the many injustices of this life shall be possible. But it goes without saying that, although desires such as these are often sufficient to cause belief in a future life, they constitute no evidence at all that it is a fact.

In this connection, it may be well to point out that, although both the belief in survival and the belief in the existence of a god or gods are found in most religions, nevertheless there is no necessary connection between the two beliefs. No contradiction would be involved in supposing either that there is a God but no life after death or that there is a life after death but no God. The belief that there is a life after death may be tied to a religion, but it is no more intrinsically religious than would be a belief that there is life on the planet Mars. The after-death world, if it exists, is just another region or dimension of the universe.

But although belief in survival of death is natural and easy and has always been held in one form or another by a large majority of mankind, critical reflection quickly brings forth a number of apparently strong reasons to regard that belief as quite illusory. Let us now review them.

THE ARGUMENTS AGAINST SURVIVAL

There are, first of all, a number of facts which definitely suggest that both the existence and the nature of consciousness wholly depend on the presence of a functioning nervous system. It is pointed out, for example, that wherever

"Man's Concern with Life after Death"

Arnold Toynbee

Death is the price paid by life for an enhancement of the complexity of a live organism's structure. Biological research has demonstrated that even the simplest live organisms are complex to a degree that astonishes a layman. However, relatively simple species perpetuate themselves without either dying or begetting progeny; instead, they divide periodically into separate specimens of the species, and then each separated specimen redivides in its turn. But life has not succeeded in attaining higher degrees of complexity without having to discard each specimen of a higher species and to replace it by a new one which is produced by sexual intercourse and procreation. A specimen that has ripened for mating with a specimen of the opposite sex to reproduce their kind and that has then duly performed this function becomes expendable. The formula in the genealogical verses of Chapter 12 of the *Book of Genesis* implies that an individual human being lives, not for his own sake, but for the sake of perpetuating his race by begetting children.

Nevertheless, every living being that is subject to death exerts itself to stay alive, whether or not it has produced progeny. Some non-human species grieve, as human beings grieve, at the loss of their mates, and also at the loss of other members of their community in the case of some social, non-human animals. But human beings appear to be unique among the fauna inhabiting the 'biosphere' that coats the planet earth in being aware that they themselves and all their living contemporaries are going to die, and that death has already overtaken countless earlier generations. The Greek historian Herodotus reports that the Persian emperor Xerxes wept after he had reviewed his immense expeditionary force, because he realized that not a single member of it would still be alive one hundred years later.

consciousness is observed, it is found associated with a living and functioning body. Further, when the body dies, or the head is struck a heavy blow, or some anesthetic is administered, the familiar outward evidences of consciousness terminate, permanently or temporarily. Again, we know well that drugs of various kinds—alcohol, caffein, opium, heroin, and many others—cause specific changes at the time in the nature of a person's mental states. Also, by stimulating in appropriate ways the body's sense organs, corresponding states of consciousness—namely, the various kinds of sensations—can be caused at will. On the other hand, cutting a sensory nerve immediately eliminates a whole range of sensations.

Again, the contents of consciousness, the mental powers, or even the personality, are modified in characteristic ways when certain regions of the brain are destroyed by disease or injury or are disconnected from the rest by such an operation as prefrontal lobotomy. And that the nervous system is the indispensable basis of mind is further suggested by the fact that, in the evolutionary scale, the degree of intelligence of various species of animals keeps pace closely with the degree of development of their brain.

That continued existence of mind after death is impossible has been argued also on the basis of theoretical considerations. It has been contended, for instance, that what we call states of consciousness—or more particularly, ideas, sensations, volitions, feelings, and the like—are really nothing but the minute physical or chemical events which take place in the tissues of the brain. For, it is urged, it would be absurd to suppose that an idea or a volition, if it is not itself a material thing or process, could cause material effects such as contractions of muscles.

Moreover, it is maintained that the possibility of causation of a material event by an immaterial, mental cause is ruled out *a priori* by the principle of the conservation of energy; for such causation would mean that an additional quantity of energy suddenly pops into the nervous system out of nowhere.

Another conception of consciousness, which is more often met with today than the one just mentioned, but which also implies that consciousness cannot survive death, is that "consciousness" is only the name we give to certain types of behavior, which differentiate the higher animals from all other things in nature. According to this view, to say, for example, that an animal is conscious of a difference between two stimuli means nothing more than that it responds to each by different behavior. That is, the difference of *behavior* is what consciousness of difference between the stimuli *consists in;* and is not, as is commonly assumed, only the behavioral sign of something mental and not public, called "consciousness that the stimuli are different."

Or again, consciousness, of the typically human sort called thought, is identified with the typically human sort of behavior called speech; and this, again not in the sense that speech *expresses* or *manifests* something different from itself, called "thought," but in the sense that speech—whether uttered or only whispered—*is* thought itself. And obviously, if thought, or any mental activity, is thus but some mode of behavior of the living body, the mind cannot possibly survive death.

Still another difficulty confronting the hypothesis of survival becomes evident when one imagines in some detail what survival would have to include in order to satisfy the desires which cause man to crave it. It would, of course, have to include persistence not alone of consciousness, but also of personality; that is, of the individual's character, acquired knowledge, cultural skills and interests, memories, and awareness of personal identity. But even this would not be enough, for what man desires is not bare survival, but to go on living in some objective way. And this means to go on meeting new situations and, by exerting himself to deal with them, to broaden and deepen his experience and develop his latent capacities.

But it is hard to imagine this possible without a body and an environment for it, upon which to act and from which to receive impressions.

And, if a body and an environment were supposed, but not material and corruptible ones, then it is paradoxical to think that, under such radically different conditions, a given personality could persist.[2]

To take a crude but telling analogy, it is past belief that, if the body of any one of us were suddenly changed into that of a shark or an octopus, and placed in the ocean, his personality could, for more than a very short time, if at all, survive intact so radical a change of environment and of bodily form.

THE ARGUMENTS EXAMINED

Such, in brief, are the chief reasons commonly advanced for holding that survival is impossible. Scrutiny of them, however, will, I think, reveal that they are not as strong as they first seem and far from strong enough to show that there can be no life after death.

Let us consider first the assertion that "thought," or "consciousness," is but another name for subvocal speech, or for some other form of behavior, or for molecular processes in the tissues of the brain. As Paulsen and others have pointed out,[3] no evidence ever is or can be offered to support that assertion, because it is in fact but a disguised proposal to make the words "thought," "feeling," "sensation," "desire," and so on, denote facts quite different from those which these words are commonly employed to denote. To say that those words are but other names for certain chemical or behavioral events is as grossly arbitrary as it would be to say that "wood" is but another name for glass, or "potato" but another name for cabbage. What thought, desire, sensation, and other mental states are like, each of us can observe directly by introspection; and what introspection reveals is that they do not in the least resemble muscular contraction, or glandular secretion, or any other known bodily events. No tampering with language can alter the observable fact that thinking is one thing and muttering quite another; that the feeling called anger has no resemblance to the bodily behavior which usually goes with it; or that an act of will is not in the least like anything we find when we open the skull and examine the brain. Certain mental events are doubtless connected in some way with certain bodily events, but they are not those bodily events themselves. The connection is not identity.

This being clear, let us next consider the arguments offered to show that mental processes, although not identical with bodily processes, nevertheless depend on them. We are told, for instance, that some head injuries, or anesthetics, totally extinguish consciousness for the time being. As already pointed out, however, the strict fact is only that the usual bodily signs of consciousness are then absent. But they are also absent when a person is asleep; and yet, at the same time, dreams, which are states of consciousness, may be occurring.

It is true that when the person concerned awakens, he often remembers his dreams, whereas the person that has been anesthetized or injured has usually no memories relating to the period of apparent blankness. But this could mean that his consciousness was, for the first time, dissociated from its ordinary channels of manifestation, as was reported of the co-conscious personalities of some of the patients of Dr. Morton Prince.[4] Moreover, it sometimes occurs that a person who has been in an accident reports lack of memories not only for the period during which his body was unresponsive but also for a period of several hours *before* the accident, during which he had given to his associates all the ordinary external signs of being conscious as usual.

2. Cf. Gardner Murphy, "Difficulties Confronting the Survival Hypothesis," *Journal of the American Society for Psychical Research* for April, 1945, p. 72; Corliss Lamont, "The Illusion of Immortality" (New York, 1935), pp. 26 ff.

3. F. Paulsen, "Introduction to Philosophy" (trans. by F. Thilly, 2d ed.), pp. 82–83.

4. "My Life as a Dissociated Personality" (edited by Morton Prince; Boston: Badger).

But, more generally, if absence of memories relating to a given period proved unconsciousness for that period, this would force us to conclude that we were unconscious during the first few years of our lives, and indeed have been so most of the time since; for the fact is that we have no memories whatever of most of our days. That we were alive and conscious on any long past specific date is, with only a few exceptions, not something we actually remember, but only something which we infer must be true.

EVIDENCE FROM PSYCHICAL RESEARCH

Another argument advanced against survival was, it will be remembered, that death must extinguish the mind, since all manifestations of it then cease. But to assert that they invariably then cease is to ignore altogether the considerable amount of evidence to the contrary, gathered over many years and carefully checked by the Society for Psychical Research. This evidence, which is of a variety of kinds, has been reviewed by Professor Gardner Murphy in an article published in the Journal of the Society.[5] He mentions first the numerous well-authenticated cases of apparition of a dead person to others as yet unaware that he had died or even been ill or in danger. The more strongly evidential cases of apparition are those in which the apparition conveys to the person who sees it specific facts until then secret. An example would be that of the apparition of a girl to her brother nine years after her death, with a conspicuous scratch on her cheek. Their mother

5. "An Outline of Survival Evidence," *Journal of the American Society for Psychical Research,* January, 1945.

"Buddha's No-Self Doctrine"

Buddhist Scripture

"Your majesty, I am called Nāgasena; my fellow-priests, your majesty, address me as Nāgasena: but whether parents give one the name Nāgasena, or Sūrasena, or Vīrasena, or Sīhasena, it is, nevertheless, your majesty, but a way of counting, a term, an appellation, a convenient designation, a mere name, this Nāgasena; for there is no Self here to be found." . . .

"Bhante Nāgasena, if there is no Self to be found, who is it then furnishes you priests with the priestly requisites,—robes, food, bedding, and medicine, the reliance of the sick? who is it makes use of the same? who is it keeps the precepts? who is it applies himself to meditation? . . . who is it commits immorality? who is it tells lies? . . .

In that case, there is no merit; there is no demerit; there is no one who does or causes to be done meritorious or demeritorious deeds; neither good nor evil deeds can have any fruit or result. Bhante Nāgasena, neither is he a murderer who kills a priest, nor can you priests, bhante Nāgasena, have any teacher, preceptor, or ordination. When you say, 'My fellow-priests, your majesty, address me as Nāgasena,' what then is this Nāgasena? Pray, bhante, is the hair of the head Nāgasena?"

"Nay, verily, your majesty."

"Is the hair of the body Nāgasena?"

"Nay, verily, your majesty."

"Are nails . . . teeth . . . skin . . . flesh . . . sinews . . . bones . . . marrow of the bones . . . kidneys . . . heart . . . liver . . . blood . . . sweat . . . fat . . . tears . . . saliva . . . snot . . . urine . . . brain of the head Nāgasena?"

"Nay, verily, your majesty."

"Is now, bhante, form Nāgasena?"

"Nay, verily, your majesty."

"Is sensation Nāgasena?" . . .

then revealed to him that she herself had made that scratch accidentally while preparing her daughter's body for burial, but that she had then at once covered it with powder and never mentioned it to anyone.

Another famous case is that of a father whose apparition some time after death revealed to one of his sons that existence and location of an unsuspected second will, benefiting him, which was then found as indicated. Still another case would be the report by General Barter, then a subaltern in the British Army in India, of the apparition to him of a lieutenant he had not seen for two or three years. The lieutenant's apparition was riding a brown pony with black mane and tail. He was much stouter than at their last meeting, and, whereas formerly clean-shaven, he now wore a peculiar beard in the form of a fringe encircling his face. On inquiry the next day from a person who had known the lieutenant at the time he died, it turned out that he had indeed become very bloated before his death; that he had grown just such a beard while on the sick list; and that he had some time before bought and eventually ridden to death a pony of that very description.

Other striking instances are those of an apparition seen simultaneously by several persons. It is on record that an apparition of a child was perceived first by a dog, that the animal's rushing at it, loudly barking, interrupted the conversation of the seven persons present in the room, thus drawing their attention to the apparition, and that the latter then moved through the room for some fifteen seconds, followed by the barking dog.[6]

6. The documents obtained by the Society for Psychical Research concerning this case, that of the lieutenant's apparition, and that of the girl with the scratch, are reproduced in Sir Ernest Bennett's "Apparitions and Haunted Houses" (London: Faber and Faber, 1945), pp. 334–337, 28–35, and 145–150 respectively.

"Is consciousness Nāgasena?"

"Nay, verily, your majesty."

"Are, then, bhante, form, sensation, perception, the predispositions, and consciousness unitedly Nāgasena?"

"Nay, verily, your majesty."

"Is it, then, bhante, something besides form sensation, perception, the predispositions, and consciousness, which is Nāgasena?"

"Nay, verily, your majesty."

"Bhante, although I question you very closely, I fail to discover any Nāgasena. Verily, now, bhante, Nāgasena is a mere empty sound. What Nāgasena is there here? Bhante, you speak a falsehood, a lie: there is no Nāgasena." . . .

* * *

"How, bhante Nāgasena, does rebirth take place without anything transmigrating? Give an illustration."

"Suppose, your majesty, a man were to light a light from another light; pray, would the one light have passed over [transmigrated] to the other light?"

"Nay, verily, bhante."

"In exactly the same way, your majesty, does rebirth take place without anything transmigrating."

"Give another illustration."

"Do you remember, your majesty, having learnt, when you were a boy, some verse or other from your professor of poetry? . . . did the verse pass over [transmigrate] to you from your teacher?"

"Nay, verily, bhante."

"In exactly the same way, your majesty, does rebirth take place without anything transmigrating."

"You are an able man, bhante Nāgasena."

From H. C. Warren, *Buddhism in Translation* (1963), (*Milindapañha,* 71) with a few editorial emendations.

Another type of empirical evidence of survival consists of communications, purporting to come from the dead, made through the persons commonly called sensitives, mediums, or automatists. Some of the most remarkable of these communications were given by the celebrated American medium, Mrs. Piper, who for many years was studied by the Society for Psychical Research, London, with the most elaborate precautions against all possibility of fraud. Twice, particularly, the evidences of identity supplied by the dead persons who purportedly were thus communicating with the living were of the very kinds, and of the same precision and detail, which would ordinarily satisfy a living person of the identity of another living person with whom he was not able to communicate directly, but only through an intermediary, or by letter or telephone.[7]

Again, sometimes the same mark of identity of a dead person, or the same message from him, or complementary parts of one message, are obtained independently from two mediums in different parts of the world.

Of course, when facts of these kinds are recounted, as I have just done, only in abstract summary, they make little if any impression upon us. And the very word "medium" at once brings to our minds the innumerable instances of demonstrated fraud perpetrated by charlatans to extract money from the credulous bereaved. But the modes of trickery and sources of error, which immediately suggest themselves to us as easy, natural explanations of the seemingly extraordinary facts, suggest themselves just as quickly to the members of the research committees of the Society for Psychical Research. Usually, these men have had a good deal more experience than the rest of us with the tricks of conjurers and fraudulent mediums, and take against them precautions far more strict and ingenious than would occur to the average skeptic.[8]

But when, instead of stopping at summaries, one takes the trouble to study the detailed, original reports, it then becomes evident that they cannot all be just laughed off; for to accept the hypothesis of fraud or malobservation would often require more credulity than to accept the facts reported.

To *explain* those facts, however, is quite another thing. Only two hypotheses at all adequate to do so have yet been advanced. One is that the communications really come, as they purport to do, from persons who have died and have survived death. The other is the hypothesis of telepathy—that is, the supposition, itself startling enough, that the medium is able to gather information directly from the minds of others, and that this is the true source of the information communicated. To account for all the facts, however, this hypothesis has to be stretched very far, for some of them require us to suppose that the medium can tap the minds even of persons far away and quite unknown to him, and can tap even the subconscious part of their minds.

Diverse highly ingenious attempts have been made to devise conditions that would rule out telepathy as a possible explanation of the communications received; but some of the most critical and best-documented investigators still hold that it has not yet been absolutely excluded. Hence, although some of the facts recorded by psychical research constitute, prima facie, strong empirical evidence of survival, they cannot be said to establish it beyond question. But they do show that we need to revise rather radically in some respects our ordinary ideas of what is and is not possible in nature.

7. A summary of some of the most evidential facts may be found in the book by M. Sage, entitled "Mrs. Piper and the Society for Psychical Research" (New York: Scott-Thaw Co., 1904); others of them are related in some detail in Sir Oliver Lodge's "The Survival of Man," Sec. IV (New York: Moffat, Yard and Co., 1909) and in A. M. Robbins' "Both Sides of the Veil," Part II (Boston: Sherman, French, and Co., 1909). The fullest account is in the *Proceedings of the Society for Psychical Research.*

8. Cf. H. Carrington, "The Physical Phenomena of Spiritualism, Fraudulent and Genuine" (Boston: Small, Maynard & Co., 1908).

CAN MENTAL STATES CAUSE BODILY EVENTS?

Let us now turn to another of the arguments against survival. That states of consciousness entirely depend on bodily processes, and therefore cannot continue when the latter have ceased, is proved, it is argued, by the fact that various states of consciousness—in particular, the several kinds of sensations—can be caused at will by appropriately stimulating the body.

Now, it is very true that sensations and some other mental states can be so caused: but we have just as good and abundant evidence that mental states can cause various bodily events. John Laird mentions, among others, the fact that merely willing to raise one's arm normally suffices to cause it to rise; that a hungry person's mouth is caused to water by the idea of food; that feelings of rage, fear or excitement cause digestion to stop; that anxiety causes changes in the quantity and quality of the milk of a nursing mother; that certain thoughts cause tears, pallor, blushing or fainting; and so on.[9] The evidence we have that the relation is one of cause and effect is exactly the same here as where bodily processes cause mental states.

It is said, of course, that to suppose something non-physical, such as thought, to be capable of causing motion of a physical object, such as the body, is absurd. But I submit that if the heterogeneity of mind and matter makes this absurd, then it makes equally absurd the causation of mental states by stimulation of the body. Yet no absurdity is commonly found in the assertion that cutting the skin causes a feeling of pain, or that alcohol, caffein, bromides, and other drugs, cause characteristic states of consciousness. As David Hume made clear long ago, no kind of causal connection is intrinsically absurd. Anything might cause anything; and only observation can tell us what in fact can cause what.

9. John Laird, "Our Minds and Their Bodies" (London, 1925), pp. 16–19.

Somewhat similar remarks would apply to the allegation that the principle of the conservation of energy precludes the possibility of causation of a physical event by a mental event. For if it does, then it equally precludes causation in the converse direction, and this, of course, would leave us totally at a loss to explain the occurrence of sensations. But, as Keeton and others have pointed out,[10] that energy is conserved is not something observation has revealed or could reveal, but only a postulate—a defining postulate for the notion of an "isolated physical system."

That is, conservation of energy is something one has to have if, but only if, one insists on conceiving the physical world as wholly self-contained, independent, isolated. And just because the metaphysics which the natural sciences tacitly assume does insist on so conceiving the physical world, this metaphysics compels them to save conservation by postulations *ad hoc* whenever dissipation of energy is what observation reveals. It postulates, for instance, that something else, which appears at such times but was not until then regarded as energy, is energy too, but it is then said, "in a different form."

Furthermore, as Broad has emphasized, all that the principle of conservation requires is that when a quantity Q of energy disappears at one place in the physical world an equal quantity of it should appear at some other place there. And the supposition that, in some cases, what causes it to disappear here and appear there is some mental event, such perhaps as a volition, does not violate at all the supposition that energy is conserved.[11]

A word, next, on the parallelism between the degree of development of the nervous systems of various animals and the degree of their intelligence. This is alleged to prove that the latter is the product of the former. But the facts lend themselves equally well to the supposition

10. M. T. Keeton, "Some Ambiguities in the Theory of the Conservation of Energy," *Philosophy of Science*, Vol. 8, No. 3, July 1941.

11. C. D. Broad, "The Mind and Its Place in Nature," pp. 103 ff.

that, on the contrary, an obscurely felt need for greater intelligence in the circumstances the animal faced was what brought about the variations which eventually resulted in a more adequate nervous organization.

In the development of the individual, at all events, it seems clear that the specific, highly complex nerve connections which become established in the brain and cerebellum of, for instance, a skilled pianist are the results of his will over many years to acquire the skill.

We must not forget in this context that there is a converse, equally consistent with the facts, for the theory, called epiphenomenalism, that mental states are related to the brain much as the halo is to the saint, that is, as effects but never themselves as causes. The converse theory, which might be called hypophenomenalism, and which is pretty well that of Schopenhauer, is that the instruments which the various mechanisms of the body constitute are the objective products of obscure cravings for the correspond-

Buddhist Reincarnation

Why would a Buddhist who does not believe in selves think that anyone is "reincarnated?" That is, why would a Buddhist think that there is survival of any kind going on? A major part of the answer seems to be that some people have experiences which they take to be memories of previous lives. In a Western view of what memory involves, it is easy to see why such an experience would encourage a belief in reincarnation. What's more difficult to see is why in the Buddhist view such experiences would encourage belief in reincarnation. Consider, for instance, the following dialogue from Buddhist scripture:

VATSIPUTRIYA: If there is no soul, who is it that remembers?
VASUBANDIHU: What is the meaning of the word, 'to remember'?
VATSIPUTRIYA: It means to grasp an object by memory.
VASUBANDIHU: Is this 'grasping by memory' something different from memory?
VATSIPUTRIYA: It is an agent who acts through memory.
VASUBANDIHU: . . . The cause productive of a recollection is a suitable state of mind, nothing more.
VATSIPUTRIYA: But when we use the expression, 'Caitra remembers,' what does it mean?
VASUBANDIHU: In the current of phenomena which is designated by the name, *Caitra*, a recollection appears.

Thus experiences remembered are not a reincarnated person's memories because the so-called reincarnated person was never a person in the first place but only a pattern, just as stellar constellations, such as the Big Dipper and the Little Dipper, are not entities but only perceived patterns.

ing powers; and, in particular, that the organization of the nervous system is the effect and material isomorph of the variety of mental functions exercised at a given level of animal or human existence.

THE INITIAL ASSUMPTION BEHIND THE ARGUMENTS AGAINST SURVIVAL

We have now scrutinized all but the last of the reasons mentioned earlier for rejecting the possibility of survival, and we have found them all logically weak. Before examining the one which remains, it will be useful for us to pause a moment and inquire why so many of the persons who advance those reasons nevertheless think them convincing.

It is, I believe, because these persons approach the question of survival with a certain unconscious metaphysical bias. It derives from a particular initial assumption which they tacitly make. It is that *to be real is to be material.* And to be material, of course, is to be some process or part of the perceptually public world, that is, of the world we all perceive by means of our so-called five senses.

Now the assumption that to be real is to be material is a useful and appropriate one for the purpose of investigating the material world and of operating upon it; and this purpose is a legitimate and frequent one. But those persons, and most of us, do not realize that the validity of that assumption is strictly relative to that specific purpose. Hence they, and most of us, continue making the assumption, and it continues to rule judgment, even when, as now, the purpose in view is a different one, for which the assumption is no longer useful or even congruous.

The point is all-important here and therefore worth stressing. Its essence is that the conception of the nature of reality that proposes to define the real as the material is not the expression of an observable fact to which everyone would have to bow, but is the expression only of a certain direction of interest on the part of the persons who so define reality—of interest, namely, which they have chosen to center wholly in the material, perceptually public world. This specialized interest is of course as legitimate as any other, but it automatically ignores all the facts, commonly called facts of mind, which only introspection reveals. And that specialized interest is what alone compels persons in its grip to employ the word "mind" to denote, instead of what it commonly does denote, something else altogether, namely, the public behavior of bodies that have minds.

Only so long as one's judgment is swayed unawares by that special interest do the logically weak arguments against the possibility of survival, which we have examined, seem strong.

The Buddha Sakyamuni in Abhaya-mudra. North India. Gupta period, sixth century A.D., bronze.

It is possible, however, and just as legitimate, as well as more conducive to a fair view of our question, to center one's interest at the start on the facts of mind as introspectively observable, ranking them as most real in the sense that they are the facts the intrinsic nature of which we most directly experience, the facts which we most certainly know to exist; and moreover, that they are the facts without the experiencing of which we should not know any other facts whatever—such, for instance, as those of the material world.

The sort of perspective one gets from this point of view is what I propose now to sketch briefly. For one thing, the material world is then seen to be but one among other objects of our consciousness. Moreover, one becomes aware of the crucially important fact that it is an object postulated rather than strictly given. What this means may be made clearer by an example. Suppose that, perhaps in a restaurant we visit for the first time, an entire wall is occupied by a large mirror and we look into it without realizing that it is a mirror. We then perceive, in the part of space beyond it, various material objects, notwithstanding that in fact they have no existence there at all. A certain set of the vivid color images which we call visual sensations was all that was strictly given to us, and these we construed, automatically and instantaneously, but nonetheless erroneously, as signs of appearances of the existence of certain material objects at a certain place.

Again, and similarly, we perceive in our dreams various objects which at the time we take as physical but which eventually we come to believe were not so. And this eventual conclusion, let it be noted, is forced upon us not because we then detect that something, called "physical substance," was lacking in those objects, but only because we notice, as we did not at the time, that their behavior was erratic—

Karma

According to the Buddhist view of self, the connections between people from one life to the next are not, strictly speaking, between people (since ultimately there aren't any) but between the elements out of which people are composed—various bodily and psychological units in perpetual flux. These elements are the only real things. In that sense, people are like stellar constellations: imaginary patterns. *Karma* connects the impermanent elements out of which people are composed in one lifetime to the impermanent elements out of which people are composed in a future lifetime.

But what is karma? Is it a substance, or a mechanism, and if it is, how is it different from a soul? Buddhists tend to answer in similes—karmic influence between lifetimes is like lighting one candle with another.

Whatever the official Buddhist view, karma would not have to be a substance or a mechanism, but could just be the name for a certain kind of causal relationship. One pattern person—the imaginary person we would ordinarily call "you right now"—merely by existing and having the characteristics it has, incoherent with their ordinary one. That is, their appearance was a *mere* appearance, deceptive in the sense that it did not then predict truly, as ordinarily it does, their later appearances. This, it is important to notice, is the *only* way in which we ever discover that an object we perceive was not really physical, or was not the particular sort of physical object we judged it to be.

These two examples illustrate the fact that our perception of physical objects is sometimes erroneous. But the essential point is that, even when it is veridical instead of erroneous, *all* that is literally and directly given to our minds is still only *some set of sensations*. These, on a given occasion, may be only color sensations; but they often include also tactual sensations, sounds, odors, and so on. It is especially interesting, however, to remark here in passing that, with respect to almost all the many thousands of persons and other "physical" objects we have perceived in a lifetime, *vivid color images* were the only data our perceiving strictly had to go by; so that, if the truth should happen to have been that those objects, like ghosts or images in a mirror, were actually intangible—that is, were *only* color images—we should never have discovered that this was the fact. For all we *directly* know, it *may* have been the fact!

To perceive a physical object, then, instead of merely experiencing passively certain sensations (something which perhaps hardly ever occurs, is always to *interpret,* that is to *construe,* given sensations as signs of, and appearances to us of, a postulated something other than themselves, which we believe is causing them in us and is capable of causing in us others of specific kinds. We believe this because we believe that our sensations too must have some cause, and we find none for them among our other mental states.

Such a postulated extramental something we call "a physical object." We say that we ob-

---

might affect the characteristics of another pattern person, say, the imaginary person who a thousand years from now will inherit your karma. The cause and effect could be by action at a distance, with no intervening causal mechanism. In that case, karma would just be a name for this fact about how the cosmos works.

Why, though, according to the Buddhist view, would karma work this way? Buddhists could respond that it just does: That's the way the cosmos works in accordance with a kind of cosmic moral law. In the same way, if we were to ask scientists for an explanation of why the most basic physical laws that are currently known work the way they do, they would say they don't know—that that's just the way the cosmos works, in accordance with a kind of cosmic natural law.

But how could karma "know" which elements to connect with which elements? That is, if "karma" were the name for the fact that influence is transmitted from one lifetime to the next, what could determine which elements get configured into a pattern that is affected one way rather than another?

---

serve physical objects, and this is true. But it is important for the present purpose to be clear that we "observe" them never in any more direct or literal manner than is constituted by the process of interpretive postulation just described—never, for example, in the wholly direct and literal manner in which we are able to observe our sensations themselves and our other mental states. . . .

Terence Penelhum

"LIFE AFTER DEATH"

TERENCE PENELHUM teaches philosophy at the University of Alberta at Calgary, where he has been dean of arts and sciences. He has written extensively on the philosophy of religion, personal identity, and the survival of bodily death.

TWO CONCEPTS OF SURVIVAL

The doctrine of the immortality of the soul certainly predates Christianity. It finds its classic expression in Plato's dialogue, the *Phaedo.* This dialogue has as its dramatic setting the last day in the life of Socrates. Socrates has been condemned to death by the Athenians for allegedly corrupting the youth of the city with his philosophical questioning, and when the sun sets he must drink the cup of poison that will kill him. As Plato portrays his last day in prison before the carrying out of the sentence, Socrates devotes his final hours to discussion of whether the soul can survive the death of the body and whether death is to be feared. His conclusion is that the soul will survive and that the wise man need have no fear of death but should welcome it as a release of the soul from the bondage of the body. The arguments that Plato puts into the mouth of Socrates are based upon his belief that the human soul shows an awareness of a higher and nonmaterial realm of forms or ideas, of which it could not learn through the body and its sensory apparatus alone. The soul shows this awareness through its capacity to use general concepts and in particular through its powers of mathematical and moral reflection. It is thus identified primarily with the reason of man and is held to be alien to the body and essentially imprisoned within it. The philosopher is the man who is able to recognize the soul's higher kinship and attempts as far as he can to free the soul from the shackles of physical concerns. For him, at least, death will complete what he has partially succeeded in achieving during his lifetime. It is clear from the doctrine of the parts of the soul in the *Republic* that Plato recognizes the desires as parts of the soul also and not merely as functions of bodily states; but he thinks of the satisfaction of physical desires as alien to the natural concerns of the soul, which has its own, immaterial objects to seek after.

This doctrine has been enormously influential, and many have thought that it, or something like it, is also the Christian doctrine. Certain

Reprinted by permission of the author from *Religion and Rationality* (New York: Random House, 1971), pp. 334–355.

elements in the Platonic view (such as Plato's suggestion that the soul's higher aspirations reveal its preexistence and his belief that matter is a fundamentally negative, and even evil, principle) would have to be abandoned or amended for the two doctrines to be assimilated. But many Christians have thought that their belief is in essence the same as the doctrine we find in Plato. This obscures the fact that the doctrine of the resurrection of the body clearly seems to be a distinctively Christian contribution. When this fact is emphasized, it becomes important to decide how far the two beliefs are irreconcilable.

Some thinkers certainly hold that they are. Professor Oscar Cullmann, for example, has recently argued that there is a fundamental divergence between the Platonic and Christian doctrines and that this can be seen when we compare the serenity with which Socrates' doctrines enable him to face his approaching death in the *Phaedo,* with the agony that Jesus undergoes when faced with the approach of death in the Gospel narratives.[1] The primitive Christian tradition, he argues, does not present death as a welcome passage from one realm to another, but as the most elemental and horrifying reality that man confronts, because death is the destruction of the person, not his release. The distinctive Christian hope, expressed in the doctrines of the Resurrection of Christ and the final resurrection of men, is the hope that God will literally re-create what he has permitted death to destroy. This interpretation has been challenged by H. A. Wolfson, who has argued that the early Christian Church believed both in the survival of the soul and in the resurrection of the body, and that this combination of beliefs can readily accommodate all the original New Testament attitudes toward death.[2] The final doctrinal issue between them seems to be whether or not the soul continues in a disembodied state between death and resurrection. If so, then at the resurrection the person is made whole again by the soul's being reunited with the body (or, perhaps, by its being united with another body). If not, then the resurrection is indeed the reappearance of a person from annihilation.

I cannot comment profitably on the historical question that Cullmann and Wolfson debate; though some of the later discussion will bear on the logic of the two competing alternatives. There can be no doubt that the doctrine of the immortality of the soul, even though Greek in origin, has been held by many members of the Christian tradition, whether it belonged originally to that tradition or not. The doctrine of the resurrection of the body, certainly authentically a part of the Christian tradition (since some form of it is clearly held by St. Paul),[3] is part of the most widely used creed of the Christian Church. Let us leave aside their historical relationship and look at the logical possibilities they present. I shall begin with the doctrine of the immortality of the soul, or, as I prefer to word it, the doctrine of disembodied survival. Before doing so, however, I shall attempt to clear the ground a little by indicating the major sources of difficulty that philosophers have discovered in these doctrines.

These difficulties divide themselves naturally into two groups. There are, first of all, difficulties about envisaging the kind of life that survivors of death in either sense could be said to lead. It is not enough to say that the nature of this life is totally unknown, for if this is taken seriously to the extent of our being unable to say that these beings will possess personal characteristics as we now understand these, it seems to leave the belief that they will survive without any content. If one wishes to avoid this pitfall, one has to ascribe to the survivors some characteristics that persons as we know them possess. This does not seem impossible in the case

1. Oscar Cullmann, *Immortality of the Soul or Resurrection of the Dead?* (London: Epworth, 1958).

2. H. A. Wolfson, "Immortality and Resurrection in the Philosophy of the Church Fathers," in *Religious Philosophy* (Cambridge: Harvard University Press, 1961).

3. See I Corinthians, Chapter 15.

of the doctrine of the resurrection of the body; though it can be made impossible if unlimited stress is placed on the claim that the body of the survivor is transformed. Radical transformation is to be expected as part of such a doctrine, but total transformation would rob the notion of survival of all clear meaning, for it is part of that notion that the *person* survives, and this seems to entail that the resulting being is a person also. But if the doctrine of the resurrection of the body is expressed in ways that avoids this danger, it is clearly possible for us to form a rough notion (which is all one can reasonably demand) of what such a future state would be like.

The difficulty seems much greater, however, when we consider the doctrine of disembodied survival. For it is not obviously intelligible to ascribe personal characteristics to a being that is denied to have any physical ones. The notion of human intelligence, for example, seems closely bound up with the things men can be seen to

"I Think of Socrates"

Kim Malthe-Bruun

During the holocaust, a young philosopher wrote the following letter on the eve of his execution by a Nazi firing squad. The letter is dated April 4, 1945.

My own little sweetheart: Today I was put on trial and condemned to death. What terrible news for a little girl only twenty years old! I obtained permission to write this farewell letter. And what words shall I write now? How shall they, my swan song, sound?

We sailed upon the wild sea, we met each other in the trustful way of playing children, and we loved each other. We still love each other and we shall continue to do so. But one day a storm tore us asunder; I struck a reef and went down, but you were washed up on another shore, and you will live on in a new world. You are not to forget me, I do not ask that: why should you forget something that is so beautiful? But you must not cling to it. You must live on as gay as ever and doubly happy, for life has given you on your path the most beautiful of all beautiful things. . . .

I think of Socrates. Read about him—you will find Plato telling about what I am now experiencing. I love you boundlessly, but not more now than I have always loved you. The stab I feel in my heart is nothing. That is simply the way things are, and you must understand this. Something lives and burns within me—love, inspiration, call it what you will, but it is something for which I have not yet found a name. Now I am to die, and I do not know whether I have kindled a little flame in another heart, a flame that will outlive me; nonetheless I am calm, for I have seen and I know that nature is so rich that no one takes note when a few isolated little sprouts are crushed underfoot and die. Why then should I despair, when I see all the wealth that lives on?

Lift up your head, you my heart's most precious core, lift up your head and look about you. The sea is still blue—the sea that I have loved so much, the sea that has enveloped both of us. Live on now for the two of us. . . . Remember, and I swear to you that it is true, that every sorrow turns into happiness—but very few people will in retrospect admit this to themselves. They wrap themselves in their sorrow, and habit leads them to believe that it continues to be sorrow, and they go on wrapping themselves in it. The truth is that after sorrow comes a maturation, and after maturation comes fruit. . . . I should like to breathe into you all the life that is in me, so that thereby it could perpetuate itself and as little as possible of it be lost. That is what my nature demands.

Yours, but not forever,
Kim

From *Voices of Death* by Edwin Shneidman (1980).

do and heard to say; the notion of human emotion seems closely bound up with the way men talk and behave; and the notion of human action seems closely bound up with that of physical movement. There is plenty of room for disagreement over the nature of these connections, but they cannot even exist in the case of an allegedly disembodied being. So can we understand what is meant by talk of disembodied intelligences, or disembodied sufferers of emotion, or disembodied agents? A natural answer to our present problem is: Disembodied survivors might have mental lives. They might, that is, think, imagine, dream, or have feelings. This looks coherent enough. On the other hand, for them to have anything to think *about* or have feelings *toward,* it might be necessary for them also to have that which supplies us with our objects of reflection or emotion, namely, perception. Some might also want to add the notion of agency (especially if they wish to use the doctrine of disembodied survival to offer explanations of the phenomena of psychical research). We must bear in mind, further, that disembodied persons could, of course, never perceive or meet each other, in any normal sense of these words. What we need to do, even at the risk of spinning fantasies, is to see how severely the belief in their disembodiment restricts the range of concepts that we can apply to them.

The second group of difficulties affects both doctrines, though in different ways. These are difficulties about the self-identity of the survivors. The belief that people survive is not merely the belief that after people's deaths there will be personal beings in existence. It is the belief that those beings will be the same ones that existed before death. One of the reasons for concern about the nature of the life a disembodied person might lead is that if this mode of life were *too* radically different from the sort of life we lead, those beings leading it could not be identified with us. This difficulty is critical, for even if we can readily understand what the future life that is spoken of would be like, its coming to pass would only be an interesting cosmic hypothesis, lacking any personal relevance, if the beings living that life were not ourselves.[4] This requirement connects with another. We have to be able to form some concept of what it is for the future, post-mortem being to remain the same through time in the future life, quite apart from his also being identifiable with some previous person who existed in *this* life. If, for instance, our being able to identify a person whom we meet now as some person we knew previously depends on our being able to discern some feature that he still possesses; and if that feature is something that a being in the future life could not possess, then it needs to be shown that there could be post-mortem persons who persist through time at all. There would have to be some substitute, in the case of post-mortem persons, for the feature that establishes identity for pre-mortem persons. If we are not able to indicate what this would be, we have no adequately clear concept of what talk of post-mortem persons means.

These problems about identity arise in quite different ways for the two doctrines of disembodied survival and bodily resurrection. A proponent of the doctrine of disembodied survival has to face the problem of the continuing identity of the disembodied person through time, by showing that what makes that person identical though time could be some wholly *mental* feature and that the absence of a body does not render the notion of a body inapplicable. (He may or may not do this by claiming that we use mental rather than physical features to identify pre-mortem beings through time.) This task may not be hopeless, though it looks as though we depend on the physical continuity of people for our ability to reidentify them. He must also succeed in showing that some purely mental feature will serve to identify the post-mortem person with his pre-mortem predecessor.

4. The emphasis on the importance of this is a most valuable feature of Antony Flew's contributions to this subject. See *A New Approach to Psychical Research* (London: Watts & Co., 1953) and his article "Immortality," in Paul Edwards (ed.), *Encyclopedia of Philosophy* (New York: Macmillan and Free Press, 1967), Vol. 4, pp. 139–150.

In the case of the doctrine of the resurrection of the body, the problem of how the post-mortem, resurrected person can remain identical through time in the future state does not look very difficult, since the sort of life envisaged for this being is an embodied one, similar in enough respects (one may suppose) to our own. So even if we decided that the continuity of the body is a necessary condition of the continuance of a person through time, this condition could easily be said to be satisfied in the case of a resurrected person. Yet we still have a difficulty: Could a post-mortem person, even in this embodied state, be identified with any pre-mortem person? For if the doctrine of resurrection is presented in a form that entails the annihilation of a person at death, it could reasonably be argued that what is predicted as happening at the resurrection is not, after all, the reappearance of the original person but the (first) appearance of a *duplicate* person—no doubt resembling the former one but not numerically identical with him. If this can be argued and cannot be refuted, we are in the odd position of being unsure whether or not to say that the future persons are the former ones. Philosophers have often noted the extent to which problems of identity seem to involve not discoveries but decisions—decisions on what to *call* a particular situation. The literature of personal identity is full of actual and imagined stories introduced to help us discover, by deciding how to talk of them, what the conditions of application of our concepts are. The doctrine of the resurrection of the body seems to present us with just such a matter of decision—namely, would this admittedly conceivable future state properly be described as the reappearance of a former person or as the first appearance of a duplicate of him?

DISEMBODIED PERSONALITY

Let us now look at the first group of difficulties, those connected with the possibility of applying our normal concepts of personal life to post-

"A Hindu Experience of Death"

When this self gets to weakness, gets to confusedness, as it were, then the breaths gather round him. He takes to himself those particles of light and descends into the heart. When the person in the eye turns away, then he becomes non-knowing of forms. He is becoming one, he does not see, they say; he is becoming one, he does not smell, they say; he is becoming one, he does not taste, they say; he is becoming one, he does not speak, they say; he is becoming one, he does not hear, they say; he is becoming one, he does not think, they say; he is becoming one, he does not touch, they say; he is becoming one, he does not know, they say.

The point of his heart becomes lighted up and by that light the self departs either through the eye or through the head or through other apertures of the body. And when he thus departs, life departs after him. And when life thus departs, all the vital breaths depart after him. He becomes one with intelligence. What has intelligence departs with him. His knowledge and his work take hold of him as also his past experience.

Verily, when a person departs from this world, he goes to the air. It opens out there for him like the hole of a chariot wheel. Through that he goes upwards. He goes to the sun. It opens out there for him like the hole of a *lambara.* Through that he goes upwards. He reaches the moon. It opens out there for him like the hole of a drum. Through that he goes upwards. He goes to the world free from grief, free from snow. There he dwells eternal years.

From *The Upanishads.* Translated by S. Radhakrishnan.

The goddess Kali devouring her husband, the god Siva. Wood. Nepal. Eighteenth or nineteenth century.

mortem beings. These seem to arise, as we have seen already, only in connection with the belief that men survive without their bodies, and I shall therefore only discuss them in this connection.

These difficulties raise the most fundamental issues in the philosophy of mind. There is no doubt that the belief that the soul continues after physical death is one of the major causes of the famous "Cartesian dualism" of mind and matter. The dualist position, formulated by Descartes in the seventeenth century, restated a metaphysical position very close in many ways to that of Plato. Descartes' position is, roughly, that the soul (or mind) and the body are two distinct substances that have no common properties and have a purely causal and contingent relationship with one another. The mind occupies no space, is free, and indivisible; whereas the body does occupy space, is incapable of spontaneous motion, and can be divided. Further, each person cannot fail to be aware of the contents of his own mind, whereas the possibility of knowledge of the external physical world needs philosophical demonstration in view of the fact that our senses sometimes deceive us.

In the *Meditations* Descartes argues for his metaphysical dualism on epistemological grounds like these. But whatever its surface and deep causes are, its strengths and weaknesses as a theory about the composition of the human person have dominated philosophical discussion for over two centuries. Only recently, through the work of Wittgenstein and Ryle, have philosophers freed themselves from this dominance.[5] It is not necessary to hold the dualistic view of the nature of embodied persons in order to maintain the post-mortem existence of *dis*embodied persons, but a combination of the two is natural and is very common on a popular level. If we can make sense of the view that the mind or soul is essentially independent of the body it is "in," then there would seem to be no real difficulty about understanding the belief that it can continue when its occupancy of that body ceases. It has become very clear, however, that the dualistic picture of the structure of a person forces its adherents into the view that a person's mental life and mental qualities are features of the history of his mind and have at best a causal relationship with what his body is seen to do. In fact the greater part of what we say about people commits us to certain expectations about their physical performances. This does not mean, as some overenthusiastic behaviorists seem at times to suggest, that people do not have private mental images, wishes, and thoughts. It means rather that their intelligence, will, and emotions do not consist only, or even mainly, in the occurrence

5. See Ludwig Wittgenstein, *Philosophical Investigations,* trans. by G. E. M. Anscombe (Oxford: Basil Blackwell, 1953); Gilbert Ryle, *The Concept of Mind* (London: Hutchinson, 1949).

of those private experiences. It is therefore very doubtful indeed that dualism could hope to do justice to the variety of people's mental lives; it is also doubtful that this mental life could continue without a body. The only way of seeing whether or not the latter can be made plausible seems to be the slow and tedious process of wondering, case by case, how much of what we now can ascribe to embodied persons could be ascribed to disembodied ones without absurdity. If little or nothing can be so ascribed, we cannot attach any content to the phrase "disembodied person." If some characteristics can be ascribed to such a person, we may be able to attach some content to this notion, although the concept of a person will be much attenuated in the process.

Disembodied persons can conduct no physical performances. They cannot walk or talk (or, therefore, converse), open and close their eyes or peer (or, therefore, look), turn their heads and incline their ears (or, therefore, listen), raise their hands in anger or weep (or, therefore, give bodily expression to their emotions), or touch or feel physical objects. Hence they cannot perceive each other or be perceived by us. Can they, still, be said without absurdity to perceive physical things? Perhaps we could say so if we were prepared to allow that a being having a set of visual images corresponding to the actual disposition of some physical things was thereby *seeing* those things. We could say so if we were prepared to allow that a being having a sequence of auditory experiences that made him think correctly that a certain object was giving off a particular sound was thereby *hearing* that object. The notions of seeing and hearing would be attenuated, since they would not, if applied in such cases, entail that the person who saw was physically in front of the object he saw with his face turned toward it or that the person who heard was receiving sound waves from the object that was giving them off. On the other hand, many philosophers hold that such implications are at most informal ones that are not essential to the concepts in question. Perhaps we could also say even that disembodied percipients could *do* things to the objects (or persons) they see and hear. We might be able to say this if we imagined that

"A Buddhist Experience of Death"

('Saddharma-smrityupasthāna Sūtra,' from Chapter XXXIV)

When a human being dies and is going to be reincarnated as a human being . . . when the time of his death is approaching he sees these signs: he sees a great rocky mountain lowering above him like a shadow. He thinks to himself, 'The mountain might fall down on top of me,' and he makes a gesture with his hand as though to ward off this mountain. His brothers and kinsmen and neighbours see him do this; but to them it seems that he is simply pushing out his hand into space. Presently the mountain seems to be made of white cloth and he clambers up this cloth. Then it seems to be made of red cloth. Finally, as the time of his death approaches he sees a bright light, and being unaccustomed to it at the time of his death he is perplexed and confused. He sees all sorts of things such as are seen in dreams, because his mind is confused. He sees his (future) father and mother making love, and seeing them a thought crosses his mind, a perversity arises in him. If he is going to be reborn as a man he sees himself making love with his mother and being hindered by his father; or if he is going to be reborn as a woman, he sees himself making love with his father and being hindered by his mother. It is at that moment that the Intermediate Existence is destroyed and life and consciousness arise and causality begins once more to work. It is like the imprint made by a die; the die is then destroyed but the pattern has been imprinted.

Chinese text dates from A.D. 542. Translated by Arthur Waley.

sometimes these percipients had wishes that were immediately actualized in the world, without any natural explanation for the strange things that occurred; though obviously such fantasies would involve the ascription of occult powers to the spirits.[6] We might prefer to avoid all talk of interaction between the world of the spirits and ours, however, by denying that a disembodied being can see or hear or act in our world at all. Perhaps their lives consist exclusively of internal processes—acts of imagination and reflection. Such a life would be life in a dream world; and each person would have his own private dream. It might include dream images "of" others, though the accuracy of any reflections they occasioned would be purely coincidental.[7]

These informal suggestions indicate that it might be possible, given a good deal of conceptual elasticity, to accord to disembodied persons at least some of the forms of mental life with which we are familiar. It therefore seems over-doctrinaire to refuse to admit that such beings could be called persons. We must bear in mind, however, that they could hardly be said to have an *inter*personal existence. Not only would we be unable to perceive a disembodied person; but a disembodied person, being unable to perceive another disembodied person, could have no more reason than we have to believe that others besides himself existed. Only if he can perceive embodied persons would he be in a position to know from anything other than memory that they exist or that they act in particular ways. The logic of the concept of disembodied persons clearly rules out the possibility of there being a community of such persons, even though by exercising conceptual care and tolerance we do seem able to ascribe some sort of life to disembodied individuals. In response to this, a verificationist might demand that before we can understand the ascriptions we have considered we should be able to say how we would *know* that a disembodied individual was having some experience or performing some act. But since we are dealing with a possible use of predicates that we have already learned, this verificationist demand seems too stringent.

We have also had to put aside another question whose bearing cannot be disputed, since it casts doubt on our ability to think of disembodied individuals. In asking whether some of the notions of a personal mental life can be applied, we have had to assume that there is a continuing, nonphysical subject to whom they can be applied, who has the experience or who does the action. This notion is essential to our understanding of the suggestion that there is a plurality of distinct individuals (whether they form a community or not), that on some occasion an experience is had by one of them rather than another, and that on another occasion a second experience is had by the same individual (or, indeed, a different individual) as had the first. In daily life the distinction between individuals and the continuing identity of individuals through time seems to depend upon the fact that each individual person has a distinguishable and persisting body. In the absence of a body are we able to form any notion of what has the experience or does the actions, has certain other experiences or actions in its past, and will have others in its future? In what follows, in order to retain some degree of clarity and simplicity in a philosophical area where obscurity is especially easy, I shall concentrate on trying to provide some account of what it might be for a disembodied person to retain identity through time. The philosophical theories we shall look at are usually also intended to offer some answer to the problem of distinguishing between two or more contemporaries—the problem, that is, of individuation. It is in any case hard to see how that question could have an answer if the problem of identity through time does not. I shall

6. These suggestions and alternatives to some of them are discussed in Chapters 2, 3, and 4 of my book *Survival and Disembodied Existence* (London: Routledge & Kegan Paul, 1970).

7. See H. H. Price, "Survival and the Idea of 'Another World,'" *Proceedings of the Society for Psychical Research,* 50 (1952); reprinted in J. R. Smythies (ed.), *Brain and Mind* (London: Routledge & Kegan Paul, 1965). For comments on Price see the Smythies volume and Penelhum, *Survival and Disembodied Existence,* Chapter 4.

now turn, then, to the second, and more fundamental, of our two problems in the logic of the concept of survival.

THE PROBLEM OF IDENTITY: HUME'S SKEPTICISM

The logical problems one has to contend with when examining the concept of survival are to a large extent extensions of those that have puzzled philosophers when they have tried to analyze the notion of personal identity.[8] We all recognize one another; we are all familiar enough with the experience of wondering who someone is; and most of us know the embarrassment that follows when one makes a mistake about who someone is. Our day-to-day thinking about these matters suggests that we take it for granted that there are clearly understood factors that determine whether the man before us is Smith or not, or is who he says he is or not, even though we may be unable to decide sometimes, through lack of information, whether these factors obtain. Philosophers have been puzzled, however, when they have tried to say what these factors are. Skeptical philosophers have even wondered whether any such factors can be isolated; and if they cannot be, they have suggested, our assumption that people do retain their identities from one period of time to the next may be an illusion.

We do not need to spend much time here on this sort of skepticism. Its most famous exponent is Hume, who confessed himself unable to detect any stability in the mental life of men and therefore thought that the incessant changes that human minds undergo make it plainly false that they retain any identity at all.[9] Our belief that they do retain an identity is a convenient fiction but nothing better. This skepticism rests on an unstated assumption that there is some sort of logical conflict between the notions of sameness and change. If this were so, then in order to be sure that any type of being retained identity through time, we would have to be sure that it, or at least the essential part of it, remained unchanged through that time. If this is true, then of course Hume would be quite justified in relapsing into skepticism about personal identity. But once the assumption is exposed, its gratuitousness becomes apparent. Sameness or identity is an ambiguous notion; borrowing vocabulary found in Hume himself, we can distinguish between "numerical identity" and "specific identity." Two things are identical in the specific sense if they are exactly alike in some or all respects. This can only be true if they are, nevertheless, two distinct things—if, that is, they are *not* identical in the numerical sense. Two numerically different things may or may not be the same in the specific sense. One and the same thing (in the numerical sense) may be the same at one time as it was at an earlier time, or it may not. If it is not, it has changed. To say that just because it has changed it cannot be numerically the same is to confuse the two sorts of identity.

Certain changes, however, may destroy a thing—that is, whatever remains of it is no longer sufficient to entitle us to say that that thing has continued in existence, and we are forced to say that something else is there, as when a house crumbles and a mere heap of stones remains. Even though Hume is wrong in thinking that the mere fact of change destroys numerical identity, it is still the case that for each *sort* of thing, certain changes will destroy that identity and certain others will not. Reducing all parts of a chair to ashes in a fire will destroy its identity,

8. For a general discussion of the problems of personal identity, see my article of that title in *Encyclopedia of Philosophy,* Vol. 6. This contains, besides a more rigorous treatment of issues raised briefly here, some extended discussion of the implications of the "puzzle cases," which I have had to omit from a short treatment of these topics. The latter part of my *Survival and Disembodied Existence* is intended to be a more thorough examination of the issues introduced here.

9. See Hume's *Treatise of Human Nature,* Book I, Part 4, Section 6. The criticisms I make here are more informal versions of those I raised in "Hume on Personal Identity," *The Philosophical Review,* 44, No. 4 (1955), 571–589, reprinted in V. C. Chappell (ed.), *Hume* (New York: Doubleday, 1967), pp. 213–239.

whereas changing the color of its surface by painting it will not. This suggests, once again, that the proper philosophical task is to discover, at least in the case of those classes of things that are of philosophical interest to us, what factors have to remain for a thing of that sort to continue in being and which ones do not. The problem of personal identity consists, in part, of trying to clarify this in the case of persons.

When we try to do this we are confronted with another oddity in a discussion like Hume's. He restricts himself, without any apparent recognition of the need to justify this restriction, to a consideration of only the mental factors that make up the being of a person and ignores the physical ones. If one makes this restriction, one is immediately confronted with the following facts that Hume stresses: first, he notes that the changes we can introspect within the mind succeed one another very rapidly; and second, he points out that one cannot detect any more stable element. Since we usually conceive of *things* as entities that change fairly slowly unless catastrophe strikes them and do not normally change nearly as rapidly as the contents of the mind seem to do, our ascription of identity to the person is apt to seem puzzling. But what needs to be questioned here is Hume's restriction. One of the major reasons for it is that Hume inherits the dualism that Descartes passed down from Plato into modern philosophy. It is a characteristic part of that tradition not merely to divide the human person into two parts but to identify the real person with the mind and assume that the body is merely a place that this person inhabits. If this identification is presupposed, then Hume's bewilderment in the face of the rapidity of mental change is understandable enough.

MENTAL AND BODILY CRITERIA OF IDENTITY

One way of trying to avoid this confusion is to resort to a doctrine that Hume recognizes to be without value: the doctrine of spiritual substance. This is the doctrine that in spite of the changingness of our mental lives, there is some hidden core to it that persists unchanged throughout, thus providing a backdrop against which the changes occur. This backdrop need not be *un*changing: It could be subject only to gradual change. The tacit assumption that it cannot change at all is only the result of assuming that identity and change are always inconsistent. But even if we allow that the spiritual substance to which the occurrences in our mental lives belong might itself be subject to gradual change, the doctrine is without value. For if the doctrine implies that we can find this relatively permanent core within by looking into ourselves, then it is false; for we cannot, as Hume emphasizes. If on the other hand, it is admitted that the doctrine postulates something that is not accessible to observation, there is another difficulty: It can at best be a matter of happy accident that when we judge someone before us to be the same person as someone we knew before, we are right. For the only thing that would make this judgment reliable is the knowledge that the features possessed by the present and the past person belonged to the same substance. Yet when the substance is inaccessible even to the person himself, how could we ever know that an identity judgment was true? It is obvious that our basis for such judgments must be something other than what the doctrine requires it to be, for how, otherwise, could we learn to make such judgments in the first place?

We base our identity judgments, at least of others, upon the observation of their physical appearance. This fact, plus the mysteriousness of the doctrine of spiritual substance, has made it very tempting for philosophers to say that what makes a person the same from one period to the next is the continuance of his body throughout the two periods. The human body has the relative stability that we associate with a great many observable material objects and is not usually subject to the rapid changes that go on in the human mind. The plausibility of the claim that bodily continuity is a necessary and sufficient condition of personal identity derives also from the fact that our judgments about the identity of persons are in the vast majority of cases based on our having looked at them, talked to them, and recognized them. This may be why even philosophers who have tacitly identified the person with his mind have assumed that a person cannot consist only of thoughts, feelings, images, and other fleeting and changing phenomena, but must consist, beneath this, of something more stable. For they have, perhaps, been looking within the mind itself for something that has the relative stability of the body, even though they have officially abandoned any belief that the body provides persons with their continuing identity.

Suppose, however, that they were to abandon body surrogates like spiritual substance. Suppose they were not to assume that the identity of a person consists in the persistence of some relatively stable element such as his body, but were to concentrate their attention solely upon what they consider to be the contents of his mental life. If they were to do this, it would seem that their only hope of giving an account of the self-identity of persons would be to suggest the existence of some relationship among the fleeting elements of which human mental life is composed. An appropriate relationship does seem available. Some of the later experiences in a man's life history are, the story might go, memories of the earlier ones. And only the same person who had the earlier experiences could have a memory of one of them among his later experiences. So we have here the possibility of a purely mental standard of identity: that person A at time T_2 is the same as person B at some earlier time T_1 if and only if, among the experiences that person A has at T_2 there are memories of experiences that person B had at T_1. In the literature of the subject these two criteria of identity (bodily continuity and memory) have contended for priority.

The claim that personal identity can be understood solely in terms of memory can be accepted by someone who does not believe that a person can be identified with his mind or that anyone ever survives physical death. A philosopher who does not believe these things might still believe that the embodied person before him can be identified with Smith, whom he used to know, only if the person before him has the appropriate memories. But it is clear that some-

"A Tibetan Buddist Experience of Death"

When the expiration hath ceased, the vital-force will have sunk into the nerve-centre of Wisdom and the Knower will be experiencing the Clear Light of the natural condition. . . . Now thou art experiencing the Radiance of the Clear Light of Pure Reality. Recognize it. . . . thy present intellect, in real nature void, not formed into anything as regards characteristics or colour, naturally void, is the very Reality, the All-Good.

Thine own intellect, which is now voidness, yet not to be regarded as of the voidness of nothingness, but as being the intellect itself, unobstructed, shining, thrilling, and blissful, is the very consciousness, the All-good Buddha.

Thine own consciousness, not formed into anything, in reality void, and the intellect, shining and blissful,—these two,—are inseparable. The union of them is . . . Perfect Enlightenment.

Thine own consciousness, shining, void, and inseparable from the Great Body of Radiance, hath no birth, nor death, and is the Immutable Light. . . .

Knowing this is sufficient. Recognizing the voidness of thine own intellect to be Buddhahood, and looking upon it as being thine own consciousness, is to keep thyself in the divine mind of the Buddha. . . .

From *The Tibetan Book of the Dead.* Translated by W. Y. Evans-Wentz.

one who does believe those things must reject the thesis that only bodily continuity can be a criterion of personal identity. For if it is a necessary condition of a person's continuing that his body should continue, no one could survive in a disembodied form. Someone who accepts the doctrine of disembodied survival, therefore, will naturally incline toward the view that memory is the one necessary and sufficient condition of personal identity, since he must reject the traditional alternative position.

There is an artificiality about speaking, as I have, about two competing positions here. For in daily life it looks as though we use both standards of identity, resorting to one or the other depending on circumstances. Sometimes we decide who someone is by ascertaining facts about their physical appearance, height, weight, and the rest. Sometimes we decide who someone is by trying to determine whether or not they can remember certain past events that the person they claim to be could not fail, we think, to recall. Indeed, the barrier between these two methods becomes less clear than it first seems, when we reflect that we might try to reach our decision by seeing what skills a person has retained or what performances he can carry out. But although both standards are used, one might still have priority over the other. This would be the case if the other would not be available to us if the one were not or if the description of the one required some reference to the other.

It might look as though the use of the bodily criterion of identity presupposes that of memory in some way. For we cannot know, without resorting to our own or someone else's memory of the person in question, whether the body before us is the same one that the person we think he is had in the past. This is true, but it does not show that the man's own memories determine who he is. It only shows that other people could not determine the necessary physical facts about him unless they could rely on their own memories to do it, and this is not the same thing.

There are two arguments that tend to show, I think, that the bodily criterion has priority over the memory criterion. The first one, which is the less fundamental, rests on the fact that people forget things. We cannot say that the man before us is the man who performed some past action if and only if he remembers doing that action, for people forget actions they have done. But one might object on two counts that this need not refute the claim that his having the memory of that action is what makes that action his rather than someone else's. For, first, all we mean by this is that he *could* remember doing it, not that he *does* remember doing it; and, second, all we need is that he be able to remember doing some action or having some experience that the person who did the original action also did, or had.

Let us take these objections in order. The first will not do, for what do we mean when we say that he could remember doing the action in question? If we mean that it is in practice possible to get him to recall doing it, for instance, by psychoanalysis, then the retort is that all practicable methods might fail without thereby showing that the action was not done by him. If, on the other hand, we merely mean that it is in theory possible, then this requires further elucidation: Something that is possible in theory but not in practice is possible in virtue of some condition that in practice cannot bring it about. And this condition can only be the very fact that we are trying to elucidate, namely, the fact that the action was done by him and not by someone else. The other objection does not hold either, for a similar sort of reason. If we say that although the man before us cannot remember doing the action in question, he did do it because he can remember having some experience that the past person who did that action had, this presupposes that we understand what makes the past person who had that experience the same past person who did the original action. There must therefore be some standard of identity, actually satisfied, that we are appealing to in order to presuppose this. To say that this standard is itself that of memory is to raise our original question all over again.

The second and more fundamental argument rests on the fact that the notion of remembering is ambiguous. To say that someone remembers some action or event may mean merely that he believes he did it or witnessed it (without, at least consciously, basing this belief upon being told about it). It is possible, of course, for someone to remember something in this sense without what he remembers having happened at all and without its having happened to *him* even if it did occur. The more common use of the notion of remembering, however, concedes the truth of the man's belief, so that to say that the man remembers some action or event is to say that his claim to know about it is correct. Let us call these sense (i) and sense (ii) of "remember." Then we can say that to remember in sense (i) is to believe that one remembers in sense (ii).

It is apparent that memory in sense (i) cannot provide a criterion of personal identity. It is certainly not a sufficient condition of a man before us being the person that he claims to be that he remembers, in sense (i), doing or experiencing something done or experienced by the man he claims to be. For he could believe that he remembered doing something in this sense, even if nobody had done it. So we have to lean on sense (ii) of "remember." But this leads into a deeper problem. Let us simplify our discussion by concentrating solely upon a person's remembering doing an action or having an experience or witnessing an event and leave aside the complexities involved in someone's remembering some fact, such as that Cáesar was murdered. To say that someone, in sense (ii), remembers, is not merely to report that he believes something, but to accept his belief to be true. But an integral part of his belief is not only that some action was done, some experience had, or some event witnessed, but that it was done or had or witnessed *by him*. In other words, to say that he remembers in sense (ii) is not just to say that he now has some mental image or some conviction, even though it is likely to include this; it is to say that the past action, experience, or event that he refers to is part of his own past. But it now becomes clear that we cannot even state the memory criterion of identity without having some prior (and therefore independent) notion of the identity of the person. So the identity of the person must in the end rest upon some other condition, and the claim that it could rest solely upon memory must be false. The bodily criterion of identity is the natural one to refer to here. If, because of some commitment to dualism, one refuses to resort to it, it becomes wholly mysterious what the criterion of personal identity can be.[10]

IDENTITY AND SURVIVAL

We can now return to the problem of survival. We were considering how far it is possible to make sense of the notion of the persistence of a disembodied person through time and of the claim that some particular future disembodied person will be identical with one of us in this world here and now. We can also ask how far the doctrine of the resurrection of the body frees us from the difficulties that the doctrine of disembodied survival encounters.

If bodily continuity is a necessary condition of the persistence of a person through time, then we cannot form any clear conception of the persistence of a person through time without a body nor of the identity of such a person with some previous embodied person. The previous reflections about the notion of personal identity leave us with two results: first, that to attempt to understand the self-identity of a person solely in terms of memory is impossible and, second, that when we are considering the case of flesh-and-blood persons there seems no alternative but to conclude that bodily continuity is a necessary condition of personal identity. These conclusions by themselves do not show that no sub-

10. On this topic see Antony Flew, "Locke and the Problem of Personal Identity," *Philosophy,* 26 (1951), 53–68, and Sydney Shoemaker, "Personal Identity and Memory," *Journal of Philosophy,* 56 (1959), 868–882.

stitute for bodily continuity could be invented when discussing the case of disembodied personality. But some substitute for it would have to be supplied by invention, and until it is, the notion of disembodied personal identity makes no sense.

The main line of argument is now plain, but for greater completeness it may be desirable to apply it to the doctrine of disembodied survival in a little more detail. An adherent of this doctrine, anxious to avoid admitting the necessity of the bodily criterion of personal identity, might perhaps claim that a survivor of death would intelligibly be said to be identical with someone who had died, because he remembered the actions and experiences of that person. And he might be said intelligibly to persist through time in his disembodied state because later and earlier experiences in the afterlife could be similarly connected by memories.

Let us take the latter suggestion first. It is that the disembodied person who has some experience at some future time FT_2 will be identical with the disembodied person who will have had some experience at an earlier future time FT_1 if, along with the experience at FT_2, there is a memory of the one he had at FT_1. The difficulty is to make sense not only of a phrase like "along with the experience there is a memory," but also, of what it means to speak of a memory here at all. For it will have to be a memory in sense (ii). And to say that the disembodied person has a memory at FT_2 in sense (ii) of some experience had at FT_1 is to assume that the two experiences will have been had by the same person; and this time, since we have no bodily criterion of identity to fall back on, we have no way of interpreting this claim.

If we turn now to the problem of identifying the disembodied person with some person who has died, we find the same difficulty. To say that he can be so identified because he remembers the deeds or experiences of that person is once again to use the notion of remembering in sense (ii). But to do this is to presuppose that we understand what it is for the remembering to be identical with the person who did those deeds or had those experiences. And we do not actually understand this. For although the person who did those deeds had a body, the rememberer, by hypothesis, does not have one and therefore cannot have the same body. It does not seem possible, therefore, to find any answer to the problem of self-identity for disembodied persons.

What about the doctrine of the resurrection of the body? Given that we are talking of the future existence of persons with bodies, the notion of their lasting through time in their future state does not seem to present any logical difficulties. But what of their identity with ourselves? If we assume some one-to-one correspondence between the inhabitants of the next world and of this (that is, assume at least that the inhabitants of the next world each resemble, claim to be, and claim to remember the doings of inhabitants of this one), it might seem foolish to deny that they will be identical with ourselves. But foolishness is not logical absurdity. It is conceivable that there might be a future existence in which there were large numbers of persons each resembling one of us and having uncanny knowledge of our pasts. And if that world does come to be in the future, we shall not be in it. What would make it a world with us in it, rather than a world with duplicates of us in it and not ourselves? Unless we can give a clear answer to this, it seems, very paradoxically, to be a matter of arbitrary choice whether to say these future people are us or not.

Surely, the answer might run, they will have the same bodies that we now have. But this is precisely what is not obvious. Apart from questions about whether the future bodies are like ours in youth, maturity, or old age, the dissolution of the earthly body means that the future body will be in some sense new. To say that it is the old one re-created is merely to say it is the same one without giving any reason for saying it is identical with the original body rather than one very much like it. To answer this way, then, seems merely to face the same puzzle again.

To say that the future beings will remember in sense (ii) our doings and feelings is to raise the same questions here as before. The only possible solution seems to be to insist that in spite of the time gap between the death of the old body and the appearance of the new one, something persists in between. But what? The person disembodied? If so, then the doctrine of the resurrection of the body does not avoid the difficulties that beset the doctrine of disembodied survival, for the simple reason that it falls back upon that very doctrine when its own implications are understood.

This argument does not show that the doctrine of the resurrection of the body is absurd in the way in which the doctrine of disembodied survival is. It shows rather that the doctrine of resurrection is merely one way, and a question-begging way, of describing a set of circumstances that can be described equally well in another fashion. Yet the difference between the two alternative descriptions is a vital one. For it comes to no less than the original question, namely, do we survive? It is a question that the doctrine provides an answer to but one that seems to have no conclusive grounds, even if the circum-

"Death and Aloneness"

Jiddu Krishnamurti

If one is afraid then one cannot possibly find out what this immense thing called death is. It must be the most extraordinary thing. To find out what death is one must also enquire into what life is before death. One never does that. One never enquires what living is. Death is inevitable; but what is living? Is this living, this enormous suffering, fear, anxiety, sorrow, and all the rest of it—is this living? Clinging to that one is afraid of death. If one does not know what living is one cannot know what death is—they go together. If one can find out what the full meaning of living is, the totality of living, the wholeness of living, then one is capable of understanding the wholeness of death. But one usually enquires into the meaning of death without enquiring into the meaning of life.

. . . So, before one enquires into the meaning of death one is asking what living is. Is the life one is living, living? The constant struggle with each other? . . .

Death comes and with that one cannot argue; one cannot say: "Wait a few minutes more"—it is there. When it comes, can the mind meet the end of everything while one is living, while one has vitality and energy, while one is full of life? When one's life is not wasted in conflicts and worries one is full of energy, clarity. Death means the ending of all that one knows, of all one's attachments, of one's bank accounts, of all one's attainments—there is a complete ending. Can the mind, while living, meet such a state? Then one will understand the full meaning of what death is. If one clings to the idea of 'me', that me which one believes must continue, the me that is put together by thought, including the me in which one believes there is the higher consciousness, the supreme consciousness, then one will not understand what death is in life.

Thought lives in the known; it is the outcome of the known; if there is not freedom from the known one cannot possibly find out what death is, which is the ending of everything, the physical organism with all its ingrained habits, the identification with the body, with the name, with all the memories it has acquired. One cannot carry it all over when one goes to death. One cannot carry there all one's money; so, in the same way one has to end in life everything that one knows. That means there is absolute aloneness; not loneliness but aloneness, in the sense there is nothing else but that state of mind that is completely whole. Aloneness means all one.

From *The Wholeness of Life,* 1982.

stances envisaged in the doctrine were admitted to be forthcoming.

The belief in survival, then, at least in this version, does not run into insuperable difficulties of logic. But it does not seem possible to describe a set of future circumstances that will unambiguously show it to be true. . . . If the doctrine is agreed to be coherent, it can offer a suitable answer to the difficulties about the verification of religious beliefs. I do not consider the present puzzle to show that it is not coherent. But it does show its status to be very baffling.

Raymond Martin

"SURVIVAL OF BODILY DEATH: A QUESTION OF VALUES"

RAYMOND MARTIN teaches at the University of Maryland and writes primarily on philosophical psychology and the philosophy of history. Among his books are *Wisdom without Answers, The Experience of Philosophy, Self and Identity,* and *The Past within Us.*

Does anyone ever survive his or her bodily death? *Could* anyone? No speculative questions are older than these, or have been answered more frequently or more variously. None have been laid to rest more often, or, in our times, with more claimed decisiveness. Jay Rosenberg, for instance, no doubt speaks for many contemporary philosophers when he claims, in his recent book, to have *"demonstrated"* that "we cannot [even] make *coherent sense* of the supposed possibility that a person's history might continue beyond that person's [bodily] death."[1]

It may seem preposterous at this late date—after thousands of years of debate—to try to add anything radically new to the philosophical discussion of survival. Surely by now it has all been said. Surprisingly, though, there is something new to add—a realization that has emerged from the recent debate over personal identity that makes it much easier to argue successfully for meaningful personal survival. This realization is that for many people the preservation of personal identity does not matter primarily in survival. What this means to the debate over survival of bodily death is that now the person who would argue for survival does not have to presuppose any particular criterion of identity and has much more latitude in terms of how the evidence for survival might be explained. The purpose of the present paper is to illustrate these claims. I shall do this by arguing for a kind of minimalist reincarnation.

Traditional arguments for reincarnation are invariably burdened with unnecessary and questionable assumptions: The vehicle for survival is some sort of metaphysical substance or soul; there are connections of an unverifiable kind (say, karmic connections) between earlier and later people; personal survival requires identity.

Reprinted from *Religious Studies,* v. 28 (1992), by permission of the publisher and the author.

1. *Thinking Clearly About Death* (Englewood Cliffs, NJ: Prentice-Hall, 1983), p. 96, emphasis added.

The argument that I shall present, by contrast, is compatible with materialism or physicalism, stands or falls on straightforward empirical grounds, and dispenses with the assumption that meaningful personal survival requires identity. It is modest also in being only for the *temporary* survival of *some* (so, not for immortality or even for the temporary survival of everyone) and in resting on admittedly *incomplete and fragmentary data,* so that even if the argument is successful as far as it goes, it shows no more than that there is a *prima facie* case for actual survival that could easily be undermined later by more and better data. Even with all of these qualifications, however, the argument is still ambitious in that it is for *actual* personal survival of bodily death, something that most contemporary philosophers regard as completely beyond the pale.

I shall rely heavily on the hard work of others: On the philosophical side, on the arguments and examples of Derek Parfit and, to a lesser extent, on those of Sydney Shoemaker and Robert Nozick—none of whom, of course, has argued for *actual* personal survival of bodily death; and, on the empirical side, on the data that Ian Stevenson and his associates have collected in their investigations of children who apparently remember previous lives.[2] The argument is what I regard as the best defense of the claim that the most likely explanation of Stevenson's data implies meaningful personal survival. Although Stevenson has already used his data to argue for reincarnation, my argument will be so much more modest than Stevenson's own argument that those who find his persuasive (a group that probably does not include many professional philosophers) may well feel that I have thrown out the baby with the bathwater. No matter, both arguments could be correct.

I

From 1694, when John Locke added a chapter on personal identity to his *Essay Concerning Human Understanding,* until the late 1960s, British and American philosophers concerned with personal identity concentrated on a central question: What are the necessary and sufficient conditions under which *personal identity* is preserved (over time)? In 1967 the univocal focus of this nearly 300-year-old debate was shattered, probably irrevocably. What changed things was the introduction into the debate, by David Wiggins, of so-called fission examples, in which a person somehow divides (in Wiggin's account, amoeba-like) into two or more qualitatively similar persons.[3] Consideration of these examples forced philosophers to face the possibility that one might survive *as* someone else whose existence one values as much as one's own and, hence, also forced them, appropriately enough, to divide two questions they had previously treated as one: The traditional question, mentioned above, and the new one, what are the conditions under which *what matters primarily in survival* is preserved (over time)? This new question was never raised earlier probably because it was simply assumed that personal identity must be what matters primarily in survival, an assumption that, if true, would guarantee that both questions have the same answer.

In the 1970s and 1980s, several philosophers—including Parfit, Shoemaker, and No-

2. See especially Derek Parfit, "Personal Identity," *The Philosophical Review* 80 (1971): 3–27, and his *Reasons and Persons* (Oxford: Clarendon Press, 1984), Part III; Sydney Shoemaker, "Persons and Their Pasts," *American Philosophical Quarterly* 7 (1970): 269–285, and his "Personal Identity: A Materialist Account," in Sydney Shoemaker and Richard Swinburne, *Personal Identity* (Oxford: Basil Blackwell, 1984), pp. 69–152; and Robert Nozick, *Philosophical Explanations* (Cambridge, MA: Harvard University Press, 1981), Ch. 1. Stevenson's early investigations are summarized in *Twenty Cases Suggestive of Reincarnation* (Charlottesville: University Press of Virginia, 1966; Second Edition, 1974), but he has since (with associates) published additional data in four thick volumes: *Cases of the Reincarnation Type,* Vol. 1 (1975), Vol. 2 (1977), Vol. 3 (1980), and Vol. 4 (1983), as well as in his *Unlearned Language: New Studies in Xenoglossy* (1984) and *Children Who Remember Previous Lives* (1987), all of which were published by University Press of Virginia. *Children Who Remember* contains a bibliography of Stevenson's many additional articles on cases suggestive of reincarnation, including ones in *International Journal of Comparative Sociology* (1970), *Journal of Nervous and Mental Disease* (1983), and *American Journal of Psychiatry* (1979).

3. David Wiggins, *Identity and Spatio-Temporal Continuity* (Oxford: Basil Blackwell, 1967), p. 50.

zick—argued persuasively that other things matter more in survival than identity. If their arguments are correct, then there are ways of surviving (or, quasi-surviving) that do not preserve identity that are as good, or almost as good, from a person's own egoistic or self-regarding point of view, as survival that does preserve identity. This is not a new idea. In the Vedic traditions that led to Hinduism, for instance, the idea that there can be meaningful survival not as oneself but as part of a larger psychic entity is as old as recorded history. But, hardheaded Western thinkers have for the most part summarily dismissed such possibilities as either not responsive to Western interests in personal survival or as so much mystical mumbo-jumbo. Antony Flew, for instance, who has written more extensively on survival of bodily death than perhaps any other analytic philosopher, nicely captures this dismissive attitude:

> Confronted by such an obstacle [the inevitability of bodily death] how is any such doctrine [of personal survival] to get started? Before trying to suggest an answer I wish to make a sharp, simplifying move . . . I shall . . . be taking it for granted, first, that what we are interested in is our personal post-mortem futures, if any. 'Survival', through our children and our children's children after we ourselves are irrecoverably dead, 'immortality' through the memories of others thanks to our great works, or even our immersion in some universal world-soul—whatever that might mean—may be as much as, or much more than, most of us will in fact be getting. And it may be lamentably self-centered, albeit humanly altogether understandable, that we should be concerned about more than these thin substitutes. But, for better or for worse, what we are discussing now is the possibility of our post-mortem survival as persons identifiable as those we are here and now.[4]

The sort of quick, dismissive move expressed in Flew's remarks is now obsolete. Although the seeming possibility of meaningful personal survival without identity may be illusory, it will no longer do simply to *assume* that it is. The point must be argued.

My argument for reincarnation will stake its claim in the territory that Flew (and most other analytic philosophers) have vacated. Whether its conclusion—that some have survived *as* others to whom they are not (or may not be) identical—is a "thin substitute" for ordinary survival (with identity) remains to be seen. It depends partly on which alternatives to ordinary survival one has in mind. (The ones I consider will be much closer to ordinary survival than those Flew mentions, particularly in that one might reasonably anticipate the future experiences of those he survives *as* in the same ways as he anticipates his own future experiences.) It depends also on how "thick" ordinary survival is. I think, along with Parfit and some others (although for somewhat different reasons), that ordinary survival is much "thinner" than we usually suppose, a point to which I shall return.

One of the things that makes the change of focus that comes with arguing for meaningful personal survival without identity theoretically interesting is that virtually all of the arguments that Flew and Rosenberg and others have presented against either the possibility or the actuality of survival with identity are not even relevant as objections. A plausible argument for meaningful personal survival without identity, then, can provide us with a fresh approach (at least within the context of Western philosophy) to an old and relatively tired set of issues. Of course, it is controversial whether other things do in fact matter more in survival than identity. To find out, one has to consider hypothetical situations—such as the fission examples—in which one is forced to choose between survival with identity and survival without it. I shall illustrate such choice situations shortly. The outcome of a full consideration of them, as I have argued at length elsewhere, is the realization that for many people some kinds of survival

4. *The Presumption of Atheism* (New York: Harper & Row, 1976), p. 104; Flew repeats this dismissive move in almost the same words in his Gifford Lectures, published as *The Logic of Mortality* (Oxford: Basil Blackwell, 1987), pp. 2–3.

without identity matter as much, or almost as much, as survival with identity.[5] If this is the outcome, then to address the values *of these people* the debate over personal survival will have to shift away from its traditional focus and toward three questions that philosophers have only recently begun to discuss: What matters most importantly in survival? Under what conditions is *this* (whatever it turns out to be) preserved (over time)? Is there good evidence that *this* has ever persisted beyond someone's bodily death?

This last question is the crucial one. As indicated, I answer that, yes, for many people the persistence of their psychologies under favorable conditions (whether or not this preserves identity) may well be—if not now, at least on reflection—among the things that matter most importantly to them in survival, and there is a good enough *prima facie* case that enough of the psychologies of some people have persisted beyond their bodily deaths to make the claim of meaningful personal survival in their cases plausible.

II

The kind of fission examples that have preoccupied philosophers are, for the most part, science fiction scenarios far removed from the practical realities of day-to-day life (and death). But, these scenarios are not completely removed. In the late 1930s, some psychosurgeons began severing the corpus callosums of severe epileptics in an effort to reduce the severity and frequency of their seizures, a procedure that had the bizarre side effect, not discovered until many years later, of creating two independent centers of consciousness within the same human skull.[6] These centers not only lacked introspective access to each other, but they could also be made to acquire information about the world and express it behaviorally, independently of each other. Most dramatically, they sometimes differed volitionally, expressing their differences using alternate sides of the same human bodies that they jointly shared. In one frequently cited example, a patient was reported to have hugged his wife with one arm while he pushed her away with the other; in another, a patient tried with his right hand (controlled by his left, verbal hemisphere) to hold a newspaper in front of himself, thereby blocking his view of the television, while he tried with his left hand to knock the paper out of the way.

The fission (and nonfission) examples that have preoccupied philosophers concerned with the possibility of survival without identity are tidier and more complete than these real life cases. They have the disadvantage of being hypothetical but the advantage of bringing the issue of egoistic survival values into much sharper focus. Consider, for instance, an example, based on one originally presented by Shoemaker, in which you are asked to imagine that you have a health problem that will result soon in your sudden and painless death unless you receive one of two available treatments.[7] The first is to have your brain removed and placed into the empty cranium of a body that is otherwise qualitatively identical to your own. The second is to have your brain removed, divided into functionally identical halves (each of which is capable of sustaining your full psychology), and then to have each of these halves put into the empty cranium of a body of its own, again one that is brainless but otherwise qualitatively identical to your own.

In the first treatment there is a ten percent chance that the transplantation will take. If it does take, the survivor who wakes up in the recovery room will be physically and psycholog-

5. See my "Identity, Transformation, and What Matters in Survival," in Daniel Kolak and Raymond Martin, eds., *Self and Identity* (New York: Macmillan, 1991), pp. 289–301.

6. See ibid., for a sample of the literature on commissurotomy.

7. Shoemaker, "Personal Identity: A Materialist Account, p. 119.

ically like you just prior to the operation except that he will know he has had the operation and he will be healthy. In the second, there is a ninety-five percent chance both transplantations will take. If they do, the survivors who wake up in the recovery room will be physically and psychologically like you just prior to the operation except that each of them will know he has had the operation and each will be healthy. If the transplantation in the first treatment does not take, the would-be survivor will die painlessly on the operating table. If either transplantation in the second treatment does not take, then the other will not either, and both of the would-be survivors will die painlessly on the operating table. Suppose everything else about the treatments is the same and as attractive to you as possible: For instance, both are painless and free of charge and, if successful, result in survivors who recover quickly.

Many philosophers believe that identity would be retained in the first (nonfission) treatment but lost in the second (fission) treatment. The reason for its loss in the second treatment is that identity is a transitive relationship, which implies that if one of the survivors were the same person as the brain donor, and the donor were the same person as the other survivor, then the former survivor would be the same person as the latter survivor. Yet the survivors, at least once they begin to lead independent lives, are not plausibly regarded as the same people as each other. And, since it would be arbitrary to regard just one of the survivors, but not the other, as the same person as the brain donor (in the beginning they are equally qualified), it is more plausible to regard each of the survivors as a different person from the donor.

But if you would persist through the first treatment but not the second, then only by sacrificing your identity can you greatly increase the chances of someone surviving for years who is qualitatively just like you. Would it be worth it—that is, would it be worth it for selfish (or self-regarding) reasons? Most people who consider this example feel strongly that it would be, hence (apparently) that survival without identity can matter as much, or almost as much, as survival with identity.

Some have questioned whether fission undermines identity and, hence, whether such examples can support the view that survival without identity matters as much as survival with identity. Since I have argued elsewhere that the same point can be made with nonfission examples, nothing hinges, in my view, on the debate over whether fission undermines identity, and I shall here, for expository reasons, stick to the fission case as my central example, asking the reader to focus on what is crucial about this case—not fission, but the apparently selfishly motivated trading of continued identity for other benefits.[8]

I want now to illustrate how these theoretical developments make it much easier to make a case for meaningful personal survival by considering the data that Stevenson has collected in his investigations of children who apparently remember past lives. I am using Stevenson's data because I believe it is the best evidence we have of the survival of human personality beyond the grave. The theoretical point I want to illustrate, though, is a general one that could be illustrated as well with other data, such as those gleaned from reports of mediumistic communications.

III

To begin with a specific case, consider that of Jasbir, who was born in Rasulpur, India, in 1950, and who, when he was three and one-half years

8. David Lewis has questioned whether fission undermines identity by arguing for a multiple occupancy view of persons, in "Survival and Identity," in Amelie Rorty, ed., *The Identities of Persons* (Berkeley: University of California Press, 1976), reprinted, along with "Postscripts," in *Philosophical Papers,* Vol. 1 (New York: Oxford University Press, 1983), and in Kolak and Martin, *Self and Identity.* John Perry has questioned the transitivity of identity in "Can the Self Divide?" *Journal of Philosophy* 69 (1972): 463–488. I have argued that, so far as the importance of identity is concerned, not much depends on whether identity is lost in fission (see "Identity, Transformation, and What Matters in Survival," op. cit.).

old, was thought to have died of smallpox.[9] According to Stevenson's report, Jasbir's father made preparations to bury him but because of darkness postponed the burial until morning. That night he noticed stirrings in his son's body. Over a period of several weeks the boy gradually recovered enough to talk. When he did talk it was evident that he had undergone a remarkable transformation. He then stated that he was the son of Shanker of Vehedi — a person unknown to Jasbir's parents and from a relatively remote village; and he communicated many details of "his" life and death in Vehedi, including how, during a wedding procession, he had eaten poisoned sweets given him by a man who owed him money, fell from a chariot he was riding, injured his head, and died.

Stevenson claims that Jasbir's father tried to hide Jasbir's strange claims and behavior but news of it leaked out and about three years later came to the attention of a woman from Jasbir's village who had married a native of Vehedi. On rare occasions, at intervals of several years, she returned to Rasulpur. On one such trip in 1957, Jasbir saw her and "recognized" her as his aunt. She then reported the incident and what she had learned of Jasbir's claims to her husband's family and also to the Tyagi family of Vehedi whose son, Sobha Ram Tyagi, had died in May, 1954, at the age of twenty-two, in a chariot accident, in the manner described by Jasbir. The Tyagis knew nothing, though, of any poisoning or debt owed Sobha Ram.

When Sobha Ram's father and other members of his family later went to Rasulpur, Jasbir reportedly recognized them and correctly identified their relationships to Sobha Ram. Jasbir was then brought to Vehedi, put down near the railway station, and asked to lead the way to the Tyagi quadrangle, which he did without difficulty. Then, over a period of several days, he demonstrated to the Tyagis and other villagers a detailed knowledge of the Tyagis and their affairs. He returned to Rasulpur reluctantly, afterward complaining that he felt isolated and lonely there and wanted to live in Vehedi, which he continued to visit from time to time, usually for several weeks in the summer.

According to Stevenson, Jasbir made twenty-two checkable statements about "himself," almost all of which were true of Sobha Ram. For instance, Jasbir said that he was the son of Shankar of Vehedi, that he was a Brahmin (not, as Jasbir was, a Jat), that there was a peepal tree in front of his house, and that the house had a well that was half in and half outside the house (the only well of this kind in Vehedi). He said that his wife belonged to the village of Molna, that his mother was named Kela, his son Baleshwar, his aunt Ram Kali, and his mother-in-law Kirpi. And, as indicated, Jasbir explained the circumstances of Sobha Ram's death.

Stevenson claims that Jasbir recognized a total of sixteen relatives and friends of Sobha Ram and correctly identified their relationships to Sobha Ram, sometimes adding relevant details. For instance, when a man named Birbal Singh, who was teasingly called "Gandhiji" (because he had large ears that resembled those of Mahatma Gandhi), appeared at the door, Jasbir said, "Come in, Gandhiji." Someone present reportedly corrected Jasbir by saying, "This is Birbal," to which Jasbir replied, "We call him "Gandhiji." For their part, the Tyagis accepted Jasbir as a full member of the family and consulted him about the marriage of Sobha Ram's son and daughter. And the man Jasbir claimed killed Sobha Ram to avoid paying a debt later paid Jasbir (not Sobha Ram's family) 600 rupees.

Stevenson reports that Jasbir, after his change in personality, did not retain his original Jasbir-personality. Instead, Jasbir claimed that he was Sobha Ram, behaved like Sobha Ram, and only gradually (and never fully) accepted the body and life situations of Jasbir. He continued to think of himself as a Brahmin, added Sobha Ram's Brahmin name to his Jat family name, and refused employment that was appropriate to his

9. The Jasbir case is described in Stevenson's *Twenty Cases* and also in his *Children Who Remember*.

Jat status because he considered it beneath his dignity. Yet he continued to live most of the time with his natural parents and planned to marry in the Jat caste.

Jasbir's case differs importantly from most of the other cases Stevenson has investigated, first, in that the person whose personality Jasbir apparently took over did not die until after Jasbir was born (normally the previous personality dies first); second, in that Jasbir's personality was virtually replaced by that of Sobha Ram's (normally there is a blending of the two personalities)[10]; and, third, in that Jasbir's apparent memories of Sobha Ram's life and his identification with Sobha Ram continued into adulthood (normally the apparent memories and identification last only a few years). Otherwise, Jasbir's case closely resembles Stevenson's other cases.

Stevenson claims, as of 1987, to have investigated about 250 "cases suggestive of reincarnation" thoroughly and to have investigated at least another thousand cases in enough detail to include them in an analysis of recurrent features. Additional cases have been investigated by Stevenson's associates. Usually Stevenson and his associates have arrived on the scene only after the families involved have attempted to verify the child's statements. Stevenson then has gathered his information after the fact, so to speak, in (apparently) carefully conducted interviews (usually involving re-interviews and cross-examination of key informants). However, in twenty-four cases (the number is continually growing) Stevenson claims that someone made a written record of what the child had said *before* anyone attempted to verify the child's statements and before the two families concerned had met.[11]

Stevenson reports that the children usually began speaking about "their previous lives" as soon as they could speak—between two and four years old—and then stopped talking about them between the ages of five and eight. (In only a few cases, one of which is Jasbir's, did the apparent memories of the previous life continue into adulthood.) Stevenson claims that in the cases he has investigated thoroughly about ninety percent of the children's checkable statements about "their previous lives" are correct.

In many cases the previous personality met a violent and early death, and events connected with or just preceding his or her death tend to be prominent among the children's apparent memories. And, Stevenson reports that in fifty percent of the cases in which the previous personality died violently, phobias related to the previous personality's mode of death were present. For instance, if the previous personality died of drowning (or, from being shot), the subject might have a phobia of water (or, of firearms). Stevenson claims that the subjects sometimes had skills, such as sewing or the ability to repair engines, that the previous personalities also had and that the children had no normal opportunities to acquire. He also claims that birthmarks on the children corresponding closely to marks on the previous personality, often to the wounds from which the previous personality met death, are not uncommon—but, curiously, are more common in some cultures, such as the Eskimos, the Tlingits, and the Burmese, than in others.

Cultural differences are also reflected in other ways in the data—most importantly, perhaps, in that reported cases are much more common in cultures in which reincarnation is a widely shared

10. Interestingly, philosophers sometimes argue on *a priori* grounds, apparently without considering the empirical evidence to the contrary from the psychological study of dissociation, that the blending of memories from different psychologies is impossible. See, for instance, Richard Wollheim, *The Thread of Life* (Cambridge, MA: Harvard University Press, 1984), pp. 112 ff. (to which I responded in "Memory, Connecting, and What Matters in Survival," *Australasian Journal of Philosophy* 24 [1987]: 82–97) and Marya Schechtman, "Personhood and Personal Identity," *Journal of Philosophy* 87 (1990): 71–92.

11. In addition to the references in note 2, see Stevenson's "Three New Cases of the Reincarnation Type in Sri Lanka with Written Records Made before Verifications," summarized in *The Journal of Nervous and Mental Disease* 176 (1988): 741, and presented fully in *Journal of Scientific Exploration* 2 (1988): 217–238.

belief than in ones in which it is not, even when the two are side by side. So, for instance, there are many more reported cases from Asia and Western Africa than from Europe and (nontribal) North America and many more from the Druses of Lebanon than from the Christians of Lebanon. [Stevenson says he has investigated at least thirty-five (nontribal) cases from the continental United States.] The interval between the death of the previous personality and the birth of the subject is also linked to culturally determined beliefs.

With this brief indication of the rich array of descriptive data that have been, and still are being, collected by Stevenson and his associates, I want now to turn to the more theoretically interesting question of how dispensing with the assumption that meaningful personal survival requires identity affects the evaluation of competing explanations of Stevenson's data.

IV

Stevenson considers six different possible explanations of his data: fraud, cryptomnesia, paramnesia, genetic memory, extrasensory perception, and survival. Among survival explanations he distinguishes between possession and reincarnation, a distinction I shall ignore since both involve the persistence of a mind or soul that is distinct from a person's physical body and which transmigrates somehow from the deceased person to the child who apparently remembers that person's life.

Fraud

I know of no specific evidence for fraud in connection with Stevenson's data, other than what Stevenson himself mentions. Even so, it is always a possibility, either on the part of the investigators or those they investigate. And judgments about how likely it is, made ultimately against the backdrop of unstated and often unconscious assumptions about what is plausible and what is not, are bound to vary from person to person. In my own admittedly subjective view, if Stevenson is as honest as he appears to be, then fraud on a scale sufficient to undermine his data is quite unlikely.

As for Stevenson himself, since 1966 he has conducted his research as a highly visible public figure, often in conjunction with research assistants, and from a relatively high profile base of operations at the University of Virginia. None of Stevenson's by now voluminous publications on these cases have the internal earmarks of investigative fraud—indeed just the opposite. Stevenson consistently comes across as one who is willing and open to the idea of other investigators checking his cases, although few of them have actually been checked.[12] There are, of course, independent anecdotal reports of the same phenomenon and many reports of closely related phenomena, such as adults who claim to remember previous lives.[13] (Given how common it is for adults under hypnosis to claim to remember past lives, perhaps it should not be surprising that so many children should make such claims.) Still, even if everything else about my argument for reincarnation is persuasive, one should not regard it as anything more than a *prima facie* case for survival unless and until Stevenson's data has survived the most rigorous checking by *independent* investigators.

Assuming, then, that the data as Stevenson presents them are accurate, Stevenson himself argues persuasively (at least to me) that large scale fraud on the part of his informants is unlikely. While he admits that fraud has occurred occasionally (he claims to know of three cases) he doubts it has happened often because the sort

12. Criticism of Stevenson may be found in Ian Wilson, *Mind Out of Time* (London: Victor Gollancz, 1981), pp. 58–60; William G. Roll, "The Changing Perspectives on Life after Death," in Stanley Krippner, ed., *Advances in Parapsychological Research* (New York: Plenum, 1982), vol. 3; C.T.K. Chari, "Reincarnation Research: Method and Interpretation," in M. Ebon, ed., *Signet Handbook of Parapsychology* (New York: New American Library, 1978); and Paul Edwards, "The Case Against Reincarnation," a four-part article in *Free Inquiry*, vols. 6–7, 1986–87.

13. See, for instance, A.S. Pringle Patterson, *The Idea of Immortality* (Oxford: Oxford University Press, 1922), p. 107, and Alan Gauld, *Mediumship and Survival* (London: Heinemann, 1982), pp. 172–187.

of peasant villagers that are frequently the subjects of his investigations usually lack both the time and motivation to prepare an elaborate hoax and because a successful hoax generally would require an extraordinary conspiracy involving numerous witnesses, including children, that, he thinks, his usual practice of multiple interviews would probably detect.[14] Stevenson says he has occasionally heard adults prompting the subjects, which he says he strongly discourages, but claims that it has never seemed to him to be more than an expression of adult eagerness not to have the children let the adults down by failing to say to Stevenson what the children have often said to them.

Stevenson also cites the difficulties of directing and staging some of the highly emotional scenes he claims to have witnessed.

> I cannot believe that simple villagers would have the time or inclination to rehearse such dramas as occurred in Chhatta when the family of Prakash thought—or said they thought—I favored his returning to the other family. The complexity of the [behavioral] features of these cases alone seems to make fraud virtually out of the question, and I prefer to pass on to other more plausible explanations of them.[15]

And we should as well. My purpose is not to put the argument for reincarnation in its most convincing form but merely to put it fully and plausibly enough that it can be used to illustrate the ways in which the dynamic of the traditional debate over survival of bodily death should change.

Cryptomnesia would occur if the children acquired the information that they thought they remembered in a normal way, forgot how they acquired it, and then subsequently honestly mistook memories of this information for memories of a previous life. Stevenson claims that despite persistent trying he has generally been unable to find any significant link between the pairs of families involved in these cases and, hence, doubts that cryptomnesia could often be the explanation. He also thinks it is unlikely that young children, many of whom could barely talk when they first began relating their apparent memories, could assimilate so much information on the basis of a few overheard conversations. And, he claims that many of the children investigated have revealed private information that was not known outside of the immediate families of the previous personalities. For instance, one child knew of the previous personality's attempt to borrow money from his wife, another of an occasion when the previous personality and a woman had gone to a wedding in a village (which she named) where they had had difficulty finding a latrine. Finally, Stevenson notes that it is not just information but also behavioral features of the cases that must be explained—such as the strong identifications that the subjects often make with the previous personalities.

Paramnesia

This occurs when there are certain other sorts of honest distortions and inaccuracies in the memories of those who provide information on the cases. A possible scenario, that Stevenson thinks may have obtained in a few of the cases he has investigated, involves the parents unwittingly giving their child's first few statements about the previous personality more coherence than the statements actually had:

> [The subject's parents] think of the sort of person about whom the child might be talking. Then they start searching for such a person. They find a family having a deceased member whose life seems to correspond to the child's statements. They explain to this family what their child has been saying about the previous life. The second family agrees that the child's statements might refer to the deceased member of their family. The two families exchange detailed information about the deceased person and about

14. *Children Who Remember*, p. 147.

15. *Twenty Cases* (2d ed.), p. 333; see also Stevenson's discussion of fraud in *Cases*, Vol. 3, pp. 343–345.

> what the child has been saying. From enthusiasm and carelessness, they may then credit the child with having stated numerous details about the identified deceased person, when in fact he said very little, and perhaps nothing specific, before the two families met.[16]

Thus, a myth of what the child apparently remembered might develop and come to be accepted by both the families.

But this sort of scenario—and paramnesia generally—is not easily applicable in those cases in which someone had made a written record of what the child said before the accuracy of his or her statements were checked and before the two families had met. And, paramnesia is unlikely also in many other cases in which Stevenson claims that he or his associates reached the scene within a few weeks or months of the initial meeting between the families and before memories of the child's previous remarks had much of a chance to fade. Add to this that the children often repeated their apparent memories many times before the families involved met and that in some cases many people's memories of the child's statements would have had to become distorted in the same ways, and paramnesia begins to seem less plausible as a general explanation of the data.

There is also the question of motive. Stevenson claims that many parents are reluctant to have the child's statements verified: Some believe that the child could be harmed by remembering a past life; some think that they could lose the child to the other family; some are reluctant to have anyone verify the child's statements about another life that was either much poorer or much more prosperous than their own; and some simply dislike encouraging behavior that they find unattractive in the child.[17] In addition, Stevenson claims that the families of the previous personalities often have their own reasons for being reluctant to endorse the case: Some, particularly wealthy families, are afraid that the subject's family means to exploit them; some dread embarrassing revelations that the subject may make about the family; still others—somewhat paradoxically—do not wish to reawaken the grief they continue to have for the deceased person.[18] Paramnesia, then, whether from ordinary forgetfulness or from motivated distortion seems an unlikely explanation of much of the data.

Genetic Memory

Another possibility, at least for those cases in which the subject might be a descendant of the previous personality, is genetic (or inherited) memory. But much of the information apparently remembered is about events, such as the deaths of previous personalities, that occurred after the previous personalities' children were conceived, and, in any case, most of the children investigated were not even genetic descendants of the previous personalities.

Extrasensory Perception

Stevenson claims that ESP by itself cannot account for the behavioral features of the richer cases, including the fact that the subjects characteristically attribute their apparent memories to a previous personality with whom they identify (personation). He therefore considers ESP-with-personation as the hypothesis that most plausibly competes with survival (hereafter, I shall use the label ESP to mean ESP-with-personation). Even so, Stevenson does not think ESP would explain the selection of the person whose experiences are apparently remembered, or how—in those cases where we would have to suppose that the information apparently remembered was obtained telepathically from more than one living person who remembered it—the informa-

16. *Children Who Remember*, pp. 150–151.

17. Ibid., p. 152.

18. Ibid., p. 153.

tion came to be organized in the minds of the children who apparently remembered it in the same ways it was organized in the minds of the previous personalities, or, particularly in cultures hostile to the idea of reincarnation, why the information came to the children in the form of apparent memories, or, how, in some cases, the children exhibited special skills or birthmarks appropriate to the previous personalities. In short, Stevenson claims that if ESP were the explanation, it would have to be ESP "of a very extensive and extraordinary kind."

Second, Stevenson claims that the cases suggestive of reincarnation differ in various ways from what one would expect if ESP were the explanation. Other than their apparent memories of previous lives, these children rarely exhibit any additional evidence of ESP; the phenomenology of the children's apparent memories is the same as that of ordinary memory—not, say, trance-like. Most of the children experience the apparent memories not as disconnected but as continuous with their present lives; the children's access to information about, and identification with, the previous lives sometimes lasts more or less continuously for a long time—usually for years and occasionally even for decades; and the children and also their parents often lack a plausible motive for the children to identify with the previous personalities.

In what must be one of the most knowledgeable reviews of Stevenson's data, the British psychologist Alan Gauld claims that it is "extremely unlikely that either fraud or cryptomnesia have been more than marginal factors in producing the correct statements and recognitions" and remarks that he is "quite at one with Stevenson over his doubts concerning the ESP (or super-ESP) theory." Gault concludes that he does "not find it easy to dissent" from Stevenson's claim that his data sustain "a rational belief in reincarnation."[19]

19. Gauld, p. 185.

V

I assume that *something* explains Stevenson's data. If his data are accurate, then I agree with Stevenson that fraud, cryptomnesia, paramnesia and genetic memory are unlikely as explanations. That leaves ESP and survival. There are, of course, scientific objections to ESP. Those who weight these more heavily than I do will perhaps give the nod to one of the explanations, such as cryptomensia, that I would pass over. But if they do, it is probably because they feel that one of those explanations *must* be correct, not because there is much independent evidence that one of them actually is correct. Currently, so far as I know, there is almost no such evidence.

Even those who weight scientific objections to ESP more heavily than I do would probably agree that if we had more and better data on cases suggestive of reincarnation, data of a sort that counts against normal explanations and toward ESP or survival, that would at least make those latter explanations *more* likely. So long as one admits that *enough* good data of this sort *could* make either ESP or survival the *most* likely explanation, then disagreement over how much evidence that would take is a matter of judgment about which it is difficult and probably pointless to argue. It would be dogmatic, it seems to me, for someone to take the view that *no matter how good* the data were, they could *never* tip the balance far enough that it actually favored either the ESP or survival explanations. As long as one agrees with that, the prudent course is simply to wait and see how good the evidence actually gets.

Whatever objections one might have to ESP as an alternative to normal explanations, these are not likely to be objections to it as an alternative to the survival explanation. So, to focus on those aspects of the argument that illustrate how the traditional debate over survival should change, I am going to set scientific qualms about ESP to one side and consider just the relative merits of ESP and survival. In my opinion, Stevenson is not in a position to dismiss ESP so easily as a possible explanation of his data. The reason is that we have virtually no basis for opinions about how ESP, if it exists, might work and, hence, no basis for claiming that it could not have produced the results Stevenson has reported. This would be so even if there were no evidence in parapsychological research that ESP might be as extraordinary and extensive as it would have to be to account for Stevenson's data. But, there is *some.*

The French physician E. Osty, Director from 1926 to 1938 of the Institut Metapsychique of Paris, reported incidents that would amount (according to Gauld) "to what could justifiably be called 'super-ESP' . . . without any suggestion that the information originated from spirits."[20] And, S.G. Soal, former president of the British Society for Psychical Research, reported on sittings with the famous medium Mrs. Blanche Cooper in which Soal claims she thought (as did Soal) that she was communicating with a dead Gordon Davis, but instead telepathically got information from a living Gordon Davis while simultaneously exhibiting impressive evidence of precognition. Gauld remarks that "'super-ESP' seems an appropriate term to describe what was going on; and if it could occur in this case, why not in others, indeed in all the others that have been presented as evidence for survival?"[21] Why not indeed?

Gauld has his reasons why not—which include the fact that Osty was careless in writing up his reports and that Gauld suspects Soal of having "improved" the Gordon Davis case. But even if the outcome of Gauld's assessment was—which it is not—that our evidence for ESP is *always* evidence for more modest results than would be required to account for Stevenson's data, because we do not know how ESP works, if we concede that it has to be taken seriously as a possible explanation (which we should *when* the competing explanation is survival), then we do not have a right to say that ESP could not be powerful enough to account for Stevenson's data. This should be clear from an analogy.

Idiot savants sometimes have extraordinary memories and equally impressive behavioral skills, such as the ability to make complicated mathematical computations quickly and accurately or to play a musical instrument proficiently with little or no training. Imagine an investigator of a hundred and fifty years ago who did not have much of an idea what genes were or how they worked but who believed that he had evidence that there were genes and that a certain kind of gene, which he called a memory gene, exercised a powerful influence on the quality and scope of every normal person's memory. Suppose he denied that memory genes might account for the extraordinary memories and skills of idiot savants on the grounds that for a memory gene to produce such results it would have to be not an ordinary memory gene but a super-memory gene—something for which, he claimed correctly, there was no evidence except in the cases of idiot savants. Imagine that he urged, instead, that the extraordinary powers of these idiot savants are more likely explained on the supposition that they draw directly on the powers of immaterial souls (many of whom were once incarnated in people who were musical or mathematical) that have somehow survived bodily death.

No one should be convinced, first, because until the investigator knows more about genes, and about memory genes in particular, he has no business putting such limits on what genes are capable of producing, and, second, because no matter how mysterious it might seem—and a hundred and fifty years ago it might have seemed mysterious to the point of being almost miraculous—that genes could produce the extraordinary powers observed in some idiot savants, it could hardly be less mysterious to explain these powers by appeal to the survival of dead people.

Even Stevenson admits that ESP might have produced the results he has observed if, as he

20. Ibid., p. 131.

21. Ibid., p. 136.

says, it were of a very extensive and extraordinary kind—for instance, if it were a kind of ESP that produced both informational and behavioral results in an organized way, so as to mimic the arrangement in a previous personality, and even produced physical effects such as the birthmarks. But *how* could ESP do all this? It could if something about the previous personality directly caused the result in the subjects, who were "selected" simply due to their unusual receptivity. The "transmissions" could either be without intervening links (so-called action at a distance) or in the form of something like a radio wave. We can suppose that the subjects' receptivity was such that it caused them to experience the informational aspects of these transmissions as if they were ordinary memory, which, then, in some of them did and in some did not become firmly enough implanted to resist erosion by competing influences that came later. Finally, we can suppose that this receptivity in the subjects was a special capacity distinct from the more ordinary and diffuse powers of ESP that are sometimes exhibited by others and, hence, not likely to manifest itself as a generalized capacity for ESP.

Fantastic? I agree. But if we accept Stevenson's data at face value and reject fraud, cryptomnesia, paramnesia, and genetic memory as explanations, then all of the remaining explanations are fantastic. I do not say that the explanation I have just sketched is preferable to Stevenson's survival explanation, only that—based on what we know—it is at least as likely, and that it would be arbitrary to reject it in favor of Stevenson's explanation. In sum, if the case for meaningful personal survival based on Stevenson's data depends on survival being the best explanation, then it fails, since for all we know his data can be explained by super-ESP.

But there is no reason that I know of to suppose that the case for meaningful personal survival based on Stevenson's data does depend on survival being the best explanation. Stevenson may feel that if ESP were the best explanation, then the identities of the people whose lives the children apparently remembered would not have been preserved. Whether he is right about that is debatable, just as it is debatable, and for much the same reasons, whether the identities would have been preserved even on Stevenson's dualistic hypothesis—Rosenberg, for instance, does not think that they would have been.

The deeper point is that it may not matter as much as survivalists, such as Stevenson, and skeptics, such as Flew and Rosenberg, seem to think whether the *identities* of the previous personalities in these cases have or have not been preserved. The new developments in personal identity theory, as illustrated in the fission example, suggest that meaningful personal survival may not require the preservation of identity. And, since we have no *evidence* to support a view about *how* either a disincarnate mind or ESP (whatever these might be) could account for Stevenson's data, it is arbitrary, in our current state of ignorance, to assume that if ESP accounted for them, that would be inferior—from the point of view either of preserving identity or of sustaining meaningful personal survival—to the ways in which souls would account for his data. If this is not obvious, consider another analogy.[22]

Imagine that you are a resident of Earth at some time in the technologically distant future and that you have urgent business on Mars. You can conduct this business only by activating a Star Trek–style beamer that records exact and complete information about your body, brain, and psychology at the same time as it dematerializes you on Earth and sends the information to a receiving station on Mars. A few minutes later, the information is used on Mars to create an exact replica of you out of new, but qualitatively similar, matter. In short, the beamer is, in effect, a reincarnation machine. Suppose further that even though no one in your culture has ever known exactly how the beamer works,

22. This sort of example is discussed by Parfit, *Reasons and Persons*, pp. 199–200, and by Nozick, p. 41.

since it obviously preserves a person's psychology and bodily form its use is widely accepted as a way of preserving identity. You share this belief, though with some hesitation. Remembering that there are philosophers who argue that the beamer does not preserve identity—but also remembering the fission examples—you reason that whether or not the beamer preserves identity, it at least preserves what matters most to you in survival. So you drive to the transmitting station to be beamed. Once there, however, you learn that scientists have recently discovered that the beamer works in exactly the same way that super-ESP works, which, as it happens, is one of the ways I sketched above.

Would this new information make any difference to you, so far as your decision to enter the beamer is concerned? If you were satisfied that the beamer probably preserves identity, would you feel now that its claim to preserve identity had been sullied by the revelation that the information is transmitted from Earth to Mars by means of a process that also underlies super-ESP? If you were satisfied that whether or not the beaming process preserves identity it at least preserves what matters to you in survival, would you feel that it would preserve what matters to you any less if the information were transmitted by a process that also underlies super-ESP? Probably not—to both questions. But, then, super-ESP may be as good a way of ensuring meaningful personal survival as the process, whatever it is, that underlies Stevenson's survival hypothesis.

What I am suggesting is that assuming that Stevenson's data are as he presents them, then they may well provide the basis for a good argument for meaningful personal survival *whether or not* the super-ESP explanation or his survival explanation best explains them and *whether or not* the actual processes involved in either explanation preserve personal identity. They *will* provide such a case for anyone for whom what matters primarily in survival is simply the singular reemergence of his or her psychology—beliefs, memories, intentions, personality, and so on—after bodily death.

VI

In philosophical discussions of survival of bodily death, values often masquerade as facts, and facts are often portrayed as being more substantial than they actually are. For instance, how "thick" or "thin" something is as a substitute for ordinary survival, which may seem to be a factual question, depends not on how *much*—physically or psychologically—has been lost in the substitution, not even, necessarily, on whether identity has been lost, but, rather, on how much *of what matters* in survival has been lost. That is, the relevant senses of "thick" and "thin" have more to do in the first instance with our values than with either our identities or our normal circumstances, which are relevant only to the extent that we value preserving them. So even though a great deal (quantitatively) may have been lost in some transformation, if what was lost is trivial from the vantage point of our concern for meaningful personal survival, then what emerged from the transformation is not, in the relevant sense, a thin substitute for survival, but, rather, a robust one.

The ways philosophers argue for one criterion of identity over another are also often covertly evaluative in that they rely heavily on idiosyncratic and controversial intuitive judgments about whether identity would be preserved through various sorts of bizarre transformations (the infamous puzzle cases of the personal identity literature), which are controversial in the first place because our conventions, which were formed to apply to cases that arise in normal circumstances, underdetermine what we should say about these extraordinary examples. Thus, the suspicion is unavoidable that the ways philosophers try to extend the conventions to cover the extraordinary examples generally has more to do with their personal values than with objective social facts; in particular, they seem to have more to do with their feelings about whether *what matters in survival* has been preserved through the transformations depicted in the examples. If this is right, then disputes over criteria of personal identity are often simply disguised disputes over what matters in survival.

Even if it were possible, which it does not seem to be, to determine objectively how our linguistic conventions regarding personal identity should extend to cover the puzzle cases, our linguistic conventions are just that—conventions; they are not necessarily deep ontological truths. Before thinking much about how personal identity may be conventional, our identities may seem quite substantial; after thinking about it, they are likely to seem more ephemeral. Nozick was right to call the puzzle cases in the personal identity literature "a koan for philosophers." Even the so-called facts of identity may be thinner than they first appear.

This "lightness" of identity is surprisingly bearable. Consider, for instance, Shoemaker's example of an environmentally polluted society of the technologically distant future in which people, to keep from getting very sick, have to replace their bodies every several years with qualitatively identical ones, a procedure that in their society is regarded as routine—no more of a threat to maintaining one's identity than, say, getting one's teeth cleaned is in our society. Projecting ourselves imaginatively into such a society, it is easy for many of us to see ourselves (or our replicas) conforming without much strain to their conventions. This suggests that we could simply, and sensibly, take the view that any ways in which our social conventions might differ from those of the polluted society are not that important. By analogy, when one sees that various moral prohibitions in one's own society (for instance, against public nudity or extra-marital sex) are not shared by other societies with which one can identify without much strain, there is a natural tendency to downplay the importance of the conventions of one's own society. In the same way, when one sees that certain of our conventions regarding personal identity are not present in other (possible) societies with which one can identify without much strain, there is a natural tendency to downplay the importance of our own conventions. There is nothing inevitable about shedding such parochial values, but it is a natural and often reasonable response to exposure to attractive alternatives.

In sum, the fission examples and the other examples that have motivated the belief that identity may not be what matters primarily in survival suggest that identity, even under normal circumstances, has been overrated. In particular, they suggest that identity is not a condition of reasonably anticipating experiences in the same ways we would ordinarily anticipate our own future experiences. These suggestions may or may not be correct. To decide we will have to look freshly at—that is, *reevaluate*—what it means to survive under ordinary as well as hypothetical circumstances. Yet among those who have tried to do this there is not now, and probably never will be, a univocal response; to some identity seems to matter a great deal, to others much less.

Whatever the outcome of this process of reevaluation, as soon as we admit, as it seems we must, its relevance to the assessment of arguments for meaningful personal survival of bodily death, the cat is out of the bag. For then no argument for meaningful personal survival is dismissible merely on the grounds that because the kind of survival it postulates would not preserve identity, it is too "thin" to be responsive to our egoistic interests in survival. And this means that the standard ways many philosophers have dismissed arguments for survival will no longer work. One must now consider not just whether the kind of process postulated preserves identity but also whether it preserves enough of what matters importantly in survival. In sum, when it comes to meaningful personal survival of bodily death the key question is not simply one of metaphysics, as has been assumed traditionally, but also one of values—and values that, in the end, may well vary from person to person in quite subjective ways.

Many philosophers will not welcome this conclusion. We philosophers love to be decisive, to settle things not just for the time being and for people with certain values rather than others, but for everyone and once and for all. We want to draw straight, definite lines. Particularly when it comes to "nonsense," we like to dispatch it not just as unwarranted but as impossible. Yet the new developments in personal identity theory strongly suggest that for the bit of nonsense we have been discussing—meaningful personal survival of bodily death—the days of decisive dismissals are over. On this topic, many of the lines that most need to be drawn are now and henceforth probably always will be curved and blurry.[23]

23. I am grateful to several people who offered criticisms and suggestions when I talked on the topic of reincarnation at the University of New Mexico in March, 1991, and also to John Barresi and Ian Stevenson for written comments on an earlier version of this paper.

Douglas R. Hofstadter

"WHO SHOVES WHOM AROUND INSIDE THE CAREENIUM? *OR,* WHAT IS THE MEANING OF THE WORD 'I'?"

DOUGLAS R. HOFSTADTER is professor of cognitive science and computer science at the Center for Research on Concepts and Cognition at Indiana University. He is the author of the award-winning *Gödel, Escher, Bach* (1979), co-editor, with Daniel C. Dennett, of *The Mind's I* (1982), and author of *Metamagical Themas* (1985), a collection of essays, many of which appeared originally in a column he wrote for *Scientific American*.

The Achilles symbol and the Tortoise symbol encounter each other inside the author's cranium.

TORTOISE: . . . Am I right? Isn't there something you're just itching to tell me?

ACHILLES: Come to mention it, yes. It's related to a book I saw in the bookstore the other day, called *Molecular Gods: How Molecules Determine Our Behavior.* It was the subtitle that intrigued me.

TORTOISE: In what way?

ACHILLES: My first thought on reading it was,

"Oh, that's interesting—I didn't know that the molecules inside me could affect me that much."

TORTOISE: A classic reaction.

ACHILLES: I know it sounds dumb, but what's wrong with it?

TORTOISE: How can you say that? Molecules is all you are, my friend! Read Francis Crick's *Of Molecules and Men* someday.

ACHILLES: Oh, yes—I know I'm made of molecules. Nobody could deny *that.* It just seems to me that my molecules are at *my* beck and call—not individually, of course, but in large "chunks", such as my fingers, when I play my cello or sign a check. So that when *I* decide to do something, my molecules are forced to come along. So—haven't you really got it reversed? Isn't it *really* the case that *I* shove those molecules around, and not vice versa?

TORTOISE *(rather exasperated)***:** What do you mean, "I"? What is this "you"?

ACHILLES: How I feel—let me put it that way. My free will determines what I do.

TORTOISE: All right. Let me suggest a definition. Let me suggest that the term "free will", when you use it, is a shorthand for a complex set of predispositions of your brain to act in certain ways. Just a moment ago, you used the word "fingers" as an abbreviation for a whole bunch of molecules. In a similar way, the phrase "free will" could be thought of as an abbreviation for a whole bunch of natural tendencies and constraints. So . . . your free will—your set of preferred pathways for neural activity to flow along—constrains the motions of molecules inside your brain, and those motions in turn are reflected in the patterns that your fingers will trace out.

ACHILLES: Are you saying that when I say "free will", I'm really using a shorthand for a kind of "hedge maze", like the ones on the grounds of Victorian palaces, a maze that allows some pathways and disallows others?

TORTOISE: Yes, that's the idea—only of course this "hedge maze" is inside your skull, and is a bit more abstract. For instance, it's a little oversimplified to imagine that pathways are *rigidly* allowed or disallowed. It would be more accurate to think of the set of predispositions in terms of a set of pins in a pinball machine. You know what I mean by "pins"?

ACHILLES: Those stationary round things with rubber "bumpers" that the shiny marbles bounce off of?

TORTOISE: Correct. Were you to take an average over a million marbles, you could find out how each pin statistically affects the way the marbles descend to the bottom. Pathways aren't just *allowed* or *disallowed;* rather, some are more likely, some are less likely, depending on how the pins are arrayed. But if you still like the image of the maze of hedges, that's not a bad one to hold in your head. The hedges make more rigid constraints—things are more black-and-white than with the pins. There are fewer degrees of freedom for the motions in a maze. But I can make the maze image richer. Suppose that in your maze, one of the effects of the people moving through the maze were that the hedges gradually shifted position. It's somehow as if the maze were formed of movable partitions that constrain the maze runners, yet the maze runners' paths gradually move the partitions, thus changing the maze.

ACHILLES: You mean the maze runners could just decide—by free will—that they want to pick up a partition and plop it down somewhere else?

TORTOISE: Not like that. It's got to be a deterministic outcome of the act of maze running itself. Let me go back to the pinball analogy. It's more as if the pins, instead of being fastened on the board, were *slidable* objects like hockey pucks, objects that as they get banged around from above and below and all sides, slightly slip and change positions. The pins need not be circular; they could be longish so that two or more located near each other could act like a channel or a funnel for marbles. In any case, they are jounced around by the rapidly moving pinballs.

ACHILLES: As in Brownian motion?

TORTOISE: Exactly. There are really *two scales* in time and space operating here, each affecting the other. The heavy hockey-puck-like pins appear almost stationary to the light marbles. To a casual observer who's following the motions of the marbles, the massive pins would appear to be *determining* the light marbles' motions, to be telling the marbles where to go—or in Sperry's words, to be "shoving them around".

ACHILLES: I like that image. It agrees with my earlier view that *I* shove my molecules around.

TORTOISE: True—provided you identify "yourself" with the configuration of the pins.

ACHILLES: That's a little strange, I admit.

TORTOISE: Now imagine a second observer, who's watching a *film* of the whole thing speeded up by a factor of a thousand or more. To *her,* there is a smooth, interesting patterned motion of a bunch of large, variously shaped pucks. She says to herself, "Wonder why they're moving that way—I can't see anything visible causing any of it."

ACHILLES: She doesn't see the marbles?

TORTOISE: No—they are shooting around so fast in this time scale that their tracks all blur together into one uniform background color with no apparent motion.

ACHILLES: Ah, yes . . . Now the facts about Brownian motion begin to come back to me. I remember how people were mystified by the jostling motions of colloidal particles in solutions when they looked at them under a microscope. They couldn't figure out what was causing such motions. The molecules that were battering them constantly were too small to be visible, and besides, they were moving too quickly.

TORTOISE: Exactly. An observer on this time scale might start to develop a sense for the slow drifting patterns of the pucks, even without having any clear notion of what's *causing* the pucks to move about.

ACHILLES: It's a natural human tendency. Why not?

TORTOISE: The observer could anthropomorphize: "Oh, those two little ones don't like to be close together, and those two long thin ones are trying to be parallel"—and so on. So she develops a teleology, or a way of describing the heavy pucks' motions all on their own. She's quite unaware that they are being bombarded constantly by teeny objects, as in Brownian motion. (Let's pretend that the marbles are more like BB's—really small.) She doesn't know that something smaller is *making* the pucks swim around in those patterns.

ACHILLES: So you can turn a knob on your movie projector and flip back and forth between the fast and slow views? Or even smoothly go between them? That's neat! At first, at the slowest setting, the immobile pucks seem to determine the paths of the many little bouncing marbles. As you speed up the film, the marbles become harder and harder to track, and pretty soon they become just a big blur. Meanwhile, you begin to notice that the pucks actually *aren't* immobile, after all. They're being shoved about by the marbles. So—who's shoving whom around *really?* Well, it's mutual, I now see.

TORTOISE: Good. Now let me add some more richness to this whole metaphor. Let's say that marbles are constantly being shot in from all sides of the table, and also leaving on all sides. You can envision something like a pool table, with a lot of little marble-launching stations mounted on the walls, and a lot of pockets that act as exits for stray marbles that land in them. The inflow and outflow are equal, so there's no net gain or loss of marbles. And the bombardment is pretty uniform, but not exactly. The marbles are launched according to conditions *outside* the table. For example, if there's a red light near a marble-launching station, that station slows down its firing rate; if a green light is near it, it speeds it up. So you have a set of *transducers* from *external light* to *internal marble-shooting.* Now if the puck observer watches both the lights *and* the pucks, she'll be able to draw some causal connections between light patterns outside and the puck-patterns inside. Using mentalistic language will become quite natural. For instance, it would sound quite reasonable to say, "It saw the green light—it's moving away from it—I guess it doesn't like green." And so on.

ACHILLES: Now you've got me thinking. I too want to add some strange features. I'll propose a physical linkage between one partic-

Free Will

The competition between science and religion (see Part VIII) and between history and religion (see Part IX) is not just over conflicting explanations of important phenomena and events, but also over broader conceptual issues. A scientific account of human behavior challenges the traditional religious idea that people have free will. Ironically, the threat to this religious idea arose independently of science from within religion itself—in the debates over whether God's supposed foreknowledge is compatible with human free will (see Pike and Kolak selections). The debate over the compatibility of causal determinism and free will is the naturalized version of that theological challenge.

Science challenges the idea that people have free will by encouraging us to look for natural causes of human behavior, ultimately for causes that are beyond the control of the people whose behavior is being explained. To whatever extent such causes are found—and as the sciences of biology and psychology progress, they are found increasingly—it is difficult to continue to feel that people are genuinely free in the same pristine and vigorous sense in which religion and common sense have traditionally supposed that they are.

What sort of freedom could it be that can coexist happily with the idea that our thought and behavior are caused by conditions beyond our control? Perhaps there is room for a conception of human freedom that satisfies this constraint (many philosophers have argued that there is), but surely it is a thin kind of freedom by comparison with the robust, self-originating powers that are attributed to people by almost every religious tradition. If the idea that humans are ultimately free is discarded, or weakened, the weakening of the idea that they are ultimately responsible cannot be far behind.

It may seem that modern science, with its emphasis on indeterminism, has come to the aid of traditional religious belief in free will. But indeterminism, or randomness, is just as corrosive of the idea that people are ultimately in control of their behavior as determinism is. You are no more responsible for an event that takes place in your brain and is uncaused (random) than you are for an event that is caused by conditions beyond your control.

ular puck and an external "arm" that can move toward or away from the lights. So, when that puck moves a certain way on the table, the arm may push a light away or pull it closer. Of course this is primitive—there are no fingers or anything, but at least there's now a two-way link between the pucks and the lights. Gosh! I'm almost completely forgetting about those marbles careening around down there! I'm just *relying* on the marble-shooters to keep on doing their job without much maintenance or attention needed . . . All I see now is the seemingly animate interplay—a sort of dance—among the pucks, the lights, and the arms . . .

TORTOISE: We're really jumping from one metaphor to another, aren't we? And each time, we escalate in complexity . . . Oh, well, that's fine with me. No matter how complex the scene gets, you can always slow down the projector, unblur the marbles and no longer see the pucks moving at all.

ACHILLES: Of course. But there's now something that bothers me. In the brain, there *aren't* these large- and small-sized units—everything's uniform, right? I mean, it's all just a dense packing of neurons. So where do the two scales come from? If we go back to the maze and partitions, there too we had two levels of objects (maze people and maze walls), each kind pushing the other around. But in the brain, this isn't so—or is it? What else is there besides neural activity?

TORTOISE: Let's add, then, a level of detail to our picture that we didn't have before. Let's say there are no pucks at all. There are only marbles and a number of larger stiff yet malleable mobile metal strips, which I'll also describe as "stiff yet malleable membranes" (and you'll soon see why). They can be bent into *U*'s or *S*'s or circles . . .

ACHILLES: So these things are swimming in the soup of marbles, now, but there are no more pucks, eh?

TORTOISE: Right. Can you guess what might happen now?

ACHILLES: I can imagine that these strips—

TORTOISE: Would you mind calling them "stiff yet malleable membranes", just to please me?

ACHILLES: Are you going to pull some acronymic trick off in a moment? Let's see—"SYMM" doesn't spell anything, does it? Is that really what you want me to call them, Mr. T?

TORTOISE: In fact you anticipated me, Achilles. Go ahead and do call them "SYMM's".

ACHILLES: All right. So these SYMM's will now be knocked around along with the marbles that are bashing into one another. Will the SYMM's occasionally get wrapped around some group of marbles and form a circular membrane, separating out a group of marbles from the rest?

TORTOISE: Just call the circular structure so formed a "SYMM-ball", if you please.

ACHILLES: Oh . . . I should have seen it coming. All right. Now I see that in this way, structures like pucks are emerging again, only this time as *composite structures* made up out of many, many marbles. So now, my old question of who pushes whom around in the cranium—er, should I say "in the *careenium*"?—becomes one of *symmballs* versus *marbles*. Do the marbles push the symmballs around, or vice versa? And I can twiddle the speed control on the projector and watch the film fast or slow.

TORTOISE: I should mention that once a symmball is formed, it might have quite a bit of stability, because the marbles inside it get fairly densely packed together, and jostle each other around only a little bit when the symmball gets hit by a fast marble from the outside. The impact gets spread around and shared among the marbles inside, and the symmball won't tend to break up—at least not when you watch the film at either of the two speeds we've already mentioned. Perhaps the *fission* of a symmball would occur on a longer time scale than the *motions* of symmballs. And the same for the formation of a symmball.

ACHILLES: Would it be fair to liken a symmball's emergence to the solidifying of water into a cube of ice?

TORTOISE: An excellent analogy. Symmballs are constantly forming and unforming, like blocks of ice melting down into chaotically bouncing water molecules—and then new ones can form, only to melt again. This kind of "phase transition" view of the activity is very apt. And it introduces yet a third time scale for the projector, one where it is running much faster and even the motions of the symmballs would start to blur. Symmballs have a dynamics, a way of forming, interacting, and splitting open and disintegrating, all their own. Symmballs can be seen as reflecting, internally to the careenium, the patterns of lights outside of it. They can store "images" of light patterns long after the light patterns are gone—thus the configurations of symmballs can be interpreted as *memory, knowledge,* and *ideas.*

ACHILLES: It seems to me that although you got rid of the pucks, you added another structure—the SYMM's. So how is this new system any improvement, as a model of a brain, over the old one? Don't you still have two levels of basic physical constituents and activity?

TORTOISE: The SYMM's are there only to provide a way for marbles to join up and form clusters. There are other conceivable ways I could have done this. I could have said, "Imagine that each marble is magnetic, or Velcro-coated, so that they all attract each other and stick together (unless jostled too hard)." That suggestion would have had a similar effect—namely, of making much larger units grow out of smaller ones—and so you would have only *one* kind of basic physical constituent. Would that be more satisfying to you, Achilles?

ACHILLES: Yes, but then you'd have lost your pun on "symbols", which would be too bad.

TORTOISE: Not at all! I'd cleverly rename the marbles themselves this time, as "small yellow magnetic marbles"—"SYMM's"—and a magnetically bound cluster of them would form a "SYMM-ball". No loss.

ACHILLES: That's a relief! I would hate to see a good metaphor go down the drain for lack of a pun to illustrate it.

TORTOISE: Hofstadter would never let *that* happen! You can take it from me. Anyway, you can conceive of the larger units however you want, as long as you have it clear in your mind that starting with just *one* level, you wind up with *two* levels and *two* time scales—three time scales, in fact, when you take into account the slow formation, fission, fusion, and fizzling of the symmballs.

ACHILLES: Now can we go back and talk about whether *I* control my molecules, or my molecules control *me?* That's where this all started, after all.

TORTOISE: Certainly! Why don't you try to answer the question yourself?

ACHILLES: The problem is that in all those pulsations inside a careenium, I just don't see a "me". I see a lot of activity—I see a lot of internalized representations of things "out there"—I mean of light patterns, in this case. And with fancier transducers, we could have a careenium in which symmball patterns reflected such things as sounds, touches, smells, temperatures, and so on.

TORTOISE: Let your imagination run wild, Achilles!

ACHILLES: All right. If I stretch my imagination, I can even see a gigantic three-dimensional careenium, hundreds of feet on a side, filled with billions upon billions of marbles floating in zero gravity, shooting back and forth, and all over forming short-lived and long-lived symmballs, and with those symmballs in turn governing the marbles' paths. I can see all that, and yet I don't see free will or "I". I guess I can't see how *I myself* could be a system like this inside my cranium. *I* feel alive! *I* have thoughts, feelings, desires, sensations!

TORTOISE: Hold on, hold on! One at a time. These are all related, but let's try to talk about just one—say, thoughts. Let me propose that the word "thought" is a shorthand for the activity of the symmballs that you see when you run the movie fast: the way they interact and trigger patterns of motions among themselves (mediated, of course, by the constant background swarming of marbles too fast to make out).

ACHILLES: But I *feel* myself thinking. There's no one *inside* a careenium to *feel* those "thoughts". It's all just a bunch of silly yellow magnetic marbles bashing into each other! It's all impersonal and unalive. How can you call that "thought"?

TORTOISE: Well, isn't it equally true of the molecules running around in *your* brain? Where's the soul of Achilles that "shoves *them* around"?

ACHILLES: Oh, Mr. T, that's not a good enough answer. I've just heard it said too many times that we're made out of atoms, so there's no

"The Self and Free Will"

C. A. Campbell

Now if one chooses thus to limit one's self to the rôle of external observer, it is, I think, perfectly true that one can attach no meaning to an act which is the act of something we call a 'self' and yet follows from nothing in that self's character. But then *why should we* so limit ourselves, when what is under consideration is a subjective activity? For the apprehension of subjective acts there is *another* standpoint available, that of *inner experience,* of the practical consciousness in its actual functioning. If our free will should turn out to be something to which we can attach a meaning from *this* standpoint, no more is required. And no more ought to be expected. For I must repeat that only from the inner standpoint of living experience *could* anything of the nature of 'activity' be directly grasped. Observation from without is in the nature of the case impotent to apprehend the active *qua* active. We can from without observe sequences of states. If into these we read activity (as we sometimes do), this can only be on the basis of what we discern in ourselves from the inner standpoint. It follows that if anyone insists upon taking his criterion of the meaningful simply from the standpoint of external observation, he is really deciding in advance of the evidence that the notion of activity, and *a fortiori* the notion of a free will, is 'meaningless'. He looks for the free act through a medium which is in the nature of the case incapable of revealing it, and then, because inevitably he doesn't find it, he declares that it doesn't exist!

But if, as we surely ought in this context, we adopt the inner standpoint, then (I am suggesting) things appear in a totally different light. From the inner standpoint, it seems to me plain, there is no difficulty whatever in attaching meaning to an act which is the self's act and which nevertheless does not follow from the self's character. . . . [This] is thrown into particularly clear relief where the moral decision is to make the moral effort required to rise to duty. I submit, therefore, that the self knows very well indeed—from the inner standpoint—what is meant by an act which is the *self's* act and which nevertheless does not follow from the self's *character.*

What this implies—and it seems to me to be an implication of cardinal importance for any theory of the self that aims at being more than superficial—is that the nature of the self is for itself something more than just its character as so far formed. The 'nature' of the self and what we commonly call the 'character' of the self are by no means the same thing, and it is utterly vital that they should not be confused. The 'nature' of the self comprehends, but is not without remainder reducible to, its 'character': it must, if we are to be true to the testimony of our experience of it, be taken as including *also* the authentic creative power of fashioning and refashioning 'character'.

From *On Selfhood and Godhood,* 1957.

room for souls or other things—but I know I'm there, it's an undeniable *fact,* so I need more insight than a mere reminder that my body obeys the laws of physics. *Where* does this feeling of "I" come from, a feeling that I have and you have but stones *don't* have?

TORTOISE: You're calling my bluff, eh? All right. Let's see what I can do to turn you around. Let's add one more feature to the careenium—an artificial mouth and throat, just as we added an arm. Let various parameters of them be driven by various symmballs. Now suppose we turn on a green light on the right-hand side of the careenium. New marble activity near that side begins immediately, and there follows a complex regrouping of symmballs. As it all settles down into a new steady configuration, the mouth-throat combination makes an audible sound: "There's a green light out there." Maybe it even says, "I saw a green light out there."

ACHILLES: You're trying to play on my weaknesses. You're trying to get me to identify with a careenium by making it more human-seeming, by making it simulate talking. But to me, this is merely "artificially signaling" (to borrow one of my favorite phrases from Professor Jefferson's Lister Oration). Do you expect me also to believe that somewhere out there, there is a conscious person reciting the time of day twenty-four hours a day, simply because I can dial a certain number and hear a human voice say, over the telephone, "At the tone, Pacific Daylight Time will be five forty-two"? A voice uttering sentence-like sounds doesn't necessarily signify the presence of a conscious being behind it.

TORTOISE: Granted. But this careenium voice isn't merely uttering a mechanically repetitious sequence of sentences. It is giving a dynamic description of what is perceived in the vicinity.

ACHILLES: I have a question about that. Is the thing being perceived located *outside* the careenium, or *inside* it? Why does the mouth say, "I saw a green light *out there*" rather than say something such as, "Inside me, a new symmball just formed and exchanged places with an old one"? Isn't *that* a more accurate description of what it perceived?

TORTOISE: In a way, yes, that is what it perceived, but in another way, no, it did not perceive its own activity. Think about what perception really involves. When you perceive something "out there", you cannot help but mirror that event inside you somehow. Without that internal mirroring event, there would be no perception. The trick is to know what kind of external event triggered it and to describe what you felt out loud in public language that refers to something external. You subtract one layer of transduction. You omit, in your description of what happened, one step along the way. You omit mention of the step that converted the green light into internal symmball responses. You are not even aware of that step, unless you are something of a philosopher or psychologist.

ACHILLES: Why would I or anyone else omit a real level? What's the origin of this socially conventional lie? *I* don't omit levels in *my* speech!

TORTOISE: Actually, you do. It's a universal phenomenon. If you live near a railroad track and hear a certain kind of loud noise coming from that direction—rumbling, bells dinging, and so on—do you say, "I hear a train", or do you say, "I hear the *sound* of a train"?

ACHILLES: I guess that ordinarily, I would tend to say, "I hear the train."

TORTOISE: Do you see a train, or do you see *light* hitting your eyes? When you touch a chair, do you feel the chair, or do you feel your *feeling* of the chair?

ACHILLES: I opt for the simpler alternative. I never would think those extra philosophical thoughts that go along with it. What point would it serve to say, "I hear the *sound* of the train"?

TORTOISE: Exactly my point. The most convenient language, the least obfuscatory and pedantic, omits the heavy "extra" reference to the medium carrying the signals, omits mention of the transducers, and so on. It simply gets straight to the *external source.* This seems, somehow, the most *honest* way to look at things—and the least confusing. You hear and see a *train,* not an image of a train, not the light reflected off a train, not retinal cells firing—and most definitely not your perception of a train! We are constructed in such a way as to be unaware of our brain's internal activity underlying perception, and therefore we "map it outward".

ACHILLES: Yes, I see that pretty well. I think I see why a careenium with a voice might talk about a green light rather than talk about its symmballs. But wait a minute. How would it know anything about green lights? It might *prefer* to refer to things in the outside world—but nonetheless, all it knows about is its own internal state!

TORTOISE: True, but its way of verbalizing its internal state employs words that you and I think refer to objects and facts *outside* the careenium. In fact, it too thinks so. But you could very well argue that it is just making sounds that mirror its internal state in some very complex way. It could be deluding itself. There might be nothing out there to refer to!

ACHILLES: True, but that's not exactly my question. What I want to know is, how come it uses the *right words* to describe what's out there? Where did it learn to say "green light"? The same question goes for people. How come we all say the same sounds for the same things?

TORTOISE: Oh, *that's* not so hard. I had thought you were asking whether reality exists or not. I quickly tire of such pointless quibbling over solipsism. But let me answer the question you *did* ask. When you were a tot, you saw things—say, rattles—and heard certain sounds—namely, various pronunciations of the word "rattle"—at about the same time. Those sights and sounds were transduced from your retinas and eardrums into internal symbol states inside your cranium. Now, as a member of the human race, you were constructed in such a way as to enjoy mimicry, so you made funny noises, something like "wattle", which were then automatically picked up by your eardrums, and fed back into the interior of your cranium. You heard your own voice, to your great delight and thrill! You were then able to compare the sounds *you'*d just made with your memory of the sounds you'd heard. By playing this exciting new game, you were learning the English words for objects. Of course you started with the nouns for visible objects, but quickly you built on that most concrete level and over the next few years you developed a large vocabulary including such things as "ball", "pick up", "next to", "splash", "window", "seven", "remember", "sort of", "zebra", "maze", "stretch", "of course", "by accident", "tongue-twister", "blunder", "confetti", "equilibrium", "analogy", "*vis-à-vis*", "chortle", "Picasso", "double negation", "few and far between", "neutrino"; "*Weltanschauung*", "*n*-dimensional vector space", "tRNA-amino-acyl synthetase", "solipsism", "careenium"—

ACHILLES: Wait a minute! What about "banana split"?

TORTOISE: Now how did I overlook that? A shameful oversight. But I hope you get the point.

ACHILLES: I think I see what you mean. Gradually, I internalized a huge set of external, public, aural conventions—namely the English words attached to particular states of my own brain, states that were correlated with things "out there".

TORTOISE: Not just things—actions and styles and relationships and so on.

ACHILLES: To be sure. But instead of conceiving that the words described my brain state, it was easier to conceive of them as describing things out there *directly.* In this way, by omitting a level in my interpretation of

A kiva—a religious site—in the "Cliff Palace" in Mesa Verde National Park. Used by Native Americans for rituals.

my own brain's state, I cast internal images outward.

TORTOISE: A careenium would do likewise—casting its internal symmball patterns outward, attributing them to some properties of the external worlds. And if a large number of careenia happened to be located near some specific stimulus, they could all communicate back and forth by means of a set of publicly recognizable noises that are externalizations of their internal states! So it's actually very useful to subtract out the references to the transduction, perception, and representation levels.

ACHILLES: It all makes sense now. But unfortunately, something else is bothering me! If the system projects all its states *outward,* talking about "green lights" and "red lights" and "traffic jams" and so forth, then how is there any room left for it to perceive its own *internal* state? Will it be able to say, "I'm annoyed" or "I forgot" or "I don't know" or "It's on the tip of my tongue" or "I'm in a blue funk"? Or will it project all *those* inner states outward as well, attributing weird qualities to things outside of it? Could there be inward-directed transducers that focus on *symmballs* and come up with a *representation* of symmball activity? That would be a sort of sixth sense—an inward-directed sense.

TORTOISE: You could call it the "inner eye".

ACHILLES: That's a perfect name for it.

TORTOISE: The inner eye wouldn't need to do much transducing, would it? It's the easiest thing in the world to monitor because it's right there inside you.

ACHILLES: Now, Mr. T, you always warn me

about confusing use and mention; I think you yourself are committing that error here. To have a word such as "Tortoise" in a text is enough to make somebody conjure up the image of a Tortoise, but it is not at all the same as making that person start to think about the *word* "Tortoise", is it? They may not notice it at all.

TORTOISE: Point well taken. There is a difference between *having* your symmballs in certain states, and *being aware* of that fact. It's something like the difference between using grammar correctly and knowing the rules of grammar.

ACHILLES: Now I sense I could get really confused here—things could get very tangled. How can symmballs "watch" other symmballs? The ones that react to green lights, I can imagine and understand. There are transducers—the marble shooters on the borders. But would there be some symmball that always reacts to, say, the fusion of two symmballs? How would it detect such a fusion? What would make it react that way? Would it be a sort of satellite or U-2 plane, with an overview of the whole terrain of the brain? And what purpose would it serve?

TORTOISE: Imagine that you were watching an actual careenium, and at a very slow speed—so slow that you could reach down with your hand and pick up and remove an entire symmball before getting struck by any symms careening toward your hand. All of a sudden there would be a vacuum, where before there had been a dense mass of marbles. If you switched speeds now and watched the results in the *symmballs'* time scale, you'd see a massive regrouping of symmballs all over the careenium, a kind of *shudder* passing through the whole system as all the various symmballs come to occupy slightly different positions.

ACHILLES: You could call such a shudder a "mindquake".

TORTOISE: An excellent suggestion. Various types of "mindquakes" would have characteristic qualities to them. They would have "signatures", so to speak. Now if *you,* Achilles, an observer from the outside, could learn to recognize such a signature, then why couldn't the system itself, from within, be even more able to do so? Such mindquakes would be, after all, just as tangible to the system as is an increase of marble-firings on any side. Both are simply *internal events,* even though the one is triggered by something external, while the other is set off by something internal.

ACHILLES: So would there be various "seismometer symmballs", each one sitting there waiting to feel a specific kind of mindquake, and when that happens it would react?

TORTOISE: Sure. And for each type of mindquake, there is a special symmball there just sitting there like a pencil on end—and when its type of mindquake comes along, it topples. Of course that "toppling" in itself is just *more symmball activity*—

ACHILLES: Another mindquake?

TORTOISE: Precisely—and it can set off further reactions inside the careenium. The whole thing is very circular—one shudder triggers another one, and that one sets off more, and so on.

ACHILLES: It sounds like it would never stop. There would just be constant symmball activity rippling back and forth across the careenium.

TORTOISE: Well, of course! That *is* what happens with conscious systems, isn't it? We're constantly thinking thoughts—some fresh, some stale—constantly mentally alive and aware—partly of the external world, partly of our own state—for example, how confused or tired we are, what something reminds us of, how bored we are with this long monotonous dialogue. . . .

ACHILLES: Hey, wait a minute! The *reader* may be bored, but I'm not!

TORTOISE: Only kidding, Achilles. Just trying to liven things up a bit.

ACHILLES: All right. Well anyway, I admit that everything you've been saying is true, makes sense, but how is it *useful* for us to monitor our own state?

TORTOISE: Well, think first of a simple animal. What it needs most of all is food. Its brain—if it has one—is connected to its stomach by nerves, and it transduces an emptiness in the stomach into a certain configuration of symbols in the brain. Actually, this animal might be so simple that the symmball level doesn't exist. There might just be marbles zipping around in its cranium, but no larger-scale agglomerations. In any case, the effect of this may then be a shuddering in its brain, which produces repercussions on the animal's peripheries. It may move. All this is very much at the reflex level. Mostly it involves monitoring the organism's hunger state and controlling its limbs. Every organism has to monitor itself in terms of hunger. But primitive organisms don't use much information about the external environment they're in—they just flap about and "hope"—if that isn't too strong a word!—to encounter some food. Pretty unconscious. On the other hand, take a more complex animal. It will have an elaborate representation of its environment inside itself, so it also has a lot of options when it detects internal hunger. The symbolic activity representing the empty stomach has to be dealt with in the context of all the other symbols, which might represent danger, priorities other than eating, choices of when and what to eat, and so on. The total interaction of symbols at that point we might call "consideration" or "deliberation" or "reflection"—as distinguished from "reflexes". Now after all this, let me ask you: Does this help you to see why such a careenium might have a self?

ACHILLES: Well . . . I might grant that there's reflection going on in there, I might even grant that it's *thinking*—but there's no*body* in there *doing* the thinking!

TORTOISE: Would you grant that there's *free will* inside there?

ACHILLES: Hardly!

TORTOISE: Then I can see that you will need some more persuading. All right. Let me suggest that there *is* free will, and that this notion of a careenium may help you understand more clearly what free will truly consists in. We began this discussion by talking about whether you can "shove your molecules around" or not. This is a central question—in truth, it is *the* central question, I think. So I'd like to ask you, Achilles, can you freely decide to do anything?

ACHILLES: Of course I can! That's precisely what free will is about! I can decide to do whatever I want!

TORTOISE: Really? Can you decide, say, to answer me in Sanskrit?

ACHILLES: Obviously not. But that has nothing to do with it. I don't speak Sanskrit. How could I answer you in it? Your question doesn't make sense.

TORTOISE: Not so. You can only do what your brain will allow you to do, and that is very crucial. Let me ask you another question. Can you decide to kill me right now?

ACHILLES: Mr. T! What a suggestion! How could you suggest such a thing, even in jest?

TORTOISE: Could you nevertheless decide to do it?

ACHILLES: Sure! Why not? I can certainly *imagine* myself deciding to do it.

TORTOISE: That is beside the point, Achilles. Don't confuse hypothetical or fictitious worlds with reality. I'm asking you if you *can* decide to kill me.

ACHILLES: I guess that in this world, in the *real* world, I could not *carry out* such a decision, even had I "decided"—or claimed I'd decided—to do it. So I guess I *couldn't* decide to do it, actually.

TORTOISE: That's right. That innocent-seeming trailer phrase that one tends to tack on—exactly as you did—is very telling, after all.

ACHILLES: What innocent phrase? What do you mean?

TORTOISE: Don't you remember? You insisted vehemently to me, "I can decide to do *whatever I want.*" Now that phrase "whatever I want" may *sound* like a grand, universal, all-inclusive, sweeping phrase—but in fact, it represents quite the opposite: a severe constraint. It's not true that you are able to decide to do *anything;* you are limited to being able to decide to do only things you *want.* Worse yet, you are in fact limited to doing, at any time the *one* thing that you want *most* to do! Here, "want" is a complex function of the state of the entire system.

ACHILLES: Are you saying that choice is an illusion?

TORTOISE: Only to the extent that "I" is an illusion. Let me explain. It's quite common for people to develop interests that begin to consume them—doing puzzles, doing music, thinking about philosophy . . . Sometimes such habits get so strong that they begin to interfere with the rest of their lives. A wife may pick up a bad habit—say, twiddling a cube or smoking cigars or constantly punning—and then *try* to get rid of it. Her exasperated husband may say to her, "What's this *trying?* Why can't you just *decide* to stop cubing? It is driving a wedge between you and me. Why don't you just *decide* to quit?" Yet the afflicted wife may, for all her good intentions, be unable to do so. Certainly having a modicum of desire is not enough. I would put it this way. The husband is appealing to what I would call his wife's "soul"—a coherent set of principles and tendencies and interests and personality traits and so forth that represent to him the person that he married. They have always before seemed to provide reasons or explanations for his wife's character, and he loves her for that aggregate of ways of being. So he appeals to this "soul" to put a clamp on its new obsession. But once the wife starts twiddling her cube, a *part* of her takes over. She gets obsessed—or should I say "possessed"?—by one of her own subsystems!

ACHILLES: "Possessed" is the word for it. I myself find it very hard to stop practicing a piece on my cello once I have gotten into the swing of it. Before I start, I think, "Now, I'll just play this piece *one time.*" (Or, "I'll just eat one potato chip", or "I'll just solve the cube one time".) But then, once I've let myself start, I'm no longer quite the same person—some things inside me have subtly shifted. And the *new* me thinks, "*That* guy said *he'd* do it only once. That's what *he* thought. But *I* know better!" There is a kind of inner inertia that makes me want to continue, even when there are *other* things I would also like to do. It's as if some part of you just "slips away" from a higher level of control—some subsystem gets "out of control" and won't obey the soul on top—like a bucking bronco unwilling to obey its rider.

TORTOISE: A powerful image. In such cases the wife herself may be confused and torn. Her inner turmoil is like that of a country in inner strife. There are factions battling each other—only in this case, the factions are neural firings, not people, of course. On some level, this woman may *feel* she wants to be able to decide to give up her habit—yet she may not have enough neurons on her side! And as in a country where the people won't support the government, so here: the "soul" has to have the support of its neurons! It can't just arbitrarily "shove them around", in reality.

ACHILLES: I'm all confused. Who *is* in control, here?

TORTOISE: We'd like to be able to say that the symmballs can *decide* to do arbitrary things, but they are constrained. They are in a system that "wants" its parts to move in some ways but doesn't "want" them to move in others. We could come back to the hedge-maze metaphor, to make this more vivid.

ACHILLES: Yes, but that applied to the *lower-level* objects—marbles, symms, or neural firings.

TORTOISE: Exactly. The "heavyweight" entities—hedges, pins, symmballs—constrain the "lightweight" entities—maze runners, pinballs, symms; but in revenge, the little ones, acting together, control how the high-level ones are arrayed.

ACHILLES: So *nobody*'s free here!

TORTOISE: Well, from the outside, that's the way it seems. But on the inside, the system may feel, just as you did, that it can "decide to do whatever it wants to do". But mind you, two symmballs in a careenium aren't free to *decide,* arbitrarily, on their own, to move in parallel—they have to have the cooperation of the marbles. The marbles have to do the work for them. Similarly, when the unhappy wife tries to "decide" to give up her cubing or punning habit, she can't do it without the agreement, the support, of her neurons.

ACHILLES: You make this wife's "soul" sound like a general trying to marshall unruly neurons, to force them into line when they have their *own* paths to follow. A military general has some degree of power over his soldiers, so he can coerce them to some extent—but only so far. Beyond that, they'll mutiny. So the general has to go along with the tide. He can't really dictate policy—he can only resonate with it.

TORTOISE: It's true. However, sometimes an unexpected shift at a higher level can precipitate an abrupt "phase transition" of lower levels. A million tiny things suddenly find themselves swirling around in unexpected ways, and realigning in totally novel higher-level patterns. Once in a while—just once in a while—the "general" *can* gain control of those unruly neurons—but only when they themselves don't know what they want, haven't reached any kind of consensus, and are instead in a malleable, leadable, chaotic state.

ACHILLES: It sounds like you're describing a "snap decision"—an exercise of pure will power, such as when I say to myself, "I'm going to quit cubing *right now!*", or "I'm going to stop feeling sorry for myself and go out and get something useful done." But if I understand *your* way of looking at this kind of thing, even a phrase like "snap decision" is really just a kind of shorthand for summarizing a lot of low-level activity. Is that so? It seems to me it would *have* to be so, in your picture.

TORTOISE: You're right, saying something like "snap decision" is really a coarse-grained manner of speaking about a huge cloud of neural activity, like a huge blurry cloud of symms in a careenium projected at a high speed on the screen. And sometimes the activity of neurons inside a cranium, or of symms inside a careenium, lends itself admirably to such a high-level, coarse-grained, symbolic description—or in the case of a careenium, a "symm-ball-ic" description.

ACHILLES: Not always.

TORTOISE: Are all ponds always frozen?

ACHILLES: Oh, I see what you mean. If the relevant portions of the careenium are chunked into symmballs, then a symmball-level description can be made. One set of symmballs is seen to affect other sets of symmballs regularly and predictably. Whereas if there *are* no symmballs—just a lot of stray symms careening around with nothing to constrain them except the careenium's boundary—then it's kind of chaotic, and no higher-level description applies. But when the whole careenium is "symm-ball-ic"—when the phrase transitions have taken place—then the person—I mean the *careenium!*—feels very much in control of his or her thoughts.

TORTOISE: *Its* thoughts?

ACHILLES: Yeah, yeah—that's what I meant. Its thoughts. But when not enough phase transitions have taken place, then there's an indescribable hubbub: random symms careening all over the place without orderly constraints. But I wonder what it's like when the brain is in sort of a halfway state—when there are lots of symmballs, but at the same time still a lot of stray symms that belong to no one. It reminds me of a half-frozen lake in early winter or early spring, when the molecules have only *half*-coalesced into large blocks of ice.

TORTOISE: That's a wonderful state to be in. I find I'm most creative when I feel my brain consisting of such halfway-coalesced symbols—neurons acting somewhat independently, somewhat collectively. It's a happy medium where neural bubblings cooperate with symbolic channelings and yield the most creative, fulfilling, semi-chaotic sense of aliveness.

ACHILLES: You think some of that uncoalesced freedom is essential for creativity?

TORTOISE: I was convinced of it by Hofstadter, who certainly feels that way. In *GEB,* writing about his plight as a writer, he portrayed himself as suffering from "helplessness" of the top level, for although he—or his symbol level—may in *some* sense have decided what to write, still he is entirely and utterly dependent on vast cooperating teams of neurons to come up with imagery and ideas and choices of words and sentence structures. Those lower-level items feel to the top level as if they "bubble up" from nowhere. But in reality they are somehow formed from the churning, seething masses of interacting neural sparks—just as patterns of symmball motions emerge out of the chaotic Brownian motion of the many tiny symms. And a few of those ideas make it out through the narrow channel of verbalization, like grains of sand passing through the narrow neck of an hourglass. Yet most likely Hofstadter will *insist* that he himself is responsible for this dialogue, will desire the credit to accrue to *him.*

ACHILLES: Hmm . . . to the overall system that constrained the marbles to jounce in those ways . . . It is hard to assign "credit" or "blame", once you start analyzing thought mechanistically. I see that "decision" and "choice" are very subtle concepts that somehow have to do with the ways in which constraints on two different levels affect each other reciprocally, and at two different time scales, inside a cranium, or a careenium.

TORTOISE: You're getting the idea.

ACHILLES: Every time you say "bubbling up", I can't help but think about the bubbles in ginger ale—I love the stuff. And I'm thirsty. I'm going to have some. Care for a glass yourself.

TORTOISE: Ah, ginger ale—capital suggestion.

ACHILLES *(sipping from a tall glass of cool ginger ale)***:** Did it ever occur to you that when your leg is asleep, it feels like it's full of ginger ale?

TORTOISE: Clever observation.

ACHILLES: Not really original, I have to admit. I read it once in a "Dennis the Menace" cartoon.

TORTOISE: Are you sure *you* read it—or was it Hofstadter?

ACHILLES: Spoilsport!

TORTOISE: It strikes me that having your leg fall asleep is one very weird experience. It's as if nature were giving you a chance, every once in a while, to be privy to all the tiny goings-on inside your leg, feeling the mingling tingling of trillions of cells all buzzing at once . . .

ACHILLES: Do you suppose that's what being alive *really* is like, and most of the time we're just numb to it?

TORTOISE: Precisely. Can you imagine if all of your body were always as fizzy and tingly as that? I've always wondered why people say their leg is *asleep.* We Tortoises say, "My leg is *awake.*" And French speakers say, "I've got ants in my leg." Those seem so much more accurate to me.

ACHILLES: Phooey!

TORTOISE: What's the matter now?

ACHILLES: I just realized that Hofstadter planted all of this. I mean, I'd thought I was genuinely thirsty. Now I see I was just being manipulated. He wanted to get certain remarks in here, and having me be thirsty was just a convenient avenue for him to do so. I should have known better.

TORTOISE: Oh, so your ginger ale doesn't taste any good?

ACHILLES: That's not what I mean. It tastes fine!

TORTOISE: Well then, what are you grumbling about? You're happy, he's happy. Would you have been happier if he were *unhappy?* That would seem a little perverse, even to me.

ACHILLES: I guess you have a point. You know, now that I think about it, sometimes the decisions I make seem to be slow percolating processes, things that are utterly out of my control. In fact, a rather gory image that illustrates this idea flashed before my mind's eye while we were talking about the difficulty of breaking out of mental ruts.

TORTOISE: What was that?

ACHILLES: I imagined a grim scene where a man's young wife is in a car crash and is badly mangled. He will certainly *react.* Perhaps he will react with love and devotion, perhaps with pity. Perhaps, to his own own dismay, he will even react with revulsion. But it occurred to me that in such emotionally wrenching cases, you can hardly *decide* what you will feel. Something just *happens* inside you. Subtle forces shift deep inside you, hidden, subterranean. It's quite scary, in a way, because in real crises like that, instead of being able to *decide* how you'll act, you *find out* what sort of stuff you're made of. It's more passive than active—or more accurately put, the action is on levels of yourself that are far lower—far more microscopic—than you have direct control over.

TORTOISE: Correct. You and your neurons are not on speaking terms, any more than a country could be on speaking terms with its citizens. There is, in both cases, a kind of collective action of a myriad tiny elements on low levels that swings the balance—exactly as in a country that "decides" to go to war or not. It will flip or not, depending on the polarization of its citizens. And they seem to align in larger and larger groups, aided by communication channels and rumors and so on. All of a sudden, a country that seemed undecided will just "swing" in a way that surprises everyone.

ACHILLES: Or, to shift imagery again, it's like an avalanche caused by the collective outcome of the way that billions upon billions of snow crystals are poised. One tiny event can get amplified into stupendous proportions—a chain reaction. But the crystals have to be poised in the right way, otherwise nothing will happen.

TORTOISE: In cases of judgment, whether it be of one musical composer over another, one potential title or subtitle for a book over another, or whatever, the top level pretty much has to wait for decisions to percolate up from the bottom level. The masses down below are where the decision *really* gets made, in a time of brooding and rumination. Then the top level may struggle to articulate the seething activity down below, but those verbalized reasons it comes up with are always *a posteriori.* Words alone are never rich enough to explain the subtlety of a difficult choice. Reasons may sound plausible but they are never the essence of a decision. The verbalized reason is just the tip of an iceberg. Or, to change images, conflicts of ideas are like wars, in which *every reason has its army.* When reasons collide, the real battleground is not at the verbal level (although some people would love to believe so); it's really a battle between opposing armies of neural firings, bringing in their heavy artillery of connotations, imagery, analogies, memories, residual atavistic fears, and ancient biological realities.

ACHILLES: My goodness, it sounds terrifying! You make the battlefield of the mind sound like a vast mined battlefield! Or a treacherous ice field on a steep mountain face. I never realized that a mechanistic explanation of thinking could sound so organic and living. It's sort of awful and yet it's sort of awe-inspiring as well. But I am very confused now about the "soul", the free will.

TORTOISE: I think that all these strangely evocative images have brought us back to your original perplexity, over the question of who pushes whom around in the cranium. Would you now be inclined to say, Achilles, that your molecules push *you* around, or that *you* push *them* around?

ACHILLES: Actually, I'm not sure how this "I" fits into a cranium—or a careenium. You've got my head so spinning now that I don't know what's up or down.

TORTOISE: Wonderful! At least now your mind may be malleable. Do you see how "free will" in a careenium is actually constrained—*physically* constrained, I mean—by the "wants" of the system?

ACHILLES: Yes, I see that these seemingly intangible "wants" are actually physical attributes of the overall system—tendencies to shun certain modes of behavior or to repeat certain patterns. So in a way I can see that a careenium has "free will" in this constrained sense of freedom. Maybe "free will" should be renamed *"free won't"*.

TORTOISE: Oh, my, Achilles! Did you just make that clever one up?

ACHILLES: I don't know—it just came to me. I never thought about it. It just "bubbled up from nowhere". I don't know who deserves the credit. Maybe Hofstadter made it up. Or maybe it just bubbled up inside *his* brain—although I don't quite see the difference.

TORTOISE: It sounds like the sort of thing Hofstadter's friend Scott Kim would say.

ACHILLES: Hmm . . . I still wonder, though—could a careenium's symmballs actually *decide* to do anything on their own?

TORTOISE: They certainly can't disobey the way the symms push them around—but on the other hand, the symms *are* always poised in just such a way that the *one* internal event that the symmballs *most* want to happen *will* happen. Isn't that a miraculous coincidence?

ACHILLES: Now that I understand how all this comes about, I can see that it's not at all a coincidence. By the *definition* of "want", the symmballs will get shoved around the way they want to be (*whether they like it or not*)! I guess that the real conviction of having free will would arise when, repeatedly and reliably, a collection of symmballs wants something and then watches its desire getting carried out. It must seem like magic!

TORTOISE: It's what happens when you decide, say, to sign your name. Your fingers begin obeying you, and miraculously, you watch your name just appear before you, effortlessly! Is that magic?

ACHILLES: Aha! That brings back that ultimately confusing term, "I". We say "*I* decide to sign my name." But what does that mean? I can see everything in a careenium—wants, desires, beliefs—but I just can't seem to take that last step. I simply fail to see an "I" in there.

TORTOISE: I've tried to explain that the word "I" is just a shorthand used by a system such as a careenium—a system that perceives itself in terms of symmballs and their predispositions to act in certain ways and not others—particularly a careenium that has *not* perceived that it is composed of small yellow magnetic marbles.

ACHILLES: Perceive, shmerceive, Mr. T! There's no one inside a careenium who *could* perceive such a thing. Perception requires *awareness,* which no careenium has. There's no one inside a careenium to feel and experience and *enjoy* its "free will", even if it's there, in your sense. Or maybe the best way to say it is that there's perception and free will there, but there's nobody there to have it.

TORTOISE: You mean you seriously would grant that a physical system could have *free will* but you wouldn't then feel forced to say there was *someone exercising* that free will? Or that there was perception but no *perceiver?* Perceiverless perception? Agentless, subjectless free will? Soulless, inanimate free will? That's a real doozy!

ACHILLES: I know it sounds paradoxical. I could almost agree with you—except I'm still hung up on one thing. Just *which* perceiver, *which* agent, *which* subject, *which* soul would it be? Which person gets to *be* that careenium? Or maybe I should turn the question around: Which careenium gets to have a given soul? Do you see what I mean?

TORTOISE: I think so. You seem to be envisioning a corral of souls up in the sky, into which God (or some other Grand Overarching Deity) dips, whenever a new cranium or careenium comes into existence, and from which It pulls out a soul, imbuing that careenium or cranium with *that* identity forevermore—almost as if It were putting a cherry on top of a sundae.

ACHILLES: Are you mocking me?

TORTOISE: I don't mean to be. If it sounds that way, it's only because I'm trying to take what I think your implicit notion of "soul" is and to characterize it explicitly, by putting it into as graphic terms as possible. But if you subtract out the imagery of a corral and God and cherries on sundaes, am I not putting into words the gist of your view?

ACHILLES: In a way, I suppose so—only you've made it sound so silly that I hesitate to adopt that view now.

TORTOISE: It's so tempting to think that different I's are just "out there", dormant, waiting to be attached to structures, like saddles put on horses or cherries on sundaes. Then, once they are in place, suddenly there is a consciousness that "wakes up". As if the consciousness, and the identity, the "who-ness", were provided by the cherry, and without it there would be only a hollow "pseudo-I"—a thing possessing free will but with nobody to *be!* Isn't that a little sad? Wouldn't you feel sorry for such a poor, deprived entity? Oh, no, of course you wouldn't—there would be no one to be sorry for, right?

ACHILLES: Well, it's hard to see where a sense of "who I am" could come to a bunch of marbles in a careenium, or even to a collection of firing neurons. It seems to me that the identity *has* to be imposed on top of such a structure. A careenium is a complex pinball machine—a heap of metallic machinery—even if, unlike pinball machines, some of its states represent the world and its workings. But until you add some sort of living "flame" to that heap, it's empty—soulless. You need "flame" (although I admit I don't know quite what I mean by that term) to turn a physical object into a *being,* just as you need flame to turn a pile of wood into a fire. No matter how much lighter fluid you pour on it, without a flame, it's still inert.

TORTOISE: Wait a minute! A pile of wood starts *burning* when you set flame to it—but does it acquire a *soul* at that moment? No—as you said, it simply becomes active instead of inert. Any old flame would do. The identity of a fire doesn't come from the torch that lit it, but from the combustible materials! It's the transition from inactivity to activity that makes the flame seem so critical. But a careenium doesn't need to become *more* active than it is. Yet for some reason, Achilles, you seem to balk at my suggestion that in that activity there is as much reason to see an individualized soul as in neural firing activity. But what's so special about neurons? You know what you remind me of?

ACHILLES: I don't know that I *want* to know, but tell me anyway.

TORTOISE: You remind me of somebody who runs into a pile of metal that's merrily burning away, and who declares that although it *looks* mighty like a fire, it surely *isn't* a fire (especially not a *genuine* fire!), because it's made of metal, and everyone knows that fires—especially *genuine* ones—are always made of burning wood or paper.

ACHILLES: That sounds pretty silly and narrow-minded—more so than I am, I should hope. I'm not insisting that no careenium could have a genuine soul so much as I am wondering, "*If* a careenium had a soul, *which* soul would it be? Who would be *this* careenium, who would be *that* one?" On what basis could a decision be made?

TORTOISE: Wow, have you got things upside down! (Or backwards—I'm not sure which.) The same question goes for people as much as for careenia. Who gets to be which body? Do you also have the belief that *any body* could be *anybody?* All it takes is the right flame inside? Could there be a "flame transplant", where someone else's flame—say mine—got implanted in your body, leaving your brain and body intact? Then who would be you? Or, who would you be? Or *where* would you be?

ACHILLES: And where would *you* be, Mr. T? Something seems wrong in this picture, I admit. If a careenium is actually somebody, where does the decision as to *who* it is originate?

TORTOISE: I think you've got things backwards. (Or upside down—I'm not sure which.) First of all, it's not a *decision*—it's an *outcome.* Secondly, which "who" a careenium is is an outcome of its structure, particularly the way it represents its own structure in itself. The more it is able to see itself as an independent and coherent agent, the more of a "who" there is for it to be. Eventually, by building up enough of a sense of its unique self, it has built up a complete "who" for it to be: a soul, if you will. The continuity and strength of the feeling of "being someone" come from identification with past and future versions of the same system, from the way the system sees itself as a unitary thing moving and changing through time.

ACHILLES: That's a strange idea—a thing whose identity remains stable even though that thing changes in time. Is it like a country that changes and yet remains somehow the same country? I think of Poland, for instance. If *any* country has had its soul-flame tampered with, Poland is it—yet it seems to have maintained a continuous "Polish spirit" for hundreds of years.

TORTOISE: A beautiful example. The sense of "one thing, extending through time" is very much at the root of our feeling of "being someone". And in a way it is nature's hoax: the illusion of soulsameness. Or, if you prefer not to call it an illusion, you can say that the ability of an organism to abstract, to think it sees some constant thing, over time, that it considers its self even as it changes, makes that organism's soul *not* an illusion.

ACHILLES: You mean anything that can fool itself—I mean, *see* itself—as unchanging over time has a soul?

TORTOISE: That's not such a silly notion—provided that the verb "see" has its usual abstract meaning, not some dilution of the term. If the organism is as perceptually powerful as living ones like you and me, then I would definitely say it has a soul, if it sees itself as essentially "the same organism" over time.

ACHILLES: But to see itself *as an organism* is not a trivial thing! It has to see itself as one coherent thing acting for *reasons,* not just randomly.

TORTOISE: Now you're talking! I couldn't agree more. Such a way of looking at something—namely, ascribing mental attributes to it—has been called by Daniel Dennett "adopting the intentional stance" toward that thing. In the case of you looking at a careenium, it would come down to your seeing it at the *symmball* level, and interpreting the symmball configurations and the patterns they go through over time as representing the system's beliefs, desires, needs, and so on, overlooking the underlying masses of marbles, either deliberately or out of ignorance.

ACHILLES: But you're not talking about *me*

looking at a system; you're talking about a situation where some system does that to *itself,* right?

TORTOISE: Exactly. It looks at its own behavior and, instead of seeing all the little marbles deep down there making it act as it does, it sees only its *symmballs,* acting in sensible, rational ways—

ACHILLES: The system sees itself just as observers of the fast film see it! It could say of itself, "It wants this, believes that", and so on—only now it is ascribing all these beliefs and penchants and preferences and desires and so forth to itself, so instead it says, "*I* want this, believe that", and so on. This seems peculiar to me. It makes up a bunch of hypothetical notions about itself simply out of convenience, then ascribes them to itself in all seriousness. For God's sake, though—if beliefs and desires and purposes and so on *really* existed inside itself, wouldn't the blasted careenium itself have direct access to them?

TORTOISE: What makes you think those beliefs *aren't* real? Aren't ice cubes and traffic jams and symmballs real? And what makes you think that this self-perception *isn't* direct access to its beliefs? After all, does your perception of your own feelings via your "inner eye" differ so wildly from this?

ACHILLES: I suppose not.

TORTOISE: When an *outsider* ascribes beliefs and purposes to some organism or mechanical system, he or she is "adopting the intentional stance" toward that entity. But when the organism is so complicated that it is forced to do that with respect to *itself,* you could say that the organism is "adopting the *auto*-intentional stance". This would imply that the organism's own best way of understanding itself is by attributing to itself desires, beliefs, and so on.

ACHILLES: That's a very strange sort of level-crossing feedback loop, Mr. T. The system's self-image (as a collection of symmballs) is getting recycled back into the system but of course this depends on the very concrete symms themselves to carry it out. It's like a television looking at its own screen, recycling a representation of itself over and over, building up a pattern of nested self-images on the screen.

TORTOISE: And that stable pattern becomes a real thing in and of itself. If you were a careenium, merely by adopting the auto-intentional stance toward yourself, you would create a self-perpetuating delusion. As soon as you create this illusion that there is just one thing there—a unitary self with beliefs and desires rather than a mere bunch of goalless, soulless marbles—then that illusion reenters the system as one of its own beliefs. The more that illusion of unity is cycled through the system, the more established and hardened and locked-in the whole illusion becomes. It's like a crystal whose crystallization, once started, somehow has a catalyzing effect on its further crystallization. Some sort of vicious closed loop that self-reinforces, so that even if it starts out as a delusion, by the time it has locked in, it has so deeply permeated the system's structure that no one could possibly explain how or why the system works as it does without referring to its "silly, self-deluding" belief in itself *as a self.*

ACHILLES: But by that time it isn't so silly any more, is it?

TORTOISE: No, by then it has to be taken quite seriously, because it will have a lot of explanatory power. Once the self has become so locked-in, or "reified", in the system's own set of concepts, this fact determines much of the system's own future behavior—or at least if you are restricted to watching the fast projector, to looking at the *symmball* level, that is the easiest way to understand matters. And the curious thing is that this *same* level-crossing feedback loop (of adopting the auto-intentional stance) takes place in *every* careenium of sufficient complexity. So that whichever careenium you take, the stable self-image pattern that it finally establishes in this loopy way is isomorphic to the stable self-image pattern in every *other* careenium!

ACHILLES: Bizarre! The medium is different, but the abstract phenomenon it supports is the same. It's a universal. That's sort of hard to grasp.

TORTOISE: Maybe so, but it's right. They all have isomorphic, identical senses of "I". There is just *one* sense of the word—just one referent—just one abstract pattern—yet each one seems to feel *it* knows it *uniquely!* There's a kind of fight for sole possession of something that everyone shares.

ACHILLES: *Soul* possession, Mr. T?

TORTOISE: Very astute, Achilles.

ACHILLES: Do you really believe there is just *one* "I", Mr. T?

TORTOISE: Not quite—an exaggeration for rhetorical purposes. The real point is, there's only *one mechanism* underlying "I-ness": namely, the circling-back of a complex representation of the system together with its representations of all the rest of the world. Which "I" you are is determined by the *way* you carry out that cycling, and the way you represent the world.

ACHILLES: So you mean that all that determines who "I" am is the set of experiences some organism has gone through?

TORTOISE: Not at all. I said "the *way* things are cycled", not "*which* things are so cycled and represented". You've got to distinguish between the *set* of objects represented, and the overall *style* with which they are represented. It's that *style* that determines how the loop will loop. *That's* what creates the uniqueness of each "I".

ACHILLES: Well, Mr. T, I think I am beginning to see your point. It's just *so* hard, emotionally, to acknowledge that a "soul" emerges from so physical a system as a careenium.

TORTOISE: The trick is in seeing the curious bidirectional causality operating between the levels of the system, and in integrating that vision with a sense of how symbols have representational power, including the power to recognize certain qualities of their own activity, even though only approximately. This is the crux of the mental, and the source of the enigma of "I".

Harry G. Frankfurt

"FREEDOM OF THE WILL AND THE CONCEPT OF A PERSON"

HARRY G. FRANKFURT, who received his Ph.D. from Johns Hopkins University, is a Descartes scholar and one of the leading contemporary theorists on free will. Formerly a professor of philosophy at Ohio State University, at Rockefeller University, and at Yale, he now teaches at Princeton.

What philosophers have lately come to accept as analysis of the concept of a person is not actually analysis of *that* concept at all. Strawson, whose usage represents the current standard, identifies the concept of a person as "the concept of a type of entity such that *both* predicates ascribing states of consciousness *and* predicates ascribing corporeal characteristics . . . are equally applicable to a single individual of that single type."[1] But there are many entities besides persons that have both mental and physical properties. As it happens—though it seems extraordinary that this should be so—there is no common English word for the type of entity Strawson has in mind, a type that includes not only human beings but animals of various lesser species as well. Still, this hardly justifies the misappropriation of a valuable philosophical term.

Whether the members of some animal species are persons is surely not to be settled merely by determining whether it is correct to apply to them, in addition to predicates ascribing corporeal characteristics, predicates that ascribe states of consciousness. It does violence to our language to endorse the application of the term 'person' to those numerous creatures which do have both psychological and material properties but which are manifestly not persons in any normal sense of the word. This misuse of language is doubtless innocent of any theoretical error. But although the offense is "merely verbal," it does significant harm. For it gratuitously diminishes our philosophical vocabulary, and it increases the likelihood that we will overlook the important area of inquiry with which the term 'person' is most naturally associated. It might have been expected that no problem would be of more central and persistent concern to philosophers than that of understanding what we ourselves essentially are. Yet this problem is so generally neglected that it has been possible to make off with its very name almost without being noticed and, evidently, without evoking any widespread feeling of loss.

There is a sense in which the word 'person' is merely the singular form of 'people' and in which both terms connote no more than membership in a certain biological species. In those senses of the word which are of greater philosophical interest, however, the criteria for being a person do not serve primarily to distinguish the members of our own species from the members of other species. Rather, they are designed

From Harry G. Frankfurt, "Freedom of the Will and the Concept of a Person," *The Journal of Philosophy,* LXVIII, 1 (January 14, 1971): 5–20. Reprinted by permission of the author and the publisher.

1. P. F. Strawson, *Individuals* (London: Methuen, 1959), pp. 101–102. Ayer's usage of 'person' is similar: "it is characteristic of persons in this sense that besides having various physical properties . . . they are also credited with various forms of consciousness" [A. J. Ayer, *The Concept of a Person* (New York: St. Martin's 1963), p. 82]. What concerns Strawson and Ayer is the problem of understanding the relation between mind and body, rather than the quite different problem of understanding what it is to be a creature that not only has a mind and a body but is also a person.

to capture those attributes which are the subject of our most humane concern with ourselves and the source of what we regard as most important and most problematical in our lives. Now these attributes would be of equal significance to us even if they were not in fact peculiar and common to the members of our own species. What interests us most in the human condition would not interest us less if it were also a feature of the condition of other creatures as well.

Our concept of ourselves as persons is not to be understood, therefore, as a concept of attributes that are necessarily species-specific. It is conceptually possible that members of novel or even of familiar nonhuman species should be persons; and it is also conceptually possible that some members of the human species are not persons. We do in fact assume, on the other hand, that no member of another species is a person. Accordingly, there is a presumption that what is essential to persons is a set of characteristics that we generally suppose—whether rightly or wrongly—to be uniquely human.

It is my view that one essential difference between persons and other creatures is to be found in the structure of a person's will. Human beings are not alone in having desires and motives, or in making choices. They share these things with the members of certain other species, some of whom even appear to engage in deliberation and to make decisions based upon prior thought. It seems to be peculiarly characteristic of humans, however, that they are able to form what I shall call "second-order desires" or "desires of the second order."

Besides wanting and choosing and being moved *to do* this or that, men may also want to have (or not to have) certain desires and motives. They are capable of wanting to be different, in their preferences and purposes, from what they are. Many animals appear to have the capacity for what I shall call "first-order desires" or "desires of the first order," which are simply desires to do or not to do one thing or another. No animal other than man, however, appears to have the capacity for reflective self-evaluation that is manifested in the formation of second-order desires.[2]

I

The concept designated by the verb 'to want' is extraordinarily elusive. A statement of the form "*A* wants to *X*"—taken by itself, apart from a context that serves to amplify or to specify its meaning—conveys remarkably little information. Such a statement may be consistent, for example, with each of the following statements: (a) the prospect of doing *X* elicits no sensation or introspectible emotional response in *A*; (b) *A* is unaware that he wants to *X*; (c) *A* believes that he does not want to *X*; (d) *A* wants to refrain from *X*-ing; (e) *A* wants to *Y* and believes that it is impossible for him both to *Y* and to *X*; (f) *A* does not "really" want to *X*; (g) *A* would rather die than *X*; and so on. It is therefore hardly sufficient to formulate the distinction between first-order and second-order desires, as I have done, by suggesting merely that someone has a first-order desire when he wants to do or not to do such-and-such, and that he has a second-order desire when he wants to have or not to have a certain desire of the first order.

As I shall understand them, statements of the form "*A* wants to *X*" cover a rather broad range of possibilities.[3] They may be true even when statements like (a) through (g) are true: when *A* is unaware of any feelings concerning

2. For the sake of simplicity, I shall deal only with what someone wants or desires, neglecting related phenomena such as choices and decisions. I propose to use the verbs 'to want' and 'to desire' interchangeably, although they are by no means perfect synonyms. My motive in forsaking the established nuances of these words arises from the fact that the verb 'to want', which suits my purposes better so far as its meaning is concerned, does not lend itself so readily to the formation of nouns as does the verb 'to desire'. It is perhaps acceptable, albeit graceless, to speak in the plural of someone's "wants." But to speak in the singular of someone's "want" would be an abomination.

3. What I say in this paragraph applies not only to cases in which 'to *X*' refers to a possible action or inaction. It also applies to cases in which 'to *X*' refers to a first-order desire and in which the statement that '*A* wants to *X*' is therefore a shortened version of a statement—"*A* wants to want to *X*"—that identifies a desire of the second order.

X-ing, when he is unaware that he wants to *X*, when he deceives himself about what he wants and believes falsely that he does not want to *X*, when he also has other desires that conflict with his desire to *X*, or when he is ambivalent. The desires in question may be conscious or unconscious, they need not be univocal, and *A* may be mistaken about them. There is a further source of uncertainty with regard to statements that identify someone's desires, however, and here it is important for my purposes to be less permissive.

Consider first those statements of the form "*A* wants to *X*" which identify first-order desires—that is, statements in which the term 'to *X*' refers to an action. A statement of this kind does not, by itself, indicate the relative strength of *A*'s desire to *X*. It does not make it clear whether this desire is at all likely to play a decisive role in what *A* actually does or tries to do. For it may correctly be said that *A* wants to *X* even when his desire to *X* is only one among his desires and when it is far from being paramount among them. Thus, it may be true that *A* wants to *X* when he strongly prefers to do something else instead; and it may be true that he wants to *X* despite the fact that, when he acts, it is not the desire to *X* that motivates him to do what he does. On the other hand, someone who states that *A* wants to *X* may mean to convey that it is this desire that is motivating or moving *A* to do what he is actually doing or that *A* will in fact be moved by this desire (unless he changes his mind) when he acts.

It is only when it is used in the second of these ways that, given the special usage of 'will' that I propose to adopt, the statement identifies *A*'s will. To identify an agent's will is either to identify the desire (or desires) by which he is motivated in some action he performs or to identify the desire (or desires) by which he will or would be motivated when or if he acts. An agent's will, then, is identical with one or more of his first-order desires. But the notion of the will, as I am employing it, is not coextensive with the notion of first-order desires. It is not the notion of something that merely inclines an agent in some degree to act in a certain way. Rather, it is the notion of an *effective* desire—one that moves (or will or would move) a person all the way to action. Thus the notion of the will is not coextensive with the notion of what an agent intends to do. For even though someone may have a settled intention to do *X*, he may nonetheless do something else instead of doing *X* because, despite his intention, his desire to do *X* proves to be weaker or less effective than some conflicting desire.

Now consider those statements of the form "*A* wants to *X*" which identify second-order desires—that is, statements in which the term 'to *X*' refers to a desire of the first order. There are also two kinds of situation in which it may be true that *A* wants to want to *X*. In the first place, it might be true of *A* that he wants to have a desire to *X* despite the fact that he has a univocal desire, altogether free of conflict and ambivalence, to refrain from *X*-ing. Someone might want to have a certain desire, in other words, but univocally want that desire to be unsatisfied.

Suppose that a physician engaged in psychotherapy with narcotics addicts believes that his ability to help his patients would be enhanced if he understood better what it is like for them to desire the drug to which they are addicted. Suppose that he is led in this way to want to have a desire for the drug. If it is a genuine desire that he wants, then what he wants is not merely to feel the sensations that addicts characteristically feel when they are gripped by their desires for the drug. What the physician wants, insofar as he wants to have a desire, is to be inclined or moved to some extent to take the drug.

It is entirely possible, however, that, although he wants to be moved by a desire to take the drug, he does not want this desire to be effective. He may not want it to move him all the way to action. He need not be interested in finding out what it is like to take the drug. And insofar as he now wants only to *want* to take it, and not to *take* it, there is nothing in what he now wants that would be satisfied by the drug itself. He may now have, in fact, an altogether univocal desire *not* to take the drug; and he may prudently arrange to make it impossible for him to satisfy the desire he would have if his desire to want the drug should in time be satisfied.

It would thus be incorrect to infer, from the fact that the physician now wants to desire to take the drug, that he already does desire to take it. His second-order desire to be moved to take the drug does not entail that he has a first-order desire to take it. If the drug were now to be administered to him, this might satisfy no desire that is implicit in his desire to want to take it. While he wants to want to take the drug, he may have *no* desire to take it; it may be that *all* he wants is to taste the desire for it. That is, his desire to have a certain desire that he does not have may not be a desire that his will should be at all different than it is.

Someone who wants only in this truncated way to want to X stands at the margin of preciosity, and the fact that he wants to want to X is not pertinent to the identification of his will. There is, however, a second kind of situation that may be described by 'A wants to want to X';

"Defense of Leopold and Loeb" (1924)

Clarence Darrow

I know that one of two things happened to Richard Loeb: that this terrible crime was inherent in his organism, and came from some ancestor; or that it came through his education and his training after he was born. Do I need to prove it? Judge Crowe said at one point in this case, when some witness spoke about their wealth, that "probably that was responsible."

To believe that any boy is responsible for himself or his early training is an absurdity that no lawyer or judge should be guilty of today. Somewhere this came to the boy. If his failing came from his heredity, I do not know where or how. None of us are bred perfect and pure; and the color of our hair, the color of our eyes, our stature, the weight and fineness of our brain, and everything about us could, with full knowledge, be traced with absolute certainty to somewhere. If we had the pedigree it could be traced just the same in a boy as it could in a dog, a horse or a cow.

I do not know what remote ancestors may have sent down the seed that corrupted him, and I do not know through how many ancestors it may have passed until it reached Dickie Loeb.

All I know is that it is true, and there is not a biologist in the world who will not say that I am right.

If it did not come that way, then I know that if he was normal, if he had been understood, if he had been trained as he should have been it would not have happened. Not that anybody may not slip, but I know it and Your Honor knows it, and every schoolhouse and every church in the land is an evidence of it. Else why build them?

Every effort to protect society is an effort toward training the youth to keep the path. Every bit of training in the world proves it, and it likewise proves that it sometimes fails. I know that if this boy had been understood and properly trained—properly for him—and the training that he got might have been the very best for someone; but if it had been the proper training for him he would not be in this courtroom today with the noose above his head. If there is responsibility anywhere, it is back of him; somewhere in the infinite number of his ancestors, or in his surroundings, or in both. And I submit, Your Honor, that under every principle of natural justice, under every principle of conscience, of right, and of law, he should not be made responsible for the acts of someone else.

From *Attorney for the Damned*, edited by Arthur Weinburg (1957).

and when the statement is used to describe a situation of this second kind, then it does pertain to what *A* wants his will to be. In such cases the statement means that *A* wants the desire to *X* to be the desire that moves him effectively to act. It is not merely that he wants the desire to *X* to be among the desires by which, to one degree or another, he is moved or inclined to act. He wants this desire to be effective—that is, to provide the motive in what he actually does. Now when the statement that *A* wants to want to *X* is used in this way, it does entail that *A* already has a desire to *X*. It could not be true both that *A* wants the desire to *X* to move him into action and that he does not want to *X*. It is only if he does want to *X* that he can coherently want the desire to *X* not merely to be one of his desires but, more decisively, to be his will.[4]

Suppose a man wants to be motivated in what he does by the desire to concentrate on his work. It is necessarily true, if this supposition is correct, that he already wants to concentrate on his work. This desire is now among his desires. But the question of whether or not his second-order desire is fulfilled does not turn merely on whether the desire he wants is one of his desires. It turns on whether this desire is, as he wants it to be, his effective desire or will. If, when the chips are down, it is his desire to concentrate on his work that moves him to do what he does, then what he wants at that time is indeed (in the relevant sense) what he wants to want. If it is some other desire that actually moves him when he acts, on the other hand, then what he wants at that time is not (in the relevant sense) what he wants to want. This will be so despite the fact that the desire to concentrate on his work continues to be among his desires.

II

Someone has a desire of the second order either when he wants simply to have a certain desire or when he wants a certain desire to be his will. In situations of the latter kind, I shall call his second-order desires "second-order volitions" or "volitions of the second order." Now it is having second-order volitions, and not having second-order desires generally, that I regard as essential to being a person. It is logically possible, however unlikely, that there should be an agent with second-order desires but with no volitions of the second order. Such a creature, in my view, would not be a person. I shall use the term 'wanton' to refer to agents who have first-order desires but who are not persons because, whether or not they have desires of the second order, they have no second-order volitions.[5]

The essential characteristic of a wanton is that he does not care about his will. His desires move him to do certain things, without its being true of him either that he wants to be moved by those desires or that he prefers to be moved by other desires. The class of wantons includes all nonhuman animals that have desires and all very young children. Perhaps it also includes some adult human beings as well. In any case, adult humans may be more or less wanton; they may act wantonly, in response to first-order desires concerning which they have no volitions of the second order, more or less frequently.

4. It is not so clear that the entailment relation described here holds in certain kinds of cases, which I think may fairly be regarded as nonstandard, where the essential difference between the standard and the nonstandard cases lies in the kind of description by which the first-order desire in question is identified. Thus, suppose that *A* admires *B* so fulsomely that, even though he does not know what *B* wants to do, he wants to be effectively moved by whatever desire effectively moves *B*; without knowing what *B*'s will is, in other words, *A* wants his own will to be the same. It certainly does not follow that *A* already has, among his desires, a desire like the one that constitutes *B*'s will. I shall not pursue here the questions of whether there are genuine counterexamples to the claim made in the text or of how, if there are, that claim should be altered.

5. Creatures with second-order desires but no second-order volitions differ significantly from brute animals, and, for some purposes, it would be desirable to regard them as persons. My usage, which withholds the designation 'person' from them, is thus somewhat arbitrary. I adopt it largely because it facilitates the formulation of some of the points I wish to make. Hereafter, whenever I consider statements of the form "*A* wants to want to *X*," I shall have in mind statements identifying second-order volitions and not statements identifying second-order desires that are not second-order volitions.

The fact that a wanton has no second-order volitions does not mean that each of his first-order desires is translated heedlessly and at once into action. He may have no opportunity to act in accordance with some of his desires. Moreover, the translation of his desires into action may be delayed or precluded either by conflicting desires of the first order or by the intervention of deliberation. For a wanton may possess and employ rational faculties of a high order. Nothing in the concept of a wanton implies that he cannot reason or that he cannot deliberate concerning how to do what he wants to do. What distinguishes the rational wanton from other rational agents is that he is not concerned with the desirability of his desires themselves. He ignores the question of what his will is to be. Not only does he pursue whatever course of action he is most strongly inclined to pursue, but he does not care which of his inclinations is the strongest.

Thus a rational creature, who reflects upon the suitability to his desires of one course of action or another, may nonetheless be a wanton. In maintaining that the essence of being a person lies not in reason but in will, I am far from suggesting that a creature without reason may be a person. For it is only in virtue of his rational capacities that a person is capable of becoming critically aware of his own will and of forming volitions of the second order. The structure of a person's will presupposes, accordingly, that he is a rational being.

The distinction between a person and a wanton may be illustrated by the difference between two narcotics addicts. Let us suppose that the physiological condition accounting for the addiction is the same in both men, and that both succumb inevitably to their periodic desires for the drug to which they are addicted. One of the addicts hates his addiction and always struggles desperately, although to no avail, against its thrust. He tries everything that he thinks might enable him to overcome his desires for the drug. But these desires are too powerful for him to withstand, and invariably, in the end, they conquer him. He is an unwilling addict, helplessly violated by his own desires.

The unwilling addict has conflicting first-order desires: he wants to take the drug, and he also wants to refrain from taking it. In addition to these first-order desires, however, he has a volition of the second order. He is not a neutral with regard to the conflict between his desire to take the drug and his desire to refrain from taking it. It is the latter desire, and not the former, that he wants to constitute his will; it is the latter desire, rather than the former, that he wants to be effective and to provide the purpose that he will seek to realize in what he actually does.

The other addict is a wanton. His actions reflect the economy of his first-order desires, without his being concerned whether the desires that move him to act are desires by which he wants to be moved to act. If he encounters problems in obtaining the drug or in administering it himself, his responses to his urges to take it may involve deliberation. But it never occurs to him to consider whether he wants the relations among his desires to result in his having the will he has. The wanton addict may be an animal, and thus incapable of being concerned about his will. In any event he is, in respect of his wanton lack of concern, no different from an animal.

The second of these addicts may suffer a first-order conflict similar to the first-order conflict suffered by the first. Whether he is human or not, the wanton may (perhaps due to conditioning) both want to take the drug and want to refrain from taking it. Unlike the unwilling addict, however, he does not prefer that one of his conflicting desires should be paramount over the other; he does not prefer that one first-order desire rather than the other should constitute his will. It would be misleading to say that he is neutral as to the conflict between his desires, since this would suggest that he regards them as equally acceptable. Since he has no identity apart from his first-orders desires, it is true neither that he prefers one to the other nor that he prefers not to take sides.

It makes a difference to the unwilling addict, who is a person, which of his conflicting first-order desires wins out. Both desires are his, to be sure; and whether he finally takes the drug or finally succeeds in refraining from taking it, he acts to satisfy what is in a literal sense his own desire. In either case he does something he himself wants to do, and he does it not because of some external influence whose aim happens to coincide with his own but because of his desire to do it. The unwilling addict identifies himself, however, through the formation of a second-order volition, with one rather than with the other of his conflicting first-order desires. He makes one of them more truly his own and, in so doing, he withdraws himself from the other. It is in virtue of this identification and withdrawal, accomplished through the formation of a second-order volition, that the unwilling addict may meaningfully make the analytically puzzling statements that the force moving him to take the drug is a force other than his own, and that it is not of his own free will but rather against his will that this force moves him to take it.

The wanton addict cannot or does not care which of his conflicting first-order desires wins out. His lack of concern is not due to his inability to find a convincing basis for preference. It is due either to his lack of the capacity for reflection or to his mindless indifference to the enterprise of evaluating his own desires and motives.[6] There is only one issue in the struggle to which his first-order conflict may lead: whether the one or the other of his conflicting desires is the stronger. Since he is moved by both desires, he will not be altogether satisfied by what he does no matter which of them is effective. But it makes no difference to *him* whether his craving or his aversion gets the upper hand. He has no stake in the conflict between them and so, unlike the unwilling addict, he can neither win nor lose the struggle in which he is engaged. When a *person* acts, the desire by which he is moved is either the will he wants or a will he wants to be without. When a *wanton* acts, it is neither.

III

There is a very close relationship between the capacity for forming second-order volitions and another capacity that is essential to persons—one that has often been considered a distinguishing mark of the human condition. It is only because a person has volitions of the second order that he is capable both of enjoying and of lacking freedom of the will. The concept of a person is not only, then, the concept of a type of entity that has both first-order desires and volitions of the second order. It can also be construed as the concept of a type of entity for whom the freedom of its will may be a problem. This concept excludes all wantons, both infrahuman and human, since they fail to satisfy an essential condition for the enjoyment of freedom of the will. And it excludes those suprahuman beings, if any, whose wills are necessarily free.

Just what kind of freedom is the freedom of the will? This question calls for an identification of the special area of human experience to which the concept of freedom of the will, as distinct from the concepts of other sorts of freedom, is particularly germane. In dealing with it, my aim will be primarily to locate the problem with which a person is most immediately concerned when he is concerned with the freedom of his will.

According to one familiar philosophical tradition, being free is fundamentally a matter of doing what one wants to do. Now the notion of an agent who does what he wants to do is by no means an altogether clear one: both the doing

6. In speaking of the evaluation of his own desires and motives as being characteristic of a person, I do not mean to suggest that a person's second-order volitions necessarily manifest a *moral* stance on his part toward his first-order desires. It may not be from the point of view of morality that the person evaluates his first-order desires. Moreover, a person may be capricious and irresponsible in forming his second-order volitions and give no serious consideration to what is at stake. Second-order volitions express evaluations only in the sense that they are preferences. There is no essential restriction on the kind of basis, if any, upon which they are formed.

and the wanting, and the appropriate relation between them as well, require elucidation. But although its focus needs to be sharpened and its formulation refined, I believe that this notion does capture at least part of what is implicit in the idea of an agent who *acts* freely. It misses entirely, however, the peculiar content of the quite different idea of an agent whose *will* is free.

We do not suppose that animals enjoy freedom of the will, although we recognize that an animal may be free to run in whatever direction it wants. Thus, having the freedom to do what one wants to do is not a sufficient condition of having a free will. It is not a necessary condition either. For to deprive someone of his freedom of action is not necessarily to undermine the freedom of his will. When an agent is aware that there are certain things he is not free to do, this doubtless affects his desires and limits the range of choices he can make. But suppose that someone, without being aware of it, has in fact lost or been deprived of his freedom of action. Even though he is no longer free to do what he wants to do, his will may remain as free as it was before. Despite the fact that he is not free to translate his desires into actions or to act according to the determinations of his will, he may still form those desires and make those determinations as freely as if his freedom of action had not been impaired.

When we ask whether a person's will is free we are not asking whether he is in a position to translate his first-order desires into actions. That is the question of whether he is free to do as he pleases. The question of the freedom of his will does not concern the relation between what he does and what he wants to do. Rather, it concerns his desires themselves. But what question about them is it?

It seems to me both natural and useful to construe the question of whether a person's will is free in close analogy to the question of whether an agent enjoys freedom of action. Now freedom of action is (roughly, at least) the freedom to do what one wants to do. Analogously, then, the statement that a person enjoys freedom of the will means (also roughly) that he is free to want what he wants to want. More precisely, it means that he is free to will what he wants to will, or to have the will he wants. Just as the question about the freedom of an agent's action has to do with whether it is the action he wants to perform, so the question about the freedom of his will has to do with whether it is the will he wants to have.

It is in securing the conformity of his will to his second-order volitions, then, that a person exercises freedom of the will. And it is in the discrepancy between his will and his second-order volitions, or in his awareness that their coincidence is not his own doing but only a happy chance, that a person who does not have his freedom feels its lack. The unwilling addict's will is not free. This is shown by the fact that it is not the will he wants. It is also true, though in a different way, that the will of the wanton addict is not free. The wanton addict neither has the will he wants nor has a will that differs from the will he wants. Since he has no volitions of the second order, the freedom of his will cannot be a problem for him. He lacks it, so to speak, by default.

People are generally far more complicated than my sketchy account of the structure of a person's will may suggest. There is as much opportunity for ambivalence, conflict, and self-deception with regard to desires of the second order, for example, as there is with regard to first-order desires. If there is an unresolved conflict among someone's second-order desires, then he is in danger of having no second-order volition; for unless this conflict is resolved, he has no preference concerning which of his first-order desires is to be his will. This condition, if it is so severe that it prevents him from identifying himself in a sufficiently decisive way with *any* of his conflicting first-order desires, destroys him as a person. For it either tends to paralyze his will and to keep him from acting at all, or it tends to remove him from his will so that his will operates without his participation. In both cases he becomes, like the unwilling addict though in a different way, a helpless bystander to the forces that move him.

Another complexity is that a person may have, especially if his second-order desires are in conflict, desires and volitions of a higher order than the second. There is no theoretical limit to the length of the series of desires of higher and higher orders; nothing except common sense and, perhaps, a saving fatigue prevents an individual from obsessively refusing to identify himself with any of his desires until he forms a desire of the next higher order. The tendency to generate such a series of acts of forming desires, which would be a case of humanization run wild, also leads toward the destruction of a person.

It is possible, however, to terminate such a series of acts without cutting it off arbitrarily. When a person identifies himself *decisively* with one of his first-order desires, this commitment "resounds" throughout the potentially endless array of higher orders. Consider a person who, without reservation or conflict, wants to be motivated by the desire to concentrate on his work. The fact that his second-order volition to be moved by this desire is a decisive one means that there is no room for questions concerning the pertinence of desires or volitions of higher orders. Suppose the person is asked whether he wants to want to want to concentrate on his work. He can properly insist that this question concerning a third-order desire does not arise. It would be a mistake to claim that, because he has not considered whether he wants the second-order volition he has formed, he is indifferent to the question of whether it is with this volition or with some other that he wants his will to accord. The decisiveness of the commitment he has made means that he has decided that no further question about his second-order volition, at any higher order, remains to be asked. It is relatively unimportant whether we explain this by saying that this commitment implicitly generates an endless series of confirming desires of higher orders, or by saying that the commitment is tantamount to a dissolution of the pointedness of all questions concerning higher orders of desire.

Examples such as the one concerning the unwilling addict may suggest that volitions of the second order, or of higher orders, must be formed deliberately and that a person characteristically struggles to ensure that they are satisfied. But the conformity of a person's will to his higher-order volitions may be far more thoughtless and spontaneous than this. Some people are naturally moved by kindness when they want to be kind, and by nastiness when they want to be nasty, without any explicit forethought and without any need for energetic self-

"Determinism and Free Will"

John Hospers

1. An occurrence over which we had no control is something we cannot be held responsible for.
2. Events E, occurring during our babyhood, were events over which we had no control.
3. Therefore events E were events which we cannot be held responsible for.
4. But if there is something we cannot be held responsible for, neither can we be held responsible for something that inevitably results from it.
5. Events E have as inevitable consequence Neurosis N, which in turn has inevitable consequence Behavior B.
6. Since N is the inevitable consequence of E and B is the inevitable consequence of N, B is the inevitable consequence of E.
7. Hence, not being responsible for E, we cannot be responsible for B.

From "Free Will and Psychoanalysis," *Philosophy and Phenomenological Research* (1950).

control. Others are moved by nastiness when they want to be kind and by kindness when they intend to be nasty, equally without forethought and without active resistance to these violations of their higher-order desires. The enjoyment of freedom comes easily to some. Others must struggle to achieve it.

IV

My theory concerning the freedom of the will accounts easily for our disinclination to allow that this freedom is enjoyed by the members of any species inferior to our own. It also satisfies another condition that must be met by any such theory, by making it apparent why the freedom of the will should be regarded as desirable. The enjoyment of a free will means that satisfaction of certain desires—desires of the second or of higher orders—whereas its absence means their frustration. The satisfactions at stake are those which accrue to a person of whom it may be said that his will is his own. The corresponding frustrations are those suffered by a person of whom it may be said that he is estranged from himself, or that he finds himself a helpless or a passive bystander to the forces that move him.

A person who is free to do what he wants to do may yet not be in a position to have the will he wants. Suppose, however, that he enjoys both freedom of action and freedom of the will. Then he is not only free to do what he wants to do; he is also free to want what he wants to want. It seems to me that he has, in that case, all the freedom it is possible to desire or to conceive. There are other good things in life, and he may not possess some of them. But there is nothing in the way of freedom that he lacks.

It is far from clear that certain other theories of the freedom of the will meet these elementary but essential conditions: that it be understandable why we desire this freedom and why we refuse to ascribe it to animals. Consider, for example, Roderick Chisholm's quaint version of the doctrine that human freedom entails an absence of causal determination.[7] Whenever a person performs a free action, according to Chisholm, it's a miracle. The motion of a person's hand, when the person moves it, is the outcome of a series of physical causes; but some event in this series, "and presumably one of those that took place within the brain, was caused by the agent and not by any other events." A free agent has, therefore, "a prerogative which some would attribute only to God: each of us, when we act, is a prime mover unmoved."

This account fails to provide any basis for doubting that animals of subhuman species enjoy the freedom it defines. Chisholm says nothing that makes it seem less likely that a rabbit performs a miracle when it moves its leg than that a man does so when he moves his hand. But why, in any case, should anyone *care* whether he can interrupt the natural order of causes in the way Chisholm describes? Chisholm offers no reason for believing that there is a discernible difference between the experience of a man who miraculously initiates a series of causes when he moves his hand and a man who moves his hand without any such breach of the normal causal sequence. There appears to be no concrete basis for preferring to be involved in the one state of affairs rather than in the other.[8]

It is generally supposed that, in addition to satisfying the two conditions I have mentioned, a satisfactory theory of the freedom of the will necessarily provides an analysis of one of the conditions of moral responsibility. The most common recent approach to the problem of understanding the freedom of the will has been, indeed, to inquire what is entailed by the assumption that someone is morally responsible for what he has done. In my view, however, the

7. "Freedom and Action," in K. Lehrer, ed., *Freedom and Determination* (New York: Random House, 1966), pp. 11–44.

8. I am not suggesting that the alleged difference between these two states of affairs is unverifiable. On the contrary, physiologists might well be able to show that Chisholm's conditions for a free action are not satisfied, by establishing that there is no relevant brain event for which a sufficient physical cause cannot be found.

relation between moral responsibility and the freedom of the will has been very widely misunderstood. It is not true that a person is morally responsible for what he has done only if his will was free when he did it. He may be morally responsible for having done it even though his will was not free at all.

A person's will is free only if he is free to have the will he wants. This means that, with regard to any of his first-order desires, he is free either to make that desire his will or to make some other first-order desire his will instead. Whatever his will, then, the will of the person whose will is free could have been otherwise; he could have done otherwise than to constitute his will as he did. It is a vexed question just how 'he could have done otherwise' is to be understood in contexts such as this one. But although this question is important to the theory of freedom, it has no bearing on the theory of moral responsibility. For the assumption that a person is morally responsible for what he has done does not entail that the person was in a position to have whatever will he wanted.

This assumption *does* entail that the person did what he did freely, or that he did it of his own free will. It is a mistake, however, to believe that someone acts freely only when he is free to do whatever he wants or that he acts of his own free will only if his will is free. Suppose that a person has done what he wanted to do, that he did it because he wanted to do it, and that the will by which he was moved when he did it was his will because it was the will he wanted. Then he did it freely and of his own free will. Even supposing that he could have done otherwise, he would not have done otherwise; and even supposing that he could have had a different will, he would not have wanted his will to differ from what it was. Moreover, since the will that moved him when he acted was his will because he wanted it to be, he cannot claim that his will was forced upon him or that he was a passive bystander to its constitution. Under these conditions, it is quite irrelevant to the evaluation of his moral responsibility to inquire whether the alternatives that he opted against were actually available to him.[9]

In illustration, consider a third kind of addict. Suppose that his addiction has the same physiological basis and the same irresistible thrust as the addictions of the unwilling and wanton addicts, but that he is altogether delighted with his condition. He is a willing addict, who would not have things any other way. If the grip of his addiction should somehow weaken, he would do whatever he could to reinstate it; if his desire for the drug should begin to fade, he would take steps to renew its intensity.

The willing addict's will is not free, for his desire to take the drug will be effective regardless of whether or not he wants this desire to constitute his will. But when he takes the drug, he takes it freely and of his own free will. I am inclined to understand his situation as involving the overdetermination of his first-order desire to take the drug. This desire is his effective desire because he is physiologically addicted. But it is his effective desire also because he wants it to be. His will is outside his control, but, by his second-order desire that his desire for the drug should be effective, he has made this will his own. Given that it is therefore not only because of his addiction that his desire for the drug is effective, he may be morally responsible for taking the drug.

My conception of the freedom of the will appears to be neutral with regard to the problem of determinism. It seems conceivable that it should be causally determined that a person is free to want what he wants to want. If this is conceivable, then it might be causally determined that a person enjoys a free will. There is no more than an innocuous appearance of paradox in the proposition that it is determined, ineluctably and by forces beyond their control, that certain people have free wills and that oth-

9. For another discussion of the considerations that cast doubt on the principle that a person is morally responsible for what he has done only if he could have done otherwise, see my "Alternate Possibilities and Moral Responsibility," *Journal of Philosophy,* Vol. 66, No. 23 (Dec. 4, 1969): 829–839.

ers do not. There is no incoherence in the proposition that some agency other than a person's own is responsible (even *morally* responsible) for the fact that he enjoys or fails to enjoy freedom of the will. It is possible that a person should be morally responsible for what he does of his own free will and that some other person should also be morally responsible for his having done it.[10]

On the other hand, it seems conceivable that it should come about by chance that a person is free to have the will he wants. If this is conceivable, then it might be a matter of chance that certain people enjoy freedom of the will and that certain others do not. Perhaps it is also conceivable, as a number of philosophers believe, for states of affairs to come about in a way other than by chance or as the outcome of a sequence of natural causes. If it is indeed conceivable for the relevant states of affairs to come about in some third way, then it is also possible that a person should in that third way come to enjoy the freedom of the will.

10. There is a difference between being *fully* responsible and being *solely* responsible. Suppose that the willing addict has been made an addict by the deliberate and calculated work of another. Then it may be that both the addict and this other person are fully responsible for the addict's taking the drug, while neither of them is solely responsible for it. That there is a distinction between full moral responsibility and sole moral responsibility is apparent in the following example. A certain light can be turned on or off by flicking either of two switches, and each of these switches is simultaneously flicked to the "on" position by a different person, neither of whom is aware of the other. Neither person is solely responsible for the light's going on, nor do they share the responsibility in the sense that each is partially responsible; rather, each of them is fully responsible.

PART III

Arguments for and against God

"THE FIVE WAYS"

ST. THOMAS AQUINAS (1225–1274), born of Italian nobility, began his education in Naples where he became a Dominican monk. He then went to Cologne to study under Albertus Magnus, the leading Aristotelian of the time. Aquinas later taught theology in Paris for a few years, before returning to Italy where he spent most of the rest of his life. His great theological system is a synthesis of Christian theology and Greek metaphysics. He is generally regarded as the greatest medieval philosopher, and Catholic scholars usually consider him the greatest Christian theologian of all time. His two major works are *Summa Theologica* and *Summa Contra Gentiles*.

Aquinas's famous five ways of proving the existence of God are, in simplest terms: first, that change implies the existence of an Unmoved Mover that originates it; second, that causation implies the existence of a First Cause; third, that contingency—that is, the dependence of natural objects for their existence on other things—implies the existence of something which is necessary, or incapable of coming into and going out of existence; fourth, degrees of excellence in things imply the existence of a Perfect Being; fifth, the (alleged) purposeful behavior of natural objects implies the existence of an intelligence that directs their behavior.

[PART I, QUESTION 2, ARTICLE 3]

The existence of God can be proved in five ways.

The first and more manifest way is the argument from motion. It is certain, and evident to our senses, that in the world some things are in motion. Now whatever is moved is moved by another, for nothing can be moved except it is in potentiality to that towards which it is moved; whereas a thing moves inasmuch as it is in act. For motion is nothing else than the reduction of something from potentiality to actuality. But nothing can be reduced from potentiality to actuality, except by something in a state of actuality. Thus that which is actually hot, as fire, makes wood, which is potentially hot, to be actually hot, and thereby moves and changes it. Now it is not possible that the same thing should be at once in actuality and potentiality in the same respect, but only in different respects. For what is actually hot cannot simultaneously be potentially hot; but it is simultaneously potentially cold. It is therefore impossible that in the same respect and in the same way a thing should be both mover and moved, *i.e.,* that it should move itself. Therefore, whatever is moved must be moved by another. If that by which it is moved be itself moved, then this also must needs be moved by another, and that by another again. But this cannot go on to infinity, because then there would be no first mover, and consequently no other mover, seeing that subsequent movers move only inasmuch as they are moved by the first mover; as the staff moves only because it is moved by the hand. Therefore it is necessary

The sacred Inca city of Machu Picchu, Peru, hidden away high in the Andes. Not discovered by Europeans until 1911.

to arrive at a first mover, moved by no other; and this everyone understands to be God.

The second way is from the nature of efficient cause. In the world of sensible things we find there is an order of efficient causes. There is no case known (neither is it, indeed, possible) in which a thing is found to be the efficient cause of itself; for so it would be prior to itself, which is impossible. Now in efficient causes it is not possible to go on to infinity, because in all efficient causes following in order, the first is the cause of the intermediate cause, and the intermediate is the cause of the ultimate cause, whether the intermediate cause be several, or one only. Now to take away the cause is to take away the effect. Therefore, if there be no first cause among efficient causes, there will be no ultimate, nor any intermediate, cause. But if in efficient causes it is possible to go on to infinity, there will be no first efficient cause, neither will there be an ultimate effect, nor any intermediate efficient causes; all of which is plainly false. Therefore it is necessary to admit a first efficient cause, to which everyone gives the name of God.

The third is taken from possibility and necessity, and runs thus. We find in nature things that are possible to be and not to be, since they are found to be generated, and to be corrupted, and consequently, it is possible for them to be and not to be. But it is impossible for these always to exist, for that which can not-be at some time is not. Therefore, if everything can not-be, then at one time there was nothing in existence. Now if this were true, even now there would be nothing in existence, because that which does not exist begins to exist only through something already existing. Therefore, if at one time nothing was in existence, it would have been impossible for anything to have begun to exist; and thus even now nothing would be in existence—which is absurd. Therefore, not all beings are merely possible, but there must exist something the existence of which is necessary. But every necessary thing either has its necessity caused by another, or not. Now it is impossible to go on to infinity in necessary things which have their necessity caused by another, as has been already proved in regard to efficient causes. Therefore we cannot but admit the existence of some being having of itself its own necessity, and not receiving it from another, but rather causing in others their necessity. This all men speak of as God.

The fourth way is taken from the gradation to be found in things. Among beings there are some more and some less good, true, noble, and the like. But *more* and *less* are predicated of different things according as they resemble in their different ways something which is the maximum, as a thing is said to be hotter according as it more nearly resembles that which is hottest; so that there is something which is truest, something best, something noblest, and, consequently, something which is most being, for those

Sacred plaza in Machu Picchu.

things that are greatest in truth are greatest in being, as it is written in *Metaph.* ii. Now the maximum in any genus is the cause of all in that genus, as fire, which is the maximum of heat, is the cause of all hot things, as is said in the same book. Therefore there must also be something which is to all beings the cause of their being, goodness, and every other perfection; and this we call God.

The fifth way is taken from the governance of the world. We see that things which lack knowledge, such as natural bodies, act for an end, and this is evident from their acting always, or nearly always, in the same way, so as to obtain the best result. Hence it is plain that they achieve their end, not fortuitously, but designedly. Now whatever lacks knowledge cannot move towards an end, unless it be directed by some being endowed with knowledge and intelligence; as the arrow is directed by the archer. Therefore some intelligent being exists by whom all natural things are directed to their end; and this being we call God.

Paul Edwards

"A CRITIQUE OF THE COSMOLOGICAL ARGUMENT"

PAUL EDWARDS received his Ph.D. from Columbia and taught philosophy at Brooklyn College, University of Melbourne, Columbia, City College of New York, and the University of California, Berkeley. He has written extensively in many areas of philosophy, including on religion and the meaning of life. He edited the monumental *Encyclopedia of Philosophy*.

I

The so-called "cosmological proof" is one of the oldest and most popular arguments for the existence of God. It was forcibly criticized by Hume, Kant, and Mill, but it would be inaccurate to consider the argument dead or even moribund. Catholic philosophers, with hardly any exception, appear to believe that it is as solid and conclusive as ever. Thus Father F.C. Copleston confidently championed it in his Third Programme debate with Bertrand Russell, and in America, where Catholic writers are more sanguine, we are told by a Jesuit professor of physics that "the existence of an intelligent being as the First Cause of the universe can be established by *rational scientific inference.*"[1]

> I am absolutely convinced [the same writer continues] that any one who would give the same consideration to that proof (the cosmological argument), as outlined for example in William Brosnan's *God and Reason,* as he would give to a line of argumentation found in the *Physical Review* or the *Proceedings of the Royal Society* would be forced to admit that the cogency of this argument for the existence of God far outstrips that which is found in the reasoning which Chadwick uses to prove the existence of the neutron, which today is accepted as certain as any conclusion in the physical sciences.

Mild theists like the late Professor Dawes Hicks and Dr. [A. C.] Ewing, who concede many of Hume's and Kant's criticisms, nevertheless contend that the argument possesses a certain core of truth. In popular discussions it also crops up again and again—for example, when believers address atheists with such questions as "You tell me where the universe came from!" Even philosophers who reject the cosmological proof sometimes embody certain of its confusions in the formulation of their own position. In the light of all this, it may be worthwhile to undertake a fresh examination of the argument with special attention to the fallacies that were not emphasized by the older critics.

II

The cosmological proof has taken a number of forms, the most important of which are known as the "causal argument" and "the argument from contingency," respectively. . . . The causal argument is the second of the "five ways" of Aquinas and roughly proceeds as follows: we find

Reprinted from *The Rationalist Annual,* 1959, edited by Hector Hawton. Reprinted by permission of Paul Edwards. Footnotes edited.

1. J. S. O'Connor, "A Scientific Approach to Religion," *The Scientific Monthly* (1940), p. 369; my italics.

that the things around us come into being as the result of the activity of other things. These causes are themselves the result of the activity of other things. But such a causal series cannot "go back to infinity." Hence there must be a first member, a member which is not itself caused by any preceding member—an uncaused or "first" cause.

It has frequently been pointed out that even if this argument were sound it would not establish the existence of *God.* It would not show that the first cause is all-powerful or all-good or that it is in any sense personal. Somebody believing in the eternity of atoms, or of matter generally, could quite consistently accept the conclusion. Defenders of the causal argument usually concede this and insist that the argument is not in itself meant to prove the existence of God. Supplementary arguments are required to show that the first cause must have the attributes assigned to the deity. They claim, however, that the argument, if valid, would at least be an important step towards a complete proof of the existence of God.

Does the argument succeed in proving so much as a first cause? This will depend mainly on the soundness of the premise that an infinite series of causes is impossible. Aquinas supports this premise by maintaining that the opposite belief involves a plain absurdity. To suppose that there is an infinite series of causes logically implies that nothing exists now; but we know that plenty of things do exist now; and hence any theory which implies that nothing exists now must be wrong. Let us take some causal series and refer to its members by the letters of the alphabet:

$$A \rightarrow B \ldots W \rightarrow X \rightarrow Y \rightarrow Z$$

Z stands here for something presently existing, e.g. Margaret Truman. *Y* represents the cause or part of the cause of *Z,* say Harry Truman. *X* designates the cause or part of the cause of Y, say Harry Truman's father, etc. Now, Aquinas reasons, whenever we take away the cause, we also take away the effect: if Harry Truman had never lived, Margaret Truman would never have been born. If Harry Truman's father had never lived, Harry Truman and Margaret Truman would never have been born. If *A* had never existed, none of the subsequent members of the series would have come into existence. But it is precisely *A* that the believer in the infinite series is "taking away." For in maintaining that the series is infinite he is denying that it has a first member; he is denying that there is such a thing as

Ultimate Questions

Does science always leave certain ultimate questions unanswered—for instance, why is there something at all rather than nothing—that must in the end be answered mythologically or not at all? In other words, even if the competition between science and religion is a fair one, and even if science wins that competition whenever the issue is joined, does science have to be supplemented in the end by some sort of mythology anyway? Is the alternative to avoiding mythology altogether that we simply have to admit that we have no answers—and probably never will—to our most ultimate questions about why the world exists and is the way it is?

a first cause; he is in other words denying the existence of *A*. Since without *A, Z* could not have existed, his position implies that *Z* does not exist now; and that is plainly false.

This argument fails to do justice to the supporter of the infinite series of causes. Aquinas has failed to distinguish between the two statements:

(1) *A* did not exist, and
(2) *A* is not uncaused.

To say that the series is infinite implies (2), but it does not imply (1). The following parallel may be helpful here: Suppose Captain Spaulding had said, "I am the greatest explorer who ever lived," and somebody replied, "No, you are not." This answer would be denying that the Captain possessed the exalted attribute he had claimed for himself, but it would not be denying his existence. It would not be "taking him away." Similarly, the believer in the infinite series is not "taking *A* away." He is taking away the privileged status of *A;* he is taking away its "first causiness." He does not deny the existence of *A* or of any particular member of the series. He denies that *A* or anything else *is the first member* of the series. Since he is not taking *A* away, he is not taking *B* away, and thus he is also not taking *X, Y,* or *Z* away. His view, then, does not commit him to the absurdity that nothing exists now, or more specifically, that Margaret Truman does not exist now. It may be noted in this connection that a believer in the infinite series it not necessarily denying the existence of supernatural beings. He is merely committed to denying that such a being, if it exists, is uncaused. He is committed to holding that whatever other impressive attributes a supernatural being might possess, the attribute of being a first cause is not among them.

The causal argument is open to several other objections. Thus, even if otherwise valid, the argument would not prove a *single* first cause. For there does not seem to be any good ground for supposing that the various causal series in the universe ultimately merge. Hence even if it is granted that no series of causes can be infinite the possibility of a plurality of first members has not been ruled out. Nor does the argument establish the *present* existence of the first cause. It does not prove this, since experience clearly shows that an effect may exist long after its cause has been destroyed.

III

Many defenders of the causal argument would contend that at least some of these criticisms rest on a misunderstanding. They would probably go further and contend that the argument was not quite fairly stated in the first place—or at any rate that if it was fair to some of its adherents it was not fair to others. They would in this connection distinguish between two types of causes—what they call "causes *in fieri*" and what they call "causes *in esse*." A cause *in fieri* is a factor which brought or helped to bring an effect into existence. A cause *in esse* is a factor which "sustains" or helps to sustain the effect "in being." The parents of a human being would be an example of a cause *in fieri.* If somebody puts a book in my hand and I keep holding it up, his putting it there would be the cause *in fieri,* and my holding it would be the cause *in esse* of the book's position. To quote Father [G. H.] Joyce:

> If a smith forges a horse-shoe, he is only a cause *in fieri* of the shape given to the iron. That shape persists after his action has ceased. So, too, a builder is a cause *in fieri* of the house which he builds. In both cases the substances employed act as causes *in esse* as regards the continued existence of the effect produced. Iron, in virtue of its natural rigidity, retains in being the shape which it has once received; and, similarly, the materials employed in building retain in being the order and arrangement which constitute them into a house.[2]

2. *The Principles of Natural Theology,* p. 58.

Using this distinction, the defender of the argument now reasons in the following way. To say that there is an infinite series of causes *in fieri* does not lead to any absurd conclusions. But Aquinas is concerned only with causes *in esse* and an infinite series of *such* causes is impossible. In the words of the contemporary American Thomist, R. P. Phillips:

> Each member of the series of causes possesses being solely by virtue of the actual present operation of a superior cause. . . . Life is dependent, *inter alia,* on a certain atmospheric pressure, this again on the continual operation of physical forces, whose being and operation depends on the position of the earth in the solar system, which itself must endure relatively unchanged, a state of being which can only be continuously produced by a definite—if unknown—constitution of the material universe. This constitution, however, cannot be its own cause. That a thing should cause itself is impossible: for in order that it may cause it is necessary for it to exist, which it cannot do, on the hypothesis, until it has been caused. So it must *be* in order to cause itself. Thus, not being uncaused nor yet its own cause, it must be caused by another, which produces and preserves it. It is plain, then, that as no member of this series possesses being except in virtue of the actual present operation of a superior cause, if there be no first cause actually operating none of the dependent causes could operate either. We are thus irresistibly led to posit a first efficient cause which, while itself uncaused, shall impart causality to a whole series. . . .
>
> The series of cause which we are considering is not one which stretches back into the past; so that we are not demanding a beginning of the world at some definite moment reckoning back from the present, but an actual cause now operating, to account for the present being of things.[3]

3. *Modern Thomistic Philosophy,* Vol. II, pp. 284–85.

Professor Phillips offers the following parallel to bring out his point:

> In a goods train each truck is moved and moves by the action of the one immediately in front of it. If then we suppose the train to be infinite, i.e. that there is no end to it, and so no engine which starts the motion, it is plain that no truck will move. To lengthen it out to infinity will not give it what no member of it possesses of itself, viz, the power of drawing the truck behind it. If then we see any truck in motion we know there must be an end to the series of trucks which gives causality to the whole.[4]

Father Joyce introduces an illustration from Aquinas to explain how the present existence of things may be compatible with an infinite series of causes *in fieri* but not with an infinite series of causes *in esse.*

> When a carpenter is at work, the series of efficient causes on which his work depends is necessarily limited. The final effect, e.g. the fastening of a nail is caused by a hammer: the hammer is moved by the arm: and the motion of his arm is determined by the motor-impulses communicated from the nerve centres of the brain. Unless the subordinate causes were limited in number, and were connected with a starting-point of motion, the hammer must remain inert; and the nail will never be driven in. If the series be supposed infinite, no work will ever take place. But if there is question of causes on which the work is not essentially dependent, we cannot draw the same conclusion. We may suppose the carpenter to have broken an infinite number of hammers, and as often to have replaced the broken tool by a fresh one. There is nothing in such a supposition which excludes the driving home of the nail.

The supporter of the infinite series of causes, Joyce also remarks, is

4. Ibid., p. 278.

> . . . asking us to believe that although each link in a suspended chain is prevented from falling simply because it is attached to the one above it, yet if only the chain be long enough, it will, taken as a whole, need no support, but will hang loose in the air suspended from nothing.

This formulation of the causal argument unquestionably circumvents one of the objections mentioned previously. If *Y* is the cause *in esse* of an effect, *Z,* then it must exist as long as *Z* exists. If the argument were valid in this form it would therefore prove the present and not merely the past existence of a first cause. In this form the argument is, however, less convincing in another respect. To maintain that all "natural" or "phenomenal" objects—things like tables and mountains and human beings—require a cause *in fieri* is not implausible, though even here Mill and others have argued that strictly speaking only *changes* require a causal explanation. It is far from plausible, on the other hand, to claim that all natural objects require a cause *in esse.* It may be granted that the air around us is a cause *in esse* of human life and further that certain gravitational forces are among the causes *in esse* of the air being where it is. But when we come to gravitational forces or, at any rate, to material particles like atoms or electrons it is difficult to see what cause *in esse* they require. To those not already convinced of the need for a supernatural First Cause some of the remarks by Professor Phillips in this connection appear merely dogmatic and question-begging. Most people would grant that such particles as atoms did not cause themselves, since, as Professor Phillips observes, they would in that event have had to exist before they began existing. It is not at all evident, however, that these particles cannot be uncaused. Professor Phillips and all other supporters of the causal argument immediately proceed to claim that there is something else which needs no cause *in esse.* They themselves admit thus, that there is nothing self-evident about the proposition that everything must have a cause *in esse.* Their entire procedure here lends substance to Schopenhauer's gibe that supporters of the cosmological argument treat the law of universal causation like "a hired cab which we dismiss when we have reached our destination."

But waiving this and all similar objections, the restatement of the argument in terms of causes *in esse* in no way avoids the main difficulty which was previously mentioned. A believer in the infinite series would insist that his position was just as much misrepresented now as before. He is no more removing the member of the series which is supposed to be the first cause *in esse* than he was removing the member which had been declared to be the first cause *in fieri.* He is again merely denying a privileged status to it. He is not denying the reality of the cause *in esse* labelled "A." He is not even necessarily denying that it possesses supernatural attributes. He is again merely taking away its "first causiness."

The advocates of the causal argument in either form seem to confuse an infinite series with one which is long but finite. If a book, *Z,* is to remain in its position, say 100 miles up in the air, there must be another object, say another book, *Y,* underneath it to serve as its support. If *Y* is to remain where it is, it will need another support, *X,* beneath it. Suppose that this series of supports, one below the other, continues for a long time, but eventually, say after 100,000 members, comes to a first book which is not resting on any other book or indeed on any other support. In that event the whole collection would come crashing down. What we seem to need is a first member of the series, a first support (such as the earth) which does not need another member as *its* support, which in other words is "self-supporting."

This is evidently the sort of picture that supporters of the First Cause argument have before their minds when they rule out the possibility of an infinite series. But such a picture is not a fair representation of the theory of the infinite series. A *finite* series of books would indeed come crashing down, since the first or lowest member would not have a predecessor on which it could be supported. If the series, however, were infinite this would not be the case. In that event every member *would* have a predecessor to support itself on and there would be no crash. That is to say: a crash can be avoided either by a finite series with a first self-supporting member or by an infinite series. Similarly, the present existence of motion is equally compatible with the theory of a first unmoved mover and with the theory of an infinite series of moving objects; and the present existence of causal activity is compatible with the theory of a first cause *in esse* as much as with the theory of an infinite series of such causes.

The illustrations given by Joyce and Phillips are hardly to the point. It is true that a carpenter would not, *in a finite time-span*, succeed in driving in a nail if he had to carry out an infinite number of movements. For that matter, he would not accomplish this goal in a finite time if he broke an infinite number of hammers. However,

The Anthropic Principle

John D. Barrow and Frank J. Tipler

The central problem of science and epistemology is deciding which postulates to take as fundamental. The perennial solution of the great idealistic philosophers has been to regard Mind as logically prior, and even materialistic philosophers consider the innate properties of matter to be such as to allow—or even require—the existence of intelligence to contemplate it; that is, these properties are necessary or sufficient for life. Thus the existence of Mind is taken as one of the basic postulates of a philosophical system. . . . [D]uring the past fifteen years there has grown up amongst cosmologists an interest in a collection of ideas, known as the Anthropic Cosmological Principle, which offer a means of relating Mind and observership directly to the phenomena traditionally within the encompass of physical science.

The expulsion of Man from his self-assumed position at the centre of Nature owes much to the Copernican principle that we do not occupy a privileged position in the Universe. This Copernican assumption would be regarded as axiomatic at the outset of most scientific investigations. However, like most generalizations it must be used with care. Although we do not regard our position in the Universe to be central or special in every way, this does not mean that it cannot be special in *any* way. This 'Anthropic Principle' . . . [is that] *The Universe must have those properties which allow life to develop within it at some stage in its history.*

An implication . . . is that the constants and laws of Nature must be such that life can exist. This speculative statement leads to a number of quite distinct interpretations of a radical nature: firstly, the most obvious is to continue in the tradition of the classical Design Arguments and claim that:

> (A) *There exists one possible Universe 'designed' with the goal of generating and sustaining 'observers'.*

This view would have been supported by the natural theologians of past centuries, . . . [The physicist John Archibald] Wheeler has a second possible interpretation . . . :

> (B) *Observers are necessary to bring the Universe into being.*

This statement is somewhat reminiscent of the outlook of Bishop Berkeley and we shall see that it has physical content when considered in the light of attempts to arrive at a satisfactory interpretation of quantum mechanics.

From *The Anthropic Cosmological Principle* (1986).

to make the illustrations relevant we must suppose that he has infinite time at his disposal. In that case he would succeed in driving in the nail even if he required an infinite number of movements for this purpose. As for the goods train, it may be granted that the trucks do not move unless the train has an engine. But this illustration is totally irrelevant as it stands. A relevant illustration would be that of engines, each moved by the one in front of it. Such a train would move if it were infinite. For every member of this series there would be one in front capable of drawing it along. The advocate of the infinite series of causes does not, as the original illustration suggests, believe in a series whose members are not really causally connected with one another. In the series he believes in every member is genuinely the cause of the one that follows it.

IV

No staunch defender of the cosmological argument would give up at this stage. Even if there were an infinite series of causes *in fieri* or *in esse,* he would contend, this still would not do away with the need for an ultimate, a first cause. As Father Copleston put it in his debate with Bertrand Russell:

> Every object has a phenomenal cause, if you insist on the infinity of the series. But the series of phenomenal causes is an insufficient explanation of the series. Therefore, the series has not a phenomenal cause, but a transcendent cause. . . .
>
> An infinite series of contingent beings will be to my way of thinking, as unable to cause itself as one contingent being.

The demand to find the cause of the series as a whole rests on the erroneous assumption that the series is something over and above the members of which it is composed. It is tempting to suppose this, at least by implication, because the word "series" is a noun like "dog" or "man". Like the expression "this dog" or "this man" the phrase "this series" is easily taken to designate an individual object. But reflection shows this to be an error. If we have explained the individual members there is nothing additional left to be explained. Supposing I see a group of five Eskimos standing on the corner of Sixth Avenue and 50th Street and I wish to explain why the group came to New York, investigation reveals the following stories:

> Eskimo No. 1 did not enjoy the extreme cold in the polar region and decided to move to a warmer climate.
>
> No. 2 is the husband of Eskimo No. 1. He loves her dearly and did not wish to live without her.
>
> No. 3 is the son of Eskimos 1 and 2. He is too small and too weak to oppose his parents.
>
> No. 4 saw an advertisement in the *New York Times* for an Eskimo to appear on television.
>
> No. 5 is a private detective engaged by the Pinkerton Agency to keep an eye on Eskimo No. 4.

Let us assume that we have now explained in the case of each of the five Eskimos why he or she is in New York. Somebody then asks: "All right, but what about the group as a whole; why is *it* in New York?" This would plainly be an absurd question. There is no group over and above the five members, and if we have explained why each of the five members is in New York we have *ipso facto* explained why the group is there. It is just as absurd to ask for the cause of the series as a whole as distinct from asking for the causes of individual members.

V

It is most unlikely that a determined defender of the cosmological line of reasoning would surrender even here. He would probably admit that the series is not a thing over and above its members and that it does not make sense to ask for the cause of the series if the cause of each member has already been found. He would insist, however, that when he asked for the explanation of the entire series, he was not asking for its *cause*. He was really saying that a series, finite or infinite, is not "intelligible" or "explained" if it consists of nothing but "contingent" members. To quote Father Copleston once more:

> What we call the world is intrinsically unintelligible apart from the existence of God. The infinity of the series of events, if such an infinity could be proved, would not be in the slightest degree relevant to the situation. If you add up chocolates, you get chocolates after all, and not a sheep. If you add up chocolates to infinity, you presumably get an infinite number of chocolates. So, if you add up contingent beings to infinity, you still get contingent beings, not a necessary being.

This last quotation is really a summary of the "contingency argument," the other main form of the cosmological proof and the third of the five ways of Aquinas. It may be stated more fully in these words: All around us we perceive contingent beings. This includes all physical objects and also all human minds. In calling them "contingent" we mean that they might not have existed. We mean that the universe can be *conceived* without this or that physical object, without this or that human being, however certain their actual existence may be. These contingent beings we can trace back to other contingent beings—e.g. a human being to his parents. However, since these other beings are also contingent, they do not provide a real or full explanation. The contingent beings we originally wanted explained have not yet become intelligible, since the beings to which they have been traced back are no more necessary than they were. It is just as true of our parents, for example, as it is of ourselves, that they might not have existed. We can then properly explain the contingent beings around us only by tracing them back ultimately to some necessary being, to something which exists necessarily, which has "the reason for its existence within itself." The existence of contingent beings, in other words, implies the existence of a necessary being.

This form of cosmological argument is even more beset with difficulties than the causal variety. In the first place, there is the objection, stated with great force by Kant, that it really commits the same error as the ontological argument in tacitly regarding existence as an attribute or characteristic. To say that there is a necessary being is to say that it would be a self-contradiction to deny its existence. This would mean that at least one existential statement is a necessary truth; and this in turn presupposes that in at least one case existence is contained in a concept. But only a characteristic can be contained in a concept and it has seemed plain to most philosophers since Kant that existence is not a characteristic, that it can hence never be contained in a concept, and that hence no existential statement can ever be a necessary truth. To talk about anything "existing necessarily" is in their view about as sensible as to talk about round squares, and they have concluded that the contingency-argument is quite absurd.

It would lead too far to discuss here the reasons for denying that existence is a characteristic. I will assume that this difficulty can somehow be surmounted and that the expression "necessary being," as it is intended by the champions of the contingency-argument, might conceivably apply to something. There remain other objections which are of great weight. I shall try to state these by first quoting again from the debate between Bertrand Russell and Father Copleston:

RUSSELL: . . . It all turns on this question of sufficient reason, and I must say you haven't defined "sufficient reason" in a way that I can understand—what do you mean by sufficient reason? You don't mean cause?

COPLESTON: Not necessarily. Cause is a kind of sufficient reason. Only contingent being can have a cause. God is his own sufficient reason; and he is not cause of himself. By sufficient reason in the full sense I mean an explanation adequate for the existence of some particular being.

RUSSELL: But when is an explanation adequate? Suppose I am about to make a flame with a match. You may say that the adequate explanation of that is that I rub it on the box.

COPLESTON: Well for practical purposes—but theoretically, that is only a partial explanation. An adequate explanation must ultimately be a total explanation, to which nothing further can be added.

RUSSELL: Then I can only say that you're looking for something which can't be got, and which one ought not to expect to get.

COPLESTON: To say that one has not found it is one thing; to say that one should not look for it seems to me rather dogmatic.

RUSSELL: Well, I don't know. I mean, the explanation of one thing is another thing which makes the other thing dependent on yet another, and you have to grasp this sorry scheme of things entire to do what you want, and that we can't do.

Russell's main point here may be expanded in the following way. The contingency-argument rests on a misconception of what an explanation is and does, and similarly on what it is that makes phenomena "intelligible." Or else it involves an obscure and arbitrary redefinition of "explanation," "intelligible," and related terms. Normally, we are satisfied that we have explained a phenomenon if we have found its cause or if we have exhibited some other uniform or near-uniform connection between it and something else. Confining ourselves to the former case, which is probably the most common, we might say that a phenomenon, *Z,* has been explained if it has been traced back to a group of factors, *a, b, c, d,* etc., which are its cause. These factors are the full and real explanation of *Z,* quite regardless of whether they are pleasing or displeasing, admirable or contemptible, necessary or contingent. The explanation would not be adequate only if the factors listed are not really the cause of *Z.* If they are the cause of *Z,* the explanation would be adequate, even though each of the factors is merely a "contingent" being.

Let us suppose that we have been asked to explain why General Eisenhower won the elections of 1952. "He was an extremely popular general," we might answer, "while Stevenson was relatively little known; moreover there was a great deal of resentment over the scandals in the Truman Administration." If somebody complained that this was only a partial explanation we might mention additional antecedents, such as the widespread belief that the Democrats had allowed communist agents to infiltrate the State Department, that Eisenhower was a man with a winning smile, and that unlike Stevenson he had shown the good sense to say one thing on race relations in the North and quite another in the South. Theoretically, we might go further and list the motives of all American voters during the weeks or months preceding the elections. If we could do this we would have explained Eisenhower's victory. We would have made it intelligible. We would "understand" why he won and why Stevenson lost. Perhaps there is a sense in which we might make Eisenhower's victory even more intelligible if we went further back and discussed such matters as the origin of American views on Communism or of racial attitudes in the North and South. However, to explain the outcome of the election in any ordinary sense, loose or strict, it would not be necessary to go back to prehistoric days or to the amoeba or to a first cause, if such a first cause exists. Nor would our explanation be considered in any way defective because each of the factors mentioned was a "contingent" and not a necessary being. The only thing that matters is whether the factors were really the cause of Eisenhower's election. If they were, then it has been explained although they are contingent beings. If they were not the cause of Eisenhower's victory, we would have failed to explain it even if each of the factors were a necessary being.

If it is granted that, in order to explain a phenomenon or to make it intelligible, we need not bring in a necessary being, then the contingency argument breaks down. For a series, as was already pointed out, is not something over and above its members; and every contingent member of it could in that case be explained by reference to other contingent beings. But I should wish to go further than this and it is evident from Russell's remarks that he would do so also. Even if it were granted, both that the phrase "necessary being" is meaningful and that all explanations are defective unless the phenomena to be explained are traced back to a necessary being, the conclusion would still not have been established. The conclusion follows from this premise together with the additional premise that *there are* explanations of phenomena in the special sense just mentioned. It is this further premise which Russell (and many other philosophers) would question. They do not merely question, as Copleston implies, whether human beings can ever obtain explanations in this sense, but whether they *exist.* To assume without further ado that phenomena have explanations or an explanation in this sense is to beg the very point at issue. The use of the same word 'explanation' in two crucially different ways lends the additional premise a plausibility it does not really possess. It may indeed be highly plausible to assert that phenomena have explanations, whether we have found them or not, in the ordinary sense in which this usually means that they have causes. It is then tempting to suppose, because of the use of the same word, that they also have explanations in a sense in which this implies dependence on a necessary being. But this is a gross *non sequitur.*

VI

It is necessary to add a few words about the proper way of formulating the position of those

"Is the Universe a 'Free Lunch'?"

Paul Davies

We can . . . construct a cosmic scenario that reveals the astonishing scope of the new physics to explain the physical world. . . . Recent discoveries in particle physics have suggested mechanisms whereby matter can be created in empty space by the cosmic gravitational field, which only leaves the origin of spacetime itself as a mystery. But even here there are some indications that space and time could have sprung into existence spontaneously without violating the laws of physics. . . .In this remarkable scenario, the entire cosmos simply comes out of nowhere, completely in accordance with the laws of quantum physics, and creates along the way all the matter and energy needed to build the universe we now see. It thus incorporates the creation of all physical things, including space and time. Rather than postulate an unknowable singularity to start the universe off, the quantum spacetime model attempts to explain everything entirely within the context of the laws of physics. It is an awesome claim. We are used to the idea of 'putting something in and getting something out', but getting something for nothing (or out of nothing) is alien. Yet the world of quantum physics routinely produces something for nothing. Quantum gravity suggests we might get everything for nothing. Discussing this scenario, the physicist Alan Guth remarked: 'It is often said that there is no such thing as a free lunch. The universe, however, is a free lunch.'

Does such a universe model have any need for God? . . . The 'free lunch' scenario claims that all you need are the laws — the universe can take care of itself, including its own creation.

From *God and the New Physics* (1983).

The so-called Pyramid of the Moon in Teotihuacán, near Mexico City. Situated at the end of an avenue lined with pyramids and other sacred buildings. Teotihuacán flourished from 100 B.C. to about 700 A.D.

who reject the main premise of the cosmological argument, in either of the forms we have considered. It is sometimes maintained in this connection that in order to reach a "self-existing" entity it is not necessary to go beyond the universe: the universe itself (or "Nature") is "self-existing." And this in turn is sometimes expanded into the statement that while all individual things "within" the universe are caused, the universe itself is uncaused. Statements of this kind are found in Büchner, Bradlaugh, Haeckel, and other free-thinkers of the nineteenth and early twentieth century. Sometimes the assertion that the universe is "self-existing" is elaborated to mean that *it* is the "necessary being." Some eighteenth-century unbelievers, apparently accepting the view that there is a necessary being, asked why Nature or the material universe could not fill the bill as well as or better than God.

> "Why," asks one of the characters in Hume's *Dialogues,* "may not the material universe be the necessarily existent Being? . . . We dare not affirm that we know all the qualities of matter; and for aught we can determine, it may contain some qualities, which, were they known, would make its nonexistence appear as great a contradiction as that twice two is five."

Similar remarks can be found in Holbach and several of the Encyclopedists.

The former of these formulations immediately invites the question why the universe, alone of all "things," is exempted from the universal sway of causation. "The strong point of the cosmological argument," writes Dr. Ewing, "is that after all it does remain incredible that the physical universe should just have happened . . . It calls out for some further explanation of some kind." The latter formulation is exposed to the criticism that there is nothing any more "necessary" about the existence of the universe or Nature as a whole than about any particular thing within the universe.

I hope some of the earlier discussions in this article have made it clear that in rejecting the cosmological argument one is not committed to either of these propositions. If I reject the view that there is a supernatural first cause, I am not thereby committed to the proposition that there is a *natural* first cause, and even less to the proposition that a mysterious "thing" called "the universe" qualifies for this title. I may hold that there is no "universe" over and above individual things of various sorts; and, accepting the causal principle, I may proceed to assert that all these things are caused by other things, and these other things by yet other things, and so on, *ad infinitum*. In this way no arbitrary exception is made to the principle of causation. Similarly, if I reject the assertion that God is a "necessary being," I am not committed to the view that the universe is such an entity. I may hold that it does not make sense to speak of anything as a "necessary being' and that even if there were such a thing as the universe it could not be properly considered a necessary being.

However, in saying that nothing is uncaused or that there is no necessary being, one is not committed to the view that everything, or for that matter anything, is merely a "brute fact." Dr. Ewing laments that "the usual modern philosophical views opposed to theism do not try to give any rational explanation of the world at all, but just take it as a brute fact not to be explained." They thus fail to "rationalize" the universe. Theism, he concedes, cannot completely rationalize things either since it does not show "how God can be his own cause or how it is that he does not need a cause." Now, if one means by "brute fact" something for which there *exists* no explanation (as distinct from something for which no explanation is in our possession), then the theists have at least one brute fact on their hands, namely God. Those who adopt Büchner's formulation also have one brute fact on their hands, namely "the universe." Only the position I have been supporting dispenses with brute facts altogether. I don't know if this is any special virtue, but the defenders of the cosmological argument seem to think so.

William Paley

"THE COSMIC WATCHMAKER"

WILLIAM PALEY (1743–1805), archdeacon of Carlisle, was one of the most influential apologists for Christianity in the nineteenth century. Before he became a minister in the Church of England, he taught philosophy at Cambridge University. His liberal political and religious views and acts (he worked, for instance, for the abolition of the slave trade) kept him from achieving higher office in the church. His most influential work is *Natural Theology, or Evidences of the Existence and Attributes of the Deity Collected from the Appearances of Nature* (1802).

STATEMENT OF THE ARGUMENT

In crossing a heath, suppose I pitched my foot against a *stone,* and were asked how the stone came to be there, I might possibly answer, that, for anything I knew to the contrary, it had lain there for ever; nor would it, perhaps, be very easy to show the absurdity of this answer. But suppose I found a *watch* upon the ground, and it should be inquired how the watch happened to be in that place, I should hardly think of the answer which I had given—that, for anything I knew, the watch might have always been there. Yet why should not this answer serve for the watch as well as for the stone? why is it not as admissible in the second case as in the first? For this reason, and for no other; viz., that, when we come to inspect the watch, we perceive (what we could not discover in the stone) that its several parts are framed and put together for a purpose, e.g., that they are so formed and adjusted as to produce motion, and that motion so regulated as to point out the hour of the day; that, if the different parts had been differently shaped from what they are, if a different size from what they are, or placed after any other manner, or in any other order than that in which they are placed, either no motion at all would have been carried on in the machine, or none which would have answered the use that is now served by it. To reckon up a few of the plainest of these parts, and of their offices, all tending to one result:—We see a cylindrical box containing a coiled elastic spring, which, by its endeavor to relax itself, turns round the box. We next observe a flexible chain (artificially wrought for the sake of flexure) communicating the action of the spring from the box to the fusee. We then find a series of wheels, the teeth of which catch in, and apply to, each other, conducting the motion from the fusee to the balance, and from the balance to the pointer, and, at the same time, by the size and shape of those wheels, so regulating that motion as to terminate in causing an index, by an equable and measured progression, to pass over a given space in a given time. We take notice that the wheels are made of brass, in order to keep them from rust; the springs of steel, no other metal being so elastic; that over the face of the watch there is placed a glass, a material employed in no other part of the work, but in the room of which, if there had been any other than a transparent substance, the hour could not be seen without opening the case. This mechanism being observed, (it requires indeed an examination of the instrument, and perhaps some previous knowledge of the subject, to perceive and understand it; but being once, as we have said, observed and understood,) the inference, we think, is inevitable, that the watch must have had a maker; that there must have existed, at some time, and at some place or other, an artificer or artificers who formed it for the purpose which we find it actually to answer; who comprehended its construction, and designed its use.

I. Nor would it, I apprehend, weaken the conclusion, that we had never seen a watch made; that we had never known an artist capable of making one; that we were altogether incapable of executing such a piece of workmanship ourselves, or of understanding in what manner it was performed; all this being no more than what is true of some exquisite remains of ancient art, of some lost arts, and, to the generality of mankind, of the more curious productions of modern manufacture. Does one man in a million know how oval frames are turned? Ignorance of this kind exalts our opinion of the unseen and unknown artist's skill, if he be unseen and unknown, but raises no doubt in our minds of the existence and agency of such an artist, at some former time, and in some place or other. Nor can I perceive that it varies at all the inference, whether the question arise concerning a human agent, or concerning an agent of a different spe-

From William Paley, *Natural Theology, or Evidences of the Existence and Attributes of the Deity Collected from the Appearances of Nature.* First published in 1802.

cies, or an agent possessing, in some respect, a different nature.

II. Neither, secondly, would it invalidate our conclusion, that the watch sometimes went wrong, or that it seldom went exactly right. The purpose of the machinery, the design, and the designer, might be evident, and, in the case supposed, would be evident, in whatever way we accounted for the irregularity of the movement, or whether we could account for it or not. It is not necessary that a machine be perfect, in order to show with what design it was made; still less necessary, where the only question is, whether it were made with any design at all.

III. Nor, thirdly, would it bring any uncertainty into the argument, if there were a few parts of the watch, concerning which we could not discover, or had not yet discovered, in what manner they conduced to the general effect; or even some parts, concerning which we could not ascertain whether they conduced to that effect in any manner whatever. For, as to the first branch of the case, if by the loss, or disorder, or decay of the parts in question, the movement of the watch were found in fact to be stopped, or disturbed, or retarded, no doubt would remain in our minds as to the utility or intention of these parts, although we should be unable to investigate the manner according to which, or the connection by which, the ultimate effect depended upon their action or assistance; and the more complex is the machine, the more likely is this obscurity to arise. Then, as to the second thing supposed, namely, that there were parts which might be spared without prejudice to the movement of the watch, and that he had proved this by experiment, these superfluous parts, even if we were completely assured that they were such, would not vacate the reasoning which we had instituted concerning other parts. The indication of contrivance remained, with respect to them, nearly as it was before.

IV. Nor, fourthly, would any man in his senses think the existence of the watch, with its various machinery, accounted for, by being told that it was one of possible combinations of material forms; that whatever he had found in the place where he found the watch, must have contained some internal configuration or other; and that this configuration might be the structure now exhibited, viz., of the works of a watch, as well as a different structure.

V. Nor, fifthly, would it yield his inquiry more satisfaction, to be answered, that there existed in things a principle of order, which had disposed the parts of the watch into their present form and situation. He never knew a watch made by the principle of order; nor can he even form to himself an idea of what is meant by a principle of order, distinct from the intelligence of the watchmaker.

VI. Sixthly, he would be surprised to hear that the mechanism of the watch was no proof of contrivance, only a motive to induce the mind to think so:

VII. And not less surprised to be informed, that the watch in his hand was nothing more than the result of the laws of *metallic* nature. It is a perversion of language to assign any law as the efficient, operative cause of anything. A law presupposes an agent; for it is only the mode according to which an agent proceeds; it implies a power; for it is the order according to which that power acts. Without this agent, without this power, which are both distinct from itself, the *law* does nothing, is nothing. The expression, "the law of metallic nature," may sound strange and harsh to a philosophic ear; but it seems quite as justifiable as some others which are more familiar to him such as "the law of vegetable nature," "the law of animal nature," or, indeed, as "the law of nature" in general, when assigned as the cause of phenomena in exclusion of agency and power, or when it is substituted into the place of these.

VIII. Neither, lastly, would our observer be driven out of his conclusion, or from his confidence in its truth, by being told that he knew nothing at all about the matter. He knows enough for his argument: he knows the utility of the end: he knows the subserviency and adaptation of the means to the end. These points being

The center stairway of the temple of Guetzalcoatl, "The Feathered Serpent," in Teotihuacán, Mexico.

known, his ignorance of other points, his doubts concerning other points, affect not the certainty of his reasoning. The consciousness of knowing little need not beget a distrust of that which he does know. . . .

APPLICATION OF THE ARGUMENT

Every indication of contrivance, every manifestation of design, which existed in the watch, exists in the works of nature; with the difference, on the side of nature, of being greater and more, and that in a degree which exceeds all computation. I mean that the contrivances of nature surpass the contrivances of art, in the complexity, subtilty, and curiosity of the mechanism; and still more, if possible, do they go beyond them in number and variety; yet in a multitude of cases, are not less evidently mechanical, not less evidently contrivances, not less evidently accommodated to their end, or suited to their office, than are the most perfect productions of human ingenuity. . . .

St. Anselm

"THE ONTOLOGICAL ARGUMENT"

ST. ANSELM (1033–1109), archbishop of Canterbury, formulated the ontological argument, one of the most famous of the classical arguments for the existence of God. After studying at Avranches in Burgundy and at Bec, then the leading center of learning in Europe, he entered the Benedictine order and became abbot at the Monastery of Bec. His most important philosophical works are *Monologion* (1076), in which he advances both the argument from design and the cosmological argument, and *Proslogion* (1077–1078), in which he presents the ontological argument.

. . . I began to ask myself whether there might be found a single argument which would require no other for its proof than itself alone; and alone would suffice to demonstrate that God truly exists, and that there is a supreme good requiring nothing else, which all other things require for their existence and well-being; and whatever we believe regarding the divine Being.

Although I often and earnestly directed my thought to this end, and at some times that which I sought seemed to be just within my reach, while again it wholly evaded my mental vision, at last in despair I was about to cease, as if from the search for a thing which could not be found. But when I wished to exclude this thought altogether, lest, by busying my mind to no purpose, it should keep me from other thoughts, in which I might be successful; then more and more, though I was unwilling and shunned it, it began to force itself upon me, with a kind of importunity. So, one day, when I was exceedingly wearied with resisting its importunity, in the very conflict of my thoughts, the proof of which I had despaired offered itself, so that I eagerly embraced the thoughts which I was strenuously repelling.

And so Lord, do thou, who dost give understanding to faith, give me, so far as thou knowest it to be profitable, to understand that thou art as we believe; and that thou art that which we believe. And, indeed, we believe that thou art a being than which nothing greater can be conceived. Or is there no such nature, since the fool hath said in his heart, there is no God? But, at any rate, this very fool, when he hears of this being of which I speak—a being than which nothing greater can be conceived—understands what he hears, and what he understands is in his understanding; although he does not understand it to exist.

For, it is one thing for an object to be in the understanding, and another to understand that the object exists. When a painter first conceives of what he will afterwards perform, he has it in his understanding, but he does not yet understand it to be, because he has not yet performed it. But after he had made the painting, he both has it in his understanding, and he understands that it exists, because he has made it.

From the *Proslogium,* S. N. Deane trans., Open Court, 1903.

Hence, even the fool is convinced that something exists in the understanding, at least, than which nothing greater can be conceived. For, when he hears of this, he understands it. And whatever is understood, exists in the understanding. And assuredly that, than which nothing greater can be conceived, cannot exist in the understanding alone. For, suppose it exists in the understanding alone: then it can be conceived to exist in reality; which is greater.

Therefore, if that, than which nothing greater can be conceived, exists in the understanding alone, the very being, than which nothing greater can be conceived, is one, than which a greater can be conceived. But obviously this is impossible. Hence, there is no doubt that there exists a being, than which nothing greater can be conceived, and it exists both in the understanding and in reality.

And it assuredly exists so truly, that it cannot be conceived not to exist. For, it is possible to conceive of a being which cannot be conceived not to exist, and this is greater than one which can be conceived not to exist. Hence, if that, than which nothing greater can be conceived, can be conceived not to exist, it is not that, than which nothing greater can be conceived. But this is an irreconcilable contradiction. There is, then, so truly a being than which nothing greater can be conceived to exist, that it cannot even be conceived not to exist; and this being thou art, O Lord, our God.

So truly, therefore, doest thou exist, O Lord, my God, that thou canst not be conceived not to exist; and rightly. For if a mind could conceive of a being better than thee, the creature would rise above the Creator; and this is most absurd. And, indeed, whatever else there is, except thee alone, can be conceived not to exist. To thee alone, therefore, it belongs to exist more truly than all other beings, and hence in a higher degree than all others. For, whatever else exists does not exist so truly, and hence in a less degree it belongs to it to exist. Why, then, has the fool said in his heart, there is no God, since it is so evident, to a rational mind, that thou dost exist in the highest degree of all? Why, except that he is dull and a fool?

Chalchiuhtlicue, "The Water Goddess," in Teotihuacán, Mexico.

IN BEHALF OF THE FOOL

An Answer to the Argument of Anselm by Gaunilon, a Monk of Marmoutier

. . . if it should be said that a being which cannot be even conceived in terms of any fact, is in the understanding, I do not deny that this being is, accordingly, in my understanding. But since through this fact it can in no wise attain to real existence also, I do not yet concede to it that existence at all, until some certain proof of it shall be given.

For he who says that this being exists, because otherwise the being which is greater than all will not be greater than all, does not attend strictly to what he is saying. For I do not yet say, no, I even deny or doubt that this being is greater than any real object. Nor do I concede to it any other existence than this (if it should be called existence) which it has when the mind, according to a word merely heard, tries to form the image of an object absolutely unknown to it.

How, then, is the veritable existence of that being proved to me from the assumption, by hypothesis, that it is greater than all other beings? For I should still deny this, or doubt your demonstration of it, to this extent, that I should not admit that this being is in my understanding and concept even in the way in which many objects whose real existence is uncertain and doubtful, are in my understanding and concept. For it should be proved first that this being itself really exists somewhere; and then, from the fact that it is greater than all, we shall not hesitate to infer that it also subsists in itself.

For example: it is said that somewhere in the ocean is an island, which, because of the difficulty, or rather the impossibility, of discovering what does not exist, is called the lost island. And they say that this island has an inestimable wealth of all manner of riches and delicacies in greater abundance than is told of the Islands of the Blest; and that having no owner or inhabitant, it is more excellent than all other countries, which are inhabited by mankind, in the abundance with which it is stored.

Now if someone should tell me that there is such an island, I should easily understand his words, in which there is no difficulty. But suppose that he went on to say, as if by a logical inference: "You can no longer doubt that this island which is more excellent than all lands exists somewhere, since you have no doubt that it is in your understanding. And since it is more excellent not to be in the understanding alone, but to exist both in the understanding and in reality, for this reason it must exist. For if it does not exist, any land which really exists will be more excellent than it; and so the island already understood by you to be more excellent will not be more excellent."

If a man should try to prove to me by such reasoning that this island truly exists, and that its existence should no longer be doubted, either I should believe that he was jesting, or I know not which I ought to regard as the greater fool: myself, supposing that I should allow this proof; or him, if he should suppose that he had established with any certainty the existence of this island. For he ought to show first that the hypothetical excellence of this island exists as a real and indubitable fact, and in no wise as any unreal object, or one whose existence is uncertain, in my understanding.

ANSELM'S REPLY

But, you say, it is as if one should suppose an island in the ocean, which surpasses all lands in its fertility, and which, because of the difficulty, or rather the impossibility, of discovering what does not exist, is called a lost island; and should say that there can be no doubt that this island truly exists in reality, for this reason that one who hears it described easily understands what he hears.

Now I promise confidently that if any man shall devise anything existing either in reality or in concept alone (except that than which a greater cannot be conceived) to which he can adapt the sequence of my reasoning, I will discover that thing, and will give him his lost island, not to be lost again.

But it now appears that this being than which a greater is inconceivable cannot be conceived not to be, because it exists on so assured a ground of truth; for otherwise it would not exist at all.

Hence, if any one says that he conceives this being not to exist, I say that at the time when he conceives of this either he conceives of a being than which a greater is inconceivable, or he does not conceive at all. If he does not conceive, he does not conceive of the nonexistence of that of which he does not conceive. But if he does conceive, he certainly conceives of a being which cannot be even conceived not to exist. For if it could be conceived not to exist, it could be conceived to have a beginning and an end. But this is impossible.

He, then, who conceives of this being conceives of a being which cannot be even conceived not to exist; but he who conceives of this being does not conceive that it does not exist; else he conceives what is inconceivable. The nonexistence, then, of that than which a greater cannot be conceived is inconceivable.

Immanuel Kant

"AGAINST THE ONTOLOGICAL ARGUMENT"

IMMANUEL KANT (1726–1806) was born in East Prussia, where his grandfather had emigrated from Scotland. His *Critique of Pure Reason* (1781) is considered by many philosophers to be the most profound single work of philosophy ever written. He himself considered it a philosophical innovation on a par with the Copernican scientific revolution, arguing in it that space, time, and causality are not fully objective but are to a great extent the product of the human mind.

Kant was the first of the great modern philosophers who earned his living as a university professor. But instead of having his salary set and paid by an administration, he collected it directly from his students! He got into trouble with the Prussian king, Frederick William II, for the "distortion and depreciation of many leading and fundamental doctrines of holy writ and Christianity," and was ordered not to lecture or write further on religious subjects. Kant, who even in ethics was an extreme rationalist and believed that moral principles are objectively valid commands and must be done from a sense of duty, dutifully obeyed the king's order until the king died, when he resumed his writings on these topics.

It is easily perceived, from what has been said before, that the concept of an absolutely necessary Being is a concept of pure reason, that is, a mere idea, the objective reality of which is by no means proved by the fact that reason requires it. That idea does no more than point to a certain but unattainable completeness, and serves rather to limit the understanding, than to extend its sphere. It seems strange and absurd, however, that a conclusion of an absolutely necessary existence from a given existence in general should seem urgent and correct, and that yet all the conditions under which the understanding can form a concept of such a necessity should be entirely against us.

People have at all times been talking of an *absolutely necessary* Being, but they have tried,

From *The Critique of Pure Reason* (1781). A 592–603 = B 620–31, Max Müller trans. (New York: Macmillan, 1896).

not so much to understand whether and how a thing of that kind could even be conceived, as rather to prove its existence. No doubt a verbal definition of that concept is quite easy, if we say that it is something the non-existence of which is impossible. This, however, does not make us much wiser with reference to the conditions that make is necessary to consider the non-existence of a thing as absolutely inconceivable. It is these conditions which we want to know, and whether by that concept we are thinking anything or not. For to use the word *unconditioned,* in order to get rid of all the conditions which the understanding always requires when wishing to conceive something as necessary, does not render it clear to us in the least whether, after that, we are still thinking anything or perhaps nothing, by the concept of the unconditionally necessary.

Nay, more than this, people have imagined that by a number of examples they had explained this concept, at first risked as haphazard, and afterwards become quite familiar, and that therefore all further inquiry regarding its intelligibility were unnecessary. It was said that every proposition of geometry, such as, for instance, that a triangle has three angles, is absolutely necessary, and people began to talk of an object entirely outside the sphere of our understanding, as if they understood perfectly well what, by that concept, they wished to predicate of it.

But all these pretended examples are taken without exception from *judgments* only, not from *things,* and their existence. Now the unconditioned necessity of judgments is not the same thing as an absolute necessity of things. The absolute necessity of a judgment is only a conditioned necessity of the thing, or of the predicate in the judgment. The above proposition did not say that three angles were absolutely necessary, but that under the condition of the existence of a triangle, three angles are given (in it) by necessity. Nevertheless, this pure logical necessity has exerted so powerful an illusion, that, after having formed of a thing a concept *a priori* so constituted that it seemed to include existence in its sphere, people thought they could conclude with certainty that, because existence necessarily belongs to the object of that concept, provided always that I accept the thing as given (existing), its existence also must necessarily be accepted (according to the rule of identity), and that the Being therefore must itself be absolutely necessary, because its existence is implied in a concept, which is accepted voluntarily only, and always under the condition that I accept the object of it as given.

If in an identical judgment I reject the predicate and retain the subject, there arises a contradiction, and hence, I say, that the former belongs to the latter necessarily. But if I reject the subject as well as the predicate, there is no contradiction, because there is nothing left that can be contradicted. To accept a triangle and yet to reject its three angles is contradictory, but there is no contradiction at all in admitting the non-existence of the triangle and of its three angles. The same applies to the concept of an absolutely necessary Being. Remove its existence, and you remove the thing itself, with all its predicates, so that a contradiction becomes impossible. There is nothing external to which the contradiction could apply, because the thing is not meant to be externally necessary; nor is there anything internal that could be contradicted, for in removing the thing out of existence, you have removed at the same time all its internal qualities. If you say, God is almighty, that is a necessary judgment, because almightiness cannot be removed, if you accept a deity, that is, an infinite Being, with the concept of which that other concept is identical. But if you say, God is not, then neither his almightiness, nor any other of his predicates is given; they are all, together with the subject, removed out of existence, and therefore there is not the slightest contradiction in that sentence.

We have seen therefore that, if I remove the predicate of a judgment together with its subject, there can never be an internal contradiction, whatever the predicate may be. The only way of evading this conclusion would be to say that there are subjects which cannot be removed out of existence, but must always remain. But this would be the same as to say that there exist absolutely necessary subjects, an assumption the correctness of which I have called in question, and the possibility of which you had undertaken to prove. For I cannot form to myself the smallest concept of a thing which, if it had been removed together with all its predicates, should leave behind a contradiction; and except contradiction, I have no other test of impossibility by pure concepts *a priori*. Against all these general arguments (which no one can object to) you challenge me with a case, which you represent as a proof by a fact, namely, that there is one, and this one concept only, in which the non-existence or the removal of its object would be self-contradictory, namely, the concept of the most real Being (*ens realissimum*). You say that it possesses all reality, and you are no doubt justified in accepting such a Being as possible. This for the present I may admit, though the absence of self-contradictoriness in a concept is far from proving the possibility of its object.[1] Now reality comprehends existence, and therefore existence is contained in the concept of a thing possible. If that thing is removed, the internal possibility of the thing would be removed, and this is self-contradictory.

[1] A concept is always possible, if it is not self-contradictory. This is the logical characteristic of possibility, and by it the object of the concept is distinguished from the *nihil negatium*. But it may nevertheless be an empty concept, unless the objective reality of the synthesis, by which the concept is generated, has been distinctly shown. This, however, as shown above, must always rest on principles of possible experience, and not on the principle of analysis (the principle of contradiction). This is a warning against inferring at once from the possibility of concepts (logical) the possibility of things (real).

"Proving God"

G. W. F. von Leibniz

31. Our reasons are founded on *two great principles, that of contradiction,* in virtue of which we judge that to be *false* which involves contradiction, and that *true,* which is opposed or contradictory to the false.
32. And *that of sufficient reason,* in virtue of which we hold that no fact can be real or existent, no statement true, unless there be a sufficient reason why it is so and not otherwise, although most often these reasons cannot be known to us.
33. There are also two kinds of truths, those of *reasoning* and those of *fact.* Truths of reasoning are necessary and their opposite is impossible, and those of fact are contingent and their opposite is possible. When a truth is necessary its reason can be found by analysis, resolving it into more simple ideas and truths until we reach those which are primitive. . . .
36. But there must also be a *sufficient reason* for *contingent truths,* or those *of* fact,—that is, for the series of things diffused through the universe of created objects—where the resolution into particular reason might run into a detail without limits, on account of the immense variety of objects and the division of bodies *ad infinitum.*
37. And as all this *detail* only involves other contingents, anterior or more detailed, each one of which needs a like analysis for its explanation, we make no advance: and the sufficient or final reason must be outside of the sequence or *series* of this detail of contingencies, however infinite it may be.
38. And thus it is that the final reason of things must be found in a necessary substance, in which the detail of changes exists only eminently, as in their source; and this it is which we call God.
39. Now this substance, being the sufficient reason of all this detail, which also is linked together throughout, *there is but one God, and this God suffices.*

From *The Monadology* (1714).

I answer: Even in introducing into the concept of a thing, which you wish to think in its possibility only, the concept of its existence, under whatever disguise it may be, you have been guilty of a contradiction. If you were allowed to do this, you would apparently have carried your point; but in reality you have achieved nothing, but have only committed a tautology. I simply ask you, whether the proposition, that *this or that thing* (which, whatever it may be, I grant you as possible) *exists,* is an analytical or a synthetical proposition? If the former, then by its existence you add nothing to your thought of the thing; but in that case, either the thought within you would be the thing itself, or you have presupposed existence, as belonging to possibility, and have according to your own showing deduced existence from internal possibility, which is nothing but a miserable tautology. The mere word *reality,* which in the concept of a thing sounds different from existence in the concept of the predicate, can make no difference. For if you call all accepting or positing (without determining what it is) reality, you have placed a thing, with all its predicates, within the concept of the subject, and accepted it as real, and you do nothing but repeat it in the predicate. If, on the contrary, you admit, as every sensible man must do, that every proposition involving existence is synthetical, how can you say that the predicate of existence does not admit of removal without contradiction, a distinguishing property

Leibniz's God

Although Leibniz disagreed vehemently with Newton on the nature of God, he offered (roughly) the following "proof" of God's existence. Everything you see around you did not, as far as anybody can tell, just pop in from out of nowhere. Nor do things create themselves; everything, as far as we know, comes from something else. In other words, the existence of all things in the cosmos is *contingent,* that is, dependent for its existence on something else. In the case of your own existence, for instance, there is a long causal chain stretching all the way back to as far as time goes, either to the beginning of the cosmos or forever, into infinity. But suppose we ask why this entire series of contingent events, culminating in the present state of the cosmos, which includes you right now reading this book, exists at all? Why isn't there just nothing?

At this point Leibniz relies on his *principle of sufficient reason,* according to which nothing exists without some reason, or prior cause, for its existence. So, once again we ask: Why does the cosmos as a whole exist; why isn't there just nothing? Relying on the principle of sufficient reason, itself suggested in part by our experience of the world, Leibniz claims that what is true of the part is true also of the whole; since nothing within the cosmos, as far as we know, exists without some reason, or prior cause, to explain its existence, the cosmos as a whole must have had some reason, or prior cause, for its existence. This cosmic cause, itself external to the cosmos, must, since it is not dependent

which is peculiar to analytical propositions only, the very character of which depends on it?

I might have hoped to put an end to this subtle argumentation, without many words, and simply by an accurate definition of the concept of existence, if I had not seen that the illusion, in mistaking a logical predicate for a real one (that is the predicate which determines a thing), resists all correction. Everything can become a *logical predicate,* even the subject itself may be predicated of itself, because logic takes no account of any contents of concepts. *Determination,* however, is a predicate, added to the concept of the subject, and enlarging it, and it must not therefore be contained in it.

Being is evidently not a real predicate, or a concept of something that can be added to the concept of a thing. It is merely the admission of a thing, and of certain determinations in it. Logically, it is merely the copula of a judgment. The proposition, *God is almighty,* contains two concepts, each having its object, namely, God and almightiness. The small word *is,* is not an additional predicate, but only serves to put the predicate *in relation* to the subject. If, then, I take the subject (God) with all its predicates (including that of almightiness), and say, *God is,* or there is a God, I do not put a new predicate to the concept of God, but I only put the subject by itself, with all its predicates, in relation to my concept, as its object. Both must contain exactly the same kind of thing, and nothing can

on anything in the cosmos for its existence, be noncontingent: That is, whatever brought about the cosmos must exist not contingently,but, rather, *necessarily.* The being of the ultimate cause of the cosmos must be necessary being. And, this necessary being is God.

Leibniz made a mistake, according to Kant, in extending the principle of sufficient reason outside the cosmos, beyond the realm of experience. Kant reasoned that it is appropriate to apply the principle to everything within the cosmos but not beyond because our conceptual framework—which partly structures space and time and, through them, our experience—determines the limit of the proper application of principles such as the principle of sufficient reason. Stretching principles past the domain of their proper application, according to Kant, makes them useless in proving or disproving anything. In this way, Kant helped launch the mind on its flight toward a contemporary philosophical and scientific understanding of the cosmos and everything in it.

In Kant's view, there is no bridge needed between self and cosmos because mind is the realm of concepts and our concepts help structure the cosmos; it is by our concepts that we are ourselves, directly, hooked to the universe. Even space and time, once thought of as passive containers, do not exist independently of the mind but require mind, as mind requires them, in order to exist. In this way, Kant built upon the work of his great predecessors, Descartes, Locke, Berkeley, and Hume, to build a system that removed God as an explanation in our understanding of the world.

have been added to the concept, which expresses possibility only, by my thinking its object as simply given and saying, it is. And thus the real does not contain more than the possible. A hundred real dollars do not contain a penny more than a hundred possible dollars. For as the latter signify the concept, the former the object and its position by itself, it is clear that, in case the former contained more than the latter, my concept would not express the whole object, and would not therefore be its adequate concept. In my financial position no doubt there exists more by one hundred real dollars, than by their concept only (that is their possibility), because in reality the object is not just contained analytically in my concept, but is added to my concept (which is a determination of my state), synthetically; but the conceived hundred dollars are not in the least increased through the existence which is outside my concept.

Kant and the Fall of God

In the United States, all the coins minted by the government proclaim: "In God we trust." Suppose, however, you asked for a government grant to find out what people did to make God angry enough to evoke the wrath of cancer. Would you get any funding? Would you get even one dollar? A nickel? The answer, of course, is that you would not get a penny.

Or suppose that you go to your doctor because you have been having terrible, debilitating headaches that make you collapse from pain. After examining you, the doctor says, "Let us get on our knees and ask God, who knows everything, to give us the right diagnosis." Would you get down on your knees? Or would you get another doctor?

Similarly, suppose that you are one among a group of scientists designing and building a nuclear reactor. One of them says she received instructions from God about the meltdown safety mechanism, which, God told her, should be made out of tin foil with the words "God bless this reactor" on it. Suppose you, a deeply religious person, previously had good reason to believe your colleague is a sane, competent human being. How would you treat her proposal?

People tend to believe in the God of their particular religious cultural tradition. This is more or less as true today as it was at any time in recorded history. But regardless and independently of anyone's beliefs, an important change in our thinking about God occurred in the West. The change grew out of the advent of the New Science, evolved through modern philosophy, and was finalized by Immanuel Kant. The change in our thinking is not so much religious as it is secular, and it has to do with whether, and to what extent, the concept of God functions within our explanations.

Until as late as the time of Newton, God was considered by most philosophers and scientists as an important explanatory principle in their systems.

By whatever and by however many predicates I may think a thing (even in completely determining it), nothing is really added to it, if I add that the thing exists. Otherwise, it would not be the same that exists, but something more than was contained in the concept, and I could not say that the exact object of my concept existed. Nay, even if I were to think in a thing all reality, except one, that one missing reality would not be supplied by my saying that so defective a thing exists, but it would exist with the same defect with which I thought it; or what exists would be different from what I thought. If, then, I try to conceive a being, as the highest reality (without any defect), the question still remains, whether it exists or not. For though in my concept there may be wanting nothing of the possible real content of a thing in general, something is wanted in its relation to my whole state of thinking, namely, that the knowledge of that

For some, the nature of God was derived more or less independently of their religious traditions; for others, such as Newton, the nature of God was taken directly from their traditions. Newton, for instance, not only spent a lot of time on the prophesies of Daniel but, in his famous debate with Leibniz, claimed that God was necessary, within his system of mechanics, to keep the solar system running. No contemporary scientific cosmological theory relies on God.

In other words, although the rift between science and religion today is often presented in a way that polarizes scientific explanations of the cosmos from religious explanations, until recently there was no such clear rift. Historically, what happened is that God was simply dropped out of the knowledge-seeking enterprise. How did this happen?

For Descartes, who based his theory of knowledge on rational intuition and took the self as the starting point of all inquiry, God was needed as a reliable bridge to the cosmos. For Berkeley, who based his theory of knowledge on experience, God was needed as a reliable perceiver to keep the cosmos in existence when it is not being perceived by any finite sentient beings. What followed, in the philosophy of Immanuel Kant, is—speaking rather loosely—a sort of marriage between self and cosmos, a marriage that excluded God from our understanding of the world.

From the subjective point of view, there is the inner world of the self experiencing and thinking about itself and the cosmos in which it exists. From the objective point of view, there is the outer world of matter and motion, space and time. One of the central problems of knowledge is how to connect the two. In both the rationalist and empiricist views, the bridge often turned out to be God. Kant's innovation, in a nutshell, was to explain how mind and cosmos were interrelated in such a fundamental way that no bridge was needed. So God was not needed. Kant sought to tidy things up with what, during his time, was the most sensational impact of his work: namely, the destruction of the traditional proofs for the existence of God.

"El Castillo," a pyramid with a temple on the top, and "The Temple of the Warriors" in the background, from the Maya-Toltec period (eleventh to thirteenth centuries), in Chichén Itzá, Yucatán, Mexico. The Toltec (who conquered the Maya) infused their beliefs into Mayan culture, introducing both human sacrifice on a scale not previously known to the Maya and an aggressive military attitude.

object should be possible *a posteriori* also. And here we perceive the cause of our difficulty. If we were concerned with an object of our senses, I could not mistake the existence of a thing for the mere concept of it; for by the concept the object is thought as only in harmony with the general conditions of a possible empirical knowledge, while by its existence it is thought as contained in the whole content of experience. Through this connection with the content of the whole experience, the concept of an object is not in the least increased; our thought has only received through it one more possible perception. If, however, we are thinking existence through the pure category alone, we need not wonder that we cannot find any characteristic to distinguish it from mere possibility.

Whatever, therefore, our concept of an object may contain, we must always step outside it, in order to attribute to it existence. With objects of the senses, this takes place through their connection with any one of my perceptions, according to empirical laws; with objects of pure thought, however, there is no means of knowing their existence, because it would have to be known entirely *a priori,* while our consciousness of every kind of existence, whether immediately by perception, or by conclusions which connect something with perception, belongs entirely to the unity of experience, and any existence outside that field, though it cannot be declared to be absolutely impossible, is a presupposition that cannot be justified by anything.

The concept of a Supreme Being is, in many respects, a very useful idea, but, being an idea only, it is quite incapable of increasing, by itself alone, our knowledge with regard to what exists. It cannot even do so much as to inform us any further as to its possibility. The analytical characteristic of possibility, which consists in the absence of contradiction in mere positions (realities), cannot be denied to it; but the connection of all real properties in one and the same thing is a synthesis the possibility of which we cannot judge *a priori* because these realities are not given to us as such, and because, even if this were so, no judgment whatever takes place, it being necessary to look for the characteristic of the possibility of synthetical knowledge in experience only, to which the object of an idea can never belong. Thus we see that the celebrated Leibniz is far from having achieved what he

The pyramid of "The Soothsayer" includes five temples at different levels. In Uxmál, Yucatán, Mexico. Uxmál, one of the greatest achievements of the Maya civilization, was built between 850 and 1000 A.D.

thought he had, namely, to understand *a priori* the possibility of so sublime an ideal Being.

Time and labour therefore are lost on the famous ontological (Cartesian) proof of the existence of a Supreme Being from mere concepts; and a man might as well imagine that he could become richer in knowledge by mere ideas, as a merchant in capital, if, in order to improve his position, he were to add a few noughts to his cash account.

Norman Malcolm

"ANSELM'S ONTOLOGICAL ARGUMENTS"

NORMAN MALCOLM, who received his B.A. from the University of Nebraska and his Ph.D. from Harvard University, was for years the Susan Linn Sage Professor of Philosophy at Cornell University. He was a student and close friend of the philosopher Ludwig Wittgenstein, about whom he wrote *A Memoir* (1958). His own work was primarily on epistemology and philosophy of mind, and included *Dreaming* (1959) and *Knowledge and Certainty* (1963).

I believe that in Anselm's *Proslogion* and *Responsio editoris* there are two different pieces of reasoning which he did not distinguish from one another, and that a good deal of light may be shed on the philosophical problem of "the ontological argument" if we do distinguish them. In Chapter 2 of the *Proslogion*[1] Anselm says that we believe that God is *something a greater than which cannot be conceived.* (The Latin is *aliquid quo nihil maius cogitari possit.* Anselm sometimes uses the alternative expressions *aliquid quo maius nihil cogitari potest, id quo maius cogitari nequit, aliquid quo maius cogitari non valet.*) Even the fool of the Psalm who says in his heart there is no God, when he hears this very thing that Anselm says, namely, "something a greater than which cannot be conceived," understands what he hears, and what he understands is in his understanding though he does not understand that it exists.

Apparently Anselm regards it as tautological to say that whatever is understood is in the understanding (*quidquid intelligitur in intellectu est*): he uses *intelligitur* and *in intellectu est* as interchangeable locutions. The same holds for another formula of his: whatever is thought is in thought (*quidquid cogitatur in cogitatione est*).[2]

Of course many things may exist in the understanding that do not exist in reality; for example, elves. Now, says Anselm, something a greater than which cannot be conceived exists in the understanding. But it cannot exist *only* in the understanding, for to exist in reality is greater. Therefore that thing a greater than which cannot be conceived cannot exist only in the understanding, for then a greater thing could be conceived: namely, one that exists both in the understanding and in reality.[3]

Here I have a question. It is not clear to me whether Anselm means that (a) existence in reality by itself is greater than existence in the understanding, or that (b) existence in reality and existence in the understanding together are greater than existence in the understanding alone. Certainly he accepts (b). But he might also accept (a), as Descartes apparently does in *Meditation III* when he suggests that the mode of being by which a thing is "objectively in the understanding" is *imperfect.*[4] Of course Anselm might accept both (a) and (b). He might hold that in general something is greater if it has both of these "modes of existence" than if it has either one alone, but also that existence in reality is a more perfect mode of existence than existence in the understanding.

In any case, Anselm holds that something is greater if it exists both in the understanding and in reality than if it exists merely in the understanding. An equivalent way of putting this interesting proposition, in a more current terminology, is: something is greater if it is both conceived of and exists than if it is merely conceived of. Anselm's reasoning can be expressed as follows: *id quo maius cogitari nequit* cannot be merely conceived of and not exist, for then it would not be *id quo maius cogitari nequit.* The doctrine that something is greater if it exists in addition to being conceived of, than if it is only conceived of, could be called the doctrine

Reprinted from *The Philosophical Review* 69(1960), 41–62, by permission of the publisher.

1. I have consulted the Latin text of the *Proslogion,* of *Gaunilonis pro Insipiente,* and of the *Responsio editoris,* in S. Anselmi. *Opera Omnia,* edited by F. C. Schmitt (Secovii, 1938), vol. I. With numerous modifications, I have used the English translation by S. N. Deane: *St. Anselm* (LaSalle, Illinois, 1948).

2. See *Proslogion* 1 *and Responsio* 2.

3. Anselm's actual words are: "Et certe id quo maius cogitari nequit, non potest esse in solo intellectu. Si enim vel in solo intellectu est, potest cogitari esse et in re, quod maius est. Si ergo id quo maius cogitari non potest, est in solo intellectu: id ipsum quo maius cogitari non potest, est quo maius cogitari potest. Sed certe hoc esse non potest." *Proslogion 2.*

4. Haldane and Ross, *The Philosophical Works of Descartes,* 2 vols. (Cambridge, 1931), I, 163.

that *existence is a perfection.* Descartes maintained, in so many words, that existence is a perfection,[5] and presumably he was holding Anselm's doctrine, although he does not, in *Meditation V* or elsewhere, argue in the way that Anselm does in *Proslogion 2.*

When Anselm says, "And certainly, that than which nothing greater can be conceived cannot exist merely in the understanding. For suppose it exists merely in the understanding, then it can be conceived to exist in reality, which is greater,"[6] he is claiming that if I conceived of a being of great excellence, that being would be *greater* (more excellent, more perfect) if it existed than if it did not exist. His supposition that "it exists merely in the understanding" is the supposition that it is conceived of but does not exist. Anselm repeated this claim in his reply to the criticism of the monk Gaunilo. Speaking of the being a greater than which cannot be conceived, he says:

> I have said that if it exists merely in the understanding it can be conceived to exist in reality, which is greater. Therefore, if it exists merely in the understanding obviously the very being a greater than which cannot be conceived, is one a greater than which can be conceived. What, I ask, can follow better than that? For if it exists merely in the understanding, can it not be conceived to exist in reality? And if it can be so conceived does not he who conceives of this conceive a thing greater than it, if it does exist merely in the understanding? Can anything follow better than this: that if a being a greater than which cannot be conceived exists merely in the understanding, it is something a greater than which can be conceived? What could be plainer?[7]

He is implying, in the first sentence, that if I conceive of something which does not exist then it is possible for it to exist, and *it will be greater if it exists than if it does not exist.*

5. *Op. cit.,* p. 182.
6. *Proslogion* 2; Deane, p. 8.
7. *Responsio* 2; Deane, pp. 157–58.

The doctrine that existence is a perfection is remarkably queer. It makes sense and is true to say that my future house will be a better one if it is insulated than if it is not insulated; but what could it mean to say that it will be a better house if it exists than if it does not? My future child will be a better man if he is honest than if he is not; but who would understand the saying that he will be a better man if he exists than if he does not? Or who understands the saying that if God exists He is more perfect than if He does not exist? One might say, with some intelligibility, that it would be better (for oneself or for mankind) if God exists than if He does not—but that is a different matter.

A king might desire that his next chancellor should have knowledge, wit, and resolution; but it is ludicrous to add that the king's desire is to have a chancellor who exists. Suppose that two royal councilors, A and B, were asked to draw up separately descriptions of the most perfect chancellor they could conceive, and that the descriptions they produced were identical except that A included existence in his list of attributes of a perfect chancellor and B did not. (I do not mean that B put nonexistence in his list.) One and the same person could satisfy both descriptions. More to the point, any person who satisfied A's description would *necessarily* satisfy B's description and *vice versa!* This is to say that A and B did not produce descriptions that differed in any way but rather one and the same description of necessary and desirable qualities in a chancellor. A only made a show of putting down a desirable quality that B had failed to include.

I believe I am merely restating an observation that Kant made in attacking the notion that "existence" or "being" is a "real predicate." He says:

> By whatever and by however many predicates we may think a thing—even if we completely determine it—we do not make the least addition to the thing when we further declare that this thing *is.* Otherwise, it would not be exactly the same thing that exists, but something more than

> we had thought in the concept; and we could not, therefore, say that the exact object of my concept exists.[8]

Anselm's ontological proof of *Proslogion* 2 is fallacious because it rests on the false doctrine that existence is a perfection (and therefore that "existence" is a "real predicate"). It would be desirable to have a rigorous refutation of the doctrine but I have not been able to provide one. I am compelled to leave the matter at the more or less intuitive level of Kant's observation. In any case, I believe that the doctrine does not belong to Anselm's other formulation of the ontological argument. It is worth noting that Gassendi anticipated Kant's criticism when he said, against Descartes:

> Existence is a perfection neither in God nor in anything else; it is rather that in the absence of which there is no perfection. . . . Hence neither is existence held to exist in a thing in the way that perfections do, nor if the thing lacks existence is it said to be imperfect (or deprived of a perfection), so much as to be nothing.[9]

II

I take up now the consideration of the second ontological proof, which Anselm presents in the very next chapter of the *Proslogion*. (There is no evidence that he thought of himself as offering two different proofs.) Speaking of the being a greater than which cannot be conceived, he says:

> And it so truly exists that it cannot be conceived not to exist. For it is possible to conceive of a being which cannot be conceived not to exist; and this is greater than one which can be conceived not to exist. Hence, if that, than which nothing greater can be conceived, can be conceived not to exist, it is not that than which nothing greater can be conceived. But this is a contradiction. So truly, therefore, is there something than which nothing greater can be conceived, that it cannot even be conceived not to exist. And this being thou art, O Lord, our God.[10]

Ancient Egyptian figure.

Anselm is saying two things: first, that a being whose nonexistence is logically impossible is "greater" than a being whose nonexistence is logically possible (and therefore that a being a greater than which cannot be conceived must be one whose nonexistence is logically impossible); second, that *God* is a being than which a greater cannot be conceived.

In regard to the second of these assertions, there certainly is *a* use of the word "God," and I think far the more common use, in accordance with which the statements "God is the greatest of all beings," "God is the most perfect being,"

8. *The Critique of Pure Reason,* tr. by Norman Kemp Smith (London, 1929), p. 505.

9. Haldane and Ross, II, 186.

10. *Proslogion* 3; Deane, pp. 8–9.

"God is the supreme being," are *logically* necessary truths, in the same sense that the statement "A square has four sides" is a logically necessary truth. If there is a man named "Jones" who is the tallest man in the world, the statement "Jones is the tallest man in the world" is merely true and is not a logically necessary truth. It is a virtue of Anselm's unusual phrase, "a being a greater than which cannot be conceived,"[11] to make it explicit that the sentence "God is the greatest of all beings" expresses a logically necessary truth and not a mere matter of fact such as the one we imagined about Jones.

With regard to Anselm's first assertion (namely, that a being whose nonexistence is logically impossible is greater than a being whose nonexistence is logically possible) perhaps the most puzzling thing about it is the use of the word "greater." It appears to mean exactly the same as "superior," "more excellent," "more perfect." This equivalence by itself is of no help to us, however, since the latter expressions would be equally puzzling here. What is required is some explanation of their use.

We do think of *knowledge,* say, as an excellence, a good thing. If A has more knowledge of algebra than B we express this in common language by saying that A has a *better* knowledge of algebra than B, or that A's knowledge of algebra is *superior* to B's, whereas we should not say that B has a better or superior *ignorance* of algebra than A. We do say "greater ignorance," but here the word "greater" is used purely quantitatively.

Previously I rejected *existence* as a perfection. Anselm is maintaining in the remarks last quoted, not that existence is a perfection, but that *the logical impossibility of nonexistence is a perfection.* In other words, *necessary existence* is a perfection. His first ontological proof uses the principle that a thing is greater if it exists than if it does not exist. His second proof employs the different principle that a thing is greater if it necessarily exists than if it does not necessarily exist.

Some remarks about the notion of *dependence* may help to make this latter principle intelligible. Many things depend for their existence on other things and events. My house was built by a carpenter: its coming into existence was dependent on a certain creative activity. Its continued existence is dependent on many things: that a tree does not crush it, that it is not consumed by fire, and so on. If we reflect on the common meaning of the word "God" (no matter how vague and confused this is), we realize that it is incompatible with this meaning that God's existence should *depend* on anything. Whether we believe in Him or not we must admit that the "almighty and everlasting God" (as several ancient prayers begin), the "Maker of heaven and earth, and of all things visible and invisible" (as is said in the Nicene Creed), cannot be thought of as being brought into existence by anything or as depending for His continued existence on anything. To conceive of anything as dependent upon something else for its existence is to conceive of it as a lesser being than God.

If a housewife has a set of extremely fragile dishes, then as dishes they are *inferior* to those of another set like them in all respects except that they are *not* fragile. Those of the first set are *dependent* for their continued existence on gentle handling; those of the second set are not. There is a definite connection in common language between the notions of dependency and inferiority, and independence and superiority. To say that something which was dependent on nothing whatever was superior to ("greater than") anything that was dependent in any way upon anything is quite in keeping with the everyday use of the terms "superior" and "greater." Correlative with the notions of dependence and independence are the notions of *limited* and *unlimited.* An engine requires fuel and this is a limitation. It is the same thing to say that an

11. Professor Robert Calhoun has pointed out to me that a similar locution had been used by Augustine. In *De moribus Manichaeorum* (Bk, II, ch. xi, sec. 24), he says that God is a being *quo esse aut cogitari melius nihil possit* (*Patrologiae Patrum Latinorum,* ed. by J. P. Migne, Paris, 1841–1845, vol. 32: *Augustinus,* vol. 1).

engine's operation is *dependent* on as that it is *limited* by its fuel supply. An engine that could accomplish the same work in the same time and was in other respects satisfactory, but did not require fuel, would be a *superior* engine.

God is usually conceived of as an *unlimited* being. He is conceived of as a being who *could not* be limited, that is, as an absolutely unlimited being. This is no less than to conceive of Him as *something a greater than which cannot be conceived.* If God is conceived to be an absolutely unlimited being He must be conceived to be unlimited in regard to His existence as well as His operation. In this conception it will not make sense to say that He depends on anything for coming into or continuing in existence. Nor, as Spinoza observed, will it make sense to say that something could *prevent* Him from existing.[12] Lack of moisture can prevent trees from existing in a certain region of the earth. But it would be contrary to the concept of God as an unlimited being to suppose that anything other than God Himself could prevent Him from existing, and it would be self-contradictory to suppose that He Himself could do it.

Some may be inclined to object that although nothing could prevent God's existence, still it might just *happen* that He did not exist. And if He did exist that too would be by chance. I think, however, that from the supposition that it could happen that God did not exist it would follow that, if He existed, He would have mere duration and not eternity. It would make sense to ask, "How long has He existed?," "Will He still exist next week?," "He was in existence yesterday but how about today?," and so on. It seems absurd to make God the subject of such questions. According to our ordinary conception of Him, He is an eternal being. And eternity does not mean endless duration, as Spinoza noted. To ascribe eternity to something is to exclude as senseless all sentences that imply that it has duration. If a thing has duration then it would be merely a *contingent* fact, if it was a fact, that its duration was endless. The moon could have endless duration but not eternity. If something has endless duration it will *make sense* (although it will be false) to say that it will cease to exist, and it will make sense (although it will be false) to say that something will *cause* it to cease to exist. A being with endless duration is not, therefore, an absolutely unlimited being. That God is conceived to be eternal follows from the fact that He is conceived to be an absolutely unlimited being.

I have been trying to expand the argument of *Proslogion* 3. In *Responsio* 1 Anselm adds the following acute point: if you can conceive of a certain thing and this thing does not exist then if it *were* to exist its nonexistence would be *possible.* It follows, I believe, that if the thing were to exist it would depend on other things both for coming into and continuing in existence, and also that it would have duration and not eternity. Therefore it would not be, either in reality or in conception, an unlimited being, *aliquid quo nihil maius cogitari possit.*

Anselm states his argument as follows:

> If it [the thing a greater than which cannot be conceived] can be conceived at all it must exist. For no one who denies or doubts the existence of a being a greater than which is inconceivable, denies or doubts that if it did exist its non-existence, either in reality or in the understanding, would be impossible. For otherwise it would not be a being a greater than which cannot be conceived. But as to whatever can be conceived but does not exist: if it were to exist its non-existence either in reality or in the understanding would be possible. Therefore, if a being a greater than which cannot be conceived, can even be conceived, it must exist.[13]

What Anselm has proved is that the notion of contingent existence or of contingent nonexistence cannot have any application to God. His

12. *Ethics,* pt. I, prop. 11.

13. *Responsio* 1; Deane, pp. 154–55.

existence must either be logically necessary or logically impossible. The only intelligible way of rejecting Anselm's claim that God's existence is necessary is to maintain that the concept of God, as a being a greater than which cannot be conceived, is self-contradictory or nonsensical.[14] Supposing that this is false, Anselm is right to deduce God's necessary existence from his characterization of Him as a being a greater than which cannot be conceived.

Let me summarize the proof. If God, a being a greater than which cannot be conceived, does not exist then He cannot *come* into existence. For if He did He would either have been *caused* to come into existence or have *happened* to come into existence, and in either case He would be a limited being, which by our conception of Him He is not. Since He cannot come into existence, if He does not exist His existence is impossible. If He does exist He cannot have come into existence (for the reasons given), nor can He cease to exist, for nothing could cause Him to cease to exist nor could it just happen that He ceased to exist. So if God exists His existence is necessary. Thus God's existence is either impossible or necessary. It can be the former only if the concept of such a being is self-contradictory or in some way logically absurd. Assuming that this is not so, it follows that He necessarily exists.

It may be helpful to express ourselves in the following way: to say, not that *omnipotence* is a property of God, but rather that *necessary omnipotence* is: and to say, not that omniscience is a property of God, but rather that *necessary omniscience* is. We have criteria for determining that a man knows this and that and can do this and that, and for determining that one man has greater knowledge and abilities in a certain subject than another. We could think of various tests to give them. But there is nothing we should wish to describe, seriously and literally, as "testing" God's knowledge and powers. That God is omniscient and omnipotent has not been determined by the application of criteria: rather these are requirements of our conception of Him. They are internal properties of the concept, although they are also rightly said to be properties of God. *Necessary existence* is a property of God in the *same sense* that *necessary omnipotence* and *necessary omniscience* are His properties. And we are not to think that "God necessarily exists" means that it follows necessarily from something that God exists *contingently*. The a priori proposition "God necessarily exists" entails the proposition "God exists," if and only if the latter also is understood as an a priori proposition: in which case the two propositions are equivalent. In this sense Anselm's proof is a proof of God's existence.

Descartes was somewhat hazy on the question of whether existence is a property of things that exist, but at the same time he saw clearly enough that *necessary existence* is a property of God. Both points are illustrated in his reply to Gassendi's remark, which I quoted above:

> I do not see to what class of reality you wish to assign existence, nor do I see why it may not be said to be a property as well as omnipotence, taking the word property as equivalent to any attribute or anything which can be predicted of a thing, as in the present case it should be by all means regarded. Nay, necessary existence in the case of God is also a true property in the strictest sense of the word, because it belongs to Him and forms part of His essence alone.[15]

Elsewhere he speaks of "the necessity of existence" as being "that crown of perfections without which we cannot comprehend God."[16] He is

14. Gaunilo attacked Anselm's argument on this very point. He would not concede that a being a greater than which cannot be conceived existed in his understanding (*Gaunilonis pro Insipiente*, secs. 4 and 5; Deane, pp. 148–50). Anselm's reply is: "I call on your faith and conscience to attest that this is most false" (*Responsio* 1; Deane, p. 154). Gaunilo's faith and conscience will attest that it is false that "God is not a being a greater than which is inconceivable," and false that "He is not understood (*intelligitur*) or conceived (*cogitatur*)" (*ibid.*). Descartes also remarks that one would go to "strange extremes" who denied that we understand the words "*that thing which is the most perfect that we can conceive;* for that is what all men call God" (Haldane and Ross, II, 129).

15. Haldane and Ross, II, 228.

16. *Ibid.*, I, 445.

A sculpture from ancient Egypt: the sun above a pharaoh and his family.

emphatic on the point that necessary existence applies solely to "an absolutely perfect Being."[17]

III

I wish to consider now a part of Kant's criticism of the ontological argument which I believe to be wrong. He says:

> If, in an identical proposition, I reject the predicate while retaining the subject, contradiction results; and I therefore say that the former belongs necessarily to the latter. But if we reject subject and predicate alike, there is no contradiction; for nothing is then left that can be contradicted. To posit a triangle, and yet to reject three angles, is self-contradictory; but there is no contradiction in rejecting the triangle together with its three angles. The same holds true of the concept of an absolutely necessary being. If its existence is rejected, we reject the thing itself with all its predicates and no question of contradiction can then arise. There is nothing outside it that would then be contradicted, since the necessity of the thing is not supposed to be derived from anything external; nor is there anything internal that would be contradicted, since in rejecting the thing itself we have at the same time rejected all its internal properties. "God is omnipotent" is a necessary judgment. The omnipotence cannot be rejected if we posit a Deity, that is, an infinite being; for the two concepts are identical. But if we say, "There is no God," neither the omnipotence nor any other of its predicates is given; they are one and all rejected

17. E.g., *ibid.,* Principle 15, p. 225.

> together with the subject, and there is therefore not the least contradiction in such a judgment.[18]

To these remarks the reply is that when the concept of God is correctly understood one sees that one cannot "reject the subject." "There is no God" is seen to be a necessarily false statement. Anselm's demonstration proves that the proposition "God exists" has the same a priori footing as the proposition "God is omnipotent."

Many present-day philosophers, in agreement with Kant, declare that existence is not a property and think that this overthrows the ontological argument. Although it is an error to regard existence as a property of things that have contingent existence, it does not follow that it is an error to regard necessary existence as a property of God. A recent writer says, against Anselm, that a proof of God's existence "based on the necessities of thought" is "universally regarded as fallacious: it is not thought possible to build bridges between mere abstractions and concrete existence."[19] But this way of putting the matter obscures the distinction we need to make. Does "concrete existence" mean contingent existence? Then to build bridges between concrete existence and mere abstractions would be like inferring the existence of an island from the concept of a perfect island, which both Anselm and Descartes regarded as absurd. What Anselm did was to give a demonstration that the proposition "God necessarily exists" is entailed by the proposition "God is a being a greater than which cannot be conceived" (which is equivalent to "God is an absolutely unlimited being"). Kant declares that when "I think a being as the supreme reality, without any defect, the question still remains whether it exists or not."[20] But once one has grasped Anselm's proof of the necessary existence of a being a greater than which cannot be conceived, no question remains as to whether it exists or not, just as Euclid's demonstration of the existence of an infinity of prime numbers leaves no question on that issue.

Kant says that "every reasonable person" must admit that "all existential propositions are synthetic."[21] Part of the perplexity one has about the ontological argument is in deciding whether or not the proposition "God necessarily exists" is or is not an "existential proposition." But let us look around. Is the Euclidean theorem in number theory, "There exists an infinite number of prime numbers," an "existential proposition"? Do we not want to say that *in some sense* it asserts the existence of something? Cannot we say, with equal justification, that the proposition "God necessarily exists" asserts the existence of something, *in some sense*? What we need to understand, in each case, is the particular sense of the assertion. Neither proposition has the same sort of sense as do the propositions, "A low pressure area exists over the Great Lakes," There still exists some possibility that he will survive," "The pain continues to exist in his abdomen." One good way of seeing the difference in sense of these various propositions is to see the variously different ways in which they are proved or supported. It is wrong to think that all assertions of existence have the same kind of meaning. There are as many kinds of existential propositions as there are kinds of subjects of discourse.

Closely related to Kant's view that all existential propositions are "synthetic" is the contemporary dogma that all existential propositions are contingent. Professor Gilbert Ryle tells us that "Any assertion of the existence of something, like any assertion of the occurrence of something, can be denied without logical absurdity.[22] "All existential statements are contingent," says Mr. I. M. Crombie.[23] Professor J. J. C. Smart remarks that "Existence is not a prop-

18. *Op. cit.*, p. 502.

19. J. N. Findlay, "Can God's Existence Be Disproved?," *New Essays in Philosophical Theology,"* ed. by A. N. Flew and A. MacIntyre (London, 1955), p. 47.

20. *Op. cit.*, pp. 505–6.

21. *Ibid.*, p. 504.

22. *The Nature of Metaphysics*, ed. by D. F. Pears (New York, 1957), p. 150.

23. *New Essays in Philosophical Theology*, p. 114.

erty" and then goes on to assert that "There can never be any *logical contradiction* in denying that God exists."[24] He declares that "The concept of a logically necessary being is a self-contradictory concept, like the concept of a round square. . . . No existential proposition can be logically necessary," he maintains, for "the truth of a logically necessary proposition depends only on our symbolism, or to put the same thing in another way, on the relationship of concepts" (p. 38). Professor K. E. M. Baier says, "It is no longer seriously in dispute that the notion of a logically necessary being is self-contradictory. Whatever can be conceived of as existing can equally be conceived of as not existing."[25] This is a repetition of Hume's assertion, "Whatever we conceive as existent, we can also conceive as non-existent. There is no being, therefore, whose non-existence implies a contradiction."[26]

Professor J. N. Findlay ingeniously constructs an ontological *dis*proof of God's existence, based on a "modern" view of the nature of "necessity in propositions": the view, namely, that necessity in propositions "merely reflects our use of words, the arbitrary conventions of our language."[27] Findlay undertakes to characterize what he calls "religious attitude," and here there is a striking agreement between his observations and some of the things I have said in expounding Anselm's proof. Religious attitude, he says, presumes *superiority* in its object and superiority so great that the worshiper is in comparison as nothing. Religious attitude finds it "anomalous to worship anything *limited* in any thinkable manner. . . . And hence we are led on irresistibly to demand that our religious object should have an *unsurpassable* supremacy along all avenues, that it should tower *infinitely* above all other objects" (p. 51). We cannot help feeling that "the worthy object of our worship can never be a thing that merely *happens* to exist, nor one on which all other objects merely *happen* to depend. The true object of religious reverence must not be one, merely, to which no *actual* independent realities stand opposed: it must be one to which such opposition is totally *inconceivable*. . . . And not only must the existence of *other* things be unthinkable without him, but his own non-existence must be wholly unthinkable in any circumstances" (p. 52). And now, says Findlay, when we add up these various requirements, what they entail is "not only that there isn't a God, but that the Divine Existence is either senseless or impossible" (p. 54). For on the one hand, "if God is to satisfy religious claims and needs, He must be a being in every way inescapable, One whose existence and whose possession of certain excellences we cannot possibly conceive away." On the other hand, "modern views make it self-evidently absurd (if they don't make it ungrammatical) to speak of such a Being and attribute existence to Him. It was indeed an ill day for Anselm when he hit upon his famous proof. For on that day he not only laid bare something that is of the essence of an adequate religious object, but also something that entails its necessary non-existence" (p. 55).

Now I am inclined to hold the "modern" view that logically necessary truth "merely reflects our use of words" (although I do not believe that the conventions of language are always *arbitrary*). But I confess that I am unable to see how that view is supposed to lead to the conclusion that "the Divine existence is either senseless or impossible." Findlay does not explain how this result comes about. Surely he cannot mean that this view entails that nothing can have necessary properties: for this would imply that mathematics is "senselsss or impossible," which no one wants to hold. Trying to fill in the argument that is missing from his article, the most plausible conjecture I can make is the following: Findlay thinks that the view that logical necessity "reflects the use of words" implies, not that nothing has necessary properties, but that *existence* cannot be a necessary property of any-

24. *Ibid.*, p. 34.

25. *The Meaning of Life,* Inaugural Lecture, Canberra University College (Canberra, 1957), p. 8.

26. *Dialogues Concerning Natural Religion,* pt. IX.

27. Findlay, *op. cit.*, p. 154.

thing. That is to say, every proposition of the form "*x* exists," including the proposition "God exists," must be *contingent.*[28] At the same time, our concept of God requires that His existence be *necessary,* that is, that "God exists" be a necessary truth. Therefore, the modern view of necessity proves that what the concept of God requires *cannot* be fulfilled. It proves that God *cannot* exist.

The correct reply is that the view that logical necessity merely reflects the use of words cannot possibly have the implication that every existential proposition must be contingent. That view requires us to *look at* the use of words and not manufacture a priori theses about it. In the Ninetieth Psalm it is said: "Before the mountains were brought forth, or ever thou hadst formed the earth and the world, even from everlasting to everlasting, thou art God." Here is expressed the idea of the necessary existence and eternity of God, an idea that is essential to the Jewish and Christian religions. In those complex systems of thought, those "language-games," God has the status of a necessary being. Who can doubt that? Here we must say with Wittgenstein, "This language-game is played!"[29] I believe we may rightly take the existence of those religious systems of thought in which God figures as a necessary being to be a disproof of the dogma, affirmed by Hume and others, that no existential proposition can be necessary.

Another way of criticizing the ontological argument is the following. "Granted that the concept of necessary existence follows from the concept of a being a greater than which cannot be conceived, this amounts to no more than granting the *a priori* truth of the *conditional* proposition, 'If such a being exists then it necessarily exists.' This proposition, however, does not entail the *existence* of *anything,* and one can deny its antecedent without contradiction." Kant, for example, compares the proposition (or "judgment," as he calls it) "A triangle has three angles" with the proposition "God is a necessary being." He allows that the former is "absolutely necessary" and goes on to say:

> The absolute necessity of the judgment is only a conditional necessity of the thing, or of the predicate in the judgment. The above proposition does not declare that three angles are absolutely necessary, but that, under the condition that there is a triangle (that is, that a triangle is given), three angles will necessarily be found in it.[30]

He is saying, quite correctly, that the proposition about triangles is equivalent to the conditional proposition, "If a triangle exists, it has three angles." He then makes the comment that there is no contradiction "in rejecting the triangle together with its three angles." He proceeds to draw the alleged parallel: "The same holds true of the concept of an absolutely necessary being. If its existence is rejected, we reject the thing itself with all its predicates; and no question of contradiction can then arise."[31] The priest, Caterus, made the same objection to Descartes when he said:

> Though it be conceded that an entity of the highest perfection implies its existence by its very name, yet it does not follow that that very existence is anything actual in the real world, but merely that the concept of existence is inseparably united with the concept of highest being. Hence you cannot infer that the existence of God is anything actual, unless you assume that that highest being actually exists; for then it will actually contain all its perfections, together with this perfection of real existence.[32]

28. The other philosophers I have just cited may be led to the opinion by the same thinking. Smart, for example, says that "the truth of a logically necessary proposition depends only on our symbolism, or to put the same thing in another way, on the relationship of concepts" (*supra*). This is very similar to saying that it "reflects our use of words."

29. *Philosophical Investigations* (New York, 1953), sec. 654.

30. *Op. cit.,* pp. 501–2.

31. *Ibid.,* p. 502.

32. Haldane and Ross, II, 7.

I think that Caterus, Kant, and numerous other philosophers have been mistaken in supposing that the proposition "God is a necessary being" (or "God necessarily exists") is equivalent to the conditional proposition "If God exists then He necessarily exists."[33] For how do they want the antecedent clause, "*If* God exists," to be understood? Clearly they want it to imply that it is *possible* that God does *not* exist.[34] The whole point of Kant's analysis is to try to show that it is possible to "reject the subject." Let us make this implication explicit in the conditional proposition, so that it reads: "If God exists (and it is possible that He does not) then He necessarily exists." But now it is apparent, I think, that these philosophers have arrived at a self-contradictory position. I do not mean that this conditional proposition, taken alone, is self-contradictory. Their position is self-contradictory in the following way. On the one hand, they agree that the proposition "God necessarily exists" is an a priori truth; Kant implies that it is "absolutely necessary," and Caterus says that God's existence is implied by His very name. On the other hand, they think that it is correct to analyze this proposition in such a way that it will entail the proposition "It is possible that God does not exist." But so far from its being the case that the proposition "God necessarily exists" entails the proposition "It is possible that God does not exist," it is rather the case that they are *incompatible* with one another! Can anything be clearer than that the conjunction "God necessarily exists but it is possible that He does not exist" is self-contradictory? Is it not just as plainly self-contradictory as the conjunction "A square necessarily has four sides but it is possible for a square not to have four sides"? In short, this familiar criticism of the ontological argument is self-contradictory, because it accepts *both* of two incompatible propositions.[35]

One conclusion we may draw from our examination of this criticism is that (contrary to Kant) there is a lack of symmetry, in an important respect, between the propositions "A triangle has three angles" and "God has necessary existence," although both are a priori. The former can be expressed in the conditional assertion "If a triangle exists (and it is possible that none does) it has three angles." The latter cannot be expressed in the corresponding conditional assertion without contradiction.

IV

I turn to the question of whether the idea of a being a greater than which cannot be conceived is self-contradictory. Here Leibniz made a contribution to the discussion of the ontological argument. He remarked that the argument of Anselm and Descartes

33. I have heard it said by more than one person in discussion that Kant's view was that it is really a misuse of language to speak of a "necessary being," on the grounds that necessity is properly predicated only of propositions (judgments) not of *things*. This is not a correct account of Kant. (See his discussion of "The Postulates of Empirical Thought in General," *op. cit.*, pp. 239–56, esp. p. 239 and pp. 247–48.) But if he had held this, as perhaps the above philosophers think he should have, then presumably his view would not have been that the pseudo-proposition "God is a necessary being" is equivalent to the conditional "If God exists then He necessarily exists." Rather his view would have been that the genuine proposition "'God exists' is necessarily true" is equivalent to the conditional "If God exists then He exists" (*not* "If God exists then he *necessarily* exists," which would be an illegitimate formulation, on the view imaginatively attributed to Kant).

"If God exists then He exists" is a foolish tautology which says nothing different from the tautology "If a new earth satellite exists then it exists." If "If God exists then He exists" were a correct analysis of "'God exists' is necessarily true," then "If a new earth satellite exists then it exists" would be a correct analysis of "'A new earth satellite exists' is necessarily true." If the *analysans* is necessarily true then the *analysandum* must be necessarily true, provided the analysis is correct. If this proposed Kantian analysis of "'God exists' is necessarily true" were correct, we should be presented with the consequence that not only is it necessarily true that God exists, but also it is necessarily true that a new earth satellite exists: which is absurd.

34. When summarizing Anselm's proof (in part II, *supra*) I said: "If God exists He necessarily exists." But there I was merely stating an entailment. "If God exists" did not have the implication that it is possible He does not exist. And of course I was not regarding the conditional as *equivalent* to "God necessarily exists."

35. This fallacious criticism of Anselm is implied in the following remarks by Gilson: "To show that the affirmation of necessary existence is analytically implied in the idea of God, would be . . . to show that God is necessary if He exists, but would not prove that He does exist" (E. Gilson, *The Spirit of Medieval Philosophy,* New York, 1940, p. 62).

> is not a paralogism, but it is an imperfect demonstration, which assumes something that must still be proved in order to render it mathematically evident; that is, it is tacitly assumed that this idea of the all-great or all-perfect being is possible, and implies no contradiction. And it is already something that by this remark it is proved that, assuming that God is possible, he exists, which is the privilege of divinity alone.[36]

Leibniz undertook to give a proof that God is possible. He defined a *perfection* as a simple, positive quality in the highest degree.[37] He argued that since perfections are *simple* qualities they must be compatible with one another. Therefore the concept of a being possessing all perfections is consistent.

I will not review his argument because I do not find this definition of a perfection intelligible. For one thing, it assumes that certain qualities or attributes are "positive" in their intrinsic nature, and others "negative" or "privative," and I have not been able clearly to understand that. For another thing, it assumes that some qualities are intrinsically simple. I believe that Wittgenstein has shown in the *Investigations* that nothing is *intrinsically* simple, but that whatever has the status of a simple, an indefinable, in one system of concepts, may have the status of a complex thing, a definable thing, in another system of concepts.

I do not know how to demonstrate that the concept of God—that is, of a being a greater than which cannot be conceived—is not self-contradictory. But I do not think that it is legitimate to demand such a demonstration. I also do not know how to demonstrate that either the concept of a material thing or the concept of *seeing* a material thing is not self-contradictory, and philosophers have argued that both of them are. With respect to any particular reasoning that is offered for holding that the concept of seeing a material thing, for example, is self-contradictory, one may try to show the invalidity of the reasoning and thus free the concept from the charge of being self-contradictory *on that ground.* But I do not understand what it would mean to demonstrate *in general,* and not in respect to any particular reasoning, that the concept is not self-contradictory. So it is with the concept of God. I should think there is no more of a presumption that it is self-contradictory than is the concept of seeing a material thing. Both concepts have a place in the thinking and the lives of human beings.

But even if one allows that Anselm's phrase may be free of self-contradiction, one wants to know how it can have any *meaning* for anyone. Why is it that human beings have even *formed* the concept of an infinite being, a being a greater than which cannot be conceived? This is a legitimate and important question. I am sure there cannot be a deep understanding of that concept without an understanding of the phenomena of human life that give rise to it. To give an account of the latter is beyond my ability. I wish, however, to make one suggestion (which should not be understood as autobiographical).

There is the phenomenon of feeling guilt for something that one has done or thought or felt or for a disposition that one has. One wants to be free of this guilt. But sometimes the guilt is felt to be so great that one is sure that nothing one could do oneself, nor any forgiveness by another human being, would remove it. One feels a guilt that is beyond all measure, a guilt "a greater than which cannot be conceived." Paradoxically, it would seem, one nevertheless has an intense desire to have this incomparable guilt removed. One requires a forgiveness that is beyond all measure, a forgiveness "a greater than which cannot be conceived." Out of such a storm in the soul, I am suggesting, there arises the conception of a forgiving mercy that is limitless, beyond all measure. This is one important feature of the Jewish and Christian conception of God.

I wish to relate this thought to a remark made by Kierkegaard, who was speaking about

36. *New Essays Concerning the Human Understanding,* Bk. IV, ch. 10; ed. by A. G. Langley (LaSalle, Illinois, 1949), p. 504.

37. See *Ibid.,* Appendix X, p. 714.

belief in Christianity but whose remark may have a wider application. He says:

> There is only one proof of the truth of Christianity and that, quite rightly, is from the emotions, when the dread of sin and a heavy conscience torture a man into crossing the narrow line between despair bordering upon madness—and Christendom.[38]

One may think it absurd for a human being to feel a guilt of such magnitude, and even more absurd that, if he feels it, he should *desire* its removal. I have nothing to say about that. It may also be absurd for people to fall in love, but they do it. I wish only to say that there *is* that human phenomenon of an unbearably heavy conscience and that it is importantly connected with the genesis of the concept of God, that is, with the formation of the "grammar" of the word "God." I am sure that this concept is related to human experience in other ways. If one had the acuteness and depth to perceive these connections one could grasp the *sense* of the concept. When we encounter this concept as a problem in philosophy, we do not consider the human phenomena that lie behind it. It is not surprising that many philosophers believe that the idea of a necessary being is an arbitrary and absurd construction.

What is the relation of Anselm's ontological argument to religious belief? This is a difficult question. I can imagine an atheist going through the argument, becoming convinced of its validity, acutely defending it against objections, yet remaining an atheist. The only effect it could have on the fool of the Psalm would be that he stopped saying in his heart "There is no God," because he would now realize that this is something he cannot meaningfully say or think. It is hardly to be expected that a demonstrative argument should, in addition, produce in him a living faith. Surely there is a level at which one can view the argument as a piece of logic, following the deductive moves but not being touched religiously? I think so. But even at this level the argument may not be without religious value, for it may help to remove some philosophical scruples that stand in the way of faith. At a deeper level, I suspect that the argument can be thoroughly understood only by one who has a view of that human "form of life" that gives rise to the idea of an infinitely great being, who views it from the *inside* not just from the outside and who has, therefore, at least some inclination to *partake* in that religious form of life. This inclination, in Kierkegaard's words, is "from the emotions." This inclination can hardly be an *effect* of Anselm's argument, but is rather presupposed in the fullest understanding of it. It would be unreasonable to require that the recognition of Anselm's demonstration as valid must produce a conversion.

38. *The Journals,* tr. by A. Dru (Oxford, 1938), sec. 926.

Ernest Nagel

"A DEFENSE OF ATHEISM"

ERNEST NAGEL (1901–1985), who from the 1930s through the 1970s was one of the world's most distinguished philosophers of science, was John Dewey Professor of Philosophy at Columbia University. He was opposed to speculative metaphysics and considered himself a materialist. Among his works are *On the Logic of Measurement* (1930), *Principles of the Theory of Probability* (1939), *Logic without Metaphysics* (1956), and *Godel's Proof* (1958). His *The Structure of Science* (1961) was for two decades the leading philosophy of science text in English and importantly influenced an entire generation of younger philosophers.

The essays in [*Basic Beliefs*] are devoted in the main to the exposition of the major religious creeds of humanity. It is a natural expectation that this final paper, even though its theme is so radically different from nearly all of the others, will show how atheism belongs to the great tradition of religious thought. Needless to say, this expectation is difficult to satisfy, and did anyone succeed in doing so he would indeed be performing the neatest conjuring trick of the week. But the expectation nevertheless does cause me some embarrassment, which is only slightly relieved by an anecdote Bertrand Russell reports in his recent book, *Portraits from Memory*. Russell was imprisoned during the First World War for pacifistic activities. On entering the prison he was asked a number of customary questions about himself for the prison records. One question was about his religion. Russell explained that he was an agnostic. "Never heard of it," the warden declared, "How do you spell it?" When Russell told him, the warden observed, "Well, there are many religions, but I suppose they all worship the same God." Russell adds that this remark kept him cheerful for about a week. Perhaps philosophical atheism also is a religion.

1

I must begin by stating what sense I am attaching to the word "atheism," and how I am construing the theme of this paper. I shall understand by "atheism" a critique and a denial of the major claims of all varieties of theism. And by theism I shall mean the view which holds, as one writer has expressed it, "that the heavens and the earth and all that they contain owe their existence and continuance in existence to the wisdom and will of a supreme, self-consistent, omnipotent, omniscient, righteous, and benevolent being, who is distinct from, and independent of, what he has created." Several things immediately follow from these definitions.

In the first place, atheism is not necessarily an irreligious concept, for theism is just one among many views concerning the nature and origin of the world. The denial of theism is logically compatible with a religious outlook upon life, and is in fact characteristic of some of the great historical religions. For as readers of this volume will know, early Buddhism is a religion which does not subscribe to any doctrine about a god; and there are pantheistic religions and philosophies which, because they deny that God is a being separate from and independent of the world, are not theistic in the sense of the word explained above.

The second point to note is that atheism is not to be identified with sheer unbelief, or with disbelief in some particular creed of a religious group. Thus, a child who has received no religious instruction and has never heard about God, is not an atheist—for he is not denying any theistic claims. Similarly in the case of an adult who, if he has withdrawn from the faith of his fathers without reflection or because of frank indifference to any theological issue, is also not an atheist—for such an adult is not challenging theism and is not professing any views on the subject. Moreover, though the term "atheist" has been used historically as an abusive label for those who do not happen to subscribe to some regnant orthodoxy (for example, the ancient Romans called the early Christians atheists, because the latter denied the Roman divinities), or for those who

Ernest Nagel, "Philosophical Concepts of Atheism." In J. E. Fairchild (ed.), *Basic Beliefs*. New York: Sheridan House, Inc., 1959.

engage in conduct regarded as immoral it is not in this sense that I am discussing atheism.

One final word of preliminary explanation. I propose to examine some *philosophic* concepts of atheism, and I am not interested in the slightest in the many considerations atheists have advanced against the evidences for some particular religious and theological doctrine—for example, against the truth of the Christian story. What I mean by "philosophical" in the present context is that the views I shall consider are directed against any form of theism, and have their origin and basis in a logical analysis of the theistic position, and in a comprehensive account of the world believed to be wholly intelligible without the adoption of a theistic hypothesis.

Theism as I conceive it is a theological proposition, not a statement of a position that belongs primarily to religion. On my view, religion as a historical and social phenomenon is primarily an institutionalized *cultus* or practice, which possesses identifiable social functions and which expresses certain attitudes men take toward their world. Although it is doubtful whether men ever engage in religious practices or assume religious attitudes without some more or less explicit interpretation of their ritual or some rationale for their attitude, it is still the case that it is possible to distinguish religion as a social and personal phenomenon from the theological doctrines which may be developed as justifications for religious practices. Indeed, in some of the great religions of the world the profession of a creed plays a relatively minor role. In short, religion is a form of social communion, a participation in certain kinds of ritual (whether it be a dance, worship, prayer, or the like), and a form of experience (sometimes, though

Graveyard of the Gods

In 1921 the Baltimore journalist and essayist H. L. Mencken published an article in which he asked for the location of the graveyard of dead gods, 168 of which he listed. Each of these gods once had tremendous followings and commanded enormous respect. Now they are all but forgotten, their names—El, Addu, Osiris, Gunfled, Nin, U-urugal—alien to anyone but a student of the history of religion. Who were they? What were they like? Why didn't they last? What have those dead gods got to do with God, that is, with whichever God we may acknowledge?

Most of the gods that Mencken lists were, in his words:

> . . . once gods of the highest eminence. Many of them are mentioned with fear and trembling in the Old Testament. They ranked, five or six thousand years ago, with Jahveh himself. . . . They were gods of the highest standing and dignity—gods of civilized peoples—worshiped and believed in by millions. All were theoretically omnipotent, omniscient, and immortal. And all are dead.

To us, the origins and exploits of these now dead gods are transparently mythological. For instance, Huitzilopochtli, one of the gods, who was born as a consequence of an apparently innocent flirtation that his mother, a virtuous

not invariably, directed to a personal confrontation with divine and holy things). Theology is an articulated and, at its best, a rational attempt at understanding these feelings and practices, in the light of their relation to other parts of human experience, and in terms of some hypothesis concerning the nature of things entire.

2

As I see it, atheistic philosophies fall into two major groups: 1) those which hold that the theistic doctrine is meaningful, but reject it either on the ground that, (a) the positive evidence for it is insufficient, or (b) the negative evidence is quite overwhelming; and 2) those who hold that the theistic thesis is not even meaningful, and reject it (a) as just nonsense or (b) as literally meaningless but interpreting it as a symbolic rendering of human ideals, thus reading the theistic thesis in a sense that most believers in theism would disavow. Critiques of theism falling into the second main group are usually based on some form of what is known as "the verifiability theory of meaning," and cannot be evaluated without first examining that theory. The limited space at my disposal makes such an examination impossible, so that the brief comment I will allow myself to make on these criticisms must be stated dogmatically. The versions of the verifiability theory commonly used to show that theism has no cognitive meaning also exclude most scientific theories (e.g., theories about the atomic constitution of matter) as meaningless, and are unacceptable for at least this reason. More generally, I do not find the claim credible that all theistic statements are meaningless non-

widow, carried on with the sun, developed tremendous power and a lust for human sacrifice that was virtually unlimited: "When he frowned, his father, the sun, stood still. When he roared with rage, earthquakes engulfed whole cities." But although Huitzilopochtli and his exploits may have been mythological, the response of his followers was all too real. When Huitizilopochtli thirsted, Mencken tells us, "He was watered with 10,000 gallons of human blood"; in one year alone, fifty thousand victims were sacrificed to him.

Primitive, nasty stuff. One's own God, one tends to think, is different. Real, not mythological. Humane. A permanent fixture of human history. The God of the Judeo-Christian tradition, for instance, is regarded by most people in Europe and North America as the true God, a God of mercy, a God whose name will be revered until the end of time. But, according to Judeo-Christian scriptural accounts, their own God's temperament and pedigree are not so different from Huitzilopochtli's. The Judeo-Christian God also had a taste for human blood. For instance, He ordered his agent, Moses, to slaughter thousands of Midianites; only the virgin women were spared and God gave them to the sons of Israel as part of the spoils of war. And, Jesus lacked a human father and had a human mother.

"Memorial Service," in H. L. Mencken, *A Mencken Chrestomathy* (1949).

sense, and I believe that on the contrary theism can be construed as a doctrine which is either true or false and which must therefore be assessed in the light of the arguments advanced for it. In any case, however, most of the traditional atheistic critiques of theism belong to the first rather than the second group of analyses mentioned above.

But before turning to the philosophical examination of the major classical arguments for theism, it is well to note that such philosophical critiques do not quite convey the passion with which atheists have often carried on their analyses of theistic views. For historically, atheism has been, and indeed continues to be, a form of social and political protest, directed as much against institutionalized religion as against theistic doctrine. Atheism has been, in effect, a moral revulsion against the undoubted abuses of the secular power exercised by religious leaders and religious institutions.

Religious authorities have opposed the correction of glaring injustices, and encouraged politically and socially reactionary policies. Religious institutions have been havens of obscurantist thought and centers for the dissemination of intolerance. Religious creeds have been used to set limits to free inquiry, to perpetuate inhumane treatment of the ill and the underprivileged, and to support moral doctrines insensitive to human suffering.

These indictments may not tell the whole story about the historical significance of religion; but they are at least an important part of the story. The refutation of theism has thus seemed to many as an indispensable step not only towards liberating men's minds from superstition, but also towards achieving a more equitable reordering of society. And no account of even the more philosophical aspects of atheistic thought is adequate, which does not give proper recognition to the powerful social motives that actuate many theistic arguments.

But however this may be, I want now to discuss three classical arguments for the existence of God, arguments which have constituted at least a partial basis for theistic commitments. As long as theism is defended simply as a dogma, asserted as a matter of direct revelation or as the deliverance of authority, belief in the dogma is impregnable to rational argument. In fact, however, reasons are frequently advanced in support of the theistic creed, and these reasons have been the subject of acute philosophical critiques.

One of the oldest intellectual defenses of theism is the cosmological argument, also known as the argument from a first cause. Briefly put, the argument runs as follows. Every event must have a cause. Hence an event A must have as cause some event B, which in turn must have a cause C, and so on. But if there is no end to this backward progression of causes, the progression will be infinite; and in the opinion of those who use this argument, an infinite series of actual events is unintelligible and absurd. Hence there must be a first cause, and this first cause is God, the initiator of all change in the universe.

The argument is an ancient one, and is especially effective when stated within the framework of assumptions of Aristotelian physics; and it has impressed many generations of exceptionally keen minds. The argument is nonetheless a weak reed on which to rest the theistic thesis. Let us waive any question concerning the validity of the principle that every event has a cause, for though the question is important its discussion would lead us far afield. However, if the principle is assumed, it is surely incongruous to postulate a first cause as a way of escaping from the coils of an infinite series. For if everything must have a cause, why does not God require one for His own existence? The standard answer is that He does not need any, because He is self-caused? But if God can be self-caused, why cannot the world itself be self-caused? Why do we require a God transcending the world to bring the world into existence and to initiate changes in it? On the other hand, the supposed inconceivability and absurdity of an infinite series of regressive causes will be admitted by no one who has competent familiarity with the modern mathematical analysis of infinity. The cosmological argument does not stand up under scrutiny.

The second "proof" of God's existence is usually called the ontological argument. It too has a long history going back to early Christian days, though it acquired great prominence only in medieval times. The argument can be stated in several ways, one of which is the following. Since God is conceived to be omnipotent, he is a perfect being. A perfect being is defined as one whose essence or nature lacks no attributes (or properties) whatsoever, one whose nature is complete in every respect. But it is evident that we have an idea of a perfect being, for we have just defined the idea; and since this is so, the argument continues, God who is the perfect being must exist. Why must he? Because his existence follows from his defined nature. For if God lacked the attribute of existence, he would be lacking at least one attribute, and would therefore not be perfect. To sum up, since we have an idea of God as a perfect being, God must exist.

There are several ways of approaching this argument, but I shall consider only one. The argument was exploded by the 18th century philosopher Immanuel Kant. The substance of Kant's criticism is that it is just a confusion to say that existence is an attribute, and that though the *word* "existence" may occur as the grammatical predicate in a sentence no attribute is being predicated of a thing when we say that the thing exists or has existence. Thus, to use Kant's example, when we think of $100 we are thinking of the nature of this sum of money; but the nature of $100 remains the same whether we have $100 in our pockets or not. Accordingly, we are confounding grammar with logic if we suppose that some characteristic is being attributed to the nature of $100 when we say that a hundred dollar bill exists in someone's pocket.

To make the point clearer, consider another example. When we say that a lion has a tawny color, we are predicating a certain attribute of the animal, and similarly when we say that the lion is fierce or is hungry. But when we say the lion exists, all that we are saying is that something is (or has the nature of) a lion; we are not specifying an attribute which belongs to the nature of anything that is a lion. In short, the word "existence" does not signify any attribute, and in consequence no attribute that belongs to the nature of anything. Accordingly, it does not follow from the assumption that we have an idea of a perfect being that such a being exists. For the idea of a perfect being does not involve the attribute of existence as a constituent of that idea, since there is no such attribute. The ontological argument thus has a serious leak, and it can hold no water.

3

The two arguments discussed thus far are purely dialectical, and attempt to establish God's existence without any appeal to empirical data. The next argument, called the argument from design, is different in character, for it is based on what purports to be empirical evidence. I wish to examine two forms of this argument.

One variant of it calls attention to the remarkable way in which different things and processes in the world are integrated with each other, and concludes that this mutual "fitness" of things can be explained only by the assumption of a divine architect who planned the world and everything in it. For example, living organisms can maintain themselves in a variety of environments, and do so in virtue of their delicate mechanisms which adapt the organisms to all sorts of environmental changes. There is thus an intricate pattern of means and ends throughout the animate world. But the existence of this pattern is unintelligible, so the argument runs, except on the hypothesis that the pattern has been deliberately instituted by a Supreme Designer. If we find a watch in some deserted spot, we do not think it came into existence by chance, and we do not hesitate to conclude that an intelligent creature designed and made it. But the world and all its contents exhibit mechanisms and natural adjustments that are far more complicated and subtle than are those of a watch. Must we not therefore conclude that these things too have a Creator?

The conclusion of this argument is based on an inference from analogy: the watch and the world are alike in possessing a congruence of parts and an adjustment of means to ends; the watch has a watch-maker; hence the world has a world maker. But is the analogy a good one? Let us once more waive some important issues, in particular the issue whether the universe is the unified system such as the watch admittedly is. And let us concentrate on the question what is the ground for our assurance that watches do not come into existence except through the operations of intelligent manufacturers. The answer is plain. We have never run across a watch which has not been deliberately made by someone. But the situation is nothing like this in the case of the innumerable animate and inanimate systems with which we are familiar. Even in the case of living organisms, though they are generated by their parent organisms, the parents do not "make" their progeny in the same sense in which watch-makers make watches. And once this point is clear, the inference from the existence of living organisms to the existence of a supreme designer no longer appears credible.

Moreover, the argument loses all its force if the facts which the hypothesis of a divine designer is supposed to explain can be understood on the basis of a better supported assumption. And indeed, such an alternative explanation is one of the achievements of Darwinian biology. For Darwin showed that one can account for the variety of biological species, as well as for their adaptations to their environments, without invoking a divine creator and acts of special creation. The Darwinian theory explains the diversity of biological species in terms of chance variations in the structure of organisms, and of a mechanism of selection which retains those variant forms that possess some advantages for survival. The evidence for these assumptions is considerable; and developments subsequent to Darwin have only strengthened the case for a thoroughly naturalistic explanation of the facts of biological adaptation. In any event, this version of the argument from design has nothing to recommend it.

A second form of this argument has been recently revived in the speculations of some modern physicists. No one who is familiar with the facts, can fail to be impressed by the success with which the use of mathematical methods has enabled us to obtain intellectual mastery of many parts of nature. But some thinkers have therefore concluded that since the book of nature is ostensibly written in mathematical language, nature must be the creation of a divine mathematician. However, the argument is most dubious. For it rests, among other things, on the assumption that mathematical tools can be successfully used only if the events of nature exhibit some *special* kind of order, and on the further assumption that if the structure of things were different from what they are mathematical language would be inadequate for describing such structure. But it can be shown that no matter what the world were like—even if it impressed us as being utterly chaotic—it would still possess some order, and would in principle be amenable to a mathematical description. In point of fact, it makes no sense to say that there is absolutely *no* pattern in any conceivable subject matter. To be sure, there are differences in complexities of structure, and if the patterns of events were sufficiently complex we might not be able to unravel them. But however that may be, the success of mathematical physics in giving us some understanding of the world around us does not yield the conclusion that only a mathematician could have devised the patterns of order we have discovered in nature.

4

The inconclusiveness of the three classical arguments for the existence of God was already made evident by Kant, in a manner substantially not different from the above discussion. There are, however, other types of arguments for theism that have been influential in the history of thought, two of which I wish to consider, even if only briefly.

Indeed, though Kant destroyed the classical intellectual foundations for theism, he himself invented a fresh argument for it. Kant's attempted proof is not intended to be a purely theoretical demonstration, and is based on the supposed facts of our moral nature. It has exerted an enormous influence on subsequent theological speculation. In barest outline, the argument is as follows. According to Kant, we are subject not only to physical laws like the rest of nature, but also to moral ones. These moral laws are categorical imperatives, which we must heed not because of their utilitarian consequences, but simply because as autonomous moral agents it is our duty to accept them as binding. However, Kant was keenly aware that though virtue may be its reward, the virtuous man (that is, the man who acts out of a sense of duty and in conformity with the moral law) does not always receive his just desserts in this world; nor did he shut his eyes to the fact that evil men frequently enjoy the best things this world has to offer. In short, virtue does not always reap happiness. Nevertheless, the highest human good is the realization of happiness commensurate with one's virtue; and Kant believed that it is a practical postulate of the moral life to promote this good. But what can guarantee that the highest good is realizable? Such a guarantee can be found only in God, who must therefore exist if the highest good is not to be a fatuous ideal. The existence of an omnipotent, omniscient, and omnibenevolent God is thus postulated as a necessary condition for the possibility of a moral life.

Despite the prestige this argument has acquired, it is difficult to grant it any force. It is easy enough to postulate God's existence. But as Bertrand Russell observed in another connection, postulation has all the advantages of theft over honest toil. No postulation carries with it any assurance that what is postulated is actually the case. And though we may postulate God's existence as a means to guaranteeing the possibility of realizing happiness together with virtue, the postulation establishes neither the actual realizability of this ideal nor the fact of his existence. Moreover, the argument is not made more cogent when we recognize that it is based squarely on the highly dubious conception that considerations of utility and human happiness must not enter into the determination of what is morally obligatory. Having built his moral theory on a radical separation of means from ends, Kant was driven to the desperate postulation of God's existence in order to relate them again. The argument is thus at best a *tour de force,* contrived to remedy a fatal flaw in Kant's initial moral assumptions. It carries no conviction to anyone who does not commit Kant's initial blunder.

One further type of argument, pervasive in much Protestant theological literature, deserves brief mention. Arguments of this type take their point of departure from the psychology of religious and mystical experience. Those who have undergone such experiences, often report that during the experience they feel themselves to be in the presence of the divine and holy, that they lose their sense of self-identity and become merged with some fundamental reality, or that they enjoy a feeling of total dependence upon some ultimate power. The overwhelming sense of transcending one's finitude which characterizes such vivid periods of life, and of coalescing with some ultimate source of all existence, is then taken to be compelling evidence for the existence of a supreme being. In a variant form of this argument, other theologians have identified God as the object which satisfies the commonly experienced need for integrating one's scattered and conflicting impulses into a coherent unity, or as the subject which is of ultimate concern to us. In short, a proof of God's existence is found in the occurrence of certain distinctive experiences.

It would be flying in the face of well-attested facts were one to deny that such experiences frequently occur. But do these facts constitute evidence for the conclusion based on them? Does the fact, for example, that an individual experiences a profound sense of direct contact with an alleged transcendent ground of all reality, constitute competent evidence for the claim that there is such a ground and that it is the immediate cause of the experience? If well-established canons for evaluating evidence are accepted, the answer is surely negative. No one will dispute that many men do have vivid experiences in which such things as ghosts or pink elephants appear before them; but only the hopelessly credulous will without further ado count such experiences as establishing the existence of ghosts and pink elephants. To establish the existence of such things, evidence is required that is obtained under controlled conditions and that can be confirmed by independent inquirers. Again, though a man's report that he is suffering pain may be taken at face value, one cannot take at face value the claim, were he to make it, that it is the food he ate which is the cause (or a contributory cause) of his felt pain—not even if the man were to report a vivid feeling of abdominal disturbance. And similarly, an overwhelming feeling of being in the presence of the Divine is evidence enough for admitting the genuineness of such feeling; it is no evidence for the claim that a supreme being with a substantial existence independent of the experience is the cause of the experience.

5

Thus far the discussion has been concerned with noting inadequacies in various arguments widely used to support theism. However, much atheistic criticism is also directed toward exposing incoherencies in the very thesis of theism. I want therefore to consider this aspect of the atheistic critique, though I will restrict myself to the central difficulty in the theistic position which arises from the simultaneous attribution of omnipotence, omniscience, and omnibenevolence to the Deity. The difficulty is that of reconciling these attributes with the occurrence of evil in the world. Accordingly, the question to which I now turn is whether, despite the existence of evil, it is possible to construct a theodicy which will justify the ways of an infinitely powerful and just God to man.

Two main types of solutions have been proposed for this problem. One way that is frequently used is to maintain that what is commonly called evil is only an illusion, or at worst only the "privation" or absence of good. Accordingly, evil is not "really real," it is only the "negative" side of God's beneficience, it is only the product of our limited intelligence which fails to plumb the true character of God's creative bounty. A sufficient comment on this proposed solution is that facts are not altered or abolished by rebaptizing them. Evil may indeed be only an appearance and not genuine. But this does not eliminate from the realm of appearance the tragedies, the sufferings, and the iniquities which men so frequently endure. And it raises once more, though on another level, the problem of reconciling the fact that there is evil in the realm of appearance with God's alleged omnibenevolence. In any event, it is small comfort to anyone suffering a cruel misfortune for which he is in no way responsible, to be told that what he is undergoing is only the absence of good. It is a gratuitous insult to mankind, a symptom of insensitivity and indifference to human suffering, to be assured that all the miseries and agonies men experience are only illusory.

Another gambit often played in attempting to justify the ways of God to man is to argue that the things called evil are evil only because they are viewed in isolation; they are not evil when viewed in proper perspective and in relation to the rest of creation. Thus, if one attends to but a single instrument in an orchestra, the sounds issuing from it may indeed be harsh and discordant. But if one is placed at a proper distance from the whole orchestra, the sounds of that single instrument will mingle with the sounds issuing from the other players to produce a marvellous bit of symphonic music. Analogously, experiences we call painful undoubtedly occur and are real enough. But the pain is judged to be an evil only because it is experienced in a limited perspective—the pain is there for the sake of a more inclusive good, whose reality eludes us because our intelligences are too weak to apprehend things in their entirety.

It is an appropriate retort to this argument that of course we judge things to be evil in a human perspective, but that since we are not God this is the only proper perspective in which to judge them. It may indeed be the case that what is evil for us is not evil for some other part of creation. However, we are not this other part of creation, and it is irrelevant to argue that were we something other than what we are, our evaluations of what is good and bad would be different. Moreover, the worthlessness of the argument becomes even more evident if we remind ourselves that it is unsupported speculation to suppose that whatever is evil in a finite perspective is good from the purported perspective of the totality of things. For the argument can be turned around: what we judge to be a good is a good only because it is viewed in isolation; when it is viewed in proper perspective, and in relation to the entire scheme of things, it is an evil. This is in fact a standard form of the argument for a universal pessimism. Is it any worse than the similar argument for a universal optimism? The very raising of this question is a *reductio ad absurdum* of the proposed solution to the ancient problem of evil.

I do not believe it is possible to reconcile the alleged omnipotence and omnibenevolence of God with the unvarnished facts of human existence. In point of fact, many theologians have concurred in this conclusion; for in order to escape from the difficulty which the traditional attributes of God present, they have assumed that God is not all powerful, and that there are limits as to what He can do in his efforts to establish a righteous order in the universe. But whether such a modified theology is better off, is doubtful; and in any event, the question still remains whether the facts of human life support the claim that an omnibenevolent Deity, though limited in power, is revealed in the ordering of human history. It is pertinent to note in this connection that though there have been many historians who have made the effort, no historian has yet succeeded in showing to the satisfaction of his professional colleagues that the hypothesis of a Divine Providence is capable of explaining anything which cannot be explained just as well without this hypothesis.

6

This last remark naturally leads to the question whether, apart from their polemics against theism, philosophical atheists have not shared a common set of positive views, a common set of phil-

Agnosticism

T. H. Huxley

. . . Agnosticism . . . is not a creed, but a method, the essence of which lies in the rigorous application of a single principle. That principle is of great antiquity; it is as old as Socrates; as old as the writer who said, "Try all things, hold fast by that which is good"; it is the foundation of the Reformation, which simply illustrated the axiom that every man should be able to give a reason for the faith that is in him; it is the great principle of Descartes; it is the fundamental axiom of modern science. Positively the principle may be expressed: In matters of the intellect, follow your reason as far as it will take you, without regard to any other consideration. And negatively: In matters of the intellect do not pretend that conclusions are certain which are not demonstrated or demonstrable. That I take to be the agnostic faith, which if a man keep whole and undefiled, he shall not be ashamed to look the universe in the face, whatever the future may have in store for him. . . .

From *Science and Christian Tradition,* 1898.

osophical convictions which set them off from other groups of thinkers. In one very clear sense of this query the answer is indubitably negative. For there never has been what one might call a "school of atheism," in the way in which there has been a Platonic school or even a Kantian school. In point of fact, atheistic critics of theism can be found among many of the conventional groupings of philosophical thinkers—even, I venture to add, among professional theologians in recent years who in effect preach atheism in the guise of language taken bodily from the Christian tradition.

Nevertheless, despite the variety of philosophic positions to which at one time or another in the history of thought atheists have subscribed, it seems to me that atheism is not simply a negative standpoint. At any rate, there is a certain quality of intellectual temper that has characterized, and continues to characterize, many philosophical atheists. (I am excluding from consideration the so-called "village atheist," whose primary concern is to twit and ridicule those who accept some form of theism, or for that matter those who have any religious convictions.) Moreover, their rejection of theism is based

"What Is Religion?

Jiddu Krishnamurti

First of all, let us find out what is *not* religion. Isn't that the right approach? If we can understand what is *not* religion, then perhaps we shall begin to perceive something else. It is like cleaning a dirty window—one begins to see through it very clearly. So let us see if we can understand and sweep out of our minds that which is not religion; don't let us say, "I will think about it" and just play around with words. Perhaps you can do it, but most of the older people are already caught; they are comfortably established in that which is not religion and they do not want to be disturbed.

So, what is not religion? Have you ever thought about it? You have been told over and over again what religion is supposed to be—belief in God and a dozen other things—but nobody has asked you to find out what is *not* religion and now you and I are going to find out for ourselves.

In listening to me, or to anyone else, do not merely accept what is said, but listen to discern the truth of the matter. If once you perceive for yourself what is not religion, then throughout your life no priest or book can deceive you, no sense of fear will create an illusion which you may believe and follow. To find out what is not religion you have to begin on the everyday level, and then you can climb. To go far you must begin near, and the nearest step is the most important one. So, what is not religion? Are ceremonies religion? Doing *puja* over and over again—is that religion?

True education is to learn *how* to think, not what to think. If you know how to think, if you really have that capacity, then you are a free human being—free of dogmas, superstitions, ceremonies—and therefore you can find out what religion is.

Ceremonies are obviously not religion, because in performing ceremonies you are merely repeating a formula which has been handed down to you. You may find a certain pleasure in performing ceremonies, just as others do in smoking or drinking; but is that religion? In performing ceremonies you are doing something about which you know nothing. Your father and your grandfather do it, therefore you do it, and if you don't they will scold you. That is not religion, is it?

And what is in a temple? A graven image fashioned by a human being according to his own imagination. The image may be a symbol, but it is still only an image, it is not the real thing. A symbol, a word, is not the thing it represents. The word 'door' is not the door, is it? The word is not the thing. We go to the temple to worship—what? An image which is supposed to be

not only on the inadequacies they have found in the arguments for theism, but often also on the positive ground that atheism is a corollary to a better supported general outlook upon the nature of things. I want therefore to conclude this discussion with a brief enumeration of some points of positive doctrine to which, by and large, philosophical atheists seem to me to subscribe. These points fall into three major groups.

In the first place, philosophical atheists reject the assumption that there are disembodied spirits, or that incorporeal entities of any sort can exercise a causal agency. On the contrary, atheists are generally agreed that if we wish to achieve any understanding of what takes place in the universe, we must look to the operations of organized bodies. Accordingly, the various processes taking place in nature, whether animate or inanimate, are to be explained in terms of the properties and structures of identifiable and spatiotemporally located objects. Moreover, the present variety of systems and activities found in the universe is to be accounted for on the basis of the transformations things undergo when they enter into different relations with one another—transformations which often result in the

a symbol; but the symbol is not the real thing. So why go to it? These are facts; I am not condemning; and, since they are facts, why bother about who goes to the temple, whether it be the touchable or the untouchable, the brahman or the non-brahman? Who cares? You see, the older people have made the symbol into a religion for which they are willing to quarrel, fight, slaughter; but God is not there. God is never in a symbol. So the worship of a symbol or of an image is not religion.

And is belief religion? This is more complex. We began near, and now we are going a little bit farther. Is belief religion? The Christians believe in one way, the Hindus in another, the Moslems in another, the Buddhists in still another, and they all consider themselves very religious people; they all have their temples, gods, symbols, beliefs. And is that religion? Is it religion when you believe in God, in Rama, Sita, Ishwara, and all that kind of thing? How do you get such a belief? You believe because your father and your grandfather believe; or having read what some teacher like Shankara or Buddha is supposed to have said, you believe it and say it is true. Most of you just believe what the *Gita* says, therefore you don't examine it clearly and simply as you would any other book; you don't try to find out what is true.

We have seen that ceremonies are not religion, that going to a temple is not religion, and that belief is not religion. Belief divides people. The Christians have beliefs and so are divided both from those of other beliefs and among themselves; the Hindus are everlastingly full of enmity because they believe themselves to be brahmans or non-brahmans, this or that. So belief brings enmity, division, destruction, and that is obviously not religion.

Then what *is* religion? If you have wiped the window clean—which means that you have actually stopped performing ceremonies, given up all beliefs, ceased to follow any leader or *guru*—then your mind, like the window, is clean, polished, and you can see out of it very clearly. When the mind is swept clean of image, of ritual, of belief, of symbol, of all words, *mantrams* and repetitions, and of all fear, then what you see will be the real, the timeless, the everlasting, which may be called God; but this requires enormous insight, understanding, patience, and it is only for those who really inquire into what is religion and pursue it day after day to the end. Only such people will know what is true religion. The rest are merely mouthing words, and all their ornaments and bodily decorations their *pujas* and ringing of bells—all that is just superstition without any significance. It is only when the mind is in revolt against all so-called religion that it finds the real.

emergence of novel kinds of objects. On the other hand, though things are in flux and undergo alteration, there is no all-encompassing unitary pattern of change. Nature is ineradicably plural, both in respect to the individuals occurring in it as well as in respect to the processes in which things become involved. Accordingly, the human scene and the human perspective are not illusory; and man and his works are no less and no more "real" than are other parts or phases of the cosmos. At the risk of using a possibly misleading characterization, all of this can be summarized by saying that an atheistic view of things is a form of materialism.

In the second place, atheists generally manifest a marked empirical temper, and often take as their ideal the intellectual methods employed in the contemporaneous empirical sciences. Philosophical atheists differ considerably on important points of detail in their account of how responsible claims to knowledge are to be established. But there is substantial agreement among them that controlled sensory observation is the court of final appeal in issues concerning matters of fact. It is indeed this commitment to the use of an empirical method which is the final basis of the atheistic critique of theism. For at bottom this critique seeks to show that we can understand whatever a theistic assumption is alleged to explain, through the use of the proved methods of the positive sciences and without the introduction of empirically unsupported *ad hoc* hypotheses about a Deity. It is pertinent in this connection to recall a familiar legend about the French mathematical physicist Laplace. According to the story, Laplace made a personal presentation of a copy of his now famous book on celestial mechanics to Napoleon. Napoleon glanced through the volume, and finding no reference to the Deity asked Laplace whether God's existence played any role in the analysis. "Sire, I have no need for that hypothesis," Laplace is reported to have replied. The dismissal of sterile hypotheses characterizes not only the work of Laplace; it is the uniform rule in scientific inquiry. The sterility of the theistic assumption is one of the main burdens of the literature of atheism both ancient and modern.

And finally, atheistic thinkers have generally accepted a utilitarian basis for judging moral issues, and they have exhibited a libertarian attitude toward human needs and impulses. The conceptions of the human good they have advocated are conceptions which are commensurate with the actual capacities of mortal men, so that it is the satisfaction of the complex needs of the human creature which is the final standard for evaluating the validity of a moral ideal or moral prescription.

In consequence, the emphasis of atheistic moral reflection has been this-worldly rather than other-worldly, individualistic rather than authoritarian. The stress upon a good life that must be consummated in this world, has made atheists vigorous opponents of moral codes which seek to repress human impulses in the name of some unrealizable other-worldly ideal. The individualism that is so pronounced a strain in many philosophical atheists has made them tolerant of human limitations and sensitive to the plurality of legitimate moral goals. On the other hand, this individualism has certainly not prevented many of them from recognizing the crucial role which institutional arrangements can play in achieving desirable patterns of human living. In consequence, atheists have made important contributions to the development of a climate of opinion favorable to pursuing the values of a liberal civilization and they have played effective roles in attempts to rectify social injustices.

Atheists cannot build their moral outlook on foundations upon which so many men conduct their lives. In particular, atheism cannot offer the incentives to conduct and the consolations for misfortune which theistic religions supply to their adherents. It can offer no hope of personal immortality, no threats of Divine chastisement, no promise of eventual recompense for injustices suffered, no blueprints to sure salvation. For on its view of the place of man in nature, human excellence and human

The Sorrow of the Bereaved, as depicted in a tombstone sculpture from the late nineteenth century in a cemetery in Stuttgart, Germany.

dignity must be achieved within a finite lifespan, or not at all, so that the rewards of moral endeavor must come from the quality of civilized living, and not from some source of disbursement that dwells outside of time. Accordingly, atheistic moral reflection at its best does not culminate in a quiescent ideal of human perfection, but is a vigorous call to intelligent activity—activity for the sake of realizing human potentialities and for eliminating whatever stands in the way of such realization. Nevertheless, though slavish resignation to remediable ills is not characteristic of atheistic thought, responsible atheists have never pretended that human effort can invariably achieve the heart's every legitimate desire. A tragic view of life is thus an uneliminable ingredient in atheistic thought. This ingredient does not invite or generally produce lugubrious lamentation. But it does touch the atheist's view of man and his place in nature with an emotion that makes the philosophical atheist a kindred spirit to those who, within the frameworks of various religious traditions, have developed a serenely resigned attitude toward the inevitable tragedies of the human estate.

PART IV

Evil and Other Problems

H. J. McCloskey

"GOD AND EVIL"

H. J. McCLOSKEY, after training to become a minister, got his Ph.D. from the University of Melbourne, where he also taught for many years before moving to Latrobe University as one of its first chairs in philosophy. He has written extensively on ethics and political theory. The essay that follows has become one of the classic contemporary presentations of the problem of evil.

A. THE PROBLEM STATED

Evil is a problem for the theist in that a contradiction is involved in the fact of evil on the one hand, and the belief in the omnipotence and perfection of God on the other. God cannot be both all-powerful and perfectly good if evil is real. This contradiction is well set out in its detail by Mackie in his discussion of the problem.[1] In his discussion Mackie seeks to show that this contradiction cannot be resolved in terms of man's free will. In arguing in this way Mackie neglects a large number of important points, and concedes far too much to the theist. He implicitly allows that whilst physical evil creates a problem, this problem is reducible to the problem of moral evil and that therefore the satisfactoriness of solutions of the problem of evil turns on the compatibility of free will and absolute goodness. In fact physical evils create a number of distinct problems which are not reducible to the problem of moral evil. Further, the proposed solution of the problem of moral evil in terms of free will renders the attempt to account for physical evil in terms of moral good, and the attempt thereby to reduce the problem of evil to the problem of moral evil, completely untenable. Moreover, the account of moral evil in terms of free will breaks down on more obvious and less disputable grounds than those indicated by Mackie. Moral evil can be shown to remain a problem whether or not free will is compatible with absolute goodness. I therefore propose in this paper to reopen the discussion of "the problem of evil," by approaching it from a more general standpoint, examining a wider variety of solutions than those considered by Mackie and his critics.

The fact of evil creates a problem for the theist; but there are a number of simple solutions available to a theist who is content seriously to modify his theism. He can either admit a limit to God's power, or he can deny God's moral perfection. He can assert either (1) that God is not powerful enough to make a world that does not contain evil, or (2) that God created only the good in the universe and that some other power created the evil or (3) that God is all-powerful but morally imperfect, and chose to create an imperfect universe. Few Christians accept these solutions, and this is no doubt partly because such 'solutions' ignore the real inspiration of religious beliefs, and partly because they introduce embarrassing complications for the theist in his attempts to deal with other serious problems. However, if any one of these 'solutions' is accepted, then the problem of evil is avoided, and a weakened version of theism is

1. "Evil and Omnipotence", *Mind,* 1955.

H. J. McCloskey, "God and Evil," *Philosophical Quarterly,* 10 (1960), 97–114. Reprinted by permission of the publisher and the author.

made secure from attacks based upon the fact of the occurrence of evil.

For more orthodox theism, according to which God is both omnipotent and perfectly good, evil creates a real problem; and this problem is well-stated by the Jesuit, Father G. H. Joyce. Joyce writes:

> The existence of evil in the world must at all times be the greatest of all problems which the mind encounters when it reflects on God and His relation to the world. If He is, indeed, all-good and all-powerful, how has evil any place in the world which He has made? Whence came it? Why is it here? If He is all-good why did He allow it to arise? If all-powerful why does He not deliver us from the burden? Alike in the physical and moral order creation seems so greviously marred that we find it hard to understand how it can derive in its entirety from God.[2]

The facts which give rise to the problem are of two general kinds, and give rise to two distinct types of problem. These two general kinds of evil are usually referred to as 'physical' and as 'moral' evil. These terms are by no means apt—suffering for instance is not strictly physical evil—and they conceal significant differences. However, this terminology is too widely accepted, and too convenient to be dispensed with here, the more especially as the various kinds of evil, whilst important as distinct kinds, need not for our purposes be designated by separate names.

Physical evil and moral evil then are the two general forms of evil which independently and jointly constitute conclusive grounds for denying the existence of God in the sense defined, namely as an all-powerful, perfect Being. The acuteness of these two general problems is evident when we consider the nature and extent of the evils of which account must be given. To take physical evils, looking first at the less important of these.

2. Joyce: *Principles of Natural Theology,* ch. XVII. All subsequent quotations from Joyce in this paper are from this chapter of this work.

(a) Physical Evils

Physical evils are involved in the very constitution of the earth and animal kingdom. There are deserts and icebound areas, there are dangerous animals of prey, as well as creatures such as scorpions and snakes. There are also pests such as flies and fleas and the hosts of other insect pests, as well as the multitude of lower parasites such as tapeworms, hookworms and the like. Secondly, there are the various natural calamities and the immense human suffering that follows in their wake—fires, floods, tempests, tidal-waves, volcanoes, earthquakes, droughts and famines. Thirdly, there are the vast numbers of diseases that torment and ravage man. Diseases such as leprosy, cancer, poliomyelitis, appear *prima facie* not to be creations which are to be expected of a benevolent Creator. Fourthly, there are the evils with which so many are born—the various physical deformities and defects such as misshapen limbs, blindness, deafness, dumbness, mental deficiency and insanity. Most of these evils contribute towards increasing human pain and suffering; but not all physical evils are reducible simply to pain. Many of these evils are evils whether or not they result in pain. This is important, for it means that, unless there is one solution to such diverse evils, it is both inaccurate and positively misleading to speak of *the* problem of physical evil. Shortly I shall be arguing that no one 'solution' covers all these evils, so we shall have to conclude that physical evils create not one problem but a number of distinct problems for the theist.

The nature of the various difficulties referred to by the theist as the problem of physical evil is indicated by Joyce in a way not untypical among the more honest, philosophical theists, as follows:

> The actual amount of suffering which the human race endures is immense. Disease has store and to spare of torments for the body: and disease and death are the lot to which we must all look forward. At all times, too, great numbers of the race are pinched by want. Nor is the world

> ever free for very long from the terrible sufferings which follow in the track of war. If we concentrate our attention on human woes, to the exclusion of the joys of life, we gain an appalling picture of the ills to which the flesh is heir. So too if we fasten our attention on the sterner side of nature, on the pains which men endure from natural forces—on the storms which wreck their ships, the cold which freezes them to death, the fire which consumes them—if we contemplate this aspect of nature alone we may be led to wonder how God came to deal so harshly with His Creatures as to provide them with such a home.

Many such statements of the problem proceed by suggesting, if not by stating, that the problem arises at least in part by concentrating one's attention too exclusively on one aspect of the world. This is quite contrary to the facts. The problem is not one that results from looking at only one aspect of the universe. It may be the case that over-all pleasure predominates over pain, and that physical goods in general predominate over physical evils, but the opposite may equally well be the case. It is both practically impossible and logically impossible for this question to be resolved. However, it is not an unreasonable presumption, with the large bulk of mankind inadequately fed and housed and without adequate medical and health services, to suppose that physical evils at present predominate over physical goods. In the light of the facts at our disposal, this would seem to be a much more reasonable conclusion than the conclusion hinted at by Joyce and openly advanced by less cautious theists, namely, that physical goods in fact outweigh physical evils in the world.

However, the question is not, Which predominates, physical good or physical evil? The problem of physical evil remains a problem whether the balance in the universe is on the side of physical good or not, because the problem is that of accounting for the fact that physical evil occurs at all.

(b) Moral Evil

Physical evils create one of the groups of problems referred to by the theist as 'the problem of evil'. Moral evil creates quite a distinct problem. Moral evil is simply immorality—evils such as selfishness, envy, greed, deceit, cruelty, callousness, cowardice and the larger scale evils such as wars and the atrocities they involve.

Moral evil is commonly regarded as constituting an even more serious problem than physical evil. Joyce so regards it, observing:

> The man who sins thereby offends God. . . . We are called on to explain how God came to create an order of things in which rebellion and even final rejection have such a place. Since a choice from among an infinite number of possible worlds lay open to God, how came He to choose one in which these occur? Is not such a choice in flagrant opposition to the Divine Goodness?

Some theists seek a solution by denying the reality of evil or by describing it as a 'privation' or absence of good. They hope thereby to explain it away as not needing a solution. This, in the case of most of the evils which require explanation, seems to amount to little more than an attempt to sidestep the problem simply by changing the name of that which has to be explained. It can be exposed for what it is simply by describing some of the evils which have to be explained. That is why a survey of the data to be accounted for is a most important part of the discussion of the problem of evil.

In *The Brothers Karamazov,* Dostoievsky introduces a discussion of the problem of evil by reference to some then recently committed atrocities. Ivan states the problem:

> "By the way, a Bulgarian I met lately in Moscow," Ivan went on . . . "told me about the crimes committed by Turks in all parts of Bulgaria through fear of a general rising of the Slavs. They burn villages, murder, outrage women and children, and nail their prisoners by the ears to the fences, leave them till morning, and in the

> morning hang them—all sorts of things you can't imagine. People talk sometimes of bestial cruelty, but that's a great injustice and insult to the beasts; a beast can never be so cruel as a man, so artistically cruel. The tiger only tears and gnaws and that's all he can do. He would never think of nailing people by the ears, even if he were able to do it. These Turks took a pleasure in torturing children too, cutting the unborn child from the mother's womb, and tossing babies up in the air and catching them on the points of their bayonets before their mothers' eyes. Doing it before the mother's eyes was what gave zest to the amusement. Here is another scene that I thought very interesting. Imagine a trembling mother with her baby in her arms, a circle of invading Turks around her. They've planned a diversion: they pet the baby to make it laugh. They succeed; the baby laughs. At that moment, a Turk points a pistol four inches from the baby's face. The baby laughs with glee, holds out its little hands to the pistol, and he pulls the trigger in the baby's face and blows out its brains. Artistic, wasn't it?"[3]

Ivan's statement of the problem was based on historical events. Such happenings did not cease in the nineteenth century. *The Scourge of the Swastika* by Lord Russell of Liverpool contains little else than descriptions of such atrocities; and it is simply one of a host of writings giving documented lists of instances of evils, both physical and moral.

Thus the problem of evil is both real and acute. There is a clear *prima facie* case that evil and God are incompatible—both cannot exist. Most theists admit this, and that the onus is on them to show that the conflict is not fatal to theism; but a consequence is that a host of proposed solutions are advanced.

The mere fact of such a multiplicity of proposed solutions, and the widespread repudiation of each other's solutions by theists, in itself suggests that the fact of evil is an insuperable obstacle to theism as defined here. It also makes it impossible to treat of all proposed solutions, and all that can be attempted here is an examination of those proposed solutions which are most commonly invoked and most generally thought to be important by theists.

Some theists admit the reality of the problem of evil, and then seek to sidestep it, declaring it to be a great mystery which we poor humans cannot hope to comprehend. Other theists adopt a rational approach and advance rational arguments to show that evil, properly understood, is compatible with, and even a consequence of God's goodness. The arguments to be advanced in this paper are directed against the arguments of the latter theists; but in so far as these arguments are successful against the rational theists, to that extent they are also effective in showing that the non-rational approach in terms of great mysteries is positively irrational.

B. PROPOSED SOLUTIONS TO THE PROBLEM OF PHYSICAL EVIL

Of the large variety of arguments advanced by theists as solutions to the problem of physical evil, five popularly used and philosophically significant solutions will be examined. They are, in brief: (i) Physical good (pleasure) requires physical evil (pain) to exist at all; (ii) Physical evil is God's punishment of sinners; (iii) Physical evil is God's warning and reminder to man; (iv) Physical evil is the result of the natural laws, the operations of which are on the whole good; (v) Physical evil increases the total good.

(i) Physical Good Is Impossible without Physical Evil

Pleasure is possible only by way of contrast with pain. Here the analogy of colour is used. If every-

3. P. 244, Garnett translation, Heinemann.

thing were blue we should, it is argued, understand neither what colour is nor what blue is. So with pleasure and pain.

The most obvious defect of such an argument is that it does not cover all physical goods and evils. It is an argument commonly invoked by those who think of physical evil as creating only one problem, namely the problem of human pain. However, the problems of physical evils are not reducible to the one problem, the problem of pain; hence the argument is simply irrelevant to much physical evil. Disease and insanity are evils, but health and sanity are possible in the total absence of disease and insanity. Further, if the argument were in any way valid even in respect of pain, it would imply the existence of only a speck of pain, and not the immense amount of pain in the universe. A speck of yellow is all that is needed for an appreciation of blueness and of colour generally. The argument is therefore seen to be seriously defective on two counts even if its underlying principle is left unquestioned. If its underlying principle is questioned, the argument is seen to be essentially invalid. Can it seriously be maintained that if an individual were born crippled and deformed and never in his life experienced pleasure, that he could not experience pain, not even if he were severely injured? It is clear that pain is possible in the absence of pleasure. It is true that it might not be distinguished by a special name and called 'pain' but the state we now describe as a painful state would nonetheless be possible in the total absence of pleasure. So too the converse would seem to apply. Plato brings this out very clearly in Book 9 of the *Republic* in respect of the pleasures of taste and smell. These pleasures seem not to depend for their existence on any prior experience of pain. Thus the argument is unsound in respect of its main contention; and in being unsound in this respect, it is at the same time ascribing a serious limitation to God's power. It maintains that God cannot create pleasure without creating pain, although as we have seen, pleasure and pain are not correlatives.

(ii) Physical Evil Is God's Punishment for Sin

This kind of explanation was advanced to explain the terrible Lisbon earthquake in the 18th century in which 40,000 people were killed. There are many replies to this argument, for instance Voltaire's. Voltaire asked: "Did God in this earthquake select the 40,000 least virtuous of the Portuguese citizens?" The distribution of disease and pain is in no obvious way related to the virtue of the persons afflicted, and popular saying has it that the distribution is slanted in the opposite direction. The only way of meeting the fact that evils are not distributed proportionately to the evil of the sufferer is by suggesting that all human beings, including children, are such miserable sinners, that our offences are of such enormity, that God would be justified in punishing all of us as severely as it is possible for humans to be punished; but even then, God's apparent caprice in the selection of His victims requires explanation. In any case it is by no means clear that young children who very often suffer severely are guilty of sin of such an enormity as would be necessary to justify their sufferings as punishment.

Further, many physical evils are simultaneous with birth—insanity, mental defectiveness, blindness, deformities, as well as much disease. No crime or sin of *the child* can explain and justify these physical evils as punishment; and, for a parent's sin to be punished in the child is injustice or evil of another kind.

Similarly, the sufferings of animals cannot be accounted for as punishment. For these various reasons, therefore, this argument must be rejected. In fact it has dropped out of favour in philosophical and theological circles, but it continues to be invoked at the popular level.

(iii) Physical Evil is God's Warning to Men

It is argued, for instance of physical calamities, that "they serve a moral end which compensates the physical evil which they cause. The awful nature of these phenomena, the overwhelming power of the forces at work, and man's utter helplessness before them, rouse him from the religious indifference to which he is so prone. They inspire a reverential awe of the Creator who made them, and controls them, and a salutary fear of violating the laws which He has imposed" (Joyce). This is where immortality is often alluded to as justifying evil.

This argument proceeds from a proposition that is plainly false; and that the proposition from which it proceeds is false is conceded implicitly by most theologians. Natural calamities do not necessarily turn people to God, but rather present the problem of evil in an acute form; and the problem of evil is said to account for more defections from religions than any other cause. Thus if God's object in bringing about natural calamities is to inspire reverence and awe, He is a bungler. There are many more reliable methods of achieving this end. Equally important, the use of physical evil to achieve this object is hardly the course one would expect a benevolent God to adopt when other, more effective, less evil methods are available to Him, for example, miracles, special revelation, etc.

(iv) Evils Are the Results of the Operation of Laws of Nature

This fourth argument relates to most physical evil, but it is more usually used to account for animal suffering and physical calamities. These evils are said to result from the operation of the natural laws which govern these objects, the relevant natural laws being the various causal laws, the law of pleasure-pain as a law governing sentient beings, etc. The theist argues that the non-occurrence of these evils would involve either the constant intervention by God in a miraculous way, and contrary to his own natural laws, or else the construction of a universe with different components subject to different laws of nature; for God, in creating a certain kind of being, must create it subject to its appropriate law; He cannot create it and subject it to any law of His own choosing. Hence He creates a world which has components and laws good in their total effect, although calamitous in some particular effects.

Against this argument three objections are to be urged. First, it does not cover all physical evil. Clearly not all disease can be accounted for along these lines. Secondly, it is not to give a reason against God's miraculous intervention simply to assert that it would be unreasonable for Him constantly to intervene in the operation of His own laws. Yet this is the only reason that theists seem to offer here. If, by intervening in respect to the operation of His laws, God could thereby eliminate an evil, it would seem to be unreasonable and evil of Him not to do so. Some theists seek a way out of this difficulty by denying that God has the power miraculously to intervene; but this is to ascribe a severe limitation to His power. It amounts to asserting that when His Creation has been effected, God can do nothing else except contemplate it. The third objection is related to this, and is to the effect that it is already to ascribe a serious limitation to God's omnipotence to suggest that He could not make sentient beings which did not experience pain, nor sentient beings without deformities and deficiencies, nor natural phenomena with different laws of nature governing them. There is no reason why better laws of nature governing the existing objects are not possible on the divine hypothesis. Surely, if God is all-powerful, He could have made a better universe in the first place, or one with better laws of nature governing it, so that the operation of its laws did not produce calamities and pain. To maintain this is not to suggest that an omnipotent God should be capable of achieving what is logically impossible. All that has been indicated here is logically possible, and therefore not beyond the powers of a being Who is really omnipotent.

This fourth argument seeks to exonerate God by explaining that He created a universe sound on the whole, but such that He had no direct control over the laws governing His creations, and had controls only in His selection of His creations. The previous two arguments attribute the detailed results of the operations of these laws directly to God's will. Theists commonly use all three arguments. It is not without significance that they betray such uncertainty as to whether God is to be *commended* or *exonerated.*

(v) The Universe Is Better with Evil in It

This is the important argument. One version of it runs:

> Just as the human artist has in view the beauty of his composition as a whole, not making it his aim to give to each several part the highest degree of brilliancy, but that measure of adornment which most contributes to the combined effect, so it is with God (Joyce).

Another version of this general type of argument explains evil not so much as *a component* of a good whole, seen out of its context as a mere component, but rather as *a means* to a greater good. Different as these versions are,

Soulmaking

The problem of evil arises from the conviction that since a God with unlimited knowledge, power, and goodness would not have created a world as full of suffering and misfortune as this one, therefore, there is no such God. Theists have responded primarily by trying to explain why a world that includes suffering and misfortune—or at least is structured so that it is prone to result in suffering and misfortune—is actually *better,* all things considered, than one that does not.

How could that be? It could be, some claim, that a world such as ours, whatever else may be said against it, provides humans with the opportunities and challenges they need to develop their finest qualities, such as courage, compassion, generosity, kindness, prudence, and unselfishness. For instance, in a world from which all possibility of suffering and misfortune had been excluded, there would be no great or even minor disasters and no human wrongdoing that caused harm to others: no devastating floods, no merciless earthquakes, no one who ever succeeded in intentionally (or unintentionally) injuring anyone else, no one who ever suffered injury through accident.

Suppose, though, that in a world without suffering and misfortune, someone *tried* to injure someone else. Then something would always go wrong with the attempt. For instance, the would-be murderer's bullet would swerve off course at the last minute. Or, if someone behaved recklessly, then his or her behavior would never come to a bad end. For instance, the drunken driver who drove his car off a cliff would discover that it floated safely to the ground. As John Hick, a champion of this response to the problem of evil points out,

> To make possible this continual series of individual adjustments, nature would have to work by "special providences" instead of running according to general laws which men must learn to respect on penalty of pain or death. The laws of nature

they may be treated here as one general type of argument for the same criticisms are fatal to both versions.

This kind of argument if valid simply shows that some evil may enrich the Universe; it tells us nothing about *how much* evil will enrich this particular universe, and how much will be too much. So, even if valid in principle—and shortly I shall argue that it is not valid—such an argument does not in itself provide a justification for the evil in the universe. It shows simply that the evil which occurs might have a justification. In view of the immense amount of evil the probabilities are against it.

This is the main point made by Wisdom in his discussion of this argument. Wisdom sums up his criticism as follows:

> It remains to add that, unless there are independent arguments in favour of this world's being the best logically possible world, it is probable that some of the evils in it are not logically

---

> would have to be extremely flexible: sometimes gravity would operate, sometimes not; sometimes an object would be hard and solid, sometimes soft. There could be no sciences, for there would be no enduring world structure to investigate. In eliminating the problems and hardships of an objective environment, with its own laws, life would become like a dream in which, delightfully but aimlessly, we would float and drift at ease. (*Philosophy of Religion*, 3rd ed., Prentice-Hall, 1983, p. 45)

According to Hick, there would be a heavy price to pay for this bliss:

> In such a world human misery would not evoke deep personal sympathy or call forth organised relief and sacrifical help and service. For it is presupposed in these compassionate reactions both that the suffering is deserved and that it is *bad* for the sufferer. We do not acknowledge a moral call to sacrificial measures to save a criminal from receiving his just punishment or a patient from receiving the painful treatment that is to cure him. But men and women often act in true compassion and massive generosity and self-giving in the face of unmerited suffering, especially when it comes in such dramatic forms as an earthquake, a famine, or a mining disaster. It seems, then, that in a world that is to be the scene of compassionate love and self-giving for others, suffering must fall upon mankind with something of the haphazardness and inequity that we now experience. It must be apparently unmerited, pointless, and incapable of being morally rationalized. For it is precisely this feature of our common human lot that creates sympathy between man and man and evokes the unselfishness, kindness, and goodwill which are among the highest values of personal life. (*Evil and the God of Love*, Macmillan, 1966, pp. 370–71)

Hick concludes that a world without suffering and misfortune would not be suitable for promoting the divine objective of *soulmaking*.

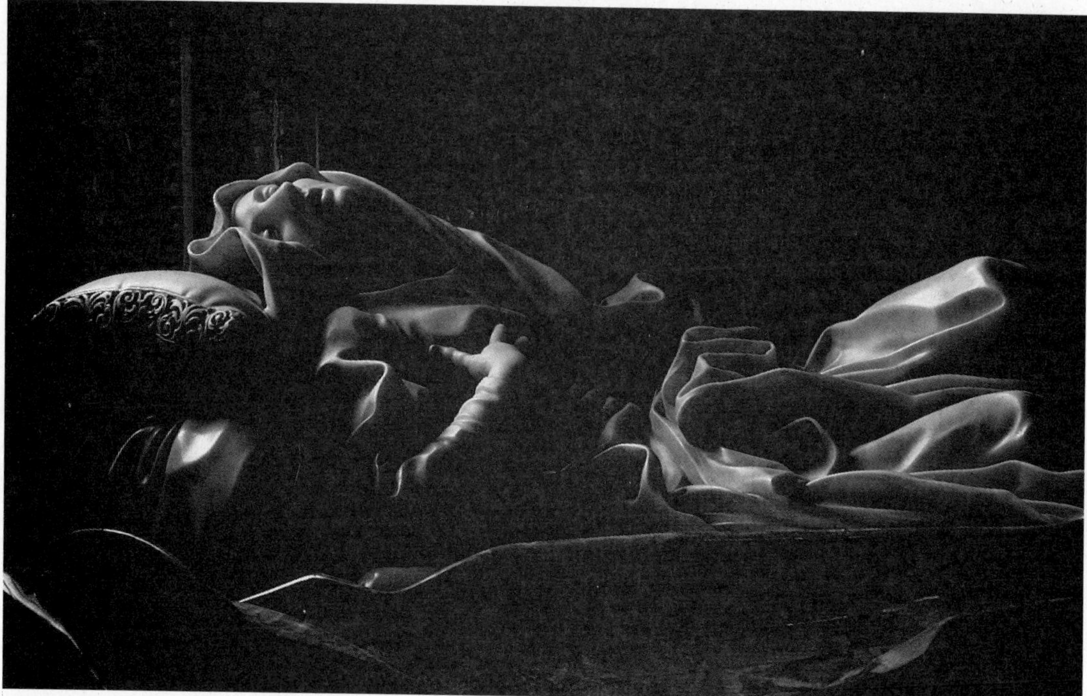

The great Roman baroque sculptor Bernini carved (in 1674) this marble statute of the Blessed Ludovica Albertoni in a state of religious ecstasy, experiencing a union with Jesus (S. Francesco a Ripa in Rome).

> necessary to a compensating good; it is probable because there are so many evils.[4]

Wisdom's reply brings out that the person who relies upon this argument as a conclusive and complete argument is seriously mistaken. The argument, if valid, justifies only some evil. A belief that it justifies all the evil that occurs in the world is mistaken, for a second argument, by way of a supplement to it, is needed. This supplementary argument would take the form of a proof that all the evil that occurs is *in fact* valuable and necessary as a means to greater good. Such a supplementary proof is in principle impossible; so, at best, this fifth argument can be taken to show only that some evil *may be* necessary for the production of good, and that the evil in the world may perhaps have a justification on this account. This is not to justify a physical evil, but simply to suggest that physical evil might nonetheless have a justification, although we may never come to know this justification.

Thus the argument even if it is valid as a general form of reasoning is unsatisfactory because inconclusive. It is, however, also unsatisfactory in that it follows on the principle of the argument that, just as it is possible that evil in the total context contributes to increasing the total ultimate good, so equally, it will hold that good in the total context may increase the ultimate evil. Thus if the principle of the argument were sound, we could never know whether evil is really evil, or good really good. (Aesthetic analogies may be used to illustrate this point.) By implication it follows that it would be dangerous to eliminate evil because we may thereby introduce a discordant element into the divine symphony of the universe; and, conversely, it may be wrong to condemn the elimination of what

4. *Mind,* 1931.

In the Abbey Church of Echternach, Luxembourg.

is good, because the latter may result in the production of more, higher goods.

So it follows that, even if the general principle of the argument is not questioned, it is still seen to be a defective argument. On the one hand, it proves too little—it justifies only some evil and not necessarily all the evil in the universe; on the other hand it proves too much because it creates doubts about the goodness of apparent goods. These criticisms in themselves are fatal to the argument as a solution of the problem of physical evil. However, because this is one of the most popular and plausible counts of physical evil, it is worthwhile considering whether it can properly be claimed to establish even the very weak conclusion indicated above.

Why, and in what way, is it supposed that physical evils such as pain and misery, disease and deformity, will heighten the total effect and add to the value of the moral whole? The answer given is that physical evil enriched the whole by giving rise to moral goodness. Disease, insanity, physical suffering and the like are said to bring into being the noble moral virtues—courage, endurance, benevolence, sympathy and the like. This is what the talk about the enriched whole comes to. W. D. Niven makes this explicit in his version of the argument:

> Physical evil has been the goad which has impelled men to most of those achievements which made the history of man so wonderful. Hardship is a stern but fecund parent of invention. Where life is easy because physical ills are at a minimum we find man degenerating in body, mind, and character.

And Niven concludes by asking:

> Which is preferable—a grim fight with the possibility of splendid triumph; or no battle at all?[5]

5. W. D. Niven, *Encyclopedia of Religion and Ethics.*
Joyce's corresponding argument runs:
"Pain is the great stimulant to action. Man no less than animals is impelled to work by the sense of hunger. Experience shows that, were it not for this motive the majority of men would be content to live in indolent ease. Man must earn his bread.
"One reason plainly why God permits suffering is that man may rise to a height of heroism which would otherwise have been beyond his scope. Nor are these the only benefits which it confers. That sympathy for others which is one of the most precious parts of our experience, and one of the most fruitful sources of well-doing, has its origin in the fellow-feeling engendered by endurance of similar trials. Furthermore, were it not for these trials, man would think little enough of a future existence, and of the need of striving after his last end. He would be perfectly content with his existence and would reck little of any higher good. These considerations here briefly advanced suffice at least to show how important is the office filled by pain in human life, and with what little reason it is asserted that the existence of so much suffering is irreconcilable with the wisdom of the Creator."
And:
"It may be asked whether the Creator could not have brought man to perfection without the use of suffering. Most certainly He could have conferred upon him a similar degree of virtue without requiring any effort on his part. Yet it is easy to see that there is a special value attaching to a conquest of difficulties such as man's actual demands, and that in God's eyes this may well be an adequate reason for assigning this life to us in preference to another. . . . Pain has value in respect to the next life but also in respect to this. The advance of scientific discovery, the gradual improvement of the organization of the community, the growth of material civilization are due in no small degree to the stimulus afforded by pain".

The argument is: Physical evil brings moral good into being, and in fact is an essential precondition for the existence of some moral goods. Further, it is sometimes argued in this context that those moral goods which are possible in the total absence of physical evils are more valuable in themselves if they are achieved as a result of a struggle. Hence physical evil is said to be justified on the grounds that moral good plus physical evil is better than the absence of physical evil.

A common reply, and an obvious one, is that urged by Mackie.[6] Mackie argues that whilst it is true that moral good plus physical evil together are better than physical good alone, the issue is not as simple as that, for physical evil also gives rise to and makes possible many moral evils that would not or could not occur in the absence of physical evil. It is then urged that it is not clear that physical evils (for example, disease and pain) plus some moral goods (for example, courage) plus some moral evil (for example, brutality) are better than physical good and those moral goods which are possible and which would occur in the absence of physical evil.

This sort of reply, however, is not completely satisfactory. The objection it raises is a sound one, but it proceeds by conceding too much to the theist, and by overlooking two more basic defects of the argument. It allows implicitly that the problem of physical evil may be reduced to the problem of moral evil; and it neglects the two objections which show that the problem of physical evil cannot be so reduced.

The theist therefore happily accepts this kind of reply, and argues that, if he can give a satisfactory account of moral evil he will then have accounted for both physical and moral evil. He then goes on to account for moral evil in terms of the value of free will and/or its goods. This general argument is deceptively plausible. It breaks down for the two reasons indicated here, but it breaks down at another point as well. If free will alone is used to justify moral evil, then even if no moral good occurred, moral evil would still be said to be justified; but physical evil would have no justification. Physical evil is not essential to free will; it is only justified if moral good actually occurs, and if the moral good which results from physical evils outweighs the moral evils. This means that the argument from free will cannot alone justify physical evil along these lines; and it means that the argument from free will and its goods does not justify physical evil, because such an argument is incomplete, and necessarily incomplete. It needs to be supplemented by factual evidence that it is logically and practically impossible to obtain.

The correct reply, therefore, is first that the argument is irrelevant to many instances of physical evil, and secondly that it is not true that physical evil plus the moral good it produces is better than physical good and its moral goods. Much pain and suffering, in fact much physical evil generally, for example in children who die in infancy, animals and the insane passes unnoticed; it therefore has no morally uplifting effects upon others, and cannot by virtue of the examples chosen have such effects on the sufferers. Further, there are physical evils such as insanity and much disease to which the argument is inapplicable. So there is a large group of significant cases not covered by the argument. And where the argument is relevant, its [premise] is plainly false. It can be shown to be false by exposing its implications in the following way.

We either have obligations to lessen physical evil or we have not. If we have obligations to lessen physical evil then we are thereby reducing the total good in the universe. If, on the other hand, our obligation is to increase the total good in the universe it is our duty to prevent the reduction of physical evil and possibly even to increase the total amount of physical evil. Theists usually hold that we are obliged to reduce the physical evil in the universe; but in maintaining this, the theist is, in terms of this account of physical evil, maintaining that it is his duty to

6. Mackie, "Evil and Omnipotence", *Mind,* 1955.

reduce the total amount of real good in the universe, and thereby to make the universe worse. Conversely, if by eliminating the physical evil he is not making the universe worse, then that amount of evil which he eliminates was unnecessary and in need of justification. It is relevant to notice here that evil is not always eliminated for morally praiseworthy reasons. Some discoveries have been due to positively unworthy motives, and many other discoveries which have resulted in a lessening of the sufferings of mankind have been due to no higher a motive than a scientist's desire to earn a reasonable living wage.

This reply to the theist's argument brings out its untenability. The theist's argument is seen to imply that war plus courage plus the many other moral virtues war brings into play are better than peace and its virtues; that famine and its moral virtues are better than plenty; that disease and its moral virtues are better than health. Some Christians in the past, in consistency with this mode of reasoning, opposed the use of anaesthetics to leave scope for the virtues of endurance and courage, and they opposed state aid to the sick and needy to leave scope for the virtues of charity and sympathy. Some have even contended that war is a good in disguise, again in consistency with this argument. Similarly the theist should, in terms of this fifth argument, in his heart if not aloud regret the discovery of the Salk polio vaccine because Dr. Salk has in one blow destroyed infinite possibilities of moral good.

There are three important points that need to be made concerning this kind of account of physical evil. (*a*) We are told, as by Niven, Joyce and others, that pain is a goad to action and that part of its justification lies in this fact. This claim is empirically false as a generalization about all people and all pain. Much pain frustrates action and wrecks people and personalities. On the other hand many men work and work well without being goaded by pain or discomfort. Further, to assert that men need goading is to ascribe another evil to God, for it is to claim that God made men naturally lazy. There is no reason why God should not have made men naturally industrious; the one is no more incompatible with free will than the other. Thus the argument from physical evil being a goad to man breaks down on three distinct counts. Pain often frustrates human endeavour, pain is not essential as a goad with many men, and where pain is a goad to higher endeavours, it is clear that less evil means to this same end are available to an omnipotent God. (*b*) The real fallacy in the argument is in the assumption that all or the highest moral excellence results from physical evil. As we have already seen, this assumption is completely false. Neither all moral goodness nor the highest moral goodness is triumph in the face of adversity or benevolence towards others in suffering. Christ Himself stressed this when He observed that the two great commandments were commandments to love. Love does not depend for its possibility on the existence and conquest of evil. (*c*) The 'negative' moral virtues which are brought into play by the various evils—courage, endurance, charity, sympathy and the like—besides not representing the highest forms of moral virtue, are in fact commonly supposed by the theist and atheist alike not to have the value this fifth argument ascribes to them. We—theists and atheists alike—reveal our comparative valuations of these virtues and of physical evil when we insist on state aid for the needy; when we strive for peace, for plenty, and for harmony within the state.

In brief, the good man, the morally admirable man, is he who loves what is good knowing that it is good and preferring it because it is good. He does not need to be torn by suffering or by the spectacle of another's sufferings to be morally admirable. Fortitude in his own sufferings, and sympathetic kindness in others' may reveal to us his goodness; but his goodness is not necessarily increased by such things.

Five arguments concerning physical evil have now been examined. We have seen that the problem of physical evil is a problem in its own right, and one that cannot be reduced to the problem of moral evil; and further, we have seen that physical evil creates not one but a number of problems to which no one nor any combination of the arguments examined offers a solution.

C. PROPOSED SOLUTIONS TO THE PROBLEM OF MORAL EVIL:

The problem of moral evil is commonly regarded as being the greater of the problems concerning evil. As we shall see, it does create what appears to be insuperable difficulties for the theist; but so too, apparently, do physical evils.

For the theist moral evil must be interpreted as a breach of God's law and as a rejection of God Himself. It may involve the eternal damnation of the sinner, and in many of its forms it involves the infliction of suffering on other persons. Thus it aggravates the problem of physical evil, but its own peculiar character consists in the fact of sin. How could a morally perfect, all-powerful God create a universe in which occur such moral evils as cruelty, cowardice and hatred, the more especially as these evils constitute a rejection of God Himself by His creations, and as such involve them in eternal damnation?

The two main solutions advanced relate to free will and to the fact that moral evil is a consequence of free will. There is a third kind of solution more often invoked implicitly than as an explicit and serious argument, which need not be examined here as its weaknesses are plainly evident. This third solution is to the effect that moral evils and even the most brutal atrocities have their justification in the moral goodness they make possible or bring into being.

(i) Free Will Alone Provides a Justification for Moral Evil

This is perhaps the more popular of the serious attempts to explain moral evil. The argument in brief runs: men have free will; moral evil is a consequence of free will; a universe in which men exercise free will even with lapses into moral evil is better than a universe in which men become *automata* doing good always because predestined to do so. Thus on this argument it is the mere fact of the supreme value of free will itself that is taken to provide a justification for its corollary moral evil.

(ii) The Goods Made Possible by Free Will Provide a Basis for Accounting for Moral Evil

According to this second argument, it is not the mere fact of free will that is claimed to be of such value as to provide a justification of moral evil, but the fact that free will makes certain goods possible. Some indicate the various moral virtues as the goods that free will makes possible, whilst others point to beatitude, and others again to beatitude achieved by man's own efforts or the virtues achieved as a result of one's own efforts. What all these have in common is the claim that the good consequences of free will provide a justification of the bad consequences of free will, namely moral evil.

Each of these two proposed solutions encounters two specific criticisms, which are fatal to their claims to be real solutions.

(i) To consider first the difficulties to which the former proposed solution is exposed. (*a*) A difficulty for the first argument—that it is free will alone that provides a justification for moral evil—lies in the fact that the theist who argues in this way has to allow that it is logically possible on the free will hypothesis that all men should always will what is evil, and that even so, a universe of completely evil men possessing free will is better than one in which men are predestined to virtuous living. It has to be contended that the value of free will itself is so immense that it more than outweighs the total moral evil, the eternal punishment of the wicked, and the sufferings inflicted on others by the sinners in their evilness. It is this paradox that leads to the formulation of the second argument; and it is to be noted that the explanation of moral evil switches to the second argument or to a combination of the first and second argument, immediately the theist refuses to face the logical possibility of complete wickedness, and insists instead that in fact men do not always choose what is evil.

(*b*) The second difficulty encountered by the first argument relates to the possibility that free will is compatible with less evil, and even with no evil, that is, with absolute goodness. If it could be shown that free will is compatible with absolute goodness, or even with less moral evil than actually occurs, then all or at least some evil will be left unexplained by free will alone.

Mackie, in his recent paper, and Joyce, in his discussion of this argument, both contend that free will is compatible with absolute goodness. Mackie argues that if it is not possible for God to confer free-will on men and at the same time ensure that no moral evil is committed He cannot really be omnipotent. Joyce directs his argument rather to fellow-theists, and it is more of an *ad hominem* argument addressed to them. He writes:

> Free will need not (as is often assumed) involve the power to choose wrong. Our ability to misuse the gift is due to the conditions under which it is exercised here. In our present state we are able to reject what is truly good, and exercise our power of preference in favour of some baser attraction. Yet it is not necessary that it should be so. And all who accept Christian revelation admit that those who attain their final beatitude exercise freedom of will, and yet cannot choose aught but what is truly good. They possess the knowledge of Essential Goodness; and to it, not simply to good in general, they refer every choice. Moreover, even in our present condition it is open to omnipotence so to order our circumstances and to confer on the will such instinctive impulses that we should in every election adopt the right course and not the wrong one.

To this objection, that free will is compatible with absolute goodness and that therefore a benevolent, omnipotent God would have given man free will and ensured his absolute virtue, it is replied that God is being required to perform what is logically impossible. It is logically impossible, so it is argued, for free will and absolute goodness to be combined, and hence, if God lacks omnipotence only in this respect, He cannot be claimed to lack omnipotence in any sense in which serious theists have ascribed it to Him.

Quite clearly, if free will and absolute goodness are logically incompatible, then God, in not being able to confer both on man does not lack omnipotence in any important sense of the term. However, it is not clear that free will and absolute goodness are logically opposed; and Joyce does point to considerations which suggest that they are not logical incompatibles. For my own part I am uncertain on this point; but my uncertainty is not a factual one but one concerning a point of usage. It is clear that an omnipotent God could create rational agents predestined always to make virtuous 'decisions'; what is not clear is whether we should describe such agents as having free will. The considerations to which Joyce points have something of the status of test cases, and they would suggest that we should describe such agents as having free will. However, no matter how we resolve the linguistic point, the question remains—Which is more desirable, free will and moral evil and the physical evil to which free will gives rise, or this special free will or pseudo-free will which goes with absolute goodness? I suggest that the latter is clearly preferable. Later I shall endeavour to defend this conclusion; for the moment I am content to indicate the nature of the value judgement on which the question turns at this point.

The second objection to the proposed solution of the problem of moral evil in terms of free will alone, related to the contention that free will is compatible with less moral evil than occurs, and possibly with no moral evil. We have seen what is involved in the latter contention. We may now consider what is involved in the former. It may be argued that free will is compatible with less moral evil than in fact occurs on various grounds.

1. God, if He were all-powerful, could miraculously intervene to prevent some or perhaps all moral evil; and He is said to do so on occa-

sions in answer to prayers, (for example, to prevent wars) or His own initiative (for instance, by producing calamities which serve as warnings, or by working miracles, etc.).

2. God has made man with a certain nature. This nature is often interpreted by theologians as having a bias to evil. Clearly God could have created man with a strong bias to good, whilst still leaving scope for a decision to act evilly. Such a bias to good would be compatible with freedom of the will.

3. An omnipotent God could so have ordered the world that it was less conducive to the practice of evil.

These are all considerations advanced by Joyce, and separately and jointly, they establish that God could have conferred free will upon us, and at least very considerably *reduced* the amount of moral evil that would have resulted from the exercise of free will. This is sufficient to show that *not all* the moral evil that exists can be justified by reference to free will alone. This conclusion is fatal to the account of moral evil in terms of free will alone. The more extreme conclusion that Mackie seeks to establish is that absolute goodness is compatible with free will—is not essential as a basis for refuting the free will argument. The difficulty is as fatal to the claims of theism whether all moral evil or only some moral evil is unaccountable. However, whether Mackie's contentions are sound is still a matter of logical interest, although not of any real moment in the context of the case against theism, once the fact that less moral evil is compatible with free will has been established.

(ii) The second free will argument arises out of an attempt to circumvent these objections. It is not free will, but the value of the goods achieved through free will that is said to be so great as to provide a justification for moral evil.

(*a*) This second argument meets a difficulty in that it is now necessary for it to be supplemented by a proof that the number of people who practice moral virtue or who attain beatitude or who attain beatitude and/or virtue after a struggle is sufficient to outweigh the evilness of moral evil, the evilness of their eternal damnation and the physical evil they cause to others. This is a serious defect in the argument, because it means that the argument can at best show that moral evil *may have* a justification, and not that is has a justification. It is both logically and practically impossible to supplement and complete the argument. It is necessarily incomplete and inconclusive even if its general principle is sound.

(*b*) This second argument is designed also to avoid the other difficulty of the first argument—that free will may be compatible with no evil and certainly with less evil. It is argued that even if free will is compatible with absolute goodness it is still better that virtue and beatitude be attained after a genuine personal struggle; and this, it is said, would not occur if God in conferring free will nonetheless prevented moral evil or reduced the risk of it. Joyce argues in this way:

> To receive our final beatitude as the fruit of our labours, and as the recompense of a hard-worn victory, is an incomparably higher destiny than to receive it without any effort on our part. And since God in His wisdom has seen fit to give us such a lot as this, it was inevitable that man should have the power to choose wrong. We could not be called to merit the reward due to victory without being exposed to the possibility of defeat.

There are various objections which may be urged here. First, this argument implies that the more intense the struggle, the greater is the triumph and resultant good, and the better the world; hence we should apparently, on this argument, court temptation and moral struggles to attain greater virtue and to be more worthy of our reward. Secondly, it may be urged that God is being said to be demanding too high a price for the goods produced. He is omniscient. He knows that many will sin and not attain the goods or the Good free will is said to make possible. He creates men with free will, with the natures men have, in the world as it is constituted, knowing that in His doing so He is committing many to moral evil and eternal damnation. He could avoid all this evil by creating men with rational wills predestined to virtue, or He could eliminate much of it by making men's natures and the conditions in the world more conducive to the practice of virtue. He is said not to choose to do this. Instead, at the cost of the sacrifice of the many, He is said to have ordered things so as to allow fewer men to attain this higher virtue and higher beatitude that result from the more intense struggle.

In attributing such behaviour to God, and in attempting to account for moral evil along these lines, theists are, I suggest, attributing to God immoral behaviour of a serious kind—of a kind we should all unhesitatingly condemn in a fellow human being.

We do not commend people for putting temptation in the way of others. On the contrary, anyone who today advocated, or even allowed where he could prevent it, the occurrence of evil and the sacrifice of the many—even as a result of their own freely chosen actions—for the sake of the higher virtue of the few, would be condemned as an immoralist. To put severe temptation in the way of the many, knowing that many and perhaps even most will succumb to the temptation, for the sake of the higher virtue of the few, would be blatant immorality; and it would be immoral whether or not those who yielded to the temptation possessed free will. This point can be brought out by considering how a conscientious moral agent would answer the question: Which should I choose for other people, a world in which there are intense moral struggles and the possibility of magnificent triumphs and the certainty of many defeats, or a world in which there are less intense struggles, less magnificent triumphs but more triumphs and fewer defeats, or a world in which there are no struggles, no triumphs and no defeats? We are constantly answering less easy questions than this in a way that conflicts with the theist's contentions. If by modifying our own behaviour we can save someone else from an intense moral struggle and almost certain moral evil, for example if by refraining from gambling or excessive drinking ourselves we can help a weaker person not to become a confirmed gambler or an alcoholic, or if by locking our car and not leaving it unlocked and with the key in it we can prevent people yielding to the temptation to become car thieves, we feel obliged to act accordingly, even though the persons concerned would freely choose the evil course of conduct. How much clearer is the decision with which God is said to be faced—the choice between the higher virtue of some and the evil of others, or the higher but less high virtue of many more, and the evil of many fewer. Neither alternative denies free will to men.

These various difficulties dispose of each of the main arguments relating to moral evil. There are in addition to these difficulties two other objections that might be urged.

If it could be shown that man has not free will both arguments collapse and even if it could be shown that God's omniscience is incompatible with free will they would still break down. The issues raised here are too great to be pursued in this paper; and they can simply be noted as possible additional grounds from which criticisms of the main proposed solutions of the problem of moral evil may be advanced.

The other general objection is by way of a follow-up to points made in objections (*b*) to both arguments (i) and (ii). It concerns the relative value of free will and its goods and evils and the value of the best of the alternatives to free will and its goods. Are free will and its goods so much more valuable than the next best alternatives that their superior value can really justify the immense amount of evil that is introduced into the world by free will?

Theologians who discuss this issue ask, Which is better—men with free will striving to work out their own destinies, or automata-machine-like creatures, who never make mistakes because they never make decisions? When put in this form we naturally doubt whether free will plus moral evil plus the possibility of the eternal damnation of the many and the physical evil of untold billions are quite so unjustified after all; but the fact of the matter is that the question has not been fairly put. The real alternative is, on the one hand, rational agents with free wills making many bad and some good decisions on rational and non-rational grounds, and 'rational' agents predestined always 'to choose' the right things for the right reasons—that is, if the language of automata must be used, rational automata. Predestination does not imply the absence of rationality in all senses of that term. God, were He omnipotent, could preordain the decisions and the reasons upon which they were based; and such a mode of existence would seem to be in itself a worthy mode of existence, and one preferable to an existence with free will, irrationality and evil.

D. CONCLUSION

In this paper it has been maintained that God, were He all-powerful and perfectly good, would have created a world in which there was no unnecessary evil. It has not been argued that God ought to have created a perfect world, nor that He should have made one that is in any way logically impossible. It has simply been argued that a benevolent God could, and would, have created a world devoid of superfluous evil. It has been contended that there is evil in this world—unnecessary evil—and that the more popular and philosophically more significant of the many attempts to explain that evil are completely unsatisfactory. Hence we must conclude from the existence of evil that there cannot be an omnipotent, benevolent God.

Nelson Pike

"DIVINE OMNISCIENCE AND VOLUNTARY ACTION"

NELSON PIKE, a graduate of Harvard, taught at Cornell before accepting his current position as professor of philosophy at the University of California, Irvine. A frequent contributor to *The Philosophical Review* (and author of *God and Time*, 1970), he has made many important contributions to the philosophy of religion.

In Book V, sec. 3 of his *Consolatio Philosophiae,* Boethius entertained (though he later rejected) the claim that if God is omniscient, no human action is voluntary. This claim seems intuitively false. Surely, given only a doctrine describing God's *knowledge,* nothing about the voluntary status of human actions will follow. Perhaps such a conclusion would follow from a doctrine of divine omnipotence or divine providence, but what connection could there be between the claim that God is *omniscient* and the claim that human actions are determined? Yet Boethius thought he saw a problem here. He thought that if one collected together just the right assumptions and principles regarding God's knowledge, one could derive the conclusion that

Reprinted from *The Philosophical Review* 74 (1965): 27–46, by permission of the publisher and the author.

if God exists, no human action is voluntary. Of course, Boethius did not think that all the assumptions and principles required to reach this conclusion are true (quite the contrary), but he thought it important to draw attention to them nonetheless. If a theologian is to construct a doctrine of God's knowledge which does not commit him to determinism, he must first understand that there is a way of thinking about God's knowledge which would so commit him.

In this paper, I shall argue that although his claim has a sharp counterintuitive ring, Boethius was right in thinking that there is a selection from among the various doctrines and principles clustering about the notions of knowledge, omniscience, and God, which, when brought together, demand the conclusion that if God exists, no human action is voluntary. Boethius, I think, did not succeed in making explicit all of the ingredients in the problem. His suspicions were sound, but his discussion was incomplete. His argument needs to be developed. This is the task I shall undertake in the pages to follow. I should like to make clear at the outset that my purpose in rearguing this thesis is not to show that determinism is true, not to show that God does not exist, nor to show that either determinism is true or God does not exist. Following Boethius, I shall not claim that the items needed to generate the problem are either philosophically or theologically adequate. I want to concentrate attention on the implications of a certain set of assumptions. Whether the assumptions are themselves acceptable is a question I shall not consider.

I

A. Many philosophers have held that if a statement of the form "*A* knows *X*" is true, then "*A* believes *X*" is true and "*X*" is true. As a first assumption, I shall take this partial analysis of "*A* knows *X*" to be correct. And I shall suppose that since this analysis holds for all knowledge claims, it will hold when speaking of God's knowledge. "God knows *X*" entails "God believes *X*" and "'*X*' is true."

Secondly, Boethius said that with respect to the matter of knowledge, God "cannot in anything be mistaken."[1] I shall understand this doctrine as follows. Omniscient beings hold no false beliefs. Part of what is meant when we say that a person is omniscient is that the person in question believes nothing that is false. But, further, it is part of the "essence" of God to be omniscient. This is to say that any person who is not omniscient could not be the person we usually mean to be referring to when using the name "God." To put this last point a little differently: if the person we usually mean to be referring to when using the name "God" were suddenly to lose the quality of omniscience (suppose, for example, He came to believe something false), the resulting person would no longer be God. Although we might call this second person "God" (I might call my cat "God"), the absence of the quality of omniscience would be sufficient to guarantee that the person referred to was not the same as the person formerly called by that name. From this last doctrine it follows that the statement "If a given person is God, that person is omniscient" is an a priori truth. From this we may conclude that the statement "If a given person is God, that person holds no false beliefs" is also an a priori truth. It would be conceptually impossible for God to hold a false belief. "'*X*' is true" follows from "God believes *X*." These are all ways of expressing the same principle—the principle expressed by Boethius in the formula "God cannot in anything be mistaken."

A second principle usually associated with the notion of divine omniscience has to do with the scope or range of God's intellectual gaze. To say that a being is omniscient is to say that he knows everything. "Everything" in this statement is usually taken to cover future, as well as present and past, events and circumstances. In fact, God is usually said to have had foreknowl-

1. Boethius, *Consolatio Philosophiae*, Bk., V, sec. 3, par. 6.

edge of everything that has ever happened. With respect to anything that was, is, or will be the case, God knew, *from eternity,* that it would be the case.

The doctrine of God's knowing everything from eternity is very obscure. One particularly difficult question concerning this doctrine is whether it entails that with respect to everything that was, is, or will be the case, God knew *in advance* that it would be the case. In some traditional theological texts, we are told that God is *eternal* in the sense that He exists "outside of time," that is, in the sense that He bears no temporal relations to the events or circumstances of the natural world.[2] In a theology of this sort, God could not be said to have known that a given natural event was going to happen before it happened. If God knew that a given natural event was going to occur *before* it occurred, at least one of God's cognitions would then have occurred before some natural event. This, surely, would violate the idea that God bears no temporal relations to natural events.[3] On the other hand, in a considerable number of theological sources, we are told that God *has always* existed—that He existed long *before* the occurrence of any natural event. In a theology of this sort, to say that God is eternal is not to say that God exists "outside of time" (bears no temporal relations to natural events); it is to say, instead, God has existed (and will continue to exist) at each moment.[4] The doctrine of omniscience which goes with this second understanding of the notion of eternity is one in which it is affirmed that God *has always* known what was going to happen in the natural world. John Calvin wrote as follows:

> When we attribute foreknowledge of God, we mean that all things have ever been and perpetually remain before, his eyes, so that to his knowledge nothing is future or past, but all things are present; and present in such manner, that he does not merely conceive of them from ideas formed in his mind, as things remembered by us appear to our minds, but really he holds and sees them as if (*tanquam*) actually placed before him.[5]

All things are "present" to God in the sense that He "sees" them as if (*tanquam*) they were actually before Him. Further, with respect to any given natural event, not only is that event "present" to God in the sense indicated, it has *ever been and has perpetually remained* "present" to Him in that sense. This latter is the point of special interest. Whatever one thinks of the idea that God "sees" things as if "actually placed before him," Calvin would appear to be committed to the idea that God has *always known* what was going to happen in the natural world. Choose an event (E) and a time (t_2) at which E occurred. For any time (t_1) prior to t_2 (say, five thousand, six hundred, or eighty years prior to t_2), God knew at t_1 that E would occur at t_2. It will follow from this doctrine, of course, that with respect to any human action, God knew well in advance of its performance that the action would be performed. Calvin says, "when God created man, He foresaw what would happen concerning him." He adds, "little more than five thousand years have elapsed since the creation of the world."[6] Calvin seems to have thought that God foresaw the outcome of every human action well over five thousand years ago.

In the discussion to follow, I shall work only with this second interpretation of God's knowing everything *from eternity.* I shall assume that if

2. This position is particularly well formulated in St. Anselm's *Proslogium,* ch. xix, and *Monoloquium,* chs. xxi–xxii; and in Frederich Schleiermacher's *The Christian Faith,* Pt. I, sec. 2, par. 51. It is also explicit in Boethius, *Consolatio,* secs. 4–6, and in St. Thomas Aquinas's *Summa Theologicae,* Pt. I, q. 10.

3. This point is explicit in Boethius, *Consolatio,* secs. 4–6.

4. This position is particularly well expressed in William Paley's *Natural Theology,* ch. xxiv. It is also involved in John Calvin's discussion of predestination, *Institutes of the Christian Religion,* Bk. III, ch. xxi; and in some formulations of the first cause argument for the existence of God, e.g., John Locke's *An Essay Concerning Human Understanding,* Bk. v, ch. x.

5. Calvin, *Institutes of the Christian Religion,* Bk. III, ch. xxi; this passage trans. by John Allen (Philadelphia, 1813), II, p. 145.

6. Ibid., p. 144.

a person is omniscient, that person has always known what was going to happen in the natural world—and, in particular, has always known what human actions were going to be performed. Thus, as above, assuming that the attribute of omniscience is part of the "essence" of God, the statement "For any natural event (including human actions), if a given person is God, that person would always have known that the event was going to occur at the time it occurred" must be treated as an a priori truth. This is just another way of stating a point admirably put by St. Augustine when he said: "For to confess that God exists and at the same time to deny that He has foreknowledge of future things is the most manifest folly. . . . One who is not prescient of all future things is not God."[7]

B. Last Saturday afternoon, Jones mowed his lawn. Assuming that God exists and is (essentially) omniscient in the sense outlined above, it follows that (let us say) eighty years prior to last Saturday afternoon, God knew (and thus believed) that Jones would mow his lawn at that time. But from this it follows, I think, that at the time of action (last Saturday afternoon) Jones was not *able*—that is, it was not *within Jones's power*—to refrain from mowing his lawn.[8] If at the time of action, Jones had been able to refrain from mowing his lawn, then (the most obvious conclusion would seem to be) at the time of action, Jones was able to do something which would have brought it about that God held a false belief eighty years earlier. But God cannot in anything be mistaken. It is not possible that some belief of His was false. Thus, last Saturday afternoon, Jones was not able to do something which would have brought it about that God held a false belief eighty years ago. To suppose that it was would be to suppose that, at the time of action, Jones was able to do something having a conceptually incoherent description, namely something that would have brought it about that one of God's beliefs was false. Hence, given that God believed eighty years ago that Jones would mow his lawn on Saturday, if we are to assign Jones the power on Saturday to refrain from mowing his lawn, this power must not be described as the power to do something that would have rendered one of God's beliefs false. How then should we describe it vis-à-vis God and His belief? So far as I can see, there are only two other alternatives. First, we might try describing it as the power to do something that would have brought it about that God believed otherwise than He did eighty years ago; or, secondly, we might try describing it as the power to do something that would have brought it about that God (Who, by hypothesis, existed eighty years earlier) did not exist eighty years earlier—that is, as the power to do something that would have brought it about that any person who believed eighty years ago that Jones would mow his lawn on Saturday (one of whom was, by hypothesis, God) held a false belief, and thus was not God. But again, neither of these latter can be accepted. Last Saturday afternoon, Jones was not able to do something that would have brought it about that God believed otherwise than He did eighty years ago. Even if we suppose (as was suggested by Calvin) that eighty years ago God knew Jones would mow his lawn on Saturday in the sense that He "saw" Jones mowing his lawn as if this action were occurring before Him, the fact remains that God knew (and thus believed) eighty years prior to Saturday that Jones would mow his lawn. And if God held such a belief eighty years prior to Saturday, Jones did not have the power on Saturday to do something that would

7. Augustine, *City of God,* Bk, V, sec. 9.

8. The notion of someone being *able* to do something and the notion of something being *within one's power* are essentially the same. Traditional formulations of the problem of divine foreknowledge (e.g., those of Boethius and Augustine) made use of the notion of what is (and what is not) *within one's power.* But the problem is the same when framed in terms of what one is (and one is not) *able* to do. Thus, I shall treat the statements "Jones was able to do *X*," "Jones had the ability to do *X*," and "It was within Jones's power to do *X*" as equivalent. Richard Taylor, in "I Can," *Philosophical Review,* 69(1960):78–89, has argued that the notion of ability or power involved in these last three statements is incapable of philosophical analysis. Be this as it may, I shall not here attempt such an analysis. In what follows I shall, however, be careful to affirm only those statements about what is (or is not) within one's power that would have to be preserved on any analysis of this notion having even the most distant claim to adequacy.

have made it the case that God did not hold this belief eighty years earlier. No action performed at a given time can alter the fact that a given person held a certain belief at a time prior to the time in question. This last seems to be an a priori truth. For similar reasons, the last of the above alternatives must also be rejected. On the assumption that God existed eighty years prior to Saturday, Jones on Saturday was not able to do something that would have brought it about that God did not exist eighty years prior to that time. No action performed at a given time can alter the fact that a certain person existed at a time prior to the time in question. This, too, seems to me to be an a priori truth. But if these observations are correct, then, given that Jones mowed his lawn on Saturday, and given that God exists and is (essentially) omniscient, it seems to follow that at the time of action, Jones did not have the power to refrain from mowing his lawn. The upshot of these reflections would appear to be that Jones's mowing his lawn last Saturday cannot be counted as a voluntary action. Although I do not have an analysis of what it is for an action to be *voluntary,* it seems to me that a situation in which it would be wrong to assign Jones the *ability* or *power* to do *other* than he did would be a situation in which it would also be wrong to speak of his action as voluntary. As a general remark, if God exists and is (essentially) omniscient in the sense specified above, no human action is voluntary.[9]

As the argument just presented is somewhat complex, perhaps the following schematic representation of it will be of some use.

1. "God existed at t_1" entails "If Jones did X at t_2, God believed at t_1 that Jones would do X at t_2."
2. "God believes X" entails "'X' is true."
3. It is not within one's power at a given time to do something having a description that is logically contradictory.
4. It is not within one's power at a given time to do something that would bring it about that someone who held a certain belief at a time prior to the time in question did not hold that belief at the time prior to the time in question.
5. It is not within one's power at a given time to do something that would bring it about that a person who existed at an earlier time did not exist at that earlier time.
6. If God existed at t_1 and if God believed at t_2 that Jones would do X at t_2, then if it was within Jones's power at t_2 to refrain from doing X, then (1) it was within Jones's power at t_2 to do something that would have brought it about that God held a false belief at t_1, or (2) it was within Jones's power at t_2 to do something which would have brought it about that God did not hold the belief He held at t_1, or (3) it was within Jones's power at t_2 to do something that would have brought it about that any person who believed at t_1 that Jones would do X at t_2 (one of whom was, by hypothesis, God) held a false-belief and thus was not God—that is, that God (who by hypothesis existed at t_1) did not exist at t_1.
7. Alternative 1 in the consequent of item 6 is false. (from 2 and 3)
8. Alternative 2 in the consequent of item 6 is false. (from 4)
9. Alternative 3 in the consequent of item 6 is false. (from 5)
10. Therefore, if God existed at t_1 and if God believed at t_1 that Jones would do X at t_2, then it was not within Jones's power at t_2 to retrain from doing X. (from 6 through 9)
11. Therefore, if God existed at t_1, and if Jones did X at t_2, it was not within Jones's power at t_2 to refrain from doing X. (from 1 and 10)

In this argument, items 1 and 2 make explicit the doctrine of God's (essential) omniscience with

9. In Bk. II, ch. xxi, secs. 8–11 of *An Essay,* Locke says that an agent is not *free* with respect to a given action (i.e., that an action is done "under necessity") when it is not within the agent's power to do otherwise. Locke allows a special kind of case, however, in which an action may be *voluntary* though done under necessity. If a man chooses to do something without knowing that it is not within his power to do otherwise (e.g., if a man chooses to stay in a room without knowing that the room is locked), his action may be voluntary though he is not free to forbear it. If Locke is right in this (and I shall not argue the point one way or the other), replace "voluntary" with (let us say) "free" in the above paragraph and throughout the remainder of this paper.

which I am working. Items 3, 4, and 5 express what I take to be part of the logic of the concept of ability or power as it applies to human beings. Item 6 is offered as an analytic truth. If one assigns Jones the power to refrain from doing X at t_2 (given that God believed at t_1 that he would do X at t_2), so far as I can see, one would have to describe this power in one of the three ways listed in the consequent of item 6. I do not know how to argue that these are the only alternatives, but I have been unable to find another. Item 11, when generalized for all agents and actions, and when taken together with what seems to me to be a minimal condition for the application of "voluntary action," yields the conclusion that if God exists (and is essentially omniscient in the way I have described) no human action is voluntary.

C. It is important to notice that the argument given in the preceding paragraphs avoids use of two concepts that are often prominent in discussions of determinism.

In the first place, the argument makes no mention of the *causes* of Jones's action. Say (for example, with St. Thomas)[10] that God's foreknowledge of Jones's action was, itself, the cause of the action (though I am really not sure what this means). Say, instead, that natural events or circumstances caused Jones to act. Even say that Jones's action had no cause at all. The argument outlined above remains unaffected. If eighty years prior to Saturday, God believed that Jones would mow his lawn at that time, it was not within Jones's power at the time of action to refrain from mowing his lawn. The reasoning that justifies this assertion makes no mention of a causal series preceding Jones's action.

Secondly, consider the following line of thinking. Suppose Jones mowed his lawn last Saturday. It was then *true* eighty years ago that Jones would mow his lawn at that time. Hence, on Saturday, Jones was not able to refrain from mowing his lawn. To suppose that he was would

10. Aquinas, *Summa Theologicae,* Pt. 1, q. 14, a. 8.

Bar mitzvah in Jerusalem; young Jewish boy carries the Torah from the Western (wailing) Wall.

be to suppose that he was able on Saturday to do something that would have made false a proposition that was *already true* eighty years earlier. This general kind of argument for determinism is usually associated with Leibniz, although it was anticipated in chapter ix of Aristotle's *De Interpretatione.* It has been used since, with some modification, in Richard Taylor's article, "Fatalism."[11] This argument, like the one I have offered above, makes no use of the notion of causation. It turns, instead, on the notion of its being *true eighty years ago* that Jones would mow his lawn on Saturday.

I must confess that I share the misgivings of those contemporary philosophers who have wondered what (if any) sense can be attached to a statement of the form "It was true at t_1 that E would occur at t_2."[12] Does this statement mean

11. Richard Taylor, "Fatalism," *Philosophical Review,* 71(1962):56–66. Taylor argues that if an event E fails to occur at t_2, then at t_1 it was true that E would fail to occur at t_2. Thus, at t_1, a necessary condition of anyone's performing an action sufficient for the occurrence of E at t_2 is missing. Thus at t_1, no one could have the power to perform an action that would be sufficient for the occurrence of E at t_2. Hence, no one has the power at t_1 to do something sufficient for the occurrence of an event at t_2 that is not going to happen. The parallel between this argument and the one recited above can be seen very clearly if one reformulates Taylor's argument, pushing back the time at which it was true that E would not occur at t_2.

12. For a helpful discussion of difficulties involved here, see Rogers Albritton's "Present Truth and Future Contingency," a reply to Richard Taylor's "The Problem of Future Contingency," both in *Philosophical Review,* 66(1957):1–28.

that had someone believed, guessed, or asserted at t_1 that E would occur at t_2, he would have been right?[13] (I shall have something to say about this form of determinism later in this paper.) Perhaps it means that at t_1 there was sufficient evidence upon which to predict that E would occur at t_2.[14] Maybe it means neither of these. Maybe it means nothing at all.[15] The argument presented above presupposes that it makes straightforward sense to suppose that God (or just anyone) held a true belief eighty years prior to Saturday. But this is not to suppose that *what* God believed *was true eighty years prior to Saturday.* Whether (or in what sense) it was true eighty years ago that Jones would mow his lawn on Saturday is a question I shall not discuss. As far as I can see, the argument in which I am interested requires nothing in the way of a decision on this issue.

II

I now want to consider three comments on the problem of divine foreknowledge which seem to be instructively incorrect.

A. Leibniz analyzed the problem as follows:

> They say that what is foreseen cannot fail to exist and they say so truly; but it follows not that what is foreseen is necessary. For necessary truth is that whereof the contrary is impossible or implies a contradiction. Now the truth which states that I shall write tomorrow is not of that nature, it is not necessary. Yet, supposing that God foresees it, it is necessary that it come to pass, that is, the consequence is necessary, namely that it exist, since it has been foreseen; for God is infallible. This is what is termed a *hypothetical necessity.* But our concern is not this necessity; it is an *absolute* necessity that is required, to be able to say that an action is necessary, that it is not contingent, that it is not the effect of free choice.[16]

The statement "God believed at t_1 that Jones would do X at t_2" (where the interval between t_1 and t_2 is, for example, eighty years) does not entail "'Jones did X at t_2' is necessary." Leibniz is surely right about this. All that will follow from the first of these statements concerning "Jones did X at t_2" is that the latter is *true,* not that it is *necessarily true.* But this observation has no real bearing on the issue at hand. The following passage from St. Augustine's formulation of the problem may help to make this point clear.

> Your trouble is this. You wonder how it can be that these two propositions are not contradictory and incompatible, namely that God has foreknowledge of all future events, and that we sin voluntarily and not by necessity. For if, you say, God foreknows that a man will sin, he must necessarily sin. But if there is necessity there is no voluntary choice of sinning, but rather fixed and unavoidable necessity.[17]

In this passage, the term "necessity" (or the phrase "by necessity") is not used to express a modal-logical concept. The term "necessity" is here used in contrast with the term "voluntary," not (as in Leibniz) in contrast with the term "contingent." If one's action is necessary (or by necessity), this is to say that one's action is not voluntary. Augustine says that if God has foreknowledge of human actions, the actions are necessary. But the form of this conditional is "p implies q," not "p implies n (q)." "q" in the consequent of this conditional is the claim that human actions are not voluntary—that is, that one is not able, or does not have the power, to do other than he does.

Perhaps I can make this point clearer by

13. Gilbert Ryle interprets it this way. See "It Was to Be," in *Dilemmas* (Cambridge, Engl., 1954).

14. Richard Gale suggests this interpretation in "Endorsing Predictions," *Philosophical Review,* 70(1961):376–85.

15. This view is held by John Turk Saunders in "Sea Fight Tomorrow?," *Philosophical Review,* 67(1958):367–78.

16. G. W. Leibniz, *Théodicée,* Pt. I, sec. 37. This passage trans. by E. M. Huggard (New Haven, 1952), p. 144.

17. *De Libero Arbitrio,* Bk. III. This passage trans. by J. H. S. Burleigh, *Augustine's Earlier Writings* (Philadelphia, 1955).

reformulating the original problem in such a way as to make explicit the modal operators working within it. Let it be *contingently* true that Jones did X at t_2. Since God holds a belief about the outcome of each human action well in advance of its performance, it is then *contingently* true that God believed at t_1 that Jones would do X at t_2. But it follows from this that it is *contingently* true that at t_2 Jones was not able to refrain from doing X. Had he been (contingently) able to refrain from doing X at t_2, then either he was (contingently) able to do something at t_2 that would have brought it about that God held a false belief at t_1, or he was (contingently) able to do something at t_2 that would have brought it about that God believed otherwise than He did at t_1, or he was (contingently) able to do something at t_2 that would have brought it about that God did not exist at t_1. None of these latter is an acceptable alternative.

B. In *Concordia Liberi Arbitrii,* Luis de Molina wrote as follows:

> It was not that since He foreknew what would happen from those things which depend on the created will that it would happen; but, on the contrary, it was because such things would happen through the freedom of the will, that He foreknew it; and that He would foreknow the opposite if the opposite was to happen.[18]

Remarks similar to this one can be found in a great many traditional and contemporary theological texts. In fact, Molina assures us that the view expressed in this passage has always been "above controversy"—a matter of "common opinion" and "unanimous consent"—not only among the Church fathers, but also, as he says, "among all catholic men."

One claim made in the above passage seems to me to be truly "above controversy." With respect to any given action foreknown by God, God would have foreknown the opposite if the opposite was to happen. If we assume the notion of omniscience outlined in the first section of this paper, and if we agree that omniscience is part of the "essence" of God, this statement is a conceptual truth. I doubt if anyone would be inclined to dispute it. Also involved in this passage, however, is at least the suggestion of a doctrine that cannot be taken as an item of "common opinion" among *all* catholic men. Molina says it is not because God foreknows what He foreknows that men act as they do: it is because men act as they do that God foreknows what He foreknows. Some theologians have rejected this claim. It seems to entail that men's actions determine God's cognitions. And this latter, I think, has been taken by some theologians to be a violation of the notion of God as self-sufficient and incapable of being affected by events of the natural world.[19] But I shall not develop this point further. Where the view put forward in the above passage seems to me to go wrong in an interesting and important way is in Molina's claim that God can have foreknowledge of things that will happen "through the freedom of the will." It is this claim that I here want to examine with care.

What exactly are we saying when we say that God can know in advance what will happen *through the freedom of the will?* I think that what Molina has in mind is this. God can know in advance that a given man is going to *choose* to perform a certain action sometime in the future. With respect to the case of Jones mowing his lawn, God knew at t_1 that Jones would *freely decide* to mow his lawn at t_2. Not only did God know at t_1 that Jones would mow his lawn at t_2, He also knew at t_1 that this action would be performed *freely.* In the words of Emil Brunner, "God knows that which will take place in freedom in the future as something which happens in freedom."[20] What God knew at t_1 is that Jones would *freely* mow his lawn at t_2.

18. Luis de Molina, *Concordia Liberi Arbitrii.* This passage trans. by John Mourant, *Readings in the Philosophy of Religion* (New York, 1954), p. 426.

19. Cf. Boethius's *Consolatio,* Bk. V, sec. 3, par. 2.

20. Emil Brunner, *The Christian Doctrine of God,* trans. by Olive Wyon (Philadelphia, 1964), p. 262.

I think that this doctrine is incoherent. If God knew (and thus believed) at t_1 that Jones would *do* X at t_2,[21] I think it follows that Jones was not able to do other than X at t_2 (for reasons already given). Thus, if God knew (and thus believed) at t_1 that Jones would *do* X at t_2, it would follow that Jones did X at t_2, but *not freely.* It does not seem to be possible that God could have believed at t_1 that Jones would freely do X at t_2. If God believed at t_1 that Jones would do X at t_2, Jones's action at t_2 was not free; and if God *also* believed at t_1 that Jones would freely act at t_2, it follows that God held a false belief at t_1—which is absurd.

C. Frederich Schleiermacher commented on the problem of divine foreknowledge as follows:

> In the same way, we estimate the intimacy between two persons by the foreknowledge one has of the actions of the other, without supposing that in either case, the one or the other's freedom is thereby endangered. So even the divine foreknowledge cannot endanger freedom.[22]

St. Augustine made this same point in *De Libero Arbitrio.* He said:

> Unless I am mistaken, you would not directly compel the man to sin, though you knew beforehand that he was going to sin. Nor does your presence in itself compel him to sin even though he was certainly going to sin, as we must assume if you have real prescience. So there is no contradiction here. Simply you know beforehand what another is going to do with his own will. Similarly God compels no man to sin, though he sees beforehand those who are going to sin by their own will.[23]

If we suppose (with Schleiermacher and Augustine) that the case of an intimate friend having foreknowledge of another's action has the same implications for determinism as the case of God's foreknowledge of human actions, I can imagine two positions which might then be taken. First, one might hold (with Schleiermacher and Augustine) that God's foreknowledge of human actions cannot entail determinism—since it is clear that an intimate friend can have foreknowledge of another's voluntary actions. Or, secondly, one might hold that an intimate friend cannot have foreknowledge of another's voluntary actions—since it is clear that God cannot have foreknowledge of such actions. This second position could take either of two forms. One might hold that since an intimate friend *can* have foreknowledge of another's actions, the actions in question cannot be voluntary. Or, alternatively, one might hold that since the other's actions *are* voluntary, the intimate friend cannot have foreknowledge of them.[24] But what I propose to argue in the remaining pages of this paper is that Schleiermacher and Augustine were mistaken in supposing that the case of an intimate friend having foreknowledge of another's actions has the same implications for determinism as the case of God's foreknowledge of human actions. What I want to suggest is that the argument I used above to show that God cannot have foreknowledge of voluntary actions cannot be used to show that an intimate friend cannot have foreknowledge of another's actions. Even if one holds that an intimate friend *can* have foreknowledge of another's voluntary actions, one ought not to think that the case is the same when dealing with the problem of divine foreknowledge.

Let Smith be an ordinary man and an intimate friend of Jones. Now, let us start by supposing that Smith believed at t_1 that Jones would do X at t_2. We make no assumption concerning the truth or falsity of Smith's belief, but assume only that Smith held it. Given only this much, there appears to be no difficulty in supposing that at t_2 Jones was able to do X and that at t_2 Jones was able to do not-X. So far as the above

21. Note: no comment here about *freely* doing X.

22. Schleiermacher, *The Christian Faith,* Pt. I, sec. 2, par. 55. This passage trans. by W. R. Matthew (Edinburgh, 1928), p. 228.

23. *De Libero Arbitrio,* Bk. III.

24. This last seems to be the position defended by Richard Taylor in "Deliberation and Foreknowledge," *American Philosophical Quarterly,* 1(1964):73–80.

description of the case is concerned, it might well have been within Jones's power at t_2 to do something (namely, X) which would have brought it about that Smith held a true belief at t_1, and it might well have been within Jones's power at t_2 to do something (namely, not-X) which would have brought it about that Smith held a false belief at t_1. So much seems apparent.

Now let us suppose that Smith *knew at* t_1 that Jones would do X at t_2. This is to suppose that Smith correctly believed (with evidence) at t_1 that Jones would do X at t_2. It follows, to be sure, that Jones *did* X at t_2. But now let us inquire about what Jones was *able* to do at t_2. I submit that there is nothing in the description of this case that requires the conclusion that it was not within Jones's power at t_2 to refrain from doing X. By hypothesis, the belief held by Smith at t_1 was true. Thus, by hypothesis, Jones did X at t_2. But even if we assume that the belief held by Smith at t_1 was *in fact* true, we can add that the belief held by Smith at t_1 *might have* turned out to be false.[25] Thus, even if we say that Jones *in fact* did X at t_2, we can add that Jones *might not* have done X at t_2—meaning by this that it was within Jones's power at t_2 to refrain from doing X. Smith held a true belief which might have turned out to be false, and, correspondingly, Jones performed an action which he was able to refrain from performing. Given that Smith correctly believed at t_1 that Jones would do X at t_2, we can still assign Jones the *power* at t_2 to refrain from doing X. All we need add is that the power in question is one which Jones *did not exercise.*

These last reflections have no application, however, when dealing with God's foreknowledge. Assume that God (being essentially omniscient) existed at t_1, and assume that He believed at t_1 that Jones would do X at t_2. It follows, again, that Jones did X at t_2. God's beliefs are true. But now, as above, let us inquire into what Jones was *able* to do at t_2. We cannot claim now, as in the Smith case, that the belief held by God at t_1, was *in fact* true but *might have* turned out to be false. No sense of "might have" has application here. It is a conceptual truth that God's beliefs are true. Thus, we cannot claim, as in the Smith case, that Jones *in fact* acted in accordance with God's beliefs but had the *ability* to refrain from so doing. The ability to refrain from acting in accordance with one of God's beliefs would be the ability to do something that would bring it about that one of God's beliefs was false. And no one could have an ability of this description. Thus, in the case of God's foreknowledge of Jones's action at t_2, if we are to assign Jones the ability at t_2 to refrain from doing X, we must understand this ability in some way other than the way we understood it when dealing with Smith's foreknowledge. In this case, either we must say that it was the ability at t_2 to bring it about that God believed otherwise than He did at t_1; or we must say that it was the ability at t_2 to bring it about that any person who believed at t_1 that Jones would do X at t_2 (one of whom was, by hypothesis, God) held a false belief and thus was not God. But, as pointed out earlier, neither of these last alternatives can be accepted.

The important thing to be learned from the study of Smith's foreknowledge of Jones's action is that the problem of divine foreknowledge has as one of its pillars the claim that truth is *analytically* connected with God's being. No problem of determinism arises when dealing with human knowledge of future actions. This is because truth is not analytically connected with human belief even when (as in the case of human knowledge) truth is contingently conjoined to belief. If we suppose that Smith knows at t_1 that Jones will do X at t_2, what we are supposing is that Smith believes at t_1 that Jones will do X at t_2 and (as an additional, contingent, fact) that the belief in question is true. Thus having supposed that Smith knows at t_1 that Jones will do

25. The phrase "might have" as it occurs in this sentence does not express mere *logical* possibility. I am not sure how to analyze the notion of possibility involved here, but I think it is roughly the same notion as is involved when we say, "Jones might have been killed in the accident (had it not been for the fact that at the last minute he decided not to go)."

X at t_2, when we turn to a consideration of the situation of t_2 we can infer (1) that Jones *will* do X at t_2 (since Smith's belief is true), and (2) that Jones does not have the power at t_2 to do something that would bring it about that Smith did not *believe* as he did at t_1. But paradoxical though it may seem (and it seems paradoxical only at first sight), Jones can have the power at t_2 to do something that would bring it about that Smith did not have *knowledge* at t_1. This is simply to say that Jones can have the *power* at t_2 to do something that would bring it about that the belief held by Smith at t_1 (which was, in fact, true) was (instead) false. We are required only to add that since Smith's belief was in fact true (that is, was knowledge) Jones *did not* (in fact) *exercise* that power. But when we turn to a consideration of God's foreknowledge of Jones's action at t_2 the elbowroom between belief and truth disappears and, with it, the possibility of assigning Jones even the *power* of doing other than he does at t_2. We begin by supposing that God *knows* at t_1 that Jones will do X at t_2. As above, this is to suppose that God believes at t_1 that Jones will do X at t_2, and it is to suppose that this belief is true. But it is *not* an additional, contingent fact that the belief held by God is true. "God believes X" entails "X is true." Thus, having supposed that God knows (and thus believes) at t_1 that Jones will do X at t_2, we can infer (1) that Jones *will do X* at t_2 (since God's belief is true); (2) that Jones does not have the power at t_2 to do something that would bring it about that God did not hold the belief He held at t_1, and (3) that Jones does not have the power at t_2 to do something that would bring it about that the belief held by God at t_1 was false. This last is what we could *not* infer when truth and belief were only factually connected—as in the case of Smith's knowledge. To be sure, "Smith knows at t_1 that Jones will do X at t_2" and "God knows at t_1 that Jones will do X at t_2" both entail "Jones will do X at t_2" ("A knows X" entails "'X' is true"). But this similarity between "Smith knows X" and "God knows X" is not a point of any special interest in the present discussion. As Schleiermacher and Augustine rightly insisted (and as we discovered in our study of Smith's foreknowledge), the mere fact that someone knows in advance how another will act in the future is not enough to yield a problem of the sort we have been discussing. We begin to get a glimmer of the knot involved in the problem of divine foreknowledge when we shift attention away from the *similarities* between "Smith knows X" and "God knows X" (in particular, that they both entail "'X' is true") and concentrate instead on the logical *differences* which obtain between Smith's knowledge and God's knowledge. We get to the difference which makes the difference when, after analyzing the notion of knowledge as true belief (supported by evidence) we discover the radically dissimilar relations between truth and belief in the two cases. When truth is only factually connected with belief (as in Smith's knowledge) one can have the power (though, by hypothesis, one will not exercise it) to do something that would make the belief false. But when truth is analytically connected with belief (as in God's belief) no one can have the power to do something which would render the belief false.

To conclude: I have assumed that any statement of the form "A knows X" entails a statement of the form "A believes X" as well as a statement of the form "'X' is true." I have then supposed (as an analytic truth) that if a given person is omniscient, that person (1) holds no false beliefs, and (2) holds beliefs about the outcome of human actions in advance of their performance. In addition, I have assumed that the statement "If a given person is God that person is omniscient" is an a priori statement. (This last I have labeled the doctrine of God's essential omniscience.) Given these items (plus some premises concerning what is and what is not within one's power), I have argued that if God exists, it is not within one's power to do other than he does. I have inferred from this that if God exists, no human action is voluntary.

As emphasized earlier, I do not want to claim that the assumptions underpinning the argument are acceptable. In fact, it seems to me that a theologian interested in claiming both that God is omniscient and that men have free will could deny any one (or more) of them. For example, a theologian might deny that a statement of the form "*A* knows *X*" entails a statement of the form "*A* believes *X*" (some contemporary philosophers have denied this), or alternatively, he might claim that this entailment holds in the case of human knowledge but fails in the case of God's knowledge. This latter would be to claim that when knowledge is attributed to God, the term "knowledge" bears a sense other than the one it has when knowledge is attributed to human beings. Then again, a theologian might object to the analysis of "omniscience" with which I have been working. Although I doubt if any Christian theologian would allow that an omniscient being could believe something false, he might claim that a given person could be omniscient although he did not hold beliefs about the outcome of human actions *in advance* of their performance. (This latter is the way Boethius escaped the problem.) Still again, a theologian might deny the doctrine of God's essential omniscience. He might admit that if a given person is God that person is omniscient, but he might deny that this statement formulates an a priori truth. This would be to say that although God is omniscient, He is not *essentially* omniscient. So far as I can see, within the conceptual framework of theology employing any one of these adjustments, the problem of divine foreknowledge outlined in this paper could not be formulated. There thus appears to be a rather wide range of alternatives open to the theologian at this point. It would be a mistake to think that commitment to determinism is an unavoidable implication of the Christian concept of divine omniscience.

But having arrived at this understanding, the importance of the preceding deliberations ought not to be overlooked. There is a pitfall in the doctrine of divine omniscience. That knowing involves believing (truly) is surely a tempting philosophical view (witness the many contemporary philosophers who have affirmed it). And the idea that God's attributes (including omniscience) are essentially connected to His nature, together with the idea that an omniscient being would hold no false beliefs and would hold beliefs about the outcome of human actions in advance of their performance, might be taken by some theologians as obvious candidates for inclusion in a finished Christian theology. Yet the theologian must approach these items critically. If they are embraced together, then if one affirms the existence of God, one is committed to the view that no human action is voluntary.

Robert Merrihew Adams

"MUST GOD CREATE THE BEST?"

ROBERT MERRIHEW ADAMS, a Presbyterian minister, taught philosophy at the University of Michigan before accepting his current position as professor of philosophy at the University of California, Los Angeles. He has written extensively on

Reprinted from *The Philosophical Review* 74 (1965): 27–46, by permission of the publisher and the author.

metaphysics, ethics, the history of philosophy, and contemporary philosophy of religion. He recently published his collected papers under the title *The Virtue of Faith* (1987).

Many philosophers and theologians have accepted the following proposition:

> *(P)* If a perfectly good moral agent created any world at all, it would have to be the very best world that he could create.

The best world that an omnipotent God could create is the best of all logically possible worlds. Accordingly, it has been supposed that if the actual world was created by an omnipotent, perfectly good God, it must be the best of all logically possible worlds.

In this paper I shall argue that ethical views typical of the Judeo-Christian religious tradition do not require the Judeo-Christian theist to accept *(P)*. He must hold that the actual world is a good world. But he need not maintain that it is the best of all possible worlds, or the best world that God could have made.[1]

The position which I am claiming that he can consistently hold is that *even if* there is a best among possible worlds, God could create another instead of it, and still be perfectly good. I do not in fact see any good reason to believe that there is a best among possible worlds. Why can't it be that for every possible world there is another that is better? And if there is no maximum degree of perfection among possible worlds, it would be unreasonable to blame God, or think less highly of His goodness, because He created a world less excellent than He could have created.[2] But I do not claim to be able to prove that there is no best among possible worlds, and in this essay I shall assume for the sake of argument that there is one.

Whether we accept proposition *(P)* will depend on what we believe are the requirements for perfect goodness. If we apply an act-utilitarian standard of moral goodness, we will have to accept *(P)*. For by act-utilitarian standards, it is a moral obligation to bring about the best state of affairs that one can. It is interesting to note that the ethics of Leibniz, the best-known advocate of *(P)*, is basically utilitarian.[3] In his *Theodicy* (Part I, Section 25) he maintains, in effect, that men, because of their ignorance of many of the consequences of their actions, ought to follow a rule-utilitarian code, but that God, being omniscient, must be a perfect act utilitarian in order to be perfectly good.

I believe that utilitarian views are not typical of the Judeo-Christian ethical tradition, although Leibniz is by no means the only Christian utilitarian. In this essay I shall assume that we are working with standards of moral goodness which are not utilitarian. But I shall not try either to show that utilitarianism is wrong or to justify the standards that I take to be more typical of Judeo-Christian religious ethics. To attempt either of these tasks would unmanageably enlarge the scope of the paper. What I can hope to establish here is therefore limited to the claim that the rejection of *(P)* is consistent with Judeo-Christian religious ethics.

Assuming that we are not using utilitarian standards of moral goodness, I see only two types of reason that could be given for *(P)*. (1) It might be claimed that a creator would necessarily wrong someone (violate someone's rights), or be less kind to someone than a perfectly good moral agent must be, if he knowingly created a less excellent world instead of the best that he could. Or (2) it might be claimed that even if no one would be wronged or treated unkindly by the

---

1. What I am saying in this paper is obviously relevant to the problem of evil. But I make no claim to be offering a complete theodicy here.

2. Leibniz held (in his *Theodicy,* pt. I, sec. 8) that if there were no best among possible worlds, a perfectly good God would have created nothing at all. But Leibniz is mistaken if he supposes that in this way God could avoid choosing an alternative less excellent than others He could have chosen. For the existence of no created world at all would surely be a less excellent state of affairs than the existence of some of the worlds that God could have created.

3. See Gaston Grua, *Jurisprudence universelle et théodicée selon Leibniz* (Paris, 1953), pp. 210–218.

creation of an inferior world, the creator's choice of an inferior world must manifest a defect of character. I will argue against the first of these claims in Section II. Then I will suggest, in Section III, that God's choice of a less excellent world could be accounted for in terms of His grace, which is considered a virtue rather than a defect of character in Judeo-Christian ethics. A counterexample, which is the basis for the most persuasive objections to my position that I have encountered, will be considered in Sections IV and V.

II

Is there someone *to* whom a creator would have an obligation to create the best world he could? Is there someone whose rights would be violated, or who would be treated unkindly, if the creator created a less excellent world? Let us suppose that our creator is God, and that there does not exist any being, other than Himself, which He has not created. It follows that if God has wronged anyone, or been unkind to anyone, in creating whatever world He has created, this must be one of His own creatures. To which of His creatures, then, might God have an obligation to create the best of all possible worlds? (For that is the best world He could create.)

Might He have an obligation to the creatures in the best possible world, to create them? Have they been wronged, or even treated unkindly, if God has created a less excellent world, in which they do not exist, instead of creating them? I think not. The difference between actual beings and merely possible beings is of fundamental moral importance here. The moral community consists of actual beings. It is they who would have actual rights, and it is to them that there are actual obligations. A merely possible being cannot be (actually) wronged or treated unkindly. A being who never exists is not wronged by not being created, and there is no obligation to any possible being to bring it into existence.

Perhaps it will be objected that we believe we have obligations to future generations, who are not yet actual and may never be actual. We do say such things, but I think what we mean is something like the following. There is not merely a logical possibility, but a probability greater than zero, that future generations will really exist; and *if* they will in fact exist, we will have wronged them if we act or fail to act in certain ways. On this analysis we cannot have an obligation to future generations to bring them into existence.

I argue, then, that God does not have an obligation to the creatures in the best of all possible worlds to create them. If God has chosen to create a world less excellent than the best possible, He has not thereby wronged any creatures whom He has chosen not to create. He has not even been unkind to them. If any creatures are wronged, or treated unkindly, by such a choice of the creator, they can only be creatures that exist in the world He has created.

I think it is fairly plausible to suppose that God could create a world which would have the following characteristics:

(1) None of the individual creatures in it would exist in the best of all possible worlds.
(2) None of the creatures in it has a life which is so miserable on the whole that it would be better for that creature if it had never existed.
(3) Every individual creature in the world is at least as happy on the whole as it would have been in any other possible world in which it could have existed.

It seems obvious that if God creates such a world He does not thereby wrong any of the creatures in it, and does not thereby treat any of them with less than perfect kindness. For none of them would have been benefited by His creating any other world instead.[4]

If there are doubts about the possibility of God's creating such a world, they will probably have to do with the third characteristic. It may

4. Perhaps I can have a right to something which would not benefit me (e.g., if it has been promised to me). But if there are such non-beneficial rights, I do not see any plausible reason for supposing that a right not to be created could be among them.

be worthwhile to consider two questions, on the supposition (which I am not endorsing) that no possible world less excellent than the best would have characteristic (3), and that God has created a world which has characteristics (1) and (2) but not (3). In such a case must God have wronged one of His creatures? Must He have been less than perfectly kind to one of His creatures?

I do not think it can reasonably be argued that in such a case God must have wronged one of His creatures. Suppose a creature in such a case were to complain that God had violated its rights by creating it in a world in which it was less happy on the whole than it would have been in some other world in which God could have created it. The complaint might express a claim to special treatment: "God ought to have created *me* in more favorable circumstances (even though that would involve His creating some *other* creature in less favorable circumstances than He could have created it in)." Such a complaint would not be reasonable, and would not establish that there had been any violation of the complaining creature's rights.

Alternatively, the creature might make the more principled complaint, "God has wronged me by not following the principle of refraining from creating any world in which there is a creature that would have been happier in another world He could have made." This also is an unreasonable complaint. For if God followed the stated principle, He would not create any world that lacked characteristic (3). And we are assuming that no world less excellent than the best possible would have characteristic (3). It follows that if God acted on the stated principle He would not create any world less excellent than the best possible. But the complaining creature would not exist in the best of all possible worlds; for we are assuming that this creature exists in a world which has characteristic (1). The complaining creature, therefore, would never have existed if God had followed the principle that is urged in the complaint. There could not possibly

In ancient Greece, religion, art, literature, and philosophy were one; the theater in Epidaurus (built in approximately 300 B.C.), which seated twelve thousand people.

be any advantage to this creature from God's having followed that principle; and the creature has not been wronged by God's not following the principle. (It would not be better for the creature if it had never existed; for we are assuming that the world God created has characteristic [2].)

The question of whether in the assumed case God must have been unkind to one of His creatures is more complicated than the question of whether He must have wronged one of them. In fact it is too complicated to be discussed adequately here. I will just make three observations about it. The first is that it is no clearer that the best of all possible worlds would possess characteristic (3) than that some less excellent world would possess it. In fact it has often been supposed that the best possible world might not possess it. The problem we are now discussing can therefore arise also for those who believe that God has created the best of all possible worlds.

My second observation is that if kindness to a person is the same as a tendency to promote his happiness, God has been less than perfectly

"God's Compassion"

William J. Wainwright

Anselm argued that God is compassionate in the sense that He acts *as if* He felt compassion although He doesn't actually do so. . . .

Bernard of Clairvaux (1090–1153) maintained that while God can't grieve or suffer in His *own* nature, He became incarnate so that He might "learn by his own experience how to commiserate and sympathize with those who are . . . suffering and tempted." . . .

Thomas Aquinas (1225–74) has a more adequate solution. Love and joy are pure perfections. Hence, God literally has them although the mode in which He loves and rejoices differs from the mode in which we do so. (Human love and joy are often partly voluntary. We willingly embrace what we love or rejoice in. But they are also "passions"—externally induced modifications of our animal nature over which we have little control. God has no animal nature. His love and joy are wholly active, an expression only of His will.)

Anger and sorrow differ from love and joy because they entail suffering. Hence, even when these emotions are appropriate, they are only mixed perfections. They can therefore only be ascribed to God metaphorically. Nevertheless, anger and sorrow aren't *equally* metaphorical. Anger is ascribed to God because He produces effects similar to those which an angry person might produce. But no internal modification of God corresponds to anger in us. By contrast, God "is said to be saddened in so far as certain things take place contrary to what He loves and approves." While God doesn't literally grieve, there is something *in* God (an internal modification of God) that we apprehend as sorrow, namely, His love. That is, when our awareness of God's love is coupled with our recognition that creatures disobey God and suffer, we construe the divine love as sorrow.

Like Bernard, Thomas implicitly recognizes that there is no compassion without sympathetic feeling or emotion. But unlike many modern theologians, Thomas thinks the emotion in question is simply love—not tender sorrow. This has two advantages. Love is compatible with unalloyed joy while sympathetic sorrow is not. Furthermore, love can be a purely active emotion—a spontaneous expression of the lover's own inner richness. By contrast, sympathetic sorrow is essentially a reaction rather than an action. Love thus coheres better with God's independence.

Thomas's solution is superior to Anselm's and Bernard's. Whether it is fully satisfactory depends on whether a compassion that doesn't literally involve sympathetic suffering is really compassion and thus adequately meets the demands of religious consciousness.

From *Philosophy of Religion*, 1988.

(completely, unqualifiedly) kind to any creature whom He could have made somewhat happier than He has made it. (I shall not discuss here whether kindness to a person is indeed the same as a tendency to promote his happiness; they are at least closely related.)

But in the third place I would observe that such qualified kindness (if that is what it is) toward some creatures is consistent with God's being perfectly good, and with His being very kind to all His creatures. It is consistent with His being very kind to all His creatures because He may have prepared for all of them a very satisfying existence even though some of them might have been slightly happier in some other possible world. It is consistent with His being perfectly good because even a perfectly good moral agent may be led, by other considerations of sufficient weight, to qualify his kindness or beneficence toward some person. It has sometimes been held that a perfectly good God might cause or permit a person to have less happiness than he might otherwise have had, in order to punish him, or to avoid interfering with the freedom of another person, or in order to create the best of all possible worlds. I would suggest that the desire to create and love all of a certain group of possible creatures (assuming that all of them would have satisfying lives on the whole) might be an adequate ground for a perfectly good God to create them, even if His creating *all* of them must have the result that some of them are less happy than they might otherwise have been. And they need not be the best of all possible creatures, or included in the best of all possible worlds, in order for this qualification of His kindness to be consistent with His perfect goodness. The desire to create *those* creatures is as legitimate a ground for Him to qualify His kindness toward some, as the desire to create the best of all possible worlds. This suggestion seems to me to be in keeping with the aspect of the Judeo-Christian moral ideal which will be discussed in Section III.

These matters would doubtless have to be discussed more fully if we were considering whether the *actual* world can have been created by a perfectly good God. For our present purposes, however, enough may have been said—especially since, as I have noted, it seems a plausible assumption that God could make a world having characteristics (1), (2), and (3). In that case He could certainly make a less excellent world than the best of all possible worlds without wronging any of His creatures or failing in kindness to any of them. (I have, of course, *not* been arguing that there is *no* way in which God could wrong anyone or be less kind to anyone than a perfectly good moral agent must be.)

III

Plato is one of those who held that a perfectly good creator would make the very best world he could. He thought that if the creator chose to make a world less good than he could have made, that could be understood only in terms of some defect in the creator's character. Envy is the defect that Plato suggests.[5] It may be thought that the creation of a world inferior to the best that he could make would manifest a defect in the creator's character even if no one were thereby wronged or treated unkindly. For the perfectly good moral agent must not only be kind and refrain from violating the rights of others, but must also have other virtues. For instance, he must be noble, generous, high-minded, and free from envy. He must satisfy the moral ideal.

There are differences of opinion, however, about what is to be included in the moral ideal. One important element in the Judeo-Christian moral ideal is *grace*. For present purposes, grace may be defined as a disposition to love which is not dependent on the merit of the person loved. The gracious person loves without worrying about whether the person he loves is worthy of his love. Or perhaps it would be better to say that the gracious person sees what is valuable in the person he loves, and does not worry about whether

5. *Timaeus*, 29E–30A.

it is more or less valuable than what could be found in someone else he might have loved. In the Judeo-Christian tradition it is typically believed that grace is a virtue which God does have and men ought to have.

A God who is gracious with respect to creating might well choose to create and love less excellent creatures than He could have chosen. This is not to suggest that grace in creation consists in a preference for imperfection as such. God could have chosen to create the best of all possible creatures, and still have been gracious in choosing them. God's graciousness in creation does not imply that the creatures He has chosen to create must be less excellent than the best possible. It implies, rather, that even if they are the best possible creatures, that is not the ground for His choosing them. And it implies that there is nothing in God's nature or character which would require Him to act on the principle of choosing the best possible creatures to be the object of His creative powers.

Grace, as I have described it, is not part of everyone's moral ideal. For instance, it was not part of Plato's moral ideal. The thought that it may be the expression of a virtue, rather than a defect of character, in a creator, *not* to act on the principle of creating the best creatures he possibly could, is quite foreign to Plato's ethical viewpoint. But I believe that thought is not at all foreign to a Judeo-Christian ethical viewpoint.

This interpretation of the Judeo-Christian tradition is confirmed by the religious and devotional attitudes toward God's creation which prevail in the tradition. The man who worships God does not normally praise Him for His moral rectitude and good judgment in creating *us.* He thanks God for his existence as for an undeserved personal favor. Religious writings frequently deprecate the intrinsic worth of human beings, considered apart from God's love for them, and express surprise that God should concern Himself with them at all.

Jerusalem, holy city to three religions: the Western (wailing) Wall, one of the most sacred Jewish religious sites, is the sole remnant of Solomon's temple, built around 960 B.C. and rebuilt around 515 B.C. Looming directly above the Western Wall is the Dome of the Rock on the Temple Mount, one of the holiest Muslim shrines.

> When I look at thy heavens, the work of thy fingers, the moon and the stars which thou hast established;
> What is man that thou art mindful of him, and the son of man that thou dost care for him?
> Yet thou hast made him little less than God, and dost crown him with glory and honor.
> Thou hast given him dominion over the works of thy hands; thou hast put all things under his feet [Psalm 8:3–6].

Such utterances seem quite incongruous with the idea that God created us because if He had not He would have failed to bring about the best possible state of affairs. They suggest that God has created human beings and made them dominant on this planet although He could have created intrinsically better states of affairs instead.

I believe that in the Judeo-Christian tradition the typical religious attitude (or at any rate the attitude typically encouraged) toward the fact of our existence is something like the following. "I am glad that I exist, and I thank God for the life He has given me. I am also glad that other people exist, and I thank God for them. Doubtless there could be more excellent creatures than we. But I believe that God, in His grace, created us and loves us; and I accept that gladly and

"The Doctrine of Analogy"

St. Thomas Aquinas

Since it is possible to find in God every perfection of creatures, but in another and more eminent way, whatever names unqualifiedly designate a perfection without defect are predicated of God and of other things: for example, goodness, wisdom, being, and the like. But when any name expresses such perfections along with a mode that is proper to a creature, it can be said of God only according to likeness and metaphor. According to metaphor, what belongs to one thing is transferred to another, as when we say that a man is a *stone* because of the hardness of his intellect. Such names are used to designate the species of a created thing, for example, *man* and *stone;* for to each species belongs its own mode of perfection and being. The same is true of whatever names designate the properties of things, which are caused by the proper principles of their species. Hence, they can be said of God only metaphorically. But the names that express such perfections along with the mode of supereminence with which they belong to God are said of God alone. Such names are the *highest good, the first being,* and the like.

I have said that some of the aforementioned names signify a perfection without defect. This is true with reference to that which the name was imposed to signify; for as to the mode of signification, every name is defective. For by means of a name we express things in the way in which the intellect conceives them. For our intellect, taking the origin of its knowledge from the senses, does not transcend the mode which is found in sensible things in which the form and the subject of the form are not identical owning to the composition of form and matter. Now, a simple form is indeed found among such things, but one that is imperfect because it is not subsisting; on the other hand, though a subsisting subject of a form is found among sensible things, it is not simple but rather concreted. Whatever our intellect signifies as subsisting, therefore, it signifies in concretion; but what it signifies as simple, . . .

Now, the mode of supereminence in which the abovementioned perfections are found in God can be signified by names used by us only through negation, as when we say that God is *eternal* or *infinite,* or also through a relation of God to other things, as when He is called the *first cause* or the *highest good.* For we cannot grasp what God is, but only what He is not and how other things are related to Him, as is clear from what we said above.

From *Summa Theologica.*

gratefully." (Such an attitude need not be complacent; for the task of struggling against certain evils may be seen as precisely a part of the life that the religious person is to accept and be glad in.) When people who have or endorse such an attitude say that God is perfectly good, we will not take them as committing themselves to the view that God is the kind of being who would not create any other world than the best possible. For they regard grace as an important part of perfect goodness.

IV

On more than one occasion when I have argued for the positions I have taken in Sections II and III above, a counterexample of the following sort has been proposed. It is the case of a person who, knowing that he intends to conceive a child and that a certain drug invariably causes severe mental retardation in children conceived by those who have taken it, takes the drug and conceives a severely retarded child. We all, I imagine, have a strong inclination to say that such a person has done something wrong. It is objected to me that our moral intuitions in this case (presumably including the moral intuitions of religious Jews and Christians) are inconsistent with the views I have advanced above. It is claimed that consistency requires me to abandon those views unless I am prepared to make moral judgments that none of us are in fact willing to make.

I will try to meet these objections. I will begin by stating the case in some detail, in the most relevant form I can think of. Then I will discuss objections based on it. In this section I will discuss an objection against what I have said in Section II, and a more general objection against the rejection of proposition *(P)* will be discussed in Section V.

Let us call this Case *(A)*. A certain couple become so interested in retarded children that they develop a strong desire to have a retarded child of their own—to love it, to help it realize its potentialities (such as they are) to the full, to see that it is as happy as it can be. (For some reason it is impossible for them to *adopt* such a child.) They act on their desire. They take a drug which is known to cause damaged genes and abnormal chromosome structure in reproductive cells, resulting in severe mental retardation of children conceived by those who have taken it. A severely retarded child is conceived and born. They lavish affection on the child. They have ample means, so that they are able to provide for special needs, and to insure that others will never be called on to pay for the child's support. They give themselves unstintedly, and do develop the child's capacities as much as possible. The child is, on the whole, happy, though incapable of many of the higher intellectual, aesthetic, and social joys. It suffers some pains and frustrations, of course, but does not feel miserable on the whole.

The first objection founded on this case is based, not just on the claim that the parents have done something wrong (which I certainly grant), but on the more specific claim that they have *wronged the child.* I maintained, in effect, in Section II that a creature has not been wronged by its creator's creating it if both of the following conditions are satisfied.[6] (4) The creature is not, on the whole, so miserable that it would be better for him if he had never existed. (5) No being who came into existence in better or happier circumstances would have been the same individual as the creature in question. If we apply an analogous principle to the parent-child relationship in Case *(A)*, it would seem to follow that the retarded child has not been wronged by its parents. Condition (4) is satisfied: the child is happy rather than miserable on the whole. And condition (5) also seems to be satisfied. For the retardation in Case *(A)*, as described, is not due to prenatal injury but to the genetic con-

6. I am not holding that these are necessary conditions, but only that they are jointly sufficient conditions, for a creature's not being wronged by its creator's creating it. I have numbered these conditions in such a way as to avoid confusion with the numbered characteristics of worlds in sec. II.

stitution of the child. Any normal child the parents might have conceived (indeed any normal child at all) would have had a different genetic constitution, and would therefore have been a different person, from the retarded child they actually did conceive. But—it is objected to me—we do regard the parents in Case *(A)* as having wronged the child, and therefore we cannot consistently accept the principle that I maintained in Section II.

My reply is that if conditions (4) and (5) are really satisfied the child cannot have been wronged by its parents' taking the drug and conceiving it. If we think otherwise we are being led, perhaps by our emotions, into a confusion. If the child is not worse off than if it had never existed, and if *its* never existing would have been a sure consequence of its not having been brought into existence as retarded, I do not see how *its* interests can have been injured, or *its* rights violated, by the parents' bringing it into existence as retarded.

It is easy to understand how the parents might come to feel that they had wronged the child. They might come to feel guilty (and rightly so), and the child would provide a focus for the guilt. Moreover, it would be easy, psychologically, to assimilate Case *(A)* to cases of culpability for prenatal injury, in which it is more reasonable to think of the child as having been wronged.[7] And we often think very carelessly about counterfactual personal identity, asking ourselves questions of doubtful intelligibility, such as, "What if I had been born in the Middle Ages?" It is very easy to fail to consider the objection, "But that would not have been the same person."

It is also possible that an inclination to say that the child has been wronged may be based, at least in part, on a doubt that conditions (4) and (5) are really satisfied in case *(A)*. Perhaps one is not convinced that in real life the parents could ever have a reasonable confidence that the child would be happy rather than miserable. Maybe it will be doubted that a few changes in chromosome structure, and the difference between damaged and undamaged genes, are enough to establish that the retarded child is a different person from any normal child that the couple could have had. Of course, if conditions (4) and (5) are not satisfied, the case does not constitute a counterexample to my claims in Section II. But I would not rest any of the weight of my argument on doubts about the satisfaction of the conditions on Case *(A)*, because I think it is plausible to suppose that they would be satisfied in Case *(A)* or in some very similar case.

V

Even if the parents in Case *(A)* have not wronged the child, I assume that they have done something wrong. It may be asked *what* they have done wrong, or *why* their action is regarded as wrong. And these questions may give rise to an objection, not specifically to what I said in Section II, but more generally to my rejection of proposition *(P)*. For it may be suggested that what is wrong about the action of the parents in Case *(A)* is that they have violated the following principle:

> *(Q)* It is wrong to bring into existence, knowingly, a being less excellent than one could have brought into existence.[8]

If we accept this principle we must surely agree that it would be wrong for a creator to make a world that was less excellent than the best he could make, and therefore that a perfectly good creator would not do such a thing. In other words, *(Q)* implies *(P)*.

7. I may be questioned whether even the prenatally injured child is the same person as any unimpaired child that might have been born. I am inclined to think it is the same person. At any rate there is *more* basis for regarding it as the same person as a possible normal child than there is for so regarding a child with abnormal genetic constitution.

8. Anyone who was applying this principle to human actions would doubtless insert an "other things being equal" clause. But let us ignore that, since such a clause would presumably provide no excuse for an agent who was deciding an issue so important as what world to create.

I do not think *(Q)* is a very plausible principle. It is not difficult to think of counterexamples to it.

Case *(B)*: A man breeds goldfish, thereby bringing about their existence. We do not normally think it is wrong, or even prima facie wrong, for a man to do this, even though he could equally well have brought about the existence of more excellent beings, more intelligent and capable of higher satisfactions. (He could have bred dogs or pigs, for example.) The deliberate breeding of human beings of subnormal intelligence is morally offensive; the deliberate breeding of species far less intelligent than retarded human children is not morally offensive.

Case *(C)*: Suppose it has been discovered that if intending parents take a certain drug before conceiving a child, they will have a child whose abnormal genetic constitution will give it vastly superhuman intelligence and superior prospects of happiness. Other things being equal, would it be wrong for intending parents to have normal children instead of taking the drug? There may be considerable disagreement of moral judgment about this. I do not think that parents who chose to have normal children rather than take the drug would be doing anything wrong, nor that they would necessarily be manifesting any weakness or defect of moral character. Parents' choosing to have a normal rather than a superhuman child would not, at any rate, elicit the strong and universal or almost universal disapproval that would be elicited by the action of the parents in Case *(A)*. Even with respect to the offspring of human beings, the principle we all confidently endorse is not that it is wrong to bring about, knowingly and voluntarily, the procreation of offspring less excellent than could have been procreated, but that it is wrong to bring about, knowingly and voluntarily, the procreation of a human offspring which is deficient by comparison with normal human beings.

Such counterexamples as these suggest that our disapproval of the action of the parents in Case *(A)* is not based on principle *(Q)*, but on a less general and more plausible principle such as the following:

> *(R)* It is wrong for human beings to cause, knowingly and voluntarily, the procreation of an offspring of human parents which is notably deficient, by comparison with normal human beings, in mental or physical capacity.

One who rejects *(Q)* while maintaining *(R)* might be held to face a problem of explanation. It may seem arbitrary to maintain such a specific moral principle as *(R)*, unless one can explain it as based on a more general principle, such as *(Q)*. I believe, however, that principle *(R)* might well be explained in something like the following way in a theological ethics in the Judeo-Christian tradition, consistently with the rejection of *(Q)* and *(P)*.[9]

God, in His grace, has chosen to have human beings among His creatures. In creating us He has certain intentions about the qualities and goals of human life. He has these intentions for us, not just as individuals, but as members of a community which in principle includes the whole human race. And His intentions for human beings as such extend to the offspring (if any) of human beings. Some of these intentions are to be realized by human voluntary action, and it is our duty to act in accordance with them.

It seems increasingly possible for human voluntary action to influence the genetic constitution of human offspring. The religious believer in the Judeo-Christian tradition will want to be extremely cautious about this. For he is to be thankful that we exist as the beings we are, and will be concerned lest he bring about the procreation of human offspring who would be deficient in their capacity to enter fully into the purposes that God has for human beings as such. We are not God. We are His creatures, and we belong to Him. Any offspring we have will belong to Him in a much more fundamental way than they can belong to their human parents. We have

9. I am able to give here, of course, only a very incomplete sketch of a theological position on the issue of "biological engineering."

not the right to try to have as our offspring just any kind of being whose existence might on the whole be pleasant and of some value (for instance, a being of very low intelligence but highly specialized for the enjoyment of aesthetic pleasures of smell and taste). If we do intervene to affect the genetic constitution of human offspring, it must be in ways which seem likely to make them *more* able to enter fully into what we believe to be the purposes of God for human beings as such. The deliberate procreation of children deficient in mental or physical capacity would be an intervention which could hardly be expected to result in offspring more able to enter fully into God's purposes for human life. It would therefore be sinful, and inconsistent with a proper respect for the human life which God has given us.

On this view of the matter, our obligation to refrain from bringing about the procreation of deficient human offspring is rooted in our obligation to God, as His creatures, to respect His purposes for human life. In adopting this theological rationale for the acceptance of principle *(R)*, one in no way commits oneself to proposition *(P)*. For one does not base *(R)* on any principle to the effect that one must always try to bring into existence the most excellent things that one can. And the claim that, because of His intentions for human life, we have an obligation to God not to try to have as our offspring beings of certain sorts does not imply that it would be wrong for God to create such beings in other ways. Much less does it imply that it would be wrong for God to create a world less excellent than the best possible.

In this essay I have argued that a creator would not necessarily wrong anyone, or be less kind to anyone than a perfectly good moral agent must be, if he created a world of creatures who would not exist in the best world he could make. I have also argued that from the standpoint of Judeo-Christian religious ethics, a creator's choice of a less excellent world need not be regarded as manifesting a defect of character. It could be understood in terms of his *grace,* which (in that ethics) is considered an important part of perfect goodness. In this way I think the rejection of proposition *(P)* can be seen to be congruous with the attitude of gratitude and respect for human life as God's gracious gift which is encouraged in the Judeo-Christian religious tradition. And that attitude (rather than any belief that one ought to bring into existence only the best beings one can) can be seen as a basis for the disapproval of the deliberate procreation of deficient human offspring.

Daniel Kolak

CAUSALITY, RESPONSIBILITY, AND THE FREE WILL DEFENSE

DANIEL KOLAK received his Ph.D. from the University of Maryland and teaches philosophy at William Paterson College. Among his books are *The Search for God* (1993), *The Philosophy of Mind* (1993), *Wisdom without Answers* (1991), *The*

Experience of Philosophy (1990), *Self and Identity* (1991), and *Mathematical Thought* (1993), as well as the forthcoming titles, *Zeno's Paradox Refined: An Eleatic Model of Rationality*, and *I Am You: Dissolving the Boundaries of Personal Identity*.

Imagine a huge, perhaps infinite, casino with billions of roulette wheels in it, which are all spun together at the same time when the appropriate signal is given to the croupiers. Suppose, further, that the outcome of a spin of any one wheel is causally indeterminate: That is, at the moment of the spin, given all possible data available—the momentum of the ball, the position of the air molecules, the torque on the wheel, friction, and so on—one could not, on the basis of this alone, predict the outcome. In other words, no matter how much data we tabulate about the ball and the wheel, we would not be able to predict with absolute certainty the numbered slot in which the ball will land (though a perfect knower might be able to somehow "see" the future outcome beforehand).

On any one wheel there are forty possible outcomes: the ball can land in any one of the slots (1 through 36, 0, 00), or can be knocked out of the wheel, or can be a "floater," that is, can remain in equilibrium above the numbered slots. So, at a certain time, say at noon, the pit boss gives the order, and all the croupiers spin their wheels and set the balls rolling. The balls roll until each lands in a slot, or is knocked out, or reaches equilibrium. If the casino is big enough, statistics tells us, every possible outcome will occur. In the present case, each outcome, we are assuming, will occur by pure chance.

Let us take each roulette wheel as representing one possible world so that, for our purposes, there are only forty possible worlds. The number 23 represents our world. The pit master in charge of the casino is God. Each of the outcomes on each of the wheels represents one of the forty possible worlds God knows God can create. The time (in God's reference frame) is 11:55—that is, before, or outside, "creation" (the spinning of the wheel at noon). God is making a choice as to which one of the wheels is to be spun; God knows what the outcome of any one wheel will be, even though immediate interactions of the ball against the partitions of the slots is not directly controlled by God but, rather, is the result of the roulette wheel's own matrix of causal and random quantum interactions; God could have created the wheels in such a way that they were self-contained causal (and noncausal) systems. God then points to one of the croupiers and says, "You are the one who gets to spin your wheel." The wheel is spun, and the number that comes up is 23.

Now, God, by hypothesis, knew the outcomes of all possible wheel spins, not due to prediction (by calculating) but, rather, by "seeing" the outcomes beforehand, and God had to choose among all of the possible outcomes as to which one was to be instantiated. By doing so, God *predetermined* the outcome. But the predetermined outcome, in our example, *could have been the result of random (i.e., noncausal) processes.* That is, God in no way has to fix the wheels or push the ball along its path, in which case we would have said that pure chance had not been involved within the system and that God had causally and directly been involved with the outcome. Rather, the result of any one wheel comes up of its own accord. Divine foreknowledge of these events predetermines them, even though the events themselves occur as a result of complete causal randomness. In other words, regardless of whether the events are directly brought about by God, or whether they come about "of their own accord," God is responsible for the outcome.

Consider a related analogy. I (God) write a novel in which Jones murders Smith on Tuesday. That is, the day of the week within the book on which Jones murders Smith comes before Wednesday, when Jones is captured and taken to jail, and after Monday, the day when Jones prepares for the murder by purchasing a gun. (Assume, too, that the characters in the novel feel pain, suffer, experience joy, and so on.) The novel is contained in my reality although I, the author, am not *in* the book at any point, even though I might choose to write myself in as a character (i.e., Buddha, Christ) and when I meet Jones refer to myself as "I." Properly speaking, I am always outside the book. But there is a chronology within the book itself; Jones murders Smith on Tuesday, which comes after Monday in the sequence of Jones's temporal ordering; but the murder can be marked as occurring on page 32, which puts it within my ordering system. Although I know that Jones murders Smith on page 32, I do not know, properly speaking, *on* (in) page 32 that Jones murders Smith. For I do not exist on page 32, even though it would be proper to say that I knew, during the reading of page 32, that Jones murders Smith. Now, as long as I am the reader, not the author, of the novel, my knowledge of the murder in no way makes me responsible for Jones's act of murdering Smith on Tuesday. But while the case of a perfect predictor (or worldly omniscient being) is analogous to the case of the reader who has read the book and knows everything in it, the case of God is analogous to the *author* of the book; God's knowledge of the events in the world created by God makes God responsible.

Consider God before the act of creation. God is imagining the world in its potentiality, not in its actuality, along with an infinite number of other possible worlds. This would follow from God's essential properties, since God would know what would transpire *if* God did such and such. That is, God, unlike human authors who rarely, if ever, know exactly every detail of how their novels will turn out, knows exactly how God's creation—the actual world—will turn out. This

The Nature of God

Many Jews and Christians do not believe their own scriptural stories. God's real characteristics, these nonorthodox believers claim, are different and much more intellectually respectable than those ascribed to God in their own holy books. For instance, while the God of Judeo-Christian scriptural accounts may sometimes have behaved viciously, almost all contemporary Christians and Jews believe that God is loving and sanctions only a humane morality.

How do the nonorthodox Jews and Christians know what their God is like? If their own scriptural accounts are not to be taken literally (assuming that they could unambiguously be taken literally, something many claim is impossible), then how should they be taken? If they need to be corrected and interpreted, what rules ought to govern this process? How do the people doing the interpreting know that these rules, rather than some others, ought to be followed? More generally, what ought to be the relationship between reason and revelation?

And, once we have decided, by whatever means, what God is really like, do we need to suspend reason in order to believe our own account, or can the claim that there is a God with the characteristics we attribute to God survive rational scrutiny? For instance, the Judeo-Christian God is often said to exist outside of space and time and also to love us. But do we have the slightest

would hold not only for the actual world God creates, but for every possible world that God might create. Indeed, God would know in advance of making the first move in any act of creation exactly how any world God could ever create would turn out. Since God chooses among an infinite number of possible worlds to actualize one world, the responsibility for everything that happens in the world created by God thus belongs to God.

Suppose I am an omniscient father who is immortal and who knows what all possible children fathered by me would be like if I fathered them. How many possible variations of children might I have? An infinite number. Suppose, then, that I wish to father one billion children. Since I am the omniscient father of all my children, I can, if I choose, father only those children who I know will, of their own free will, choose to do good. I know that if I father Jack, for instance, Jack will, of his own free will, be a mass murderer. I know that if instead of Jack I father Joe, Joe will, of his own free will, be a writer. Suppose that in all other respects Joe and Jack are alike; given that I have an infinite number of children to choose from, this would not be an unlikely situation (for reasons similar to why, given enough time and enough monkeys banging on typewriters, the monkeys would, sooner or later, of their own accord produce every conceivable combination of letters, including this article, all the works of Shakespeare, and everything that has ever been written). Since it is at my disposal to choose to father a finite set of human beings from an infinite variety of human beings—since I have an infinite number of children to choose from—and since I will choose from among the infinity of possible children to create a finite

---

understanding of what the love of such a being might be like? Human love is a complex emotion, the experience of which unfolds over time; it also involves various dispositions to behave in certain ways rather than others on appropriate occasions, for instance, to go to the aid of those we love when they are in trouble. All of this also takes time. But God's love, if God exists outside of space and time, cannot be anything like this. Such a God, it would seem, cannot experience love that takes time to experience or do actions that take time to perform. Indeed, it seems difficult, if not impossible, to imagine how a timeless being could have *any* experiences, period—even consciousness.

What of other characteristics, such as omnipotence and omniscience, that are often attributed to God? Do we understand what these involve? Consider, for instance, the following puzzle? Can we explain plausibly why God's omnipotence either does (as René Descartes and St. John of the Cross thought) or does not (as many contemporary theologians think) give God the power to create a stone so heavy that it cannot be lifted even by God? (If God can lift the stone, then there is at least one thing God cannot do, namely make a stone so heavy that it cannot be lifted even by God, and then God is not omnipotent. Or, if God cannot create a stone that cannot be lifted even by God, then there is at least one thing God cannot do, and so once again God is not omnipotent.) Similarly, can we explain how God's omniscience is compatible with our having free will?

---

number, I can choose to father only those children that I know will be good. (This would be akin to stepping into the monkey house and picking from the infinite variety of monkey books only those books that are "good books" and stocking my library with them. I did not cause the monkeys to write any of the books. The monkeys caused the books to be written. But since I, being omniscient and immortal, must choose from among an infinity of possible books which ones actually go into my library, I am responsible for any and all actual books being in my library rather than some other books, even though I did not causally bring about those books rather than some other books—the monkeys caused them.) Thus if I, an omniscient and immortal father, choose to father Jack rather than Joe, to whatever extent Jack is responsible for the murders he commits and is therefore evil, I am also responsible for the murders Jack commits and am in a sense even more evil than Jack.

Consider the case of Bill the Novelist. We read Bill's novel in which the characters, by and large, suffer horribly and live terrible lives full of pain and sorrow. Let us assume, once again, that the painful events described in the novel are experienced by the characters as pain, and so on. (In that respect, then, Bill's novel might be thought of as an elaborate computer program in which the software functions in the ways in which our minds function so that, "viewed from the inside," the computer program world appears to the computer-generated characters as our world appears to us.) We are supposing that Bill can create any sort of characters he wishes, and that Bill is omniscient so that he knows in advance what the characters he creates will be like and what they will do, and that he must choose to create a finite set of characters from an infinite set. Who then is responsible for the events in Bill's novel? Even if the characters created by Bill have their own built-in randomizing programs within their "minds," given that Bill the omniscient novelist (computer programmer) foresees in advance what any possible character would do if actualized into the novel (program), Bill is responsible for their (random) actions being one way rather than another.

"The Black Death"

Vernon Reynolds and Ralph E. Tanner

. . . The Black Death was widely regarded as a Holy punishment for the sins of the world.

There was no consistent secular search for the cause of the disease and the cure was left to the clergy, who in some areas, notably Germany, advised extreme penitence, giving rise to the Flagellant movement. The rationale behind the movement was that since the pestilence was God's wrath the only cure lay in demonstrating penitence, and this could best be demonstrated by public acts of self-punishment. Flagellants on the march moved in a long crocodile from 200 to 1,000 strong. Arriving at their destination, they formed a circle around the market place and into this circle came sick people from the area. Self-scourging then took place, until the flagellants were in a state of near hysteria, using whips with nails in them to tear at their flesh and occasionally actually killing themselves. One of the promises Brethren had to make on joining the movement was not to change their clothes—they wore long skirts to their ankles. It is hard to think of a more efficient method of spreading the plague than the practices of these people, which were specifically designed to eliminate it.

From *The Biology of Religion* (1983).

Now consider a spectrum of possible worlds about which God has foreknowledge,[1] at one end of which is a world, Wd, consisting in fully determined events, and at the other end of which is a world, Wr, consisting in completely random events. A possible world about which God has foreknowledge and which also contains free will, Wf, would be somewhere between the two endpoint worlds, Wd and Wr. At the Wd end of the spectrum, God's foreknowledge may or may not be incompatible with free will, but let us assume that at the Wd end that there just isn't any: World Wd thus contains a bunch of robots whose every action is directly controlled by God in the way a puppet master controls the actions of puppets. The relevant question, then, is about the possible worlds in the spectrum somewhere between Wd and Wf and in which there is human free will. But even at the extreme end of the spectrum, Wr, where the possible world consists in complete randomness (perfect unpredictability), God's foreknowledge *still* predetermines the events of that perfectly random world, even though, individually, they are noncausal events. No event in any possible world could be more free of God's influence than a perfectly random, noncaused event. But if God, an essentially omniscient creator of the world, exists, then the responsibility for the outcome of even this perfectly random, noncaused event belongs with God.

Let us substitute for the words *pure chance* the words *free will.* In terms of free will, then, the argument is this. God, before creating the world, has to decide among the infinite possible worlds; knowing how each would turn out if actualized, by actualizing any one possible world at the exclusion of all others, God had to decide, for instance, whether Adam is to eat the forbidden apple or not. That is, God could have created a world where Adam decides, of his own free will, not to eat the apple, just as God could have created a world in which Adam decides, of his own free will, to eat the apple. For whatever be the reasons, or the inclinations, of Adam's conscious or unconscious choice making, Adam's reasons and inclinations could have been different than they actually were, and their existence requires of God many choices (since we can at least make certain causal connections about a person by his or her environment, upbringing, genes, physical stature, brain chemicals, and so on, which require much less of God than is required in the setting of all the various universal constants, etc.). But even if the human mind is as unfathomable as a random sequence of purely indeterministic forces (which it is not, since we can at least make guesses about what choices a particular person of such and such a disposition will make), God is still *responsible* for the outcome existing as an actual outcome. God would have to have predetermined Adam's choice just as surely as God would have had to predetermine the number 23 in the casino example—and this in spite of the fact that Adam's choice can still be said to be a free one, just as the outcome of the roulette wheel was, in and of itself, pure chance even though it was predetermined.

(The reason I claim that if God can determine the outcome of a random process, then God can determine the outcome of free will, is as follows. We have seen how God can determine the outcome of a purely random event simply by being the creator of the world in which that event occurs and by being omniscient. But in

1. It might be claimed that, strictly speaking, the argument here is not about divine *fore*knowledge—God's knowledge of what *will* happen in the actual world—but about so-called divine "middle" knowledge—God's knowledge of what each possible free creature *would* do if created. I have chosen, for the sake of simplicity and to keep the focus on the main issue, to use "foreknowledge" to cover both cases; as long as it is kept in mind that we are talking about a supposedly omnipotent God who can do anything that would actually be possible when such a God is (prior to creation) selecting the one actual world from infinitely many and infinitely diverse possible worlds, we can substitute "middle knowledge" for "foreknowledge" and the same difficulties posed by my examples will apply as before. Indeed, I would claim, in the so-called middle knowledge case, it is even harder to get God off the hook in my examples. For discussions of middle knowledge, see Alfred Freddoso, introduction to Luis de Molina, *On Divine Foreknowledge, Part IV of the Concordia* (Cornell, 1988); Robert Adams, "Middle Knowledge and the Problem of Evil," *American Philosophical Quarterly* (April 1977); Edward Wierenga, *The Nature of God: An Inquiry into Divine Attributes* (Cornell, 1989), Chapter 5; William Hasker, *God, Time, and Knowledge* (Cornell, 1989), Chapter 2; and Linda Zagzebski, *The Dilemma of Freedom and Foreknowledge* (Oxford, 1991), Chapter 5.

Split, Croatia, was built within the walls of the vast palace of Emperor Diocletian (circa 300 A.D.). His mausoleum became a church alongside which, nearly a thousand years later, a romanesque bell tower was erected.

Adam's case, God has, in *addition* to what God has in the purely random chance example to be fixed by God, many *causal* factors to fix. God has to make the Tree of Knowledge a certain distance away, etc. Perhaps on the fateful day Adam and Eve had great sex, and so Adam is more predisposed to listen to her. Or Adam could be hungry, or have an inbred dislike [or like] of apples. And so on.)

Consider two means of foreknowledge: foreknowledge by calculation and foreknowledge by seeing the future. In a case of worldly foreknowledge, a computer monitors me from a glass-enclosed booth, successfully predicting all my actions, which it reports to a team of scientists who, in turn, are observing me. All the computer's predictions are, without exception, always correct. Say the test is, once a minute, my choosing whether or not to touch my nose. We now ask *how* the computer makes its prediction. Suppose a man walks into the room, points a gun at me, and says, "Touch your nose at the next minute mark or I'll blow your head off." I wait until the minute mark and do as he says. Meanwhile, the predicting computer has already predicted that I would touch my nose. In this case we would clearly say that I did not act of my own free will. It was at least partially coerced (for I could have chosen not to touch my nose, thereby forefeiting my life), and we can easily imagine the man tying me up and at the appropriate time lifting my hand to my nose, in which case I would have had no say whatsoever in the action, and we could conclude that my action was not free. If, after the police took the man away and at the next minute mark I touch my nose, we could then say that in *that* case (as opposed to when I was at gunpoint) I acted freely—regardless of the fact that the computer had, a few moments earlier, once again correctly predicted that I would touch my nose.

In other words, on one plausible conception of free will, to say that an act is free is not to say that in principle the act is unpredictable.[2] The use of "free will" would always be at least linguistically valid as a distinction between coerced and uncoerced behavior. Thus the existence of the predicting computer, prima facie, has no import concerning the freedom of my actions.

Returning now to the nature of the computer's predictions, either the computer some-

2. For instance, Anthony Flew, in "Divine Omnipotence and Human Freedom," in Peter Angeles, ed., *Critiques of God* (New York, 1976), p. 230, writes: "And if it is the case that one day a team of psychologists will be able to predict a person's behavior . . . even up to 100 percent completely and successfully, still this will not show that he never acts freely, can never choose between alternatives, deciding for himself on the one which most appeals to him (or the one which is the most uncongenial for that matter, if that is what he chooses to do). Unless they produce evidence that there was obstruction or pressure or an absence of alternatives, their discoveries will not even be relevant to questions about his freedom of choice, much less a decisive disproof of the manifest fact that sometimes he has complete, sometimes restricted, and sometimes no freedom."

how "sees" the future or, on the basis of given information, calculates each outcome. If the latter were the case, we would have causal determinism. In that case, those who have faith in our most successful physical theory of all time—quantum mechanics—would have to amend their views, since quantum mechanics implies that there exists in nature a fundamental indeterminacy which is not simply a measure of our ignorance. If, on the other hand, the computer "sees" the future, those who feel that reverse causation is logically impossible would have to amend their views. For if the computer sees what I will do at the minute mark thirty seconds before I do it, then clearly the cause of the computer's prediction is the future event: My touching my nose at the minute mark causes the computer to predict thirty seconds earlier that I will touch my nose at the minute mark. In this case, the foreknowledge in no way causes the (let us assume, free) action; in fact the (free) action causes the foreknowledge. Yet doing as predicted is logically entailed by the predictions; *not* doing as predicted would, in this case, be doing in fact otherwise than one did in fact do—which is a logical contradiction. It is this second kind of foreknowledge, foreknowledge by "seeing" rather than by "predicting," that is relevant to the divine case.[3]

In terms of our predicting computer, if at thirty seconds before the minute mark the computer sees me touch my nose at the minute mark, then my touching my nose at the minute mark—my *choosing* to touch my nose at the minute mark—*causes* the computer to predict, at thirty seconds before the minute mark, that I will touch my nose at the minute mark. This in no way restricts my freedom, provided we make one important qualification: Namely, the prediction, or belief, must not enter the causal matrix of the agent about whom the prediction is being made. For imagine what would happen if the computer's predictions became known to me before the minute mark: the prediction occurs at thirty seconds before the minute mark, I learn of it at fifteen seconds before the minute mark, and the prediction (about what I will do at the minute mark) either is, or is not, realized at the minute mark. Four outcomes are possible, three of which are relevant. Say the prediction is that at the minute mark I will touch my nose:

a. I will do as the prediction says;
b. I will not do as the prediction says;
c. I will *try* not to do what the prediction says, but fail;
d. (irrelevant) I will try to do as predicted but fail.

It is extremely unlikely that once I received the prediction (a) would occur. Although it is conceivable that, for some unknown reason I would, upon learning of the prediction, decide to do as predicted, probably I would wish to frustrate the prediction. Thus (b) is a more likely choice; I would probably, out of desire to prove the computer wrong, do just the opposite. But (c) is a possibility also, for although I would probably decide to *try* and do the opposite of what the computer predicted, I could become paralyzed in my arms for a moment, followed by a spasmodic twitch during which I find myself touching my nose. And so on.

There is a paradox here, which can be illuminated most clearly by constructing a "Perfect No Machine." A Perfect No Machine always does exactly the opposite of what it is told it will do; that is, if the input is, "You will turn off the light," the No Machine leaves the light on. The Perfect Predictor now makes its prediction (whether by seeing the future or by forecasting) and tells the Perfect No Machine, at thirty seconds before the top of the minute, whether or not it will turn on its light at the top of the minute. If the Perfect Predictor predicts "You will turn off your light," the light stays on, in which case the Perfect Predictor was not perfect, and if the Perfect Predictor predicts "You will leave your light on," the light goes off, with the same problematic implications (assuming that

3. See Pike, *God and Timelessness,* for various discussions of the theological doctrines that agree on this point.

the Perfect No Machine is a successful Perfect No Machine). We can draw three conclusions:

x. The concept of a Perfect No Machine is impossible;
y. The concept of a Perfect Predictor is impossible;
z. The prediction about the Perfect No Machine's actions cannot be communicated to the Perfect No Machine's causal matrix.

Surely (x) cannot be so; we could easily build such a machine. That leaves (y) and (z). Already, however, we have seen that the existence of a Perfect Predictor (divine or otherwise) may be questionable, but our discussion now hinges on our assuming that a Perfect Predictor (knower) does exist, so, if we want to keep our discussion intact, we must accept (z). The situation, then, is this: Unless we want to construct an "impossible possible world," we have to say that,

> *Z*) If a Perfect Predictor exists, then, assuming that there are agents (or entities) disposed to, and able to, frustrate the Perfect Predictor's predictions if only the agents knew what they were, the Perfect Predictor's predictions cannot be made known to the agents.

The clause about "frustrating agents" is included because the Perfect Predictor could, of course, make perfect predictions to a Perfect "Yes Machine" without paradox. Note, however, that (*Z*) does *not* preclude the possibility of a perfect *knower*. A perfect knower could exist, without paradox, so long as the knower did not become a predictor by uttering or communicating the knowledge to the agents which are disposed to, and able to, frustrate the predictions.

Suppose God appears before me and tells me that, in one minute, I will touch my nose. Again, we have three relevant possibilities:

a′. I will do as God says I will;
b′. I will not do as God says I will;
c′. I will *try* not to do what God says but fail.

Since God is essentially omniscient and infallible, (b′) is not possible. If I were a Perfect No Machine, (a′) would also be impossible, and I think I would be as predisposed to frustrate God's prediction as would a No Machine. So, at best, (c′) would happen. But then we could insert the words "free will" or "without coercion from God or from any of God's acts" into God's predictive statement, so that God's prediction becomes "At the top of the minute you will touch your nose of your own free will." In that case, if I try not to touch my nose but somehow feel my hand forced toward my nose by some invisible power, and so on, the prediction would still be frustrated. In this case, we would have to say that this last move—inserting "free will" into the Perfect Prediction—is not allowed, but this would suggest one of two results in the example: Either free will does not exist, or God cannot predict the outcome of free actions (though God might be able to know about them in advance). As long as we are not given the information, no paradox arises.

In the casino example, for instance, God's foreknowledge cannot be communicated to the croupiers. For suppose that it is. God tells the croupier, "You may now spin your wheel, and the number that will come up is 23." Immediately, the croupier, who happens to be evil, places a tiny metal covering plate over the 23 slot, thereby excluding the possibility of 23 coming up. So, of course, in *that* case God, who is essentially omniscient and thus would have known that the croupier would cover the 23 slot, would not have said "23" to the croupier. But what other number could God have given? Whichever number God would have given, the evil croupier would then have covered that slot. Therefore, God, if God is to keep the "pure chance" of the wheel intact, cannot communicate the knowledge to the croupier and thereby allow it to enter the causal matrix of the system. But as long as we respect condition (*Z*), or some such condition for possible worlds analyses, such that certain essential information about the system is kept outside the causal matrix of the system (or is restricted to being within the mind of the omniscient being) no actual paradox occurs: God gets to predetermine the outcome, and yet the outcome occurs by pure chance.

We have here a plausible analysis by which God—if God exists, is omniscient, and is the creator of the actual world—must, by virtue of God's having those properties essentially, have predetermined the world. This allows for free will among the inhabitants of the world, just as "pure chance" is allowed both in the world and in our analogous casino. That this free will is predetermined makes it no less free, just as its being free makes it no less predetermined. This result, however, has grave implications for the free will defense to the argument from evil.

The problem is that, by our analysis, the sort of free will that would be compatible with a divine creator's foreknowledge firmly places the responsibility of human choices on God. Ordinarily, we would assume that if I do an action freely in a world created by God then I, not God, am responsible for that action. The surprising conclusion, however, is that God is responsible, not I! The reason, as we have seen in the examples, is that God must choose among an infinite number of possible worlds to actualize one possible world rather than another.

Consider the nonbelievers' claim that God, if God is all-good and all-powerful, could have created a world in which there were no (moral) evil; but, the nonbeliever points out, there *is* (moral) evil in the world. Thus either God could have created a world without evil but wouldn't—in which case God is not all-good and is therefore not God–or else God would have created a world without evil but couldn't, in which case God is not all-powerful and is therefore not God. Part of the believer's most persistent defense against this argument from evil has been that God created a world with free human creatures in it such that whether these creatures choose good over evil is up to the creatures, not God, in such a way that the burden of responsibility for human actions falls firmly on humans, not on God.

A religious pilgrimage in a village near Dubrovnik, Croatia.

But our examples show that God could have created free creatures who, as a matter of fact, always freely choose good over evil, on the grounds that God can predetermine the outcome of free actions. Consider, for instance, the case of the Omniscient Coinflipper. A coin is flipped at noon and, by pure chance, it comes up "tails." The coin is flipped again at 12:05 and, say again by pure chance, it turns up "heads." It is 11:55 and you are the Omniscient Coinflipper. You know that *if* you flip the coin at noon it will come up tails and that *if* you flip the coin at five past noon it will come up heads. So, simply by deciding at what time to flip the coin, you determine the outcome. You could choose to flip the coin only at those times when you knew the outcome would be heads. Thus by choosing to flip the coin only at those times when the coin would, by pure chance, come up heads, you could bring it about that heads, and only heads, occurred for all flips of the coin—without fixing the coin itself. Indeed, the motions of the coin can, as specified, be the result of purely random processes. It would be like creating a randomizing machine whose internal workings were random quantum processes but then, by virtue of being able to see not only the future but all possible futures, turning the randomizer on (actualizing any outcome) only at those times when you have already foreseen the result of the noncausal process. Who would be responsible? The randomizing machine or the actualizer of the randomizing machine? The actualizer.

Suppose Jones holds a gun to my head and demands that you, the Omniscient Coinflipper, flip the coin within the next half hour. Heads, Jones will blow my head off; tails, she will give up and turn herself in. It is 11:55. You know that if you flip the coin at noon it will be tails and my life will be spared. If you flip the coin at five past, it will be heads and I will die. You wait until five past and flip the coin. Of its own accord, it comes up—freely, unforced by you, but exactly as you the Omniscient Coinflipper knew it would—heads. Jones kills me. All else being equal, this is a case in which your epistemic status in relation to the coin, omniscience, makes you as guilty of murder as Jones. Indeed, the conclusion to be drawn from such an example would be that, arguably, you are even more evil and malicious than Jones.

My claim, then, is that the sort of free will that would be compatible with divine foreknowledge is incompatible with the existence of evil in such a way that the responsibility for moral evil lies with the actualizer of those free human agents: God. Some philosophers have argued to the contrary,[4] claiming, for instance, that the free will defense works against the argument from evil because there are certain possible worlds that God cannot actualize; in particular, God cannot actualize a world containing moral good without moral evil. A statement like "If God brings it about that I refrain from touching my nose, then I do not freely refrain from touching my nose," expresses, some would claim, a necessary truth. But does it? Consider, "If G, an omniscient coinflipper, brings it about that the result of a coinflip is heads, then heads was not the result of a random occurrence." This does not express a necessary truth; in fact, by my analysis, it is false. For, as I have argued, God can determine the outcome of purely random processes, just as an omniscient coinflipper can determine the outcome of a purely random coin flip. The Omniscient Coinflipper does not force the coin along its trajectory, nor cause it to bounce against air molecules in such and such a way; rather, the coin's movements are the result, ultimately, of random (and fundamentally indeterminate) quantum processes. If God can determine the outcome of purely random processes, it stands to reason that God can determine (fix) the outcomes of free choices, no matter what traditional concept of free will one espouses; for there are so many more factors (genetic makeup, environment, brain chemicals, etc., plus cosmological constants and so on) that can be influenced by God in the case of free will.

Consider pure chance again. One thing we mean when we say that heads was the result of a random process, or pure chance, is that *given the very same* antecedent conditions, tails *could have* occurred. That is, there is a possible world just like *this* one in which heads occurred, in which the result of the coin flip is tails. Part of what we mean by saying of an outcome that it occurred by pure chance is that it was not fixed causally by antecedent conditions: Those particular antecedent conditions occurring do not make it more probable that the "random" result will occur one way (heads) rather than another (tails). So, possible worlds W1 and W2 share antecedent conditions up to the time they branch, but in W1 at the time of the branch the flip results

4. Alvin Plantinga, *The Nature of Necessity* (Oxford University Press, 1974).

(randomly) in tails, whereas in W2 at the time of the branch the flip results in heads. If our having shown that God's being able to determine the outcome of purely random actions assures God's being able to determine the outcome of free actions, then it is plausible to suppose that God is responsible for the outcome insofar as God must actualize one of the possible worlds.

In other words, the believer's claim that God created this world, a world containing moral evil, because God wanted us to have free will rather than predetermining our choices, is predicated on two assumptions: (1) the sort of free will we plausibly have is not predetermined by God, and (2) God could not have created a world containing both free will and creatures who always choose to do good. Both of these assumptions are false.

A believer could respond by claiming that perhaps some evil people go wrong in every possible world in which they exist. That is, perhaps God cannot make a world in which, say, Hitler freely chooses to do good. Perhaps Hitler is "transworldly depraved," that is, depraved in all possible worlds[5] in which he exists. However, we might ask, then, why God would want to create such creatures. Perhaps Hitler, aside from being transworldly depraved, has *some* good qualities in addition to his depraved qualities that God desires to bring into the world, and this is something God cannot do without creating a world with Hitler in it. But then, could not God have created a creature like Hitler who had those very same good qualities and without the evil qualities? Unless Hitler's good qualities are somehow dependent on Hitler's evil qualities, I do not see why not. Supposedly God has no trouble creating angels, for instance, who always freely choose to do good. Why would God not create a world of angels?[6] Does Hitler have some qualities admired by God that God could not bring about by creating an angelic version of Hitler? Indeed, if God were all-good, one could argue that God would in that case have created a universe populated not with subservient lesser creatures but, rather, populated by angelic colleagues—fellow gods.[7]

In any case, and more to the point, such exotic possibilities—that is, Hitler being such that he always, *of his own free will,* wreaks havoc

5. Ibid., p. 177.

6. One might also use the Catholic view of the Blessed Virgin Mary as an example against Plantinga: Since there has already been one such sinless human, why not many?

7. I owe this example to my colleague Angelo Juffras.

"Suffering"

W. Somerset Maugham

At that time (a time to most people of sufficient ease, when peace seemed certain and prosperity secure) there was a school of writers who enlarged upon the moral value of suffering. They claimed that it was salutary. They claimed that it increased sympathy and enhanced the sensibilities. They claimed that it opened to the spirit new avenues of beauty and enabled it to get into touch with the mystical kingdom of God. They claimed that it strengthened the character, purified it from its human grossness, and brought to him who did not avoid but sought it a more perfect happiness . . . I set down in my note-books, not once or twice, but in a dozen places, the facts that I had seen. I knew that suffering did not ennoble; it degraded. It made men selfish, mean, petty, and suspicious. It absorbed them in small things. It did not make them more than men; it made them less than men; and I wrote ferociously that we learn resignation not by our own suffering, but by the suffering of others.

upon his fellow human beings—fails to put the responsibility of the actions on the agent, where it must be if the free will defense is to work against the argument from evil and leave the responsibility firmly on God's shoulders. Consider again our Omniscient Coinflipper example. The "transworld depravity" claim would, by analogy, amount to saying this: A regular, untampered with coin, by pure chance, lands tails; furthermore, no matter how many times—whenever and wherever—you flip this coin, the coin will, by pure chance land tails; therefore, not even God could bring it about that the coin, by pure chance, lands heads. This, however, is counterintuitive, since at least one sense of "pure chance" is that, if we say A occurred by pure chance we imply that A could have happened otherwise than it did. If we surreptitiously tag onto this a phrase like, "but in fact it never, under any possible circumstances, happens otherwise," we seem to be contradicting ourselves. What we have is not a fair, but a fixed coin.

The claim that God could have created humans who always, of their own free will, choose good over evil has been argued against by Alvin Plantinga on the grounds that such arguments imply that

> [X] If God is omnipotent He can create or bring about any logically possible state of affairs.[8]
>
> And,
>
> [A] *That there is a state of affairs that is not created by God* is a logically possible state of affairs,[9]

is true; hence (X) and (A) together entail

> [B] If God is omnipotent, God can create a state of affairs that is not created by God,[10]

which, claims Plantinga, is false.

But my examples have shown that (B), when properly understood, is not false. For we gave meaning to how God in fact *could* bring about states of affairs that were themselves not created, or brought about, by God: The (indeterminate) actions of the roulette ball, in our casino example, and the (pure chance, or random) outcome of the coin flip are both examples of states of affairs that were created by God but were not, strictly speaking, causally brought about by God. Thus I claim that what (B) means is

> B′) If God is omnipotent, God can create a state of affairs that is not causally brought about by God.

Hence (X) can be given a consistent interpretation and we can hold that God could have created a world of moral good without moral evil. A world of moral good without moral evil does not exist (given that God is, by hypothesis, essentially all-good). Therefore, God does not exist.

Plantinga claims that

> [Y] God can create free men such that they always do what is right[11]

is true only if

> [Y′] God creates free men such that they always do what is right[12]

is consistent. But Y′, claims Plantinga, is equivalent to

> [Y″] God creates free men and brings it about that they always freely do what is right[13]

which he claims is *not* consistent and that, therefore, Y′ is also not consistent. But Plantinga is mistaken: Y′ *is* consistent. Consider:

> Y‴) God creates random processes and brings it about that their outcomes always (without God having *caused* them) do what God intended.

8. Alvin Plantinga, *God and Other Minds* (New York: Cornell University Press, 1967), p. 137.

9. Ibid.

10. Ibid.

11. Ibid., p. 138.

12. Ibid.

13. Ibid.

Y‴ is consistent. And if Y‴ is consistent, then there is no reason to deny that Y″ is consistent (since God's being able to determine the outcomes of purely random actions assures God's being able to determine the outcomes of free actions).

In conclusion, then, the sort of free will that is compatible with divine foreknowledge fails as a defense against the argument from evil. In the actual world that exists, a world containing moral evil, there is no room for God as conceived of in traditional Christian doctrine, namely, a God who is a supreme being (nonidentical to the individual beings in God's world), essentially omniscient, omnipotent, and an all-good creator of the world. I conclude, therefore, that such a God does not exist.[14]

14. I am extremely grateful to Raymond Martin, Nelson Pike, Dennis Ahern, Jerrold Levinson, Hugh LaFollette, and Marshall Missner for their helpful comments on earlier drafts of this paper.

PART V

Miracles

David Hume

"OF MIRACLES"

A brief biography of Hume appears on pages 23–24.

PART I

There is, in Dr. Tillotson's writings, an argument against the *real presence,* which is as concise, and elegant, and strong as any argument can possibly be supposed against a doctrine, so little worthy of a serious refutation. It is acknowledged on all hands, says that learned prelate, that the authority, either of the scripture or of tradition, is founded merely in the testimony of the apostles, who were eye-witnesses to those miracles of our Savior, by which he proved his divine mission. Our evidence, then, for the truth of the *Christian* religion is less than the evidence for the truth of our senses; because, even in the first authors of our religion, it was no greater; and it is evident it must diminish in passing from them to their disciples; nor can any one rest such confidence in their testimony, as in the immediate object of his senses. But a weaker evidence can never destroy a stronger; and therefore, were the doctrine of the real presence ever so clearly revealed in scripture, it were directly contrary to the rules of just reasoning to give our assent to it. It contradicts sense, though both the scripture and tradition, on which it is supposed to be built, carry not such evidence with them as sense; when they are considered merely as external evidences, and are not brought home to every one's breast, by the immediate operation of the Holy Spirit.

Nothing is so convenient as a decisive argument of this kind, which must at least *silence* the most arrogant bigotry and superstition, and free us from their impertinent solicitations. I flatter myself, that I have discovered an argument of a like nature, which, if just, will, with the wise and learned, be an everlasting check to all kinds of superstitious delusion, and consequently, will be useful as long as the world endures. For so long, I presume, will the accounts of miracles and prodigies be found in all history, sacred and profane.

Though experience be our only guide in reasoning concerning matters of fact; it must be acknowledged, that this guide is not altogether infallible, but in some cases is apt to lead us into errors. One, who in our climate, should expect better weather in any week of June than in one of December, would reason justly, and conformably to experience; but it is certain, that he may happen, in the event, to find himself mistaken. However, we may observe, that, in such a case, he would have no cause to complain of experience; because it commonly informs us beforehand of the uncertainty, by that contrariety of events, which we may learn from a diligent observation. All effects follow not with like certainty from their supposed causes. Some events are found, in all countries and ages, to have been constantly conjoined together. Others are found to have been more variable, and sometimes to disappoint our expectations; so that, in our reasonings concerning matter of fact, there are all imaginable degrees of assurance, from the highest certainty to the lowest species of moral evidence.

A wise man, therefore, proportions his belief to the evidence. In such conclusions as are

From section 10 of *Enquiry Concerning Human Understanding,* first published in 1748.

founded on an infallible experience, he expects the event with the last degree of assurance, and regards his past experience as a full *proof* of the future existence of that event. In other cases, he proceeds with more caution: He weighs the opposite experiments: He considers which side is supported by the greater number of experiments: to that side he inclines, with doubt and hesitation; and when at last he fixed his judgment, the evidence exceeds not what we properly call *probability*. All probability, then, supposes an opposition of experiments and observations, where the one side is found to overbalance the other, and to produce a degree of evidence, proportioned to the superiority. A hundred instances or experiments on one side, and fifty on another, afford a doubtful expectation of any event; though a hundred uniform experiments, with only one that is contradictory, reasonably begets a pretty strong degree of assurance. In all cases, we must balance the opposite experiments, where they are opposite, and deduce the *smaller number* from the greater, in order to know the exact force of the superior evidence.

To apply these principles to a particular instance; we may observe, that there is no species of reasoning more common, more useful, and even necessary to human life, than that which is derived from the testimony of men, and the reports of eye-witnesses and spectators. This species of reasoning, perhaps, one may deny to be founded on the relation of cause and effect. I shall not dispute about a word. It will be sufficient to observe that our assurance in any argument of this kind is derived from no other principle than our observation of the veracity of human testimony, and of the usual conformity of facts to the reports of the witnesses. It being a general maxim, that no objects have any discoverable connexion together, and that all the inferences, which we draw from one to another, are founded merely on our experience of their constant and regular conjunction; it is evident, that we ought not to make an exception of this maxim in favor of human testimony, whose connexion with any event seems, in itself, as little necessary as any other. Were not the memory tenacious to a certain degree; had not men commonly an inclination to truth and a principle of probity, were they not sensible to shame, when detected in a falsehood: Were not these, I say, discovered by *experience* to be qualities, inherent in human nature, we should never repose the least confidence in human testimony. A man delirious, or noted for falsehood and villany, has no manner of authority with us.

And as the evidence, derived from witnesses and human testimony, is founded on past experience, so it varies with the experience, and is regarded either as *proof* or a *probability,* according as the conjunction between any particular kind of report and any kind of object has been found to be constant or variable. There are a number of circumstances to be taken into consideration in all judgments of this kind; and the ultimate standard, by which we determine all disputes, that may arise concerning them, is always derived from experience and observation. Where this experience is not entirely uniform on any side, it is attended with an unavoidable contrariety in our judgments, and with the same opposition and mutual destruction of argument as in every other kind of evidence. We frequently hesitate concerning the reports of others. We balance the opposite circumstances, which cause any doubt or uncertainty; and when we discover a superiority on one side, we incline to it; but still with a diminution of assurance, in proportion to the force of its antagonist.

This contrariety of evidence, in the present case, may be derived from several different causes; from the opposition of contrary testimony; from the character or number of the witnesses; from the manner of their delivering their testimony; or from the union of all these circumstances. We entertain a suspicion concerning any matter of fact, when the witnesses contradict each other; when they are but few, or of a doubtful character; when they have an interest in what they affirm; when they deliver their testimony with hesitation, or, on the contrary, with too violent asseverations. There are many other particulars of the same kind, which may diminish or destroy the force of any argument, derived from human testimony.

Suppose, for instance, that the fact, which the testimony endeavors to establish, partakes of the extraordinary and the marvelous; in that case, the evidence, resulting from the testimony, admits of a diminution, greater or less, in proportion as the fact is more or less unusual. The reason why we place any credit in witnesses and historians is not derived from any *connexion,* which we perceive *a priori,* between testimony and reality, but because we are accustomed to find a conformity between them. But when the fact attested is such a one as has seldom fallen under our observation, here is a contest of two opposite experiences; of which the one destroys the other, as far as its force goes, and the superior can only operate on the mind by the force which remains. The very same principle of experience, which gives us a certain degree of assurance in the testimony of witnesses, gives us also, in this case, another degree of assurance against the fact, which they endeavor to estab-

"Lourdes"

Patrick Marnham

On the first occasion Bernadette saw a soft glow in the grotto above a rose bush, and then a beautiful girl appeared, dressed in white. Bernadette afterwards referred to the girl as '*Aquero*', meaning 'that one' in the local Bigourdan dialect. Feeling frightened on the first occasion, Bernadette said her rosary. The vision beckoned her. She did not respond and it suddenly disappeared. . . . On Sunday, after High Mass, the children . . . took some holy water with them and the original party of three was accompanied by seven other girls. As Bernadette prayed she saw the second apparition and sprinkled it with the water. *Aquero* smiled. None of the children could see anything. . . . It had been decided that *Aquero* should be invited to write her own name. Accordingly, when the third apparition began, Bernadette was handed the inkstand before she advanced into the cave. . . . When the vision was over they asked Bernadette why she had not requested the name. Bernadette replied that she had asked, but *Aquero* had replied 'It is not necessary.' . . .

This was the beginning of what is now known as 'the fortnight of apparitions'. In the fifteen days between 18 February and 4 March, Bernadette saw *Aquero* thirteen times. During this fortnight her audience increased from two people to eight thousand, and she eventually had to be escorted to the grotto by armed soldiers. During this time, too, *Aquero* entrusted her with various secrets which she never revealed; she discovered a spring in the grotto, a number of allegedly miraculous cures took place . . . and the popular idea grew that Massabielle was a place chosen by the Mother of God to appear to a peasant girl of Lourdes.

In 1862 Monseigneur Laurence, Bishop of Tarbes, recognized the apparitions. His *mandat* stated: 'We judge that Mary Immaculate, Mother of God, really appeared to Bernadette Soubirous on 11 February, 1858, and on subsequent days, eighteen times in all. . . . The faithful are justified in believing this to be certain. . . . We authorize the cult of the Our Lady of the Grotto of Lourdes in our diocese . . . [and] in conformity with the wishes of the Blessed Virgin, expressed more than once in the course of the apparitions, we propose to build a shrine on the land of the Grotto, which has now been acquired by the Bishops of Tarbes.' The same document proclaimed seven of the cures which had taken place at the Grotto in 1858 to be 'miraculous'.*

From *Lourdes: A Modern Pilgrimage* (1980). *Eds. note: Mr. Marnham does not necessarily endorse the supernatural aspects of the story he is reporting.

lish; from which contradiction there necessarily arises a counterpoize, and mutual destruction of belief and authority.

I should not believe such a story were it told me by Cato, was a proverbial saying in Rome, even during the lifetime of that philosophical patriot.[1] The incredibility of a fact, it was allowed, might invalidate so great an authority.

The Indian prince, who refused to believe the first relations concerning the effects of frost, reasoned justly; and it naturally required very strong testimony to engage his assent to facts, that arose from a state of nature, with which he was unacquainted, and which bore so little analogy to those events, of which he had had constant and uniform experience. Though they were not contrary to his experience, they were not conformable to it.[2]

But in order to [increase] the probability against the testimony of witnesses, let us suppose, that the fact, which they affirm, instead of being only marvelous, is really miraculous; and suppose also, that the testimony considered apart and in itself, amounts to an entire proof; in that case, there is proof against proof, of which the strongest must prevail, but still with a diminution of its force, in proportion to that of its antagonist.

A miracle is a violation of the laws of nature; and as a firm and unalterable experience has established these laws, the proof against a miracle, from the very nature of the fact, is as entire as any argument from experience can possibly be imagined. Why is it more than probable, that all men must die; that lead cannot, of itself, remain suspended in the air; that fire consumes wood, and is extinguished by water; unless it be, that these events are found agreeable to the laws of nature, and there is required a violation of these laws, or in other words, a miracle to prevent them? Nothing is esteemed a miracle, if it ever happen in the common course of nature. . . . It is no miracle that a man, seemingly in good health, should die of a sudden: because such a kind of death, though more unusual than any other, has yet been frequently observed to happen. But it is a miracle, that a dead man should come to life; because that has never been observed in any age or country. There must, therefore, be a uniform experience against every miraculous event, otherwise the event would not merit that appellation. And as a uniform experience amounts to a proof, there is here a direct and full *proof,* from the nature of the fact, against the existence of any miracle; nor can such a proof be destroyed, or the miracle rendered credible, but by an opposite proof, which is superior.[3]

1. Plutarch, in vita Catonis.

2. No Indian, it is evident, could have experience that water did not freeze in cold climates. This is placing nature in a situation quite unknown to him; and it is impossible for him to tell *a priori* what will result from it. It is making a new experiment, the consequence of which is always uncertain. One may sometimes conjecture from analogy what will follow; but still this is but conjecture. And it must be confessed, that, in the present case of freezing, the event follows contrary to the rules of analogy, and is such as a rational Indian would not look for. The operations of cold upon water are not gradual, according to the degrees of cold; but whenever it comes to the freezing point, the water passes in a moment, from the utmost liquidity to perfect hardness. Such an event, therefore, may be denominated *extraordinary,* and requires a pretty strong testimony, to render it credible to people in a warm climate: But still it is not *miraculous,* nor contrary to uniform experience of the course of nature in cases where all the circumstances are the same. The inhabitants of Sumatra have always seen water fluid in their own climate, and the freezing of their rivers ought to be deemed a prodigy: But they never saw water in Muscovy during the winter; and therefore they cannot reasonably be positive what would there be the consequence.

3. Sometimes an event may not, *in itself, seem* to be contrary to the laws of nature, and yet, if it were real, it might, by reason of some circumstances, be denominated a miracle; because, *in fact,* it is contrary to these laws. Thus if a person, claiming a divine authority, should command a sick person to be well, a healthful man to fall down dead, the clouds to pour rain, the winds to blow, in short, should order many natural events, which immediately follow upon his command; these might justly be esteemed miracles, because they are really, in this case, contrary to the laws of nature. For if any suspicion remain, that the event and command concurred by accident, there is no miracle and no transgression of the laws of nature. If this suspicion be removed, there is evidently a miracle, and a transgression of these laws; because nothing can be more contrary to nature than that the voice or command of a man should have such an influence. A miracle may be accurately defined, *a transgression of a law of nature by a particular volition of the Deity, or by the interposition of some invisible agent.* A miracle may either be discoverable by men or not. This alters not its nature and essence. The raising of a house or ship into the air is a visible miracle. The raising of a feather, when the wind wants ever so little of a force requisite for that purpose, is as real a miracle, though not so sensible with regard to us.

The plain consequence is (and it is a general maxim worthy of our attention), "That no testimony is sufficient to establish a miracle, unless the testimony be of such a kind, that its falsehood would be more miraculous, than the fact, which it endeavors to establish; and even in that case there is a mutual destruction of arguments, and the superior only gives us an assurance suitable to that degree of force, which remains, after deducting the inferior." When anyone tells me, that he saw a dead man restored to life, I immediately consider with myself, whether it be more probable, that this person should either deceive or be deceived, or that the fact, which he relates, should really have happened. I weigh the one miracle against the other; and according to the superiority, which I discover, I pronounce my decision, and always reject the greater miracle. If the falsehood of his testimony would be more miraculous, than the event which he relates; then, and not till then, can he pretend to command my belief or opinion.

PART II

In the foregoing reasoning we have supposed, that the testimony, upon which a miracle is founded, may possibly amount to an entire proof, and that the falsehood of that testimony would be a real prodigy: But it is easy to show, that we have been a great deal too liberal in our concession, and that there never was a miraculous event established on so full an evidence.

For *first,* there is not to be found, in all history, any miracle attested by a sufficient number of men, of such unquestioned good sense, education, and learning, as to secure us against all delusion in themselves; of such undoubted integrity, as to place them beyond all suspicion of any design to deceive others; of such credit and reputation in the eyes of mankind, as to have a great deal to lose in case of their being detected in any falsehood; and at the same time, attesting facts performed in such a public manner and in so celebrated a part of the world, as to render the detection unavoidable: All which circumstances are requisite to give us a full assurance in the testimony of men.

Secondly. We may observe in human nature a principle which, if strictly examined, will be found to diminish extremely the assurance, which we might, from human testimony, have, in any kind of prodigy. The maxim, by which we commonly conduct ourselves in our reasonings, is, that the objects, of which we have no experience, resemble those, of which we have; that what we have found to be most usual is always most probable; and that where there is an opposition of arguments, we ought to give the preference to such as are founded on the greatest number of past observations. But though, in proceeding by this rule, we readily reject any fact which is unusual and incredible in an ordinary degree; yet in advancing farther, the mind observes not always the same rule; but when anything is affirmed utterly absurd and miraculous, it rather the more readily admits of such a fact, upon account of that very circumstance, which ought to destroy all its authority. The passion of *surprise* and *wonder,* arising from miracles, being an agreeable emotion, gives a sensible tendency towards the belief of those events, from which it is derived. And this goes so far, that even those who cannot enjoy this pleasure immediately, nor can believe those miraculous events, of which they are informed, yet love to partake of the satisfaction at second-hand or by rebound, and place a pride and delight in exciting the admiration of others.

With what greediness are the miraculous accounts of travelers received, their descriptions of sea and land monsters, their relations of wonderful adventures, strange men, and uncouth manners? But if the spirit of religion join itself to the love of wonder, there is an end of common sense; and human testimony, in these circumstances, loses all pretensions to authority. A religionist may be an enthusiast, and imagine he sees what has no reality: he may know his narrative to be false, and yet persevere in it, with the best intentions in the world, for the sake of promoting so holy a cause: or even where this delusion has not place, vanity, excited by so strong a temptation, operates on him more powerfully than on the rest of mankind in any other circumstances; and self-interest with equal force. His auditors may not have, and commonly have not, sufficient judgment to canvass his evidence: what judgment they have, they renounce by principle, in these sublime and mysterious subjects: or if they were ever so willing to employ it, passion and a heated imagination disturb the regularity of its operations. Their credulity increases his impudence: and his impudence overpowers their credulity.

Eloquence, when at its highest pitch, leaves little room for reason or reflection; but addressing itself entirely to the fancy or the affections, captivates the willing hearers, and subdues their understanding. Happily, this pitch it seldom attains. But what a Tully or a Demosthenes could scarcely effect over a Roman or Athenian audience, every *Capuchin,* every itinerant or stationary teacher can perform over the generality of mankind, and in a higher degree, by touching such gross and vulgar passions.

The many instances of forged miracles, and prophecies, and supernatural events, which, in all ages, have either been detected by contrary

"The Shroud of Turin"

Kenneth E. Stevenson and Gary R. Habermas

The scientists on the investigating team are unanimous in concluding that the Shroud is an actual archaeological artifact. Facts such as the exact anatomical and pathological data, the first-century date of the cloth, and the absence of fakery, its correspondence to other archaeological and historical facts even in areas unknown to an ancient artist, have led to the conclusion that it is genuine. . . .

. . . [And] it was found to be highly probable that the man buried in the Shroud is the same man described in the gospels as Jesus of Nazareth. This conclusion was reached through a comparison of the areas of agreement between the Shroud and Jesus' death, points which are irregularities in normal crucifixion procedure. These irregularities include the severe beating, the crown of thorns, the absence of broken ankles, the post-mortem lance wound, and the presence of blood and watery fluid. Other irregularities are the individual burial, the fine linen shroud, the hasty burial, and the absence of decomposition. The Shroud not only agrees with the gospel accounts on these and other irregularities, but it also does not contradict the gospels at any particular point. This leads to a high probability that Jesus of Nazareth and the man buried in the Shroud are the same person. . . . This is made much more highly probable by the empirical witness of history, which also verifies Jesus' resurrection from the dead. An important consideration here is that the Shroud would then constitute scientifically empirical evidence for Jesus' resurrection. This is a type of evidence which has always seemed to elude religious belief since the first century.

. . . Although the Shroud may somehow still turn out to be inauthentic, . . . the evidence before us indicates that it is very probably the actual burial garment of Jesus, an object which gives insights into Jesus' physical death and scientific evidence for his resurrection from the dead. . . .

Some skeptical philosophers have long raised the question of whether there is any strong empirical evidence for theistic beliefs. . . . What better validation could God have left than this highly probable, empirical, and historical evidence for Jesus' resurrection and the possibility of eternal life for each of us?

From *Verdict on the Shroud* (1981).

evidence, or which detect themselves by their absurdity, prove sufficiently the strong propensity of mankind to the extraordinary and the marvelous, and ought reasonably to beget a suspicion against all relations of this kind. This is our natural way of thinking, even with regard to the most common and most credible events. For instance: There is no kind of report which rises so easily, and spreads so quickly, especially in country places and provincial towns, as those concerning marriages; insomuch that two young persons of equal condition never see each other twice, but the whole neighborhood immediately join them together. The pleasure of telling a piece of news so interesting, of propagating it, and of being the first reporters of it, spreads the intelligence. And this is so well known, that no man of sense gives attention to these reports, till he find them confirmed by some greater evidence. Do not the same passions, and others still stronger, incline the generality of mankind to believe and report, with the greatest vehemence and assurance, all religious miracles?

Thirdly. It forms a strong presumption against all supernatural and miraculous relations, that they are observed chiefly to abound among ignorant and barbarous nations; or if a civilized people has ever given admission to any of them, that people will be found to have received them from ignorant and barbarous ancestors, who transmitted them with that inviolable sanction and authority, which always attend received opinions. When we peruse the first histories of all nations, we are apt to imagine ourselves transported into some new world; where the whole frame of nature is disjointed, and every element performs its operations in a different manner, from what it does at present. Battles, revolutions, pestilence, famine and death, are never the effect of those natural causes, which we experience. Prodigies, omens, oracles, judgments, quite obscure the few natural events, that are intermingled with them. But as the former grow thinner every page, in proportion as we advance nearer the enlightened ages, we soon learn, that there is nothing mysterious or supernatural in the case, but that all proceeds from the usual propensity of mankind towards the marvelous, and that, though this inclination may at intervals receive a check from sense and learning, it can never be thoroughly extirpated from human nature.

It is strange, a judicious reader is apt to say, upon the perusal of these wonderful historians, *that such prodigious events never happen in our days.* But it is nothing strange, I hope, that men should lie in all ages. You must surely have seen instances enough of that frailty. You have yourself heard many such marvelous relations started, which, being treated with scorn by all the wise and judicious, have at last been abandoned even by the vulgar. Be assured, that those renowned lies, which have spread and flourished to such a monstrous height, arose from like beginnings; but being sown in a more proper soil, shot up at last into prodigies almost equal to those which they relate.

It was a wise policy in that false prophet, Alexander, who though now forgotten, was once so famous, to lay the first scene of his impostures in Paphlagonia, where, as Lucian tells us, the people were extremely ignorant and stupid, and ready to swallow even the grossest delusion. People at a distance, who are weak enough to think the matter at all worth enquiry, have no opportunity of receiving better information. The stories come magnified to them by a hundred circumstances. Fools are industrious in propagating the imposture; while the wise and learned are contented, in general, to deride its absurdity, without informing themselves of the particular facts, by which it may be distinctly refuted. And thus the impostor above mentioned was enabled to proceed, from his ignorant Paphlagonians, to the enlisting of votaries, even among the Grecian philosophers, and men of the most eminent rank and distinction in Rome; nay, could engage the attention of that sage emperor Marcus Aurelius; so far as to make him trust the success of a military expedition to his delusive prophecies.

The advantages are so great, of starting an imposture among an ignorant people, that, even though the delusion should be too gross to impose on the generality of them (*which, though seldom, is sometimes the case*) it has a much better chance for succeeding in remote countries, than if the first scene had been laid in a city renowned for arts and knowledge. The most ignorant and barbarous of these barbarians carry the report abroad. None of their countrymen have a large correspondence, or sufficient credit and authority to contradict and beat down the delusion. Men's inclination to the marvelous has full opportunity to display itself. And thus a story, which is universally exploded in the place where it was first started, shall pass for certain at a thousand miles distance. But had Alexander fixed his residence at Athens, the philosophers of that renowned mart of learning had immediately spread, throughout the whole Roman empire, their sense of the matter; which, being supported by so great authority, and displayed by all the force of reason and eloquence, had entirely opened the eyes of mankind. It is true; Lucian, passing by chance through Paphlagonia, had an opportunity of performing this good office. But, though much to be wished, it does not always happen, that every Alexander meets with Lucian, ready to expose and detect his impostures.

I may add as a *fourth* reason, which diminishes the authority of prodigies, that there is no testimony for any, even those which have not been expressly detected, that is not opposed by an infinite number of witnesses; so that not only the miracle destroys the credit of testimony, but the testimony destroys itself. To make this the better understood, let us consider, that, in matters of religion, whatever is different is contrary; and that it is impossible the religions of ancient Rome, of Turkey, of Siam, and of China should, all of them, be established on any solid foundation. Every miracle, therefore, pretended to have been wrought in any of these religions (and all of them abound in miracles), as its direct scope is to establish the particular system to which it is attributed; so has it the same force, though more indirectly, to overthrow every other system. In destroying a rival system, it likewise destroys the credit of those miracles, on which that system was established; so that all the prodigies of different religions are to be regarded as contrary facts; and the evidences of these prodigies, whether weak or strong, as opposite to each other. According to this method of reasoning, when we believe any miracle of Mahomet or his successors, we have for our warrant the testimony of a few barbarous Arabians: And on the other hand, we are to regard the authority of Titus Livius, Plutarch, Tacitus, and, in short, of all the authors and witnesses, Grecian, Chinese, and Roman Catholic, who have related any miracle in their particular religion; I say, we are to regard their testimony in the same light as if they had mentioned that Mahometan miracle, and had in express terms contradicted it, with the same certainty as they have for the miracle they relate. This argument may appear over subtile and refined; but is not in reality different from the reasoning of a judge, who supposes, that the credit of two witnesses, maintaining a crime against any one, is destroyed by the testimony of two others, who affirm him to have been two hundred leagues distant, at the same instant when the crime is said to have been committed.

One of the best attested miracles in all profane history, is that which Tacitus reports of Vespasian, who cured a blind man in Alexandria, by means of his spittle, and a lame man by the mere touch of his foot; in obedience to a vision of the god Serapis, who had enjoined them to have recourse to the Emperor, for these miraculous cures. The story may be seen in that fine historian;[4] where every circumstance seems to add weight to the testimony, and might be displayed at large with all the force of argument and eloquence, if any one were now concerned to enforce the evidence of that exploded and idolatrous superstition. The gravity, solidity, age, and probity of so great an emperor, who, through

4. Hist. lib. v. cap. 8. Suetonius gives nearly the same account *in vita* Vesp.

the whole course of his life, conversed in a familiar manner with his friends and courtiers, and never affected those extraordinary airs of divinity assumed by Alexander and Demetrius. The historian, a contemporary writer, noted for candor and veracity, and withal, the greatest and most penetrating genius, perhaps, of all antiquity; and so free from any tendency to credulity, that he even lies under the contrary imputation, of atheism and profaneness: The persons, from whose authority he related the miracle, of established character for judgment and veracity, as we may well presume; eye-witnesses of the fact, and confirming their testimony, after the Flavian family was despoiled of the empire, and could no longer give any reward, as the price of a lie. . . . To which if we add the public nature of the facts, as related, it will appear, that no evidence can well be supposed stronger for so gross and so palpable a falsehood.

There is also a memorable story related by Cardinal de Retz, which may well deserve our consideration. When that intriguing politician fled into Spain, to avoid the persecution of his enemies, he passed through Saragossa, the capital of Arragon, where he was shown, in the cathedral, a man, who had served seven years as a doorkeeper, and was well known to everybody in town, that had ever paid his devotions at the church. He had been seen, for so long a time, wanting a leg; but recovered that limb by the rubbing of holy oil upon the stump; and the cardinal assures us that he saw him with two legs. This miracle was vouched by all the canons of the church; and the whole company in town were appealed to for a confirmation of the fact: whom the cardinal found, by their zealous devotion, to be thorough believers of the miracle. Here the relater was also contemporary to the supposed prodigy, of an incredulous and libertine character, as well as of great genius; the miracle of so *singular* a nature as could scarcely admit of a counterfeit, and the witnesses very numerous, and all of them, in a manner, spectators of the fact, to which they gave their testimony. And what adds mightily to the force of the evidence, and may double our surprise on this occasion, is, that the cardinal himself, who relates the story, seems not to give any credit to it, and consequently cannot be suspected of any concurrence in the holy fraud. He considered justly, that it was not requisite, in order to reject a fact of this nature, to be able accurately to disprove the testimony, and to trace its falsehood, through all the circumstances of knavery and credulity which produced it. He knew, that, as this was commonly altogether impossible at any small distance of time and place; so it was extremely difficult, even where one was immediately present, by reason of the bigotry, ignorance, cunning, and roguery of a great part of mankind. He therefore concluded, like a just reasoner, that such evidence carried falsehood upon the very face of it, and that a miracle, supported by any human testimony, was more properly a subject of derision than of argument.

There surely never was a greater number of miracles ascribed to one person, than those, which were lately said to have been wrought in France upon the tomb of Abbé Paris, the famous Jansenist, with whose sanctity the people were so long deluded. The curing of the sick, giving hearing to the deaf, and sight to the blind, were everywhere talked of as the usual effects of that holy sepulchre. But what is more extraordinary; many of the miracles were immediately proved upon the spot, before judges of unquestioned integrity, attested by witnesses of credit and distinction, in a learned age, and on the most eminent theatre that is now in the world. Nor is this all: a relation of them was published and dispersed everywhere; nor were the *Jesuits,* though a learned body, supported by the civil magistrate, and determined enemies to those opinions, in whose favor the miracles were said to have been wrought, ever able distinctly to refute or detect them. Where shall we find such a number of circumstances, agreeing to the corroboration of one fact? And what have we to oppose to such a cloud of witnesses, but the absolute impossibility or miraculous nature of the events, which they relate? And this surely, in the eyes of all reasonable people, will alone be regarded as a sufficient refutation.

Is the consequence just, because some human testimony has the utmost force and authority in some cases, when it relates the battle of Philippi or Pharsalia for instance; that therefore all kinds of testimony must, in all cases, have equal force and authority? Suppose that the Caesarean and Pompeian factions had, each of them, claimed the victory in these battles, and that the historians of each party had uniformly ascribed the advantage to their own side; how could mankind at this distance, have been able to determine between them? The contrariety is equally strong between the miracles related by Herodotus or Plutarch, and those delivered by Mariana, Bede, or any monkish historian.

The wise lend a very academic faith to every report which favors the passion of the reporter; whether it magnifies his country, his family, or himself, or in any other way strikes in with his natural inclinations and propensities. But what greater temptation than to appear a missionary, a prophet, an ambassador from heaven? Who would not encounter many dangers and difficulties, in order to attain so sublime a character? Or if, by the help of vanity and a heated imagination, a man has first made a convert of himself, and entered seriously into the delusion; who ever scruples to make use of pious frauds, in support of so holy and meritorious a cause?

The smallest spark may here kindle into the greatest flame; because the materials are always prepared for it. The *avidum genus auricularum,*[5] the gazing populace, receive greedily, without examination, whatever soothes superstition, and promotes wonder.

How many stories of this nature have, in all ages, been detected and exploded in their infancy? How many more have been celebrated for a time, and have afterwards sunk into neglect and oblivion? Where such reports, therefore, fly about, the solution of the phenomenon is obvious; and we judge in conformity to regular experience and observation, when we account for it by the known and natural principles of credulity and delusion. And shall we, rather than have a recourse to so natural a solution, allow of a miraculous violation of the most established laws of nature?

I need not mention the difficulty of detecting a falsehood in any private or even public history, at the place, where it is said to happen; much more when the scene is removed to ever so small a distance. Even a court of judicature, with all the authority, accuracy, and judgment, which they can employ, find themselves often at a loss to distinguish between truth and falsehood in the most recent actions. But the matter never comes to any issue, if trusted to the common method of altercations and debate and flying rumors; especially when men's passions have taken part on either side.

In the infancy of new religions, the wise and learned commonly esteem the matter too inconsiderable to deserve their attention or regard. And when afterwards they would willingly detect the cheat, in order to undeceive the deluded multitude, the season is now past, and the records and witnesses, which might clear up the matter, have perished beyond recovery.

No means of detection remain, but those which must be drawn from the very testimony itself of the reporters: and these, though always sufficient with the judicious and knowing, are commonly too fine to fall under the comprehension of the vulgar.

Upon the whole, then, it appears, that no testimony for any kind of miracle has ever amounted to a probability, much less to a proof; and that, even supposing it amounted to a proof, it would be opposed by another proof; derived from the very nature of the fact, which it would endeavor to establish. It is experience only, which gives authority to human testimony; and it is the same experience, which assures us of the laws of nature. When, therefore, these two kinds of experience are contrary, we have nothing to

5. Lucret.

do but subtract the one from the other, and embrace an opinion, either on one side or the other, with that assurance which arises from the remainder. But according to the principle here explained, this substraction, with regard to all popular religions, amounts to an entire annihilation; and therefore we may establish it as a maxim, that no human testimony can have such force as to prove a miracle, and make it a just foundation for any such system of religion.

I beg the limitations here made may be remarked, when I say, that a miracle can never be proved, so as to be the foundation of a system of religion. For I own, that otherwise, there may possibly be miracles, or violations of the usual course of nature, of such a kind as to admit of proof from human testimony, though, perhaps, it will be impossible to find any such in all the records of history. Thus, suppose, all authors, in all languages, agree, that, from the first of January 1600, there was a total darkness over the whole earth for eight days: suppose that the tradition of this extraordinary event is still strong and lively among the people: that all travelers, who return from foreign countries, bring us accounts of the same tradition, without the least variation or contradiction: it is evident, that our present philosophers, instead of doubting the fact, ought to receive it as certain, and ought to search for the causes whence it might be derived. The decay, corruption, and dissolution of nature, is an event rendered probable by so many analogies, that any phenomenon, which seems to have a tendency towards that catastrophe, comes within the reach of human testimony, if that testimony be very extensive and uniform.

But suppose, that all the historians who treat of England, should agree, that, on the first of January 1600, Queen Elizabeth died; that both before and after her death she was seen by her physicians and the whole court, as is usual with persons of rank; that her successor was acknowledged and proclaimed by the Parliament; and that, after being interred a month, she again appeared, resumed the throne, and governed England for three years: I must confess that I should be surprised at the occurrence of so many odd circumstances, but should not have the least inclination to believe so miraculous an event. I should not doubt of her pretended death, and of those other public circumstances that followed it: I should only assert it to have been pretended, and that it neither was, nor possibly could be real. You would in vain object to me the difficulty, and almost impossibility of deceiving the world in an affair of such consequence; the wisdom and solid judgment of that renowned queen; with the little or no advantage which she could reap from so poor an artifice: All this might astonish me; but I would still reply, that the knavery and folly of men are such common phenomena, that I should rather believe the most extraordinary events to arise from their concurrence, than admit of so signal a violation of the laws of nature.

But should this miracle be ascribed to any new system of religion; men, in all ages, have been so much imposed on by ridiculous stories of that kind, that this very circumstance would be a full proof of a cheat, and sufficient, with all men of sense, not only to make them reject the fact, but even reject it without farther examination. Though the Being to whom the miracle is ascribed, be, in this case, Almighty, it does not, upon that account, become a whit more probable; since it is impossible for us to know the attributes or actions of such a Being, otherwise than from the experience which we have of his productions, in the usual course of nature. This still reduces us to past observation, and obliges us to compare the instances of the violation of truth in the testimony of men, with those of the violation of the laws of nature by miracles, in order to judge which of them is most likely and probable. As the violations of truth are more common in the testimony concerning religious miracles, than in that concerning any other matter of fact; this must diminish very much the authority of the former testimony, and make us form a general resolution, never to lend any attention to it, with whatever specious pretence it may be covered.

Old Jewish cemetery near the Mount of Olives in Jerusalem.

Lord Bacon seems to have embraced the same principles of reasoning. "We ought," says he, "to make a collection or particular history of all monsters and prodigious births or productions, and in a word of every thing new, rare, and extraordinary in nature. But this must be done with the most severe scrutiny, lest we depart from truth. Above all, every relation must be considered as suspicious, which depends in any degree upon religion, as the prodigies of Livy: And no less so, every thing that is to be found in the writers of natural magic or alchimy, or such authors, who seem, all of them, to have an unconquerable appetite for falsehood and fable.[6]

I am the better pleased with the method of reasoning here delivered, as I think it may serve to confound those dangerous friends or disguised enemies to the *Christian Religion,* who have undertaken to defend it by the principles of human reason. Our most holy religion is founded on *Faith,* not on reason; and it is a sure method of exposing it to put it to such a trial as it is, by no means, fitted to endure. To make this more evident, let us examine those miracles, related in scripture; and not to lose ourselves in too wide a field, let us confine ourselves to such as we find in the *Pentateuch,* which we shall examine, according to the principles of these pretended Christians, not as the word or testimony of God himself, but as the production of a mere human writer and historian. Here then we are first to consider a book, presented to us by a barbarous and ignorant people, written in an age when they were still more barbarous, and in all probability long after the facts which it relates, corroborated by no concurring testimony, and resembling those fabulous accounts, which every nation gives of its origin. Upon reading this book, we find it full of prodigies and miracles. It gives an account of a state of the

6. Nov. Org. lib. ii. aph. 29.

world and of human nature entirely different from the present: Of our fall from that state: Of the age of man, extended to near a thousand years: Of the destruction of the world by a deluge: Of the arbitrary choice of one people, as the favorites of heaven; and that people the countrymen of the author: Of their deliverance from bondage by prodigies the most astonishing imaginable: I desire any one to lay his hand upon his heart, and after a serious consideration declare, whether he thinks that the falsehood of such a book, supported by such a testimony, would be more extraordinary and miraculous than all the miracles it relates; which is, however, necessary to make it be received, according to the measures of probability above established.

What we have said of miracles may be applied, without any variation, to prophecies; and indeed, all prophecies are real miracles, and as such only, can be admitted as proofs of any revelation. If it did not exceed the capacity of human nature to foretell future events, it would be absurd to employ any prophecy as an argument for a divine mission or authority from heaven. So that, upon the whole, we may conclude, that the *Christian Religion* not only was at first attended with miracles, but even at this day cannot be believed by any reasonable person without one. Mere reason is insufficient to convince us of its veracity: And whoever is moved by *Faith* to assent to it, is conscious of a continued miracle in his own person, which subverts all the principles of his understanding, and gives him a determination to believe what is most contrary to custom and experience.

Richard Swinburne

"MIRACLES"

RICHARD SWINBURNE, the Nolloth Professor of Philosophy of Religion at Oxford University, is one of the main twentieth-century philosophical apologists for Christianity. His prolific writings in philosophy of science and philosophy of religion include his *Existence of God* (1979), considered by many to be one of the best defenses of the traditional arguments for the existence of God since the Middle Ages, and *Faith and Reason* (1981).

In this article I wish to investigate whether there could be strong historical evidence for the occurrence of miracles, and contrary to much writing which has derived from Hume's celebrated chapter "Of Miracles," I shall argue that there could be. I understand by a miracle a violation of a law of Nature by a god, that is, a very powerful rational being who is not a material object (viz., is invisible and intangible). My definition of a miracle is thus approximately the same as Hume's: "a transgression of a law of nature by a particular volition of the Deity or by the interposition of some invisible agent."[1] It has been questioned by many biblical scholars

Reprinted from Richard Swinburne, "Miracles," *Philosophical Quarterly* 18 (1968), by permission of the publisher and the author.

1. David Hume, *An Enquiry Concerning Human Understanding,* ed. L. A. Selby-Bigge (Oxford, 2nd ed., 1902), p. 115, footnote.

whether this is what the biblical writers understood by the terms translated into English 'miracle'. I do not propose to enter into this controversy. Suffice it to say that many subsequent Christian theologians have understood by 'miracle' roughly what I understand by the term and that much medieval and modern apologetic which appeals to purported miracles as evidence of the truth of the Christian revelation has had a similar understanding of miracle to mine.

I shall take the question in two parts. I shall enquire first whether there could be evidence that a law of nature has been violated, and secondly, if there can be such evidence, whether there could be evidence that the violation was due to a god.

First, then, can there be evidence that a law of nature has been violated? It seems natural to understand, as Ninian Smart[2] does, by a violation of a law of nature, an occurrence of a non-repeatable counter-instance to a law of nature. Clearly, as Hume admitted, events contrary to predictions of formulae which we had good reason to believe to be laws of nature often occur. But if we have good reason to believe that they have occurred and good reason to believe that similar events would occur in similar circumstances, then we have good reason to believe that the formulae which we previously believed to be the laws of nature were not in fact such laws. Repeatable counter-instances do not violate laws of nature, they just show propositions purporting to state laws of nature to be false. But if we have good reason to believe that an event *E* has occurred contrary to predictions of a formula *L* which we have good reason to believe to be a law of nature, and we have good reason to believe that events similar to *E* would not occur in circumstances as similar as we like in any respect to those of the original occurrence, then we do not have reason to believe that *L* is not a law of nature. For any modified formula which allowed us to predict *E* would allow us to predict similar events in similar circumstances and hence, we have good reason to believe, would give false predictions. Whereas if we leave the formula *L* unmodified, it will, we have good reason to believe, give correct predictions in all other conceivable circumstances. Hence if we are to say that any law of nature is operative in the field of question we must say that it is *L*. This seems a natural thing to say rather than to say that no law of nature operates in the field. Yet *E* is contrary to the predictions of *L*. Hence, for want of a better expression, we say that *E* has violated the law of nature *L*. If the use of the word 'violated' suggests too close an analogy between laws of nature and civil or moral laws, that is unfortunate. Once we have explained, as above, what is meant by a violation of a law of nature, no subsequent confusion need arise.

The crucial question, not adequately discussed by Smart, however, is what would be good reason for believing that an event *E*, if it occurred, was a non-repeatable as opposed to a repeatable counter-instance to a formula *L* which we have on all other evidence good reason to believe to be a law of nature. The evidence that *E* is a repeatable counter-instance would be that a new formula L^1 fairly well confirmed by the data as a law of nature can be set up. A formula is confirmed by data, if the data obtained so far are predicted by the formula, if new predictions are successful and if the formula is a simple and coherent one relative to the collection of data.

Compatible with any finite set of data, there will always be an infinite number of possible formulae from which the data can be predicted. We can rule out many by further tests, but however many tests we make we shall still have only a finite number of data and hence an infinite number of formulae compatible with them.

But some of these formulae will be highly complex relative to the data, so that no scientist would consider that the data were evidence that those formulae were true laws of nature. Others are very simple formulae such that the data can be said to provide evidence that they are true

2. Ninian Smart, *Philosophers and Religious Truth* (London, 1964), Ch. II.

laws of nature. Thus suppose the scientist's task is to find a formula accounting for marks on a graph, observed at (1, 1), (2, 2), (3, 3), and (4, 4), the first number of each pair being the x co-ordinate and the second the y co-ordinate. One formula which would predict these marks is $x = y$. Another one is $(x - 1)(x - 2)(x - 3)(x - 4) + x = y$. But clearly we would not regard the data as supporting the second formula. It is too clumsy a formula to explain four observations. Among simple formulae supported by the data, the simplest is the best supported and regarded, provisionally, as correct. If the formula survives further tests, that increases the evidence in its favour as a true law.

Now if for E and for all other relevant data we can construct a formula L^1 from which the data can be derived and which either makes successful predictions in other circumstances where L makes bad predictions, or is a fairly simple formula, so that from the fact that it can predict E, and L cannot, we have reason to believe that its predictions, if tested, would be better than those of L in other circumstances, then we have good reason to believe that L^1 is the true law in the field. The formula will indicate under what circumstances divergencies from L similar to E will occur. The evidence thus indicates that they will occur under these circumstances and hence that E is a repeatable counter-instance to the original formula L.

Suppose, however, that for E and all the other data of the field we can construct no new formula L^1 which yields more successful predictions than L in other examined circumstances, nor one which is fairly simple relative to the data; but for all the other data except E the simple formula L does yield good predictions. And suppose that as the data continue to accumulate, L remains a completely successful predictor and there remains no reason to suppose that a simple formula L^1 from which all the other data and E can be derived can be constructed. The evidence then indicates that the divergence from L will not be repeated and hence that E is a non-repeatable counter-instance to a law of nature L.

Here is an example. Suppose E to be the levitation (viz., rising into the air and remaining floating on it) of a certain holy person. E is a counter-instance to otherwise well substantiated laws of mechanics L. We could show E to be a repeatable counter-instance if we could construct a formula L^1 which predicted E and also successfully predicted other divergences from L, as well as all other tested predictions of L; or if we could construct L^1 which was comparatively simple relative to the data and predicted E and all the other tested predictions of L, but predicted divergences from L which had not yet been tested. L^1 might differ from L in that, according to it, under certain circumstances bodies exercise a gravitational repulsion on each other, and the circumstance in which E occurred was one of those circumstances. If L^1 satisfied either of the above two conditions, we would adopt it, and we would then say that under certain circumstances people do levitate and so E was not a counter-instance to a law of nature. However, it might be that any modification which we made to the laws of mechanics to allow them to predict E might not yield any more successful predictions than L and they [might] be so clumsy that there was no reason to believe that their predictions not yet tested would be successful. Under these circumstances we would have good reasons to believe that the levitation of the holy person violated the laws of nature.

If the laws of nature are statistical and not deterministic, it is not in all cases so clear what counts as a counter-instance to them. How improbable does an event have to be to constitute a counter-instance to a statistical law? But this problem is a general one in the philosophy of science and does not raise any issues peculiar to the topic of miracles.

It is clear that all claims about what does or does not violate the laws of nature are corrigible. New scientific knowledge may force us to revise any such claims. But all claims to knowledge about matters of fact are corrigible, and we must reach provisional conclusions about them on the evidence available to us. We have to some extent good evidence about what are the laws of nature, and some of them are so well established and account for so many data that any modifications to them which we could suggest to account for the odd counter-instance would be so clumsy and *ad hoc* as to upset the whole structure of science. In such cases the evidence is strong that if the purported counter-instance occurred it was a violation of the laws of nature. There is good reason to believe that the following events, if they occurred, would be violations of the laws of nature: levitation; resurrection from the dead in full health of a man whose heart has not been beating for twenty-four hours and who was, by other criteria also, dead; water turning into wine without the assistance of chemical apparatus or catalysts; a man getting better from polio in a minute.

So then we could have the evidence that an event *E* if it occurred was a non-repeatable counter-instance to a true law of nature *L*. But Hume's argument here runs as follows. The evidence, which *ex hypothesi* is good evidence, that *L* is a true law of nature is evidence that *E* did not occur. We have certain other evidence that *E* did occur. In such circumstances, writes Hume, the wise man "weighs the opposite experiments.

The Scientific Mythod

We have scientific accounts of the origins of the universe that were arrived at and tested so differently than religious myths (most of which are either not subject to any sort of empirical test or else blatantly fail such tests), that it hardly seems appropriate to lump science and mythology into the same category. The point of science, most people think, is to replace mythology: A good scientific answer is not mythological but simply true.

Surely scientific explanations are in general more worthy of belief than nonscientific ones. But perhaps science goes too far by encouraging habits of mind that unfairly prejudice the evaluation of competing explanations in favor of currently acceptable ones, thus insulating its most general theories from competition with nonscientific alternatives. For instance, scientific habits of mind encourage us always to prefer natural to supernatural explanations of unusual phenomena, and among natural explanations those that fit into current scientific theory to those that do not.

In the battle among competing explanations of unusual phenomena, does this scientific mind-set load the deck in favor of current scientific theory? Does it tend to perpetuate its own outlook regardless of what evidence might turn up? If the answers to these questions are "yes," then perhaps science has a mythological element, a kind of *methodological* mythology that ensures the perpetuation of its own current outlook and theories.

He considers which side is supported by the greater number of experiments."[3] Since he supposes that the evidence that *E* occurred would be that of testimony, Hume concludes "that no testimony is sufficient to establish a miracle, unless the testimony be of such a kind, that its falsehood would be more miraculous, than the fact which it endeavours to establish."[4] He considers that this condition is not in fact satisfied by any purported miracle, though he seems at times to allow that it is logically possible that it might be.

One wonders here at Hume's scale of evidence. Suppose two hundred witnesses claiming to have observed some event *E*, an event which, if it occurred, would be a non-repeatable counter-instance to a law of nature. Suppose these to be witnesses able and anxious to show that *E* did not occur if there were grounds for doing so. Would not their combined evidence give us good reason to believe that *E* occurred? Hume's answer which we can see from his discussion of two apparently equally well authenticated miracles is—No. But then, one is inclined to say, is not Hume just being bigoted, refusing to face facts? It would be virtually impossible to draw up a table showing how many witnesses and of what kind we need to establish the occurrence of an event which, if it occurred, would be a non-repeatable counter-instance to a law of nature. Each purported instance has to be considered on its merits. But certainly one feels that Hume's standards of evidence are too high. What, one wonders, would Hume himself say if he saw such an event?

But behind Hume's excessively stringent demands on evidence there may be a philosophical point which he has not fully brought out. This is a point made by Flew in justification of Hume's standards of evidence: "The justification for giving the 'scientific' this ultimate precedence here over the 'historical' lies in the nature of the propositions concerned and in the evidence which can be displayed to sustain them . . . the candidate historical proposition will be particular, often singular, and in the past tense. . . . But just by reason of this very pastness and particularly it is no longer possible for anyone to examine the subject directly for himself . . . the law of nature will, unlike the candidate historical proposition, be a general nomological. It can thus in theory, though obviously not always in practice, be tested at any time by any person."[5]

Flew's contrast is, however, mistaken. Particular experiments on particular occasions only give a certain and far from conclusive support to claims that a purported scientific law is true. Any person can test for the truth of a purported scientific law, but a positive result to one test will only give limited support to the claim. Exactly the same holds for purported historical truths. Anyone can examine the evidence, but a particular piece of evidence only gives limited support to the claim that the historical proposition is true. But in the historical as in the scientific case, there is no limit to the amount of evidence. We can go on and on testing for the truth of historical as well as scientific propositions. We can look for more and more data which can only be explained as effects of some specified past event, and data incompatible with its occurrence, just as we can look for more and more data for or against the truth of some physical law. Hence the truth of the historical proposition can also "be tested at any time by any person."

What Hume seems to suppose is that the only evidence about whether an event *E* happened is the written or verbal testimony of those who would have been in a position to witness it, had it occurred. And as there will be only a finite number of such pieces of testimony, the evidence about whether or not *E* happened would be finite. but this is not the only testimony which is relevant—we need testimony about the char-

3. Op. cit., p. 111.
4. Op. cit., p. 116.
5. Antony Flew, *Hume's Philosophy of Belief* (London, 1961), pp. 207 *ff.*

acter and competence of the original witnesses. Nor is testimony the only type of evidence. All effects of what happened at the time of the alleged occurrence of *E* are also relevant. Far more than in Hume's day we are today often in a position to assess what occurred by studying the physical traces of the event. Hume had never met Sherlock Holmes with his ability to assess what happened in the room from the way in which the furniture lay, or where the witness was yesterday from the mud on his boot. As the effects of what happened at the time of the occurrence of *E* are always with us in some form, we can always go on examining them yet more carefully. Further, we need to investigate whether *E*, if it did occur, would in fact have brought about the present effects, and whether any other cause could have brought about just these effects. To investigate these issues involves investigating which scientific laws operate (other than the law *L* of which it is claimed that *E* was a violation), and this involves doing experiments *ad lib.* Hence there is no end to the amount of new evidence which can be had. The evidence that the event *E* occurred can go on mounting up in the way that evidence that *L* is a law of nature can do. The wise man in these circumstances will surely say that he has good reason to believe that *E* occurred, but also that *L* is a true law of nature and so that *E* was a violation of it.

So we could have good reason to believe that a law of nature has been violated. But for a violation of a law of nature to be a miracle, it has to be caused by a god, that is, a very powerful rational being who is not a material object. What could be evidence that it was?

To explain an event as brought about by a rational agent with intentions and purposes is to give an entirely different kind of explanation of its occurrence from an explanation by scientific laws acting on precedent causes. Our normal grounds for attributing an event to the agency of an embodied rational agent *A* is that we or others perceived *A* bringing it about *or* that it is the sort of event that *A* typically brings about and that *A*, and no one else of whom we have knowledge, was in a position to bring it about. The second kind of ground is only applicable when we have prior knowledge of the existence of *A*. In considering evidence for a violation *E* of a law of nature being due to the agency of a god, I will distinguish two cases, one where we have good reason on grounds other than the occurrence of violations of laws of nature to believe that there exists at least one god, and one where we do not.

Let us take the second case first. Suppose we have no other good reason for believing that a god exists, but an event *E* then occurs which, our evidence indicates, is a non-repeatable counter-instance to a true law of nature. Now we cannot attribute *E* to the agency of a god by seeing the god's body bring *E* about, for gods do not have bodies. But suppose that *E* occurs in ways and circumstances *C* strongly analogous to those in which occur events brought about by human agents, and that other violations occur in such circumstances. We would then be justified in claiming that *E* and other such violations are, like effects of human actions, brought about by agents, but ones unlike men in not being material objects. This inference would be justified because, if an analogy between effects is strong enough, we are always justified in postulating slight difference in causes to account for slight difference in effects. Thus if because of its other observable behaviour we say that light is a disturbance in a medium, then the fact that the medium, if it exists, does not, like other media, slow down material bodies passing through it, is not by itself (viz., if there are no other disanalogies) a reason for saying that the light is not a disturbance in a medium, but only for saying that the medium in which light is a disturbance has the peculiar property of not resisting the passage of material bodies. So if, because of very strong similarity between the ways and circumstances of the occurrence of *E* and other violations of laws of nature to the ways and circumstances in which effects are produced by human agents, we postulate a similar cause—a rational agent, the fact that there are certain disanalogies (viz., we cannot point to the agent, say where his body is) does not mean that our explanation is wrong. It only means that the agent is unlike humans in not having a body. But this move is only justified if the similarities are otherwise strong. Nineteenth-century scientists eventually concluded that for light the similarities were not strong enough to outweigh the dissimilarities and justify postulating the medium with the peculiar property.

Now what similarities in the ways and circumstances *C* of their occurrence could there be between *E* (and other violations of laws of nature) and the effects of human actions to justify the postulation of similar causes? Suppose that *E* occurred in answer to a request. Thus *E* might be an explosion in my room, totally inexplicable by the laws of nature, when at the time of its occurrence there were in a room on the other side of the corridor men in turbans chanting "O God of the Sikhs, may there be an explosion in Swinburne's room." Suppose, too, that when *E* occurs a voice, but not the voice of an embodied agent, is heard giving reasonable reasons for granting the request. When the explosion occurs in my room, a voice emanating from no man or animal or man-made machine is heard saying "Your request is granted. He deserves a lesson." Would not all this be good reason for postulating a rational agent other than a material object who brought about *E* and the other violations, an agent powerful enough to change instantaneously by intervention the properties of things, viz., a god? Clearly if the analogy were strong enough between the ways and circumstances in which violations of laws of nature and effects of human action occur, it would be. If furthermore the prayers which were answered by miracles were prayers for certain kinds of events (e.g., relief of suffering, punishment of ill-doers) and those which were not answered by miracles were for events of different kinds, then this would show something about the character of the god. Normally, of course, the evidence adduced by theists for the occurrence of miracles is not as strong as I have indicated that very strong evidence would be. Violations are often reported as occurring subsequent to prayer for them to occur, and seldom otherwise; but voices giving reason for answering such a request are rare indeed. Whether in cases where voices are not heard but the occurrence of a violation *E* and of prayer for its occurrence were both well confirmed, we would be justified in concluding that the existence of a god who brought *E* about is a matter of whether the analogy is strong enough as it stands. The question of exactly when an analogy is strong enough to justify an inference based on it is a difficult one. But my only point here is that if the analogy were strong enough, the inference would be justified.

Suppose now that we have other evidence for the existence of a god. Then if *E* occurs in the circumstances *C*, previously described, that *E* is due to the activity of a god is more adequately substantiated, and the occurrence of *E* gives further support to the evidence for the existence of a god. But if we already have reason to believe in the existence of a god, the occurrence of *E* not under circumstances as similar as *C* to those under which human agents often bring about results, could nevertheless sometimes be justifiably attributed to his activity. Thus, if the occurrence of *E* is the sort of thing that the only god of whose existence we have evidence would wish to bring about if he has the character suggested by the other evidence for his existence, we can reasonably hold him responsible for the occurrence of *E* which would otherwise be unexplained. The healing of a faithful blind Christian contrary to the laws of nature could reasonably be attributed to the God of the Christians, if there were other evidence for his existence, whether or not the blind man or other Christians had ever prayed for that result.

For these reasons I conclude that we can have good reason to believe that a violation of a law of nature was caused by a god, and so was a miracle.

I would like to make two final points, one to tidy up the argument and the other to meet a further argument put forward by Hume which I have not previously discussed.

Entia non sunt multiplicanda praeter necessitatem.—Unless we have good reason to do so we ought not to postulate the existence of more than one god, but to suppose that the same being answers all prayers. But there could be good reason to postulate the existence of more than one god, and evidence to this effect could be provided by miracles. One way in which this could happen is that prayers for a certain kind of result, for example, shipwreck, which began "O, Neptune" were often answered, and also prayers for a different kind of result, for example, success in love, which began "O, Venus" were also often answered, but prayers for a result of the first kind beginning "O, Venus," and for a result of the second beginning "O, Neptune" were never answered. Evidence for the existence of one god would in general support, not oppose, evidence for the existence of a second one since, by suggesting that there is one rational being other than those whom we can see, it makes more reasonable the postulation of another one.

The second point is that there is no reason at all to suppose that Hume is in general right to claim that "every miracle . . . pretended to have been wrought in any . . . (religion) . . . as its direct scope is to establish the particular system to which it is attributed; so it has the same force, though more indirectly, to overthrow every other system. In destroying a rival system it likewise destroys the credit of those miracles on which that system was established."[6] If Hume were right to claim that evidence for the miracles of one religion was evidence against the miracles of any other, then indeed evidence for miracles in each would be poor. But in fact evidence for a miracle "wrought in one religion" is only evidence against the occurrence of a miracle "wrought in another religion" if the two miracles, if they occurred, would be evidence for propositions of the two religious systems incompatible with each other. It is hard to think of pairs of alleged miracles of this type. If there were evidence for a Roman Catholic miracle which was evidence for the doctrine of transubstantiation and evidence for a Protestant miracle which was evidence against it, here we would have a case of the conflict of evidence which, Hume claims, occurs generally with alleged miracles. But it is enough to give this example to see that most alleged miracles do not give rise to conflicts of this kind. Most alleged miracles, if they occurred, would only show the power of god or gods and their concern for the needs of men, and little else.

My main conclusion, to repeat it, is that there are no logical difficulties in supposing that there could be strong historical evidence for the occurrence of miracles. Whether there is such evidence is, of course, another matter.

6. Op. cit., pp. 121 *ff.*

J. L. Mackie

"MIRACLES AND TESTIMONY"

J. L. MACKIE (1917–1981), who received his B.A. from the University of Sydney and his M.A. from Oxford University, taught at the University of York (England), the University of Otago (New Zealand), and the University of Sydney (Australia), before becoming Reader in Philosophy at Oxford University and Fellow of University College. He wrote extensively in metaphysics, ethics, philosophy of science, and the history of philosophy. *The Miracle of Theism* (1982), from which all four of his selections in the present text are taken, is regarded by many as a classic contemporary assessment of the central issues in philosophy of religion.

(a) HUME'S ARGUMENT—EXPOSITION

Traditional theism does not explicitly include any contrast between the natural and the supernatural. Yet there is a familiar, if vague and undeveloped, notion of the natural world in contrast with which the theistic doctrines stand out as asserting a supernatural reality. The question whether and how there can be evidence for what, if real, would be supernatural is therefore one of central significance. Besides, explicit assertions about supernatural occurrences, about miracles or divine interventions which have disrupted the natural course of events, are common in early all religions: alleged miracles are often cited to validate religious claims. Christianity, for example, has its share of these. In the life of Christ we have the virgin birth, the turning of water into wine, Christ's walking on the water, his healing of the sick, his raising of Lazarus from the dead, and, of course, the resurrection. The Roman Catholic church will not recognize anyone as a saint unless it is convinced that at least two miracles have been performed by the supposed saint, either in his or her life or after death.

The usual purpose of stories about miracles is to establish the authority of the particular figures who perform them or are associated with them, but of course these stories, with their intended interpretation, presuppose such more general religious doctrines as that of the existence of a god. We can, therefore, recognize, as one of the supports of traditional theism, an argument from miracles: that is, an argument whose main premiss is that such and such remarkable events have occurred, and whose conclusion is that a god of the traditional sort both exists and intervenes, from time to time, in the ordinary world.

Hume, however, in his essay on miracles, Section 10 of his *Enquiry Concerning Human Understanding,* makes the bold claim that he has discovered an argument which refutes all such stories about the occurrence of miracles.[1] 'I flatter myself,' he says, 'that I have discovered

From J. L. Mackie, *The Miracle of Theism,* Clarendon Press, 1982, pp. 13–29. Reprinted by permission of Oxford University Press.

1. D. Hume, *Enquiries Concerning the Human Understanding and Concerning the Principles of Morals,* edited by L. A. Selby-Bigge (Oxford University Press, 1902). References in the text are to pages in this edition.

an argument . . . which, if just, will, with the wise and learned, be an everlasting check to all kinds of superstitious delusion, and consequently, will be useful as long as the world endures. For so long, I presume, will the accounts of miracles and prodigies be found in all history, sacred and profane.' (p. 110) In this fairly early work, as in the much later remarks quoted in the Introduction, Hume does not expect the popular belief in the supernatural to die out: it is only with the 'wise and learned' that rational criticism can be expected to carry much weight. But how sound is the argument in which he felt this modest confidence? What is its substance?

We should distinguish the central argument which Hume discovered, and which he states in Part I of this section, from various secondary reasons which he gives in Part II for doubting the stories about miracles. Let us run through these secondary reasons first, and then come back to the main argument.

First, Hume says that there are no really well-attested miracles: none, that is, 'attested by a sufficient number of men, of such unquestioned good-sense, education, and learning, as to secure us against all delusion in themselves; of such undoubted integrity, as to place them beyond all suspicion of any design to deceive others; of such credit and reputation in the eyes of mankind, as to have a great deal to lose in case of their being detected in any falsehood; and at the same time attesting facts, performed in such a public manner, and in so celebrated a part of the world, as to render the detection unavoidable' (pp. 116–17). These are high standards. But such high standards are appropriate in an area where deceit, self-deception, and mistake are so easy. Unfortunately, it is a matter of controversy whether they have ever been met. At least Hume's remarks here specify questions that we might well ask when we encounter any reports of alleged miracles.

Hume points out, secondly, that the human mind has a positive tendency to believe what is strange and marvellous in an extreme degree. 'The passion of *surprise* and *wonder*, arising from miracles, being an agreeable emotion, gives a sensible tendency towards the belief of those events from which it is derived.' (p. 117) The willingness of many people today to believe accounts of flying saucers and their crews illustrates this tendency: such reports are, paradoxically, made more believable by the very divergence from the ordinary which in fact makes them less worthy of belief.

Thirdly, reports of miracles 'are observed chiefly to abound among ignorant and barbarous nations'. Where they are believed by civilized peoples, these 'will be found to have received them from ignorant and barbarous ancestors', so that the stories will have acquired the authority of received opinions before the nations in question have developed powers of criticism and traditions of rational inquiry. (p. 119)

Fourthly, different religions are in conflict: their claims therefore undermine and destroy one another. The truth of any report of a miracle which would tend to establish the religious authority of Christ or his followers would require the falsity of any report of a miracle which would tend to establish the authority of Mahomet. Thus the miracle reports of any one religion are implicitly or in effect contradicted by the miracle reports of many other religions: it is as if a law-court were presented with, say, twenty witnesses, each of whom was denounced as a liar by the other nineteen. (pp. 121–2)

This argument, however, has less force now than it had when Hume was writing. Faced with influential bodies of atheist or sceptical opinion, the adherents of different religions have toned down their hostility to one another. The advocate of one religion will now often allow that a number of others have at least some elements of truth and even, perhaps, some measure of divine authorization. It is no longer 'The heathen in his blindness . . .', but rather 'We worship the same god, but under different names and in different ways'. Carried far enough, this modern tendency would allow Christian miracles to support, not undermine, belief in the supernatural achievements of stone-age witch doctors and medicine men, and vice versa. It is as if someone had coined the slogan, 'Miracle-workers of the world, unite!'

Fifthly, Hume says, the very fact that a miracle story is used to introduce a new religion or to support an existing one is an additional reason for scepticism. Many people have an intense desire to believe in some religious object, and experience shows that large numbers are constantly deluded by such claims. (pp. 125–6) This is in itself a strong point. But we might add to it the fact that in a religious context credulity is often thought to be meritorious, while doubt or critical caution is felt to be sinful. Consequently, once even a modicum of belief arises in a group of people in communication with one another, it tends to reinforce itself and so develop into total conviction. No doubt this appears to the members of such a group as a virtuous spiral, but it has no valid claim to be regarded as a rational process.

These five points, then, are of unequal force, but between them they certainly provide grounds for a high degree of initial caution and scepticism about every alleged miracle. But they are secondary considerations, additional and subordinate to Hume's main argument.

This main argument rests upon a principle that governs the acceptance of testimony, believing what one is told, about any matter at all. If someone tells you something, you are in general disposed to believe him; but why? Why should you give any credence at all to what he says? Your basic reason must be that it is unlikely that he would have told you this if it were not so. His report—assuming that you have understood it correctly—could be false only in either of two ways: he might be mistaken, or he might be deceiving you. Is it likely that he is mistaken? Is it likely that he is insincere? If both of these are unlikely, then it is unlikely that he would be telling you this if it were not so. Since he *is* telling you this, it is unlikely that it is not so; that is, so far as these considerations are concerned, it is likely that it is so. But these are not the only relevant considerations: you must weigh along with them the intrinsic likelihood or unlikelihood of whatever it is that your informant reports. The less intrinsically likely this is, the more reliable the testimony needs to be, if it is to deserve acceptance. The question to be answered is this: 'Which of these two is the more unlikely as a whole: that he should be telling you this and it not be so—and therefore that he should be mistaken or dishonest—or that he should be telling this and it be so—that is, that the event he reports, despite whatever intrinsic unlikeliness attaches to it, should have happened?' So if the event reported is something intrinsically improbable, the crucial question is whether the reporter's being either deceived or a deceiver is intrinsically more improbable still. Further, the magnitude of each of these unlikelihoods or improbabilities must be determined with reference to the way the world goes on, that is, with reference to the laws of nature so far as we know them. In deciding how the world goes on, we can rely only on past experience: we must reason inductively from what we have observed. Now if the event reported is a miracle, it must be literally contrary to the laws of nature, it must contradict the conclusion of an induction of maximum strength. That is, it must be as unlikely as anything could be. The competing unlikelihood of the reporter's being deceived or a deceiver cannot exceed this, but can at most equal it. Indeed Hume thinks it will never even equal it, for it will not be contrary to a law of nature that your informant should have made a mistake or that he should be dishonest. But if the two unlikelihoods are equal, they will simply cancel one another out: we shall still have, on balance, no positive reason for accepting the report of the miracle.

That, at least, seems to be what Hume is saying. However, at the end of Part I of this Section he hesitates. 'The plain consequence', he says, 'is "That no testimony is sufficient to establish a miracle, unless the testimony be of such a kind, that its falsity would be more mi-

The Church of the Holy Sepulchre in Jerusalem was built over the tomb where Jesus supposedly was buried.

raculous, than the fact, which it endeavours to establish; and even in that case there is a mutual destruction of arguments, and the superior only gives us an assurance suitable to that degree of force, which remains, after deducting the inferior".' (pp. 115–16) This comment seems to allow that the balance of probabilities could be in favour of our accepting the miracle report, though with no very high degree of confidence; it will also entail something that Hume seems not to have noticed, that if the force of testimony is pretty strong, though not strong enough to make it reasonable for us to accept the miracle report, it will significantly lower the degree of confidence with which we reject it.

In fact, Hume's conclusion needs to be tidied up and restated as follows. There are three conceivable cases. In the first, the unlikelihood of the testimony's being false (either mistaken or dishonest) is less than the intrinsic unlikelihood of the miracle's having occurred: in this case, we must reject the miracle report, with a degree of confidence that corresponds to the difference between these unlikelihoods. In the second, the two unlikelihoods are equal: now we must simply suspend our judgement until some fresh consideration tips the balance either way; but in the meantime we cannot rationally accept the report. In the third case the occurrence of the miracle is intrinsically less unlikely than the testimony's being false: in this, we are rationally bound to accept the miracle report, but again with a degree of conviction that corresponds to the difference between the two unlikelihoods. This degree of conviction can never be high, on account of the great intrinsic improbability of the miracle. Where the falsity of the report would itself be a miracle in the sense of a violation of what we take to be the laws of nature, we must, Hume says, 'weigh the one miracle against the other', and 'reject the greater miracle'. 'If the falsity of his testimony would be more miraculous than the event which he relates; then, and not till then, can he pretend to command my belief or opinion.' (p. 116)

Thus tidied up, the conclusion of Part I clearly allows, in principle, cases where the testimony would establish a miracle, at least tentatively, with no great preponderance of rational support, and also cases where we ought to suspend judgement. But we can now understand the argumentative function of the secondary considerations offered in Part II. They are meant to show that neither of these two conceivable cases is ever actually realized, that the unlikelihood that the testimony brought in favour of a miracle should be false is never in practice very great, so that it will always in fact be less than the unlikelihood of the miracle's having occurred.

(b) HUME'S ARGUMENT—DISCUSSION

What Hume has been expounding are the principles for the rational acceptance of testimony, the rules that ought to govern our believing or not believing what we are told. But the rules that govern people's actual acceptance of testimony are very different. We are fairly good at detecting dishonesty, insincerity, and lack of conviction, and we readily reject what we are told by someone who betrays these defects. But we are strongly inclined simply to accept, without question, statements that are obviously assured and sincere. As Hume would say, a firm association of ideas links someone else's saying, with honest conviction, that *p,* and its being the case that *p,* and we pass automatically from the perception of the one to belief in the other. Or, as he might also have said, there is an intellectual sympathy by which we tend automatically to share what we find to be someone else's belief, analogous to sympathy in the original sense, the tendency to share what we see to be someone else's feelings. And in general this is a useful tendency. People's beliefs about ordinary matters are right, or nearly right, more often than they are wildly wrong, so that intellectual sympathy enables fairly correct information to be passed on more smoothly than it could be if we were habitually cautious and constantly checked testimony against the principles for its rational acceptance. But what is thus generally useful can sometimes be misleading, and miracle reports are a special case where we need to restrain our instinctive acceptance of honest statements, and go back to the basic rational principles which determine whether a statement is really reliable or not. Even where we are cautious, and hesitate to accept what we are told—for example by a witness in a legal case—we often do not go beyond the question 'How intrinsically reliable is this witness?', or, in detail, 'Does he seem to be honest? Does he have a motive for misleading us? Is he the sort of person who might tell plausible lies? Or is he the sort of person who, in the circumstances, might have made a mistake?' If we are satisfied on all these scores, we are inclined to believe what the witness says, without weighing very seriously the question 'How intrinsically improbable is what he has told us?' But, as Hume insists, this further question is highly relevant. His general approach to the problem of when to accept testimony is certainly sound.

Hume's case against miracles is an epistemological argument: it does not try to show that miracles never do happen or never could happen, but only that we never have good reasons for believing that they have happened. It must be clearly distinguished from the suggestion that the very concept of a miracle is incoherent. That suggestion might be spelled out as follows. A miracle is, by definition, a violation of a law of nature, and a law of nature is, by definition, a regularity—or the statement of a regularity—about what happens, about the way the world works; consequently, if some event actually occurs, no regularity which its occurrence infringes (or, no regularity-statement which it falsifies) can really be a law of nature; so this event, however unusual or surprising, cannot after all be a miracle. The two definitions together entail that whatever happens is not a miracle, that is, that miracles never happen. This, be it noted, is not Hume's argument. If it were correct, it would make Hume's argument unnecessary. Before we discuss Hume's case, then, we should consider whether there is a coherent concept of a miracle which would not thus rule out the occurrence of miracles *a priori.*

If miracles are to serve their traditional function of giving spectacular support to religious claims—whether general theistic claims, or the authority of some specific religion or some particular sect or individual teacher—the concept must not be so weakened that anything at all unusual or remarkable counts as a miracle. We must keep in the definition the notion of a violation of natural law. But then, if it is to be even possible that a miracle should occur, we must modify the definition given above of a law of nature. What we want to do is to contrast the order of nature with a possible divine or supernatural intervention. The laws of nature, we must say, describe the ways in which the world—including, of course, human beings—works when left to itself, when not interfered with. A miracle occurs when the world is not left to itself, when something distinct from the natural order as a whole intrudes into it.

This notion of ways in which the world works is coherent and by no means obscure. We know how to discover causal laws, relying on a principle of the uniformity of the course of nature—essentially the assumption that there are some laws to be found—in conjunction with suitable observations and experiments, typically varieties of controlled experiment whose underlying logic is that of Mill's 'method of difference'. Within the laws so established, we can further mark off basic laws of working from derived laws which hold only in a particular context or contingently upon the way in which something is put together. It will be a derived law that a particular clock, or clocks of a particular sort, run at such a speed, and this will hold only in certain conditions of temperature, and so on; but this law will be derived from more basic ones which describe the regular behaviour of certain kinds of material, in view of the way in which the clock is put together, and these more basic laws of materials may in turn be derived from yet more basic laws about sub-atomic particles, in view of the ways in which those materials are made up of such particles. In so far as we advance towards a knowledge of such a system of basic and derived laws, we are acquiring an understanding of ways in which the world works. As well as what we should ordinarily call causal laws, which typically concern interactions, there are similar laws with regard to the ways in which certain kinds of things simply persist through time, and certain sorts of continuous process just go on. These too, and in particular the more basic laws of these sorts, help to constitute the ways in which the world works. Thus there are several kinds of basic 'laws of working'.[2] For our present purpose, however, it is not essential that we should even be approaching an understanding of how the world works; it is enough that we have the concept of such basic laws of working, that we know in principle what it would be to discover them. Once we have this concept, we have moved beyond the definition of laws of nature merely as (statements of) what always happens. We can see how, using this concept and using the assumption that there are some such basic laws of working to be found, we can hope to determine what the actual laws of working are by reference to a restricted range of experiments and observations. This opens up the possibility that we might determine that something *is* a basic law of working of natural objects, and yet also, independently, find that it was occasionally violated. An occasional violation does not in itself necessarily overthrow the independently established conclusion that this *is* a law of working.

Equally, there is no obscurity in the notion of intervention. Even in the natural world we have a clear understanding of how there can be for a time a closed system, in which everything that happens results from factors within that system in accordance with its laws of working, but how then something may intrude from outside it, bringing about changes that the system would not have produced of its own accord, so that things go on after this intrusion differently from how they would have gone on if the system had remained closed. All we need do, then, is to regard the whole natural world as being, for most of the time, such a closed system; we can then think of a supernatural intervention as something that intrudes into that system from outside the natural world as a whole.

If the laws by which the natural world works are deterministic, then the notion of a violation of them is quite clear-cut: such a violation would be an event which, given that the world was a closed system working in accordance with these laws, and given some actual earlier complete state of the world, simply could not have happened at all. Its occurrence would then be clear proof that either the supposed laws were not the real laws of working, or the earlier state was not as it was supposed to have been, or else the system was not closed after all. But if the basic laws of working are statistical or probabilistic, the notion of a violation of them is less precise. If something happens which, given those statistical laws and some earlier complete state of the world, is extremely improbable—in the sense of physical probability: that is, something such that there is a strong propensity or tendency for it *not* to happen—we still cannot say firmly that the laws have been violated: laws of this sort explicitly allow that what is extremely improbable may occasionally come about. Indeed it is highly probable (both physically and epistemically) that some events, each of which is very improbable, will occur at rare intervals.[3] If tosses of a coin were governed by a statistical law that

2. The notion of basic laws of working is fully discussed in Chapters 8 and 9 of my *The Cement of the Universe: A Study of Causation* (Oxford University Press, 1974 and 1980).

3. The distinction between physical and epistemic probability has been drawn in the Introduction; the exact form of statistical laws is discussed in Chapter 9 of *The Cement of the Universe.*

gave a 50 per cent propensity to heads at each toss, a continuous run of ten heads would be a highly improbable occurrence; but it would be highly probable that there would be some such runs in a sequence of a million tosses. Nevertheless, we can still use the contrast between the way of working of the natural world as a whole, considered as a normally closed system, and an intervention or intrusion into it. This contrast does not disappear or become unintelligible merely because we lack decisive tests for its application. We can still define a miracle as an event which would not have happened in the course of nature, and which came about only through a supernatural intrusion. The difficulty is merely that we cannot now say with certainty, simply by reference to the relevant laws and some antecedent situation, that a certain event would not have happened in the course of nature, and therefore must be such an intrusion. But we may still be able to say that it is very probable—and this is now an epistemic probability—that it would not have happened naturally, and so is likely to be such an intrusion. For if the laws made it physically improbable that it would come about, this tends to make it epistemically improbable that it did come about through those laws, if there is any other way in which it could have come about and which is not equally improbable or more improbable. In practice the difficulty mentioned is not much of an extra difficulty. For even where we believe there to be deterministic laws and an earlier situation which together would have made an occurrence actually impossible in the course of nature, it is from our point of view at best epistemically very probable, not certain, that those are the laws and that that was the relevant antecedent situation.

Consequently, whether the laws of nature are deterministic or statistical, we can give a coherent definition of a miracle as a supernatural intrusion into the normally closed system that works in accordance with those laws, and in either case we can identify conceivable occurrences, and alleged occurrences, which if they were to occur, or have occurred, could be believed with high probability, though not known with certainty, to satisfy that definition.

However, the full concept of a miracle requires that the intrusion should be purposive, that it should fulfil the intention of a god or other supernatural being. This connection cannot be sustained by any ordinary causal theory; it presupposes a power to fulfil intentions directly, without physical means, which . . . is highly dubious; so this requirement for a miracle will be particularly hard to confirm. On the other hand it is worth noting that successful prophecy could be regarded as a form of miracle for which there could in principle be good evidence. If someone is reliably recorded as having prophesied at t_1 an event at t_2 which could not be predicted at t_1 on any natural grounds, and the event occurs at t_2, then at any later time t_3 we can assess the evidence for the claims both that the prophecy was made at t_1 and that its accuracy cannot be explained either causally (for example, on the ground that it brought about its own fulfilment) or as accidental, and hence that it was probably miraculous.

There is, then, a coherent concept of miracles. Their possibility is not ruled out *a priori,* by definition. So we must consider whether Hume's argument shows that we never have good reason for believing that any have occurred.

Hume's general principle for the evaluation of testimony, that we have to weigh the unlikelihood of the event reported against the unlikelihood that the witness is mistaken or dishonest, is substantially correct. It is a corollary of the still more general principle of accepting whatever hypothesis gives the best overall explanation of all the available and relevant evidence. But some riders are necessary. First, the likelihood or unlikelihood, the epistemic probability or improbability, is always relative to some body of information, and may change if additional information comes in. Consequently, any specific decision in accordance with Hume's principle must be provisional. Secondly, it is one thing to decide which of the rival hypotheses in the field at any time should be provisionally accepted in the light of the evidence then available; but it is quite another to estimate the weight of this evidence, to say how well supported this favoured hypothesis is, and whether it is likely that its claims will be undermined either by additional information or by the suggesting of further alternative hypotheses. What is clearly the best-supported view of some matter at the moment may still be very insecure, and quite likely to be overthrown by some further considerations. For example, if a public opinion poll is the only evidence we have about the result of a coming election, this evidence may point, perhaps decisively, to one result rather than another; yet if the poll has reached only a small sample of the electorate, or if it was taken some time before the voting day, it will not be very reliable. There is a dimension of reliability over and above that of epistemic probability relative to the available evidence. Thirdly, Hume's description of what gives support to a prediction, or in general to a judgement about an unobserved case that would fall under some generalization, is very unsatisfactory. He seems to say that if *all* so far observed As have been Bs, then this amounts to a 'proof' that some unobserved A will be (or is, or was) a B, whereas if some observed As have been Bs, but some have not, there is only a 'probability' that an unobserved A will be a B (pp. 110–12). This mixes up the

Science and the Occult

Suppose you had a vivid, lifelike vision of a godlike figure who delivered a checkable prophesy to you and a message on how to lead your life. Days later the prophesy came true. How would science, that is, scientific habits of mind, encourage you to explain these unusual events? Probably in two ways: first, by preferring natural explanations to supernatural ones; and, second, by preferring natural explanations that fit into current scientific theory over natural explanations that do not.

Thus you would be encouraged, say, to dismiss the vision as hallucinatory rather than accept it as veridical; that is, to dismiss it as due just to the activity of your own brain rather than to the operation of any outside agency. You would be encouraged to attribute the correctness of the prophesy to coincidence, rather than to some unexplainable form of veridical precognition. Or, if it was just too improbable that the correctness of the prophesy could be coincidence, then you would be encouraged to deny that it ever really happened—say, by attributing your apparent memory of the prophesy to some kind of memory breakdown. In such a scientific mind-set, what are regarded as acceptable scientific explanations are effectively insulated from competition with nonscientific or even radically unconventional explanations. Thus current science might be said to encourage a methodology that effectively insulates it from serious challenges from without. In other words, like many religious myths, science may encourage a way of evaluating its own general outlook on the world that effectively perpetuates that outlook.

reasoning *to* a generalization with the reasoning *from* a generalization to a particular case. It is true that the premisses 'All As are Bs' and 'This is an A' constitute a proof of the conclusion 'This is a B', whereas the premisses 'x per cent of As are Bs' and 'This is an A' yield—if there is no other relevant information—a probability of x per cent that this is a B: they *probabilify* the conclusion to this degree, or, as we can say, the probability of the conclusion 'This is a B' relative to that evidence is x per cent. But the inductive argument from the observation 'All so far observed As have been Bs' to the generalization 'All As are Bs' is far from secure, and it would be most misleading to call this a proof, and therefore misleading also to describe as a proof the whole line of inference from 'All so far observed As have been Bs' to the conclusion 'This as yet unobserved A is a B'. Similarly, the inductive argument from 'x per cent of observed As have been Bs' to the statistical generalization 'x per cent of As are Bs' is far from secure, so that we cannot say that 'x per cent of observed As have been Bs' even probabilifies to the degree x per cent the conclusion 'This as yet unobserved A is a B'. A good deal of other information and background knowledge is needed, in either case, before the generalization, whether universal or statistical, is at all well supported, and hence before the stage is properly set for either proof or probabilification about an as yet unobserved A. It is harder than Hume allows here to arrive at well-supported generalizations of either sort about how the world works.

These various qualifications together entail that what has been widely and reasonably thought to be a law of nature may not be one, perhaps in ways that are highly relevant to some supposed miracles. Our present understanding of psychosomatic illness, for example, shows that it is not contrary to the laws of nature that someone who for years has seemed, to himself as well as to others, to be paralysed should rapidly regain the use of his limbs. On the other hand, we can still be pretty confident that it is contrary to the laws of nature that a human being whose heart has stopped beating for forty-eight hours in ordinary circumstances—that is, without any special life-support systems—should come back to life, or that what is literally water should without addition or replacement turn into what is literally good-quality wine.

However, any problems there may be about establishing laws of nature are neutral between the parties to the present debate, Hume's followers and those who believe in miracles; for both these parties need the notion of a well-established law of nature. The miracle advocate needs it in order to be able to say that the alleged occurrence is a miracle, a violation of natural law by supernatural intervention, no less than Hume needs it for his argument against believing that this event has actually taken place.

It is therefore not enough for the defender of a miracle to cast doubt (as he well might) on the certainty of our knowledge of the law of nature that seems to have been violated. For he must himself say that this *is* a law of nature: otherwise the reported event will not be miraculous. That is, he must in effect *concede* to Hume that the antecedent improbability of this event is as high as it could be, hence that, apart from the testimony, we have the strongest possible grounds for believing that the alleged event did not occur. This event must, by the miracle advocate's own admission, be contrary to a genuine, not merely a supposed, law of nature, and therefore maximally improbable. It is this maximal improbability that the weight of the testimony would have to overcome.

One further improvement is needed in Hume's theory of testimony. It is well known that the agreement of two (or more) *independent* witnesses constitutes very powerful evidence. Two independent witnesses are more than twice as good as each of them on his own. The reason for this is plain. If just one witness says that p, one explanation of this would be that it was the case that p and that he has observed this, remembered it, and is now making an honest report; but there are many alternative explanations, for example that he observed something else which he mistook for its being that *p,* or is misremembering what he observed, or is telling a lie. But if two witnesses who can be shown to be quite independent of one another both say that *p,* while again one explanation is that each of them has observed this and remembered it and is reporting honestly, the alternative explanations are not now so easy. They face the question 'How has there come about this *agreement* in their reports, if it was not the case that *p?* How have the witnesses managed to misobserve to the same effect, or to misremember in the same way, or to hit upon the same lie?' It is difficult for even a single liar to keep on telling a *consistent* false story; it is much harder for two or more liars to do so. Of course if there is any collusion between the witnesses, or if either has been influenced, directly or indirectly, by the other, or if both stories have a common source, this question is easily answered. That is why the independence of the witnesses is so important. This principle of the improbability of coincident error has two vital bearings upon the problem of miracles. On the one hand, it means that a certain sort of testimony can be more powerful evidence than Hume's discussion would suggest. On the other, it means that where we seem to have a plurality of reports, it is essential to check carefully whether they really are independent of one another; the difficulty of meeting this requirement would be an important supplement to the points made in Part II of Hume's essay. Not only in remote and barbarous times, but also in recent ones, we are usually justified in suspecting that what look like distinct reports of a remarkable occurrence arise from different strands of a single tradition between which there has already been communication.

We can now put together the various parts of our argument. Where there is some plausible testimony about the occurrence of what would appear to be a miracle, those who accept this as a miracle have the double burden of showing both that the event took place and that it violated the laws of nature. But it will be very hard to sustain this double burden. For whatever tends to show that it would have been a violation of natural law tends for that very reason to make it most unlikely that it actually happened. Correspondingly, those who deny the occurrence of a miracle have two alternative lines of defence. One is to say that the event may have occurred, but in accordance with the laws of nature. Perhaps there were unknown circumstances that made it possible; or perhaps what were thought to be the relevant laws of nature are not strictly laws; there may be as yet unknown kinds of natural causation through which this event might have come about. The other is to say that this event would indeed have violated natural law, but that for this very reason there is a very strong presumption against its having happened, which it is most unlikely that any testimony will be able to outweigh. Usually one of these defences will be stronger than the other. For many supposedly miraculous cures, the former will be quite a likely sort of explanation, but for such feats as the bringing back to life of those who are really dead the latter will be more likely. But the *fork,* the disjunction of these two sorts of explanation, is as a whole a very powerful reply to any claim that a miracle has been performed.

However, we should distinguish two different contexts in which an alleged miracle might be discussed. One possible context would be where the parties in debate already both accept some general theistic doctrines, and the point at issue is whether a miracle has occurred which would enhance the authority of a specific sect or teacher. In this context supernatural intervention, though *prima facie* unlikely on any particular occasion, is, generally speaking, on the cards: it is not altogether outside the range of reasonable expectation for these parties. Since they agree that there is an omnipotent deity, or at any rate one or more powerful supernatural beings, they cannot find it absurd to suppose that such a being will occasionally interfere with the course of nature, and this *may* be one of these occasions. For example, if one were already a theist and a Christian, it would not be unreasonable to weigh

The Dome of the Rock was built in 691 A.D. over the rock from which Mohammed is believed to have leapt into heaven.

seriously the evidence of alleged miracles as some indication whether the Jansenists or the Jesuits enjoyed more of the favour of the Almighty. But it is a very different matter if the context is that of fundamental debate about the truth of theism itself. Here one party to the debate is initially at least agnostic, and does not yet concede that there is a supernatural power at all. From this point of view the intrinsic improbability of a genuine miracle, as defined above, is very great, and one or other of the alternative explanations in our fork will always be much more likely—that is, either that the alleged event is not miraculous, or that it did not occur, that the testimony is faulty in some way.

This entails that it is pretty well impossible that reported miracles should provide a worthwhile argument for theism addressed to those who are initially inclined to atheism or even to agnosticism. Such reports can form no significant part of what, following Aquinas, we might call a *Summa contra Gentiles,* or what, following Descartes, we could describe as being addressed to infidels. Not only are such reports unable to carry any rational conviction on their own, but also they are unable even to contribute independently to the kind of accumulation or battery of arguments referred to in the Introduction. To this extent Hume is right, despite the inaccuracies we have found in his statement of the case.

One further point may be worth making. Occurrences are sometimes claimed to be literally, and not merely metaphorically, miracles, that is, to be genuine supernatural interventions into the natural order, which are not even *prima facie* violations of natural law, but at most rather unusual and unexpected, but very welcome. Thus the combination of weather conditions which facilitated the escape of the British army from Dunkirk in 1940, making the Luftwaffe less than usually effective but making it easy for ships of all sizes to cross the Channel, is sometimes called a miracle. However, even if we accepted theism, and could plausibly assume that a benevolent deity would have favoured the British rather than the Germans in 1940, this explanation would still be far less probable than that which treats it as a mere meteorological coincidence: such weather conditions can occur in the ordinary course of events. Here, even in the context of a debate among those who already accept theistic doctrines, the interpretation of the event as a miracle is much weaker than the rival natural explanation. *A fortiori,* instances of this sort are utterly without force in the context of fundamental debate about theism itself.

There is, however, a possibility which Hume's argument seems to ignore—though, as we shall see, he did not completely ignore it. The argument has been directed against the acceptance of miracles on testimony; but what, it may be objected, if one is not reduced to reliance on testimony, but has observed a miracle for oneself? Surprisingly, perhaps, this possibility does not make very much difference. The first of the above-mentioned lines of defence is still available: maybe the unexpected event that one has oneself observed did indeed occur, but in accordance with the laws of nature. Either the relevant circumstances or the operative laws were not what one had supposed them to be. But at least a part of the other line of defence is also available. Though one is not now relying literally on another witness or other witnesses, we speak not inappropriately of the evidence of our senses, and what one takes to be an observation of one's own is open to questions of the same sort as is the report of some other person. I may have misobserved what took place, as anyone knows who has ever been fooled by a conjurer or 'magician', and, though this is somewhat less likely, I may be misremembering or deceiving myself after an interval of time. And of course the corroboration of one or more independent witnesses would bring in again the testimony of others which it was the point of this objection to do without. Nevertheless, anyone who is fortunate enough to have carefully observed and carefully recorded, for himself, an apparently miraculous occurrence is no doubt rationally justified in taking it very seriously; but even here it will be in order to entertain the possibility of an alternative natural explanation.

As I said, Hume does not completely ignore this possibility. The Christian religion, he says, cannot at this day be believed by any reasonable person without a miracle. 'Mere reason is insufficient to convince us of its veracity: And whoever is moved by *Faith* to assent to it, is conscious of a continued miracle in his own person, which subverts all the principles of his understanding . . .' (p. 131) But of course this is only a joke. What the believer is conscious of in his own person, though it may be a mode of thinking that goes against 'custom and experience', and so is contrary to the ordinary rational principles of the understanding, is not, as an occurrence, a violation of natural law. Rather it is all too easy to explain immediately by the automatic communication of beliefs between persons and the familiar psychological processes of wish fulfilment. . . .

PART VI

Mysticism and Religious Experience

William James

"THE SIGNIFICANCE OF MYSTICISM"

WILLIAM JAMES (1842–1910), brother of the novelist Henry James, was born in New York City and educated at Harvard University. He taught physiology and psychology at Johns Hopkins University and in 1880 became a professor of philosophy at Harvard. His *The Principles of Psychology* (1890) is a classic. James's main contribution to philosophy of religion was the synthesis of religion with an empiricist theory of knowledge employing the "pragmatic" theory of truth, which he took over from another American philosopher, Charles Peirce. *The Varieties of Religious Experience*, from which the following selection is taken, is the classic treatment of religious experience.

LECTURES XVI AND XVII: MYSTICISM

Over and over again in these lectures I have raised points and left them open and unfinished until we should have come to the subject of Mysticism. Some of you, I fear, may have smiled as you noted my reiterated postponements. But now the hour has come when mysticism must be faced in good earnest, and those broken threads wound up together. One may say truly, I think, that personal religious experience has its root and centre in mystical states of consciousness; so for us, who in these lectures are treating personal experience as the exclusive subject of our study, such states of consciousness ought to form the vital chapter from which the other chapters get their light. Whether my treatment of mystical states will shed more light or darkness, I do not know, for my own constitution shuts me out from their enjoyment almost entirely, and I can speak of them only at second hand. But though forced to look upon the subject so externally, I will be as objective and receptive as I can; and I think I shall at least succeed in convincing you of the reality of the states in question, and of the paramount importance of their function.

First of all, then, I ask, What does the expression 'mystical states of consciousness' mean? How do we part off mystical states from other states?

The words 'mysticism' and 'mystical' are often used as terms of mere reproach, to throw at any opinion which we regard as vague and vast and sentimental, and without a base in either facts or logic. For some writers a 'mystic' is any person who believes in thought-transference, or spirit-return. Employed in this way the word has little value: there are too many less ambiguous synonyms. So, to keep it useful by restricting it, I . . . propose to you four marks which, when an experience has them, may justify us in calling it mystical for the purpose of the present lectures. In this way we shall save verbal disputation, and the recriminations that generally go therewith.

From William James, *The Varieties of Religious Experience*. First published in 1902.

1. *Ineffability.*—The handiest of the marks by which I classify a state of mind as mystical is negative. The subject of it immediately says that it defies expression, that no adequate report of its contents can be given in words. It follows from this that its quality must be directly experienced; it cannot be imparted or transferred to others. In this peculiarity mystical states are more like states of feeling than like states of intellect. No one can make clear to another who has never had a certain feeling, in what the quality or worth of it consists. One must have musical ears to know the value of a symphony; one must have been in love one's self to understand a lover's state of mind. Lacking the heart or ear, we cannot interpret the musician or the lover justly, and are even likely to consider him weak-minded or absurd. The mystic finds that most of us accord to his experiences an equally incompetent treatment.
2. *Noetic quality.*—Although so similar to states of feeling, mystical states seem to those who experience them to be also states of knowledge. They are states of insight into depths of truth unplumbed by the discursive intellect. They are illuminations, revelations, full of significance and importance, all inarticulate though they remain; and as a rule they carry with them a curious sense of authority for after-time.

   These two characters will entitle any state to be called mystical, in the sense in which I use the word. Two other qualities are less sharply marked, but are usually found. These are:—
3. *Transiency.*—Mystical states cannot be sustained for long. Except in rare instances, half an hour, or at most an hour or two, seems to be the limit beyond which they fade into the light of common day. Often, when faded, their quality can but imperfectly be reproduced in memory; but when they recur it is recognized; and from one recurrence to another it is susceptible of continuous development in what is felt as inner richness and importance.
4. *Passivity.*—Although the oncoming of mystical states may be facilitated by preliminary voluntary operations, as by fixing the attention, or going through certain bodily performances, or in other ways which manuals of mysticism prescribe; yet when the characteristic sort of consciousness once has set in, the mystic feels as if his own will were in abeyance, and indeed sometimes as if he were grasped and held by a superior power. This latter peculiarity connects mystical states with certain definite phenomena of secondary or alternative personality, such as prophetic speech, automatic writing, or the mediumistic trance. When these latter conditions are well pronounced, however, there may be no recollection whatever of the phenomenon, and it may have no significance for the subject's usual inner life, to which, as it were, it makes a mere interruption. Mystical states, strictly so called, are never merely interruptive. Some memory of their content always remains, and a profound sense of their importance. They modify the inner life of the subject between the times of their recurrence. Sharp divisions in this region are, however, difficult to make, and we find all sorts of gradations and mixtures.

   These four characteristics are sufficient to mark out a group of states of consciousness peculiar enough to deserve a special name and to call for careful study. Let it then be called the mystical group.

Our next step should be to gain acquaintance with some typical examples. Professional mystics at the height of their development have often elaborately organized experiences and a philosophy based thereupon. But you remember what I said in my first lecture: phenomena are best understood when placed within their series, studied in their germ and in their over-ripe decay, and compared with their exaggerated and degenerated kindred. The range of mystical experience is very wide, much too wide for us to cover in the time at our disposal. Yet the method of serial study is so essential for interpretation that if we really wish to reach conclusions we must use it. I will begin, therefore, with phenomena which claim no special religious significance, and end with those of which the religious pretensions are extreme.

The simplest rudiment of mystical experience would seem to be that deepened sense of the significance of a maxim or formula which occasionally sweeps over one. "I've heard that said all my life," we exclaim, "but I never realized its full meaning until now." . . . This sense of deeper significance is not confined to rational propositions. Single words,[1] and conjunctions of words, effects of light on land and sea, odors and musical sounds, all bring it when the mind is tuned aright. Most of us can remember the strangely moving power of passages in certain poems read when we were young, irrational doorways as they were through which the mystery of fact, the wildness and the pang of life, stole into our hearts and thrilled them. The words have now perhaps become mere polished surfaces for us; but lyric poetry and music are alive and significant only in proportion as they fetch these vague vistas of a life continuous with our own, beckoning and inviting, yet ever eluding our pursuit. We are alive or dead to the eternal inner message of the arts according as we have kept or lost this mystical susceptibility.

A more pronounced step forward on the mystical ladder is found in an extremely frequent phenomenon, that sudden feeling, namely, which sometimes sweeps over us, of having 'been here before,' as if at some indefinite past time, in just this place, with just these people, we were already saying just these things. As Tennyson writes:

> Moreover, something is or seems,
> That touches me with mystic gleams,
> Like glimpses of forgotten dreams—
>
> Of something felt, like something here;
> Of something done, I know not where;
> Such as no language may declare.[2]

Sir James Crichton-Browne has given the technical name of 'dreamy states' to these sudden invasions of vaguely reminiscent consciousness.[3] They bring a sense of mystery and of the metaphysical duality of things, and the feeling of an enlargement of perception which seems imminent but which never completes itself. In Dr. Crichton-Browne's opinion they connect themselves with the perplexed and scared disturbances of self-consciousness which occasionally precede epileptic attacks. I think that this learned alienist takes a rather absurdly alarmist view of an intrinsically insignificant phenomenon. He follows it along the downward ladder, to insanity; our path pursues the upward ladder chiefly. The divergence shows how important it is to neglect no part of a phenomenon's connections, for we make it appear admirable or dreadful according to the context by which we set if off.

Somewhat deeper plunges into mystical consciousness are met with in yet other dreamy states. Such feelings as these which Charles Kingsley describes are surely far from being uncommon, especially in youth:—

1. 'Mesopotamia' is the stock comic instance.—An excellent old German lady, who had done some traveling in her day, used to describe to me her *Sehnsucht* that she might yet visit 'Phīladelphiā,' whose wondrous name had always haunted her imagination. . . .

2. The Two Voices. In a letter to Mr. B. P. Blood, Tennyson reports of himself as follows:—

"I have never had any revelations through anaesthetics, but a kind of waking trance—this for lack of a better word—I have frequently had, quite up from boyhood, when I have been all alone. This has come upon me through repeating my own name to myself silently, till all at once, as it were out of the intensity of the consciousness of individuality, individuality itself seemed to dissolve and fade away into boundless being, and this not a confused state but the clearest, the surest of the surest, utterly beyond words—where death was an almost laughable impossibility—the loss of personality (if so it were) seeming no extinction, but the only true life. I am ashamed of my feeble description. Have I not said the state is utterly beyond words?"

Professor Tyndall, in a letter, recalls Tennyson saying of this condition: "By God Almighty! there is no delusion in the matter! It is no nebulous ecstasy, but a state of transcendent wonder, associated with absolute clearness of mind." Memoirs of Alfred Tennyson, ii. 473.

3. The Lancet, July 6 and 13, 1895, reprinted as the Cavendish Lecture, on Dreamy Mental States, London, Baillière, 1895. . . .

When I walk the fields, I am oppressed now and then with an innate feeling that everything I see has a meaning, if I could but understand it. And this feeling of being surrounded with truths which I cannot grasp amounts to indescribable awe sometimes. . . . Have you not felt that your real soul was imperceptible to your mental vision, except in a few hallowed moments?[4]

A much more extreme state of mystical consciousness is described by J. A. Symonds; and probably more persons than we suspect could give parallels to it from their own experience.

. . . One reason why I disliked this kind of trance was that I could not describe it to myself. I cannot even now find words to render it intelligible. It consisted in a gradual but swiftly progressive obliteration of space, time, sensation, and the multitudinous factors of experience which seem to qualify what we are pleased to call our Self. In proportion as these conditions of ordinary consciousness were subtracted, the sense of an underlying or essential consciousness acquired intensity. At last nothing remained but a pure, absolute, abstract Self. The universe became without form and void of content. But Self persisted, formidable in its vivid keenness, feeling the most poignant doubt about reality, ready, as it seemed, to find existence break as breaks a bubble round about it. And what then? The apprehension of a coming dissolution, the grim conviction that this state was the last state of the conscious Self, the sense that I had followed the last thread of being to the verge of the abyss, and had arrived at demonstration of eternal Maya or illusion, stirred or seemed to stir me up again. The return to ordinary conditions of sentient existence began by my first recovering the power of touch, and then by the gradual though rapid influx of familiar impressions and diurnal interests. At last I felt myself once more a human being; and though the riddle of what is meant by life remained unsolved, I was thankful for this return from the abyss—this deliverance from so awful an initiation into the mysteries of skepticism.

"This trance recurred with diminishing frequency until I reached the age of twenty-eight. It served to impress upon my growing nature the phantasmal unreality of all the circumstances which contribute to a merely phenomenal consciousness. Often have I asked myself with anguish, on waking from that formless state of denuded, keenly sentient being, Which is the unreality?—the trance of fiery, vacant, apprehensive, skeptical Self from which I issue, or these surrounding phenomena and habits which veil that inner Self and build a self of flesh-and-blood conventionality? Again, are men the factors of some dream, the dream-like unsubstantiality of which they comprehend at such eventful moments? What would happen if the final stage of the trance were reached.?"[5]

In a recital like this there is certainly something suggestive of pathology.[6] The next step into mystical states carries us into a realm that public opinion and ethical philosophy have long since branded as pathological, though private practice and certain lyric strains of poetry seem still to bear witness to its ideality. I refer to the consciousness produced by intoxicants and anæsthetics, especially by alcohol. The sway of alcohol over mankind is unquestionably due to its power to stimulate the mystical faculties of human nature, usually crushed to earth by the cold facts and dry criticisms of the sober hour.

4. Charles Kingsley's Life, i. 55, quoted by Inge: Christian Mysticism, London, 1899, p. 341.

5. H. F. Brown: J. A. Symonds, a Biography, London, 1895, pp. 29–31, abridged.

6. Crichton-Browne expressly says that Symonds's "highest nerve centres were in some degree enfeebled or damaged by these dreamy mental states which afflicted him so grievously." Symonds was, however, a perfect monster of many-sided cerebral efficiency, and his critic gives no objective grounds whatever for his strange opinion, save that Symonds complained occasionally, as all susceptible and ambitious men complain, of lassitude and uncertainty as to his life's mission.

Sobriety diminishes, discriminates, and says no; drunkeness expands, unites, and says yes. It is in fact the great exciter of the *Yes* function in man. It brings its votary from the chill periphery of things to the radiant core. It makes him for the moment one with truth. Not through mere perversity do men run after it. To the poor and the unlettered it stands in the place of symphony concerts and of literature; and it is part of the deeper mystery and tragedy of life that whiffs and gleams of something that we immediately recognize as excellent should be vouchsafed to so many of us only in the fleeting earlier phases of what in its totality is so degrading a poisoning. The drunken consciousness is one bit of the mystic consciousness, and our total opinion of it must find its place in our opinion of that larger whole.

Nitrous oxide and ether, especially nitrous oxide, when sufficiently diluted with air, stimulate the mystical consciousness in an extraordinary degree. Depth beyond depth of truth seems revealed to the inhaler. This truth fades out, however, or escapes, at the moment of coming to; and if any words remain over in which it seemed to clothe itself, they prove to be the veriest nonsense. Nevertheless, the sense of a profound meaning having been there persists;

"The History of Mysticism"

Abraham Maslow

I see in the history of many organized religions a tendency to develop two extreme wings: the "mystical" and individual on the one hand, and the legalistic and organizational on the other. The profoundly and authentically religious person integrates these trends easily and automatically. The forms, rituals, ceremonials, and verbal formulae in which he was reared, remain for him experientially rooted, symbolically meaningful, archetypal, unitive. Such a person may go through the same motions and behaviors as his more numerous coreligionists, but he is never *reduced* to the behavioral, as most of them are. Most people lose or forget the subjectively religious experience, and redefine Religion as a set of habits, behaviors, dogmas, forms, which at the extreme becomes entirely legalistic and bureaucratic, conventional, empty, and in the truest meaning of the word, anti-religious. The mystic experience, the illumination, the great awakening, along with the charismatic seer who started the whole thing, are forgotten, lost, or transformed into their opposites. Organized Religion, the churches, finally may become the major enemies of the religious experience and the religious experiencer.

But on the other wing, the mystical (or experiential) also has its traps which I have not stressed sufficiently. . . . Out of the joy and wonder of his ecstasies and peak-experiences he may be tempted to *seek* them, *ad hoc,* and to value them exclusively, as the only or at least the highest goods of life, giving up other criteria of right and wrong. Focused on these wonderful subjective experiences, he may run the danger of turning away from the world and from other people in his search for triggers to peak-experiences, *any* triggers. In a word, instead of being temporarily self-absorbed and inwardly searching, he may become simply a selfish person, seeking his own personal salvation, trying to get into "heaven" even if other people can't, and finally, even perhaps *using* other people as triggers, as means to his sole end of higher states of consciousness. In a word, he may become not only selfish but also evil. My impression, from the history of mysticism, is that this trend can sometimes wind up in meanness, nastiness, loss of compassion, or even in the extreme of sadism.

From *Religions, Values, and Peak Experiences* (1970).

and I know more than one person who is persuaded that in the nitrous oxide trance we have a genuine metaphysical revelation.

Some years ago I myself made some observations on this aspect of nitrous oxide intoxication, and reported them in print. One conclusion was forced upon my mind at that time, and my impression of its truth has ever since remained unshaken. It is that our normal waking consciousness, rational consciousness as we call it, is but one special type of consciousness, whilst all about it, parted from it by the filmiest of screens, there lie potential forms of consciousness entirely different. We may go though life without suspecting their existence; but apply the requisite stimulus, and at a touch they are there in all their completeness, definite types of mentality which probably somewhere have their field of application and adaptation. No account of the universe in its totality can be final which leaves these other forms of consciousness quite disregarded. How to regard them is the question,—for they are so discontinuous with ordinary consciousness. Yet they may determine attitudes though they cannot furnish formulas, and open a region though they fail to give a map. At any rate, they forbid a premature closing of our accounts with reality. Looking back on my own experiences, they all converge towards a kind of insight to which I cannot help ascribing some metaphysical significance. The keynote of it is invariably a reconciliation. it is as if the opposites of the world, whose contradictoriness and conflict make all our difficulties and troubles, were melted into unity. Not only do they, as contrasted species, belong to one and the same genus, but *one of the species,* the nobler and better one, *is itself the genus, and so soaks up and absorbs its opposite into itself.* This is a dark saying, I know, when thus expressed in terms of common logic, but I cannot wholly escape from its authority. I feel as if it must mean something, something like what the Hegelian philosophy means, if one could only lay hold of it more clearly. Those who have ears to hear, let them hear; to me the living sense of its reality only comes in the artificial mystic state of mind. . . .[7]

In India, training in mystical insight has been known from time immemorial under the name of yoga. Yoga means the experimental union of the individual with the divine. It is based on persevering exercise; and the diet, posture, breathing, intellectual concentration, and moral discipline vary slightly in the different systems which teach it. The yogi, or disciple, who has by these means overcome the obscurations of his lower nature sufficiently, enters into the condition termed *samâdhi,* "comes face to face with facts which no instinct or reason can ever know." He learns—

> That the mind itself has a higher state of existence, beyond reason, a superconscious state, and that when the mind gets to that higher state, then this knowledge beyond reasoning comes. . . . All the different steps in yoga are intended to bring us scientifically to the superconscious state or samâdhi. . . . Just as unconscious work is beneath consciousness, so there is another work which is above consciousness, and which, also, is not accompanied with the feeling of *I,* and yet the mind works, desireless, free from restlessness, objectless, bodiless. Then the Truth shines in its full effulgence, and we know ourselves—for Samâdhi lies potential in us all—for what we truly are, free, immortal, omnipotent, loosed from the finite, and its contrasts of good and evil altogether, and identical with the Atman or Universal Soul.[8]

The Vedantists say that one may stumble into superconsciousness sporadically, without the previous discipline, but it is then impure.

7. What reader of Hegel can doubt that that sense of a perfected Being with all its otherness soaked up into itself, which dominates his whole philosophy, must have come from the prominence in his consciousness of mystical moods like this, in most persons kept subliminal? . . .

8. My quotations are from Vivekananda, Raja Yoga, London, 1896. The completest source of information on Yoga is the work translated by Vihari Lala Mitra; Yoga Vasishta Maha Ramayana, 4 vols., Calcutta, 1891–99.

Their test of its purity, like our test of religion's value, is empirical: its fruits must be good for life. When a man comes out of Samâdhi, they assure us that he remains "enlightened, a sage, a prophet, a saint, his whole character changed, his life changed, illumined."[9]

The Buddhists use the word 'samâdhi' as well as the Hindus; but 'dhyâna' is their special word for higher states of contemplation. There seem to be four stages recognized in dhyâna. The first stage comes through concentration of the mind upon one point. It excludes desire, but no discernment or judgment: it is still intellectual. In the second stage the intellectual functions drop off, and the satisfied sense of unity remains. In the third stage the satisfaction departs, and indifference begins, along with memory and self-consciousness. In the fourth stage the indifference, memory, and self-consciousness are perfected. [Just what 'memory' and 'self-consciousness' mean in this connection is doubtful. They cannot be the faculties familiar to us in the lower life.] Higher stages still of contemplation are mentioned—a region where there exists nothing, and where the meditator says: "There exists absolutely nothing," and stops. Then he reaches another region where he says: "There are neither ideas nor absence of ideas," and stops again. Then another region where, "having reached the end of both idea and perception, he stops finally." This would seem to be, not yet Nirvâna, but as close an approach to it as this life affords.[10]

In the Mohammedan world the Sufi sect and various dervish bodies are the possessors of the mystical tradition. The Sufis have existed in Persia from the earliest times, and as their pantheism is so at variance with the hot and rigid monotheism of the Arab mind, it has been suggested that Sufism must have been inoculated into Islam by Hindu influences. We Christians know little of Sufism, for its secrets are disclosed only to those initiated. To give its existence a certain liveliness in your minds, I will quote a Moslem document, and pass away from the subject.

Al-Ghazzali, a Persian philosopher and theologian, who flourished in the eleventh century, and ranks as one of the greatest doctors of the Moslem church, has left us one of the few autobiographies to be found outside of Christian literature. Strange that a species of book so abundant among ourselves should be so little represented elsewhere—the absence of strictly personal confessions is the chief difficulty to the purely literary student who would like to become acquainted with the inwardness of religions other than the Christian.

M. Schomölders has translated a part of Al-Ghazzali's autobiography into French:[11]

> "The Science of the Sufis," says the Moslem author, "aims at detaching the heart from all that is not God, and at giving to it for sole occupation the meditation of the divine being. Theory being more easy for me than practice, I read [certain books] until I understood all that can be learned by study and hearsay. Then I recognized that what pertains most exclusively to their method is just what no study can grasp, but only transport, ecstasy, and the transformation of the soul. How great, for example, is the difference between knowing the definition of health, of satiety, and their causes and conditions, and being really healthy or filled. How different to know in what drunkenness consists,—as being a state occasioned by a vapor that rises from the stomach,—and *being* drunk

9. A European witness, after carefully comparing the results of Yoga with those of the hypnotic or dreamy states artificially producible by us, says: "It makes of its true disciples good, healthy, and happy men. . . . Through the mastery which the yogi attains over his thoughts and his body, he grows into a 'character.' By the subjection of his impulses and propensities to his will, and the fixing of the latter upon the ideal of goodness, he becomes a 'personality' hard to influence by others, and thus almost the opposite of what we usually imagine a 'medium' so-called, or 'psychic subject' to be." Karl Kellner: Yoga: Eline Skizze, München, 1896, p. 21.

10. I follow the account in C. F. Koeppen: Die Religion des Buddha, Berlin, 1857, i. 585 ff.

11. For a full account of him, see D. B. Macdonald: The Life of Al-Ghazzali, in the Journal of the American Oriental Society, 1899, vol. xx. p. 71.

effectively. Without doubt, the drunken man knows neither the definition of drunkenness nor what makes it interesting for science. Being drunk, he knows nothing; whilst the physician, although not drunk, knows well in what drunkenness consists, and what are its predisposing conditions. Similarly there is a difference between knowing the nature of abstinence, and *being* abstinent or having one's soul detached from the world.—Thus I had learned what words could teach of Sufism, but what was left could be learned neither by study nor through the ears, but solely by giving one's self up to ecstasy and leading a pious life.

"Reflecting on my situation, I found myself tied down by a multitude of bonds—temptations on every side. Considering my teaching, I found it was impure before God. I saw myself struggling with all my might to achieve glory and to spread my name. [Here follows an account of his six months' hesitation to break away from the conditions of his life at Bagdad, at the end of which he fell ill with a paralysis of the tongue.] Then, feeling my own weakness, and having entirely given up my own will, I repaired to God like a man in distress who has no more resources. He answered, as he answers the wretch who invokes him. My heart no longer felt any difficulty in renouncing glory, wealth, and my children. So I quitted Bagdad, and reserving from my fortune only what was indispensable for my subsistence, I distributed the rest. I went to Syria, where I remained about two years, with no other occupation than living in retreat and solitude, conquering my desires, combating my passions, training myself to purify my soul, to make my character perfect, to prepare my heart for meditating on God—all according to the methods of the Sufis, as I had read of them.

"This retreat only increased my desire to live in solitude, and to complete the purification of my heart and fit it for meditation. But the vicissitudes of the times, the affairs of the family, the need of subsistence, changed in some respects my primitive resolve, and interfered with my plans for a purely solitary life. I had never yet found myself completely in ecstasy, save in a few single hours; nevertheless, I kept the hope of attaining this state. Every time that the accidents led me astray, I sought to return; and in this situation I spent ten years. During this solitary state things were revealed to me which it is impossible either to describe or to point out. I recognized for certain that the Sufis are assuredly walking in the path of God. Both in their acts and in their inaction, whether internal or external, they are illumined by the light which proceeds from the prophetic source. The first condition for a Sufi is to purge his heart entirely of all that is not God. The next key of the contemplative life consists in the humble prayers which escape from the fervent soul, and in the meditations on God in which the heart is swallowed up entirely. But in reality this is only the beginning of the Sufi life, the end of Sufism being total absorption in God. The intuitions and all that precede are, so to speak, only the threshold for those who enter. From the beginning, revelations take place in so flagrant a shape that the Sufis see before them, whilst wide awake, the angels and the souls of the prophets. They hear their voices and obtain their favors. Then the transport rises from the perception of forms and figures to a degree which escapes all expression, and which no man may seek to give an account of without his words involving sin.

"Whoever has had no experience of the transport knows of the true nature of prophetism nothing but the name. He may meanwhile be sure of its existence, both by experience and by what he hears the Sufis say. As there are men endowed only with the sensitive faculty who reject what is offered them in the way of objects of the pure understanding, so there are intellectual men who reject and avoid the things perceived by the prophetic faculty. A blind man can understand nothing of colors save what he has learned by narration and hearsay. Yet God has brought prophetism near to men in giving them all a state analogous to it in its principal characters. This state is sleep. If you were to tell a man who was himself without experience of such a phenomenon that there are people who at times swoon away so as to resemble dead men, and who [in dreams] yet perceive things that are hidden, he would deny it [and give his reasons]. Nevertheless, his arguments would be refuted by actual experience. Wherefore, just as the understanding is a stage of human life in which an eye opens to discern various intellectual objects uncomprehended by sensation; just so in the prophetic the sight is illumined by a light which uncovers hidden things and objects which the intellect fails to reach. The chief properties of prophetism are perceptible only during the transport, by those who embrace the Sufi life. The prophet is endowed with qualities to which you possess nothing analogous, and which consequently you cannot possibly understand. How should you know their true nature, since one knows only what one can comprehend? But the transport which one attains by the method of the Sufis is like an immediate perception, as if one touched the objects with one's hand."[12]

This incommunicableness of the transport is the keynote of all mysticism. Mystical truth exists for the individual who has the transport, but for no one else. In this, as I have said, it resembles the knowledge given to us in sensations more than that given by conceptual thought. Thought, with its remoteness and abstractness, has often enough in the history of philosophy been contrasted unfavorably with sensation. It is a commonplace of metaphysics that God's knowledge cannot be discursive but must be intuitive, that is, must be constructed more after

12. A. Schmölders: Essai sur les écoles philosophiques chez les Arabes, Paris, 1842, pp. 54–68, abridged.

"Mystical Experience vs. Religious Visions"

Walter Stace

Suppose someone sees a vision of the Virgin Mary. What he sees has shape, the shape of a woman, and color—white skin, blue raiment, a golden halo, and so on. But these are all images or sensations. They are therefore composed of elements of our sensory-intellectual consciousness. The same is true of voices. Or suppose one has a precognition of a neighbor's death. The components one is aware of—a dead man, a coffin, etc.—are composed of elements of our sensory-intellectual consciousness. The only difference is that these ordinary elements are arranged in unfamiliar patterns which we have come to think cannot occur, so that if they do occur they seem supernormal. Or the fact that such elements are combined in an unusual way so as to constitute the figure of a woman up in the clouds, perhaps surrounded by other humanlike figures with wings added to them—all this does not constitute a different *kind* of consciousness at all. And just as sensory elements of any sort are excluded from the mystical consciousness, so are conceptual elements. It is not that the thoughts in the mystical consciousness are different from those we are accustomed to. It does not include any thoughts at all. The mystic, of course, expresses thoughts about his experience after that experience is over, and he remembers it when he is back again in his sensory-intellectual consciousness. But there are no thoughts *in* the experience itself. . . .

The most important, the central characteristics in which all *fully developed* mystical experiences agree, and which in the last analysis is definitive of them and serves to mark them off from other kinds of experiences, is that they involve the apprehension of *an ultimate nonsensuous unity in all things,* a oneness or a One to which neither the senses nor the reason can penetrate. In other words, it entirely transcends our sensory-intellectual consciousness.

From *The Teachings of the Mystics* (1960).

the pattern of what in ourselves is called immediate feeling, than after that of proposition and judgment. But *our* immediate feelings have no content but what the five senses supply; and we have seen and shall see again that mystics may emphatically deny that the senses play any part in the very highest type of knowledge which their transports yield.

In the Christian church there have always been mystics. Although many of them have been viewed with suspicion, some have gained favor in the eyes of the authorities. The experiences of these have been treated as precedents, and a codified system of mystical theology has been based upon them, in which everything legitimate finds its place.[13] The basis of the system is 'orison' or meditation, the methodical elevation of the soul towards God. Through the practice of orison the higher levels of mystical experience may be attained. It is odd that Protestantism, especially evengelical Protestantism, should seemingly have abandoned everything methodical in this line. Apart from what prayer may lead to, Protestant mystical experience appears to have been almost exclusively sporadic. It has been left to our mind-curers to reintroduce methodical meditation into our religious life.

The first thing to be aimed at in orison is the mind's detachment from outer sensations, for these interfere with its concentration upon ideal things. Such manuals as Saint Ignatius's Spiritual Exercises recommend the disciple to expel sensation by a graduated series of efforts to imagine holy scenes. The acme of this kind of discipline would be a semi-hallucinatory mono-ideism—an imaginary figure of Christ, for example, coming fully to occupy the mind. Sensorial images of this sort, whether literal or symbolic, play an enormous part in mysticism.[14]

13. Görres's Christliche Mystik gives a full account of the facts. So does Ribet's Mystique Divine, 2 vols., Paris, 1890. . . .

14. M. Récéjac, in a recent volume, makes them essential. Mysticism he defines as "the tendency to draw near to the Absolute morally, *and by the aid of Symbols.*" See his Fondements de la Connaissance mystique, Paris, 1897, p. 66. But there are unquestionably mystical conditions in which sensible symbols play no part.

But in certain cases imagery may fall away entirely, and in the very highest raptures it tends to do so. The state of consciousness becomes then insusceptible of any verbal description. Mystical teachers are unanimous as to this. Saint John of the Cross, for instance, one of the best of them, thus describes the condition called the 'union of love,' which, he says, is reached by 'dark contemplation.' In this the Deity compenetrates the soul, but in such a hidden way that the soul—

> finds no terms, no means, no comparison whereby to render the sublimity of the wisdom and the delicacy of the spiritual feeling with which she is filled. . . . We receive this mystical knowledge of God clothed in none of the kinds of images, in none of the sensible representations, which our mind makes use of in other circumstances. Accordingly in this knowledge, since the senses and the imagination are not employed, we get neither form nor impression, nor can we give any account or furnish any likeness, although the mysterious and sweet-tasting wisdom comes home so clearly to the inmost parts of our soul. Fancy a man seeing a certain kind of thing for the first time in his life. He can understand it, use and enjoy it, but he cannot apply a name to it, nor communicate any idea of it, even though all the while it be a mere thing of sense. How much greater will be his powerlessness when it goes beyond the senses! This is the peculiarity of the divine language. The more infused, intimate, spiritual, and supersensible it is, the more does it exceed the senses, both inner and outer, and impose silence upon them. . . . The soul then feels as if placed in a vast and profound solitude, to which no created thing has access, in an immense and boundless desert, desert the more delicious the more solitary it is. There, in this abyss of wisdom, the soul grows by what it drinks in from the wellsprings of the comprehension of love, . . . and recognizes, however sublime and learned may be the terms we employ, how ut-

> terly vile, insignificant, and improper they are, when we seek to discourse of divine things by their means.[15]

I cannot pretend to detail to you the sundry stages of the Christian mystical life.[16] Our time would not suffice, for one thing; and moreover, I confess that the subdivisions and names which we find in the Catholic books seem to me to represent nothing objectively distinct. So many men, so many minds: I imagine that these experiences can be as infinitely varied as are the idiosyncrasies of individuals.

The cognitive aspects of them, their value in the way of revelation, is what we are directly concerned with, and it is easy to show by citation how strong an impression they leave of being revelations of new depths of truth. Saint Teresa is the expert of experts in describing such conditions, so I will turn immediately to what she says of one of the highest of them, the 'orison of union.'

> "In the orison of union," says Saint Teresa, "the soul is fully awake as regards God, but wholly asleep as regards things of this world and in respect of herself. During the short time the union lasts, she is as it were deprived of every feeling, and even if she would, she could not think of any single thing. Thus she needs to employ no artifice in order to arrest the use of her understanding: it remains so stricken with inactivity that she neither knows what she loves, nor in what manner she loves, nor what she wills. In short, she is utterly dead to the things of the world and lives solely in God. . . . I do not even know whether in this state she has enough life left to breathe. It seems to me she has not; or at least that if she does breathe, she is unaware of it. Her intellect would fain understand something of what is going on within her, but it has so little force now that it can act in no way whatsoever. So a person who falls into a deep faint appears as if dead. . . .
>
> "Thus does God, when he raises a soul to union with himself, suspend the natural action of all her faculties. She neither sees, hears, nor understands, so long as she is united with God. But this time is always short, and it seems even shorter than it is. God establishes himself in the interior of this soul in such a way, that when she returns to herself, it is wholly impossible for her to doubt that she has been in God, and God in her. This truth remains so strongly impressed on her that, even though many years should pass without the condition returning, she can neither forget the favor she received, nor doubt of its reality. If you, nevertheless, ask how it is possible that the soul can see and understand that she has been in God, since during the union she has neither sight nor understanding, I reply that she does not see it then, but that she sees it clearly later, after she has returned to herself, not by any vision, but by a certitude which abides with her and which God alone can give her. I knew a person who was ignorant of the truth that God's mode of being in everything must be either by presence, by power, or by essence, but who, after having received the grace of which I am speaking, believed this truth in the most unshakable manner. So much so that, having consulted a half-learned man who was as ignorant on this point as she had been before she was enlightened, when he replied that God is in us only by 'grace,' she disbelieved his reply, so sure she was of the true answer; and when she came to ask wiser doctors, they confirmed her in her belief, which much consoled her. . . .
>
> "But how, you will repeat, *can* one have such certainty in respect to what one does not see? This question, I am powerless to answer. These are secrets of God's omnipotence which it does not appertain to me to penetrate. All that I know is that I tell the truth; and I shall never believe

15. Saint John of the Cross: The Dark Night of the Soul, book ii. ch. xvii., in Vie et Œuvres, 3me édition, Paris, 1893, iii. 428–432. Chapter xi. of book ii. of Saint John's Ascent of Carmel is devoted to showing the harmfulness for the mystical life of the use of sensible imagery.

16. In particular I omit mention of visual and auditory hallucinations, verbal and graphic automatisms, and such marvels as 'levitation,' stigmatization, and the healing of disease. These phenomena, which mystics have often presented (or are believed to have presented), have no essential mystical significance, for they occur with no consciousness of illumination whatever, when they occur, as they often do, in persons of non-mystical mind. Consciousness of illumination is for us the essential mark of 'mystical' states.

that any soul who does not possess this certainty has ever been really united to God."[17]

The kinds of truth communicable in mystical ways, whether these be sensible or supersensible, are various. Some of them relate to this world,—visions of the future, the reading of hearts, the sudden understanding of texts, the knowledge of distant events, for example; but the most important revelations are theological or metaphysical.

> Saint Ignatius confessed one day to Father Laynez that a single hour of meditation at Manresa had taught him more truths about heavenly things than all the teachings of all the doctors put together could have taught him. . . . One day in orison, on the steps of the choir of the Dominican church, he saw in a distinct manner the plan of divine wisdom in the creation of the world. On another occasion, during a procession, his spirit was ravished in God, and it was given him to contemplate, in a form and images fitted to the weak understanding of a dweller on the earth, the deep mystery of the holy Trinity. This last vision flooded his heart with such sweetness, that the mere memory of it in after times made him shed abundant tears.[18]

Similarly with Saint Teresa. "One day, being in orison," she writes, "it was granted me to perceive in one instant how all things are seen and contained in God. I did not perceive them in their proper form, and nevertheless the view I had of them was of a sovereign clearness, and has remained vividly impressed upon my soul. It is one of the most signal of all the graces which the Lord has granted me. . . . The view was so subtile and delicate that the understanding cannot grasp it."[19]

She goes on to tell how it was as if the Deity were an enormous and sovereignly limpid diamond, in which all our actions were contained in such a way that their full sinfulness appeared evident as never before. On another day, she relates, while she was reciting the Athanasian Creed,—

> Our Lord made me comprehend in what way it is that one God can be in three Persons. He made me see it so clearly that I remained as extremely surprised as I was comforted, . . . and now, when I think of the holy Trinity, or hear It spoken of, I understand how the three adorable Persons form only one God and I experience an unspeakable happiness.

On still another occasion, it was given to Saint Teresa to see and understand in what wise the Mother of God had been assumed into her place in Heaven.[20]

The deliciousness of some of these states seems to be beyond anything known in ordinary consciousness. It evidently involves organic sensibilities, for it is spoken of as something too extreme to be borne, and as verging on bodily pain.[21] But it is too subtle and piercing a delight for ordinary words to denote. God's touches, the

17. The Interior Castle, Fifth Abode, ch. i., in Œuvres, translated by Bouix, iii. 421–424.

18. Bartoli-Michel: Vie de Saint Ignace de Loyola, i. 34–36. Others have had illuminations about the created world, Jacob Boehme, for instance. At the age of twenty-five he was "surrounded by the divine light, and replenished with the heavenly knowledge; insomuch as going abroad into the fields to a green, at Görlitz, he there sat down, and viewing the herbs and grass of the field, in his inward light he saw into their essences, use, and properties, which was discovered to him by their lineaments, figures, and signatures." Of a later period of experience he writes: "In one quarter of an hour I saw and knew more than if I had been many years together at an university. For I saw and knew the beings of all things, the Byss and the Abyss, and the eternal generation of the holy Trinity, the descent and original of the world and of all creatures through the divine wisdom. I knew and saw in myself all the three worlds, the external and visible world being of a procreation or extern birth from both the internal and spiritual worlds; and I saw and knew the whole working essence, in the evil and in the good, and the mutual original and existence; and likewise how the fruitful bearing womb of eternity brought forth. So that I did not only greatly wonder at it, but did also exceedingly rejoice, albeit I could very hardly apprehend the same in my external man and set it down with the pen. For I had a thorough view of the universe as in a chaos, wherein all things are couched and wrapt up, but it was impossible for me to explicate the same." Jacob Boehme's Theosophic Philosophy, etc., by Edward Taylor, London, 1691, pp. 425, 427, abridged. . . .

19. Vie, pp. 581. 582.

20. Loc. cit., p. 574.

21. Saint Teresa discriminates between pain in which the body has a part and pure spiritual pain (Interior Castle, 6th Abode, ch. xi.). As for the bodily part in these celestial joys, she speaks of it as "penetrating to the marrow of the bones, whilst earthly pleasures affect only the surface of the senses. I think," she adds, "that this is a just description, and I cannot make it better." Ibid., 5th Abode, ch. i.

wounds of his spear, references to ebriety and to nuptial union have to figure in the phraseology by which it is shadowed forth. Intellect and senses both swoon away in these highest states of ecstasy. "If our understanding comprehends," says Saint Teresa, "it is in a mode which remains unknown to it, and it can understand nothing of what it comprehends. For my own part, I do not believe that it does comprehend, because, as I said, it does not understand itself to do so. I confess that it is all a mystery in which I am lost."[22] In the condition called *raptus* or ravishment by theologians, breathing and circulation are so depressed that it is a question among the doctors whether the soul be or be not temporarily dissevered from the body. One must read Saint Teresa's descriptions and the very exact distinctions which she makes, to persuade one's self that one is dealing, not with imaginary experiences, but with phenomena which, however rare, follow perfectly definite psychological types.

To the medical mind these ecstasies signify nothing but suggested and imitated hypnoid states, on an intellectual basis of superstition, and a corporeal one of degeneration and hysteria. Undoubtedly these pathological conditions have existed in many and possibly in all the cases, but that fact tells us nothing about the value for knowledge of the consciousness which they induce. To pass a spiritual judgment upon these states, we must not content ourselves with superficial medical talk, but inquire into their fruits for life.

Their fruits appear to have been various. Stupefaction, for one thing, seems not to have been altogether absent as a result. You may remember the helplessness in the kitchen and schoolroom of poor Margaret Mary Alacoque. Many other ecstatics would have perished but for the care taken of them by admiring followers. The 'otherworldliness' encouraged by the mystical consciousness makes this over-abstraction from practical life peculiarly liable to befall mystics in whom the character is naturally passive and the intellect feeble; but in natively strong minds and characters we find quite opposite results. The great Spanish mystics, who carried the habit of ecstasy as far as it has often been carried, appear for the most part to have shown indomitable spirit and energy, and all the more so for the trances in which they indulged.

Saint Ignatius was a mystic, but his mysticism made him assuredly one of the most powerfully practical human engines that ever lived. Saint John of the Cross, writing of the intuitions and 'touches' by which God reaches the substance of the soul, tells us that—

> They enrich it marvelously. A single one of them may be sufficient to abolish at a stroke certain imperfections of which the soul during its whole life had vainly tried to rid itself, and to leave it adorned with virtues and loaded with supernatural gifts. A single one of these intoxicating consolations may reward it for all the labors undergone in its life—even were they numberless. Invested with an invincible courage, filled with an impassioned desire to suffer for its God, the soul then is seized with a strange torment—that of not being allowed to suffer enough.[23]

Saint Teresa is as emphatic, and much more detailed. You may perhaps remember a passage I quoted from her in my first lecture.[24] There are many similar pages in her autobiography. Where in literature is a more evidently veracious account of the formation of a new centre of spiritual energy than is given in her description of the effects of certain ecstasies which in departing leave the soul upon a higher level of emotional excitement?

> Often, infirm and wrought upon with dreadful pains before the ecstasy, the soul emerges from it full of health and admirably disposed for action . . . as if God had willed that the body itself,

22. Vie, p. 198.

23. Œuvres, ii. 320.

24. Above, p. 34 [1902 edition].

already obedient to the soul's desires, should share in the soul's happiness. . . . The soul after such a favor is animated with a degree of courage so great that if at that moment its body should be torn to pieces for the cause of God, it would feel nothing but the liveliest comfort. Then it is that promises and heroic resolutions spring up in profusion in us, soaring desires, horror of the world, and the clear perception of our proper nothingness. . . . What empire is comparable to that of a soul who, from this sublime summit to which God has raised her, sees all the things of earth beneath her feet, and is captivated by no one of them? How ashamed she is of her former attachments! How amazed at her blindness! What lively pity she feels for those whom she recognizes still shrouded in the darkness! . . . She groans at having ever been sensitive to points of honor, at the illusion that made her ever see as honor what the world calls by that name. Now she sees in this name nothing more than an immense lie of which the world remains a victim. She discovers, in the new light from above, that in genuine honor there is nothing spurious, that to be faithful to this honor is to give our respect to what deserves to be respected really, and to consider as nothing, or as less than nothing, whatsoever perishes and is not agreeable to God. . . . She laughs when she sees grave persons, persons of orison, caring for points of honor for which she now feels profoundest contempt. It is suitable to the dignity of their rank to act thus, they pretend, and it makes them more useful to others. But she knows that in despising the dignity of their rank for the pure love of God they would do more good in a single day than they would effect in ten years by preserving it. . . . She laughs at herself that there should ever have been a time in her life when she made any case of money, when she ever desired it. . . . Oh! if human beings might only agree together to regard it as so much useless mud, what harmony would then reign in the world! With what friendship we would all treat each other if our interest in honor and in money could but disappear from earth! For my own part, I feel as if it would be a remedy for all our ills.[25]

Mystical conditions may, therefore render the soul more energetic in the lines which their inspiration favors. But this could be reckoned an advantage only in case the inspiration were a true one. If the inspiration were erroneous, the energy would be all the more mistaken and misbegotten. So we stand once more before that problem of truth which confronted us at the end of the lectures on saintliness. You will remember that we turned to mysticism precisely to get some light on truth. Do mystical states establish the truth of those theological affections in which the saintly life has its root?

In spite of their repudiation of articulate self-description, mystical states in general assert a pretty distinct theoretic drift. It is possible to give the outcome of the majority of them in terms that point in definite philosophical directions. One of these directions is optimism, and the other is monism. We pass into mystical states from out of ordinary consciousness as from a less into a more, as from a smallness into a vastness, and at the same time as from an unrest to a rest. We feel them as reconciling, unifying states. They appeal to the yes-function more than to the no-function in us. In them the unlimited absorbs the limits and peacefully closes the account. Their very denial of every adjective you may propose as applicable to the ultimate truth,—He, the Self, the Atman, is to be described by 'No! no!' only, say the Upanishads,[26] though it seems on the surface to be a no-function, is a denial made on behalf of a deeper yes. Whoso calls the Absolute anything in particular, or says that it is *this,* seems implicitly to shut it off from being *that*—it is as if he lessened it. So we deny the 'this,' negating the negation which it seems to us to imply, in the interests of the higher affirmative attitude by which we are possessed. The fountainhead of Christian mysticism is

25. Vie, pp. 200, 229, 231–233, 243.

26. Müller's translation, part ii. p. 180.

Dionysius the Areopagite. He describes the absolute truth by negatives exclusively.

> "The cause of all things is neither soul nor intellect; nor has it imagination, opinion, or reason, or intelligence; nor is it reason or intelligence; nor is it spoken or thought. It is neither number, nor order, nor magnitude, nor littleness, nor equality, nor inequality, nor similarity, nor dissimilarity. It neither stands, nor moves, nor rests. . . . It is neither essence, nor eternity, nor time. Even intellectual contact does not belong to it. It is neither science nor truth. It is not even royalty or wisdom; not one; not unity; not divinity or goodness; nor even spirit as we know it," etc., *ad libitum.*[27]

But these qualifications are denied by Dionysius, not because the truth falls short of them, but because it so infinitely excels them. It is above them. It is *super*-lucent, *super*-splendent,

27. T. Davidson's translation, in Journal of Speculative Philosophy, 1893, vol. xxii. p. 399.

"The Perennial Philosophy"

Frank C. Happold

Not only have mystics been found in all ages, in all parts of the world and in all religious systems, but also mysticism has manifested itself in similar or identical forms wherever the mystical consciousness has been present. Because of this it has sometimes been called the Perennial Philosophy. Out of their experience and their reflection on it have come the following assertions:

1. This phenomenal world of matter and individual consciousness is only a partial reality and is the manifestation of a Divine Ground in which all partial realities have their being.
2. It is of the nature of man that not only can he have knowledge of this Divine Ground by inference, but also he can realize it by direct intuition, superior to discursive reason, in which the knower is in some way united with the known.
3. The nature of man is not a single but a dual one. He has not one but two selves, the phenomenal *ego,* of which he is chiefly conscious and which he tends to regard as his true self, and a non-phenomenal, eternal self, an inner man, the spirit, the spark of divinity within him, which is his true self. It is possible for a man, if he so desires and is prepared to make the necessary effort, to identify himself with his true self and so with the Divine Ground, which is of the same or like nature.
4. It is the chief end of man's earthly existence to discover and identify himself with his true self. By so doing, he will come to an intuitive knowledge of the Divine Ground and so apprehend Truth as it really is, and not as to our limited human perceptions it appears to be. Not only that, he will enter into a state of being which has been given different names, eternal life, salvation, enlightenment, etc.

Further, the Perennial Philosophy rests on two fundamental convictions:

1. Though it may be to a great extent atrophied and exist only potentially in most men, men possess an organ or faculty which is capable of discerning spiritual truth, and, in its own spheres, this faculty is as much to be relied on as are other organs of sensation in theirs.
2. In order to be able to discern spiritual truth men must in their essential nature be spiritual; in order to know That which they call God, they must be, in some way, partakers of the divine nature; . . .

From *The Perennial Philosophy* (1970).

super-essential, *super*-sublime, *super* everything that can be named. Like Hegel in his logic, mystics journey towards the positive pole of truth only by the 'Methode der Absoluten Negativität.'[28]

Thus come the paradoxical expressions that so abound in mystical writings. As when Eckhart tells of the still desert of the Godhead, "where never was seen difference, neither Father, Son, nor Holy Ghost, where there is no one at home, yet where the spark of the soul is more at peace than in itself."[29] As when Boehme writes of the Primal Love, that "it may fitly be compared to Nothing, for it is deeper than any Thing, and is as nothing with respect to all things, forasmuch as it is not comprehensible by any of them. And because it is nothing respectively, it is therefore free from all things, and is that only good, which a man cannot express or utter what it is, there being nothing to which it may be compared, to express it by."[30] . . .

To this dialectical use, by the intellect, of negation as a mode of passage towards a higher kind of affirmation, there is correlated the subtlest of moral counterparts in the sphere of the personal will. Since denial of the finite self and its wants, since asceticism of some sort, is found in religious experience to be the only doorway to the larger and more blessed life, this moral mystery intertwines and combines with the intellectual mystery in all mystical writings.

> "Love," continues Behmen, is Nothing, for "when thou art gone forth wholly from the Creature and from that which is visible, and art become Nothing to all that is Nature and Creature, then thou art in that eternal One, which is God himself, and then thou shalt feel within thee the highest virtue of Love. . . . The treasure of treasures for the soul is where she goeth out of the Somewhat into that Nothing out of which all things may be made. The soul here saith, *I have nothing,* for I am utterly stripped and naked; *I can do nothing,* for I have no manner of power, but am as water poured out; *I am nothing,* for all that I am is no more than an image of Being, and only God is to me I AM; and so, sitting down in my own Nothingness, I give glory to the eternal Being, and *will nothing* of myself, that so God may will all in me, being unto me my God and all things."[31]

In Paul's language, I live, yet not I, but Christ liveth in me. Only when I become as nothing can God enter in and no difference between his life and mine remain outstanding.[32]

This overcoming of all the usual barriers between the individual and the Absolute is the great mystic achievement. In mystic states we both become one with the Absolute and we become aware of our oneness. This is the everlasting and triumphant mystical tradition, hardly altered by differences of clime or creed. In Hinduism, in Neoplatonism, in Sufism, in Christian mysticism, in Whitmanism, we find the same

28. "Deus propter excellentiam non immerito Nihil vocatur." Scotus Erigena, quoted by Andrew Seth: Two Lectures on Theism, New York, 1897, p. 55.

29. J. Royce: Studies in Good and Evil, p. 282.

30. Jacob Boehme's Dialogues on the Supersensual Life, translated by Bernard Holland, London, 1901, p. 48.

31. Op. cit., pp. 42, 74, abridged.

32. From a French book I take this mystical expression of happiness in God's indwelling presence:—

"Jesus has come to take up his abode in my heart. It is not so much a habitation, as association, as a sort of fusion. Oh, new and blessed life! life which becomes each day more luminous. . . . The wall before me, dark a few moments since, is splendid at this hour because the sun shines on it. Wherever its rays fall they light up a conflagration of glory; the smallest speck of glass sparkles, each grain of sand emits fire; even so there is a royal song of triumph in my heart because the Lord is there. My days succeed each other; yesterday a blue sky; to-day a clouded sun; a night filled with strange dreams; but as soon as the eyes open, and I regain consciousness and seem to begin life again, it is always the same figure before me, always the same presence filling my heart. . . . Formerly the day was dulled by the absence of the Lord. I used to wake invaded by all sorts of sad impressions, and I did not find him on my path. To-day he is with me; and the light cloudiness which covers things is not an obstacle to my communion with him. I feel the pressure of his hand, I feel something else which fills me with a serene joy; shall I dare to speak it out? Yes, for it is the true expression of what I experience. The Holy Spirit is not merely making me a visit; it is no mere dazzling apparition which may from one moment to another spread its wings and leave me in my night, it is a permanent habitation. He can depart only if he takes me with him. More than that; he is not other than myself: he is one with me. It is not a juxtaposition, it is a penetration, a profound modification of my nature, a new manner of my being." Quoted from the MS. 'of an old man' by Wilfred Monod: Il Vit: six méditations sur le mystère chrétien, pp. 280–283.

recurring note, so that there is about mystical utterances an eternal unanimity which ought to make a critic stop and think, and which brings it about that the mystical classics have, as has been said, neither birthday nor native land. Perpetually telling of the unity of man with God, their speech antedates languages, and they do not grow old.[33]

'That art Thou!' say the Upanishads, and the Vedantists add: 'Not a part, not a mode of That, but identically That, that absolute Spirit of the World.' "As pure water poured into pure water remains the same, thus, O Gautama, is the Self of a thinker who knows. Water in water, fire in fire, ether in ether, no one can distinguish them; likewise a man whose mind has entered into the Self."[34] "'Every man,' says the Sufi Gulshan-Râz, 'whose heart is no longer shaken by any doubt, knows with certainty that there is no being save only One. . . . In his divine majesty the *me,* the *we,* the *thou,* are not found, for in the One there can be no distinction. Every being who is annulled and entirely separated from himself, hears resound outside of him this voice and this echo: *I am God:* he has an eternal way of existing, and is no longer subject to death.'"[35] In the vision of God, says Plotinus, "what sees is not our reason, but something prior and superior to our reason. . . . He who thus sees does not properly see, does not distinguish or imagine two things. He changes, he ceases to be himself, preserves nothing of himself. Absorbed in God, he makes but one with him, like a centre of a circle coinciding with another centre."[36] "Here," writes Suso, "the spirit dies, and yet is all alive in the marvels of the Godhead . . . and is lost in the stillness of the glorious dazzling obscurity and of the naked simple unity. It is in this modeless *where* that the highest bliss is to be found."[37]

33. Compare M. Maeterlinck: L'Ornement des Noces spirituelles de Ruysbroeck, Bruxelles, 1891, Introduction, p. xix.

34. Upanishads, M. Müller's translation, ii. 17, 334.

35. Schmölders: Op. cit., p. 210.

36. Enneads, Bouillier's translation, Paris, 1861, iii. 561. Compare pp. 473–477, and vol. i. p. 27.

37. Autobiography, pp. 309, 310.

"Ich bin so gross als Gott," sings Angelus Silesius again, "Er ist als ich so klein; Er kann nicht über mich, ich unter ihm nicht sein."[38]

In mystical literature such self-contradictory phrases as 'dazzling obscurity,' 'whispering silence,' 'teeming desert,' are continually met with. They prove that not conceptual speech, but music rather, is the element through which we are best spoken to by mystical truth. Many mystical scriptures are indeed little more than musical compositions.

> He who would hear the voice of Nada, 'the Soundless Sound,' and comprehend it, he has to learn the nature of Dhâranâ. . . . When to himself his form appears unreal, as do on waking all the forms he sees in dreams; when he has ceased to hear the many, he may discern the ONE—the inner sound which kills the outer. . . . For then the soul will hear, and will remember. And then to the inner ear will speak THE VOICE OF THE SILENCE. . . . And now thy *Self* is lost in SELF, *thyself* unto THYSELF, merged in that SELF from which thou first didst radiate. . . . Behold! thou hast become the Light, thou hast become the Sound, thou art the Master and thy God. Thou art THYSELF the object of thy search: the VOICE unbroken, the resounds throughout eternities, exempt from change, from sin exempt, the seven sounds in one, the VOICE OF THE SILENCE. *Om tat Sat.*[39]

These words, if they do not awaken laughter as you receive them, probably stir chords within you which music and language touch in common. Music gives us ontological messages which non-musical criticism is unable to contradict, though it may laugh at our foolishness in minding them. There is a verge of the mind which these things haunt; and whispers therefrom mingle with the operations of our understanding, even as the waters of the infinite ocean send their waves to break among the pebbles that lie upon our shores.

38. Op. cit., Strophe 10.

39. H. P. Blavatsky: The Voice of the Silence.

Here begins the sea that ends not till the world's end.
Where we stand,
Could we know the next high sea-mark set beyond these waves that gleam,
We should know what never man hath known, nor eye of man hath scanned. . . .
Ah, but here man's heart leaps, yearning towards the gloom with venturous glee,
From the shore that hath no shore beyond it, set in all the sea.[40]

That doctrine, for example, that eternity is timeless, that our 'immortality,' if we live in the eternal, is not so much future as already now and here, which we find so often expressed to-day in certain philosophic circles, finds its support in a 'hear, hear!' or an 'amen,' which floats up from that mysteriously deeper level.[41] We recognize the passwords to the mystical region as we hear them, but we cannot use them ourselves; it alone has the keeping of 'the password primeval.'[42]

I have now sketched with extreme brevity and insufficiency, but as fairly as I am able in the time allowed, the general traits of the mystic range of consciousness. *It is on the whole pantheistic and optimistic, or at least the opposite of pessimistic. It is anti-naturalistic, and harmonizes best with twice-bornness and so-called otherworldly states of mind.*

My next task is to inquire whether we can invoke it as authoritative. Does it furnish any *warrant for the truth* of the twice-bornness and supernaturality and pantheism which it favors? I must give my answer to this question as concisely as I can.

In brief my answer is this,—and I will divide it into three parts:—

(1) Mystical states, when well developed, usually are, and have the right to be, absolutely authoritative over the individuals to whom they come.

(2) No authority emanates from them which should make it a duty for those who stand outside of them to accept their revelations uncritically.

(3) They break down the authority of the non-mystical or rationalistic consciousness, based upon the understanding and the senses alone. They show it to be only one kind of consciousness. They open out the possibility of other orders of truth, in which, so far as anything in us vitally responds to them, we may freely continue to have faith.

I will take up these points one by one.

I

As a matter of psychological fact, mystical states of a well-pronounced and emphatic sort *are* usually authoritative over those who have them.[43] They have been 'there,' and know. It is vain for rationalism to grumble about this. If the mystical truth that comes to a man proves to be a force that he can live by, what mandate have we of the majority to order him to live in another way? We can throw him into prison or a madhouse, but we cannot change his mind—we commonly attach it only the more stubbornly to its beliefs.[44] It mocks our utmost efforts, as a matter of fact, and in point of logic it absolutely escapes our jurisdiction. Our own more 'rational' beliefs are based on evidence exactly similar in nature to that which mystics quote for theirs. Our senses, namely, have assured us of certain states of fact; but mystical experiences are as direct perceptions of fact for those who have them as any sensations ever were for us.

40. Swinburne: On the Verge, in 'A Midsummer Vacation.'

41. Compare the extracts from Dr. Bucke, quoted on p. 136.

42. As serious an attempt as I know to mediate between the mystical region and the discursive life is contained in an article on Aristotle's Unmoved Mover, by F. C. S. Schiller, in Mind, vol. ix., 1900.

43. I abstract from weaker states, and from those cases of which the books are full, where the director (but usually not the subject) remains in doubt whether the experience may not have proceeded from the demon.

44. Example: Mr. John Nelson writes of his imprisonment for preaching Methodism: "My soul was as a watered garden, and I could sing praises to God all day long; for he turned my captivity into joy, and gave me to rest as well on the boards, as if I had been on a bed of down. Now could I say, 'God's service is perfect freedom,' and I was carried out much in prayer that my enemies might drink of the same river of peace which my God gave so largely to me." Journal, London, no date, p. 172.

The records show that even though the five senses be in abeyance in them, they are absolutely sensational in their epistemological quality, if I may be pardoned the barbarous expression,—that is, they are face to face presentations of what seems immediately to exist.

The mystic is, in short, *invulnerable,* and must be left, whether we relish it or not, in undisturbed enjoyment of his creed. Faith, says Tolstoy, is that by which men live. And faith-state and mystic state are practically convertible terms.

II

But I now proceed to add that mystics have no right to claim that we ought to accept the deliverance of their peculiar experiences, if we are ourselves outsiders and feel no private call thereto. The utmost they can ever ask of us in this life is to admit that they establish a presumption. They form a consensus and have an unequivocal outcome; and it would be odd, mystics might say, if such a unanimous type of experience should prove to be altogether wrong. At bottom, however, this would only be an appeal to numbers, like the appeal of rationalism the other way; and the appeal to numbers has no logical force. If we acknowledge it, it is for 'suggestive,' not for logical reasons: we follow the majority because to do so suits our life.

But even this presumption from the unanimity of mystics is far from being strong. In characterizing mystic states as pantheistic, optimistic, etc., I am afraid I over-simplified the truth. I did so for expository reasons, and to keep the closer to the classic mystical tradition. The classic religious mysticism, it now must be confessed, is only a 'privileged case.' It is an *extract,* kept true to type by the selection of the fittest specimens and their preservation in 'schools.' It is carved out from a much larger mass; and if we take the larger mass as seriously as religious mysticism has historically taken itself, we find that the supposed unanimity largely disappears. To begin with, even religious mysticism itself, the kind that accumulates traditions and makes schools, is much less unanimous than I have allowed. It has been both ascetic and antinomianly self-indulgent within the Christian church.[45] It is dualistic in Sankhya, and monistic in Vedanta philosophy. I called it pantheistic; but the great Spanish mystics are anything but pantheists. They are with few exceptions non-metaphysical minds, for whom 'the category of personality' is absolute. The 'union' of man with God is for them much more like an occasional miracle than like an original identity.[46] How different again, apart from the happiness common to all, is the mysticism of Walt Whitman, Edward Carpenter, Richard Jefferies, and other naturalistic pantheists, from the more distinctively Christian sort.[47] The fact is that the mystical feeling of enlargement, union, and emancipation has no specific intellectual content whatever of its own. It is capable of forming matrimonial alliances with material furnished by the most diverse philosophies and theologies, provided only they can find a place in their framework for its peculiar emotional mood. We have no right, therefore, to invoke its prestige as distinctively in favor of any special belief, such as that in absolute idealism, or in the absolute monistic identity, or in the absolute goodness, of the world. It is only relatively in favor of all these things—it passes out of common human consciousness in the direction in which they lie.

So much for religious mysticism proper. But more remains to be told, for religious mysticism is only one half of mysticism. The other half has no accumulated traditions except those which the text-books on insanity supply. Open any one of these, and you will find abundant cases in which 'mystical ideas' are cited as characteristic

45. Ruysbroeck, in the work which Maeterlinck has translated, has a chapter against the antinomianism of disciples. . . .

46. Compare Paul Rousselot: Les Mystiques Espagnols, Paris, 1869, ch. xii.

47. See Carpenter's Towards Democracy, especially the latter parts, and Jefferies's wonderful and splendid mystic rhapsody, The Story of my Heart.

symptoms of enfeebled or deluded states of mind. In delusional insanity, paranoia, as they sometimes call it, we may have a *diabolical* mysticism, a sort of religious mysticism turned upside down. The same sense of ineffable importance in the smallest events, the same texts and words coming with new meanings, the same voices and visions and leadings and missions, the same controlling by extraneous powers; only this time the emotion is pessimistic: instead of consolations we have desolations; the meanings are dreadful; and the powers are enemies to life. It is evident that from the point of view of their psychological mechanism, the classic mysticism and these lower mysticisms spring from the same mental level, from that great subliminal or transmarginal region of which science is beginning to admit the existence, but of which so little is really known. That region contains every kind of matter: 'seraph and snake' abide there side by side. To come from thence is no infallible credential. What comes must be sifted and tested, and run the gauntlet of confrontation with the total context of experience, just like what comes from the outer world of sense. Its value must be ascertained by empirical methods, so long as we are not mystics ourselves.

Once more, then, I repeat that non-mystics are under no obligation to acknowledge in mystical states a superior authority conferred on them by their intrinsic nature.[48]

Yet, I repeat once more, the existence of mystical states absolutely overthrows the pretension of non-mystical states to be the sole and ultimate dictators of what we may believe. As a

48. In chapter i. of book ii. of his work Degeneration, 'Max Nordau' seeks to undermine all mysticism by exposing the weakness of the lower kinds. Mysticism for him means any sudden perception of hidden significance in things. He explains such perception by the abundant uncompleted associations which experiences may arouse in a degenerate brain. These give to him who has the experience a vague and vast sense of its leading further, yet they awaken no definite or useful consequent in his thought. The explanation is a plausible one for certain sorts of feeling of significance. . . . But the higher mystical flights, with their positiveness and abruptness, are surely products of no such merely negative condition. It seems far more reasonable to ascribe them to inroads from the subconscious life, of the cerebral activity correlative to which we as yet know nothing.

"Cosmic Religious Feeling"

Albert Einstein

It is easy to see why the churches have always fought science and persecuted its devotees. On the other hand, I maintain that the cosmic religious feeling is the strongest and noblest motive for scientific research. Only those who realize the immense efforts and, above all, the devotion without which pioneer work in theoretical science cannot be achieved are able to grasp the strength of the emotion out of which alone such work, remote as it is from the immediate realities of life, can issue. What a deep conviction of the rationality of the universe and what a yearning to understand, were it but a feeble reflection of the mind revealed in this world. Kepler and Newton must have had to enable them to spend years of solitary labor in disentangling the principles of celestial mechanics! Those whose acquaintance with scientific research is derived chiefly from its practical results easily develop a completely false notion of the mentality of the men who, surrounded by a skeptical world, have shown the way to kindred spirits scattered wide through the world and the centuries. Only one who has devoted his life to similar ends can have a vivid realization of what has inspired these men and given them the strength to remain true to their purpose in spite of countless failures. It is cosmic religious feeling that gives a man such strength. A contemporary has said, not unjustly, that in this materialistic age of ours the serious scientific workers are the only profoundly religious people.

From *Religion and Science* (1950).

rule, mystical states merely add a supersensuous meaning to the ordinary outward data on consciousness. They are excitements like the emotions of love or ambition, gifts to our spirit by means of which facts already objectively before us fall into a new expressiveness and make a new connection with our active life. They do not contradict these facts as such, or deny anything that our senses have immediately seized.[49] It is the rationalistic critic rather who plays the part of denier in the controversy, and his denials have no strength, for there never can be a state of facts to which new meaning may not truthfully be added, provided the mind ascend to a more enveloping point of view. It must always remain an open question whether mystical states may not possibly be such superior points of view, windows through which the mind looks out upon a more extensive and inclusive world. The difference of the views seen from the different mystical windows need not prevent us from entertaining this supposition. The wider world would in that case prove to have a mixed constitution like that of this world, that is all. It would have its celestial and its infernal regions, its tempting and its saving moments, its valid experiences and its counterfeit ones, just as our world has them; but it would be a wider world all the same. We should have to use its experiences by selecting and subordinating and substituting just as is our custom in this ordinary naturalistic world; we should be liable to error just as we are now; yet the counting in of that wider world of meanings, and the serious dealing with it, might, in spite of all the perplexity, be indispensable stages in our approach to the final fullness of the truth.

In this shape, I think, we have to leave the subject. Mystical states indeed wield no authority due simply to their being mystical states. But the higher ones among them point in directions to which the religious sentiments even of nonmystical men incline. They tell of the supremacy of the ideal, of vastness, of union, of safety, and of rest. They offer us *hypotheses,* hypotheses which we may voluntarily ignore, but which as thinkers we cannot possibly upset. The supernaturalism and optimism to which they would persuade us may, interpreted in one way or another, be after all the truest of insights into the meaning of this life.

"Oh, the little more, and how much it is; and the little less, and what worlds away!" It may be that possibility and permission of this sort are all that the religious consciousness requires to live on. In my last lecture I shall have to try to persuade you that this is the case.*

49. They sometimes add subjective *audita et visa* to the facts, but as these are usually interpreted as transmundane, they oblige no alteration in the facts of sense.

* See James's "Conclusion," in part XI.

J. L. Mackie

"RELIGIOUS EXPERIENCE"

A brief biography of Mackie appears on page 322.

Since the early nineteenth century, and particularly through Kant's influence, the traditional 'proofs' of theistic doctrines have been widely rejected or abandoned—though, among Christian thinkers, such abandonment is less characteristic of Catholics than of Protestants. Also, . . . the problem of evil poses a very awkward question for anyone who wants to assert, literally, the full traditional set of theistic doctrines. A widespread response to these difficulties has been a shift of emphasis away from proofs and even from doctrines of a metaphysical sort, and a growing reliance instead upon religious experience.

This reliance, however, can take either of two very different forms. First, it may be held that religious experience itself is all that really matters. Believers, and, significantly, people at the moment of conversion, of transition from unbelief to belief, have experiences which are, to them, intrinsically valuable and all-important, which shape and colour their whole lives. It is of this, it may be said, that religion fundamentally consists: any formulated doctrines, biblical or metaphysical, whether they are the peculiar teachings of a particular faith or sect or a very general theism or supernaturalism, are simply beside the point. Although they may seem, to this or that group of believers, to be vital, the experiences would be essentially unchanged even if the associated doctrines were different, and whether those doctrines are true or false the experiences remain valid in their own right. But,

From J. L. Mackie, *The Miracle of Theism,* Clarendon Press, 1982, pp. 177–187. Reprinted by permission of Oxford University Press.

In the Cathedral of Reims, France, the mysticism of the Middle Ages became architectural reality.

alternatively, it may be held that the religious experience, as well as being valuable in itself, is also evidence, or even proof, of the objective truth of some associated beliefs. That is, there may be an argument *from* religious experience *to* something further. But there are sub-divisions of this second alternative. The something further may be taken to be the central doctrines of traditional theism, which we have been examining in relation to many other arguments. Or the something further may be the special teachings of a particular faith, for example the divinity of Jesus Christ and the availability of salvation through him alone. Or it may indeed by just *something further,* the reality of *some* higher but potentially friendly power.

The contrast between these two approaches may be drawn in another way. The verb 'to experience' is indeed transitive: any experience must have an object, it must be *of* something. But it may have an intentional object only, as does a dream experience or the experience of pain. The pain, or the dream, will no doubt have causes; but the pain itself has no existence apart from the experience of it, nor do the events which constitute the manifest dream content. Alternatively, an experience may have a real object: we ordinarily suppose our normal perceptual experience to be or to include awareness of independently existing material spatio-temporal things. The question then is whether specifically religious experiences should be taken to have real objects, to give us genuine information about independently existing supernatural entities or spiritual beings, or whether all that matters is their intrinsic character, their intentional objects, and, of course, their influence on the rest of the lives of those who have them.

In considering either approach, it will be essential to have some understanding of what sorts of experiences these are. For this, we can hardly do better than resort to William James's classical work, *The Varieties of Religious Experience.*[1] Like Hume's *Dialogues,* this is one of the few masterpieces among books *about* religion. Drawing upon a great many first-hand reports, both published and unpublished, it not only surveys very different sorts of experience that can all be counted as religious, but also considers, in a balanced, tentative, and yet enterprising way, how they should be explained and evaluated, and what arguments can in the end be properly based upon them.

James's interest is particularly focused on the experiences, especially the solitary experiences, of individual men and women, and on their more extreme, rather than their milder and more conventional forms. He assumes—though this, as we shall see, is controversial—that all organized, institutional, religion, and all theology, are secondary outgrowths from these solitary experiences: the gods of the churches, the gods of tribes and states, as well as the god of the philosophers, are derived from and ultimately dependent upon the god encountered in solitude by the individual worshipper or convert or mystic. Religions, James thinks, are both founded and repeatedly revived by those who have overwhelming personal experiences of some religious sort. (See Lectures II, XIV, and XV, especially p. 328.)

Being a psychologist, and sub-titling his work 'A Study in Human Nature', James is greatly concerned with the causal origin of these peculiar states of mind and their resemblances to other mental phenomena. But he insists (in Lecture II) that the question of the 'value' of these experiences—in which he includes the question whether what they reveal is an otherwise inaccessible realm of truth—is quite independent of the question of their origin, and in the end (in Lecture XX) he defends not only what *we* would call their value but also, tentatively and in some measure, their objective truth.

One of James's main themes, as his title suggests, is just how varied religious experiences are. He describes (in Lectures IV and V) 'the religion of healthy-mindedness' which 'looks on all things and sees that they are good', perhaps to the point of denying evil, in the style of Christian Science and other forms of 'mind-cure'. Radically different from this is the deeper sort of experience in which a 'sick soul' is miraculously healed, where someone is first overwhelmed by a sense of sin or guilt or inner conflict or perhaps, like Tolstoy, of the sheer meaninglessness of life, and then experiences a revelation, a conversion, in which he feels saved, free, unified, and happy. Different again are the experiences of mystics, whose content is commonly said to be inexpressible and uncommun-

1. W. James, *The Varieties of Religious Experience* (Collins, Fontana, London, 1960). References in the text to this work are to the numbered Lectures and to pages in this edition.

icable, but which nevertheless seem to those who have them to be states not only of intense emotion but also of profound knowledge; the knowledge in question can, for many cases at least, be roughly expressed as an awareness of the cosmos as unified and beautiful and of the mystic's own unity with it. And experiences of these varied sorts may or may not involve the literal seeing of visions, either of bright lights or of supernatural beings, the hearing of voices, or the sense of being guided about what to do.

But from this bewildering complexity we can, with James's help, sort out some leading themes and principles. One of these is the close resemblances between religious experiences and other well-known mental phenomena. We are all familiar with dreams. Waking visions and hallucinations are relatively infrequent, but still common enough. Many people have occasionally had the impression of hearing words spoken when there have been no such physical sounds in the neighbourhood. Many religious experiences closely resemble, even in their sequences of contrasting phases, the almost universal human experience of being in love. Hysteria, delusions, cycles of mania and depression are known and reasonably well understood psychopathic phenomena in innumerable cases where there is no religious component; but experiences which have such components, which count as religious *par excellence,* share many features with these pathological ones. Experiences of the mystical kind are often induced by certain drugs. Some of the experiences reported by mystics almost irresistibly invite interpretation as expressions of violent sexual passion. From a psychological point of view, as James himself makes clear, the phenomena of conversion, 'mind-cure', sensory or motor automatisms (such as hearing voices), inspiration, mysticism, and so on lend themselves very readily to being understood in terms of the operation of unconscious or subconscious parts of the mind. 'Let me propose', he says, therefore, 'as an hypothesis, that whatever it may be on its *farther* side, "more" with which in religious experience we feel ourselves connected is on its *hither* side the subconscious continuation of our conscious life' (Lecture XX, p. 487; but see also pp. 125, 237, 267, and 462).

Also, despite James's own insistence that the question of the origin of a religious experience is quite distinct from those of its value and truth, there is an important indirect connection between them. Since these experiences are of kinds which are psychologically understandable without the help of any specifically religious assumptions, they do not in themselves carry any guarantee of a supernatural source. There is nothing intrinsically very remarkable or distinctive about them. This obviously holds for any single 'religious' experience. Peter Sutcliffe, the 'Yorkshire Ripper', who recently murdered at least thirteen women, heard voices which he took to be of divine origin urging him to kill. Theologians themselves have long recognized that it is not easy to decide, about particular visions and messages, whether they come from God or from the devil. As James says, reporting both Jonathan Edwards and St. Theresa, 'No appearances whatever are infallible proofs of grace . . . The good dispositions that a vision, voice, or other apparently heavenly favor leave behind them are the only marks by which we may be sure that they are not possible deceptions of the tempter' (Lecture I, pp. 41–2). Admittedly these alternatives, God and the devil, would both fall under the broad heading of 'some supernatural source'. But it will be fairly readily admitted today that the experiences initially ascribed to the devil are fully explicable in terms of purely human but subconscious motives; since it is also admitted that those which the theologian would ascribe to God are not *intrinsically* distinguishable from those which he would initially ascribe to the devil, it follows that even what he classes as genuinely religious experiences do not intrinsically resist explanation in purely human terms. And this in itself seems fatal to any argument *from* religious experience *to* any supernatural conclusions whatever.

We distinguished, above, three different forms that such supernatural conclusions might take:

the central theistic doctrines, the special teachings of a particular faith, and the existence merely of *some* higher but potentially friendly power. But any argument from religious experience to a conclusion of the second of these kinds would be extremely weak. It is true that the detailed content, the intentional objects, of particular experiences often involve or presuppose such special beliefs. When St. Paul, on the road to Damascus, heard the question 'Saul, Saul, why persecutest thou me?', he was told, within the vision, who was addressing him. James's 'Oxford graduate' (like innumerable others who have experienced conversion) was equally sure that it was both Jesus Christ and God the Father who had worked on him (pp. 222–4). When George Fox saw a channel of blood running down the streets of Lichfield, he was able to connect this with the martyrdom of a thousand Christians there in the time of Diocletian (pp. 30–1). But it is obvious that such interpretations depend either on the context of the experiences or on the believer's independently acquired knowledge and beliefs. Even if the special doctrines are somehow represented in the content of the experiences, it is all too easy to understand them as having been fed in from the religious tradition by which the experiencer has been influenced. Visions of the Virgin Mary may come to those who already pray to her; those who focus on the Bible as the word of God may find new meaning and force in a biblical phrase (pp. 195–8). James also refers to a number of cases of conversion which, though otherwise like religious ones, are purely ethical, involving no theological beliefs or content (Lecture IX, p. 207). Indeed, J. S. Mill's *Autobiography* records a sequence of depression followed by regeneration which had all the marks of religious conversion except that, not having been brought up in any theistic tradition, Mill read no theistic import into his experiences.[2] Kierkegaard says that one who, living in an idolatrous community, prays to an idol *in the right spirit* thereby prays, after all, to the true god.[3] But this cuts both ways. It entails that one who prays, intentionally, to a specifically Christian god, and who has an experience as of Christ or the Virgin Mary, may, by the same token, be receiving a response from some quite different true god who is sufficiently broad-minded to make allowances for the trivial errors of his worshippers. When the Christian says 'I know that my redeemer liveth', we must reply 'No, you don't: certainly not if you mean, by "my redeemer," Jesus as distinct from Osiris or Ashtaroth or Dionysus or Baldur or Vishnu or Amida'. But equally the response may be coming from no god beyond the experiencer's own unconscious mind.

Religious experience is also essentially incapable of supporting any argument for the traditional central doctrines of theism. Nothing in an experience as such could reveal a creator of the world, or omnipotence, or omniscience, or perfect goodness, or eternity, or even that there is just one god. On this James is very firm and obviously right: 'I feel bound to say that religious experience, as we have studied it, cannot be cited as unequivocally supporting the infinitist belief. The only thing that it unequivocally testifies to is that we can experience union with *something* larger than ourselves and in that union find our greatest peace . . . It need not be infinite, it need not be solitary' (p. 499). Thus he is prepared to return to 'a sort of polytheism', which, he remarks, 'has always been the real religion of common people, and is so still today' (pp. 499–500). Moreover, it is a 'piecemeal supernaturalism' that, on his view, these experiences support. God, or the gods, do not merely create and sustain the whole natural world; the supernatural must enter into 'transactions of detail' with the natural—in other words, the sorts of interventions that we have defined miracles to be (pp. 496–8). Here James's empiricism is at work. It is only

2. J. S. Mill, *Autobiography* [edited by Jack Stillinger (Oxford University Press, 1969)], Chapter 5.

3. S. Kierkegaard, *Concluding Unscientific Postscript,* translated by D. F. Swenson and W. Lowrie (Princeton University Press, 1941). Book I, Part II, Chapter 2.

if the supernatural makes some such specific differences that a supernaturalist hypothesis could be confirmed in contrast with a purely naturalistic rival.

The very most, then, that an argument from religious experience could give us is much less than either the philosophical theist or the adherent of any specific faith demands. Even if these experiences were witnesses to some further truth, it could only be, as James says, the existence of *some* greater friendly power, whose precise identity and character are left wholly indeterminate. But this, James thinks, is enough for religion. He finds a common core of intellectual content underlying all the discrepancies of the varied and conflicting creeds, namely the combination of an 'uneasiness' and a 'solution'. The uneasiness is that 'there is *something wrong about us* as we naturally stand'; the solution is that '*we are saved from the wrongness* by making proper connection with the higher powers'. The individual finds in himself a better part which is '*continuous with a* MORE *of the same quality which is operative in the universe outside of him, and which he can . . . in a fashion get on board of and save himself when all his lower being has gone to pieces in the wreck*' (pp. 483–4). All the phenomena, he says, 'are accurately describable in these very simple general terms. They allow for the divided self and the struggle; they involve the change of personal center and the surrender of the lower self; they express the appearance of exteriority of the helping power and yet account for our sense of union with it; and they fully justify our feelings of security and joy. There is probably no autobiographic document, among all those which I have quoted, to which the description will not well apply' (pp. 484–5).

However, 'So far . . . as this analysis goes, the experiences are only psychological phenomena' (p. 485). Whether their content has any objective truth is the crucial further question. Certainly no demonstrative argument will establish this. The issue is whether the hypothesis that there objectively is a something more gives a better explanation of the whole range of phenomena than can be given without it. James himself thinks that it does; yet he gives no real argument to support this opinion. This is, obviously, a less economical hypothesis than its naturalistic rival, and in fact such argument as James gives undermines it: 'the theologian's contention that the religious man is moved by an external power is vindicated, for it is one of the peculiarities of invasions from the subconscious region to take on objective appearances, and to suggest to the Subject an external control. In the religious life the control is felt as "higher'; but since on our hypothesis it is pri-

"The Extraordinary Ordinary"

Abraham Maslow

The search for the exotic, the strange, the unusual, the uncommon has often taken the form of pilgrimages, of turning away from the world, the "Journey to the East," to another country or to a different Religion. The great lesson from the true mystics, from the Zen monks, and now also from the Humanistic and Transpersonal psychologists—that the sacred is *in* the ordinary, that it is to be found in one's daily life, in one's neighbors, friends, and family, in one's backyard, and that travel may be a *flight* from confronting the sacred—this lesson, can be easily lost. To be looking elsewhere for miracles is to me a sure sign of ignorance that *everything* is miraculous.

The rejection of a priestly caste who claimed to be exclusive custodians of a private hot line to the sacred was, in my opinion, a great step forward in the emancipation of mankind, and we have the mystics—among others—to thank for this achievement. . . .

marily the higher faculties of our own hidden mind which are controlling, the sense of union with the power beyond us is a sense of something, not merely apparently, but literally true' (p. 488). But clearly this 'vindicates' the theologian's contention only by reducing it to the rival naturalistic view. Our 'ideal impulses', James says, originate in 'an altogether other dimension of existence form the sensible and merely "understandable" world . . . we find them possessing us in a way for which we cannot articulately account', and this region 'is not merely ideal, for it produces effects in this world' (p. 490). However, all that has been shown goes against even this modest and indeterminate supernaturalism. The undeniably real causal source of these impulses may be normally 'unseen' and not understood or articulately reported; but it is eminently understandable, and it belongs well within the same 'dimensions of existence' as other, wholly familiar, mental phenomena.

This conclusion is corroborated by an examination of what James says about the question whether 'the mystic range of consciousness' furnishes 'any *warrant for the truth* of the twice-bornness and supernaturality and pantheism which it favors'. Mystical states, he says, are 'absolutely authoritative over the individuals to whom they come'; yet 'No authority emanates from them which should make it a duty for those who stand outside of them to accept their revelations uncritically'; nevertheless, 'They break down the authority of the non-mystical or rationalistic consciousness, based upon the understanding and the senses alone. They show it to be only one kind of consciousness. They open out the possibility of other orders of truth, in which, so far as anything in us vitally responds to them, we may freely continue to have faith' (p. 407). But this is incoherent. Since, as he rightly says, no authority emanates from mystical experiences—because they can be so easily explained in purely natural, psychological, terms—for anyone who stands outside them to accept their revelations (the word 'uncritically' is redundant: to accept them at all in these circumstances would be uncritical), they cannot be authoritative in an objective sense even for those who have them. Though such people commonly do subjectively take their revelations as authoritative, this is no more than a sign that they are insufficiently critical. There is no reason why they too, in their more sober moments, should not realize that their experiences are open to explanations which accord them no veridical force. Consequently, these experiences do not show that what is based on the understanding and the senses is only one 'order of truth' among others: there may indeed be more than one kind of consciousness, but the one familiar order of truth can accommodate them all.

We may now turn to the other issue, whether we can take religious experience as sufficient in itself, without attempting to base on it any argument for any further, supernatural, reality. What sort of value have these experiences in themselves? Here, too, however, there are several more specific questions. First, what value is found in these experiences by those who take them as what they purport to be, revelations of a deeper, supernatural, realm? Secondly, what value should *we* assign to these experiences, if we abandon any truth-claims that they involve, but still consider the experiences as they are, containing those truth-claims? Thirdly, are these experiences more valuable as they are than otherwise similar ones that lacked those truth-claims would be? Fourthly, would they remain valuable if they had still the very same religious content, the same intentional objects, but those who had them no longer believed this content to be objectively true?

Undoubtedly those who have these experiences and take them seriously find immense value in them. Yet even they will sometimes allow that this value is conditional upon their further fruits. St. Theresa herself argues that her visions are genuinely heavenly ones, not the work of the devil or the sport of her own imagination, on the ground that they have yielded 'a harvest of ineffable spiritual riches, and an admirable renewal of bodily strength' (quoted, pp. 41–2). But James's assessment is rather different:

> She had a powerful intellect of the practical order. She wrote admirable descriptive psychology, possessed a will equal to any emergency, great talent for politics and business, a buoyant disposition, and a first-rate literary style. She was tenaciously aspiring, and put her whole life at the service of her religious ideals. Yet so paltry were these, according to our present way of thinking, that (although I know that others have been moved differently) I confess that my only feeling in reading her has been pity that so much vitality of soul should have found such poor employment.
>
> . . . in the main her idea of religion seems to have been that of an endless amatory flirtation . . . between the devotee and the deity. (pp. 338–9)

In other words, St. Theresa's experiences fail by the very test that she herself proposed: the harvest was not, in James's opinion, one of spiritual riches. Similarly, James describes St. John of the Cross as 'a Spanish mystic who flourished—or rather who existed, for there was little that suggested flourishing about him—in the sixteenth century' (p. 300), and he shows how the 'characteristic practical consequences' of saintliness, namely devoutness, asceticism, strength of soul, purity, charity, and the cult of poverty and obedience, while some measure of them may be valuable, can all run to absurd extremes (pp. 270–320 and 333–65). 'When their intellectual outlook is narrow, [the saints] fall into all sorts of holy excesses, fanaticism or theopathic absorption, self-torment, prudery, scrupulosity, gullibility, and morbid inability to meet the world. By the very intensity of his fidelity to the paltry ideals with which an inferior intellect may inspire him, a saint can be even more objectionable and damnable than a superficial carnal man would be in the same situation' (p. 358). Yet James also allows (p. 364) that the greatest saints are immediate successes. In short, once we give up the assumption that the content of religious experience is true, we cannot reach any unequivocal estimate of their worth: whether their fruits are good or evil depends very much on other, surrounding factors.

Our third question, whether these experiences would be more or less valuable without the specifically religious truth-claims that they contain, is also hard to answer. We have noted that J. S. Mill and others display non-religious analogues of the sequence of depression followed by an inspiring conversion. There can be little doubt that John Bunyan would have undergone cycles of misery and elevation even if he had not been caught up in the movement of religious thought that gave his experiences their specific character (pp. 163–5, 191–3). On the other hand the religious tradition itself, like the medical one, often helps to create the diseases that it boasts of curing. Religious teachings, taken all

"You are God"

Leo Tolstoy

God is the unlimited spiritual source, complete in Himself, which I am aware of as my "I" and which I acknowledge in all that lives. . . .

God breathes through our lives and through all life in the world. He and I are one and the same. As soon as I understood this, I became God.

From *Diaries* (1910).

too literally by some who are exposed to them, help to generate the extreme sense of sin and failure which characterizes the sick soul and gives it an overwhelming need for salvation. Without the associated religious beliefs, both the antecedent misery and the subsequent relief would probably be, in general, less extreme. On balance, this might be a gain more often than a loss.

The answers to both our second and third questions must also be affected by this consideration: if the religious experiences do not yield any argument for a further supernatural reality, and if, as we have seen in previous chapters, there is no other good argument for such a conclusion, then these experiences include in their content beliefs that are probably false and in any case unjustified. This, it seems, must be scored as a disvalue against them. However, this judgement must remain provisional until we have considered . . . whether belief without reason, without intellectual justification, can nevertheless be defended.

Our fourth question was whether these experiences would remain valuable if the experiences themselves were more critical about them, and abandoned the belief that their specifically religious content is objectively true. Could they keep them just as experiences, but still with significance for and power over the rest of their lives? That seems unlikely. Such a change is more likely to be equivalent to replacing these experiences with their non-religious counterparts, as envisaged in our third question. Systematically to withdraw the claim to objective truth would in time significantly alter the internal quality of the experiences, and reduce, though not necessarily cancel, their influence. . . .

Robert Nozick

"BEYOND"

ROBERT NOZICK is a professor of philosophy and the chair of the department at Harvard University. He has written on nearly every area of philosophy but is perhaps most widely known for his controversial contribution to political philosophy, *Anarchy, State and Utopia* (1974). He is one of the few leading analytic philosophers who has written sympathetically about Eastern philosophy and mystical traditions. His books include *Philosophical Explanations* (1981) and *Philosophical Meditations*.

The important hymn from the Vedas, the Hymn of Creation, begins "Nonbeing then existed not nor being". This is the translation by Radhakrishnan and Moore.[1] In the Griffith translation, we find this as "Then was not nonexistent nor existent"; in the Max Muller translation, "There was then neither what is nor what is not."

How can what there was "then", that is, in the beginning or before everything else, be neither nonbeing nor being, neither nonexistent nor existent, neither is nor is not? For being and nonbeing, existent and nonexistent, is and is not, seem exhaustive. There does not seem to be any

1. Sarvepalli Radhakrishnan and Charles Moore, *Sourcebook in Indian Philosophy* (Princeton University Press, Princeton, 1957), p. 23.

other possibility. In accordance with the law of the excluded middle, everything is either one or the other.

However, sometimes things that seem to exhaust the possibilities do not, rather they do so only within a certain realm. Consider color. Everything is either colored (singly colored or multicolored) or uncolored, that is, transparent. Either a thing is colored or it is uncolored, what other possibility is there? Yet the number 5, and Beethoven's Quartet Number 15, are neither colored nor uncolored. These are not the sort of things that can have or fail to have colors—they are not physical or spatial objects or events. (Do not confuse them with numerals or written musical scores, which can be colored.)

Let us say that this pair of terms (colored, uncolored) has a presupposition; it presupposes that the thing or subject to which the terms 'colored' or 'uncolored' are applied is a physical or spatial object or event. When the presupposition 'X is a physical or spatial object or event' is satisfied, then 'X is colored' and 'X is uncolored' exhaust the possibilities. When the presupposition is satisfied, X cannot be neither colored nor uncolored. However, when that presupposition is not satisfied, then X may be neither colored nor uncolored.[2]

Similarly, the pair of terms (loud, not loud) presupposes that X is a sound or a possible sound source, that is, a physical object or event. The number 5 is neither loud nor not-loud. The pair of terms (harmonious, unharmonious) presupposes that a thing has parts related in a certain way. An elementary particle itself is neither harmonious nor unharmonious.

2. The topic of presupposition as giving rise to truth value gaps was introduced into recent philosophy by P. F. Strawson, "On Referring," *Mind,* Vol. 59, 1950, pp. 320–344. For an indication of the various approaches in the literature since then, see the following: B. C. Van Fraassen. "Presuppositions, Supervaluations and Free Logic" in K. Lambert, ed., *The Logical Way of Doing Things,* Yale University Press, New Haven, 1969, pp. 67–92; Robert Stalnaker, "Presuppositions," *Journal of Philosophical Logic,* Vol. 2, 1973, pp. 447–457; L. Karttunen, "Presuppositions of Compound Sentences," *Linguistic Inquiry,* Vol. 4, 1973, pp. 169–193; J. Katz, *Propositional Structure and Illocutionary Force,* Harvard University Press, Cambridge, 1980, pp. 88–112; G. Gazdar, *Pragmatics,* Academic Press, New York, 1979, chs. 5, 6.

Might it be that every pair of predicates that seems to exhaust the possibilities, apparently contradictory, has a presupposition beyond which neither of the terms applies? We might picture a presuppositional situation as follows (Figure 1). A rectangle represents all the things there are. Encircled things are the things that satisfy the presupposition. The pair of terms t_1 and t_2 divides up everything that satisfies the presupposition; each such thing is one or the other. Outside the set of things that satisfies the presupposition are all the things that are neither, things to which neither one of these terms applies. The crosshatched area contains those things that are neither t_1 nor t_2.

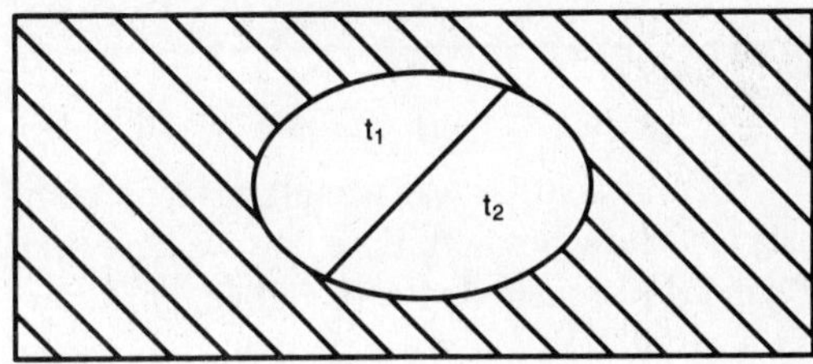

FIGURE 1

There are two ways we can try to avoid there being any presupposition. Where the rectangle is everything that exists, everything there is, we can simply draw a line across it, across all of it, letting t_1 apply to one resulting part and t_2 to the other (Figure 2). Nothing is left outside.

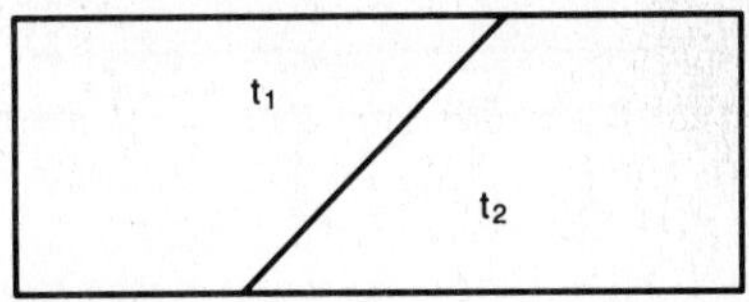

FIGURE 2

However, this assumes that 'exists' exhausts everything, that there is nothing that doesn't exist. This need not faze us; if there are things that do not exist, Santa Claus, golden mountains, and so on, let our large rectangle be all those things that do or could exist, and let our line then distinguish those things that exist from those that do not. Surely, there is no presupposition now.

This assumes, however, that the pair of terms (exists, doesn't exist) does not itself have a presupposition, that it does not apply just to a certain range of things with something outside. It assumes that we do not have the situation shown in Figure 3, with the crosshatched area being those things that neither exist nor don't exist.

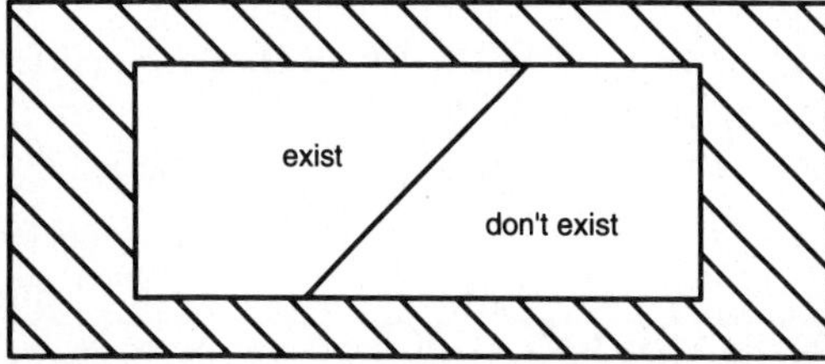

FIGURE 3

There is another way we might try to eliminate any presupposition. Until now we have been specifying a domain by the rectangle, and drawing a distinction within it. (I now use a wavy line for the distinction.) But we had worries that there was something outside the domain, as in Figure 4. Why do we not instead just draw the

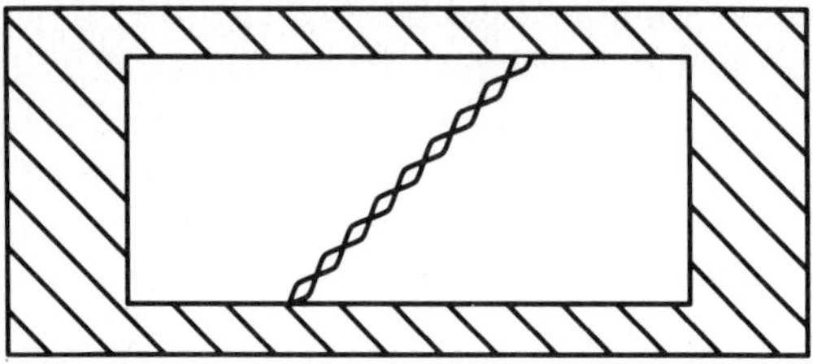

FIGURE 4

distinction? In Figure 5 we mark t_1 off against everything else. There appears to be no further worry that there are things outside; t_1 is distinguished from whatever else there is.

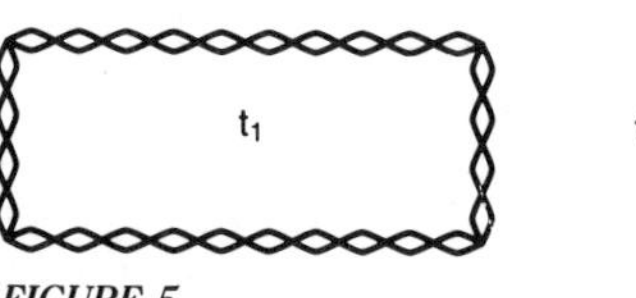

FIGURE 5

However, there are reasons for thinking we encounter paradoxes and contradictions if we proceed without first specifying the domain and then drawing distinctions within it.* Also, we said "it is distinguished from whatever else there is." But why think *is* does not itself have a presupposition? We distinguish t_1 from whatever else ______________. If the blank itself has a presupposition, then the structure of the situation is as represented by Figure 6.

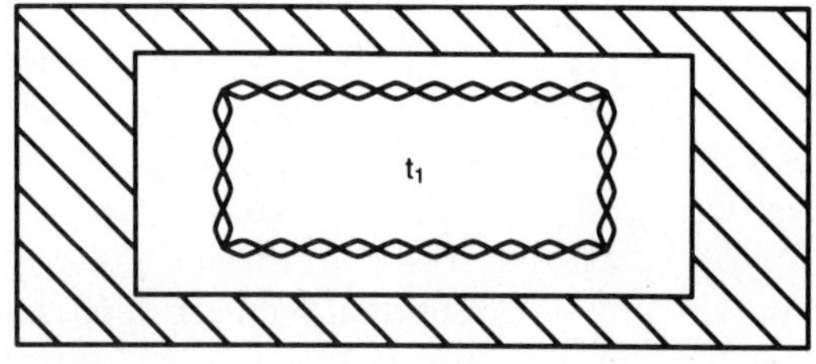

FIGURE 6

I suggest we understand the beginning of the Hymn of Creation, "nonbeing then existed not nor being", as saying that the pairs being and nonbeing, existent and nonexistent, and is and isn't have presuppositions, that the terms within these pairs apply and exhaust the possibilities only within a certain domain, while outside this domain a thing may be neither. Such theories are not unknown in the West: Plato says God is "beyond being" (*Republic* VI, 509b), and Plotinus makes this central to his theory of the One; Judah Halevi (*Kuzari* II, 2) holds that neither of a pair of contrasting terms applies to God; and there are other examples.

It is plausible that whatever every existent thing comes from, their source, falls outside the categories of existence and nonexistence. Moreover, we then avoid the question: why does *that* exist? It doesn't *exist.* Strictly, that which is beyond those categories neither exists nor doesn't exist. But if you had to say one, you would men-

*This is the usual moral drawn from the set-theoretical paradoxes. So set theory is done without a universal set which contains everything, or with a class which does but is ontologically different from what is within it and so not subject to the same manipulations as sets. Or, most securely, set theory is done in iterative fashion, starting the null set and iterating operations to generate new and always limited sets.

tion whichever of existence and nonexistence was closer to its status. If both were equally close or distant, if it was equidistant from both, you might say: it exists *and* it doesn't exist. We read this as: strictly speaking neither holds, and it is no more distant from one than from the other. This provides us with a possible explanation of the tendency to utter contradictions on the part of those who talk about such things.[3]

There are at least four questions to ask about a theory that holds that the pair existence and nonexistence has a presupposition that can fail to be satisfied. First, what is the presupposition, what is the condition which all things that exist and all that nonexist satisfy, yet which need not be satisfied? Second, what reason is there to believe that something does fail to satisfy the presupposition, that there is something beyond existence and nonexistence? Third, is there a biggest box, with nothing outside it? And fourth, if there is, how can one tell one has reached it, that there is not still some hidden transcendable presupposition, outside of which is another realm that fits none of the previous categories?

This chapter is not the place to deal with all of these questions. Let me say just a few words about the first. Is the presupposition statable? Well, we can coin a short word. We can say that only those things which *th* exist or nonexist, that the presupposition of the pair exist and nonexist is that there be (this is a verb coming up) *thing.** We can coin this word to denote the presupposition, but can we explain it in terms we already understand?

It seems we can only come to understand the presupposition ostensively. We can state the boundaries and understand what they are only by standing outside them. If this is so, and if experience of what is outside the boundary is necessary to get one to see what the presupposition of the boundary is and to understand what can transcend it, then such experience will be necessary to understand the position, to grasp its content. The experiences can function not only to support the position (in the next section we shall consider the intricate question of whether they do so) but also to ostensively explain it. The ostensive route to understanding the position may be the only route we have, raising the possibility that all those who understand it realize that it is true. (Shouldn't some accounts of a priori knowledge be revised, then, to exclude this realization as a priori?)

Persons who have had such experiences struggle to describe them; they say all descriptions are inadequate, that strictly the experience is ineffable. This goes beyond saying that we cannot describe it in terms already available to us, that an ostensive encounter with it is needed to know what it is like and what any term applying to it means. Perhaps such ostensive acquaintance is needed to understand what sounds or sights are, an understanding which a blind or deaf person would lack (in the absence of direct stimulation of the brain to produce the experience). Still, those of us who do have the experience can produce a descriptive vocabulary to describe them. Sights and sounds are not ineffable. Perhaps those who call the experience of what is beyond existence and nonexistence ineffable merely mean that they cannot adequately describe it to those who have not had it. If so, their use of "ineffable" is misleading. Perhaps they mean something more, however, namely that there is a presupposition to the application of terms, that we normally live within the realm where the presupposition is satisfied and hence never consider the possibility that there is such a presupposition, and finally, that their experience has taken them beyond the realm of the presupposition to where terms, all terms,

3. Dale Gottlieb has suggested to me another view, that contradictions do fit some situations (via the existing rules of the language), and the mystic realizes this after his experience. Different mystics use the same contradictions, so perhaps what the mystic experiences is effable, and is effed by contradictions. See G. K. Pletcher, "Mysticism, Contradiction, and Ineffability," *American Philosophy Quarterly,* Vol. 10, 1973, pp. 201–211.

*We can continue with a verb-form theory that goes beyond merely the presuppositional view. We might view "nothing" as the present continuous of the verb 'to noth', and "something" as the present continuous of the verb 'to someth'. Clearly, an x noths or someths, it is nothing or something only if it ths. What 'to noth' and 'to someth' have in common is 'to th'. (The following sentence contains three present continuous verbs, and no nouns except insofar as the quantificational structure does duty for them.) Only thing is nothing or something.

just do not apply. This raises problems of a familiar sort: what about second-level terms such as "ineffable" or "is such that first-level terms do not apply to it"? We can leave these problems aside now.

Of something that does not satisfy the presupposition of the pair exists and nonexists, and so neither exists nor nonexists, we cannot ask why it exists. But though it does not exist, it does ______________. Some verb must describe its status; so let us just coin a verb, 'to aum', to fill in the blank. Auming is what that which is beyond existence and nonexistence does. It aums. Now it seems we can ask: why does it aum? Why does it aum rather than not?

If the ineffability doctrine were true and the presuppositions for the application of terms were not satisfied, then of course we could not coin a term for what it does and then ask why it does that. (But couldn't we just wonder "why?" and mentally gesture in the direction of the ineffable? Or does the term "why" fail to get a grip, along with the other terms?) To keep the possibility of saying something further, I shall proceed on the assumption that a term can be applied so that a question can be asked. It aums, and we ask why.

Without knowing more about what is beyond existence and nonexistence, and about auming, it is difficult to see how to begin to discuss the question. There is one structural possibility worth mentioning, however. Various versions of the ontological argument (for the existence of God) founder on their treatment of 'exists'. By treating existence or necessary existence as a property or perfection, they allow us to consider the nth most perfect being ($n = 1,2,3, \ldots$), and so to overpopulate our universe. What the ontological argument wanted to discuss, though, was a being whose essence included existence; it is a structural possibility similar to this, rather than the deduction of existence from the concept of a thing, that I want to take up. Can the nature of whatever is beyond existence and nonexistence include auming, so that there is no possibility that *it* does not aum? We need not suppose that we are (or aren't) speaking of God here; when it says "nonbeing then existed not, nor being" the Hymn to Creation is not speaking of God. Nor am I constructing an ontological argument from the concept of what is beyond existence and nonexistence to its auming. Perhaps auming is part of its essence without being part of the concept of it. Indeed it is difficult to suppose we have presented a determinate concept of it here at all, if the only route to knowing what is beyond existence and nonexistence and about auming is through an experience of it. My intention here is merely to raise the possibility that there is no room for the question "why does it aum?"

Consider, as an analogy, the structure of all possibilities. A particular possibility is realized or is actual or exists, and another is not realized and so nonexists. What exists and nonexists are particular possibilities. The structure of all possibilities underlies existence and nonexistence. That structure itself doesn't exist and it doesn't nonexist. A presupposition for the application of this pair of terms (exists, nonexists) is not satisfied by the structure of all possibilities. Now suppose we coin a verb for the status of the structure of all possibilities, saying that it *modes.* Is it clear that there is room for the question, why does the structure of all possibilities mode? Can *it* fail to mode?

I do not claim that the structure of all possibilities is what the Hymn of Creation begins with, or is what is found in experience. I believe that the Hymn of Creation means to speak of what underlies and gives rise to the structure of possibilities. What that might be we shall pursue in a later chapter. My purpose here is to give an example of something that does not satisfy the presupposition of the pair exists and nonexists, yet about whose status there may be no room for the question why it does that, why the structure of all possibilities modes. All this is to give one some feeling for how there might be no room for the question of why what aums does aum. Even so, there still would remain the question of how and why existence and nonexistence arise from what aums.

Huston Smith

"DO DRUGS HAVE RELIGIOUS IMPORT?"

HUSTON SMITH was a professor of philosophy at Syracuse University, the Massachusetts Institute of Technology, and Washington University. Among his books are *Forgotten Truth: The Primordial Tradition* (1977) and *The Religions of Man* (1958).

Until six months ago, if I picked up my phone in the Cambridge area and dialed KISS-BIG, a voice would answer, "If-if." These were coincidences: KISS-BIG happened to be the letter equivalents of an arbitrarily assigned telephone number, and I.F.I.F. represented the initials of an organization with the improbable name of the International Federation for Internal Freedom. But the coincidences were apposite to the point of being poetic. "Kiss big" caught the euphoric, manic, life-embracing attitude that characterized this most publicized of the organizations formed to explore the newly synthesized consciousness-changing substances; the organization itself was surely one of the "iffyest" phenomena to appear on our social and intellectual scene in some time. It produced the first firings in Harvard's history, an ultimatum to get out of Mexico in five days, and "the miracle of Marsh Chapel," in which, during a two-and-one-half-hour Good Friday service, ten theological students and professors ingested psilocybin and were visited by what they generally reported to be the deepest religious experiences of their lives.

Despite the last of these phenomena and its numerous if less dramatic parallels, students of religion appear by and large to be dismissing the psychedelic drugs that have sprung to our attention in the '60s as having little religious relevance. The position taken in one of the most forward-looking volumes of theological essays to have appeared in recent years—*Soundings,* edited by A. R. Vidler[1]—accepts R. C. Zaehner's *Mysticism Sacred and Profane* as having "fully examined and refuted" the religious claims for mescalin which Aldous Huxley sketched in *The Doors of Perception.* This closing of the case strikes me as premature, for it looks as if the drugs have light to throw on the history of religion, the phenomenology of religion, the philosophy of religion, and the practice of the religious life itself.

1. DRUGS AND RELIGION VIEWED HISTORICALLY

In his trial-and-error life explorations man almost everywhere has stumbled upon connections between vegetables (eaten or brewed) and actions (yogi breathing exercises, whirling-dervish dances, flagellations) that alter states of consciousness. From the psychopharmacological standpoint we now understand these states to be the products of changes in brain chemistry. From the sociological perspective we see that they tend to be connected in some way with

Reprinted from Huston Smith, "Do Drugs Have Religious Import?" *The Journal of Philosophy* LXI, 18 (1964), 517–530, by permission of the publisher and the author.

1. *Soundings: Essays Concerning Christian Understandings,* A. R. Vidler, ed. (Cambridge: University Press, 1962). The statement cited appears on page 72, in H. A. William's essay on "Theology and self-awareness."

religion. If we discount the wine used in Christian communion services, the instances closest to us in time and space are the peyote of The Native American [Indian] Church and Mexico's 2000-year-old "sacred mushrooms," the latter rendered in Aztec as "God's Flesh"—striking parallel to "the body of our Lord" in the Christian eucharist. Beyond these neighboring instances lie the *soma* of the Hindus, the *haoma* and hemp of the Zoroastrians, the Dionysus of the Greeks who "everywhere . . . taught men the culture of the vine and the mysteries of his worship and everywhere [was] accepted as a god,"[2] the *benzoin* of Southeast Asia, Zen's tea whose fifth cup purifies and whose sixth "calls to the realm of the immortals,"[3] the *pituri* of the Australian aborigines, and probably the mystic *kykeon* that was eaten and drunk at the climactic close of the sixth day of the Eleusinian mysteries.[4] There is no need to extend the list, as a reasonably complete account is available in Philippe de Félice's comprehensive study of the subject, *Poisons sacrés, ivresses divines.*

More interesting than the fact that consciousness-changing devices have been linked with religion is the possibility that they actually initiated many of the religious perspectives which, taking root in history, continued after their psychedelic origins were forgotten. Bergson saw the first movement of Hindus and Greeks toward "dynamic religion" as associated with the "divine rapture" found in intoxicating beverages;[5] more recently Robert Graves, Gordon Wasson, and Alan Watts have suggested that most religions arose from such chemically induced theophanies. Mary Barnard is the most explicit proponent of this thesis. "Which . . . was more likely to happen first," she asks,[6] "the spontaneously generated idea of an afterlife in which the disembodied soul, liberated from the restrictions of time and space, experiences eternal bliss, or the accidental discovery of hallucinogenic plants that give a sense of euphoria, dislocate the center of consciousness, and distort time and space, making them balloon outward in greatly expanded vistas?" Her own answer is that "the [latter] experience might have had . . . an almost explosive effect on the largely dormant minds of men, causing them to think of things they had never thought of before. This, if you like, is direct revelation." Her use of the subjunctive "might" renders this formulation of her answer equivocal, but she concludes her essay on a note that is completely unequivocal: "Looking at the matter coldly, unintoxicated and unentranced, I am willing to prophesy that fifty theobotanists working for fifty years would make the current theories concerning the origins of much mythology and theology as out-of-date as pre-Copernican astronomy."

This is an important hypothesis—one which must surely engage the attention of historians of religion for some time to come. But as I am concerned here only to spot the points at which the drugs erupt onto the field of serious religious study, not to ride the geysers to whatever heights, I shall not pursue Miss Barnard's thesis. Having located what appears to be the crux of the historical question, namely the extent to which drugs not merely duplicate or simulate theologically sponsored experiences but generate or shape theologies themselves, I turn to phenomenology.

2. DRUGS AND RELIGION VIEWED PHENOMENOLOGICALLY

Phenomenology attempts a careful description of human experience. The question the drugs pose for the phenomenology of religion, therefore, is whether the experiences they induce differ from religious experiences reached naturally, and if so how.

2. Edith Hamilton, *Mythology* (New York: Mentor, 1953), p. 55.

3. Quoted in Alan Watts, *The Spirit of Zen* (New York: Grove Press, 1958), p. 110.

4. George Mylonas, *Eleusis and the Eleusinian Mysteries* (Princeton, N.J.: Princeton Univ. Press, 1961), p. 284.

5. *Two Sources of Morality and Religion* (New York: Holt, 1935), pp. 206–212.

6. "The God in the Flowerpot," *The American Scholar* 32, No. 4 (Autumn 1963), 584, 586.

Even the Bible notes that chemically induced psychic states bear *some* resemblance to religious ones. Peter had to appeal to a circumstantial criterion—the early hour of the day—to defend those who were caught up in the Pentecostal experience against the charge that they were merely drunk: "These men are not drunk, as you suppose, since it is only the third hour of the day" (Acts 2:15); and Paul initiates the comparison when he admonishes the Ephesians not to "get drunk with wine . . . but [to] be filled with the spirit" (Ephesians 5:18). Are such comparisons, paralleled in the accounts of virtually every religion, superficial? How far can they be pushed?

Not all the way, students of religion have thus far insisted. With respect to the new drugs, Prof. R. C. Zaehner has drawn the line emphatically. "The importance of Huxley's *Doors of Perception,*" he writes, "is that in it the author clearly makes the claim that what he experienced under the influence of mescalin is closely comparable to a genuine mystical experience. If he is right, . . . the conclusions . . . are alarming."[7] Zaehner thinks that Huxley is not right, but I fear that it is Zaehner who is mistaken.

There are, of course, innumerable drug experiences that have no religious feature; they can be sensual as readily as spiritual, trivial as readily as transforming, capricious as readily as sacramental. If there is one point about which every student of the drugs agrees, it is that there is no such thing as the drug experience *per se*—no experience that the drugs, as it were, merely secrete. Every experience is a mix of three ingredients: drug, set (the psychological make-up of the individual), and setting (the social and

7. *Mysticism Sacred and Profane* (New York: Oxford, 1961), p. 12.

"A Zen Diagnosis: The Sickness of the Mind"

Yasutani-Roshi

Between a supremely perfected Buddha and us, who are ordinary, there is no difference as to substance. This "substance" can be likened to water. One of the salient characteristics of water is its conformability: when put into a round vessel it becomes round, when put into a square vessel it becomes square. We have this same adaptability, but as we live bound and fettered through ignorance of our true nature, we have forfeited this freedom. To pursue the metaphor, we can say that the mind of a Buddha is like water that is calm, deep, and crystal clear, and upon which the "moon of truth" reflects fully and perfectly. The mind of the ordinary man, on the other hand, is like murky water, constantly being churned by the gales of delusive thought and no longer able to reflect the moon of truth. The moon nonetheless shines steadily upon the waves, but as the waters are roiled we are unable to see its reflection. Thus we lead lives that are frustrating and meaningless.

How can we fully illumine our life and personality with the moon of truth? We need first to purify this water, to calm the surging waves by halting the winds of discursive thought. In other words, we must empty our minds of what the Kegon (Avatamsaka) sutra calls the "conceptual thought of man." Most people place a high value on abstract thought, but Buddhism has clearly demonstrated that discriminative thinking lies at the root of delusion. I once heard someone say: "Thought is the sickness of the human mind." From the Buddhist point of view this is quite true. To be sure, abstract thinking is useful when wisely employed—which is to say, when its nature and limitations are properly understood—but as long as human beings remain slaves to their intellect, fettered and controlled by it, they can well be called sick.

From Phillip Kapleau, *The Three Pillars of Zen* (1980).

physical environment in which it is taken). But given the right set and setting, the drugs can induce religious experiences indistinguishable from experiences that occur spontaneously. Nor need set and setting be exceptional. The way the statistics are currently running, it looks as if from one-fourth to one-third of the general population will have religious experiences if they take the drugs under naturalistic conditions, meaning by this conditions in which the researcher supports the subject but does not try to influence the direction his experience will take. Among subjects who have strong religious inclinations to begin with, the proportion of those having religious experiences jumps to three-fourths. If they take the drugs in settings that are religious too, the ratio soars to nine in ten.

How do we know that the experiences these people have really are religious? We can begin with the fact that they say they are. The "one-fourth to one-third of the general population" figure is drawn from two sources. Ten months after they had had their experiences, 24 per cent of the 194 subjects in a study by the Californian psychiatrist Oscar Janiger characterized their experiences as having been religious.[8] Thirty-two per cent of the 74 subjects in Ditman and Hayman's study reported, looking back on their LSD experience, that it looked as if it had been "very much" or "quite a bit" a religious experience; 42 per cent checked as true the statement that they "were left with a greater awareness of God, or a higher power, or ultimate reality."[9] The statement that three-fourths of subjects having religious "sets" will have religious experiences comes from the reports of sixty-nine religious professionals who took the drugs while the Harvard project was in progress.[10]

In the absence of (a) a single definition of religious experience acceptable to psychologists of religion generally and (b) foolproof ways of ascertaining whether actual experiences exemplify any definition, I am not sure there is any better way of telling whether the experiences of the 333 men and women involved in the above studies were religious than by noting whether they seemed so to them. But if more rigorous methods are preferred, they exist; they have been utilized, and they confirm the conviction of the man in the street that drug experiences can indeed be religious. In his doctoral study at Harvard University, Walter Pahnke worked out a typology of religious experience (in this instance of the mystical variety) based on the classic cases of mystical experiences as summarized in Walter Stace's *Mysticism and Philosophy.* He then administered psilocybin to ten theology students and professors in the setting of a Good Friday service. The drug was given "double-blind," meaning that neither Dr. Pahnke nor his subjects knew which ten were getting psilocybin and which ten placebos to constitute a control group. Subsequently the reports the subjects wrote of their experiences were laid successively before three college-graduate housewives who, without being informed about the nature of the study, were asked to rate each statement as to the degree (strong, moderate, slight, or none) to which it exemplified each of the nine traits of mystical experience enumerated in the typology of mysticism worked out in advance. When the test of significance was applied to their statistics, it showed that "those subjects who received psilocybin experienced phenomena which were indistinguishable from, if not identical with . . . the categories defined by our typology of mysticism."[11]

With the thought that the reader might like to test his own powers of discernment on the question being considered, I insert here a simple test I gave to a group of Princeton students fol-

8. Quoted in William H. McGlothlin, "Long-lasting Effects of LSD on Certain Attitudes in Normals," printed for private distribution by the RAND Corporation, May 1962, p. 16.

9. *Ibid.*, pp. 45, 46.

10. Timothy Leary, "The Religious Experience: Its Production and Interpretation," *The Psychedelic Review,* 1, No. 3 (1964), 325.

11. "Drugs and Mysticism: An Analysis of the Relationship between Psychedelic Drugs and the Mystical Consciousness," a thesis presented to the Committee in Higher Degrees in History and Philosophy of Religion, Harvard University, June 1963.

lowing a recent discussion sponsored by the Woodrow Wilson Society:

Below are accounts of two religious experiences. One occurred under the influence of drugs, one without their influence. Check the one you think *was* drug-induced.

I

Suddenly I burst into a vast, new, indescribably wonderful universe. Although I am writing this over a year later, the thrill of the surprise and amazement, the awesomeness of the revelation, the engulfment in an overwhelming feeling-wave of gratitude and blessed wonderment, are as fresh, and the memory of the experience is as vivid, as if it had happened five minutes ago. And yet to concoct anything by way of description that would even hint at the magnitude, the sense of ultimate reality . . . this seems such an impossible task. The knowledge which has infused and affected every aspect of my life came instantaneously and with such complete force of certainty that it was impossible, then or since, to doubt its validity.

II

All at once, without warning of any kind, I found myself wrapped in a flame-colored cloud. For an instant I thought of fire . . . the next, I knew that the fire was within myself. Directly afterward there came upon me a sense of exultation, of immense joyousness accompanied or immediately followed by an intellectual illumination impossible to describe. Among other things, I did not merely come to believe, but I saw that the universe is not composed of dead matter, but is, on the contrary, a living Presence; I became conscious in myself of eternal life. . . . I saw that all men are immortal: that the cosmic order is such that without any preadventure all things work together for the good of each and all; that the foundation principle of the world . . . is what we call love, and that the happiness of each and all is in the long run absolutely certain.

On the occasion referred to, twice as many students (46) answered incorrectly as answered correctly (23). I bury the correct answer in a footnote to preserve the reader's opportunity to test himself.[12]

Why, in the face of this considerable evidence, does Zaehner hold that drug experiences cannot be authentically religious? There appear to be three reasons:

1. His own experience was "utterly trivial." This of course proves that not all drug experiences are religious; it does not prove that no drug experiences are religious.
2. He thinks the experiences of others that appear religious to them are not truly so. Zaehner distinguishes three kinds of mysticism: nature mysticism, in which the soul is united with the natural world; monistic mysticism, in which the soul merges with an impersonal absolute; and theism, in which the soul confronts the living, personal God. He concedes that drugs can induce the first two species of mysticism, but not its supreme instance, the theistic. As proof, he analyzes Huxley's experience as recounted in *The Doors of Perception* to show that it produced at best a blend of nature and monistic mysticism. Even if we were to accept Zaehner's evaluation of the three forms of mysticism, Huxley's case, and indeed Zaehner's entire book, would prove only that not every mystical experience induced by the drugs is theistic. Insofar as Zaehner goes beyond this to imply that drugs do not and cannot induce theistic mysticism, he not only goes beyond the evidence but proceeds in the face of it. James Slotkin reports that the peyote Indians "see visions, which may be of Christ Himself. Sometimes they hear the voice of the Great Spirit. Sometimes they become aware of the presence of God and of those personal shortcomings which

12. The first account is quoted anonymously in "The Issue of the Consciousness-expanding Drugs," *Main Currents in Modern Thought,* 20, No. 1 (September-October 1963), 10–11. The second experience was that of Dr. R. M. Bucke, the author of *Cosmic Consciousness,* as quoted in William James, *The Varieties of Religious Experience* (New York Modern Library, 1902), pp. 390–391. The former experience occurred under the influence of drugs: the latter did not.

must be correct if they are to do His will.[13] And G. M. Carstairs, reporting on the use of psychedelic *bhang* in India, quotes a Brahmin as saying, "It gives good bhakti. . . . You get a very good bhakti with bhang," *bhakti* being precisely Hinduism's theistic variant.[14]

3. There is a third reason why Zaehner might doubt that drugs can induce genuinely mystical experiences. Zaehner is a Roman Catholic, and Roman Catholic doctrine teaches that mystical rapture is a gift of grace and as such can never be reduced to man's control. This may be true; certainly the empirical evidence cited does not preclude the possibility of a genuine ontological or theological difference between natural and drug-induced religious experiences. At this point, however, we are considering phenomenology rather than ontology, description rather than interpretation, and on this level there is no difference. Descriptively, drug experiences cannot be distinguished from their natural religious counterpart. When the current philosophical authority on mysticism, W. T. Stace, was asked whether the drug experience is similar to the mystical experience, he answered, "It's not a matter of its being *similar* to mystical experience; it *is* mystical experience."

What we seem to be witnessing in Zaehner's *Mysticism Sacred and Profane* is a reenactment of the age-old pattern in the conflict between science and religion. Whenever a new controversy arises, religion's first impulse is to deny the disturbing evidence science has produced. Seen in perspective, Zaehner's refusal to admit that drugs can induce experiences descriptively indistinguishable from those which are spontaneously religious is the current counterpart of the seventeenth-century theologians' refusal to look through Galileo's telescope or, when they did, their persistence on dismissing what they saw as machinations of the devil. When the fact that drugs can trigger religious experiences becomes incontrovertible, discussion will move to the more difficult question of how this new fact is to be interpreted. The latter question leads beyond phenomenology into philosophy.

3. DRUGS AND RELIGION VIEWED PHILOSOPHICALLY

Why do people reject evidence? Because they find it threatening, we may suppose. Theologians are not the only professionals to utilize this mode of defense. In his *Personal Knowledge,*[15] Michael Polanyi recounts the way the medical profession ignored such palpable facts as the painless amputation of human limbs, performed before their own eyes in hundreds of successive cases, concluding that the subjects were impostors who were either deluding their physicians or colluding with them. One physician, Esdaile, carried out about 300 major operations painlessly under mesmeric trance in India, but neither in India nor in Great Britain could he get medical journals to print accounts of his work. Polanyi attributes this closed-mindedness to "lack of a conceptual framework in which their discoveries could be separated from specious and untenable admixtures."

The "untenable mixture" in the fact that psychotomimetic drugs can induce religious experience is its apparent implicate: that religious disclosures are no more veridical than psychotic ones. For religious skeptics, this conclusion is obviously not untenable at all; it fits in beautifully with their thesis that *all* religion is at heart an escape from reality. Psychotics avoid reality by retiring into dream worlds of make-believe; what better evidence that religious visionaries do the same than the fact that identical changes in brain chemistry produce both states of mind? Had not Marx already warned us that religion is the "opiate" of the people?—apparently he was

13. James S. Slotkin, *Peyote Religion* (New York: Free Press of Glencoe, 1956).

14. "Daru and Bhang," *Quarterly Journal of the Study of Alcohol,* 15 (1954), 229.

15. Chicago: Univ. of Chicago Press, 1958.

more literally accurate than he supposed. Freud was likewise too mild. He "never doubted that religious phenomena are to be understood only on the model of the neurotic symptoms of the individual."[16] He should have said "psychotic symptoms."

So the religious skeptic is likely to reason. What about the religious believer? Convinced that religious experiences are not fundamentally delusory, can he admit that psychotomimetic drugs can occasion them? To do so he needs (to return to Polanyi's words) "a conceptual framework in which [the discoveries can] be separated from specious and untenable admixtures," the "untenable admixture" being in this case the conclusion that religious experiences are in general delusory.

One way to effect the separation would be to argue that, despite phenomenological similarities between natural and drug-induced religious experiences, they are separated by a crucial *ontological* difference. Such an argument would follow the pattern of theologians who argue for the "real presence" of Christ's body and blood in the bread and wine of the Eucharist despite their admission that chemical analysis, confined as it is to the level of "accidents" rather than "essences," would not disclose this presence. But this distinction will not appeal to many today, for it turns on an essence-accident metaphysics which is not widely accepted. Instead of fighting a rear-guard action by insisting that if drug and non-drug religious experiences cannot be distinguished empirically there must be some transempirical factor that distinguishes them and renders the drug experience profane, I wish to explore the possibility of accepting drug-induced experiences as religious without relinquishing confidence in the truth-claims of religious experience generally.

To begin with the weakest of all arguments, the argument from authority: William James did not discount *his* insights that occurred while his brain chemistry was altered. The paragraph in which he retrospectively evaluates his nitrous oxide experiences has become classic, but it is so pertinent to the present discussion that it merits quoting once again.

> One conclusion was forced upon my mind at that time, and my impression of its truth has ever since remained unshaken. It is that our normal waking consciousness, rational consciousness as we call it, is but one special type of consciousness, whilst all about it, parted from it by the filmiest of screens, there lie potential forms of consciousness entirely different. We may go through life without suspecting their existence; but apply the requisite stimulus, and at a touch they are there in all their completeness, definite type of mentality which probably somewhere have their field of application and adaptation. No account of the universe in its totality can be final which leaves these other forms of consciousness quite disregarded. How to regard them is the question—for they are so discontinuous with ordinary consciousness. Yet they may determine attitudes though they cannot furnish formulas, and open a region though they fail to give a map. At any rate, they forbid a premature closing of our accounts with reality. Looking back on my own experiences, they all converge toward a kind of insight to which I cannot help ascribing some metaphysical significance (*op. cit.*, 378–379).

To this argument from authority, I add two arguments that try to provide something by way of reasons. Drug experiences that assume a religious cast tend to have fearful and/or beatific features, and each of my hypotheses relates to one of these aspects of the experience.

Beginning with the ominous, "fear of the Lord," awe-ful features, Gordon Wasson, the New York banker-turned-mycologist, describes these as he encountered them in his psilocybin experience as follows: "Ecstasy! In common parlance . . . ecstasy is fun. . . . But ecstasy is not fun. Your very soul is seized and shaken until it tingles. After all, who will choose to feel undi-

16. *Totem and Taboo* (New York: Modern Library, 1938).

luted awe? . . . The unknowing vulgar abuse the word; we must recapture its full and terrifying sense."[17] Emotionally the drug experience can be like having forty-foot waves crash over you for several hours while you cling desperately to a life-raft which may be swept from under you at any minute. It seems quite possible that such an ordeal, like any experience of a close call, could awaken rather fundamental sentiments respecting life and death and destiny and trigger the "no atheists in fox holes" effect. Similarly, as the subject emerges from the trauma and realizes that he is not going to be insane as he had feared, there may come over him an intensified appreciation like that frequently reported by patients recovering from critical illness. "It happened on the day when my bed was pushed out of doors to the open gallery of the hospital," reads one such report:

> I cannot now recall whether the revelation came suddenly or gradually; I only remember finding myself in the very midst of those wonderful moments, beholding life for the first time in all its young intoxication of loveliness, in its unspeakable joy, beauty, and importance. I cannot say exactly what the mysterious change was. I saw no new thing, but I saw all the usual things in a miraculous new light—in what I believe is their true light. I saw for the first time how wildly beautiful and joyous, beyond any words of mine to describe, is the whole of life. Every

17. "The Hallucinogenic Fungi of Mexico: An Inquiry into the Origins of the Religious Idea among Primitive Peoples," *Harvard Botanical Museum Leaflets,* 19, 7 (1961).

"NIRVĀNA"

Walpola Rahula

Elsewhere the Buddha unequivocally uses the word Truth in place of Nibbāna: 'I will teach you the Truth and the Path leading to the Truth.' Here Truth definitely means Nirvāna.

Now, what is Absolute Truth? According to Buddhism, the Absolute Truth is that there is nothing absolute in the world, that everything is relative, conditioned and impermanent, and that there is no unchanging, everlasting, absolute substance like Self, Soul or *Ātman* within or without. This is the Absolute Truth. Truth is never negative, though there is a popular expression as negative truth. The realization of this Truth, i.e., to see things as they are (*yathābhūtam*) without illusion or ignorance (*avijjā*), is the extinction of craving 'thirst' (*Tanhakkhaya*), and the cessation (*Nirodha*) of *dukkha,* which is Nirvāna. It is interesting and useful to remember here the Mahāyāna view of Nirvāna as not being different from *Samsāra.* The same thing is Samsāra or Nirvāna according to the way you look at it—subjectively or objectively. This Mahāyāna view was probably developed out of the ideas found in the original Theravāda Pali texts, to which we have just referred in our brief discussion.

It is incorrect to think that Nirvāna is the natural result of the extinction of craving. Nirvāna is not the result of anything. If it would be a result, then it would be an effect produced by a cause. It would be *samkhata* 'produced' and 'conditioned'. Nirvāna is neither cause nor effect. It is beyond cause and effect. Truth is not a result nor an effect. It is not produced like a mystic, spiritual, mental state, such as *dhyāna* or *samādhi.* TRUTH IS. NIRVĀNA IS. The only thing you can do is to see it, to realize it. There is a path leading to the realization of Nirvāna. But Nirvāna is not the result of this path. You may get to the mountain along a path, but the mountain is not the result, not an effect of the path. You may see a light, but the light is not the result of your eyesight.

From Walpola Rahula, *What the Buddha Taught* (1974).

> human being moving across that porch, every sparrow that flew, every branch tossing in the wind, was caught in and was a part of the whole mad ecstasy of loveliness, of joy, of importance, of intoxication of life.[18]

If we do not discount religious intuitions because they are prompted by battlefields and *physical* crises; if we regard the latter as "calling us to our senses" more often than they seduce us into delusions, need comparable intuitions be discounted simply because the crises that trigger them are of an inner, *psychic* variety?

Turning from the hellish to the heavenly aspects of the drug experience, *some* of the latter may be explainable by the hypothesis just stated; that is, they may be occasioned by the relief that attends the sense of escape from higher danger. But this hypothesis cannot possibly account for *all* the beatific episodes, for the simple reason that the positive episodes often come first, or to persons who experience no negative episodes whatever. Dr. Sanford Unger of the National Institute of Mental Health reports that among his subjects "50 to 60% will not manifest any real disturbance worthy of discussion," yet "around 75% will have at least one episode in which exaltation, rapture, and joy are the key descriptions."[19] How are we to account for the drug's

18. Margaret Prescott Montague, *Twenty Minutes of Reality* (St. Paul, Minn.: Macalester Park, 1947), pp. 15, 17.

19. "The Current Scientific Status of Psychedelic Drugs Research," read at the Conference on Methods in Philosophy and the Sciences, New School for Social Research, May 3, 1964, and scheduled for publication in David Solomon, ed., *The Conscious Expanders* (New York: Putnam, fall of 1964).

Edward Conze

We are, however, nowadays, if only through the writings of Aldous Huxley, familiar with the difference between God and Godhead . . . When we compare the attributes of the Godhead as they are understood by the more mystical tradition of Christian thought, with those of Nirvana, we find almost no difference at all. It is indeed true that Nirvana has no cosmological functions, that this is not God's world, but a world made by our own greed and stupidity. It is indeed true that through their attitude the Buddhists express a more radical rejection of the world in all its aspects than we find among many Christians. At the same time, they are spared a number of awkward theological riddles and have not been under the necessity to combine, for instance, the assumption of an omnipotent and all-loving God with the existence of a great deal of suffering and muddle in this world. Buddhists also have never stated that God is *Love,* but that may be due to their preoccupation with intellectual precision, which must have perceived that the word "Love" is one of the most unsatisfactory and ambiguous terms one could possibly use.

But, on the other hand, we are told that Nirvana is permanent, stable, imperishable, immovable, ageless, deathless, unborn, and unbecome, that it is power, bliss and happiness, the secure refuge, the shelter, and the place of unassailable safety; that it is the real Truth and the supreme Reality; that it is the *Good,* the supreme goal and the one and only consummation of our life, the eternal, hidden and incomprehensible Peace.

Similarly, the Buddha who is, as it were, the personal embodiment of Nirvana, becomes the object of all those emotions which we are wont to call religious.

There has existed throughout Buddhist history a tension between the Bhaktic and the Gnostic approach to religion, such as we find also in Christianity. There is, however, the difference that in Buddhism the Gnostic vision has always been regarded as the more true one, while the Bhaktic, devotional, type was regarded more or less as a concession to the common people.

From Edward Conze, *Buddhism* (1951).

capacity to induce peak experiences, such as the following, which are *not* preceded by fear?

> A feeling of great peace and contentment seemed to flow through my entire body. All sound ceased and I seemed to be floating in a great, very very still void or hemisphere. It is impossible to describe the overpowering feeling of peace, contentment, and being a part of goodness itself that I felt. I could feel my body dissolving and actually becoming a part of the goodness and peace that was all around me. Words can't describe this. I feel an awe and wonder that such a feeling could have occurred to me.[20]

Consider the following line of argument. Like every other form of life, man's nature has become distinctive through specialization. Man has specialized in developing a cerebral cortex. The analytic powers of this instrument are a standing wonder, but the instrument seems less able to provide man with the sense that he is meaningfully related to his environment: to life, the world, and history in their wholeness. As Albert Camus describes the situation, "If I were . . . a cat among animals, this life would have a meaning, or rather this problem would not arise, for I should belong to this world. I would *be* this world to which I am now opposed by my whole consciousness."[21] Note that it is Camus' consciousness that opposes him to his world. The drugs do not knock this consciousness out, but while they leave it operative they also activate areas of the brain that normally lie below its threshold of awareness. One of the clearest objective signs that the drugs are taking effect is the dilation they produce in the pupils of the eyes, and one of the most predictable subjective signs is the intensification of visual perception. Both of these responses are controlled by portions of the brain that lie deep, further to the rear than the mechanisms that govern consciousness. Meanwhile we know that the human organism is interlaced with its world in innumerable ways it normally cannot sense—through gravitational fields, body respiration, and the like: the list could be multiplied until man's skin began to seem more like a thoroughfare than a boundary. Perhaps the deeper regions of the brain which evolved earlier and are more like those of the lower animals—"If I were . . . a cat . . . I should belong to this world"—can sense this relatedness better than can the cerebral cortex which now dominates our awareness. If so, when the drugs rearrange the neurohumors that chemically transmit impulses across synapses between neurons, man's consciousness and his submerged, intuitive, ecological awareness might for a spell become interlaced. This is, of course, no more than a hypothesis, but how else are we to account for the extraordinary incidence under the drugs of that kind of insight the keynote of which James described "invariably a reconciliation"? "It is as if the opposites of the world, whose contradictoriness and conflict make all our difficulties and troubles, were melted into one and the same genus, but *one of the species,* the nobler and better one, *is itself the genus, and so soaks up and absorbs its opposites into itself*" (op. cit., 279).

4. DRUGS AND RELIGION VIEWED "RELIGIOUSLY"

Suppose that drugs can induce experiences indistinguishable from religious experiences and that we can respect their reports. Do they shed any light, not (we now ask) on life, but on the nature of the religious life?

One thing they may do is throw religious experience itself into perspective by clarifying its relation to the religious life as a whole. Drugs appear able to induce religious experiences; it is less evident that they can produce religious lives. It follows that religion is more than religious experiences. This is hardly news, but it may be a useful reminder, especially to those who incline toward "the religion of religion experi-

20. Quoted by Dr. Unger in the paper just mentioned.

21. *The Myth of Sisyphus* (New York: Vintage, 1955), p. 38.

ence"; which is to say toward lives bent on the acquisition of desired states of experience irrespective of their relation to life's other demands and components.

Despite the dangers of faculty psychology, it remains useful to regard man as having a mind, a will, and feelings. One of the lessons of religious history is that, to be adequate, a faith must rouse and involve all three components of man's nature. Religions of reason grow arid; religions of duty, leaden. Religions of experience have their comparable pitfalls, as evidenced by Taoism's struggle (not always successful) to keep from degenerating into quietism, and the vehemence with which Zen Buddhism has insisted that once students have attained *satori,* they must be driven out of it, back into the world. The case of Zen is especially pertinent here, for it pivots on an enlightenment experience—*satori,* or *kensho*—which some (but not all) Zennists say resembles LSD. Alike or different, the point is that Zen recognizes that unless the experience is joined to discipline, it will come to naught:

> Even the Buddha . . . had to sit. . . . Without *joriki,* the particular power developed through *zazen* [seated meditation], the vision of oneness attained in enlightenment . . . in time becomes clouded and eventually fades into a pleasant memory instead of remaining an omnipresent reality shaping our daily life. . . . To be able to live in accordance with what the Mind's eye has revealed through *satori* requires, like the purification of character and the development of personality, a ripening period of *zazen.*[22]

If the religion of religious experience is a snare and a delusion, it follows that no religion that fixes its faith primarily in substances that induce religious experiences can be expected to come to a good end. What promised to be a short cut will prove to be a short circuit; what began as a religion will end as a religion surrogate. Whether chemical substances can be helpful *adjuncts* to faith is another question. The peyote-using Native American Church seems to indicate that they can be; anthropologists give this church a good report, noting among other things that members resist alcohol and alcoholism better than do nonmembers.[23] The conclusion to which evidence currently points would seem to be that chemicals *can* aid the religious life, but only where set within a context of faith (meaning by this conviction that what they disclose is true) and discipline (meaning diligent exercise of the will in the attempt to work out the implications of the disclosures for the living of life in the everyday, common-sense world).

Nowhere today in Western civilization are these two conditions jointly fulfilled. Churches lack faith in the sense just mentioned; hipsters lack discipline. This might lead us to forget about the drugs, were it not for one fact: the distinctive religious emotion and the emotion that drugs unquestionably can occasion—Otto's *mysterium tremendum, majestas, mysterium fascinans;* in a phrase, the phenomenon of religious awe—seems to be declining sharply. As Paul Tillich said in an address to the Hillel Society at Harvard several years ago:

> The question our century puts before us [is]: Is it possible to regain the lost dimension, the encounter with the Holy, the dimension which cuts through the world of subjectivity and objectivity and goes down to that which is not world but is the mystery of the Ground of Being?

Tillich may be right; this may be the religious question of our century. For if (as we have insisted) religion cannot be equated with religious experiences, neither can it long survive their absence.

22. Phillip Kapleau, *Zen Practice and Attainment,* a manuscript in process of publication.

23. Slotkin, *op. cit.*

Robert Nozick

"MYSTICAL EXPERIENCE"

A brief biography of Nozick appears on page 366.

Assertions of something beyond existence and nonexistence, infinite and unbounded, appear in the writings of (some) mystics, not as hypotheses to answer questions of cosmogony but to describe what they have experienced and encountered.[1]

How much credence should we give to these experiences? Undoubtedly such experiences are had and are sincerely reported, and they strike the mystic as revelatory of reality, of a deeper reality. Why deeper? What is experienced is different, but this does not show that it is deeper, rather than more superficial even than the reality we normally know. The experiences come as revelatory of something deeper. Should we believe the report of mystics that there is this reality? Should the mystics themselves believe it?

There are two major approaches to these experiences: first, to explain them away, to offer an explanation of why they occur that doesn't introduce (as an explanatory factor) anything like what the mystics claim to experience; and second, to see them as revelatory of a reality that is as it is encountered. To notice that there are special conditions under which such experiences occur, for example, after yogic practice or ingestion of certain drugs, does not settle which approach should be taken. What the first approach treats as a cause of the experience, the second will see as removing the veil from reality so that it can be perceived as it really is. Does the unusual physiochemical state of the brain produce an illusion, or does it enable us to experience reality?

We might think there is an evolutionary reason why the unusual brain states should not be trusted; our tendency to have the normal ones has been selected for in a process wherein too gross a failure to cognize reality led to extinction. However, if the underlying reality is as the mystics report, and if knowing it (as opposed to knowing the more superficial features of macrophysical objects) had no adaptive value, then we should not expect these normal brain states selected for in the evolutionary process to be ones that reveal the underlying reality as it is.

The procedure often used to induce the unusual experience, yogic or zen meditation, aims at "quieting thoughts," stopping our usual chatter of thoughts so that, as some say, we can experience the true self or at any rate a reality which the thoughts mask and cover. (And this sometimes may be an effect of other means, such as chemical ones, not consciously aimed at this result.) It is surprisingly difficult to stop thoughts from flitting about, but the difficulties of accomplishing this should not distract us from won-

1. A useful reminder that the mystics within different traditions differ in their experiences, and not merely in how they interpret them, is presented by Steven Katz, "Language, Epistemology and Mysticism," in S. Katz,. ed., *Mysticism and Philosophical Analysis* (Oxford University Press, 1978), pp. 22–74. However, not all experiences are equally theory-laden, and sometimes people are catapulted into experiences, for example, by drugs, without previous theoretical preparation. Furthermore, even if the experiences are shaped by theoretical traditions and expectations, we who know of these differing traditions can ask whether mystics of different traditions are experiencing the same thing, whether the object of their experiences is the same, even though they are not experiencing it in the same way.

Useful books on mysticism by philosophers are William James, *The Varieties of Religious Experience* (Modern Library, New York, 1929); W. T. Stace, *Mysticism and Philosophy* (Lippincott, Philadelphia, 1960); Fritz Staal, *Exploring Mysticism* (University of California Press, Berkeley, 1975); Ben-Ami Scharfstein, *Mystical Experience* (Penguin Books, London, 1974); and (these are also works of mysticism) Aurobindo, *The Life Divine, Synthesis of Yoga,* and *Savitri* (each Pondicherry, India, 1973).

dering what success shows. Supposing the procedure, when it succeeds in quieting the thoughts, does lead to an experience of the sort described, should we think this reveals something fitting the experience? That depends on what experience we think the procedure would produce even if there was no such unusual underlying reality to be perceived.

The following analogy may help make the point: Consider a phonograph system as an apparatus of experience. With the amplifier on, turntable turning, speakers on, a record on the turntable and the stylus moving in its grooves, sound is experienced; it (we are temporarily imagining) has the experience of sound. Now let us do the equivalent of quieting thoughts, namely, removing the record, perhaps also turning off the speakers and the turntable. When only the amplifier is on (with no ordinary "objects of experience" given it), what is the experience like? We do not know; perhaps infinite, unbounded and so on, is what it feels like when the amplifier switch (of consciousness) is on, yet nothing is being experienced. Nothing differentiated is present to consciousness to produce a differentiated experience. It would be a mistake to think there is an unusual reality being encountered, when that merely is what it feels like when the experience-mechanism is turned on yet nothing is present to be experienced. None of the literature I know describes what experience the quieting meditative procedure would produce in the absence of any unusual reality or self, so we don't know whether the unusual experience is a revelation of an unusual reality or self, or instead an artifact of an unusual procedure of experiencing wherein most but not all functions are damped down. (Will this debunking explanation have more difficulty in explaining the surprising and often momentous changes in the people who have the experiences?)[2]

Empiricist methodology, presumably, would have us treat the mystics' experiences as on a par with all other experiences, to be fed into some procedure of theory generation and support. The question is whether the resulting theory explaining (or explaining away) the mystics' experience that p will itself incorporate p or something like it. The answer will be interesting, however, only if the procedure itself is unbiased toward the mystics' claim; for example, it must not give it an almost zero a priori probability or degree of initial credibility, or give the mystics' individual experiences lesser weight than others in fixing either what is to be accounted for or how theories are evaluated.[3]

We are far from knowing whether the mystics' p will be preserved as (*roughly*) true by the empiricists' account, even if we suppose it a maxim that the resulting explanatory theory incorporate (as true) as many q's as possible from the experiences that q for which it tries to account. As much as possible, the theory is to save the appearances, including the experiences that p.[4] Perhaps this is not merely a maxim but a necessary component of any (unbiased) confirmatory and explanatory procedure we can wield. That we don't yet know whether the empiricists' explanatory theory will endorse the mystics' claim does not mean it is not an important question to raise.

Does the empiricist methodology distinguish between the mystic and the nonmystic? One has the experience while the other only hears it reported, but should this make a difference to what they believe? Certainly, a higher percentage of those who have had mystical experiences that p than of those who have not

2. One also might view the categorization of remarkable LSD experiences in analogy to stages of the birth process, presented in Stanislav Grof, *Realms of the Human Unconscious: Observations from LSD Research* (Viking Press, New York, 1975), as a matrix for an alternative 'explaining away' of the experience.

3. Thus, we are imagining that the mystics' position is not discriminated against in an application of Bayesian procedures, or Israel Scheffler's justificatory procedure ("On Justification and Commitment," *Journal of Philosophy,* Vol. 51, 1954, pp. 180–190), or N. Rescher's coherentist confirmation (*The Coherence Theory of Truth,* Oxford University Press, 1973).

4. For an interesting discussion of the origin of the phrase "saving the phenomena or appearances," which (contrary to what I had thought) does not appear in the extant writings of Plato, see Gregory Vlastos, *Plato's Universe* (University of Washington Press, Seattle, 1975), appendix M. pp. 111–112.

believe that p is true. Some of this difference in percentages will stem from the fact that many of those without the mystical experience will not know that such experiences are had by anyone or know of the probity of those who report them; or they simply spend less time thinking about the matter because, not having had the experiences that p themselves, the question of the truth of p is less salient to them. However, I believe there will remain a difference in the percentages after we control for all such facts. A higher percentage of the mystical-experiencers will believe in the veridicality of the experience, will believe that reality is as it then was experienced.

Why should this be so? The experiences are very powerful, but the person without the experiences is told this and can weigh this in as evidence about veridicality. It is merely that the person having (had) the mystical experience cannot help believing its veridicality, or does he have reason to differ? We can imagine that a nongullible person has a powerful mystical experience, not easily dismissed, and wonders whether he should believe that reality is as it apparently has been revealed to be. What weight should he give to the fact that he himself had the experience?

Do I rationally give my experiences that q different weight than yours that r in constructing my picture of the world? My accepting that you have had the experience that r will be based on my experiences (of your reports), and so my experiences seem primary in that way. Once I have accepted the fact that you have had the experience, though, do I try to save your appearances any less than mine, your r's less than my q's?

If somehow we were telepathically connected with a creature in another galaxy or universe, having its experiences, then we must give those some credence as our access into what that world is like. Must we give more credence to them than to the experiences of other denizens of that realm (which we come to know of via our telepathic contact)? Apart from the earlier point about primacy, apparently not. And aren't we each in our own world simply in special telepathic communication with ourselves, as it were, so that it would be similarly inappropriate to give our own experiences that q special weight or credence as compared to other's experience that r?

Alternatively, imagine an amnesia victim who is being told of the experiences of different persons, including some people's mystical experiences. He comes to hold a general picture of the world which, let us suppose, rejects the mystics' claim that p. Should it make any difference to his belief if now he is told: you were one of the people who had that mystical experience. Surely not. He has already considered how much evidential weight to give the fact that such an experience was had (under certain conditions with a certain frequency), how much weight to give to the fact that *someone* had the experience; it is irrelevant further information that the someone was himself (rather than another of the same specified degree of probity, sincerity, and so on).

Yet there remains something special about the mystical experience whereby it evades this general argument. Because this mystical experience is ineffable, powerfully (if not indelibly) remembered but inadequately described, the mystic knows something the hearer of his reports does not. The hearer does know something, though, for later if he does have the experience he will know that must be what the other was reporting.* We need not hold that nothing can be transmitted by imagery, metaphor, and so on; only that something significant evades the description.

The experiencer knows what the mystical experience is like in a way and to an extent the attentive listener does not, and in a way and to an extent the amnesiac does not who is told he once had a certain sort of experience which he

* Though even this may be unclear. For example, Madhyamika Buddhists report experiences of emptiness, of a "vibrant void," while Vedantists report an experience of the fullest possible pure infinite existence: existence-consciousness-bliss. Are they experiencing the same thing? It would help to have someone who reported (in the suitable language) having both experiences (and that they were different), rather than all reporting only one or the other.

doesn't remember. Relevant is not simply the fact that the experiencer had the experience, for the amnesiac also had it, but the way this fact normally shows itself in the person's evidential base. There is evidence available to the experiencer (who remembers) that is not available to the hearer or the amnesiac. So there is a reason for him to reach a different conclusion than they do. We can see how he *might* reasonably believe that *p* (that there is an infinite underlying reality transcending existence and nonexistence) while they could not. This explanation does not show that the person with mystical experience does reasonably differ in his view that *p*; but it does leave room for such a difference, showing how such a reasonable difference might be possible.

What should a person without mystical experience, who realizes all that has been said thus far, believe? He knows that almost all those who have mystically experienced that *p* believe that *p*, and that something about their experience, which eludes telling and so is unknown to him, may (properly) play a role in their belief. This additional information may make it somewhat more reasonable for him to believe that *p*, but he still is not in the position of the experiencers. For he will face the question of whether the (unknown) character of the experience was such as to make it reasonable to believe *p*. Perhaps the experiencers are especially gullible, either because there is selective entry into the class of experiencers, the mystical experience coming only to the already especially gullible and credulous, or because the experience makes people gullible, causing them to become gullible and credulous, either generally or just about the import of this particular experience. (Should the mystics not be concerned about this, too?) Certainly mystics often appear gullible and credulous in the rest of what they accept. But is this because of a general gullibility, new or old, or rather because they reasonably have shifted their general picture of the constitution of the universe which leads to a shift in other a priori probabilities or expectations, so that some things previously excluded as impossible now will seem possible, and less evidence, is needed to establish them as actual?

Lacking firsthand acquaintance with the mystical experience, and so having an ineradicably different evidence base, the nonexperiencer may reasonably reject the mystics' claim that *p*, while admitting the mystic may be reasonable in believing that *p*. The mystic may now claim one further bit of support for the truth of *p*, other than mystical experiences that *p*. If *p*, as a hypothesis, provides an answer to the question of why there is something rather than nothing, then performing this function provides it some support. Thus we have two independent routes to *p*, each reinforcing the other: the experiential route of the mystic and the explanatory route in philosophical cosmogony.

That the (purported) fact that *p* is the right sort of thing to explain why there is something rather than nothing does not show how it does this; it does not show what the particular connection is between the fact that *p* and our universe, or its contents, in detail. Here we must be careful about the mystic's claims,

"Final Words"

Chuang Tzu

The fish trap exists because of the fish; once you've gotten the fish, you can forget the trap. The rabbit snare exists because of the rabbit; once you've gotten the rabbit, you can forget the snare. Words exist because of meaning; once you've gotten the meaning, you can forget the words. Where can I find a man who has forgotten words so I can have a word with him?

From Chuang Tzu, trans. Burton Watson (Columbia Univ. Press).

Fourteenth-century stained glass window depicting the Annunciation.

distinguishing those p's for which he claims or reports an experience that p from other statements that he introduces as hypotheses to connect the deep underlying reality he experiences with the superficial one he normally inhabits. These connections the mystic does not himself (even claim to) experience, and they have lesser authority than his experiences. The mystic's special knowledge of his experience does not extend to a special authority about its (and its object's) connection to ordinarily perceivable reality; for this connection does not link with, much less get revealed in, the ineffable character of the experience.

For this reason we find many theorists of the connection, even among mystics; some see our world as an illusion (to whom?), others as like a work of fiction, others as a thought, others an an emanation, others as a creation, and so on, views all based on the fundamental underlying reality described in p. The fact is, I think, that what is experienced by the mystic is so different from our ordinary world, yet is experienced as underlying that world and as more real, that the mystic gropes or leaps for some explanation, for some theory of how it underlies the world, of how the two might be connected. Similarly, the mystic who experiences himself as the infinite perfect underlay of everything, neither existing nor nonexisting, whether in the experience that Atman = Brahman or in the experience of being the void, has to explain why he did not always realize this, his own true nature. Since he didn't experience himself becoming ignorant, his explanation of his (recent) ignorance is always (only) a hypothesis. So mystics present different theories here as well. Greater credence should be given to the mystic's experiences than to his hypotheses, both by the nonmystic and by the mystic.*

More than clarifying the issues somewhat, I wish I could resolve the question of whether reality is as the mystic describes it. I take the question, and the mystics' experiences, very seriously, which some will think immediately is a great mistake. (But do they think this only because they already assume a background theory that discounts the mystics' experiences; if so, what led them to that theory?) For the purposes of philosphical explaining and understanding, we need not resolve the question; it suffices to consider, elaborate, and keep track of the hypotheses. Yet there remains the question of how to act, of what path to follow.**

---

* Though, perhaps some mystical experiences can (seem to) indicate something about the character of the connection, even if not the details.

Some of the yogic mystical experiences are of the self as being the underlying substance of the universe or an infinite purity; also, I think, of it as turned back onto itself, creating itself, the experiential analogue of self-subsuming.

The practitioner of Hatha Yoga develops extraordinary suppleness and physical capabilities, and the yoga manuals are explicitly dark and mysterious about some of the practices. In these classic manuals, the practitioner of yoga is warned to keep some things very secret and to do them only in private. For example, *Gheranda Samhita,* i, 13–44, contains five admonitions that different practices are very secret; *Siva Samhita,* iv, 41–44, says the "wise Yogi" should "practice this . . . in secret, in a retired place." See the passages quoted in Theos Bernard, *Hatha Yoga* (Columbia University Press, 1943, reprinted by Samuel Weiser, New York 1950), pp. 34 and 69. For an indication of the suppleness of body developed, see the photographs there.

Printed interpretations and explanations of what is involved leave the practice innocuous. (For example, M. Eliade, *Yoga,* Princeton University Press, 1969, ch. 6. For discussion of reading esoteric texts, see Leo Strauss, *Persecution and the Art of Writing,* Free Press, Glencoe, 1952.) They leave it wholly mysterious why secrecy is enjoined, why if that is all that is involved, the manuals do not say it straight out. It is a general principle in interpreting texts which announce they hold secrets, however, that the secret doctrine should turn out to be something the writer would go to great lengths to keep secret.

In these yoga manuals the actions and postures of the practitioner are meant to lead him to the secret. When the doctrine itself is to be conveyed by the text, though, the writer has a special problem: having announced that a secret is embedded in the work, how can he prevent its detection by the very ones from whom he wishes to keep it secret, who have been told explicitly that there is some secret to be found? The writer has to bury something that can be ferreted out to satisfy the unwelcome seeker, a decoy secret. This must be something the writer plausibly would want to keep secret; otherwise it will not be a successful cover. How will one know if one has found the valuable silver or the more deeply hidden gold? If only one thing has been uncovered, being the easier to find, it is not the real secret. But has any author buried a secret doctrine underneath two covers? (Or flashed the fact of contained secrets, without announcing it, by discussing esoteric devices, I mean doctrines, rambunctiously?)

What are the yoga manuals keeping hidden, which the practitioner is expected to come to himself? What does the cutting of the fraenum linguae aid? What nectar is brought upwards and drunk What is the mouth of the well of nectar over which the tongue is placed and what ambrosia is drunk daily? (These are the terms used in the yoga manuals. See Bernard, *Hatha Yoga,* pp. 30, 65–67.)

I conjecture that one of the acts the (male) yogis perform, during their experiences of being identical with infinitude, is autofellatio, wherein they have an intense and escstatic experience of self-generation, of the universe and themselves turned back upon itself in a self-creation. (Compare the mythological theme of creation from an ouroboros, a serpent with its tail in its mouth.)

Here I have only conjecture to go on, and this conjecture may well be mistaken. But it does specify something the yogis in their altered consciousness might seek and regard as a pinnacle, yet, even with their disdain for the ordinary practices and opinions of the world, also seek to keep a secret.

What tantric yoga involves, we won't conjecture.

** However, perhaps there is less urgency to the decision than we think. Siddhartha Gautama's statement notwithstanding, is the house on fire? If the theories centering on such experiences are correct, we live a sequence of lives, and so we can hope that in a later one the matter will become clearer. While if we have only this life, then these theories are incorrect and we should not follow them. So in either case, we should not follow an arduous Eastern path now. Unless, of course, the Eastern theories are correct, and the karmic consequences of acting on this argument, having come so close to realizing the truth, push one further away from it for innumerable future lifetimes.

Ronald C. Pine

"MYSTICISM AND THE CONVERGENCE THESIS"

RONALD C. PINE teaches philosophy at Honolulu Community College and wrote *Science and the Human Prospect* (1989), one of the best, although little known, philosophically oriented explanations of science for students in the humanities, from which the following selection is taken.

One more interpretation of quantum physics deserves some comment. It is a very controversial interpretation, in part because it has attracted a faddish and cultlike following, which claims that the results of modern science have validated a particular religious orientation. The possibility of such a development is one of the reasons scientists are often reluctant to communicate with the general public. An idea, however, cannot be responsible for its misuse by uncritical followers, and the misuse of an idea does not prove the idea false.

For the purpose of identification let's refer to this final interpretation as the *convergence thesis*. Essentially, this view argues that our confrontation with the quantum has demonstrated that Western science, founded upon the logic and philosophy of the ancient Greeks, has, after traveling a much different philosophical path, converged with the philosophy of the East, especially the mystical philosophies of Hinduism and Buddhism. This view was popularized in the 1970s by Fritjof Capra in *The Tao of Physics* and by Gary Zukav in *The Dancing Wu Li Masters*. According to Capra, "What Buddhists have realized through their mystical experience of nature has now been rediscovered through the experiments and mathematical theories of modern science." Zukav says, "Hindu mythology is virtually a large scale projection into the psychological realm of microscopic scientific discoveries."

For many thousands of years, it is argued, the mystics have had a cosmological, ontological, and epistemological view of things that the Western world is just beginning to understand. Cosmologically, Western science has understood only recently that the universe is extremely old. In 1965 the temperature of the universe was measured for the first time, resulting in our present estimate of the age of the universe as 15 billion years old. In the ancient literature of the East one does not, of course, find such precise figures. Instead there are analogies such as the following. Imagine an immortal eagle flying over the Himalayas only once every 1,000 years; it carries a feather in its beak and each time it passes, it lightly brushes the tops of the gigantic mountain peaks. The amount of time it would take the eagle to completely erode the mighty Himalayas is said to be the age of the present manifestation of the universe. Such a conception of time, which predates modern science by thousands of years, is thought to be remarkable, especially when it is compared to the slow realization of Western science and religion to the possibility of a less humanlike time scale.

Ontologically, Eastern mysticism is also consistent with the results of quantum physics. The mystics have always rejected the idea of a hidden clocklike mechanism, sitting out there, independent of human observation. The number one truth is that reality does not consist of separate things, but is an indescribable, interconnected oneness. Each object of our normal experience is seen to be but a brief disturbance of a universal ocean of existence. *Maya* is the illusion that the phenomenal world of separate objects and people is the only reality. For the mystics this manifestation is real, but it is a fleeting reality; it is a mistake, although a natural one, to believe that maya represents a fundamental reality. Each person, each physical object, from the perspective of eternity is like a brief, disturbed drop of water from an unbounded ocean. The goal of enlightenment is to understand this—more precisely, to experience this: to see intuitively that the distinction between me and the universe is a false dichotomy. The distinction between consciousness and physical matter, between mind and body, is the result of an unenlightened perspective.

Consciousness and the Cosmos

Life, we tend to think, is extremely rare, consciousness even rarer, and the rest of the cosmos is but lifeless matter in motion, purposeless and unaware of the universe of which it is a blind and silent part—each of us but a tiny island of conscious experience in a vast and mostly lifeless universe.

This view of ourselves as conscious beings and the rest of nature as nonconscious can seem like such an obvious tenet of scientifically informed common sense that we may need to be reminded that there has always been significant dissent. Not only in religious traditions, such as Hinduism and Buddhism, but even among secular thinkers, the view that the cosmos is conscious has been remarkably persistent.

The Greek philosopher Thales who stated, "Everything is made of water," and who many regard as the first scientist, also said, "Everything is full of gods." Spinoza, the seventeenth-century Jewish philosopher, who was widely branded as an atheist, thought that everything—the entire cosmos—is God and, as such, has a conscious aspect running through it. The seventeenth-century German philosopher Leibniz, unlike his contemporary Isaac Newton, who thought that everything is made of lifeless atoms, believed that everything is made of conscious atoms he called *monads*. In recent times, Einstein, when asked whether he believed in God, answered that he believed in the God of Spinoza. The contemporary physicist Freeman Dyson views quantum particles, like Leibnizian monads, as each having something like consciousness. And the Nobel Prize winner neurophysiologist R. W. Sperry espouses *panpsychism*, the view that everything is conscious.

Epistemologically, our so-called knowledge of the world is actually only a projection or creation of thoughts. Reality is ambiguous. It requires thoughts for distinctions to become manifest. We have seen that in the realm of the quantum, dynamic particle attributes such as "spin," "location," and "velocity" are best thought of as relational or phenomenal realities. It is a mistake to think of these properties as sitting out there; rather, they are the result of experimental arrangements and ultimately the thoughts of experimenters. Quantum particles have a partial appearance of individuality, but experiments show that the true nature of the quantum lies beyond description in human terms. Our filters produce the manifestations we see, and the result is just incomplete enough to point to another kind of reality, an ambiguous reality of "not this, not that."

For the mystic, the paradoxes of quantum physics are just another symptom of humankind's attempt to describe what can only be experienced. We are like a man with a torch surrounded by darkness. The man wants to experience the darkness, but keeps running senselessly at the darkness with his torch still in hand. He does not realize that he must drop the torch and plunge into the darkness. The proliferation of philosophical interpretations of quantum physics is a symptom of the shipwreck of a traditional Western way of understanding, of our inability to "let go" of our Western torch—our traditional logic, epistemology, and ontology. It is also a symptom of our inability to let go of our egocentricity, our persistent attempt to define everything in purely human terms, as if we were somehow special and separate from the rest of the universe. Like a nervous, self-centered teenager at a party, concerned only with what others think of him, our entire field of vision and understanding is narrowly defined in terms of "me." Because of our fear of letting go, we are missing much that is right in front of us.

According to this interpretation, the mathematics is complete just as it is. What the Schrödinger equation depicts for microscopic objects is also true for any macroscopic object. The universe is not full of separate objects, people, and

"Mind and Physics"

Freeman Dyson

It is remarkable that mind enters into our awareness of nature on two separate levels. At the highest level, the level of human consciousness, our minds are somehow directly aware of the complicated flow of electrical and chemical patterns in our brains. At the lowest level, the level of single atoms and electrons, the mind of an observer is again involved in the description of events. Between lies the level of molecular biology, where mechanical models are adequate and mind appears to be irrelevant. But I, as a physicist, cannot help suspecting that there is a logical connection between the two ways in which mind appears in my universe. I cannot help thinking that our awareness of our own brains has something to do with the process which we call "observation" in atomic physics. That is to say, I think our consciousness is not just a passive epiphenomenon carried along by the chemical events in our brains, but is an active agent forcing the molecular complexes to make choices between one quantum state and another. In other words, mind is already inherent in every electron, and the processes of human consciousness differ only in degree but not in kind from the processes of choice between quantum states which we call "chance" when they are made by electrons.

From *Disturbing the Universe* (1988).

An early Christian mosaic in S. Costanza, Rome.

places. Rather, it is an unbounded field of entangled possibilities. Because of the level of our conscious awareness, we fail to realize that duality, ambiguity, and interdependence are the rule rather than the exception. Mathematics may be one of the closest ways we can come to representing this in terms of a human language. All languages, however, are ultimately inadequate. Myths, stories, analogies, pictures, mathematical equations—all such symbol systems can just point to what can only be fully understood through a visionary experience.

In the episode entitled "The Edge of Forever" in the "Cosmos" television series, Carl Sagan visits India, and by way of introducing some of the bizarre ideas of modern physics, he acknowledges that of all the world's philosophies and religions those originating in India are remarkably consistent with contemporary scenarios of space, time, and existence. However, adamantly skeptical of the knowledge value of a nonrational mystical intuition, he concludes that although these religious ideas are worthy of our deep respect, this is obviously a "coincidence." Using natural selection as a model, Sagan proposes that this consistency is "no doubt an accident" because given enough time and possible proposals, given enough creative responses to the great mystery of existence, some ideas will fit the truth just right.

Other critics of the convergence thesis have not been as charitable. They argue that it is just plain silly to interpret an ancient belief system, founded upon certain psychological needs and within a historical context, in terms of any modern perspective. It is obvious, they argue, how the Hindu and Buddhist beliefs could soothe people living under extreme conditions. If our day-to-day reality is but a fleeting manifestation, then the vicious misfortune and meaningless suffering of this world are not real. For these critics, the methodology of psychological need as an origin of these ideas implies there is no connection. By revealing the obvious psychological motivation for a set of beliefs, it is argued, one can question the truth of these beliefs. To further suggest that there is any connection between these beliefs and the results of rigorous experimental science is ludicrous.

Both of these arguments are flawed. If the ideas of Hinduism and Buddhism are simply the result of a lot of guessing, and the serendipitous contingency of evolutionary processes the appropriate model, then shouldn't all the guessing that takes place over time be consistent with a macroscopic environment, not a microscopic environment with which a primitive people have no experience? And even if it is true that a belief system serves a set of psychological needs, does this prove the belief system false? Many scientists are also surely motivated for many reasons to hold the beliefs they do: a philosophical perspective, the need for certainty, or the need for security (be it a government grant or tenure at a prestigious university). That scientists have biases and motivations to believe what they do does not prove that what they finally believe is false.

Both of these arguments, however, do reveal a sobering point. The philosophical consistency between Hinduism and Buddhism and the results of modern science does not prove much by itself. Historically, we have seen many instances of a philosophy or a religious view being consistent with the science of a time, and a consequent rush to claim that the new science validates a religion or a philosophy. For both Copernicus and Kepler, the heliocentric system of the planets was consistent with their Neoplatonism and the idea that the sun was the "material domicile" of God. Similarly, for Bruno the heliocentric system was consistent with a larger universe and a greater God. For Newton a universe based upon the laws of universal gravitation was consistent with a conception of God as a master craftsman, a creator of an almost perfect machine who left a few defects to give Himself something to do. For some of the initial supporters of Darwin, natural selection was interpreted as a vindication of a philosophy of inevitable progress based upon a capitalistic economic system.

Perhaps the more pertinent question, applicable to all the interpretations of quantum physics, is not which offered paradigm is the truth, but which one will give us the most mileage? Which one, if followed as a guide, will be the most fruitful in stimulating the imagination of the next generation of scientists in devising new ideas, mathematical relationships, and experiments? In this [discussion] we have not given much attention to the area of modern physics

"Cosmos Created by Mind"

Paul Davies

In 1979, John Wheeler, speaking at a symposium in Princeton celebrating Einstein's centenary, drew a mind-boggling conclusion. He pointed out that our decisions to make a hybrid world can be delayed until after that world has come into existence! The precise nature of reality, Wheeler claims, has to await the participation of a conscious observer. In this way, mind can be made responsible for the retroactive creation of reality—even a reality that existed before there were people . . . .John Wheeler represents the universe as a self-observing system. Wheeler's astonishing modification of Young's two-slit experiment reveals that an observer today can be made partially responsible for generating the reality of the remote past. . . . The early stages of the universe [are] promoted to concrete reality through its later observation by consciousness which itself depends on that reality.

From *God and the New Physics* (1983).

that recently has gotten the most notoriety. In spite of the overwhelming success of the experimental demonstration that a traditional metaphysics of reductionism is inadequate, most physicists, concerned with the daily demands of obtaining research grants and Nobel Prizes, have simply filed such demonstrations away and continued with the Einsteinian quest, searching for more and more exotic particles, new "things" that will prove the supersymmetry theories, unifying all the known forces of nature and catapulting our understanding to the first microseconds of the universe and perhaps beyond.

Yet in spite of Nobel Prizes for the discovery of some of these new particles and public pronouncements that the end of the Einsteinian quest is near, one senses that all is not well with this approach. Physicists themselves complain that the proliferation of particles necessary to explain everything is too complex to be consistent with a simple universe. One senses many ad hoc approaches and a situation not unlike followers of Ptolemy adding epicycle after epicycle to make the data fit. Some experiments reveal serious anomalies. Particles that allegedly consist of a "bag" of quarks are not supposed to pass through each other, but in some cases, if the spins are just right, they do! One senses that nature is not yet ready to succumb completely to our latest gestures of understanding.

Every past success at understanding has produced new mysteries. Why should it be any different now? Perhaps the results of quantum physics discussed in this chapter are revealing to us a great discovery after all. This great partner we call the universe is not a static personality, but grows and is formed by us, as we are by it. There is every reason to believe that our romance will continue, that there are many mysteries left for a new generation of physicists. Although there have been many pretenders since the time of Kepler, no one has yet read the mind of God.

PART VII

Faith and Reason

Søren Kierkegaard

"TRUTH AND SUBJECTIVITY"

SØREN KIERKEGAARD (1813–1855), Danish philosopher and religious thinker, was a pastor in the Lutheran Church until he left because of deep personal differences over what it means to have faith: "Pastors are royal officials; royal officials have nothing to do with Christianity." He saw not only the church but his entire world as lacking in the passion required for a full synthesis of intellectual and spiritual understanding. Often considered one of the first existentialists, Kierkegaard's religious and philosophical views are expressed in a number of influential works, including *Either/Or: A Fragment of Life* (1843), *The Concept of Dread* (1844), and *Concluding Unscientific Postscript* (1846).

In an attempt to make clear the difference of way that exists between an objective and a subjective reflection, I shall now proceed to show how a subjective reflection makes its way inwardly in inwardness. Inwardness in an existing subject culminates in passion; corresponding to passion in the subject the truth becomes a paradox; and the fact that the truth becomes a paradox is rooted precisely in its having a relationship to an existing subject. Thus the one corresponds to the other. By forgetting that one is an existing subject, passion goes by the board and the truth is no longer a paradox; the knowing subject becomes a fantastic entity rather than a human being, and the truth becomes a fantastic object for the knowledge of this fantastic entity.

When the question of truth is raised in an objective manner, reflection is directed objectively to the truth, as an object to which the knower is related. Reflection is not focussed upon the relationship, however, but upon the question of whether it is the truth to which the knower is related. If only the object to which he is related is the truth, the subject is accounted to be in the truth. When the question of the truth is raised subjectively, reflection is directed subjectively to the nature of the individual's relationship; if only the mode of this relationship is in the truth, the individual is in the truth even if he should happen to be thus related to what is not true.[1] Let us take as an example the knowledge of God. Objectively, reflection is directed to the problem of whether this object is the true God; subjectively, reflection is directed to the question whether the individual is related to a something *in such a manner* that his relationship is in truth a God-relationship. On which side is the truth now to be found? Ah, may we not here resort to a mediation, and say: It is on neither side, but in the mediation of both? Excellently well said, provided we might have it explained how an existing individual manages to be in a state of mediation. For to be in a state of mediation is to be finished, while to exist is to become. Nor can an existing individual be in

1. The reader will observe that the question here is about essential truth, or about the truth which is essentially related to existence, and that it is precisely for the sake of clarifying it as inwardness or as subjectivity that this contrast is drawn.

two places at the same time—he cannot be an identity of subject and object. When he is nearest to being in two places at the same time he is in passion; but passion is momentary; and passion is also the highest expression of subjectivity.

The existing individual who chooses to pursue the objective way enters upon the entire approximation-process by which it is proposed to bring God to light objectively. But this is in all eternity impossible, because God is a subject, and therefore exists only for subjectivity in inwardness. The existing individual who chooses the subjective way apprehends instantly the entire dialectical difficulty involved in having to use some time, perhaps a long time, in finding God objectively; and he feels this dialectical difficulty in all its painfulness, because every moment is wasted in which he does not have God. That very instant he has God, not by virtue of any objective deliberation, but by virtue of the infinite passion of inwardness. The objective inquirer, on the other hand, is not embarrassed by such dialectical difficulties as are involved in devoting an entire period of investigation to finding God—since it is possible that the inquirer may die tomorrow; and if he lives he can scarcely regard God as something to be taken along if convenient, since God is precisely that which one takes *a tout prix,* which in the understanding of passion constitutes the true inward relationship to God.

It is at this point, so difficult dialectically, that the way swings off for everyone who knows what it means to think, and to think existentially; which is something very different from sitting at a desk and writing about what one has never done, something very different from writing *de omnibus dubitandum* and at the same time being as credulous existentially as the most sensuous of men. Here is where the way swings off, and the change is marked by the fact that while objective knowledge rambles comfortably on by way of the long road of approximation without being impelled by the urge of passion, subjective knowledge counts every delay a deadly peril, and the decision so infinitely important and so instantly pressing that it is as if the opportunity had already passed.

Now when the problem is to reckon up on which side there is most truth, whether on the side of one who seeks the true God objectively, and pursues the approximate truth of the God-idea; or on the side of one who, driven by the infinite passion of his need of God, feels an infinite concern for his own relationship to God in truth (and to be at one and the same time on both sides equally, is as we have noted not possible for an existing individual, but is merely the happy delusion of an imaginary I-am-I): the answer cannot be in doubt for anyone who has not been demoralized with the aid of science. If one who lives in the midst of Christendom goes up to the house of God, the house of the true God, with the true conception of God in his knowledge, and prays, but prays in a false spirit; and one who lives in an idolatrous community prays with the entire passion of the infinite, although his eyes rest upon the image of an idol: where is there most truth? The one prays in truth to God though he worships an idol; the other prays falsely to the true God, and hence worships in fact an idol.

When one man investigates objectively the problem of immortality, and another embraces an uncertainty with the passion of the infinite: where is there most truth, and who has the greater certainty? The one has entered upon a never-ending approximation, for the certainty of immortality lies precisely in the subjectivity of the individual; the other is immortal, and fights for his immortality by struggling with the uncertainty. Let us consider Socrates. Nowadays everyone dabbles in a few proofs; some have several such proofs, others fewer. But Socrates! He puts the question objectively in a problematic manner: *if* there is an immortality. He must therefore be accounted a doubter in comparison with one of our modern thinkers with the three proofs? By no means. On this "if" he risks his entire life, he has the courage to meet death and he has with the passion of the infinite so determined the pattern of his life that it must be found acceptable—*if* there is an immortality. Is any better proof capable of being given for the immortality of the soul? But those who have the three proofs do not at all determine their lives in conformity therewith; if there is an immortality it must feel disgust over their manner of life: can any better refutation be given of the three proofs? The bit of uncertainty that Socrates had, helped him because he himself contributed the passion of the infinite; the three proofs that the others have do not profit them at all, because they are dead to spirit and enthusiasm, and their three proofs, in lieu of proving anything else, prove just this. A young girl may enjoy all the sweetness of love on the basis of what is merely a weak hope that she is beloved, because she rests everything on this weak hope; but many a wedded matron more than once subjected to the strongest expressions of love, has in so far indeed had proofs, but strangely enough has not enjoyed *quod erat demonstrandum.* The Socratic ignorance, which Socrates held fast with the entire passion of his inwardness, was thus an expression for the principle that the eternal truth is related to an existing individual, and that this truth must therefore be a paradox for him as long as he exists; and yet it is possible that there was more truth in the Socratic ignorance as it was in him, than in the entire objective truth of the System, which flirts with what the times demand and accommodates itself to *Privatdocents.*

The objective accent falls on WHAT is said, the subjective accent on HOW it is said. This distinction holds even in the aesthetic realm, and receives definite expression in the principle that what is in itself true may in the mouth of such and such a person become untrue. In these times this distinction is particularly worthy of notice, for if we wish to express in a single sentence the difference between ancient times and our own, we should doubtless have to say: "In ancient times only an individual here and there knew the truth; now all know it, except that the inwardness of its appropriation stands in an inverse relationship to the extent of its dissemination." Aesthetically the contradiction that truth becomes untruth in this or that person's mouth,

"Abraham and Isaac"

Genesis

As it came to pass after these things, that God did tempt Abraham, and said unto him, "Abraham": and he said, "Behold, here I am."

And he said, "Take now thy son, thine only son Isaac, whom thou lovest, and get thee into the land of Moriah; and offer him there for a burnt offering upon one of the mountains which I will tell thee of."

And Abraham rose up early in the morning, and saddled his ass, and took two of his young men with him, and Isaac his son, and clave the wood for the burnt offering, and rose up, and went unto the place of which God had told him.

Then on the third day Abraham lifted up his eyes, and saw the place afar off.

And Abraham said unto his young men, "Abide ye here with the ass; and I and the lad will go yonder and worship, and come again to you."

And Abraham took the wood of the burnt offering, and laid it upon Isaac his son; and he took the fire in his hand, and a knife; and they went both of them together.

And Isaac spake unto Abraham his father, and said, "My father": and he said, "Here am I, my son." And he said, "Behold the fire and the wood: but where is the lamb for a burnt offering?"

And Abraham said, "My son, God will provide himself a lamb for a burnt offering": so they went, both of them together.

And they came to the place which God had told him of; and Abraham built an altar there,

is best construed comically: In the ethico-religious sphere, accent is again on the "how." But this is not to be understood as referring to demeanor, expression, or the like; rather it refers to the relationship sustained by the existing individual, in his own existence, to the content of his utterance. Objectively the interest is focussed merely on the thought-content, subjectively on the inwardness. At its maximum this inward "how" is the passion of the infinite, and the passion of the infinite is the truth. But the passion of the infinite is precisely subjectivity, and thus subjectivity becomes the truth. Objectively there is no infinite decisiveness, and hence it is objectively in order to annul the difference between good and evil, together with the principle of contradiction, and therewith also the infinite difference between the true and the false. Only in subjectivity is there decisiveness, to seek objectivity is to be in error. It is the passion of the infinite that is the decisive factor and not its content, for its content is precisely itself. In this manner subjectivity and the subjective "how" constitute the truth.

But the "how" which is thus subjectively accentuated precisely because the subject is an existing individual, is also subject to a dialectic with respect to time. In the passionate moment of decision, where the road swings away from objective knowledge, it seems as if the infinite decision were thereby realized. But in the same moment the existing individual finds himself in the temporal order, and the subjective "how" is transformed into a striving, a striving which receives indeed its impulse and a repeated renewal from the decisive passion of the infinite, but is nevertheless a striving.

When subjectivity is the truth, the conceptual determination of the truth must include an expression for the antithesis to objectivity, a memento of the fork in the road where the way swings off; this expression will at the same time serve as an indication of the tension of the subjective inwardness. Here is such a definition of truth: *An objective uncertainty held fast in an appropriation-process of the most passionate inwardness is the truth,* the highest truth attainable for an *existing* individual. At the point where

and laid the wood in order, and bound Isaac his son, and laid him on the altar upon the wood.

And Abraham stretched for his hand, and took the knife to slay his son.

And the Angel of the Lord called unto him out of heaven, and said, "Abraham, Abraham": and he said, "Here am I."

And said, "Lay not thine hand upon the lad, neither do thou any thing unto him: for now I know that thou fearest God, seeing thou has not withheld thy son, thine only son, from me."

And Abraham lifted up his eyes, and looked, and behold behind him a ram caught in a thicket by his horns: and Abraham went and took the ram, and offered him up for a burnt offering in the stead of his son.

And Abraham called the name of that place Jehovah-jireh: as it is said to this day, in the mount of the Lord it shall be seen.

And the angel of Lord called unto Abraham out of heaven the second time,

And said, "By myself I have sworn," saith the Lord, "for because thou has done this thing, and has not withheld thy son, thine only son, that in blessing I will bless thee, and in multiplying I will multiply thy seed as the stars of the heaven, and as the sand which is upon the seashore; and thy seed shall possess the gate of his enemies.

And in thy seed shall all the nations of the earth be blessed; because thou has obeyed my voice."

So Abraham returned unto his young men, and they rose up and went together to Beer-sheba; and Abraham dwelt at Beer-sheba.

Genesis 22, in the authorized (King James) translation of 1611.

Detail from the floor mosaic of the Betha Alpha Synagogue, near Galilea, depicting the sacrifice of Isaac. Sixth century A.D.

the way swings off (and where this is cannot be specified objectively, since it is a matter of subjectivity), there objective knowledge is placed in abeyance. Thus the subject merely has, objectively, the uncertainty; but it is this which precisely increases the tension of that infinite passion which constitutes his inwardness. The truth is precisely the venture which chooses an objective uncertainty with the passion of the infinite. I contemplate the order of nature in the hope of finding God, and I see omnipotence and wisdom; but I also see much else that disturbs my mind and excites anxiety. The sum of all this is an objective uncertainty. But it is for this very reason that the inwardness becomes as intense as it is, for it embraces this objective uncertainty with the entire passion of the infinite. In the case of a mathematical proposition the objectivity is given, but for this reason the truth of such a proposition is also an indifferent truth.

But the above definition of truth is an equivalent expression for faith. Without risk there is no faith. Faith is precisely the contradiction between the infinite passion of the individual's inwardness and the objective uncertainty. If I am capable of grasping God objectively, I do not believe, but precisely because I cannot do this I must believe. If I wish to preserve myself in faith I must constantly be intent upon holding fast the objective uncertainty, so as to remain out upon the deep, over seventy thousand fathoms of water, still preserving my faith.

In the principle that subjectivity, inwardness, is the truth, there is comprehended the Socratic wisdom, whose everlasting merit it was to have become aware of the essential significance of existence, of the fact that the knower is an existing individual. For this reason Socrates was in the truth by virtue of his ignorance, in the highest sense in which this was possible within paganism. To attain to an understanding of this, to comprehend that the misfortune of speculative philosophy is again and again to have forgotten that the knower is an existing individual, is in our objective age difficult enough. But to have made an advance upon Socrates without even having understood what he understood, is at any rate not "Socratic."

Let us now start from this point, and as was attempted in the *Fragments,* seek a determination of thought which will really carry us further. I have nothing here to do with the question of whether this proposed thought-determination is true or not, since I am merely experimenting; but it must at any rate be clearly manifest that the Socratic thought is understood within the new proposal, so that at least I do not come out behind Socrates.

When subjectivity, inwardness, is the truth, the truth becomes objectively a paradox; and the fact that the truth is objectively a paradox shows in its turn that subjectivity is the truth. For the objective situation is repellant; and the expression for the objective repulsion constitutes the tension and the measure of the corresponding inwardness. The paradoxical character of the truth is its objective uncertainty; this uncertainty is an expression for the passionate inwardness, and this passion is precisely the truth. So far the Socratic principle. The eternal and essential truth, the truth which has an essential relationship to an existing individual because it pertains essentially to existence (all other knowledge being from the Socratic point of view accidental, its scope and degree a matter of indifference), is a paradox. But the eternal essential truth is by no means in itself a paradox; but it becomes paradoxical by virtue of its relationship to an existing individual. The Socratic ignorance gives expression to the objective uncertainty attaching to the truth, while his inwardness in existing is the truth. To anticipate here what will be developed later, let me make the following remark. The Socratic ignorance is an analogue to the category of the absurd, only that there is still less of objective certainty in the absurd, and in the repellent effect that the absurd exercises. It is certain only that it is absurd, and precisely on that account it incites to an infinitely greater tension in the corresponding inwardness. The Socratic inwardness in existing is an analogue to faith; only that the inwardness of faith, corresponding as it does, not to the repulsion of the Socratic ignorance, but to the repulsion exerted by the absurd, is infinitely more profound.

Socratically the eternal essential truth is by no means in its own nature paradoxical, but only in its relationship to an existing individual. This finds expression in another Socratic proposition, namely, that all knowledge is recollection. This proposition is not for Socrates a cue to the speculative enterprise, and hence he does not follow it up; essentially it becomes a Platonic principle. Here the way swings off; Socrates concentrates essentially upon accentuating existence, while Plato forgets this and loses himself in speculation. Socrates' infinite merit is to have been an *existing* thinker, not a speculative philosopher who forgets what it means to exist. For Socrates therefore the principle that all knowledge is recollection has at the moment of his leave-taking and as the constantly rejected possibility of engaging in speculation, the following two-fold significance: (1) that the knower is essentially *integer,* and that with respect to the knowledge of the eternal truth he is confronted with no other difficulty than the circumstance that he exists; which difficulty, however, is so essential and decisive for him that it means that existing, the process of transformation to inwardness in existing and by existing, is the truth; (2) that existence in time does not have any decisive significance, because the possibility of taking oneself back into eternity through recollection is always there, though this possibility is constantly nullified by utilizing the time, not for speculation, but for the transformation to inwardness in existing.

The infinite merit of the Socratic position was precisely to accentuate the fact that the knower is an existing individual, and that the task of existing is his essential task. Making an advance upon Socrates by failing to understand this, is quite a mediocre achievement. This Socratic principle we must therefore bear in mind, and then inquire whether the formula may not be so altered as really to make an advance beyond the Socratic position.

Subjectivity, inwardness, has been posited as the truth; can any expression for the truth be found which has a still higher degree of inwardness? Aye, there is such an expression, provided the principle that subjectivity or inwardness is the truth begins by positing the opposite principle: that subjectivity is untruth. Let us not at this point succumb to such haste as to fail in making the necessary distinctions. Speculative philosophy also says that subjectivity is untruth, but says it in order to stimulate a movement in precisely the opposite direction, namely, in the direction of the principle that objectivity is the truth. Speculative philosophy determines subjectivity negatively as tending toward objectivity. This second determination of ours, however, places a hindrance in its own way while proposing to begin, which has the effect of making the inwardness far more intensive. Socratically speaking, subjectivity is untruth if it refuses to understand that subjectivity is truth, but, for example, desires to become objective. Here, on the other hand, subjectivity in beginning upon the task of becoming the truth through a subjectifying process, is in the difficulty that it is already untruth. Thus, the labor of the task is thrust backward, backward, that is, in inwardness. So far is it from being the case that the way tends in the direction of objectivity, that the beginning merely lies still deeper in subjectivity.

"Religion"

Paul Tillich

Some Christian theologians will ask whether religion is here considered as a creative element of the human spirit rather than as gift of divine revelation. And if one replies that religion is an aspect of man's spiritual life, they will turn away. And some secular scientists will ask whether religion is to be considered a lasting quality of the human spirit instead of an effect of changing psychological and sociological conditions. And if one answers that religion is a necessary aspect of man's spiritual life, they turn away like the theologians, but in an opposite direction.

This situation shows an almost schizophrenic split in our collective consciousness, a split which threatens our spiritual freedom by driving the contemporary mind into irrational and compulsive affirmations or negations of religion. And there is as much compulsive reaction to religion on the scientific side as there is on the religious side. . . .

If we analyze carefully these two groups . . . we discover the surprising fact that although they come from opposite directions, they have something definite in common. Both . . . define religion as man's relation to divine beings, whose existence the theological critics assert and the scientific critics deny. But it is just this idea of religion which makes any understanding of religion impossible. If you start with the question whether God does or does not exist, you can never reach Him; and if you assert that He does exist, you can reach Him even less than if you assert that He does not exist. A God about whose existence or nonexistence you can argue is a thing beside others within the universe of existing things. And the question is quite justified whether such a thing does exist, and the answer is equally justified that it does not exist. It is regrettable that scientists believe that they have refuted religion when they rightly have shown that there is no evidence whatsoever for the assumption that such a being exists. Actually, they have not only not refuted religion, but they have done it a considerable service. They have forced it to reconsider and to restate the meaning of the tremendous word *God.* Unfortunately, many theologians make the same mistake. They begin their message with the assertion that there is a highest being called God, whose authoritative revelations they have received. They are more dangerous for religion than the so-called atheistic scientists. They take the first step on the road which inescapably leads to what is called atheism. Theologians who make of God a highest being who has given some people information about Himself, provoke inescapably the resistance of those who are told they must subject themselves to the authority of this information.

From *Man's Right to Knowledge* (1955).

But the subject cannot be untruth eternally, or eternally be presupposed as having been untruth; it must have been brought to this condition in time, or here become untruth in time. The Socratic paradox consisted in the fact that the eternal was related to an existing individual, but now existence has stamped itself upon the existing individual a second time. There has taken place so essential an alteration in him that he cannot now possibly take himself back into the eternal by way of recollection. To do this is to speculate; to be able to do this, but to reject the possibility by apprehending the task of life as a realization of inwardness in existing, is the Socratic position. But now the difficulty is that what followed Socrates on his way as a rejected possibility, has become an impossibility. If engaging in speculation was a dubious merit even from the point of view of the Socratic, it is now neither more nor less than confusion.

The paradox emerges when the eternal truth and existence are placed in juxtaposition with one another; each time the stamp of existence is brought to bear, the paradox becomes more clearly evident. Viewed Socratically the knower was simply an existing individual, but now the existing individual bears the stamp of having been essentially altered by existence.

Let us now call the untruth of the individual *Sin*. Viewed eternally he cannot be sin, nor can he be eternally presupposed as having been in sin. By coming into existence therefore (for the beginning was that subjectivity is untruth), he becomes a sinner. He is not born as a sinner in the sense that he is presupposed as being a sinner before he is born, but he is born in sin and as a sinner. This we might call *Original Sin*. But if existence has in this manner acquired a power over him, he is prevented from taking himself back into the eternal by way of recollection. If it was paradoxical to posit the eternal truth in relationship to an existing individual, it is now absolutely paradoxical to posit it in relationship to such an individual as we have here defined. But the more difficult it is made for him to take himself out of existence by way of recollection, the more profound is the inwardness that his existence may have in existence; and when it is made impossible for him, when he is held so fast in existence that the back door of recollection is forever closed to him, then his inwardness will be the most profound possible. But let us never forget that the Socratic merit was to stress the fact that the knower is an existing individual; for the more difficult the matter becomes, the greater the temptation to hasten along the easy road of speculation, away from fearful dangers and crucial decisions, to the winning of renown and honors and property, and so forth. If even Socrates understood the dubiety of taking himself speculatively out of existence back into the eternal, although no other difficulty confronted the existing individual except that he existed, and that existing was his essential task, now it is impossible. Forward he must, backward he cannot go.

Subjectivity is the truth. By virtue of the relationship subsisting between the eternal truth and the existing individual, the paradox came into being. Let us now go further, let us suppose that the eternal essential truth is itself a paradox. How does the paradox come into being? By putting the eternal essential truth into juxtaposition with existence. Hence when we posit such a conjunction within the truth itself, the truth becomes a paradox. The eternal truth has come into being in time: this is the paradox. If in accordance with the determinations just posited, the subject is prevented by sin from taking himself back into the eternal, now he need not trouble himself about this; for now the eternal essential truth is not behind him but in front of him, through its being in existence or having existed, so that if the individual does not existentially and in existence lay hold of the truth, he will never lay hold of it.

Existence can never be more sharply accentuated than by means of these determinations. The evasion by which speculative philosophy attempts to recollect itself out of existence has been made impossible. With reference to this, there is nothing for speculation to do except to arrive at an understanding of this impossibility; every speculative attempt which insists on being speculative shows *eo ipso* that it has not understood it. The individual may thrust all this away from him, and take refuge in speculation; but it is impossible first to accept it, and then to revoke it by means of speculation, since it is definitely calculated to prevent speculation.

When the eternal truth is related to an existing individual it becomes a paradox. The paradox repels in the inwardness of the existing individual, through the objective uncertainty and the corresponding Socratic ignorance. But since the paradox is not in the first instance itself paradoxical (but only in its relationship to the existing individual), it does not repel with a sufficient intensive inwardness. For without risk there is no faith, and the greater the risk the greater the faith; the more objective security the less inwardness (for inwardness is precisely subjectivity), and the less objective security the more profound the possible inwardness. When the paradox is paradoxical in itself, it repels the individual by virtue of its absurdity, and the corresponding passion of inwardness is faith. But subjectivity, inwardness, is the truth; for otherwise we have forgotten what the merit of the Socratic position is. But there can be no stronger expression for inwardness than when the retreat out of existence into the eternal by way of recollection is impossible; and when, with truth confronting the individual as a paradox, gripped in the anguish and pain of sin, facing the tremendous risk of the objective insecurity, the individual believes. But without risk no faith, not even the Socratic form of faith, much less the form of which we here speak.

When Socrates believed that there was a God, he held fast to the objective uncertainty with the whole passion of his inwardness, and it is precisely in this contradiction and in this risk, that faith is rooted. Now it is otherwise. Instead of the objective uncertainty, there is here a certainty, namely, that objectively it is absurd; and this absurdity, held fast in the passion of inwardness, is faith. The Socratic ignorance is as a witty jest in comparison with the earnestness of facing the absurd; and the Socratic existential inwardness is as Greek light-mindedness in comparison with the grave strenuosity of faith.

What now is the absurd? The absurd is—that the eternal truth has come into being in time, that God has come into being, has been born, has grown up, and so forth, precisely like any other individual human being, quite indistinguishable from other individuals.

Blaise Pascal

"THE WAGER"

BLAISE PASCAL (1623–1662), born in Clermont in Auvergne, France, was a child prodigy who became a theologian, scientist, philosopher, inventor, and mathematician. He made major contributions to probability theory, number theory, and

---

From Blaise Pascal, *Thoughts,* trans. W. F. Trotter (New York: P. F. Collier & Son, 1910), p. 233.

geometry. In this selection he argues that it is in one's rational self-interest to believe that God exists.

Infinite—nothing.—Our soul is cast into a body, where it finds number, time, dimension. Thereupon it reasons, and calls this nature, necessity, and can believe nothing else.

Unity joined to infinity adds nothing to it, no more than one foot to an infinite measure. The finite is annihilated in the presence of the infinite, and becomes a pure nothing. So our spirit before God, so our justice before divine justice. There is not so great disproportion between our justice and that of God, as between unity and infinity.

The justice of God must be vast like His compassion. Now, justice to the outcast is less vast, and ought less to offend our feelings than mercy towards the elect.

We know that there is an infinite, and are ignorant of its nature. As we know it to be false that numbers are finite, it is therefore true that there is an infinity in number. But we do not know what it is. It is false that it is even, it is false that it is odd; for the addition of a unit can make no change in its nature. Yet it is a number, and every number is odd or even (this is certainly true of every finite number). So we may well know that there is a God without knowing what He is. Is there not one substantial truth, seeing there are so many things which are not the truth itself?

We know then the existence and nature of the finite, because we also are finite and have extension. We know the existence of the infinite, and are ignorant of its nature, because it has extension like us, but not limits like us. But we know neither the existence nor the nature of God, because He has neither extension nor limits.

But by faith we know His existence; in glory we shall know His nature. Now, I have already shown that we may well know the existence of a thing, without knowing its nature.

Let us now speak according to natural lights.

If there is a God, He is infinitely incomprehensible, since, having neither part nor limits, He has no affinity to us. We are then incapable of knowing either what He is or if He is. This being so, who will dare to undertake the decision of the question? Not we, who have no affinity to Him.

Who then will blame Christians for not being able to give a reason for their belief, since they profess a religion for which they cannot give a reason? They declare, in expounding it to the world, that it is a foolishness, *stultitiam*; and then you complain that they do not prove it! If they proved it, they would not keep their words; it is in lacking proofs, that they are not lacking in sense. "Yes, but although this excuses those who offer it as such, and [takes] away from them the blame of putting it forward without reason, it does not excuse those who receive it." Let us then examine this point, and say, "God is, or He is not." But to which side shall we incline? Reason can decide nothing here. There is an infinite chaos which separates us. A game is being played at the extremity of this infinite distance where heads or tails will turn up. What will you wager? According to reason, you can do neither the one thing nor the other; according to reason, you can defend neither of the propositions.

Do not then reprove for error those who have made a choice; for you know nothing about it. "No, but I blame them for having made, not this choice, but a choice; for again both he who chooses heads and he who chooses tails are equally at fault, they are both in the wrong. The true course is not to wager at all."

—Yes; but you must wager. It is not optional. You are embarked. Which will you choose then; Let us see. Since you must choose, let us see which interests you least. You have two things to lose, the true and the good; and two things to stake, your reason and your will, your knowledge and your happiness; and your nature has two things to shun, error and misery. Your reason is no more shocked in choosing one rather than the other, since you must of necessity choose. This is one point settled. But your happiness? Let us weigh the gain and the loss in wagering that God is. Let us estimate these two chances. If you gain, you gain all; if you lose, you lose nothing. Wager them without hesitation that He is.—"That is very fine. Yes, I must wager; but I may perhaps wager too much."—Let us see. Since there is an equal risk of gain and of loss, if you had only to gain two lives, instead of one, you might still wager. But if there were three lives to gain, you would have to play (since you are under the necessity of playing), and you would be imprudent, when you are forced to play, not to chance your life to gain three at a game where there is an equal risk of loss and gain. But there is an eternity of life and happiness. And this being so, if there were an infinity of chances, of which one only would be for you, you would still be right in wagering one to win two, and you would act stupidly, being obliged to play, by refusing to stake one life against three at a game in which out of an infinity of [chances there is one for you, if there were an infinity of] happy lifes to gain. But there is here an infinity of an infinitely happy life to gain, a chance of gain against a finite number of chances of loss, and what you stake is finite. It is all divided; wherever the infinite is and there is not an infinity of chances of loss against that of gain, there is no time to hesitate, you must give all. And thus, when one is forced to play, he must renounce reason to preserve his life, rather than risk it for infinite gain, as likely to happen as the loss of nothingness.

For it is no use to say it is uncertain if we will gain, and it is certain that we risk, and that the infinite distance between the *certainty* of what is staked and the *uncertainty* of what will be gained, equals the finite good which is certainly staked against the uncertain infinite. It is not so, as every player stakes a certainty to gain an uncertainty, and yet he stakes a finite certainty to gain a finite uncertainty, without transgressing against reason. There is not an infinite distance between the certainty staked and the uncertainty of the gain; that is untrue. In truth, there is an infinity between the certainty of gain and the certainty of loss. But the uncertainty of the gain is proportioned to the certainty of the stake according to the proportion of the chances of gain and loss. Hence it comes that, if there are as many risks on one side as on the other, the course is to play even; and then the certainty of the stake is equal to the uncertainty of the gain, so far is it from the fact that there is an infinite distance between them. And so our proposition is of infinite force, when there is the finite to stake in a game where there are equal risks of gain and of loss, and the infinite to gain. This is demonstrable; and if men are capable of any truths, this is one.

"I confess it, I admit it. But still is there no means of seeing the faces of the cards?"—Yes, Scripture and the rest, &c.—"Yes, but I have my hands tied and my mouth closed; I am forced to wager, and am not free. I am not released, and am so made that I cannot believe. What then would you have me do?"

"True. But at least learn your inability to believe, since reason brings you to this, and yet you cannot believe. Endeavour then to convince yourself, not by increase of proofs of God, but by the abatement of your passions. You would like to attain faith, and do not know the way; you would like to cure yourself of unbelief, and ask the remedy for it. Learn of those who have been bound like you, and who now stake all their possessions. These are people who know the way which you would follow, and who are cured of an ill of which you would be cured. Follow the way by which they began; by acting as if they believe, taking the holy water, having masses said, &c. Even this will naturally make you believe, and deaden your acuteness.—"But this is what I am afraid of."—And why? What have you to lose?

But to show you that this leads you there, it is this which will lessen the passions, which are your stumbling-blocks.

The end of this discourse.—Now what harm will befall you in taking this side? You will be faithful, honest, humble, grateful, generous, a sincere friend, truthful. Certainly you will not have those poisonous pleasures, glory and luxury; but will you not have others? I will tell you that you will thereby gain in this life, and that, at each step you take on this road, you will see so great certainty of gain, so much nothingness in what you risk, that you will at last recognize that you have wagered for something certain and infinite, for which you have given nothing.

"Ah! This discourse transports me, charms me," &c.

If this discourse pleases you and seems impressive, know that it is made by a man who has knelt, both before and after it, in prayer to that Being, infinite and without parts, before whom he lays all he has, for you also to lay before Him all you have for your own good and for His glory, so that strength may be given to lowliness.

Robert Merrihew Adams

"KIERKEGAARD'S ARGUMENTS AGAINST OBJECTIVE REASONING IN RELIGION"

A brief biography of Adams appears on page 275.

It is sometimes held that there is something in the nature of religious faith itself that renders it useless or undesirable to reason objectively in support of such faith, even if the reasoning should happen to have considerable plausibility. Søren Kierkegaard's *Concluding Unscientific Postscript* is probably the document most commonly cited as representative of this view. In the present essay I shall discus three arguments for the view. I call them the Approximation Argument, the Postponement Argument, and the Passion Argument; and I suggest they can all be found in the *Postscript.* I shall try to show that the Approximation Argument is a bad argument. The other two will not be so easily disposed of, however. I believe they show that Kierkegaard's conclusion, or something like it, does indeed follow from a certain conception of religiousness—a conception which has some appeal, although for reasons which I shall briefly suggest, I am not prepared to accept it.

Kierkegaard uses the word 'objective' and its cognates in several senses, most of which need not concern us here. We are interested in the sense in which he uses it when he says, "it is precisely a misunderstanding to seek an objective assurance," and when he speaks of "an objective uncertainty held fast in the appropriation-process of the most passionate inward-

Robert Merrihew Adams, "Kierkegaard's Arguments against Objective Reasoning in Religion," *The Monist,* 60 (1977), 228–243. Reprinted by permission of the publisher and the author.

ness" (pp. 41, 182).[1] Let us say that a piece of reasoning, *R,* is *objective reasoning* just in case every (or almost every) intelligent, fairminded, and sufficiently informed person would regard *R* as showing or tending to show (in the circumstances in which *R* is used, and to the extent claimed in *R*) that *R*'s conclusion is true or probably true. Uses of 'objective' and 'objectively' in other contexts can be understood from their relation to this one; for example, an objective uncertainty is a proposition which cannot be shown by objective reasoning to be certainly true.

I. THE APPROXIMATION ARGUMENT

"Is it possible to base an eternal happiness upon historical knowledge?" is one of the central questions in the *Postscript,* and in the *Philosophical Fragments* to which it is a "postscript." Part of Kierkegaard's answer to the question is that it is not possible to base an eternal happiness on objective reasoning about historical facts.

> For nothing is more readily evident than that the greatest attainable certainty with respect to anything historical is merely an *approximation.* And an approximation, when viewed as a basis for an eternal happiness, is wholly inadequate, since the incommensurability makes a result impossible (p. 25).

Kierkegaard maintains that it is possible, however, to base an eternal happiness on a belief in historical facts that is independent of objective evidence for them, and that that is what one must do in order to be a Christian. This is the Approximation Argument for the proposition that Christian faith cannot be based on objective reasoning.[2] (It is assumed that some belief about historical facts is an essential part of Christian faith, so that if religious faith cannot be based on objective historical reasoning, then Christian faith cannot be based on objective reasoning at all.) Let us examine the argument in detail.

Its first premise is Kierkegaard's claim that "the greatest attainable certainty with respect to anything historical is merely an approximation." I take him to mean that historical evidence, objectively considered, never completely excludes the possibility of error. "It goes without saying," he claims, "that it is impossible in the case of historical problems to reach an objective decision so certain that no doubt could disturb it" (p. 41). For Kierkegaard's purposes it does not matter how small the possibility of error is, so long as it is finitely small (that is, so long as it is not literally infinitesimal). He insists (p. 31) that his Approximation Argument makes no appeal to the supposition that the objective evidence for Christian historical beliefs is weaker than the objective evidence for any other historical belief. The argument turns on a claim about *all* historical evidence. The probability of error in our belief that there was an American Civil War in the nineteenth century, for instance, might be as small as $1/10^{2,000,000}$; that would be a large enough chance of error for Kierkegaard's argument.

It might be disputed, but let us assume for the sake of argument that there is some such finitely small probability of error in the objective grounds for all historical beliefs, as Kierkegaard held. This need not keep us from saying that we "know," and it is "certain," that there was an American Civil War. For such an absurdly small possibility of error is as good as no possibility

1. Søren Kierkegaard, *Concluding Unscientific Postscript,* trans. David F. Swenson; introduction, notes, and completion of translation by Walter Lowrie (Princeton, N.J.: Princeton University Press, 1941). Page references in parentheses in the body of the present paper are to this work.

2. The argument is not original with Kierkegaard. It can be found in works of G. E. Lessing and D. F. Strauss that Kierkegaard had read. See especially Thulstrup's quotation and discussion of a passage from Strauss in the commentary portion of Søren Kierkegaard, *Philosophical Fragments,* trans. David F. Swenson, 2d ed., translation revised by Howard V. Hong, with introduction and commentary by Niels Thulstrup (Princeton, N.J.: Princeton University Press, 1962), pp. 149–51.

of error at all, "for all practical intents and purposes," as we might say. Such a possibility of error is too small to be worth worrying about.

But would it be too small to be worth worrying about if we had an *infinite* passionate interest in the question about the Civil War? If we have an infinite passionate interest in something, there is no limit to how important it is to us. (The nature of such an interest will be discussed more fully in section III.) Kierkegaard maintains that in relation to an infinite passionate interest *no* possibility of error is too small to be worth worrying about. "In relation to an eternal happiness, and an infinite passionate interest in its behalf (in which latter alone the former can exist), an iota is of importance, of infinite importance . . ." (p. 28). This is the basis for the second premise of the Approximation Argument, which is Kierkegaard's claim that "an approximation, when viewed as a basis for an eternal happiness, is wholly inadequate" (p. 25). "An approximation is essentially incommensurable with an infinite personal interest in an eternal happiness" (p. 26).

John the Baptist baptizing the people. Depiction on a door to the baptistry in Florence. By Andrea Pisano, c. 1330.

At this point in the argument it is important to have some understanding of Kierkegaard's conception of faith, and the way in which he thinks faith excludes doubt. Faith must be decisive; in fact it seems to consist in a sort of decision-making. "The conclusion of belief is not so much a conclusion as a resolution, and it is for this reason that belief excludes doubt."[3] The decision of faith is a decision to disregard the possibility of error—to act on what is believed, without hedging one's bets to take account of any possibility of error.

To disregard the possibility of error is not to be unaware of it, or fail to consider it, or lack anxiety about it. Kierkegaard insists that the believer must be keenly *aware* of the risk of error. "If I wish to preserve myself in faith I must constantly be intent upon holding fast the objective uncertainty, so as to remain out upon the deep, over seventy thousand fathoms of water, still preserving my faith" (p. 182).

For Kierkegaard, then, to ask whether faith in a historical fact can be based on objective reasoning is to ask whether objective reasoning can justify one in disregarding the possibility of error which (he thinks) historical evidence always leaves. Here another aspect of Kierkegaard's conception of faith plays its part in the argument. He thinks that in all genuine religious faith the believer is *infinitely* interested in the object of his faith. And he thinks it follows that objective reasoning cannot justify him in disregarding *any* possibility of error about the object of faith, and therefore cannot lead him all the way to religious faith where a historical fact is concerned. The farthest it could lead him is to the conclusion that *if* he had only a certain finite (though very great) interest in the matter,

3. Kierkegaard, *Philosophical Fragments,* p. 104; cf. pp. 102–3.

the possibility of error would be too small to be worth worrying about and he would be justified in disregarding it. But faith disregards a possibility of error that *is* worth worrying about, since an infinite interest is involved. Thus faith requires a "leap" beyond the evidence, a leap that cannot be justified by objective reasoning (cf. p. 90).

There is something right in what Kierkegaard is saying here, but his Approximation Argument is a bad argument. He is right in holding that grounds of doubt which may be insignificant for most practical purposes can be extremely troubling for the intensity of a religious concern, and that it may require great decisiveness, or something like courage, to overcome them religiously. But he is mistaken in holding that objective reasoning could not justify one in disregarding any possibility of error about something in which one is infinitely interested.

The mistake, I believe, lies in his overlooking the fact that there are at least two different reasons one might have for disregarding a possibility of error. The first is that the possibility is too small to be worth worrying about. The second is that the risk of not disregarding the possibility of error would be greater than the risk of disregarding it. Of these two reasons only the first is ruled out by the infinite passionate interest.

I will illustrate this point with two examples, one secular and one religious. A certain woman has a very great (though not infinite) interest in her husband's love for her. She rightly judges that the objective evidence available to her renders it 99.9 percent probable that he loves her truly. The intensity of her interest is sufficient to cause her some *anxiety* over the remaining 1/1,000 chance that he loves her not; for her this chance is not too small to be worth worrying about. (Kierkegaard uses a similar example to support his Approximation Argument; see p. 511). But she (very reasonably) wants to *disregard* the risk of error, in the sense of not hedging her bets, if he does love her. This desire is at least as strong as her desire not to be deceived if he does not love her. Objective reasoning should therefore suffice to bring her to the conclusion that she ought to disregard the risk of error, since by not disregarding it she would run 999 times as great a risk of frustrating one of these desires.

Or suppose you are trying to base your eternal happiness on your relation to Jesus, and therefore have an infinite passionate interest in the question whether he declared Peter and his episcopal successors to be infallible in matters of religious doctrine. You want to be committed to whichever is the true belief on this question, disregarding any possibility of error in it. And suppose, just for the sake of argument, that objective historical evidence renders it 99 percent probable that Jesus did declare Peter and his successors to be infallible—or 99 percent probable that he did not—for our present discussion it does not matter which. The 1 percent chance of error is enough to make you *anxious,* in view of your infinite interest. But objective reasoning leads to the conclusion that you ought to commit yourself to the more probable opinion, *disregarding* the risk of error, if your strongest desire in the matter is to be so committed to the true opinion. For the only other way to satisfy this desire would be to commit yourself to the less probable opinion, disregarding the risk of error in it. The first way will be successful if and only if the more probable opinion is true, and the second way if and only if the less probable opinion is true. Surely it is prudent to do what gives you a 99 percent chance of satisfying your strong desire, in preference to what gives you only a 1 percent chance of satisfying it.

In this argument your strong desire to be committed to the true opinion is presupposed. The reasonableness of this desire may depend on a belief for which no probability can be established by purely historical reasoning, such as the belief that Jesus is God. But any difficulties arising from this point are distinct from those urged in the Approximation Argument, which itself presupposes the infinite passionate interest in the historical question.

There is some resemblance between my arguments in these examples and Pascal's famous Wager argument. But whereas Pascal's argument turns on weighing an infinite interest against a finite one, mine turn on weighing a large chance of success against a small one. . . .

The reader may well have noticed in the foregoing discussion some unclarity about what sort of justification is being demanded and given for religious beliefs about historical facts. There are at least two different types of question about a proposition which I might try to settle by objective reasoning: (1) Is it probable that the proposition is true? (2) In view of the evidence which I have for and against the proposition, and my interest in the matter, is it prudent for me to have faith in the truth of the proposition, disregarding the possibility of error? Correspondingly, we may distinguish two ways in which a belief can be *based on* objective reasoning. The proposition believed may be the conclusion of a piece of objective reasoning, and accepted because it is that. We may say that such a belief is *objectively probable.* Or one might hold a belief or maintain a religious faith because of a piece of objective reasoning whose conclusion is that it would be prudent, morally right, or otherwise desirable for one to hold that belief or faith. In this latter case let us say that the belief is *objectively advantageous.* It is clear that historical beliefs can be objectively probable; and in the Approximation Argument, Kierkegaard does not deny Christian historical beliefs can be objectively probable. His thesis is, in effect, that in view of an infinite passionate interest in their subject matter, they cannot be objectively advantageous, and therefore cannot be fully justified objectively, even if they are objectively probable. It is this thesis that I have attempted to refute. I have not been discussing the question whether Christian historical beliefs are objectively probable.

II. THE POSTPONEMENT ARGUMENT

The trouble with objective historical reasoning, according to the Approximation Argument, is that it cannot yield complete certainty. But that is not Kierkegaard's only complaint against it as a basis for religious faith. He also objects that objective historical inquiry is never completely finished, so that one who seeks to base his faith on it postpones his religious commitment forever. In the process of historical research "new difficulties arise and are overcome, and new difficulties again arise. Each generation inherits from its predecessor the illusion that the method is quite impeccable, but the learned scholars have not yet succeeded . . . and so forth. . . . The infinite personal passionate interest of the subject . . . vanishes more and more, because the decision is postponed, and postponed as following directly upon the result of the learned inquiry" (p. 28). As soon as we take "an historical document" as "our standard for the determination of Christian truth," we are "involved in a parenthesis whose conclusion is everlastingly prospective" (p. 28)—that is, we are involved in a religious digression which keeps religious commitment forever in the future.[4]

Kierkegaard has such fears about allowing religious faith to rest on *any* empirical reasoning. The danger of postponement of commitment arises not only from the uncertainties of historical scholarship, but also in connection with the design argument for God's existence. In the *Philosophical Fragments* Kierkegaard notes some objections to the attempt to prove God's existence from evidence of "the wisdom in nature, the goodness, the wisdom in the governance of the world," and then says, "even if I

4. Essentially the same argument can be found in a plea, which has had great influence among more recent theologians, for making Christian faith independent of the results of critical historical study of the Bible: Martin Kähler's famous lecture, first delivered in 1892, *Der sogenannte historische Jesus und der geschichtliche biblische Christus* (Munich: Christus Kaiser Verlag, 1961), p. 50f.

began I would never finish, and would in addition have to live constantly in suspense, lest something so terrible should suddenly happen that my bit of proof would be demolished."[5] What we have before us is a quite general sort of objection to the treatment of religious beliefs as empirically testable. On this point many analytical philosophers seem to agree with Kierkegaard. Much discussion in recent analytical philosophy of religion has proceeded from the supposition that religious beliefs are not empirically testable. I think it is far from obvious that that supposition is correct; and it is interesting to consider arguments that may be advanced to support it.

Kierkegaard's statements suggest an argument that I call the Postponement Argument. Its first premise is that one cannot have an authentic religious faith without being totally committed to it. In order to be totally committed to a belief, in the relevant sense, one must be determined not to abandon the belief under any circumstances that one recognizes as epistemically possible.

The second premise is that one cannot yet be totally committed to any belief which one bases on an inquiry in which one recognizes any possibility of a future need to revise the results. Total commitment to any belief so based will necessarily be postponed. I believe that this premise, suitably interpreted, is true. Consider the position of someone who regards himself as committed to a belief on the basis of objective evidence, but who recognizes some possibility that future discoveries will destroy the objective justification of the belief. We must ask how he is disposed to react in the event, however unlikely, that the objective basis of his belief is overthrown. Is he prepared to abandon the belief in that event? If so, he is not totally committed to the belief in the relevant sense. But if he is determined to cling to his belief even if its objective justification is taken away, then he is not basing the belief on the objective justification—or at least he is not basing it solely on the justification.[6]

The conclusion to be drawn from these two premises is that authentic religious faith cannot be based on an inquiry in which one recognizes any possibility of a future need to revise the results. We ought to note that this conclusion embodies two important restrictions on the scope of the argument.

In the first place, we are not given an argument that authentic religious faith cannot *have* an objective justification that is subject to possible future revision. What we are given is an argument that the authentic believer's holding of his religious belief cannot *depend* entirely on such a justification.

In the second place, this conclusion applies only to those who *recognize* some epistemic possibility that the objective results which appear to support their belief may be overturned. I think it would be unreasonable to require, as part of total commitment, a determination with regard to one's response to circumstances that one does not recognize as possible at all. It may be, however, that one does not recognize such a possibility when one ought to.

Kierkegaard needs one further premise in order to arrive at the conclusion that authentic religious faith cannot without error be based on any objective empirical reasoning. This third premise is that in every objective empirical inquiry there is always, objectively considered, some epistemic possibility that the results of the inquiry will need to be revised in view of new evidence or new reasoning. I believe Kierkegaard makes this assumption; he certainly makes it with regard to historical inquiry. From this premise it follows that one is in error if in any objective empirical inquiry one does not rec-

5. Kierkegaard, *Philosophical Fragments,* p. 52.

6. Kierkegaard notes the possibility that in believing in God's existence "I make so bold as to defy all objections, even those that have not yet been made." But in that case he thinks the belief is not really based on the evidence of God's work in the world; "it is not from the works that I make my proof" (*Philosophical Fragments,* p. 52).

ognize any possibility of a future need to revise the results. But if one does recognize such a possibility, then according to the conclusion already reached in the Postponement Argument, one cannot base an authentic religious faith on the inquiry.

Some philosophers might attack the third premise of this argument; and certainly it is controversial. But I am more inclined to criticize the first premise. There is undoubtedly something plausible about the claim that authentic religious faith must involve a commitment so complete that the believer is resolved not to abandon his belief under any circumstances that he regards as epistemically possible. If you are willing to abandon your ostensibly religious beliefs for the sake of objective inquiry, mightn't we justly say that objective inquiry is your real religion, the thing to which you are most deeply committed?

There is also something plausible to be said on the other side, however. It has commonly been thought to be an important part of religious ethics that one ought to be humble, teachable, open to correction, new inspiration, and growth of insight, even (and perhaps especially) in important religious beliefs. That view would have to be discarded if we were to concede to Kierkegaard that the heart of commitment in religion is an unconditional determination not to change in one's important religious beliefs. In fact I think there is something radically wrong with this conception of religious commitment. Faith ought not to be thought of as unconditional devotion to a belief. For in the first place the object of religious devotion is not a belief or attitude of one's own, but God. And in the second place it may be doubted that religious devotion to God can or should be completely unconditional. God's love for sinners is sometimes said to be completely unconditional, not being based on any excellence or merit of theirs. But religious devotion to God is generally thought to be based on his goodness and love. It is the part of the strong, not the weak, to love unconditionally. And in relation to God we are weak.

III. THE PASSION ARGUMENT

In Kierkegaard's statements of the Approximation Argument and the Postponement Argument it is assumed that a system of religious beliefs might be objectively probable. It is only for the sake of argument, however, that Kierkegaard allows this assumption. He really holds that religious faith, by its very nature, needs objective *im*probability. "Anything that is almost probable, or probable, or extremely and emphatically probable, is something [one] can almost know, or as good as know, or extremely and emphatically almost *know*—but it is impossible to *believe*" (p. 189). Nor will Kierkegaard countenance the suggestion that religion ought to go beyond belief to some almost-knowledge based on probability. "Faith is the highest passion in a man. There are perhaps many in every generation who do not even reach it, but no one gets further."[7] It would be a betrayal of religion to try to go beyond faith. The suggestion that faith might be replaced by "probabilities and guarantees" is for the believer "a temptation to be resisted with all his strength" (p. 15). The attempt to establish religious beliefs on a foundation of objective probability is therefore no service to religion, but inimical to religion's true interests. The approximation to certainty which might be afforded by objective probability is rejected, not only for the reasons given in the Approximation Argument and Postponement Argument, but also from a deeper motive, "since on the contrary it behooves us to get rid of introductory guarantees of security, proofs from consequences, and the whole mob of public pawnbrokers and guarantors, so as to permit the absurd to stand out in all its clarity—in order that the individual may believe if he wills it; I merely say that it must be strenuous in the highest degree so to believe" (p. 190).

7. Søren Kierkegaard, *Fear and Trembling*, trans. Walter Lowrie, 2d ed. (Princeton, N.J.: Princeton University Press, 1970; published in one volume with *The Sickness unto Death*), p. 131. Cf. *Postscript*, p. 31f.

As this last quotation indicates, Kierkegaard thinks that religious belief ought to be based on a strenuous exertion of the will—a passionate striving. His reasons for thinking that objective probability is religiously undesirable have to do with the place of passion in religion, and constitute what I call the Passion Argument. The first premise of the argument is that the most essential and the most valuable feature of religiousness is passion, indeed an infinite passion, a passion of the greatest possible intensity. The second premise is that an infinite passion requires objective improbability. And the conclusion therefore is that that which is most essential and most valuable in religiousness requires objective improbability.

My discussion of this argument will have three parts. (a) First I will try to clarify, very briefly, what it is that is supposed to be objectively improbable. (b) Then we will consider Kierkegaard's reasons for holding that infinite passion requires objective improbability. In so doing we will also gain a clearer understanding of what a Kierkegaardian infinite passion is. (c) Finally I will discuss the first premise of the argument—although issues will arise at that point which I do not pretend to be able to settle by argument.

(a) What are the beliefs whose improbability is needed by religious passion? Kierkegaard will hardly be satisfied with the improbability of just any one belief; it must surely be at least an important belief. On the other hand it would clearly be preposterous to suppose that every belief involved in Christianity must be objectively improbable. (Consider, for example, the belief that the man Jesus did indeed live.) I think that what is demanded in the Passion Argument is the objective improbability of at least one belief which must be true if the goal sought by the religious passion is to be attained.

(b) We can find in the *Postscript* suggestions of several reasons for thinking that an infinite passion needs objective improbability. The two that seem to be most interesting have to do with (i) the risks accepted and (ii) the costs paid in pursuance of a passionate interest.

(i) One reason that Kierkegaard has for valuing objective improbability is that it increases the *risk* attaching to the religious life, and risk is so essential for the expression of religious passion that "without risk there is no faith" (p. 182). About the nature of an eternal happiness, the goal of religious striving, Kierkegaard says "there is nothing to be said . . . except that it is the good which is attained by venturing everything absolutely" (p. 382).

> But what then does it mean to venture? A venture is the precise correlative of an uncertainty; when the certainty is there the venture becomes impossible. . . . If what I hope to gain by venturing is itself certain, I do not risk or venture, but make an exchange. . . . No, if I am in truth resolved to venture, in truth resolved to strive for the attainment of the highest good, the uncertainty must be there, and I must have room to move, so to speak. But the largest space I can obtain, where there is room for the most vehement gesture of the passion that embraces the infinite, is uncertainty of knowledge with respect to an eternal happiness, or the certain knowledge that the choice is in the finite sense a piece of madness: now there is room, now you can venture! (pp. 380–82)

How is it that objective improbability provides the largest space for the most vehement gesture of infinite passion? Consider two cases. (A) You plunge into a raging torrent to rescue from drowning someone you love, who is crying for help. (B) You plunge into a raging torrent in a desperate attempt to rescue someone you love, who appears to be unconscious and *may* already have drowned. In both cases you manifest a passionate interest in saving the person, risking your own life in order to do so. But I think Kierkegaard would say there is more passion in the second case than in the first. For in the second case you risk your life on what is, objectively considered, a smaller chance that you will be able to save your loved one. A greater passion is required for a more desperate attempt.

A similar assessment may be made of the following pair of cases. (A′) You stake everything on your faith in the truth of Christianity, knowing that it is objectively 99 percent probable that Christianity is true. (B′) You stake everything on your faith in the truth of Christianity, knowing that the truth of Christianity is, objectively, possible but so improbable that its probability is, say, as small as $1/10^{2,000,000}$. There is passion in both cases, but Kierkegaard will say that there is more passion in the second case than in the first. For to venture the same stake (namely, everything) on a much smaller chance of success shows greater passion.

Acceptance of risk can thus be seen as a *measure* of the intensity of passion. I believe this provides us with one way of understanding what Kierkegaard means when he calls religious passion "infinite." An *infinite* passionate interest in x is an interest so strong that it leads one to make the greatest possible sacrifices in order to obtain x, on the smallest possible chance of success. The infinity of the passion is shown in that there is no sacrifice so great one will not make it, and no chance of success so small one will not act on it. A passion which is infinite in this sense requires, by its very nature, a situation of maximum risk for its expression.

It will doubtless be objected that this argument involves a misunderstanding of what a passionate interest is. Such an interest is a disposition. In order to have a great passionate interest it is not necessary actually to make a great sacrifice with a small chance of success; all that is necessary is to have such an intense interest that one *would* do so if an appropriate occasion should arise. It is therefore a mistake to say that there *is* more passion in case (B) than in case (A), or in (B′) than in (A′). More passion is *shown* in (B) than in (A), and in (B′) than in (A′); but an equal passion may exist in cases in which there is no occasion to show it.

This objection may well be correct as regards what we normally mean by "passionate interest." But that is not decisive for the argument. The crucial question is what part dispositions, possibly unactualized, ought to play in religious devotion. And here we must have a digression about the position of the *Postscript* on this question—a position that is complex at best and is not obviously consistent.

In the first place I do not think that Kierkegaard would be prepared to think of passion, or a passionate interest, as primarily a disposition that might remain unactualized. He seems to conceive of passion chiefly as an intensity in what one actually does and feels. "Passion is momentary" (p. 178), although capable of continual repetition. And what is momentary in such a way that it must be repeated rather than protracted is presumably an occurrence rather than a disposition. It agrees with this conception of passion that Kierkegaard idealizes a life of "persistent striving," and says that the religious task is to "exercise" the God-relationship and to give "existential expression" to the religious choice (pp. 110, 364, 367).

All of this supports the view that what Kierkegaard means by "an infinite passionate interest" is a pattern of actual decision-making in which one continually exercises and expresses one's religiousness by making the greatest possible sacrifices on the smallest possible chance of success. In order to actualize such a pattern of life one needs chances of success that are as small as possible. That is the room that is required for "the most vehement gesture" of infinite passion.

But on the other hand Kierkegaard does allow a dispositional element in the religious life, and even precisely in the making of the greatest possible sacrifices. We might suppose that if we are to make the greatest possible sacrifices in our religious devotion, we must do so by abandoning all worldly interests and devoting all our time and attention to religion. That is what monasticism attempts to do, as Kierkegaard sees it; and (in the *Postscript,* at any rate) he rejects the attempt, contrary to what our argument to this point would have led us to expect of him. He holds that "resignation" (pp. 353, 367) or "renunciation" (pp. 362, 386) of *all* finite ends is precisely the first thing that religiousness requires; but he means a renunciation that is compatible with pursuing and enjoying finite ends (pp. 362–71). This renunciation is the practice of a sort of detachment; Kierkegaard uses the image of a dentist loosening the soft tissues around a tooth, while it is still in place, in preparation for pulling it (p. 367). It is partly a matter of not treating finite things with a desperate seriousness, but with a certain coolness or humor, even while one pursues them (pp. 368, 370).

This coolness is not just a disposition. But the renunciation also has a dispositional aspect. "Now if for any individual an eternal happiness is his highest good, this will mean that all finite satisfactions are volitionally relegated to the status of what may have to be renounced in favor of an eternal happiness" (p. 350). The volitional relegation is not a disposition but an act of choice. The object of this choice, however, appears to be a dispositional state—the state of being such that one *would* forgo any finite satisfaction *if* it *were* religiously necessary or advantageous to do so.

It seems clear that Kierkegaard, in the *Postscript,* is willing to admit a dispositional element at one point in the religious venture, but not at another. It is enough in most cases, he thinks, if one is *prepared* to cease for the sake of religion from pursuing some finite end; but it is not enough that one *would* hold to one's belief in the face of objective improbability. The belief must actually be improbable, although the pursuit of the finite need not actually cease. What is not clear is a reason for this disparity. The following hypothesis, admittedly somewhat speculative as interpretation of the text, is the best explanation I can offer.

The admission of a dispositional element in the religious renunciation of the finite is something to which Kierkegaard seems to be driven by the view that there is no alternative to it except idolatry. For suppose one actually ceases from all worldly pursuits and enters a monastery. In the monastery one would pursue a number of particular ends (such as getting up in the middle of the night to say the offices) which, although religious in a way ("churchy," one might say), are still finite. The absolute *telos* or end of religion is no more to be identified with them than with the ends pursued by an alderman (pp. 362–71). To pretend otherwise would be to make an idolatrous identification of the absolute end with some finite end. An existing person cannot have sacrificed everything by actually having ceased from pursuing *all* ends. For as long as he lives and acts he is pursuing some finite end. Therefore his renouncing *everything* finite must be at least partly dispositional.

Kierkegaard does not seem happy with this position. He regards it as of the utmost importance that the religious passion should come to expression. The problem of finding an adequate expression for a passion for an infinite end, in the face of the fact that in every concrete action one will be pursuing some finite end, is treated in the *Postscript* as the central problem of religion (see especially pp. 386–468). If the sacrifice of everything finite must remain largely dispositional, then perhaps it is all the more important to Kierkegaard that the smallness of the chance for which it is sacrificed should be fully actual, so that the infinity of the religious passion may be measured by an actuality in at least one aspect of the religious venture.

(ii) According to Kierkegaard, as I have argued, the intensity of a passion is measured in part by the smallness of the chances of success that one acts on. It can also be measured in part by its *costliness*—that is, by how much one gives up or suffers in acting on those chances. This second measure can also be made the basis of an argument for the claim that an infinite passion requires objective improbability. For the objective improbability of a religious belief, if recognized, increases the costliness of holding it. The risk involved in staking everything on an objectively improbable belief gives rise to an anxiety and mental suffering whose acceptance is itself a sacrifice. It seems to follow that if one is not staking everything on a belief one sees to be objectively improbable, one's passion is not infinite in Kierkegaard's sense, since one's sacrifice could be greater if one did adhere to an improbable belief.

Kierkegaard uses an argument similar to this. For God to give us objective knowledge of himself, eliminating paradox from it, would be "to lower the price of the God-relationship."

> And even if God could be imagined willing, no man with passion in his heart could desire it. To a maiden genuinely in love it could never occur that she had bought her happiness too dear, but rather that she had not bought it dear enough. And just as the passion of the infinite was itself the truth, so in the case of the highest value it holds true that the price is the value, that a low price means a poor value . . . (p. 207).

Kierkegaard here appears to hold, first, that an increase in the objective probability of religious belief would reduce its costliness, and second, that the value of a religious life is measured by its cost. I take it his reason for the second of these claims is that passion is the most valuable thing in a religious life and passion is measured by its cost. If we grant Kierkegaard the requisite conception of an infinite passion, we seem once again to have a plausible argument for the view that objective improbability is required for such a passion.

(c) We must therefore consider whether infinite passion, as Kierkegaard conceives of it, ought to be part of the religious ideal of life. Such a passion is a striving, or pattern of decision-making, in which, with the greatest possible intensity of feeling, one continually makes the greatest possible sacrifices on the smallest possible chance of success. This seems to me an impossible ideal. I doubt that any human being could have a passion of this sort, because I doubt that one could make a sacrifice so great that a greater could not be made, or have a (nonzero) chance of success so small that a smaller could not be had.

But even if Kierkegaard's ideal is impossible, one might want to try to approximate it. Intensity of passion might still be measured by the greatness of sacrifices made and the smallness of chances of success acted on, even if we cannot hope for a greatest possible or a smallest possible here. And it could be claimed that the most essential and valuable thing in religiousness is a passion that is very intense (though it cannot be infinite) by this standard—the more intense the better. This claim will not support an argument that objective improbability is absolutely required for religious passion. For a passion could presumably be very intense, involving great sacrifices and risks of some other sort, without an objectively improbable belief. But it could still be argued that objectively improbable religious beliefs enhance the value of the religious life by increasing its sacrifices and diminishing its chances of success, whereas objective probability detracts from the value of religious passion by diminishing its intensity.

The most crucial question about the Passion Argument, then, is whether maximization of sacrifice and risk are so valuable in religion as to make objective improbability a desirable characteristic of religious beliefs. Certainly much religious thought and feeling places a very high value on sacrifice and on passionate intensity. But the doctrine that it is desirable to increase without limit, or to the highest possible degree (if there is one) the cost and risk of a religious life is less plausible (to say the least) than the view that *some* degree of cost and risk may add to the value of a religious life. The former doctrine would set the religious interest at enmity with all other interests, or at least with the best of them. Kierkegaard is surely right in thinking that it would be impossible to live without pursuing some finite ends. But even so it would be possible to exchange the pursuit of better finite ends for the pursuit of worse ones—for example, by exchanging the pursuit of truth, beauty, and satisfying personal relationships for the self-flagellating pursuit of pain. And a way of life would be the costlier for requiring such an exchange. Kierkegaard does not, in the *Postscript,* demand it. But the presuppositions of his Passion Argument seem to imply that such a sacrifice would be religiously desirable. Such a conception of religion is demonic. In a tolerable religious ethics some way must be found to conceive of the religious interest as inclusive rather than exclusive of the best of other interests—including, I think, the interest in having well-grounded beliefs.

IV. PASCAL'S WAGER AND KIERKEGAARD'S LEAP

Ironically, Kierkegaard's views about religious passion suggest a way in which his religious beliefs could be based on objective reasoning—not on reasoning which would show them to be objectively probable, but on reasoning which shows them to be objectively advantageous. Consider the situation of a person whom Kierkegaard would regard as a genuine Christian believer. What would such a person want most of all? He would want above all else to attain the truth through Christianity. That is, he would desire both that Christianity be true and that he himself be related to it as a genuine believer. He would desire that state of affairs (which we may call *S*) so ardently that he would be willing to sacrifice everything else to obtain it, given only the smallest possible chance of success.

We can therefore construct the following argument, which has an obvious analogy to Pascal's Wager. Let us assume that there is, objectively, some chance, however small, that Christianity is true. This is an assumption which Kierkegaard accepts (p. 31), and I think it is plausible. There are two possibilities, then: either Christianity is true, or it is false. (Others might object to so stark a disjunction, but Kierkegaard will not.) If Christianity is false it is impossible for anyone to obtain *S,* since *S* includes the truth of Christianity. It is only if Christianity is true that anything one does will help one or hinder one in obtaining *S.* And if Christianity is true, one will obtain *S* just in case one becomes a genuine Christian believer. It seems obvious that one would increase one's chances of becoming a genuine Christian believer by becoming one now (if one can), even if the truth of Christian beliefs is now objectively uncertain or improbable. Hence it would seem to be advantageous for anyone who can to become a genuine Christian believer now, if he wants *S* so much that he would be willing to sacrifice everything else for the smallest possible chance of obtaining *S.* Indeed I believe that the argument I have given for this conclusion is a piece of objective reasoning, and that Christian belief is therefore *objectively* advantageous for anyone who wants *S* as much as a Kierkegaardian genuine Christian must want it.

Of course this argument does not tend at all to show that it is objectively probable that Christianity is true. It only gives a practical, prudential reason for believing, to someone who has a certain desire. Nor does the argument do anything to prove that such an absolutely overriding desire for *S* is reasonable.[8] It does show, however, that just as Kierkegaard's position has more logical structure than one might at first think, it is more difficult than he probably realized for him to get away entirely from objective justification.

8. It is worth noting, though, that a similar argument might still provide some less overriding justification of belief to someone who had a strong, but less overriding, desire for *S.*

W. K. Clifford

"THE ETHICS OF BELIEF"

WILLIAM K. CLIFFORD (1845–1879), English mathematician and philosopher, began his studies at Kings College, London, at the age of fifteen, where he quickly established a reputation as an unusually original and clear-minded thinker. Three years later he went on to Trinity College, Cambridge. His early religious interests, inspired by Aquinas, were on the side of Catholic dogma, but he became an agnostic and, in the end, under the influence of Spencer and Darwin, turned against religion altogether, developing a scientific epistemology based on the idea of knowledge as a biological response to the environment.

A shipowner was about to send to sea an emigrant ship. He knew that she was old, and not over-well built at the first; that she had seen many seas and climes, and often had needed repairs. Doubts had been suggested to him that possibly she was not seaworthy. These doubts preyed upon his mind and made him unhappy; he thought that perhaps he ought to have her thoroughly overhauled and refitted, even though this should put him to great expense. Before the ship sailed, however, he succeeded in overcoming these melancholy reflections. He said to himself that she had gone safely through so many voyages and weathered so many storms that it was idle to suppose she would not come safely home from this trip also. He would put his trust in Providence, which could hardly fail to protect all these unhappy families that were leaving their fatherland to seek for better times elsewhere. He would dismiss from his mind all ungenerous suspicions about the honesty of builders and contractors. In such ways he acquired a sincere and comfortable conviction that his vessel was thoroughly safe and seaworthy; he watched her departure with a light heart, and benevolent wishes for the success of the exiles in their strange new home that was to be; and he got his insurance money when she went down in midocean and told no tales.

What shall we say of him? Surely this, that he was verily guilty of the death of those men. It is admitted that he did sincerely believe in the soundness of his ship; but the sincerity of his conviction can in no wise help him, because he had no right to believe on such evidence as was before him. He had acquired his belief not by honestly earning it in patient investigation, but by stifling his doubts. And although in the end he may have felt so sure about it that he could not think otherwise, yet inasmuch as he had knowingly and willingly worked himself into that frame of mind, he must be held responsible for it.

Let us alter the case a little, and suppose that the ship was not unsound after all; that she made her voyage safely, and many others after it. Will that diminish the guilt of her owner? Not one jot. When an action is once done, it is right or wrong forever; no accidental failure of its good or evil fruits can possibly alter that. The man would not have been innocent, he would only have been not found out. The question of right or wrong has to do with the origin of his belief, not the matter of it; not what it was, but how he got it; not whether it turned out to be

From W. K. Clifford, *Lectures and Essays* (London: Macmillan, 1879).

true or false, but whether he had a right to believe on such evidence as was before him.

There was once an island in which some of the inhabitants professed a religion teaching neither the doctrine of original sin nor that of eternal punishment. A suspicion got abroad that the professors of this religion had made use of unfair means to get their doctrines taught to children. They were accused of wresting the laws of their country in such a way as to remove children from the care of their natural and legal guardians; and even of stealing them away and keeping them concealed from their friends and relations. A certain number of men formed themselves into a society for the purpose of agitating the public about this matter. They published grave accusations against individual citizens of the highest position and character, and did all in their power to injure those citizens in the exercise of their professions. So great was the noise they made, that a Commission was appointed to investigate the facts; but after the Commission had carefully inquired into all the evidence that could be got, it appeared that the accused were innocent. Not only had they been accused on insufficient evidence, but the evidence of their innocence was such as the agitators might easily have obtained, if they had attempted a fair inquiry. After these disclosures the inhabitants of that country looked upon the members of the agitating society, not only as persons whose judgment was to be distrusted, but also as no longer to be counted honorable men. For although they had sincerely and conscientiously believed in the charges they had made, yet they had no right to believe on such evidence as was before them. Their sincere convictions, instead of being honestly earned by patient inquiring, were stolen by listening to the voice of prejudice and passion.

Let us vary this case also, and suppose, other things remaining as before, that a still more accurate investigation proved the accused to have been really guilty. Would this make any difference in the guilt of the accusers? Clearly not; the question is not whether their belief was true or false, but whether they entertained it on wrong grounds. They would no doubt say, "Now you see that we were right after all; next time perhaps you will believe us." And they might be believed, but they would not thereby become honorable men. They would not be innocent, they would only be not found out. Every one of them, if he chose to examine himself *in foro conscientiae,* would know that he had acquired and nourished a belief, when he had no right to believe on such evidence as was before him; and therein he would know that he had done a wrong thing.

It may be said, however, that in both of these supposed cases it is not the belief which is judged to be wrong, but the action following upon it. The shipowner might say, "I am perfectly certain that my ship is sound, but still I feel it my duty to have her examined, before trusting the lives of so many people to her." And it might be said to the agitator, "However convinced you were of the justice of your cause and the truth of your convictions, you ought not to have made a public attack upon any man's character until you had examined the evidence on both sides with the utmost patience and care."

In the first place, let us admit that, so far as it goes, this view of the case is right and necessary; right, because even when a man's belief is so fixed that he cannot think otherwise, he still has a choice in regard to the action suggested by it, and so cannot escape the duty of investigating on the ground of the strength of his convictions; and necessary, because those who are not yet capable of controlling their feelings and thoughts must have a plain rule dealing with overt acts.

But this being premised as necessary, it becomes clear that it is not sufficient, and that our previous judgment is required to supplement it. For it is not possible so to sever the belief from the action it suggests as to condemn the one without condemning the other. No man holding a strong belief on one side of a question, or even wishing to hold a belief on one side, can investigate it with such fairness and completeness as if he were really in doubt and unbiassed; so that the existence of a belief not founded on fair inquiry unfits a man for the performance of this necessary duty.

Nor is that truly a belief at all which has not some influence upon the actions of him who holds it. He who truly believes that which prompts him to an action has looked upon the action to lust after it, he has committed it already in his heart. If a belief is not realized immediately in open deeds, it is stored up for the guidance of the future. It goes to make a part of that aggregate of beliefs which is the link between sensation and action at every moment of all our lives, and which is so organized and compacted together that no part of it can be isolated from the rest, but every new addition modifies the structure of the whole. No real belief, however trifling and fragmentary it may seem, is ever truly insignificant; it prepares us to receive more of its like, confirms those which resembled it before, and weakens others; and so gradually it lays a stealthy train in our inmost thoughts, which may some day explode into overt action, and leave its stamp upon our character forever.

And no one man's belief is in any case a private matter which concerns himself alone. Our lives are guided by that general conception of the course of things which has been created by society for social purposes. Our words, our phrases, our forms and processes and modes of thought, are common property, fashioned and perfected from age to age; an heirloom which every succeeding generation inherits as a precious deposit and a sacred trust to be handed on to the next one, not unchanged but enlarged and purified, with some clear marks of its proper handiwork. Into this, for good or ill, is woven every belief of every man who has speech of his fellows. An awful privilege, and an awful responsibility, that we should help to create the world in which posterity will live.

In the two supposed cases which have been considered, it has been judged wrong to believe on insufficient evidence, or to nourish belief by suppressing doubts and avoiding investigation. The reason of this judgment is not far to seek: it is that in both these cases the belief held by one man was of great importance to other men. But for as much as no belief held by one man, however seemingly trivial the belief, and however obscure the believer, is ever actually insignificant or without its effect on the fate of mankind, we have no choice but to extend our judgment to all cases of belief whatever. Belief, that sacred faculty which prompts the decisions of our will, and knits into harmonious working all the compacted energies of our being, is ours not for ourselves, but for humanity. It is rightly used on truths which have been established by long experience and waiting toil, and which have stood in the fierce light of free and fearless questioning. Then it helps to bind men together, and to strengthen and direct their common action. It is desecrated when given to unproved and unquestioned statements, for the solace and private pleasure of the believer; to add a tinsel splendor to the plain straight road of our life and display a bright mirage beyond it; or even to drown the common sorrows of our kind by a self-deception which allows them not only to cast down, but also to degrade us. Whoso would deserve well of his fellows in this matter will guard the purity of his belief with a very fanaticism of jealous care, lest at any time it should rest on an unworthy object, and catch a stain which can never be wiped away.

It is not only the leader of men, statesman, philosopher, or poet, that owes this bounden duty to mankind. Every rustic who delivers in the village alehouse his slow, infrequent sentences, may help to kill or keep alive the fatal superstitions which clog his race. Every hard-worked wife of an artisan may transmit to her children beliefs which shall knit society together, or rend it in pieces. No simplicity of mind, no obscurity of station, can escape the universal duty of questioning all that we believe.

It is true that this duty is a hard one, and the doubt which comes out of it is often a very bitter thing. It leaves us bare and powerless where we thought that we were safe and strong. To know all about anything is to know how to deal with it under all circumstances. We feel much happier and more secure when we think we know precisely what to do, no matter what happens, than when we have lost our way and do not know where to turn. And if we have supposed ourselves to know all about anything, and to be capable of doing what is fit in regard to it, we naturally do not like to find that we are really ignorant and powerless, that we have to begin again at the beginning, and try to learn what the thing is and how it is to be dealt with—if indeed anything can be learned about it. It is the sense of power attached to a sense of knowledge that makes men desirous of believing, and afraid of doubting.

This sense of power is the highest and best of pleasures when the belief on which it is founded is a true belief, and has been fairly earned by investigation. For then we may justly feel that it is common property, and holds good for others as well as for ourselves. Then we may be glad, not that *I* have learned secrets by which I am safer and stronger, but that *we men* have got mastery over more of the world; and we shall be strong, not for ourselves, but in the name of Man and in his strength. But if the belief has been accepted on insufficient evidence, the pleasure is a stolen one. Not only does it deceive ourselves by giving us a sense of power which we do not really possess, but it is sinful, because it is stolen in defiance of our duty to mankind. That duty is to guard ourselves from such beliefs as from a pestilence, which may shortly master our own body and then spread to the rest of the town. What would be thought of one who, for the sake of a sweet fruit, should deliberately run the risk of bringing a plague upon his family and his neighbors?

And, as in other such cases, it is not the risk only which has to be considered; for a bad action is always bad at the time when it is done, no matter what happens afterwards. Every time we let ourselves believe for unworthy reasons, we weaken our powers of self-control, of doubting, of judicially and fairly weighing evidence. We all suffer severely enough from the maintenance and support of false beliefs and the fatally wrong actions which they lead to, and the evil born when one such belief is entertained is great and wide. But a greater and wider evil arises when the credulous character is maintained and supported, when a habit of believing for unworthy reasons is fostered and made permanent. If I steal money from any person, there may be no harm done by the mere transfer of possession; he may not feel the loss, or it may prevent him from using the money badly. But I cannot help doing this great wrong towards Man, that I make myself dishonest. What hurts society is not that it should lose its property, but that it should become a den of thieves; for then it must cease to be society. This is why we ought not to do evil that good many come; for at any rate this great evil has come, that we have done evil and are made wicked thereby. In like manner, if I let myself believe anything on insufficient evidence, there may be no great harm done by the mere belief; it may be true after all, or I may never have occasion to exhibit it in outward acts. But I cannot help doing this great wrong toward Man, that I make myself credulous. The danger to society is not merely that it should believe wrong things, though that is great enough; but that it should become credulous, and lose the habit of testing things and inquiring into them; for then it must sink back into savagery.

The harm which is done by credulity in a man is not confined to the fostering of a credulous character in others, and consequent support of false beliefs. Habitual want of care about what I believe leads to habitual want of care in others about the truth of what is told to me. Men speak the truth to one another when each reveres the truth in his own mind and in the other's mind; but how shall my friend revere the truth in my mind when I myself am careless about it, when I believe things because I want to believe them, and because they are comforting and pleasant? Will he not learn to cry, "Peace," to me, when there is no peace? By such a course I shall surround myself with a thick atmosphere of falsehood and fraud, and in that I must live. It may matter little to me, in my cloud-castle of sweet illusions and darling lies; but it matters much to Man that I have made my neighbors ready to deceive. The credulous man is father to the liar and the cheat; he lives in the bosom of this his family, and it is no marvel if he should become even as they are. So closely are our duties knit together, that whoso shall keep the whole law, and yet offend in one point, he is guilty of all.

To sum up: it is wrong always, everywhere, and for anyone, to believe anything upon insufficient evidence.

If a man, holding a belief which he was taught in childhood or persuaded of afterwards, keeps down and pushes away any doubts which arise about it in his mind, purposely avoids the reading of books and the company of men that call in question or discuss it, and regards as impious those questions which cannot easily be asked without disturbing it—the life of that man is one long sin against mankind. . . .

Inquiry into the evidence of a doctrine is not to be made once for all, and then taken as finally settled. It is never lawful to stifle a doubt; for either it can be honestly answered by means of the inquiry already made, or else it proves that the inquiry was not complete.

"But," says one, "I am a busy man; I have no time for the long course of study which would be necessary to make me in any degree a competent judge of certain questions, or even able to understand the nature of the arguments." Then he should have no time to believe. . . .

William James

"THE WILL TO BELIEVE"

A brief biography of James appears on page 338.

. . . I have brought with me to-night something like a sermon on justification by faith to read to you,—I mean an essay in justification *of* faith, a defence of our right to adopt a believing attitude in religious matters, in spite of the fact that our merely logical intellect may not have been coerced. . . .

I.

Let us give the name of *hypothesis* to anything that may be proposed to our belief; and just as the electricians speak of live and dead wires, let us speak of any hypothesis as either *live* or *dead*. A live hypothesis is one which appeals as a real possibility to him to whom it is proposed. If I ask you to believe in the Mahdi, the notion makes no electric connection with your nature,—it refuses to scintillate with any credibility at all. As an hypothesis it is completely dead. To an Arab, however (even if he be not one of the Mahdi's followers), the hypothesis is among the mind's possibilities: it is alive. This shows that deadness and liveness in an hypothesis are not intrinsic properties, but relations to the individual thinker. They are measured by his willingness to act. The maximum of liveness in an hypothesis means

Published in *New World,* June 1896.

Christ carrying the cross. Fifteenth-century statue in Weil der Stadt, a small town in southern Germany where Johannes Kepler was born.

willingness to act irrevocably. Practically, that means belief; but there is some believing tendency wherever there is willingness to act at all.

Next, let us call the decision between two hypotheses an *option.* Options may be of several kinds. They may be—1, *living* or *dead;* 2, *forced* or *avoidable;* 3, *momentous* or *trivial;* and for our purposes we may call an option a *genuine* option when it is of the forced, living, and momentous kind.

1. A living option is one in which both hypotheses are live ones. If I say to you: "Be a theosophist or be a Mohammedan," it is probably a dead option, because for you neither hypothesis is likely to be alive. But if I say: "Be an agnostic or be a Christian," it is otherwise: trained as you are, each hypothesis makes some appeal, however small, to your belief.
2. Next, if I say to you: "Choose between going out with your umbrella or without it," I do not offer you a genuine option, for it is not forced. You can easily avoid it by not going out at all. Similarly, if I say, "Either love me or hate me," "Either call my theory true or call it false," your option is avoidable. You may remain indifferent to me, neither loving nor hating, and you may decline to offer any judgment as to my theory. But if I say, "Either accept this truth or go without it," I put on you a forced option, for there is no standing place outside of the alternative. Every dilemma based on a complete logical disjunction, with no possibility of not choosing, is an option of this forced kind.
3. Finally, if I were Dr. Nansen and proposed to you to join my North Pole expedition, your option would be momentous; for this would probably be your only similar opportunity, and your choice now would either exclude you from the North Pole sort of immortality altogether or put at least the chance of it into your hands. He who refuses to embrace a unique opportunity loses the prize as surely as if he tried and failed. *Per contra,* the option is trivial when the opportunity is not unique, when the stake is insignificant, or when the decision is reversible if it later prove unwise. Such trivial options abound in the scientific life. A chemist finds an hypothesis live enough to spend a year in its verification: he believes in it to that extent. But if his experiments prove inconclusive either way, he is quit for his loss of time, no vital harm being done.

It will facilitate our discussion if we keep all these distinctions well in mind.

II.

The next matter to consider is the actual psychology of human opinion. When we look at certain facts, it seems as if our passional and volitional nature lay at the root of all our convictions. When we look at others, it seems as if they could do nothing when the intellect had once said its say. Let us take the latter facts up first.

Does it not seem preposterous on the very face of it to talk of our opinions being modifiable at will? Can our will either help or hinder our intellect in its perceptions of truth? Can we, by just willing it, believe that Abraham Lincoln's existence is a myth, and that the portraits of him in *McClure's Magazine* are all of some one else? Can we, by any effort of our will, or by any strength of wish that it were true, believe ourselves well and about when we are roaring with rheumatism in bed, or feel certain that the sum of the two one-dollar bills in our pocket must be a hundred dollars? We can *say* any of these things, but we are absolutely impotent to believe them; and of just such things is the whole fabric of the truths that we do believe in made up,—matters of fact, immediate or remote, as Hume said, and relations between ideas, which are either there or not there for us if we see them so, and which if not there cannot be put there by any action of our own.

In Pascal's *Thoughts* there is a celebrated passage known in literature as Pascal's wager. In it he tries to force us into Christianity by reasoning as if our concern with truth resembled our concern with the stakes in a game of chance. Translated freely his words are these: You must either believe or not believe that God is—which will you do? Your human reason cannot say. A game is going on between you and the nature of things which at the day of judgment will bring out either heads or tails. Weight what your gains and your losses would be if you should stake all you have on heads, or God's existence: if you win in such case, you gain eternal beatitude; if you lose, you lose nothing at all. If there were an infinity of chances, and only one for God in this wager, still you ought to stake your all on God; for though you surely risk a finite loss by this procedure, any finite loss is reasonable, even a certain one is reasonable, if there is but the possibility of infinite gain. Go, then, and take holy water, and have masses said; belief will come and stupefy your scruples,—*Cela vous fera croire et vous abêtira.* Why should you not? At bottom, what have you to lose?

You probably feel that when religious faith expresses itself thus, in the language of the gaming-table, it is put to its last trumps. Surely Pascal's own personal belief in masses and holy water had far other springs; and this celebrated page of his is but an argument for others, a last desperate snatch at a weapon against the hardness of the unbelieving heart. We feel that a faith in masses and holy water adopted wilfully after such a mechanical calculation would lack the inner soul of faith's reality; and if we were ourselves in the place of the Deity, we should probably take particular pleasure in cutting off believers of this pattern from their infinite reward. It is evident that unless there be some pre-existing tendency to believe in masses and holy water, the option offered to the will by Pascal is not a living option. Certainly no Turk ever took to masses and holy water on its account; and even to us Protestants these means of salvation seem such foregone impossibilities that Pascal's logic, invoked for them specifically leaves us unmoved. As well might the Mahdi write to us, saying, "I am the Expected One whom God has created in his effulgence. You shall be infinitely happy if you confess me; otherwise you shall be cut off from the light of the sun. Weigh, then, your infinite gain if I am genuine against your finite sacrifice if I am not!" His logic would be that of Pascal; but he would vainly use it on us, for the hypothesis he offers us is dead. No tendency to act on it exists in us to any degree.

The talk of believing by our volition seems, then, from one point of view, simply silly. From another point of view it is worse than silly, it is vile. When one turns to the magnificent edifice of the physical sciences, and sees how it was reared; what thousands of disinterested moral lives of men lie buried in its mere foundations; what patience and postponement, what choking down of preference, what submission to the icy laws of outer fact are wrought into its very stones and mortar; how absolutely impersonal it stands in its vast augustness,—then how besotted and contemptible seems every little sentimentalist who comes blowing his voluntary smoke-wreaths, and pretending to decide things from out of his private dream! Can we wonder if those bred in the rugged and manly school of science should feel like spewing such subjectivism out of their mouths? The whole system of loyalties which grow up in the schools of science go dead against its toleration; so that it is only natural that those who have caught the scientific fever should pass over to the opposite extreme, and write sometimes as if the incorruptibly truthful intellect ought positively to prefer bitterness and unacceptableness to the heart in its cup.

> It fortifies my soul to know
> That, though I perish, Truth is so—

sings Clough, while Huxley exclaims: "My only consolation lies in the reflection that, however bad our posterity may become, so far as they hold by the plain rule of not pretending to believe what they have no reason to believe, because it may be to their advantage so to pretend [the word 'pretend' is surely here redundant], they will not have reached the lowest depth of immorality." And that delicious *enfant terrible* Clifford writes: "Belief is desecrated when given to unproved and unquestioned statements for the solace and private pleasure of the believer. . . . Whoso would deserve well of his fellows in this matter will guard the purity of his belief with a very fanaticism of jealous care, lest at any time it should rest on an unworthy object, and catch a stain which can never be wiped away. . . . If [a] belief has been accepted on insufficient evidence [even though the belief be true, as Clifford on the same page explains] the pleasure is a stolen one. . . . It is sinful because it is stolen in defiance of our duty to mankind. That duty is to guard ourselves from such beliefs as from a pestilence which may shortly master our own body and then spread to the rest of the town. . . . It is wrong always, everywhere, and for every one, to believe anything upon insufficient evidence."

III.

All this strikes one as healthy, even when expressed, as by Clifford, with somewhat too much of robustious pathos in the voice. Free-will and simple wishing do seem, in the matter of our credences, to be only fifth wheels to the coach. Yet if any one should thereupon assume that intellectual insight is what remains after wish and will and sentimental preference have taken wing, or that pure reason is what then settles

"Faith and Reciprocity"

Martin Buber

Philosophy errs in thinking of religion as founded in a noetical act, even if an inadequate one, and in therefore regarding the essence of religion as the knowledge of an object which is indifferent to being known. As a result, philosophy understands faith as an affirmation of truth lying somewhere between clear knowledge and confused opinion. Religion, on the other hand, insofar as it speaks of knowledge at all, does not understand it as a noetic relation of a thinking subject to a neutral object of thought, but rather as mutual contact, as the genuinely reciprocal meeting in the fullness of life between one active existence and another. Similarly, it understands faith at the entrance into this reciprocity; as binding oneself in relationship with an undemonstrable and unprovable, yet even so, in relationship, knowable Being, from whom all meaning comes.

From *The Eclipse of God* (1952).

our opinions, he would fly quite as directly in the teeth of the facts.

It is only our already dead hypotheses that our willing nature is unable to bring to life again. But what has made them dead for us is for the most part a previous action of our willing nature of an antagonistic kind. When I say "willing nature," I do not mean only such deliberate volitions as may have set up habits of belief that we cannot now escape from,—I mean all such factors of belief as fear and hope, prejudice and passion, imitation and partisanship, the circumpressure of our caste and set. As a matter of fact we find ourselves believing, we hardly know how or why. Mr. Balfour gives the name of "authority" to all those influences, born of the intellectual climate, that make hypotheses possible or impossible for us, alive or dead. Here in this room, we all of us believe in molecules and the conservation of energy, in democracy and necessary progress, in Protestant Christianity and the duty of fighting for "the doctrine of the immortal Monroe," all for no reasons worthy of the name. We see into these matters with no more inner clearness, and probably with much less, than any disbeliever in them might possess. His unconventionality would probably have some grounds to show for its conclusions; but for us, not insight, but the *prestige* of the opinions, is what makes the spark shoot from them and light up our sleeping magazines of faith. Our reason is quite satisfied, in nine hundred and ninety-nine cases out of every thousand of us, if it can find a few arguments that will do to recite in case our credulity is criticised by some one else. Our faith is faith in some one else's faith, and in the greatest matters this is most the case. Our belief in truth itself, for instance, that there is a truth, and that our minds and it are made for each other,—what is it but a passionate affirmation of desire, in which our social system backs us up? We want to have a truth; we want to believe that our experiments and studies and discussions must put us in a continually better and better position towards it; and on this line we agree to fight out our thinking lives. But if a pyrrhonistic sceptic asks us *how we know* all this, can our logic find a reply? No! certainly it cannot. It is just one volition against another,—we willing to go in for life upon a trust or assumption which he, for his part, does not care to make.[1]

As a rule we disbelieve all facts and theories for which we have no use. Clifford's cosmic emotions find no use for Christian feelings. Huxley belabors the bishops because there is no use for sacerdotalism in his scheme of life. Newman, on the contrary, goes over to Romanism, and finds all sorts of reasons good for staying there, because a priestly system is for him an organic need and delight. Why do so few "scientists" even look at the evidence for telepathy, so called? Because they think, as a leading biologist, now dead, once said to me, that even if such a thing were true, scientists ought to band together to keep it suppressed and concealed. It would undo the uniformity of Nature and all sorts of other things without which scientists cannot carry on their pursuits. But if this very man had been shown something which as a scientist he might *do* with telepathy, he might not only have examined the evidence, but even have found it good enough. This very law which the logicians would impose upon us—if I may give the name of logicians to those who would rule out our willing nature here—is based on nothing but their own natural wish to exclude all elements for which they, in their professional quality of logicians, can find no use.

Evidently, then, our non-intellectual nature does influence our convictions. There are passional tendencies and volitions which run before and others which come after belief, and it is only the latter that are too late for the fair; and they are not too late when the previous passional work has been already in their own direction. Pascal's argument, instead of being powerless, then seems a regular clincher, and is the last

1. Compare the admirable page 310 in S. H. Hodgson's "Time and Space," London, 1865.

stroke needed to make our faith in masses and holy water complete. The state of things is evidently far from simple; and pure insight and logic, whatever they might do ideally, are not the only things that really do produce our creeds.

IV.

Our next duty, having recognized this mixed-up state of affairs, is to ask whether it be simply reprehensible and pathological, or whether, on the contrary, we must treat it as a normal element in making up our minds. The thesis I defend is, briefly stated, this: *Our passional nature not only lawfully may, but must, decide an option between propositions, whenever it is a genuine option that cannot by its nature be decided on intellectual grounds; for to say, under such circumstances, "Do not decide, but leave the question open," is itself a passional decision,—just like deciding yes or no,—and is attended with the same risk of losing the truth.* The thesis thus abstractly expressed will, I trust, soon become quite clear. But I must first indulge in a bit more of preliminary work.

It will be observed that for the purposes of this discussion we are on "dogmatic" ground,—ground, I mean, which leaves systematic philosophical scepticism altogether out of account. The postulate that there is truth, and that it is the destiny of our minds to attain it, we are deliberately resolving to make, though the sceptic will not make it. We part company with him, therefore, absolutely, at this point. But the faith that truth exists, and that our minds can find it, may be held in two ways. We may talk of the *empiricist* way and of the *absolutist* way of believing in truth. The absolutists in this matter say that we not only can attain to knowing truth, but we can *know when* we have attained to knowing it; while the empiricists think that although we may attain it, we cannot infallibly know when. To *know* is one thing, and to know for certain *that* we know is another. One may hold to the first being possible without the second; hence the empiricists and the absolutists, although neither of them is a sceptic in the usual philosophic sense of the term, show very different degrees of dogmatism in their lives. . . .

VI.

But now, since we are all such absolutists by instinct, what in our quality of students of philosophy ought we to do about the fact? Shall we espouse and indorse it? Or shall we treat it as a weakness of our nature from which we must free ourselves, if we can?

I sincerely believe that the latter course is the only one we can follow as reflective men. Objective evidence and certitude are doubtless very fine ideals to play with, but where on this moonlit and dream-visited planet are they found? I am, therefore, myself a complete empiricist so far as my theory of human knowledge goes. I live, to be sure, by the practical faith that we must go on experiencing and thinking over our experience, for only thus can our opinions grow more true; but to hold any of them—I absolutely do not care which—as if it never could be reinterpretable or corrigible, I believe to be a tremendously mistaken attitude, and I think that the whole history of philosophy will bear me out. There is but one indefectibly certain truth, and that is the truth that pyrrhonistic scepticism itself leaves standing,—the truth that the present phenomenon of consciousness exists. That, however, is the bare starting-point of knowledge, the mere admission of a stuff to be philosophized about. The various philosophies are but so many attempts at expressing what this stuff really is. And if we repair to our libraries what disagreement do we discover! Where is a certainly true answer found? Apart from abstract propositions of comparison (such as two and two are the same as four), propositions which tell us nothing by themselves about concrete reality, we find no proposition ever regarded by any one as evidently certain that has not either been called a falsehood, or at least had its truth sincerely questioned by some one else. The transcending of the axioms of geometry, not in play but in earnest, by certain of our contemporaries (as Zöllner and Charles H. Hinton), and the rejection of the whole Aristotelian logic by the Hegelians, are striking instances in point.

No concrete test of what is really true has ever been agreed upon. Some make the criterion external to the moment of perception, putting it either in revelation, the *consensus gentium,* the instincts of the heart, or the systematized experience of the race. Others make the perceptive moment its own test,—Descartes, for instance, with his clear and distinct ideas guaranteed by the veracity of God; Reid with his "common-sense"; and Kant with his forms of synthetic judgment *a priori.* The inconceivability of the opposite; the capacity to be verified by sense; the possession of complete organic unity or self-relation, realized when a thing is its own other,—are standards which, in turn, have been used. The much lauded objective evidence is never triumphantly there; it is a mere aspiration or *Grenzbegriff,* marking the infinitely remote ideal of our thinking life. To claim that certain truths now possess it, is simply to say that when you think them true and they *are* true, then their evidence is objective, otherwise it is not. But practically one's conviction that the evidence one goes by is of the real objective brand, is only one more subjective opinion added to the lot. For what a contradictory array of opinions have objective evidence and absolute certitude been claimed! The world is rational through and through,—its existence is an ultimate brute fact; there is a personal God,—a personal God is inconceivable; there is an extra-mental physical world immediately known,—the mind can only know its own ideas; a moral imperative exists,—obligation is only the resultant of desires; a permanent spiritual principle is in every one,—there are only shifting states of mind; there is an endless chain of causes,—there is an absolute first cause; an eternal necessity,—a freedom; a purpose,—no purpose; a primal One,—a primal Many; a universal continuity,—an essential discontinuity in things; an infinity,—no infinity. There is this,—there is that; there is indeed nothing which some one has not thought absolutely true, while his neighbor deemed it absolutely false; and not an absolutist among them seems ever to have considered that the trouble may all the time be essential, and that the intellect, even with truth directly in its grasp, may have no infallible signal for knowing whether it be truth or no. When, indeed, one remembers that the most striking practical application to life of the doctrine of objective certitude has been the conscientious labors of the Holy Office of the Inquisition, one feels less tempted than ever to lend the doctrine a respectful ear.

But please observe, now, that when as empiricists we give up the doctrine of objective certitude, we do not thereby give up the quest or hope of truth itself. We still pin our faith on its existence, and still believe that we gain an ever better position towards it by systematically continuing to roll up experiences and think. Our great difference from the scholastic lies in the way we face. The strength of his system lies in the principles, the origin, the *terminus a quo* of his thought; for us the strength is in the outcome, the upshot, the *terminus ad quem.* Not where it comes from but what it leads to is to decide. It matters not to an empiricist from what quarter an hypothesis may come to him: he may have acquired it by fair means or by foul; passion may have whispered or accident suggested it; but if the total drift of thinking continues to confirm it, that is what he means by its being true.

VII.

One more point, small but important, and our preliminaries are done. There are two ways of looking at our duty in the matter of opinion,—ways entirely different, and yet ways about whose difference the theory of knowledge seems hitherto to have shown very little concern. *We must know the truth;* and *we must avoid error,*—these are our first and great commandments as would-be knowers; but they are not two ways of stating an identical commandment, they are two separable laws. Although it may indeed happen that when we believe the truth *A,* we escape as an incidental consequence from believing the falsehood *B,* it hardly ever happens that by merely disbelieving *B* we necessarily believe *A.* We may in escaping *B* fall into believing other falsehoods, *C* or *D,* just as bad as *B;* or we may escape *B* by not believing anything at all, not even *A.*

Believe truth! Shun error!—these, we see, are two materially different laws; and by choosing between them we may end by coloring differently our whole intellectual life. We may regard the chase for truth as paramount, and the avoidance of error as secondary; or we may, on the other hand, treat the avoidance of error as more imperative, and let truth take its chance. Clifford, in the instructive passage which I have quoted, exhorts us to the latter course. Believe nothing, he tells us, keep your mind in suspense forever, rather than by closing it on insufficient evidence incur the awful risk of believing lies. You, on the other hand, may think that the risk of being in error is a very small matter when compared with the blessings of real knowledge, and be ready to be duped many times in your investigation rather than postpone indefinitely the chance of guessing true. I myself find it

"Between Faith and Skepticism"

James W. Woelfel

Why persons interpret various life-experiences as encounters with a transcendent reality, and more specifically as encounters with "God" as interpreted by a particular religious tradition, is a very complex question. I want here to look at only one aspect of "experience of God"—albeit I think a significant one—using my own shift from believing to unbelieving theologian as illustration. What my experience has suggested to me is this: The name "God," when used to refer to an experienced reality by those who believe they experience such a reality, appears to derive its indicative power and meaning entirely from its use within a particular context of religious world-orientation. When that interpretative context as a whole becomes too problematic—no longer hangs together—for someone, then we may expect that that person will no longer be able to interpret her or his experience of the world using the name "God," at least in the forms in which it is articulated in that context.

That is just what has happened in my own case. When I was a "faithful" theologian, I believed that I encountered the reality of God in and through varied sorts of experiences and events in my life. The use of the name "God" in connection with such experiences and events arose and derived its meaning and legitimacy from the Christian context of world-interpretation which I accepted and in which I participated together with other members of the Christian community. In my case the progressive breakdown of the Christian framework of interpretation and the non-viability to me of alternative theistic contexts of meaning have brought with them a decreasing ability on my part to apply the name "God" in connection with events and experiences in my life, until now I am no longer able to speak of my experience in terms of God at all. In this sense God has "died" for me—although as the whole drift of my essay indicates, by no means do I regard the "death of God" as a universalizeable declaration on my part.

I am suggesting, then, that talk about God as a personally experienced reality appears to function typically as an aspect of a particular religious tradition or context of interpretation, and to stand or fall for individuals together with the plausibility or implausibility of that context.

From "Between Faith and Skepticism: A Case Study" (1982).

impossible to go with Clifford. We must remember that these feelings of our duty about either truth or error are in any case only expressions of our passional life. Biologically considered, our minds are as ready to grind out falsehood as veracity, and he who says, "Better go without belief forever than believe a lie!" merely shows his own preponderant private horror of becoming a dupe. He may be critical of many of his desires and fears, but this fear he slavishly obeys. He cannot imagine any one questioning its binding force. For my own part, I have also a horror of being duped; but I can believe that worse things than being duped may happen to a man in this world: so Clifford's exortation has to my ears a thoroughly fantastic sound. It is like a general informing his soldiers that it is better to keep out of battle forever than to risk a single wound. Not so are victories either over enemies or over nature gained. Our errors are surely not such awfully solemn things. In a world where we are so certain to incur them in spite of all our caution, a certain lightness of heart seems healthier than this excessive nervousness on their behalf. At any rate, it seems the fittest thing for the empiricist philosopher.

VIII.

. . . I fear here that some of you my hearers will begin to scent danger, and lend an inhospitable ear. Two first steps of passion you have indeed had to admit as necessary,—we must think so as to avoid dupery, and we must think so as to gain truth; but the surest path to those ideal consummations, you will probably consider, is from now onwards to take no further passional step.

Well, of course, I agree as far as the facts will allow. Wherever the option between losing truth and gaining it is not momentous, we can throw the chance of *gaining truth* away, and at any rate save ourselves from any chance of *believing falsehood,* by not making up our minds at all till objective evidence has come. In scientific questions, this is almost always the case; and even in human affairs in general, the need of acting is seldom so urgent that a false belief to act on is better than no belief at all. Law courts, indeed, have to decide on the best evidence attainable for the moment, because a judge's duty is to make law as well as to ascertain it, and (as a learned judge once said to me) few cases are worth spending much time over: the great thing is to have them decided on *any* acceptable principle, and got out of the way. But in our dealings with objective nature we obviously are recorders, not makers, of the truth; and decisions for the mere sake of deciding promptly and getting on to the next business would be wholly out of place. Throughout the breadth of physical nature facts are what they are quite independently of us, and seldom is there any such hurry about them that the risks of being duped by believing a premature theory need be faced. The questions here are always trivial options, the hypotheses are hardly living (at any rate not living for us spectators), the choice between believing truth or falsehood is seldom forced. The attitude of sceptical balance is therefore the absolutely wise one if we would escape mistakes. What difference, indeed, does it make to most of us whether we have or have not a theory of the Röntgen rays, whether we believe or not in mind-stuff, or have a conviction about the causality of conscious states? It makes no difference. Such options are not forced on us. On every account it is better not to make them, but still keep weighing reasons *pro et contra* with an indifferent hand. . . .

The most useful investigator, because the most sensitive observer, is always he whose eager interest in one side of the question is balanced by an equally keen nervousness lest he become deceived.[2] Science has organized this nervousness into a regular *technique,* her so-called method of verification; and she has fallen so deeply in love with the method that one may

2. Compare Wilfrid Ward's Essay, "The Wish to Believe," in his *Witnesses to the Unseen,* Macmillan, 1893.

even say she has ceased to care for truth by itself at all. It is only truth as technically verified that interests her. The truth of truths might come in merely affirmative form, and she would decline to touch it. Such truth as that, she might repeat with Clifford, would be stolen in defiance of her duty to mankind. Human passions, however, are stronger than technical rules. "Le coeur a ses raisons," as Pascal says, "que la raison ne connaît pas;" and however indifferent to all but the bare rules of the game the umpire, the abstract intellect, may be, the concrete players who furnish him the materials to judge of are usually, each one of them, in love with some pet "live hypothesis" of his own. Let us agree, however, that wherever there is no forced option, the dispassionately judicial intellect with no pet hypothesis, saving us, as it does, from dupery at any rate, ought to be our ideal.

The question next arises: Are there not somewhere forced options in our speculative questions, and can we (as men who may be interested at least as much in positively gaining truth as in merely escaping dupery) always wait with impunity till the coercive evidence shall have arrived? It seems *a priori* improbable that the truth should be so nicely adjusted to our needs and powers as that. In the great boarding-house of nature, the cakes and the butter and the syrup seldom come out so even and leave the plates so clean. Indeed, we should view them with scientific suspicion if they did.

IX.

Moral questions immediately present themselves as questions whose solution cannot wait for sensible proof. A moral question is a question not of what sensibly exists, but of what is good, or would be good if it did exist. Science can tell us what exists; but to compare the *worths,* both of what exists and of what does not exist, we must consult not science, but what Pascal calls our heart. Science herself consults her heart when she lays it down that the infinite ascertainment of fact and correction of false belief are the supreme goods for man. Challenge the statement, and science can only repeat it oracularly, or else prove it by showing that such ascertainment and correction bring man all sorts of other goods which man's heart in turn declares. The question of having moral beliefs at all or not having them is decided by our will. Are our moral preferences true or false, or are they only odd biological phenomena, making things good or bad for *us,* but in themselves indifferent? How can your pure intellect decide? If your heart does not *want* a world of moral reality, your head will assuredly never make you believe in one. Mephistophelian scepticism, indeed, will satisfy the head's play-instincts much better than any rigorous idealism can. . . .

A social organism of any sort whatever, large or small, is what it is because each member proceeds to his own duty with a trust that the other members will simultaneously do theirs. Wherever a desired result is achieved by the co-operation of many independent persons, its existence as a fact is a pure consequence of the precursive faith in one another of those immediately concerned. A government, an army, a commercial system, a ship, a college, an athletic team, all exist on this condition, without which not only is nothing achieved, but nothing is even attempted. A whole train of passengers (individually brave enough) will be looted by a few highwaymen, simply because the latter can count on one another, while each passenger fears that if he makes a movement of resistance, he will be shot before any one else backs him up. If we believe that the whole car-full would rise at once with us, we should each severally rise, and train-robbing would never even be attempted. There are, then, cases where a fact cannot come at all unless a preliminary faith exists in its coming. *And where faith in a fact can help create the fact,* that would be an insane logic which should say that faith running ahead of scientific evidence is the "lowest kind of immorality," into which a thinking being can fall. Yet such is the logic by which our scientific absolutists pretend to regulate our lives!

X.

In truths dependent on our personal action, then, faith based on desire is certainly a lawful and possibly an indispensable thing.

But now, it will be said, these are all childish human cases, and have nothing to do with great cosmical matters, like the question of religious faith. Let us then pass on to that. Religions differ so much in their accidents that in discussing the religious question we must make it very generic and broad. What then do we now mean by the religious hypothesis? Science says things are; morality says some things are better than other things; and religion says essentially two things.

First, she says that the best things are the more eternal things, the overlapping things, the things in the universe that throw the last stone, so to speak, and say the final word. "Perfection is eternal,"—this phrase of Charles Secrétan seems a good way of putting this first affirmation of religion, an affirmation which obviously cannot yet be verified scientifically at all.

The second affirmation of religion is that we are better off even now if we believe her first affirmation to be true.

Now, let us consider what the logical elements of this situation are *in case the religious hypothesis in both its branches be really true.* (Of course, we must admit that possibility at the outset. If we are to discuss the question at all, it must involve a living option. If for any of you religion be a hypothesis that cannot, by any living possibility, be true, then you need go no farther. I speak to the "saving remnant" alone.) So proceeding, we see, first, that religion offers itself as a *momentous* option. We are supposed to gain, even now, by our belief, and to lose by our nonbelief, a certain vital good. Secondly, religion is a *forced* option, so far as that good goes. We cannot escape the issue by remaining sceptical and waiting for more light, because, although we do avoid error in that way *if religion be untrue,* we lose the good, *if it be true,* just as certainly as if we positively chose to disbelieve. It is as if a man should hesitate indefinitely to ask a certain woman to marry him because he was not perfectly sure that she would prove an angel after he brought her home. Would he not cut himself off from that particular angel-possiblity as decisively as if he went and married some one else? Scepticism, then, is not avoidance of option; it is option of a certain particular kind of risk. *Better risk loss of truth than chance of error,*—that is your faith-vetoer's exact position. He is actively playing his stake as much as the believer is; he is backing the field against the religious hypothesis, just as the believer is backing the religious hypothesis against the field. To preach scepticism to us as a duty until "sufficient evidence" for religion be found, is tantamount therefore to telling us, when in presence of the religious hypothesis, that to yield to our fear of its being error is wiser and better than to yield to our hope that it may be true. It is not intellect against all passions, then; it is only intellect with one passion laying down its law. And by what, forsooth, is the supreme wisdom of this passion warranted? Dupery for dupery, what proof is there that dupery through hope is so much worse than dupery through fear? I, for one, can see no proof; and I simply refuse obedience to the scientist's command to imitate his kind of option, in a case where my own stake is important enough to give me the right to choose my own form of risk. If religion be true and the evidence for it be still insufficient, I do not wish, by putting your extinguisher upon my nature (which feels to me as if it had after all some business in this matter), to forfeit my sole chance in life of getting upon the winning side,—that chance depending, of course, on my willingness to run the risk of acting as if my passional need of taking the world religiously might be prophetic and right.

All this is on the supposition that it really may be prophetic and right, and that, even to us who are discussing the matter, religion is a live hypothesis which may be true. Now, to most of us religion comes in a still further way that makes a veto on our active faith even more illogical. The more perfect and more eternal aspect of the universe is represented in our religions as having personal form. The universe is no longer a mere *It* to us, but a *Thou,* if we are religious, and any relation that may be possible from person to person might be possible here. For instance, although in one sense we are passive portions of the universe, in another we show a curious autonomy, as if we were small active centres on our own account. We feel, too, as if the appeal of religion to us were made to our own active good-will, as if evidence might be forever withheld from us unless we met the hypothesis half-way. To take a trivial illustration: just as a man who in a company of gentlemen made no advances, asked a warrant for every concession, and believed no one's word without proof, would cut himself off by such churlishness from all the social rewards that a more trusting spirit would earn,—so here, one who should shut himself up in snarling logicality and try to make the gods exhort his recognition willy-nilly, or not get it at all, might cut himself off forever from his only opportunity of making the gods' acquaintance. This feeling, forced on us we know not whence, that by obstinately believing that there are gods (although not to do so would be so easy both for our logic and our life) we are doing the universe the deepest service we can, seems part of the living essence of the religious hypothesis. If the hypothesis *were* true in all its parts, including this one, then pure intellectualism, with its veto on our making willing advances, would be an absurdity; and some participation of our sympathetic nature would be logically required. I, therefore, for one, cannot see my way to accepting the agnostic rules for truth-seeking, or wilfully agree to keep my willing nature out of the game. I cannot do so for this plain reason, that *a rule of thinking which would absolutely prevent me from acknowledging certain kinds of truth if those kinds of truth were really there, would be an irrational rule.* That for me is the long and short of the formal logic of the situation, no matter what the kinds of truth might materially be.

I confess I do not see how this logic can be escaped. But sad experience makes me fear that some of you may still shrink from radically saying with me, *in abstracto,* that we have the right to believe at our own risk any hypothesis that is live enough to tempt our will. I suspect, however that if this is so, it is because you have got away from the abstract logical point of view altogether, and are thinking (perhaps without realizing it) of some particular religious hypothesis which for you is dead. The freedom to "believe what we will" you apply to the case of some patent superstition; and the faith you think of is the faith defined by the schoolboy when he said, "Faith is when you believe something that you know ain't true." I can only repeat that this is misapprehension. *In concreto,* the freedom to believe can only cover living options which the intellect of the individual cannot by itself resolve; and living options never seem absurdities to him who has them to consider. When I look at the religious question as it really puts itself to concrete men, and when I think of all the possibilities which both practically and theoretically it involves, then this command that we shall put a stopper on our heart, instincts, and courage, and *wait*—acting of course meanwhile more or less as if religion were *not* true[3]—till doomsday, or till such time as our intellect and senses working together may have raked in evidence enough,— this command, I say, seems to

3. Since belief is measured by action, he who forbids us to believe religion to be true, necessarily also forbids us to act as we should if we did believe it to be true. The whole defence of religious faith hinges upon action. If the action required or inspired by the religious hypothesis is in no way different from that dictated by the naturalistic hypothesis, then religious faith is a pure superfluity, better pruned away, and controversy about its legitimacy is a piece of idle trifling, unworthy of serious minds. I myself believe, of course, that the religious hypothesis gives to the world an expression which specifically determines our reactions, and makes them in a large part unlike what they might be on a purely naturalistic scheme of belief.

me the queerest idol ever manufactured in the philosophic cave. Were we scholastic absolutists, there might be more excuse. If we had an infallible intellect with its objective certitudes, we might feel ourselves disloyal to such a perfect organ of knowledge in not trusting to it exclusively, in not waiting for its releasing word. But if we are empricists, if we believe that no bell in us tolls to let us know for certain when truth is in our grasp, then it seems a piece of idle fantasticality to preach so solemnly our duty of waiting for the bell. Indeed we *may* wait if we will,—I hope you do not think that I am denying that,—but if we do so, we do so at our peril as much as if we believed. In either case we *act,* taking our life in our hands.

J. L. Mackie

"BELIEF WITHOUT REASON"

A brief biography of Mackie appears on page 322.

It would appear . . . that the central doctrines of theism, literally interpreted, cannot be rationally defended. Even those who have enjoyed what they take to be religious experiences have no good reason to interpret them as they do, as direct contacts with literally divine or supernatural beings, nor can any sort of revelation justify such beliefs. There may be enough flexibility in those central doctrines for even the conjunction of them to escape conclusive disproof by the problem of evil, but the overall balance of evidence and argument is against each of those doctrines on its own, and strongly against the conjunction of them.

But does this matter? 'Our most holy religion', Hume said 'is founded on *faith,* not on reason,' and though Hume meant this ironically, there have been many religious believers who have held this literally.[1] Can theism, then, dispense with rational support, and rely on faith alone?

Obviously it can, since for many believers it does so rely. There are any number of adherents not only of Christianity but also of many other religions who just accept their various faiths, never thinking seriously of the possibility that they might be mistaken, and therefore never feeling any need for rational support for the central doctrines of those religions. No doubt their belief has causes: it has been taken over from parents or teachers or a whole cultural tradition; but these causes do not involve reasons. They may be traced by a natural history of religion which shows how belief can flourish not merely without rational support but even in opposition to the weight of the evidence.

It is, therefore, not in doubt for a moment that belief without reason is causally possible. What is of interest is rather the paradoxical question whether belief without reason may none the less be intellectually respectable, whether, although there are no reasons which would give a balance of direct support of theistic doctrines,

From J.L. Mackie, *The Miracle of Theism,* Clarendon Press, 1982, pp. 199–216. Reprinted by permission of Oxford University Press.

1. *Enquiry Concerning Human Understanding,* Section 10, Part 2.

there are reasons for not demanding any such reasons. Various arguments for this initially surprising thesis have been advanced by Pascal, Kierkegaard, and William James.

(a) PASCAL'S WAGER[2]

Either God exists or he does not; but reason, Pascal says, is unable to decide the question either way. So you are forced to play a game of chance: you must, in effect, bet on one or the other. You cannot simply suspend judgement. Since it is a practical choice, you should consider what your various interests are. What you may stand to gain is knowledge of the truth and happiness; what you risk, if you should lose, is error and misery; the resources with which you wager are your reason and your will. There is no more damage to your reason if you bet one way rather than another, so it does not count. If you bet on God's existing, then, if it turns out that he does exist, you gain infinite happiness; while, if it turns out that he does not exist, you lose nothing. But if you bet on God's not existing, then, if it turns out that he does exist, you will have lost your chance of everlasting happiness; while, if it turns out that he does not exist, you gain nothing. So it is overwhelmingly practically reasonable to bet on God's existing, although you have no more intellectual reason to suppose that he exists than that he does not.

This is Pascal's first formulation of the choice before us; but he adds others. Perhaps it is not true that you lose *nothing* in betting on God's existing: you lose the worldly happiness that you could gain in this life if you were free from religious commitments. So, if you bet on God's existing, then, if you lose, you will have lost one happy life, while, if you win, you will have won an infinity of happy lives. But if you bet against God's existing, then, whether you win or lose, you will have only one happy life, while, if you lose, you will have lost the opportunity of an infinity of happiness. Pascal adds that he does not need to assume that the chance of God's existing is equal to the chance of his not existing. Even if the odds against his existing are n to I, your expectation is betting on his existing, measured in units of happy lives, is infinity divided by $n + 1$, which is still infinity, while your expectation in betting on his not existing is one such unit; so long as n is finite, the former is infinitely greater than the latter: 'il y a ici une infinité de vie infiniment heureuse à gagner, un hasard de gain contre un nombre fini de hasards de perte, et ce que vous jouez est fini'. The decision would become problematic only if n equalled infinity—that is, only if the odds against God's existing were infinite—so that the expectation in betting on God's existing were infinity divided by infinity, which is indeterminate.

The accompanying table, therefore, would express Pascal's final view of the betting problem. (Results and expectations are here measured in happy life units.)

Bet on God's existing		*Bet against God's existing*	
Chance of winning $\frac{1}{n+1}$	Chance of losing $\frac{n}{n+1}$	Chance of winning $\frac{n}{n+1}$	Chance of losing $\frac{1}{n+1}$
Result of winning ∞	Result of losing 0	Result of winning I	Result of losing I
Expectation $\frac{\infty}{n+1} + 0 = \frac{\infty}{n+1}$		Expectation $\frac{n}{n+1} + \frac{1}{n+1} = 1$	

2. Pascal, *Pensées,* in Œuvres, edited by L. Brunschvigg (Hachette, Paris, 1925), Section III, No. 233.

All this is a paraphrase of Pascal's argument, not an exact translation. It is clear that, given his assumptions, the argument goes through. Everything turns, therefore, on the acceptability of those assumptions. Of these the most basic is the very formulation of the problem as one of a practical decision in uncertainty. What, one might ask, would it be to wager that God exists? One can decide, on the grounds of various probable advantages and disadvantages, to act in one way or another, but can one, for such practical reasons, decide to believe something? Although there are voluntary actions, there seems to be no possibility of voluntary belief. However, Pascal has anticipated this objection. Perhaps, for the reasons he has given, you would like to believe in God but find yourself initially unable to do so. Since it is not reason that is now an obstacle to belief—for, by hypothesis, intellectual considerations were unable to settle the question either way, and practical reason, in view of the wager argument, favours belief—the obstacle must lie in your passions. You can work on these as others have done who have found the way to faith, by using holy water, having masses said, and so on: 'Naturellement même cela vous fera croire et vous abêtira'. Although you cannot believe by simply deciding to do so, you can come to believe by deciding to cultivate belief. Indirectly voluntary belief is possible, though directly voluntary belief is not.

No doubt Pascal is right about this; but it goes against his earlier claim that to bet one way or the other about God will do no injury to your reason. Deliberately to make oneself believe, by such techniques as he suggests—essentially by playing tricks on oneself that are found by experience to work upon people's passions and to give rise to belief in non-rational ways—*is* to do violence to one's reason and understanding. As Pascal himself says, 'cela . . . vous abêtira': it will make you stupid. Others have put it more mildly: to acquire faith, you must become as a little child. But, however it is expressed, the point remains: in deliberately cultivating non-rational belief, one would be suppressing one's critical faculties. Of course it will be said that to do this is to reject only a false reason, a superficial understanding, in order to attain a true wisdom, a deeper understanding. But to say this is to beg the question. We have as yet no reason to suppose that this 'true wisdom' is anything but a hopeful delusion, a self-deception. Nor could we come to have any reason to suppose this except by exercising those despised critical faculties.

Here, too, we should remember that in his discussion of the wager Pascal moves from the assumption that the odds for and against the existence of God are equal to the assumption that the odds against his existence are n to one, where n is any finite number. With the latter assumption, he is still able to argue that the expectation of happiness is greater in betting for than in betting against God's existence; but he can no longer argue that there is no greater cost to one's reason in the former than in the latter. To decide to cultivate belief in God, when, epistemically, the odds are n to one against his existing, and n is some large number, is deliberately to reject all rational principles of belief in uncertainty. There is, in Pascal's proposal, a real cost which he has tried to conceal.

Still, it may be thought that even if this cost is properly allowed for, the case for a practical choice based on comparative expectations holds good. But here we must bring out, and challenge, his other assumptions. He considers only these alternatives: first, that there is a god who will reward with everlasting happiness all those who believe in him for whatever reason, and, secondly, that there is no god and that one's existence simply ends completely when one dies. But obviously there are other possibilities. One, to which a Christian thinker might well have paid some attention, is that people are predestined to salvation or to non-salvation—perhaps to damnation—no matter what they now decide, or try to decide, to do. If so, nothing one does now will make any difference with regard to one's prospects for an afterlife, so one should try to do whatever gives the best chance that the present life will be happy. Another possibility is that there might be a god who looked with more favour on honest doubters or atheists who, in Hume's words, proportioned their belief to the evidence, than on mercenary manipulators of their own understandings. Indeed, this would follow from the ascription to God of moral goodness in any sense that we can understand. The sort of god required for Pascal's first alternative is modelled upon a monarch both stupid enough and vain enough to be pleased with self-interested flattery. Again, even if there were a god of Pascal's sort, there are various sub-possibilities to be taken into account: perhaps this god is not satisfied with the mere belief that there is *a* god, but adopts the principle *nulla salus extra ecclesiam,* where the church within which alone salvation is to be found is not necessarily the Church of Rome, but perhaps that of the Anabaptists or the Mormons or the Muslim Sunnis or the worshippers of Kali or of Odin. Who can say? From the position of initial ignorance and non-reliance on reason in which Pascal starts, no such possibility is more likely than any other.

Once the full range of such possibilities is taken into account, Pascal's argument from comparative expectations falls to the ground. The cultivation of non-rational belief is not even practically reasonable. Indeed, the true position is the exact opposite of what he has presented. Whereas Pascal says that speculative reason is neutral with regard to the existence of a god, and that belief must therefore, and can, be based on practical reason alone, the truth is rather that practical reason is here neutral, and that we can and must therefore do the best we can with speculative reason after all.

(b) WILLIAM JAMES AND THE WILL TO BELIEVE[3]

William James's discussion in his essay 'The Will to Believe' is both intellectually and morally far superior to Pascal's. Indeed, he anticipates one of our criticisms of Pascal: 'if we were ourselves in the place of the Deity, we should probably take particular pleasure in cutting off believers of this pattern [that is, those who follow Pascal's advice] from their infinite reward'. But he also develops some of Pascal's ideas, and he, too, sees the problem as one of rational choice in uncertainty.

James distinguishes the options with which he is most concerned, which he calls 'genuine' options, as those which are (for the agent or thinker in question) *living, forced,* and *momentous.* A living option is one where the agent sees both the alternatives as serious possibilities. A momentous one is one that matters, and in particular one where the agent has a unique opportunity, where his decision is not easily reversible, and if he lets this chance go it will not recur. An option is forced where the choice is between two exclusive and exhaustive alternatives, where there is no real third possibility such as suspense of judgement. For choices in the area thus defined, he argues against the view of W. K. Clifford, that 'It is wrong always, everywhere, and for every one, to believe anything upon insufficient evidence'.[4] He maintains, on the contrary, that '*Our passional nature not only lawfully may, but must, decide an option between propositions, whenever it is a genuine option that cannot by its nature be decided on intellectual grounds*'.

To show this, James first insists, and rightly, that 'our non-intellectual nature does influence our convictions'. Though 'talk of believing by our volition seems . . . simply silly', the truth is that 'It is only our already dead hypotheses that our willing nature is unable to bring to life again. But what has made them dead for us is for the most part a previous action of our willing nature . . . ' 'There are passional tendencies and volitions which run before and others which come after belief, and it is only the latter that are too

3. W. James, *The Will to Believe and Other Essays* (Longmans, London, 1896).

4. Quoted by James from W. K. Clifford, *Lectures and Essays* (Macmillan, London, 1886).

late for the fair; and they are not too late when the previous passional work has been already in their own direction.'

He combines this with another correct thesis, that most of what anyone believes, he believes on authority, through the influence of the intellectual climate around him. He could say, at Brown University, and again at Yale, 'Here in this room, we all of us believe in molecules and the conservation of energy, in democracy and necessary progress, in Protestant Christianity and the duty of fighting for "the doctrine of the immortal Monroe", all for no reasons worthy of the name'.

Secondly, James distinguishes between absolutism or dogmatism—the view that we can achieve not merely knowledge but certainty, that we can know when we know—and empiricism, that is, fallibilism, the view that objective certainty is in general unattainable. While firmly endorsing empiricism, he says that this does not mean giving up the quest for truth and the hope of gradually getting closer to it. This is correct, though we must query his characteristically pragmatist remark that 'if the total drift of thinking continues to confirm [a hypothesis], that is what [the empiricist] means by its being true'. We may well hope that the results of investigation will converge upon the truth, and their convergence with one another will be evidence for their truth, but the truth of a hypothesis does not consist in convergence, but rather in things simply being as the hypothesis supposes that they are.

James's third step is to distinguish between the two purposes of knowing the truth and avoiding error, and to say that he himself regards 'the chase for truth as paramount, and the avoidance of error as secondary'. Clifford's view, by contrast, treats the avoidance of error as more important than the attaining of truth. 'Clifford's exhortation . . . is like a general informing his soldiers that it is better to keep out of battle forever than to risk a single wound. Not so are victories either over enemies or over nature gained. Our errors are surely not such awfully solemn things. In a world where we are so certain to incur them in spite of all our caution, a certain lightness of heart seems healthier than this excessive nervousness on their behalf.' But he admits that this principle bears differently upon questions of various sorts.

In the consideration of scientific questions, James allows that suspense of judgement may be in order: here options are not forced. But even here less caution, more passionate involvement, is favourable for discovery. 'The most useful investigator, because the most sensitive observer, is always he whose eager interest in one side of the question is balanced by an equally keen nervousness lest he become deceived. Science has organized this nervousness into a regular *technique* . . . ' What James says here is closely related to some of Karl Popper's doctrines. James speaks of 'verification,' whereas Popper speaks only of 'corroboration' when a hypothesis stands up to severe tests and resists attempts to falsify it; but James rightly assumes what Popper is very reluctant to concede: this outcome tells positively in favour of a hypoth-

"Faith and Reason"

Hans Küng

No, theology cannot evade the demands for confirmation of belief in God: *Not a blind, but a justifiable belief: a person should not be abused, but convinced by arguments, so that he can make a responsible decision of faith. Not a belief devoid of reality, but a belief related to reality.*

From *Does God Exist?* (1980).

esis, and gives us some reason to believe that it is at least approaching the truth.[5] James's account of the typical motives of the good investigator is also sounder than Popper's.

Moral questions, unlike scientific ones, 'present themselves as questions whose solutions cannot wait for sensible proof'. James wants to hold on to the objectivity of morals, while denying that moral questions can be empirically settled. I would agree with his dictum, but for a different reason, namely that categorically imperative statements, purporting to give people directives to do this or to refrain from that, directives that are unconditional and in no way dependent upon the desires or purposes of the agent, are not capable of being simply true, nor are statements about what is good or bad in senses that would entail such directives.[6]

There are also 'truths dependent upon our personal action'. 'Whenever a desired result is achieved by the co-operation of many independent persons, its existence as a fact is a pure consequence of the precursive faith in one another of those immediately concerned.' Hence there are 'cases where a fact cannot come at all unless a preliminary faith exists in its coming'; in such cases 'it would be an insane logic' to forbid faith to run ahead of evidence.

Almost all of these initial steps in James's argument are not only eloquently expressed but also correct and important. Most of our beliefs do rest on authority, and our 'passional nature' does play some part in many, perhaps all, of them. In almost all areas judgements are fallible in varying degrees, and while we aim at truth we can claim at most that tested and confirmed hypotheses are likely to come close to the truth. In science it is reasonable not only to make enterprising guesses but also to combine critical testing of them with the hope and tentative belief that they are not too far from truth. In social and political affairs it is reasonable—since it is a necessary condition for co-operation—to trust others in advance of any certainty that they are trustworthy. Moral judgements of some central sorts are not capable of being true, and *a fortiori* cannot be shown to be true; but it is not contrary to reason to make them, and the sentiments and ways of thinking that they express are essential to any tolerable human and especially social life. In all these ways we must at least qualify Clifford's dictum; but the crucial question is, How do these principles relate to religion and in particular to theistic belief?

According to James himself, religion says essentially two things. 'First, she says that the best things are the more eternal things, the overlapping things, the things in the universe that throw the last stone, so to speak, and say the final word . . . The second affirmation of religion is that we are better off even now if we believe her first affirmation to be true.' Now two things are plain about this summary. The first affirmation is extremely vague, and the main content of both affirmations is evaluative, though the first may presuppose some factual claims. James goes on to say that 'The more perfect and more eternal aspect of the universe is represented in our religions as having personal form'. From this he concludes that the only practical way of taking the religious hypothesis seriously is to meet it half way. One who refused to make advances until he had proof 'might cut himself off forever from his only opportunity of making the gods' acquaintance'.

The problem of religious belief is thus assimilated on the one hand to that of morality (in a broad sense) and on the other to the need, in social co-operation, to trust others before one is sure that they are to be trusted—that is, to two spheres in which we have already agreed that it is reasonable for decision to run ahead of evidence. That is why James rejects 'the agnostic rules for truth-seeking', saying that '*a rule of thinking which would absolutely prevent me from acknowledging certain kinds of truth if those kinds of truth were really there, would be*

5. See, in P. A. Schilpp, editor, *The Philosophy of Karl Popper* (Open Court, La Salle, Illinois, 1974), Popper's 'Replies to My Critics', especially pp. 1013–41.

6. See my *Ethics: Inventing Right and Wrong* (Penguin, Harmondsworth, 1977). Chapter 1.

an irrational rule.'. In this field, therefore, as in some others, not only is it a fact that 'our passional nature' influences our opinions, it is also legitimate that it should do so. In effect, James is saying about faith, as the Samnite, Gaius Pontius (in Livy, Book IX) said about war, that it is justified when you cannot avoid it: *Iusta est fides, quibus necessaria.*

This is a persuasive and powerful case. But three strands can be distinguished within it. One concerns what are essentially moral choices. These are, indeed, free in the sense that they need not and cannot wait for the intellect to determine them. They escape Clifford's rigid agnosticism. But this fact leaves us with, as yet, no guidance about what choices to make. Whatever choice lies concealed in the obscure claim that the best things are the more eternal things, we should have to test this by seeing how it fits in and coheres with our other moral views and our purposes as a whole. . . .

The second theme is that of passion as a tiebreaker. Even on factual questions, issues of truth and falsehood, James says that where intellectual considerations are evenly balanced—and where the option is living, forced, and momentous, so that suspense of judgement is impossible—passion can lawfully decide. This is more questionable. It is all too close to Pascal's view that, when speculative reason cannot decide, self-seeking practical reason can act as a tiebreaker. Admittedly passion *will* frequently so decide in an impasse; we must accept this as inevitable, and we can do so with the less unease when we admit, as we must, that at all times many of our beliefs rest partly on passion. But James has exaggerated the dependence of belief on passion by putting under this heading the very many beliefs which we hold on authority. Some of these, I grant, belong under the heading of passion, where our acceptance of a supposed authority itself rests on nothing more than custom and our tendency to go along with other people. But sometimes what passes for an authority really is an authority; that is, we may have good reason to suppose that the 'authority' has knowledge, or a well-founded opinion, about the matter and has no strong motive for deceiving us. Sometimes we even have evidence from our own experience that the 'authority' is generally reliable in the area in question. In such cases, what we accept on authority is thereby given, though only indirectly, some degree of rational support. No doubt we still are constantly deceived in many ways, often on matters of the greatest importance. But this is no reason for happily accepting the determination of belief by passion; rather it is a reason for trying to be more critical, and for extending into other fields, if possible, those practices of mutual criticism and testing which in lawsuits and in science, for example, provide some check on error and deceit. In any case, we need a tiebreaker only where there is a tie to be broken; and it is far from clear that rational consideration about what is the best overall explanatory hypothesis does reach such an impasse with regard to the central questions of theism.

The third strand in James's argument is the most important. Given that there is, inevitably, a 'passional' component in thought, and, equally inevitably, a great and constant risk of error, and given also that, about many matters, the chance of being right has a value not outweighed by the disvalue of the chance of being wrong, we must reject Clifford's principle of never believing anything on insufficient evidence. We must be willing not only to frame hypothesis and test them, but also to give a tentative acceptance to hypotheses which have some plausibility and have received some confirmation through testing. This is a principle which an atheist can endorse as readily and whole-heartedly as any theist. It is James's next step that is crucial: there may be for us a live hypothesis that 'the more perfect and more eternal aspect of the universe' is personal in form, and then the only proper way to test this hypothesis will be to try to enter into conversation with this person (or persons): to have a chance of 'making the gods' acquaintance', we must be prepared to meet them halfway. In view of all that has been said in earlier chapters, I doubt whether this should still be a live hypothesis for us. But let us suppose that it is. Let us agree with James that a rule of thinking which would absolutely prevent me from acknowledging certain kinds of truth if those kinds of truth were really there would be an irrational rule. What follows is that we shall be intellectually better placed in relation to theism—whether in the end we accept it or reject it—if we have at least once made the experiment of playing along with it, if we have genuinely opened not only the intellectual but also the passional side of our minds to the possibility of conversing with 'the gods', if there are any gods and they are willing to converse with us. But it follows also that since our object is to ascertain whether 'those kinds of truth are really there', we must maintain in this area also the tension of which James himself has spoken (with reference to science) between the eager interest of the optimistic speculator and the critical 'nervousness lest he become deceived', the balanced consideration whether our observations really confirm our hypothesis or disconfirm it. An experiment whose aim is to ascertain the truth must be so conducted as to allow the hypothesis in question to be falsified or at least disconfirmed. A hypothesis is confirmed only by surviving severe tests, that is, tests which, if it is false, are likely to show that it is false. While we must, as James says, reject as irrational a rule of thinking which would prevent us from acknowledging certain kinds of truth even if they were really here, we must equally reject as irrational a rule of thinking which would prevent us from denying such supposed truths even if they were not really there. And this is not only in order to avoid error: it is an essential part of the method of confirming truth. If faith is to be defended as an experiment, it must conform to the general principles of experimental inquiry. The result of any such experiment, of trying to converse with 'the gods', will presumably be some 'religious experience'. But . . . , the credentials of any such experience are themselves doubtful. A favourable result of the experiment would have to be a series of experiences which somehow resisted the kinds of psychological explanation indicated in [our earlier discussions].

With this proviso, we can accept this third strand in James's argument, his case for what we may call an experimental faith. But how different this is from anything that would ordinarily be advocated as religious faith! In particular, how different this is from the way in which Pascal proposes that we should cultivate religious belief—'cela . . . vous abêtira'—and also, as we shall see, from Kierkegaard's view that reason has no place in the sphere of faith. According to this third strand in James's argument, a kind of tentative faith is a move in the game of rational investigation. It may be objected that such employment is inconsistent with the very spirit of religious belief, that the latter requires an intellectual unconditional surrender, an abandonment of autonomous investigation. That is, it may be said that "experimental faith' is a contradiction in terms. I shall argue, against Kierkegaard, that this is not so; but if it were so, its effect would be to destroy James's case for antecedent belief. We could not retain his argument for faith while rejecting the empiricist assumptions and the experimental principles on which that whole argument depends.

(c) KIERKEGAARD AND THE PRIMACY OF COMMITMENT[7]

In Kierkegaard the move from reason to faith is more extreme than in either Pascal or James. 'The inquiring subject,' he says, 'must be in one or the other of two situations. *Either* he is in faith convinced of the truth of Christianity, and in faith assured of his own relationship to it; in which case he cannot be infinitely interested in all the rest, since faith itself is the infinite interest of Christianity, and since every other interest may readily come to constitute a temp-

7. S. Kierkegaard, *Concluding Unscientific Postscript*, translated by D. F. Swenson and W. Lowrie (Princeton University Press, 1941), Book I, Part II, Chapter 2.

tation. *Or* the inquirer is, on the other hand, not in an attitude of faith, but objectively in an attitude of contemplation, and hence not infinitely interested in the determination of the question.' From this he concludes that 'the problem cannot in this manner decisively arise; which means that it does not arise at all, since decisiveness is of the essence of the problem'.

If this were sound, it would mean that the rational discussion of theism, at least in the form of Christianity, is impossible, and (for example) that all the arguments, on either side, reported or offered in our previous chapters have failed to come to grips with any real issue. But is it sound? Let us try to spell out Kierkegaard's argument more fully. In saying that decisiveness is of the essence of the problem, he is claiming, first, that the question of the truth of Christianity is such that it is part of the question itself that the questioner should be infinitely interested in the determination of it. But secondly, he alleges, one cannot be infinitely interested in this determination unless one is infinitely interested in Christianity, and, thirdly, one can be infinitely interested in Christianity only if one is already convinced of its truth, that is, if one is already in a state of faith which precludes the *consideration* of the question. Thus expanded, the argument is valid: given the premisses, the conclusion follows. But there is no reason why we should accept any one of these premisses, let alone all three. The second and third are just dubious empirical assertions; the first of the three is more discussable. How *could* a questioner's interest in a question be part of the essence of the question itself? If there is an issue of truth and falsity about Christianity, that is, if there is any such thing as even the possibility that Christianity is true, then there must be the two possible states of affairs, its being so and its not

"Religion and Art"

R. G. Collingwood

Now religion is essentially assertion, belief. To believe this is to deny that. Therefore religion by its very nature is pledged to selectiveness, to a discrimination between the utterances of the spirit, to a dualism between true vision and false vision. At first, when religion in its most primitive phase is as yet ignorant of its own nature, and asserts without understanding what assertion means, it thinks it can assert every fantasy that arises in the mind; and in this phase anything may be an object of worship. Here it is only the attitude of worship that distinguishes religion from art; in the indiscriminateness of their fancy they are identical. But when the religious mind discovers that to assert one fantasy means denying another, primitive religion and its easy polytheism are doomed. . . .

The effect of this principle is to produce for the first time a world or cosmos of imagination. Art has no cosmology, it gives us no view of the universe; every distinct work of art gives us a little cosmology of its own, and no ingenuity will combine all these into a single whole. But religion is essentially cosmological, though its cosmology is always an imaginative cosmology:. . . . Now assertion or the logical function of the mind is the recognition of reality as such, and reality is that which is real for all minds. If a number of minds are engaged in imagining, they have no common ground, for each man's imaginations are his own. But if they are engaged in asserting, they at once become a society, for each asserts what he believes to be not his own but common property, objective reality. And even when their assertions are different, they are not merely different, like different works of art, but contradictory; and contradiction, even in its extreme forms of persecution and war, is a function of sociability. It is the explicitly national character of religion that necessitates religious controversy and persecution, for these are only corollaries of its cosmological social nature.

From *Principles of Art*.

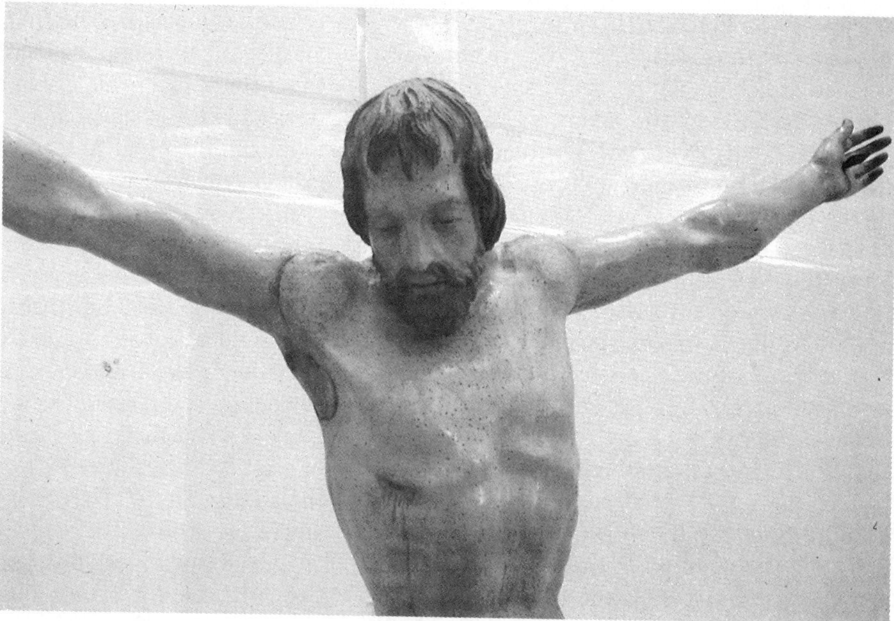

Crucifix by the great Italian artist Donatello. Fifteenth century, Florence.

being so. Then anyone who can think about or envisage these two possibilities can consider also the possibility of a decision between them, and to do this is to raise the question. Thus the question of the truth of Christianity arises for such a thinker, quite irrespectively of his degree of interest in the question or of his commitment to either side. To deny this is to cast serious doubt on whether there is any question of truth here at all; and, as we shall see, Kierkegaard's argument drives him in that direction.

He develops his thesis by contrasting 'objective' and 'subjective' reflections, or ways of raising the question of truth. '*When the question of truth is raised in an objective manner, reflection is directed objectively to the truth, as an object to which the knower is related . . . When the question of the truth is raised subjectively, reflection is directed subjectively to the nature of the individual's relationship; if only the mode of this relationship is in the truth, the individual is in the truth even if he should happen to be thus related to what is not true.*' Again, 'subjectively, reflection is directed to the question whether the individual is related to a something *in such a manner* that his relationship is in truth a God relationship'. He contrasts one who prays in the house of the true God and with the true conception of God in his knowledge, but prays in a false spirit, with one who, living in an idolatrous community, prays with the entire passion of the infinite, although his eyes rest upon the image of an idol: 'The one prays in truth to God though he worships an idol; the other prays falsely to the true God, and hence worships in fact an idol.'

This suggests that according to Kierkegaard what matters is not the truth or falsity of *what anyone believes*—that would be 'objective truth'—but rather the nature of the believing relationship.

'Objectively *what* is said is stressed; subjectively *how* it is said.' But what is it for this relationship to be 'in the truth'? Apparently all that is required is that it should be one of infinitely passionate personal interest and commitment. But if the nature of this relationship is all that matters, does not the second term of the relationship simply drop out? Is it not a loose cog that does no work? And might it not then be anything at all, or indeed a mere fantasy object? This is strongly suggested by Kierkegaard's thesis that 'truth is subjectivity'; but it seems not to be what he intends. For (as quoted above) he contrasts 'the true God' with 'an idol'; he takes the life of Christ quite literally as a revelation given to men by this true God; and he even speaks of the Christian as being passionately interested *on behalf of his own eternal happiness;* one so interested would be a victim of deception (perhaps self-deception), if the Christian doctrines were not literally true. When someone prays in (subjective) truth to an idol, this is somehow converted into prayer to the 'true God'; the proper second term of the relationship is there, and the worshipper is related to it, after all. Again, 'The object of faith is the reality of another . . . it is the reality of the teacher, that the teacher really exists'. Yet there is also support for the 'loose cog' interpretation: Kierkegaard also speaks of one who 'embraces an uncertainty with the passion of the infinite', and uses Socrates as an illustration. Although Socrates regards immortality as problematic, 'On this "if" he risks his entire life, he has the courage to meet death, and he has with the passion of the infinite so determined the pattern of his life that it must be found acceptable—*if* there is an immortality'. This *might* be read as saying that Socrates had based his plan of life on an anticipation of Pascal's wager; but this would be so fantastic a distortion of Socrates' thoughts and motives, as Plato presents them, that I cannot believe that it is what Kierkegaard meant. He must have meant rather that Socrates' total commitment to philosophical, especially moral, inquiry, and to the criticism of unfounded claims to knowledge, itself involved 'the passion of the infinite'. If so, there must be a great deal of free play with respect to the intentional object of commitment.

The two interpretations between which we are hesitating, and between which Kierkegaard himself seems to oscillate, reflect upon his attempt to show that the problem of the truth of Christianity, or perhaps of theism in general, cannot arise. If *all* that matters is the mode of relationship, and it can have almost any object at all, including an imaginary one, then, indeed, although a question may arise above the reality of this or that specific object, it will be trivial and it will not be the problem of the truth of Christianity in general, or of theism in general: there will, indeed, be no such problem. But if Christianity, or theism, essentially involves some literal claims about the existence of a god and his relationship to and dealings with men, then, even if the mode of relationship *also* matters—so that the relationship's being 'in truth' can somehow forge a connection with its proper object even where the believer is himself unaware of that object or uncertain about it—there is a real question which arises and can be investigated, and which is not foreclosed by Kierkegaard's dilemma.

More important, however, to Kierkegaard than the claim that this question cannot arise is his view that even if it arises the 'objective' consideration of it is worse than useless. Not, apparently, because it cannot establish the truth of religion, but rather because it might come close to doing so. The 'objective approximation-process' is incompatible with faith. 'Anything that is almost probable, or probable, or extremely and emphatically probable, is something he can almost know, or as good as know, or extremely and emphatically almost *know*—but it is impossible to believe. For the absurd is the object of faith, and the only object that can be believed.' Kierkegaard stresses and welcomes the paradoxical character of Christianity—especially in its claim that God has literally existed as an individual human being—and explicitly rejects any interpretations that would make it more rationally acceptable: 'Christianity is therefore not a doctrine, but the fact that God has existed.' It is vital for him that the absurd should 'stand out in all its clarity—in order that the individual may believe if he so wills'.

Like Pascal in his wager, and like James with his experimental faith, Kierkegaard makes belief a matter of will. But unlike both of these, he is not arguing on any general grounds in favour of such belief. He seems to be arguing *from* a position, not *to* a position. His dominant aim is expository, to show what Christianity is. Of course this means that he is really showing what Christianity as *he conceives it* is, although he would not concede this qualification. Rather, he would insist that this is what Christianity *really* is, and this would include—but would not be exhausted by—the historical claim that his is the original type of Christianity. Since Christianity was in his day, and still is, in a very broad sense an *established* religion, since many people think that it is good to be Christian, and many more give Christianity formal adherence or lip service or at least some considerable degree of respect, it is in practice a way of recommending a position to say that it is the truly Christian one. (This is an instance of the propaganda device that Charles L. Stevenson analysed under the name of 'persuasive definition'.[8]) Perhaps, then, Kierkegaard is, after all, arguing for a position, but only by trading upon that conventional, respectable, nominal Christianity which he despises and condemns.

Leaving this piece of trickery aside, we can say that what Kierkegaard does is to present for his readers' acceptance a picture of a purely voluntary faith, a faith which relies on no intellectual support and spurns intellectual questioning and criticism. 'Faith constitutes a sphere all by itself, and every misunderstanding of Christianity may at once be recognized by its transforming it into a doctrine, transferring it to the sphere of the intellectual.'

This contrasts sharply with a view which Anselm, for example, summed up in the phrase 'faith seeking understanding': *fides quaerens intellectum.* Anselm begins from a position of faith. He believes in a god, and indeed addresses God as a person. Nevertheless he would like to add understanding and intellectual conviction, or even logical proof, to that initial belief. This project is not incoherent or misguided. We saw . . . that it fails; but that does not mean that it was misconceived. And in fact there are plenty of other reasonable and in some cases successful instances of *fides quaerens intellectum:* many of the philosophical replies to various forms of scepticism come under this heading. Our beliefs in an external world, in other minds, and in the general reliability of inductive reasoning are all initially non-rational. We merely find ourselves believing these things, as James would say, for no reasons worthy of the name. That is why, when the sceptical doubts are raised, we at first, and perhaps for quite a long time, find them unanswerable. Not having reached these beliefs by any process of reasoning, we have no arguments prepared and ready with which we could reply to the sceptic. Nevertheless, such arguments can in the end be found. In these cases faith can seek and find the understanding to support it. And when understanding has thus supported it, our belief in these matters is not thereby undermined or corrupted.

For all that anyone could have told in advance, the same might have been true of Anselm's project. He, of course, was looking for, and thought he had found, an *a priori* demonstration of God's existence. But the same might equally have been true of Swinburne's project of seeking an empirical, inductive, argument for this conclusion, or of James's project of seeking experimental confirmation. Indeed, the two latter are, at least today, more sensible projects than Anselm's, in so far as we have good general ground for denying that demonstration is possible about such a matter of fact as the existence of a god. But the main point is that faith can seek for understanding, whether demonstrative or inductive or experimental. One does not abandon one's initial belief when one sets out to look

8. C. L. Stevenson 'Persuasive Definitions' in *Mind* 47(1938).

for confirmation, nor, if one found it, would one have to give up the belief. A test pilot, flying a new type of plane for the first time, must have plenty of faith in its designers and manufacturers. None the less, his task is to confirm what he initially believes, and he does so only by taking the risk of disproving it, and only by being on the lookout for any weaknesses and faults. And Kierkegaard himself, in his commendation of Socrates, implicitly admits that a commitment of the kind he values can be shown in an inquiry that sees its own outcome as uncertain.

Why, then, does Kierkegaard also take the contrary view, that commitment must be uncritical, and that the absurd is the only possible object of faith? Is he, perhaps, falling into the fallacy of supposing that because someone would need a particularly strong commitment or will to believe in order to accept an absurd or paradoxical belief with no objective reasons in its favour, it is only a belief of this sort that can retain the commitment that he values? Or is he finding a special merit in *gratuitous* faith, which would be lost if the faith were supported by reason, or even if it sought such support? There are, indeed, some analogous judgements of value. We may admire someone whose loyalty to a friend lets him go on believing that the friend is innocent of some crime although all the evidence seems to show that he is guilty; we might even admire the patriot whose slogan is 'My country, right or wrong'. Certainly there is merit in loyalty that does not give way too easily; but there is also room for the concept of misplaced loyalty and misguided devotion. Or is Kierkegaard looking at the matter from what he takes to be God's point of view? Would God want an unquestioning faith in himself, and value it the more highly the more resistant it was to adverse evidence? But this suggestion, like Pascal's, presupposes a god to whom we cannot ascribe moral goodness in any sense that we can understand. We are, in effect, back with the god of the Book of Job, and, whatever we may think of Job himself, there can be no doubt that Jehovah comes out of that story very badly.

At the same time, we cannot deny the psychological attraction of Kierkegaard's emphasis on gratuitous faith. His writings have fathered a whole family of existentialisms, whose common quality is just this advocacy of the making of dramatic choices unbacked by reasons. Here we find a practical analogue of the human mind's tendency (pointed out by Hume . . .) to believe what is strange and marvellous in an extreme degree, just because surprise or wonder is such an agreeable emotion. Just as we may believe reports for the very reason that makes them less worthy of belief, so we may choose actions for reasons that might well rather warn us against them. It is fun to take risks, and there is a thrill in making an indefensible and apparently unmotivated choice. But this can hardly be recommended as a general plan of life, and what Kierkegaard himself is advocating is a sort of intellectual Russian roulette.

We set out to inquire whether belief without reason could, paradoxically, be intellectually respectable. Kierkegaard has certainly not shown that it is. Though he disdains rational considerations, he is, nevertheless, exposed to rational criticism. As we have seen, he is not free from inconsistencies. He hesitates over the question whether faith is compatible with a critical outlook, and also over the question whether it matters that theism, or Christianity, should be true. If it does matter, then we cannot dismiss as irrelevant the only sorts of inquiry that could determine its truth. If it does not matter, then it would be better to admit this openly, and try to defend religion as a form of commitment that does not require belief.

Annette Baier

"SECULAR FAITH"

ANNETTE BAIER is a professor of philosophy at the University of Pittsburgh. She has written extensively on the history of philosophy and on ethics and is a recent president of the American Philosophical Association

1. THE CHALLENGE

Both in ethics and in epistemology one source of scepticism in its contemporary version is the realization, often belated, of the full consequences of atheism. Modern non-moral philosophy looks back to Descartes as its father figure, but disowns the *Third Meditation.* But if God does not underwrite one's cognitive powers, what does? The largely unknown evolution of them, which is just a version of Descartes' unreliable demon? "Let us . . . grant that all that is here said of God is a fable, nevertheless in whatever way they suppose that I have arrived at the state of being that I have reached, whether they attribute it to fate or to accident, or make out that it is by a continual succession of antecedents, or by some other method—since to err and deceive oneself is a defect, it is clear that the greater will be the probability of my being so imperfect as to deceive myself ever, as is the Author to whom they assign my being the less powerful" (Meditation I, Haldane and Ross, tr.). Atheism undermines a solitary thinker's single-handed cognitive ambitions, as it can determine his expectation that unilateral virtue will bring happiness. The phenomenon of atheism in unacknowledged debt to theism can be seen both in ethical theory and in epistemology, and the threat of scepticism arises in a parallel manner.

Annette Baier, "Secular Faith," *Canadian Journal of Philosophy,* Volume X, No. 1, March 1980, pp. 131–148. Reprinted by permission of the author and publisher.

In a provocative article, David Gauthier[1] has supported the charge made two decades ago by Anscombe,[2] that modern secular moral philosophers retain in their theories concepts which require a theological underpinning. "The taking away of God . . . in thought dissolves all," said Locke, and Gauthier agrees that it dissolves all those duties or obligations whose full justification depends upon a general performance of which one has no assurance. He quotes Hobbes: "He that would be modeste and tractable and perform all he promises in such time and place where no man els should do so, should but make himself the prey to others, and procure his own ruin, contrary to all Lawes of Nature, which tend to Nature's preservation" (*Leviathan,* chap. 15). The problem arises not merely when "no man els" does his[3] duty, but when a significant number do not, so that the rest, even a majority, make themselves prey to the immoral ones, and pro-

1. "Why Ought One Obey God, Reflections on Hobbes and Locke," *Canadian Journal of Philosophy 7* (1977), pp. 425–46.

2. G. E. M. Anscombe, in "Modern Moral Philosophy," (*Philosophy,* 1958, pp. 1–18, reprinted in *The Definition of Morality,* ed. Wallace and Walker, London) 1970 claimed that all deontological moral concepts are empty words unless there is a divine lawgiver and duty-determiner. Gauthier's thesis concerns not *all* moral laws and duties, but only those involving "moral convention," where mutual benefits depend upon general observance. I accept his assumption that all moral duties require some rational basis, that we do not simply intuit moral absolutes.

3. Throughout this paper I use 'his' to mean 'his or her' and sometimes use 'man' to mean 'person'. This is especially regrettable in a paper about justice, but needed allusions to the words of Hobbes and other sexists dictated my usage. I am not, it seems, willing to make the sacrifices in communication needed to help gain as much currency for 'the one just woman' as already gained for the one just man.

Light as seen through stained glass windows in the Sainte-Chapelle in Paris—to many, a manifestation of the divine spirit.

cure their own exploitation, if not their own ruin. The theist can believe, in his cool hour, that unilateral, or minority, or exploited majority morality will not procure his ultimate ruin, that all things work together for good, but what consolation can a secular philosopher offer for the cool thoughtful hour, in the absence of God? If Gauthier is right, either false or insufficient consolation. He says that in those modern theories which preserve some vestige of a duty to do what others are not known to be doing, or known to be failing to do, "God is lurking unwanted, even unconceived, but not unneeded."[4]

I shall suggest that the secular equivalent of faith in God, which we need in morality as well as in science or knowledge acquisition, is faith in the human community and its evolving procedures—in the prospects for many-handed cognitive ambitions and moral hopes. Descartes had deliberately shut himself away from other thinkers, distrusting the influence of his teachers and the tradition in which he had been trained. All alone, he found he could take no step beyond a sterile self certainty. Some other mind must come to his aid before he could advance. Descartes sought an absolute assurance to replace the human reassurance he distrusted, and I suggest that we can reverse the procedure. If we distrust the theist's absolute assurance we can return to what Descartes spurned, the support of human tradition, of a cross-generational community. This allows us to avoid the narrow and self-destructive self seeking which is the moral equivalent of solipsism. But Gauthier's challenge is precisely to the reasonableness of com-

4. Gauthier, op.cit., p. 428.

munity-supportive action when we have no guarantee of reciprocal public-spirited or communally-minded action from others. Not only may we have no such guarantee, we may have evidence which strongly *dis*confirms the hypothesis that others are doing their part. We may have neither knowledge nor inductively well based belief that others are doing their part. Faith and hope I take to involve acceptance of belief on grounds other than deductive or inductive evidence of its truth. Faith is the evidence of things unseen. It will be faith, not knowledge, which will replace religious faith. I shall try to make clear exactly what that faith is faith in, and what it would be for it to be (a) ill-founded or unreasonable, (b) reasonable, but in vain. I shall be defending the thesis that the just must live by faith, faith in a community of just persons.

2. FAITH: THE SUBSTANCE OF THINGS HOPED FOR

Faith, not knowledge, was and is needed to support those "plain duties" whose unilateral observation sometimes appears to procure the dutiful person's ruin. But faith, for rational persons, must appear reasonable before it can be attained. If it is to be reasonable, it must not fly in the face of inductive evidence, but it may go beyond it, when there are good reasons of another sort to do so. We may have such good reasons to hope for an empirically very unlikely but not impossible eventuality. Reasonableness is relative to the alternative beliefs or policies one might adopt, or be left with, if one rejected the candidate for the status of reasonable belief. One of the chief arguments for the moral faith I shall present is the great unreasonableness of any alternative to it. The *via negativa* which leads to secular faith has been clearly indicated in Hobbes' description of the state of nature, the state of persons without the constraint of justice. Hobbes' modern commentators, including Gauthier, have underlined the futility of the alternatives to morality. Yet if everyone insisted on knowing in advance that any sacrifice of independent advantage which they personally make, in joining or supporting a moral order, will be made up for by the returns they will get from membership in that moral order, that order could never be created nor, if miraculously brought about, sustained. Only by conquest could a Hobbesian *Leviathan* ever be created, if the rational man must have secure knowledge that others are doing likewise before he voluntarily renounces his right to pursue independent advantage. How, except by total conquest, could one ever know for sure that other would-be war makers will lay down their arms when one does so?

In fact Hobbes' first Law of Nature requires every man to endeavor peace, not when he has certainty of attaining it, but "as fare as he has *hope* of attaining it" (*Leviathan,* chap. 14, emphasis added). Hope had been previously defined as "appetite with opinion of attaining" (op.cit., chap. 6) and opinion is contrasted with science (op.cit., chap. 7), which alone is the outcome of correct reckoning or calculation. It is then, for Hobbes, a Law of Nature, or a counsel of rational prudence, to act on hope when what is at stake is escape from the Hobbesian state of nature.

Faith, Hobbes tells us "is in the man, Beleefe both of the man and of the truth of what he says" (ibid.). It is faith in its Hobbesian sense, in men, not merely belief in the truth of what they say which I shall argue is the only 'substance' of the hoped-for cooperation which avoids the futility and self destructiveness of its alternatives. Faith, in a non-Hobbesian sense, that is a belief which runs beyond the inductive evidence for it, when it is faith in the possibility of a just cooperative scheme being actualized, is the same as that hope whose support is trust "in the man."

Trust in people, and distrust, tends to be self-fulfilling. Faith or lack of faith in any enterprise, but especially one requiring trust in fellow-workers, can also be self-fulfilling. Confidence can produce its own justification, as William James[5] persuasively argued. The question whether to support a moral practice without guarantee of full reciprocity is, in James' terminology, live, momentous, and forced, and the choice made can be self-verifying whichever way we choose. Every new conversion to moral scepticism strengthens the reason for such scepticism, since, if acted on, it weakens the support of moral practices and so diminishes their returns to the morally faithful. Similarly, every person who continues to observe those practices provides some reason for belief that they are supported, and so strengthens the foundation for his own belief that their support is sufficient, and provides some justification for his own dependence on that support. *Some* justification, but not enough, surely, to be decisive, since he is unlikely to be the critical straw to save or break the camel's back. The case for the self-confirmation of moral faith is less clear than for the self-confirmation, the band wagon effect, of moral scepticism. Immorality breeds immorality, but need moral action, especially if *unilateral,* breed more of the same? The sense in which the exemplary unilateral act *does* provide its own support, even if the example it gives is not followed by one's contemporaries, will be explored later. For the moment the best one can say for the reasonableness of willing to belief in the value of (possibly) unilateral moral action is that the alternative, giving up on that crucial part of the moral enterprise which secures cooperation, must lead eventually to an outcome disastrous to all, although those with a taste for gun-running may make a good profit before doomsday dawns. There are different styles of shoring fragments against one's ruin, and some choose to exploit the presumed failure of morality, while others or even the same ones, retreat into a narrow circle where virtues can still be cultivated. But when, even granted the badness of its alternatives, would it be unreasonable to keep faith in the moral enterprise, in particular in the attempt to achieve a fair scheme of human cooperation? I turn next to consider the coherence of the ideal of justice.

3. MORE OR LESS JUST SOCIETIES

When would an actual cooperative scheme between persons be a just one, one which gave its participants the *best reasons* to support it? When the goods, for each, gained by cooperation outweigh the individual advantage any sacrificed, and where all partakers in the benefits make their fair contribution, pay their dues, observe the rules which ensure production and fair distribution of benefits. Even in a society where this was true, there would still be a place for a descendant of Hobbes' *Leviathan,* to enforce rules, since there may still be persons who act irrationally, and who have a perverse taste for bucking the system, whatever the system. A stable, efficient, equitable[6] and democratic scheme of cooperation would give its conforming members security, delectation, non-exploitation and freedom, but some may still try to get a free ride, or to break the rules out of what Hobbes called "the stubbornness of their passions." His fifth Law of Nature commands "compleasance," that every man strive to accommodate himself to the rest, and unilateral breach of this rule is contrary to Hobbesian reason whose dictates include the laws of nature, since it calculates that the in-

5. William James, "The Will to Believe," in *The Will to Believe and Other Essays in Popular Philosophy* (New York and London, 1897). In this paper I am really saying no more than James said about moral faith. I suppose the justification for saying it again, and adapting it to a Hobbesian context, is the perennial character of the issue. I have benefited from discussion with Richard Gale on James' position, and from his comments on an earlier version of this paper.

6. It is not an easy matter to formulate an acceptable criterion of the equitable, but I have assumed that we can get a stronger test for justice than that provided by Hobbes—"What all men have accepted, no man can call unjust." If we cannot, then maybe only the fool says in his heart that there is more to justice than fidelity to possibly forced agreement. If the ideal of the equitable or fair is empty or incoherent, then the more inclusive ideal of justice in a strong sense, which I am invoking, will also be empty or incoherent.

dividual can count on preserving himself only if steps are taken to ensure the conservation of men in multitudes, and so to ensure peace. "He that having sufficient security, that others observe the same laws towards him, observes them not himself, seeketh not peace, but war; and consequently the destruction of his own nature by violence" (*Leviathan,* chap. 15, immediately following the passage quoted by Gauthier, which points out the folly of unilateral conformity to the laws of nature).

Both unilateral conformity and unilateral non-conformity are, according to Hobbes, contrary to reason, but man's natural intractability inclines him to the latter. In any state of affairs short of perfect and perfectly secure justice such intractability provides a healthy challenge to an imperfect *status quo,* but if a satisfactory form of cooperation were attained such a character trait would serve no useful function. And even if Hobbes is wrong in claiming that one who refuses to do his part thereby irrationally seeks his own violent destruction, his claim that only a fool believes he can profit by breaking the rules his fellows keep is plausible to this extent, that if those rules were just in a stronger sense than any Hobbes can provide, then however attractive the promised gains of a free ride, or of exploiting others, only a fool would believe that he has more to gain by risking the enmity of his fellows by such a policy than by cultivating a taste for the pleasures of cooperation and regulated fair competition. It may not be positively irrational to break the fifth Law of Nature, especially in a would-be totalitarian Leviathan state, but it would be against reason to think one would do better by breaking the rules of a decent just scheme of cooperation. There is no reason *not* to be sociable in a decent society, and nothing to be gained there by non-irrational unsociability, by going it alone, by entering into a state of war with one's fellows. But some will act contrary to reason, "by asperity of Nature," and be "Stubborn, Insociable, Forward, Intractable." Such stubbornness is perversity, not superior rationality, when the rules are just. We could define a perfectly just society as one where it takes such intractability to motivate disobedience.

How do we measure how close an actual society is to the adequately just society? Unless we can do this it would seem impossible ever to judge a society so unjust that its institutions merit disrespect, or to have confidence that any change made in existing institutions is a change for the better. Yet there are grave problems in establishing any coherent measure of comparative justice. These problems arise because of the tension between two ways in which an existing state of things may approximate the just society. In one sense an institution is just to the extent that it *resembles* one we expect to be part of the adequately just society. In another sense an institution is better to the extent that it is instrumental in moving the society closer in time to that adequacy. But the institutions a society needs, to change itself, may be quite other than those it needs, once improvement is no longer needed. Yet if we opt for this dynamic measure of relative justice, and say that institutions are good to the extent that they facilitate movement towards adequate justice, we run up against the possibility, explored by Hegel and developed by Marx, that historical movement towards a social ideal may be dialectical, that the institutions which best facilitate movement towards an ideal may be ones which least embody that ideal.

The ideal of *justice,* however, is one which cannot generate a sense of 'more just than' in which intolerable exploitation is counted more just than a lesser degree of exploitation, merely because it is more likely to precipitate rebellion and change. Those who advocate making things worse in order that they may get better cannot claim that what their strategies increase is justice. Is justice then an ideal which is committed to a perhaps groundless liberal faith in progress, faith in its own gradual attainment by moves, each of which represents *both* an increase in qualitative approximation to the ideal, and *also* a step closer, historically and causally, to its attainment? If these two measures of approximation are both proper, yet can come apart, can come into irresolvable conflict with one another, then the ideal of justice may be confused and incoherent,[7] may rest on a faith which is false. I think there is a genuine issue here, but it is not one which I shall discuss further. Social science, not philosophy, would shore up the liberal's faith, or show it to be false. If it is false, if there is no coherent measure of relative justice, then the modern moral philosophy Gauthier criticises is in even worse straits than he claims. But I shall proceed within the limits of the comforting liberal faith which I take Gauthier to share, faith that some institutions can be judged less just than others, and that improving them can count as progress towards a just society. It is worth pointing out that this is part of the *faith* the just live by, but it is not that part of it which is controversial to Gauthier and those he criticises, none of whom embrace the radical moral scepticism to which the Marxist argument leads, nor the new non-moral revolutionary faith which can fill the vacuum it creates.

Where else does faith enter into the motivation to act, in a less than fully just society, for the sake of justice, to conform to more or less just institutions which not all conform to, or to act, possibly unilaterally to reform salvageable institutions, and to protest corrupt ones? What must the just person believe, which must turn out to be true if his action is not to be pointless or futile? Before we can discuss the question of whether and when personal advantage is pointlessly sacrificed, we must first discuss the nature and varieties of advantage and personal good. I shall in this discussion adopt a hedonist terminology, to stay as close as possible to the Hobbesian point of departure.

4. GOODS: SECURE AND INSECURE

Hobbes speaks not of advantage but of *power*, namely "present means to obtain some future apparent good." Advantage strictly is advantage over, or against, others, and Hobbes' emphasis on man's "diffidence" or need to assure himself that there is "no other power great enough to endanger him" (op.cit., chap 13) turns power-seeking into the attempt to attain advantage, competitive edge, a position superior to one's fellows, since even in civil society he believes that men "can relish nothing but what is eminent" (op.cit., chap. 17). I shall keep the term 'advantage' for this competitive good, superiority over others, and use Hobbes' word 'power' for the more generic concept of possession of present means to obtain some future, apparent, possibly noncompetitive, good. (I think that when Gauthier speaks of 'advantage' he is using it in a looser way, more equivalent simply to 'good', that is to a combination of possession of present good and power or present means to attain a future good, whether or not these goods are scarce and competed for.)

Hobbes says that prudence, the concern for power rather than for immediate good, is concern for the future, which is "but a fiction of the mind" (op.cit., chap. 3), and moreover is based on an uncertain presumption that we can learn, from the past, what to expect in the future. "And though it be called Prudence, when the Event answereth our Expectation; yet in its own nature is but Presumption" (ibid.). Hobbes is surely correct in pointing out the risks inherent in prudence. One may invest in a form of power which turns out to be a passing not a lasting one. Hobbes (op.cit., chap. 10) catalogs the many forms power takes, and it is fairly obvious that accidents of chance and history may add to, and

7. As has been pointed out by a reader for this journal, coherence could be preserved by letting one test apply on some occasions, the other on others, whenever the two tests would give conflicting decisions if both were applied. This would preserve only a weak formal coherence, unless some clear principle could be formulated which selects which test is applicable, and unless this principle itself expressed some component element in our hazy intuitive idea of justice.

subtract from, this list, as well as determine the relative importance of different items on it. Even if one's choice of a form of power to obtain is a lucky one, one may not live into that future where the power could be spent in delectation, or even in misery-avoidance. At some point, in any case, the restless pursuit of power after power must end in death, so *some* future good for which the prudent person saved is bound, if he remains prudent to the end, not to be enjoyed by him. In theory one might, when imminent death is anticipated, make a timely conversion to imprudence, cash one's power in for delectation and die gratified and powerless, but persons with Hobbesian, or with our actual, psychology are not likely to be capable of such a feat. One may have advantage, and have power, which is no good to one, or no longer any good to one, if to be good it must be cashed in delectation.

How are we to judge what is and what is not good to a person? Must good, to be such, be converted, eventually, from apparent good into real indubitable good, and from future into present good? These are hard questions, and it would take a full theory of the good of a person, the place in it of pleasure, interest, power, advantage, to answer them. I have no such theory,[8] and will offer only a few remarks about the complexity of all goods other than present simple pleasures. In all human motivation, other than the gratification of current appetite, there is a potential multi-tier structure. In the case of action designed to make possible the gratification of future desires, that is in prudent action, the good for the sake of which one acts is the expected future gratification, but usually also, derivatively, the present satisfaction of feeling secure, of believing that one has taken thought for the future, secured its needs. So even if the prudent investor does not live into that future for which he provided, he may still enjoy a sense of security while he lives. Prudence, like virtue, may be, and sometimes has to be, its own reward. It is possible, but unlikely, that prudent persons take no present satisfaction in their prudent action, that they develop no taste for a sense of security. The normal accompaniment of prudence is the pleasure of a sense of security. I shall call such pleasures, which make reference to other, possibly non-present pleasures, 'higher' pleasures (Hobbes' "pleasures of the mind"). By calling these pleasures 'higher' I do not mean to imply that they should necessarily be preferred to lower ones. The special class of them which makes reference to future pleasures are power-derivative higher pleasures (Hobbes' "glory"). Such pleasures can coexist with regret that the cost of prudence was renunciation of a present available lower pleasure, and even with doubt whether such costs were unavoidable, and whether one will live to enjoy the future for which one has saved. It would be incorrect to say that the prudent person trades in present lower pleasure for higher pleasure—the higher pleasure is merely a bonus which can come with the power for which the lower pleasure was traded. But hedonic bonuses count for *something,* when the rationality of the action is to be judged.

When one acts for the sake of some good for others, be that good pleasure or power, present or future, there is a similar immediate bonus or "glory" possible, the pleasure of believing that someone else's present or future is improved by one's action. Persons who perform such altruistic acts usually do develop a taste for altruism, a fellow-feeling whereby they share in the good they do others. Just as the sense of personal security usually pleases the prudent person, the awareness of others' pleasure and the sense of their security usually pleases the altruist. It may be possible to do good to others because the moral law is thought to require it, without thereby getting any satisfaction for oneself, but such bonus-refusing psychology seems

8. Although in what follows I try to depart as little as possible from the hedonism of Hobbes and Locke (not because I agree with it, but because of the context of the present discussion), I do however depart very significantly from Hobbes in accepting, as rational motivation, not only self-preservation of the natural man, or "nature's preservation" but also preservation, not of Leviathan, but of a moral community, and of the very idea of such a community. A special 'pleasure of the mind' would have to be added to Hobbes' list to accommodate such Kantian motivation.

neither likely nor desirable. It is best if virtue is at least *part* of its own reward, and a waste if it is not.

5. ARTIFICES TO SECURE THE INSECURE

To be a normal human person is to be capable of higher pleasures, both self-derived and other-derived, to be able to make the remote in time and the remote from oneself close enough in thought and concern not merely to affect present action but to give present pleasure. Hume explored the mechanisms whereby concern for the remote, both from the present, and from oneself and one's family, can be strengthened by its coincidence with concern for the contiguous, so that the "violent propension to prefer the contiguous to the remote," (*Treatise,* p. 537) may be combatted, its unfortunate and sometimes violent effects avoided. These mechanisms include not merely psychological ones, imagination and sympathy, which turn the useful into the also agreeable, and the agreeable for others into the agreeable for oneself also, but also social practices of training and education, and social artifices. Such artifices—promise, property, allegiance—turn the useful for people in general into what is useful for oneself, and this requires both convention, or agreement between people as to *what* the artifice is, and general conformity to its constitutive rules. Convention requires both communication and coordination. Hume believed, perhaps wrongly, that all of justice was in this sense artificial and that only with respect to the artificial virtues did a person risk being "the cully of his integrity" (*Treatise,* p. 535) if he acted unilaterally, without assurance that others were similarly virtuous. Since the actions of a kind or a generous person do the good they do, to individual others, case by case, whereas just or honest actions *need* do no good to any specified individual, and do what good they do, for people in general, for the public interest, only when they are supported by other just acts, it is an easy but false move from this valid contrast between the ways the natural and the artificial virtues do good, to a contrast at the level of motivation for the agent, and to the claim that an individual always has good reason to display a natural virtue whether or not others do, while one has no reason to display an artificial virtue, unless others are displaying the same version of it. Non-violence, or gentleness, is a natural virtue, but non-violence toward the violent can be as self-destructive as unilateral promise-keeping. Moreover, the higher pleasure of knowing that one's attacker has not suffered at one's hands is not merely insufficient to outweigh the loss of life or limb, it will also be lessened by the awareness that, when violence is the rule, the good to the violent man done by one's own non-violence is shortlived and insignificant, unless it inspires others to non-violence.

The natural virtues can, in individual cases, lose most of their point if the degree of non-virtuousness of others is great enough. They still contrast with the artificial virtues, however, in that their good-promoting power will vary from case to case, given the same degree of general conformity. When there is general conformity to non-violence, one may still have reason not to trust individual persons, if there is reason to believe that those ones reciprocate non-violence with violence. When there is general violence, one may still have reason to expect a non-violent response to non-violence in selected cases, so that isolated pockets of gentleness and mutual trust can grow up within a climate of general violence. The same is true, up to a point, of the artificial virtues, in that respect for property rules, or promise keeping, or allegiance, may be dependable within a restricted circle—say among members of the mafia—although they do not observe rules outside the group. The artificial virtues differ from the natural ones, however, in that there is never excuse for *selective non-observance,* within a generally conforming circle, as there can be reason for selective non-observance of non-violence, generosity, helpfulness. A debt owed to a vicious man, a miser, a profligate debauchee, or a dishonest man, is still owed. "Justice, in her decisions never regards the fitness or unfitness of objects to particular persons, but conducts herself by more extensive views. Whether a man be generous, or a miser, he is equally well receiv'd by her, and obtains with the same facility or decision in her favor, even for what is entirely useless to him" (Hume, *Treatise,* p. 502). To grant that the conformity of others does affect the value of the natural as well as the artificial virtues is not to deny Hume's point here, that selective non-observance, based on "fitness or unfitness of objects to particular persons," is reasonable with natural but not with artificial virtues. "Taking any single act, my justice may be pernicious in every respect; and 'tis only on the supposition, that others are to imitate my example; that I can be persuaded to embrace that virtue; since nothing but this combination can render justice advantageous or afford me any motives to conform myself to its rules" (op.cit., p. 498).

6. THE PLEASURES OF CONFORMITY

One must suppose, then, that enough others will imitate one's just action if a just act is to be "advantageous," is to advance any interest or give anyone, however altruistic or public-spirited, rational motive to perform it. When the supposition or faith is reasonable, then there will be a new higher pleasure obtainable by virtuous persons, the satisfaction of knowing that they have contributed to the preservation of the condition of general conformity needed for justice to deliver its utility. This higher pleasure of conformity will be obtainable not only from acts conforming to established more or less just artifices, but also from acts displaying those natural virtues whose full point requires the reasonable expectation that others will not return vice for virtue. The higher pleasure of conformity can, in those latter cases, be added to those of altruism and prudence, and it exceeds them in 'height'. As prudence and altruism facilitate delectation, so conformity facilitates prudence and altruism, as well as extending their range through artifices.

There are, then, a series of hedonic bonus pleasures which we can enjoy, if we cultivate our spiritual palates and develop a relish for them, as Locke puts it (*Essay,* Bk. II, 21, 69). They can accompany the non-hedonic goods which are powers, the non-self directed goods, and conformity to those artifices which create public "powers" to increase the powers and pleasures of individuals. Such present occurrent pleasures, once obtained, cannot be taken away from the prudent man, the altruist, or the conformist, even if the non-present or other-dependent good *in* which the pleasure is taken does not eventuate. Bonus pleasures are non-negligible contributors to the goodness of a life. As pains are indicators of other ills, these pleasures are indicators, not guarantees, of other presumed goods, and they add to them as well as indicate them. But the indication may be false, the glory may be vainglory. Only insofar as one can reasonably hope for the success of one's prudent policy, altruistic project, or for the successful achievement of *general* conformity to an institution, can one derive a higher pleasure from prudent, altruistic or conforming action. Should the hopes on which they were, reasonably, based become later known to be false, the already obtained bonus pleasures may be devalued. They cannot be cancelled, but they may count for less, perhaps count negatively, in the person's proper assessment of the goodness of the life. If hopes turn out to have been what Hobbes calls vain "presumptions," the pleasures dependent on them may come to have been vainglory. If, on one's deathbed, one were persuaded that the person whose apparent love and devotion had given one much pleasure had really been uncaring, perhaps even had despised one, it would not, I think, be reasonable to react with the thought 'thank God I didn't know till now'. False pleasures, pleasures based on what comes to be seen as a lie, can, if the lie is serious and has reverberating implications for many of one's concerns, be worse than the absence of pleasure. Better no glory than vainglory.

Would the prudent man's bonus pleasure of feeling secure come to have been, like the friend's trusting pleasure, fool's gold, if he comes to realize that he will not live into the future for which he saved? If the bonus pleasure had been pleasure in the anticipated spendings of his savings, it would certainly be degraded by realization that he will not spend it, but to the extent that his bonus pleasure in his sense of security was in that which freed him from anxiety about his future, that bonus pleasure is not devalued by any knowledge he may acquire about his imminent early death. The power he had was a good, even if not exercised, because its absence would have been an ever present felt evil. One might say, of the trusting friend, that his trust that his love was reciprocated was a good similar to the prudent man's security, in that its absence would have been an evil for him. But could the evil of suspicion or distrust, or of the absence of affection, be as great as the evil the friend suffers if he bases his life on a false trust? The difference, I think, lies in the fact the unnecessarily prudent man is not *betrayed* by events, as the friend is by the false friend. The prudent man saves, because of the *possibility* that he may live long, but the friend loved in the confidence that love was returned. Prudence is, and knows itself to be, a reaction to risk and uncertainty, so its goods are not devalued if the possibility the prudent man provided for does not come about. But friendship does not, typically, see itself as content with the mere *possibility* of returned trust and love.

Can the man who acts for the sake of justice, when he knows or suspects that others are *not* conforming, get any bonus pleasures which are not fool's gold? We need to distinguish the cases where most but not all others are conforming from the cases where the conformists are in a minority, and, within the latter class, between the few who are trying to *inaugurate* a needed practice, and the few who are clinging to a once accepted but now imperilled institution. The last case, of fidelity to a once supported practice, faces less severe problems than those of the moral innovator, who must both get agreement on *what* should be conformed to, and also try to get sufficient conformity to it to secure the rewards of conformity. At least the moral conservative, the wound-be supporter of a once established practice, does not face what have been called[9] the isolation and coordination problems, he faces only the problem of assurance of compliance. I shall not discuss the problems, faced by Hobbesian natural men, of simultaneously achieving communication, agreeing on what institutions are desirable (what coordination scheme to adopt) and also getting assured compliance to them. Let us, optimistically, assume that we have got, by the fact of past established conventions, their later reform, and their agreed need for specific further reforms, a solution to the isolation and coordination problems, that is, we have agreement on how we *should* all be acting. The compliance problem then arises—namely whether to act as we all should if we all are to get the best state of things for us, when there is no assurance that the rest of us are going to comply. If I comply and the rest of you don't, then the main good, for the sake of which that cooperative scheme was seen to be acceptable, will not be fully obtained, by any of us. To the extent it is partially attained it will be attained by noncompliers as well as compliers. I will have been the cully of my integrity. So, it seems, the pleasure of conformity is fool's gold unless others do in fact conform in sufficient numbers.

One thing which might save those pleasures from becoming false is the psychological taste of the individual for conformity. Not everyone can enjoy gun-running. Just as the prudent man who doesn't live to enjoy his savings may nevertheless have been saved by his prudence from unpleasant anxiety, so conformity to the old ways

9. Kurt Baier, "Rationality and Morality," *Erkenntnis* 11 (1977), p. 197, where the 'isolation', 'coordination', and 'assurance' problems are distinguished.

may soothe the timid who would be alarmed, not gratified, by the immoralists' life style.

But suppose I *could* develop a relish for gun-running, would it be irrational for me to decide to stick by, not to abandon, the threatened moral practices? Can unilateral, (or minority-wide) conformity to just, or potentially just, institutions have any genuine lure for me?

7. THE HIGHER PLEASURE OF QUALIFYING FOR MEMBERSHIP IN THE KINGDOM OF ENDS

Hume's point, a valid one, is that only a fool supports widely unsupported institutions whose only good depends on their getting wide support. But support from whom? My contemporaries and only them? It is fairly evident, I think, that the support of the majority of his contemporaries is not *sufficient* to guard the conformist from being taken in by fool's gold, especially when the institution is one which *conserves* goods for future generations. Whole generations can be retroactively made into cullies of their joint integrity by later generations' waste and destruction. What I want to stress is that conformity by the majority of one's contemporaries is not *necessary* to save the moral man from having been a fool.

Here, at last, I turn to the obvious source of a reply to Gauthier: Kant. He spelled out more clearly than any other modern philosopher the wholly secular basis for a strong set of plain duties. It is wholly secular, and it is also faith-requiring.

Kant says that although a rational being, when he acts on the maxim he can will as a universal law, "cannot for that reason expect every other rational being to be true to it; nor can he expect the realm of nature and its orderly design to harmonize with him as a fitting member of a realm of ends which is possible through himself. That is, he cannot count on its favoring his expectation of happiness. Still the law: Act according to the maxims of a universally legislative member of a merely potential realm of

"Blind Faith"

Helen Keller

Faith has such might because next to love it is the force most inherent in one's own awareness. It directs to the light when darkness prevails; it supplies incentive to action and converts ideas into realities. It fires the imagination, and this is essential, for one must envision the higher life and behave as if it were a fact before it can unfold. But though faith belongs to the future, its energy irradiates the present, just as the green leaf pigment—the delicate link between the sun and life—permeates the vegetable world.

Faith, like philosophy, endows me with a unity I miss in the chaos of material experience devoid of sight and hearing. But like everyone else I have eyes in my soul. Through faith I create the world I gaze upon; I make my own day and night, tint the clouds with iridescent fires, and behold! a midnight is strewn with other stars. It is faith which lights us into sustaining realities beyond those perceived by the physical senses. . . .

The reason, I am sure, why God permitted me to lose both sight and hearing seems clear now—that through me He might cleave a rock unbroken before and let quickening streams flow through other lives desolate as my own once was. I believe that life is given to us so we may glow in love, and I believe that God is in me as the sun is in the color and fragrance of a flower—the Light in my darkness, the Voice in my silence.

From "In the Garden of the Lord" (1948).

ends, remains in full force, because it commands categorically. And just in this lies the paradox, that merely the dignity of humanity as rational nature without any end or advantage to be gained by it, and thus respect for a mere idea, should serve as the inflexible precept of the will. There is the further paradox that the sublimity and worthiness of every rational subject to be a legislative member in the realm of ends consists precisely in independence of maxims from all such incentives" (Kant, *Foundation of the Metaphysics of Morals,* trs. Lewis White Beck). In this remarkable passage Kant appears to be claiming that the willingness to act *as if* one were a member of an actual kingdom of ends, when one knows that one is in fact a member of a society which falls short of the ideal, alone makes one worthy to be a legislating member of an actual kingdom of ends, or just society. But unless there can be such sublime and worthy persons, no just society is possible. The kingdom of ends is "possible through oneself." The existence of persons with the ability to act from respect for that "mere idea," is, then, the condition of the idea's actualization. Apparently just institutions would not guarantee a just society, if those persons living under them fail Kant's motivational test. A just society must be comprised of just men whose lives are ordered by just institutions.

On this account, apparently futile unilateral and possibly self-sacrificing action is neither futile not unilateral. Not futile, because it keeps alive the assurance of the possibility of qualified members for a just society. Not unilateral, because the one just man has a 'cloud of witnesses,' all those others whose similar acts in other times kept alive the same hope. The actions of individuals who, unsupported by their contemporaries, act for the sake of justice do not necessarily hasten the coming of a just society, but they do rule out one ground on which it might be feared impossible. In this very modest way the just man's actions confirm his faith, demonstrate that *one* condition of the existence of a just society can be met, that human psychology can be a psychology for sovereigns. And the one just man is not alone, his isolation problem is solved if he recalls that enough others have already acted as he is acting. Thus every action in conformity to a just but threatened institution or in protest against an unjust but supported one, furthers the cause, keeps the faith. The highest pleasure or 'relish' of all is that of qualifying for membership in the kingdom of ends.[10] It is not just a priggish pleasure if the demonstration that there are and can be qualified members has the role which Kant as I interpret him claimed for it. (The blood of the martyrs is the seed of the church.)

8. THE FAITH THE JUST LIVE BY

The secular faith which the just live by is, then, a faith in the possibility of a society for membership in which their just action theoretically qualifies them. They believe, in part, because of the previous demonstration that there can be such qualified members, so they join a movement already started. Each new member gives other potential members new assurance that the faith is not in vain, and it also confirms the faith of that new member himself, in that, after his act, the club of which he is an 'honorary' member is the larger by one, and its point depends on the size and persistence of its membership.

The qualified, so honorary, member of the kingdom of ends, usually hopes that some actual society, perhaps long after his death, will embody the kingdom of ends on earth, that the possible will become actual. Such a society would, in general intention, honor all those who acted for the sake of justice, who qualified for membership but did not survive to be members. They would be participants in the secular variant of the communion of the saints. This higher pleas-

10. I have not discussed the question, raised by Gauthier's example of unilateral abstention from preemptive nuclear strike, of what should be done when the decision taken may commit others besides the decision-maker to the higher pleasures of martyrdom for a good cause. This is the *really* difficult question.

ure is a variant of that pleasure of imagination, delight in the prospect of posthumous recognition, which even Hobbes allows as a real pleasure. "Though after death there be no sense of the praise given us on earth, as being joys that are either swallowed up in the unspeakable joys of heaven or extinguished in the extreme torments of hell, yet is not such fame vain; because men have a present delight therein from the foresight of it and of the benefit that may redound thereby to their prosperity, which, though they see not, yet they imagine; and anything that is pleasure to the sense, the same is also pleasure in the imagination" (*Leviathan,* chap. 11). Hobbes would not be content with anonymous recognition—presumably only the foresight that one's name will live on, preserved on some honor roll, could give Hobbesian man this pleasure of imagination. Fame is one thing, membership in the faceless communion of the saints quite another for one who values nothing but what is eminent. Still, the qualification for praise and recognition by a posterity to whom benefits redound is at least part of what the Hobbesian can glory in, and for a Kantian it suffices for glory.

Does this pleasure of imagination require expectation that posterity *will* benefit? Does the faith the just live by include confidence that some society on earth will some day actually be just? As already acknowledged, the ideal of justice includes a demand, which may be Utopian, that its historical approximation coincide with its qualitative approximation. In addition to this demand, which the just person must, for the moment at least, merely *hope* can be met, there is another more serious difficulty in the idea of an actual just society which would meet the Kantian requirements. This is that, to the extent that there *is* conformity among one's contemporaries to apparently just practices, to precisely that extent none of the conformers can be assured that they, each of them, qualify for membership in the kingdom of ends. If they are acting, not for a mere idea, but in support of an actual practice, they cannot be sure they meet Kant's paradoxical test for qualification for membership in a just society, that is they cannot be sure how they *would* act if there were not general conformity. But the apparently just conforming society will not *be* just, in Kant's sense, if its sovereign-subjects are not qualified to be members. Kant's paradox is real, and so, once again, the ideal of a just society threatens to become incoherent. The threat, this time, is not one which can be allayed by sociological and historical findings, but is more fundamental—a *necessary* conflict between the criteria for qualification as the just society comprised of qualified members, and the criteria for its actualization.

Must the just man then conclude *'credo quia absurdum est?'* He might—as he might develop a relish for acting for necessarily lost causes—but he can keep his faith from being the absurd hope for the impossible, by acceptance of the fact that one can live without certainty. As the just man *now,* in an unjust world, has no certainty, only faith and hope, that there really can and will be a just society of the living, so, in any apparently attained just society, that is in one with just institutions, its members will rely on the faith and hope that they could if necessary act for a mere idea, and so that they really qualify for membership. A new variant of Hobbesian faith in man will be needed. Both in the absence and in the presence of an actual just society, then, the just will live by faith.[11]

11. I have tried, throughout this paper, to evoke some Biblical echoes, to show how the secular faith I describe parallels its theological forerunners. The effort to speak both the language of Hobbes and that of the King James Bible has resulted in a style which some readers have found obscure. This I regret, but I do want to keep, for those in a position to recognize them, allusions to, e.g., St. Paul's Epistle to the Hebrews chaps. 10 and 11.

Norman Malcolm

"THE GROUNDLESSNESS OF BELIEF"

A brief biography of Malcolm appears on page 219.

I

In his final notebooks Wittgenstein wrote that it is difficult "to realize the groundlessness of our believing."[1] He was thinking of how much mere acceptance, on the basis of no evidence, forms our lives. This is obvious in the case of small children. They are told the names of things. They accept what they are told. They do not ask for grounds. A child does not demand a proof that the person who feeds him is called "Mama." Or are we to suppose that the child reasons to himself as follows: "The others present seem to know this person who is feeding me, and since they call her 'Mama' that probably is her name"? It is obvious on reflection that a child cannot consider evidence or even doubt anything until he has already learned much. As Wittgenstein puts it: "The child learns by believing the adult. Doubt comes *after* belief" (*OC,* 160).

What is more difficult to perceive is that the lives of educated, sophisticated adults are also formed by groundless beliefs. I do not mean eccentric beliefs that are out on the fringes of their lives, but fundamental beliefs. Take the belief that familiar material things (watches, shoes, chairs) do not cease to exist without some physical explanation. They don't "vanish in thin air." It is interesting that we do use that very expression: "I *know* I put the keys right here on this table. They must have vanished in thin air!" But this exclamation is hyperbole; we are not speaking in literal seriousness. I do not know of any adult who would consider, in all gravity, that the keys might have inexplicably ceased to exist.

Yet it is possible to imagine a society in which it was accepted that sometimes material things do go out of existence without having been crushed, melted, eroded, broken into pieces, burned up, eaten, or destroyed in some other way. The difference between those people and ourselves would not consist in their *saying* something that we don't say ("It vanished in thin air"), since we say it too. I conceive of these people as acting and thinking differently from ourselves in such ways as the following: If one of them could not find his wallet he would give up the search sooner than you or I would; also he would be less inclined to suppose that it was stolen. In general, what we would regard as convincing circumstantial evidence of theft those people would find less convincing. They would take fewer precautions that we would to protect their possessions against loss or theft. They would have less inclination to save money, since it too can just disappear. They would not tend to form

---

Reprinted from Norman Malcolm, "The Groundlessness of Belief," in *Reason and Religion,* edited by Stuart C. Brown.

1. Ludwig Wittgenstein, *On Certainty,* ed. G. E. M. Anscombe and G. H. von Wright; English translation by D. Paul and G. E. M. Anscombe (Oxford, 1969), paragraph 166. Henceforth I include references to this work in the text, employing the abbreviation *"OC"* followed by paragraph number. References to Wittgenstein's *The Blue and Brown Books* (Oxford, 1958) are indicated in the text by *"BB"* followed by page number. References to his *Philosophical Investigations,* ed. G. E. M. Anscombe and R. Rhees; English translation by Anscombe (Oxford, 1967) are indicated by *"PI"* followed by paragraph number,. In *OC* and *PI,* I have mainly used the translations of Paul and Anscombe but with some departures.

strong attachments to material things, animals, or other people. Generally, they would stand in a looser relation to the world than we do. The disappearance of a desired object, which would provoke us to a frantic search, they would be more inclined to accept with a shrug. Of couse, their scientific theories would be different; but also their attitude toward experiment, and inference from experimental results, would be more tentative. If the repetition of a familiar chemical experiment did not yield the expected result this *could* be because one of the chemical substances had vanished.

The outlook I have sketched might be thought to be radically incoherent. I do not see that this is so. Although those people consider it to be possible that a wallet might have inexplicably ceased to exist, it is also true that they regard that as unlikely. For things that are lost usually do turn up later; or if not, their fate can often be accounted for. Those people use pretty much the same criteria of identity that we do; their reasoning would resemble ours quite a lot. Their thinking would not be incoherent. But it would be different, since they would leave room for some possibilities that we exclude.

If we compare their view that material things do sometimes go out of existence inexplicably, with our own rejection of that view, it does not appear to me that one position is supported by *better evidence* than is the other. Each position is compatible with ordinary experience. On the one hand it is true that familiar objects (watches, wallets, lawn chairs) occasionally disappear without any adequate explanation. On the other hand it happens, perhaps more frequently, that a satisfying explanation of the disappearance is discovered.

Our attitude in this matter is striking. We would not be willing to consider it as even improbable that a missing lawn chair had "just ceased to exist." We would not entertain such a suggestion. If anyone proposed it we would be sure he was joking. It is no exaggeration to say that this attitude is part of the foundations of our thinking. I do not want to say that this attitude is *un*reasonable; but rather that it is something that we do not *try* to support with grounds. It could be said to belong to "the framework" of our thinking about material things.

Wittgenstein asks: "Does anyone ever test whether this table remains in existence when no one is paying attention to it?" (*OC,* 163). The answer is: Of course not. Is this because we would not call it "a table" if that were to happen? But we do call it "a table" and none of us makes the test. Doesn't this show that we do not regard that occurrence as a possibility? People who did so regard it would seem ludicrous to us. One could imagine that they made ingenious experiments to decide the question; but this research would make us smile. Is this because experiments were conducted by our ancestors that settled the matter once and for all? I don't believe it. The principle that material things do not cease to exist without physical cause is an unreflective part of the framework within which physical investigations are made and physical explanations arrived at.

Wittgenstein suggests that the same is true of what might be called "the principle of the continuity of nature":

> Think of chemical investigations. Lavoisier makes experiments with substances in his laboratory and now concludes that this and that takes place when there is burning. He does not say that it might happen otherwise another time. He has got hold of a world-picture—not of course one that he invented: he learned it as a child. I say world-picture and not hypothesis, because it is the matter-of-course *(selbstverständliche)* foundation for his research and as such also goes unmentioned (*OC,* 167).

> But now, what part is played by the presupposition that a substance A always reacts to a substance B in the same way, given the same circumstances? Or is that part of the definition of a substance? (*OC,* 168).

Framework principles such as the continuity of nature or the assumption that material things do not cease to exist without physical cause belong to what Wittgenstein calls a "system." He makes the following observation, which seems to me to be true: "All testing, all confirmation and disconfirmation of a hypothesis takes place already within a system. And this system is not a more or less arbitrary and doubtful point of departure for all our arguments: no, it belongs to the nature of what we call an argument. The system is not so much the point of departure, as the element in which arguments have their life" (*OC,* 105).

A "system" provides the boundaries within which we ask questions, carry out investigations, and make judgments. Hypotheses are put forth, and challenged, *within* a system. Verification, justification, the search for evidence, occur *within* a system. The framework propositions of the system are not put to the test, not backed up by evidence. This is what Wittgenstein means when he says: "Of course there is justification; but justification comes to an end" (*OC,* 192); and when he asks: "Doesn't testing come to an end?" (*OC,* 164); and when he remarks that "whenever we test anything we are already presupposing something that is not tested" (*OC,* 163).

That this is so is not to be attributed to human weakness. It is a conceptual requirement that our inquiries and proofs stay within boundaries. Think, for example, of the activity of calculating a number. Some steps in a calculation we will check for correctness, but others we won't: for example, that $4 + 4 = 8$. More accurately, some beginners might check it, but grown-ups won't. Similarly, some grown-ups would want to determine by calculation whether $25 \times 25 = 625$, whereas others would regard that as laughable. Thus the boundaries of the system within which *you* calculate may not be exactly the same as *mine.* But we do calculate; and, as Wittgenstein remarks, "In certain circumstances . . . we regard a calculation as sufficiently checked. What gives us a right to do so? . . . Somewhere we must be finished with justification, and then there remains the proposition that *this* is how we calculate" (*OC,* 212). If someone did not accept any boundaries for calculating this would mean that he had not learned *that* language-game: "If someone supposed that *all* our calculations were uncertain and that we could rely on none of them (justifying himself by saying that mistakes are always possible) perhaps we would say he was crazy. But can we say he is in error? Does he not just react differently? We rely on calculations, he doesn't; we are sure, he isn't" (*OC,* 217). We are taught, or we absorb, the systems within which we raise doubts, make inquiries, draw conclusions. We grow into a framework. We don't question it. We accept it trustingly. But this acceptance is not a consequence of reflection. We do not decide to accept framework propositions. We do not decide that we live on the earth, any more than we decide to learn our native tongue. We do come to adhere to a framework proposition, in the sense that it forms the way we think. The framework propositions that we accept, grow into, are not idiosyncrasies but common ways of speaking and thinking that are pressed on us by our human community. For our acceptances to have been withheld would have meant that we had not learned how to count, to measure, to use names, to play games, or even *to talk.* Wittgenstein remarks that "a language game is only possible if one trusts something." Not *can,* but *does* trust something (*OC,* 509). I think he means by this trust or acceptance what he calls belief "in the sense of religious belief" (*OC,* 459). What does he mean by belief "in the sense of religious belief"? He explicitly distinguishes it from *conjecture* (*Vermutung:* ibid.) I think this means that there is nothing tentative about it; it is not adopted as a hypothesis that might later be withdrawn in the light of new evidence. This also makes explicit an important feature of Wittgenstein's understanding of belief, in the sense of "religious belief," namely, that it does not rise or fall on the basis of evidence or grounds: it is "groundless."

II

In our Western academic philosophy, religious belief is commonly regarded as unreasonable and is viewed with condescension or even contempt.

It is said that religion is a refuge for those who, because of weakness of intellect or character, are unable to confront the stern realities of the world. The objective, mature, *strong* attitude is to hold beliefs solely on the basis of *evidence*.

It appears to me that philosophical thinking is greatly influenced by this veneration of evidence. We have an aversion to statements, reports, declarations, beliefs, that are not based on grounds. There are many illustrations of this philosophical bent.

For example, in regard to a person's report that he has an image of the Eiffel Tower we have an inclination to think that the image must *resemble* the Eiffel Tower. How else could the person declare so confidently what his image is *of? How could he know?*

Another example: A memory-report or memory-belief must be based, we think, on some mental *datum* that is equipped with various features to match the corresponding features of the memory-belief. This datum will include an image that provides the *content* of the belief, and a peculiar feeling that makes one refer the image to a *past* happening, and another feeling that makes one believe that the image is an *accurate* portrayal of the past happening, and still another feeling that informs one that it was *oneself* who witnessed the past happening. The presence of these various features makes memory-beliefs thoroughly reasonable.

Another illustration: If interrupted in speaking one can usually give a confident account, later on, of what one had been *about* to say. How is this possible? Must not one remember *a feeling of tendency to say just those words?* This is one's basis for knowing what one had been about to say. It justifies one's account.

Still another example: After dining at a friend's house you announce your intention to go home. How do you know your intention? One theory proposes that you are presently aware of a particular mental state or bodily feeling which, as you recall from your past experience, has been highly correlated with the behavior of going home; so you infer that *that* is what you are going to do now. A second theory holds that you must be aware of some definite mental state or event which reveals itself, not by experience but *intrinsically,* as the intention to go home. Your awareness of that mental item *informs* you of what action you will take.

Yet another illustration: This is the instructive case of the man who, since birth, has been immune to sensations of bodily pain. On his thirtieth birthday he is kicked in the shins and for the first time he responds by crying out, hopping around on one foot, holding his leg, and exclaiming, "The pain is terrible!" We have an overwhelming inclination to wonder, "How could he tell, *this first time,* that what he felt was *pain?*" Of course, the implication is that *after* the first time there would be *no* problem. Why not? Because his first experience with pain would provide him with a sample that would be preserved in memory; thereafter he would be equipped to determine whether any sensation he feels is or isn't pain; he would just compare it with the memory-sample to see whether the two match! Thus he will have a justification for believing that what he feels is pain. But the *first time* he will not have this justification. This is why the case is so puzzling. Could it be that this first time he *infers* that he is in pain from his own behavior?

A final illustration: Consider the fact that after a comparatively few examples and bits of instruction a person can go on to carry out a task, apply a word correctly in the future, continue a numerical series from an initial segment, distinguish grammatical from ungrammatical constructions, solve arithmetical problems, and so on. These correct performances will be dealing with new and different examples, situations, combinations. The performance output will be far more varied than the instruction input. How is this possible? What carries the person from the meager instruction to his rich performance? The explanation has to be that an effect of his training was that he abstracted the Idea, perceived the Common Nature, "internalized" the Rule, grasped the Structure. What else could

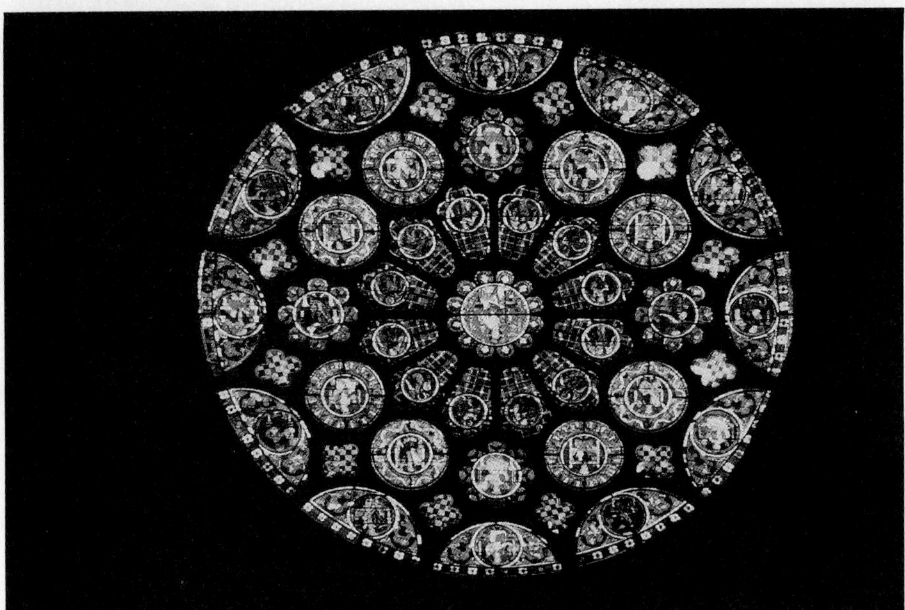

A rose window in one of the largest Gothic cathedrals: Chartres, France, which is famous for its complete set of medieval stained glass windows.

bridge the gap between the poverty of instruction and the wealth of performance? Thus we postulate an intervening mental act or state which removes the inequality and restores the balance.

My illustrations belong to what could be called the *pathology* of philosophy. Wittgenstein speaks of a "general disease of thinking" which attempts to explain occurrences of discernment, recognition, or understanding, by postulating mental states or processes from which those occurrences flow "as from a reservoir" (*BB,* p. 143). These mental intermediaries are assumed to contribute to the causation of the various cognitive performances. More significantly for my present purpose, they are supposed to *justify* them; they provide our *grounds* for saying or doing this rather than that; they *explain how we know.* The Image, or Cognitive State, or Feeling, or Idea, or Sample, or Rule, or Structure, *tells* us. It is like a road map or a signpost. It guides our course.

What is "pathological" about these explanatory constructions and pseudoscientific inferences? Two things at least. First, the movement of thought that demands these intermediaries is circular and empty, unless it provides criteria for determining their presence and nature *other than* the occurrence of the phenomena they are postulated to explain—and, of course, no such criteria are forthcoming. Second, there is the great criticism by Wittgenstein of this movement of philosophical thought: namely, his point that no matter what kind of state, process, paradigm, sample, structure, or rule, is conceived as giving us the necessary guidance, *it* could be taken, or understood, as indicating a *different* direction from the one in which we actually did go. The assumed intermediary Idea, Structure, or Rule, does not and cannot reveal that because of it we went in the only direction it was reasonable to go. Thus the internalized intermediary we are tempted to invoke to bridge the gap between training and performance, as being that which shows us what we must do or say if we are to be rational, cannot do the job it was invented to do. It cannot fill the epistemological gap. It cannot provide the bridge of justification. It cannot put to rest the How-do-we-know? question. Why not? Because it cannot tell us how *it itself* is to be taken, understood, applied. Wittgenstein puts the point briefly and powerfully: "Don't always think that you read off your words from facts; that you portray these in words according to rules. For even so you would have to apply the rule in the particular case without guidance" (*PI,* 292). Without guidance! Like Wittgenstein's signpost arrow that cannot tell us whether to go in the direction of the arrow tip or in the opposite direction, so too the Images, Ideas, Cognitive Structures, or Rules, that we philosophers imagine as devices for guidance, cannot interpret themselves to us. The signpost does not tell the traveler how to read it. A second signpost might tell him how to read the first one; we can imagine such a case. But this can't go on. If the traveler is to continue his journey he will have to do something on his own, without guidance.

The parable of the traveler speaks for *all* of the language-games we learn and practice; even those in which there is the most disciplined instruction and the most rigorous standards of conformity. Suppose that a pupil has been given thorough training in some procedure, whether it is drawing patterns, building fences, or proving theorems. But then he has to carry on by himself in new situations. How does he know what to do? Wittgenstein presents the following dialogue: "'However you instruct him in the continuation of a pattern—how can he *know* how he is to continue by himself?'—Well, how do *I* know?—If that means 'Have I grounds?', the answer is: the grounds will soon give out. And then I shall act, without grounds" (*PI,* 211). Grounds come to an end. Answers to How-do-we-know? questions come to an end. Evidence comes to an end. We must speak, act, live, without evidence. This is so, not just on the fringes of life and language, but at the center of our most regularized activities. We do learn rules and learn to follow them. But our training was in the past! We had to leave it behind and proceed on our own.

It is an immensely important fact of nature that as people carry on an activity in which they have received a common training, they do largely *agree* with one another, accepting the same examples and analogies, taking the same steps. We agree in what to say, in how to apply language. We agree in our responses to particular cases.

As Wittgenstein says: "That is not agreement in opinions but in form of life" (*PI,* 241). We cannot explain this agreement by saying that we are just doing what the rules tell us—for our agreement in applying rules, formulae, and signposts is what gives them their *meaning.*

One of the primary pathologies of philosophy is the feeling that we must *justify* our language-games. We want to establish them as well-grounded. But we should consider here Wittgenstein's remark that a language-game "is not based on grounds. It is there—like our life" (*OC,* 559).

Within a language-game there is justification and lack of justification, evidence and proof, mistakes and groundless opinions, good and bad reasoning, correct measurements and incorrect ones. One cannot properly apply these terms to a language-game itself. It may, however, be said to be "groundless," not in the sense of a groundless opinion, but in the sense that we accept it, we live it. We can say, "This is what we do. This is how we are."

In this sense religion is groundless; and so is chemistry. Within each of these two systems of thought and action there is controversy and argument. Within each there are advances and recessions of insight into the secrets of nature or the spiritual condition of humankind and the demands of the Creator, Savior, Judge, Source. Within the framework of each system there is criticism, explanation, justification. But we should not expect that there might be some sort of rational justification of the framework itself.

A chemist will sometimes employ induction. Does he have evidence for a Law of Induction?

Wittgenstein observes that it would strike him as nonsense to say, "I know that the Law of Induction is true." ("Imagine such a statement made in a law court.") It would be more correct to say, "I believe in the Law of Induction" (*OC,* 500). This way of putting it is better because it shows that the attitude toward induction is belief in the sense of "religious" belief—that is to say, an acceptance which is not conjecture or surmise and for which there is no reason—it is a groundless acceptance.

It is intellectually troubling for us to conceive that a whole system of thought might be groundless, might have no rational justification. We realize easily enough, however, that grounds soon give out—that we cannot go on giving reasons for our reasons. There arises from this realization the conception of a reason that is *self-justifying*—something whose credentials as a reason cannot be questioned.

This metaphysical conception makes its presence felt at many points—for example, as an explanation of how a person can tell what his mental image is *of.* We feel that the following remarks, imagined by Wittgenstein, are exactly right: "'The image must be more similar to its object than any picture. For however similar I make the picture to what it is supposed to represent, it can always be the picture of something else. But it is essential to the image that it is the image of *this* and of nothing else'" (*PI,* 389). A pen and ink drawing represents the Eiffel Tower; but it could represent a mine shaft or a new type of automobile jack. Nothing prevents this drawing from being taken as a representation of something other than the Eiffel Tower. But my mental image of the Eiffel Tower is *necessarily* an image of the Eiffel Tower. Therefore it must be a "remarkable" kind of picture. As Wittgenstein observes: "Thus one might come to regard the image as a super-picture" *(ibid.).* Yet we have no intelligible conception of how a super-picture would differ from an ordinary picture. It would seem that it has to be a *super-likeness*—but what does this mean?

There is a familiar linguistic practice in which one person *tells* another what his image is of (or what he intends to do, or what he was about to say) and no question is raised of how the first one *knows* that what he says is true. This question is imposed from outside, artificially, by the philosophical craving for justification. We can see here the significance of these remarks: "It isn't a question of explaining a language-game by means of our experiences, but of noting a language-game" (*PI,* 655). "Look on the language-game as the *primary* thing" (*PI,* 656). Within a system of thinking and acting there occurs, *up to a point,* investigation and criticism of the reasons and justifications that are employed in that system. This inquiry into whether a reason is good or adequate cannot, as said, go on endlessly. We stop it. We bring it to an end. We come upon something that *satisfies* us. It is as if we made a decision or issued an edict: "*This* is an adequate reason!" (or explanation, or justification). Thereby we fix a boundary of our language-game.

There is nothing wrong with this. How else could we have disciplines, systems, games? But our fear of groundlessness makes us conceive that we are under some logical compulsion to terminate at *those particular* stopping points. We imagine that we have confronted the self-evident reason, the self-justifying explanation, the picture or symbol whose meaning cannot be questioned. This obscures from us the *human* aspect of our concepts—the fact that what we call "a reason," "evidence," "explanation," "justification," is what appeals to and satisfies *us.*

III

The desire to provide a rational foundation for a form of life is especially prominent in the philosophy of religion, where there is an intense preoccupation with purported proofs of the existence of God. In American universities there must be hundreds of courses in which these proofs are the main topic. We can be sure that nearly always the critical verdict is that the proofs are invalid and consequently that, up to the present time at least, religious belief has received no rational justification.

Well, of course not! The obsessive concern with the proofs reveals the assumption that in order for religious belief to be intellectually respectable it *ought* to have a rational justification. *That* is the misunderstanding. It is like the idea that we are not justified in relying on memory until memory has been proved reliable.

Roger Trigg makes the following remark: "To say that someone acts in a certain way because of his belief in God does seem to be more than a redescription of his action. . . . It is to give a *reason* for it. The belief is distinct from the commitment which may follow it, and is the justification for it."[2] It is evident from other remarks that by "belief in God" Trigg means "belief in the existence of God" or "belief that God exists." Presumably by the *acts* and *commitments* of a religious person Trigg refers to such things as prayer, worship, confession, thanksgiving, partaking of sacraments, and participation in the life of a religious group.

For myself I have great difficulty with the notion of belief in *the existence* of God, whereas the idea of belief *in* God is to me intelligible. If a man did not ever pray for help or forgiveness, or have any inclination toward it; nor ever felt that it is "a good and joyful thing" to thank God for the blessings of this life; nor was ever concerned about his failure to comply with divine commandments—then, it seems clear to me, he could not be said to believe in God. Belief in God is not an all or none thing; it can be more or less; it can wax and wane. But belief in God in any degree does require, as I understand the words, some religious action, some commitment, or if not, at least a bad conscience.

According to Trigg, if I take him correctly, a man who was entirely devoid of any inclination toward religious action or conscience, might believe in *the existence* of God. What would be the marks of this? Would it be that the man knows some theology, can recite the Creeds, is well-read in Scripture? Or is his belief in the existence of God something different from this? If so, what? What would be the difference between a man who knows some articles of faith, heresies, scriptural writings, and in addition believes in the existence of God, and one who knows these things but does not believe in the existence of God? I assume that both of them are indifferent to the acts and commitments of religious life.

I do not comprehend this notion of belief in *the existence* of God which is thought to be distinct from belief *in* God. It seems to me to be an artificial construction of philosophy, another illustration of the craving for justification.

Religion is a form of life; it is language embedded in action—what Wittgenstein calls a "language-game." Science is another. Neither stands in need of justification, the one no more than the other.

Present-day academic philosophers are far more prone to challenge the credentials of religion than of science, probably for a number of reasons. One may be the illusion that science can justify its own framework. Another is the fact that science is a vastly greater force in our culture. Still another may be the fact that by and large religion is to university people an alien form of life. They do not participate in it and do not understand what it is all about.

Their nonunderstanding is of an interesting nature. It derives, at least in part, from the inclination of academics to suppose that their employment as scholars demands of them the most severe objectivity and dispassionateness. For an academic philosopher to become a religious believer would be a stain on his professional competence! Here I will quote from Nietzsche, who was commenting on the relation of the German scholar of his day to religious belief; yet his remarks continue to have a nice appropriateness for the American and British scholars of our own day:

2. *Reason and Commitment* (Cambridge, 1973), p. 75.

Pious or even merely church-going people seldom realize *how much* good will, one might even say wilfulness, it requires nowadays for a German scholar to take the problem of religion seriously; his whole trade . . . disposes him to a superior, almost good-natured merriment in regard to religion, sometimes mixed with a mild contempt directed at the "uncleanliness" of spirit which he presupposes wherever one still belongs to the church. It is only with the aid of history (thus *not* from his personal experience) that the scholar succeeds in summoning up a reverent seriousness and a certain shy respect towards religion; but if he intensifies his feelings towards it even to the point of feeling grateful to it, he has still in his own person not got so much as a single step closer to that which still exists as church or piety; perhaps the reverse. The practical indifference to religious things in which he was born and raised is as a rule sublimated in him into a caution and cleanliness which avoids contact with religious people and things: . . . Every age has its own divine kind of naïvety for the invention of which other ages may envy it—and how much naïvety, venerable, childlike and boundlessly stupid naïvety there is in the scholar's belief in his superiority, in the good conscience of his tolerance, in the simple unsuspecting certainty with which his instinct treats the religious man as an inferior and lower type which he himself has grown beyond and above.[3]

3. Friedrich Nietzsche, *Beyond Good and Evil,* trans. R. J. Hollingdale, para. 58.

Philip Quinn

"IN SEARCH OF THE FOUNDATIONS OF THEISM"

PHILIP QUINN has taught at the University of Michigan, Princeton University, and Brown University, where he held an endowed chair. Currently he is John A. O'Brien Professor of Philosophy at the University of Notre Dame. He has published extensively on the philosophy of science and philosophy of religion, including *Divine Commands and Moral Requirements* (1978).

Foundationalism comes in two varieties. Descriptive foundationalism is a thesis about the structure of a body of beliefs, and normative foundationalism is a thesis about the structure of epistemic justification for a body of beliefs. Both varieties partition a body of beliefs into two subclasses, a foundational class and a founded class. For descriptive foundationalism, the foundational class is the class of basic beliefs. A belief is basic for a person at a time provided it is accepted by that person at that time but is not accepted by that person at that time on the basis

Philip Quinn, "In Search of the Foundations of Theism." Reprinted from *Faith and Philosophy* 2 (1985): 469–486, with permission of the author and the editors.

Michelangelo designed the dome of St. Peter's Basilica in Rome, which is directly above the grave of St. Peter.

of any of his or her other beliefs at that time. For normative foundationalism, the foundational class is the class of properly basic beliefs. A belief is properly basic for a person at a time just in case it is basic for the person at the time and its being basic for the person at the time is contrary to no correct canon of epistemic propriety and results from no epistemic deficiency on his or her part at that time. For descriptive foundationalism, the founded class is the class of beliefs based on basic beliefs, and for normative foundationalism, the founded class is the class of beliefs properly based on properly basic beliefs.

It surely is possible that, for some human persons at some times, certain propositions that self-evidently entail that God exists are basic. But is it also possible that, for some human persons at some times, certain propositions that self-evidently entail that God exists are *properly* basic? In other words, could such propositions *be,* or at least *be among,* the normative foundations of theism, at least for some people at some times? The answers to these questions depend, of course, on what the correct criteria for proper basicality turn out to be.

Recently Alvin Plantinga has been arguing that it is in order for a religious epistemologist to return affirmative answers to these questions.[1] There are two prongs to Plantinga's argument. The first is destructive: It is an attempt to show that certain criteria for proper basicality,

1. Alvin Plantinga, "Is Belief in God Properly Basic?" *Nous* 15 (1981). Additional discussion related to the charge that modern foundationalism is self-referentially incoherent may be found in Alvin Plantinga, "Is Belief in God Rational?" *Rationality and Religious Belief,* edited by C. F. Delaney (Notre Dame: Univ. of Notre Dame Press, 1979). Material from both these papers has subsequently been incorporated into Alvin Plantinga, "Rationality and Religious Belief," *Contemporary Philosophy of Religion,* edited by Steven M. Cahn and David Shatz (New York: Oxford Univ. Press, 1982). And some of the same themes are further amplified in Alvin Plantinga, "Reason and Belief in God," *Faith and Rationality,* edited by Alvin Plantinga and Nicholas Wolterstorff (Notre Dame: Univ. of Notre Dame Press, 1983).

according to which propositions that self-evidently entail the existence of God could not be properly basic, are seriously defective and must be rejected. The second is constructive: It is an attempt to elaborate a procedure for justifying criteria for proper basicality that will allow that some propositions self-evidently entailing that God exists could turn out to be properly basic.

This paper has two aims. The first is to criticize Plantinga's argument. In the first section of the paper, I argue for two claims: (1) that Plantinga has failed to show that the criteria for proper basicality he proposes to reject are in any way defective; and (2) that Plantinga's procedure for justifying criteria for proper basicality provides no better reason for adopting criteria according to which some propositions that self-evidently entail the existence of God can be properly basic than for adopting a criterion according to which no such propositions can be properly basic. The paper's second aim is exploratory. Although Plantinga's argument is unsuccessful, it may nevertheless be true that some propositions that self-evidently entail that God exists could be properly basic. And so, in the second section of the paper, I go on to argue, on the hypothesis that this is true, for two additional claims: (1) that actually being properly basic would be a relatively unimportant feature of such propositions because they would be at least as well justified if properly based on other properly basic propositions and could always be so based; and (2) that such propositions would seldom, if ever, be properly basic for intellectually sophisticated adult theists in our culture.

The criteria for proper basicality Plantinga proposes to reject are those of classical foundationalism. Classical foundationalism is the disjunction of ancient or medieval foundationalism and modern foundationalism. The criterion for proper basicality of ancient or medieval foundationalism is the triply universal claim:

"Proper Basicality"

Alvin Plantinga

Criteria for proper basicality must be reached from below rather than above; they should not be presented *ex cathedra* but argued and tested by a relevant set of examples. But there is no reason to assume, in advance, that everyone will agree on the examples. The Christian or Jew will of course suppose that belief in God is entirely proper and rational; if he doesn't accept this belief on the basis of other propositions, he will conclude that it is basic for him and quite properly so. Followers of Bertrand Russell and Madelyn Murray O'Hare may disagree, but how is that relevant? Must my criteria, or those of the believing community, conform to their examples? Surely not. The theistic community is responsible to *its* set of examples, not to theirs.

Accordingly, the Reformed epistemologist can properly hold that belief in the Great Pumpkin is not properly basic, even though he holds that belief in God *is* properly basic, and even if he has no full-fledged criterion of proper basicality. Of course he is committed to supposing that there is a relevant *difference* between belief in God and belief in the Great Pumpkin, if he holds that the former but not the latter is properly basic. But this should prove no great embarrassment; there are plenty of candidates. These candidates are to be found in the neighborhood of the conditions I mentioned that justify and ground belief in God. Thus, for example, the Reformed epistemologist may concur with Calvin in holding that God has implanted in us a natural tendency to see his hand in the world around us; the same cannot be said for the Great Pumpkin, there being no Great Pumpkin and no natural tendency to accept beliefs about the Great Pumpkin. . . .

From *Rationality and Religious Belief* (1978).

> (1) For any proposition *p*, person *S*, and time *t*, *p* is properly basic for *S* at *t* if and only if *p* is self-evident to *S* at *t* or is evident to the senses of *S* at *t*.

And the criterion for proper basicality of modern foundationalism is this triply universal claim:

> (2) For any proposition *p*, person *S*, and time *t*, *p* is properly basic for *S* at *t* if and only if *p* is incorrigible for *S* at *t* or is self-evident to *S* at *t*.

Although Plantinga thinks the propositions expressed by both (1) and (2) should be rejected on grounds of self-referential incoherence, he actually discusses only the latter proposition at any length. However, it is clear that if his argument for self-referential incoherence succeeds against the proposition expressed by (2), a similar argument will, *mutatis mutandis,* work equally well against the proposition expressed by (1). But what exactly is the argument? And how much does it really prove?

Consider the proposition expressed by (2). What place does it have in the modern foundationalist's own structure of epistemic justification? Is it in the foundational class? Does the modern foundationalist suppose that it is ever properly basic for anyone? If he or she does, then he or she must hold that for someone at some time it is either incorrigible or self-evident. Plantinga believes it to be "neither self-evident nor incorrigible."[2] I agree. I think the proposition expressed by (2) is never incorrigible for or self-evident to me. Are Plantinga and I idiosyncratic in this respect? Could the modern foundationalist claim with any plausibility that we are just plain mistaken on this point? I think the answer to these questions has to be negative. It seems to me perfectly clear that the proposition expressed by (2) is never incorrigible for or self-evident to anyone. Hence, no one, not even a modern foundationalist, is entitled to suppose that the proposition expressed by (2) is ever properly basic for anyone.

2. Plantinga, "Is Belief in God Properly Basic?" 49.

Does this suffice to show that modern foundationalism is self-referentially incoherent? Obviously it does not. What would be self-referentially incoherent would be to affirm the proposition expressed by (2), to assert that it is itself never incorrigible for or self-evident to anyone, and also to claim that it is itself properly basic for someone at some time. But this leaves the modern foundationalist with the option of continuing to affirm the proposition expressed by (2) while conceding that it is itself never properly basic for anyone. For all that has been said so far, the proposition expressed by (2), though never properly basic for anyone, is for some people at some times properly based on propositions that, by its own lights, are properly basic for those people at those times. In discussion, Plantinga has claimed that no modern foundationalist has ever given a good argument for the view that the proposition expressed by (2) is, for some people at some times, properly based on propositions that by its own lights, are properly basic for them then. Maybe this is so. But, even if it is, this does not show that modern foundationalism is self-referentially incoherent. All it shows is that the modern foundationalist has so far not completed the task of justifying the proposition expressed by (2) in the only way that remains open to him or her, namely, by showing how it can, for some people at some times, be properly based on propositions that are, by its own lights, properly basic for them at those times. Can this be done, and, if so, how? More generally, how could any criterion for proper basicality be justified?

Plantinga offers us an explicit answer to the more general question. He says:

> . . . the proper way to arrive at such a criterion is, broadly speaking, *inductive.* We must assemble examples of beliefs and conditions such that the former are obviously properly basic in the latter, and examples of beliefs and conditions such that the former are obviously *not* properly basic in the latter. We must then frame hypotheses as to the necessary and sufficient conditions of

> proper basicality and test these hypotheses by reference to those examples.[3]

As I understand the proposed procedure, it requires that we do two things. First, we are to assemble the data upon which the induction will be based. A datum may be represented as an ordered pair whose first member is a belief and whose second member is a condition. Positive data are data such that the beliefs that are their first members are obviously properly basic in the conditions that are their second members; negative data are data such that the beliefs that are their first members are obviously not properly basic in the conditions that are their second members. Call the set of data, presumably finite, so assembled 'the initial set'. Second, we are to frame hypotheses stating necessary and sufficient conditions for proper basicality and test them against the data in the initial set. A hypothesis will pass the test posed by the data in the initial set if and only if all of the positive data in the initial set and none of the negative data in that set satisfy its necessary and sufficient conditions for proper basicality. So far, so good.

However, two questions about this procedure quickly arise. First, how do we know that there will be *any* hypothesis at all stating nontrivial necessary and sufficient conditions for proper basicality that will pass the test posed by the data in the initial set? Maybe the initial set will itself be inconsistent or in some other way subtly incoherent. So perhaps we should be allowed to throw data out of the initial set should we discover that it is in some fashion incoherent. But, second, how do we know that there will be *only one* hypothesis stating nontrivial necessary and sufficient conditions for proper basicality that will pass the test posed by the data in the initial set? If the initial set is finite and our hypotheses are universally quantified, as the classical foundationalist's criteria are, then the data in the initial set will underdetermine the truth of hypotheses. In that case, there may very well be several interesting hypotheses that all pass the test posed by the data in the initial set and yet disagree radically about the proper basicality of examples outside the initial set. So perhaps we should also be allowed to add data to the initial set if this will help us to eliminate at least some of those hypotheses that have passed the test posed by the data in the initial set. These considerations make one thing very clear. Plantinga has so far given us only the rough outlines of the first stage of a broadly inductive procedure for arriving at a uniquely justified criterion of proper basicality. Many more details would need to be filled in before we could have any rational assurance that correct application of the procedure would yield exactly one hypothesis about conditions necessary and sufficient for proper basicality inductively best supported by, or most firmly based upon, the data in the initial set in some suitable revision of the initial set.

But, rough though it be, Plantinga's sketch of the first stage of a procedure for justifying criteria of proper basicality is nonetheless well enough developed to permit us to see that it confronts at the outset at least one important difficulty. This is because, as Plantinga himself acknowledges, there is no reason to assume in advance that everyone will agree on what is to go into the initial set. Plantinga says:

> The Christian will of course suppose that belief in God is entirely proper and rational; if he doesn't accept this belief on the basis of other propositions, he will conclude that it is basic for him and quite properly so. Followers of Bertrand Russell and Madelyn Murray O'Hare (*sic!*) may disagree, but how is that relevant! Must my criteria, or those of the Christian community, conform to their examples? Surely not. The Christian community is responsible to *its* set of examples, not to theirs.[4]

The difficulty if, of course, that this is a game any number can play. Followers of Muhammed, followers of Buddha, and even followers of the Reverend Moon can join in the fun. Even the modern foundationalist can play. When a mod-

3. Ibid., 50.

4. Idem.

ern foundationalist, under optimal conditions for visual perception, seems to see a green beach ball in front of her, she can claim that one thing that is obviously properly basic for her then is this:

(3) I am being appeared to greenly.

And one thing that is obviously not properly basic for her then, she can say, is this:

(4) I am seeing a green beachball.

After all, as she sees it, the proposition expressed by the latter sentence is for her then properly based, at least in part, on the proposition expressed by the former. And she can then mimic Plantinga's own argument in this fashion: "Followers of G. E. Moore and Alvin Plantinga may disagree, but how is that relevant? Must my criteria, or those of the community of modern foundationalists, conform to their examples? Surely not. The community of modern foundationalists is responsible to *its* set of examples, not to theirs." It would seem that what is sauce for Russell's goose should also be sauce for Plantinga's gander. Turnabout *is,* in this case, fair play.

Ad hominem arguments to one side, the problem is that fidelity to the data in an initial set constructed from intuitions about what is obvious is a very weak constraint on the justification of a criterion for proper basicality. The modern foundationalist can easily choose the data in his or her initial set so that his or her criterion for proper basicality passes the test they pose by making sure (1) that the only beliefs that nearly everyone would admit are, in the associated conditions, incorrigible or self-evident are the first members of positive data, and (2) that all beliefs that nearly everyone would, in the associated conditions, not consider incorrigible or self-evident are either the first members of negative data or outside the initial set altogether. How is this to be accomplished?

Suppose a modern foundationalist is contemplating believing that she is being appeared to redly in conditions optimal for visual experience in which she is being appeared to redly. Surely she can plausibly say that it is self-evident to her that that belief would be properly basic for her in those conditions, and clearly she can also reasonably claim that it is self-evident to her that the belief would be self-evident to her in those conditions. Now suppose the same foundationalist is contemplating belief that Jove is expressing disapproval in conditions optimal for auditory experience in which she is being appeared to thunderously. Surely she can plausibly say that it is self-evident to her that that belief would not be properly basic for her in those conditions, and clearly she can also reasonably claim that it is self-evident to her that that belief would be neither incorrigible nor self-evident to her in those conditions. After having assembled a rich initial set of positive and negative data by ringing the changes on these two thought experiments, the modern foundationalist is then in a position to claim and properly so, that his or her criterion, though not itself properly basic, is properly based, in accord with what Plantinga has told us about proper procedures for justifying criteria for proper basicality, on beliefs that are properly basic by its own lights.

It is important to understand that the data I am supposing the modern foundationalist might use to justify his or her criterion of proper basicality derive from thought experiments about hypothetical situations. My claim is not that when, for instance, a person in fact believes that Jove is expressing disapproval in conditions optimal for auditory experience in which she is being appeared to thunderously, it will then in fact be self-evident to her that the belief is not properly basic for her in those conditions. After all, she may not even wonder whether that belief is properly basic for her in those conditions when she happens to have the belief in the conditions. Rather my claim is that when a modern foundationalist contemplates the hypothetical situation of believing that Jove is expressing disapproval in conditions optimal for auditory experience in which she is being appeared to thunderously, then she can with plausibility maintain that it is self-evident to her that that belief would not in those conditions be properly basic for her.

Moses holding the Ten Commandments, a statue by Michelangelo in Rome. Michelangelo put horns on Moses's head because he and other artists of the time relied on a misinterpretation of the original biblical text.

Because I hold that our intuitions about such hypothetical situations often provide the ultimate and decisive test of philosophical generalizations, I think the role of such beliefs about hypothetical situations in confirming or disconfirming philosophical generalizations is best explained on the supposition that they can be, in the right circumstances, self-evident.

In discussion, Plantinga has objected to this line of argument. If I understand his objection, it goes as follows. To say that a belief is properly basic in a set of circumstances is to say, among other things, that in those circumstances a person could accept the belief without displaying some kind of noetic defect. But what constitutes a noetic defect depends upon what constitutes the proper working of one's noetic equipment. So a proposition to the effect that a certain person on a certain occasion is displaying no such defect cannot possibly be self-evident because it cannot be self-evident to one that all one's noetic equipment is in proper working order. Hence, a proposition to the effect that a certain belief is properly basic on a certain occasion cannot possibly be self-evident either.

I concede, of course, that it is not usually self-evident to one that all one's noetic equipment is in proper working order. But if Plantinga's objection is to have any force against my argument, it must apply to the particular hypothetical case I have described above. I believe it does not. Our modern foundationalist is supposed to be contemplating believing that she is being appeared to redly in conditions optimal for visual experience in which she is being appeared to redly. It seems quite clear to me that it could be self-evident to her that she would display no noetic defect in accepting that belief in those conditions. To be sure, her noetic equipment might then have some defects of which she was unaware. She might then, for example,, not be able to recognize the taste of ordinary table salt. But that is irrelevant provided she would display none of these defects in accepting the belief that she is being appeared to redly in the specified circumstances. For all that is required is that it could be self-evident to her that she would display no such defect in accepting that belief in those circumstances. Because I believe this requirement can be met, I conclude that Plantinga's objection fails. In short, it can be self-evident to one that one is displaying no noetic defect in accepting a certain belief on a certain occasion without it also being self-evident to one then that all one's noetic equipment is in proper working order.

I do not expect that this reply will bring Plantinga's objections to an end. I suspect Plantinga will continue to think the modern foundationalist has made some mistake if he or she proceeds in this fashion to justify his or her criterion for proper basicality. But it is not obvious that this is so; nor is it obvious what precisely the mistake might be. After all, one of the rules of the game specifies that the community of modern foundationalists is permitted to be responsible to *its* set of examples. Hence, absent a good argument by Plantinga that establishes that a mistake must occur in such a procedure, I think we are entitled to hold that Plantinga's own procedure for justifying criteria for proper basicality provides no better reason for adopting criteria according to which some propositions that self-evidently entail the existence of God can be properly basic than for adopting a criterion, namely, the one proposed by the modern foundationalist, according to which no such propositions can be properly basic.

Of course, nothing I have said rules out the possibility that Plantinga could use the inductive procedure he advocates to justify a criterion of proper basicality according to which some propositions that self-evidently entail that God exists can be properly basic. Indeed, if, as his talk about being responsible to the examples of the Christian community suggests, he would take some such propositions to be the first members of positive data in his initial set and thereafter not delete all such positive data in revising his initial set, it is pretty obvious that Plantinga can succeed in this task, though success at so cheap a price may be thought by some to come uncomfortably close to question begging. But if Plantinga does succeed in performing this exercise, then I think the conclusion we should draw is that his fight with classical foundationalism has resulted in a standoff.

If my critique of Plantinga has been successful, I have shown that he fails to prove that belief in propositions that self-evidently entail God's existence could ever be properly basic for anyone. But it might be true that belief in such propositions could be properly basic, even if Plantinga has not proved it. And if it were, what would be the consequences for religious epistemology? I now turn to an exploration of this issue.

Plantinga's examples of beliefs that could be properly basic in the right conditions include the following items:

(5) God is speaking to me.

(6) God disapproves of what I have done. and

(7) God forgives me for what I have done.

And according to Plantinga, the right conditions include a component that is, broadly speaking, experiential. He says,

> Upon reading the Bible, one may be impressed with a deep sense that God is speaking to him. Upon having done what I know is cheap, or wrong, or wicked I may feel guilty in God's sight and form the belief that *God disapproves of what I've done.* Upon confession and repentence, I may feel forgiven, forming the belief *God forgives me for what I've done.*[5]

It strikes me that part of what makes the suggestion that beliefs like those expressed by (5)–(7) could be properly basic in conditions like those partially described in the quoted passage seem attractive is an analogy with an extremely plausible view about how certain Moorean commonsense beliefs are often justified. When I have the experience of seeming to see a hand in front of me in the right conditions, I may be justified in believing that

(8) I see a hand in front of me.

This justification may be direct in the sense of being grounded directly in the experience itself without passing through the intermediary of a belief about the way I am being appeared to such as

(9) It seems to me that I see a hand in front of me.

For I may not in the circumstances have entertained, much less accepted, the proposition expressed by (9), but, on the view under consideration, my justification for believing the proposition expressed by (8) is in no way defective on that account. Hence, the proposition expressed by (8) may be basic, and quite

5. Ibid., 46.

properly so, in the right conditions. And if this is, as I believe it to be, an attractive view about how believing the proposition expressed by (8) can be, and sometimes is, justified, then there is an argument from analogy for supposing that propositions like those expressed by (5)–(7) may also be properly basic in conditions that include an experiential component of the right sort for grounding such beliefs. To be sure, there are significant disanalogies. The direct justification of the belief expressed by (8) is grounded in a mode of sensory experience that is now generally believed by nonskeptical epistemologists to be reliable in the right conditions. By contrast, the direct justification of the beliefs expressed by (5)–(7) is grounded in a mode of experience that, though it may be reliable in the right conditions, is not now generally believed by nonskeptical epistemologists to be so. But, although such considerations might be taken to show that the analogical argument is not very strong, it does not deprive the positive analogy of heuristic and explanatory capabilities. I am going to make use of these capabilities in the remainder of the discussion.

When I have the experience of seeming to see a hand in front of me in the right conditions, though the proposition expressed by (8) could then be properly basic for me, it could instead be the case that the proposition expressed by (9) is then properly basic for me and the proposition expressed by (8) is then properly based, at least in part, on the proposition expressed by (9). For when I have that experience in those conditions, I might well be attending mainly to the qualitative aspects of my visual experience with the result that the proposition expressed by (9) is then basic for me. If this happens, the proposition expressed by (9) would clearly be properly basic for me. I might well also then base the proposition expressed by (8) in part on the proposition expressed by (9). And, if this too happens, then the proposition expressed by (8) would be properly based, in part, on the proposition expressed by (9) because the latter proposition does nothing more than serve to articulate that part of the content of my visual experience that is relevant to justifying the former. If the proposition expressed by (8) were indirectly justified by being properly based on the proposition expressed by (9), it would be no less well justified than if it were directly justified by being directly grounded in visual experience. Since, by hypothesis, my visual experience in those conditions suffices to confer a certain degree of justification on the proposition expressed by (8), the amount of justification that reaches the proposition expressed by (8) from that experience will not be less in those conditions if it passes by way of the proposition expressed by (9) than if it is transmitted directly without intermediary. But neither would its justification be any better if indirect in this way. Moreover, it could happen that at a certain time the proposition expressed by (8) is properly basic for me and at a later time it is no longer properly basic, though still justified, for me because in the interval it has come to be properly based on the proposition expressed by (9). For in the interval I might, for example, have come to wonder whether I was justified in believing the proposition expressed by (8) and as a result come to believe the proposition expressed by (9) and to base properly on this belief my belief in the proposition expressed by (8). And if such a process did occur, I think the degree to which the proposition expressed by (8) was justified for me would, other things remaining unaltered, stay constant through it.

By analogy, similar things seem true of the examples that are Plantinga's prime candidates for religious beliefs that could be properly basic. When I am impressed with a deep sense that God is speaking to me, if the proposition expressed by (5) could then be properly basic for me, then it could instead be the case that some other proposition is among those then properly basic for me and the proposition expressed by (5) is then properly based in part on it. Such a proposition is:

(10) It seems to me that God is speaking to me.

If the proposition expressed by (5) were indirectly justified for me by being properly based on the proposition expressed by (10), its justification would be no better, and no worse, than if it were properly basic and directly justified for me by being directly grounded in my experiential sense that God is speaking to me, other things remaining the same. And it could happen that in the course of time the proposition expressed by (5) changes from being properly basic for me to being properly based in part for me on the proposition expressed by (10) without gain or loss of degree of justification.

So, oddly enough, if certain propositions that self-evidently entail the existence of God can be properly basic for a person at a time, it is epistemically unimportant whether such propositions actually are properly basic for that person at that time. Without loss of degree of justification, such theistic propositions can just as well be properly based, at least in part, on others that are descriptive of the person's experience at the time and are then properly basic for the person. Although such theistic propositions would not need to be based on the evidence of other propositions, they always could be so based. So the cautious philosopher who did so base them would be every bit as justified in believing in the existence of God as the reckless mystic who did not.

There is another salient feature of directly justified Moorean beliefs like the one expressed by (8) which would have an analogue in the case of religious beliefs like those expressed by (5)–(7) if they could be properly basic in the right conditions. This is that the kind of justification conferred on such Moorean beliefs by direct grounding in experience of the right sort is defeasible. So, for example, a potential defeater for the proposition expressed by (8) is this:

(11) I am now hallucinating a hand.

If propositions such as (8) are taken to be properly basic in the right conditions, then a full specification of those conditions must include reference to the status of potential defeaters such as (11). What would it be reasonable to say about potential defeaters when specifying in fuller detail the right conditions for proper basicality of the proposition expressed by (8)? Several possibilities come to mind.

It might be suggested that conditions are right for the proposition expressed by (8) to be properly basic for me only if none of its potential defeaters is true. This suggestion clearly misses the mark. When I have the experience of seeming to see a hand in front of me, it may be that the proposition expressed by (8) is true and the proposition expressed by (11) is false, and yet I am justified in rejecting the former and accepting the latter because, for instance, I remember taking a large dose of some hallucinogen only an hour ago and hallucinating wildly in the interval. Merely to insist that potential defeaters be false in order for conditions to be right for proper basicality is to require much too little.

Alternatively, it might be suggested that conditions are right for the proposition expressed by (8) to be properly basic for me only if each of its potential defeaters is such that I have some reason to think it is false. Clearly this suggestion errs in the direction of demanding too much. I have never exhaustively enumerated the potential defeaters of the proposition expressed by (8), and I am inclined to doubt that I would ever complete such a task if I began it. I have certainly never mobilized or acquired a reason against each of them. No one I know has ever tried to do such a thing in defense of all of his or her Moorean commonsense beliefs. So if such beliefs frequently are properly basic in virtue of being directly grounded in sensory experience, as I think they are, conditions are often right for proper basicality without such an elaborate structure of reasons for the falsity of potential defeaters having been mobilized.

It does, however, seem initially plausible to suppose that conditions are right for the proposition expressed by (8) to be properly basic for me only if I have no sufficiently substantial reasons to think that any of its potential defeaters is true and this is not due to epistemic negligence on my part. Two features of this claim require a bit of explanation. First, if the only reason I have to think that some potential defeater of the proposition expressed by (8) is true is, for instance, that I remember once, long ago, having mistaken a tree's branches for a hand, then that will not usually suffice to undermine the *prima facie* justification the proposition expressed by (8) has in the right experiential conditions to such an extent that that proposition is not properly basic. More generally, since *prima facie* justification comes in degrees, although any good reason one has for thinking one of a proposition's potential defeaters is true will undermine that proposition's *prima facie* justification to some degree, slight reasons will usually not singly undermine it to the extent that it is no longer *prima facie* justified. Instead, it will usually remain *prima facie* justified in the presence of one or a few such reasons but to a lesser degree than it would be in their absence. It takes a sufficiently substantial reason for thinking one of its potential defeaters is true to rob a proposition of proper basicality in conditions in which it would otherwise be properly basic.[6] Second, if I happen to lack sufficiently substantial reasons to think that any potential defeater of the proposition expressed by (8) is true merely because, for example, I have negligently failed to recall that I ingested some hallucinogenic substance only an hour ago and have been hallucinating wildly in the interval, then clearly conditions are not right for the proposition expressed by (8) to be properly basic for me, even though it may in fact be basic for me. More generally, a proposition is not *prima facie* justified if one negligently ignores good reasons for thinking one of its potential defeaters is true that would be sufficiently substantial to undermine the proposition's *prima facie* justification to such an extent that it would not be *prima facie* justified. Such epistemic negligence would constitute an epistemic deficiency.

6. I came to appreciate this point as a result of reflecting on comments by Jonathan Malino and William P. Alston.

By analogy, it also seems initially plausible to say that conditions are right for the propositions expressed by (5)–(7) to be properly basic for me only if I have no sufficiently substantial reason to think that any of their potential defeaters is true and this is not due to epistemic negligence on my part. But there is the rub. A potential defeater of the propositions expressed by (5)–(7) is this:

(12) God does not exist.

And, unfortunately, I do have very substantial reasons for thinking that the proposition expressed by (12) is true. My reasons derive mainly from one of the traditional problems of evil. What I know, partly from experience and partly from testimony, about the amount and variety of nonmoral evil in the universe confirms highly for me the proposition expressed by (12). Of course, this is not indefeasible confirmation of the proposition expressed by (12). It could be defeated by other things I do not know. Perhaps it is not even undefeated confirmation. Maybe it is even defeated by other things I do know. Nevertheless, it does furnish me with a very substantial reason for thinking that the proposition expressed by (12) is true. Moreover, I dare say that many, perhaps most, intellectually sophisticated adults in our culture are in an epistemic predicament similar to mine. As I see it, an intellectually sophisticated adult in our culture would have to be epistemically negligent not to have very substantial reasons for thinking that what (12) expresses is true. After all, nontrivial atheological reasons, ranging from various problems of evil to naturalistic theories according to which theistic belief is illusory or merely projective, are a pervasive, if not obtrusive, component of the rational portion of our cultural heritage.

But, even if such reasons are very substantial, are they sufficiently substantial to make it the case that the propositions expressed by (5)–(7) would no longer be properly basic in conditions of the sort described by Plantinga in which, we are supposing, they could have been properly basic but for the presence of such substantial reasons? On reflection, I am convinced that such reasons are, taken collectively, sufficiently substantial, though I confess with regret that I cannot at present back up my intuitive conviction with solid arguments. But I conjecture that many, perhaps most, intellectually sophisticated adults in our culture will share my intuitive conviction on this point. And so I conclude that many, perhaps most, intellectually sophisticated adult theists in our culture are seldom, if ever, in conditions that are right for propositions like those expressed by (5)–(7) to be properly basic for them.

It does not follow from this conclusion that intellectually sophisticated adult theists in our culture cannot be justified in believing propositions like those expressed by (5)–(7). For all that I have said, some such propositions are such that, for every single one of their potential defeaters that is such that there is some very substantial reason to think it is true, there is an even better reason to think it is false. And so, for all I know, some intellectually sophisticated adult theists in our culture could be, or perhaps even are, in the fortunate position, with respect to some such propositions and their potential defeaters, of having, for each potential defeater that some epistemically nonnegligent, intellectually sophisticated adult in our culture has a very substantial reason to think is true, an even better reason to think it is false. But if there are such fortunate theists in our culture, they are people who have already accomplished at least one of the main tasks traditionally assigned to natural theology. Although they may know of no proof of the existence of God, they possess reasons good enough to defend some proposition that self-evidently entails the existence of God against all of its potential defeaters that epistemically nonnegligent, intellectually sophisticated adults in our culture have very substantial reasons to believe. I tend to doubt that many intellectually sophisticated adult theists in our culture are in this fortunate position for any appreciable portion of their lives.

But suppose someone were in this fortunate position. Such a person would have reasons good enough to defend theistic belief against all of its potential defeaters that epistemically nonnegligent, intellectually sophisticated adults in our culture have very substantial reasons to believe, and such reasons would be parts of such a person's total case for the rationality of theistic belief. But would such a person's theistic belief have to based on such reasons? That depends, of course, on exactly what is involved in basing one belief on others. Plantinga is prudently reticent about describing the basing relation; he says only that, "although this relation isn't easy to characterize in a revealing and nontrivial fashion, it is nonetheless familiar."[7] On the basis of the examples Plantinga gives, I once conjectured in discussion that he thinks the relation is characterized by something like the following principle:

> (13) For any person *S* and distinct propositions *p* and *q*, *S* believes *q* on the basis of *p* only if *S* entertains *p*, *S* accepts *p*, *S* infers *q* from *p*, and *S* accepts *q*.[8]

If Plantinga does have in mind some such narrow conception of the basing relation, then our hypothetical fortunate person's theistic belief clearly need not be based on all the reasons, including defenses against potential defeaters that have very substantial support, in the person's total case for the rationality of theistic belief. After all, some such defenses may consist only of considerations that show that certain atheological arguments are unsound or otherwise defective, and our fortunate person's belief need not be based, in this narrow sense, on such con-

7. Plantinga, "Is Belief in God Properly Basic?" 41.

8. In a more thorough treatment, it would be important to worry about the temporal references in this principle. If I have just looked up the spelling of *umbrageous* in my dictionary, then my belief about how that word is spelled may now be based on belief about what *my* dictionary says. But if I last looked up its spelling many months ago, then my belief about how *umbrageous* is spelled may now only be based on my belief that I seem to remember seeing it spelled that way in *some dictionary or other*. Presumably bases of the sort specified by this principle can and sometimes do shift with time.

siderations. Indeed, for all I know, it is possible that all our fortunate person's successful defenses against potential defeaters that have substantial support are of this sort. Hence, for all I know, our fortunate person could have a successful total case for the rationality of theistic belief made up entirely of reasons such that belief in some proposition that self-evidently entails the existence of God needs none of them for a basis. Thus, for all I know, on this narrow conception of the basing relation, our fortunate person's theistic belief might be properly basic in the right conditions.

If I were to endorse some such narrow conception of the basing relation, I would have to revise my earlier proposal about when it is plausible to suppose conditions are right for propositions to be properly basic for me. I am inclined to believe that the appropriate thing to say, in light of the line of reasoning developed in the previous paragraph, is that it seems plausible to suppose that conditions are right for propositions like those expressed by (5)–(7) to be, in the narrow sense, properly basic for me if (i) either I have no sufficiently substantial reason to think that any of their potential defeaters is true, or I do have some such reasons but, for each such reason I have, I have an even better reason for thinking the potential defeater in question is false, and (ii), in either case, my situation involves no epistemic negligence on my part. I could then put the point I am intent on pressing by saying that, depending on which of the two disjuncts in the first clause of this principle one imagines my satisfying, I would have to be nonnegligently either rather naive and innocent or quite fortunate and sophisticated in order for conditions to be right for propositions like those expressed by (5)–(7) to be, in the narrow sense, properly basic for me. When I examine my epistemic predicament, I find myself forced to conclude that I am in neither of those extreme situations. Since I have very substantial reasons for thinking the proposition expressed by (12) is true, innocence has been lost. But, because I have not yet done enough to defend theistic belief against potential defeaters that have substantial support, I have not reached the position of our hypothetical fortunate person. Innocence has not, so to speak, been regained. Hence, conditions are not now right for propositions like those expressed by (5)–(7) to be, in the narrow sense, properly basic for me. My conjecture is that many, perhaps most, intellectually sophisticated persons in our culture are in an epistemic predicament similar to mine in this respect for most of their adult lives.

There is, of course, nothing wrong with construing the basing relation in some such narrow fashion provided one is tolerably clear about what one is doing. Surely there is such a relation, and Plantinga is free to use it in his theories if he wishes But I think it may be more perspicuous, or at least equally illuminating, to look at matters in a slightly different way. Consider again our hypothetical fortunate person who has reasons good enough to defend theistic belief against all of its potential defeaters that epistemically nonnegligent, intellectually sophisticated adults in our culture have very substantial reasons to believe. I would say that, for such a person, theistic belief would be based, in a broad sense, on all the reasons that are parts of the person's total case for the rationality of theistic belief. In employing this broad conception of the basing relation, I am aiming to draw attention to the fact that, if the person did not have all those reasons and were like many, perhaps most, intellectually sophisticated adults in our culture, theistic belief would not be rational for the person, or at least its rationality would be diminished to an appreciable extent if some of those reasons were absent. On this broad conception of the basing relation, I would not need to revise the principle concerning the right conditions for certain propositions to be, in the broad sense, properly basic for me, to which I had ascribed initial plausibility, in order to accommodate the hypothetical fortunate person, for the fortunate person's theistic belief would be, in the broad sense, properly based on all the reasons that comprise his or her total case for the rationality of theistic belief. Reasons that are, in the broad sense, part of a basis for theistic belief need not be related to a proposition that self-evidently entails the existence of God in the same way that the premises of an inference are related to its conclusion. They may instead provide part of a basis for theistic belief roughly in the same way a physicist's demonstration that the so-called "clock paradox" does not reveal an inconsistency in special relativity provides part of a basis for special relativity. Or, to cite what may be a more helpful analogy in the present context, they may provide part of a basis for theistic belief in much the same way Richard Swinburne's argument in *The Coherence of Theism* that the claim that God exists is not demonstrably incoherent provides part of the basis for Swinburne's claim in *The Existence of God* that God's existence is more probable than not.[9] And if I am right about the epistemic predicament of many, perhaps most, intellectually sophisticated adult theists in our culture, for them theistic belief stands in need of at least some basis of this kind if it is to be rational. This may, in the end, be a point on which Plantinga and I have a disagreement that is not merely verbal. I would insist, and Plantinga, for all I know, might not, that many, perhaps most, intellectually sophisticated adult theists in our culture must, if their belief in God is to be rational, have a total case for the rationality of theistic belief that includes defenses against defeaters that have very substantial support.

If theistic belief can be *prima facie* justified by experience at all, then there may be less difference between Plantinga and his opponents than one might at first have thought.[10] Plantinga locates a proper doxastic foundation for theistic belief at the level of propositions like that expressed by (5); a modern foundationalist would wish to claim that there is a subbasement in the truly proper doxastic structure at the level of propositions like that expressed by (10).

Plantinga's view has the advantage of psychological realism. I doubt that most theists generate their doxastic structures by first entertaining and accepting propositions like that expressed by (10) and then inferring from them, together perhaps with some epistemic principles, propositions like that expressed by (5). Nonetheless, I think there is something to be said on behalf of what I take to be an important insight captured by the modern foundationalist's position, though perhaps not perfectly articulated there. Although it may be a mistake to suppose that a phenomenological belief like the one expressed by (10) must always mediate between experience and a belief like the one expressed by (5), experience of the sort that could serve to ground a belief like the one expressed by (5) is itself so thoroughly shaped and penetrated by conceptual elements that, if it grounds a belief like the one expressed by (5) directly, then that belief is based on a cognitive state of the believer, even if that state is not an explicit belief with a phenomenological proposition for its object. Perhaps it is at the level of such cognitive states that we may hope to discover the real evidential foundations in experience for theistic belief.

9. See Richard Swinburne, *The Coherence of Theism* (Oxford: Clarendon Press, 1977) and Richard Swinburne, *The Existence of God* (Oxford: Clarendon Press, 1979).

10. A recent defense of the view that theistic belief can be *prima facie* justified by experience of certain kinds may be found in William P. Alston, "Religious Experience and Religious Belief," *Nous* 16 (1982).

PART VIII

The Scientific Challenge

Creation Myths

The authors of the following creation myths are unknown.

INDIA: "RIG VEDA"

1. Then even nothingness was not, nor existence.
   There was no air then, nor the heavens beyond it.
   What covered it? Where was it? In whose keeping?
   Was there then cosmic water, in depths unfathomed?
2. Then there were neither death nor immortality,
   nor was there then the torch of night and day.
   The One breathed windlessly and self-sustaining.
   There was that One then, and there was no other.
3. At first there was only darkness wrapped in darkness.
   All this was only unillumined water.
   That One which came to be, enclosed in nothing,
   arose at last, born of the power of heat.
4. In the beginning desire descended on it—
   that was the primal seed, born of the mind.
   The sages who have searched their hearts with wisdom
   know that which is, is kin to that which is not.
5. And they have stretched their cord across the void,
   and know what was above, and what below.
   Seminal powers made fertile mighty forces.
   Below was strength, and over it was impulse.
6. But, after all, who knows, and who can say
   whence it all came, and how creation happened?
   The gods themselves are later than creation,
   so who knows truly whence it has arisen?
7. Whence all creation had its origin,
   he, whether he fashioned it or whether he did not,
   he, who surveys it all from highest heaven,
   he knows—or maybe even he does not know.

GREECE: HESIOD, "THEOGONY," 116

First of all, the Void (*Chaos*) came into being, next broad-bosomed Earth, the solid and eternal home of all, and Eros [Desire], the most beautiful of the immortal gods, who in every man and every god softens the sinews and overpowers the prudent purpose of the mind. Out of Void came Darkness and black Night, and out of Night came Light and Day, her children conceived after union in love with Darkness. Earth first produced starry Sky, equal in size with herself, to cover her on all sides. Next she produced the tall mountains, the pleasant haunts of the gods, and also gave birth to the barren waters, sea with its raging surges—all this without the passion of love. Thereafter she lay with Sky and gave birth to Ocean with its deep current.

Translation by N. O. Brown.

ISRAEL: "GENESIS"

CHAPTER 1

In the beginning God created the heaven and the earth.
2 And the earth was without form, and void; and darkness *was* upon the face of the deep. And the Spirit of God moved upon the face of the waters.
3 And God said, Let there be light: and there was light.
4 And God saw the light, that *it was* good: and God divided the light from the darkness.
5 And God called the light Day, and the darkness he called Night. And the evening and the morning were the first day.
6 And God said, Let there be a firmament in the midst of the waters, and let it divide the waters from the waters.
7 And God made the firmament, and divided the waters which *were* under the firmament from the waters which *were* above the firmament: and it was so.
8 And God called the firmament Heaven. And the evening and the morning were the second day.
9 And God said, Let the waters under the heaven be gathered together unto one place, and let the dry *land* appear: and it was so.
10 And God called the dry *land* Earth; and the gathering together of the waters called he Seas: and God saw that *it was* good.
11 And God said, Let the earth bring forth grass, the herb yielding seed, *and* the fruit tree yielding fruit after his kind, whose seed *is* in itself, upon the earth: and it was so.
12 And the earth brought forth grass, *and* herb yielding seed after his kind, and the tree yielding fruit, whose seed *was* in itself, after his kind: and God saw that *it was* good.
13 And the evening and the morning were the third day.
14 And God said, Let there be lights in the firmament of the heaven to divide the day from the night; and let them be for signs, and for seasons, and for days, and years:
15 And let them be for lights in the firmament of the heaven to give light upon the earth: and it was so.
16 And God made two great lights; the greater light to rule the day, and the lesser light to rule the night: *he made* the stars also.
17 And God set them in the firmament of the heaven to give light upon the earth,
18 And to rule over the day and over the night, and to divide the light from the darkness: and God saw that *it was* good.
19 And the evening and the morning were the fourth day.
20 And God said, Let the waters bring forth abundantly the moving creature that hath life, and fowl *that* may fly above the earth in the open firmament of heaven.
21 And God created great whales, and every living creature that moveth, which the waters brought forth abundantly, after their kind, and every winged fowl after his kind: and God saw that *it was* good.
22 And God blessed them, saying. Be fruitful, and multiply, and fill the waters in the seas, and let fowl multiply in the earth.
23 And the evening and the morning were the fifth day.
24 And God said, Let the earth bring forth the living creature after his kind, cattle, and creeping thing, and beast of the earth after his kind: and it was so.
25 And God made the beast of the earth after his kind, and cattle after their kind, and every thing that creepeth upon the earth after his kind: and God saw that *it was* good.
26 And God said, Let us make man in our image, after our likeness: and let them have dominion over the fish of the sea, and over the fowl of the air, and over the cattle, and over all the earth, and over every creeping thing that creepeth upon the earth.

From the authorized (King James) translation of 1611.

27 So God created man in his *own* image, in the image of God created he him; male and female created he them.
28 And God blessed them, and God said unto them, Be fruitful, and multiply, and replenish the earth, and subdue it: and have dominion over the fish of the sea, and over the fowl of the air, and over every living thing that moveth upon the earth.
29 And God said, Behold, I have given you every herb bearing seed, which *is* upon the face of all the earth, and every tree, in the which is the fruit of a tree yielding seed; to you it shall be for meat.
30 And to every beast of the earth, and to every fowl of the air, and to every thing that creepeth upon the earth, wherein *there* is life, *I have given* every green herb for meat: and it was so.
31 And God saw every thing that he had made, and, behold, *it was* very good. And the evening and the morning were the sixth day.

CHAPTER 2

Thus the heavens and the earth were finished, and all the host of them.
2 And on the seventh day God ended his work which he had made; and he rested on the seventh day from all his work which he had made.
3 And God blessed the seventh day, and sanctified it: because that in it he had rested from all his work which God created and made.
4 These *are* the generations of the heavens and of the earth when they were created, in the day that the LORD God made the earth and the heavens,
5 And every plant of the field before it was in the earth, and every herb of the field before it grew: for the LORD God had not caused it to rain upon the earth, and *there was* not a man to till the ground.
6 But there went up a mist from the earth, and watered the whole face of the ground.

Cosmic Myths

According to a creation myth of the Winnebago Indians of Wisconsin, Earthmaker cried, and, looking down, noticed that his tears had become seas. Then he wished for light and there was light. Then for earth and there was earth. Surveying his creation he reached down and picked up a piece of earth, which he fashioned into an image of himself. But when he talked to it, it did not answer. So he made a mind for it, but still it did not answer. So he made a tongue for it. Still it did not answer. So he made a soul for it. Then he talked to it again and it very nearly said something. But the sounds it made were not intelligible. So Earthmaker breathed into its mouth and talked to it again. This time, it answered.

What did it say? The myth does not tell us. But having just sprung to consciousness it would have been natural, looking at its creator, had the first human said, "Where am I? Who am I? Who are you?"

The cosmogenic myths of the world's cultures, which are designed to answer questions such as where the world came from and how we got here, come in a great variety of forms. In some of them a god creates the world by thought or word, or by some ritualistic act, say, by heating himself in a steam hut. In others, a god or one of his emissaries—say, an aquatic bird—dives to

7 And the LORD God formed man *of* the dust of the ground, and breathed into his nostrils the breath of life, and man became a living soul.
8 And the LORD God planted a garden eastward in Eden; and there he put the man whom he had formed.
9 And out of the ground made the LORD God to grow every tree that is pleasant to sight, and good for food; the tree of life also in the midst of the garden, and the tree of knowledge of good and evil.
10 And a river went out of Eden to water the garden; and from thence it was parted, and became into four heads.
11 The name of the first *is* Pí-son: that *is* it which compasseth the whole land of Hav-i-lah, where *there is* gold,
12 And the gold of that land is good: there *is* bdellium and the onyx stone.
13 And the name of the second river *is* Gíhon: the same is it that compasseth the whole land of E-thi-ó-pi-a.
14 And the name of the third river is Hid′-de-kel: that *is* it which goeth toward the east of Assyria. And the fourth river *is* Eu-phrá-tes.
15 And the LORD God took the man, and put him into the garden of Eden to dress it and to keep it.
16 And the LORD God commanded the man, saying, Of every tree of the garden thou mayest freely eat:
17 But of the tree of the knowledge of good and evil, thou shalt not eat of it: for in the day that thou eatest thereof thou shalt surely die.
18 And the LORD God said, *It is* not good that the man should be alone; I will make him an help meet for him.

the bottom of the primordial ocean to retrieve a piece of earth from which land grows. In others, a primordial unity divides, amoebalike, to create a heaven and earth. In still others, a fantastic being is dismembered, perhaps in battle, and his parts supply the original material for the earthly world we inhabit.

The ancient myths satisfy the curiosity only of those for whom they were invented. For us, such myths are poetic. Poetry may satisfy us aesthetically, but it does not satisfy our curiosity about the origins of things. When we contemplate these ancient myths, it may even be hard for us to understand how they ever stilled anyone's curiosity, for it is difficult for us to project ourselves into a mentality in which such myths would not have raised as many questions as they answered.

Do our religious myths do any better? Because our myths are so familiar and we have become accustomed to using them to mask the unknown, they may seem to answer more. But do they?

Our situation is quite different from that of primitive peoples who were satisfied by such myths. They knew only their own myths, and, unless they were shamans or visionaries, they had only two choices: accept the official myth or sink into an abyss of unknowing. But we know both our myths and theirs. So we not only have a choice of myths, but also the insecurity that comes with the suspicion that our myths may be make-believe.

19 And out of the ground the LORD God formed every beast of the field, and every fowl of the air; and brought *them* unto Adam to see what he would call them: and whatsoever Adam called every living creature, that *was* the name thereof.
20 And Adam gave names to all cattle, and to the fowl of the air, and to every beast of the field; but for Adam there was not found an help meet for him.
21 And the LORD God caused a deep sleep to fall upon Adam, and he slept: and he took one of his ribs, and closed up the flesh instead thereof;
22 And the rib which the LORD God had taken from man, made he a woman, and brought her unto the man.
23 And Adam said, "This *is* now bone of my bones, and flesh of my flesh: she shall be called Woman, because she was taken out of Man.
24 Therefore shall a man leave his father and his mother, and shall cleave unto his wife: and they shall be one flesh.
25 And they were both naked, the man and his wife, and were not ashamed.

JAPAN: "KO-JI-KI"[1]

Hereupon all the Heavenly Deities commanded the two Deities His Augustness the Male-Who-Invites and Her Augustness the Female-Who-Invites, ordering them to 'Make, consolidate and give birth to this drifting land.' Granting to them an heavenly jewelled spear, they (thus) deigned to charge them. So the two Deities, standing upon the Floating Bridge of Heaven, pushed down the jewelled spear and stirred with it, whereupon, when they had stirred the brine till it went curdlecurdle, and drew (the spear) up, the brine that dripped down from the end of the spear was piled up and became an island. This is the Island of Onogoro. (*Ko-ji-ki,* p. 19)

Translated by B. H. Chamberlain.

1. Eighth century A.D.

"The World Is Not What It Seems"

Bertrand Russell

Consider this table in front of us, which has hitherto roused but the slightest thought in us. It is full of surprising possibilities. The one thing we know is that it is not what it seems. Beyond this modest result, we have the most complete liberty of conjecture. Leibniz tells us it is a community of souls; Bishop Berkeley tells us it is an idea in the mind of God; sober science, scarcely less wonderful, tells us it is a vast collection of electric charges in violent motion.

From *The Problems of Philosophy* (1912).

COLUMBIA (UIOTO): "NAINEMA"

In the beginning there was nothing but mere appearance, nothing really existed. It was a phantasm, an illusion that our father touched; something mysterious it was that he grasped. Nothing existed. Through the agency of a dream our father, He-who-is-appearance-only, Nainema, pressed the phantasm to his breast and then was sunk in thought.

Not even a tree existed that might have supported this phantasm and only through his breath did Nainema hold this illusion attached to the thread of a dream. He tried to discover what was at the bottom of it, but he found nothing. 'I have attached that which was non-existent,' he said. There was nothing.

Then our father tried again and investigated the bottom of this something and his fingers sought the empty phantasm. He tied the emptiness to the dream-thread and pressed the magical glue-substance upon it. Thus by means of his dream did he hold it like the fluff of raw cotton.

He seized the bottom of the phantasm and stamped upon it repeatedly, allowing himself finally to rest upon the earth of which he had dreamt.

The earth-phantasm was now his. Then he spat out saliva repeatedly so that the forests might arise. He lay upon the earth and set the covering of heaven above it. He drew from the earth the blue and white heavens and placed them above.

Paul Radin, *Monotheism Among Primitive Peoples* (Basel, 1954), pp. 13–14.

GUATEMALA (MAYA): "POPOL VUH"

Written after the introduction of Christianity.

Admirable is the account—so the narrative opens—admirable is the account of the time in which it came to pass that all was formed in heaven and upon earth, the quartering of their signs, their measure and alignment, and the establishment of parallels to the skies and upon the earth to the four quarters thereof, as was spoken by the Creator and Maker, the Mother, the Father of life and of all existence, that one by whom all move and breathe, father and sustainer of the peace of peoples, by whose wisdom was premediated the excellence of all that doth exist in the heavens, upon the earth, in lake and sea.

Lo, all was in suspense, all was calm and silent; all was motionless, all was quiet, and wide was the immensity of the skies.

Lo, the first word and the first discourse. There was not yet a man, not an animal; there were no birds nor fish nor crayfish; there was no wood, no stone, no bog, no ravine, neither vegetation nor marsh; only the sky existed.

The face of the earth was not yet to be seen; only the peaceful sea and the expanse of the heavens.

Nothing was yet formed into a body; nothing was joined to another thing; naught held itself poised; there was not a rustle, not a sound beneath the sky. There was naught that stood upright; there were only the quiet waters of the sea, solitary within its bounds; for as yet naught existed.

There were only immobility and silence in the darkness and in the night. Alone was the Creator, the Maker, Tepeu, the Lord, and Gucumatz, the Plumed Serpent, those who engender, those who give being, alone upon the waters like a growing light.

They are enveloped in green and azure, whence is the name Gucumatz, and their being is great wisdom. Lo, how the sky existeth, how the Heart of the Sky existeth—for such is the name of God, as He doth name Himself!

NEW ZEALAND (MAORI): "IO"

Io, the Supreme Being of the Maori of New Zealand, is regarded as eternal, omniscient, and the creator of the universe.

Io dwelt within the breathing-space of immensity.
The Universe was in darkness, with water everywhere.
There was no glimmer of dawn, no clearness, no light.
And he began by saying these words,—
That He might cease remaining inactive:
'Darkness become a light-possessing darkness.'
And at once light appeared.
(He) then repeated those self-same words in this manner.
That He might cease remaining inactive:
'Light, become a darkness-possessing light.'
And again an intense darkness supervened.
Then a third time He spake saying:
'Let there be one darkness above,
Let there be one darkness below.
. . . .
Let there be one light above,
Let there be one light below,
. . . .
A dominion of light,
A bright light.'
And now a great light prevailed.
(Io) then looked to the waters which compassed him about, and spake a fourth time, saying:
'Ye waters of Tai-kama, be ye separate.
Heaven, be formed.' Then the sky became suspended.
'Bring forth thou Tupua-horo-nuku.'
And at once the moving earth lay stretched abroad.

Gregory Vlastos

"THE GREEKS DISCOVER THE COSMOS"

GREGORY VLASTOS, one of the foremost twentieth-century authorities on Greek philosophy, was for most of his career Stuart Professor of Philosophy at Princeton University. Appointed to the Institute for Advanced Study at Princeton and twice the recipient of a Guggenheim fellowship, Vlastos was awarded the prestigious MacArthur grant while in retirement. He died in 1992.

In English *cosmos* is a linguistic orphan, a noun without a parent verb. Not so in Greek which has the active, transitive verb, *kosmeō:* to set in order, to marshal, to arrange. It is what the military commander does when he arrays men and horses for battle; what a civic official does in preserving the lawful order of a state; what a cook does in putting foodstuffs together to make an appetizing meal; what Odysseus' servants have to do to clean up the gruesome mess in the palace after the massacre of the suitors.[1] What we get in all of these cases is not just any sort of arranging, but one that strikes the eye or the mind as pleasingly fitting: as setting, or keeping, or putting back, things in their proper order. There is a marked aesthetic component here, which leads to a derivative use of *kosmos* to mean not *order* as such, but *ornament, adornment;* this survives in the English derivative, *cosmetic,* which, I dare say, no one, without knowledge of Greek, would recognize as a blood-relation of *cosmic.* In the Greek the affinity with the primary sense is perspicuous since what *kosmos* denotes is a crafted, composed, beauty-enhancing order. Now for the Greeks the moral sense merges with the aesthetic: they commonly say *kalos,* "beautiful" or *aischros,* "ugly," to mean *morally admirable* or *repugnant.* We would then expect moral, not less than military, civic, domestic, and architectural applications of *kosmos.* And this is what we find. In Homer we see it used adverbially (κόσμι. κατὰ κόσμον) for speech or action conducted in a socially decent, morally proper way.[2] Later we see it even used to signify the general observance of morality and justice, as when Theognis in mid-sixth century, lamenting the corruption of morals, exclaims,

> They seize property by violence; *kosmos* has perished;
> Equitable distribution no longer obtains.
>
> [Vv. 677–78]

What then could have led men who had used *kosmos* in these ways since their childhood to give it a physical application—to use it as a name for a physical system composed of earth, moon, sun, stars, and everything in or on or between these objects, so that if they believed that there was only one such system in existence they would speak of it as "the cosmos" or "this cosmos," while if they thought there were many such they

Reprinted from Gregory Vlastos, *Plato's Universe,* Seattle: University of Washington Press, 1975, by permission of the publisher. Footnotes edited.

1. For illustrative texts and illuminating remarks on the meaning of *kosmeō,* see Charles Kahn, *Anaximander and the Origins of Greek Cosmology,* pp. 219ff.

2. Good examples in ibid.

The ascent to the Acropolis in Athens, the most impressive temple area in classical Greece.

would speak of *kosmoi* in the plural? For the answer I shall look to the fragments of Heraclitus (first third of the fifth century B.C.). These are the earliest surviving sentences in which the word is used with this new sense, and it is sound historical method to work so far as possible with original source-materials. Throughout this part of my discussion it would be well to bear in mind that Heraclitus is not a typical *physiologos*—he is too much a mystic, a poet, and a metaphysician to fit the general pattern. But though a maverick, he is more, not less, than a *physiologos;* in any case, he is enough of one—he has a theory of the constitution of the physical universe and many explanations of natural phenomena—to make his own use of the term representative.

I begin with fragment B30.[3]

> This cosmos, the same for all, no god or man has made, but it was, is, and will be for ever: ever-living fire, kindling according to measure and being extinguished according to measure.[4]

As everyone knows, fire is Heraclitus' universal substance: the whole world, he thinks, consists of fire, though only that part of it which is in the "kindled" state is recognizable as fire and is

3. The numbering of Heraclitean and Presocratic fragments is that in H. Diels and W. Kranz, *Die Fragmente der Vorsokratiker* (subsequently cited as DK). "B" prefaces the number when the editors judge that the fragment retains the original wording.

4. For a discussion of the text and meaning of this fragment see my paper, "On Heraclitus," pp. 344–47. . . .

generally so called. The two other world-masses which must be added to account for the whole of his material universe, water and earth, must then be fire "extinguished": water is fire liquefied, earth is fire solidified. Holding that everyting is in constant change—this is his most famous doctrine, the one which makes him for all subsequent ages the philosopher of flux—he takes the world-process to consist of the ceaseless intertransformations of these three conponents. In each of these interchanges one element assures its own existence by destroying another; in his own language (B76) each "lives the other's death."

To conjure up a physical model that would fall within his own experience, let us take an oil lamp. Its flame exists ("lives") by the constant extinction ("death") of the oil (liquid, hence "water"); so fire "lives the death of water." The same would be true of a wood or charcoal fire, where the victims are solids, and would probably count as "earth" for Heraclitus. So "fire kindling" is water or earth turning into fire, and "fire being extinguished" would be the converse, fire turning into water or earth, thus "living" its own "death." This is happening always, and always "according to measure." If the "measures" of the converse processes, fire kindling and fire extinguished, were the same in all occurrences of fire in the universe, fire would indeed be "everliving." For then as much of fire would be turning into water and earth at any given time, as of water and of earth into fire at the same time, and then the quantity of fire would remain constant. And if the corresponding thing happened in the case of water and of earth, their quantities too would remain constant. And since these three compose all the matter there is, its distribution as between fire, water, and earth would remain invariant, and the universe as a whole would be eternal, in spite of incessant change throughout its length and breadth.

The Parthenon on the Acropolis, a temple dedicated to the goddess Athena.

This would be a striking innovation in natural philosophy. From its beginnings in the sixth century, in Thales, Anaximander, and Anaximenes, its dominant pattern had been cosmogonic: physical theory centered in the question, "What is the source and origin of our world? What is that from which our world began and to which it will eventually return?" The reasoning I have just sketched in Heraclitus would break with this tradition. It would show him how the world could be everlasting, birthless and deathless as a whole, because birth and death keep balancing out within its parts. Here, for the first time in Greek history, we have a cosmology without a cosmogony.

To return to our fragment: "ever-living fire" at the start of the second colon stands in apposition to "this cosmos" at the start of the first.[5] So the two phrases have the same denotation. And since the second refers to the whole world, so must the former. "Cosmos" then cannot mean here simply *order, arrangement,* as many scholars have thought,[6] but that which *has* this order, this arrangement; it must mean the world in its aspect of order.[7] And we can see what kind of order Heraclitus is thinking of here: not the static order or architectonic pattern—no reference, here or elsewhere in Heraclitus, to the shape or structural design of the universe—but to the dynamic order which marks the intertransformations of its elements. In the world picture of his predecessor, Anaximander, spatial, architectonic symmetries have been conspicuous: there sun, moon, stars were a sequence of huge concentric fire-rings around a central earth, with equal intervals between successive pairs in the sequence; and the infinitely many worlds in his universe were at equal intervals from one another.[8] In Heraclitus the symmetries are exclusively temporal: they are causal sequences. The order of his world reveals itself in the constancy of the "measures" of its balanced kindlings and extinguishings.

And if the aesthetic and moral nuances in *kosmos* are recalled, it is not surprising to see Heraclitus refer to the world-order as "Justice," on one hand, as "Harmony," on the other:

> We should know that war is common, and strife is justice and that all things happen according to strife and just necessity.[B80]
>
> The adverse is concordant; from discord the fairest harmony.[B8]

Fire, water, and earth are in deadly opposition. They are at war. They are annihilating each other. But the dynamic symmetries of their intertransformations harmonize the warring opposites, make them perpetuate each other through their very strife and thus compose a world which is everlasting because all through it life is perpetually renewed by death. If you believe that "from discord [comes] the fairest harmony," what could be fairer than this? And why should it be "just"? Because of the same pattern, now viewed in its aspect of the even-handed reciprocity that insures to each of the three elements its equal share of living and of dying; what each loses in dying into its peers it invariably recoups in living their death.[9]

Now look at the phrase which follows "This cosmos" in B30: "This cosmos, *the same for all. . . .*" If you wonder, what is the point of saying that, look at the next three fragments:

5. If we keep the punctuation I have used above (favored by many scholars, including Kirk and Marcovich). Alternatively the colon could be deleted, in which case "ever-living fire" would be the predicate nominative of the verbs in the immediately preceding clause; then Heraclitus would be saying that "this world . . . *is* . . . ever-living fire," but the meaning would not be substantially affected, since in that case the "is" expresses simple identity.

6. Notably Kirk, *Heraclitus,* pp. 307ff., and again in *The Presocratic Philosophers,* p. 199. Rebuttal by Marcovich, *Heraclitus,* pp. 269–70.

7. Cf. my remark in the paper cited in n. 4 above: in this fragment "*kosmos,* though it implies, does not just mean, 'order,' for what is in question here is not merely that nobody made the *order* of the world, but that nobody made this orderly *world;* this world is fire, and nobody made the fire, for it is 'ever-living'" (p. 346).

8. For the references see Vlastos, "Equality and Justice in Early Greek Cosmologies" in Furley and Allen, eds., *Studies in Presocratic Philosophy,* 1:75–76 (corrected reprint of the original in *Classical Philology,* 1947).

9. See my paper cited in n. 4 above, pp. 356–57.

> For those who are awake the cosmos is one and common. But those who are asleep turn aside each into a private cosmos.[B89][10]
>
> We should not act and speak like men asleep.[B73]
>
> One should follow the common. But while the Logos is common, the many live as though they had a private understanding.[B2]

"Same for all" in B30, "one and common for all" in B89 are obviously equivalent expressions. Now who are those for whom the cosmos is "one and common" in B89? They are men wide awake in contrast to dreamers, to men asleep. Brooding on that bizarre mode of consciousness into which we all sink in our sleep, Heraclitus finds the key to its enfeebled intelligence in its privacy—its anarchic subjectivity. In sleep he sees us cutting ourselves off from the common world which sets the norms of veridical perception, coherent speech, and effective action. That he has both speech and action in view is clear from B73: "We should not act and speak like men asleep." If we talk in our sleep we babble; and the actions we dream we are doing are impotent to achieve their end.[11] So when Heraclitus exhorts his fellows *not* to act and speak like that, he is implying that this is their present condition: they are living in a world as false as that of the dream. And in the next fragment, B2, he laments that "while the Logos is common, the many live as though they had a private understanding." "Logos" here is not only his own discourse but, no less, what his discourse is meant to reveal, that is, the intelligible pattern of the world process. "That is what you must understand and follow," he is telling his contemporaries, "else you will not be able to think, speak, or act straight." He is thus claiming that his teaching about the cosmos conveys a truth whose apprehension will change their mode of consciousness, their very lives—that, if they but grasp what he is talking about, their perceptions, their speech, their actions will alter as dramatically as would those of a sleepwalker if he were to be suddenly jarred awake.

What could have prompted him to make such an extraordinary claim? A full answer to that question would take me well beyond the limits of my present theme: it would require me to reckon with Heraclitus' mysticism, that is to say, with that very strain in his thought which makes him untypical of Ionian *physiologia.* So I must content myself with a partial answer which, however, will do for my present purposes, for it takes account of just that part of his outlook which he shares fully with the *physiologoi* and throws good light on their discovery of the cosmos. For this I go to fragment B94:

> The Sun will not overstep his measures, else the Furies, the adjutants of Justice, will find him out.

What "measures" could he have had in view here? Each of the following regularities would have qualified:

1. That of the sun's diurnal motion, proceeding always from east to west, and at a constant rate, with never a slow-down along the way.
2. That of the times and places at which this daily motion starts and ends: sunrise and sunset occur at fixed times, at fixed points of the horizon, the same for the same day of the year in any two years, with seasonal variations whose pattern is invariant from year to year.
3. That of the size of the sun and of the outflow of its radiant energy: these too remain constant, so that for any given day what it gives off in light and heat will be the same from year to year.

Now let us note that regardless of the extent to which other *physiologoi* might differ from Heraclitus, every single one of them would join him in two affirmations:

10. On the authenticity of this fragment (rejected in whole or in part by some scholars: e.g., Kirk, *Heraclitus,* pp. 63–64, who thinks it a Plutarchean paraphrase) see Kerschensteiner, "Kosmos," pp. 99ff., and Marcovich, *Heraclitus,* pp. 369–70.

11. As in the famous simile in the *Iliad* (bk. 22, vv. 199–200): "As in a dream we cannot run down one who flees;/Powerless he is to escape, and we to pursue."

The ancient Greek Temple of Poseidon in Paestum, Italy, circa 500 B.C.

1. Solar regularities are either themselves absolutely unbreachable or else any given breach of them will admit of a natural explanation as a special case of some other, still more general, regularity which is itself absolutely unbreachable.
2. What makes the world a cosmos is the existence of such highest-level, absolutely unbreachable, regularities.

Let me explain my reason for putting that first affirmation in disjunctive form. Most of the *physiologoi*—probably all except Heraclitus himself—would have denied that the regularities of the sun's behavior are so inexorably fixed that they can never fail. An obvious example would be an eclipse. This could be regarded as a temporary stoppage of the radiant energy that streams out from the sun: this is in fact Anaximander's explanation, as a blocking of the aperture in the sun ring from which normally light and heat rush out. Heraclitus' theory is that, on the contrary, the sun is a bowl-shaped container filled with fire, and that eclipses occur when the bowl turns away from the earth.[12] This would enable him to hold that the outflow of heat and light from the bowl remained constant, eclipse or no eclipse, and that the reason why the sky was darkened in an eclipse is that while this lasted the sun's light was emitted in another direction, away from the earth, instead of toward it. But this sort of difference of opinion would leave undisturbed the conviction which Heraclitus shared with Anaximander and with every other believer in the cosmos: that the failure of this, or any other, observable regularity implies no disturbance of the more massive constancies which constitute the order of nature and, if known, would yield the ultimate explanation of every natural phenomenon, no matter how unusual and surprising. On this point Heraclitus, Anaximander, and all the *physiologoi* would stand united—a handful of intellectuals against the world. Everyone else, Greek and barbarian alike, would take it for granted that any regularity you

12. On Heraclitus' theory of the sun see Kirk, *Heraclitus*, pp. 269ff.

care to mention could fail, and for a reason which ruled out *a priori* a natural explanation of the failure: because it was caused by supernatural intervention.

Let us look at a couple of examples: Herodotus (7.37.2) relates that as Xerxes' army was starting off from Sardis for the invasion of Greece, "the sun, leaving his place in the heavens, disappeared, though there were no clouds and the sky was absolutely clear; and there was night instead of day." It is not only Xerxes and his courtiers who take the eclipse as "an apparition" (φάσμα), a sign from the gods. So does Herodotus himself. Child of the enlightenment though he was,[13] he kept a foot in both worlds; time and again in his story of the Persian wars we see him underwriting some tale of divine intervention—"god" or *a* god causing a flood, for instance, flooding the land, or causing a savage gale (8.129; 8.13).[14] In this case, though he does not actually say so, the language he uses strongly suggests the supernatural view of the eclipse: no naturalistic view, no matter how eccentric, could have involved the sun's "leaving his place in the heavens," and doing so out of a blue sky (i.e., without winds or clouds, which might have suggested a natural explanation).[15]

The same language is used by Pindar in his Ninth Paean:

Far-seeing beam of the sun, mother of sight,
Star supreme, robbed from our sight by day,
Why have you made impotent the power of man, the path of wisdom
By rushing forth on a darkened path? . . .

And here the interpretation of the event as a prodigy is explicit and long-winded:

Are you bringing a sign of war,
Or of failure to the crops,
Or of an excessively violent snow-storm,
Or of dire civil strife,
Or of the emptying of the sea,
Or of a freeze-up of the soil,
Or of a heat-wave from the south
Streaming with raging rain?
Or will you, by flooding the land,
Set a new start for the human race?

Convinced that the order of nature has been breached at this point, Pindar feels that almost anything can happen now: heat wave or frost are equally possible, and any number of other calamities, from crop failure and floods to war and civil strife. His conviction that it would be hopeless to look for any sort of rational explanation is voiced plainly when he asks, "Why have you made impotent the power of man, the path of wisdom?" Here "wisdom" (σοφία, intelligence) stands for the human power of rational explanation and prediction; this is what has been stymied, rendered "helpless," left without resource. All you can do in such a pass is to turn to the soothsayers—to those whose wisdom is "divine."

Now at last we are within sight of understanding why Heraclitus, and all the *physiologoi,* would have good cause to think that their discovery of the cosmos would revolutionize men's outlook. If you believe that the gods have power to make the sun drop out of his course in the sky, there will be no limit to the number of ways in which you will credit them with the ability to break into your world; and this will affect your whole attitude to what is going on around you and even, as I shall explain directly, to what is going on in you, in your very thoughts and feelings. That the area of possible divine intervention is traditionally unlimited becomes obvious

13. For his links with *physiologoi* and sophists see, e.g., W. Nestlé, *Vom Mythos zum Logos,* the chapter on Herodotus, pp. 503ff.

14. In 8.129 the Persians attacking Potidaea are overwhelmed by an unusually high tide which floods the swamp they are trying to cross; Herodotus says he agrees with the Potidaeans that this must have been caused by Poseidon because the Persians had desecrated his temple. . . . For other examples of references to miracles and portents by Herodotus with no apparent skepticism see, e.g., Nestlé *Vom Mythos zum Logos,* p. 505, no. 9.

15. How different is the language he uses when doing his own homespun *physiologia* one can see from his discussion of the summer risings of the Nile (2.24.1 and 2.53.3): he speaks of the sun in Egypt as "driven from his old [i.e., established] course by storms" during the winter and "returning to the middle of the sky" as the winter comes to an end. Here there is not the slightest hint of supernatural intervention: he is evidently thinking of the strong winds in the winter as the natural cause of the variation in the sun's customary behavior.

The interior of the Poseidon Temple in Paestum, Italy.

when we recall the variety of things the gods were expected to do in a relatively routine matter, like policing an oath. Here is the formula of the oath of the Amphictyonic league, quoted in a speech by Aeschines (*Against Ctesiphon,* 111) in 330 B.C.:

> The curse is that their land bear no fruit;
> that their women bear children which are not like their parents, but monsters;
> that their flocks produce no offspring according to nature;
> that they be beaten in war, in law court, and in the market;
> that they perish utterly, themselves, their household, and their clan.

Apollo, Artemis, and Athena Pronaea are being credited with the ability to manipulate not only the reproductive process in man, beast, and land, but also men's mental processes. For only so could they have been expected to punish a perjurer by bringing on him a streak of losses in the law courts and in the market: to do this the gods would either have to tone up the wits of his adversaries and competitors, so that they would be more likely to come out on top in litigation and business deals, or else to impair those of the perjurer himself so as to make him do the foolish things that would prove his undoing. The latter is the course of which we hear most often in Greek literature. The phenomenon is labeled *atē*—a word whose primary sense is "bewilderment, infatuation, caused by blindness or delusion sent by the gods," with "bane, ruin, disaster" as an extended, derivative, sense. E. R. Dodds has a full acount of *atē* in his beautiful book, *The Greeks and the Irrational*—an account which has already become a classic. Acknowledging the great debt I owe it myself, I must none the less register some differences from Dodds, for they affect importantly the theme of the present chapter.

First of all, belief in *atē,* though more conspicuous in the Homeric poems than anywhere else in Greek literature, is by no means as centered in the heroic and archaic age as Dodds seems to suggest. It is a permanent feature of the traditional Greek world-view; it persists into the fifth and even the fourth centuries, so that it is held by contemporaries of the *physiologoi,* and of Plato and Aristotle as well. Thus the Athenian orator, Lycurgus, a contemporary of Aristotle, subscribes to it himself, and expects that it would be widely shared by his public, or he would not have risked alienating the jury (501 Athenians selected by lot) by building it into his speech *Against Leocrates* (92):

> The first thing the gods do to wicked men is to subvert their reason. I value as I would an oracle these lines, bequeathed by ancient poets to posterity:
>
> When the wrath of the gods is deployed to someone's harm

> The first thing it does is to take away good sense
> From his wits, and give his judgment a worse
> turn,
> So that he knows not when he errs.

Sophocles was no less sure of the popular acceptance of this belief in his own time; he puts it into the mouth of the fifteen Theban elders who form the Chorus in the *Antigone* (vv. 621–24):

> Wisely someone uttered the famous word
> That evil at times will be thought to be good
> By one whom God draws to *atē*.[16]

And now for my second, and more important point: belief in *atē* embroils the believer in a logical predicament whose seriousness does not seem to be fully appreciated by Dodds and other classical scholars who have discussed this topic in recent years. This is the crux of it: believing that someone is acting under the influence of *atē* is logically incompatible with holding him responsible for his action. To hold a man responsible for an act, it must be *his*—it must be the action chosen by someone with his disposition, his perceptions of the world and of himself, his fund of memories, his present desires and aspirations. But an act described as done under the influence of *atē* cannot satisfy this condition: the whole point of so describing it is to call attention to the supposed fact that, but for the intervention of the deity, the agent *would not have acted in that way.* How then could we speak of it as his act? Yet speak of it as his we must, since it is not only physically his own behavior, but psychologically as well: *atē* is not supposed to have turned him into a human puppet, going through motions without accompanying perceptions, desires, and intentions; the intruding deity is not supposed to be just moving the man's muscles and bones, but to have reached into his innermost being. His private experience—his feelings, aspirations, his sense of good and evil[17]—the whole of his psyche is supposed to have been invaded by the deity, so that the agent's mind is at that moment just what the god has wanted it to be. So the act *is* the man's own: he says, "I do thus and so," and later, "I did it," and others say, "You are doing it, you did it." Yet it is *not* his, since *he would not have chosen to do it* if he were acting in accordance with those habits and purposes which characterize him, those established personality traits, interests, and commitments which constitute his social identity. Here then is a muddle, a contradiction, which cannot be avoided, or even palliated, in either of the two ways which have proved popular among scholars:

One of these is the line taken by Dodds, followed with modifications by A. W. H. Adkins in his influential books.[18] This line is predicated on the claim that archaic morality and jurisprudence impute responsibility solely on the basis of the act with no regard for what lawyers call *mens rea,* that is, the mental state of the agent. "Early Greek justice," writes Dodds, "cared nothing for intent; it was the act that mattered."[19] If this claim could be made good the contradiction would be resolved, for then the question of whether an act was chosen by the agent or forced on him by a god or goddess could be ignored: on that hypothesis he could be held responsible for the act simply because he did it. I submit that this resolution will not work, for the claim on which it is based is demonstrably false. There are cases in both the *Iliad* and the *Odyssey* in which a man is cleared of responsibility when it is established that the offending act was done in ignorance or under duress. For example, in Book 22 of the *Odyssey,*

16. Dodds, *The Greeks and the Irrational,* p. 49, quotes these lines (and the whole of the lyric in which they occur) to illustrate "the beauty and terror of the old beliefs." I know of no reason to believe that they would be denied contemporary acceptance (the *Antigone* was probably produced in 441 B.C.).

17. Cf. the citations from Aeschines and Sophocles in the preceding paragraphs of the text above.

18. A. W. H. Adkins, *Merit and Responsibility; From the Many to the One; Moral Values and Political Behaviour in Ancient Greece.*

19. Dodds, *The Greeks and the Irrational,* p. 3.

when Odysseus has just slaughtered the suitors and is about to do the same to the bard, Phemius, for having connived in their *hybris,* Phemius pleads that he had associated with the suitors only under duress, hence "with no will or desire of [his] own" (οὔ τι ἑκων . . . οὐδὲ χατίζων, v. 351). He calls on Telemachus to corroborate his plea; and when Telemachus does so, Phemius is absolved, declared free of culpable responsibility (ἀναίτιος v. 356); he goes scot free. By the same token everyone who believes himself, or is believed by others, to have acted under the influence of *atē* would have to be cleared of responsibility, since *atē* would be even stronger—totally irresistible—duress. This is in fact how Agamemnon in Book 19 of the *Iliad* represents that act of his which had wronged Achilles and had provoked the hero's "baneful wrath":

I am not responsible (ἐγώ δ᾽οὐχ αἴτιός εἰμι)
But Zeus is, and Fate, and the Erinys that walks
in darkness:
These put into my wits a savage *atē* in the assembly
When I despoiled Achilles of his prize.
So what could I do? Deity will always have its way
[Vv. 86–89].[20]

But nonetheless he is held responsible and he holds himself responsible and proceeds to make amends for his misdeed exactly as if he had been, and had thought himself, responsible. This is the contradiction I have been talking about, and you can see it here stark and unresolved.

Nor can this contradiction be resolved by way of the principle, now widely accepted among classicists, that in the case of *atē* a double causation—by the god *and* by the human agent—is being supposed, hence dual responsibility.[21] This principle is indeed true,[22] and we see it dramatically instantiated in the Embassy scene in the *Iliad* (Book 9): there, in a speech by Ajax, which is in every other way sane and wise, Achilles' wrath is represented, first as what *he,* Achilles, "has put into his breast," and then, just eight lines later, as what "the gods put in Achilles' breast." The contradiction is blatant. But neither the speaker, nor Achilles, nor anyone else there makes any allusion to it: it is just one aspect of the predicament that all who believe in *atē* have learned to live with. If you are struck by *atē,* the god who strikes you puts thoughts and feelings into you heart—yet you too put them there, for otherwise the resulting act would not be yours, and what the god did to you would not be *atē.*

I have dwelt so long on *atē* because it dramatizes the perception of an *ir*rational universe which the *physiologoi* inherited as did everyone else in their time. But, of course, it is only one of the many possible examples. For just one more, I shall revert to the perception of an eclipse, illustrating by the most famous and fateful eclipse in the whole of Greek history. The scene is the plain before Syracuse, where the Athenian expeditionary force and that of its allies—the largest ever committed by Athens in a military engagement—has been encamped. Its position has become indefensible and immediate withdrawal is mandatory: further delay would be criminal folly. Let Thucydides continue the story:

> The preparations for the departure were made and they were on the point of sailing, when the moon, being just then at the full, was eclipsed. The mass of the army was greatly moved and called upon the generals to remain. Nicias himself, who was too much under the influence of divination and the like, refused even to discuss the question of the evacuation until they had remained 27 days, as the soothsayers prescribed. This was the reason why the departure of the Athenians was finally delayed. [*History,* 7.50.4]

And the result? The whole of Nicias' army was wiped out—killed or sold into slavery. Nicias was not an ignorant man. He must have fancied himself an intellectual. We see him in one of Plato's

20. The translation owes much to that in Dodds, *The Greeks and the Irrational.*

21. A. Lesky, "Göttliche und menschliche Motivation im homerischen Epos," followed, e.g., by H. Lloyd-Jones, *The Justice of Zeus,* pp. 9ff.

22. I.e., as a description of Greek belief. What I am denying is only that it helps in the slightest to resolve, or even mitigate, the contradiction in the state of mind which it reports.

dialogues, the *Laches,* taking a leading part in a Socratic elenchus, acting as a partisan of the highly intellectualized Socratic view of courage (194Dff.). But he was still a prisoner of the traditional world-view where the sun and the moon *could* "overstep their measures" and would at the behest of supernatural powers.

In using the term "supernatural" here, and a little earlier, to identify the factor whose agency made the crucial difference between the world of traditional belief and the cosmos of the *physiologoi* I may be exposing myself to the charge of anachronism: Nicias and his soothsayers could not have said that the eclipse had a supernatural cause—they had no such word. That compound has no counterpart in classical Greek: *hyperphysikos* is not in Nicias' or Thucydides' or Plato's language. But what their language does have are the counterparts—indeed the true originals—of one of that term's components: the words for *natural.* and *nature, physikos, physis.*[23] And this gives me all I need. For *physis* is the key term in the transition from the world of Homer, Hesiod, Archilochus, Sappho, Aeschylus, Sophocles, Aristophanes, Herodotus, and the orators—that is to say, from the world of common belief and imagination throughout the archaic and classical periods—to the world of the *physiologoi* and of a few tough, hard-bitten, intellectuals like Thucydides and the Hippocratics—the world which was cosmos. That *physis* is even more basic than *kosmos* is evident from the fact that the discoverers of the cosmos came to be called *physiologoi,* not *kosmologoi,* and that "nature" occurs much more frequently in titles of their treatises than does "cosmos."[24] The beauty of *physis* is that it shows what it was in the traditional conception of the world that gave the *physiologoi* the building materials for their new construction. The cosmos they had to invent. *Physis* they found ready-made in the inherited conceptual scheme; all they needed to do with *physis* was to make a new use of it.

To explain this, let me point out how *physis* is used by Herodotus. In his prose the *physis* of any given thing is that cluster of stable characteristics by which we can recognize that thing and can anticipate the limits within which it can act upon other things or be acted upon by them. Thus in his chapter on Egypt, Herodotus introduces his Greek readers to two of its unfamiliar animals through descriptions which begin "The *physis* of the crocodile is of this sort . . ." (2.68.1); "The hippopotamus has a *physis* of this form . . ." (2.71). Now from the fact that a given thing has a *physis* Herodotus would not allow us to infer that we will always see it in full possession of that *physis.* Thus it is the *physis* of a crocodile to have a tail; but it does not follow that this crocodile will have one; he may have lost it in a fight, or in some other way. The one thing that is certain for Herodotus is that, barring supernatural intervention, whenever things interact their *physeis* set limits to what can happen. Thus when he hears the story that Hercules, when he came to Egypt, was seized by a mob and marched up to an altar to be sacrificed, whereupon "he put forth his strength and slew them all" (2.45.3), Herodotus asks, "If Hercules was a man, as they admit, how would it be natural (κῶς φύσιν ἔχει) for [this one man] to kill many thousands?" Note the force of the conditional. If Hercules were not a man, but the demigod he became after his death, that question would not have been raised. In this Herodotus stays within the traditional view, where *physis* fixes the limits of the possible for everything *except* the supernatural.

What the *physiologoi* do is to drop that exception. They make the world a cosmos by keeping what was already there in the form of *physis* and cleaning out everything else. They do so without saying so. They could not say so in a society whose public cult, saturated with the supernatural, was ensconced in the state establishment and enjoyed the protection of the law.

23. For a fundamental study of the concept of *physis* in early Greek thought see W. A. Heidel, "Peri physeōs." For an important subsequent monograph which collects illustrative passages see D. Holwerda, *Physis.*

24. For the titles see the Word Index in Diels-Kranz, Vol. 3, *s.v. Physis, Kosmos.*

To attack the supernatural head-on would turn them into outlaws. So they do the next best thing. They proceed by indirection. They so fill up the universe with *physis* as to leave no room for anything else. This is a two-pronged operation. The first prong invades the heartland of the supernatural: the heavens, whose sun and moon had been thought gods; and the *meteōra,* between the heavens and the earth, whose rain, clouds, lightning and thunder, mists, winds, rainbows, storms were so closely associated with divine control that the formulaic epithet for Zeus in Homer had been "cloud-gatherer" and the Greek expansion of "raining" would be, not "it is raining," but "he—Zeus—is raining." The other prong of the operation produces theories of the *physis* of the universe as a whole. These are at first genetic (they tell of a primordial substance from which our world and any others, if such there be, arise, and to which they eventually return), but then become increasingly theories of the invariants of change (fire, water, earth in Heraclitus; the dark and bright forms in the cosmology of Parmenides; the four "roots" in Empedocles; the infinitely numerous qualitatively multiform seeds in Anaxagoras; and the infinitely numerous qualitatively uniform atoms in Leucippus and Democritus).

On both of these operations the demolition of the supernatural is accomplished without a single word about the victim. In the first the job is done just by implementing a single tacit axiom of rational explanation: that whatever happens in any region of the universe—in the heavens, beyond it, or under it—involves only interactions between material entities whose *physis* is always the same wherever it turns up and conforms to the same highest-level regularities. So long as that axiom is observed theories of the same phenomena may vary wildly while making

"The Origin of the Universe from Nothing"

Isaac Asimov

Quantum mechanics is a way of treating the behavior of subatomic particles according to mathematical equations worked out in the 1920s by such scientists as the Austrian physicist Erwin Schrodinger (1887–1961) and the German physicist Werner Karl Heisenberg (1901–1976). Since then, quantum mechanics has proved phenomenally successful and has met every test.

In 1973 the American physicist Edward P. Tryon showed that according to quantum mechanics, it was possible for a Universe to appear, as a tiny object, out of *nothing.* Ordinarily, such a Universe would quickly disappear again, but there were circumstances under which it might not.

In 1982 Alexander Vilenkin combined Tryon's notion with the inflationary Universe and showed that the Universe, after it appeared, would inflate, gaining enormous energies at the expense of the original gravitational field, and would not disappear. However, it would eventually slow its expansion, come to a halt, begin to contract and return to its original tiny size and enormous temperature, and then, in a "Big Crunch," disappear into the nothingness from which it came.

Of course, somewhere in the infinite sea of Nothingness (which somehow reminds one of the infinite sea of Chaos that the Greeks imagined as a starting point) there may be an infinite number of Universes of all sizes beginning and ending—some having done so unimaginably long before our own, and some that will do so unimaginably long after our own.

It does not seem likely, however, that we'll ever know of any other Universes. We may be doomed to know only our own, and we have now traced it back to what may well be its absolute beginning some 15,000 million years ago, together with a forecast of what may well be an absolute ending at some undetermined time in the future.

From *Beginnings* (1987).

the same contribution to the perception of a rational universe. What could be more different than the two theories of the sun we noticed above: Anaximander's, that the sun is a huge annular body filled with fire, revolving around the earth throughout the years, all of it totally invisible except for a small part of it, an orifice from which fire keeps streaming out—and Heraclitus', that the sun is a bowl-shaped container, containing fire "maintained by moist exhalations or evaporations from the sea, which are somehow collected in [it] and burned as fuel."[25]

And there were other theories too, as different from the one as from the other—Anaximenes' sun, for example, a disk of fire, "flat as a leaf," floating on air, as durable as Anaximander's, but no larger than was the aperture in the latter's fire-ring. Anaximander's sun impresses us by its imaginative grandeur; the suns of Anaximenes and Heraclitus depress us by their crudeness and naïveté. But the fact is that while in none of the three cases do we have anything we can begin to call a *scientific* explanation of the sun, all three provide an explanation that would be *rational* in a comfortably pragmatic sense (any one of the three would have sufficed to put out of business soothsayer specialists on eclipses) and also in a more reflective sense (highest-level natural uniformities would be secure in all three; the fire in each would be as certain to behave according to its *physis* as would the fire in your hearth).

In the second operation the spectrum of variations is even wider. Although I have mentioned most of the major ones, I cannot bring this [paper] to a close without alluding to two more which are particularly significant for Heraclitus' place within that spectrum. On one hand, there is the question of whether or not the orderliness of the physical universe should be described in moral terms. In the earlier phase of *physiologia* we see strong answers in the affirmative. So, for example, in Anaximander (fragment B1), who sees in cycles of natural changes "injustice" followed invariably by reparation.[26] So too in Heraclitus to whose faith that "strife is justice" I referred above. But two generations later, in the atomists, the universe is as severely nonmoral as the human imagination has ever made it. Leucippus and Democritus would no more think of reading justice into the cosmos than would Thucydides or Camus. On the other hand, there is the question of whether or not the *physiologoi* can find a home for deity within their cosmos. Some do and some do not. Heraclitus apparently does. He writes: "The One, the only wise, will and will not be named 'Zeus'" (B32). It will not, because it is the fire dispersed throughout the universe in measured kindlings and extinguishings. Yet it will, for this same fire is somehow also mind—"the thought which steers all things through all things" (B41)—and thus discharges in the universe, though on a vastly grander scale, the role of supreme ruler traditionally ascribed to Zeus. And there are others, like Anaxagoras and Diogenes of Apollonia, who postulate a mind that is ultimately responsible for the order which makes a cosmos of the world; the latter speaks quite explicitly of this cosmic intelligence as "god." At the other extreme, we have the rigorous materialism of the atomists, where order is inherent in matter, and an ordering cosmic mind is too incongruous a notion to be even worth arguing against.

What unites these men, in spite of these and other differences, is that for all of them nature remains the inviolate all-inclusive principle of explanation. In the Heraclitean cosmos a god-sent eclipse in the heavens is as unthinkable as in the Democritean. *Atē* is equally unthinkable in both. Heraclitus can say, "a man's fate is his character" (B119), with the same conviction as would Democritus. For the first time in history man has achieved a perception of a rational universe which leaves his own destiny to be determined solely by *physis*—his own and that of the world.

25. Kirk in G. S. Kirk and J. E. Raven, *The Presocratic Philosophers*, p. 203.

26. B1. For my interpretation of this much discussed fragment see my "Equality and Justice in Early Greek Cosmologies" in Furley and Allen, eds., *Studies in Presocratic Philosophy*, 1:73 ff.

PLATO'S COSMOS, I: THEORY OF CELESTIAL MOTIONS

In Book 10 of the *Laws* Plato drafts a statute against impiety which is without parallel in any surviving code of ancient Greece.[1] The mildest of its penalties is five years' solitary confinement, to be followed by execution if the prisoner is still unreformed. A man of irreproachable character would get this sentence if it were proved that he believed that there are no gods or that they do not care for men (888C). As one reads the philosophical preamble (885Bff.) it dawns on one that the Ionian discoverers of the cosmos, the *physiologoi,* are in Plato's eyes the main fomenters of the heresies from which his utopia must be purged. His punitive measures are directed first and foremost against men who hold that the original constituents of the universe are material entities like earth, air, water, and fire, which exist "by nature" and "by chance"—that is to say, things whose existence did not come about by design or, as Plato puts it, "by art": things which just happened to exist. And they teach that this cosmos of ours, with all of the "art" in it, is the chance outcome of the natural interactions of these soulless bodies.[2]

Some of our *physiologoi,* arraigned for impiety before the Court for Capital Offences in Plato's utopia, would have protested this account of their system: Heraclitus and Diogenes of Apollonia, for example, for, as I have pointed out, both of them endowed their universal substance with intelligence and even thought of it as a god. In other ways too we might fault the exact applicability of Plato's indictment to each of the systems of the *physiologoi.*[3] But if we see in Plato's diatribe against them not historical reportage, but a philosopher's diagnosis of the basic difference between his own world-view and theirs, what he says is profoundly true: it gets at the root of the matter. Regardless of many disagreements among themselves, the *physiologoi* are united in the assumption that the order which makes our world a cosmos is natural, that is to say, that it is immanent in nature; all of them would account for this order by the natures of the components of the universe without appeal to anything else, hence without appeal to a transcendent ordering intelligence. Plato is dead right on this point—obviously so in the case of the last and most mature product of Ionian *physiologia,* the atomistic system, where our own cosmos and infinitely many others are produced within the infinite universe by purely mechanical causes, when atoms colliding at random in the void happen to fall into a particular mechanical pattern, a vortex. Even those other systems where one of the constituents of the universe is made the producer of order and is endowed with the attributes of reason—as is fire in Heraclitus, air in Anaximenes and Diogenes—even they would bear out the Platonic diagnosis: for they too assume that order is inherent in nature and does not need to be imposed upon it by a supernatural ordering mind.[4] The differ-

1. See the comments by G. R. Morrow, *Plato's Cretan City,* pp. 488–89: "Plato becomes the first political thinker to propose that errors of opinion be made crimes punishable by law . . . with fateful consequences to Western history, for henceforth the punishment of errors of opinion could claim the sanction of one of the highest authorities."

2. The crucial passage, retranslated:
By nature and by chance, they say, fire and water and earth and air all exist—none of them exist by art—and the bodies which come next—the earth, the sun, the moon, and the stars—were generated by these totally soulless means: things moved by chance, each by its own power, as they happened to combine fittingly somehow with one another—the hot with the cold or the dry with the moist or the hard with the soft, and all those things which through the mingling of opposites chanced into forced intermixture. In such a way and by such means the whole of the heavens and everything pertaining to it has been generated, and moreover all animals and all plants, all of the seasons having been generated from these same things, not by intelligence, they say, not by a god, nor by art, but by what we are talking about: by nature and by chance. [889B1-C6]. . . .

3. Cf. my "Equality and Justice in Early Greek Cosmologies," pp. 176–77.

4. For Heraclitus and Diogenes see above. The real exception, of course, is Anaxagoras. He starts off the cosmogonic vortex with an extramundane "Mind" which exists apart (B12) from matter in its primordial, undifferentiated, state, yet somehow manages to get the vortical motion started (B13) and even to "dominate" it (B12) thereafter. Plato knows all about this effort by a *physiologos* to make Mind the ordering agency of nature. But he indicts the effort as abortive (*Phaedo* 97C–99C): in spite of that attempt, Anaxagoras' cosmogony remains for all practical purposes mechanistic, explaining the main features of the universe by material causes, without reference to the purposes Mind was bent on realizing in and through these mindless things.

A Greek temple in Segesta, Sicily. Where there are now only pastoral hills, there was once a thriving city (c. 430 B.C.).

ence on this point Plato considers so irreconcilable with his own view and so momentous in its moral and political implications as to justify the removal from the body politic of anyone who holds it. What does he offer in return? A theological cosmogony.

What Heraclitus had denied when he wrote, "this world, the same for all, no man or god has made," Plato makes the first principle of cosmology in the *Timaeus*. He undertakes to depict the origin of the cosmos as the work of a god who takes over matter in a chaotic state and moulds it in the likeness of an ideal model, the Platonic Idea of Living Creature (30Cff.). That this god is supernatural in the literal sense of the term is plain enough: he stands outside of nature and above it; he is not himself a member of the system of interacting entities which constitutes nature; he acts upon that system, but the system does not act on him. But how far would Plato go in assimilating this god to the supernaturals of popular belief? Would this divine world-creator have the power to violate the regularities of nature? The answer is not clear. What *is* clear is that, if he does have such power, he will never choose to exercise it. This follows, I think, from the conception of his character in the *Timaeus*.

It would be hard to think of two more sharply divergent ideas of the supreme deity than Plato's and the traditionalists'—this in spite of the fact that intelligence is a dominant attribute in each case. Zeus had always been thought brainier than the other gods, with the possible exception of Athena who, after all, had been his brain-child. But the Olympian's wisdom had been that of a deep-scheming, far-sighted, monarch, while the high god of the *Timaeus* is not so much a governor as a philosopher, a mathematician, an engineer, and, above all, an artist. That he is Reason personified is taken for granted; Plato alludes to this from time to time, but feels no need to say so formally. He does not call his deity "Nous" or "Logos," but "Demiourgos"—literally, "Craftsman." The name is surprising. In Plato's Athens the craftsman is often a slave and as often a free-man working shoulder to shoulder with slaves in the same kind of work. So the scorn which the leisure classes feel for the slave tends to rub off on the craftsman too: he becomes the victim of stigma by association, and in all but the most advanced forms of democracy his civic status is precarious. Plato denies him political participation in the *Republic* and robs him even of citizenship in the *Laws*. So does Aristotle in his "polity" which is meant to be a very moderate constitution, a "mixed" one, a compromise between aristocracy and democracy. That the supreme god of Plato's cosmos should wear the mask of a manual worker is a triumph of the philosophical imagination over ingrained social prejudice.

To be sure the images of "king" and "father" are also invoked; but they are marginal—traditional hang-overs that do not dictate the working imagery of the dialogue. Neither the sexual nor the domestic associations of paternity are followed out in the creation story, nor yet the political ones of kingship, but only those prompted by the Craftsman metaphor. It is phrases like "contriving," "moulding," "measuring out," "pouring into a mixing-bowl," "cutting up," and "splicing together" that carry the bulk of the narrative. But this divine mechanic is not a drudge. He is an artist or, more precisely, what an artist would have to be in Plato's conception of art: not the inventor of new form, but the imposer of pre-existing form on as yet formless material. The Demiurge chooses the Idea of Living Creature for this purpose because he has the artist's longing to create a thing of beauty, and that model is the most beautiful he can find; and, further, because, says Plato, "he was good and in the good there can be no envy at any time about anything" (29E).

Here is another striking deviation from established patterns. The envy of the gods had been one of the deepest convictions in Greek theology, and one of the most persistent: it is more in evidence in Herodotus and Euripides than in Homer.[5] Greek gods are so defensive of their privileged status *vis à vis* men that they grudge humanity any benefit, however innocent in itself, that would narrow the gap between the splendor of their own existence and the wretchedness of the human estate. To exalt themselves they abase men. That is why they punish Prometheus so savagely. His motive, *philanthropia,*[6] does not extenuate his crime in bringing man the gift of fire, but rather aggravates it. The Olympians can no more forgive this "man-loving" god than an aristocratic white caste could forgive one of its members who turns into a "nigger-lover." That is why Plutus, the god of wealth, is blinded by Zeus in Aristophanes' comedy.[7] While he could see, he brought prosperity only to good and wise men. Zeus blinded me, says Plutus, because he was "envious of mankind": Zeus could not tolerate the improvement of the human lot that would ensue if Plutus were allowed the ability to insure that wealth will always match virtue in man's life.

Unlike the cruel tyrant of the *Prometheus Vinctus* and the *Plutus,* Plato's Craftsman is driven by the desire to share his excellence with

5. For Herodotus and Euripides see, e.g., S. Ranulf, *The Jealousy of the Gods and Criminal Law at Athens,* chap. 5. For brief and penetrating comment see Dodds, *The Greeks and the Irrational,* pp. 30–31.

6. That this is what he is being punished for is stressed from the start of the *Prometheus Vinctus* of Aeschylus: his theft of the fire he brought to mortals is "the sin for which he must pay just penalty to the gods that he may learn to welcome the tyranny of Zeus and cease his man-loving disposition" (vv. 9–11).

7. *Plutus,* vv. 86ff. Dodds points out that in writers like Aeschylus and Herodotus "divine *phthonos* [envy] is sometimes though not always, moralized as nemesis, 'righteous indignation'" (*The Greeks and the Irrational,* p. 31 and notes). Lloyd-Jones goes further; he holds that for these and other fifth-century writers divine *phthonos* "actually formed part of justice" (*The Justice of Zeus,* pp. 69–70). I cannot follow him on this point. . . .

others; the more beauty and goodness outside of him, the better his unenvious nature is pleased. This is the noblest image of the deity ever projected in classical antiquity and it opens the way to a radically new idea of piety for the intellectual which the traditionalists would have thought impious: that of striving for similitude to God (ὁμοίωσις θεῷ). If I were in a position here to trace out the implications of this idea, I think I could show how inspiring it is and yet disquieting, for it connects with the ominous notion of the philosopher king in the *Republic.* But here my concern is not with Plato's contribution to religion and morality, but to cosmology. So let me proceed to that.

The accomplishments of the Demiurge fall into two categories:

The accomplishments of the Demiurge fall into two categories:

I. Triumphs of Pure Teleology (Part I of the Creation Story, 29E–47D).
II. Compromises of Teleology with Necessity (Part II, from 47E to the end).

Category I comprises two classes of propositions: those which admit of teleological *derivation,* on one hand, those which admit of teleological *explanation,* on the other. To begin with the first, here Plato startles us, claiming to discover facts about our universe by deducing their existence from the postulates of his cosmology, that is, from the hypothesis that the universe is produced by a god whose benevolence and love of beauty prompt him to create a physical likeness of the Ideal Form of Living Creature. Here are some of these supposed facts:

1. The cosmos must have a soul. Why so? Because the Ideal Form of Living Creature has a soul (30B).
2. The cosmos must be unique. Why so? Because the Ideal model is unique, and the world would be more like that model if it too were unique (31A–B).[8]
3. The cosmos must be spherical. Why so? Because the sphere is the most homogeneous (ὁμοιότατον) shape there is, and the homogeneous, says Plato, is "ten thousand times more beautiful" (33B7) than the heterogeneous.
4. The cosmos must be characterized by time. Why so? Because time, as Plato thinks of it, is "a moving image of eternity" (37D5); it brings a dimension of ordered constancy to the inconstancy of flux, and thus makes the changing image more like the unchanging model than it would otherwise be.

I am not disposed to linger on this part of the creation story. But a historian would be derelict in his duty if he failed to acknowledge the retrograde turn which Plato gives to cosmological inquiry when he converts so blatantly preconceptions of value into allegations of fact. To be sure, he was not the first to do this, Pythagoras had done so openly long before.[9] Even the *physiologoi* were not completely immune to that tendency: Anaximander and Heraclitus . . . had projected into the physical cosmos their faith in justice. But there is a vast difference between their practice and Plato's. Suppose we could have asked the *physiologoi*—any of them, from Anaximander down—the following question: 'In your inquiries into nature, when you have to decide whether or not something is thus and so, would you think it right to settle the issue by arguing, "It would be better, more beautiful, if things were thus and so; *ergo,* they are thus and so?"'[10] There can be little doubt, I think, that we would have got an emphatic, 'No,' from each. Certainly that is how Plato thinks of them: he denounces them in the *Phaedo* (97Cff.) for failing to invoke the principle of the good in their natural inquiries; he reproaches them for deciding such a question as whether the earth is flat or round without first asking which of the two would be the "better" (97E). It would have gone against

8. For a curious error in Plato's reasoning see D. Keyt, "The Mad Craftsman of the *Timaeus,*" pp. 230–35.

9. On this feature of his system all scholars would agree in spite of their disagreement over his other doctrines.

10. I put first-instance imaginary quotations in single quotes, reserving first-instance double quotes for quotations from cited sources.

the grain of Ionian *physiologia* to concede such a principle; and in its final, atomistic, chapter the principle is ejected root and branch. When Leucippus declares, "Nothing happens at random, but everything from reason and necessity" (B2), the "reason" to which he refers is the reason *of* necessity—the reasoning of mechanistic explanation which excludes rigorously and systematically considerations of value from the determination of matter of fact. This is, in good part, why the atomistic system proved so congenial to the founders of modern science in the seventeenth century—why they welcomed it as a haven from the Aristotelian system which had consolidated the teleological methodology championed by Plato.

But there is more to this part of the *Timaeus.* Plato fortunately does not stay stuck in this shady area where one gets one's facts by deducing them from theological and metaphysical premises. He soon comes within sight of *facts derived from a scientific discipline,* and then, with those facts in hand, invokes the teleological framework of his creation story to structure them in a coherent scheme. Let us look at this scheme. In some ways it is more fantastic than anything we have seen so far. But let us not prejudge it until we have seen what is the work which it will do for Plato.

Since a soul must be provided for the cosmos, the Demiurge proceeds to its creation. Plato now implements one of his long-standing tenets, namely, that soul straddles the two disparate realms of his ontology—that of the abstract Forms, on one hand, which constitute the world of eternal Being, and that of sensible things, on the other, which constitute the ever-changing world of Becoming. Soul has a leg in each of these.In rational thought, whose objects are pure Forms, it has contact with the world of Being. In sense-perception, whose objects are changing things, it has contact with the world of Becoming. Plato, therefore, pictures the creation of soul as a blending of Being and Becoming.[11]

11. I take this to be the main point of the complicated psychogony at 35Aff.

Mixing these up in his mixing-bowl, the Demiurge produces a new kind of stuff—or, should I say, super-stuff?— which contains no physical matter (no fire, air, water, earth) and has none of the properties of physical matter (such as temperature, density, weight) except one: it can move. But even in its capacity for motion it differs radically from physical matter. For Plato the latter is inert—any part of it moves only when it is moved by something other than itself; soul, and only soul, can move itself:[12] by thinking and willing it can move the body to which it is attached and, through this, other bodies. So in creating soul the Demiurge does something which will have vast physical consequences: the self-caused movement of the World Soul and of the souls of the stars will account for every movement in the heavens: all celestial motion is to be explained as psychokinesis.

The Demiurge creates the World Soul by cutting up into strips the soul-stuff he has produced, and joining the ends to make "circles," that is, mobile circular bands. Why circular? Because of another Platonic doctrine: that rotary motion is the one "most appropriate for reason and intelligence" (34A); only thus, Plato thinks, can the absolute invariance of the eternal Forms be approximated within the ceaseless variance which is inherent in motion. The first of the soul-circles the Demiurge puts at the circumference of the cosmos to produce "the movement of the Same," a movement which Plato thinks runs through the whole universe: everything in the cosmos, from its extreme periphery down to the center of our earth, is subject to this motion,[13] though this is counteracted by other motions everywhere[14] except in the region of the fixed stars. In their case we can see it pure and

12. Self-motion is said to be "the essence and definition" of soul in *Phaedrus* 245C–E; soul is "the thing that is self-moved" in *Timaeus* 37B5.

13. He speaks of the movement of the Same as "everywhere inwoven from the center to the outermost heaven and enveloping the heaven all around on the outside" (36E2–3, Cornford's translation).

14. It follows that it has to be counteracted in the earth, for otherwise the earth would share the diurnal motion of the fixed stars, and this would cancel out their motion relative to the earth. . . .

unimpeded: it is the diurnal revolution from east to west parallel to the plane of the celestial equator[15]—the World Soul's self-caused "movement of the Same," communicated to each of the fixed stars, so that it becomes *their* motion in turn.[16]

But Plato must also account for another set of celestial motions: those peculiar to the "wandering" stars, the moon, the sun, and the five planets.[17] Each of these exhibits a long-term motion of its own from which the fixed stars are totally exempt. For if the successive positions of any member of the septet are plotted against those of the fixed stars over extended periods of time, they will be found to keep shifting eastward, so that eventually they will have made a complete circuit of the sky. These slow eastward orbits differ conspicuously from the diurnal westward revolution which predominates in the sky. Three of the differences are specially noteworthy:

In the first place, all of their periods are much longer, with wide variations in length among them. The moon takes a lunar month to return to her original position; the sun a solar year and Venus and Mercury the same (on the average); Mars 1 year plus 322 days; Jupiter 11 years plus 315 days; Saturn 29 years plus 166 days.

In the second place, these orbits proceed in different planes from those of the fixed stars. Instead of running parallel to the plane of the celestial equator, all of the eastward orbits of the septet move in planes which intersect the latter obliquely. Thus the sun moves in the plane of the ecliptic which intersects the plane of the celestial equator at an angle of 23.5°.[18] The moon and the five planets move in varying degrees of proximity to the ecliptic, their orbits falling almost entirely within "the Zodiac circle"—a narrow band of fixed stars on either side of the ecliptic, conveniently figured in a sequence of twelve distinctive constellations.

In the third place, all of these orbits exhibit the phenomenon which is so marked in the seasonal behavior of the sun: all of them have "turnings" (τροπαί), points of maximum deviation north and south at which they turn back and proceed in the reverse direction until the opposite point of "turning" has been reached.[19]

To account for all these features of "wandering" motion Plato postulates another "circle" in the World Soul which he calls "the movement of the Different"[20] and describes it as "slanting" (πλαγίαν 39A) in an inverse direction, "toward the left by the way of the diagonal," while the motion of the Same is "toward the right by way of the side."[21] This second circle is broken up into seven circles of unequal length with appropriately different angular velocities which are distributed to the moon, the sun, and the five planets to become their individual, characteristic, motions, and account for the eastward movement of each in, or close to, the plane of the ecliptic.

Thus before coming around to the creation of humanity the Demiurge has brought into the world a huge population of "everlasting gods" (37B6): the World Soul; the countless multitude

15. Speaking, as always in this chapter, from the geocentric viewpoint of ancient astronomy.

16. This is their "forward" motion; as each is "mastered by the revolution of the Same and uniform" (40B). They have an additional motion which is all their own: axial rotation ("uniform motion in the same place," 40B).

17. A terminological point: my use of the term "planet" will follow Plato's. In the only two passages in which he refers to the term πλανητόν as a name for celestial bodies—38C5–6, ἐπίκλην ἔχοντα "πλανητά," and *Laws* 821B9, ἐπονομάζοντες "πλανητὰ" αὐτά—he is clearly restricting it to the five planets of Greek astronomy. . . .

18. Reckoned at 24° (the angle subtended at the center of a circle by the side of a regular fifteen-sided polygon) in the fourth century B.C. . . .

19. At least as far back as Hesiod (*Works and Days,* vv. 479, 564, 663), probably even in Homer (*Odyssey,* bk. 15, v. 404), "turnings of the sun" (τροπαὶ ἠελίου) is the common label for the summer and winter solstices. When the planets are discovered, the term is naturally extended to them, since they too exhibit similar "turnings."

20. Plato's term, θατερον, could also be translated "the Other," and is often so rendered in the literature. . . .

21. "By way of the diagonal" (κατὰ διαμετρον *vs.* κατὰ πλευράν, 36C). Plato has in view a geometrical diagram: a rectangle inscribed in a circle, whose upper side represents the summer tropic, its base the winter tropic, and the diagonal the ecliptic. . . .

of fixed stars,[22] whose visible motion[23] is exclusively the movement of the Same; and the sun, the moon, and the five planets, whose visible motions exhibit also diversifications of the movement of the Different. Because of the invariant periodicity of their motions the stars provide visible measures of time: they are celestrial chronometers.[24] Here the sun's contribution is outstanding: the spectacular alternations of light and darkness caused by his rising and setting (μέτρον ἐναργές) of all the heavenly motions. But the moon's eastward circuit of the heavens also affords us with a serviceable temporal yardstick, the lunar month.[25] So does the annual circuit of the sun. The periods of the five planets too, if they had been determined, would have provided further units of time reckoning. And while the like contribution of the fixed stars is not mentioned, it is acknowledged by implication when Plato speaks of all the stars—not just the "wandering" septet—as "instruments of time,"[26] and again when he says that "time and the heavens were generated together" (38B6), for the fixed stars make up the overwhelming majority of the constituents of the heavens.[27]

Where in all this, the reader may wonder, is the coherent scheme organizing scientifically ascertained facts that I promised a few pages back? I shall come to this, but not before attending to two preliminary tasks: (A) I must make clear what I understand by "scientifically ascertained facts"; (B) I must establish that facts of this sort were now available in Greek astronomy and that Plato himself was taking full advantage of their availability. Task A can be quickly disposed of. By "scientifically ascertained facts" I understand facts satisfying three basic requirements:

1. They are established by observation or by inference from it: they are derived, directly or indirectly, by the use of the senses.
2. They have theoretical significance: they provide answers to questions posed by theory.
3. They are shareable and corrigible: they are the common property of qualified investigators who are aware of possible sources of observational error and are in a position to repeat or vary the observation to eliminate or reduce suspected error.

Task B will take longer. What I would like to do here is to give the reader some sense of the progress which Greek astronomy had already made as an observational science and show that Plato was well abreast of this progress by the time he came to write the *Timaeus*. To document this progress in any detail is not possible. The record is too fragmentary, and often vague and unreliable as well. But even so, meager though it is, the record yields matter enough to document essential points.

We happen to know that in the thirties of the fifth century B.C.—two thirds of a century or so before the writing of the *Timaeus*—two Athenian astronomers, Euctemon and Meton,[28]

22. The fact that their creation is mentioned only at 40A–B, after the creation of sun, moon, and five planets (38C–39D), is an accident of the exposition; it has no chronological import, since chronology starts with the creation of the heavens ("time and the heavens were generated together," 38B6), and "the heavens" *is* the fixed stars along with the "wandering" septet.

23. I.e., their translatory "forward" (40B1) motion. They have another motion as well—axial rotation—invisible to us (40A7–B1), as must all the celestial bodies, including the ones that "wander": . . .

24. "Instruments of time": ὄργανα χρόνων, 41E5; ὄργανα χρόνου, 42D.

25. I.e., the lunar synodic month: the interval from new moon to new moon, in which "the moon traverses its own circuit and overtakes the sun" (39C3–4).

26. See n. 24 above for the references. There can be no doubt here that all the stars are meant: souls "equal in number" (ἰσαρίθμους) to the stars have been created, and each soul gets one star for its habitation.

27. As Plato uses the term in the *Timaeus*, "the heavens" (οὐρανός) is nothing but the stars which make it up.

28. Otherwise known for their contributions to the reform of the calendar (for references see Heath, *Aristarchus of Samos*, p. 293). Meton was the author of a "Great Year" of nineteen years, named after him, which aligned the lunar month with the solar year by intercalating seven months in the course of the nineteen-year period and by using months varying in length between twenty-nine and thirty days. "This would give a mean lunar month less than two minutes too long" (Dicks, *Early Greek Astronomy*, p. 88). A similar intercalation cycle (seven intercalations in nineteen years) comes also into use in Babylonia during the fifth century (O. Neugebauer, *The Exact Sciences in Antiquity*, p. 97), but there is no evidence that Meton derived his own cycle thence. According to Theophrastus (*de Sign.* 4) he derived it from a certain Phaenus, an astronomer who was a resident alien in Athens.

A view from Micenae, the palace of Agamemnon, to the bay where the Greek fleet assembled before sailing to Troy.

had made observations[29] which disclosed the inequality of the astronomical seasons. Their figures were as follows:

From summer solstice to autumnal equinox, 90 days.

From autumnal equinox to winter solstice, 90 days.

From winter solstice to vernal equinox, 92 days.

From vernal equinox to summer solstice, 93 days.[30]

What is remarkable about these findings is not their accuracy. As Heath (*Aristarchus of Samos,* pp. 215–16) points out, compared with modern figures they show errors ranging from 1.23 to 2.01 days, while the error in the corresponding figures reached a century later by Callippus (92, 89, 90, 91 days, respectively)[31] ranges only from 0.08 to 0.44 days. The truly memorable thing here is that Euctemon and Meton were prepared to allow observation to supersede the assumptions that the two intersolstitial intervals are strictly equal and that both equinoxes fall at their exact midpoints—assumptions so very plausible in themselves and so seductive in their own time and place, given the Greek obsession with symmetry. Banking on these assumptions, Euctemon and Meton might have spared themselves the trouble of reaching by observation figures for equinoxes and winter solstices: they might have got these by simply counting days between successive summer solstices and dividing by four—which is what Babylonian astronomers were doing down to the end of the fourth century B.C.[32] That they chose instead the harder,

29. By rare good luck we have an exact date for one of these: Ptolemy, writing half a millennium later, refers to their observation of a summer solstice in 432 B.C. (*Syntaxis Mathematica* ["The Almagest"] 3.1 [Claudii Ptolemaei *Opera Omnia,* J. L. Heiberg, ed., vol. 1, part 1, p. 205]).

30. These figures are preserved in the papyrus entitled "Ars Eudoxi," Column 23 (F. Blass, ed., Eudoxi *Ars Astronomica,* p. 25). . . .

31. Also preserved in the papyrus cited in the preceding note.

32. Neugebauer (*The Exact Sciences in Antiquity,* p. 102), describing Babylonian practice: "It is the summer solstices which are systematically computed, whereas the equinoxes and the winter solstices are simply placed at equal intervals."

observational way, and that they stuck by its results when it turned up inequalities in lieu of the expected equalities, is striking testimony to the observational orientation to which practicing Greek astronomers were now committed.

And what is involved here is not simple, but theory-charged, observation which, as Dicks has claimed, "presupposes, at the very least, the theory of a spherical earth at the center of the celestial sphere" (*Early Greek Astronomy,* p. 88).[33] The argument for this claim need not be premised on the assumption that Euctemon's observational procedures were the same as those in use in subsequent, more highly developed, stages of Greek astronomy.[34] This assumption would be hard to justify in the face of the much higher accuracy in Callippus' figures, which suggests drastic improvements in observational methods in the course of the next hundred years. The substance of Dicks's claim can be supported by arguments which bypass this risky assumption: Euctemon's and Meton's acceptance of the sphericity of the earth may be inferred with a measure of probability from their peregrinations north and south in carrying out their observations:[35] they are not likely to have done this if they had been unable to handle latitude;[36] and the concept of latitude certainly presupposes a spherical earth.[37] Moreover, there can be little doubt that the obliquity of the ecliptic was known to their contemporary, Oenopides.[38] It therefore would not be unreasonable to assume that they too had assimilated this discovery[39] and its implied conceptual machinery: the heavenly sphere with its equator as a great circle at right angles to its north-south axis; the tropics as two circles on the sphere, parallel to the equator and equidistant from it; and the ecliptic as another great circle on the sphere, intersecting the equator at a sharp angle and touching the tropics at its northern and southern extremities.

Even if we had missed this information about Euctemon and Meton, we could still have inferred with confidence that well before Plato's time—by the last third of the fifth century at the latest—the role of observation had changed drastically in Greek astronomy since the days when rational inquiry into the heavens had begun in Miletus as a branch of *physiologia.* We could have inferred this directly from the intervening changes in the reported content of astronomical doctrine. To mark the contrast let me refer again to that grandiose model of the cosmos to which I alluded in the preceding chapter: Anaximander's. Here the sun, it will be recalled, is an enormous ring or hoop of fire at the periphery of our world, invisible save for an orifice from which the fire escapes; the moon is another fire-ring, similar in design, but smaller, its diameter two thirds that of the sun; this is followed in turn, after another interval of vacancy, by the countless multitude of star-rings whose visible orifices are tiny and whose diameters are half that of the moon, a third that

33. A very substantial claim, for the question whether the earth is flat or spherical remains in dispute among philosophical astronomers down to the end of the fifth century and even beyond. . . .

34. In "Solstices, Equinoxes, and the Presocratics" (p. 32) Dicks had listed a complex set of theoretical assumptions (including the celestial and terrestrial spheres), claiming that these were presupposed in the earliest equinoctial calculations by Greek astronomers, buttressing up the claim with the remark that this "is clear from the methods used by Hipparchus and Ptolemy."

35. See n. 30 above.

36. Their meteorological observations are dated by risings and settings of fixed stars which would be affected by variations of latitude.

37. A powerful argument for the sphericity of the earth in Aristotle is the observed variation of celestial phenomena that results from changes in the observer's latitude: "Certain stars visible in Egypt and in Cyprus are not visible in northern locations, and some stars which never set in northern areas do set in the aforenamed places" (*de Caelo* 298A3–6). This is a standard argument in later authors; see, e.g., Theo Smyrnaeus, pp. 191–92.

38. From the testimonia in DK 41A7 we learn the following: Oenipides claimed "as his own invention" the discovery of the ecliptic (Aetius, *de Placitis Reliquiae* [hereafter to be cited by author's name only]). . . .

39. Proclus (p. 66) speaks of Oenipides as "a little younger" than Anaxagoras (who was born around 500 B.C.). If he were, say, fifteen years younger, it would be reasonable to place his astronomical discoveries in the forties of the fifth century (or, at any rate, not much later), hence likely to be known in Athens by the time Euctemon and Meton were making their observations (cf. n. 33 above). . . .

of the sun.[40] A mere glance at this construct will show that it is a work of imagination whose departure from the inherited world-view could not have been justified by a single scientifically ascertained fact meeting the conditions [I have previously noted]. Anaximander is said by a late author to have discovered the gnomon—that simple, but enormously useful, instrument consisting of a rod fixed upright on a flat base on which seasonal variations in the length of the sun's shadow may be measured.[41] The veracity of the report is dubious.[42] But suppose it were conceded: suppose Anaximander did have a gnomon and used it to his heart's content. Nothing he could have learned with its help could have

40. For the textual data on which this account is based see, e.g., Kirk in Kirk and Raven, *The Presocratic Philosophers,* pp. 135–37: the main doxographical texts, with translation and commentary; fuller treatment in Kahn, *Anaximander,* pp. 58–63. The picture is conjectural to a degree, the figures for the stars wholly so, being due to Paul Tannery's ingenious inferences (*Pour l'Histoire de la Science Hellène,* pp. 90ff.), and their soundness has been vigorously disputed . . . but they have been accepted by the overwhelming majority of historians.

41. Diogenes Laertius, *Vitae Philosophorum* (hereafter to be cited by author's name only) 2.2 (in DK 12A1): "He was the first to discover the gnomon and he set it up at the Skiathera in Sparta, as is stated by Favorinus in his *Universal History.*" And Herodotus states that "the Greeks" learned "the *polos* and the gnomon and the twelve parts of the day from the Babylonians" (2.109.3). Later testimonia simply repeat or conflict these two reports. . . .

42. Taken as a whole it would be rendered suspect by its tale that Anaximander set up his gnomon in Sparta, of all places (notoriously unfriendly to philosophical and scientific imports) and its representation as equipped to indicate "solstices and equinoxes" (unlikely at this earliest phase of Greek astronomy: Dicks, "Solstices, Equinoxes," pp. 29–30), even if Favorinus had a more consistent record of historical credibility. However, when all the objections to his testimony have been given full weight, we cannot be sure that there is no fire behind his smoke. For all we know to the contrary, Anaximander may have made use of some simple form of the gnomon.

"The First Hundredth of a Second"

Steven Weinberg

In the beginning there was an explosion. Not an explosion like those familiar on earth, starting from a definite center and spreading out to engulf more and more of the circumambient air, but an explosion which occurred simultaneously everywhere, filling all space from the beginning, with every particle of matter rushing apart from every other particle. "All space" in this context may mean either all of an infinite universe, or all of a finite universe which curves back on itself like the surface of a sphere. Neither possibility is easy to comprehend, but this will not get in our way; it matters hardly at all in the early universe whether space is finite or infinite.

At about one-hundredth of a second, the earliest time about which we can speak with any confidence, the temperature of the universe was about a hundred thousand million (10^{11}) degrees Centigrade. This is much hotter than in the center of even the hottest star, so hot, in fact, that none of the components of ordinary matter, molecules, or atoms, or even the nuclei of atoms, could have held together. Instead, the matter rushing apart in this explosion consisted of various types of the so-called elementary particles. . . .

In addition to electrons and positrons, there were roughly similar numbers of various kinds of neutrinos, ghostly particles with no mass or electric charge whatever. Finally, the universe was filled with light. . . .

These particles—electrons, positrons, neutrinos, photons—were continually being created out of pure energy, and then after short lives being annihilated again. Their number therefore was not preordained, but fixed instead by a balance between processes of creation and annihilation.

From *The First Three Minutes: A Modern View of the Origin of the Universe* (1976).

yielded the slightest observational support for the sun-moon-stars-earth order in his model.[43] Conversely, had he troubled to observe the starlit sky over extended periods of time he would have been virtually certain to pick up facts irreconcilable with that order, for example, facts of celestial occultation.[44] These are the very ones to which Aristotle refers as observational evidence for the moon's being nearer the earth than are the planets or fixed stars:

> For we have seen the moon at the half-full approaching on its own darkened side the star of Mars which is thereupon screened from our view to reappear on the moon's bright and shiny side. About the other stars too similar accounts have been given by Egyptians and Babylonians who had observed them for very many years in the past and from whom we have received many trustworthy reports about each.[45]

Aristotle's mention of "the star of Mars" and his allusion to similar records about other planets points up another feature of Anaximander's astronomical theory symptomatic of the scarcity of scientifically ascertained data available to its author: its world-model makes no special place for planets in contradistinction to the fixed stars.[46] It is doubtful that it even took explicit notice of the existence of any celestial body which would have answered to what the Greeks understood by "planet"—stars (other than the sun and moon) distinguished from the fixed stars by their apparently erratic ("wandering" or "roaming") motion. From our (admittedly meager) sources we cannot even be sure that any star had been identified in Greece as a planet before Parmenides (first third of the fifth century B.C.). Though Venus was known and observed in Babylonia even before 1,500 B.C.,[47] there is no sign of it in Homer or Hesiod—no indication in those poems that "Dawnbringer" (Ἑωσφόρος) and "Evening Star" (Ἕσπερος) are named for the same star and that what each names is a "roamer."[48] As late as the fourth century B.C. there are parts of Greece where the identity is unknown: the Cretan interlocutor in Plato's *Laws* has no suspicion of it.[49]

The identification is assigned to Parmenides in a doxographic text of respectable authenticity.[50] "First in the aether Parmenides places the Dawnstar (τὸνυ Ἑῷιον) which he thinks identical with the Evening Star; following this, the sun, under which he puts the stars in the fiery region which he calls 'heaven'" (Aetius 2.15.7 [=DK 28A40a].[51] The text does not state that Parmenides thought of the Dawnstar as a "roamer." But the fact that he makes of it a

43. For the sort of reason Anaximander might have had for hitting on this perplexing order, see Kahn's ingenious surmise (*Anaximander,* p. 90): he might have been counting on "a general tendency for fire to collect more abundantly near the periphery of the heavens" (typical theorizing in the style of Ionian *physiologia*).

44. Cf. Dreyer's remark on Anaximander's placing the stars between the earth and the moon: "This shows at once how little the celestial phenomena had been watched, as the frequent occultation of a bright star by the moon must have been unkown to Anaximander" (*A History of Astronomy from Thales to Kepler,* p. 14).

45. *De Caelo* 292A3–9. The dating of the influx from Babylonia into Greece of extensive tables of observations of planetary motions has long been in dispute. . . .

46. Statements to the contrary in accounts of his astronomical theory in some histories of Greek philosophy and science are without foundation. . . .

47. A. Pannekoek, *A History of Astronomy,* pp. 33–35. All five planets are known and observed in the Assyrian period (eighth to seventh century B.C.): ibid., pp. 39–41, citing texts of the seventh century B.C.

48. Cf. F. Cumont "Les noms des planètes et l'astrolatrie chez les Grecs," *Antiquité Classique,* pp. 5–6; Dicks, *Early Greek Astronomy,* pp. 32–33. That the identification had been missed is certain. What is uncertain is whether or not either of these putatively separate stars is thought of as a planet in the epic. The answer turns on whether or not we are entitled to assume that the marked differences between the motion of each and that of the fixed stars had been noticed. . . .

49. 821C: "In my own lifetime I have often observed that both the Dawnbringer and the Evening Star and certain other stars never travel on the same course but wander about in every way; and that this is how the sun and the moon behave we all know." The grammar of the speaker's allusion to the first-named stars . . . gives away his lack of awareness of their identity.

50. In addition to this text see also Diogenes Laertius, 9.23 (in DK 28A1): "He is believed to have been the first to state that the Evening Star and the Lightbringer are the same." Diogenes' authority being Favorinus, the report may not be worth much (cf. n. 46 above); but it does at least show that neither Diogenes nor Favorinus knew of any ascription of the discovery to an earlier thinker.

51. The use of Ἑῷιος instead of the customary Ἑωσφόρος suggests that Aetius here is using a source which reproduces Parmenidean diction, which is also suggested by the terminal clause (probably an allusion to B10, 5). . . .

distinct "garland" (στεφάνη)[52] separated from the fixed stars by the "garland" of the sun,[53] suggests that he recognizes that its own pattern of motion is very different from theirs.[54] So we should probably reckon Parmenides the first Greek to identify one of the five planets of Greek astronomy.

Thereafter progress was rapid: the other four, and their approximately correct order,[55] were discovered within two generations of the identification of the first. This solid achievement of observational astronomy was won in spite of some continuing addiction to highly speculative hypotheses, projected with no apparent concern for observational controls. In that vein Anaxagoras and Democritus postulate the existence of an unspecified multitude of planets, claiming that the conjunction (σύμφασις) of such bodies is what accounts for the appearance of comets;[56] and Democritus' Pythagorean contemporary, Philolaus, turns the earth itself into a star revolving about an invisible fire at the center of the universe and interpolates another star, a mysterious "counter-earth," in between.[57] Yet side by side with these fanciful flights,[58] observationally grounded theory was advancing apace. The true quintet of planets is known to Philolaus[59] and possibly also to Democritus. In any case, it must have been well established by the time Plato came to write the *Republic* (probably late in the second decade of the fourth century),[60] for he builds it into the world-model of the myth of Er: there the earth is at the center of the cosmos, the fixed stars are at its periphery, and in between these two extremes come seven stars which could only be moon, sun, and five planets. The last are identified by color, not by name, but there can be no doubt as to which is which and that they are placed in the right order.[61]

I have taken the time to trace the discovery of the planets because a finding of this nature establishes conclusively the coming of age of Greek astronomy[62]—its transformation from the speculative exercise it had been throughout its origins in Milesian *physiologia* and for at least a generation thereafter[63] into a discipline where theory, continuing to be as boldly imaginative

---

52. As has long been recognized, these "garlands" or "bands" are a variation on Anaximander's conception of celestial bodies as great rings or hoops. . . .

53. In placing the fixed stars under the sun he appears to be following Anaximander, while breaking with him in giving the moon the lowest place in the heavens (Aetius 2.7.1 [= DK 28A37]), which would allow, as the Anaximandrian model would not, for occultations of stars by the moon.

54. Indeed he could scarcely have failed to recognize this in the course of making the observations and inferences which led him to discover the identity of the Morning and the Evening Star.

55. I.e., their correct order in radial distance of their orbits from the earth (which is Mercury—Venus—Mars—Jupiter—Saturn) except that Venus is thought to precede Mercury by most Greek astronomers (as by Plato in *Republic* 616E–617B and *Ti.* 38D) down to the second century B.C. (for the references see A. E. Taylor, *Commentary on Plato's "Timaeus,"* 192–94). The contrast with Babylonian astronomy is striking. It had got off to a much earlier start (cf. n. 52 above)—all five planets had been identified by the seventh century at the latest (i.e., at least two centuries before Parmenides)—but the discovery of their correct order was missed down to the end of the fourth century B.C.: "In the cuneiform texts of the Seleucid period the standard arrangement is

Jupiter—Venus—Mercury—Saturn—Mars.

The reason for this arrangement is unknown . . . " (Neugebauer, *The Exact Sciences,* pp. 168–69).

56. Aristotle, *Meteorologica* 342B27–29. . . .

57. In Aristotle these remarkable doctrines are ascribed to "those in Italy who are called "Pythagoreans" (*de Caelo* 293A20–25). In doxographic reports they are credited by name to Philolaus (Aetius 2.7.7 and 3.11.3 [= DK 44A16, 17]). . . .

58. Quite apart from the mysterious counter-earth, even the notion of the earth's orbiting around a central point of the planetary system could hardly have been supported by facts observed, or observable, at this time. . . .

59. Five planets are ascribed to him explicitly in the first of the doxographic reports cited in n. 57 above. . . .

60. Though much in Plato's biography is uncertain and controversial, there is fairly wide agreement among scholars that the *Republic* was composed at a date close to that of his first journey to Syracuse, which is known to have occurred when he was "nearly forty" (Epistle VII, 324A6), i.e., at, or just before, 387 B.C.

61. *Republic* 616B–617D. See Heath, *Aristarchus of Samos,* pp. 155–58.

62. More so than does the more sensational discovery of the cause of eclipses: this is a triumph of inventive inference rather than of observationally controlled theory. . . .

63. Dicks's remark (*Early Greek Astronomy,* p. 60) about the astronomical theories of "the earlier Presocratics," that "they are the dream children of the speculative thinker in his study intoxicated by the novelty and daring of the new intellectual atmosphere," would be entirely correct of the Milesians, Heraclitus, and Alcmaeon. . . .

as ever, had now entered into productive teamwork with observation, its hypotheses now being informed by a growing body of scientifically established data. To say that those five planets were discovered is *ipso facto* to refer to a multitude of observations brought into systematic unity by theory. It is to assert that at particular places in the sky at particular hours of the night in particular periods of the year shining objects of a certain order of brilliance had been seen and would be always there to be seen by anyone who cares to look; and that these five sets of visibilia represent as many stars, each set answering to the same star making appearances widely separated in time and space—as widely, for example, as would be those of Mercury in a given year, brightly visible as morning star during September and October, and then dropping out of sight to reappear once again months later as evening star in the western horizon. Even if we knew nothing more than that the existence of the five planets had been discovered by Plato's time, we would know that in the area of astronomy the Greeks had now succeeded where they had failed in every other major area of empirical investigation:[64] they had managed to break out of the style of free-wheeling speculation so characteristic of *physiologia* and to discover another mode of natural inquiry where theorizing was to be controlled by factual subject matter meeting the requirements of scientific observation I laid down above. . . .

64. Some distinguished historians of Greek philosophy and science have looked to medicine for the Greek paradigm of empirically oriented science. In my review of Cornford . . . I have tried to explain why this is a mistake. Certainly the subject-matter of the medical writers is only too plainly—and grossly—empirical. But their theoretical treatment of it suffers from the same flaw which afflicts the *physiologoi:* the conceptual design of their theories is not made with a view to confirmation or disconfirmation by empirical data.

"The End of Science"

Richard Feynman

What of the future of this adventure? What will happen ultimately? We are going along guessing the laws; how many laws are we going to have to guess? I do not know. Some of my colleagues say that this fundamental aspect of our science will go on; but I think there will certainly not be perpetual novelty, say for a thousand years. This thing cannot keep on going so that we are always going to discover more and more new laws. If we do, it will become boring that there are so many levels one underneath the other. It seems to me that what can happen in the future is either that all the laws become known—that is, if you had enough laws you could compute consequences and they would always agree with experiment, which would be the end of the line—or it may happen that the experiments get harder and harder to make, more and more expensive, so you get 99.9 per cent of the phenomena, but there is always some phenomenon which has just been discovered, which is very hard to measure, and which disagrees; and as soon as you have the explanation of that one there is always another one, and it gets slower and slower and more and more uninteresting. That is another way it may end. But I think it has to end in one way or another.

From *The Character of Physical Law.*

Candles burning against the glow of stained glass (Reims Cathedral in France.

Charles Darwin

"THE DESCENT OF MAN"

CHARLES DARWIN (1809–1882), British biologist, revolutionized our scientific, philosophical, and theological views of ourselves and the world as profoundly as had Copernicus. *The Origin of Species* (1859) and *The Descent of Man* (1871) argued that all living things on earth developed from basic, simple forms through evolution; they also presented to a disbelieving public the then-shocking theory of natural selection. Darwin began his studies with a firm belief in Genesis, convinced that

From *The Descent of Man and Selection in Relation to Sex.* First published in 1871.

each species was fixed as described in the story of original creation. But his observations of fossils and organism distribution across a wide part of the globe drove him to formulate his unorthodox new position. He did not rush into print, however, remaining deeply skeptical for a long time, as did most of the leading scientists of his day, many of whom found his argument "repugnant." Supported by radical intellectuals hostile to the Establishment, attacked by reactionaries and fundamentalists, Darwin avoided the debates provoked by his theses while his friend T. H. Huxley, the famous scientist and critic of religion, defended Darwin against the Bible thumpers. Having finally given up his Christian beliefs, Darwin expressed wonder at how any intelligent person could even wish them to be true.

Natural Selection

We have now seen that man is variable in body and mind; and that the variations are induced, either directly or indirectly, by the same general causes, and they obey the same general laws, as with the lower animals. Man has spread widely over the face of the earth, and must have been exposed, during his incessant migrations, to the most diversified conditions. The inhabitants of Tierra del Fuego, the Cape of Good Hope, and Tasmania in the one hemisphere, and of the Arctic regions in the other, must have passed through many climates, and changed their habits many times, before they reached their present homes. The early progenitors of man must also have tended, like all other animals, to have increased beyond their means of subsistence; they must, therefore, occasionally have been exposed to a struggle for existence, and consequently to the rigid law of natural selection. Beneficial variations of all kinds will thus, either occasionally or habitually, have been preserved and injurious ones eliminated. I do not refer to strongly marked deviations of structure, which occur only at long intervals of time, but to mere individual differences. We know, for instance, that the muscles of our hands and feet, which determine our powers of movement, are liable, like those of the lower animals, to incessant variability. If then the progenitors of man inhabiting any district, especially one undergoing some change in its conditions, were divided into two equal bodies, the one-half which included all the individuals best adapted by their powers of movement for gaining subsistence, or for defending themselves, would on an average survive in greater numbers, and procreate more offspring than the other and less well endowed half.

Man in the rudest state in which he now exists is the most dominant animal that has ever appeared on this earth. He has spread more widely than any other highly organized form: and all others have yielded before him. He manifestly owes this immense superiority to his intellectual faculties, to his social habits, which lead him to aid and defend his fellows, and to his corporeal structure. The supreme importance of these characters has been proved by the final arbitrament of the battle for life. Through his powers of intellect, articulate language has been evolved; and on this his wonderful advancement has mainly depended. As Mr. Chauncey Wright remarks: "a psychological analysis of the faculty of language shows, that even the smallest proficiency in it might require more brain power than the greatest proficiency in any other direction." He has invented and is able to use various weapons, tools, traps, etc., with which he defends himself, kills or catches prey, and otherwise obtains food. He has made rafts or canoes for fishing or crossing over to neighboring fertile islands. He has discovered the art of making fire, by which hard and stringy roots can be rendered digestible, and poisonous roots or herbs innocuous. This discovery of fire, probably the greatest ever made by man, excepting language, dates from before the dawn of history. These several inventions, by which man in the rudest state has become so pre-eminent, are the direct results of the development of his powers of observation, memory, curiosity, imagination, and reason. I cannot, therefore, understand how it is that Mr. Wallace maintains, that "natural selection could only have endowed the savage with a brain a little superior to that of an ape."

Although the intellectual powers and social habits of man are of paramount importance to him, we must not underrate the importance of his bodily structure. . . .

If it be an advantage to man to stand firmly on his feet and to have his hands and arms free, of which, from his pre-eminent success in the battle of life, there can be no doubt, then I can see no reason why it should not have been advantageous to the progenitors of man to have become more and more erect or bipedal. They would thus have been better able to defend themselves with stones or clubs, to attack their prey, or otherwise to obtain food. The best built individuals would in the long run have succeeded best and survived in larger numbers. If the gorilla and a few allied forms had become extinct, it might have been argued, with great force and apparent truth, that an animal could not have been gradually converted from a quadruped into a biped, as all the individuals in an intermediate condition would have been miserably ill-fitted for progression. But we know (and this is well worthy of reflection) that the anthropomorphous apes are now actually in an intermediate condition; and no one doubts that they are on the whole well adapted for their conditions of life. Thus the gorilla runs with a sidelong shambling gait, but more commonly progresses by resting on its bent hands. The long-armed apes occasionally use their arms like crutches, swinging their bodies forward between them, and some kinds of Hylobates, without having been taught, can walk or run upright with tolerable quickness, yet they move awkwardly and much less securely than man. We see, in short, in existing monkeys a manner of progression intermediate between that of a quadruped and a biped; but, as an unprejudiced judge insists, the anthropomorphous apes approach in structure more nearly to the bipedal than to the quadrupedal type.

As the progenitors of man became more and more erect, with their hands and arms more and more modified for prehension and other purposes, with their feet and legs at the same time transformed for firm support and progression, endless other changes of structure would have become necessary. The pelvis would have to be broadened, the spine peculiarly curved, and the head fixed in an altered position, all of which changes have been attained by man. . . .

The free use of the arms and hands, partly the cause and partly the result of man's erect position, appears to have led in an indirect manner to other modifications of structure. The early male forefathers of man were, as previously stated, probably furnished with great canine teeth; but as they gradually acquired the habit of using stones, clubs, or other weapons for fighting with their enemies or rivals they would use their jaws and teeth less and less. In this case the jaws, together with the teeth, would become reduced in size, as we may feel almost sure from innumerable analogous cases. . . . [W]e shall meet with a closely parallel case in the reduction or complete disappearance of the canine teeth in male ruminants, apparently in relation with the development of their horns; and in horses in relation to their habits of fighting with their incisor teeth and hoofs. . . .

Another most conspicuous difference between man and the lower animals is the nakedness of his skin. Whales and porpoises (Cetacea), dugongs (Sirenia) and the hippopotamus are naked; and this may be advantageous to them for gliding through the water; nor would it be injurious to them from the loss of warmth, as the species which inhabit the colder regions are protected by a thick layer of blubber, serving the same purposes as the fur of seals and otters. Elephants and rhinoceroses are almost hairless; and as certain extinct species, which formerly lived under an Arctic climate, were covered with long wool or hair, it would almost appear as if the existing species of both genera had lost their hairy covering from exposure to heat. This appears the more probable, as the elephants in India which live on elevated and cool districts are more hairy than those on the lowlands. May we then infer that man became divested of hair from having aboriginally inhabited some tropical land? That the hair is chiefly retained in the male sex on the chest and face, and in both sexes at the junction of all four limbs with the trunk, favors this inference—on the assumption that the hair was lost before man became erect; for the parts which now retain most hair would then have been most protected from the heat of the sun. The crown of the head, however, offers a curious exception, for at all times it must have been one of the most exposed parts, yet is thickly clothed with hair. The fact, however, that the other members of the order of Primates, to which man belongs, although inhabiting various hot regions, are well clothed with hair, generally thickest on the upper surface, is opposed to the supposition that man became naked through the action of the sun. Mr. Belt believes that within the tropics it is an advantage to man to be destitute of hair, as he is thus enabled to free himself of the multitude of ticks (acari) and other parasites, with which he is often infested, and which sometimes cause ulceration. But whether this evil is of sufficient magnitude to have led to the denudation of his body through natural selection, may be doubted, since none of the many quadrupeds inhabiting the tropics have, as far as I know, acquired any specialized means of relief. The view which seems to me the most probable is that man, or rather primarily woman, became divested of hair for ornamental purposes, . . . ; and, according to this belief, it is not surprising that man should differ so greatly in hairiness from all other Primates, for characters, gained through sexual selection, often differ to an extraordinary degree in closely related forms. . . .

I have now endeavored to show that some of the most distinctive characters of man have in all probability been acquired, either directly, or more commonly indirectly, through natural selection. We should bear in mind that modifications in structure or constitution which do not serve to adapt an organism to its habits of life, to the food which it consumes, or passively to the surrounding conditions, cannot have been thus acquired. We must not, however, be too confident in deciding what modifications are of service to each being; we should remember how little we know about the use of many parts, or what changes in the blood or tissues may serve to fit an organism for a new climate or new kinds of food. Nor must we forget the principle of correlation, by which, as Isidore Geoffroy has shown in the case of man, many strange deviations of structure are tied together. Independently of correlation, a change in one part often leads, through the increased or decreased use of other parts, to other changes of a quite unexpected nature. It is also well to reflect on such facts, as the wonderful growth of galls on plants caused by the poison of an insect, and on the remarkable changes of color in the plumage of parrots when fed on certain fishes, or inoculated with the poison of toads; for we can thus see that the fluids of the system, if altered for some special purpose, might induce other changes. We should especially bear in mind that modifications acquired and continually used during past ages for some useful purpose, would probably become firmly fixed, and might be long inherited. . . .

Conclusion

. . . [W]e have seen that as man at the present day is liable, like every other animal, to multiform individual differences or slight variations, so no doubt were the early progenitors of man; the variations being formerly induced by the same general causes, and governed by the same general and complex laws as at present. As all animals tend to multiply beyond their means of subsistence, so it must have been with the progenitors of man, and this would inevitably lead to a struggle for existence and to natural selection. The latter process would be greatly aided by the inherited effects of the increased use of parts, and these two processes would incessantly react on each other. It appears, also, . . . that various unimportant characters have been acquired through sexual selection. An unexplained residuum of change must be left to the assumed uniform action of those unknown agencies, which occasionally induce strongly marked and abrupt deviations of structure in our domestic productions.

Judging from the habits of savages and of the greater number of the Quadrumana, primeval men, and even their ape-like progenitors, probably lived in society. With strictly social animals, natural selection sometimes acts on the individual, through the preservation of variations which are beneficial to the community. A community which includes a large number of well-endowed individuals increases in number, and is victorious over other less favored ones; even although each separate member gains no advantage over the others of the same community. Associated insects have thus acquired many remarkable structures, which are of little or no service to the individual, such as the pollen-collecting apparatus, or the sting of the worker-bee, or the great jaws of soldier-ants. With the higher social animals, I am not aware that any structure has been modified solely for the good of the community, though some are of secondary service to it. For instance, the horns of ruminants and the great canine teeth of baboons appear to have been acquired by the males as weapons for sexual strife, but they are used in defense of the herd or troop. In regard to certain mental powers the case . . . is wholly different; for these faculties have been chiefly, or even exclusively, gained for the benefit of the community, and the individuals thereof have at the same time gained an advantage indirectly.

It has often been objected to such views as the foregoing, that man is one of the most helpless and defenseless creatures in the world; and that during his early and less well developed condition he would have been still more helpless. The Duke of Argyll, for instance, insists that "the human frame has diverged from the structure of brutes in the direction of greater physical helplessness and weakness. That is to say, it is a divergence, which of all others it is most impossible to ascribe to mere natural selection." He adduces the naked and unprotected state of the body, the absence of great teeth or claws for defense, the small strength and speed of man, and his slight power of discovering food or of avoiding danger by smell. To these deficiencies

"The Biology of Religion"

Vernon Reynolds and Ralph E. Tanner

The 'instructions' religions give to individuals concern people's obligations to reproduce a lot or a little; whether or not to contracept; whether or not to practise abortion or infanticide; whether to devote massive care to those who are born throughout their lives or to be more resigned to the facts of death; whether to marry young or to postpone marriage; whether to divorce easily or regard divorce as impossible; whether to regard sex as holy or sinful; whether to equate personal hygiene with religious purity and piety, or not to connect the two. These rules and the actions resulting from them are adaptive in the sense that they are found in countries where the results they produce will tend to enhance the reproductive success of individuals following them.

Religions thus act as culturally phrased biological messages.

From *The Biology of Religion* (1983).

there might be added one still more serious, namely, that he cannot climb quickly and so escape from enemies. The loss of hair would not have been a great injury to the inhabitants of a warm country. For we know that the unclothed Fuegians can exist under a wretched climate. When we compare the defenseless state of man with that of apes we must remember that the great canine teeth with which the latter are provided are possessed in their full development by the males alone, and are chiefly used by them for fighting with their rivals, yet the females, which are not thus provided, manage to survive.

In regard to bodily size or strength, we do not know whether man is descended from some small species, like the chimpanzee, or from one as powerful as the gorilla; and, therefore, we cannot say whether man has become larger and stronger, or smaller and weaker than his ancestors. We should, however, bear in mind that an animal possessing great size, strength and ferocity, and which, like the gorilla, could defend itself from all enemies, would not perhaps have become social; and this would most effectually have checked the acquirement of the higher mental qualities, such as sympathy and the love of his fellows. Hence it might have been an immense advantage to man to have sprung from some comparatively weak creature.

The small strength and speed of man, his want of natural weapons, etc., are more than counterbalanced, firstly, by his intellectual powers, through which he has formed for himself weapons, tools, etc., though still remaining in a barbarous state, and secondly, by his social qualities which lead him to give and receive aid from his fellow-men. No country in the world abounds in a greater degree with dangerous beasts than Southern Africa; no country presents more fearful physical hardships than the Arctic regions; yet one of the puniest of races, that of the Bushmen, maintains itself in Southern Africa, as do the dwarfed Esquimaux in the Arctic regions. The ancestors of man were, no doubt, inferior in intellect, and probably in social disposition to the lowest existing savages; but it is quite conceivable that they might have existed, or even flourished, if they had advanced in intellect, while gradually losing their brute-like powers, such as that of climbing trees, etc. But these ancestors would not have been exposed to any special danger, even if far more helpless and defenseless than any existing savages, had they inhabited some warm continent or large island, such as Australia, New Guinea, or Borneo, which is now the home of the orang. And natural selection arising from the competition of tribe with tribe in some such large area as one of these, together with the inherited effects of habit, would, under favorable conditions, have sufficed to raise man to his present high position in the organic scale.

Philip Kitcher

"ABUSING SCIENCE: THE CASE AGAINST CREATIONISM"

PHILIP KITCHER was a professor of philosophy at the University of Minnesota and director of the Minnesota Center for the Philosophy of Science before accepting his current position at the University of California, San Diego. He has written extensively on the philosophy of mathematics, the philosophy of science, and the philosophy of biology, including *The Nature of Mathematical Knowledge* and *Abusing Science*, from which the following selection is taken.

The central idea of strict Creationism is that all kinds of organisms presently existing, and perhaps some more, were formed on the earth in a single event. Some people hold this view purely as an article of religious faith, making no claim that it is a part of science supported by scientific evidence. Such people accept strict Creationism because its central doctrine follows from two other beliefs that they hold: (i) The Bible is to be read literally; (ii) When the Bible is read literally, it says that all kinds of organisms were formed on the earth in a single event. I disagree with this view, because I do not believe it is possible, let alone reasonable, to read the Bible literally. (Nor do I think that Christians and Jews are compelled, as sincere believers, to read the Bible literally.) However, I have no intention of criticizing Creationism insofar as it is held as an explicitly religious belief, a belief that is recognized as running counter to the scientific evidence.

There is another way to be a Creationist. One might offer Creationism as a scientific theory: Life did not evolve over millions of years; rather all forms were created at one time by a particular Creator. Although pure versions of Creationism were no longer in vogue among scientists by the end of the eighteenth century, they had flourished earlier (in the writings of Thomas Burnet, William Whiston, and others). Moreover, *variants* of Creationism were supported by a number of eminent nineteenth-century scientists—William Buckland, Adam Sedgwick, and Louis Agassiz, for example. These Creationists trusted that their theories would accord with the Bible, interpreted in what they saw as a correct way. However, that fact does not affect the scientific status of those theories. Even postulating an unobserved Creator need be no more unscientific than postulating unobservable particles. What matters is the character of the proposals and the ways in which they are articulated and defended. The great scientific Creationists of the eighteenth and nineteenth centuries offered problem-solving strategies for many of the questions addressed by evolutionary theory. They struggled hard to explain the observed distribution of fossils. Sedgwick, Buckland, and others practiced genuine science. They stuck their necks out and volunteered information about the catastrophes that they invoked to explain biological and geological findings. Because their theories offered definite proposals, those theories were refutable. Indeed, the the-

Philip Kitcher, *Abusing Science: The Case Against Creationism*, Cambridge, Massachusetts: The MIT Press. Footnotes edited.

ories actually achieved refutation. In 1831, in his presidential address to the Geological Society, Adam Sedgwick publicly announced that his own variation of Creationism had been refuted:

> Having been myself a believer, and, to the best of my power, a propagator of what I now regard as a philosophic heresy . . . I think it right, as one of my last acts before I quit this Chair, thus publicly to read my recantation.
>
> We ought, indeed, to have paused before we first adopted the diluvian theory, and referred all our old superficial gravel to the action of the Mosaic Flood. For of man, and the works of his hands, we have not yet found a single trace among the remnants of a former world entombed in these ancient deposits. In classing together distant unknown formations under one name; in giving them a simultaneous origin, and in determining their data, not by the organic remains we had discovered, but by those we expected hypothetically hereafter to discover, in them; we have given one more example of the passion with which the mind fastens upon general conclusions, and of the readiness with which it leaves the consideration of unconnected truths. . . .

Since they want Creationism taught in public schools, contemporary Creationists cannot present their view as based on religious faith. On the other hand, the doctrine is too dear to be subjected to the possibility of outright defeat. What is wanted, then, is a version of Creationism that is not vulnerable to refutation, but that appears to enjoy the objective status that can only be conferred by evidential support. This is an impossible demand. A theory cannot drink at the well of evidential support without running the risk of being poisoned by future data. What emerges from the conflict of goals is the pseudoscience promulgated by the Institute for Creation Research. It is vaguely suggested that the central Creationist idea could be used to solve some problems. But the details are never given, the links to nature never forged. Oddly, "scientific" Creationism fails to be a science not because of what it says (or, in its "public school" editions, very carefully omits) about a Divine Creator, but because of what it does not say about the natural world. The theory has no infrastructure, no ways of articulating its vague central idea, so that specific features of living forms can receive detailed explanations.

Despite my best efforts, I have found only two problem-solving strategies in the writing of "scientific" Creationists. Most of the literature is negative, a set of variations on . . . antievolutionary themes. . . . The positive proposals of Creation "science" are remarkably skimpy. Even *Scientific Creationism* (the work that is intended to enable teachers to present the "creation model") spends far more pages attacking evolutionary theory than in developing the Creationist account. Nevertheless, there are passages where a positive doctrine seems to flicker among the criticisms. Similarly, the much earlier book *The Genesis Flood* (Whitcomb and Morris 1961), mixes attempts at constructing Creation "science" with its explicit Biblical interpretation. Because of the uniformly negative character of most other Creationist writings, my evaluation of the positive theory presented by "scientific" Creationists will be based primarily on these two works. The two problem-solving strategies of "scientific" Creationism are the attempt to use Flood Geology to answer questions about the ordering of fossils and an appeal to a mix of "design" and historical narrative to account for the properties, relationships, and distributions of organisms. I shall document my remarks about pseudoscience by taking a closer look at how these explanatory vehicles operate.

ROOM AT THE TOP FOR THE UPWARDLY MOBILE?

Creationists recognize that the fossil record is ordered. All over the earth we find a regular succession of organisms through the rock strata. At the lowest levels, we find only small marine invertebrates. As we move up, other groups of animals are encountered: Fish join the marine invertebrates: then come the amphibians, reptiles, and, finally, the mammals and birds. Of course, within each of these groups there is also an order. The first reptiles diversify, giving rise at later times to several different groups, some of which, like the dinosaurs, die out, while others of which, like the snakes, turtles, lizards, and crocodilians, persist to the present. Even without evolutionary assumptions, it is possible to offer a simple explanation of this order. The different strata all contain remains of the distinctive organisms that were alive at the time at which those strata were deposited, and the order reflects the fact that different groups of animals have existed at different times. In other words, the animals who have inhabited the earth were not all contemporaries.

Although this simple explanation makes no commitment to the *evolution* of organisms, Creationists cannot accept it. For they believe that all the animals that have ever existed were formed in one original event of Creation. Nor can they abandon this belief without forswearing the theological payoff of their "science." So how are they to explain the order of the fossil record? Some antievolutionists of the late nineteenth century ascended to new levels of ad hoc explanation with two transparent ruses: (i) The Devil placed the fossils in the rocks to deceive us; (ii) God put the fossils there to test us. Contemporary Creationists are more subtle. They invoke the Flood. They hypothesize a worldwide, cataclysmic deluge, which destroyed virtually all the animals of the earth and deposited almost all the fossil-bearing rocks, thereby producing the fossil record.

Here is an outline of their major ideas. The primeval earth was a very pleasant place, consisting of land masses divided by "narrow seas." It was surrounded by a canopy of water vapor, producing a "greenhouse effect." In the Flood, water came from two directions; primitive waters inside the earth burst through the crust, and, at the same time, the vapor canopy was broken up to cause torrential rain. Some humans and animals escaped in boats (including, presumably, Noah, his family, and a pair of [land] animals of every kind). Others, less lucky, were drowned or destroyed, and some of them were engulfed by mud and other debris that were later deposited as sediments. (The latter animals are the ones that became fossilized.) Finally, the Flood came to an end, partly as the result of evaporation, partly because mountains erupted, producing basins in which the residual waters were entrapped. At this point, the remaining animals dispersed, bred, multiplied, and spread themselves over the new earth.

The attempt to explain geological formations by reference to the Flood is not new. Contemporary Creationists are heirs to a long tradition, begun by Thomas Burnet (whose *Sacred Theory of the Earth* was published in 1681). The idea of invoking a *single* cataclysm (and a single period of Creation) had been abandoned by the wiser geologists by the end of the eighteenth century, at which time the enterprise appeared hopeless. Nineteenth-century Catastrophists—Cuvier, Buckland, Sedgwick, and their followers—preferred to think of Noah's Flood as the last in a series of catastrophes. But "scientific" Creationists will have none of these newfangled compromises. So their account is vexed by all the questions that arose for their illustrious predecessors—as well as other questions inspired by the discoveries of the past 150 years. Here are just a few. How exactly did the land reemerge? (In traditional terms, how was "the pond drained"?) Did *all* kinds of land animals go on Noah's ship? If so, why are there so many kinds that are unrecorded in "post-Deluge" strata? How were the domestic economies managed during the voyage of the Ark? Obviously, the *mechanisms* of the whole episode could stand considerably more description. Creationists sometimes admit the point; Morris exhorts teachers to prepare geology students who can help with the task of working out the details. However, neither he nor any other Creationist I have read seems to have any definite conception of where or how to begin this Herculean task.

Those disposed to take a charitable attitude toward Flood Geology might offer the following appraisal. Flood Geology is really only the sketch of a theory. Much further work is required to make a full-fledged theory. Still, in 1859, Darwin presented only a sketch of a theory, so really the sketchiness of Flood Geology does not doom the Creationist enterprise. They simply need time.

This apparently apt analogy comes apart when one compares Darwin's offering with the wares of the Institute for Creation Research. Darwin's theory and Flood Geology (in its contemporary version) are both "theory sketches" only in the same sense that a Leonardo drawing and a Rorschach inkblot are both sketches of works of art. Unlike Darwin's theory, Flood Geology offers no detailed explanation of any aspect of the fossil record. It provides nothing even remotely analogous to Darwin's studies of barnacles and South American mammals. Unlike Darwin's theory, Flood Geology shows no promise of fruitful interchange with other sciences. Darwin built upon the existing science of his day, and his proposals stimulated fruitful work throughout biology and geology. By contrast, as we shall see below, "scientific" Creationism would force us to abandon well-developed related theories, without any hint of how to construct replacements. Another important difference is that Flood Geology, as currently practiced, does not aim at advancing science—it does not seek to extend the range of phenomena that are open to scientific investigation. The goal is to fight a rearguard action, not to open up new areas of inquiry. Moreover, as we shall see, Flood Geology is very vague. Where Darwin explained carefully how he proposed to address biological questions, making clear how the application of his problem-solving strategy was to be made, Flood Geology is indefinite. Finally, Flood Geology is now a new proposal, daring and untried. There is little room to think that further efforts will enable the "theory" to emerge as a detailed solution to the problems it hopes to resolve. If Creationists do succeed in luring some talented geologists to their cause, I am inclined to mourn the waste of ability. Their program has no more to offer than it had when Thomas Burnet wrote the original script.

To see why Flood Geology deserves an obituary, let us watch it in action. The most ambitious attempt at detailed problem solving is presented by Henry Morris. Morris is very emphatic that Flood Geology accounts for the order of the fossils. After announcing fourteen "obvious predictions" of his story, he concludes, "Now there is no question that all of the above predictions from the cataclysmic model are explicitly confirmed in the geologic column. The general order from simple to complex in the fossil record in the geologic column, considered by evolutions to be the main proof of evolution, is thus likewise predicted by the rival model, only with more precision and detail. But it is the exceptions that are inimical to the evolution model." Bold words. Before we take up the large claims made for Flood Geology, let us consider the swipes at the evolutionary account. First, the "general order from simple to complex" in the fossil record is not considered "the main proof" of evolution. Evolutionary theory rests on its ability to subsume a vast number of diverse phenomena—including the *details* of biogeography, adaptive characteristics, relationships among organisms, and the sequence of fossils—under a single type of historical reasoning. To say that "the general order from simple to complex" in the fossil record is the primary evidence for evolution is like saying that the fact that most bodies tend to fall is the primary evidence for the Newtonian theory. Second, those "inimical exceptions" are our old friends the overthrusts, the cave drawings—and, of course, Paluxy. As I have already pointed out, these are not genuine problems for evolutionary theory.

How exactly does Morris propose to "predict" the order of the fossils from his model? Let us look at some of his "predictions" and their justifications:

3. In general, animals living at the lowest elevations would tend to be buried at the lowest elevations,

and so on, with elevations in the strata thus representing elevations of habitat or ecological zones.

4. Marine invertebrates would normally be found in the bottom rocks of any local geologic column, since they live on the sea bottom.
5. Marine vertebrates (fishes) would be found in higher rocks than the bottom-dwelling invertebrates. They live at higher elevations and also could escape burial longer.
6. Amphibians and reptiles would tend to be found at still higher elevations, in the commingled sediments at the interface between land and water. . . .
9. In the marine strata where invertebrates were fossilized, these would tend locally to be sorted hydrodynamically into assemblages of similar size and shape. Furthermore, as the turbulently upwelling waters and sediments settled back down, the simpler animals, more nearly spherical or streamlined in shape, would tend to settle out first because of lower hydraulic drag. Thus each kind of marine invertebrate would tend to appear in its simplest form at the lowest elevation, and so on.
10. Mammals and birds would be found in general at higher elevations than reptiles and amphibians, both because of their habitat and because of their greater mobility. However, few birds would be found at all, only occasional exhausted birds being trapped and buried in sediments.

It is hard to know where to start. Morris appears to have three possible explanatory factors: (1) *habitat* (lower dwelling animals were deposited first), (2) *hydraulic characteristics* (the order of deposition depends on the animal's resistance to the downward waters), (3) *mobility* (more mobile animals will be deposited later). The passages I have quoted juggle these three methods so as to obtain the desired results.

Now, for all the extravagant claims about "prediction" with "more precision and detail," the account Morris offers is extremely vague. Puzzles begin to appear in large numbers when we start to consider the details of the fossil record. Why are bottom-dwelling marine invertebrates found at *all* levels of the strata? Why are some very delicate marine invertebrates, which would have been likely to sink more slowly, found at the very lowest levels? Why are all the "modern" fishes (the *teleostean* fishes, which, on the standard account, emerged only in the age of dinosaurs and became spectacularly successful as the reign of the dinosaurs came to its end) found only in Morris's "late Flood" deposits? Why do these particular fishes not occur, as other fishes do, at lower levels? Why are whales and dolphins only found at higher levels, while marine reptiles of similar size are found only much lower? Why do lumbering creatures like ground sloths appear only in Morris's post-Flood depos-

"Christian Science"

Mary Baker Eddy

Christian Science reveals incontrovertibly that mind is all-in-all, that the only realities are the divine Mind and idea. (p. 109)

Christian Science explains all cause and effect as mental, not physical. (p. 114)

Christian Science eschews what is called natural science, in so far as this is built on the false hypotheses that matter is its own lawgiver, that law is founded on material conditions. (p. 127)

We must abandon pharmaceutics, and take up ontology—'the science of real being'. (p. 129)

Treatises on anatomy, physiology, and health, sustained by what is termed material law, are the promoters of sickness and disease (p. 179)

From *Science and Health* (1906).

its, while much more agile mammals (such as the ancestors of contemporary carnivores and ungulates) appear much lower? Why are the *flying* reptiles found "in the commingled sediments at the interface between land and water"? Why were not *most* of the birds "exhausted," since perching places would have been hard to find in the raging Deluge? The sequence of questions could go on and on.

Morris does not consider the particularities. So the idea that we get *more* detail from his account is simply bluster. In fact, given that the problems raised for evolutionary theory are spurious—the "inimical exceptions" do not present any difficulty—the question we must ask is whether Flood Geology can *emulate* the ability of evolutionary theory to explain the fossil record. There are two ways in which Creationists might elaborate their proposals. One would be to acknowledge that the account so far given is programmatic and incomplete and to face up to the task of working out the details. The second would be to deny that there are residual questions for "scientific" Creationism to answer.

In the spirit of Morris's exhortation to young paleontologists, Creationists might concede that Flood Geology is only a "sketch." However, it is hardly a matter of adding a bit of detail to the main lines of the account. Problems are everywhere, solutions nowhere. What were the mechanics of the Flood? How were the animals preserved? Why are the details of the fossil ordering as we find them to be? It is reasonable to wonder what Flood Geology does have going for it that inspires people to work further on it. Wonderment increases when we realize that Creationists have abandoned the position of the most enlightened nineteenth-century Catastrophists. . . .

Here is a different "theory sketch" about the history of life on earth. For a very long time, the earth has been a laboratory for clever aliens who live in outer space. Periodically, they have "seeded" our planet with living organisms. In the beginning, they were only able to produce rather simple terrestrial organisms. So they started off with some marine invertebrates. After a while, they came for a visit to see how things were going. At this time, a dreadful thing happened. Something about the alien spacecraft caused a cataclysm on the earth; volcanoes erupted, there were massive earthquakes, enormous tidal waves, and so forth. Perhaps the spacecraft emitted some peculiar type of radiation that triggered all these unfortunate events. In any case, all the first crop of organisms was destroyed and buried in the cataclysm. The whole experiment was spoiled. However, since they understood the moral of Kipling's "If," the aliens decided to try again. Their technology had now improved, and they were able to manufacture more complicated animals. Some of those that had not performed well on the first round were dropped from the cast. The experiment went very well again—until they came to take another look. Once again, their presence led to disaster, and they were forced to start over from scratch. So it has gone for a number of trials. (How many would you like?) The aliens are very persevering. They still have not figured out what it is about their presence that makes the earth go into convulsions. But their technology is clearly improving by leaps and bounds. After all, last time they made us.

My brief acquaintance with the "theory sketch" of the last paragraph has not yet led to a deep attachment. (It took me about ten minutes to make it up.) So I shall not exhort others to join me in working out the details. However, I do want to suggest that, *from a scientific point of view,* my silly proposal is no worse than Morris's Flood Geology. It would not be difficult to mimic the "fourteen predictions." ("What evolutionists call *trends* are really the aliens' progress in fine tuning already workable designs." Notice, too, that my theory, like Morris's vague account of Flood Geology, has plenty of "wiggle room.") The point of the comparison should be obvious. There is utterly no reason to take either my proposal or Flood Geology seriously—or to exhort promising students to waste their careers in the pursuit of such obvious folly.

The second way in which the Creationists can respond to questions about the details is even worse. Instead of taking the problems of detail seriously, they can contend that we can never know how the Flood worked. All that can be done is to lay down some general considerations, which hold "as a rule," and suggest that, given some unknowable distribution of upwelling waters, torrential rains, and trapped animals, everything sorted out as it did. So, for example, the questions I have raised about teleostean fishes, whales, flying reptile, and giant sloths can just be ducked. These are "the exceptional cases."

Some passages suggest that, when push comes to shove, Morris and his fellow Creationists will slide in this direction:

> 14. All the above predictions would be expected statistically but, because of the cataclysmic nature of the phenomena, would also admit of many exceptions in every case. In other words, the cataclysmic model predicts the general order and character of the deposits but also allows for occasional exceptions.

> In other localities, and perhaps somewhat later in the period of the rising waters of the Flood, in general, land animals and plants would be expected to be caught in the sediments and buried; and this, of course, is exactly what the strata show. Of course, this would be only a general rule and there would be many exceptions, as currents would be intermingling from all directions, particularly as the lands became increasingly submerged and more and more amphibians, reptiles and mammals were overtaken by the waters.

The remarkable point about these passages is not the *number* of qualifying phrases, but their *variable strength.* Are there "many exceptions in every case" or are the exceptions "occasional"? I do not know what Morris or Whitcomb intends. Yet one thing is clear. Such passages can be used to maintain that the anomalies I have mentioned are not genuine problems for Flood Geology. Morris and Whitcomb have carefully provided an all-purpose escape clause. So while (alleged) exceptions are "inimical" to evolutionary theory—they would mean refutation—exceptions, even hordes of exceptions, in no way weaken the case for Creation "science." For Creation "scientists" data has only one function; it is a potential source of problems for evolution. Counterexamples to the "theory" of Creation "science" do not count.

To see how severe the anomalies are, let us look at one example in more detail. Fossils of teleostean fishes (this class comprises just about all contemporary types from sardines to swordfish) are found only from late Triassic times (roughly 200 million years ago), and they show increasing abundance in the fossil record. Now recall that a leading principle of Flood Geology is that "animals living at the lowest elevations would tend to be buried at the lowest elevations." Overlooking such niceties as the fact that some teleosteans are deep-sea fish, let us ask what accounts for their success in resisting the Flood. Were they hydraulically special, less "streamlined" than other fish? No, as a group, there is more variation of shape *within* the teleosteans than there is between teleosteans and the groups of fish that were buried beneath them. So perhaps the answer is that they found room at the top because they were upwardly mobile? But this explanation loses its attractiveness when we realize that the teleosts "range from speedy swimmers to slow swimmers to almost sedentary forms, from dwellers in the open ocean to bottom-living types to lake and river fishes." Yet all these lucky teleostean fishes managed to resist the flood waters for a long time, while large numbers of speedy fish are buried beneath them.

By considering this one example, I hope to have explained what lies behind my charge that Flood Geology faces serious anomalies. But my principal purpose is to illustrate the impotence of the idea that worrisome details can be written off as "exceptional cases." Were *all* the teleosts exceptional? Was there no single unlucky sardine, salmon, or swordfish who was buried in the early deposits? Is it enough to remind ourselves that there are bound to be exceptions "because of the cataclysmic nature of the phenomena"? The case of teleosts is only one among many. Ground sloths, flying reptiles, whales, trilobites, and a host of other creatures prove similarly embarrassing. . . .

Writing in 1961, Whitcomb and Morris made it clear what their last resort would be if the difficult questions began to threaten: "It is because the Bible itself teaches us these things that we are fully justified in appealing to *the power of God,* whether or not He used means amenable to our scientific understanding, for the gathering of two of every kind of animal into the Ark and for the care and preservation of those animals in the Ark during the 371 days of the Flood." Today, "scientific" Creationists have pledged themselves to argue on the scientific evidence. So this last refuge is—officially, at least—out of bounds.

The second major biological problem-solving strategy offered by Creationism attempts to answer questions about adaptation, relationships among organisms, and biogeographical distribution. . . .

The basic idea is straightforward. When we recognize a characteristic of an organism as unmodified, the Creationist explanation of its presence will be to show how the feature manifests the Creator's design. The account of similarities among distinct "basic kinds" will identify the similar needs of organisms of those distinct kinds. Here are some sample "explanations." Bats have wings because the Creator endowed them with wings, and He did so because they need to fly. Chimps and humans have similar hemoglobins (and other biological molecules) because the Creator gave them similar molecules from the start, and He did so because their physical requirements are similar. Some (perfectly palatable) butterflies mimic unpalatable butterflies of the same region because the Creator saw that they had to have some defense against predators. To each according to his need.

If one wants to believe in Creationism, this picture can easily lull critical faculties. Yet, if we think about it, it is bizarre. Surely we should not imagine the Creator contemplating a wingless bat, recognizing that it would be defective, and so equipping it with the wings it needs. Rather, if we take the idea of a single creative event seriously, we must view it as the origination of an entire system of kinds of organisms, *whose needs themselves are in large measure from the character of the system.* Why were bats created at all? Why were any defenses against predation needed? Why did the Creator form this system of organisms, with their interrelated needs, needs that are met in such diverse and complicated ways?

Invocation of the word "design," or the passing reference to the satisfaction of "need," explains nothing. The needs are not given in advance of the design of structures to accommodate them, but are themselves encompassed in the design. Nor do we achieve any understanding of the adaptations and relationships of organisms until we see, at least in outline, what the Grand Plan of Creation might have been. This point has been clear at least since the seventeenth century. At the beginning of the *Discourse on Metaphysics,* Leibniz gave a beautiful exposition of it. He recognized that unless there are independent criteria of design, then praise of the Creator's design is worthless: "In saying, therefore, that things are not good according to any standard of goodness, but simply by the will of God, it seems to me that one destroys, without realizing it, all the love of God and all his glory; for why praise him for what he has done, if he would be equally praiseworthy in doing the contrary?" For Leibniz, to invoke "design" without saying what counts as good design is not only vacuous but blasphemous. Later in the same work, Leibniz developed the theme with a striking analogy. *Any* world can be conceived as regular ("designed") just as *any* array of points can be joined by a curve with some algebraic formula.

Why are contemporary Creationists silent about the Design? Because things did not go so well for their predecessors who tried to show how each kind of organism had been separately created with a special design. They found it hard to reconcile the observed features of some organisms with the attributes of the Creator. Contemporary Creationists have learned from these heroic—but fruitless—efforts.

So we encounter the strategy exemplified by Morris: Talk generally about design, pattern, purpose, and beauty in nature. There are many examples of adaptations that can be used—the wings of bats or "the amazing circulatory system," for example. But what happens if we press some more difficult cases? Well, if there seems to be no design or purpose to a feature (and if its presence cannot be understood as a modification of ancestral characters), one can always point out that some parts of the Creator's plan may be too vast for human understanding. *We* do not see what the design is, but there *is* design, nonetheless.

Since no plan of design has been specified, Creationists have available another all-purpose escape clause. But it is precisely this feature of Creation "science" that impugns its scientific credentials. To mumble that "the ways of the Creator are many and mysterious" may excuse one from identifying design in unlikely places. It is not to do science.

To provide scientific explanations, a Creationist would have to identify the plan implemented in the Creation. The trouble is that there are countless examples of properties of organisms that are hard to integrate into a coherent theory of design. There are two main types of difficulty, stemming from the frequent tinkerings of evolution and the equally common nastiness of nature. Let us begin with evolutionary tinkering. Structures already present are modified to answer to the organism's current needs. The result may be clumsy and inefficient, but it gets the job done. A beautiful example is the case of the Panda's thumb. Although they belong to the order Carnivora, giant pandas subsist on a diet of bamboo. In adapting to this diet, they needed a means to grasp the shoots. Like other carnivores, they lack an opposable thumb. Instead, a bone in the wrist has become extended to serve as part of a device for grasping. It does not work well. Any component engineer who wanted to design a giant panda could have done better. But it works well enough.

It is easy to multiply examples. Orchids have evolved complicated structures that discourage self-fertilization. These baroque contraptions are readily understood if we understand them as built out of the means available. Ruminants have acquired very complicated stomachs and a special digestive routine. These characteristics have enabled them to break down the cellulose layers that encase valuable proteins in many grasses. Their inner life could have been so much simpler had they been given the right enzymes from the start.

The second class of cases covers those in which, to put it bluntly, nature's ways are rather repulsive. There is nothing intrinsically beautiful about the scavenging of vultures, the copulatory behavior of the female praying mantis (who tries to bite off the head of the "lucky" male), or the ways in which some insects paralyze their prey. Let me describe one example in more detail. Some animals practice *coprophagy*. They produce feces that they eat. Rabbits, for example, devour their morning droppings. From an evolutionary perspective, the phenomenon is understood. Rabbits have solved the problem of breaking down cellulose by secreting bacteria toward the end of their intestinal tracts. Since the cellulose breakdown occurs at the end of the tract, much valuable protein and many valuable bacteria are liable to be lost in the feces. Hence the morning feces are eaten, the protein is metabolized, and the supply of bacteria is kept up. Creationists ought to find such phenomena puzzling. Surely an all-powerful, all-loving Creator, who *separately designed* each kind of living thing, could have found some less repugnant (and, I might add, more efficient) way to get the job done. (These examples are, of course, far less problematic for those who believe simply that the Creator set the universe in motion billions of years ago and that contemporary organisms are the latest product of the laws and conditions instituted in that original creative event.)

So far, I have concentrated on Creationist resources for answering questions about the characteristics of organisms and the similarities and differences among kinds of organisms. Let us now take a brief look at Creationist biogeography. Discussions of the distribution of animals are not extensive, but the following passage lays down the ground rules of the enterprise: "If the Flood was geographically universal, then all the air-breathers of the animal kingdom which were not in the Ark perished; and present-day animal distribution must be explained on the basis of migrations from the mountains of Ararat." One's

Science vs. Religion: The Role of Authority

When the Athenians brought Socrates to trial for questioning the accepted gods, Plato tells us that Socrates was given the opportunity to cross-examine his principal accuser, and that when he did, the following exchange took place:

SOCRATES: What an extraordinary statement! Why do you think, Meletus that I am an atheist? Do you mean that I do not believe in the god-head of the sun or moon, like the rest of mankind?

MELETUS: I assure you, judges, that he does not, for he says that the sun is stone, and the moon earth.

This was perhaps the first recorded legal battle between science and religion.

Historically, science and religion arose out of the same quest to understand the unknown. From the very beginnings of science, however, they have often been in conflict with each other, a conflict that religious authorities have usually tried to win not by refuting scientific theories but by silencing them. For instance, the authorities tried to intimidate Socrates into silence. When they failed, he was sentenced to death. This pattern of intolerance is a familiar one, and often successful in the short run. Socrates was put to death, and when the Inquisitors tried to silence Galileo, they succeeded. However, suppression has not worked in the long run.

One by one religious authorities have witnessed their mythological explanations—of consciousness, of humanity, of life, of the earth, of the universe—replaced by scientific ones. But the competition between science and religion continues. Even today, in the United States, conservative Christians are trying to defuse the explosive myth-destroying power of modern evolutionary theory by lobbying to have it put side by side in high school textbooks with so-called creation science, that is, with their own favored mythological accounts of the origins of life and of the various species.

first response is surely to ask: Why only one Ark? Why Ararat? (Why not New Jersey?) Of course, we know the answers to these questions. But what *scientific* evidence is there for supposing that there was just one vehicle for preserving land animals during the Deluge and that the subsequent radiation began from Mount Ararat? Creationists tie their hands behind their backs when they approach problems of biogeography with such gratuitous assumptions. There are obvious difficulties posed by the existence of peculiar groups of animals in particular places. The most striking example is the presence of marsupials as the dominant mammals of Australia. Given that all the land animals reemerged at the same place at the same time, why did Australia become a stronghold for marsupial mammals?

Whitcome and Morris consider precisely this question. Much of their discussion is directed against claims made by one of their evangelical rivals, a geologist who advocated only a "local flood." However, they do indicate the main lines of their answer. In essence, they propose to accelerate the migration of organisms described in a standard evolutionary account. Here is the standard explanation of how the marsupials came to dominate Australia.

One central hypothesis is *placental chauvinism:* Marsupials are competitively inferior to the recent eutherian (placental) mammals. This hypothesis is confirmed by evidence of the consequences of introducing eutherian competitors into marsupial populations. It is usually suggested that the marsupials arose in North America about 130 million years ago and that they were able to compete successfully with the *early* eutherian mammals. The marsupials radiated extensively, established themselves in South America, and crossed over to Australia by way of Antarctica. (Australia, Antarctica, and South America became separated about 70 million years ago.) Their eutherian contemporaries did not reach Australia, so the marsupials were able to diversify and attain their modern forms without competition from eutherians. Other marsupial strongholds (for example, South America) became vulnerable when new continental connections (the Isthmus of Panama) made it possible for the high successful *recent* eutherians to invade. But Australia was sufficiently isolated, and a rich marsupial fauna developed there.

What Creationists propose to do is to squash something like this sequence of events into less than 100 centuries. Here, then, is the scenario. Noah's Ark lands on Mount Ararat. Out come the animals. They begin to compete for resources. Because they are inferior competitors, the poor marsupials are forced to disperse ever more widely. Spreading southward, they eventually manage to reach Australia. By the time the placentals have given chase, the land connection with Australia is severed. The marsupials are safe in their stronghold.

This is an exciting story, worthy of the best cowboy tradition. The trouble is that it has the marsupials arising in the wrong place, going by the wrong route, and competing with the wrong animals. Apart from that, the pace is just a bit too quick. If Creationists are going to explain fossil findings that, by their own lights, are post-Flood, they had better suppose that the marsupials reached Australia by travelling through Europe, North America, and South America. If they are going to insist that *contemporary* kinds of eutherian mammals emerged from the Ark, then they will have to explain why competition was not so severe that the marsupials were completely vanquished. Waiving these difficulties, let us consider the rate of the migration. When we think of marsupials, we naturally think of kangaroos—so we have the vision of successive generations of kangaroos hopping toward Australia. But kangaroos are relatively speedy. Some marsupials—wombats, koalas, and marsupial moles, for example—move very slowly. Koalas are sedentary animals, and it is difficult to coax them out of the eucalyptus trees on which they feed. Wombats, like marsupial moles, construct elaborate burrows, in which they spend their time and carry on their social relations. The idea of *any* of these animals engaging in a hectic dash around the globe is patently absurd. (On the evolutionary account, of course, they are all descendants of ancestral marsupials who had millions of years to reach their destination.)

Next we must face the question of why all the lucky refugees were *marsupials.* Surely, large numbers of animals would have found it prudent to disperse widely from the Ark. Why is it that the marsupials, almost *alone* among the mammals, were able to find the land connection to Australia and scurry across before other mammals in need of *Lebensraum* could catch up with them? And what about the conveniently disappearing land connection itself? Creationists seem to assume very rapid movements of land masses. Unlike orthodox geologists, who have independent evidence for slow separation of the continents, they maintain that, in a matter of centuries, a land connection that would support a full-scale exodus of marsupials presented an insuperable barrier to the pursuing eutherians. Indeed, if the marsupials were really *driven* across by eutherian competition, then we would expect the competition to be snapping at their heels—otherwise would not the wombat have stopped to dig a burrow, the koala have settled in a convenient tree? In that case, the bridge would have to be cut *very* quickly?

Once again, when the Creationist story is pressed for details, anomalies appear in droves. . . . What are the rules of the Creationist game? What constraints govern hypotheses about past land connections? Since the Creationists have foresworn the apparatus of modern geology, their claims about the past relations of land masses seem invulnerable to independent checks. No worries about mechanisms for rapid land subsidence need perturb them, for they may always appeal to the after effects of the great cataclysm. Anything goes.

When Whitcome and Morris wrote *The Genesis Flood* in 1961, Creationist strategy was somewhat different from that currently in vogue. Those were halcyon days, when Creationists did not mind admitting their reliance on unfathomable supernatural mechanisms. Perhaps they even hoped that a version of Creationism, explicitly based on the Genesis account, might find its place in science education. The following passage is far less guarded than more recent statements:

> The more we study the fascinating story of animal distribution around the earth, the more convinced we have become that this vast river of variegated life forms, moving ever outward from the Asiatic mainland, across the continents and seas, has not been a chance and haphazard phenomenon. Instead, *we see the hand of God guiding and directing these creatures in ways that man, with all his ingenuity, has never been able to fathom,* in order that the great commission to the postdiluvian animal kingdom might be carried out, and "that they may breed abundantly in the earth, and be fruitful, and multiply upon the earth" (Gen. 8 : 17).

There is the all-purpose escape clause. If the way in which the animals might have managed to leave the Ark and distribute themselves around the globe boggles your mind, do not tax yourself. They were guided, directed in ways that we are not able to understand.

Morris's subsequent writings take a different line about biogeographical questions. The subject is not discussed. Hence it is impossible to be sure that current Creationists would invoke the actions of the Creator to help out when the going gets tough. Nevertheless, this is one more instance of the phenomenon that we have seen repeatedly. The alleged rival to evolutionary theory provides no definite problem-solving strategies that can be applied to give detailed answers to specific questions. . . .

Creation "science" is spurious science. To treat it as science we would have to overlook its intolerable vagueness. We would have to abandon large parts of well-established sciences (physics, chemistry, and geology, as well as evolutionary biology, are all candidates for revision). We would have to trade careful technical procedures for blind guesses, unified theories for motley collections of special techniques. Exceptional cases, whose careful pursuit has so often led to important turnings in the history of science, would be dismissed with a wave of the hand. Nor would there be any gains. There is not a single scientific question to which Creationism provides its own detailed problem solution. In short, Creationism could take a place among the sciences only if the substance and methods of contemporary science were mutilated to make room for a scientifically worthless doctrine. What price Creationism?

Paul Feyerabend

"HOW TO DEFEND SOCIETY AGAINST SCIENCE"

PAUL FEYERABEND, born in 1924 and one of the best known, staunchest, and most scientifically sophisticated advocates of the view that science is just one of many ways to properly apprehend reality, is a professor of philosophy at the University of California, Berkeley and a professor of philosophy of science at the Federal Institute of Technology at Zurich. He is the author of *Against Method* and *Knowledge without Foundations*.

FAIRYTALES

I want to defend society and its inhabitants from all ideologies, science included. All ideologies must be seen in perspective. One must not take them too seriously. One must read them like fairytales which have lots of interesting things to say but which also contain wicked lies, or like ethical prescriptions which may be useful rules of thumb but which are deadly when followed to the letter.

Now—is this not a strange and ridiculous attitude? Science, surely, was always in the forefront of the fight against authoritarianism and superstition. It is to science that we owe our increased intellectual freedom vis-à-vis religious beliefs; it is to science that we owe the liberation of mankind from ancient and rigid forms of thought. Today these forms of thought are nothing but bad dreams—and this we learned from science. Science and enlightenment are one and the same thing—even the most radical critics of society believe this. Kropotkin wants to overthrow all traditional institutions and forms of belief, with the exception of science. Ibsen criticises the most intimate ramifications of nineteenth century bourgeois ideology, but he leaves science untouched. Levi-Strauss has made us realise that Western Thought is not the lonely peak of human achievement it was once believed to be, but he excludes science from his relativization of plays in education. Scientific "facts" are taught at a very early age and in the very same manner in which religious "facts" were

Paul Feyerabend, "How to Defend Society against Science," *Radical Philosophy* 2 (1975): 4–8. Reprinted by permission of the author and the publisher.

taught only a century ago. There is no attempt to waken the critical abilities of the pupil so that he may be able to see things in perspective. At the universities the situation is even worse, for indoctrination is here carried out in a much more systematic manner. Criticism is not entirely absent. Society, for example, and its institutions, are criticised most severely and often most unfairly and this already at the elementary school level. But science is excepted from the criticism. In society at large the judgement of bishops and cardinals was accepted not too long ago. The move towards "demythologization," for example, is largely motivated by the wish to avoid any clash between Christianity and scientific ideas. If such a clash occurs, then science is certainly right and Christianity wrong. Pursue this investigation further and you will see that science has now become as oppressive as the ideologies it had once to fight. Do not be misled by the fact that today hardly anyone gets killed for joining a scientific heresy. This has nothing to do with science. It has something to do with the general quality of our civilization. Heretics in science are still made to suffer from the *most severe* sanctions this relatively tolerant civilization has to offer.

But—is this description not utterly unfair? Have I not presented the matter is a very distorted light by using tendentious and distorting terminology? Must we not describe the situation in a very different way? I have said that science has become *rigid,* that it has ceased to be an instrument of *change* and *liberation* without adding that it has found the *truth,* or a large part thereof. Considering this additional fact we realise, so the objection goes, that the rigidity of science is not due to human willfulness. It lies in the nature of things. For once we have discovered the truth—what else can we do but follow it?

This trite reply is anything but original. It is used whenever an ideology wants to reinforce the faith of its followers. "Truth" is such a nicely neutral word. Nobody would deny that it is commendable to speak the truth and wicked to tell lies. Nobody would deny that—and yet nobody knows what such an attitude amounts to. So it is easy to twist matters and to change allegiance to truth in one's everyday affairs into allegiance to the Truth of ideology which is nothing but the dogmatic defence of that ideology. And it is of course *not* true that we *have* to follow the truth. Human life is guided by many ideas. Truth is one of them. Freedom and mental independence are others. If Truth, as conceived by some ideologists, conflicts with freedom then we have a *choice.* We may abandon freedom. But we may also abandon Truth. (Alternatively, we may adopt a more sophisticated idea of truth that no longer contradicts freedom; that was Hegel's solution.) My criticism of modern science is that it inhibits freedom of thought. If the reason is that it has found the truth and now follows it then I would say that there are better things than first finding, and then following such a monster.

This finishes the general part of my explanation.

There exists a more specific argument to defend the exceptional position science has in society today. Put in a nutshell the argument says (1) that science has finally found the correct *method* for achieving results and (2) that there are many *results* to prove the excellence of the method. The argument is mistaken—but most attempts to show this lead into a dead end. Methodology has by now become so crowded with empty sophistication that it is extremely difficult to perceive the simple errors at the basis. It is like fighting the hydra—cut off one ugly head, and eight formalizations take its place. In this situation the only answer is superficiality: when sophistication loses content then the only way of keeping in touch with reality is to be crude and superficial. This is what I intend to be.

AGAINST METHOD

There is a method, says part (1) of the argument. What is it? How does it work?

One answer which is no longer as popular as it used to be is that science works by collecting facts and inferring theories from them. The answer is unsatisfactory as theories never *follow* from facts in the strict logical sense. To say that they may yet be *supported* by facts assumes a notion of support that (a) does not show this defect and is (b) sufficiently sophisticated to permit us to say to what extent, say, the theory of relativity is supported by the facts. No such notion exists today nor is it likely that it will be found (one of the problems is that we need a notion of support in which grey ravens can be said to support "All Ravens are Black"). This was realised by conventionalists and transcendental idealists who pointed out that theories *shape* and *order* facts and can therefore be retained come what may. They can be retained because the human mind either consciously or unconsciously carried out its ordering function. The trouble with these views is that they assume for the mind what they want to explain for the world, viz, that it works in a regular fashion. There is only one view which overcomes all these difficulties. It was invented twice in the nineteenth century, by Mill, in his immortal essay *On Liberty,* and by some Darwinists who extended Darwinism to the battle of ideas. This view takes the bull by the horns: theories cannot be justified and their excellence cannot be shown without reference to other theories. We may explain the *success* of a theory by reference to a more comprehensive theory (we explain the success of Newton's theory by using the general theory of relativity); and we may explain our *preference* for it by comparing it with other theories. Such a comparison does not establish the intrinsic excellence of the theory we have chosen. As a matter of fact, the theory we have chosen may be pretty lousy. It may contain contradictions, it may conflict with well-known facts, it may be cumbersome, unclear, ad hoc in decisive places and so on. But it may still be better than any other theory that is available at the time. It may in fact be the best lousy theory there is. Nor are the standards of judgement chosen in an absolute manner. Our sophistication increases with every choice we make, and so do our standards. Standards compete just as theories compete and we choose the standards most appropriate to the historical situation in which the choice occurs. The rejected alternatives (theories; standards; "facts") are not eliminated. They serve as correctives (after all, we may have made the wrong choice) and they also explain the content of the preferred views (we understand relativity better when we understand the structure of its competitors; we know the full meaning of freedom only when we have an idea of life in a totalitarian state, of its advantages—and there are many advantages—as well as of its disadvantages). Knowledge so conceived is an ocean of alternatives channelled and subdivided by an ocean of standards. It forces our mind to make imaginative choices and thus makes it grow. It makes our mind capable of choosing, imagining, criticising.

Today this view is often connected with the name of Karl Popper. But there are some very decisive differences between Popper and Mill. To start with, Popper developed his view to solve a special problem of epistemology—he wanted to solve "Hume's problem." Mill, on the other hand, is interested in conditions favourable to human growth. His epistemology is the result of a certain theory of man, and not the other way around. Also Popper, being influenced by the Vienna Circle, improves on the logical form of a theory before discussing it while Mill uses every theory in the form in which it occurs in science. Thirdly, Popper's standards of comparison are rigid and fixed while Mill's standards are permitted to change with the historical situation. Finally, Popper's standards eliminate competitors once and for all: theories that are either not falsifiable, or falsifiable and falsified have no place in science. Popper's criteria are clear, unambiguous, precisely formulated: Mill's criteria are not. This would be an advantage if science itself were clear, unambiguous, and precisely formulated. Fortunately, it is not.

To start with, no new and revolutionary scientific theory is ever formulated in a manner that permits us to say under what circumstances we must regard it as endangered: many revolutionary theories are unfalsifiable. Falsifiable versions do exist, but they are hardly ever in agreement with accepted basic statements: every moderately interesting theory is falsified. Moreover, theories have formal flaws, many of them contain contradictions, ad hoc adjustments, and so on and so forth. Applied resolutely, Popperian criteria would eliminate science without replacing it by anything comparable. They are useless as an aid to science.

In the past decade this has been realised by various thinkers, Kuhn and Lakatos among them. Kuhn's ideas are interesting but, alas, they are much too vague to give rise to anything but lots of hot air. If you don't believe me, look at the literature. Never before has the literature on the philosophy of science been invaded by so many creeps and incompetents. Kuhn encourages people who have no idea why a stone falls to the ground to talk with assurance about scientific method. Now I have no objection to incompetence but I do object when incompetence is accompanied by boredom and self-righteousness. And this is exactly what happens. We do not get interesting false ideas, we get boring ideas or words connected with no ideas at all. Secondly, wherever one tries to make Kuhn's ideas more definite one finds that they are *false.* Was there ever a period of normal science in the history of thought? No—and I challenge anyone to prove the contrary.

Lakatos is immeasurably more sophisticated than Kuhn. Instead of theories he considers research programmes which are sequences of theories connected by methods of modification, so-called heuristics. Each theory in the sequence may be full of faults. It may be beset by anomalies, contradictions, ambiguities. What counts is not the shape of the single theories, but the tendency exhibited by the sequence. We judge historical developments, achievements over a period of time, rather than the situation at a particular time. History and methodology are combined into a single enterprise. A research programme is said to progress if the sequence of theories leads to novel predictions. It is said to degenerate if it is reduced to absorbing facts that have been discovered without its help. A decisive feature of Lakatos's methodology is that such evaluations are no longer tied to methodological rules which tell the scientist to either retain or to abandon a research programme. Scientists may stick to a degenerating programme, they may even succeed in making the programme overtake its rivals and they therefore proceed rationally with whatever they are doing (provided they continue calling degenerating programmes degenerating and progressive programmes progressive). This means that Lakatos offers *words* which *sound* like the elements of a methodology; he does not offer a methodology. This is no method according to the most advanced and sophisticated methodology in existence today. This finishes my reply to part (1) of the specific argument.

AGAINST RESULTS

According to part (2), science deserves a special position because it has produced *results.* This is an argument only if it can be taken for granted that nothing else has ever produced results. Now it may be admitted that almost everyone who discusses the matter makes such an assumption. It may also be admitted that it is not easy to show that the assumption is false. Forms of life different from science have either disappeared or have degenerated to an extent that makes a fair comparison impossible. Still, the situation is not as hopeless as it was only a decade ago. We have become acquainted with methods of medical diagnosis and therapy which are effective (and perhaps even more effective than the corresponding parts of Western medicine) and which are yet based on an ideology that is radically different from the ideology of Western science. We have learned that there are phenomena such as telepathy and telekinesis which are obliterated by a scientific approach and which could be used to do research in an entirely novel way (earlier thinkers such as Agrippa of Nettesheim, John Dee, and even Bacon were aware of these phenomena). And then—is it not the case that the Church saved souls while science often does the very opposite? Of course, nobody now believes in the ontology that underlies this judgement. Why? Because of ideological pressures identical with those which today make us listen to science to the exclusion of everything else. It is also true that phenomena such as telekinesis and acupuncture may eventually be absorbed into the body of science and may therefore be called "scientific." But note that this happens only *after* a long period of resistance during which a science *not yet* containing the phenomena wants to get the upper hand over forms of life that contain them. And this leads to a further objection against part (2) of the specific argument. The fact that science has results counts in its favour only if these results were achieved by science alone, and without any outside help. A look at history shows that science hardly ever gets its results in this way. When Copernicus introduced a new view of the universe, he did not consult *scientific* predecessors, he consulted a crazy Pythagorean such as Philolaos. He adopted his ideas and he maintained them in the face of all sound rules of scientific method. Mechanics and optics owe a lot to artisans, medicine to midwives and witches. And in our own day we have seen how the interference of the state can advance science: when the Chinese Communists refused to be intimidated by the judgement of experts and ordered traditional medicine back into universities and hospitals there was an outcry all over the world that science would now be ruined in China. The very opposite occurred: Chinese science advanced and Western science learned from it. Wherever we look we see that great scientific advances are due to outside interference which is made to prevail in the face of the most basic and most "rational" methodological rules. The lesson is plain: there does not exist a single argument that could be used to support the exceptional role which science today plays in society. Science has done many things, but so have other ideologies. Science often proceeds systematically, but so do other ideologies (just consult the records of the many doctrinal debates that took place in the Church) and, besides, there are no overriding rules which are adhered to under any circumstances: there is no "scientific methodology" that can be used to separate science from the rest. *Science is just one of the many ideologies that propel society and it should be treated as such* (this statement applies even to the most progressive and most dialectical sections of science). What consequences can we draw from this result?

The most important consequence is that there must be a *formal separation between state and science* just as there is now a formal separation between state and church. Science may influence society but only to the extent to which any political or other pressure group is permitted to influence society. Scientists may be consulted on important projects but the final judgement must be left to the democratically elected consulting bodies. These bodies will consist mainly of laymen. Will the laymen be able to come to a correct judgement? Most certainly, for the competence, the complications and the successes of science are vastly exaggerated. One of the most exhilarating experiences is to see how a lawyer, who is a layman, can find holes in the testimony, the technical testimony of the most advanced expert and thus prepare the jury for its verdict. Science is not a closed book that is understood only after years of training. It is an intellectual discipline that can be examined and criticised by anyone who is interested and that looks difficult and profound only because of a systematic campaign of obfuscation carried out by many scientists (though, I am happy to say, not by all). Organs of the state should never hesitate to reject the judgement of scientists when they have reason for doing so. Such rejection will educate the general public, will make it more confident and it may even lead to improvement. Considering the sizeable chauvinism of the scientific establishment we can say: the more Lysenko affairs the better (it is not the *interference* of the state that is objectionable in the case of Lysenko, but the *totalitarian* interference which kills the opponent rather than just neglecting his advice). Three cheers to the fundamentalists in California who succeeded in having a dogmatic formulation of the theory of evolution removed from the text books and an account of Genesis included (but I know that they would become as chauvinistic and totalitarian as scientists are today when given the chance to run society all by themselves. Ideologies are marvelous when used in the company of other ideologies. They become boring and doctrinaire as soon as their merits lead to the removal of their opponents). The most important change, however, will have to occur in the field of *education.*

EDUCATION AND MYTH

The purpose of education, so one would think, is to introduce the young into life, and that means: into the *society* where they are born and into the *physical universe* that surrounds the society. The method of education often consists in the teaching of some *basic myth.* The myth is available in various versions. More advanced versions may be taught by initiation rites which firmly implant them into the mind. Knowing the myth the grown-up can explain almost everything (or else he can turn to experts for more detailed information). He is the master of Nature and of Society. He understands them both and he knows how to interact with them. However, *he is not the master of the myth that guides his understanding.*

Such further mastery was aimed at, and was partly achieved, by the Pre-Socratics. The Pre-Socratics not only tried to understand the *world.* They also tried to understand, and thus to become the masters of, the *means of understanding the world.* Instead of being content with a single myth they developed many and so diminished the power which a well-told story has over the minds of men. The Sophists introduced still further methods for reducing the debilitating effect of interesting, coherent, "empirically adequate" etc. etc. tales. The achievements of these thinkers were not appreciated and they certainly are not understood today. When teaching a myth we want to increase the chance that it will be understood (i.e. no puzzlement about any feature of the myth), believed, *and accepted.* This does not do any harm when the myth is counterbalanced by other myths: even the most dedicated (i.e. totalitarian) instructor in a certain version of Christianity cannot prevent his pupils from getting in touch with Buddhists, Jews and other disreputable people. It is very different in the case of science, or of rationalism where the field is almost completely dominated by the believers. In this case it is of paramount importance to strengthen the minds of the young and "strengthening the minds of the young" means strengthening them *against* any easy acceptance of comprehensive views. What we need here is an education that makes people *contrary, countersuggestive without* making them incapable of devoting themselves to the elaboration of any single view. How can this aim be achieved?

It can be achieved by protecting the tremendous imagination which children possess and by developing to the full the spirit of contradiction that exists in them. On the whole children are much more intelligent than their teachers. They succumb, and give up their intelligence because they are bullied, or because their teachers get the better of them by emotional means. Children can learn, understand, and keep separate two to three different languages ("children" and by this I mean 3 to 5 years old, NOT eight years old who were experimented upon quite recently and did not come out too well: why? because they were already loused up by incompetent teaching at an earlier age). Of course, the languages must be introduced in a more interesting way than is usually done. There are marvellous writers in all languages who have told marvellous stories—let us begin our language teaching with *them* and not with "der Hund hat einen Schwanz" and similar inanities. Using stories we may of course also introduce "scientific" accounts, say, of the origin of the world and thus make the children acquainted with science as well. But science must not be given any special position except for pointing out that there are lots of people who believe in it. Later on the stories which have been told will be supplemented with "reasons" where by reasons I mean further accounts of the kind found in the tradition to which the story belongs. And, of course, there will also be contrary reasons. Both reasons and contrary reasons will be told by the experts in the fields and so the young generation becomes acquainted with all kinds of sermons and all types of wayfarers. It becomes acquainted with them, it becomes acquainted with their stories and every individual can make up his mind which way to go. By now everyone knows that you can earn a lot of money and respect and perhaps even a Nobel Prize by becoming a scientist, so, many will become scientists. They will *become* scientists *without having been taken in by the ideology of science,* they will *be* scientists *because they have made a free choice.* But has not much time been wasted on unscientific subjects and will this not detract from their competence once they have become scientists? Not at all! The progress of science, of good science, depends on novel ideas and on intellectual freedom; science has very often been advanced by outsiders (remember that Bohr and Einstein regarded themselves as outsiders). Will not many people make the wrong choice and end up in a dead end? Well, that depends on what you mean by a "dead end." Most scientists today are devoid of ideas, full of fear, intent on producing some paltry result so that they can add to the flood of inane papers that now constitutes "scientific progress" in many areas. And, besides, what is more important? To lead a life which one has chosen with open eyes, or to spend one's time in the nervous attempt of avoiding what some not so intelligent people call "dead ends"? Will not the number of scientists decrease so that in the end there is nobody to run our precious laboratories? I do not think so. Given a choice many people may chose science, for a science that is run by free agents looks much more attractive than the science of today which is run by slaves, slaves of institutions and slaves of "reason." And if there is a temporary shortage of scientists the situation may always be remedied by various kinds of incentives. Of course, scientists will not play any predominant role in the society I envisage. They will be more than balanced by magicians, or priests, or astrologers. Such a situation is unbearable for many people, old and young, right and left. Almost all

Today's Truths, Tomorrow's Falsehoods

Looking back at several scientific revolutions since the seventeenth century, we see that nearly every view that has ever been held by anybody has turned out to be either false or deeply questionable. At the time it was held, however, the (now defunct) view was taken, by the people who held it, to be the final truth. Today, we are in the same boat! Truth is heavily biased toward the ever-receding present—and, apparently, recedes with it! Based on what has happened to past truth, we have, it seems, good reason to believe that very much of what we now believe to be true will someday be unmasked and revealed as false by views that will *also*, at some future time, themselves be revealed as false!

of you have the firm belief that at least *some* kind of truth has been found, that it must be preserved, and that the method of teaching I advocate and the form of society I defend will dilute it and make it finally disappear. You have this firm belief; many of you may even have reasons. *But what you have to consider is that the absence of good contrary reasons is due to a historical accident;* it does *not* lie in the nature of things. Build up the kind of society I recommend and the views you now despise (without knowing them, to be sure) will return in such splendour that you will have to work hard to maintain your own position and will perhaps be entirely unable to do so. You do not believe me? Then look at history. Scientific astronomy was firmly founded on Ptolemy and Aristotle, two of the greatest minds in the history of Western Thought. Who upset their well-argued, empirically adequate and precisely formulated system? Philolaos the mad and antediluvian Pythagorean. How was it that Philolaos could stage a comeback: Because he found an able defender: Copernicus. Of course, you may follow your intuitions as I am following mine. But remember that your intuitions are the result of your "scientific" training where by science I also mean the science of Karl Marx. My training, or, rather, my non-training, is that of a journalist who is interested in strange and bizarre events. Finally, it is not utterly irresponsible, in the present world situation, with millions of people starving, others enslaved, downtrodden, in abject misery of body and mind, to think luxurious thoughts such as these? Is not freedom of choice a luxury under such circumstances; Is not the flippancy and the humour I want to see combined with the freedom of choice a luxury under such circumstances? Must we not give up all self-indulgence and *act?* Join together, and *act?* That is the most important objection which today is raised against an approach such as the one recommended by me. It has tremendous appeal, it has the appeal of unselfish dedication. Unselfish dedication—to what? Let us see!

We are supposed to give up our selfish inclinations and dedicate ourselves to the liberation of the oppressed. And selfish inclinations are what? They are our wish for maximum liberty of thought in the society in which we live *now,* maximum liberty not only of an abstract kind, but expressed in appropriate institutions and methods of teaching. This wish for concrete intellectual and physical liberty in our own surroundings is to be put aside, for the time being. This assumes, first, that we do not need this liberty for our task. It assumes that we can carry out our task with a mind that is firmly closed to some alternatives. It assumes that the correct way of liberating others *has already been found* and that all that is needed is to carry it out. I am sorry, I cannot accept such doctrinaire self-assurance in such extremely important matters. Does this mean that we cannot act at all? It does not. But it means that *while acting we have to try to realise as much of the freedom I have recommended so that our actions may be corrected in the light of the ideas we get while increasing our freedom.* This will slow us down, no doubt, but are we supposed to charge ahead simply because some people tell us that they have found an explanation for all the misery and an excellent way out of it? Also we want to liberate people not to make them succumb to a new kind of slavery, *but to make them realise their own wishes,* however different these wishes may be from our own. Self-righteous and narrow-minded liberators cannot do this. As a rule they soon impose a slavery that is worse, because more systematic, than the very sloppy slavery they have removed. And as regards humour and flippancy the answer should be obvious. Why would anyone want to liberate anyone else? Surely not because of some *abstract* advantage of liberty but because liberty is the best way to free development *and thus to happiness.* We want to liberate people *so that they can smile.* Shall we be able to do this if we ourselves have forgotten how to smile and are frowning on those who still remember? Shall we then not spread another disease, comparable to the one we want to remove, the disease of puritanical self-righteousness? Do not object that dedication and humour do not go together—Socrates is an excellent example to the contrary. *The hardest task needs the lightest hand or else its completion will not lead to freedom but to a tyranny much worse than the one it replaces.*

Wallace Matson

"THE PIOUS GENE"

WALLACE MATSON teaches philosophy at the University of California, Berkeley, and is the author of many publications on the philosophy of religion, including *The Existence of God* (1965), a penetrating attack on the traditional arguments for God. The selection that follows, previously unpublished, is the opening salvo in what Matson believes will be his magnum opus.

Whatever is believed always, everywhere, and by everyone, is true;
Everyone, always, everywhere, believes that God exists;
Therefore, God exists.

So goes the Argument *ex consensu gentium.* It didn't make the Big Three. Theologians and philosophers have paid it relatively scant attention. What, after all, is there to say about it other than that it begs the question and that both its premisses are false?

However, it is worth asking why an intellect of the caliber of Cicero's would endorse this reasoning. I do not propose to defend the argument. Nevertheless it has to be admitted that there is an *almost* universal propensity in humankind to believe in the existence of *some* sort(s) of transcendental anthropoid(s). Part of the explanation, of course, might be that the belief is true.

One might argue this way: A true proposition is one that describes the way things really are. Now, a creature that does not believe that things are as in fact they are, is at a biological disadvantage. For actions are based on beliefs. (I am not assuming a behavioristic account of belief. One can not read off beliefs straightway from actions. But it is obvious that there is a fairly tight correlation, statistically speaking.) Thus erroneous beliefs will tend to instigate activities that do not efficiently attain the goals aimed at, which is to say they will have negative survival value. The result then will be that we should expect evolution to favor the holding of true beliefs. Given enough time, error ought to be bred out.

I expect everyone will agree that this conclusion is wildly at variance with observation. Excepting me and thee, everyone's mind is an aviary stocked with specimens of all varieties of misconceptions, heresies, and absurdities. And

 This is the first publication of a paper delivered at the conference, "Christianity Challenges the Universities," held in Dallas, Texas, under the auspicies of the International Academy of Philosophy, in February 1985.

every newspaper apprises of the continued proliferation of the breeds. So something must be wrong with the evolutionary argument.

The error is obvious. While there is a connection between belief and action, it is not a simple one, and in particular it is not the case in general that the success of an action is a monotonic function of the truth of the beliefs that instigate it. Nature does not care about what we believe, only what we do. False beliefs may have survival value. Suppose that one soldier, being about to go into battle for the Faith, believes that if he is killed that is the end of him. And another soldier believes that his so-called death would be really the beginning of an eternity of sensuous delights of inconceivable intensity and duration. Which of the two is likelier to perform in such a way as to insure, if not his personal survival, at any rate the advancement of the Cause and the proliferation of the faithful?

II

Agriculture has been known for about two hundred generations, and has been the predominant way of human life for not more than half that time. In a hundred, or even two hundred, generations no very profound evolutionary changes come about. The life style we are all primarily adapted to is still that of hunter-gatherers, existing in tribes of seldom less than thirty individuals nor more than forty.

A hard life. To succeed at it two things are essential: individual skills, and teamwork. What sorts of beliefs go with them?

The tribesman has to deal with his world appropriately, that is, he has to have the right beliefs about which plants are edible and which poisonous, he has to believe that fire burns and water quenches, that insults breed enmity while flattery wins allies—in short he has to have the right beliefs about matters where, in acting on the beliefs, he constantly runs into reality. Beliefs of the class I am talking about are frequently put to the test; if they turn out not to correspond to the way things really are, the believer will suffer the frustration of his purpose in acting; he may run a risk of injury or death. We should expect, then, that natural selection will insure that these commonplace beliefs about the properties of things and the ways of animals including other human beings, will be true. Those whose beliefs don't jibe will pass on their idiosyncrasies to a diminished posterity. In the not too long run false beliefs about matters that are commonly put to the test will become abnormal in the sense of rare.

The beliefs I am now talking about need not be explicitly formulated. Few people ever bother to announce that fire burns or that here is one hand and here is another. Indeed these kinds of beliefs may safely be ascribed to all conscious animals, whether they have language or not. The dog who trots to the door at the sound of the family car turning into the driveway believes that Master is about to appear. I am using the word belief as roughly synonymous to anticipation of experience. Dogs and cats may be right or wrong in their anticipations, and so—at any rate as I am using the term—they may have true or false beliefs. The kind of anticipation of experience that is frequently revealed in the event to be correct or incorrect, I shall dub *low belief.* All beliefs of non-human animals, and many of ours, are low.

The class of low beliefs, as thus characterized, is not to be identified either extensionally or intentionally with the "empirically verifiable," though there is much overlap. Mathematical and logical propositions, though necessary truths, impinge constantly on reality, and the creature who too often adds up seven and five to give eleven, or affirms the consequent, will be in practical trouble. According to a plausible speculation the origin of human language is to be found in the signalling incident to cooperative hunting. What descriptive language primarily makes possible is the communication of beliefs: the speaker, in uttering *p,* intends the hearer to believe *p* on the basis of his knowledge that the speaker has that intention. (Note that the Gricean* analysis presupposes, as I do also, that beliefs antedate speech.) Language capability is a tremendous evolutionary advantage for a gregarious species, making possible the passing on from one generation to the next of acquired beliefs. The new generation no longer needs to start from scratch (as it were) or from a repertoire of instincts but can be educated to hold, from the outset, beliefs that the ancestors had to acquire the hard way. This advantage accrues on condition that the children tend to believe what they are told by their elders—a condition that is of course necessary for the effectiveness of language as such. Doubt and skepticism in hearers, as well as dissimulation in speakers, must be parasitic [on] sophisticated later developments.

With the invention of language it becomes possible to tell *stories.* Like music, story-telling is a universal human activity the theoretical basis of which is still a puzzle: to this day no one has come up with an account, commanding general agreement, of "the ontological status of fictional entities." The workaday task of language is to communicate beliefs about how (real) things (really, literally) are. And as we learn from dealing with young children, the naive human impulse is to take anything said as having that intent.

Now, an anticipation of experience is a "set," such as a tensing of the body in preparation for combat, salivating for eating, fleeing the scene where the tiger is expected to show up. This set involves imagination (not necessarily visual or indeed sensuous at all). A creature with language can describe his set—I mean merely that he can say "I expect such-and-such to happen." The set will then be duplicated, more or less, in the auditors; that is, the belief about what is going to happen will have been communicated. This makes possible the detachment of belief from immediate experience. (Remember that beliefs are anticipations and thus basically about the future. Historical and present-tense descriptions derive their interest initially only as they bear on what we are *going* to do.) Without language, conscious beliefs are concerned with the specious present only; they may persist as habits, i.e., established sets; but when not in the context of imminent action they are merely latent. With language, beliefs may be enunciated and consciously held (which perhaps are the same thing) at any time. Cats and dogs live only in the present; man takes thought for the morrow.

Thus language makes possible the holding of a belief that is *not* confronted forthwith with experimental verification or falsification. The language user can hold beliefs about what will happen in the remote future, or in hypothetical circumstances, or about what went on in past times and distant places not accessible to observation. That is, he can hold beliefs that are not low—not subject to frequent, or even any, direct confrontation with experience. Let us call these beliefs *high.* Examples: death will not be the end of experience; the Chief is the great-great-great-grandson of the Sun; We will survive and They will perish; everybody is secretly out to get me; somebody up there likes (or has it in for) me.

High beliefs include the unverifiable propositions of Positivism, but are a broader class: they are those beliefs that in fact, in a given cultural context, are not put to unambiguous test: either because they are logically unverifiable, or because it is impossible with available technology or difficult or expensive or dangerous or bothersome or boring or prohibited to try. "The gods live on Olympus" is a high belief where mountaineering is undeveloped.

Once language and hence imagination are developed, high beliefs may occur and be communicated in random fashion, inasmuch as reality (merely as such) imposes no limit on their formation. But there may be causes why some survive and some perish.

Both high and low beliefs influence action. Low beliefs do it directly: belief that *amanita phalloides* is toxic inhibits eating of that vege-

* After Paul Grice, *Studies in the Way of Words,* 1989. Eds. note.

table. The high belief that cows are sacred has a like effect on cows. The former belief has survival value; and so does the latter, as Marvin Harris has shown. (*Cows, Pigs, Wars, and Witches.*) We should expect high beliefs with this advantageous characteristic to survive and be passed on accordingly.

Returning to the hunter-gatherer band of forty members, can we say with any specificity what sorts of high beliefs we might expect to become established among them? Other things being equal, chances for survival will be enhanced by beliefs that reinforce industry, communal loyalty, cooperation, willingness to sacrifice immediate personal self-interest for the good of the group, subordination to leaders, and other civic virtues; and a conviction that the struggle to maintain the group is worthwhile. Without appropriate high beliefs these virtues and attitudes will constantly be in jeopardy. The facts of the case only too often tempt to despair, and the possibility of satisfying personal self-interest at group expense is omnipresent. The high belief is nature's way of resolving the prisoner's dilemma.

A survey of the stories told and believed—the high beliefs—in all cultures will show them to have these effects, at any rate before sophistication and decadence set in. The high beliefs taken together constitute a view of how things are, according to which it is in everybody's individual long-run interest to be a good citizen, to observe the rules, obey the powers that be, and contribute all one can to the communal good. And the individual believer is—in a higher sense—not deceived: it *is* this kind of behavior that makes life worth living, that wards off the ever-present danger of its becoming solitary, poor, nasty, brutish, and short. And, it seems, nothing else but high beliefs will do the job with the human species. One might think that rational beings would intellectually perceive the advantages of a social contract and enact one forthwith, or behave as if they or their ancestors had done so. But rational beings can hardly be prevented from seeing sooner or later that each has only one life to live and in its allotted time, the short run, the chance of its quality's being enhanced by fudging the contract (supposing it to exist) from time to time is too favorable to be passed up.

And so we can say that the evolutionarily stable human situation with regard to beliefs is this:

Members of the stable social unit, the forty hunter-gatherers, have in common two sets of beliefs:

The first, the low beliefs, are those that directly impinge on reality: that is, when the propositions believed are true, people who believe them are (on the whole) likelier to achieve those of their goals that are directly concerned with the objects of the beliefs, than if they do not believe them. These are the humdrum commonplaces about edibility and toxicity, the habits of animals, the succession of the seasons, how to build fires, smelt ores, set broken bones, prepare curare, how your fellows will probably behave in various kinds of situations, and so on and on. With rare exceptions all these low beliefs will be true. They constitute *knowledge.*

The second set, the high beliefs, do not directly impinge on reality, that is to say, if the proposition that is the object of a high belief happens to be false, it does not follow that one whose action is influenced by the (erroneous) belief that it is true, is put at a disadvantage. Nor, needless to say, if the proposition is true is there a disadvantage in disbelieving it. *The effects of high beliefs are independent of the truth values of the propositions believed.* Evolution therefore does not tend to reinforce true over false high beliefs, but rather those that have survival value, i.e., are such that those who believe them behave so as to favor the proliferation of their gene pool more than they would if they did not believe them.

As we have seen, low beliefs arise out of practical transactions between people and the world, and at least the simpler kinds do not presuppose language. High beliefs on the other hand are not with any plausibility to be ascribed to non-lingual creatures; they are the productions of imagination, which is a faculty available only to animals that can detach belief from present context; and that, we have argued, can only be done via language.

III

Thus high and low beliefs have distinct origins and quite different epistemologies. However, if high beliefs are to have the social function we have ascribed to them, *it is essential that the believers make no epistemological distinction between high and low.* That 'Zeus hurls the thunderbolt' must be taken as completely on a par with 'Fire burns.' Various expressions of high beliefs may be admitted to be metaphorical or otherwise imaginatively colored, but the conviction must be firm that there is some literal meaning behind them, however obscure it may be; and in particular, that the entities postulated in the high beliefs must really exist, in a straightforward sense. This necessity follows immediately from the fact that beliefs can influence conduct in only one way, namely in causing us to modify our behavior to take account of their (certain or probable) *truth.*

In the ideal steady state, then, high and low beliefs must never get in each other's way. And if there were a sharp, fixed line between them, they never could. If for example low/high corresponded to verifiable/unverifiable in the strict logical sense there could be no trouble; for low beliefs would all be expressed as singular propositions, universal generalizations being unverifiable. But 'all men are mortal' expresses a low belief, while 'The angel Gabriel appeared to Mary on 25 March, 1 B.C.' is high. And what happens when somebody at last climbs Olympus and finds it uninhabited?

It is marvelous how Nature managed to produce mechanisms that avoided these problems for countless eons. Here are some:

1. First and foremost, built-in credulousness, which as we have seen has a sound evolutionary reason for being.
2. For the most part, high beliefs, so far from clashing with low, purport to explain and systematize them. Roughly speaking, low beliefs are about phenomena, high beliefs get at the noumena alleged to be behind the facade.
3. The noumenal powers postulated by high beliefs are usually modelled on human agency and thus are endowed with free will or inscrutability that protects them against suspicion of non-existence when they do not perform as advertised. When, however, they "come through," they get full credit.
4. Although the noumenal powers are supposed to be omnipotent, that is, capable of performing any task, they are never called upon to do it by themselves, unless it is something (like parting the sea) that human beings cannot even *try* to do by themselves. In all other cases the believers are expected to exert their utmost efforts on their own behalf, whereupon the powers, if they see fit, may come to their aid. However differently the powers may be conceived, "God(s) help (only) those who help themselves" is an axiom in every system. This has to be so, since to rely on the transcendental powers to do what human effort might accomplish on its own, would be to subvert the original purpose of high beliefs, which is to encourage human effort. Evolution would abhor those who practised such a custom.
5. Emotions focus almost exclusively on high beliefs. Low beliefs for the most part are concerned only with the means of getting on with life; high beliefs are what make life worth living. They are typically enunciated by persons of special dignity, reinforced by impressive costumes and operating in surroundings enhanced by all the resources of art. High beliefs are frequently inscribed in marble, versified, set to music; low beliefs, seldom if ever.
6. Preeminent among high beliefs is belief in the reprehensibility of questioning high beliefs. In all cultures the high skeptic is a pariah, assumed to be wickeder than the merely behavioral criminal, seldom allowed to live within the confines of the tribe or even to live at all. The low skeptic, if (as is doubtful) one ever occurs, is merely pitied. And just to the extent that peoples outside

the group fail to share its high beliefs, they are held to be inferior or even subhuman.

7. *In extremis,* high beliefs take refuge in metaphorization. "Olympus" is discovered to have signified not the mountain in Thessaly but a high place outside merely human ken—or even outside space.

These are some of the factors operating to protect high beliefs, once they have been established, from doubt and revision. In primitive circumstances at least, all beliefs are high that express the people's conceptions of the hang of things, (what we should call) the general causal structure of the world. While the experience of being a causal agent insures that some beliefs of the form "C causes (is responsible for, is the way to produce) E" will be low, this lore is not generalized into a world-view except insofar as it affords the model for the purported modus operandi of the noumena.

IV

Nevertheless systems of high beliefs, like everything else human except low beliefs, are mortal. They begin and end with the cultures of which they form the backbones. They get superseded by, or amalgamated into, other systems as the primitive units of forty coalesce after the discovery of agriculture. And new systems appropriate to that advanced way of life develop: fertility gods, divine kings, sanctification of serfdom and so on. Some new limitations develop as well: for example with the invention of writing, the past, to the extent that it becomes documented, is made accessible to low beliefs and is no longer wide open to high scenarios. But the wall between low and high remains unbreached.—until the first half of the sixth century B.C., in the Ionian cities.

There and then occurred the most momentous event in intellectual history: the birth of science, which we are now in a position to define as *the extension of low beliefs into the domain previously reserved exclusively to the high:* that is to say, a world-view rooted in beliefs that survive frequent testing by confrontation with the reality out there. Thales of Miletus gave an account of the underlying nature of things and of cosmic processes that was couched in terms derived from ordinary experiences such as the silting up of harbors, and of commonly observed properties of things such as the ability of water to exist in all three phases, solid, liquid, and gaseous (as we should say). Perhaps Thales' account was hardly nearer the literal truth about the world than what the Babylonian priests had said before him. That was not the important thing; the revolution consisted in having produced the first element in a *convergent* series. For the new view was accessible to criticism and modification in the light of experience-based data. Thus the series was continued first by Anaximander who criticized and improved on his teacher's account both by logical argumentation and by calling attention to the significance of data not incorporated into it; and by Anaximenes who similarly (though not so happily) dealt with Anaximander's account in turn. And from that day to this the advance of the objective, scientific conception of the nature of things, though frequently slowed, sometimes stopped, and once or twice even pushed back, has proved inexorable. This is the triumph of low belief.

We can see in hindsight some of the factors that made possible this mutation in thought. On the one hand, the high belief systems in this part of the world were many, jostling up against each other; complicated, hard to make into a coherent whole (though Hesiod tried, with more or less success); and devoid of the crucial support of a professional class with personal interests identified with their protection, such as existed in Egypt, Babylon, and nearly everywhere else. On the other hand, the collection of observations of nature and technological expertise seems to have reached a critical mass; the people involved had, it seems, a special acuity for logical connections and systematizations, as shown not only by the example of Hesiod but by their simultaneous invention of the first structured deductive corpus of mathematical truths. Egyptians and Babylonians knew many mathematical propositions and could make sophisticated calculations, but they seem to have had no conception of arrangement into a deductive system of theorems explicitly derived from primitive propositions. And as the contemporary flowering of lyric poetry shows, individuality was developing and finding expression to an unprecedented extent. Anyway, it happened; and never—independently—anywhere else.

It took these extraordinary Greeks scarcely five generations to work out the objective view of the world, culminating in Democritus's atomic theory, that in its essential structure endures to the present day: the view, that is to say, that sees the world as a dynamic material structure in which alteration occurs in accord with formulable regularities inherent in the entities—not imposed on lumpishly inert stuff from outside. And we find this conception supported not by inspiration or tradition but by explicit argumentation appealing to sensible phenomena and logical inferences based thereon. Perhaps the uniqueness and unexpectedness of the beginning of science caused the partisans of high beliefs among the Greeks—of course they constituted the vast majority—to respond tardily to it. Although it was noticed as early as Xenophanes that the new view of things was irreconcilable with many current high beliefs, not until the prosecution of Anaxagoras in the middle of the fifth century—well over a hundred years after Thales—is there evidence of popular awareness of the conflict, and not until Aristophanes' *Clouds* does the high reaction achieve literary expression. By that time the new outlook was too firmly established to be obliterated; the best that could be done in defense of high belief systems is illustrated by Plato's philosophy, which used pseudo-scientific argumentation, not in a crude attempt to reinstate the old high system, but to produce a new one deemed adequate to generate the piety essential to a stable social order.

For Aristophanes and Plato were perfectly well aware of the consequences of the damage to high beliefs done by the scientific view of things: Unjust Logos and Thrasymachus are taking over. One beats one's father, and, realizing that the laws and customs are merely restraints invented by the powerful and clever to make others serve their interests, one devotes one's ingenuity to their circumvention. One prospers, for a while; then the deluge.

Plato thought he had discovered a class of entities, the Ideas, that were at once the objects of true scientific study and of moral allegiance. Noticing, rightly, that our mathematical beliefs are the securest and most objective that we have, and understandably supposing them to be *about* intelligible but not sensible things, he concluded that every meaningful universal term must, like a numeral, name a fixed intelligible entity, and in particular Justice must. Consequently, he thought, real Knowledge is not about sensible things at all; in our terms, low beliefs cannot aspire to objective scientific status, and Ionian subversion is frustrated. Real science is vindicated as being, after all, high: its objects are never encountered in vulgar sensible experience. Plato's mistake can be diagnosed as a failure to note that mathematical beliefs are low, impinging on experience constantly. Whatever the answer may be to the vexed question of what they are *about,* it cannot affect this fact.

Abandoning the Ideas, Aristotle attempted to found objective ethics and politics on the facts (confirmed low beliefs) of human nature. Perhaps he succeeded, or at least showed the way to success.

V

The problem that so worried Plato, of how to protect the belief structure basic to a viable society from undermining by science, cannot be said to have been a terribly serious practical one for his times. The very existence of science was known only to a few, and it had little effect on technology. The disintegration of the moral system noted by Thucydides was due mostly to other causes. And it was still possible without abandoning reason simply to reject the scientific outlook altogether. It was an alternative, a rival, to the traditional high belief system, but no more; the Greek could still pay his money and take his choice. But *we* cannot—not since Galileo and Darwin, who first presented evidence that *directly* controverted the system of high beliefs. And the knowledge that this has happened can no longer be concealed from the vulgar.

As anthropologists and geneticists have noted, there is an important sense in which every kind of life other than that of the small hunter-gatherer band is unnatural to our species: we are not evolutionarily adapted to it. In consequence we experience various tensions and are the victims of a certain kind of irrationality: the attitudes, the propensities to behavior built into our genes as appropriate to the hunter-gatherer band, keep on being manifested in circumstances where they are at best no longer appropriate and at worst may prove lethal.

In this paper I have been concerned with one aspect of the general problem presented by our so rapid progress. (I do not put scare quotes around the word, for I believe in a real ascent of man. But:) The beliefs we need for getting around in the world must correspond to the way things are. The beliefs we need in order to form viable social units (without which we would perish utterly) on the other hand must persuade us that there is a tight fit between behavior in the short-run individual interest and in the long-run social interest. Since that proposition seems to be objectively false, it cannot in logic be supported by true propositions alone. So to get along, we need some beliefs that are true, and some that are false.

Evolution took care of the problem of keeping the disparate classes of beliefs separate, while blinding us to their difference in kind, as long as our life was the 'natural' human one. The solution proved adequate for five millennia or so in which the conditions of human existence underwent the most astounding alterations in every respect.

The Greeks changed all that. Almost all the old high beliefs have either vanished altogether or are moribund. The human propensity for high believing is of course still there in full force, and in our time is being satisfied, if that is the word, by political creeds, which tend to command the emotional allegiances lavished on religion in the old days. (Religion and politics are of course one.) But whether this expedient can keep us afloat, is the question.

PART IX

The Historical Challenge

Ignatius of Loyola founded the Jesuit order, the spearhead of the Counter-Reformation. After he was sainted in 1622 the Jesuits built the church of S. Ignazio in Rome; the ceiling depicts the saint entering heaven.

J. L. Mackie

"NATURAL HISTORIES OF RELIGION"

A brief biography of Mackie appears on page 322.

William James thought that the religious experiences of individuals were the nucleus and root of all religion, and that all factual claims going beyond what such experiences themselves contain, all metaphysical theology, and all socially organized and institutionalized religion, are merely secondary outgrowths from this root.

From J. L. Mackie, *The Miracle of Theism,* Clarendon Press, 1982, pp. 187–198. Reprinted by permission of Oxford University Press.

But this is controversial. . . [P]articular religious experiences are in general very much coloured by or even parasitic upon, the traditions in or near which they occur. This *might* mean only that each single experience is affected by a residue from earlier religious experiences; but it leaves not merely open but far more likely the alternative possibility that religion has sources other than any such experiences, that experiences in the sense in which James has surveyed them interact with other currents of thought and feeling to generate religion as a whole.

. . . [T]he general character of religious and mystical experiences invites us to assimilate them to otherwise familiar and explicable mental phenomena; but such an explanation of their *general* character would leave unaccounted for just those elements in their content which make them *specifically* religious. For any single experience, it is easy to explain these further elements as having been drawn in from a surrounding religious tradition—even a convert like St. Paul or Alphonse Ratisbonne (see James, pp. 225–8) will already be in touch with, although hostile to, the movement to which he is converted, and is likely to have been brought up in some related tradition. But this explanation obviously cannot account for these elements in the whole body of religious experience, unless we postulate some source for them other than those experiences themselves. If no other source could be found, there would be more plausibility in James's view that although 'on the hither side' the supposed objects of these experiences can be understood as belonging to the subconscious continuation of our conscious life, we need to postulate something 'on the farther side' as well, that the natural psychological mechanisms may be a route by which we have access to an otherwise unseen supernatural reality, and that 'If there were such

History vs. Religion

Strictly speaking, it is not science, narrowly construed, but rather scientific habits of mind that invariably come into conflict with religious orthodoxy. Socrates, for instance, was not a scientist in the modern sense, but one of several influential Greek philosophers who laid the groundwork for scientific thinking. In our own times, modern historical methodology, while also clearly not a science, is imbued with the spirit of scientific inquiry and may in the end be as corrosive as science of the historical myths that are so crucial to many of the adherents of religious traditions.

Religious authorities who give great importance to historical myths of what happened, and why, at some crucial time in the past are increasingly challenged by modern historians who approach the same periods and events not as an exercise in the elaboration of mythology but rather with an eye to constructing interpretations to be evaluated in the sobering light of publicly available evidence. Were it not for the fact, for instance, that high schools in the United States typically do not teach any scientifically inspired historical accounts of early Christianity, there would no doubt be a movement in some states to try to force the schools to teach Christian history side by side with regular nonmythological history.

a thing as inspiration from a higher realm, it might well be that the neurotic temperament would furnish the chief condition of the requisite receptivity' (p. 45).

In fact, several other sources have been proposed, most notably perhaps by Hume (in association with whom we can take such anthropologists as E. B. Tylor, Sir James Frazer, and R. R. Marett), Feuerbach, Marx, and Freud. Hume entitled his work on this topic *The Natural History of Religion,*[1] implying that he would describe religion as a natural phenomenon, with an origin in human nature, in much the same way as botanists describe plants or zoologists describe animals in their branches of 'natural history'. We can borrow this title as a general name for the whole class of projects of this sort.

In the *Natural History,* which was published soon after it was written, not held in reserve, like the *Dialogues,* until after Hume's death, Hume pretends to take as established truth a philosophical theism rationally based on the argument for design. But, he argues, this pure theism is not the ordinary religion of mankind. The first religion was, he says, polytheism or idolatry. Literary records show that (apart from Judaism, which he rather surprisingly ignores) 'about 1700 years ago all mankind were idola-

1. D. Hume, *The Natural History of Religion,* edited by A. W. Colver in *David Hume on Religion* (Oxford University Press, 1976). References in the text are to pages in this edition.

"Religion as Wish Fulfillment"

Sigmund Freud

At this point one must expect to meet with an objection. "Well then if even obdurate sceptics admit that the assertions of religion cannot be refuted by reason, why should I not believe in them, since they have so much on their side—tradition, the agreement of mankind, and all the consolations they offer?" Why not, indeed? Just as no one can be forced to believe, so no one can be forced to disbelieve. But do not let us be satisfied with deceiving ourselves that arguments like these take us along the road of correct thinking. If ever there was a case of a lame excuse we have it here. Ignorance is ignorance; no right to believe anything can be derived from it. In other matters no sensible person will behave so irresponsibly or rest content with such feeble grounds for his opinions and for the line he takes. It is only in the highest and most sacred things that he allows himself to do so. In reality these are only attempts at pretending to oneself or to other people that one is still firmly attached to religion, when one has long since cut oneself loose from it. Where questions of religion are concerned, people are guilty of every possible sort of dishonesty and intellectual misdemeanor. Philosophers stretch the meaning of words until they retain scarcely anything of their original sense. They give the name of "God" to some vague abstraction which they have created for themselves; having done so they can pose before all the world as deists, as believers in God, and they can even boast that they have recognized a higher, purer concept of God, notwithstanding that their God is now nothing more than an insubstantial shadow and no longer the mighty personality of religious doctrines. Critics persist in describing as "deeply religious" anyone who admits to a sense of man's insignificance or impotence in the face of the universe, although what constitutes the essence of the religious attitude is not this feeling but only the next step after it, the reaction to it which seeks a remedy for it. The man who goes no further, but humbly acquiesces in the small part which human beings play in the great world—such a man is, on the contrary, irreligious in the truest sense of the word.

From *The Future of an Illusion* (1927).

ters'; but he also argues *a priori* that theism could not have been the primary religion of the human race, because the sort of reasoning that would lead to it does not come naturally to most people. They do not in general look for a cause or explanation of the overall order in the world, or of the 'marks of design' in plants and animals, for these are all familiar and are so taken for granted. It is irregularities, prodigies, and unpredictable calamities that suggest supernatural powers, and still more the particular needs and uncertainties in human life: 'the first ideas of religion arose not from a contemplation of the works of nature, but . . . from the incessant hopes and fears, which actuate the human mind', and these lead men to acknowledge 'several limited and imperfect deities' (pp. 30–1). And although monotheism has now arisen and spread very widely, Hume argues that its success is due not to the (supposedly) cogent reasoning in the design argument, but to a curious development from polytheism. A nation comes to give special adoration to some one tutelary deity chosen from the pantheon, or, modelling the society of gods and goddesses on human monarchies, it makes one the ruler over the rest. In either case, competition in flattery of this chosen god elevates him ultimately to the status of a perfect being, creator and absolute monarch of the universe (pp. 51–3). Yet there is, Hume says, 'a kind of flux and reflux in the human mind'; contrary tendencies lead from idolatry to theism but also back again from theism to idolatry (pp. 56–7). The one trend could be illustrated by the transition from 'Thou shalt not make unto thee any graven image . . . Thou shalt not bow down thyself to them, nor serve them' and 'Thou shalt have no other gods before me' to the dictum that 'There is no god but God'. In the opposing trend, men seek particular objects of devotion, closer to them than the one perfect and universal god, and more attentive to their special needs: this is illustrated by the role of the saints in Catholicism. Whereas William James *advocates* 'piecemeal supernaturalism', Hume thinks that it is rationally much less defensible than monotheism, but in some ways better adapted to the emotional needs of mankind.

Hume's main purpose in this work is to drive a wedge between the religions that actually flourish and secure people's allegiance—whether polytheist or monotheist, or, by recognizing saints, angels, and so on, a compromise between the two—and the pure philosophical theism, verging on deism, that alone seemed to him likely to command any rational support. He wants to show that philosophy cannot be used to defend any ordinary popular religion. If philosophy is incorporated into a theology, 'instead of regulating each principle, as they'—that is, philosophy and theology—'advance together, she is at every turn perverted to serve the purposes of superstition' (p. 65). He concludes:

> What a noble privilege it is of human reason to attain the knowledge of the supreme being; and, from the visible works of nature, be enabled to infer so sublime a principle as its supreme Creator. But turn the reverse of the medal . . . Examine the religious principles, which have, in fact, prevailed in the world. You will scarcely be persuaded, that they are other than sick men's dreams: Or perhaps will regard them more as the playsome whimsies of monkeys in human shape, than the serious, positive, dogmatical asseverations of a being, who dignifies himself with the name of rational. (p. 94)

'Playsome whimsies', however, describes only some of the less important embroideries on religious thought, and 'sick men's dreams' sums up rather that side of religion that is based on the sorts of experience that James has surveyed. Neither phrase is adequate to the most important themes in Hume's own discussion, the way in which piecemeal supernaturalism expresses and satisfies needs that arise from all the varied uncertainties of human life, from hopes and fears about events which are largely uncontrollable and whose causes are largely unknown, and the way in which a special relation to a particular chosen deity may lead from idolatry to monotheism.

It is surely beyond question that these are real tendencies in human thinking, and that they have contributed, along with the religious or mystical experiences of individuals, to the religious tradition. Moreover, these tendencies naturally find expression in social, organized, forms of religion. It is in groups that people commonly face and try to cope with life's uncertainties or significant changes—birth, adolescence, marriage, and death—and it was, notably, a tribe or nation which having first seen itself as his chosen people, then turned Jehovah into a universal god.

Later anthropologists inserted animism and magical belief as a stage preceding the worship of departmental deities (though still later workers in this field have cast doubt on any simple evolutionary pattern). This would not seriously affect Hume's argument; but it lends itself to exaggerations which are open to criticism. Tylor and Frazer saw magic as essentially a kind of pseudo-science and pseudo-technology, the imagining of causal relationships in many places where there are none (based on just those principles of resemblance and contiguity which Hume saw as the principles of the association of ideas) and the attempt to use these imagined causal connections to bring about desired results. But D. Z. Phillips, following Wittgenstein, protests that such an account 'asks us to believe that so-called primitive men were ignorant of elementary natural facts and elementary causal connections', whereas 'the facts easily refute this suggestion. The peoples concerned possessed considerable technical skills and knowledge. They had a thriving agriculture and . . . had to take advantage of the regularity of the seasons . . . They were also skilled hunters. They made their own weapons, knew where to look for their prey and how to stalk it . . . how could any of this be possible if they were imprisoned by the kind of ignorance ascribed to them by Tylor and Frazer?'[2] This comment would apply only to a suggestion that among these peoples the belief in

2. D. Z. Phillips, *Religion without Explanation* (Basil Blackwell, Oxford, 1976), pp. 32–3.

"Freud's View of Religion"

John Hick

In *Totem and Taboo,* Freud uses his distinctive concept of the Oedipus complex (which rests on concurrent ambivalent feelings) to account for the tremendous emotional intensity of religious life and the associated feelings of guilt and of obligation to obey the behests of the deity. He postulates a stage of human prehistory in which the unit was the "primal horde" consisting of father, mother, and offspring. The father, as the dominant male, retained to himself exclusive rights over the females and drove away or killed any of the sons who challenged his position. Finding that individually they could not defeat the father-leader, the sons eventually banded together to kill (and also, being cannibals, to eat) him. This was the primal crime, the patricide that has set up tensions within the human psyche out of which have developed moral inhibitions, totemism, and the other phenomena of religion. Having slain their father, the brothers are struck with remorse. They also find that they cannot all succeed to his position and that there is a continuing need for restraint. The dead father's prohibition accordingly takes on new ("moral") authority as a taboo against incest. This association of religion with the Oedipus complex, which is renewed in each individual (for Freud believed the Oedipus complex to be universal), is held to account for the mysterious authority of God in the human mind and the powerful guilt feelings which make people submit to such a fantasy.

From *Philosophy of Religion,* 3d ed. (1983).

magical pseudocausation replaced and excluded all recognition of genuine causal relations; otherwise there is no problem. These peoples, like the rest of us, knew of some genuine causal connections but not others, and like us often felt the need to control things that they could not control by natural means. As Phillips himself admits, 'Tylor and Frazer saw [the rituals] as supplementations to the purposive activities . . . which we have already referred to'. There is no implausibility in supposing that people who use rational and efficient methods of achieving their purposes *also* believe in, and *to some extent* rely upon, the direct causal efficacy of magical devices or religious ceremonies. We need only recall the extent to which quack medicine, fringe medicine, and indeed large parts of respectable medicine have constantly flourished and been relied upon, in the most civilized societies, even where there has been no significant causal connection, by the intended routes, between their treatments and recovery. They are believed to be efficacious in ways in which they are not, partly because we very much want help and reassurance that are not otherwise available, and partly because, either by chance or through the psychological effect of the comfort they give, their treatments are followed by recovery often enough to yield apparent confirmations of their claims. And exactly the same has been true of the causal claims of magic and of primitive (and not so primitive) religion.

The real mistake made by these anthropologists was to suggest that magic functioned *only* as pseudo-science and pseudo-technology. No doubt the rituals had genuinely beneficial, if not explicitly intended, effects in sustaining morale and co-operation. Also, as Phillips says, they would have an expressive character. But he is quite wrong in saying that 'When rituals are seen as expressions of this kind, it can also be seen that in no sense are they based on hypotheses or opinions' (p. 36). They can easily be *both* expressive *and* causally purposive. And, curiously, Phillips is equally critical of R. R. Marett's view that these rituals have the function of relieving emotional stress (pp. 49–55). Yet when he says 'the ritual is not performed in *order* to express anything; it *is* the expression of something' (p. 52), he is not denying anything that Marett, or any similar theorist, asserts: of course it is not being suggested that the savage first recognizes his emotional stress as such and then deliberately invents a ritual to discharge it. Phillips's other criticism is that the emotions cannot explain the religious (or magical) thinking, because they themselves arise only within a religious or magical tradition; but again all that is being criticized here is an absurdly oversimplified causal model. Of course there is interaction between the emotions and the religious thought. But this in no way tells against the hypothesis that feelings which have their sources partly in other aspects of life contribute, both as originating and as sustaining causes, along with mistaken but understandable causal beliefs, to the tradition of magical or religious practice and thought.

Men's hopes and fears, their practical and emotional needs, supply most of the force and help to determine the character of religion; but we must look elsewhere for the source of what we may call its pictorial or descriptive content. Magical relations are, perhaps, merely pseudo-causal and impersonal; but the supernatural, whether in animism or polytheism or monotheism, has usually been conceived as personal. Men have made not only their first but also their last gods in their own image. Being conscious of personality in themselves and in one another, they imagined innumerable spirits as persons with thoughts, desires, and purposes somewhat like their own, responding to men somewhat as men respond to one another, and actively fulfilling intentions through such control over material things as men sometimes have and more often wish to have. Ludwig Feuerbach argues that what was thus obviously true of earlier religions remains true of the most sophisticated, for example of Christianity with its metaphysical concepts of infinite perfection, of the *ens realissimum,* and the doctrines of the incarnation and the trinity.[3] All such descriptive content is borrowed from human nature. 'Man—this is the mystery of religion—projects his being into objectivity, and then again makes himself an object to this projected image of himself' (p. 29). 'What was at first religion becomes at a later period idolatry; man is seen to have adored his own nature . . . But every particular religion, while it pronounces its predecessors idolatrous, excepts itself . . . it imputes only to other religions what is the fault, if fault it be, of religion in general' (p. 13). Anthropomorphism is not really, Feuerbach thinks, a fault, for its complete avoidance would be a denial of religion; a thoroughgoing negative theology 'is simply a subtle, disguised atheism' (p. 15). 'Religious anthropomorphisms . . . are in contradiction with the understanding; it repudiates their application to God . . . But this God, free from anthropomorphisms, impartial, passionless, is nothing less than the nature of the understanding itself regarded as objective' (p. 35). 'Thus the understanding is the *ens realissimum* . . . What . . . is the nature conceived without limits, but the nature of the understanding releasing, abstracting itself from all limits' (pp. 38–9). Again, 'God as a morally perfect being is nothing else than the realised idea, the fulfilled law of morality, the moral nature of man posited as the absolute being'; but by adding the notion of God as love man 'delivers himself from this state of disunion between himself and the perfect being, from the painful consciousness of sin, from the distressing sense of his own nothingness' (pp. 46–8). The incarnation and the trinity represent human tenderness and social union. Thus various aspects of the Christian god are projections of human understanding, will, and affection. In the end, 'God is the self-consciousness of man freed from all discordant elements' (pp. 97–8).

Feuerbach is, indeed, concerned not only to explain religion but also to recommend a religion of his own. He suggests that we can find in humanity as a whole, in man as a species, the freedom from the limitations of individuals which traditional religions have fictionally postulated in God. We can find a satisfying religious object by eliminating the errors of supernaturalism and making explicit the human aspirations of which previous religions have been distorted expressions. But this proposal is unpersuasive. Though mankind as a whole may be free from many of the limitations of individuals, it is certainly not free from all limitations, it is not omnipotent or omniscient or morally perfect, and many of the needs that religion expresses and purports to fulfil will not be satisfied by mankind as a whole, even on the most optimistic view of its future. But such defects in Feuerbach's proposal do not entail that there are errors in his explanation. No doubt it, like others, only *helps* to account for religion; but the projection of human nature, especially of the moral aspirations which themselves arise from the social interactions between human beings, certainly contributes significantly to the content of religious ideas.

An important variant of Feuerbach's approach is to see religion less as a projection of forms of individual thought and feeling than as a representation of human society. A body of religious practice, with its associated beliefs, is a way in which a social group copes as a unit with the various crises that confront it or its members. Taking the beliefs as being essentially subordinate to this function, we can think of Jehovah as a personification of a certain movement or tradition or spirit (in the metaphorical sense) in which the Israelites were to some extent caught up, though other tendencies repeatedly drew them away from this one. Similarly, we can think of Pallas Athene not just as the tutelary deity of Athens, but as a personification of the spirit of political unity and joint purpose in the Athenian people. In John Anderson's phrase, God is the social movement.[4] Such movements, traditions, and institutions are both

3. L. Feuerbach, *The Essence of Christianity,* translated by Marian Evans (Kegan Paul, London, 1893). References in the text are to pages in this edition.

4. John Anderson, Professor of Philosophy at the University of Sydney, 1927–58, made this remark more than once in discussion, though I have not been able to find it in his published works.

external and internal to the individual, as God in religious experience is felt to be. They are larger, independent, realities, objectively existent though not directly perceivable. The individual is not merely governed by them but also caught up in them: they enter into him and help to constitute his nature. This is, therefore, another way in which we can not merely explain but make true the believer's conviction that he is moved by an external power, that (in James's summary) he finds in himself a part which is 'continuous with a MORE of the same quality which is operative in the universe outside of him'. But, obviously, we must add that the god or gods of traditional religion are distorted representations of such social realities: we must still account otherwise—by reference to the other side of Feuerbach's theory, or to Freud's—for the element of personification.

Any adequate social explanation of religion must take account of social division and conflict as well as co-operation. Here the classic statement is that of Karl Marx:

> Religion . . . is the self-consciousness and the self-feeling of the man who either has not yet found himself, or else (having found himself) has lost himself once more. But man is not an abstract being . . . Man is the world of men, the State, society. This State, this society, produce religion, produce a perverted world consciousness, because they are a perverted world . . . Religion is the sigh of the oppressed creature, the feelings of a heartless world, just as it is the spirit of unspiritual conditions. It is the opium of the people.
>
> The people cannot be really happy until it has been deprived of illusory happiness by the abolition of religion. The demand that the people should shake itself free of illusion as to its own condition is the demand that it should abandon a condition which needs illusion.[5]

This is echoed by Engels:

> All *religion* . . . is nothing but the fantastic reflection in men's minds of those external forces which control their daily life, a reflection in which the terrestrial forces assume the form of supernatural forces . . . when *society, by taking possession of all means of production and using them on a planned basis,* has freed itself and all its members from the bondage in which they are now held by these means of production which they themselves have produced but which confront them as an irrestible alien force . . . only then *will the last alien force which is still reflected in religion vanish; and with it will also vanish the religious reflection itself,* for the simple reason that then there will be nothing left to reflect.[6]

This view has several different facets. Most directly, it means that those who are deprived and exploited find, or are given, an illusory consolation in religion (either in the prospect of happiness in an afterlife or in the immediate joys of corporate religious experience) which reconciles them to their material poverty and helplessness, and so weakens their resistance to oppression and prevents them from resorting to revolution. Less directly, it means that the system of religious thought is part of an ideology through which the ruling class sees its position and procedures as justified, and, insofar as this ideology is transmitted to the lower classes, they too are encouraged to accept the existing order as right and proper, and to see any revolt against it as being also a rebellion against God. In particular, some of the typical Christian virtues, such as meekness, humility, obedience, non-resistance, and non-retaliation are well adapted to keeping subordinates in their place, while their betters are content to recommend these virtues rather than practice them. More generally still, it means that religion is an expression of an alienated human nature, of a situation where

5. K. Marx, *Introduction to a Critique of the Hegelian Philosophy of Right,* in K. Marx and F. Engels, *Collected Works* (Lawrence & Wishart, London, 1975 onwards), Vol. 3.

6. F. Engels, *Anti-Dühring* (Lawrence & Wishart, London, 1969), pp. 374–6.

some success for the material betterment of oppressed and deprived classes, and have not merely provided other-worldly consolations. Equally, the men are cut off both from one another and from the economic resources and forces which they have brought into existence, and can be expected to disappear when such alienation ceases.

There are elements of truth in this view, and it too is a contribution to a natural history of religion. But it also contains wild exaggerations. It is easy to point out that there have been revolutionary religions as well as ones that have defended the established order, and that religiously influenced movements have worked with some success for the material betterment of oppressed and deprived classes, and have not merely provided other-worldly consolations. Equally, the 'sighs' that religion expresses arise not only from economic deprivation and political oppression, but also from psychological tensions with various other causes. Again, Engels's theory of 'reflection' is far too crude, and if it were seen merely as a metaphor it would not sustain the conclusion he draws from it. Once the religious tradition has arisen—and obviously it arose long before class conflicts took their present form—it has naturally a force and a history of its own: it is not a mere epiphenomenon but interacts with the politico-economic order: nor is it merely used by other social forces. There is therefore little reason to suppose that religion would disappear if politico-economic alienation were removed. What is more, the characteristic Marxist over-optimism of expecting social conflict and alienation themselves to disappear after a proletarian revolution is itself best understood as a kind of secularized salvationism, the expression of a consoling illusion different, indeed, in specific content but not in general character from the vision of a supernatural ideal realm.

"The Conflict between Religion and Science"

Morris R. Cohen

Consider the attitude of a simple man or woman to anyone who offers to prove that we come from an inferior stock, or that our country is inferior in merit to its traditional rivals. Who can doubt that the first and most patent reaction will be resentment rather than intellectual curiosity? And the same is bound to be our attitude as regards religion, so long as the latter integrates in simple piety all traditional and habitual loyalties to the sources of our being. Thus arises the fierce intolerance of religion as contrasted with the cultivated open-mindedness of science. To religion, agreement is a practical and emotional necessity, and doubt is a challenge and an offense. We cannot tolerate those who will interfere with or break up the hallowed customs of our group. Science, on the other hand, is a game in which opposing claims only add zest and opportunity. If the foundations of Euclidean geometry or Newtonian physics are suddenly questioned, some individual scientists may show their human limitations. But science as a whole has its field widened thereby, great enthusiasm is created for new investigations, and the innovators are objects of grateful general homage. Science does not need, therefore, to organize crusades to kill off heretics or unbelievers. Science, like art, enjoys its own activity and this enjoyment is not interfered with by anyone who obstinately refuses to join the game or scoffs at what the scientist has proved. The scientific banquet is not spoiled by our neighbors' refusing to enjoy it.

Thus it comes to pass that religion passionately clings to traditional beliefs which science light-heartedly overthrows in order to satisfy its insatiable curiosity or its desire for logical consistency.

The conflict between science and religion is thus a conflict between loyalty to the old, and disinterested and morally irresponsible curiosity about everything.

From *The Faith of a Liberal* (1946).

Another influential natural history of religion is that proposed by Freud and other psychoanalysts. The central theme in psychoanalysis is that a great many phenomena—dreams, neuroses, psychoses, mistakes and slips, but also large parts of culture, including religion—can be understood in terms of the fulfillment of unconscious and often repressed wishes. Freud saw an analogy between religious rituals and the elaborate and repeated performances of obsessional neurotics. In *Totem and Taboo* he explained both these primitive systems of thought and later religions, especially Christianity, as having arisen from events in the Darwinian 'primal horde', where the sons killed the father whom they not only hated but also loved and admired.[7] He saw religion as one expression among others of the Oedipus complex, the relic of an infant son's ambivalent attitude to his father: man's relation to a god is modelled on the infantile state of helpless dependence on a father who is both a benefactor and a tyrant. Thus religious ideas are 'illusions, fulfillments of the oldest, strongest, and most urgent wishes of mankind'.[8]

The details of Freud's speculations are open to many doubts and criticisms. On the other hand, the general theses that religion expresses and seems to fulfil very strong and persistent wishes, both conscious and unconscious, and that the believer's supposed relation to God (or the gods) is significantly like that of a child to its parents, and is probably influenced by the adult's memory of that relation, will hardly be disputed. What is disputable is the claim that individual psychology (even aided by a very dubious sort of race memory) can *on its own* provide a full explanation of religious phenomena.

Two main conclusions emerge from this survey of some proposed natural histories of religion. First, it would be a mistake to think that any one of them, by itself, can fully account for religion; but it is very likely that each of them correctly identifies factors which have contributed to some extent to religion, whether to the content of its beliefs, or to its emotional power, or to its practices and organization, both as originating and as sustaining causes. But, secondly, even an adequate, unified, natural history which incorporated all these factors would not in itself amount to a disproof of theism. As William James and many others have insisted, no account of the origin of a belief can settle the question whether that belief is or is not true. Not that any of our theorists thought that it did. Hume, in his *Natural History,* pretended to assume that a pure theism, and only a pure theism, was true; his aim was to separate popular, living, religion from this defensible philosophical view of the world. Feuerbach, Marx, and Freud all assumed that the explicit doctrines of religion, taken literally, were false; but they also assumed that this falsity had been established already, before they offered their accounts of the origin of religion. Marx was an atheist long before he became a socialist or communist or economic theorist; Freud was an atheist long before he discovered psychoanalysis. This whole natural-history approach neither is nor purports to be a *primary* case against theism.

Nevertheless, as we have already noted, it contributes indirectly and subordinately to the case against theism. Our reply to the argument from religious experience to further, supernaturalists, claims, even when these are as tentative and unorthodox as those put forward by William James, was that we need not postulate any supernatural source or sources for these experiences, since they can be fully explained on purely natural grounds, by reference to otherwise familiar psychological processes and forces. But this explanation, as we originally sketched it, was incomplete. Any single religious experience could be understood, given the context and background of the religious tradition within (or in the neighbourhood of) which it occurred. But

7. S. Freud, *Standard Edition of the Complete Psychological Works* (Hogarth Press, London, 1953 onwards); see especially *Totem and Taboo* (Vol. XIII, 1957) and *The Future of an Illusion* (Vol. XXI, 1961).

8. *The Future of an Illusion,* p. 30.

such traditions themselves were in need of further explanation. If no independent further explanation were on offer, there would be some plausibility in James's suggestion that the whole body of religious experience should be seen as a series of contacts with an objective unseen realm, the 'neurotic temperament' merely providing 'receptivity' to messages from that realm. But if there is, as we have seen, a set of factors which between them provide an adequate explanation of all those elements in the religious tradition which are not covered by the familiar psychological analogues of religious experience, then James's suggestion loses all its plausibility. Here, as elsewhere, the supernaturalist hypothesis fails because there is an adequate and much more economical naturalistic alternative.

It is, indeed, surprising that popular defenders of religion so often argue that man has a natural, psychological, need for religious belief. For, insofar as this is so, it tells not for but against the truth of theism, by explaining why religious beliefs would arise and persist, and why they would be propagated and enforced and defended as vigorously as they are, even if there were no good reason to suppose them to be true.

There is, however, one further loose end to be tied up. We have noted D. Z. Phillip's criticisms of such thinkers as Tylor, Frazer, and Marett. He is similarly critical of Feuerbach, Durkheim, and Freud. But we have not yet examined his main objection to all such explanations of religion, which underlies his contrary advocacy of 'religion without explanation'. They all presuppose that what is essential to religion, and is therefore in need of explanation, is belief in an objective supernatural reality. Phillips is ready to concede, as his opponents hold, that such beliefs would be either false or meaningless, or at least ungrounded: this, he admits, has been established by Hume and his successors, provided that the religious statements are interpreted, as Hume and his successors have assumed, as making literal, factual, claims. But Phillips, following Wittgenstein, thinks that religion need not and should not be thus understood. If he is right, then our natural histories do, indeed, miss the mark. What they seek to explain is at any rate not the vital heart of religion. . . .

Raymond Martin

"HISTORICAL JUDGMENT: THE DEBATE OVER THE SYNOPTIC PROBLEM"

A brief biography of Martin appears on p. 141.

The Synoptic Problem is the problem of explaining why there are certain agreements and disagreements among the texts of the New Testament Gospels of St. Matthew, St. Mark and St. Luke. The agreements and disagreements at issue are legion. In examining them, I shall use the expressions, "St. Matthew," "St. Mark," and so on, to refer respectively to the *authors* of the several gospels—whoever these authors may be—and the expressions, "Matthew," "Mark," and so on, to refer to the *Gospels* themselves.

Some of the more significant of these agreements and disagreements are the following: (1) Most of the subject matter of Mark is also in Matthew, and much of it is also in Luke. There is little of the subject matter of Mark that is not also in either Matthew or Luke; Matthew and Luke, on the other hand, contain much subject matter that is not in Mark. (2) Subject matter that is in all three Gospels usually occurs in the same order. When common subject matter is ordered differently in Matthew than it is in Mark, Luke's order tends to agree with the order in Mark. When it is ordered differently in Luke than it is in Mark, Matthew's order tends to agree with the order of Mark. (3) Matthew and Luke, in the subject matter they share with Mark, are often similar in wording, and Matthew and Luke tend not to have significant words in common unless Mark has them also. Frequently, Mark and Matthew will share the same wording, while Luke diverges, or Mark and Luke will do so, while Matthew diverges.

The agreements and disagreements that need to be explained, as these examples illustrate, are primarily of subject matter, of the order in which subject matter is presented, and of wording. Virtually all New Testament scholars feel that these agreements and disagreements are not coincidental, but are explicable only if there are relationships of literary dependency among these three Gospels. The debate over the Synoptic Problem is the debate over what these relationships of literary dependency are.

The modern discussion of the Synoptic Problem began in the latter half of the eighteenth century in Germany, when scholars such as Lessing, Herder and Eichhorn subjected the traditional account of the relationships among the New Testament Gospels to vigorous criticism.[1] During the next hundred years, scholars proposed literally hundreds of hypotheses to account for these relationships, but no clear consensus emerged. However, with the publication in 1863 of the work of Holtzmann, attention began to be focused on a narrower range of alternatives. The history of the debate subsequent to 1863 is largely the history of the triumph of what came to be called "the two-document hypothesis" and the evolution of that hypothesis into the form in which it received its classic defense in B. H. Streeter's *The Four Gospels,* published in 1924.

Throughout the twentieth century a near consensus of New Testament scholars have felt that the best solution to the Synoptic Problem is the two-document hypothesis. This hypothesis consists of two claims: first, that St. Matthew and St. Luke each used a written version of Mark virtually identical with our own from which they drew much of the subject matter for their own Gospels; secondly, that St. Matthew and St. Luke made large additions to their reproductions of Marcan material, which they drew from a common source (which historians have named "Q"). I shall call the first of these two claims, "the priority of Mark," and the second, "the existence of Q."

The two-document hypothesis is still the dominant view, but since the early 1950s, scholars have argued increasingly for competing solutions to the Synoptic Problem. Some scholars, for instance, have revived the so-called Griesbach hypothesis, according to which St. Matthew wrote first, St. Luke wrote second and used Matthew as a source, St. Mark wrote third and used both Matthew and Luke as sources, and there is no Q. But there is no consensus among recent critics of the two-document hypothesis as to how the Synoptic Problem should be solved.

I want now to consider several examples of kinds of arguments that have played a significant part in the debate over the Synoptic Problem. . . . For this purpose I am asking you to understand the expression "historical judgment" to mean an assessment, on grounds that are not made explicit, of the relative likelihood of competing historical claims. Numerous examples

1. W. R. Farmer, *The Synoptic Problem* (New York: Macmillan, 1964) contains a fascinating history of the debate over the Synoptic Problem.

follow. What makes historical judgments methodologically interesting is not that historians do not confirm them explicitly, but rather that often historians cannot confirm them explicitly. Historians of the Synoptic Problem, for instance, often use arguments that depend on historical judgments even though they cannot confirm those judgments explicitly. Thus, historians often use arguments that depend on judgments that they cannot defend.

. . . In the debate over the Synoptic Problem, proponents of every solution to the Problem use such arguments so routinely, and in such crucial ways, that it is difficult to see how they can effectively reduce their dependence on them without undermining the cases they make for their respective solutions. In other words, historians cannot conduct the debate over the Synoptic Problem as they do or continue it as a viable historical debate in the absence of arguments that depend essentially on historical judgments. I shall explain why by considering three sources of arguments that have figured importantly in the debate over the Synoptic Problem. [I do not claim that historians should stop using such arguments, or even that similar arguments are absent from the sciences. I want simply to illustrate how historians of this Problem actually do argue.]

STYLE AND THE MODE OF COMPOSITION

Throughout the modern discussion of the Synoptic Problem, scholars have placed great weight on the literary styles in which the Gospels are written. E. A. Abbott, for instance, in an article published in 1879, claims to have "proved by reductio ad absurdum" that St. Mark did not use Matthew and Luke as sources:

> For suppose that he did so copy, it follows that he must not only have constructed a narrative based upon two others, borrowing here a piece from Matthew and here a piece from Luke, but that he must have deliberately determined to insert, and must have adopted his narrative so as to insert, every word that was common to Matthew and Luke. The difficulty of doing this is enormous, and will be patent to anyone who will try to perform a similar feat himself. To embody the whole of even one document in a narrative of one's own, without copying it verbatim, and to do this in a free and natural manner, requires no little care. But to take two documents, to put them side by side and analyze their common matter, then to write a narrative, graphic, abrupt, and in all respects the opposite of artificial, which shall contain every phrase and word that is common to both—this would be a *tour de force* even for a skillful literary forger of these days, and may be dismissed as an impossibility for the writer of the Second Gospel.[2]

Several influential New Testament scholars accepted Abbott's argument. Their acceptance of it was, in the opinion of one historian of the Synoptic Problem, "one of the most important contributing factors to the eventual consensus that the priority of Mark was firmly established by nineteenth-century criticism."[3]

Streeter, in 1924, also appeals to the style in which Mark is written in order to argue for the priority of Mark:

> The difference between the style of Mark and of the other two is not merely that they both write better Greek. It is the difference which always exists between the spoken and the written language. Mark reads like a shorthand account of a story by an impromptu speaker—with all the repetitions, redundancies, and digressions which are characteristic of living speech . . . Matthew and Luke use the more succinct and carefully chosen language of one who writes and then revises an article for publication.[4]

Finally, G. M. Styler, in a well-known paper published in 1966, claims that "of all the arguments

2. Abbott's argument is quoted in Farmer, *ibid.*, p. 75.
3. Farmer, op. cit., p. 77.
4. B. H. Streeter, *The Four Gospels* (New York: Macmillan, 1924).

for the priority of Mark, the strongest is that based on the freshness and circumstantial character of his narrative."[5]

There are differences among these arguments. But it is what they have in common that is most important. Each draws attention to a feature of the style in which Mark is written. Each claims, at least implicitly, that it is more likely that St. Mark would have written in that style if he had written first than if he had used either Matthew or Luke as a source. The scholars who use these arguments do not defend this historical judgment.

THE ABSENCE OF PLAUSIBLE MOTIVATION

One of the main arguments for the priority of Mark is that St. Mark would have no plausible motive to write his Gospel as he did had he not written first. Streeter put this point colorfully. In responding to the Augustinian view that St. Mark was an epitomizer of Matthew, Streeter notes that Matthew is generally more concise than Mark, and that this is hard to explain unless one assumes the priority of Mark:

> Now there is nothing antecedently improbable in the idea that for certain purposes an abbreviated version of the Gospel might be desired; but only a lunatic would leave out Matthew's account of the Infancy, the Sermon on the Mount, and practically all the parables, in order to get room for purely verbal expansion of what was retained. On the other hand, if we suppose Mark to be the older document, the verbal compression and omission of minor detail seen in the parallels in Matthew has an obvious purpose in that it gives more room for the introduction of a mass of highly important teaching material not found in Mark.[6]

The historical judgment underlying this argument is that it is more likely that St. Mark wrote before St. Matthew than that he used Matthew as a source, since had St. Mark used Matthew as a source it is unlikely that he would have been motivated to write his Gospel as he did. Streeter does not defend this historical judgment.

Scholars often support the existence of Q in a similar fashion. Werner Kümmel, for instance, in the 14th edition of his *Introduction to the New Testament,* notes that the existence of Q proceeds from the insight that Matthew and Luke have an extensive amount of common material that neither St. Luke could have taken directly out of Matthew nor St. Matthew directly out of Luke.[7] Kümmel argues that it is "completely untenable" to suppose that St. Luke used Matthew as a source. Part of his reason is this:

> What could have moved Luke to break up Matthew's Sermon on the Mount and to embody part of it in his Sermon on the Plain, to distribute part over the various chapters of his Gospel, and to omit part?[8]

The question is rhetorical. Kümmel's argument depends on the historical judgment that it is more likely that St. Luke did not use Matthew as a source than that he did, since it is unlikely that had St. Luke used Matthew as a source he would have been motivated to break up St. Matthew's version of the Sermon on the Mount in the way described. Kümmel does not defend this historical judgment.

INAPPROPRIATE ORDER OR CONTENT AND MODE OF COMPOSITION

Sometimes scholars claim that because the order in which material is presented in a Gospel, or even the material itself, is inappropriate, it is more likely that the Gospel was written using

5. "Excursus IV: The Priority of Mark," p. 230, in C. F. D. Moule, ed., *The Birth of the New Testament,* 2nd ed. (London: Adams and Charles Black, 1966), pp. 223–232.

6. Streeter, op. cit., p. 158.

7. (Nashville, Tennessee: Abingdon Press, 1966), p. 50.

8. *Ibid.*

certain sources than that it was written without those sources. Kümmel, for instance, argues on the basis of inappropriate order that St. Luke probably used Mark as a source:

> Luke 4:23 speaks of miracles which took place in Capernaum, about which Luke, however, does not report until 4:31ff., because Mark 6:1ff. is placed before Mark 1:21ff par. Luke 4:31ff. In 4:38ff. Simon is named, whose calling Luke does not relate until 5:1ff. (put in a different place from Mark 1:16ff.).[9]

And Kümmel uses a similar strategy to argue that St. Matthew probably used Mark as a source:

> Both controversy discourses (Mt. 9:9–17) are out of place in the miracle cycle of Matthew and are to be explained only by the fact that these pericopes in Mark followed here.[10]

Kümmel does not defend his historical judgments that the explanations which he prefers of these features of Luke and Matthew are more likely than competing explanations of them.

Styler, on the other hand, argues on the basis of inappropriate content that St. Matthew probably used Mark as a source.

> We have passed on to an argument which to the present writer puts the priority of Mk beyond serious doubt, *viz.* that there are passages where Matt goes astray through misunderstanding, yet betrays a knowledge of the authentic version—the version which is given by Mk. The two accounts of the death of the Baptist (Mk vi. 17–29, Matt xiv. 3–12) contain clear examples of this. Mk states fully the attitude of Herod to John; he respected him, but was perplexed; and it was Herodias who was keen to kill him. And the story that follows explains how in spite of the king's reluctance she obtained her desire. Matt, whose version is much briefer, states that Herod wanted to kill John. But this must be an error; the story, which perfectly fits Mk's setting, does not fit Matt's introduction; and at xiv. 9 Matt betrays the fact that he really knows the full version by slipping in the statement that "the king" was sorry. It is surely clear that Matt, in a desire to abbreviate, has oversimplified his introduction.[11]

Styler does not defend his historical judgment that the explanation which he prefers of these differences between Mark and Matthew is more plausible than competing explanations of them.

The arguments quoted above, although they differ from each other in interesting ways, have three things in common. First, they are no more persuasive than the historical judgments on which they depend. To whatever extent one does not find the historical judgments persuasive, to at least that extent one ought not to find the arguments themselves persuasive. Secondly, the scholars who use these arguments do not defend the historical judgments on which they depend (nor, so far as I know, does anyone else). Thirdly, it would be difficult to argue convincingly, via arguments that do not themselves depend on historical judgments, that the historical judgments on which these arguments depend ought to be accepted. A closer look at these arguments reveals why this is so.

The historical judgments that underlie the three groups of examples mentioned are roughly these: Arguments in the first group depend on the historical judgment that it is more likely that St. Mark would have written his Gospel with the stylistic features that it has, had he written first, than had he used either Matthew or Luke as a source. Arguments in the second group depend on the historical judgment that it is more likely that St. Mark (or St. Luke) would have been motivated to write his Gospel as he did, had he written his Gospel without using Matthew as a source, than had he used Matthew as a source. Arguments in the third group depend on the historical judgment that it is more likely that Matthew (or Luke) would include certain

9. *Ibid,* p. 47.
10. *Ibid.*
11. Styler, *op. cit.,* p. 229.

A modern expressionist stained glass rendition of Christ.

inappropriate features that it includes, had St. Matthew (or St. Luke) used Mark as a source, than had he not used Mark as a source.

Consider the historical judgment that underlies arguments in the first group. Of the three, this would seem to be the easiest, by far, to defend without appeal to historical judgment. But how could one defend it? One could to some extent specify those stylistic features of Mark, such as its pleonasms, which are widely regarded as symptomatic of the priority of Mark. But how would one specify properties such as "fresh" and "non-artificial" that have played such an important role in the debate, particularly since it is not just the presence of certain detachable stylistic features, but rather the way in which they are embedded in various specific contexts, that is thought to support the priority of Mark? And the mere specification of general stylistic features of Mark would not thereby avoid dependence on a historical judgment. The only way to avoid such dependence is first, to formulate a generalization that correlates types of stylistic features with types of circumstances under which documents are composed, and secondly, to confirm this generalization by suitable statistical data, and thirdly, to give good reason to think that this generalization is applicable to the times and circumstances under which Mark was composed.

Neither Abbott nor Streeter nor Styler attempt to defend their historical judgment in this or any other manner. So far as I know, no other New Testament scholar attempts to defend it either, in spite of the long and venerable career of the arguments that depend on it. Furthermore, the prospects for defending the historical

"The Historian as Philosopher"

Nancy Murphy

The historian is consciously or unconsciously a philosopher. It is quite obvious that every task of the historian beyond the finding of facts is dependent on evaluations of historical factors, especially the nature of man, his freedom, his determination, his development out of nature, etc. It is less obvious but also true that even in the act of finding historical facts philosophical presuppositions are involved. This is especially true in deciding, out of the infinite number of happenings in every infinitely small moment of time, which facts shall be called historically relevant facts. The historian is further forced to give his evaluation of sources and their reliability, a task which is not independent of his interpretation of human nature. Finally, in the moment in which a historical work gives implicit or explicit assertions about the meaning of historical events for human existence, the philosophical presuppositions of history are evident.

From *Theology in the Age of Scientific Reasoning* (1990).

judgment underlying this first group of arguments were not bright when Abbott wrote and are at best only slightly brighter today. If Abbott (or Streeter, or Styler) had tried to defend the historical judgment underlying his argument in the way sketched, he probably would have failed. . . .

I could easily extend my discussion of the historical judgments that underlie arguments in the first group of examples to include the even more troublesome historical judgments underlying arguments in the second and third groups of examples. It is instructive to consider, for instance, what generalizations would have to be made explicit and defended in order to defend the arguments based on considerations of inappropriate order and content in ways which eliminate their dependence on historical judgments—say, in order to defend Styler's claim that St. Matthew betrays the fact that he really knows St. Mark's version of the death of John the Baptist since he slips in the statement that the king was sorry. I leave this task to the reader.

One might object to my assumption that if Abbott or Streeter or Styler had tried to defend the historical judgment underlying his argument in ways which eliminate his dependence on a historical judgment, he would have failed. The only way to prove that this historical judgment cannot be defended would be to make an appropriate attempt to defend it and fail. So far as I know, no one has ever tried to defend it, a fact that is significant. Remember, though, that the case for the two-document hypothesis, as well as the cases for competing solutions to the Synoptic Problem, do not gather their strength from just a handful of arguments that individually or collectively are thought to be decisive. They depend rather upon literally hundreds of detailed textual interpretations, almost all of which depend on historical judgments. These arguments provide relatively strong support for a particular solution to the Synoptic Problem, if they do, only in a cumulative fashion. Thus, nothing that is significant hinges on my being right in thinking that each of the specific arguments mentioned above or that figures importantly in the debate over the Synoptic Problem depends essentially on a historical judgment. In the debate over the Synoptic Problem, arguments that depend on historical judgments are as plentiful as blackberries. . . .

E. P. Sanders

"JESUS AND JUDAISM"

E. P. SANDERS, Dean Ireland's Professor of Exegesis at Oxford University and a professor of religious studies at McMaster University, Canada, is the author of several books on early Christianity, two of which have won National Religious Book Awards. His *Jesus and Judaism* (1985), from which the following selection is taken, is included here to help us appreciate how slender and ambiguous the evidence is from which an historian must proceed in trying to understand what Jesus was up to and why he provoked the reactions he did.

THE PROBLEM

It is the purpose of the present work to take up two related questions with regard to Jesus: his intention and his relationship to his contemporaries in Judaism.[1] These questions immediately involve us in two others: the reason for his death (did his intention involve an opposition to Judaism which led to death?) and the motivating force behind the rise of Christianity (did the split between the Christian movement and Judaism originate in opposition during Jesus' lifetime?).[2] These are questions on which there are numerous viewpoints, and gathered about which are enormous bodies of scholarly literature, so that it is with some trepidation that one advances another essay in an attempt to answer them. . . .

The Securest Evidence

No one will dispute the principle that, given the conglomeration of evidence about Jesus and the early church which one finds in the Gospels, one should begin with what is relatively secure and work out to more uncertain points. But finding agreement about the ground rules by which what is relatively secure can be identified is very difficult. One of the reasons for this is, I believe, that most studies of Jesus focus on Jesus as a teacher or preacher—at any rate, primarily a messenger—and thus move immediately to try to establish the center of his message.[3] One may start with what comes first in the Gospels (repentance in view of the coming of the kingdom), with what strikes one as most characteristic (such as the call of sinners), with the sayings material which seems to have been least subject to alteration (often held to be the parables), or with the sayings which could not conceivably have been created in the early church ('Jesus said to him, "Why do you call me good" ', Mark 10.18); but in any case one starts with a core of sayings material and proceeds to a depiction of Jesus' message and, sometimes, his intention and the cause of the conflict with Judaism.

There are two considerations which make us look elsewhere for the most secure and the best evidence if we wish to understand Jesus. The first is simply that scholars have not and, in my judgment, will not agree on the authenticity of the sayings material, either in whole or in part. There are a few sayings on which there is wide consensus, but hardly enough to allow a full depiction of Jesus. . . .

Secondly, when the study of Jesus is equated with the study of his sayings, there is the unspoken assumption that what he really was, was a teacher. He is then either a clear, straightforward teacher whose parables make his message about God and the kingdom plain, or, as in some recent studies, a difficult, riddling teacher, whose meaning is not and was not altogether clear, or even one who intended to be ambiguous.[4] Whatever sort of teacher he is held to have been, it is difficult to move from 'Jesus the teacher' to 'Jesus, a Jew who was crucified, who was the leader of a group which survived his death, which in turn was persecuted, and which formed a messianic sect which was finally successful'. It is difficult to make his teaching offensive enough to lead to execution or sectarian enough to lead to the formation of a group which eventually separated from the main body of Judaism. This is not to say that scholars have not tried to find links between Jesus' teaching, his death, and the rise of the Christian movement; but only that the links are difficult to establish. Further, the

1. 'Relationship to his contemporaries in Judaism' is the correct way to phrase the matter, but I shall sometimes use the abbreviation 'Jesus and Judaism'. The short phrase is not intended to cast doubt on the fact that Jesus was thoroughly Jewish.

2. These questions have lately received more attention than they did for some decades after the rise of form criticism. They are explicitly posed, for example, by C. K. Barrett in *Jesus and the Gospel Tradition*, 1967.

3. The almost exclusive concentration on Jesus as a teacher will be familiar to most readers. For two recent examples, see Bernard Brandon Scott, *Jesus, Symbol-Maker for the Kingdom*, 1983 (see esp. p. 153); James Breech, *The Silence of Jesus. The Authentic Voice of the Historical Man*, 1983. Some exceptions to the rule will be discussed below.

4. See the works of Scott and Breech, just cited.

most common ones (e.g., he directly opposed Moses and this aroused opposition) are, at best, dubious. . . .

We see, then, that the enormous labour which for generations has been expended on the investigation of the teaching material in the Gospels has not yielded a convincing historical depiction of Jesus—one which sets him firmly in Jewish history, which explains his execution, and which explains why his followers formed a persecuted messianic sect. What is needed is more secure evidence, evidence on which everyone can agree and which at least points towards an explanation of these historical puzzles. Such evidence, if it is produced, could then be supplemented in various ways; but the first goal of this study is to seek and establish that evidence. I think that it exists. There are *facts* about Jesus, his career, and its consequences which are very firm and which do point towards solutions of historical questions; and the present study is based primarily on facts about Jesus and only secondarily on a study of some of the sayings material.

Fuchs some years ago proposed placing first Jesus' behaviour and using that as a framework for the sayings.[5] The concrete behaviour which he had in mind was Jesus' association with sinners, which correlates with the sayings which call sinners and promise them the kingdom. In common with many modern interpreters, I shall later argue that such behaviour and sayings were characteristic of Jesus and become important for understanding him and his relationship to his contemporaries. To understand the importance of Jesus' calling sinners to be with him, however, we must understand rather a lot about who the sinners were and about what Jesus meant by the kingdom, which in turn requires the very understanding of Jesus and Judaism which we are trying to illuminate. The discussion which proceeds from Jesus' association with sinners, to understanding his intention in calling them, to making inferences about his relationship to Judaism (made up of the sinners and the righteous alike) is a fruitful one; but it turns out not to be a good starting-point. . . .

Recently two scholars have pointed to the existence of facts about Jesus, and they use them in different ways to derive a full picture of him. Morton Smith has pointed out that ' . . . the external framework of Jesus' life—the what, when, and where—is reasonably certain.'[6] He notes another important fact: 'Whatever else Jesus may or may not have done, he unquestionably started the process that became Christianity.'[7] Anthony Harvey similarly comments that 'the evidence for at least the main facts of the life and death of Jesus is as abundant, circumstantial and consistent as is the case with any other figure of ancient history.'[8] Harvey mentions as beyond reasonable doubt the following facts:

> that Jesus was known in both Galilee and Jerusalem; that he was a teacher; that he carried out cures of various illnesses, particularly demon-possession, and that these were widely regarded as miraculous; that he was involved in controversy with fellow Jews over questions of the law of Moses: and that he was crucified in the governship of Pontius Pilate.[9]

These two scholars come to different views about Jesus, though agreeing on the whole about these facts. Smith argues that the first and surest fact about Jesus is that he was a miracle worker, and he is confident that in Jesus' own ministry it was healing which attracted the crowds to whom he preached.[10] The crowds began to think of him as the Messiah. The expectations thus aroused, if they affected enough people, might lead the authorities to fear him (p. 16; cf. 43f.). Thus Smith can trace a reasonable line of development from 'miracle worker' to 'messianic pretender'

5. E. Fuchs, 'The Quest of the Historical Jesus' (1956), *Studies of the Historical Jesus,* ET 1964, pp. 21f.

6. M. Smith, *Jesus the Magician,* 1978, p. 17.
7. Ibid., p. 5.
8. Harvey, *Constraints,* pp. 5f.
9. Ibid., p. 6.
10. Smith, *Magician,* pp. 11, 14.

to the crucifixion. He also argues that the title 'son of God' arose because of Jesus' miracles (pp. 80–83; 101–3; cf. 14). Finally, he points out that a lot of teachers and some prophets were known in Israel, but that there was no tendency to make them miracle workers. It is comprehensible, however, that one first known for the latter activity became known for the others: 'the rest of the tradition about Jesus can be understood if we begin with the miracles, but the miracles cannot be understood if we begin with a purely didactic tradition' (p. 16; cf. 129). . . .

I take it that Smith has struck a blow for redressing the balance in the study of Jesus; that is, for moving us away from the almost exclusive concentration on him as a teacher. Further, building on the undoubted fact that Jesus was known as a miracle worker, he has brought forward evidence for showing that, in this activity, Jesus followed some of the standard practices of magicians. Third, he has made a substantial contribution to methodology. We should study the facts about Jesus and try to understand their significance in his context. I depart from Smith because I think that there are other facts which fit Jesus unmistakably into a context other than that of magic.

Harvey also constructs his book by setting known activities of Jesus into their context, which in turn sets definite limits to their significance.

Interpreting Jesus

When we know what Jesus said, in the sense that we know what words he uttered, how should we interpret what he meant? Should we interpret his remarks as those of a first-century Jew, which is the only way they can be interpreted by secular scholars? Or should we interpret his remarks as those of God, hence as the remarks of someone who might have known all sorts of things and had all sorts of insights and motivations that it would be absurd to attribute to a first-century Jew?

The first way is to treat Jesus like any other historical figure, for instance, Socrates or Galileo, and to base one's interpretation on the best available historical evidence. The advantage of this way is that disputes about how Jesus' remarks should be interpreted can be settled, at least in principle, by an appeal to evidence. The problem with this way, at least from the point of view of a Christian, is that one must presuppose that Jesus was neither a god nor divinely inspired and interpret his remarks accordingly.

The second way is to treat Jesus as God. The advantage of this way, at least from the point of view of a believing Christian, is that one does not need to presuppose the denial of something one believes to be true. The problem with this way is that disputes about how Jesus' remarks should be interpreted cannot be settled by an appeal to (ordinary) evidence. But isn't it then largely arbitrary, using this second approach, how one interprets Jesus' remarks?

Thus the title, *Jesus and the Constraints of History*. His procedure may be exemplified by quoting him on the question of Jesus as teacher.

> . . . we shall find that those bare biographical statements, which are established with a high degree of historical certainty but which seem at first to convey little information that is of interest to the theologian, take on considerable significance. The statement, for example, that Jesus was a teacher, when set in the context of the constraints which bore upon any teacher of his time and culture and of the relatively small number of options which was open to anyone who wished to give a new lead in religious understanding while remaining intelligible to the majority of his hearers—such a statement is capable of yielding a surprising amount of information about the kind of person Jesus must have been and the kind of achievement at which he

Christian History

How many Christians are aware of the tenuousness with which any contemporary historian who does not begin by making religious assumptions—whether or not the historian happens also, in his personal life, to be a Christian—approaches the events of Jesus' life and the first few centuries of Christianity? The facts on which such a historian has to peg an interpretation are so disputable that it is difficult for the historian even to get his or her interpretation off the ground.

How many contemporary Christians are aware that the earliest Christians had radically different ideas about Jesus and his message and even produced alternative gospels to sustain their interpretations? Even if we confine our attention just to the New Testament gospels, how many Christians know that the earliest New Testament gospel was probably not written before 50 A.D., and that the latest—that of John, who claims to be giving an eyewitness account—may have been written as late as 120 A.D.?

How many ordinary Christians know that the gospels of Matthew, Mark, and Luke were not written independently of each other—thus do not provide independent corroboration of the events they jointly depict—but that many parts of the two later accounts were copied verbatim from the earliest account? That is, how many know about the historical debate over the synoptic problem, the problem of determining the relations of literary dependency among the gospels of Matthew, Mark, and Luke (all scholars agree that John was written later), and of the ways in which historians must rely on guesswork to support *any* solution to this problem.

One final question: Given how saturated our culture is with Christian ideology and encouragement to read the Bible, why aren't the facts we have mentioned in the questions just posed *common knowledge* among all educated Christians?

> aimed; and this information is of great relevance to the ultimate question of Christology: who and what was Jesus?[11]

I shall confess to the reader that, when I read those words, I thought that Harvey had succeeded in publishing first a book on which I had been engaged, off and on, for almost ten years. That turned out not to be the case, and I now recall the moment in order to indicate how appropriate to the problem of how to describe Jesus his procedure is. . . .

There is, as is usual in dealing with historical questions, no opening which does not involve one in a circle of interpretation, that is, which does not depend on points which in turn require us to understand others. Historians always work in this kind of circle, moving from evidence to tentative conclusions, then back to the evidence with renewed insight, and so on. In discussing Smith's book, I have already mentioned a circle of interpretation which I have followed and which will be presented fully below: enough evidence points towards Jewish eschatology as the general framework of Jesus' ministry that we may examine the particulars in the light of that framework. One must be careful to enter the circle at the right point, that is, to choose the best starting place. This, in turn, is a point which is secure historically and whose meaning can be established with some degree of independence from the rest of the evidence. One must also, of course, avoid circular arguments, the basing of two points each on the other. These occur with surprising frequency, and we shall see an important one in discussing Matt. 12.28//Luke 11.20. They result not so much from deficiencies in knowledge of logic as from lack of attention to what is and is not bedrock in the tradition. Conclusions about Jesus are based on passages, especially sayings, whose authenticity and meaning depend on a context which is, in turn, provided by the conclusion. Thus the conclusion that Jesus thought that in his exorcisms the kingdom was shown to be or was made present depends on Matt. 12.28 and par. The verse is known to be both authentic and meaningful because it reflects Jesus' feeling of eschatological power. But Jesus' feeling of eschatological power is known to us only through conclusions and arguments based on Matt. 12.28 and one or two other sayings. . . .

The simplest way to avoid these and other special problems of argumentation is to found the study on bedrock, and especially to begin at the right point. Once a beginning is made, a context is set which will influence the interpretation of subsequent evidence.

We start by determining the evidence which is most secure. There are several facts about Jesus' career *and its aftermath* which can be known beyond doubt.[12] Any interpretation of Jesus should be able to account for these. The almost indisputable facts, listed more or less in chronological order, are these:

1. Jesus was baptized by John the Baptist.
2. Jesus was a Galilean who preached and healed.
3. Jesus called disciples and spoke of there being twelve.
4. Jesus confined his activity to Israel.
5. Jesus engaged in a controversy about the temple.
6. Jesus was crucified outside Jerusalem by the Roman authorities.
7. After his death Jesus' followers continued as an identifiable movement.
8. At least some Jews persecuted at least parts of the new movement (Gal. 1.13, 22; Phil. 3.6), and it appears that this persecution endured at least to a time near the end of Paul's career (II Cor. 11.24; Gal. 5.11; 6.12; cf. Matt. 23.34; 10.17).

In the course of the present work I have tried several starting points, working them out either mentally or on paper, in an effort to find the one which is most satisfactory. The aim is

11. Harvey, *Constraints*, p. 7.

12. I do not regard any items in the following as dubious, but some may. . . . There are other facts about Jesus about which I have no doubts (e.g. that he had a brother named James) but which are not relevant to the present discussion.

always to move from the evidence which is most secure and least ambiguous to more uncertain evidence. If we knew enough about any of the eight points it would serve as an adequate beginning point. If we knew, for example, whether or not there was a direct connection between the Roman execution of Jesus and the Jewish persecution of some of his followers, many of the puzzles about early Christianity and its relationship to Judaism would be solved. If we knew enough about the reported trials and the motives for the execution of Jesus, we would have a firm clue to start the unravelling of the interrelated themes which are under discussion here.[13] But on the one point our information is non-existent, on the other uncertain and unreliable. A sound answer to the question of the cause of Jesus' death requires us to solve a lot of other problems, and the fact of his execution cannot be the starting point for our study. Similarly, if we could definitely establish whether or not there was an intrinsic connection between the preaching of Jesus and the subsequent formation of his disciples into a group with its own distinctive identity, we could safely begin our study there. Yet this question remains one of the most debated points in the study of Christian origins. I have chosen to begin with the temple controversy, about which our information is a little better and which offers almost as good an entry for the study of Jesus' intention and his relationship to his contemporaries as would a truly eyewitness account of the trial.[14] The temple controversy can also be isolated to some degree from other questions. It thus gives a point of entry for the study of Jesus' career and historical setting, and it will also open the way to re-examine the question of 'Jesus and the Kingdom'. . . .

13. The very fact that the execution was by the Romans seems to have been determinative for several scholars, such as Winter and Brandon, whose views are discussed below. N. A. Dahl argued that the starting point for the study of the life of Jesus is his death, specifically his death as king of the Jews. See *The Crucified Messiah and Other Essays,* 1974, pp. 10–36, 68, 72–4.

14. Also in favour of beginning with the temple controversy is R. Pesch, 'Der Anspruch Jesu', *Orientierung* 35, 1971.

The Sayings

Although the sayings material has just been assigned a relatively secondary role, especially considering the dominance which it has generally enjoyed, it remains important in this study. A full examination of the reliability and authenticity of the sayings material is beyond the bounds of the present work,[15] but I shall explain in brief form the general stance towards the sayings material which is taken here.

I belong to the school which holds that a saying attributed to Jesus can seldom be proved beyond doubt to be entirely authentic or entirely non-authentic, but that each saying must be tested by appropriate criteria and assigned (tentatively) to an author—either to Jesus or to an anonymous representative of some stratum in the early church. . . .[16]

. . . [W]e must conclude that the material was subject to change and may have changed, but we do not know just how it changed.[17] It is not the case that I am decisively convinced that Jesus did not say the bulk of the things attributed to him in the synoptic Gospels, but rather that I regard the material as having been subject to changes in ways that cannot be precisely assessed. Thus the sayings material alone does not offer us enough firm ground to explore successfully the problems which we have set ourselves. . . .

The principal test which scholars have recently used for assessing authenticity is the test

15. There is now available a rich and illuminating body of literature on the criteria for assessing authenticity. I have found the following to be the most useful: M. D. Hooker, 'Christology and Methodology', *NTS* 17, 1970–71, pp. 480–7; 'On Using the Wrong Tool', *Theology* 75, 1972, pp. 570–81; R. S. Barbour, *Traditio-Historical Criticism of the Gospels* (Studies in Creative Criticism 4), 1972; F. G. Downing, *The Church and Jesus,* SBT II 10, 1968, esp. ch. VI; D. G. A. Calvert, 'An Examination of the Criteria for Distinguishing the Authentic Words of Jesus', *NTS* 18, 1971–72, pp. 209–19; David L. Mealand, 'The Dissimilarity Test', *SJT* 31, 1978, pp. 41–50.

16. The clearest statement of the position is by Hooker, 'Christology and Methodology', pp. 484–7; cf. Barbour, *Traditio-Historical Criticism,* p. 11.

17. Cf. Downing, *The Church and Jesus,* pp. 108f.

of double 'dissimilarity', and to that test we now turn.[18]

The test is this: material which can be accounted for neither as traditional Jewish material nor as later church material can be safely attributed to Jesus. There are well-known difficulties in applying the test. We know first-century Judaism very imperfectly, and knowledge about the interests of the church between 70 and 100 CE (when the Gospels were completed) is slender indeed.[19] Nevertheless, the test can occasionally be successfully applied, and it is used below in the discussion of Matt. 8.21f.//Luke 9.59f. Yet a problem remains. The test rules out too much. We should assume that part of what Jesus said and did became constitutive of Christian preaching, so that the elimination of all Christian motifs would result in the elimination of material which also tells us something about Jesus. Similarly, we should be prepared to assume a broad ground of positive relationships between Jesus and his contemporaries in Judaism. Another way of stating this problem with the test of double dissimilarity is to observe that it provides too little material to allow a satisfactory reconstruction of the life and teaching of Jesus. The material which remains after the test is applied is biased towards uniqueness.

Secondly, the remaining material does not interpret itself or necessarily answer historical questions. It must still be placed in a meaningful context, and that context is not automatically provided by summarizing sayings which are atypical, as far as we know, of both Judaism and the Christian church.

We have earlier agreed that, in dealing with Jesus, one has to begin with relatively secure evidence. That is not to say, however, that a summary of the most nearly certain sayings of Jesus will provide a satisfactory depiction of his career. If our assumption is true that Jesus also said things which were in agreement with the contemporary Judaism or with the views of the later church, a summary of the sayings which pass the test of double dissimilarity would be inadequate for a meaningful presentation of his teaching.

The inadequacy remains even if the list of sayings which are held to be authentic is expanded by employing other criteria, such as attestation in more than one source or attestation in more than one form.[20] No matter what criteria for testing the sayings are used, scholars still need to move beyond the sayings themselves to a broader context than a summary of their contents if they are to address historical questions about Jesus.[21]

Since historical reconstruction requires that data be fitted into a context, the establishment of a secure context, or framework of interpretation, becomes crucial. There are basically three kinds of information which provide help in this endeavour: such facts about Jesus as those outlined above (p. 11, nos. 1–6); knowledge about the outcome of his life and teaching (cf. nos. 7 and 8); knowledge of first-century Judaism.

Different scholars have tried to correlate sayings and other information in various ways.

18. The first formulation of the test, as far as I know, is R. Bultmann's in discussing parables (*Gleichnisse*) and related materials: *Die Geschichte der synoptischen Tradition*, ⁷1967, p. 222; *The History of the Synoptic Tradition*, ET 1963, p. 205. It has been widely used and often discussed. See, for example, N. Perrin, *Rediscovering the Teaching of Jesus*, 1967, pp. 39–43 (it is 'the basis for all contemporary attempts to reconstruct the teaching of Jesus'). For a rigid application of one-half of what became of the double test, see P.W. Schmiedel, 'Gospels', *Encyclopaedia Biblica* II, 1901, cols. 1765–1896, esp. 1881–3: five passages could not have been invented by the post-resurrection church.

19. Some would shift the outside dates for the composition of the Gospels earlier, for example to 66 and 90. The present point, which is that they were written during a 'tunnel" period, about which we have little knowledge, is not affected. I must with some regret leave aside the proposals of John A. T. Robinson (*Redating the New Testament*, 1976) to press the dates of composition earlier yet. His analysis of the weakness of some of the traditional arguments, while usually penetrating, does not lead to the radical revision which he proposes.

20. On multiple attestation, see Calvert, 'An Examination of the Criteria'; Barbour, *Traditio-Historical Criticism*, pp. 3f.

21. Cf. Barbour, *Traditio-Historical Criticism*, p. 18: if one starts with individual sayings it is necessary, after testing each one, to try to work it 'into an overall hypothesis'. See also Meyer, *Aims*. p. 19. Bruce Chilton puts the point sharply: 'It may be questioned whether or not the application of *a priori* criteria to data constitutes historical knowledge at all' (*God in Strength. Jesus' Announcement of the Kingdom*, 1979, p. 20; cf. p. 288).

I have already indicated that in the present work emphasis will be placed on unassailable facts about Jesus, their possible significance in his own time, and the outcome of his life and work. Once the context is established and integrated with sayings which are very probably authentic, it will be possible to draw in other material in the synoptics. . . .

A Good Hypothesis

In the first place, a good hypothesis with regard to Jesus' intention and his relationship to Judaism should meet Klausner's test: it should situate Jesus believably in Judaism and yet explain why the movement initiated by him eventually broke with Judaism. That a hypothesis should meet both these expectations will not be conceded on all sides, and a few comments should be made about each point.

Earlier generations of scholars sometimes made Jesus so unique (and Judaism so inferior) that the reader is now forced to wonder how it could be that Jesus grew up on Jewish soil. Thus Bousset, for example, while conceding some formal similarities between Jesus and his contemporaries (e.g., the use of parables), denied any similarity at all on essentials. 'In the one case we have mere exposition of the Scriptures, in the other a living piety. There the parables are designed to illustrate the distorted ideas of a dead learning. . . . Here the parable was handled by one whose whole soul was set . . . upon the real.'[22] Although many of Bousset's basic views about Judaism are still unhesitatingly repeated by New Testament scholars,[23] the crudity of his description of Judaism has pretty well disappeared, and with it the stark contrast between Jesus, who represents everything good, pure and enlightened, and Judaism, which represents everything distorted, hypocritical and misleading. There is still an appreciable drive on the part of New Testament scholars to depict Jesus as transcending the bounds of Judaism (which in this context is always considered a good thing to do), but the inclination to have Jesus so superior to his contemporaries that he is deprived of a living context in Judaism seems to have been overcome by better judgment and better historical understanding. There is today virtually unanimous consent to the first of Klausner's propositions: Jesus lived as a Jew.[24] The question which remains is how to determine what Jesus' relationship to his contemporaries was, and there is wider disagreement on how to answer that question. . . .

The second half of Klausner's position—that something in Jesus' own activity should have prepared in some way for the eventual split of Christianity from Judaism—is more controversial. . . .

The situation seems to be this: those who presumably know the most about Judaism, and about the law in particular—Jewish scholars—do not find any substantial points of disagreement between Jesus and his contemporaries, and certainly not any which would lead to death.[25] Christian scholars, on the other hand, seem to have become increasingly convinced that there was a fundamental opposition between Jesus and Judaism and that the opposition was *intentional* on Jesus' part. It is difficult to know precisely what has led to the greater willingness on the part of Christian scholars to hold this view. It does not seem to be based on fresh information about Judaism and the tolerable limits of dissent.

22. W. Bousset, *Jesus,* ET (ed. W. D. Morrison) 1911, p. 44.

23. See *Paul and Palestinian Judaism,* pp. 33–59.

24. There are a few exceptions. See the discussion above of Breech, *Silence.*

25. So also Solomon Zeitlin, 'Jesus and the Pharisees', repr. in Weiss-Rosmarin, ed., *Jewish Expressions,* pp. 148–56 (= *The Rise and Fall of the Second Judaean State* I, 1962); Ben Zion Bokser, 'Jesus: Jew or Christian?' *Jewish Expressions,* pp. 201–29 (= *Judaism and the Christian Predicament* [ed. B. Z. Bokser], 1967); A. Finkel, *The Pharisees and the Teacher of Nazareth,* 1964. See also Helmut Merkel, 'Jesus im Widerstreit', *Glaube and Gesellschaft. Festschrift für W. F. Kasch,* 1981, pp. 207–17. Merkel disputes the view of P. Lapide, who has frequently argued that Jesus did not break the law, and concludes that Jesus in fact directly contradicted Moses on the questions of Sabbath, purity and divorce. Both are simply repeating positions which we have sketched already.

It may stem, rather, from the motive which we mentioned earlier: a hypothesis is on *a priori* grounds superior if it draws a line of connection between Jesus' teaching and activity, his death, and the rise of Christianity. There are really just two possible lines of connection. . . . One is Jesus' self-consciousness. If he made a strong personal claim which was sufficient to lead to his execution, that fact would help account for several elements of his teaching, his death and the rise of Christianity. The difficulty here is finding a sufficiently strong personal claim to account for execution, especially as long as one stays within the confines of traditional terminological studies. The claim to be Messiah, if Jesus made it, would not seem to be an indictable offence (unless construed, as some have suggested, as a challenge to Rome). The claim to be the Son of man, or to know that he was coming, is not blasphemy. Stauffer, to be sure (followed by Schoeps), finds in Jesus' words a claim of divinity which might be construed as blasphemy, but the evidence cannot be considered persuasive.[26]

Thus most scholars who wish to find the thread to which we have referred have turned to Jesus' attitude towards the law. If he opposed the validity of the Mosaic code, his doing so would account for his meeting opposition during his public ministry, it might well account for an opposition to the death (although this is not the charge in the trial accounts), and it would account for a new sect which broke with Judaism. The trouble with this thread is that the apostles in Jerusalem apparently did not know that the

26. E. Stauffer, *Jesus and His Story,* ET 1960, pp. 149–59. Cf. H.-J. Schoeps, *Paul: The Theology of the Apostle in the Light of Jewish Religious History,* ET 1961, pp. 160–62.

"Historical Method in the Study of Religion"

Morton Smith

. . . The science of religion, for which these histories of particular religions are prerequisites, is still far in the future. But, when and if it comes, both it, and the individual histories already developing, will be shaped by a basic supposition of sound historical method.

This supposition, in classical terms, is "atheism." I say "in classical terms" because the adjective "atheist" was regularly used in classical times to describe, for instance, the Epicureans, who insisted that there were gods, but denied that they ever descended to any special intervention in the world's affairs. It is precisely this denial which is fundamental to any sound historical method. Whether or not supernatural beings exist is a question for metaphysics. Even if they exist and exercise some regular influence on the world, some influence of which the consequences are taken to be a part of the normal course of natural events—let us say, for instance, that they determine the motion of the sphere of fixed stars, or that the whole of nature, including its regular operation, is a manifestation of some unchanging divine nature or will—even this is of no concern to history, since it is not history's task to inquire into the causes of the normal phenomena of nature. But the historian does require a world in which these normal phenomena are not interfered with by arbitrary and *ad hoc* divine interventions to produce abnormal events with special historical consequences. This is not a matter of personal preference, but of professional necessity, for the historian's task, . . . is to calculate the most probable explanation of the preserved evidence. Now the minds of the gods are inscrutable and their actions, consequently, incalculable. Therefore, unless the possibility of their special intervention be ruled out, there can be no calculation of most probable causes—there would always be an unknown probability that a deity might have intervened.

From *History and Theory* (1968).

Torah had been abrogated: that was the contribution of Paul and possibly other apostles to the Gentiles. In Paul's case, the issue was argued on the ground that faith in Christ, not keeping the Torah, is the basis of salvation and that Gentiles must be admitted on equal footing with Jews (Rom. 3.28–30; 4.24f; 10.4–17; 11.20–23 and elsewhere). Paul does not seem to be able to refer to Jesus' attitude to the law for support (contrary to Klausner).

The fact that the early disciples did not know that Jesus had opposed the law has led some to suggest that he did so only implicitly, without knowing, or fully knowing, that he was doing so. It is hard to know what this amounts to as an historical explanation. It does not explain Christianity's subsequent break with Judaism. If neither Jesus nor the early apostles knew that he implicitly opposed the law, there would be no chain of transmission which would permit Jesus' words and deeds to influence Paul and the ultimate outcome. The implication would become clear only after the outcome had been achieved. The break would not be based on any *intention* on the part of Jesus, although, after the break had been made, support from Jesus' lifetime might be found for it. At any rate, implicit rejection seems to explain nothing; neither Paul's rejection nor the Jerusalem apostles' maintenance of the law.

Further, and more important, it is intrinsically unlikely that Jesus could have opposed the law in principle but without knowing what he was doing. If, for example, he did say that the dietary laws should not be observed, he could not have seen this as a dismissal of what is irrelevant to true religion. The explanation that Jesus did not know what he was doing, though repeated in the twentieth century, is essentially a nineteenth-century explanation, being determined by the view that Jesus' intention was to purge Judaism of crass materialism and externalities. The understanding was that Jesus *intended* to oppose only a few externalities, but that since these are part of the Mosaic code, which is one, he actually opposed the law itself. What must be recognized is that Jesus could not possibly have seen things in the way this proposal requires. It is unrealistic to regard Jesus as a modern man[27] or as someone who did not know the standard Jewish view that the law is unitary. And even if he (an untutored Galilean) could have been ignorant of this, the error would have been quickly pointed out by his adversaries. *For the principle on which the law rests is perfectly clear: God gave the Torah to Israel by the hand of Moses; obedience to the Torah is the condition for retaining the covenant promises; intentional and unrepenting disobedience implies rejection of the law, rejection of the covenant for which it is the condition, and rejection of the God who gave the law and the covenant.* This is an understanding which is so uniform in the literature which survives from the approximate period[28] that Jesus and his followers could not possibly have been ignorant of it. Thus we must reject the hypothesis that Jesus opposed the law but did not know that he was doing so. Either he opposed the law and intended something by it, or he did not oppose it. (It remains possible that he accepted it but still debated points within its framework, even to the point of using one scriptural passage against another. This device was well known to the Rabbis, for example.[29] We shall see below that most of the reputed disputes about the law are not outside the bounds of Jewish debate.)

We said earlier that many scholars are prepared to find a thread between Jesus' intention and his death and the subsequent rise of the church. There are difficulties with all the main proposals: (1) the threat is his self-assertion (the evidence is weak); (2) the threat is implicit abrogation of the law (no evident chain of transmission); (3) the threat is explicit abrogation of part of the law, which leads to rejection of all

27. Above, p. 34, on Käsemann.

28. *Paul and Palestinian Judaism,* chs. I-III.

29. See the discussion of how the clear intent of Exod. 20.7 is avoided by different Rabbis in *Paul and Palestinian Judaism,* pp. 159f.

(those who know the law best see no crucial break).

This situation seems to make it easy to return to another large option: there was no link between the content of Jesus' teaching in Galilee and the cause of his death in Jerusalem: Jesus opposed the scribes and Pharisees during his teaching activity (whether basically or only marginally), but he was killed either because the Romans (perhaps on the advice of the Jerusalem leaders) took him to be a Zealot or because he offended and threatened the Jewish hierarchy by his challenge to the temple. We have thus far said that this theory, in its turn, suffers from an *a priori* difficulty: it would be preferable to find a thread from Jesus' intention to his death to the church. We may now observe that, in addition to this deficiency, there are even graver objections. It presupposes that Jesus' activity in the temple had no intrinsic connection with the teaching. This presupposition rests on the same misapprehension which we pointed out in connection with the theory that Jesus did not know that he opposed the law: that he did not know that interrupting the temple arrangements could be seen only as a direct affront not merely to the priests' authority, but to Moses, and thus to God, who commanded the daily performance of the sacrifices. The view that Jesus went about Galilee healing, calling for repentance, and rousing the ire of the Pharisees, and that he then went to Jerusalem and interfered with the temple, rousing the ire of the priests, but that there is no connection between the two, supposes that Jesus acted with a lack of coherence that is almost incredible. Could it be that Jesus encouraged his disciples to think that something was to come of his ministry, that he was inconveniently killed along the way for reasons unconnected with his teaching, but that the cause which seemed lost was rescued by the resurrection? What is wrong with this possibility is that it supposes that Jesus intended something different when he 'cleansed' the temple from what he intended to achieve by his teaching. Or, alternatively, it supposes that Jesus intended throughout to abolish external inessentials in the name of true religion, without intending directly to oppose the law of Moses. We have already seen the improbability of the second alternative. The first is equally unlikely, for it equally requires us to believe that Jesus did not really know what he was doing or what the significance of his actions was. How could it be that something as serious as interfering with the temple sacrifices could have been seen by him as something different from his teaching and as unconnected with his calling disciples? How could it be that his activity in Jerusalem alarmed a quite different set of opponents, and for different reasons, from those whom he met in Galilee? One would have to think that Jesus quite literally did not know what he was doing. He called disciples simply to be with him, he taught simply to promote repentance, he interfered with temple practice because of a dislike of business dealings in the temple area, he was executed as a rebel or rabble rouser; and the disciples, who expected nothing in particular to come of his ministry, were galvanized into unity and activity solely by the resurrection experiences: it is possible, but it is not likely.

That the problem we have posed is not susceptible of a rock-hard answer which absolutely excludes all others is shown not only by the difficulties which can be brought against any hypothesis, but also by the very large number of hypotheses. It is almost a foregone conclusion that a fresh attempt to unravel the problem—or rather set of problems—which we have posed will not come up with a totally new answer. There are no totally new answers (except for fictional constructions) to be offered. We shall, however, investigate the most pertinent points in an effort to come up with the *best* answer. One is looking for a hypothesis which explains more (not everything), which gives a good account (not the only one) of what happened, which fits Jesus realistically into his environment, and which has in view cause and effect. . . .

Elaine Pagels

"THE GNOSTIC GOSPELS"

ELAINE PAGELS is the Harrington Spear Paine Professor of Religion at Princeton University. She is the author of *The Johannine Gospel in Gnostic Exegesis, The Gnostic Paul,* and *Adam, Eve, and the Serpent.* In her *The Gnostic Gospels,* which won a National Book Award and from which the following selection is taken, she tells the story of an extraordinary archeological discovery, in December of 1945, near the town of Nag Hammadi in Upper Egypt. Muhammad 'Ali-al-Samman, an Arab peasant, uncovered a red earthenware jar about a meter high that contained thirteen papyrus books, bound in leather. After burning some of the books in lieu of firewood, he eventually sold the remaining ones on the black market. Years later the books found their way to scholars who discovered, among other things, that some of them claimed to be secret gospels of Jesus and contained many astonishing passages. One of them, *The Gospel of Thomas,* which some scholars think is based on traditions older than those of the earliest New Testament gospels, contains sayings of Jesus that portray him as an Eastern-style spiritual teacher; for instance, Jesus says, "If you bring forth what is within you, what you bring forth will save you. If you do not bring forth what is within you, what you do not bring forth will destroy you," and, speaking to Thomas, "I am not your master. Because you have drunk, you have become drunk from the bubbling stream which I have measured out . . . He who will drink from my mouth will become as I am: I myself shall become he, and the things that are hidden will be revealed to him." Other Gnostic gospels also contain unfamiliar sketches of Jesus; for instance, in one it is written that " . . . the companion of the (Savior is) Mary Magdalene. (But Christ loved) her more than (all) the disciples, and used to kiss her (often) on her (mouth). The rest of (the disciples were offended) . . . The Savior . . . said to them, "Why do I not love you as (I love) her?" Such material, often juxtaposed with material that is familiar from the New Testament, suggests dramatically different interpretations of Jesus and his message.

One of Pagels's disturbing themes in the following selection is her searing account of the development of patriarchy in the institutional Church. Another is her thesis that the Church fathers had a self-serving, political motive for selecting the gospels that they chose to include in the New Testament and, hence, that their claim to have chosen them simply on grounds of historical accuracy is highly suspect.

I. THE CONTROVERSY OVER CHRIST'S RESURRECTION: HISTORICAL EVENT OR SYMBOL?

"Jesus Christ rose from the grave." With this proclamation, the Christian church began. This may be the fundamental element of Christian faith; certainly it is the most radical. Other religions celebrate cycles of birth and death: Christianity insists that in one unique historical moment, the cycle reversed, and a dead man came back to life! For Jesus' followers this was the turning point in world history, the sign of its coming end. Orthodox Christians since then have confessed in the creed that Jesus of Nazareth, "crucified, dead, and buried," was raised "on the third day."[1] Many today recite that creed without thinking about what they are saying, much less actually believing it. Recently some ministers, theologians, and scholars have challenged the literal view of resurrection. To account for this doctrine, they point out its psychological appeal to our deepest fears and hopes; to explain it, they offer symbolic interpretations.

But much of the early tradition insists literally that a man—Jesus—had come back to life. What makes these Christian accounts so extraordinary is not the claim that his friends had "seen" Jesus after his death—ghost stories, hallucinations, and visions were even more commonplace then than now—but that they saw an actual human being. At first, according to Luke, the disciples themselves, in their astonishment and terror at the appearance of Jesus among them, immediately assumed that they were seeing his ghost. But Jesus challenged them: "Handle me and see, for a spirit does not have flesh and bones, as you see that I have."[2] Since they remained incredulous, he asked for something to eat; as they watched in amazement, he ate a piece of broiled fish. The point is clear: no ghost could do that.

1. K. Stendahl, *Immortality and Resurrection* (New York, 1968).

2. Luke 24:36–43.

Had they said that Jesus' spirit lived on, surviving bodily decay, their contemporaries might have thought that their stories made sense. Five hundred years before, Socrates' disciples had claimed that their teacher's soul was immortal. But what the Christians said was different, and, in ordinary terms, wholly implausible. The finality of death, which had always been a part of the human experience, was being transformed. Peter contrasts King David, who died and was buried, and whose tomb was well known, with Jesus, who, although killed, rose from the grave, "because it was not possible for him to be held by it"—that is, by death.[3] Luke says that Peter excluded metaphorical interpretation of the event he said he witnessed: "[We] ate and drank with him after he rose from the dead."[4]

Tertullian, a brilliantly talented writer (A.D. C. 190), speaking for the majority, defines the orthodox position: as Christ rose bodily from the grave, so every believer should anticipate the resurrection of the flesh. He leaves no room for doubt. He is not, he says, talking about the immortality of the soul: "The salvation of the soul I believe needs no discussion: for almost any heretics, in whatever way they accept it, at least do not deny it."[5] What is raised is "this flesh, suffused with blood, built up with bones, interwoven with nerves, entwined with veins, (a flesh) which . . . was born, and . . . dies, undoubtedly human."[6] Tertullian expects the idea of Christ's suffering, death and resurrection to shock his readers; he insists that "it must be believed, because it is absurd!"[7]

Yet some Christians—those he calls heretics—dissent. Without denying the resurrection, they reject the literal interpretation; some find it "extremely revolting, repugnant, and impossible." Gnostic Christians interpret res-

3. Acts 2:22—36.

4. *Ibid.*, 10:40—41.

5. Tertullian, *De Resurrectione Carnis* 2.

6. Tertullian, *De Carne Christi* 5.

7. *Ibid.*

urrection in various ways. Some say that the person who experiences the resurrection does not meet Jesus raised physically back to life; rather, he encounters Christ on a spiritual level. This may occur in dreams, in ecstatic trance, in visions, or in moments of spiritual illumination. But the orthodox condemn all such interpretations; Tertullian declares that anyone who denies the resurrection *of the flesh* is a heretic, not a Christian.

Why did orthodox tradition adopt the literal view of resurrection? The question becomes even more puzzling when we look at what the New Testament says about it. Some accounts, like the story we noted from Luke, tell how Jesus appears to his disciples in the form they know from his earthly life; he eats with them, and invites them to touch him, to prove that he is "not a ghost." John tells a similar story: Thomas declares that he will not believe that Jesus had actually risen from the grave unless he personally can see and touch him. When Jesus appears, he tells Thomas, "Put your finger here, and see my hands; and put out your hand, and place it in my side; do not be faithless, but believing."[8] But other stories, directly juxtaposed with these, suggest different views of the resurrection. Luke and Mark both relate that Jesus appeared "in another form"[9]—*not* his former earthly form—to two disciples as they walked on the road to Emmaus. Luke says that the disciples, deeply troubled about Jesus' death, talked with the stranger, apparently for several hours. They invited him to dinner; when he sat down with them to bless the bread, suddenly they recognized him as Jesus. At that moment "he vanished out of their sight."[10] John, too, places directly before the story of "doubting Thomas" another of a very different kind: Mary Magdalene, mourning for Jesus near his grave, sees a man she takes to be the gardener. When he speaks her name, suddenly she recognizes the presence of Jesus—but he orders her *not* to touch him.[11]

So if some of the New Testament stories insist on a literal view of resurrection, others lend themselves to different interpretations. One could suggest that certain people, in moments of great emotional stress, suddenly felt that they experienced Jesus' presence. Paul's experience can be read this way. As he traveled on the Damascus road, intent on arresting Christians, "suddenly a light from heaven flashed about him. And he fell to the ground," hearing the voice of Jesus rebuking him for the intended persecution.[12] One version of this story says, "The men who were traveling with him stood speechless, hearing the voice, but seeing no one";[13] another says the opposite (as Luke tells it, Paul said that "those who were with me saw the light, but did not hear the voice of the one who was speaking to me").[14] Paul himself, of course, later defended the teaching on resurrection as fundamental to Christian faith. But although his discussion often is read as an argument for bodily resurrection, it concludes with the words "I tell you this, brethren: flesh and blood cannot inherit the kingdom of God, nor does the perishable [that is, the mortal body] inherit the imperishable."[15] Paul describes the resurrection as "a mystery,"[16] the transformation from physical to spiritual existence.

If the New Testament accounts could support a range of interpretations, why did orthodox Christians in the second century insist on a literal view of resurrection and reject all others as heretical? I suggest that we cannot answer this question adequately as long as we consider the doctrine only in terms of its religious content. But when we examine its practical effect on the

8. John 20:27.
9. Mark 16:12; Luke 24:13–32.
10. Luke 24:31.
11. John 20:11–17.
12. Acts 9:3–4.
13. *Ibid.*, 9:7.
14. *Ibid.*, 22:9.
15. I. Corinthians 15:50.
16. *Ibid.*, 15:51–53.

Christian movement, we can see, paradoxically, that the doctrine of bodily resurrection also serves an essential *political* function: it legitimizes the authority of certain men who claim to exercise exclusive leadership over the churches as the successors of the apostle Peter. From the second century, the doctrine has served to validate the apostolic succession of bishops, the basis of papal authority to this day. Gnostic Christians who interpret resurrection in other ways have a lesser claim to authority: when they claim priority over the orthodox, they are denounced as heretics.

Such political and religious authority developed in a most remarkable way. As we have noted, diverse forms of Christianity flourished in the early years of the Christian movement. Hundreds of rival teachers all claimed to teach the "true doctrine of Christ" and denounced one another as frauds. Christians in churches scattered from Asia Minor to Greece, Jerusalem, and Rome split into factions, arguing over church leadership. All claimed to represent "the authentic tradition."

How could Christians resolve such contrary claims? Jesus himself was the only authority they all recognized. Even during his lifetime, among the small group traveling through Palestine with him, no one challenged—and no one matched—the authority of Jesus himself. Independent and assertive a leader as he was, Jesus censured such traits among his followers. Mark relates that when James and John came to him privately to ask for special positions in his administration, he spoke out sharply against their ambition:

> You know that those who are supposed to rule over the Gentiles lord it over them, and their great men exercise authority over them. But it shall not be so among you; but whoever would be great among you must be your servant, and whoever would be first among you must be slave of all.[17]

17. Mark 10:42–44.

After Jesus' execution his followers scattered, shaken with grief and terrified for their own lives. Most assumed that their enemies were right—the movement had died with their master. Suddenly astonishing news electrified the group. Luke says that they heard that "the Lord has risen indeed, and has appeared to Simon [Peter]!"[18] What had he said to Peter? Luke's account suggested to Christians in later generations that he named Peter as his successor, delegating the leadership to him. Matthew says that during his lifetime Jesus already had decided that Peter, the "rock," was to found the future institution.[19] Only John claims to tell what the risen Christ said: he told Peter that he was to take Jesus' place as "shepherd" for the flock.[20]

Whatever the truth of this claim, we can neither verify nor disprove it on historical grounds alone. We have only secondhand testimony from believers who affirm it, and skeptics who deny it. But what we do know as historical fact is that certain disciples—notably, Peter—claimed that the resurrection had happened. More important, we know the result: shortly after Jesus' death, Peter took charge of the group as its leader and spokesman. According to John, he had received his authority from the only source the group recognized—from Jesus himself, now speaking from beyond the grave.

What linked the group gathered around Jesus with the world-wide organization that developed within 170 years of his death into a three-rank hierarchy of bishops, priests, and deacons? Christians in later generations maintained that it was the claim that Jesus himself had come back to life! The German scholar Hans von Campenhausen says that because "Peter was the first to whom Jesus appeared after his res-

18. Luke 24:34.
19. Matthew 16:13–19.
20. John 21:15–19.

urrection,"[21] Peter became the first leader of the Christian community. One can dispute Campenhausen's claim on the basis of New Testament evidence: the gospels of Mark and John both name Mary Magdalene, not Peter, as the first witness of the resurrection.[22] But orthodox churches that trace their origin to Peter developed the tradition—sustained to this day among Catholic and some Protestant churches—that Peter had been the "first witness of the resurrection," and hence the rightful leader of the church. As early as the second century, Christians realized the potential political consequences of having "seen the risen Lord": in Jerusalem, where James, Jesus' brother, successfully rivaled Peter's authority, one tradition maintained that James, not Peter (and certainly not Mary Magdalene) was the "first witness of the resurrection."

New Testament evidence indicates that Jesus appeared to many others besides Peter—Paul says that once he appeared to five hundred people simultaneously. But from the second century, orthodox churches developed the view that only *certain* resurrection appearances actually conferred authority on those who received them. These were Jesus' appearances to Peter and to "the eleven" (the disciples minus Judas Iscariot, who had betrayed Jesus and committed suicide).[23] The orthodox noted the account in Matthew, which tells how the resurrected Jesus announced to "the eleven" that his own authority now has reached cosmic proportions: "All authority, on heaven and on earth, has been given to me." Then he delegated that authority to "the eleven disciples."[24] Luke, too, indicates that although many others had known Jesus, and even had witnessed his resurrection, "the eleven" alone held the position of *official* witnesses—and hence became official leaders of the whole community. Luke relates that Peter, acting as spokesman for the group, proposed that since Judas Iscariot had defected, a twelfth man should now "take the office" that he vacated, restoring the group as "the twelve."[25] But to receive a share in the disciples' authority, Peter declared that he must be

> one of the men who have accompanied us during all the time that the Lord Jesus went in and out among us, beginning from the baptism of John until the day he was taken up from us—*one of these men must become with us a witness to his resurrection.*[26]

Matthias, who met these qualifications, was selected and "enrolled with the eleven apostles."[27]

After forty days, having completed the transfer of power, the resurrected Lord abruptly withdrew his bodily presence from them, and ascended into heaven as they watched in amazement.[28] Luke, who tells the story, sees this as a momentous event. Henceforth, for the duration of the world, no one would ever experience Christ's actual presence as the twelve disciples had during his lifetime—and for forty days after his death. After that time, as Luke tells it, others received only less direct forms of communication with Christ. Luke admits that Stephen saw a vision of Jesus "standing at the right hand of God"[29]; that Paul first encountered Jesus in a dramatic vision, and later in a trance[30] (Luke claims to record his words: "When I had returned to Jerusalem and was praying in the temple, I fell into a trance and saw him speaking to me"[31]). Yet Luke's account implies that these incidents cannot compare with the original events attested by the Twelve. In the first place, they occurred

21. H. von Campenhausen, *Ecclesiastical Authority and Spiritual Power* (London, 1969), trans. by J. A. Baker (original title: *Kirchliches Amt und geistliche Vollmacht,* Tübingen, 1953), 17 (see discussion in Ch. 1).

23. Mark 16:9; John 20:11–17.

23. Matthew 28:16–20; Luke 24:36–49; John 20:19–23.

24. Matthew 28:18.

25. Acts 1:15–20.

26. *Ibid.,* 1:22. Emphasis added.

27. *Ibid.,* 1:26.

28. *Ibid.,* 1:6–11.

29. *Ibid.,* 7:56.

30. Acts 9:1–6.

31. *Ibid.,* 22:17–18; cf. also Acts 18:9–10.

to persons *not* included among the Twelve. Second, they occurred only *after* Jesus' bodily ascension to heaven. Third, although visions, dreams, and ecstatic trances manifested traces of Christ's spiritual presence, the experience of the Twelve differed entirely. They alone, having known Jesus throughout his lifetime, could testify to those unique events which they knew firsthand—and to the resurrection of one who was dead to his complete, physical presence with them.[32]

Whatever we think of the historicity of the orthodox account, we can admire its ingenuity. For this theory—that all authority derives from certain apostles' experience of the resurrected Christ, an experience now closed forever—bears enormous implications for the political structure of the community. First, as the German scholar Karl Holl has pointed out, it restricts the circle of leadership to a small band of persons whose members stand in a position of incontestable authority.[33] Second, it suggests that only the apostles had the right to ordain future leaders as their successors.[34] Christians in the second century used Luke's account to set the groundwork for establishing specific, restricted chains of command for all future generations of Christians. Any potential leader of the community would have to derive, or claim to derive, authority from the same apostles. Yet, according to the orthodox view, none can ever claim to equal their authority—much less challenge it. What the apostles experienced and attested their successors cannot verify for themselves; instead, they must only believe, protect, and hand down to future generations the apostles' testimony.[35]

This theory gained extraordinary success: for nearly 2,000 years, orthodox Christians have accepted the view that the apostles alone held definitive religious authority, and that their only legitimate heirs are priests and bishops, who trace their ordination back to that same apostolic succession. Even today the pope traces his—and the primacy he claims over the rest—to Peter himself, "first of the apostles," since he was "first witness of the resurrection."

But the gnostic Christians rejected Luke's theory. Some gnostics called the literal view of resurrection the "faith of fools."[36] The resurrection, they insisted, was not a unique event in the past: instead, it symbolized how Christ's presence could be experienced in the present. What mattered was not literal seeing, but spiritual vision.[37] They pointed out that many who witnessed the events of Jesus' life remained blind to their meaning. The disciples themselves often misunderstood what Jesus said: those who announced that their dead master had come back physically to life mistook a spiritual truth for an actual event.[38] But the true disciple may never have seen the earthly Jesus, having been born at the wrong time, as Paul said of himself.[39] Yet this physical disability may become a spiritual advantage: such persons, like Paul, may encounter Christ first on the level of inner experience.

How is Christ's presence experienced? The author of the *Gospel of Mary,* one of the few gnostic texts discovered before Nag Hammadi, interprets the resurrection appearances as visions received in dreams or in ecstatic trance. This gnostic gospel recalls traditions recorded in Mark and John, that Mary Magdalene was the first to see the risen Christ.[40] John says that Mary saw Jesus on the morning of his resurrection,

32. See J. Lindblom, *Gesichte und Offenbarungen: Vorstellungen von göttlichen Weisungen und übernatürlichen Erscheinungen im ältesten Christentum* (Lund, 1968), 32–113.

33. See H. Holl, *Der Kirchenbegriff des Paulus in seinem Verhältnis zu dem der Urgemeinde,* in *Gesammelte Aufsätze zur Kirchengeschichte* (Tübingen, 1921), II, 50–51.

34. G. Blum, *Tradition und Sukzession: Studium zum Normbegriff des Apostolischen von Paulus bis Irenaeus* (Berlin, 1963), 48.

35. Campenhausen, *Ecclesiastical Authority and Spiritual Power,* 14–24. For discussion, see E. Pagels, "Visions, Appearances, and Apostolic Authority," 415–430.

36. Origen, *Commentarium in I Corinthians,* in *Journal of Theological Studies* 10 (1909), 46–47.

37. Tertullian, *De Resurrectione Carnis,* 19–27.

38. Irenaeus, AH 1.30.13.

39. I Corinthians 15:8.

40. Mark 16:9.

and that he appeared to the other disciples only later, on the evening of the same day.[41] According to the *Gospel of Mary,* Mary Magdalene, seeing the Lord in a vision, asked him, "How does he who sees the vision see it? [Through] the soul, [or] through the spirit?"[42] He answered that the visionary perceives through the mind. The *Apocalypse of Peter,* discovered by Nag Hammadi, tells how Peter, deep in trance, saw Christ, who explained that "I am the intellectual spirit, filled with radiant light."[43] Gnostic accounts often mention how the recipients respond to Christ's presence with intense emotions—terror, awe, distress, and joy.

Yet these gnostic writers do not dismiss visions as fantasies or hallucinations. They respect—even revere—such experiences, through which spiritual intuition discloses insight into the nature of reality. . . .

What interested these gnostics far more than past events attributed to the "historical Jesus" was the possibility of encountering the risen Christ in the present. . . . [44]

These gnostics recognized that their theory, like the orthodox one, bore political implications. It suggests that whoever "sees the Lord" through inner vision can claim that his or her own authority equals, or surpasses, that of the Twelve—and of their successors. Consider the political implications of the *Gospel of Mary:* Peter and Andrew, here representing the leaders of the orthodox group, accuse Mary—the gnostic—of pretending to have seen the Lord in order to justify the strange ideas, fictions, and lies she invents and attributes to divine inspiration. Mary lacks the proper credentials for leadership, from the orthodox viewpoint: she is not one of the "twelve." But as Mary stands up to Peter, so the gnostics who take her as their prototype challenge the authority of those priests and bishops who claim to be Peter's successors.

We know that gnostic teachers challenged the orthodox in precisely this way. While, according to them, the orthodox relied solely on the public, esoteric teaching which Christ and the apostles offered to "the many," gnostic Christians claimed to offer, in addition, their *secret* teaching, known only to the few.[45] The gnostic teacher and poet Valentinus (c. 140) points out that even during his lifetime, Jesus shared with his disciples certain mysteries, which he kept secret from outsiders.[46] According to the New Testament gospel of Mark, Jesus said to his disciples,

> . . . "To you has been given the secret of the kingdom of God, but for those outside everything is in parables; so that they may indeed see but not perceive, and may indeed hear but not understand; lest they should turn again, and be forgiven."[47]

Matthew, too, relates that when Jesus spoke in public, he spoke only in parables; when his disciples asked the reason, he replied, "To you it has been given to know the secrets [*mysteria;* literally, "mysteries"] of the kingdom of heaven, but to them it has not been given."[48] According to the gnostics, some of the disciples, following his instructions, kept secret Jesus' esoteric teaching: this they taught only in private, to certain persons who had proven themselves to be spiritually mature, and who therefore qualified for "initiation into *gnosis*"—that is, into secret knowledge.

Following the crucifixion, they allege that the risen Christ continued to reveal himself to

41. John 20:11–19.

42. *Gospel of Mary* 10.17–21, in NHL 472.

43. *Apocalypse of Peter* 83.8–10, in NHL 344. For discussion of Peter in gnostic traditions, see P. Perkins, "Peter in Gnostic Revelations," in *Proceedings of SBL: 1974 Seminar Papers II* (Washington, 1974), 1–13.

44. Cf. H. Koester, "One Jesus and Four Primitive Gospels," in J. M. Robinson and H. Koester, *Trajectories through Early Christianity* (Philadelphia, 1971), 158–204, and Robinson, "The Johannine Trajectory," *ibid.,* 232–268.

45. Irenaeus, AH 3.2.1–3.3.1. See also M. Smith, *Clement of Alexandria and a Secret Gospel of Mark* (Cambridge, 1973), 197–278.

26. *Ibid.,* 3.4.1–2.

47. Mark 4:11.

48. Matthew 13:11.

certain disciples, opening to them, through visions, new insights into divine mysteries. Paul, referring to himself obliquely in the third person, says that he was "caught up to the third heaven—whether in the body or out of the body I do not know." There, in an ecstatic trance, he heard "things that cannot be told, which man may not utter."[49] Through his spiritual communication with Christ, Paul says he discovered "hidden mysteries" and "secret wisdom," which, he explains, he shares only with those Christians he considers "mature"[50] but not with everyone. Many contemporary Biblical scholars, themselves orthodox, have followed Rudolph Bultmann, who insists that Paul does not mean what he says in this passage.[51] They argue that Paul does *not* claim to have a secret tradition; such a claim would apparently make Paul sound too "gnostic." Recently Professor Robin Scroggs has taken the opposite view, pointing out that Paul clearly says that he *does* have secret wisdom.[52] Gnostic Christians in ancient times came to the same conclusion. Valentinus, the gnostic poet who traveled from Egypt to teach in Rome (c. 140), even claimed that he himself learned Paul's secret teaching from Theudas, one of Paul's own disciples.

Followers of Valentinus say that only their own gospels and revelations disclose those secret teachings. These writings tell countless stories about the risen Christ—the spiritual being whom Jesus represented—a figure who fascinated them far more than the merely human Jesus, the obscure rabbi from Nazareth. For this reason, gnostic writings often reverse the pattern of the New Testament gospels. Instead of telling the history of Jesus biographically, from birth to death, gnostic accounts begin where the others end—with stories of the spiritual Christ appearing to his disciples. . . .

The controversy over resurrection, then, proved critical in shaping the Christian movement into an institutional religion. All Christians agreed in principle that only Christ himself—or God—can be the ultimate source of spiritual authority. But the immediate question, of course, was the practical one: Who, in the present, administers that authority?

Valentinus and his followers answered: Whoever comes into direct, personal contact with the "living One." They argued that only one's own experience offers the ultimate criterion of truth, taking precedence over all secondhand testimony and all tradition—even gnostic tradition! They celebrated every form of creative invention as evidence that a person has become spiritually alive. On this theory, the structure of authority can never be fixed into an institutional framework: it must remain spontaneous, charismatic, and open.

Those who rejected this theory argued that all future generations of Christians must trust the apostles' testimony—even more than their own experience. For, as Tertullian admitted, whoever judges in terms of ordinary historical experience would find the claim that a man physically returned from the grave to be incredible. What can never be proven or verified in the present, Tertullian says, "must be believed, because it is absurd." Since the death of the apostles, believers must accept the word of the priests and bishops, who have claimed, from the second century, to be their only legitimate heirs. . . .

II. "ONE GOD, ONE BISHOP": THE POLITICS OF MONOTHEISM

The Christian creed begins with the words "I believe in one God, Father Almighty, Maker of heaven and earth." Some scholars suggest that this credal statement was originally formulated to exclude followers of the heretic Marcion (c. 140) from orthodox churches. A Christian from

49. II Corinthians 12:2–4.

50. I Corinthians 2:6.

51. R. Bultmann, *Theology of the New Testament,* trans. by K. Grobel (London, 1965), I, 327; U. Wilckens, *Weisheit und Torheit* (Tübingen, 1959), 44 f., 214–224.

52. R. Scroggs, "Paul: Σόφος and πνευμάτικος," *New Testament Studies* 14, 33–55. See also E. Pagels, *The Gnostic Paul* (Philadelphia, 1975), 1–10; 55–58; 157–164.

Asia Minor, Marcion was struck by what he saw as the contrast between the creator-God of the Old Testament, who demands justice and punishes every violation of his law, and the Father whom Jesus proclaims—the New Testament God of forgiveness and love. Why, he asked, would a God who is "almighty"—all-powerful—create a world that includes suffering, pain, disease—even mosquitoes and scorpions? Marcion concluded that these must be two different Gods. The majority of Christians early condemned this view as dualistic, and identified themselves as orthodox by confessing one God, who is both "Father Almighty" and "Maker of heaven and earth."

When advocates of orthodoxy confronted another challenge—the gnostics—they often attacked them as "Marcionites" and "dualists." Irenaeus states as his major complaint against the gnostics that they, like the Marcionites, say that "there is another God besides the creator." . . .

Irenaeus himself tells us that the creed which effectively screened out Marcionites from the church proved useless against the Valentinians. In common with other Christians, they recited the orthodox creed. But Irenaeus explains that although they did "verbally confess one God," they did so with private mental reservations, "saying one thing, and thinking another."[53] While the Marcionites openly blasphemed the creator, the Valentinians, he insists, did so covertly. . . .

What made their position heretical? Why did Irenaeus find such a modification of monotheism so crucial—in fact, so utterly reprehensible—that he urged his fellow believers to expel the followers of Valentinus from the churches as heretics? He admitted that this question puzzled the gnostics themselves:

> They ask, when they confess the same things and participate in the same worship . . . how is it that we, for no reason, remain aloof from them; and how is it that when they confess the same things, and hold the same doctrines, *we call them heretics!*[54]

53. Irenaeus, AH 4.33.3.

I suggest that here again we cannot fully answer this question as long as we consider this debate exclusively in terms of religious and philosophical arguments. But when we investigate how the doctrine of God actually functions in gnostic and orthodox writings, we can see how this religious question also involves social and political issues. Specifically, by the latter part of the second century, when the orthodox insisted upon "one God," they simultaneously validated the system of governance in which the church is ruled by "one bishop." Gnostic modification of monotheism was taken—and perhaps intended—as an attack upon that system. For when gnostic and orthodox Christians discussed the nature of God, they were at the same time debating the issue of *spiritual authority.*

This issue dominates one of the earliest writings we have from the church at Rome—a letter attributed to Clement, called Bishop of Rome (c. 90–100). As spokesman for the Roman church, Clement wrote to the Christian community in Corinth at a time of crisis: certain leaders of the Corinthian church had been divested of power. Clement says that "a few rash and self-willed people" drove them out of office: "those of no reputation [rose up] against those with reputation, the fools against the wise, the young against the old."[55] Using political language, he calls this "a rebellion"[56] and insists that the deposed leaders be restored to their authority: he warns that they must be feared, respected, and obeyed.

On what grounds? Clement argues that God, the God of Israel, alone rules all things:[57] he is the lord and master whom all must obey; he is the judge who lays down the law, punishing rebels and rewarding the obedient. But how is God's

54. Irenaeus, AH 3.15.2. Emphasis added.
55. Clemens Romanus, *I Clement* 3.3.
56. *Ibid.,* 1.1.
57. *Ibid.,* 14.19–20; 60.

rule actually administered? Here Clement's theology becomes practical: God, he says, delegates his "authority of reign" to "rulers and leaders on earth."[58] Who are these designated rulers? Clement answers that they are bishops, priests, and deacons. Whoever refuses to "bow the neck"[59] and obey the church leaders is guilty of insubordination against the divine master himself. Carried away with his argument, Clement warns that whoever disobeys the divinely ordained authorities "receives the death penalty!"[60]

This letter marks a dramatic moment in the history of Christianity. For the first time, we find here an argument for dividing the Christian community between "the clergy" and "the laity." The church is to be organized in terms of a strict order of superiors and subordinates. Even within the clergy, Clement insists on ranking each member, whether bishop, priest, or deacon, "in his own order":[61] each must observe "the rules and commandments" of his position at all times.

Many historians are puzzled by this letter.[62] What, they ask, was the basis for the dispute in Corinth? What *religious* issues were at stake? The letter does not tell us that directly. But this does not mean that the author ignores such issues. I suggest that he makes his own point—his religious point—entirely clear: he intended to establish the Corinthian church on the model of the divine authority. As God reigns in heaven as master, lord, commander, judge, and king, so on earth he delegates his rule to members of the church hierarchy, who serve as generals who command an army of subordinates; kings who rule over "the people"; judges who preside in God's place.

Clement may simply be stating what Roman Christians took for granted[63]—and what Christians outside of Rome, in the early second century, were coming to accept. The chief advocates of this theory, not surprisingly, were the bishops themselves. Only a generation later, another bishop, Ignatius of Antioch in Syria, more than a thousand miles from Rome, passionately defended the same principle. But Ignatius went further than Clement. He defended the three ranks—bishop, priests, and deacons—as a hierarchical order that mirrors the divine hierarchy in heaven. As there is only one God in heaven, Ignatius declares, so there can be only one bishop in the church. "One God, one bishop"—this became the orthodox slogan. Ignatius warns "the laity" to revere, honor, and obey the bishop "as if he were God." For the bishop, standing at the pinnacle of the church hierarchy, presides "in the place of God."[64] Who, then stands below God? The divine council, Ignatius replies. And as God rules over that council in heaven, so the bishop on earth rules over a council of priests. The heavenly divine council, in turn, stands above the apostles; so, on earth, the priests rule over the deacons—and all three of these rule over "the laity."[65]

Was Ignatius merely attempting to aggrandize his own position? A cynical observer might suspect him of masking power politics with religious rhetoric. But the distinction between religion and politics, so familiar to us in the twentieth century, was utterly alien to Ignatius' self-understanding. For him, as for his contemporaries, pagan and Christian alike, religious convictions necessarily involved political relationships—and vice versa. Ironically, Ignatius himself shared this view with the Roman officials who condemned him to death, judging his religious convictions as evidence for treason

58. *Ibid.,* 60.4–61.2; 63.1–2.

59. *Ibid.,* 63.1.

60. *Ibid.,* 41.3.

61. *Ibid.,* 41.1.

62. See, for example, Campenhausen, *Ecclesiastical Authority and Spiritual Power,* 86–87; "Dogmatic issues are nowhere mentioned. We can no longer discern the background and the real point of the quarrel."

63. So says H. Beyschlag, *Clemens Romanus und der Frühkatholizismus* (Tübingen, 1966), 339–353.

64. Ignatius, *Magnesians* 6:1; *Trallians* 3.1; *Ephesians* 5.3.

65. *Magnesians* 6.1–7.2; *Trallians* 3.1; *Smyrneans* 8.1–2. For citations and discussion, see Pagels, "The Demiurge and his Archons," 306–307.

against Rome. For Ignatius, as for Roman pagans, politics and religion formed an inseparable unity. He believed that God became accessible to humanity *through the church*—and specifically, through the bishops, priests, and deacons who administer it: "without these, there is nothing which can be called a church!"[66] For the sake of their eternal salvation he urged people to submit themselves to the bishop and priests. Although Ignatius and Clement depicted the structure of the clergy in different ways,[67] both bishops agreed that this human order mirrors the divine authority in heaven. Their religious views, certainly, bore political implications; yet, at the same time, the practice they urged was based on their beliefs about God.

What would happen if someone challenged their doctrine of God—as the one who stands at the pinnacle of the divine hierarchy and legitimizes the whole structure? We do not have to guess: we can see what happened when Valentinus went from Egypt to Rome (c. 140). Even his enemies spoke of him as a brilliant and eloquent man:[68] his admirers revered him as a poet and spiritual master. One tradition attributes to him the poetic, evocative *Gospel of Truth* that was discovered at Nag Hammadi. Valentinus claims that besides receiving the Christian tradition that all believers hold in common, he has received from Theudas, a disciple of Paul's, initiation into a secret doctrine of God.[69] Paul himself taught this secret wisdom, he says, not to everyone, and not publicly, but only to a select few whom he considered to be spiritually mature.[70] Valentinus offers, in turn, to initiate "those who are mature"[71] into his wisdom, since not everyone is able to comprehend it.

What this secret tradition reveals is that the one whom most Christians naively worship as creator, God, and Father is, in reality, only the image of the true God. According to Valentinus, what Clement and Ignatius mistakenly ascribe to God actually applies only to the *creator.*[72] Valentinus, following Plato, uses the Greek term for "creator" (*demiurgos*),[73] suggesting that he is a lesser divine being who serves as the instrument of the higher powers.[74] It is not God, he explains, but the demiurge who reigns as king and lord,[75] who acts as a military commander,[76] who gives the law and judges those who violate it[77]—in short, he is the "God of Israel."

Through the initiation Valentinus offers, the candidate learns to reject the creator's authority and all his demands as foolishness. What gnostics know is that the creator makes false claims to power ("I am God, and there is no other")[78] that derive from his own ignorance. Achieving *gnosis* involves coming to recognize the true source of divine power—namely, "the depth" of all being. Whoever has come to know that source simultaneously comes to know himself and discovers his spiritual origin: he has come to know his true Father and Mother.

Whoever comes to this *gnosis*—this insight—is ready to receive the secret sacrament called the redemption (*apolytrosis;* literally, "release").[79] Before gaining *gnosis,* the candidate worshiped the demiurge, mistaking him for the true God: now, through the sacrament of redemption, the candidate indicates that he has been released from the demiurge's power. . . .

What are the practical—even political—implications of this religious theory? Consider how Valentinus or one of his initiates might respond to Clement's claim that the bishop rules over

66. *Trallians* 3.i; *Smyrneans* 8.2.

67. See, for example, Campenhausen, *Ecclesiastical Authority and Spiritual Power,* 84–106.

68. Tertullian, *Adversus Valentinianos* 4.

69. Clemens Alexandrinus, *Stromata* 7.7.

70. Irenaeus, AH 3.2.1–3.1.

71. *Ibid., Praefatio* 2; 3.15.1–2.

72. Clemens Alexandrinus, *Stromata* 4.89.6–90.1.

73. Cf. Plato, *Timaeus* 41. For discussion, see G. Quispel, "The Origins of the Gnostic Demiurge," in *Kyriakon: Festschrift Johannes Quasten* (Münster, 1970), 252–271.

74. Heracleon, Frag. 40, in Origen, COMM. JO. 13.60.

75. *Lord:* Irenaeus, AH 4.1–5.

76. *commander: Ibid.,* 1.7.4.

77. *judge:* Heracleon, Frag. 48, in Origen, COMM. JO. 20.38.

78. Irenaeus, AH 3.12.6–12.

79. *Ibid.,* 1.21.1–4.

the community "as God rules in heaven"—as master, king, judge, and lord. Would not an initiate be likely to reply to such a bishop: "You claim to represent God, but, in reality, you represent only the demiurge, whom you blindly serve and obey. I, however, have passed beyond the sphere of his authority—and so, for that matter, beyond yours!"

Irenaeus, as bishop, recognized the danger to clerical authority. The redemption ritual, which dramatically changed the initiate's relation to the demiurge, changed simultaneously his relationship to the bishop. Before, the believer was taught to submit to the bishop "as to God himself," since, he was told, the bishop rules, commands, and judges "in God's place." But now he sees that such restrictions apply only to naïve believers who still fear and serve the demiurge.[80] *Gnosis* offers nothing less than a theological justification for refusing to obey the bishops and priests! The initiate now sees them as the "rulers and powers" who rule on earth in the demiurge's name. The gnostic admits that the bishop, like the demiurge, exercises legitimate authority over most Christians—those who are uninitiated.[81] But the bishop's demands, warnings, and threats, like those of the demiurge himself, can no longer touch the one who has been "redeemed." . . .

The candidate receives from his initiation into *gnosis* an entirely new relation to spiritual authority. Now he knows that the clerical hierarchy derives its authority from the demiurge—not from the Father. When a bishop like Clement commands the believer to "fear God" or "to confess that you have a Lord," or when Irenaeus warns that "God will judge" the sinner, the gnostic may hear all of these as their attempt to reassert the false claims of the demiurge's power, and of his earthly representatives, over the believer. In the demiurge's foolish assertion that "I am God, and there is no other," the gnostic could hear the bishop's claim to exercise exclusive power over the community. . . .

80. *Ibid.*, 3.15.2.
81. *Ibid.*, 1.7.4.

Tertullian traces such arrogance to the example of their teacher Valentinus, who, he says, refused to submit himself to the superior authority of the bishop of Rome. For what reason? Tertullian says that Valentinus wanted to become bishop himself. But when another man was chosen instead, he was filled with envy and frustrated ambition, and cut himself off from the church to found a rival group of his own.[82]

Few historians believe Tertullian's story. In the first place, it follows a typical polemic against heresy which maintains that envy and ambition lead heretics to deviate from the true faith. Second, some twenty years after this alleged incident, follower of Valentinus considered themselves to be fully members of the church and indignantly resisted orthodox attempts to expel them.[83] This suggests that the orthodox, rather than those they called heretics, initiated the break.

Yet Tertullian's story, even—perhaps especially—if untrue, illustrates what many Christians saw as one of the dangers of heresy: it encourages insubordination to clerical authority. And, apparently, the orthodox were right. Bishop Irenaeus tells us that followers of Valentinus "assemble in unauthorized meetings"[84]—that is, in meetings that he himself, as bishop, has not authorized. At these meetings they attempted to raise doubts in the minds of their hearers: Does the church's teaching really satisfy them, or not?[85] Have the sacraments which the church dispenses—baptism and the eucharist—given them a complete initiation into Christian faith, or only the first step?[86] Members of the inner circle suggested that what the bishop and priests taught publicly were only *elementary* doctrines. They themselves claimed to offer more—the secret mysteries, the higher teachings.

82. Tertullian, *Adversus Valentinianos* 4.
83. Irenaeus, AH 3.15.2.
84. *Ibid.*, 3.3.2.
85. *Ibid.*, 3.15.2.
86. *Ibid.*, 1.21.1–2.

This controversy occurred at the very time when earlier, diversified forms of church leadership were giving away to a unified hierarchy of church office.[87] For the first time, certain Christian communities were organizing into a strict order of subordinate "ranks" of bishops, priests, deacons, laity. In many churches the bishop was emerging, for the first time, as a "monarch" (literally, "sole ruler"). Increasingly, he claimed the power to act as disciplinarian and judge over those he called "the laity." . . .

If gnostic Christians criticized the development of church hierarchy, how could they themselves form a social organization? If they rejected the principle of rank, insisting that all are equal, how could they even hold a meeting? Irenaeus tells us about the practice of one group that he knows from his own congregation in Lyons—the group led by Marcus, a disciple of Valentinus'.[88] Every member of the group had been initiated: this meant that every one had been "released" from the demiurge's power. For this reason, they dared to meet without the authority of the bishop, whom they regarded as the demiurge's spokesman—Irenaeus himself! Second, every initiate was assumed to have received, through the initiation ritual, the charismatic gift of direct inspiration through the Holy Spirit.[89]

How did members of this circle of "pneumatics" (literally, "those who are spiritual") conduct their meetings? Irenaeus tells us that when they met, all the members first participated in drawing lots.[90] Whoever received a certain lot apparently was designated to take the role of *priest;* another was to offer the sacrament, as *bishop;* another would read the Scriptures for worship, and others would address the group as a *prophet,* offering extemporaneous spiritual instruction. The next time the group met, they would throw lots again so that the persons taking each role changed continually.

This practice effectively created a very different structure of authority. At a time when the orthodox Christians increasingly discriminated between clergy and laity, this group of gnostic Christians demonstrated that, among themselves, they refused to acknowledge such distinctions. Instead of ranking their members into superior and inferior "orders" within a hierarchy, they followed the principle of strict equality. All initiates, men and women alike, participated equally in the drawing; anyone might be selected to serve as *priest, bishop,* or *prophet.* Furthermore, because they cast lots at each meeting, even the distinctions established by lot could never become permanent "ranks." Finally—most important—they intended, through this practice, to remove the element of human choice. A twentieth-century observer might assume that the gnostics left these matters to random chance, but the gnostics saw it differently. They believed that since God directs everything in the universe, the way the lots fell expressed his choice.

Such practices prompted Tertullian to attack "the behavior of the heretics":

> How frivolous, how worldly, how merely *human* it is, without seriousness, without authority, without discipline, as fits their faith! To begin with, it is uncertain who is a catechumen, and who a believer: they all have access equally, they listen equally, they pray equally—even pagans, if any happen to come. . . . They also share the kiss of peace with all who come, for they do not care how differently they treat topics, if they meet together to storm the citadel of the one only truth. . . . *All* of them are arrogant . . . *all* offer you *gnosis!*[91]

87. For a detailed discussion of this process, see Campenhausen, *Ecclesiastical Authority and Spiritual Power*, 76 ff.

88. Irenaeus, AH 1.13.1–6.

89. *Ibid.,* 1.13.3.

90. *Ibid.,* 1.13.4; for technical discussion of the lot (*kleros*), see Pagels, "The Demiurge and his Archons," 316–318.
Irenaeus tries to deny this: AH 1.13.4.
Such use of lots had precedent both in ancient Israel, where God was thought to express His choice through the casting of lots, and also among the apostles themselves, who selected by lot the twelfth apostle to replace Judas Iscariot (Acts 1:17-20). Apparently the followers of Valentinus intended to follow their example.

91. Tertullian, DE PRAESCR. 41. Emphasis added.

The principle of equal access, equal participation, and equal claims to knowledge certainly impressed Tertullian. But he took this as evidence that the heretics "overthrow discipline": proper discipline, in his view, required certain degrees of distinction between community members. Tertullian protests especially the participation of "those women among the heretics" who shared with men positions of authority: "They teach, they engage in discussion; they exorcise; they cure"[92]—he suspects that they might even baptize, which meant that they also acted as bishops!

Tertullian also objected to the fact that

> their ordinations are carelessly administered, capricious, and changeable. At one time they put novices in office; at another, persons bound by secular employment. . . . Nowhere is promotion easier than in the camp of rebels, where even the mere fact of being there is a foremost service. So today one man is bishop and tomorrow another; the person who is a deacon today, tomorrow is a reader; the one who is a priest today is a layman tomorrow; for even on the laity they impose the functions of priesthood![93]

This remarkable passage reveals what distinctions Tertullian considered essential to church order—distinctions between newcomers and experienced Christians; between women and men; between a professional clergy and people occupied with secular employment; between readers, deacons, priests, and bishops—and above all, between the clergy and the laity. Valentinian Christians, on the other hand, followed a practice which insured the equality of all participants. Their system allowed no hierarchy to form, and no fixed "orders" of clergy. Since each person's role changed every day, occasions for envy against prominent persons were minimized. . . .

To defend the church against these self-styled theologians, Irenaeus realized that he must forge theological weapons. He believed that if he could demolish the heretical teaching of "another God besides the creator," he could destroy the possibility of ignoring or defying—on allegedly theological grounds—the authority of the "one catholic church" and of its bishop. Like his opponents, Irenaeus took for granted the correlation between the structure of divine authority and human authority in the church. If God is One, then there can be only one true church, and only one representative of the God in the community—the bishop.

Irenaeus declared, therefore, that orthodox Christians must believe above all that God is One—creator, Father, lord, and judge. He warned that it is this one God who established the catholic church, and who "presides with those who exercise moral discipline"[94] within it. . . .

As the doctrine of Christ's bodily resurrection establishes the initial framework for clerical authority, so the doctrine of the "one God" confirms, for orthodox Christians, the emerging institution of the "one bishop" as monarch ("sole ruler") of the church. We may not be surprised, then, to discover next how the orthodox description of God (as "Father Almighty," for example) serves to define who is included—and who excluded—from participation in the power of priests and bishops.

III. GOD THE FATHER/GOD THE MOTHER

Unlike many of his contemporaries among the deities of the ancient Near East, the God of Israel shared his power with no female divinity, nor was he the divine Husband or Lover of any.[95] He can scarcely be characterized in any but masculine epithets: king, lord, master, judge, and

92. *Ibid.,* 41.

93. *Ibid.,* 41.

94. *Ibid.,* 3.25.1.

95. Where the God of Israel is characterized as husband and lover in the Old Testament, his spouse is described as the community of Israel (e.g., Isaiah 50:1, 54:1–8, Jeremiah 2:2–3; 20–25; 3:1–20; Hosea 1–4, 14) or as the land of Israel (Isaiah 62:1–5).

father.[96] Indeed, the absence of feminine symbolism for God marks Judaism, Christianity, and Islam in striking contrast to the world's other religious traditions, whether in Egypt, Babylonia, Greece, and Rome, or in Africa, India, and North America, which abound in feminine symbolism. Jewish, Christian, and Islamic theologians today are quick to point out that God is not to be considered in sexual terms at all.[97] Yet the actual language they use daily in worship and prayer conveys a different message: who, growing up with Jewish or Christian tradition, has escaped the distinct impression that God is *masculine?* And while Catholics revere Mary as the mother of Jesus, they never identify her as divine in her own right: if she is "mother of God," she is not "God the Mother" on an equal footing with God the Father!

Christianity, of course, added the trinitarian terms to the Jewish description of God. Yet of the three divine "Persons," two—the Father and the son—are described in masculine terms, and the third—the Spirit—suggests the sexlessness of the Greek neuter term for spirit, *pneuma.* Whoever investigates the early history of Christianity (the field called "patristics"—that is, study of "the fathers of the church") will be prepared for the passage that concludes the *Gospel of Thomas:*

> Simon Peter said to them [the disciples]: "Let Mary leave us, for women are not worthy of Life." Jesus said, "I myself shall lead her, in order to make her male, so that she too may become a living spirit, resembling you males. For every woman who will make herself male will enter the Kingdom of Heaven."[98]

Strange as it sounds, this simply states what religious rhetoric assumes: that the men form the legitimate body of the community, while women are allowed to participate only when they assimilate themselves to men. Other texts discovered at Nag Hammadi demonstrate one striking difference between these "heretical" sources and orthodox ones: gnostic sources continually use sexual symbolism to describe God. One might expect that these texts would show the influence of archaic pagan traditions of the Mother Goddess, but for the most part, their language is specifically Christian, unmistakably related to a Jewish heritage. Yet instead of describing a monistic and masculine God, many of these texts speak of God as a dyad who embraces both masculine and feminine elements.

One group of gnostic sources claims to have received a secret tradition from Jesus through James and through Mary Magdalene. Members of this group prayed to both the divine Father and Mother: "From Thee, Father, and through Thee, Mother, the two immortal names, Parents of the divine being, and thou, dweller in heaven, humanity, of the mighty name . . . "[99] Other texts indicate that their authors had wondered to whom a single, masculine God proposed, "Let us make man [*adam*] in our image, after our likeness" (Genesis 1:26). Since the Genesis account goes on to say that humanity was created "male and female" (1:27), some concluded that the God in whose image we are made must also be both masculine and feminine—both Father and Mother.

How do these texts characterize the divine Mother? I find no simple answer, since the texts themselves are extremely diverse. Yet we may sketch out three primary characterizations. In the first place, several gnostic groups describe the divine mother as part of an original couple. Valentinus, the teacher and poet, begins with the premise that God is essentially indescribable. But he suggests that the divine can be imagined as a dyad; consisting, in one part, of the Ineffable, the Depth, the Primal Father;

96. One may note several exceptions to this rule: Deuteronomy 32:11; Hosea 11:1; Isaiah 66:12 ff.; Numbers 11:12.

97. Formerly, as Professor Morton Smith reminds me, theologians often used the masculinity of God to justify, by analogy, the roles of men as rulers of their societies and households (he cites, for example, Milton's *Paradise Lost* IV.296 ff., 635 ff.).

98. *Gospel of Thomas* 51.19–26, in NHL 130.

99. Hippolytus, REF 5.6.

and, in the other, of Grace, Silence, the Womb and "Mother of the All."[100] Valentinus reasons that Silence is the appropriate complement of the Father, designating the former as feminine and the latter as masculine because of the grammatical gender of the Greek words. He goes on to describe how Silence receives, as in a womb, the seed of the Ineffable Source; from this she brings forth all the emanations of divine being, ranged in harmonious pairs of masculine and feminine energies. . . .

Another gnostic writing, called the *Great Announcement,* quoted by Hippolytus in his *Refutation of All Heresies,* explains the origin of the universe as follows: From the power of Silence appeared "a great power, the Mind of the Universe, which manages all things, and is a male . . . the other . . . a great Intelligence . . . is a female which produces all things."[101] Following the gender of the Greek words for "mind" (*nous*—masculine) and "intelligence" (*epinoia*—feminine), this author explains that these powers, joined in union, "are discovered to be duality . . . This is Mind in Intelligence, and these are separable from one another, and yet are one, found in a state of duality." . . .

A second characterization of the divine Mother describes her as Holy Spirit. The *Apocryphon of John* relates how John went out after the crucifixion with "great grief" and had a mystical vision of the Trinity. As John was grieving, he says that

> the [heavens were opened and the whole] creation [which is] under heaven shone and "the world] trembled. [And I was afraid, and I] saw in the light . . . a likeness with multiple forms . . . and the likeness had three forms.[102]

To John's question the vision answers: "He said to me, 'John, Jo[h]n, why do you doubt, and why are you afraid? . . . I am the one who [is with you] always. I [am the Father]; I am the Mother; I am the Son."[103] This gnostic description of God—as Father, Mother and Son—may startle us at first, but on reflection, we can recognize it as another version of the Trinity. The Greek terminology for the Trinity, which includes the neuter term for spirit (*pneuma*) virtually requires that the third "Person" of the Trinity be asexual. But the author of the *Secret Book* has in mind the Hebrew term for spirit, *ruah,* a feminine word; and so concludes that the feminine "Person" conjoined with the Father and Son must be the Mother. . . .

In addition to the eternal, mystical Silence and the Holy Spirit, certain gnostics suggest a third characterization of the divine Mother: as Wisdom. Here the Greek feminine term for "wisdom," *sophia,* translates a Hebrew feminine term, *bokbmah.* Early interpreters had pondered the meaning of certain Biblical passages—for example, the saying in Proverbs that "God made the world in Wisdom." Could Wisdom be the feminine power in which God's creation was "conceived"? According to one teacher, the double meaning of the term conception—physical and intellectual—suggests this possibility: "The image of thought [*ennoia*] is feminine, since . . . [it] is a power of conception."[104] The *Apocalypse of Adam,* discovered at Nag Hammadi, tells of a feminine power who wanted to conceive by herself:

> . . . from the nine Muses, one separated away. She came to a high mountain and spent time seated there, so that she desired herself alone in order to become androgynous. She fulfilled her desire, and became pregnant from her desire . . . [105]

The poet Valentinus uses this theme to tell a famous myth about Wisdom: Desiring to con-

100. Irenaeus, AH 1.11.1.

101. Hippolytus, REF 6. 18.

102. *Apocryphon of John* 1.31–2.9, in NHL 99.

103. *Ibid.,* 2.9–14, in NHL 99.

104. Hippolytus, REF 6.38.

105. *Apocalypse of Adam* 81.2–9, in NHL 262. See note #42 for references.

ceive by herself, apart from her masculine counterpart, she succeeded, and became the "great creative power from whom all things originate," often called Eve, "Mother of all living." But since her desire violated the harmonious union of opposites intrinsic in the nature of created being, what she produced was aborted and defective;[106] from this, says Valentinus, originated the terror and grief that mar human existence.[107] To shape and manage her creation, Wisdom brought forth the demiurge, the creator-God of Israel, as her agent.[108] . . .

Even more remarkable is the gnostic poem called the *Thunder, Perfect Mind.* This text contains a revelation spoken by a feminine power:

> I am the first and the last, I am the honored one and the scorned one. I am the whore, and the holy one. I am the wife and the virgin. I am (the mother) and the daughter. . . . I am she whose wedding is great, and I have not taken a husband. . . . I am knowledge, and ignorance. . . . I am shameless; I am ashamed. I am strength, and I am fear. . . . I am foolish, and I am wise. . . . I am godless, and I am one whose God is great.[109]

What does the use of such symbolism imply for the understanding of human nature? one text, having previously described the divine Source as a "bisexual Power," goes on to say that "what came into being from that Power—that is, humanity, being one—is discovered to be two: a male-female being that bears the female within it."[110] . . .

Yet all the sources cited so far—secret gospels, revelations, mystical teachings—are among those not included in the select list that constitutes the New Testament collection. Every one of the secret texts which gnostic groups revered was omitted from the canonical collection, and branded as heretical by those who called themselves orthodox Christians. By the time the process of sorting the various writings ended—probably as late as the year 200—virtually all the feminine imagery for God had disappeared from orthodox Christian tradition.

What is the reason for this total rejection? The gnostics themselves asked this question of their orthodox opponents and pondered it among themselves. Some concluded that the God of Israel himself initiated the polemics which his followers carried out in his name. For, they argued, this creator was a derivative, merely instrumental power whom the Mother had created to administer the universe, but his own self-conception was far more grandiose. They say that he believed that he had made everything by himself, but that, in reality, he had created the world because Wisdom, his Mother, "infused him with energy" and implanted into him her own ideas. . . .

Yet all of these are mythical explanations. Can we find any actual, historical reasons why these gnostic writings were suppressed? This raises a much larger question: By what means, and for what reasons, did certain ideas come to be classified as heretical, and others as orthodox, by the beginning of the third century? We may find one clue to the answer if we ask whether gnostic Christians derive any practical, social consequences from their conception of God—and of humanity—in terms that included the feminine element. Here, clearly, the answer is *yes.*

Bishop Irenaeus notes with dismay that women especially are attracted to heretical groups. "Even in our own district of the Rhône valley," he admits, the gnostic teacher Marcus had attracted "many foolish women" from his own congregation, including the wife of one of Irenaeus' own deacons.[111] Professing himself to be at a

106. Irenaeus, AH 1.2.2–3.

107. *Ibid.,* 1.4.1.–1.5.4.

108. *Ibid.,* 1.5.1–3. For discussion of the figure of Sophia, see the excellent articles of G. S. Stead, "The Valentinian Myth of Sophia," in *Journal of Theological Studies* 20 (1969), 75–104; and G. W. MacRae, "The Jewish Background of the Gnostic Sophia Myth," in *Novum Testamentum* 12.

109. *Thunder, Perfect Mind* 13.16–16.25, in NHL 271–274.

110. Hippolytus, REF 6.18.

111. Irenaeus, AH 1.13.5.

loss to account for the attraction that Marcus' group held, he offers only one explanation: that Marcus himself was a diabolically clever seducer, a magician who compounded special aphrodisiacs to "deceive, victimize, and defile" his prey. . . . Worst of all, from Irenaeus' viewpoint, Marcus invited women to act as priests in celebrating the eucharist with him: he "hands the cups to women"[112] to offer up the eucharistic prayer, and to pronounce the words of consecration.

Tertullian expresses similar outrage at such acts of gnostic Christians:

> These heretical women—how audacious they are! They have no modesty; they are bold enough to teach, to engage in argument, to enact exorcisms, to undertake cures, and, it may be, even to baptize![113]

. . . One of the Tertullian's prime targets, the heretic Marcion, had, in fact, scandalized his orthodox contemporaries by appointing women on an equal basis with men as priests and bishops. The gnostic teacher Marcellina traveled to Rome to represent the Carpocratian group,[114] which claimed to have received secret teaching from Mary, Salome, and Martha. The Montanists, a radical prophetic circle, honored two women, Prisca and Maximilla, as founders of the movement.

Our evidence, then, clearly indicates a correlation between religious theory and social practice.[115] Among such gnostic groups as the Valentinians, women were considered equal to men; some were revered as prophets; others acted as teachers, traveling evangelists, healers, priests, perhaps even bishops. . . .

This is an extraordinary development, considering that in its earliest years the Christian movement showed a remarkable openness toward women. Jesus himself violated Jewish convention by talking openly with women, and he included them among his companions. Even the gospel of Luke in the New Testament tells his reply when Martha, his hostess, complains to him that she is doing housework alone while her sister Mary sits listening to him: "Do you not care that my sister has left me to serve alone? Tell her, then, to help me." But instead of supporting her, Jesus chides Martha for taking upon herself so many anxieties, declaring that "one thing is needful: Mary has chosen the good portion, which shall not be taken away from her."[116] Some ten to twenty years after Jesus' death, certain women acted as prophets, teachers, and evangelists. Professor Wayne Meeks suggests that, at Christian initiation, the person presiding ritually announced that "in Christ . . . there is neither male nor female."[117] Paul quotes this saying, and endorses the work of women he recognizes as deacons and fellow workers; he even greets one, apparently, as an outstanding apostle, senior to himself in the movement.[118]

Yet Paul also expressed ambivalence concerning the practical implications of human equality. Discussing the public activity of women in the churches, he argues from his own—traditionally Jewish—conception of a monistic, masculine God for a divinely ordained hierarchy of social subordination: as God has authority over Christ, he declares, citing Genesis 2–3, so man has authority over woman:

> . . . a man . . . is the image and glory of God; but woman is the glory of man. (For man was

112. Hippolytus, REF 6.35; Irenaeus, AH 1.13.1–2.

113. Tertullian, DE PRAESCR. 41.

114. Irenaeus, AH 1.25.6.

115. This general observation is not, however, universally applicable. At least two circles where women acted on an equal basis with men—the Marcionites and the Montanists—retained a traditional doctrine of God. I know of no evidence to suggest that they included feminine imagery in their theological formulations. For discussion and references, see J. Leipoldt, *Die Frau in der antiken Welt und im Urchristentum* (Leipzig, 1955), 187 ff.; E. S. Fiorenza, "Word, Spirit, and Power: Women in Early Christian Communities," in *Women of Spirit,* ed. R. Reuther and E. McLaughlin (New York, 1979), 39 ff.

116. Luke 10:38–42. Cf. Romans 16:1–2; Colossians 4:15; Acts 2:25; 21:9; Romans 16:6; 16:12; Philippians 4.2–3.

117. See W. Meeks, "The Image of the Androgyne," 180 f. Most scholars agree with Meeks that in Galatians 3:38, Paul quotes a saying that itself belongs to pre-Pauline tradition.

118. Romans 16:7.

This was first pointed out to me by Cyril C. Richardson, and confirmed by recent research of B. Brooten, "Junia . . . Outstanding Among the Apostles," in *Women Priests,* ed. L. and A. Swidler (New York, 1977), 141–144.

> not made from woman, but woman from man. Neither was man created for woman, but woman for man.)[119]

While Paul acknowledged women as his equals "in Christ," and allowed for them a wider range of activity than did traditional Jewish congregations, he could not bring himself to advocate their equality in social and political terms. . . .

Such contradictory attitudes toward women reflect a time of social transition, as well as the diversity of cultural influences on churches scattered throughout the known world.[120] In Greece and Asia Minor, women participated with men in religious cults, especially the cults of the Great Mother and of the Egyptian goddess Isis.[121] While the leading roles were reserved for men, women took part in the services and professions. Some women took up education, the arts, and professions such as medicine. In Egypt, women had attained, by the first century A.D., a relatively advanced state of emancipation, socially, politically, and legally. In Rome, forms of education had changed, around 200 B.C., to offer to some children from the aristocracy the same curriculum for girls as for boys. Two hundred years later, at the beginning of the Christian era, the archaic, patriarchal forms of Roman marriage were increasingly giving way to a new legal form in which the man and woman bound themselves to each other with voluntary and mutual vows. The French scholar Jérôme Carcopino, in a discussion entitled "Feminism and Demoralization," explains that by the second century A.D., upper-class women often insisted upon "living their own life."[122] Male satirists complained of their aggressiveness in discussions of literature, mathematics, and philosophy, and ridiculed their enthusiasm for writing poems, plays, and music.[123] Under the Empire,

> women were everywhere involved in business, social life, such as theaters, sports events, concerts, parties, travelling—with or without their husbands. They took part in a whole range of athletics, even bore arms and went to battle . . . [124]

and made major inroads into professional life. Women of the Jewish communities, on the other hand, were excluded from actively participating in public worship, in education, and in social and political life outside the family.[125]

Yet despite all of this, and despite the previous public activity of Christian women, the majority of Christian churches in the second century went with the majority of the middle class in opposing the move toward equality, which found its support primarily in rich or what we would call bohemian circles. By the year 200, the majority of Christian communities endorsed as canonical the *pseudo*-Pauline letter of Timothy, which stresses (and exaggerates) the antifeminist element in Paul's views: "Let a woman learn in silence with all submissiveness. I permit no woman to teach or to have authority over men; she is to keep silent."[126] Orthodox Chris-

119. I. Corinthians 11:7–9.

For discussion of I Corinthians 11:7–9, see R. Scroggs, "Paul and the Eschatological Woman," in *Journal of the American Academy of Religion* 40 (1972), 283–303, and the critique by Pagels, "Paul and Women: A Response to Recent Discussion," in *Journal of the American Academy of Religion* 42 (1974), 538–549. Also see references in Fiorenza, "Word, Spirit, and Power," 62, n. 24 and 25.

120. See Leipoldt, *Die Frau;* also C. Schneider, *Kulturgeschichte des Hellenismus* (Munich, 1967), I, 78 ff.; S. A. Pomeroy, *Goddesses, Whores, Wives, and Slaves* (New York, 1975).

121. Cf. C. Vatin, *Recherches sur le mariage et la condition de la femme mariée à l'époque hellénistique* (Paris, 1970).

122. J. Carcopino, *Daily Life in Ancient Rome,* trans. by E. O. Lorimer (New Haven, 1951), 95–100.

123. *Ibid.,* 90–95.

124. L. Swidler, "Greco-Roman Feminism and the Reception of the Gospel," in *Traditio–Krisis–Renovatio,* ed. B. Jaspert (Marburg, 1976), 41–55; see also J. Balsdon, *Roman Women, Their History and Habits* (London, 1962); L. Friedländer, *Roman Life and Manners under the Early Empire* (Oxford, 1928); B. Förtsch, *Die politische Rolle der Frau in der römischen Republik* (Stuttgart, 1935). On women in Christian communities, see Fiorenza, "Word, Spirit, and Power"; R. Gryson, *The Ministry of Women in the Early Church* (Minnesota, 1976); K. Thraede, "Frau," *Reallexikon für Antike und Christentum* VIII (Stuttgart, 1973), 197–269.

125. Leipoldt, *Die Frau,* 72 ff.; R. H. Kennet, *Ancient Hebrew Social Life and Custom* (London, 1933); G. F. Moore, *Judaism in the First Centuries of the Christian Era* (Cambridge, 1932).

126. I Timothy 2:11–12.

tians also accepted as Pauline the letters to the Colossians and to the Ephesians, which order that women "be subject in everything to their husbands."[127]

Clement, Bishop of Rome, writes in his letter to the unruly church in Corinth that women are to "remain in the rule of subjection"[128] to their husbands. While in earlier times Christian men and women sat together for worship, in the middle of the second century—precisely at the time of struggle with gnostic Christians—orthodox communities began to adopt the synagogue custom, segregating women from men.[129] By the end of the second century, women's participation in worship was explicitly condemned: groups in which women continued on to leadership were branded as heretical.

What was the reason for these changes? The scholar Johannes Leipoldt suggests that the influx of many Hellenized Jews into the movement may have influenced the church in the direction of Jewish traditions, but, as he admits, "this is only an attempt to explain the situation: *the reality itself is the only certain thing.*"[130] Professor Morton Smith suggests that the change may have resulted from Christianity's move up in social scale from lower to middle class. He observes that in the lower class, where all labor was needed, women had been allowed to perform any services they could (so today, in the Near East, only middle-class women are veiled). . . .

We can see, then, two very different patterns of sexual attitudes emerging in orthodox and gnostic circles. In simplest form, many gnostic Christians correlate their description of God in both masculine and feminine terms with a complementary description of human nature. Most often they refer to the creation account of Genesis I, which suggests an equal or androgynous human creation. Gnostic Christians often take the principle of equality between men and women into the social and political structures of their communities. The orthodox pattern is strikingly different; it describes God in exclusively masculine terms, and typically refers to Genesis 2 to describe how Eve was created from Adam, and for his fulfillment. Like the gnostic view, this translates into social practice: by the late second century, the orthodox community came to accept the domination of men over women as the divinely ordained order, not only for social and family life, but also for the Christian churches. . . .

127. Ephesians 5:24; Colossians 3:18.

128. *I Clement* 1.3.

129. Leipoldt, *Die Frau,* 192; *Hippolytus of Rome,* 43.1, ed. Paul de Lagarder (*Aegyptiaca,* 1883), 253.

130. Leipoldt, *Die Frau,* 193. Emphasis added.

PART X

Morality and Values

"EUTHYPHRO"

A brief biography of Plato appears on page 64.

EUTHYPHRO: But what is the charge which he [Meletus] brings against you?

SOCRATES: What is the charge? Well, rather a grand one, which implies a degree of discernment far from contemptible in a young man. He says he knows how the youth are corrupted and who are their corruptors. I fancy that he must be a wise man, and seeing that I am the reverse of a wise man, he has found me out, and is going to accuse me of corrupting his generation. And of this our mother the state is to be the judge. Of all our political men he is the only one who seems to me to begin in the right way, with the cultivation of virtue in youth; like a good husbandman, he makes the young shoots his first care, and clears away us whom he accuses of destroying them. This is only the first step; afterwards he will assuredly attend to the elder branches; and if he goes on as he has begun, he will be a very great public benefactor.

EUTH.: I hope that he may; but I rather fear, Socrates, that the opposite will turn out to be the truth. My opinion is that in attacking you he is simply aiming a blow at the heart of the state. But in what way does he say that you corrupt the young?

SOC.: In a curious way, which at first hearing excites surprise: he says that I am a maker of gods, and that I invent new gods and deny the existence of the old ones; this is the ground of his indictment.

EUTH.: I understand, Socrates; he means to attack you about the familiar sign which occasionally, as you say, comes to you. He thinks that you are a neologian, and he is going to have you up before the court for this. He knows that such a charge is readily received by the world, as I myself know too well; for when I speak in the assembly about divine things, and foretell the future to them, they laugh at me and think me a madman. Yet every word that I say is true. But they are jealous of us all; and we must be brave and go at them.

SOC.: Their laughter, friend Euthyphro, is not a matter of much consequence. For a man may be thought clever; but the Athenians, I suspect, do not much trouble themselves about him until he begins to impart his wisdom to others; and then for some reason or other, perhaps, as you say, from jealousy, they are angry.

EUTH.: I have no great wish to try their temper towards me in this way.

SOC.: No doubt they think you are reserved in your behaviour, and unwilling to impart your wisdom. But I have a benevolent habit of pouring out myself to everybody, and would even pay for a listener, and I am afraid that the Athenians may think me too talkative. Now if, as I was saying, they would only laugh at me, as you say that they laugh at you, the time might pass gaily enough with jokes and merriment in the court; but per-

From *The Dialogues of Plato,* Benjamin Jowett trans., 4th ed., 1953.

haps they may be in earnest, and then what the end will be you soothsayers only can predict.

EUTH.: I dare say that the affair will end in nothing, Socrates, and that you will win your cause; and I think that I shall win my own.

SOC.: And what is your suit, Euthyphro? are you the pursuer or the defendant?

EUTH.: I am pursuer.

SOC.: Of whom?

EUTH.: When I tell you, you will perceive another reason why I am thought mad.

SOC.: Why, has the fugitive wings?

EUTH.: Nay, he is not very volatile at his time of life.

SOC.: Who is he?

EUTH.: My father.

SOC.: My dear Sir! Your own father?

EUTH.: Yes.

SOC.: And of what is he accused?

EUTH.: Of murder, Socrates.

SOC.: Good heavens! How little, Euthyphro, does the common herd know of the nature of right and truth! A man must be an extraordinary man, and have made great strides in wisdom, before he could have seen his way to bring such an action.

EUTH.: Indeed, Socrates, he must.

SOC.: I suppose that the man whom your father murdered was one of your family—clearly he was; for if he had been a stranger you would never have thought of prosecuting him.

EUTH.: I am amused, Socrates, at your making a distinction between one who is a member of the family and one who is not; for surely the pollution is the same in either case, if

"God's Commands and Man's Duties"

Jonathan Harrison

When we consider the relation between God's commands and man's duties, it seems to be a fairly good rough approximation to the truth to say that there are three possible views about the nature of this relation. In the *first* place, it is possible to say that God, since he is omniscient, always knows what is right and wrong, and, since he is perfectly good, always commands us to do what is right and prohibits us from doing what is wrong; he is pleased with us when we obey his commands, and do what is right, and displeased with us when we disobey his commands, and do what is wrong. On this view, God's will is determined by his knowledge of right and wrong. *Secondly,* it is possible to say that what makes right actions right and what makes wrong actions wrong is that God has commanded the right actions and prohibited the wrong ones, and that being commanded by God is the only thing which makes an action right and being prohibited by God is the *only* thing which makes an action wrong. On this view, it is impossible for God, in commanding some actions and prohibiting others, to be guided by the fact that the actions he commands are right and the actions he prohibits are wrong, because, before he has commanded them, no actions are right, and before he has prohibited them, no actions are wrong. The *third* possible view is that there are not two pairs of different facts, being commanded by God and being right, and being prohibited by God and being wrong: to say that an action is right just *means* that it is commanded by God, and to say that an action is wrong just *means* that it is prohibited by God. . . . On the third view there are not two different facts, being commanded by God and being right, such that we can ask whether the first is dependent upon the second or whether the second is dependent upon the first. There is just one single fact, which may be put indifferently by saying either that God has commanded something or that it is right.

From *Our Knowledge of Right and Wrong* (1971).

you knowingly associate with the murderer when you ought to clear yourself and him by proceeding against him. The real question is whether the murdered man has been justly slain. If justly, then your duty is to let the matter alone; but if unjustly, then proceed against the murderer, if, that is to say, he lives under the same roof with you and eats at the same table. In fact, the man who is dead was a poor dependant of mine who worked for us as a field labourer on our farm in Naxos, and one day in a fit of drunken passion he got into a quarrel with one of our domestic servants and slew him. My father bound him hand and foot and threw him into a ditch, and then sent to Athens to ask an expositor of religious law what he should do with him. Meanwhile he never attended to him and took no care about him, for he regarded him as a murderer; and thought that no great harm would be done even if he did die. Now this was just what happened. For such was the effect of cold and hunger and chains upon him, that before the messenger returned from the expositor, he was dead. And my father and family are angry with me for taking the part of the murderer and prosecuting my father. They say that he did not kill him, and that if he did, the dead man was but a murderer, and I ought not to take any notice, for that son is impious who prosecutes a father for murder. Which shows, Socrates, how little they know what the gods think about piety and impiety.

SOC.: Good heavens, Euthyphro! and is your knowledge of religion and of things pious and impious so very exact, that, supposing the circumstances to be as you state them, you are not afraid lest you too may be doing an impious thing in bringing an action against your father?

EUTH.: The best of Euthyphro, that which distinguishes him, Socrates, from the common herd, is his exact knowledge of all such matters. What should I be good for without it?

SOC.: Rare friend! I think that I cannot do better than be your disciple. . . . And therefore, I adjure you to tell me the nature of piety and impiety, which you said that you knew so well, in their bearing on murder and generally on offenses against the gods. Is not piety in every action always the same? and impiety, again—is it not always the opposite of piety, and also the same with itself, having, as impiety, one notion or form which includes whatever is impious?

EUTH.: To be sure, Socrates.

SOC.: And what is piety, and what is impiety?

EUTH.: Piety is doing as I am doing; that is to say, prosecuting anyone who is guilty of murder, sacrilege, or of any similar crime—whether he be your father or mother, or whoever he may be—that makes no difference; and not to prosecute them is impiety. And please to consider, Socrates, what a notable proof I will give you that this is the law, a proof which I have already given to others:—of the principle, I mean, that the impious, whoever he may be, ought not to go unpunished. For do not men acknowledge Zeus as the best and most righteous of the gods?—and yet they admit that he bound his father (Cronos) because he wickedly devoured his sons, and that he too had punished his own father (Uranus) for a similar reason, in a nameless manner. And yet when I proceed against my father, they are angry with me. So inconsistent are they in their way of talking when the gods are concerned, and when I am concerned.

SOC.: May not this be the reason, Euthyphro, why I am charged with impiety—that I cannot away with these stories about the gods? that, I suppose is where people think I go wrong. But as you who are well informed about them approve of them, I cannot do better than assent to your superior wisdom. What else can I say, confessing as I do, that I know nothing about them? Tell me, for the love of Zeus, whether you really believe that they are true.

EUTH.: Yes, Socrates; and things more wonderful still, of which the world is in ignorance.

SOC.: And do you really believe that the gods fought with one another, and had dire quarrels, battles, and the like, as the poets say, and as you see represented in the works of great artists? The temples are full of them; and notably the robe of Athene, which is carried up to the Acropolis at the great Panathenaea, is embroidered with them throughout. Are all these tales of the gods true, Euthyphro?

EUTH.: Yes, Socrates; and, as I was saying, I can tell you, if you would like to hear them, many other things about the gods which would quite amaze you.

SOC.: I dare say; and you shall tell me them at some other time when I have leisure. But just at present I would rather hear from you a more precise answer, which you have not as yet given, my friend, to the question, 'What is "piety"?' When asked, you only replied, 'Doing as you do, charging your father with murder'.

EUTH.: And what I said was true, Socrates.

SOC.: No doubt, Euthyphro; but you would admit that there are many other pious acts?

EUTH.: There are.

SOC.: Remember that I did not ask you to give me two or three examples of piety, but to explain the general form which makes all pious things to be pious. Do you not recollect saying that one and the same form made the impious impious, and pious pious?

EUTH.: I remember.

SOC.: Tell me what is the nature of this form, and then I shall have a standard to which I may look, and by which I may measure actions, whether yours or those of anyone else, and then I shall be able to say that such and such an action is pious, such another impious.

EUTH.: I will tell you, if you like.

SOC.: I should very much like.

EUTH.: Piety, then, is that which is dear to the gods, and impiety is that which is not dear to them.

SOC.: Very good, Euthyphro; you have now given me the sort of answer which I wanted. But

"Morality and Obedience"

Patrick Nowell-Smith

It is this premise, that being moral consists in obedience to commands, that I deny. There is an argument, familiar to philosophers but of which the force is not always appreciated, which shows that this premise cannot be right. Suppose that I have satisfied myself that God has commanded me to do this or that thing—in itself a large supposition, but I will waive objections on this score in order to come quickly to the main point—it sill makes *sense* for me to ask whether or not I *ought* to do it. God, let us say, is an omnipotent, omniscient creator of the universe. Such a creator might have evil intentions and might command me to do wrong; and if that were the case though it would be imprudent to disobey, it would not be wrong. There is nothing in the idea of an omnipotent, omniscient creator which, by itself, entails his goodness or his right to command, unless we are prepared to assent to Hobbes' phrase, "God, who by right, *that is by irresistible power,* commandeth all things." Unless we accept Hobbes' consistent but repugnant equation of God's right with his might, we must be persuaded *independently* of his goodness before we admit his right to command. We must judge for ourselves whether the Bible is the inspired word of a just and benevolent God or a curious amalgam of profound wisdom, and gross superstition. To judge this is to make a moral decision, so that in the end, so far from morality being based on religion, religion is based on morality.

From "Morality: Religious and Secular" (1961).

whether what you say is true or not I cannot as yet tell, although I make no doubt that you will go on to prove the truth of your words.

EUTH.: Of course.

SOC.: Come, then, and let us examine what we are saying. That thing or person which is dear to the gods is pious, and that thing or person which is hateful to the gods is impious, these two being the extreme opposites of one another. Was not that said?

EUTH.: It was. . . .

SOC.: And further, Euthyphro, the gods were admitted to have enmities and hatreds and differences?

EUTH.: Yes, that was also said.

SOC.: And what sort of difference creates enmity and anger? Suppose for example that you and I, my good friend, differ on the question which of two groups of things is more numerous; do differences of this sort make us enemies and set us at variance with one another? Do we not proceed at once to counting, and put an end to them?

EUTH.: True.

SOC.: Or suppose that we differ about magnitudes, do we not quickly end the difference by measuring?

EUTH.: Very true.

SOC.: And we end a controversy about heavy and light by resorting to a weighing machine?

EUTH.: To be sure.

SOC.: But what are the matters about which differences arise that cannot be thus decided, and therefore make us angry and set us at enmity with one another? I dare say the answer does not occur to you at the moment, and therefore I will suggest that these enmities arise when the matters of difference are the just and unjust, good and evil, honourable and dishonourable. Are not these the subjects about which men differ, and about which when we are unable satisfactorily to decide our differences, you and I and all of us quarrel, when we do quarrel?

EUTH.: Yes, Socrates, the nature of the differences about which we quarrel is such as you describe.

SOC.: And the quarrels of the gods, noble Euthyphro, when they occur, are of a like nature?

EUTH.: Certainly they are.

SOC.: They have differences of opinion, as you say, about good and evil, just and unjust, honourable and dishonourable: there would be no quarrels among them, if there were not such differences—would there now?

EUTH.: You are quite right.

SOC.: Does not each party of them love that which they deem noble and just and good, and hate the opposite? . . .

Then the same things are hated by the gods and loved by the gods, and are both hateful and dear to them?

EUTH.: It appears so.

SOC.: And upon this view the same things, Euthyphro, will be pious and also impious?

EUTH.: So I should suppose.

SOC.: Then, my friend, I remark with surprise that you have not answered the question which I asked. For I certainly did not ask you to tell me what action is both pious and impious; but now it would seem that what is loved by the gods is also hated by them. And therefore, Euthyphro, in thus chastising your father you may very likely be doing what is agreeable to Zeus but disagreeable to Cronos or Uranus, and what is acceptable to Hephaestus but unacceptable to Hera, and there may be other gods who have similar differences of opinion.

EUTH.: But I believe, Socrates, that all the gods would be agreed as to the propriety of punishing a murderer: there would be no difference of opinion about that.

SOC.: Well, but speaking of men, Euthyphro, did you ever hear anyone arguing that a murderer or any sort of evil-doer ought to be let off?

EUTH.: I should rather say that these are the questions which they are always arguing, especially in courts of law: they commit all sorts of crimes, and there is nothing which they will not do or say in their own defence.

SOC.: But do they admit their guilt, Euthyphro, and yet say that they ought not to be punished?

EUTH.: No, they do not.

SOC.: Then there are some things which they do not venture to say and do: for they do not venture to argue that if guilty they are to go unpunished, but they deny their guilt, do they not?

EUTH.: Yes.

SOC.: Then they do not argue that the evil-doer should not be punished, but they argue about the fact of who the evil-doer is, and what he did and when?

EUTH.: True.

SOC.: And the gods are in the same case, if as you assert they quarrel about just and unjust, and some of them say while others deny that injustice is done among them. For surely neither god nor man will ever venture to say that the doer of injustice is not to be punished?

EUTH.: That is true, Socrates, in the main.

SOC.: But they join issue about the particulars—gods and men alike, if indeed the gods dispute at all; they differ about some act which is called in question, and which by some is affirmed to be just, by others to be unjust. Is not that true?

EUTH.: Quite true.

SOC.: Well then, my dear friend Euthyphro, do tell me, for my better instruction and information, what proof have you that in the opinion of all the gods a servant who is guilty of murder, and is put in chains by the master of the dead man, and dies because he is put in chains before he who bound him can learn from the expositors of religious law what he ought to do with him, is killed unjustly; and that on behalf of such an one a son ought to proceed against his father and accuse him of murder. How would you show that all the gods absolutely agree in approving of his act? Prove to me that they do, and I will applaud your wisdom as long as I live.

EUTH.: No doubt it will be a difficult task; though I could make the matter very clear indeed to you.

SOC.: I understand; you mean to say that I am not so quick of apprehension as the judges: for to them you will be sure to prove that the act is unjust, and hateful to all the gods.

EUTH.: Yes indeed, Socrates; at least if they will listen to me.

SOC.: But they will be sure to listen if they find that you are a good speaker. There was a notion that came into my mind while you were speaking; I said to myself: 'Well, and what if Euthyphro does prove to me that all the gods regarded the death of the serf as unjust, how do I know anything more of the nature of piety and impiety? for granting that this action may be hateful to the gods, still piety and impiety are not adequately defined by these distinctions, for that which is hateful to the gods has been shown to be also dear to them.' And therefore, Euthyphro, I do not ask you to prove this; I will suppose, if you like, that all the gods condemn and abominate such an action. But I will amend the definition so far as to say that what all the gods hate is impious, and what they love pious or holy; and what some of them love and others hate is both or neither. Shall this be our definition of piety and impiety?

EUTH.: Why not, Socrates?

SOC.: Why not! certainly, as far as I am concerned, Euthyphro, there is no reason why not. But whether this premiss will greatly assist you in the task of instructing me as you promised, is a matter for you to consider.

EUTH.: Yes, I should say that what all the gods love is pious and holy, and the opposite which they all hate, impious.

SOC.: Ought we to inquire into the truth of this, Euthyphro, or simply to accept it on

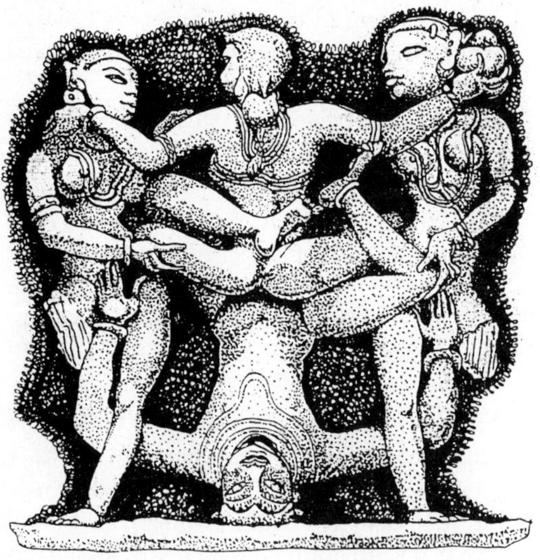

From a Hindu temple at Khajuraho, India. Tenth century A.D.

our own authority and that of others—echoing mere assertions? What do you say?

EUTH.: We should inquire; and I believe that the statement will stand the test of inquiry.

SOC.: We shall soon be better able to say, my good friend. The point which I should first wish to understand is whether the pious or holy is beloved by the gods because it is holy, or holy because it is beloved of the gods.

EUTH.: I do not understand your meaning, Socrates.

SOC.: I will endeavour to explain: . . . is not that which is beloved distinct from that which loves?

EUTH.: Certainly. . . .

SOC.: And what do you say of piety, Euthyphro: is not piety, according to your definition, loved by all the gods?

"Divine Sex"

Vernon Reynolds and Ralph E. Tanner

The exposure to adult sexuality in adolescence in the Western world is . . . opposed by all the churches as pornographic, indecent or immoral and is, in certain forms, against the law. . . .

In Hinduism it is not possible for the growing child to be unaware of adult sexuality, indeed it has an approved place in the religion since the male and female sexual organs are central in some temples and are a focus of worship. Some Hindu temples, such as Khajuraho are covered externally with copulating figures displaying a 'languid and calculated eroticism'. The well-known Hindu text, the Kama Sutra spells out in great detail the desired and approved range of sexuality and instructs lovers on how to interact with one another. . . .

Among Muslims, despite an external aloofness by women and the fierce condemnation of illegitimate sexuality, there is an equally open and divinely encouraged sexual activism for married couples. The Arab world has produced a number of erotic books, especially *The Perfumed Garden of Shaykh Nefzawi,* which has for centuries had a wide currency in Islam. [W]hat is interesting in these books is not so much the ingenious variety of the sexual practices described, but the way in which they are included within the Islamic religious doctrine.

An Egyptian book about sex thus starts with the preamble: 'Praise to the Lord who adorned the virginal bosom with breasts and who made the thighs of women for the spear handles of men' (Jalal al-Din al Siyuti 1900) while *The Perfumed Garden* starts similarly with: 'Praise be given to God, who has placed man's greatest pleasure in the natural parts of woman and has destined the natural parts of man to afford the greatest enjoyment to woman'. . . .

There is nothing in this literature to suggest that it is not read by the young. Indeed it is intended for their erudition.

From *The Biology of Religion* (1983).

EUTH.: Yes.

SOC.: Because it is pious or holy, or for some other reason?

EUTH.: No, that is the reason.

SOC.: It is loved because it is holy, not holy because it is loved?

EUTH.: Apparently.

SOC.: And it is the object of the gods' love, and is dear to them, because it is loved of them?

EUTH.: Certainly.

SOC.: Then that which is dear to the gods, Euthyphro, is not holy, nor is that which is holy dear to the gods, as you affirm; but they are two different things. . . .

EUTH.: Yes.

SOC.: But that which is dear to the gods is dear to them because it is loved by them, not loved by them because it is dear to them.

EUTH.: True.

SOC.: But, friend Euthyphro, if that which is holy were the same with that which is dear to the gods, and were loved because it is holy, then that which is dear to the gods would be loved as being dear to them; but if that which is dear to them were dear to them because loved by them, then that which is holy would be holy because loved by them. But now you see that the reverse is the case, and that the two things are quite different from one another. For one is of a kind to be loved because it is loved, and the other is loved because it is of a kind to be loved. Thus you appear to me, Euthyphro, when I ask you what is the nature of holiness, to offer an attribute only, and not the essence—the attribute of being loved by all the gods. But you still do not explain to me the nature of holiness. And therefore, if you please, I will ask you not to hide your treasure, but to start again, and tell me frankly what holiness or piety really is, whether dear to the gods or not (for that is a matter about which we will not quarrel); and what is impiety?

EUTH.: I really do not know, Socrates, how to express what I mean. For somehow or other the definitions we propound, on whatever bases we rest them, seem always to turn round and walk away from us. . . .

SOC.: Then we must begin again and ask, What is piety? That is an inquiry which I shall never be weary of pursuing as far as in me lies; and I entreat you not to scorn me, but to apply your mind to the utmost, and tell me the truth. For, if any man knows, you are he; and therefore I must hold you fast, like Proteus, until you tell. If you had not certainly known the nature of piety and impiety, I am confident that you would never, on behalf of a serf, have charged your aged father with murder. You would not have run such a risk of doing wrong in the sight of the gods, and you would have had too much respect for the opinions of men. I am sure, therefore, that you know the nature of piety and impiety. Speak out then, my dear Euthyphro, and do not hide your knowledge.

EUTH.: Another time, Socrates; for I am in a hurry, and must go now.

SOC.: Alas! my friend, and will you leave me in despair? I was hoping that you would instruct me in the nature of piety and impiety; and then I might have cleared myself of Meletus and his indictment. I would have told him that I had been enlightened by Euthyphro, and had given up rash innovations and speculations in which I had indulged only through ignorance, and that now I am about to lead a better life.

Robert Merrihew Adams

"DIVINE COMMANDS AND THE SOCIAL NATURE OF OBLIGATION"

A brief biography of Adams appears on page 275.

Divine command metaethics is one of those theories according to which the nature of obligation is grounded in personal or social relationships. In this paper I first try to show how facts about human relationships can fill some of the role that facts of obligation are supposed to play, specifically with regard to moral motivation and guilt. Then I note certain problems that arise for social theories of obligation, and argue that they can be dealt with more adequately by an expansion of our vision of the social dimension of ethics to include God as the most important participant in our system of personal relationships.

Divine command metaethics is a type of social theory of the nature of obligation. This statement makes two important points. (1) Divine command metaethics is not about the nature of all ethical properties and facts but only about the nature of those that we may call "the obligation family" of ethical properties and facts, those expressed by such terms as 'right', 'wrong', 'ought', and 'duty'. Other sorts of ethical properties and facts are not less important to Christian ethics, and theological theories may be offered about their nature too; but such theories may be expected to involve other features of God rather than his commands. For instance, we might theorize that the objectively disgusting is what disgusts God. The present paper is exclusively about divine command theories, however; and ethical properties not belonging to the obligation family will be mentioned without any inquiry being made into their nature.

(2) Divine command metaethics is one of those theories according to which the nature of obligation is *social* (in a broad sense of 'social' that encompasses intimate personal relationships as well as "impersonal," institutional relationships with larger groups). The central idea in divine command metaethics is the expansion of our vision of the social dimension of ethics to include God as the most important participant in our system of personal relationships. In this paper I will first try to show how facts about human relationships can fill some of the role that facts of obligation are supposed to play, specifically with regard to moral motivation (in section 1) and guilt (in section 2). Then (in section 3) I will note certain problems that arise for social theories of obligation, and argue that they can be dealt with more adequately by a divine command theory.

This paper presupposes a view, for which I have argued elsewhere, about the relation between conceptual analysis and theories of the

Robert Merrihew Adams, "Divine Commands and the Social Nature of Obligation." Reprinted from *Faith and Philosophy* 4 (1987): 262–275, with permission of the editors and the author.

nature of moral properties. On this view, what analysis of the concept of wrongness can tell us "is not sufficient to determine what wrongness is. What it can tell us . . . is that wrongness will be the property of actions (if there is one) that best fills" a certain role.[1] Moreover the identity of that property with wrongness will be necessary, though not discoverable by conceptual analysis. I have little to add here to my defense of this conception of the relation of metaethical theories to conceptual analysis. What I hope to illuminate is rather the roles that wrongness, and other members of the obligation family of ethical properties, are supposed to fill, and the reasons for thinking (as I do) that those roles are best filled by properties involving a relation to the commands of a loving God.

SECTION 1: HOW SOCIAL REQUIREMENTS MOTIVATE

It is essential to the point of any conception of obligation that obligations motivate—that having an obligation to do *x* is generally regarded as a reason for doing *x*. One problem about the nature of obligation is to understand this motivation.

This will not be much of a problem if we assume that one is obliged only to do things that one expects to have good results. Then the goodness of the results provides a reason, and one's desires for such good consequences a motive, for doing what one is obliged to do. Unfortunately, those who (like me) are not utilitarians cannot assume that obligations will always be so happily attuned to the value of expected results. We think we are sometimes obliged to tell the truth and to keep promises, for example, when we do not expect the consequences to be good. What would motivate us to do such a thing?

Even non-utilitarian moralists may not be satisfied with the reply that the conscientious agent has good enough reason for her action simply in the fact that it is right. This seems too abstract. John Rawls (certainly no utilitarian) writes,

> The doctrine of the purely conscientious act is irrational. This doctrine holds . . . that the highest moral motive is the desire to do what is right and just simply because it is right and just, no other description being appropriate. . . . But on this interpretation the sense of right lacks any apparent reason; it resembles a preference for tea rather than coffee.[2]

If we are to see the fact of having an obligation as itself a reason for action, we need a richer, less abstract understanding of the nature of obligation, in which we might find something to motivate us.

According to social theories of the nature of obligation, having an obligation to do something consists in being required (in a certain way, under certain circumstances), by another person or a group of persons, to do it. This opens more than one possibility for understanding obligations as reasons for action. One reason or motive for complying with a social requirement, of course, is that we fear punishment or retaliation for non-compliance. This is undoubtedly a real factor, which helps to keep morality (and other benign, and not so benign, social institutions) afloat. But here we are primarily interested in what *other* motives there may be for compliance.

The alternative explanation that I wish to pursue in this section is that *valuing one's social bonds* gives one, under certain conditions, a reason to do what is required of one by one's associates or one's community (and thus to fulfill obligations, understood as social requirements).

1. R. M. Adams, "Divine Command Metaethics Modified Again," *The Journal of Religious Ethics,* 7 (1979): 74. All my papers cited here are reprinted, some with additional notes, in my *The Virtue of Faith and Other Essays in Philosophical Theology* (New York: Oxford University Press, 1987).

2. John Rawls, *A Theory of Justice* (Cambridge, Mass: Harvard University Press, 1971), p. 477f. This passage is quoted, with approval, in James Wallace, *Virtues and Vices* (Ithaca and London: Cornell University Press, 1978), p. 116. What I have said thus far about utilitarian and nonutilitarian reasons for fulfilling an obligation largely follows Wallace's (much fuller) line of argument.

This hypothesis is not to be understood in a teleological sense. No doubt the desire to obtain or maintain a certain kind of relationship does often contribute to the motivation for complying with social requirements, but that is not all there is to social bonds as a motive. The pattern of motivation to which I wish to call attention is one in which I value the relationship which I see myself as actually having, and my complying is an *expression* of my valuing and respecting the relationship. It is one in which I act primarily *out of* a valuing of the relationship, rather than with the obtaining or maintaining of the relationship as an *end*.[3]

3. Motives that we act "out of" are interestingly and persuasively distinguished from teleological motives in Michael Stocker's paper. "Values and Purposes: The Limits of Teleology and the Ends of Friendship," *The Journal of Philosophy,* 78 (1981): 747–765.

There are at least four aspects of the relational situation that matter motivationally with regard to compliance with social requirements. (1) It matters that the demand is actually made. It is a question here of what other people do in fact (reasonably or rightly) require of me, not just of what they could reasonably require. The demand need not take the form of an explicit command or legislation; it may be an expectation more subtly communicated; but the demand must actually be made.

It is much more fashionable in ethical theory to treat moral motivation as depending on judgments about what an ideal community or authority *would* demand under certain counterfactual conditions. However, I am very skeptical of all these conditional accounts, for two reasons. First (the metaphysical reason), I doubt

"The Opium of the People"

Karl Marx

Man makes religion, religion does not make man. In other words, religion is the self-consciousness and self-feeling of man who has either not yet found himself or has already lost himself again. But *man* is no abstract being squatting outside the world. Man is *the world of man,* the state, society. This state, this society, produce religion, *a reversed world-consciousness,* because they are *a reversed world.* Religion is the general theory of that world, its encyclopaedic compendium, its logic in a popular form, its spiritualistic *point d'honneur,* its enthusiasm, its moral sanction, its solemn completion, its universal ground for consolation and justification. It is *the fantastic realization* of the human essence because the *human essence* has no true reality. The struggle against religion is therefore mediately the fight against *the other world,* of which religion is the spiritual *aroma.*

Religious distress is at the same time the *expression* of real distress and the *protest* against real distress. Religion is the sigh of the oppressed creature, the heart of a heartless world, just as it is the spirit of a spiritless situation. It is the *opium* of the people.

The abolition of religion as the *illusory* happiness of the people is required for their *real* happiness. The demand to give up the illusions about its condition is the *demand to give up a condition which needs illusions.* The criticism of religion is therefore *in embryo the criticism of the vale of woe,* the *halo* of which is religion.

Criticism has plucked the imaginary flowers from the chain not so that man will wear the chain without any fantasy or consolation but so that he will shake off the chain and cull the living flower. The criticism of religion disillusions man to make him think and act and shape his reality like a man who has been disillusioned and has come to reason, so that he will revolve round himself and therefore round his true sun. Religion is only the illusory sun which revolves round man as long as he does not revolve round himself.

From "Contribution to the Critique of Hegel's Philosophy of Right" (1844).

that the relevant counterfactuals are true, partly because they seem to be about free responses that are never actually made.[4] In the second place (the more distinctively moral or motivational reason), I do not think I care very much about whether these counterfactual conditionals are true. This is not to deny that I care about some things that are closely connected with them; it is just to say that the counterfactuals themselves are motivationally weak.

By contrast, actual demands made on us in relationships that we value are undeniably real and motivationally strong. Most actual conscientiousness rests at least partly on people's sense of such demands. Our awareness of this source of moral motivation is reflected in appeals to "be a good citizen"—or, when in a foreign country, to "remember that you are a guest."

The actual making of the demand is important, not only to the strength, but also to the character, of the motive. Not every good reason for doing something makes it intelligible that I should feel that I *have* to do it. This is one of the ways in which having even the best of reasons for doing something does not as such amount to having an obligation to do it. But the perception that something is demanded of me by other people, in a relationship that I value, does help to make it intelligible that I should feel that I have to do it.

(2) It also matters motivationally how the individual who is subject to the demand is related, and feels related, to those persons who are making the demand. Let us assume, for purposes of this discussion, that the demand is made by a community. The individual may be a member of the community, or a guest in the community; but it is essential that there be some relation, and indeed some favorably valued relation. The relation may arise through the individual's action—commonly through a history of acts of loyalty and caring within the relationship; occasionally through the action, beloved of social contract theorists, of voluntarily joining the community or consenting explicitly to its institutions and principles. But the community's attitude toward the individual is at least as important. Does the community value the individual? Is its attitude toward her supportive and respectful? It is well known that these questions have in fact a great influence on moral motivation. An individual who feels neglected, despised, abused by the community will be alienated, and will be much less inclined to comply conscientiously with society's demands. I do not mean to say that the alienated person should be exempt from blame for immoral or "anti-social" behavior, but that often such behavior should be seen, not mainly as a falling away from impersonal standards of right action, but as part of a conflict with society in which society was the first offender.

Where community prevails, rather than alienation, the sense of belonging is not to be sharply distinguished from the inclination to comply with the reasonable requirements of the community. A "community" is a group of people who live their lives to some extent—possibly a very limited extent—in common. To see myself as "belonging" to a community is to see the institution or other members of the group as "having something to say about" how I live and act—perhaps not about every department of my life, and only to a reasonable extent about any department of it, but it is part of the terms of the relationship that their demands on certain subjects are expected to have some weight with me. And valuing such a relationship—loving it or respecting it—implies some willingness to submit to reasonable demands of the community. One is willing to comply, not as a means of satisfying a desire *to* belong, but as an expression of one's sense that one *does* belong, and one's endorsement of that relationship.

(3) It also matters what are the attributes of the demander. To put it crudely and simply, one will have more reason to comply with demands made by an individual or group that one

4. Grounds for doubting the truth of such counterfactuals about free responses are given in my paper, "Middle Knowledge and the Problem of Evil," *American Philosophical Quarterly,* 14 (1977): 109–117.

admires than by one that one holds a mean opinion of.[5] If the demander is particularly impressive or admirable in any way—one will see more reason to comply than if the demander seems ill-informed, foolish, or in some other way contemptible.

(4) Finally, it matters motivationally how the demandee evaluates the demand itself.[6] It must be possible to perform such an evaluation without relying on fully developed obligation concepts, if the character of the evaluation is to shed light, without circularity, as I hope, on the nature of obligation. This requirement can be satisfied, at least in part. You can start evaluating things simply on the basis of how you value them. Is the demand one which appeals to you, or one which disgusts or revolts you? Is it one which seems to be conducive to things that you prize most, admire most, and so forth? You could ask that about your particular compliance, or you could ask it about general compliance, if that is what is being demanded. And what is the wiser social significance of the demand? Is it an expression of a project or social movement that seems good or bad to you? No obligation concepts at all are employed in these questions; yet the answers to them both will and should affect the extent to which a social requirement gives you a reason for action. More serious problems for a social theory of the nature of obligation may indeed arise from reflection on such evaluation; but consideration of them is reserved for section 3.

5. Cf. Rawls, *A Theory of Justice*, p. 465: It is favorable to "the development of the morality of authority" that the parents "be worthy objects of [the child's] admiration."

6. Cf. James D. Wallace, *Virtues and Vices* (op. cit.), p. 114: "If person A *reasonably* asks something of person B, then the reasonableness of the request gives B a *reason for complying,* quite apart from B's plans and goals. This reason for complying can be overridden by other considerations, but it is itself a consideration to be taken into account." I am much indebted to Wallace on the whole subject of the reason-giving force of social requirements, but I think that reasonableness is only one dimension of the evaluation that is needed here.

SECTION 2: GUILT AND RELATIONSHIP

The nature of obligations cannot be understood apart from the reactions that people have and are expected to have to the breach of an obligation; and central to these reactions is the notion of guilt. This is one of the main differences between obligations and other sorts of reasons for action. If I fail to do what I had the most reason to do, I am not necessarily guilty, and there is apt to be nothing offensive about my reacting quite light-heartedly to the lapse. But if I fail to do what I have an obligation to do, then (other things being equal) I am guilty, and a light-hearted reaction would normally be offensive.

The word 'guilt' is not properly the name of a feeling, but of an objective moral condition which may rightly be recognized by others even if it is not recognized by the guilty person. However, feelings of guilt, and other reactions to guilt, may reasonably be taken as a source of understanding of the objective fact of guilt to which they point. We do not have the concept of guilt merely to signify in a general way the state of having done something wrong. Such an abstract conception of guilt fails to make intelligible, for example, the fact that guilt can be expiated, discharged, or forgiven. It also results in a rather tight and empty circle in understanding, inasmuch as a major part of what distinguishes wrongness (as a member of the obligation family of properties) from other sorts of badness is precisely its connection with guilt.

It is true that one is not guilty, however unfortunate the outcome, for anything that was not in some way wrong. But there are two other aspects of guilt that are responsible for much of its human significance. One is the harm one has caused to other people by one's (wrong) action. It is wrong to drive carelessly, for example, and no less wrong when one is lucky than when an accident results. But the burden of guilt one incurs is surely heavier when one's carelessness causes the death of another person than when no damage is done. Many moralists are uncomfortable with this fact; but even if we were to define 'guilt' one-sidedly as meaning only the state of having done something wrong, the other, more complicated fact of having caused great harm through one's wrongdoing remains, and is a fact that we care about in a special way which is reflected in our actual, intuitive use of the word 'guilt'.

Harm caused to other people is not a feature of all guilt, however. One can be guilty for a violation of other people's rights that in fact harmed no one. And even if harm has been caused, it is not a serious aggravation of guilt if it does not fall heavily on some individual person or on some important project. If one is responsible for a traffic accident, for example, it would be bizarre to feel seriously guilty about a three-minute delay caused thereby to each passing motorist, even if the number of people inconvenienced is large enough for the aggregate delay to amount to a considerable cost by the standards appropriate to a traffic engineer.

A more pervasive feature of guilt is alienation from other people, or (at a minimum) a strain on one's relations with others. If I am guilty, I am out of harmony with people. Typically there is someone who is, or might well be, understandably angry at me. This feature is central to the role of guilt in human life. It is con-

"Infanticide"

Napoleon Chagnon

The Yanomamö practice infanticide, but because of the preference to have a male as their first child, they unknowingly kill more females than males. The Yanomamö have only three numbers: one, two, and more-than-two. They are accordingly, poor statisticians. They are quite unaware of the fact that they do kill more female babies, and every time I questioned them about it, they insisted that they killed both kinds—'more-than-two' of both kinds.

A child is killed at birth, irrespective of its sex, if the mother already has a nursing baby. They rationalize the practice by asserting that the new infant would probably die anyway, since its older sibling would drink most of the milk. They are most reluctant to jeopardize the health and safety of a nursing child by weaning it before it is three years old or so, preferring to kill the competitor instead. . . .

Male babies are preferred because they will grow up to be warriors and hunters. Most men make known their wishes to have a son—even to the point of insinuating that the wife ought to deliver a male or suffer the consequences. This is always done in a subtle way, usually by displaying signs of anger or resentment at the thought of having a daughter that constantly eats without being potentially an economic asset or guardian of the village. Many women will kill a female baby just to avoid disappointing their husbands. The Yanomamö also practice abortion in a very crude but effective way. The pregnant woman will lie on her back and have a friend jump on her belly to rupture the amnion. Sometimes abortions are effected because the woman does not want to kill the baby after it is born. In other cases a man will order his wife to abort if he suspects that somebody else conceived the child.

Several techniques are used to kill a newborn child. The most common method is to strangle it with a vine so as not to touch it physically. Another common method is to place a stick across the child's neck and stand on both ends of it until it chokes. In some cases the child is not given the stimulus to breathe and is simply abandoned. Finally, some women throw the child against a tree or on the ground and just abandon it without checking to see if it was killed by the injuries sustained.

From *Yanomamö: The Fierce People* (1977).

nected with such practices as punishing and apologizing. And it makes intelligible the fact that guilt can be (at least largely) removed by forgiveness.

Suppose I have done something that has offended a friend, resulting in estrangement. I think I was wrong to do it; I feel guilty. But if there is a reconciliation and my friend forgives me, I will feel released from the guilt. Indeed, I will *be* released from the guilt. The view that in such a case the guilt consists largely in an alienation produced by the wrong act is supported by the fact that the ending of the alienation ends the guilt.

This point is confirmed by reflection on an alternative scenario. Suppose I am not reconciled with my friend, but come to believe that the estrangement, though painful to him, has on the whole been good for him. Will this release me from the guilt? It will ease the burden, but not entirely remove it. In fact, I think it will not release me from guilt as completely as my friend's forgiveness (even combined with the belief that the estrangement has been bad for him) would. This suggests that alienation is not only a constituent, but a more important constituent of guilt, in this type of case, than the harm caused to the other person.

This should not surprise us if we reflect on the way in which we acquired the concept, and the sense, of guilt. In our first experience of guilt its principal significance was an action or attitude of ours that ruptured or strained our relationship with a parent. There did not have to be a failure of benevolence or a violation of a rule; perhaps we were even too young to understand rules. It was enough that something we did or expressed offended the parent, and seemed to threaten the relationship. This is the original context in which the obligation cluster of moral concepts and sentiments arise. We do not begin with a set of moral principles but with a relationship, actual in part and in part desired, which is immensely valued for its own sake. Everything that attacks or opposes that relationship seems to us bad.

Of course this starkly simple mentality is pre-moral. We do not really have obligation concepts until we can make some sort of distinction, among the things we do that strain relationships, between those in which we are at fault or wrong and those in which we are innocent or right (not to mention those in which we are partly wrong and partly right). We begin to grasp such a distinction as we learn such facts as the following: Not every demand or expectation laid on us by other people constitutes an obligation, but only demands made in certain ways in certain kinds of relationship (for instance, commands of one's parents and teachers), and expectations that arise in certain ways (for instance, from promises). An unexpressed wish is not a command. One is not guilty for anything one has not really done. The fact that somebody is angry does not necessarily imply that an obligation has been violated.

This development is compatible, however, with regarding obligations as a species of social requirement, and guilt as consisting largely in alienation from those who have required of us what we did not do. I believe it is not childish, but perceptive and correct, to persist in this way of thinking about obligation and guilt. This is a controversial position. It is generally agreed that learning about guilt begins in the way that I have indicated, and that the value we place on good relationships, not only with parents but also with peers, is crucial to moral development. But many moralists hold that in the highest stages of the moral life (perhaps not reached by many adults) the center of moral motivation is transplanted from the messy soil of concrete relationships to the pure realm of moral principles; and a corresponding development is envisaged for the sense of guilt. Thus John Rawls traces the development of the sense of justice from a "morality of authority" through a "morality of association" to a "morality of principles"; corresponding to these three stages, he speaks of "feelings of (authority) guilt," "feelings of (association) guilt," and "feeling of (principle) guilt"—only the last of these counting as "feelings of guilt in the strict sense."[7]

It is certainly possible to come to value—even to love—an ethical principle for its own sake, and this provides a motive for conforming to it. I doubt that this is ever the most powerful of ethical motives; but what I would emphasize here is that this way of relating to ethical principles has more to do with ideals than with obligations. To love truthfulness is one thing; to feel that one *has* to tell the truth is something else. Similarly, it seems to me that there is something wrong-headed about the idea of "principle guilt."

To be sure, there are *feelings* of guilt for the violation of a rule, where no person is seen as offended. But these are typically remnants of a morality of authority, and most plausibly understood as rooted in an internalization of childhood perceptions of requirements imposed by parents or other authority figures. They are part of a heteronomous, not an autonomous, reaction. The fact that the rule is seen as imposed on me, as something that I *have to* obey, is the ghost of my conception of it as sponsored by a person or persons who will be (understandably) offended if it is violated.

Feelings of "principle guilt," as Rawls conceives of them, are not like that. They are autonomous and based on one's valuing the rules, seeing them as expressing one's nature as a rational agent in a society of free and equal members. It is this non-compulsive, rational reaction to the breach of a personally valued principle that seems to me not to be a recognition of guilt, but of something different.

7. Rawls, *A Theory of Justice* (op. cit.), chs. 70–72, pp. 465, 470, and 474f. Rawls is influenced by Piaget and other developmental psychologists. One of them, heavily influenced, in turn, by Rawls, is Lawrence Kohlberg, the author of a widely discussed attempt to provide empirical support for the claim that something very like the progression that Rawls postulates is a part of normal human development. Concerning this it is interesting to note that whereas Rawls in 1971 identified "the morality of principles" with the last of Kohlberg's six stages (Rawls, op. cit., p. 462n.). Kohlberg has recently written that "We no longer claim that our empirical work has succeeded in defining the nature of a sixth and highest stage of moral judgment. The existence and nature of such a stage is, at this moment, a matter of theoretical and philosophical speculation and further empirical data collection" [Lawrence Kohlberg, *Essays on Moral Development,* Volume II: *The Psychology of Moral Development* (San Francisco: Harper & Row, 1984), p. 215; see also pp. 270–74]. It should also be noted that Kohlberg's stages are primarily stages of *reasoning* about justice; his research does not so directly address the issues on which I am focusing here, of the social or relational grounding of moral motivation and the sense of guilt. But this is not the place for the sort of thorough discussion that Kohlberg deserves.

"Religious Cruelty"

Friedrich Nietzsche

There is a great ladder of religious cruelty, with many rounds: but three of these are the most important. Once on a time men sacrificed human beings to their God, and perhaps just those they loved the best—to this category belong the firstling sacrifices of all primitive religions, and also the sacrifice of the Emperor Tiberius in the Mithra-Grotto on the Island of Capri, that most terrible of all Roman anachronisms. Then, during the moral epoch of mankind, they sacrificed to their God the strongest instincts they possessed, their "nature"; *this* festal joy shines in the cruel glances of ascetics and "anti-natural" fanatics. Finally, what still remained to be sacrificed? Was it not necessary in the end for men to sacrifice everything comforting, holy, healing, all hope, all faith in hidden harmonies, in future blessedness and justice? Was it not necessary to sacrifice God himself, and out of cruelty to themselves to worship stone, stupidity, gravity, fate, nothingness? To sacrifice God for nothingness—this paradoxical mystery of the ultimate cruelty has been reserved for the rising generation; we all know something thereof already.

From *Beyond Good and Evil* (1886).

Suppose I have done something that is simply contrary to some principle that I believe in. It is not that I have done significant harm to anyone, or alienated myself from anyone. The situation does not call for apologies or reactions to anticipated or possible or appropriate anger, because there is no one (let's suppose not even God) who might be understandably angry with me about it. It does not seem either natural or appropriate for me to feel *guilty* in such a situation. Maybe someone is entitled to think less of me for the deed. Perhaps I will see less value in my own life on account of it. I may in this way be alienated from myself, though not from anyone else. But these are reasons for feeling ashamed or degraded, rather than for feeling guilty.[8] Guilt is not necessarily worse than degradation, but they are different. And I think a main point of difference between them is that, in typical cases, guilt involves alienation from someone else who required or expected of us what we were obligated to do and have not done.

SECTION 3: THE SUPREME DEMANDER

Much can be understood about the nature of obligation in terms of human social relationships, as I have been trying to show. We even have a use for a notion of "an obligation" that can be understood purely sociologically, and therefore "naturalistically," in terms of a description of social practices such as commanding, promising, punishing, and apologizing, without any attempt to evaluate these practices as good or bad. This is a pre-moral notion in at least two ways.

(1) It is not the notion of an obligation that is "overriding" in the way that fully moral obligation is. An obligation, in this sense, must give most participants in the social system *some reason* to do what it obliges them to do; but it need not override other considerations. So no understanding is presupposed here of the nature of such an overriding.

(2) More fundamentally, the purely sociological notion is not the notion of a morally valid or binding obligation. It is just the notion of *an* obligation or duty, in the sense in which we can agree that Adolf Eichmann had *a* duty to arrange for the transportation of Jews to extermination camps. Certainly this was not a morally valid or binding duty at all, but it was in some sense *a* duty. It played a part in a system of social relationships such that there were superiors who, understandably (though immorally), would be angry if he did not do it, and in relation to whom he would feel uncomfortable if he did not do it, even if they did not know of his omission. Obligations in this pre-moral sense can be good or bad; they can even be morally repugnant, as Eichmann's was.

The nature of obligation in the pre-moral sense does not need a divine command theory to explain it. That is a good thing, because divine command metaethics itself presupposes a pre-moral, sociological conception of obligation. It is the very core of a divine command theory to think of the divine/human relationship on the model of a social relationship in which authority, commands, obedience, loyalty, and belonging play a part. But we cannot really have these things without both the reality and the concept of an obligation, in some sense. A command imposes an obligation, or is the sort of thing that could impose an obligation. And one who obeys a command sees herself as fulfilling an obligation arising out of the command. There must therefore be some sort of obligation whose nature cannot without circularity be explained in terms of anyone's commands. What divine command metaethics is meant to explain is the nature of obligation, not in the minimal, pre-moral sense, but in a stronger, fully moral sense.

8. It is significant that insofar as my reaction arises from my personally valuing a principle, or seeing it as expressing my nature, it does not seem to matter very much whether the principle is moral or aesthetic or intellectual. I could be degraded in my own eyes by doing something I regard as aesthetically or intellectually unworthy of me.

The earlier sections of this paper were meant to show something of the importance of interpersonal or social relationships for the nature of obligation in even a fully moral sense. The idea of trying to understand all obligation, including moral obligation, as constituted by some sort of social requirement has its attractions. As the Eichmann case makes clear, however, any acceptable account of the nature of moral obligation in terms of social requirements must incorporate some way of *evaluating* the requirements; and it may be doubted whether a descriptive sociological theory has the resources for the evaluation that is needed. In section 1, I described some ways in which, without appealing to any criterion of obligation as such, an individual can evaluate, and would naturally be expected to evaluate, demands made on her by other people, or by her community. That sort of evaluation is subjective, however. Its subjectivity does not keep it from being important to the motivational significance of obligation. But a definition of moral obligation in terms of social requirements that "pass" that kind of evaluation would not ascribe to moral obligation the objectivity or interpersonal validity that it is supposed to have.

The need for a standard by which to evaluate them is not the only disadvantage of human social requirements as a basis for understanding the nature of moral obligation. They also fail to cover the whole territory of moral obligation. We find that there are situations in which we would say, at least retrospectively, that none of the existing human communities demanded as much as they should have, or that there was something that really ought to have been required that was not demanded by any community, or perhaps even by any human individual, in the situation.

Moral obligation seems therefore to need a source or standard that is superior to human social requirements. Can it be found? And can it have (at least a lot of) the significance of obligations that are rooted in social requirements? In particular, how much can it have of the motivational significance of social requirements (as discussed in section 1 above)? And will it enable us to see moral guilt as something more robust than "principle guilt," and as removed by forgiveness (as discussed in section 2)? These advantages are not possessed by all the supreme sources of obligation that have been proposed in metaethical theories. I have already argued, for example, that the hypothetical deliverances of an "ideal observer" lack the motivational force of actual social demands.

Where could we find a supreme source or standard of moral obligation which has these advantages? The attempt has certainly been made to find it, after all, in a human society, in some way both actual and ideal, to which we can be seen as belonging. Emile Durkheim's lectures on *Moral Education* present a great sociologist's fascinating development of this idea. But it seems pretty clear that no actual human society is going to come close to filling this bill. To put it crudely and simply, no actual human society is good enough for that.

Where else would we look for an ideal source of moral obligation? My proposal is that we look to the set of ideas on which Durkheim quite openly and frankly modeled his secular, sociological account of morality—that is, the theistic ideas. Durkheim, following in the steps of Comte, was turning theistic ethics inside out, as it were, to get his conception of society as the source of moral obligation. I suggest that we turn the idea right side out again, and think of God as the source. More precisely, my view is that commands or requirements[9] actually issued or imposed by a loving God are the supreme standard of moral obligation. I will argue that they have much of the significance of social requirements as a source of obligation.

The pivotal role of God's forgiveness in the ethical life of theists underlines the advantages

9. The possibility of speaking of divine "requirements" here, rather than always of "commands," may serve to suggest the diversity of ways (by no means limited to explicit injunctions in sacred texts) in which God's demands may be communicated.

of divine command metaethics for the understanding of *guilt.* If the supreme standard of ethical obligation is what is required by God, then a violation of it is an offense against a person and not just against a principle, and results in something that has the full relational significance of guilt, and not just of disgrace or degradation. This relational significance enriches the possibilities for dealing with guilt—most notably by helping us to understand ethical guilt as something that can be removed by forgiveness.

Moreover, divine commands have the *motivational* significance of actual social requirements. I will point out four motivational features of divine command metaethics and of the divine commander corresponding (but in a different order) to the four motivational features of human social requirements discussed in section 1 above.

(1) One thing that matters to the motivational force of divine commands is how God is related to us. It matters that he is our creator. It matters that he loves us.[10] It matters that God has entered into covenant with us; it matters that there is a history of relationship between God and the individual and between God and the religious community—and that the divine commands play a significant role in this history, and are related to divine purposes that we see being worked out in this history and having a certain importance for our lives. It matters that all of these things about the relationship are such that,

10. In earlier papers I have made the point that the nature of moral obligation can be understood in terms of the commands only of a *loving* God. See Adams, "A Modified Divine Command Theory of Ethical Wrongness," in Gene Outka and John P. Reeder, Jr., editors, *Religion and Morality* (Garden City, N.Y.: Doubleday Anchor, 1973), pp. 318–47; and "Divine Command Metaethics Modified Again," (op. cit.).

"The Worship of Pain"

Oscar Wilde

Up to the present man has hardly cultivated sympathy at all. He has merely sympathy with pain, and sympathy with pain is not the highest form of sympathy. All sympathy is fine, but sympathy with suffering is the least fine mode. . . . One should sympathize with the entirety of life, not with life's sores and maladies merely, but with life's joy and beauty and energy and health and freedom. . . .

Upon the other hand, the terrible truth that pain is a mode through which man may realise himself exercised a wonderful fascination over the world. Shallow speakers and shallow thinkers in pulpits and on platforms often talk about the world's worship of pleasure, and whine against it, but it is rarely in the world's history that its ideal has been one of joy and beauty. The worship of pain has far more often dominated the world. Mediaevalism, with its saints and martyrs, its love of self-torture, its wild passion for wounding itself, its gashing with knives, and its whipping with rods—Mediaevalism is real Christianity and the mediaeval Christ is the real Christ. When the Renaissance dawned upon the world, and brought with it the new ideals of the beauty of life and the joy of living, men could not understand Christ. . . .

Christ had no message for the Renaissance, which was wonderful because it brought an ideal at variance with his, and to find the presentation of the real Christ we must go to mediaeval art. There, he is one maimed and marred; one who is not comely to look on, because Beauty is a joy; one who is not in fair raiment, because that may be a joy also: he is a beggar who has a marvelous soul; he is a leper whose soul is divine; he needs neither property nor health; he is a God realizing his perfection through pain.

From *The Soul of Man Under Socialism* (1891).

seeing them, we have reason to value the relationship, rather than to be alienated from it.

(2) It matters what God's attributes are. God is supremely knowledgeable and wise—he is omniscient, after all; and that is very important motivationally. It makes a difference if you think of commands as coming from someone who completely understands both us and our situation.

It matters not only that God is loving but also that he is just.[11] 'Just' is to be understood here in a sense that is quite naturalistic and largely procedural. We are applying to God a concept that has its original home in courts of law. Without any appeal to a standard of fully moral obligation we can recognize certain truths about justice: A just judge punishes people, if at all, only for things that they have actually done. Merit and demerit have some relevance to the way it is just to treat people. The just judge is interested in getting out, and acting in accordance with, the truth.[12]

Another important attribute of God is that he is beautiful or wonderful. This is a point at which Durkheim understood religious ethics rather well, and tried to exploit it for his purposes. "The good," he wrote, "is society . . . insofar as it is a reality richer than our own, to which we cannot attach ourselves without a resulting enrichment of our nature."[13] The religious root of this idea is obvious and requires no further comment, except to say that Durkheim is quite right in thinking that the richness, for us, of the being from which requirements proceed is a powerful motivating factor.

(3) It matters, for the motivation strength of divine command metaethics, what it is that is demanded of us. And it matters how what is demanded relates to our valuings. It matters motivationally, for example, that we do not believe that God demands cruelty for its own sake. Here again in thinking of our valuings we do not have to presuppose a full panoply of obligation concepts. It is enough if in some sense we love kindness and feel revolted or disgusted at cruelty. God's requirements function as an objective standard of obligation; but our subjective valuings are important to the way in which the divine requirements fulfill this function.

It is undoubtedly important that in theistic ethics the divine legislation is generally seen as upholding the binding character of a large proportion of the "obligations" defined by human institutions and practices. The divine/human relationship is not simply a superior alternative to human society as a source of obligation. Rather, God is seen as the chief member of a more comprehensive social system or "family," which is reflected, though imperfectly, in actual human relationships. Thus the motivational significance of divine and human requirements is to a large extent integrated.

(4) Finally, it matters that the requirements are actually imposed by God. Critics have argued that this does not really matter in divine command metaethics as I have expounded it. They suggest that all the work is being done by the stipulation that it is the demands of a *loving* God that bind—that really nothing would be lost if we just said that our overriding, fully moral obligation is constituted by what *would* be commanded by a loving God, whether there is one or not. I want to say why I think that that is not an adequate substitute.

My reasons on this point parallel my reasons for not being satisfied with an ideal, non-actual human authority as a source of moral obligation. First of all, I do not believe in the counterfactuals. I do not believe that there is a unique set of commands that would be issued by any loving God. There are some things that a loving God

11. The point is rightly emphasized by Alasdair MacIntyre in "Which god ought we to obey and why?" *Faith and Philosophy*, Vol. 3, No. 4 (October 1986). It was wrongly neglected in my previous papers on divine command metaethics.

12. Abraham's argument with God about the fate of Sodom, in which he asks, "Shall not the judge of all the earth do justice?" (Genesis 18:25) can be understood in terms of just such principles as these about justice. The Hebrew word for 'justice' here (*mishpat*) comes from the same root as the word for 'judge', and signifies what a judge does when he is doing his job.

13. Emile Durkheim, *L'education morale* (Paris: Félix Alcan, 1925), p. 110.

might command and might not command. In particular, among the things that I believe actually to be valid moral demands, there are some that I think might have been arranged differently by a God who would still be loving, and who would still satisfy the additional requirements of the metaethical theory. For example, a loving God could have commanded different principles regarding euthanasia from those that I believe are actually in force.[14]

14. I have discussed this issue more fully in "Moral Arguments for Theistic Belief," in C. F. Delaney, editor, *Rationality and Religious Belief* (Notre Dame and London: University of Notre Dame Press, 1979), p. 121f.

In the second place, even aside from any doubts about whether these counterfactuals about loving Gods are true, it seems to me that they are motivationally weak. They do not have anything like the motivational or reason-generating power of the belief that something actually is demanded of me by my loving creator and heavenly father. The latter belief is therefore one that metaethics cannot easily afford to exchange for the belief that such and such *would* have been demanded of me by a loving God.

Can the nature of moral obligation be adequately understood in terms of social requirements? Yes, if our system of social relationships includes God.

Susan Wolf

"MORAL SAINTS"

SUSAN WOLF, educated at Yale and Princeton, taught at Harvard and at the University of Maryland before her current position as a professor of philosophy at Johns Hopkins University. She has written many papers on ethics and the philosophy of mind and also a book, *Freedom within Reason* (1989).

I don't know whether there are any moral saints. But if there are, I am glad that neither I nor those about whom I care most are among them. By *moral saint* I mean a person whose every action is as morally good as possible, a person, that is, who is as morally worthy as can be. Though I shall in a moment acknowledge the variety of types of person that might be thought to satisfy this description, it seems to me that none of these types serve as unequivocally compelling personal ideals. In other words, I believe that moral perfection, in the sense of moral saintliness, does not constitute a model of personal well-being toward which it would be particularly rational or good or desirable for a human being to strive.

Susan Wolf, "Moral Saints," *The Journal of Philosophy,* LXXIX, 8 (1982), 419–426, 435–439. Reprinted by permission of the publisher and the author.

Outside the context of moral discussion, this will strike many as an obvious point. But, within that context, the point, if it be granted, will be granted with some discomfort. For within that context it is generally assumed that one ought to be as morally good as possible and that what limits there are to morality's hold on us are set by features of human nature of which we ought not to be proud. If, as I believe, the ideals that are derivable from common sense and philosophically popular moral theories do not support these assumptions, then something has to change. Either we must change our moral theories in ways that will make them yield more palatable ideals, or, as I shall argue, we must change our conception of what is involved in affirming a moral theory.

In this paper, I wish to examine the notion of a moral saint, first, to understand what a moral saint would be like and why such a being would be unattractive, and, second, to raise some questions about the significance of this paradoxical figure for moral philosophy. . . .

MORAL SAINTS AND COMMON SENSE

Consider first what, pretheoretically, would count for us—contemporary members of Western culture—as a moral saint. A necessary condition of moral sainthood would be that one's life be dominated by a commitment to improving the welfare of others or of society as a whole. As to what role this commitment must play in the individual's motivational system, two contrasting accounts suggest themselves to me which might equally be thought to qualify a person for moral sainthood.

First, a moral saint might be someone whose concern for others plays the role that is played in most of our lives by more selfish, or, at any rate, less morally worthy concerns. For the moral saint, the promotion of the welfare of others might play the role that is played for most of us by the enjoyment of material comforts, the opportunity to engage in the intellectual and physical activities of our choice, and the love, respect, and companionship of people whom we love, respect, and enjoy. The happiness of the moral saint, then, would truly lie in the happiness of others, and so he would devote himself to others gladly, and with a whole and open heart.

On the other hand, a moral saint might be someone for whom the basic ingredients of happiness are not unlike those of most of the rest of us. What makes him a moral saint is rather that he pays little or no attention to his own happiness in light of the overriding importance he gives to the wider concerns of morality. In other words, this person sacrifices his own interests to the interests of others, and feels the sacrifice as such.

Roughly, these two models may be distinguished according to whether one thinks of the moral saint as being a saint out of love or one thinks of the moral saint as being a saint out of duty (or some other intellectual appreciation and recognition of moral principles). We may refer to the first model as the model of the Loving Saint; to the second, as the model of the Rational Saint.

The two models differ considerably with respect to the qualities of the motives of the individuals who conform to them. But this difference would have limited effect on the saints' respective public personalities. The shared content of what these individuals are motivated to be—namely, as morally good as possible—would play the dominant role in the determination of their characters. Of course, just as a variety of large-scale projects, from tending the sick to political campaigning, may be equally and maximally morally worthy, so a variety of characters are compatible with the ideal of moral sainthood. One moral saint may be more or less jovial, more or less garrulous, more or less athletic than another. But, above all, a moral saint must have and cultivate those qualities which are apt to allow him to treat others as justly and kindly as possible. He will have the standard moral virtues to a nonstandard degree. He will be patient, considerate, even-tempered, hospitable, charitable in thought as well as in deed. He will be very reluctant to make negative judgments of other people. He will be careful not to favor some people over others on the basis of properties they could not help but have.

Perhaps what I have already said is enough to make some people begin to regard the absence of moral saints in their lives as a blessing. For there comes a point in the listing of virtues that a moral saint is likely to have where one might naturally begin to wonder whether the moral saint isn't, after all, too good—if not too good for his own good, at least too good for his own well-being. For the moral virtues, given that they are, by hypothesis, *all* present in the same individual, and to an extreme degree, are apt to crowd out the nonmoral virtues, as well as many of the interests and personal characteristics that we generally think contribute to a healthy, well-rounded, richly developed character.

In other words, if the moral saint is devoting all his time to feeding the hungry or healing the sick or raising money for Oxfam, then necessarily he is not reading Victorian novels, playing the oboe, or improving his backhand. Although no one of the interests or tastes in the category containing these latter activities could be claimed to be a necessary element in a life well lived, a life in which *none* of these possible aspects of character are developed may seem to be a life strangely barren.

The reasons why a moral saint cannot, in general, encourage the discovery and development of significant nonmoral interests and skills are not logical but practical reasons. There are, in addition, a class of nonmoral characteristics that a moral saint cannot encourage in himself for reasons that are not just practical. There is a more substantial tension between having any of these qualities unashamedly and being a moral saint. These qualities might be described as going against the moral grain. For example, a cynical or sarcastic wit, or a sense of humor that appreciates this kind of wit in others, requires that one take an attitude of resignation and pessimism toward the flaws and vices to be found in the world. A moral saint, on the other hand, has reason to take an attitude in opposition to this—he should try to look for the best in people, give them the benefit of the doubt as long as possible, try to improve regrettable situations as long as there is any hope of success. This suggests that, although a moral saint might well enjoy a good episode of *Father Knows Best,* he may not in good conscience be able to laugh at a Marx Brothers movie or enjoy a play by George Bernard Shaw.

An interest in something like gourmet cooking will be, for different reasons, difficult for a moral saint to rest easy with. For it seems to me that no plausible argument can justify the use of human resources involved in producing a *paté de canard en croute* against possible alternative beneficent ends to which these resources might be put. If there is a justification for the institution of haute cuisine, it is one which rests on the decision *not* to justify every activity against morally beneficial alternatives, and this is a decision a moral saint will never make. Presumably, an interest in high fashion or interior design will fare much the same, as will, very possibly, a cultivation of the finer arts as well.

A moral saint will have to be very, very nice. It is important that he not be offensive. The worry is that, as a result, he will have to be dull-witted or humorless or bland.

This worry is confirmed when we consider what sorts of characters, taken and refined both from life and from fiction, typically form our ideals. One would hope they would be figures who are morally good—and by this I mean more than just not morally bad—but one would hope, too, that they are not *just* morally good, but talented or accomplished or attractive in nonmoral ways as well. We may make ideals out of athletes, scholars, artists—more frivolously, out of cowboys, private eyes, and rock stars. We may strive for Katharine Hepburn's grace, Paul Newman's "cool"; we are attracted to the high-spirited passionate nature of Natasha Rostov; we admire the keen perceptiveness of Lambert Strether. Though there is certainly nothing immoral about the ideal characters or traits I have in mind, they cannot be superimposed upon the ideal of a moral saint. For although it is a part of many of these ideals that the characters set high, and not merely acceptable, moral standards for themselves, it is also essential to their power and attractiveness that the moral strengths go, so to speak, alongside of specific, independently admirable, nonmoral ground projects and dominant personal traits.

When one does finally turn one's eyes toward lives that are dominated by explicitly moral commitments, moreover, one finds oneself relieved at the discovery of idiosyncrasies or eccentricities not quite in line with the picture of moral perfection. One prefers the blunt, tactless, and opinionated Betsy Trotwood to the unfailingly kind and patient Agnes Copperfield; one prefers the mischievousness and the sense of irony in Chesterton's Father Brown to the innocence and undiscriminating love of St. Francis.

It seems that, as we look in our ideals for people who achieve nonmoral varieties of personal excellence in conjunction with or colored by some version of high moral tone, we look in our paragons of moral excellence for people whose moral achievements occur in conjunction with or colored by some interests or traits that have low moral tone. In other words, there seems to be a limit to how much morality we can stand.

One might suspect that the essence of the problem is simply that there is a limit to how much of *any* single value, or any single type of value, we can stand. Our objection then would not be specific to a life in which one's dominant concern is morality, but would apply to any life that can be so completely characterized by an extraordinarily dominant concern. The objection in that case would reduce to the recognition that such a life is incompatible with well-roundedness. If that were the objection, one could fairly reply that well-roundedness is no more supreme a virtue than the totality of moral virtues embodied by the ideal it is being used to criticize. But I think this misidentifies the objection. For the way in which a concern for morality may dominate a life, or, more to the point, the way in which it may dominate an ideal of life, is not easily imagined by analogy to the dominance an aspiration to become an Olympic swimmer or a concert pianist might have.

A person who is passionately committed to one of these latter concerns might decide that her attachment to it is strong enough to be worth the sacrifice of her ability to maintain and pursue a significant portion of what else life might offer which a proper devotion to her dominant passion would require. But a desire to be as morally good as possible is not likely to take the form of one desire among others which, because of its peculiar psychological strength, requires one to forgo the pursuit of other weaker and separately less demanding desires. Rather, the desire to be as morally good as possible is apt to have the character not just of a stronger, but of a higher desire, which does not merely successfully compete with one's other desires but which rather subsumes or demotes them. The sacrifice of other interests for the interest in morality, then, will have the character, not of a choice, but of an imperative.

Moreover, there is something odd about the idea of morality itself, or moral goodness, serving as the object of a dominant passion in the way that a more concrete and specific vision of a goal (even a concrete *moral* goal) might be imagined to serve. Morality itself does not seem to be a suitable object of passion. Thus, when one reflects, for example, on the Loving Saint easily and gladly giving up his fishing trip or his stereo or his hot fudge sundae at the drop of the moral hat, one is apt to wonder not at how much he loves morality, but at how little he loves these other things. One thinks that, if he can give these up so easily, he does not know what it *is* to truly love them. There seems, in other words, to be a kind of joy which the Loving Saint, either by nature or by practice, is incapable of experiencing. The Rational Saint, on the other hand, might retain strong nonmoral and concrete desires—he simply denies himself the opportunity to act on them. But this is no less troubling. The Loving Saint one might suspect of missing a piece of perceptual machinery, of being blind to some of what the world has to offer. The

Rational Saint, who sees it but forgoes it, one suspects of having a different problem—a pathological fear of damnation, perhaps, or an extreme form of self-hatred that interferes with his ability to enjoy the enjoyable in life.

In other words, the ideal of a life of moral sainthood disturbs not simply because it is an ideal of a life in which morality unduly dominates. The normal person's direct and specific desires for objects, activities, and events that conflict with the attainment of moral perfection are not simply sacrificed but removed, suppressed, or subsumed. The way in which morality, unlike other possible goals, is apt to dominate is particularly disturbing, for it seems to require either the lack or the denial of the existence of an identifiable, personal self.

This distinctively troubling feature is not, I think, absolutely unique to the ideal of the moral saint, as I have been using that phrase. It is shared by the conception of the pure aesthete, by a certain kind of religious ideal, and, somewhat paradoxically, by the model of the thorough-going, self-conscious egoist. It is not a coincidence that the ways of comprehending the world of which these ideals are the extreme embodiments are sometimes described as "moralities" themselves. At any rate, they compete with what we ordinarily mean by 'morality'. Nor is it a coincidence that these ideals are naturally described as fanatical. But it is easy to see that these other types of perfection cannot serve as satisfactory personal ideals; for the realization of these ideals would be straightforwardly immoral. It may come as a surprise to some that there may in addition be such a thing as a *moral* fanatic.

Some will object that I am being unfair to "common-sense morality"—that it does not really require a moral saint to be either a disgusting goody-goody or an obsessive ascetic. Admittedly, there is no logical inconsistency between having any of the personal characteristics I have mentioned and being a moral saint. It is not morally wrong to notice the faults and shortcomings of others or to recognize and appreciate nonmoral talents and skills. Nor is it immoral to be an avid Celtics fan or to have a passion for caviar or to be an excellent cellist. With enough imagination, we can always contrive a suitable history and set of circumstances that will embrace such characteristics in one or another specific fictional story of a perfect moral saint.

If one turned onto the path of moral sainthood relatively late in life, one may have already developed interests that can be turned to moral purposes. It may be that a good golf game is just what is needed to secure that big donation to Oxfam. Perhaps the cultivation of one's exceptional artistic talent will turn out to be the way one can make one's greatest contribution to society. Furthermore, one might stumble upon joys and skills in the very service of morality. If, because the children are short a ninth player for the team, one's generous offer to serve reveals a natural fielding arm or if one's part in the campaign against nuclear power requires accepting a lobbyist's invitation to lunch at Le Lion d'Or, there is no moral gain in denying the satisfaction one gets from these activities. The moral saint, then, may, by happy accident, find himself with nonmoral virtues on which he can capitalize morally or which make psychological demands to which he has no choice but to attend. The point is that, for a moral saint, the existence of these interests and skills can be given at best the status of happy accidents—they cannot be encouraged for their own sakes as distinct, independent aspects of the realization of human good.

It must be remembered that from the fact that there is a tension between having any of these qualities and being a moral saint it does not follow that having any of these qualities is immoral. For it is not part of common-sense morality that one ought to be a moral saint. Still, if someone just happened to want to be a moral saint, he or she would not have or encourage these qualities, and, on the basis of our common-sense values, this counts as a reason *not* to want to be a moral saint.

One might still wonder what kind of reason this is, and what kind of conclusion this properly allows us to draw. For the fact that the models of moral saints are unattractive does not necessarily mean that they are unsuitable ideals. Perhaps they are unattractive because they make us feel uncomfortable—they highlight our own weaknesses, vices, and flaws. If so, the fault lies not in the characters of the saints, but in those of our unsaintly selves.

To be sure, some of the reasons behind the disaffection we feel for the model of moral sainthood have to do with a reluctance to criticize ourselves and a reluctance to committing ourselves to trying to give up activities and interests that we heartily enjoy. These considerations might provide an *excuse* for the fact that we are not moral saints, but they do not provide a basis for criticizing sainthood as a possible ideal. Since these considerations rely on an appeal to the egoistic, hedonistic side of our natures, to use them as a basis for criticizing the ideal of the moral saint would be at best to beg the question and at worst to glorify features of ourselves that ought to be condemned.

The fact that the moral saint would be without qualities which we have and which, indeed, we like to have, does not in itself provide reason to condemn the ideal of the moral saint. The fact that some of these qualities are good qualities, however, and that they are qualities we *ought* to like, does provide reason to discourage this ideal and to offer other ideals in its place. In other words, some of the qualities the moral saint necessarily lacks are virtues, albeit nonmoral virtues, in the unsaintly characters who have them. The feats of Groucho Marx, Reggie Jackson, and the head chef at Lutèce are impressive accomplishments that it is not only permissible but positively appropriate to recognize as such. In general, the admiration of and striving toward achieving any of a great variety of forms of personal excellence are character traits it is valuable and desirable for people to have. In advocating the development of these varieties of excellence, we advocate nonmoral reasons for acting, and in thinking that it is good for a person to strive for an ideal that gives a substantial role to the interests and values that correspond to these virtues, we implicitly acknowledge the goodness of ideals incompatible with that of the moral saint. Finally, if we think that it is *as* good, or even better for a person to strive for one of these ideals than it is for him or her to strive for and realize the ideal of the moral saint, we express a conviction that it is good not to be a moral saint. . . .

MORAL SAINTS AND MORAL PHILOSOPHY

In pointing out the regrettable features and the necessary absence of some desirable features in a moral saint, I have not meant to condemn the moral saint or the person who aspires to become one. Rather, I have meant to insist that the ideal of moral sainthood should not be held as a standard against which any other ideal must be judged or justified, and that the posture we take in response to the recognition that our lives are not as morally good as they might be need not be defensive. It is misleading to insist that one is *permitted* to live a life in which the goals, relationships, activities, and interests that one pursues are not maximally morally good. For our lives are not so comprehensively subject to the requirement that we apply for permission, and our nonmoral reasons for the goals we set ourselves are not excuses, but may rather be positive, good reasons which do not exist *despite* any reasons that might threaten to outweigh them. In other words, a person may be *perfectly wonderful* without being *perfectly moral.*

Recognizing this requires a perspective which contemporary moral philosophy has generally ignored. This perspective yields judgments of a type that is neither moral nor egoistic. Like moral judgments, judgments about what it would be good for a person to be are made from a point of view outside the limits set by the values, interests, and desires that the person might actually have. And, like moral judgments, these judgments claim for themselves a kind of objectivity or a grounding in a perspective which any rational and perceptive being can take up. Unlike moral judgments, however, the good with which these judgments are concerned is not the good of anyone or any group other than the individual himself.

Nonetheless, it would be equally misleading to say that these judgments are made for the sake of the individual himself. For these judgments are not concerned with what kind of life it is in a person's interest to lead, but with what kind of interests it would be good for a person to have, and it need not be in a person's interest that he acquire or maintain objectively good interests. Indeed, the model of the Loving Saint, whose interests are identified with the interests of morality, is a model of a person for whom the dictates of rational self-interest and the dictates of morality coincide. Yet, I have urged that we have reason not to aspire to this ideal and that some of us would have reason to be sorry if our children aspired to and achieved it.

The moral point of view, we might say, is the point of view one takes up insofar as one takes the recognition of the fact that one is just one person among others equally real and deserving of the good things in life as a fact with practical consequences, a fact the recognition of which demands expression in one's actions and in the form of one's practical deliberations. Competing moral theories offer alternative answers to the question of what the most correct or the best way to express this fact is. In doing so, they offer alternative ways to evaluate and to compare the variety of actions, states of affairs, and so on that appear good and bad to agents from other, nonmoral points of view. But it seems that alternative interpretations of the moral point of view do not exhaust the ways in which our actions, characters, and their consequences can be comprehensively and objectively evaluated. Let us call the point of view from which we consider what kinds of lives are good lives, and what kinds of persons it would be good for ourselves and others to be, the *point of view of individual perfection.*

Since either point of view provides a way of comprehensively evaluating a person's life, each point of view takes account of, and, in a sense, subsumes the other. From the moral point of view, the perfection of an individual life will have some, but limited, value—for each individual remains, after all, just one person among others. From the perfectionist point of view, the moral worth of an individual's relation to his world will likewise have some, but limited, value—for, as I have argued, the (perfectionist) goodness of an individual's life does not vary proportionally with the degree to which it exemplifies moral goodness.

It may not be the case that the perfectionist point of view is like the moral point of view in being a point of view we are ever *obliged* to take up and express in our actions. Nonetheless, it provides us with reasons that are independent of moral reasons for wanting ourselves and others to develop our characters and live our lives in certain ways. When we take up this point of view and ask how much it would be good for an individual to act from the moral point of view, we do not find an obvious answer.[1]

The considerations of this paper suggest, at any rate, that the answer is not "as much as possible." This has implications both for the continued development of moral theories and for the development of metamoral views and for our conception of moral philosophy more generally. From the moral point of view, we have reasons to want people to live lives that seem good from outside that point of view. If, as I have argued, this means that we have reason to want people to live lives that are not morally perfect, then any plausible moral theory must make use of some conception of supererogation.

If moral philosophers are to address themselves at the most basic level to the question of how people should live, however, they must do

1. A similar view, which has strongly influenced mine, is expressed by Thomas Nagel in "The Fragmentation of Value," in *Mortal Questions* (New York: Cambridge, 1979), pp. 128–141. Nagel focuses on the difficulties such apparently incommensurable points of view create for specific, isolable practical decisions that must be made both by individuals and by societies. In focusing on the way in which these points of view figure into the development of individual personal ideals, the questions with which I am concerned are more likely to lurk in the background of any individual's life.

more than adjust the content of their moral theories in ways that leave room for the affirmation of nonmoral values. They must examine explicitly the range and nature of these nonmoral values, and, in light of this examination, they must ask how the acceptance of a moral theory is to be understood and acted upon. For the claims of this paper do not so much conflict with the content of any particular currently popular moral theory as they call into question a metamoral assumption that implicitly surrounds discussions of moral theory more generally. Specifically, they call into question the assumption that it is always better to be morally better.

The role morality plays in the development of our characters and the shape of our practical deliberations need be neither that of a universal medium into which all other values must be translated nor that of an ever-present filter through which all other values must pass. This is not to say that moral value should not be an important, even the most important, kind of value we attend to in evaluating and improving ourselves and our world. It is to say that our values cannot be fully comprehended on the model of a hierarchical system with morality at the top.

The philosophical temperament will naturally incline, at this point, toward asking, "What, then, *is* at the top—or, if there is no top, how *are* we to decide when and how much to be moral?" In other words, there is a temptation to seek a metamoral—though not, in the standard sense, metaethical—theory that will give us principles, or, at least, informal directives on the basis of which we can develop and evaluate more comprehensive personal ideals. Perhaps a theory that distinguishes among the various roles a person is expected to play within a life—as professional, as citizen, as friend, and so on—might give us some rules that would offer us, if nothing else, a better framework in which to think about and discuss these questions. I am pessimistic, however, about the chances of such a theory to yield substantial and satisfying results. For I do not see how a metamoral theory could be constructed which would not be subject to considerations parallel to those which seem inherently to limit the appropriateness of regarding moral theories as ultimate comprehensive guides for action.

This suggests that, at some point, both in our philosophizing and in our lives, we must be willing to raise normative questions from a perspective that is unattached to a commitment to any particular well-ordered system of values. It must be admitted that, in doing so, we run the risk of finding normative answers that diverge from the answers given by whatever moral theory one accepts. This, I take it, is the grain of truth in G. E. Moore's "open question" argument. In the background of this paper, then, there lurks a commitment to what seems to me to be a healthy form of intuitionism. It is a form of intuitionism which is not intended to take the place of more rigorous, systematically developed, moral theories—rather, it is intended to put these more rigorous and systematic moral theories in their place.

Robert Merrihew Adams

"SAINTS"

A brief biography of Adams appears on page 275.

One of the merits of Susan Wolf's fascinating and disturbing essay on "Moral Saints"* is that it brings out very sharply a fundamental problem in modern moral philosophy. On the one hand, we want to say that morality is of supreme value, always taking precedence over other grounds of choice, and that what is normally best must be absolutely best. On the other hand, if we consider what it would be like really to live in accordance with that complete priority of the moral, the ideal of life that emerges is apt to seem dismally grey and unattractive, as Wolf persuasively argues. I want to present a diagnosis of the problem that differs from Wolf's. Replies to Wolf might be offered on behalf of the utilitarian and Kantian moral theories that she discusses, but of them I shall have little to say. My concern here is to see that sainthood, not Kant or utilitarianism, receives its due.

WHAT ARE SAINTS LIKE?

The first thing to be said is that there *are* saints—people like St. Francis of Assisi and Gandhi and Mother Teresa—and they are quite different from what Wolf thinks a moral saint would be. In the end I will conclude that they are not exactly *moral* saints in Wolf's sense. But she writes about some of them as if they were, and discussions of moral sainthood surely owe to the real saints much of their grip on our attention. So it will be to the point to contrast the actuality of sainthood with Wolf's picture of the moral saint.

Wolf argues that moral saints will be "unattractive" (426) because they will be lacking in individuality and in the "ability to enjoy the enjoyable in life" (424), and will be so "very, very nice" and inoffensive that they "will have to be dull-witted or humorless or bland" (422). But the real saints are not like that. It is easier to think of St. Francis as eccentric than as lacking in individuality. And saints are not bland. Many have been offended at them for being very, very truthful instead of very, very nice. (Think of Gandhi—or Jesus.) Saints may not enjoy all the same things as other people, and perhaps a few of them have been melancholy; but an exceptional capacity for joy is more characteristic of them. (For all his asceticism, one thinks again of St. Francis.) There are joys (and not minor ones) that only saints can know. And as for attractiveness, the people we think of first as saints were plainly people who were intensely interesting to almost everyone who had anything to do with them, and immensely attractive to at least a large proportion of those people. They have sometimes been controversial, but rarely dull; and their charisma has inspired many to leave everything else in order to follow them.

Wolf may have set herself up, to some extent, for such contrasts, by conceiving of moral sainthood purely in terms of commitment or devotion to moral ends or principles. There are other, less voluntary virtues that are essential equipment for a saint—humility, for instance,

* *The Journal of Philosophy*. IXXIX, 8 (August 1982): 419–439. [See preceding selection.] Three-digit numbers in parentheses in the text refer to pages of Wolf's article.

Robert Merrihew Adams, "Saints," *The Journal of Philosophy,* LXXXI, 7 (1984), 392–401. Reprinted by permission of the publisher and the author.

and perceptiveness, courage, and a mind unswayed by the voices of the crowd. The last of these is part of what keeps saints from being bland or lacking in individuality.

In order to understand how Wolf arrives at her unflattering picture of the moral saint, however, we must examine her stated conception of moral sainthood.

WOLF'S ARGUMENT

Wolf states three criteria for moral sainthood; and they are not equivalent. (1) In her third sentence she says, "By *moral saint* I mean a person whose every action is as morally good as possible." (2) Immediately she adds: "a person, that is, who is as morally worthy as can be" (419). Her words imply that these two characterizations amount to the same thing, but it seems to me that the first expresses at most a very questionable test for the satisfaction of the second. The idea that only a morally imperfect person would spend half an hour doing something morally indifferent, like taking a nap, when she could have done something morally praiseworthy instead, like spending the time in moral self-examination, is at odds with our usual judgments and ought not to be assumed at the outset. The assumption that the perfection of a person, in at least the moral type of value, depends on the maximization of that type of value in every single action of the person lies behind much that is unattractive in Wolf's picture of moral sainthood; but I believe it is a fundamental error.

(3) On the next page we get a third criterion: "A necessary condition of moral sainthood would be that one's life be dominated by a commitment to improving the welfare of others or of society as a whole" (420). Here again, while it might be claimed that this is a necessary condition of a person's, or her acts', being as morally worthy as possible, the claim is controversial. It has been held as a moral thesis that the pursuit of our own perfection ought sometimes to take precedence for us over the welfare of others. The utilitarian, likewise, will presumably think that many people ought to devote their greatest efforts to their own happiness and perfection, because that is what will maximize utility. Given a utilitarian conception of moral rightness as doing what will maximize utility, why shouldn't a utilitarian say that such people, and their acts, can be as morally worthy as possible (and thus can satisfy Wolf's first two criteria of moral sainthood) when they pursue their own happiness and perfection? Presumably, therefore, Wolf is relying heavily on her third criterion, as an independent test, when she says that such cases imply "that the utilitarian would not support moral sainthood as a universal ideal" (427).

This third criterion is obviously related to Wolf's conception of morality. Later in her paper she contrasts the moral point of view with "the point of view of individual perfection," which is "the point of view from which we consider what kinds of lives are good lives, and what kinds of persons it would be good for ourselves and others to be" (437). "The moral point of view . . . is the point of view one takes up insofar as one takes the recognition of the fact that one is just one person among others equally real and deserving of the good things in life as a fact with practical consequences, a fact the recognition of which demands expression in one's actions and in the form of one's practical deliberations" (436f.). And moral theories are theories that offer "answers to the question of what the most correct or the best way to express this fact is" (437).

This account of moral theory and the moral point of view is in clear agreement with Wolf's third criterion of moral sainthood on one central issue: morality, for her, has exclusively to do with one's regard for the good (and perhaps she would add, the rights) of other persons. One's own dignity or courage or sexuality pose *moral* issues for Wolf only to the extent that they impinge on the interests of other people. Otherwise they can be evaluated from the point of view of individual perfection (and she obviously takes that evaluation very seriously) but not from the moral point of view. This limitation of the realm of the moral is controversial, but (without wishing to be committed to it in other contexts) I shall use 'moral' and 'morality' here in accordance with Wolf's conception.

It might still be doubted whether her third criterion of moral sainthood follows from her definition of the moral point of view. A utilitarian, for reasons indicated above, might argue that for many people a life not "dominated by a commitment to improving the welfare of others or of society as a whole" could perfectly express "recognition of the fact that one is just one person among others equally real and deserving of the good things of life." Dedication to the good of others is not the same as weighing their good equally with one's own. But if the former is not implied by the latter, it is the altruistic dedication that constitutes Wolf's operative criterion of moral excellence (though I suspect she looks to the equal weighing for a criterion of the morally obligatory). I do not wish to quibble about this; for what interests me most in Wolf's paper is what she says about moral devotion, and weighing one's own good equally with the good of others (demanding as that may be) is something less than devotion.

Thus Wolf's three criteria of moral sainthood seem to me to be separable. The second (maximal moral worthiness of the person, rather than the act) probably comes the closest to expressing an intuitive idea of moral sainthood in its most general form. But the other two seem to be her working criteria. I take all three to be incorporated as necessary conditions in Wolf's conception of moral sainthood.

The center of Wolf's argument can now be stated quite simply. It is that in a life perfectly "dominated by a commitment to improving the welfare of others or of society as a whole" there will not be room for other interests. In particular there will not be time or energy or attention for other good interests, such as the pursuit of aesthetic or athletic excellence. The moral saint will not be able to pursue these interests, or encourage them in others, unless "by happy accident" they have an unusual humanitarian payoff (425f.). But from the point of view of individual perfection we have to say that some of the qualities that the moral saint is thus prevented from fostering in herself or others are very desirable, and there are commendable ideals in which they have a central place. So "if we think that it is *as* good, or even better for a person to strive for one of these ideals than it is for him or her to strive for and realize the ideal of the moral saint, we express a conviction that it is good not to be a moral saint" (426f.).

SAINTHOOD AND RELIGION

While those actual saints whom I have mentioned have indeed been exceptionally devoted to improving the lives and circumstances of other people, it would be misleading to say that their lives have been "dominated by a commitment to improving the welfare of others or of society as a whole." For sainthood is an essentially religious phenomenon, and even so political a saint as Gandhi saw his powerful humanitarian concern in the context of a more comprehensive devotion to God. This touches the center of Wolf's argument, and helps to explain why actual saints are so unlike her picture of the moral saint. Wolf's moral saint sees limited resources for satisfying immense human needs and unlimited human desires, and devotes himself wholly to satisfying them as fully (and perhaps as fairly) as possible. This leaves him no time or energy for anything that does not *have* to be done. Not so the saints. The substance of sainthood is not sheer will power striving like Sisyphus (or like Wolf's Rational Saint) to accomplish a boundless task, but goodness overflowing from a boundless source. Or so, at least, the saints perceive it.

They commonly have time for things that do not *have* to be done, because their vision is not of needs that exceed any possible means of satisfying them, but a divine goodness that is more than adequate to every need. They are not in general even trying to make their *every action* as good as possible, and thus they diverge from Wolf's first criterion of moral sainthood. The humility of the saint may even require that she spend considerable stretches of time doing nothing of any great importance or excellence. Saintliness is not perfectionism, though some saints have been perfectionistic in various ways. There is an unusual moral goodness in the saints, but we shall not grasp it by asking whether any of their actions could have been morally worthier. What makes us think of a Gandhi, for example, as a saint is something more positive, which I would express by saying that goodness was present in him in exceptional power.

Many saints have felt the tensions on which Wolf's argument turns. Albert Schweitzer, whom many have honored as a twentieth-century saint, was one who felt keenly the tension between artistic and intellectual achievement on the one hand and a higher claim of humanitarian commitment on the other. Yet in the midst of his humanitarian activities in Africa, he kept a piano and spent some time playing it—even before he realized that keeping up this skill would help him raise money for his mission. Very likely that time could have been employed in actions that would have been morally worthier, but that fact by itself surely has no tendency to disqualify Schweitzer from sainthood, in the sense in which people are actually counted as saints. We do not demand as a necessary condition of sainthood that the saint's every act be the morally worthiest possible in the circumstances, nor that he try to make it so.

The religious character of sainthood also helps to explain how the saint can be so self-giving without lacking (as Wolf suggests the Loving Saint must) an interest in his own condition as a determinant of his own happiness. In fact saints have typically been intensely and frankly interested in their own condition, their own perfection, and their own happiness. Without this interest they would hardly have been fitted to lead others for whom they desired perfection and happiness. What enables them to give of themselves unstintingly is not a lack of interest in their own persons, but a trust in God to provide for their growth and happiness.

SHOULD EVERYONE BE A SAINT

Even if it can be shown that the life of a Gandhi or a St. Francis is happier and more attractive than Wolf claims that the life of a moral saint would be, we still face questions analogous to some of those she presses. Would it be good if everyone were a saint? Should we all aspire to be saints?

Not everybody *could* be a Gandhi. He himself thought otherwise. "Whatever is possible for me is possible even for a child," he wrote.[1] This is a point on which we may venture to disagree with him. A life like his involves, in religious terms, a vocation that is not given to everyone. Or to put the matter in more secular terms, not all who set themselves to do it will accomplish as much good by humanitarian endeavor as Wolf seems to assume that any utilitarian can (428). But perhaps some of us assume too easily that we could not be a Gandhi. In all probability there could be more Gandhis than there are, and it would be a very good thing if there were.

Wolf, however, will want to press the question whether there are not human excellences that could not be realized by a Gandhi, or even by someone who seriously aspired to be one, and whether it would not be good for some people to aspire to these excellences instead of aspiring to sainthood. My answer to these questions is affirmative, except for the 'instead of aspiring to sainthood'. Given the limits of human time and energy, it is hard to see how a Gandhi or a Martin Luther King, Jr., could at the same time have been a great painter or a world-class violinist.

1. M. K. Gandhi, *Gandhi's Autobiography: The Story of My Experiments with Truth,* translated by Mahadev Desai (Washington, D.C.: Public Affairs Press, 1948), p. 7.

Such saints may indeed attain and employ great mastery in the arts of speaking and writing. But there are demanding forms of excellence, in the arts and in science, for example, and also in philosophy, which probably are not compatible with their vocation (and even less compatible with the vocation of a St. Francis, for reasons of life-style rather than time and energy). And I agree that it is good that some people aspire to those excellences and attain them.

But if it is right to conclude that not everyone should aspire to be a Gandhi or a Martin Luther King or a St. Francis, it may still be too hasty to infer that not everyone should aspire to sainthood. Perhaps there are other ways of being a saint. That will depend, of course, on what is meant by 'saint'; so it is time to offer a definition.

If sainthood is an essentially religious phenomenon, as I claim, it is reasonable to seek its central feature (at least for theistic religions) in the saint's relation to God. 'Saint' means 'holy'—indeed they are the same word in most European languages. Saints are people in whom the holy or divine can be seen. In a religious view they are people who submit themselves, in faith, to God, not only loving Him but also letting His love possess them, so that it works through them and shines through them to other people. What interests a saint may have will then depend on what interests God has, for sainthood is a par-

Was Jesus Christ the Best and the Wisest of Men?

It is commonly assumed in our culture, particularly by Christians, both that we know what Jesus was like as a person and that he was one of the best and the wisest of men. Both of these assumptions are questionable. First, it is difficult on any sort of straightforward historical grounds to be confident that we know which of the sayings in the New Testament accounts that are attributed to Jesus (see the Sanders selection) were actually said by Jesus or even expressed his views. Scholars agree that many of the sayings should not be attributed to Jesus but were later additions to the text. But there is widespread disagreement both about which of the remaining sayings should be attributed to Jesus and what these sayings mean.

The historical problem has become more acute in recent times with the discovery of the Gnostic gospels (see the Pagels selection), some of which, such as the Gospel of Thomas, portray Jesus rather differently than the New Testament does and yet may well, according to some scholars, have been written earlier than Mark, supposedly the earliest New Testament gospel. Hence the historical question of what Jesus was actually like as a person is a difficult one. Suppose, though, that we just waive this question for the moment and suppose that Jesus both said the things attributed to him in the New Testament gospels and also meant what he said.

Our question, then, on this assumption, is whether *that* Jesus was one of the best and the wisest of men. Bertrand Russell, for one, did not think so, although he does concede that there are radical sayings in the New Testament that are quite to his tastes, though very few Christians either now or in former

ticipation in God's interests. And God need not be conceived as what Wolf would call a "moral fanatic" (425). He is not so limited that His moral concerns could leave Him without time or attention or energy for other interests. As the author of all things and of all human capacities, He may be regarded as interested in many forms of human excellence, for their own sake and not just for the sake of their connection with what would be classified as *moral* concerns in any narrow sense. This confirms the suggestion that Gandhi and Martin Luther King and St. Francis exemplify only certain types of sainthood, and that other types may be compatible with quite different human excellences—and in particular, with a great variety of demanding artistic and intellectual excellences. I do not see why a Fra Angelico or a Johann Sebastian Bach or a Thomas Aquinas could not have been a saint in this wider sense.

Now I suspect that Wolf will not be satisfied with the conclusion that a saint could be an Angelico or a Bach or an Aquinas. And I do not think that the sticking point here will be that the three figures mentioned all dealt with religious subjects. After all, much of Bach's and Aquinas' work is not explicitly religious, and it would be easy to make a case that a saint could have done most of Cézanne's work. The trouble, I rather expect Wolf to say, is that the forms of

---

times believe that Jesus meant any of them. For instance, Jesus said, "Resist not evil: but whosoever shall smite thee on thy right cheek, turn to him the other also," which would seem to make Jesus a pacifist, but, historically, Christians—who have written the history of their religion in blood—have not taken kindly to pacifism. Russell also noted that Jesus said, "Judge not lest ye be judged," but that this has not motivated his followers to shut down the law courts. Suppose, though, that we set aside these radical sayings and consider just those that the majority of Christians think Jesus actually meant. On the basis of just those sayings, should we conclude that Jesus was one of the best and the wisest of men?

Again Russell doesn't think so, mainly because of Jesus's doctrine of hell:

> Christ certainly as depicted in the Gospels did believe in everlasting punishment, and one does find repeatedly a vindictive fury against those people who would not listen to His preaching—an attitude which is not uncommon with preachers, but which does somewhat detract from superlative excellence. You do not, for instance, find that attitude in Socrates. You find him quite bland and urbane toward the people who would not listen to Him; and it is, to my mind, far more worthy of a sage to take that line than to take the line of indignation. You probably all remember the sort of things that Socrates was saying when he was dying, and the sort of things that he generally did say to people who did not agree with him.
>
> You will find that in the Gospels Christ said, "Ye serpents, ye generation of vipers, how can ye escape the damnation of hell?" That was said to people who did not like His preaching. It is not really to my mind quite the best tone, and there are a great many of these things about hell. . . .

(continued)

artistic and intellectual excellence typified by these figures are too sweet or too nice or too wholesome to be the only ones allowed us. There are darker triumphs of human creativity that we also admire; could a saint have produced them?

Not all of them. I admire the art of Edvard Munch, but I certainly grant that most of his work would not have been produced by a saint. I do not think that is a point against the aspiration to sainthood, however, nor even against a desire for universal sainthood. Who knows? Perhaps Munch would have painted even greater things of another sort if he had been a saint. But that is not the crucial point. Perhaps he would have given up painting and done something entirely different. The crucial point is that although I might aspire to Munch's artistic talent and skill, I certainly would not aspire to be a person who would use it to express what he did, nor would I wish that on anyone I cared about. In view not merely of the intensity of unhappiness, but also of the kind of unhappiness

---

> Then Christ says, "The Son of Man shall send forth His angels, and they shall gather out of His kingdom all things that offend, and them which do iniquity, and shall cast them into a furnace of fire; there shall be wailing and gnashing of teeth"; and He goes on about the wailing and gnashing of teeth. It comes in one verse after another. . . . Then you all, of course, remember about the sheep and the goats; how at the second coming He is going to divide the sheep from the goats, and He is going to say to the goats, "Depart from me, ye cursed, into everlasting fire." He continues, "And these shall go away into everlasting fire." Then He says again, "If thy hand offend thee, cut if off; it is better for thee to enter into life maimed, than having two hands to go into hell, into the fire that never shall be quenched; where the worm dieth not and the fire is not quenched." He repeats that again and again also. I must say that I think all this doctrine that hell-fire is a punishment for sin, is a doctrine of cruelty. . . .
>
> . . . I cannot myself feel that either in the matter of wisdom or in the matter of virtue Christ stands quite as high as some other people known to history. I think I should put Buddha and Socrates above Him in those respects. (*Why I am Not a Christian*, Watts & Co., 1927.)

Not everyone will agree with Russell's evaluation. For one thing, people disagree about what is unseemly. Some will think that Jesus' propagation of the doctrine of hell was not a defect. For another, some will doubt whether Jesus said the things to which Russell objects so strongly, or that if Jesus did say these things that Russell's interpretation expresses what Jesus really meant. But since Russell focuses on such central features of the gospel accounts and interprets the passages he quotes so straightforwardly, it would seem that a person who takes this latter line in response to Russell is obligated to tackle the difficult historical problems that we alluded to at the outset. Yet many who would take this line seem to be unaware that these problems even exist.

Nobody knows why the cliff dwellings in Mesa Verde National Park, Colorado, were abandoned around 1300 A.D. The circular structures in the foreground—so-called kivas—were places for religious ceremonies.

that comes to expression in Munch's art, it would be perverse to aspire to it, nobly as Munch expressed it. The lesson to be learned from such cases is that our ethical or religious view of life ought to allow for some ambivalence, and particularly for the appreciation of some things that we ought not to desire.

Van Gogh provides an interesting example of a different sort. There is much in his life to which one would not aspire, and his canvases sometimes express terror, even madness, rather than peace. Yet I would hesitate to say that a saint could not have painted them. The saints have not been strangers to terror, pain, and sadness; and if in Van Gogh's pictures we often see the finite broken by too close an approach of the transcendent, that is one of the ways in which the holy can show itself in human life. Certainly Van Gogh wanted to be a saint; and perhaps, in an unorthodox and sometimes despairing way, he was one.

IS MORALITY A SUITABLE OBJECT OF MAXIMAL DEVOTION?

Wolf's arguments lead her to reject an important received opinion about the nature of morality and about what it means to accept a moral theory—the opinion, namely, that it is "a test of an adequate moral theory that perfect obedience to its laws and maximal devotion to its interests be something we can whole-heartedly strive for in ourselves and wish for in those around us" (435). There are two parts to the received opinion, as it has to do with perfect obedience and with maximal devotion. I cannot see that Wolf's arguments call in question the desirability of perfect obedience to the laws of morality, unless those laws make all good deeds obligatory (as in a rigorous act of utilitarianism). Wolf seems on the whole to prefer the view that even nonmoral ideals to which it would be good to aspire ought not to involve the infringement of moral *re-*

quirements; and so she concludes that if (as she has argued) "we have reason to want people to live lives that are not morally perfect, then any plausible moral theory must make use of some conception of supererogation" (438). What she clearly rejects in the received opinion, then, is the desirability of maximal devotion to the interests of morality.

In this I agree with her. We ought not to make a religion of morality. Without proposing, like Kierkegaard and Tillich, to define religion as maximal devotion, I would say that maximal devotion (like sainthood) is essentially religious, or at least that it has its proper place only in religion. Wolf is going too far when she says that "morality itself does not seem to be a suitable object of passion" (424). But maximal devotion is much more than passion. And morality, as Wolf conceives of it, is too narrow to be a suitable object of maximal or religious devotion. Her reason (and one good reason) for thinking this is that a demand for universal maximal devotion to morality excludes too many human excellences.

Religion is richer than morality, because its divine object is so rich. He is not too narrow to be a suitable object of maximal devotion. Since He is lover of beauty, for instance, as well as commander of morals, maximal submission of one's life to Him may in some cases (as I have argued) encompass an intense pursuit of artistic excellence in a way that maximal devotion to the

"Spiritual Friend"

Chögyam Trungpa

We have to open ourselves to the suggestions of the spiritual friend at this point: he begins to mind our business a great deal. At first he may be kind and gentle with us, but nevertheless there is no privacy from him; every corner is being watched. The more we try to hide, the more our disguises are penetrated. It is not necessarily because the teacher is extremely awake or a mindreader. Rather our paranoia about impressing him or hiding from him makes our neurosis more transparent. The covering itself is transparent. The teacher acts as a mirror, which we find irritating and discomforting. It may seem at that point that the teacher is not trying to help you at all but is deliberately being provocative, even sadistic. But such overwhelming openness is real friendship. . . .

Such a spiritual friend is outrageously unreasonable simply because he minds your business so relentlessly. He is concerned about how you say hello, how you handle yourself coming into the room and so on. You want him to get out of your territory, he is too much. "Don't play games with me when I'm weak and vulnerable." Even if you see him when you feel strong, then you usually want him to recognize your strength, which is another vulnerability. You are looking for feedback in either case. He seems invulnerable and you feel threatened. He is like a beautifully built train coming toward you on solid tracks; there is no way to stop him. Or he is like an antique sword with a razor-sharp edge about to strike you. The heavy-handedness of the spiritual friend is both appreciated and highly irritating. His style is extremely forceful but so together, so right that you cannot challenge it. That is devotion. You admire his style so much, but you feel terrified by it. It is beautiful but it is going to crush you, cut you to pieces. Devotion in this case involves so much sharpness that you cannot even plead for mercy by claiming to be a wretched, nice little person who is devoted and prostrates to his teacher all the time and kisses his feet. Conmanship is ineffective in such a situation. The whole thing is very heavy-handed. The real function of a spiritual friend is to insult you.

From *The Myth of Freedom* (Shambhala, 1976).

interests of morality, narrowly understood, cannot. Many saints and other religious people, to be sure, have been quite hostile to some of the forms of human endeavor and achievement that I agree with Wolf in prizing. What I have argued is that the breadth of the Creator's interests makes possible a conception of sainthood that does not require this hostility.

There is for many (and not the least admirable) among us a strong temptation to make morality into a substitute for religion, and in so doing to make morality the object of a devotion that is maximal, at least in aspiration, and virtually religious in character. Such a devotion to morality, conceived as narrowly as Wolf conceives of it, would be, from a religious point of view, idolatry. The conclusion to which Wolf's arguments tend is that it would also be, from what she calls "the point of view of individual perfection," oppressive.

On the other hand, the loss of the possibility of sainthood, and of maximal devotion, would be a great loss. Wolf says, "A moral theory that does not contain the seeds of an all-consuming ideal of moral sainthood . . . seems to place false and unnatural limits on our opportunity to do moral good and our potential to deserve moral praise" (433). This seems right, but I do not think it is just our indefinite (not infinite) opportunities and capacities that generate the all-consuming ideal. There are other departments of human life (such as memorization) in which our potential to deserve praise is indefinite but in which it would be bizarre to adopt an all-consuming ideal. The fact is that many of the concepts that we use in morality were developed in a religious tradition; and to tear them loose entirely from a context in which something (distinct perhaps from morality but including it) claims maximal devotion seems to threaten something that is important for the seriousness of morality.

It may not, in other words, be so easy to have a satisfactory conception of morality without religion—that is, without belief in an appropriate object of maximal devotion, an object that is larger than morality but embraces it.

Mary Daly

"THE LEAP BEYOND PATRIARCHAL RELIGION"

MARY DALY, a leading feminist philosopher and theologian, teaches at Boston College and is the author of *Beyond God the Father: Toward a Philosophy of Women's Liberation, Gyn-Ecology: The Metaethics of Radical Feminism, Pure Lust: Elemental Feminist Philosophy,* and her recent *Webster's First Intergalactic Wickedary of the English Language.*

From "The Leap Beyond Patriarchal Religion," by Mary Daly from *Quest*, Vol. 1, No. 4, Spring 1975. Copyright by Mary Daly. Reprinted by permission of the author.

PROLEGOMENA

1. There exists a planetary sexual caste system, essentially the same in Saudi Arabia and in New York, differing only in degree.
2. This system is masked by sex role segregation, by the dual identity of women, by ideologies and myths.
3. Among the primary loci of sexist conditioning is grammar.
4. The "methods" of the various "fields" are not adequate to express feminist thought. Methodolatry requires that women perform Methodicide, an act of intellectual bravery.
5. All of the major world religions function to legitimate patriarchy. This is true also of the popular cults such as the Krishna movement and the Jesus Freaks.
6. The myths and symbols of Christianity are essentially sexist. Since "God" is male, the male is God. God the Father legitimates all earthly God-fathers, including Vito Corleone, Pope John II, President George Bush, the God-fathers of medicine (e.g., the American Medical Association), of science (e.g. NASA), of the media, of psychiatry, of education, and of all the -ologies.
7. The myth of feminine evil, expressed in the story of the Fall, is reinforced by the myth of salvation/redemption by a single human being of the male sex. The idea of a unique divine incarnation in a male, the God-man of the "hypostatic union," is inherently sexist and oppressive. Christolatry is idolatry.
8. A significant and growing cognitive minority of women, radical feminists, are breaking out from under the sacred shelter of patriarchal religious myths.
9. This breaking out, facing anomy when the meaning structures of patriarchy are seen through and rejected, is a communal, political event. It is a revelatory event, a creative, political ontophany.
10. The bonding of the growing cognitive minority of women who are radical feminists, commonly called *sisterhood,* involves a process of new naming, in which words are wrenched out of their old semantic context and heard in a new semantic context. For example, the "sisterhoods" of patriarchy, such as religious congregations of women, were really mini-brotherhoods. *Sisterhood* heard with new ears is bonding for women's own liberation.
11. There is an inherent dynamic in the women's revolution in Judeo-Christian society which is Antichurch, whether or not feminists specifically concern ourselves with churches. This is so because the Judeo-Christian tradition legitimates patriarchy—the prevailing power structure and prevailing world view—which the women's revolution leaves behind.
12. The women's revolution is not only Antichurch. It is a postchristian spiritual revolution.
13. The ethos of Judeo-Christian culture is dominated by The Most Unholy Trinity: Rape, Genocide, and War. It is rapism which spawns racism. It is gynocide which spawns genocide, for sexism (rapism) is fundamental socialization to objectify "the other."
14. The women's revolution is concerned with transvaluation of values, beyond the ethics dominated by The Most Unholy Trinity.

"Objective = Masculine"

George Simmel

The requirements of . . . correctness in practical judgments and objectivity in theoretical knowledge . . . belong as it were in their form and their claims to humanity in general, but in their actual historical configuration they are masculine throughout. Supposing that we describe these things, viewed as absolute ideas, by the single word 'objective', we then find that in the history of our race the equation objective = masculine is a valid one.

15. The women's revolution is not merely about equality within a patriarchal society (a contradiction in terms). It is about *power* and redefining power.
16. Since Christian myths are inherently sexist, and since the women's revolution is not about "equality" but about power, there is an intrinsic dynamic in the feminist movement which goes beyond efforts to reform Christian churches. Such efforts eventually come to be recognized as comparable to a Black person's trying to reform the Ku Klux Klan.
17. Within patriarchy, power is generally understood as power *over* people, the environment, things. In the rising consciousness of women, power is experienced as *power of presence* to ourselves and to each other, as we affirm our own being against and beyond the alienated identity (non-being) bestowed upon us within patriarchy. This is experienced as *power of absence* by those who would objectify women as "the other," as magnifying mirrors.
18. The presence of women to ourselves which is *absence* to the oppressor is the essential dynamic opening up the women's revolution to human liberation. It is an invitation to men to confront non-being and hence affirm their be-ing.

"Women Should Not Have Authority in the Church"

David Nicholas*

The idea that God desires woman to be subordinate to her husband is rooted deep in both the Old and New Testaments. . . .

Where are the indications that the woman was to be under the authority of the man? Well, the fact that man was created first and that woman originated from man is the first indication. The second is that it was Eve, who being deceived by Satan, fell into transgression. "Hold it," you protest, "doesn't the Bible say that both Adam and Eve disobeyed? Why should Eve take the rap? Does it matter which child takes the first cookie?" Now, before anyone accuses me of being an incorrigible chauvinist, let me hasten to point out that this is precisely how the Apostle Paul interprets the creation narrative in 1 Corinthians 11:7-9. . . .

Writing under the inspiration of the Holy Spirit, the Apostle Paul states in 1 Corinthians 11:7-9.

> For a man ought not to have his head covered since he is the image and glory of God; but the woman is the glory of man.
> For man does not originate from woman, but woman from man; for indeed man was not created for the woman's sake, but woman for the man's sake. . .

GENESIS AND THE FALL

Now, we must turn our attention to the effects of the Fall upon the relationship between man and woman. In Genesis 3:13, 16 we read:

> The Lord God said to the woman, "what is this you have done?" And the woman said, "The serpent deceived me and I ate" (verse 13).
> To the woman He said,
> "I will greatly multiply your pain in childbirth,
> In pain you shall bring forth children;
> Yet your desire shall be for your husband,
> And he shall rule over you" (verse 16)

With these words God initiated the curse upon the woman because of her role in the Fall. It should be observed as well, that man was also cursed because he listened to his wife and ate of the forbidden tree. The curse resulting from man's disobedience is recorded in Genesis 3: 17-19, and has to do primarily with the ground and the sentence upon man to eat bread by the sweat of his face (toil) and to do so until he returns to the dust from which he was formed (death). . . .

From *What's a Woman to Do . . . In the Church?* (1979).
*David Nicholas is a Dean at Southwest Baptist College.

19. It is unlikely that many men will accept this invitation willingly, or even be able to hear it, since they have profound vested (though self-destructive) interest in the present social arrangements.
20. The women's movement is a new mode of relating to the self, to each other, to men, to the environment—in a word—to the cosmos. It is self-affirming, refusing objectification of the self and of the other.
21. Entrance into new feminist time/space, which is moving time/space located on the boundaries of patriarchal institutions, is active participation in ultimate reality, which is de-reified, recognized as Verb, as intransitive Verb with no object to block its dynamism.
22. Entrance into radical feminist consciousness involves recognition that all male-dominated "revolutions," which do not reject the universally oppressive reality which is patriarchy, are in reality only reforms. They are "revolutions" only in the sense that they are spinnings of the wheels of the same senescent system.
23. Entrance into radical feminist consciousness implies an awareness that the women's revolution is the "final cause" (pun intended) in the radical sense that it is the cause which can move the other causes. It is the catalyst which can bring

"Why Women Should Not Be Priests"

David Stuart

Now the role of a priest is partly to be the representative of mankind (used generically) to God. Christ himself chose men to be apostles, the early church ordained men to be priests and consecrated men to be bishops. For generations the worshiper has heard the sounds of a male voice reading the prayers of consecration, for centuries the priest-confessor has been a man. Men were and continue to be the leaders, the initiators, the heads of households familial and ecclesiastical and it would be psychologically confusing as well as historically disruptive to substitute women for that office. The long history of the Holy Catholic Church has been that of a male priesthood—this tradition is not hastily or lightly to be broken.

Many women say they have been "called" to the priesthood and believe it is their God-given vocation. I do not doubt their personal talents nor their sincerity. However, unlike some denominations which permit any person "called" to be in effect self-ordained and to exercise his or her ministry according to individual whim, the Episcopal Church is part of the greater Catholic tradition which has always tested a "call" against the spirit-led wisdom of the larger church. There are many men who are both able and sincere and yet have not passed the necessary academic and psychological tests, have not gained Episcopal recognition of their call and hence have been refused ordination. Ordination to the priesthood in the Catholic Church is not and never has been a right, rather it has been a summons both by God *and* by his body on earth, the church. If we were to stray from Catholic and Orthodox tradition in such a central matter as the priesthood, some believe we will have lost the Apostolic validity of the orders we presently have, that the priesthood now given us will be cheapened, and all recognise it will greatly dim the hope of important ecumenical cooperation and progress. . . .

There are deep mysteries in Christianity and feelings are as important as rationality when we seek to probe mysteries. Many of us *feel* a positive move for ordination at this time would be wrong. Do not dismiss us, have respect for our prayerful petitions—*festina lente*. There is heartfelt confusion and doubt among us—let us not be tempted to move to a position where schism becomes for many an option and for some a necessity. Rather respecting our honest differences and the historical, theological, ecumenical, psychological and social complexity of this matter, let us now say "no" to women's ordinations.

From *The Ordination of Women*, edited by M. P. Hamiton and M. S. Montgomery (1975).

"Christ's Will"

Monsignor Arthur H. Durand

Women cannot be ordained to the priesthood of Jesus Christ in the Church for the simple reason that its founder Jesus Christ, the Source of its teachings, of its graces, of its power, and of its authority, has not included this practice in the permanent Deposit of Faith which He confided to His Apostles, and which they left us both by living Tradition and in the inspired Scriptures.

From, *The Wanderer* (1978).

"Why the Pope Is Against Women Priests"

Naomi Goldenberg

Conservative leaders of contemporary religious institutions understand that allowing women access to top positions of authority threatens the age-old composition of the institutions themselves.

In January 1977, Pope Paul VI issued a declaration affirming the Vatican's ban on allowing women to be ordained as Catholic priests. The document states that because Christ was a man and because he chose only male disciples, women can never serve as chief officials in the Catholic hierarchy.

Pope Paul used an impressive knowledge of how image and symbol operate in the human mind to build his case against female priests. "The priest," he explained, "is a sign . . . a sign that must be perceptible and which the faithful must be able to recognize with ease. The whole sacramental economy is in fact based upon natural signs, on symbols imprinted upon the human psychology. . . ."

Pope Paul reasoned that because the priest must represent Christ, i.e., God, the priest must resemble God. If the priest looked very different from Christ, a follower would not feel immediate connection between God and the priest who was supposed to embody *Him*. The Pope realized that people experience God through *His* representatives. If one were to change the sex of God's representatives, one would be changing the nature of God *Himself*. As the chief guardian of the Catholic faith, the Pope understood that he could not allow any serious tampering with the image of God. . . .

However, we must ask ourselves what will happen to Christianity when women do succeed in changing traditions so that they are treated as the equals of men. Will not this major departure from the Christian view of women radically alter the religion? Pope Paul knew it would. The Pope understood that representatives of Christianity mirror the image of God by calling to mind the male figure of Jesus Christ. If women play at being priests, they would play at being God; and Christianity, he insisted, can only afford to have men in that role. . . .

From *Changing of the Gods* (1979).

> about real change, since it is the rising up of the universally and primordially objectified "Other," discrediting the myths which legitimate rapism. Rapism is by extension the objectification and destruction of all "others" and inherently tends to the destruction of the human species and of all life on this planet.

Radical feminism, the becoming of women, is very much an Otherworld Journey. It is both discovery and creation of a world other than patriarchy. Some observation reveals that patriarchy is "everywhere." Even outer space and the future have been colonized. As a rule, even the more imaginative science fiction writers (seemingly the most foretelling futurists) cannot/will not create a space and time in which women get far beyond the role of space stewardess. Nor does this situation exist simply "outside" women's minds, securely fastened into institutions which we can physically leave behind. Rather, it is also internalized, festering inside women's heads, even feminist heads.

The journey of women *becoming,* then, involves exorcism of the internalized Godfather, in his various manifestations (His name is legion). It involves dangerous encounters with these demons. Within the Christian tradition, particularly in medieval times, evil spirits have sometimes been associated with the Seven Deadly Sins, both as personifications and as causes. A "standard" and prevalent listing of the Sins is, of course, the following: pride, avarice, anger, lust, gluttony, envy, and sloth. I am contending that these have all been radically misnamed, that is, inadequately and even perversely "understood" within Christianity. These concepts have been used to victimize the oppressed, particularly women. They are particularized expressions of the overall use of "evil" to victimize women. The feminist journey involves confrontations with the demonic distortions of evil.

"Imagine"

Marilyn Frye

Imagine—

A colony of humans established a civilization hundreds of years ago on a distant planet. It has evolved, as civilizations will. Its language is a descendant of English.

The language has personal pronouns marking the child/adult distinction, and its adult personal pronouns mark the distinction between straight and curly pubic hair. At puberty each person assumes distinguishing clothing styles and manners so others can tell what type she or he is without the closer scrutiny which would generally be considered indecent. People with straight pubic hair adopt a style which is modest and self-effacing and clothes which are fragile and confining; people with curly pubic hair adopt a style which is expansive and prepossessing and clothes which are sturdy and comfortable. People whose pubic hair is neither clearly straight nor clearly curly alter their hair chemically in order to be clearly one or the other. Since those with curly pubic hair have higher status and economic advantages, those with ambiguous pubic hair are told to make it straight, for life will be easier for a low-status person whose category might be doubted than for a high-status person whose category might be doubted.

It is taboo to eat or drink in the same room with any person of the same pubic hair type as oneself. Compulsory heterogourmandism, it is called by social critics, though most people think it is just natural human desire to eat with one's pubic-hair opposite. A logical consequence of this habit, or taboo, is the limitation to dining only singly or in pairs—a taboo against banquetism, or, as the slang expression goes, against the group gulp.

From *The Politics of Reality* (1983).

Why has it seemed "appropriate" in this culture that a popular book and film *(The Exorcist)* center around a Jesuit who "exorcises" a girl-child who is "possessed"? Why is there no book or film about a woman who exorcises a Jesuit? Within a culture possessed by the myth of feminine evil, the naming, describing, and theorizing about good and evil has constituted a web of deception, a Maya. The journey of women becoming is breaking through this web—a Fall into free space. It is reassuming the role of subject, as opposed to object, and naming good and evil on the basis of our own intuitive intellection. . . .

THE QUALITATIVE LEAP

Creative, living, political hope for movement beyond the gynocidal reign of the Fathers will be fulfilled only if women continue to make qualitative leaps in living our transcendence. A short-circuited hope of transcendence has caused many to remain inside churches, and patriarchal religion sometimes has seemed to satisfy the hunger for transcendence. The problem has been that both the hunger and the satisfaction generated within such religions have to a great extent alienated women from our deepest aspirations. Spinning in vicious circles of false needs

Erich Fromm on The Sickness of Western Society

V. Trevor Ling

In his book *The Sane Society* Erich Fromm raises the important question whether the people of the Western countries in the mid-twentieth century can now really be said to be sane. He points to some of the facts, aware that he is stating what have become truisms. In the West we have, for example, created enormous material wealth and we have also killed off millions of human beings in periodic outbursts of mass violence which we dignify by the name of war. The enemies of one year—'cruel, irrational fiends whom one must defeat to save the world from evil' are our friends a year or so later, and those nations who were previously our allies have now become our enemies. It is almost superfluous to mention the follies of the economic 'system', where a particularly bountiful crop is an economic disaster, and where, although there are millions who need what we have in abundance, we restrict productivity 'to stabilize the market'. In connection with the popular 'culture' of a society in which 90 per cent of the population are literate he points out that radio, television, movies, and newspapers are largely media to 'fill the minds of men with the cheapest trash, lacking in any sense of reality, with sadistic phantasies which a halfway cultured person would be embarrassed to entertain even once in a while'. To a prodigious extent time is saved by the most ingenious of gadgets only to have to be 'killed' in some new way.

This is a society which claims to be sane. Yet this, and other more detailed information which we possess about such matters as suicide, homicide, and alcoholism, seem to indicate pretty clearly a society which is sick. Increasing affluence is accompanied by increasing numbers of alcoholics and suicides. The countries with the worst records with regard to both suicide and alcoholism are the U.S.A., Denmark, Switzerland and Sweden; in other words they are the countries which are 'the most democratic, peaceful and prosperous'. Fromm concludes that the United States, which is the most prosperous and materially the most advanced, shows the greatest degree of mental unbalance.

and false consciousness, women caught on the patriarchal wheel have not been able to experience women's own experience.

I suggest that what is required is *ludic cerebration,* the free play of intuition in our own space, giving rise to thinking that is vigorous, informed, multi-dimensional, independent, creative, tough. *Ludic cerebration* is thinking out of experience. I do not mean the experience of dredging out All That Was Wrong with Mother, or of instant intimacy in group encounters, or of waiting at the doctoral dispensary, or of self-lobotomization in order to publish, perish, and then be promoted. I mean the experience of being. *Be-ing* is the verb that says the dimensions of depth in all verbs, such as intuiting, reasoning, loving, imaging, making, acting, as well as the couraging, hoping, and playing that are always there when one is really living.

It may be that some new things happen within patriarchy, but one thing essentially stays the same: women are always marginal beings. From this vantage point of the margin it is possible to look at what is between the margins with the lucidity of The Compleat Outsider. To change metaphors: the systems within the System do not appear so radically different from each other to those excluded by all. Hope for a qualitative leap lies in *us* by reason of that deviance from the "norm" which was first imposed but which can also be *chosen* on our own terms. This means that there has to be a shift from "acceptable" female deviance (characterized by triviality, diffuseness, dependence upon others for self-definition, low self-esteem, powerlessness) to deviance which may be unacceptable to others but which is acceptable to the self and *is* self-acceptance.

For women concerned with philosophical/theological questions, it seems to me, this implies the necessity of some sort of choice. One either tries to avoid "acceptable" deviance ("normal" female idiocy) by becoming accepted as a male-identified professional, or else one tries to make the qualitative leap toward self-acceptable deviance as ludic cerebrator, questioner of everything, madwoman, and witch.

I do mean witch. The heretic who rejects the idols of patriarchy is the blasphemous creatrix of her own thoughts. She is finding her life and intends not to lose it. The witch that smolders within every woman who cared and dared enough to become a philosophically/spiritually questing feminist in the first place seems to be crying out these days: "Light my fire!" The qualitative leap, the light of those flames of spiritual imagination and cerebral fantasy can be a new dawn. . . .

Friedrich Nietzsche

"THE PATHOLOGY OF CHRISTIANITY"

FRIEDRICH NIETZSCHE (1844–1900), German philosopher and poet, one of the most original and influential of modern thinkers, was born in Roeken, Germany, to a puritanical, religious family. The son of a minister, he studied at the University of

From *The Complete Works of Nietzsche,* 1909–11.

Bonn and the University of Leipzig before being appointed Professor of Philosophy at the University of Basel. At age twenty-four, he was promoted to associate professor even before he finished his doctoral dissertation, a completely unprecedented event at Basel. When he did finally publish he quickly became one of the most outspoken critics of religion ever, particularly of Christianity, and mounted an uncompromising attack on traditional morality. Nietzsche's philosophical stance owed much to Schopenhauer; his poetic passion was influenced by the great operatic composer, Wagner, with whom he was a close friend until their falling-out in 1875.

Nietzsche developed a comprehensive theory of the will to power and of the overman *(Übermensch)* whose power stems not from the subjugation of others (as his view is often misrepresented) but from self-control, self-understanding, creative art, and philosophy. He was opposed to the idea of an afterlife, but his theory of eternal recurrence is the now famous doctrine that everything happens again and again. Nearly every one of his books contains criticisms of religion and the idea of God; it is Nietzsche who coined the famous slogan "God is dead." He had a profound influence on twentieth-century philosophy and literature, particularly in Germany and France. Thomas Mann, Hermann Hesse, Karl Jasper, Martin Heidegger, Sigmund Freud, Jean-Paul Sartre, George Bernard Shaw, and H. L. Mencken were all influenced by him. Among his works are *Thus Spake Zarathustra* (1884), *Beyond Good and Evil* (1886), *The Genealogy of Morals* (1887), *The Antichrist* (1888), and *The Will to Power* (1806).

1. THE PATHOLOGY OF SAINTS AND SINNERS: FROM *HUMAN, ALL-TOO-HUMAN*

113. Christianity as Antiquity.

When on a Sunday morning we hear the old bells ring out, we ask ourselves, "Is it possible! This is done on account of a Jew crucified two thousand years ago who said he was the Son of God. The proof of such an assertion is wanting." Certainly in our times the Christian religion is an antiquity that dates from very early ages, and the fact that its assertions are still believed, when otherwise all claims are subjected to such strict examination, is perhaps the oldest part of this heritage. A God who creates a son from a mortal woman; a sage who requires that man should no longer work, no longer judge, but should pay attention to the signs of the approaching end of the world; a justice that accepts an innocent being as a substitute in sacrifice; one who commands his disciples to drink his blood; prayers for miraculous intervention; sins committed against a God and atoned for through a God; the fear of a future to which death is the portal; the form of the cross in an age which no longer knows the signification and the shame of the cross, how terrible all this appears to us, as if risen from the grave of the ancient past! Is it credible that such things are still believed?

114. What is Un-Greek in Christianity

The Greeks did not regard the Homeric gods as raised above them like masters, nor themselves as being under them like servants, as the Jews did. They only saw, as in a mirror, the most perfect examples of their own caste; an ideal, therefore, and not an opposite of their own nature. There is a feeling of relationship, a mutual interest arises, a kind of symmachy. Man thinks highly of himself when he gives himself such gods, and places himself in a relation like that of the lower nobility towards the higher; while the Italian nations hold a genuine peasant-faith, with perpetual fear of evil and mischievous powers and tormenting spirits. Wherever the Olympian gods retreated into the background, Greek life was more sombre and more anxious. Christianity, on the contrary, oppressed man and crushed him utterly, sinking him as if in deep mire; then into the feeling of absolute depravity it suddenly threw the light of divine mercy, so that the surprised man, dazzled by forgiveness, gave a cry of joy and for a moment believed that he bore all heaven within himself. All psychological feelings of Christianity work upon this unhealthy excess of sentiment, and upon the deep corruption of head and heart it necessitates; it desires to destroy, break, stupefy, confuse,—only one thing it does not desire, namely *moderation,* and therefore it is in the deepest sense barbaric, Asiatic, ignoble, and un-Greek.

115. To Be Religious with Advantage

There are sober and industrious people on whom religion is embroidered like a hem of higher humanity; these do well to remain religious, it beautifies them. All people who do not understand some kind of trade in weapons—tongue and pen included as weapons—become servile; for such the Christian religion is very useful, for then servility assumes the appearance of Christian virtues and is surprisingly beautiful. People to whom their daily life appears too empty and monotonous easily grow religious; this is comprehensible and excusable, only they have no right to demand religious sentiments from those whose daily life is not empty and monotonous.

116. The Commonplace Christian

If Christianity were right, with its theories of an avenging God, of general sinfulness, of redemption, and the danger of eternal damnation, it would be a sign of weak intellect and lack of character *not* to become a priest, apostle or hermit, and to work only with fear and trembling for one's own salvation; it would be senseless thus to neglect eternal benefits for temporary comfort. Taking it for granted that there *is be-*

"Religion May Be Hazardous to Your Health"

Eli S. Chesen*

Religion is actually a kind of consumer good that is without question potentially harmful to the user's mental health.

One must be impressed by the zealous concern of today's consumer for what he consumes. There has been a veritable renaissance of such interest in light of the current realization that many products do not live up to their names and claims. But it is not yet widely recognized that religion, like many of these products, also can be useless and even dangerous, at least from a psychiatric point of view. . . . I am concerned, therefore, with the effects that religion can be shown to have on mental health as well as on mental illness.

I am not espousing atheism or any other religious stance. I am merely setting down a series of conclusions based upon the observations of case histories that are representative of literally thousands of others. . . . They are, rather, typical of cases seen every day in the offices of privately practicing psychiatrists and on the wards of most mental health facilities.

The range of emotional difficulty in these patients varies from the existence of subtle disturbances to major ones in which at times the person does not know who he is but, rather, thinks that he is Jesus Christ, the Virgin Mary, or God. In each instance . . . tenacious religious beliefs can be an active thread interwoven into the tapestry of a disturbed thinking process. . . .

From *Religion May Be Hazardous to Your Health* (1972).
*Eli Chesen is a psychiatrist and family therapist.

lief, the commonplace Christian is a miserable figure, a man that really cannot add two and two together, and who, moreover, just because of his mental incapacity for responsibility, did not deserve to be so severely punished as Christianity has decreed.

117. Of the Wisdom of Christianity

It is a clever stroke on the part of Christianity to teach the utter unworthiness, sinfulness, and despicableness of mankind so loudly that the disdain of their fellow-men is no longer possible. "He may sin as much as he likes, he is not essentially different from me,—it is I who am unworthy and despicable in every way," says the Christian to himself. But even this feeling has lost its sharpest sting, because the Christian no longer believes in his individual despicableness; he is bad as men are generally, and comforts himself a little with the axiom, "We are all of one kind."

118. Change of Front

As soon as a religion triumphs it has for its enemies all those who would have been its first disciples.

War for the Glory of God

Millions have gone to their deaths in religious wars. It may not be surprising that Christianity and Islam have a history of war with each other. They have different holy books, different cultures, and different traditions that in many cases affirm absolutely what the other absolutely denies. Nor is it surprising that Hindus and Muslims have been at each other's throats for centuries. But how can there be such differences even among followers of the same book, such as the Protestants and Catholics in Ireland?

The answer is revealing. The fact is that, contrary to what we might ordinarily think, there are no clear-cut, unambiguous answers *within* the holy books that contain the so-called answers. The reason why so many different religions can spawn off the same book is that different people are in charge of interpreting the book. The interpretations are different because the people interpreting them are different.

Typically, religious authorities like followers to believe their interpretation is the one and only correct one. Followers may believe this because they are conditioned not to question—to feel that questioning their authorities is sinful, immoral, and downright *bad.* But how do the religious authorities know that their interpretation is the correct one? As we move from the various denominations within one religion to the variety of different religions, the problem is compounded. Not only do we need to ask how one is to interpret any one particular holy book, we must ask which, if any, holy book, of which religion, is the true one? How do we decide? How does anyone know? How *could* anyone know?

119. The Fate of Christianity

Christianity arose for the purpose of lightening the heart; but now it must first make the heart heavy in order afterwards to lighten it. Consequently it will perish.

120. The Proof of Pleasure

The agreeable opinion is accepted as true,—this is the proof of the pleasure (or, as the Church says, the proof of the strength), of which all religions are so proud when they ought to be ashamed of it. If Faith did not make blessed it would not be believed in; of how little value must it be, then!

132. Of the Christian Need of Redemption

With careful reflection it must be possible to obtain an explanation free from mythology of that process in the soul of a Christian which is called the need of redemption, consequently a purely psychological explanation. Up to the pre-

"Feminine Religion"

Shree Rajneesh

Lao Tzu says the nature of the existence is more like the female, more feminine. . . .

A man can also be feminine. A Buddha is feminine, a Lao Tzu is feminine, a Jesus is feminine. . . .

A man can live a feminine existence—then he becomes a mystic. That is the only way. So all mystics become in a certain way feminine. And they are the real religious men, not the founders of religion.

Remember, this is a difference. . . . Buddha is not the founder of Buddhism—no. His disciples are the founders. Jesus is not the founder of Christianity—no. His apostles, they are the founders. Mahavir is not the founder of Jainism. Gautam, his disciple, who was a scholar and great pundit, was. These are the men. . . .

You are born out of the mother's womb, and you have to find the womb again in existence. . . .

Hindus are better when they call their god "mother"—mother Kali—than Christians and Mohammedans and Jews, who go on calling their god "father." Those three religions are man-oriented, that's why they have been so violent. Mohammedans and Christians have killed so many, they have been a catastrophe on the earth. They have been murderers. In the name of religion they have been only killing and doing nothing else. This is man-oriented religion. . . .

Once a religion becomes organized, violence enters into it. Organization is going to be violent, it has to fight its way, it is bound to become male. Organization is male; religion is female.

I have heard an anecdote that a few disciples of the Devil came very worried and said and told him, "Why are you sitting here? Our whole business is at stake. A man has again become a Buddha, enlightened. We have to do something, otherwise he will transform people—and our world will be deserted, and who will come to hell? Do something immediately! No time should be lost. A man has again become a Buddha!"

The Devil said, "You don't worry. I work through the disciples. I have sent some already, the disciples are on the way. They will surround him. They will create an organization. And no need to worry: the organization will do everything that we cannot do, and they always do it better. I have learned it through history. I will create a church . . . and I will not be involved in it at all. In fact, they do it on their own. I just simply encourage and help."

Once the pope is there, Christ is forgotten; once the church is there, the Buddha is killed and murdered. It is always on the corpse of a Buddha that a religion stands.

From *Tao: The Three Treasures.*

sent, the psychological explanations of religious conditions and processes have certainly been held in some disrepute, inasmuch as a theology which called itself free carried on its unprofitable practice in this domain; for here from the beginning (as the mind of its founder, Schleiermacher, gives us reason to suppose) the preservation of the Christian religion and the continuance of Christian theology was kept in view; a theology which was to find a new anchorage in the psychological analyses of religious "facts," and above all a new occupation. Unconcerned about such predecessors we hazard the following interpretation of the phenomenon in question. Man is conscious of certain actions which stand far down in the customary rank of actions; he even discovers in himself a tendency towards similar actions, a tendency which appears to him almost as unchangeable as his whole nature. How willingly would he try himself in that other species of actions which in the general valuation are recognized as the loftiest and highest, how gladly would he feel himself to be full of the good consciousness which should follow an unselfish mode of thought! But unfortunately he stops short at this wish, and the discontent at not being able to satisfy it is added to all the other discontents which his lot in life or the consequences of those above-mentioned evil actions have aroused in him; so that a deep ill-humor is the result, with the search for a physician who could remove this and all its causes. This condition would not be felt so bitterly if man would only compare himself frankly with other men,—then he would have no reason for being dissatisfied with himself to a particular extent, he would only bear his share of the common burden of human dissatisfaction and imperfection. But he compares

"Why?"

Leo Tolstoy

[F]ive years ago something very strange began to happen with me: I was overcome by minutes at first of perplexity and then of an arrest of life, as though I did not know how to live or what to do, and I lost myself and was dejected. But that passed, and I continued to live as before. Then those minutes of perplexity were repeated oftener and oftener, and always in one and the same form. These arrests of life found their expression in ever the same questions: "Why? Well, and then?"

At first I thought that those were simply aimless, inappropriate questions. It seemed to me that that was all well known and that if I ever wanted to busy myself with their solution, it would not cost me much labour,—that now I had no time to attend to them, but that if I wanted to I should find the proper answers. But the questions began to repeat themselves oftener and oftener, answers were demanded more and more persistently, and, like dots that fall on the same spot, these questions, without any answers, thickened into one black blotch.

There happened what happens with any person who falls ill with a mortal internal disease. At first there appear insignificant symptoms of indisposition, to which the patient pays no attention; then these symptoms are repeated more and more frequently and blend into one temporally indivisible suffering. The suffering keeps growing, and before the patient has had time to look around, he becomes conscious that what he took for an indisposition is the most significant thing in the world to him,—is death.

The same happened with me. I understood that it was not a passing indisposition, but something very important, and that, if the questions were going to repeat themselves, it would be necessary to find an answer for them. And I tried to answer them. The questions seemed to be so foolish, simple, and childish. But the moment I touched them and tried to solve them, I became convinced, in the first place, that they were not childish and foolish, but very important and pro-

(continued)

himself with a being who is said to be capable only of those actions which are called unegoistic, and to live in the perpetual consciousness of an unselfish mode of thought, *i.e.* with God; it is because he gazes into this clear mirror that his image appears to him so dark, so unusually warped. Then he is alarmed by the thought of that same creature, in so far as it floats before his imagination as a retributive justice; in all possible small and great events he thinks he recognizes its anger and menaces, that he even feels its scourge-strokes as judge and executioner. Who will help him in this danger, which, by the prospect of an immeasurable duration of punishment, exceeds in horror all the other terrors of the idea?

133.

Before we examine the further consequences of this mental state, let us acknowledge that it is not through his "guilt" and "sin" that man has got into this condition, but through a series of errors of reason; that it was the fault of the mirror if his image appeared so dark and hateful to him, and that that mirror was *his* work, the very imperfect work of human imagination and power of judgment. In the first place, a nature that is only capable of purely unegoistic actions is more fabulous than the phoenix; it cannot even be clearly imagined, just because, when closely examined, the whole idea "unegoistic action" vanishes into air. No man *ever* did a thing which was done only for others and without any personal motive; how should he be *able* to do anything which had no relation to himself, and therefore without inward obligation (which must always have its foundation in a personal need)? How could the *ego* act without *ego?* A God who, on the contrary, is *all* love, as such a one is often represented, would not be capable of a single unegoistic action, whereby one is reminded of a saying of Lichtenberg's which is certainly taken from a lower sphere: "We cannot possibly *feel*

found questions in life, and, in the second, that, no matter how much I might try, I should not be able to answer them. Before attending to my Samára estate, to my son's education, or to the writing of a book, I ought to know why I should do that. So long as I did not know why, I could not do anything. I could not live. Amidst my thoughts of farming, which interested me very much during that time, there would suddenly pass through my head a question like this: "All right, you are going to have six thousand desyatínas of land in the Government of Samára, and three hundred horses,—and then?" And I completely lost my senses and did not know what to think farther. Or, when I thought of the education of my children, I said to myself: "Why?" Or, reflecting on the manner in which the masses might obtain their welfare, I suddenly said to myself: "What is that to me?" Or, thinking of the fame which my works would get me, I said to myself: "All right, you will be more famous than Gógol, Púshkin, Shakespeare, Molière, and all the writers in the world,—what of it?" And I was absolutely unable to make any reply. The questions were not waiting, and I had to answer them at once; if I did not answer them, I could not live. . . .

All that happened with me when I was on every side surrounded by what is considered to be complete happiness. I had a good, loving, and beloved wife, good children, and a large estate, which grew and increased without any labour on my part. I was respected by my neighbours and friends, more than ever before, was praised by strangers, and, without any self-deception, could consider my name famous. With all that, I was not deranged or mentally unsound,—on the contrary, I was in full command of my mental and physical powers, such as I had rarely met with in people of my age: physically I could work in a field, mowing, without falling behind a peasant; mentally I could work from eight to ten hours in succession, without experiencing any consequences from the strain. And while in such confor others, as the saying is; we feel only for ourselves. This sounds hard, but it is not so really if it be rightly understood. We do not love father or mother or wife or child, but the pleasant sensations they cause us;" or, as Rochefoucauld says: *"Si on croit aimer sa maîtresse pour l'amour d'elle, on est bien trompé."* To know the reason why actions of love are valued more than others, not on account of their nature, namely, but of their *usefulness,* we should compare the examinations already mentioned, *On the Origin of Moral Sentiments.* But should a man desire to be entirely like that God of Love, to do and wish everything for others and nothing for himself, the latter is impossible for the reason that he must do *very much* for himself to be able to do something for the love of others. Then it is taken for granted that the other is sufficiently egoistic to accept that sacrifice again and again, that living for him,—so that the people of love and sacrifice have an interest in the continuance of those who are loveless and incapable of sacrifice, and, in order to exist, the highest morality would be obliged positively to *compel* the existence of un-morality (whereby it would certainly annihilate itself). Further: the conception of a God disturbs and humbles so long as it is believed in; but as to how it arose there can no longer be any doubt in the present state of the science of comparative ethnology; and with a comprehension of this origin all belief falls to the ground. The Christian who compares his nature with God's is like Don Quixote, who under-valued his own bravery because his head was full of the marvellous deeds of the heroes of the chivalric romances,—the standard of measurement in both cases belongs to the domain of fable. But if the idea of God is removed, so is also the feeling of "sin" as a trespass against divine laws, as a stain in a creature vowed to God. Then, perhaps, there still remains that dejection which is intergrown and connected with

dition I arrived at the conclusion that I could not live, and, fearing death, I had to use cunning against myself, in order that I might not take my life.

This mental condition expressed itself to me in this form: my life is a stupid, mean trick played on me by somebody. Although I did not recognize that "somebody" as having created me, the form of the conception that some one had played a mean, stupid trick on me by bringing me into the world was the most natural one that presented itself to me.

Involuntarily I imagined that there, somewhere, there was somebody who was now having fun as he looked down upon me and saw me, who had lived for thirty or forty years, learning, developing, growing in body and mind, now that I had become strengthened in mind and had reached that summit of life from which it lay all before me, standing as a complete fool on that summit and seeing clearly that there was nothing in life and never would be. And that was fun to him—

But whether there was or was not that somebody who made fun of me, did not make it easier for me. I could not ascribe any sensible meaning to a single act, or to my whole life. I was only surprised that I had not understood that from the start. All that had long ago been known to everybody. Sooner or later there would come diseases and death (they had come already) to my dear ones and to me, and there would be nothing left but stench and worms. All my affairs, no matter what they might be, would sooner or later be forgotten, and I myself should not exist. So why should I worry about all these things? How could a man fail to see that and live,—that was surprising! A person could live only so long as he was drunk; but the moment he sobered up, he could not help seeing that all that was only a deception, and a stupid deception at that! Really, there was nothing funny and ingenious about it, but only something cruel and stupid.

From *My Confessions.* Trans. Leo Wiener (Dent, 1905).

the fear of the punishment of worldly justice or of the scorn of men; the dejection of the pricks of conscience, the sharpest thorn in the consciousness of sin, is always removed if we recognize that though by our own deed we have sinned against human descent, human laws and ordinances, still that we have not imperiled the "eternal salvation of the Soul" and its relation to the Godhead. And if man succeeds in gaining philosophic conviction of the absolute necessity of all actions and their entire irresponsibility, and absorbing this into his flesh and blood, even those remains of the pricks of conscience vanish.

134.

Now if the Christian, as we have said, has fallen into the way of self-contempt in consequence of certain errors through a false, unscientific interpretation of his actions and sensations, he must notice with great surprise how that state of contempt, the pricks of conscience and displeasure generally, does not endure, how sometimes there come hours when all this is wafted away from his soul and he feels himself once more free and courageous. In truth, the pleasure in himself, the comfort of his own strength, together with the necessary weakening through time of every deep emotion, has usually been victorious; man loves himself once again, he feels it,—but precisely this new love, this self-esteem, seems to him incredible, he can only see in it the whole, undeserved descent of a stream of mercy from on high. If he formerly believed that in every event he could recognize warning, menaces, punishments, and every kind of manifestation of divine anger, he now finds divine goodness in all his experiences,—this event appears to him to be full of love, that one a helpful hint, a third, and indeed, his whole happy mood, a proof that God is merciful. As formerly, in his state of pain, he interpreted his actions falsely, so now he misinterprets his experiences; his mood of comfort he believes to be the working of a power operating outside of himself, the love with which he really loves himself seems to him to be divine love; that which he calls mercy, and the prologue to redemption, is actually self-forgiveness, self-redemption.

135.

Therefore: A certain false psychology, a certain kind of imaginative interpretation of motives and experiences, is the necessary preliminary for one to become a Christian and to feel the need of redemption. When this error of reason and imagination is recognised, one ceases to be a Christian.

136. Of Christian Asceticism and Holiness

As greatly as isolated thinkers have endeavoured to depict as a miracle the rare manifestations of morality, which are generally called asceticism and holiness, miracles which it would be almost an outrage and sacrilege to explain by the light of common sense, as strong also is the inclination towards this outrage. A mighty impulse of nature has at all times led to a protest against those manifestations; science, in so far as it is an imitation of nature, at least allows itself to rise against the supposed inexplicableness and unapproachableness of these objections. So far it has certainly not succeeded: those appearances are still unexplained, to the great joy of the above-mentioned worshippers of the morally marvellous. For, speaking generally, the unexplained *must* be absolutely inexplicable, the inexplicable absolutely unnatural, supernatural, wonderful,—thus runs the demand in the souls of all religious and metaphysical people (also of artists, if they should happen to be thinkers at the same time); whilst the scientist sees in this demand the "evil principle" in itself. The general, first probability upon which one lights in the contemplation of holiness and asceticism is this, that their nature is a *complicated* one, for almost everywhere, within the physical world as well as in the moral, the apparently marvellous has been successfully traced back to the complicated, the many-conditioned. Let us venture, therefore, to isolate separate impulses from the soul of saints and ascetics, and finally to imagine them as intergrown.

137.

There is a *defiance of self,* to the sublimest manifestation of which belong many forms of asceticism. Certain individuals have such great need of exercising their power and love of ruling that, in default of other objects, or because they have never succeeded otherwise, they finally excogitate the idea of tyrannising over certain parts of their own nature, portions or degrees of themselves. Thus many a thinker confesses to views which evidently do not serve either to increase or improve his reputation; many a one deliberately calls down the scorn of others when by keeping silence he could easily have remained respected; others contradict former opinions and do not hesitate to be called inconsistent—on the contrary, they strive after this, and behave like reckless riders who like a horse best when it has grown wild, unmanageable, and covered with sweat. Thus man climbs dangerous paths up the highest mountains in order that he may laugh to scorn his own fear and his trembling knees; thus the philosopher owns to views of asceticism, humility, holiness, in the brightness of which his own picture shows to the worst possible disadvantage. This crushing of one's self, this scorn of one's own nature, this *spernere se sperni,* of which religion has made so much, is really a very high degree of vanity. The whole moral of the Sermon on the Mount belongs here; man takes a genuine delight in doing violence to himself by these exaggerated claims, and afterwards idolising these tyrannical demands of his soul. In every ascetic morality man worships one part of himself as a God, and is obliged, therefore, to diabolise the other parts.

2. THE DEATH OF GOD: FROM *THE JOYFUL WISDOM*

125. The Madman

Have you ever heard of the madman who on a bright morning lighted a lantern and ran to the market-place calling out unceasingly: "I seek God! I seek God!"—As there were many people standing about who did not believe in God, he caused

"The Value of Despair"

Bertrand Russell

Such, in outline, but even more purposeless, more void of meaning, is the world which Science presents for our belief. Amid such a world, if anywhere, our ideals henceforward must find a home. That Man is the product of causes which had no prevision of the end they were achieving; that his origin, his growth, his hopes and fears, his loves and his beliefs, are but the outcome of accidental collocations of atoms; that no fire, no heroism, no intensity of thought and feeling, can preserve an individual life beyond the grave; that all the labours of the ages, all the devotion, all the inspiration, all the noonday brightness of human genius, are destined to extinction in the vast death of the solar system, and that the whole temple of Man's achievement must inevitably be buried beneath the debris of a universe in ruins—all these things, if not quite beyond dispute, are yet so nearly certain, that no philosophy which rejects them can hope to stand. Only within the scaffolding of these truths, only on the firm foundation of unyielding despair, can the soul's habitation henceforth be safely built.

From "A Free Man's Worship" (1918).

a great deal of amusement. Why! is he lost? said one. Has he strayed away like a child? said another. Or does he keep himself hidden? Is he afraid of us? Has he taken a sea voyage? Has he emigrated?—the people cried out laughingly, all in a hubbub. The insane man jumped into their midst and transfixed them with his glances. "Where is God gone?" he called out. "I mean to tell you! *We have killed him,*—you and I! We are all his murderers! But how have we done it? How were we able to drink up the sea? Who gave us the sponge to wipe away the whole horizon? What did we do when we loosened this earth from its sun? Whither does it now move? Whither do we move? Away from all suns? Do we not dash on unceasingly? Backwards, sideways, forwards, in all directions? Is there still an above and below? Do we not stray, as through infinite nothingness? Does not empty space breathe upon us? Has it not become colder? Does not night come on continually, darker and darker? Shall we not have to light lanterns in the morning? Do we not hear the noise of the grave-diggers who are burying God? Do we not smell the divine putrefaction?—for even Gods putrefy! God is dead! God remains dead! And we have killed him! How shall we console ourselves, the most murderous of all murderers? The holiest and the mightiest that the world has hitherto possessed, has bled to death under our knife,—who will wipe the blood from us? With what water could we cleanse ourselves? What lustrums, what sacred games shall we have to devise? Is not the magnitude of this deed too great for us? Shall we not ourselves have to become Gods, merely to seem worthy of it? There never was a greater event,—and on account of it, all who are born after us belong to a higher history than any history hitherto!"—Here the madman was silent and looked again at his hearers; they also were silent and looked at him in surprise. At last he threw his lantern on the ground, so that it broke in pieces and was extinguished. "I come too early," he then said, "I am not yet at the right time. This prodigious event is still on its way, and is travelling,—it has not yet reached men's ears. Lightning and thunder need time, the light of the stars needs time, deeds need time, even after they are done, to be seen and heard. This deed is as yet further from them than the furthest star,—*and yet they have done it!*"—It is further stated that the madman made his way into different churches on the same day, and there intoned his *Requiem aeternam deo.* When led out and called to account, he always gave the reply: "What are these churches now, if they are not the tombs and monuments of God?"—

135. Origin of Sin

Sin, as it is at present felt wherever Christianity prevails or has prevailed, is a Jewish feeling and a Jewish invention; and in respect to this background of all Christian morality, Christianity has in fact aimed at "Judaising" the whole world. To what an extent this has succeeded in Europe is traced most accurately in the extent of our alienness to Greek antiquity—a world without the feeling of sin—in our sentiments even at present; in spite of all the good will to approximation and assimilation, which whole generations and many distinguished individuals have not failed to display. "Only when thou *repentest* is God gracious to thee"—that would arouse the laughter or the wrath of a Greek: he would say, "Slaves may have such sentiments." Here a mighty being, an almighty being, and yet a revengeful being, is presupposed; his power is so great that no injury whatever can be done to him except in the point of honor. Every sin is an infringement of respect, a *crimen laesae majestatis divinae*—and nothing more! Contrition, degradation, rolling-in-the-dust,—these are the first and last conditions on which his favour depends: the restoration, therefore, of his divine honour! If injury be caused otherwise by sin, if a profound, spreading evil be propagated by it, an evil which, like a disease, attacks and strangles one man after another—that does not trouble this honour-craving Oriental in heaven; sin is an offence against him, not against mankind!—to him on whom he has bestowed his favor he bestows also this indifference to the natural consequences of sin. God and mankind are here thought of as separated, as so antithetical that sin against the latter cannot be at all possible,—all deeds are to be looked upon *solely with respect to their supernatural consequences,* and not with respect to their natural results: it is thus that the Jewish feeling, to which all that is natural seems unworthy in itself, would have things. The *Greeks,* on the other hand, were more familiar with the thought that transgression also may have dignity,—even theft, as in the case of Prometheus, even the slaughtering of cattle as the expression of frantic jealousy, as in the case of Ajax; in their need to attribute dignity to transgression and embody it therein, they invented *tragedy,*—an art and a delight, which in its profoundest essence has remained alien to the Jew, in spite of all his poetic endowment and taste for the sublime.

343. What Our Cheerfulness Signifies

The most important of more recent events—that "God is dead," that the belief in the Christian God has become unworthy of belief—already begins to cast its first shadows over Europe. To the few at least whose eye, whose *suspecting* glance, is strong enough and subtle enough for this drama, some sun seems to have set, some old, profound confidence seems to have changed into doubt: our old world must seem to them daily more darksome, distrustful, strange and "old." In the main, however, one may say that the event itself is far too great, too remote, too much beyond most people's power of apprehension, for one to suppose that so much as the report of it could have *reached* them; not to speak of many who already knew *what* had really taken place, and what must all collapse now that this belief had been undermined,—because so much was built upon it, so much rested on it, and had become one with it: for example, our entire European morality. This lengthy, vast and uninterrupted process of crumbling, destruction, ruin and overthrow which is now imminent: who has realised it sufficiently to-day to have to stand up as the teacher and herald of such a tremendous logic of terror, as the prophet of a period of gloom and eclipse, the like of which has probably never taken place on earth before? . . . Even we, the born riddle-readers, who wait as it were on the mountains posted 'twixt to-day and to-morrow, and engirt by their contradiction, we, the firstlings and premature children of the coming century, into whose sight especially the shadows which must forthwith envelop Europe *should* already have come—how is it that even we, without genuine sympathy for this period of gloom, contemplate its advent without any *personal* solicitude or fear? Are we still, perhaps, too much under the *immediate effects* of the event—and are these effects, especially as regards *ourselves,* perhaps the reverse of what was to be expected—not at all sad and depressing, but rather like a new and indescribable variety of light, happiness, relief, enlivenment, encouragement, and dawning day? . . . In fact, we philosophers and "free spirits" feel ourselves irradiated as by a new dawn by the report that the "old God is dead"; our hearts overflow with gratitude, astonishment, presentiment and expectation. At last the horizon seems open once more, granting even that it is not bright; our ships can at last put out to sea in face of every danger; every hazard is again permitted to the discerner; the sea, *our* sea, again lies open before us; perhaps never before did such an "open sea" exist.—

3. THE ANTICHRIST: FROM *THE ANTICHRIST*

5

We must not deck out and adorn Christianity: it has waged a deadly war upon this *higher* type of man, it has set a ban upon all the fundamental instincts of this type, and has distilled evil and the devil himself out of these instincts:—the strong man as the typical pariah, the villain.

Christianity has sided with everything weak, low, and botched; it has made an ideal out of *antagonism* against all the self-preservative instincts of strong life: it has corrupted even the reason of the strongest intellects, by teaching that the highest values of intellectuality are sinful, misleading and full of temptations. The most lamentable example of this was the corruption of Pascal, who believed in the perversion of his reason through original sin, whereas it had only been perverted by his Christianity.

7

Christianity is called the religion of *pity*.—Pity is opposed to the tonic passions which enhance the energy of the feeling of life: its action is depressing. A man loses power when he pities.

"Revolt"

Jiddu Krishnamurti

Have you ever sat very quietly with closed eyes and watched the movement of your own thinking? Have you watched your mind working—or rather, has your mind watched itself in operation, just to see what your thoughts are, what your feelings are, how you look at the trees, at the flowers, at the birds, at people, how you respond to a suggestion or react to a new idea? Have you ever done this? If you have not, you are missing a great deal. To know how one's mind works is a basic purpose of education. If you don't know how your mind reacts, if your mind is not aware of its own activities, you will never find out what society is. You may read books on sociology, study social sciences, but if you don't know how your own mind works you cannot actually understand what society is, because your mind is part of society; it *is* society. Your reactions, your beliefs, your going to the temple, the clothes you wear, the things you do and don't do and what you think—society is made up of all this, it is the replica of what is going on in your own mind. So your mind is not apart from society, it is not distinct from your culture, from your religion, from your various class divisions, from the ambitions and conflicts of the many. All this is society, and you are part of it. There is no "you" separate from society.

Now, society is always trying to control, to shape, to mould the thinking of the young. From the moment you are born and begin to receive impressions, your father and mother are constantly telling you what to do and what not to do, what to believe and what not to believe; you are told that there is God, or that there is no God but the State and that some dictator is its prophet. From childhood these things are poured into you, which means that your mind—which is very young, impressionable, inquisitive, curious to know, wanting to find out—is gradually being encased, conditioned, shaped so that you will fit into the pattern of a particular society and not be a revolutionary. Since the habit of patterned thinking has already been established in you, even if you do "revolt" it is within the pattern. It is like prisoners revolting in order to have better food, more conveniences—but always within the prison. When you seek God, or try to find out what is right government, it is always within the pattern of society, which says, "This is true and that is false, this is good and that is bad, this is the right leader and these are the saints." So your revolt, like the so-called revolution brought about by ambitious or very clever people, is always limited by the past. That is not revolt, that is not revolution: it is merely heightened activity, a more valiant struggle within the pattern. Real revolt, true revolution is to break away from the pattern and to inquire outside of it.

You see, all reformers—it does not matter *who* they are—are merely concerned with bettering the conditions within the prison. They never tell you not to conform, they never say, "Break through the walls of tradition and authority, shake off the conditioning that holds the

By means of pity the drain on strength which suffering itself already introduces into the world is multiplied a thousandfold. Through pity, suffering itself becomes infectious; in certain circumstances it may lead to a total loss of life and vital energy, which is absurdly out of proportion to the magnitude of the cause (—the case of the death of the Nazarene). This is the first standpoint; but there is a still more important one. Supposing one measures pity according to the value of the reactions it usually stimulates, its danger to life appears in a much more telling light. On the whole, pity thwarts the law of development which is the law of selection. It preserves that which is ripe for death, it fights in favour of the disinherited and the condemned of life; thanks to the multitude of abortions of all kinds which it maintains in life, it lends life itself

mind." And that is real education: not merely to require you to pass examinations for which you have crammed up, or to write out something which you have learnt by heart, but to help you see the walls of this prison in which the mind is held. Society influences all of us, it constantly shapes our thinking, and this pressure of society from the outside is gradually translated as the inner; but, however deeply it penetrates, it is still from the outside, and there is no such thing as the inner as long as you do not break through this conditioning. You must know what you are thinking, and whether you are thinking as a Hindu, or a Moslem, or a Christian; that is, in terms of the religion you happen to belong to. You must be conscious of what you believe or do not believe. All this is the pattern of society and, unless you are aware of the pattern and break away from it, you are still a prisoner though you may think you are free.

But you see, most of us are concerned with revolt within the prison; we want better food, a little more light, a larger window so that we can see a little more of the sky. We are concerned with whether the outcaste should enter the temple or not; we want to break down this particular caste, and in the very breaking down of one caste we create another, a "superior" caste; so we remain prisoners, and there is no freedom in prison. Freedom lies outside the walls, outside the pattern of society; but to be free of that pattern you have to understand the whole content of it, which is "to understand your own mind. It is the mind that has created the present civilization, this tradition-bound culture or society and, without understanding your own mind, merely to revolt as a communist, a socialist, this or that, has very little meaning. That is why it is very important to have self-knowledge, to be aware of all your activities, your thoughts and feelings; and this is education, is it not? Because when you are fully aware of yourself your mind becomes very sensitive, very alert.

You try this—not someday in the far-away future, but tomorrow or this afternoon. If there are too many people in your room, if your home is crowded, then go away by yourself, sit under a tree or on the river bank and quietly observe how your mind works. Don't correct it, don't say, "This is right, that is wrong", but just watch it as you would a film. When you go to the cinema you are not taking part in the film; the actors and actresses are taking part, but you are only watching, in the same way, watch how your mind works. It is really very interesting, far more interesting than any film, because your mind is the residue of the whole world and it contains all that human beings have experienced. Do you understand? Your mind is humanity, and when you perceive this, you will have immense compassion. Out of this understanding comes great love; and then you will know, when you see lovely things, what beauty is.

a sombre and questionable aspect. People have dared to call pity a virtue (—in every *noble* culture it is considered as a weakness—); people went still further, they exalted it to *the* virtue, the root and origin of all virtues,—but, of course, what must never be forgotten is the fact that this was done from the standpoint of a philosophy which was nihilistic and on whose shield the device *The Denial of Life* was inscribed.

9

It is upon this theological instinct that I wage war. I find traces of it everywhere. Whoever has the blood of theologians in his veins, stands from the start in a false and dishonest position to all things. The pathos which grows out of this state, is called *Faith:* that is to say, to shut one's eyes once and for all, in order not to suffer at the sight of incurable falsity. People convert this faulty view of all things into a moral, a virtue, a thing of holiness. They endow their distorted vision with a good conscience,—they claim that no *other* point of view is any longer of value, once theirs has been made sacrosanct with the names "God," "Salvation," "Eternity." . . .

15

In Christianity, neither morality nor religion comes in touch at all with reality. Nothing but imaginary *causes* (God, the soul, the ego, spirit, free will—or even non-free will); nothing but imaginary *effects* (sin, salvation, grace, punishment, forgiveness of sins). Imaginary beings are supposed to have intercourse (God, spirits, souls); imaginary Natural History (anthropocentric: total lack of the notion, "natural causes"); an imaginary *psychology* (nothing but misunderstandings of self, interpretations of pleasant or unpleasant general feelings; for instance of the states of the *nervus sympathicus,* with the help of the sign language of a religio-moral idiosyncrasy,—repentance, pangs of conscience, the temptation of the devil, the presence of God); an imaginary teleology (the Kingdom of God, the Last Judgment, Everlasting Life).—This purely fictitious world distinguishes itself very unfavourably from the world of dreams: the latter *reflects* reality, whereas the former falsifies, depreciates and denies it. . . . *But this explains everything.* What is the only kind of man who has reasons for wriggling out of reality by lies? The man who suffers from reality. But in order to suffer from reality one must be a bungled portion of it. The preponderance of pain over pleasure is the *cause* of that fictitious morality and religion: but any such preponderance furnishes the formula for decadence.

PART XI

Religious Pluralism

Kwasi Wiredu

"RELIGION FROM AN AFRICAN PERSPECTIVE"

KWASI WIREDU, a professor of philosophy at the University of South Florida, was formerly professor and head of the Department of Philosophy at the University of Ghana. Educated at the universities of Ghana and Oxford, he has been a visiting professor at the University of California, Los Angeles, and has received fellowships from the Woodrow Wilson Center and the National Humanities Center. His publications are primarily in the areas of philosophy of logic and African philosophy and include his book, *Philosophy and an African Culture* (Cambridge University Press, 1980). In the selection that follows, he explains that the word *religion* may not be properly applicable to most traditional African thought.

Two assumptions that may safely be made about the human species are one, that the entire race shares some fundamental categories and criteria of thought in common and two, that, nevertheless, there are some very deep disparities among the different tribes of humankind in regard to their modes of conceptualization in some sensitive areas of thought. The first accounts for the possibility of communication among different peoples, the second for the difficulties and complications that not infrequently beset that interaction.

Is religion a field of convergence or divergence of thought among the peoples and cultures of the world? The obvious answer, in alignment with our opening reflection, is that religion is both. There is also an obvious sequel: What are the specifics? But here an obvious answer is unavailable, at least, as concerns Africa vis-à-vis, for instance, the West. In fact, it is not at all obvious in what sense the English word "religion" is applicable to any aspect of African life and thought.

This last remark, of course, amounts to discounting the frequent affirmations, in the literature of African studies, of the immanent religiosity of the African mind. What exactly are the features of life and thought that are appealed to in that characterization? In investigating this issue I am going to have to be rather particularistic. I am going to have particular, though not exclusive, recourse to the Akans of West Africa, for the considerations to be adduced presuppose a level of cultural and linguistic insight to which I cannot pretend in regard to any African peoples except that particular ethnic group which I know through birth, upbringing, reading and deliberate reflective observation. This particularism has, at least, the logical potential of all counter-examples against universal claims.

Let us return to the word "religion". It has been suggested, even by some authors by whose reckoning African life is full of religion, that there is no word in many African languages which translates this word.[1] Whether this is true of all African languages or not I do not know, but it

Kwasi Wiredu, "Universalism and Particularism in Religion from an African Perspective," *Journal of Humanism and Ethical Religion* 3(1): Fall 1990.

1. See, for example, John S. Mbiti, *African Religions and Philosophy*, London: Heinemann, 1969, p.2.

is certainly true of Akan, in the traditional use of that language, that is. Not only is there no single word for religion but there is also no periphrastic equivalent. There is, indeed, the word "Anyamesom" which many translators might be tempted to proffer. But the temptation ought to be resisted. The word is a Christian invention by which the missionaries distinguished, in Akan speech, between their own religion and what they perceived to be the religion of the indigenous "pagans". Thus, it means, not religion, pure and simple, but Christianity. Ironically, in this usage the Christian missionaries were constrained by linguistic exigencies to adapt a word which the Akans use for the Supreme Being. "Onyame" is one among several names for the Supreme Being in Akan. Another very frequent one is "Onyankopon" which literally means The Being That Is Alone Great, in other words, That Than Which a Greater Cannot Be Conceived (with apologies to Saint Anselm). The remaining component of the word "Anyamesom" is "som" which means "to serve", so that the whole word means, literally, "the service of the Supreme Being" or, if you follow Christian methods of translation, "the service of God". In turn, this was taken to mean the *worship* of God.

By way of a designation for what they saw as indigenous religion, the Christians used the word "Abosomsom". This is a combination of two words "Obosom" and "Som". Etymologically, "obosom" means the service of stones. Thus, literally, the barbarism means the service of stone service! Still, it served its Christian purpose. But why stones? That is an allusion to the fact that the Akans traditionally believe that various objects, such as certain special rocks, trees and rivers, are the abode of extra-human forces and beings of assorted grades.

Having gathered from the foregoing remarks that the Akans, in fact, believe in the existence of a supreme being and a variety of extra-human forces and beings, the reader might be disposed to wonder why I make any issue of the sense in which "religion" might be applied to any aspect of Akan culture. If so, let him or her attend to the following considerations. To begin with, religion, however it is defined, involves a certain kind of attitude. If a given religion postulates a supra-human supreme being, that belief must, on any common showing, necessarily be joined to an attitude not only of unconditional reverence but also of worship. Some will go as far as to insist that this worshipful attitude will have to be given practical expression through definite rituals, especially if the being in question is supposed to be the determiner or controller of human destiny. There is a further condition of the utmost importance; it is one which introduces an ethical dimension into the definition. Essential to any religion in the primary sense is a conception of moral uprightness. If it involves supra-human beliefs, the relevant ethic will be based logically or psychologically on the "supra" being or beings concerned. Typically, but by no means invariably, a religion will have a social framework. In that case, it will have organized hortatory and other procedures for instilling or revivifying the commitment to moral virtue.

Consider, now, the character of the Akan belief in the Supreme Being. There is, indeed, generally among the Akans a confirmed attitude of unconditional reverence for *Onyankopon,* the Supreme Being. However, there is, most assuredly, no attitude or ritual of worship directed to that being either at a social or an individual level. They regard Him as good, wise and powerful in the highest. He is the determiner of human destiny as of everything else. But in all this they see no rationale for worship. Neither is the Akan conception or practice of morality based logically or even psychologically on the belief in the Supreme Being. Being good in the highest, He disapproves of evil; but, to the Akan mind, the reason why people should not do evil is not because he disapproves of it but rather because it is contrary to human well-being, which is why He disapproves of it, in the first place.[2]

2. On this see further Kwasi Wiredu, "Morality and Religion in Akan Thought", in H. Odera Oruka and D. A. Masolo, *Philosophy and Cultures,* Nairobi: Bookwise Limited, 1983.

The early European visitors to Africa, especially the missionaries, were quick to notice the absence of any worship of God[3] among the Akans and various other African peoples. They were hardly less struck by the fact that God was not the foundation of Akan morals. On both grounds they deduced a spiritual and intellectual immaturity in the African. Notice the workings here of a facile universalism. It seems to have been assumed that belief in God must move every sound mind to worship. Perhaps, even now, such an assumption might sound plausible to many Western ears. It is, of course, not likely in this day and age that many can be found to suppose that any person of a sound mind must necessarily embrace belief in God. But given the prevailing tendencies in Western and even some non-Western cultures, it might be tempting to think that if people believe in God, then the *natural* thing for them to do is to worship Him. Yet, consider the notion of a perfect being. Why would he (she, it) need to be worshipped? What would be the point of it? It is well-known that the Judeo-Christian God *jealously* demands to be worshipped—witness The Ten Commandments—but, from an Akan point of view,[4] such clamoring for attention must be paradoxical in the extreme in a perfect being, and I confess to being an unreconstructed Akan in this regard.

There is, in their resort to the word "Abosomsom" (the worship of stones) to name what they took to be Akan religion, an odd manifestation of the special importance that the Christian missionaries attached to worship. Having seen that the Akans did not worship God, they were keen to find out what it was that they worshiped, for surely a whole people must worship something. They quickly settled on the class of what I have called extra-human forces and beings, which, as I have already hinted, is a feature of the Akan worldview. There is, indeed, a great variety of such entities postulated in the Akan ontology (as in any other African ontology that I know of). Some are relatively person-like; others somewhat automatic in their operation. The former can, it is believed, be communicated with through some special procedures, and are credited with a moral sense. Commonly, a being of this sort would be believed to be localized at a household "shrine" from where it would protect the given group from evil forces. More person-like still are the ancestors who are thought to live in a realm closely linked with the world of the living.

Actually, the ancestors are conceived of as persons who continue to be members of their pre-mortem families, watching over their affairs and generally helping them. They are regarded as persons, but not as mortal persons; for they have tasted death and transcended it. Accordingly, they are not thought to be constrained by all the physical laws which circumscribe the activities of persons with fully physical bodies. For this reason, they are supposed to be more powerful than mortals. Additionally, they are considered to be more irreversibly moral than any living mortal. All these attributes are taken to entitle the ancestors to genuine reverence. Not quite the same deference is accorded to the first group of beings, but in view of their presumed power to promote human well-being, they are approached with considerable respect.

More types of extra-human forces and beings are spoken of in the Akan ontology than we have mentioned, but these are among the most relevant, and they will suffice for the impending point; which is this: The Akan attitude to the beings in question bears closer analogy to secular esteem than religious worship. The reverence given to the ancestors is only a higher degree of the respect that in Akan society is considered to be due to the earthly elders. For all their post-mortem ontologic transformation, the ancestors are, let it be repeated, regarded as members of their families. The libations that are

3. For convenience, I am using the word "God" here. But this is subject to a rider to be entered below.

4. Abraham asserts, correctly, I think, that "if a distinction can be drawn between worship and serving, then the Akans never had a word for worship. Worship is a concept that had no place in Akan thought". (W. E. Abraham, *The Mind of Africa,* Chicago: The University of Chicago Press, 1962, p. 52.)

poured to them on ceremonial and other important occasions are simply invitations to them to come and participate in family events. Moreover, everybody hopes eventually to become an ancestor, but this is not seen as a craving for self-apotheosis. Ancestorship is simply the crowning phase of human existence.

The non-religious character of the Akan attitude to the non-ancestral forces is even more clear. Real religious devotion to a being must be unconditional. But that is the one thing that the Akan approach to those beings is not; it is purely utilitarian: if they bring help, praise be to them, and other things besides. On the other hand, if they fail, particularly if that happens consistently, they can fall into disrepute or worse. K. A. Busia and J. B. Danquah, the two most celebrated expositors of Akan thought, have borne unambiguous and, as it seems to me, reliable testimony to this fact. Busia says, "The gods are treated with respect if they deliver the goods, and with contempt if they fail. . . . Attitudes to [the gods] depend upon their success, and vary from healthy respect to sneering contempt."[5] Danquah goes somewhat further: ". . . the general tendency is to sneer at and ridicule the fetish and its priest".[6] There is an even more radical consideration. According to popular belief, these "gods" are capable of dying. Of a "god" who is finished the Akans say *nano atro,* that is, its powers have become totally blunted. This may happen through unknown causes, but it may also happen through human design. People can cause the demise of a "god" simply by permanently depriving it of attention. Or, for more rapid results, apply an antithetical substance to its "shrine". Such antidotes are known for at least some of these "gods", according to popular belief. It ought, perhaps, to be emphasized that in this matter the thought is not that a "god" has betaken itself elsewhere, but rather that it has ceased to be a force to be reckoned with at all. In light of all this, it is somewhat of a hyperbole to call the procedures designed for establishing satisfactory relations with the beings in question religious worship.

The considerations rehearsed so far should be enough, I think, to suggest the need for a review of the enthusiastic, not to say indiscriminate, attributions of religiosity to African peoples. But there are deeper reasons of the same significance. And in studying them we will see the role which the hasty universalization of certain Western categories of thought have played in the formation of the misapprehensions under scrutiny. Take, then, the Akan belief in the Supreme Being. In English discourse about Akan thought the word "God" is routinely used to refer to this being. This has led, or has been due, to the supposition that both the Akans and the Christians are talking of the same being when they speak of the Supreme Being, notwithstanding any divergences of cultural perception. This supposed identity of reference has come in handy to Christianized Africans wishing to demonstrate that they can profess Christianity and still remain basically true to their indigenous religions: There is, after all, only one God, and we are all trying to reach Him.[7]

Yet, in spite of any apparent similarities, such as the postulation of That Than Which a Greater Cannot Be Conceived in both traditions of thought, the Akan supreme being is profoundly different from the Christian one. The Christian God is a creator of the world out of nothing. In further philosophical characterization, He is said to be transcendent, supernatural and spiritual in the sense of immaterial, nonphysical. In radical contrast, the Akan supreme being is a kind of cosmic architect, a fashioner of the world order, who occupies the apex of the

5. K. A. Busia, "The Ashanti" in Daryll Forde (ed.), *African Worlds,* Oxford, 1954, p. 205.

6. J. B. Danquah, "Obligation in Akan Society", *West African Affairs,* No. 8, published by the Bureau of Current Affairs, London, 1952, for the Department of Extra-Mural Studies, University of the Gold Coast (now the University of Ghana), p. 6. (I commented on this quote from Danquah along with that from Busia cited in note 5 in my "Morality and Religion in Akan Thought" *op. cit.*)

7. See, for example, E. Bolaji Idowu, *African Traditional Religion: A Definition,* London: SCM Press, 1973, p. 146.

same hierarchy of being which accommodates, in its intermediate ranges, the ancestors and living mortals and, in its lower reaches, animals, plants and inanimate objects. This universe of being is ontologically homogenous. In other words, everything that exists exists in exactly the same sense as everything else. And this sense is empirical, broadly speaking. In the Akan language to exist is to "wo ho" which, in literal translation, means to be at some place. There is no equivalent, in Akan, of the existential "to be" or "is" of English, and there is no way of pretending in that medium to be speaking of the existence of something which is not in space. This locative connotation[8] of the Akan concept of existence is irreducible except metaphorically. Thus you might speak of there existing an explanation for something *(ne nkyerease wo ho)* without incurring any obligation of spatial specification, because an explanation is not an object in any but a metaphorical sense; and to a metaphorical object corresponds only a metophorical kind of space. The same applies to the existence of all so-called abstract entities.[9] In the Akan conceptual framework, then, existence is spatial. Now, since, whatever transcendence means in this context. it implies existence beyond space. it follows that talk of any transcendent being is not just false, but unintelligible, from an Akan point of view.

But not only transcendence goes by the board. Neither the notion of the supernatural nor that of the spiritual can convey any coherent meaning to an Akan understanding in its traditional condition.[10] No line is drawn in the Akan worldview demarcating one area of being corresponding to nature from another corresponding to supernature. Whatever is real belongs to one or another of the echelons of being postulated in that worldview. In that context it has all the explanation that is appropriate to it. An important axiom of Akan thought is that everything has its explanation, *biribiara wo nenkyerease*—a kind of principle of sufficient reason; and a clear presupposition of Akan explanations of phenomena is that there are interactions among all the orders of existents in the world. Accordingly, if an event in human affairs, for instance, does not appear explicable in human terms, there is no hesitation in invoking extra-human causality emanating from the higher or even the lower rungs of the hierarchy of beings. In doing this there is no sense of crossing an ontological chasm; for the idea is that there is only one universe of many strata wherein God, the ancestors, humans, animals, plants and all the rest of the furniture of the world have their being.

In this last connection, it might, perhaps, enhance understanding to regiment our terminology a little. Suppose we use the term "the world" to designate the totality of ordered existents fashioned out by God in the process of "creation", then, of course, God, being the author of the world, is not a part of it, in the Akan scheme of things. But we might, then, reserve the term "universe" for the totality of absolutely all existents. In this sense God would be part of the universe. Apart from regimenting our terminology, this gives us the opportunity to reinforce the point regarding the Akan sense of the inherent law-likeness of reality. And the crucial consideration is that God's relationship with the rest of the universe, that is, the world, is also conceived to be inherently law-like. This is the implication of the Akan saying that "The Creator created Death and Death killed the Creator", *Odomankoma boo Owuo na Owuo kum Odomankoma,* which, in my opinion, is one of the profoundest in the Akan corpus of metaphysical aphorisms.

But though God's relation with the world is conceived to be law-like, He is not made the

8. Kwame Gyekye insists very spiritedly on the locative connotation of the Akan concept of existence, but he does not draw the empirical implications. See his *An Essay on African Philosophical Thought,* New York: Cambridge University Press, 1987, p. 179.

9. My own explication of the concepts of existence and objecthood is essentially in conformity with Akan conception of existence. In this connection see my "Logic and Ontology" series in *Second Order: An African Journal of Philosophy,* January 1973, July 1973, July 1974, and January 1975. The definition of an object which emerged from those discussions was that an object is what can be the non-conceptual referent of a symbol. It should not strain human resources to show that any such referent will have to be in space.

10. As will become clear below, my own conceptual orientation is decidedly Akan in this respect.

basis of the explanation of any specific phenomenon, for since everything is ultimately traceable to Him, *Biribiara ne Nyame,* references to Him are incapable of helping to explain why any particular thing is what it is and not another thing. Divine law-likeness only ensures that there will be no arbitrary interferences in the course of the world-process. Thus the reason why Akan explanations of specific things do not invoke God is not because He is thought to be transcendent or supernatural or anything like that, but rather because He is too immanently implicated in the nature and happening of things to have any explanatory value.

Still, however, in facing the cognitive problems of this world all the mundane theaters of being, human and extra-human, are regarded as *equally* legitimate sources of explanation. Thus, if an Akan explains a mysterious malady in terms of, say, the wrath of the ancestors, it makes little sense to ascribe to him or her a belief in the supernatural. That characterization is intelligible only in a conceptual framework in which the natural/supernatural dichotomy has a place. But the point is that it has no place in the Akan system of thought. We may be sure, then, that the widespread notion that Africans are given to supernatural explanations is the result of the superimposition of alien categories of thought on African thought-structures, in the Akan instance, at least. There is nothing particularly insidious in the fact that Western writers on African thought have generally engaged in this practice; for, after all, one thinks most naturally in terms of the conceptual framework of one's intellectual upbringing, and the natural/supernatural distinction is very endemic, indeed, in Western thought. I do not mean by this, of course, that there is a universal belief in the supernatural in the West. The suggestion is only that this concept together with its logical complement is a customary feature of Western conceptualizations; so much so, that even the Western philosophical naturalist, in denying the existence of anything supernatural, does not necessarily dispute the coherence of that concept. It is a more striking fact that many contemporary African expositors of their own traditional systems of thought yield no ground to their Western colleagues in stressing the role of belief in the supernatural in African thinking.[11] It is hard not to see this as evidence of the fact that in some ways Christian proselytization and Western education have been over-successful in Africa.

But an interesting and important question arises. Suppose it granted that, as I have been arguing, the natural/supernatural dichotomy has no place in Akan and, perhaps, African thought generally. Does that not still leave the question of its objective validity intact? And, if it should turn out to be objectively valid, would it not be reasonable to think that it would be a good thing for Africans to learn to think along that line? My answer to both questions is affirmative; which implies a rejection of relativism. This disavowal is fully premeditated and is foreshadowed in the opening paragraph of this essay. However, for reasons of the division of preoccupation, I cannot try to substantiate my anti-relativism here.[12]

Stated baldly, my thesis is that there is such a thing as the objective validity of an idea. Were it not for the recent resurgence of relativism in Philosophy, this would have been too platitudinous for any words. Furthermore, and rather less obviously, if an idea is objectively valid (or invalid or even incoherent) in any given language or conceptual framework, both the idea and its status can, in principle,

11. K. A. Busia, for example, speaks of "the belief held among African communities that the supernatural powers and deities operate in every sphere and activity of life". *Africa in Search of Democracy,* London: Routledge and Kegan Paul, 1967, p. 9. This in spite of the fact that in his earlier work *The Challenge of Africa* (New York: Frederick A. Praeger, 1962, p. 36) he had remarked on "the apparent absence of any conceptual cleavage between the natural and the supernatural" in Akan thought. Gyekye also says that "the Akan universe is a spritual universe, one in which supernatural beings play significant roles in the thought and action of the people." *An Essay on African Philosophical Thought,* New York: Cambridge University Press, 1987, p. 69.

12. I argue against relativism in "Are There Cultural Universals?", paper presented at a Symposium of the XVIII World Congress of Philosophy, Brighton, England, August 1988.

be *represented* in, if not necessarily translated into, any other language or conceptual framework.

A corollary of the foregoing contention is that, however natural it may be to think in one's native framework of concepts, it is possible for human beings to think astride conceptual frameworks. In the absence of extended argumentation for this general claim, I will content myself with an illustration with respect to the idea of the supernatural. A relevant question, then, is: "Do the Akans need to incorporate the natural/supernatural distinction into their modes of thought?" I think not; for not only is Akan thought inhospitable to this distinction but also the distinction is, in my opinion, objectively incoherent. If this is so, it follows from our principle that it ought to be demonstrable (to the extent that such speculative matters are susceptible of demonstration) in any language and, in particular, in English. In fact, a simple argument suffices for this purpose.

In the sense pertinent to our discussion, the supernatural is that which surpasses the order of nature. In other words, a supernatural event is one whose occurrence is contrary to the laws of nature. But if the event actually happens, then any law that fails to reckon with its possibility is inaccurate and is in need of some modification, at least. However, if the law is suitably amended, even if only by means of an exceptive rider, the event is no longer contrary to natural law. Hence no event can be consistently described as supernatural.

What of the notion of the spiritual? Again, I begin with a disclaimer on behalf of Akan ontological thinking. As can be expected from the spatial character of the Akan concept of existence, the radical dualism of the material and the spiritual can find no home in the Akan scheme of reality. All the extra-human beings and powers, even including God, are spoken of in language irreducibly charged with spatial imagery. It is generally recognized by students of African eschatology that the *place* of the dead, the *abode* of the ancestors, is almost completely modelled on the world of living mortals.[13] If the replication is not complete, it is only because the ancestors are not thought of as having *fully* material bodies. Some analogue of material bodies they surely must be supposed to have, given the sorts of things that are said about them. For example, a postulated component of a person that is supposed to survive death and eventually become an ancestor, all things being equal, is believed soon after death to travel *by land and by river* before arriving at the abode of the ancestors. For this reason in traditional times coffins were stuffed with travel needs such as clothing and money for the payment of ferrying charges. I have never heard it suggested in traditional circles that this practice was purely symbolic. If it were a purely symbolic gesture, that, certainly, would have been carrying symbolism rather far. But, in any case, the practice was of a piece with the conception, and the conception is decidedly quasi-material.

I use the term "quasi-material" to refer to any being or entity conceived as spatial but lacking some of the properties of material objects. The ancestors, for instance, although they are thought of as occupying space, are believed to be invisible to the naked eye and inaudible to the normal ear, except rarely when they choose to *manifest* themselves to particular persons for special reasons. On such occasions they can, according to very widely received conceptions among the Akans, appear and disappear at will unconstrained by those limitations of speed and impenetrability to which the gross bodies of the familiar world are subject. This is held to be generally true of all the relatively personalized forms of extra-human phenomena.

It is apparent from what has just been said that if the extra-human beings of the Akan worldview are not fully material, they are not

13. See further Kwasi Wiredu, "Death and the Afterlife in African Culture" presented at Symposium on "Death and the Afterlife" at the Woodrow Wilson International Center for Scholars, Washington, D.C., June 1988. Published in Arthur S. Berger et al., eds., *Perspectives on Death and Dying: Cross-Cultural and Multi-disciplinary Views,* Philadelphia: The Charles Press, 1989.

fully immaterial either. Further to confirm this last point, we might note that, although the beings in question are not supposed to be generally visible to the *naked* eye, they are widely believed to be perceivable to the superior eyes of certain persons of special gift or training. People reputed to be of this class will sometimes tell you, "If you but had eyes to see, you would be amazed at what is going on right here around where you are standing". And here imagery tends to be so lustily spatial that, but for their selective invisibility, one would be hard put to distinguish between the quasi-material apparitions and the garden variety objects of the material world. Descriptions of human-like creatures gyrating on their heads are not unknown in such contexts. Whatever one may think of such claims, the conceptual point itself is clear, namely, that the extra-human existents of the Akan ontology do not belong to the category of the spiritual in the Cartesian sense of non-spatial, unextended. The category itself is conceptually inadmissible in this system of thought. Should the reader be curious at this stage as to whether mind too is quasi-material in the Akan way of thinking, the short answer[14] is that mind is not thought of as an entity at all but rather simply as the *capacity,* supervenient upon brain states and processes, to do various things. Hence the question whether mind is a spiritual or material or quasi-material entity does not arise.

The Akan worldview, then, involves no sharp ontological cleavages such as the Cartesian dichotomy of the material and the spiritual; what difference in nature there is between ordinary material things and those extra-human beings and forces so often called "spirits" in the literature is the difference between the fully material and the partially material. I ought, by the way, to stress that the absence of the spiritual, in the metaphysical sense, from the Akan conceptual framework does not imply the absence of spirituality, in the popular sense, from Akan life. In the latter sense spirituality is sensitivity to the less gross aspects of human experience.

But let us return to the class of quasi-material entities. A legitimate question is whether there is adequate evidence that such entities exist. Actually, this is not a question which faces Akan thought alone. All cultures, East, West and Central, abound in stories of quasi-material goings-on. In the West investigating the veridity and theoretical explicability of such stories is one of the main concerns of Parapsychology. In Africa there are any number of people who would be willing to bet their lives on the reality of such things, on the basis, reputedly, of first hand experience. Basically, the issue is an empirical one, though probably not completely; for if such phenomena were to be definitively confirmed, their explanation would be likely to have conceptual reverberations. Speaking for myself, I would say that neither in Africa nor elsewhere have I seen compelling evidence of such things; though dogmatism would be ill-advised. At all events, it is worth noting that the plausibility of specific quasi-material claims tends to dwindle in the face of advancing scientific knowledge, a consideration which any contemporary African would need to take to heart.

It is, however, interesting to note that the waning, in Africa, of belief in extra-material entities and forces would leave the indigenous orientation thoroughly empirical; for the African worldview, at any rate, the Akan one, makes room for only material and quasi-material existents. The contrary seems to be the case in the West. Here any reduction in quasi-material beliefs has not automatically resulted in gains for empirical thinking in the minds of a large mass of people; for in addition to the categories of material and quasi-material, there is that of the spiritual, i.e. the immaterial, which exercises the profoundest influence in philosophic and quasi-

14. For a longer answer see Kwasi Wiredu, "The Akan Concept of Mind", *The Ibadan Journal of Humanistic Studies,* October 1983 (University of Ibadan, Nigeria). Also in Guttorm Floistad, ed., *Contemporary Philosophy, A New Survey, Vol. 5: African Philosophy,* Dordrecht: Martinus Nijhoff Publishers (Boston: Kluwer Academic, 1987).

philosophic speculation. Not only is actual belief in immaterial entities widespread in the West but also the intelligibility of the material/immaterial contrast seems to be taken for granted even more widely. Moreover, in spite of the fact that, to say the least, quasi-material beliefs are not at all rare in the West, the tendency is for thinking to be governed by an exclusive disjunction of the material with the immaterial. Thus, for many, though, of course, not everybody, in the West, if a thing is not supposed to be material, it is necessarily immaterial. The Europeans who imposed on themselves the "burden" of bringing "salvation" to the souls of the peoples of Africa certainly had this particular either-or fixation. Consequently, those of them who made sympathetic, though not necessarily empathetic, studies of African thought could not but formulate their results in terms of that and cognate schemes of thought. A visible outcome of their assiduous evangelism is the great *flock* of faithful African converts who think in the same language, proudly attributing to their own peoples belief in sundry things spiritual and supernatural.

Yet, not only is the notion of the spiritual unintelligible within a thought system such as that of the Akans, but also it is objectively a very problematic one. One searches in vain for a useful definition of the spiritual. The sum total of the information available from Cartesian and many other spiritually dedicated sources is that the spiritual is that which is non-material. But, definition by pure negation, such as this, brings little enlightenment. The word "that" in the definition suggests that one is envisaging some *sort* of a referent, but this possibility of reference is given absolutely no grounding. How are we to differentiate between the spiritual and the void, for instance? Some negative definitions can be legitimate, but only if their context provides suitable information. In the present case the context seems to be a veritable void!

An even more unfortunate definition of the spiritual than the foregoing is sometimes encountered.[15] It is explained that the spiritual is the unperceivable, the invisible or, to adapt a phrase of Saint Paul's, the unseen. The problem with this definition is not its apparent negativeness, for the conditions of unperceivability are concrete enough; the problem is that it is so broad as to make gravity, for example, spiritual. It is, of course, not going to help to protest that although gravity is unseen, its effects are seen and felt; for exactly the same is what is claimed for the spiritual. Nor would it be of greater avail to add the condition of non-spatiality to that of invisibility, for something like the square root of four is neither spatial nor visible, and yet one wonders how spiritual it is.

Of the material/spiritual (immaterial) dichotomy, then, we can say the following. It is not a universal feature of human thinking, since the Akans, at least, do not use it. And, in any case, its coherence is questionable. It is not to be assumed, though, that if a mode of conceptualization is universal among humankind, then it is, for that reason, objectively valid. Belief in quasi-material entities, for example, seems to be universal among cultures (though not among all individuals) but the chances are that the concepts involved denote nothing.

After all the foregoing the reader is unlikely to be surprised to learn that the idea of creation out of nothing too does not make sense in the Akan framework of thinking. Avenues to that concept are blocked in Akanland from the side both of the concept of creation and that of nothingness. To take the latter first: Nothingness in the Akan language is relative to location. The idea is expressed as the absence of anything at a given location, *se whee nni ho,* literally, the circumstance of there not being something there. Note here the reappearance of the locative conception of existence. If you subtract the locative connotation from this

15. Gyekye in attributing spiritual beliefs to the Akans uses a definition of this sort: "The Supreme Being, the deities, and the ancestors are spiritual entities. They are considered invisible and unperceivable to the naked eye: This is in fact the definition of the word 'spiritual' . . ." (*An Essay on African Philosophical Thought,* p. 69.)

construal of nothingness, you have exactly nothing left, that is, nothing of the conception remains in your understanding.

The concept of creation in the Akan language is similarly non-transcendent. To create is to *bo,* and the most self-explanatory word in Akan for the creator is *Obooade. Ade* means thing, and *bo* means to make in the sense of to fashion out, which implies the use of raw materials. Any claim to *bo* and *ade* without the use of absolutely any raw material would sound decidedly self-contradictory in the language. Thus the Akan Supreme Being is a maker of things, but not out of nothing; so that if the word "Creator" is used for him, it should be clearly understood that the concept of creation involved is fundamentally different from that involved in, say, orthodox Christian talk of creation. The Akan creator is the architect of the world order, but not the *ex-nihilo* inventor of its stuff.

Interestingly, even within Western philosophy the concept of *ex nihilo* creation was not in the conceptual vocabulary of some of the greatest thinkers. It is well-known, for example, that neither Plato nor Aristotle made use of any such concept. Of course, whether it is intelligible is a separate question. On the face of it, at least, there are tremendous paradoxes in that concept, and unless its exponents can offer profound clarifications, its absence from a conceptual framework can hardly be taken as a mark of insufficiency. Be that as it may, it is clear that the word "creation" should not be used in the context of Akan cosmology without due caution. It should be apparent also that considerable semantical circumspection is called for in using the word "God" for the Akan Supreme Being. Any transcendental inferences from that usage are misplaced.

So, then, we have the following picture of the outlook of the Akans. They believe in a supreme being, but they do not worship Him. Moreover, for conceptual reasons, this being cannot be said to be a spiritual or supernatural being. Nor is He a creator out of nothing. Furthermore, the foundations of Akan ethical life and thought have no necessary reference to Him. It will be recalled also that although the Akans believe in the existence of a whole host of extra-human beings and forces, they view these as regular resources of the world order which can be exploited for good or, sometimes for ill, given appropriate knowledge and the right approach. To all this we might add the fact that the customary procedures in Akan society pertaining to important stages in life, such as naming, marriage and death, which are well-structured, elaborate and highly cherished as providing concrete occasions for the manifestation of communal caring and solidarity, have no necessary involvement with the belief in the Supreme Being. These considerations, by the way, explain why some early European students of African cosmology called the African God an absentee God. In my opinion those visitors to Africa had their finger on something real, but the pejorative tenor of the observation can only be put down to a universalistic conceit. As for the ancestors, they are called upon to come and participate in all these ceremonies, but as revered members of the family, not as gods.

If we now renew the question of the applicability of the concept of religion to any aspect of Akan culture, we must be struck by the substantial disanalogies between the Akan set-up of cosmological and moral ideas viewed in relation to practical life, on the one hand, and Western conceptions of reality and the good life viewed in the same relation. For the purpose of this discussion the most important disparity revolves round the slicing up of human experience into the categories of the religious and the secular. To start from the Western end of the comparison: whether we interpret the concept of the religious in a supernatural or non-supernatural sense, it is not a simple matter to discover an analogue of it in the traditional Akan context.

It might be thought that there is substantial common ground between Akan life and thought and that of, say, the Christian religion, since, even if the Akan Nyame is not thought of as supernatural, he is still regarded as in some sense the author of the world and determiner of its destiny. But conceptions or beliefs that do not dovetail into the fabric of practical life can hardly constitute a religion in the primary sense.

That the belief in Nyame has no essential role in the conduct of Akan life can be seen from a little exercise of the imagination. Imagine the belief in Nyame to be altogether removed from the Akan consciousness. What losses will be incurred in terms of sustenance for any institutions or procedures of practical life? The answer is, "Exactly zero." Customs and moral rules relating to the critical (or even non-critical) stages and circumstances in the lives of individuals do not have their basis in the belief in Nyame. The same is true of the institutions of traditional Akan public life. Thus neither the pursuit of moral virtue and noble ideals by individuals nor the cooperative endeavors of the community towards the common good can be said to stand or fall with the belief in Nyame; they all have a solid enough basis in considerations of human well-being, considerations, in other words, which are completely "this-worldly".

To elaborate a little on this last point: to the traditional Akan what gives meaning to life is usefulness to self, family, community and the species.[16] Nothing transcending life in human society and its empirical conditions enters into the constitution of the meaning of life. In particular, there is not, in Akan belief, in contrast, for instance, to Christian belief, any notion of an afterlife of possible salvation and eternal bliss; what afterlife there is thought to be is envisaged very much on the model of this life, as previously hinted. More importantly, that afterlife is not pictured as a life of eternal fun for the immortals but rather as one of eternal vigilance—vigilance over the affairs of the living with the sole purpose of promoting their well-being within the general constraints of Akan ethics. Indeed, this is what is taken to give meaning to their survival. From everything said (to my knowledge) about the ancestors, they are generally believed never to relent in this objective; which is one reason why they are held in such high esteem. The inhabitants of the world of the dead, then, are themselves thoroughly "this-worldly" in their orientation, according to Akan traditional conceptions.

Basically the same considerations would seem to discourage attributing to the Akans any sort of non-supernaturalistic religiosity. One great difficulty would be how to articulate such a notion within the Akan conceptual framework. Suppose we construe religion as life and thought impregnated by a sense of the sacred. Then, since the primary meaning of the word "sacred" presupposes some conception of deity, we would be in duty bound to give some notification of a broadening of meaning. Accordingly, the sacred might be understood as that in ethical life most worthy of respect, reverence and commitment. But this, in turn, would presuppose a system of values and ideals, and, in the case of the Akans, would bring us back to their irreducibly "this-worldly" ethic. Now, the remarkable thing is that in this ethic a demonstrated basic commitment to the values and ideals of the society is a component of the very concept of a person. An individual is not a person in the fullest sense unless he or she has shown a responsiveness to those ideals in confirmed habits of life. Not, of course, that an individual failing this test is denuded of human rights; for every individual, simply on the grounds of being human, is regarded as a

16. The species-wide dimensions of the Akan sense of solidarity is explicit in a number of traditional maxims. When the Akans say, for example, that *onipa hyia mmoa,* which literally means a human being needs help but is more strictly to be rendered in some such wise as "a human being, simply in virtue of being human, is deserving of help"—when the Akans say this, they mean absolutely and explicitly *any* human being. If you add to this sense of human fellowship the acute sense of the vulnerability of an individual in a strange place—the Akans say *okwantufo ye mmobo,* meaning the plight of a traveller is pitiable—then you begin to understand the ideology behind the hospitality to strangers, black or white, for which the Akans, and actually, Ghanaians generally, are famous.

center of quite extensive rights.[17] On the other hand, there is a prestige attached to the status of personhood, or more strictly, superlative personhood—for indeed the status is susceptible of degrees—to which all Akans of sound mind aspire. But this is simply the aspiration to become a responsible individual in society, an individual who, through intelligent thinking, judicious planning and hard work, is able to carve out an adequate livelihood for himself and family and make significant contributions to the well-being of the community. The problem, now, is that if this is what, in the specific context of Akan culture, living a life informed by a sense of the sacred means, then applying the concept of religion to it would scarcely pick out anything in the culture corresponding to what in, say, Western culture might be called a non-supernaturalistic religion. In Western society there are historical as well as conceptual reasons why one might want to organize one's life on the lines of what might be called a non-supernaturalist religion. In Akan society there are really none. In the West, loss of the belief in God, for example, usually results in disengagement from certain well-known institutions and practices. The consequent psychological or social void might be filled for some by a "non-theistic" religion. In the Akan situation, on the other hand, no such void is to be anticipated from a comparable belief mutation. Speaking from my own experience, failure to retain the belief in *Nyame*—I make no mention here of the Christian God, the conception of whom registers no coherent meaning upon my understanding—has caused me not the slightest alienation from any of the institutions or practices of Akan culture.

Not unexpectedly, what has cost me some dissonance with the culture is my skepticism regarding the continued existence of our ancestors. The pouring of libation, for example, is a practice in which, as previously hinted, the Akans call upon the ancestors to come and participate in important functions and lend their good auspices to any enterprise launched. This is a significant and not infrequent ceremony in Akan life. But obviously, if one does not believe that the ancestors are actually there, one cannot pretend to call them, or, what is the same thing, one can only pretend to do so. I cannot personally, therefore, participate in a custom like this with any total inwardness. In this, by the way, I do not stand alone. Any Akan Christian—and there are great numbers of them—is logically precluded from believing such things as the Akan doctrine of ancestors, for it does not cohere with Christian eschatology. As far as I am concerned, however, there is a saving consideration. This custom of libation, and many other customs of a like quasi-material basis, can be retained by simply reinterpreting the reference to the ancestors as commemoration rather than invocation. That, of course, would entail obvious verbal reformulations, but it should present no problem. What of customs that prove not to be susceptible to such revisions in the face of advancing skepticism? One hopes that they would eventually be abandoned. The culture is rich enough not to suffer any real existential deficit from such a riddance. Nor is the atrophy of custom under the pressure of changing times at all rare in the history of culture.

Be that as it may, the fact remains that as already argued, the Akan belief in the existence and power of such beings as the ancestors, and the procedures associated with that belief do not constitute a religion in any reliable sense. We are now, therefore, brought to the following conclusion: The concept of religion is not unproblematically applicable within all cultures, and Akan culture is a case in point.[18] Nevertheless,

17. On this see further, Kwasi Wiredu, "An Akan Perspective on Human Rights," in Francis Deng, et al., eds., *Human Rights in Africa: Cross-Cultural Perspectives,* Washington, D.C.: Brookings Institution, forthcoming.

18. Akan culture may not be unique in this regard. It is, for example, an open question how appropriate it is to describe the early Greek beliefs about their motley collection of gods and goddesses as a religion. It is no less an open question whether Theraveda Buddhism is a religion or a non-religious philosophy of life translated into a way of life.

there may be some justification for speaking of Akan religion in a broadened sense of the word "religion."[19] In this sense the word would refer simply to the fact that the Akans believe in Nyame, a being regarded as the architect of the world order. Certainly, this is an extremely attenuated concept of religion. As pointed out already, religion in the fullest sense, whether it be supernaturalistc or not, is not just a set of beliefs and conceptions but also a way of life based on those ideas. What we have seen, however, is that the Akan way of life is not based on the belief in Nyame. Hence, if we do use the word "religion" in the Akan context on the grounds of the belief in Nyame, we should evince some consciousness of the fact that we have made a considerable extension of meaning; otherwise we propagate a subtle misunderstanding of Akan and cognate cultures under the apparently widespread illusion that religion is a cultural universal.

Yet, surely, something must be universal. Consider the ease with which Christian missionaries have been able to convert large masses of Africans to Christianity by relaying to them "tidings" which are in some important parts most likely conceptually incoherent or, at any rate, incongruous with categories deeply embedded in indigenous ways of thinking. To be sure, it cannot be assumed that in the large majority of cases conversion has been total in terms of moral and cosmological outlook. Still there are impressive enough numbers of African converts, some in the high reaches of ecclesiastical authority, whose understanding of and dedication to the Christian religion challenges the severest comparisons among the most exalted practitioners of the same faith in the West. I take this as testimony to the malleability of the human mind which enables the various peoples of the world to share not only their insights but also their incoherences. This characteristic of the mind, being fundamental to the human status, makes our common humanity the one universal which potentially transcends all cultural particularities.

19. This does not mean, however, that the concept of religion corresponds to anything in the Akans' conceptualizations of their own experience or external existence. As one might expect from the fact, noted earlier on, that they do not, rightly, as I think, make a sharp distinction between the material and the spiritual, they do not operate with anything like the distinction between the secular and the religious. Many students of African "religion" have noted this, but have strangely drawn from it, or deduced it from, the inverted impression that in African life everything is religious. Thus Mbiti, speaking of African ways of thought, remarks that "there is no formal distinction between the sacred and the secular, between the religious and the non-religious, between the spiritual and the material areas of life". (*African Religions and Philosophy,* p. 2.) But he supposes that this is because "traditional religions permeate all the departments of life" *(loc. cit)*. And he goes on to say things like "religion is their whole system of being" (*ibid.,* p. 3). See also K. A. Busia, *Africa in Search of Democracy,* New York, Frederick A. Praeger, 1967, chap. 1: "The Religious Heritage"; Kofi Asare Opoku, *West African Traditional Religion,* London: F.E.P. International Private Ltd., 91978, chap. 1: "African Traditional Religion: A General Introduction"; Kwesi A. Dickson, *Theology in Africa,* New York: Orbis Book, 1984, chap. 2: "The African Religio-Cultural Reality". Since all these writers are Africans—actually they are all Ghanaians except Mbiti, who is an Ugandan—it might have been hoped that they would have stopped to ponder how the blanket attributions of religiosity to their peoples might be expressed within the indigenous languages. The difficulty of the experiment might well have bred caution. In any case, logic alone should have inspired doubt as to the conceptual significance of the idea of being religious in the thought of a people who, by general admission, do not have the distinction between the secular and the religious in their framework of categories.

Robert McKim

"RELIGIOUS BELIEF AND RELIGIOUS DIVERSITY"

ROBERT McKIM teaches philosophy at the University of Illinois and writes primarily on the philosophy of religion. In the selection that follows he addresses the important question of how religious plurality ought to affect a person's *attitude* toward his or her own sectarian beliefs.

I. INTRODUCTION

In this article I do not try to assess thoroughly the merits of any religious position, whether it be theism, atheism or agnosticism. I assume that these are all serious options for intelligent people, that they may all be held in an intellectually respectable way. My view, for what it is worth, is that there are reasons to be a theist and reasons not to be a theist: there are weighty considerations on each side. Which side is supported by the most reasons, and how one might go about deciding this issue, is another matter. There is a vast and ever-growing literature on this topic and here I simply sidestep most of it. Part of my reason for doing so is my wish to focus on somewhat more neglected issues. My view is that whatever may be the outcome of a full and careful scrutiny of the available evidence, there are considerations which bear on the way in which religious beliefs should be held which may be established independently.

In particular I want to focus on the fact that disagreements about religious matters are so widespread. It is obvious that on such matters intelligent, reflective, and sincere people disagree. In such disagreements there are large groups with long histories, unique traditions and practices, and deep convictions, on each side. Given the extent of the disagreement, the confidence with which people make pronouncements on matters of religious importance is striking. Almost everyone is sure that his or her beliefs about religion are right. Most atheists, Christians, Muslims, and Buddhists, to name a few of the many groups, are sure that their views are right and that the views of others are wrong, or even unintelligible or laughable. Within many groups there are smaller groups with a distinct message whose members are sure that they are the ones who are right. Almost everyone lives—and for that matter dies—in confidence that he is right. This combination of widespread disagreement and widespread confidence is striking. In this article I argue that the very fact of widespread disagreements on religious matters has important implications. In particular it is a reason why those of us who hold religious beliefs should hold them in a tentative way.

In what follows I take it for granted that many of the beliefs of different traditions really are opposed to each other. For instance, Christians and Muslims typically hold opposing views about the significance of Jesus, and about the significance of Muhammad. If Jews are right about, say, God's nature and activities, the afterlife, or the significance of the life of Jesus,

Robert McKim, "Religious Belief and Religious Diversity," *Irish Philosophical Journal,* 6 (1989), 275–302. Reprinted by permission of the publisher and the author.

then atheists, Christians, Muslims, Hindus, and others too, are wrong. And so on. I concede that there are disagreements which are merely apparent. That is, there are some claims which look as though they are inconsistent with each other, but which turn out on closer inspection to be consistent. For instance, it may be that some apparently conflicting descriptions of God are all actually true of God in virtue of God's being a complex being.[1] But there are numerous other cases in which there is genuine disagreement, and an analysis of this sort is implausible.

In considering what sorts of religious beliefs, if any, should be held, and how they should be held, I will have in mind the beliefs of an educated, intelligent, well-informed adult, who has the leisure, ability, opportunity, and so on, to subject her beliefs to scrutiny. I refer to such a person as a *privileged* person. Being privileged is a matter of degree. Being adult, well educated, well informed, and so forth, make for being privileged in the relevant sense. The greater the extent to which one has these characteristics, the more privileged one is. Among the privileged are many intellectuals, many scholars and teachers of religion as well as many priests, rabbis, ministers, and so forth. We can expect more of the privileged with respect to their beliefs, and perhaps in other areas too. We can expect them to be reflective and serious, to subject their beliefs to some scrutiny, and in general to display the intellectual characteristics which we think likely to lead to true beliefs. Let's say that we can expect them to have *intellectual integrity,* although it would be improper and elitist to suggest that this can only be expected of the privileged.

Now privileged people with intellectual integrity disagree deeply about religious matters. What this fact suggests is that there is something obscure (mysterious, puzzling) about the entire area of religion, that it is an area in which it is unclear what we ought to believe, and in which our beliefs, and the way in which our beliefs are held, ought to reflect this mysteriousness.

II. DISAGREEMENT AND MYSTERY

My central contentions are that deep and widespread disagreement suggests that we are dealing with an area of some mystery and perplexity, and that the very fact that there are widespread disagreements on religious matters is a reason why religious beliefs should be held tentatively. Actually, my view is that this is one of a number of reasons why religious beliefs should be held tentatively. In the case of theistic beliefs, I would point to the fact that, if God exists, there is a great deal of mystery about the existence and nature of God. Other reasons pertain to all religious traditions, including religions which are nontheistic. Here, for instance, I would point to the fact that it is difficult for religious experience to support uniquely the claims of a particular religion. Parts or aspects of their experience to which believers point in support of their beliefs do not have the capacity to support one rather than another such set of beliefs. Religious experience, in other words, underdetermines the various religious systems. My focus in this article, however, is almost entirely on certain implications of the widespread occurrence of religious disagreements. Consider first the claim that

> (1) if there is widespread and deep disagreement about some issue, it is likely that there is something mysterious and puzzling about that issue.

1. I explore this possibility in 'Could God have more than one nature?' (in *Faith and Philosophy,* October 1988, pp. 378–398). The claim that there are numerous issues on which religions are at odds may strike some as unwarranted. I concede that many religious statements which express the claims of a tradition should not be taken at their face value: one has to understand their point, their role in the life of those who assert them. . . . But if it is offered as an account of what people who make such assertions actually think themselves to be doing, or of what the people who make such assertions actually are doing, it is implausible. Typically people who make such assertions are attempting to describe reality and think themselves to be describing reality. They may be attempting to do more than that, and they may think themselves to be doing more than that, but that much at least. . . .

Now (1) obviously needs to be modified. If some of the disagreeing parties clearly are qualified to talk about the disputed issue, while others clearly are not, disagreement in that case does not have the same import: it may merely reflect confusion or ignorance. For disagreement to have the import I have in mind, it must be that the disagreeing parties do not include one or more which clearly has the relevant expertise and others which clearly lack that expertise. Of course, when there is widespread and deep disagreement, one of the disputed questions is likely to be the question of who has the relevant expertise.

But we can agree on some of the characteristics of an expert. An expert must have intellectual integrity, although that alone is not enough. Anyone with intellectual integrity will lack expertise on numerous issues. We need to include something like this: an expert will have reflected on the disputed issue, have made an attempt to understand it, and have worked out his or her views on it with some care. We should probably also include the requirement that at least some progress in understanding the disputed issue has been made, and perhaps we might include the requirement that an attempt has been made to understand the point of view of those who disagree. I will leave the precise nature of what it is to be an expert with respect to an issue fairly vague, and merely say that there must be some relevant expertise. So (1) should be restated as follows:

> (2) if there is widespread and deep disagreement about some issue among those with intellectual integrity and some relevant expertise, it is likely that there is something mysterious and puzzling about that issue.

Suppose there is widespread and deep disagreement about an issue, and that it is likely that there is something mysterious and puzzling about it. What are the implications of this for our beliefs? Here it is important to note that the mysterious and puzzling quality I have in mind is not just a matter of some people at some time finding an issue mysterious or puzzling. Many subjects are very puzzling, and yet there can be specialists who work out their views with care, who find that the available data supports some particular view, and who all or mostly agree that this is so. Rather it is a matter of there being something permanently and inherently puzzling and mysterious about it for beings like us in our circumstances. Of course it is not always easy to tell whether or not an issue which seems puzzling and mysterious at some time is permanently and inherently so. But the presence of a multitude of traditions with long histories of reflection, each of which disagrees with the others, strongly suggests that there is something permanently and inherently mysterious and puzzling involved.

If an issue is genuinely mysterious and puzzling, then it is more likely than it otherwise would be that people may be mistaken. The more likely it is that our beliefs in an area are mistaken, the greater is our obligation to examine those beliefs, and the more reason we have to be tentative in our believing in this area, *ceteris paribus*.

III. DISAGREEMENT AND TENTATIVE BELIEF

Here is an attempt to state the view I am advocating:

> (3) widespread and deep disagreement about some issue among those with intellectual integrity and some relevant expertise is a reason for our beliefs about that issue to be tentative.

But (3) also needs to be qualified. Maybe the beliefs of one or more disagreeing party can be explained away as the product of a defect. In that case the fact that some group holds a belief does not have the same significance. Some person or group may have intellectual integrity and some relevant expertise, and yet be unable or unwilling to accept (or unable or unwilling to reject) some belief or set of beliefs, due to some defect.

The defect might be an inability to see beyond class interests or other interests, carelessness, cowardice, conformity, stubbornness, wishful thinking, lack of imagination, sin, or something else. I do not mean that such a defect influences the person's acquisition of beliefs in its entirety: in that case the person would lack intellectual integrity. Rather, the defect pertains to the acquisition and possession of the particular belief at issue, although it would not be surprising if it pertained to other beliefs too, such as beliefs of the same type, or in the same area. Nor can the defect be a matter of, say, refusing to make any attempt to understand the issue: in that case the person lacks relevant expertise. Rather the defect must be a matter of things going wrong somehow with respect to a belief in spite of the fact that the person who has, or could have, the belief has intellectual integrity and some relevant expertise.

When (3) is modified in order to reflect this concern, we get the principle that

> (4) if the views of all but one of the disagreeing parties cannot plausibly be explained away as the product of some defect, then widespread and deep disagreement about some issue among those with intellectual integrity and with some relevant expertise is a reason for our beliefs about that issue to be tentative.

(4) says merely that if certain conditions hold, there is reason to think tentative belief to be appropriate. It should be distinguished from the stronger claim that if the conditions specified in (4) hold, tentative belief is required, and it should be distinguished from the claims that if those conditions hold, it is likely that one's own belief is mistaken, or that scepticism is required. On the other hand, I also do not wish to defend the view that in situations in which there is disagreement, tentative belief rather than, say, suspension of belief or scepticism, is what is appropriate. My claim is rather that if one continues to believe a proposition *p* in such a situation, one has a powerful reason to do so tentatively. And this is the case whether or not one ought to continue to believe *p*.

(4) says that it must not be possible to explain away plausibly the views of all but one of the disagreeing parties. The trouble is that when a disagreement is deep, each side probably has what we might call discrediting mechanisms: they have ways of discrediting or explaining away the views of those who disagree with them, for instance by appeal to an inability to see beyond class interests or to lack of imagination. Discrediting mechanisms are procedures for rendering unconvincing, and therefore unthreatening, the views of other groups. This is one case of a more general tendency to insulate entire systems of belief from attack, to resist challenge or even inspection. Thus, those with strongly held beliefs about religion tend to take steps to strengthen and confirm those beliefs: Muslims tend to read Muslim books and to associate with Muslims, Christians tend to read Christian books and to associate with Christians, and the same goes for other groups. This tendency to insulate, to seek confirmation and to avoid challenge, is hardly unique to religious belief. (And it has a number of aspects, one of which sometimes is an attempt to define the agenda for enquiry and investigation in areas for which those beliefs are seen to have implications.) Such a tendency probably is a feature of all beliefs to some extent, and especially of beliefs that matter to people. It seems pervasive in the case of large systems of beliefs which purport to explain a lot, be they religious, political, scientific, or of some other sort. Such systems of belief have ways of keeping the beliefs of others at arm's length.

So the attempt to insulate a religious system typically involves a way of accounting for the failure of non-believers to accept it. But not all discrediting mechanisms are reliable. Some can be summarily dismissed, such as those which are nothing but manifestations of prejudice, or those which attempt to discredit the views of others just because those views are at odds with the views of one's own group. Discrediting mechanisms which are at odds with widely agreed upon facts in the natural and social sciences also are implausible. In general, we can make a distinction between plausible and implausible discrediting mechanisms, although it is quite another matter to give a full account of what distinguishes the plausible from the implausible.

(4) obviously pertains to belief in general, and not just to religious belief, which is of course my main concern here. My view is that the widespread and deep disagreements that there are about religious matters, including disagreements about the nature, activities, and purposes of God, about whether or not there is an afterlife, and what its nature might be, and so forth, provide reason to hold that on such matters, tentative belief, at most, is appropriate. My view is that (4) holds primarily for those who are privileged, in the sense in which I have defined that term.

(4) may be thought of as following from a more general principle, namely one which says that if I believe *p* and then encounter significant evidence against *p,* then if I continue to believe *p,* I have reason to do so in a tentative way. Or perhaps we should state the more general principle as follows: to the extent that there is evidence against *p,* our belief that *p* ought to be tentative. If we do not think of the presence of a large community who deny *p* as *evidence* against *p,* but rather, say, as reason to think that *p* is false, then the more general principle might be stated as follows: to the extent that we have reason to believe *p* to be false, our belief that *p* ought to be tentative.

IV. TENTATIVE RELIGIOUS BELIEF

So what does tentative belief amount to, and what would tentative *religious* belief be like? There are two main components. Roughly, one has to do with the attitude to the belief in question, and the other has to do with the content of the belief. First, then, the attitude to the belief. Here what I have in mind is close to Gary Gutting's notion of 'interim assent'.[2] He distinguishes between 'decisive' and 'interim' assent as follows.

> Decisive assent to *p* is defined by the fact that it terminates the process of inquiry into the truth of *p.* This does not mean that I no longer think about *p,* but my thoughts are concerned with developing its significance (analysing its meaning, determining its implications) rather than establishing its truth. Nor does it mean that I am unconditionally committed to *p,* i.e., that I intend to maintain *p* no matter what evidence subsequently presents itself. Rather it means that I view the present case for *p* as allowing me to end the search for reasons for and against believing *p.* Interim assent, on the other hand, accepts *p* but without terminating inquiry into the truth of *p.* Its effect is to put me on the side of *p* in disputes about its truth. However, my endorsement of *p* is combined with a commitment to the epistemic need for continuing discussion of *p*'s truth. (p. 105)

I conceive of tentative belief as involving a recognition that the belief may need revision and may be mistaken, and a concomitant openness to alternative beliefs. One is open to further discussion. An exploratory attitude is involved. This is more or less what Gutting has in mind, although his term 'interim assent' may connote that one is *on the way* to decisive assent, and I mean this connotation to be absent from the notion of tentative belief. On religious questions at any rate, perhaps our assent should remain tentative: any conditions in which we find ourselves as human beings may warrant nothing

2. *Religious Belief and Religious Scepticism* (Notre Dame, 1982). In this work Gutting advances a position similar to that which I take in defence of tentative belief. . . .

more. These points about *attitude* are closely linked to some points about *content*. To say that the beliefs are open to revision is to say we may be wrong about their content. If we recognize that we may be wrong about the content, the details are likely to be less important. So tentative belief is also vague about the details. These are separate points: a willingness to revise and an openness to alternative beliefs is compatible with there being a great deal of specificity in the beliefs. There is a lack of specificity *in addition to* a willingness to revise. Some traditions might more reasonably accommodate the one, some the other.

Tentative religious belief is liberal and tolerant. Tentative theistic commitment probably will emphasize hope and trust rather than confident declaration. And there is something entirely democratic about the situation: all groups are on a par with respect to their ignorance. The same can be said for all individuals, at least those with intellectual integrity and some relevant expertise: there is a priesthood of all tentative believers. And incidentally—a thought which tends to come to mind in Ireland—tentative faith has excellent prospects for being at the heart of a tolerant and open society, which will permit, and maybe even encourage, a diversity of opinion, including opinions on religious matters. It does not fear advances in other areas of knowledge which call into question received beliefs: for instance, it will not find itself embarrassed, as some theists have been embarrassed, by discoveries in cosmology or biology.

Clearly there are degrees of tentativeness with regard to a belief, ranging from a mere suspicion, a mere inkling, that one may be wrong to something close to agnosticism about that belief. Tentativeness, in other words, is a matter of degree rather than an all-or-nothing affair. If a case can be made, as I believe it can, for the appropriateness of tentative religious belief, *how* tentative that belief should be will be determined by, among other things, how good the case in question is.

V. PART OF A CASE FOR TENTATIVE RELIGIOUS BELIEF

Some philosophers, including D. Goldstick and Lawrence Sklar, as well as Gary Gutting, have recently discussed what they call 'methodological conservatism'. What is common to methodological conservativism in its various formulations is the notion that the fact that we hold a belief gives us reason to continue to hold it. This much seems correct: the fact that one holds a belief gives at least some slight support to the claim that one ought to continue to hold it. Perhaps this is because we are confident that we are justified in holding most of our beliefs. Or perhaps it is because we are confident that most of our beliefs are true. Or perhaps it is because our beliefs have enabled us to survive, have permitted us to get this far, so that as a whole they have a lot to recommend them. In that case, the fact that some particular belief is among our beliefs is a mark in its favour. The fact that there is a *consensus* within one's own group, including among experts in that group, perhaps also provides some support for a belief. If an individual's holding a belief provides some justification for that individual to continue to hold it, then the fact that there is an entire group which holds a belief provides further justification for holding it. And the larger the group, the longer its history, the larger the number of intelligent, reflective, individuals it includes, the deeper the reflection there has been within it about the relevant issues, and so on, the more this is so. The reason why a measure of justification is to be found here is perhaps a confidence that most of the beliefs held by an entire group, especially a group with a long history, with influential members who have intellectual integrity and relevant expertise, are justified, or true, beliefs.

But if there is a plausible version of methodological conservativism, there is an equally plausible principle according to which the existence of people with intellectual integrity and some relevant expertise, who have reflected deeply on a belief and yet do not hold it, is reason to hold the belief tentatively. That is, if the fact that my group accepts a belief generates a presumption in favour of continuing to accept it, the rejection of that belief by people with intellectual integrity and some relevant expertise, and no apparent relevant defects, is at least reason to hold the belief tentatively. We might call this principle *methodological liberalism.*

A restriction of those whose views count to members of one's own group is suspect. However, if when one appeals to a consensus within one's own group, one is merely saying that one, say, has been brought up in a tradition, or that one chooses to belong to a tradition, and if claims about that tradition being the one right tradition are eschewed, there is no difficulty. Another reasonable view is that the best thing for members of each group to do is to follow the local experts, provided they seem to have intellectual integrity, some relevant expertise, and no apparent relevant defects. It may be that if claims to be the one right tradition are eschewed, many people *ought* to continue to belong to, and participate in, their religious group, provided that one can do so with intellectual integrity, and after some reflection and consideration. There can be good reasons to participate fully in one's tradition, such as a wish to express solidarity with one's community, or a wish to bring up one's children in a particular way. The extent to which participation is compatible with tentative belief will vary: it depends on what is required for being a member of one's religious community.

One reasonable approach is to say that methodological conservativism applies in certain situations and not in others. One situation in which one's holding a belief does not give reason to accept it might be characterized as a chaotic belief situation: that is, one in which there is great variety in the beliefs that are held on some topic. We might contrast that with a stable belief situation, in which there is agreement. So chaos, in the relevant sense, diminishes the extent to which holding a belief gives reason to hold it. Or perhaps the fact that one holds a belief *always* constitutes a consideration which weighs to some extent in favour of continuing to hold it, but the more chaotic the situation, the more such a consideration is likely to be outweighed by other factors. The situation with respect to religious belief is very chaotic.

There are also some reasons why *religious* belief, in particular, ought to be tentative. First, there is an obligation to respect the rationality and seriousness of other religious groups. Recognition that other groups have a history of reflection, and of refinement and development of their views, that members of those other groups are every bit as intelligent as members of one's own group, that their interest in the truth is as great as ours, and their need to find plausible explanations in crucial areas of human life as urgent as ours, is a strong reason for tentativeness in belief. The fact that views which are opposed to each other have each had a central place in enduring cultures suggests at least that there must be something valuable or worthwhile about each of them. Not to recognize this is uncharitable and parochial. This connection between tentative belief and respect for others is one of the attractive features of tentative belief. Tentative belief permits, indeed promotes, an open attitude to those who disagree with you. The respect in question is a matter of appreciating members of other groups as responsible acquirers and holders of beliefs.

Here is another consideration. Among the processes or strategies that we normally and properly use in the acquisition of beliefs is the strategy of relying on the views of those whom we judge to have intellectual integrity and some relevant expertise. But when those who can best lay claim to intellectual integrity and some relevant expertise, such as the intellectuals and religious thinkers of the various religious communities, are deeply divided, this should be reflected in the way in which beliefs about religion are held. All other things being equal, deep disagreement among experts warrants tentativeness in belief to at least the extent that consensus and unanimity among experts warrants our acceptance of a belief.

And our justified beliefs are to some extent communally and socially based. Agreement within a community is something to which one may legitimately appeal in support of a belief one holds. Two remarkable features of modern life are that we are confronted with a variety of communities, and that we can, to some extent, choose our community. To complicate matters further, in complex and mobile modern societies it is not clear what our community amounts to; we seem, if anything, to be parts of many communities, including, for instance, academic, university, church, sporting, and neighbourhood communities. Perhaps it is more accurate to think of ourselves as members of numerous social networks rather than as members of many communities: the notion of a community suggests a cohesion which is lacking from many of the arrangements in which people find themselves connected with others. The important point here is that in our chaotic situation we are in a position to choose which community or network we will align ourselves with. For that reason we have opportunities for choice with respect to beliefs in many areas, including the area of religious belief.

"Follow Your Bliss"

Joseph Campbell

[T]he man who never followed his bliss . . . may have a success in life, but then just think of it—what kind of life was it? What good was it—you've never done the thing you wanted to do in all your life. I always tell my students, go where your body and soul want to go. When you have the feeling, then stay with it, and don't let anyone throw you off. . . .

That is following your bliss. . . .

When I taught at Sarah Lawrence, I would have an individual conference with every one of my students at least once a fortnight, for a half hour or so. Now, if you're talking on about the things that students ought to be reading, and suddenly you hit on something that the student really responds to, you can see the eyes open and the complexion change. The life possibility has opened there. All you can say to yourself is, "I hope this child hangs on to that." They may or may not, but when they do, they have found life right there in the room with them. . . .

Now, I came to this idea of bliss because in Sanskrit, which is the great spiritual language of the world, there are three terms that represent the brink, the jumping-off place to the ocean of transcendence: *Sat, Chit, Ananda.* The world *"Sat"* means being. *"Chit"* means consciousness. *"Ananda"* means bliss or rapture. I thought, "I don't know whether my consciousness is proper consciousness or not; I don't know whether what I know of my being is my proper being or not; but I do know where my rapture is. So let me hang on to rapture, and that will bring me both my consciousness and my being." I think it worked. . . .

It is miraculous. I even have a superstition that has grown on me as the result of invisible hands coming all the time—namely, that if you do follow your bliss you put yourself on a kind of track that has been there all the while, waiting for you, and the life that you ought to be living is the one you are living. When you can see that, you begin to meet people who are in the field of your bliss, and they open the doors to you. I say, follow your bliss and don't be afraid, and doors will open where you didn't know they were going to be.

From *The Power of Myth* (1988).

VI. OBJECTIONS

The view that religious belief should be tentative will be perceived as a nuisance by some religious traditions: your full loyalty and devotion are called for. Tentative belief means holding back: it means thinking there to be an independent point of view from which you can assess the claims of a religion. Much religion wants to be the point of view from which you assess everything else. Many theists say that we should trust and obey God rather than examine reasons for and against belief in God. But this line of thought should not persuade us at all: for one thing, those who advocate it disagree radically about the beliefs which they take to be sacrosanct and not to be subject to assessment. In the absence of further argument there is no reason to trust any one such group rather than another.

Here is another objection. (4) says, roughly, that widespread and deep disagreement is a powerful reason to hold the relevant beliefs tentatively. In other words, roughly again, disagreement is a reason to be tentative to some extent. Consider the following situation. We have found there to be a disagreement of the sort alluded to in (4) between my group and yours. My group modifies its beliefs somewhat, becoming tentative to some extent. Whether or not your group does likewise, deep disagreement between our groups persists. The disagreement will not be as deep, especially if both sides are now somewhat tentative in their beliefs. The objection, then, is this: in the face of this new disagreement, does (4) not require both sides to go through the same process again, noting the nature of the new disagreement, and to make any changes that are required by this new disagreement, perhaps by becoming yet more tentative? And so on. Where will it all end?

There are two responses which might be offered here by the defender of (4). The first is simply to say that we should understand (4) as the claim that the beliefs of other groups should be taken into account *once*. There is no need to take them into account a second, or third, or nth time. The fact that we should respect others as responsible acquirers and holders of beliefs, for instance, provides a reason for taking their beliefs into account, and for tentativeness in our own beliefs. Once our beliefs have been modified in order to register the fact that there is disagreement, there is no need to keep modifying them. The reasons for taking the views of others into account need not be construed as reasons to continue to do so indefinitely. If we take this response, we have to accept the following outcome, an outcome that is superficially odd. Compare two believers. The first takes the beliefs of others into account and modifies her beliefs appropriately, perhaps now holding them with some particular degree of tentativeness. The second starts from that very same degree of tentativeness, and then confronts the fact that there are disagreements, and in virtue of (4), let us suppose, has reason to be yet more tentative in her beliefs. Perhaps this is not a very odd result. It might be said that what is important is that notice be taken of the fact that there are differences, that there is no particular stopping point which should be arrived at, and that the fact that, as it were, what is an appropriate stopping point for one is an inappropriate stopping point for another is beside the point.

The alternative response is to say that in some cases the new disagreement—the disagreement that remains after one or more sides have become tentative in belief in virtue of the conditions alluded to in (4)—*may* constitute a reason for further tentativeness. Whether or not this is the case will depend on some of the considerations mentioned above: for instance, are there experts on each side in this new disagreement, and are there individuals with intellectual integrity on each side? If we take this response we might be agnostic about how far we need to go, about how many times you should allow the fact of disagreement to make a difference. In any case, my general response to this objection is to say that the absence of a general formula for how many times the principle implicit in (4) should be applied is not reason to reject (4). We can leave this issue as a detail that needs to be sorted out.

Another objection. Religions help people to cope with difficulties, including tragedy, sickness, and death. How can a religion have this role if the relevant beliefs are to be held tentatively? The fact that religious beliefs satisfy deep human needs, including a need for explanation in difficult areas of human life, is indeed a reason why tentative belief is likely to be resisted. Yet the very fact that certain beliefs play a profound and important role in our lives, and perhaps even are central to our happiness, should lead us to consider the possibility that it may be what they do for us that gives them the appearance of being inescapable and clearly correct, rather than their truth. The important role that such beliefs have may tend to conceal the fact that they should be held tentatively. But I do not deny that there is a price to be paid for loss of certitude. There is great comfort and assurance in a system which provides a sure guide and interpretation in many important areas of life. Tentative belief simply will not provide the same assistance, have the same value, as untentative belief. But if loss of assurance, or even of depth of commitment, is the price of tentative faith, it is a price which may have to be paid. As things are, many people invest their hopes and confidence in points of view that are false. It is also worth observing, however, that one should not underestimate the extent to which tentative religious belief may fulfill the important social and psychological roles which have usually been played by non-tentative beliefs. It would be interesting to explore the extent to which, say, tentative theistic hope can take on the role of non-tentative theistic certitude.[3]

I concede that the belief that religions generally recommend (or in some cases require) is hardly tentative in nature, and tentative belief is unlikely to satisfy most members of most traditions. But *must* belief which is religious be more than tentative? Gary Gutting says that 'a belief is religious not only in virtue of its content . . . but also in virtue of the way it functions in the life of one who holds it'. He thinks there are at least three reasons why the way religious belief functions requires, in his terms, 'decisive rather than interim assent' (p. 106). I will look briefly at his three reasons.[4]

One reason is that

> religious belief represents the (relative) end of a quest for emotional and intellectual satisfaction. . . . [Any] religious belief worthy of the name must surely call for and legitimate a longing for God as the all-dominating longing of the believer's life, the believer's 'master passion'. (p. 107).

The important questions here are these: must religious belief 'call for and legitimate a longing for God as the all-dominating longing of the believer's life'? And to what extent is an 'all-dominating longing . . . for God' compatible with tentative belief? I take it that a longing is all-dominating not merely in virtue of its being one's greatest or strongest longing, but also in virtue both of its being a very consuming preoccupation in one's life and of its being the concern which provides the setting for all of one's other concerns. Religious belief may *call for* and *legitimate* an all-dominating longing for God, but it hardly *requires* or *presupposes* such a longing. It would be arbitrary to stipulate that belief is not to be counted as religious unless it involves such a longing. Is it not doubtful that most believers have such a longing? Perhaps this is an ideal towards which religious believers should aim rather than a requirement which must be satisfied before their beliefs may properly be classified as religious. More to the point, a longing for God, *however* dominant, seems *compatible*

3. For some explorations along these lines, see Louis P. Pojman, *Religious Belief and the Will* (London: Routledge & Kegan Paul, 1986), chapter XVI.

4. After I finished this article I read the chapter by Pojman which I refer to in note 3, in which he makes similar points in criticism of Gutting. See Pojman, pp. 230–34.

with tentative belief. Indeed, tentative theistic belief and a longing for God eminently suit each other. Both have about them the air of a quest, of something incomplete. Is there not something intellectually *unsatisfying* about neglecting the important fact of religious diversity and its implications, or about inappropriately using a discrediting mechanism to remove the challenge of other traditions?

Gutting has two further arguments, neither of which is convincing. He says that

> a merely interim assent is inconsistent with the typically religious attitude toward nonbelief. . . . [Believers] must . . . assert the superiority of their belief and see even justified nonbelief as an unfortunate fact.

It probably is true that much that has been associated with religious belief, including certain attitudes to nonbelief, would be abandoned if religious belief were to be tentative, although some of the requisite changes in attitudes to non-belief may plausibly be represented as positive ones. If I believe *p*, I believe that *p* is the superior belief in the sense that I think that it, rather than not-*p*, ought to be accepted, and that those who believe not-*p* are in an inferior state with respect to this particular belief. But all of this can be held tentatively. I can tentatively believe, say, both that God revealed the Qur'an to Muhammad, and that those who believe otherwise are mistaken. Must I also believe (tentatively or decisively) that it is unfortunate that some people believe otherwise, even if they are justified in doing so? I see no reason to think so. Once one appreciates the reasons for holding a belief tentatively, and once one recognizes the integrity of those who hold opposing beliefs, much of the point of regarding their holding their beliefs as unfortunate is lost. Their holding mistaken beliefs may be unfortunate in the sense that some such beliefs may, say, lead them to make unwise decisions. But that is not reason to think the holding of mistaken beliefs *per se* as unfortunate.

Gutting's third reason is as follows. He says that religious belief must involve decisive assent because

> what is believed religiously requires a total commitment to its implications for action that is incompatible with continuing reflection on its truth. Thus, at least as far as the fundamental content of their faith is concerned, believers should be prepared to forgo any earthly goods and to run any temporal risk for the sake of what they believe. . . . The very fact that I act so decisively on a belief requires that my assent be decisive. (pp. 107–8)

As in the case of attitudes to non-belief, I am sure that Gutting would agree that many actions which many religious believers have thought to be required by their beliefs are such that a less than total commitment to doing them would be a very good thing. And actions which are manifestations of tentative belief can be very decisive. If I know tentative belief to be appropriate, for instance, I can be very decisive in attempting to refute those who disagree. One can be decisive in taking steps to oppose those who would make a tentative approach impossible, and to oppose those who insist on non-tentative belief. And so on.

But the most important point here, and this bears on all of Gutting's points, and on other points of the same sort as his, is that if religious belief requires decisive assent, then if tentative belief really were required, we ought not to hold religious beliefs. In that case, perhaps we should hold their nearest tentative relations. That is, if belief were to be properly categorized as religious only if it is more than tentative, and if there is a convincing case for the appropriateness of tentativeness of belief in this area, then we ought not to hold religious beliefs, but rather their closest tentative cousins. To put the same point more crudely, if being tentative is not an option for the believer, it may in some cases be better to be tentative than to be a believer. But this is much too crude: it is better to say that if belief is appropriate, it is likely that tentative belief is appropriate.

VII. TENTATIVE BELIEF IN OTHER AREAS

There are many areas other than the area of religion in which there is deep and widespread disagreement. There are disputes, for instance, about whether or not Yeats's remains are buried in Drumcliff Churchyard, over whether or not a unified field theory is possible, over the causes of the destruction of the dinosaurs, over the authorship of various poems. If in such disputes the experts really are divided, and if no defect on the part of one or another side is apparent, then either the rest of us should suspend judgement or, if we continue to be on one side or the other, we have a powerful reason to be tentative in our beliefs.

And what about, for instance, various ethical and aesthetic issues. Should we be tentative on, say, controversial moral matters too? Here I will just make a few brief observations. First, there may be areas in which tentativeness is difficult, and this may include some areas of moral concern. While social policies may reflect a degree of tentativeness, perhaps by tolerating diverse ideas and ways of life, on some moral issues a decision may have to be made—at least a decision about what course of action to *take* or about what course of action to *treat* as correct, if not a decision about what course of action is correct. Societies have to make some decisions about what courses of action are to be encouraged, discouraged, prohibited, and so forth: on some moral matters tentativeness may be difficult. On religious issues, on the other hand, there seems to be more room for tentativeness.

Second, on some moral issues relativism may be the best option. We may settle for saying that different societies disagree about what position is correct on some issues, and that there is no trans-societal truth about what view is correct. On religious matters, on the other hand, there is no hope for relativism of a robust sort. Either God spoke to Moses out of the burning bush, or God did not do so; either Jesus was born of a virgin, or Jesus was not born of a virgin. And so on. The notion that it is true for one group, but false for another, that some such event occurred is unintelligible.

Third, on some moral issues on which there is deep disagreement one or more party to the dispute may not have reflected adequately, or may not have attempted to inform themselves about the issue in question, or may be in the grip of palpably mistaken beliefs. An apologist for slavery who denies that an enslaved group is fully human, for instance, is a good example of someone in the grip of a palpably mistaken belief. In some disagreements, such as disagreements over distribution of scarce resources, the views of some of the disagreeing parties may be reflections of, or influenced by, a wish of those parties to protect their own interests. To the extent that a point of view is nothing more than an expression of a wish to protect interests, it does not have the same significance.

But if on some moral issue there *has* been deep and impartial reflection on all sides, if relativism is not an option, and if tentative belief is feasible, the presence of deep and widespread disagreement is reason to think tentative belief appropriate. For it is likely that each party to the dispute has a well worked out line of thought, with arguments of some power to bring to bear. This is especially likely to be the case if the conflicting moral positions have been subscribed to by flourishing communities. Perhaps there is a compromise position which includes components taken from a number of the alternatives. It may be that more than one side reflects important values which have a claim on our allegiance, and that there is some way to reconcile them with each other. It may be fruitful to interpret in this way the enduring conflict between the right and left in politics, or the conflict between egalitarian and historical entitlement conceptions of justice, or between opponents of abortion and advocates of abortion on demand.

So although not every disagreement should be taken as an indication that the beliefs involved should be held tentatively, disagreements which satisfy the conditions specified in (4), and which are in areas where relativism is not an option (etc.) do give reason to think that beliefs on that topic should be held tentatively. With certain qualifications, therefore, it seems reasonable to accept the applicability of (4) in at least some other areas.

VIII. CONCLUSION

Most people probably are too preoccupied with matters of survival, business, family, and so forth, or are too limited in their knowledge or experience or reasoning abilities, or have too many practical difficulties to overcome, to engage in much reflection about how things appear from the point of view of others, especially others whose worldview is very different. By and large, it seems, religious diversity is not perceived as a problem for belief. No doubt the availability of discrediting mechanisms has a large role in making this to be the case. Advocates of large-scale systems of belief which include discrediting mechanisms probably are not in a position to appreciate the appeal of systems of belief they think discredited. They are not likely to give them a fair and sympathetic hearing. The majority of people get their religious beliefs from their upbringing, and they grow up to inhabit a religious world which feels as real and solid, or almost as real and solid, as the physical world. The world is a certain way, and that is that. Increased knowledge of other traditions, and more interaction with members of other traditions, tends to change this attitude; and it ought to do so.

Diversity ought to be an embarrassment to orthodoxy. In our era other traditions can no longer properly be dismissed or ignored. For their members too have wrestled with the perplexing issues, and have honestly tried to understand. But taking other traditions as seriously as they ought to be taken may shake one's tradition to the core: in particular it may require a different attitude of one's own beliefs. Perhaps there is likely to emerge from familiarity with other worldviews a spontaneous awareness that there is more than one honest attempt to grapple with something obscure, that these attempts are equally credible or close to being equally credible, or at least that one should be somewhat tentative in one's beliefs. This is an empirical matter about which it is difficult to be certain, but if one were to speculate about it, one might consider the possible survival value of being adaptable in this respect.

I take the fact of religious disagreement to be a *strong reason* to hold one's religious beliefs tentatively, a strong reason which can be overridden only by weighty considerations. Of course there are many other factors that are relevant to which beliefs one should hold and to how one should hold them, and which need to be taken into account. For instance, it might be that one of the parties who disagree on some issue has a huge body of evidence for its position and against the competing positions, and that it is clear to any impartial assessor that this is so. Perhaps one religious group enjoys religious experiences which provide decisive support for the correctness of their beliefs and others do not. Whether or not one ought, say, to be a theist, and if so whether or not one ought to hold one's theistic beliefs tentatively, all things considered, are questions which it is beyond my present purposes to answer. I think the available evidence *not* to point decisively in any particular direction. If I am right, this suggests that tentative belief is appropriate when all things *are* considered. But it is compatible with most of what I say here to agree that religious disagreement makes for the appropriateness of beliefs being held tentatively, but to contend that once certain evidence is examined and a full assessment is made, more—or less—than tentative belief will be seen to be appropriate. This is compatible with most of what I say here, although I believe it not to be the case, since I believe the evidence to be fairly neutral. At least I consider the evidence for and against a generic form of theism to be fairly neutral.

In any case the vast majority of people are not in a position to assess the evidence in a thorough way: they are much too busy with other things. Most people in modern Western societies, at any rate, are faced with a situation in which they can find weighty evidence on each side in many central religious disputes, and in which there are influential individuals with intellectual integrity on each side. They are in a situation in which they might as well take it that the evidence is neutral. A full assessment of the situation would also include considerations such as the following. It may be dangerous or self-destructive for some people to hold their religious beliefs tentatively. They may crack up, or life may lose its meaning for them.

No doubt many non-theists will say that theism is just the product of a defect of some sort such as wishful thinking, a misplaced search for security, or lack of relevant expertise. Likewise for many theists: they will say that non-belief, and in general beliefs which differ from their own beliefs, are similarly to be explained away. But everyone can play this game. Everyone can say that they alone are the experts. There seems to be no way to *prove* mistaken someone who says, for instance, 'our experts are right and those of other groups are misguided by sin', or 'I just know that my position is right and that of others is wrong', or 'we are the elect and God has bestowed knowledge of the truth solely on

"An Act for Establishing Religious Freedom"

Thomas Jefferson

Well aware that Almighty God hath created the mind free; that all attempts to influence it by temporal punishments or burdens, or by civil incapacitation, tend only to beget habits of hypocrisy and meanness, and are a departure from the plan of the Holy Author of our religion, who being Lord both of body and mind, yet chose not to propagate it by coercions on either, as was in his Almighty power to do; that the impious presumption of legislators and rulers, civil as well as ecclesiastical, who, being themselves but fallible and uninspired men have assumed dominion over the faith of others, setting up their own opinions and modes of thinking as the only true and infallible, and as such endeavoring to impose them on others, hath established and maintained false religions over the greatest part of the world, and through all time; that to compel a man to furnish contributions of money for the propagation of opinions which he disbelieves, is sinful and tyrannical; that even the forcing him to support this or that teacher of his own religious persuasion, is depriving him of the comfortable liberty of giving his contributions to the particular pastor whose morals he would make his pattern, and whose power he feels most persuasive to righteousness, and is withdrawing from the ministry those temporal rewards, which proceeding from an approbation of their personal conduct, are an additional incitement to earnest and unremitting labors for the instruction of mankind; that our civil rights have no dependence on our religious opinions, more than our opinions in physics or geometry; that, therefore, the proscribing any citizen as unworthy the public confidence by laying upon him an incapacity of being called to the offices of trust and emolument, unless he profess or renounce this or that religious opinion, is depriving him injuriously of those privileges and advantages to which in common with his fellow citizens he has a natural right; that it tends also to corrupt the principles of that very religion it is meant to encourage, by bribing, with a monopoly of worldly honors and emoluments, those who will externally profess and conform to it; that though in-our group'. But if we cannot show to be mistaken the position of someone who readily attempts to discredit the views of all other groups, perhaps by appealing to their sinfulness, we can hope that on closer inspection it will be found embarrassing by those who advocate it. I have merely tried to make a case for the attractiveness of a different approach, but I recognize that it is hardly a conclusive case.

Three final points. First, I have been discussing the claim that diversity is a reason for tentativeness in belief. But is it not also a reason for scepticism, for suspension of judgement, for agnosticism? My view is that it is a reason for scepticism, but a considerably weaker, and hence more easily overridden, reason. A change from non-tentative belief to tentative belief is a minor change in comparison with a change from non-tentative belief to, say, scepticism, so it is not surprising that a strong reason for the former should be a weak reason for the latter.

Second, throughout this article I take it for granted that we are able to exercise some control over whether or not certain beliefs are held tentatively. It seems, however, that just as we cannot suddenly adopt outlandish or even patently false beliefs, or give up certain obvious beliefs, likewise we are unable to change suddenly to holding tentatively many beliefs which we previously held non-tentatively. For instance, I seem to be unable to change suddenly to holding tentatively the belief that I have two arms or the belief that there are other people. The reason for this appears to be that everything speaks for these beliefs, and nothing against them. The situation is otherwise when there are sizeable bodies of evidence against a belief, or when there are plausible alternatives. Normally, in order

deed these are criminal who do not withstand such temptation, yet neither are those innocent who lay the bait in their way; that to suffer the civil magistrate to intrude his powers into the field of opinion and to restrain the profession or propagation of principles, on the supposition of their ill tendency, is a dangerous fallacy, which at once destroys all religious liberty, because he being of course judge of that tendency, will make his opinions the rule of judgment, and approve or condemn the sentiments of others only as they shall square with or differ from his own; that it is time enough for the rightful purposes of civil government, for its officers to interfere when principles break out into overt acts against peace and good order; and finally, that truth is great and will prevail if left to herself, that she is the proper and sufficient antagonist to error, and has nothing to fear from the conflict, unless by human interposition disarmed of her natural weapons, free argument and debate, errors ceasing to be dangerous when it is permitted freely to contradict them.

Be it therefore enacted by the General Assembly. That no man shall be compelled to frequent or support any religious worship, place or ministry whatsoever, nor shall be enforced, restrained, molested, or burthened in his body or goods, nor shall otherwise suffer on account of his religious opinions or belief; but that all men shall be free to profess, and by argument to maintain, their opinions in matters of religion, and that the same shall in nowise diminish, enlarge, or affect their civil capacities.

And though we well know this Assembly, elected by the people for the ordinary purposes of legislation only, have no power to restrain the acts of succeeding assemblies, constituted with the powers equal to our own, and that therefore to declare this act irrevocable, would be of no effect in law, yet we are free to declare, and do declare, that the rights hereby asserted are of the natural rights of mankind, and that if any act shall be hereafter passed to repeal the present or to narrow its operation, such act will be an infringement of natural right.

for tentativeness with respect to some belief to be an option, there must be something about the belief that provides a foothold for that tentativeness.

Whatever the relevant evidence may be, some people may be incapable of adopting tentative beliefs in certain areas, including religious belief. They may be so entrenched in a belief that it is pointless for them to try to hold it in a tentative way. Nothing will be changed by it. It might be said that if they cannot do so, it is false that they ought to do so, but this reflects a too narrow approach to the issue: even if one cannot change at once the way in which one holds a belief, one can perhaps gradually do so. Tentativeness might be a goal towards which we should strive. And in many cases, it may be more effective to attempt to make a change in our beliefs, whether it be a change in their content or in the way in which they are held, indirectly rather than directly. To change one's beliefs indirectly is to change them by changing something else, such as one's circumstances or brain states or friends. I take it for granted that we are able to exercise some control over our beliefs, even if in doing so we are acting in accordance with, and behaving in a way that is consonant with, others among our beliefs.

Third, disagreements about religion obviously do not occur only between those who accept different religious positions. Some reject all religious positions. The fact that there is disagreement between those who reject all religious beliefs and the defenders of one or another religious system suggests that the beliefs of those who reject all religion too should be held tentatively. Religious belief, in all of its diversity, is a challenge to those who reject it in all its forms, just as that diversity is a challenge also to orthodoxy. Partly for reasons of economy I have here usually characterized the issue of religious disagreement as a matter of disagreement between different religious groups. One way to think of my case is as a case about the sort of religious beliefs one should hold if one is going to hold religious beliefs, and to think of the question of whether or not one should accept such beliefs at all as a separate enquiry.

John Hick

"RELIGIOUS PLURALISM AND ABSOLUTE CLAIMS"

JOHN HICK, for many years a professor of theology at the University of Birmingham, England, teaches philosophy at the Claremont Graduate School. The author of many books, including *Philosophy of Religion* and *Evil and the God of Love,* Hick is a contemporary Christian theologian.

The topic that I am going to pursue under this title is that of the absolute claims made by one religion over [and] against others. Such a claim might be concerned with knowing and teaching the truth or with offering the final good of salvation/liberation. I suggest that in fact the truth-claim and the salvation-claim cohere closely together and should be treated as a single package. The valuable contents of this package, the goods conveyed, consist in salvation or liberation; and the packaging and labelling, with the identifying of the sender and the directing of the package to the recipient, are provided by the doctrine. Thus doctrines are secondary, and yet essential to the vital matter of receiving salvation, somewhat as packaging and labelling are secondary and yet essential to transmitting the contents of a parcel.

What then is an absolute claim when made on behalf of such a religious package? In this context the term 'absolute' is not, I think, being used as a precision instrument. Its operative meanings are revealed in its uses, which are in fact various. In one sense the absoluteness of, say, Christianity means the salvific sufficiency of its gospel and its way for Christians—that is, for those whose religious life is determined by that gospel and way. In this sense the absoluteness of Christianity is compatible with the absoluteness of Islam, or again of Hinduism, or Buddhism or Judaism, salvifically sufficient as these different messages and ways are for those who have been spiritually formed by them. But, since 'absolute' so strongly suggests uniqueness, and the impossibility of being surpassed or even equalled, it seems inappropriate to apply it to this pluralistic conception. And in fact this plural sense is the polar opposite of the religious absolutism that I want to discuss here. Let me approach it, however, through this opposite, namely religious pluralism.

By this I mean the view that the great world faiths embody different perceptions and conceptions of, and correspondingly different responses to, the Real or the Ultimate from within the major variant cultural ways of being human; and that within each of them the transformation of human existence from self-centredness to Reality-centredness is manifestly taking place—and taking place, so far as human observation can tell, to much the same extent. Thus the great religious traditions are to be regarded as alternative soteriological 'spaces' within which, or 'ways' along which, men and women can find salvation/liberation/fulfilment.

From this point of view the proper understanding of one's own religious faith and commitment in comparison with others' can be well expressed by adapting a phrase of Rosemary Reuther's. She speaks of her own commitment as a Roman Catholic, rather than as some other kind of Christian, as a matter of 'ecclesial ethnicity' rather than as involving a judgement that her church is superior to others.[1] Extending the idea, we may say that one's being a Muslim, or a Christian, or a Hindu, or whatever, is normally a matter of 'religious ethnicity'. That is to say, Christianity, or Buddhism, or Islam, or whatever, is the religious community into which one was born, into whose norms and insights one has been inducted, and within which (usually at least) one can therefore most satisfactorily live and grow. There are of course spiritual immigrants; but they are very few in comparison with the vast populations through which each religious tradition is transmitted from generation to generation. And having been born into, say, the Christian religious world one does not have to be able to prove (even to one's own satisfaction) that it is superior to the other religious worlds in order for it to be right and proper for one to be wholeheartedly a Christian. Realistically viewed, one's religious commitment is usually a matter of 'religious ethnicity' rather than of deliberate comparative judgement and choice.

But nevertheless each of the great traditions has long since developed a self-understanding which at some point jars, or even positively

1. *Theologians in Transition*, ed. James M. Wall (New York: Crossroad, 1981) p. 163.

clashes, with this conception of religious pluralism.

Thus in the Hindu tradition one believes that one has access to the *sanātana Dharma,* the eternal truth, incarnated in human language in the Vedas. There is a general tolerance of other ways, often however combined with the assumption that sooner or later everyone in his or her own time—and if not in the present life then in another—will come to the fullness of the Vedic understanding. Further, in advaitic philosophy it is often held that the theistic forms of religion represent a less advanced awareness of the ultimate Reality. Thus 'Hinduism' is conscious, at least in many of its adherents, of its unique superiority among the religious movements of the world; and such a consciousness does not naturally encourage a genuine acceptance of religious pluralism.

In the Hebrew tradition it is held that the Jews are God's 'chosen people,' partners in a special covenant, so that they may be God's means of revelation to all mankind. Thus, whilst to be a Jew has often involved special burdens and sufferings, sometimes of the most extreme and appalling kind, yet to be a Jew is also, from the Jewish point of view, to stand in an unique relationship to God. This does not lead to any general intolerance of other religions, nor to a feeling that their adherents must be converted to Judaism; but it does induce a sense of the privilege of having been born a Jew. However, religious pluralism implies that those who are on the other great ways of salvation are no less God's chosen people, although with different vocations; and a genuine acceptance of this is not naturally encouraged by the traditional Judaic self-understanding.

In the Buddhist tradition it is held that the true appreciation of our human situation occurs most clearly and effectively in the teachings of Gautama Buddha; and that any doctrine which denies the ceaselessly changing and insubstantial character of human life, or the possibility of attaining to the 'further shore' of *nirvāṇa,* is not conducive to liberation from the pervasive unsatisfactoriness of ordinary human existence. The Dharma is the full and saving truth, uniquely clear, effective and final among the illuminations and revelations of the world. And, again, such an assurance does not naturally encourage a full acceptance of religious pluralism.

In Islam there is the firm belief that Muhammad was 'the seal of the prophets' and that through the Qur'ān God has revealed to mankind the true religion, taking up into itself and fulfilling all previous revelations. Thus, whilst a Muslim should give friendly recognition to those within the other Abrahamic faiths and may even, in some interpretations, extend the Qur'ānic concept of the People of the Book to include those who encounter the divine through the Hindu, Buddhist, Confucian and Taoist as well as Jewish and Christian scriptures, yet he or she will retain a strong sense of the unique status of the Qurānic revelation. Here is God's final, decisive and commanding word which all must heed and obey. And such a conviction, again, does not naturally encourage a full and unqualified acceptance of religious pluralism.

And in the Christian tradition there is a powerful inbuilt basis for the sense of the unique superiority of the Christian faith in the doctrine that Jesus Christ, the founder and focus of the religion, was God himself—or more precisely, the Second Person of the divine Trinity—in human form. Given this basic dogma, it has been a natural historical consequence for Christians to see theirs as the one and only true religion, founded by God in person and the locus of God's unique saving act; with the corollary that all the other supposed ways to the Real are human constructions, not to be compared with that which God has personally provided. From this has flowed the missionary imperative (though considerably muted today within large sections of the Church) to convert all humanity to the acceptance of the Christian Gospel and to membership of the Church as the body of Christ's redeemed people.

Each of these great religious traditions, then, assumes in one way or another its own unique superiority. Psychologically, this may well only be an instance of the corporate self-respect that characterises any viable human group. The nearest parallel is national pride. What American would wish to be other than American, or what Chinese person would wish to be other than Chinese, or Nigerian other than Nigerian, or Briton other than British, or French man or woman other than French? And do not most people likewise take it unthinkingly for granted that their own mother tongue is the natural form of human speech, and that their own culture—with its familiar food, manners, art forms, and family structures, its pervasive presuppositions and atmosphere—represents the normative way of being human; so that they find it hard to see foreign ways of life as other than peculiar and, when strikingly different from their own, either laughable or bizarre. The other side of this natural parochialism, however, is that we are what we are, and are poor creatures if we do not take some satisfaction and pride in our own ethnic or national or cultural identity, however critical we may also be of some of its particular manifestations. Further, it is largely this residual tribalism that prompts us to work and sacrifice for the good of our community. And the same principle will naturally produce a corporate pride in any religious group of which we are members—both the immediate local community and the vast historical tradition which gives the latter its character and imparts to it its aura of sacredness. For we have—in most cases—been formed from infancy by our tradition, absorbing its values and presuppositions. It has become as much a part of us as our nationality, our language and our culture; and alien religious traditions can seem as peculiar or comic or bizarre as can foreign names or customs or foods.

Psychologically, then, the sense of the unique superiority of one's own religious tradition may

"Lucky to Be Born into the True Religion?"

John Hick

[I]n the great majority of cases—I should guess well over 95 per cent—the tradition within which a religious person finds his or her relationship to the Real depends to a very great extent upon where and when that person is born. For normally, in the world as a whole, the faith that a person accepts is the only faith that has been effectively made available to him or her. We can refer to this manifest dependence of spiritual allegiance upon the circumstances of birth and upbringing as the genetic and environmental relativity of religious perception and commitment. And it is an extraordinary, and to some a disturbing, thought that one's basic religious vision, which has come to seem so obviously right and true, has been largely selected by factors entirely beyond one's control—by the accidents of birth. It is not that one cannot move from one stream of religious life to another, but that this is a rare occurrence, usually presupposing privileged educational opportunities; so that the great majority of human beings live throughout their lives within the tradition by which they were formed. In view of this situation, can one be unquestioningly confident that the religion which one happens to have inherited by birth is indeed normative and that all others are properly to be graded by their likeness or unlikeness to it? Certainly, it is possible that one particular religious tradition is uniquely normative, and that I happen to have had the good fortune to be born into it. And indeed, psychologically, it is very difficult not to assume precisely this. And yet the possibility must persistently recur to any intelligent person, who has taken note of the broad genetic and environmental relativity of the forms of religious commitment, that to assess the traditions of the world by the measure of one's own tradition may merely be to be behaving, predictably, in accordance with the conditioning of one's upbringing.

From "On Grading Religions" (1982).

be simply a natural form of pride in and ingrained preference for one's own familiar group and its ways. And thus far it is to be accepted and taken into account as an inevitable feature of human life; though it must not be allowed to inhibit the spiritual travel which has been called the imaginative 'passing-over' into another religious world and then coming back with new insight to one's own.[2]

But natural pride, despite its positive contribution to human life, becomes harmful when it is elevated to the level of absolute truth and built into the belief system of a religious community. This happens when its sense of its own validity and worth is expressed in doctrines implying an exclusive or a decisively superior access to the truth or the power to save. A natural human tribal preference thereby receives the stamp of divine approval or the aura of a privileged relationship to the Divine. The resulting sense of a special status has in turn, in some cases, either spontaneously motivated or been manipulated to motivate policies of persecution, coercion, repression, conquest and exploitation, or a sense that others cannot be left to follow their own faith or insight but must be converted to one's own gospel. It is at this point, at which the sense of the superiority of one's own tradition is enshrined in formal doctrines, as an essential article of faith, that the idea of religious pluralism is felt as a challenge and may be resisted as a threat. It is also at this point however that the acceptance of religious pluralism can lead to creative doctrinal development.

It is for the adherents of each of the great traditions to look critically at their own dogmas in the light of their new experience within a religiously plural world. As a Christian I shall therefore direct my attention to Christian absolutism. In the past this has taken powerful forms, with immense human consequences, in the Roman Catholic dogma *Extra ecclesiam nulla salus* (outside the church, no salvation) and its nineteenth-century Protestant missionary equivalent: outside Christianity, no salvation. The former was expressed, for example, in the affirmation of the Council of Florence (1438–45) that

> no one remaining outside the Catholic Church, not just pagans, but also Jews or heretics or schismatics, can become partakers of eternal life; but they will go to the 'everlasting fire which was prepared for the devil and his angels', unless before the end of life they are joined to the Church (Denzinger, *Enchiridion Symbolorum Definitionum et Declarationum de Rebus Fidei et Morum,* 29th edn, no. 714).

whilst the latter was expressed in a message of the Congress on World Mission at Chicago in 1960, declaring that

> in the days since the war, more than one billion souls have passed into eternity and more than half of these went to the torment of hell fire without even hearing of Jesus Christ, who He was, or why He died on the cross of Calvary.[3]

There are today some Roman Catholic traditionalists, pre-Vatican II in outlook, who adhere to the *Extra ecclesiam* dogma in its full logical rigour; and likewise there are some Protestant fundamentalists who practice the nineteenth-century missionary faith in an unqualified form. Indeed, if we look at the entire Catholic and Protestant worlds, and not only at the parts with which we tend to be most familiar, we must say that there are today large numbers and powerful groups of Christian absolutists. But nevertheless I think that historians of twentieth-century Christianity will see as the more striking fact the progressive decay of absolutism during this period within the more active and self-critical layers of the Christian mind. The clear trend of mainline Catholic and Protestant attitudes is away from the absolutism of the past. But it is

2. John S. Dunne, *The Way of All the Earth* (New York: Macmillan; and London: Collier Macmillan, 1972) p. ix.

3. *Facing the Unfinished Task: Messages Delivered at the Congress on World Mission,* ed. J. O. Percy (Grand Rapids, Mich.: Eerdman, 1961) p. 9.

easier for this to happen at the level of practice than at the level of theological theory. For there can be no doubt that traditional Christian belief, as expressed in the scriptures, the ecumenical creeds, and the major dogmatic pronouncements and confessions, has been understood as embodying an absolute claim for the Christian Gospel and the Christian way of salvation. According to this system of belief, the historical Jesus was God the Son, the Second Person of the divine Trinity, living a human life; and by his death on the cross he has atoned for human sin, so that by responding to him in genuine repentance and faith, and gratefully accepting the benefits of his sacrifice, we may be reconciled to God and so become part of Christ's Church and heirs of eternal life.

Probably the majority of Christian theologians today want to remain loyal to the heart, at least, of this traditional teaching, centring upon the unique significance of Christ as God incarnate and as the source of human salvation, whilst however at the same time renouncing the old Christian absolutism. And so it has become common to give the old doctrines a universal rather than a restrictive meaning. It is taught that the salvation won by Christ is available to all mankind; though whenever and wherever it occurs it has been made possible only by his atoning death. His sacrifice on the cross is thus the necessary condition of human salvation; but its benefits may nevertheless be enjoyed by people who know nothing of him, or even who consciously reject the Christian interpretation of his life and death. Again, the divine Logos which became personally incarnate within the Jewish stream of religious life as Jesus of Nazareth has also been at work within other streams of religious life, inspiring spiritual leaders and thus being actively present (though no doubt in varying degrees) in Hinduism, Buddhism, Islam, and so on. Consequently there may well be significant religious lessons which Christians can learn from the people of these other traditions.

But I want to suggest that these moves, whilst admirably ecumenical in intent, only amount to epicycles added to a fundamentally absolutist structure of theory in order to obscure its incompatibility with the observed facts. In analogy with the old Ptolemaic picture of the universe, with our earth at its centre, traditional Christian theology sees the religious universe as centred in the person of Christ and his Gospel. In the history of astronomy, when new observations of the movements of the planets seemed to conflict with the Ptolemaic scheme smaller circles were added to the theory, centring on the original circles, to complicate the projected planetary paths and bring them nearer to what was observed; and these epicycles enabled the old picture to be retained for a while longer. Analogously, the Ptolemaic theology, with Christianity at the centre, is now being complicated by epicycles of theory to make it more compatible with our observations of the other great world faiths.

Purely theoretically, these moves can succeed. Further epicycles can be added indefinitely, as required, and the abandonment of the old scheme thereby indefinitely postponed. The problem is one not of logical possibility but of psychological plausibility. Natural human candidness sooner or later finds it unprofitable, and even perhaps undignified, to go on investing intellectual energy in defence of a dogma which seems to clash with the facts. And so when a simpler and more realistic model emerges there is liable to be a paradigm-shift such as took place in the Copernican revolution from the earth-centred to the helio-centric conception of the universe. In the theology of religions a comparably simpler and more realistic model is today available in the theocentric or, better, Reality-centred, conception with its pluralistic implications. Here the religious universe centres upon the divine Reality; and Christianity is seen as one of a number of worlds of faith which circle around and reflect that Reality.

A wholehearted shift to religious pluralism would mean abandoning not only the older and cruder Ptolemaic theology but also the more sophisticated versions with their new epicycles.

For to hold that divine grace reaches the other worlds of faith via our own (i.e., via the person and cross of Christ) would be like holding that the light of the sun can only fall upon the other planets by being first reflected from the earth. To take a different analogy, it is as though there were a life-saving medicine the true chemical name of which is Christ. This medicine is available in its pure form only under the brand name of Christianity. But there are other products which, unknown to their purveyors, also contain Christ, though diluted with other elements and marketed under other names. In these circumstances a knowledgeable pharmacist would always recommend Christianity if it is available. However, there may be places where it is not available; and there, for the time being at least, another product will serve as an adequate second-best. This, I would suggest, is essentially the theology of religions created by the currently favoured theological epicycles.

But, once these epicycles are seen for what they are, it is I think clear that a Christian acceptance of religious pluralism must involve the kind of rethinking of the doctrine of the Incarnation that has in fact been taking place during the last fifty years or so. Let me briefly illustrate this, first, from one of the most influential of recent Roman Catholic thinkers, Karl Rahner. Although questions were raised by traditionalists in Rome about his orthodoxy, Rahner's position as a Catholic theologian was never successfully challenged and he is widely regarded as a prime example of one who was faithful to his own tradition but who at the same time accepted a responsibility to reformulate its affirmations in ways which are relevant and intelligible to the modern world.

In his much discussed article 'Current Problems in Christology',[4] Rahner says that the Chalcedonian Definition is not to be seen as ending Christological thinking. For

> The clearest formulations, the most sanctified formulas, the classical condensations of the centuries-long work of the Church in prayer, reflexion and struggle concerning God's mysteries: all these derive their life from the fact that they are not end but beginning, not goal but means, truths which open the way to the—ever greater—Truth.[5]

Further, the traditional two-natures formula has often led in the past to

> a conception, which undoubtedly dominates the popular mind (without of course reaching the stage of consciously formulated heresy), and which could be put rather as follows: 'When our Lord (= God) walked on earth with his disciples, still humble and unrecognized. . . .'[6]

As against what Rahner sees as this popular misconception—which is however barely distinguishable from the traditional Christian conception of incarnation—we must, he writes, recognise the genuine humanity of Christ, which entails that

> the 'human nature' of the Logos possesses a genuine, spontaneous, free, spiritual, active centre, a human selfconsciousness, which as creaturely faces the eternal Word in a genuinely human attitude of adoration, obedience, a most radical sense of creaturehood.[7]

For otherwise Christ 'would only be the God who is active among us in human form, and not the true man who can be our Mediator with respect to God in genuine human freedom'.[8]

Accordingly Rahner suggests that we should see the Incarnation not as the unique exception to God's normal relationship to man but rather as the uniquely perfect instance of that relationship. For

> Christological considerations have led the way back to the more general doctrine of God's re-

4. Karl Rahner, *Theological Investigations*, vol. 1, trs. Cornelius Ernst, 2nd edn (London: Darton, Longman and Todd, 1965) ch 5.

5. Ibid., p. 149.
6. Ibid., p. 157.
7. Ibid., p. 158.
8. Ibid., p. 160.

> lation to the creature and allowed Christology to appear as the clearly unique 'specifically' distinct perfection of this relation.[9]

Accordingly, the relation of created spiritual beings to God 'reaches its absolute peak in the case of Christ.'[10] Indeed, Rahner suggests in a striking phrase, 'Christology may be studied as self-transcending anthropology, and anthropology as deficient Christology'.[11] Thus the Incarnation is not to be seen as a divine intervention which lies apart from God's creative work in human life, but as

> the *ontologically* (not merely 'morally', an afterthought) unambiguous goal of the movement of creation as a whole, in relation to which everything prior is merely a preparation of the scene. . . . Consequently it is not pure fantasy (though the attempt must be made with caution) to conceive of the 'evolution' of the world *towards Christ,* and to show how there is a gradual ascent which reaches a peak in him.[12]

Hence Rahner can even see the Incarnation as the supreme instance of the operation of divine grace. For is not grace

> the unfolding within human nature of the union of the human with Logos . . . and is therefore, and *arising thence,* something which can also be had in those who are not the ek-sistence of the Logos in time and history but who do belong to his necessary environment?[13]

And so Rahner is able to say,

> Suppose someone says: 'Jesus is the man whose life is one of absolutely unique self-surrender to God.' He may very well have stated the truth about the very depths of what Christ really is, *provided* that he has understood (a) that this self-abandonment presupposes a communication of God to the man; (b) that an absolute self-surrender implies an absolute self-communication of God to the man, one which makes what is produced by it into the reality of the producer himself; and (c) that such an existential statement does not signify something 'mental', a fiction, but is in the most radical way a statement about being.[14]

In a later paper, Rahner develops this thought that human nature is essentially endowed with the possibility of self-transcendence, and that 'The incarnation of God is therefore the unique, *supreme,* case of the total actualization of human reality, which consists of the fact that man *is* in so far as he gives up himself.'[15] For

> God has taken on human nature, because it is essentially ready and adoptable, because it alone, in contrast to what is definable without transcendence, can exist in total dispossession of itself, and comes therein to the fulfilment of its own incomprehensible meaning.[16]

In other words, divine incarnation in human life is a general human possibility. As Rahner says, in the context of a discussion of Christology in relation to the idea of evolution,

> It seems to me that we should have no particular difficulty in representing the history of the world and of the spirit to ourselves as the history of a self-transcendence into the life of God—a self-transcendence which, in this its final and highest phase, is identical with an absolute self-communication of God expressing the same process but now looked at from God's side.[17]

Thus incarnation is the ultimate human possibility, and will constitute the eschatological human reality. But in this world it has only actually happened in one unique case: 'it is only in Jesus of Nazareth that one can dare to believe such a thing has happened and happens eternally.'[18]

9. Ibid., p. 163.
10. Ibid., p. 164.
11. Ibid., p. 164. n. 1.
12. Ibid., p. 165.
13. Ibid., p. 199–200.
14. Ibid., p. 172.
15. Karl Rahner, *Theological Investigations,* vol. IV, trs. Kevin Smyth (London: Darton, Longman and Todd, 1966), p. 110.
16. Ibid.
17. Karl Rahner, *Theological Investigations,* vol. V, trans. Karl-H. Krugger (London: Darton, Longman and Todd, 1966), pp. 178–9.
18. Rahner, *Theological Investigations,* vol. IV, p. 111.

Clearly one could pursue this line of thought further by understanding incarnation as a matter of degree. We should then say that, whenever and wherever the grace of God is effective in men and women, evoking self-giving love for God and neighbour, to that extent God has become incarnate within human history. Such an enlarging—or, from a traditional point of view, metaphoricalising—of the idea of divine incarnation would have important implications for the Christian theology of religions. For, whereas an unique and absolute incarnation defines an unique stream of salvation history, incarnation understood as taking place in many degrees of human openness to the divine has no such effect.

However, Rahner is bound to the Chalcedonian tradition, according to which incarnation is unique and absolute. In Chalcedonian thinking this uniqueness and absoluteness are necessitated by the concept of substance. One is or is not of the eternal and uncreated substance of God the Father; this cannot be a matter of degree; and among all human life only Jesus Christ has been of that divine substance. Thus against the prompting of his own insights—as it must seem to the outside observer—Rahner insists that although Jesus was genuinely human yet also 'This man . . . is God.'[19] And in support of the traditional paradox that Jesus was unambiguously human and yet unambiguously God he propounds the following argument:

> only a *divine* Person can possess as its own a freedom really distinct from itself in such a way that this freedom does not cease to be truly free even with regard to the divine Person possessing it, while it continues to qualify this very person as its ontological subject. For it is only in the case of God that it is conceivable at all that he himself can constitute something in a state of distinction from himself. This is precisely an attribute of his divinity as such and his intrinsic creativity: to be able, by himself and through his *own* act *as such,* to constitute something in being which by the very fact of its being radically dependent (because *wholly* constituted in being), also acquires autonomy, independent reality and truth (precisely because it is constituted in being by the one, unique *God*), and all this precisely with respect to the God who constitutes it in being.[20]

Here Rahner attempts to render the paradox acceptable by the assertion that God, being God ('This is precisely an attribute of his divinity as such'[21]), can bring it about that, as incarnate, God is both a free, autonomous finite human person, and yet at the same time the infinite creator of all things. But the tortuous complexity of his argument conceals the simple proposition that God, being God, can do anything, and therefore can become a genuinely free and independent human being whilst remaining God. This is merely, however, to reiterate the traditional dogma without doing anything either to recommend it or to render it intelligible. Rahner's faithfulness to this tradition, with its implied absolute claim, is reflected consistently in his own theology of religions. Here it is assumed, on the basis of tradition, that redemption is through Christ alone and that outside the Church there is no salvation; but devout and godly people within the other great world traditions are to be regarded as 'anonymous Christians'. This has been Rahner's distinctive contribution to the spinning of epicycles in aid of a basically Ptolemaic theology. Given his adherence to the Chalcedonian Christology—despite exciting new insights which seem to point beyond it—the doctrine of the anonymous Christian is as far as he is able to go towards the alternative vision of religious pluralism.

However, let us turn at this point to the work of recent Protestant theologians who have also been trying to do justice to the genuinely human Jesus perceived by the modern historical reading of the Gospel records. The work of some of the more adventurous among them points to

19. Rahner, *Theological Investigations,* vol. I, p. 173.

20. Ibid., p. 162.

21. Ibid.

a way of understanding God's activity in the 'Christ-event' which does not in principle preclude an acceptance of religious pluralism. These theologians have not generally been primarily concerned with the question of other religions; and in so far as they touch upon it most of them adhere to the traditional assumption of the unique superiority of Christianity. But it is an important feature of their work—even if one which was not always noticed by these authors themselves—that whereas the Chalcedonian Christology entailed the unique superiority of Christianity these modern Christologies do not. Logically, they leave the comparative assessment of the Christian and other traditions to be determined—if it can be determined—by historical observation and spiritual judgement. Thus the superiority of Christianity loses its status as an *a priori* dogma and becomes a claim that could only be established by adequate historical evidence.

I shall illustrate this development from the work of the Presbyterian Donald Baillie and the Anglican Geoffrey Lampe, though American scholars such as John Knox and Norman Pittenger, to cite just two, would have served my purpose equally well.

The late Donald Baillie's book *God Was in Christ* was described by Rudolf Bultmann as 'the most significant book of our time in the field of Christology'.[22] Not only the title but the entire tone of Baillie's book shows that his intention was wholly orthodox. He was not criticising the idea of divine incarnation in Jesus Christ, but was trying to make it intelligible to our twentieth century. He did so by understanding incarnation in terms of what he called the paradox of grace. This is the paradoxical fact that when we do God's will it is true both that we are acting freely and responsibly, and also that God, through supernatural grace, is acting in and through us. The paradox is summed up in St Paul's words, concerning his own labours, that 'it was not I, but the grace of God which is with me'.[23] As Baillie says, the essence of the paradox

> lies in the conviction which a Christian man possesses, that every good thing in him, every good thing he does, is somehow not wrought by himself but by God. This is a highly paradoxical conviction, for in ascribing all to God it does not abrogate human personality nor disclaim personal responsibility. Never is human action more truly and fully personal, never does the agent feel more perfectly free, than in those moments of which he can say as a Christian that whatever good was in them was not his but God's.[24]

Baillie now uses this paradox of grace as the clue to the yet greater paradox of the Incarnation: that the life of Jesus was an authentically human life and yet that in and through that life God was at work on earth. Baillie says,

> What I wish to suggest is that this paradox of grace points the way more clearly and makes a better approach than anything else in our experience to the mystery of the Incarnation itself; that this paradox in its fragmentary form in our own Christian lives is a reflection of that perfect union of God and man in the Incarnation on which our whole Christian life depends, and may therefore be our best clue to the understanding of it. In the New Testament we see the man in whom God was incarnate surpassing all other men in refusing to claim anything for Himself independently and ascribing all the goodness to God. We see Him also desiring to take up other men into His own close union with God, that they might be as He was, And if these men, entering in some small measure through Him into that union, experience the paradox of grace for themselves in fragmentary ways, and are constrained to say, 'It was not I but God', may not this be a clue to the understanding of that perfect life in which the paradox is complete and absolute, that life of Jesus which, being the perfection of humanity, is also, and even in a deeper and prior sense, the very life of God Himself? If the paradox is a reality in our poor imperfect lives

22. Quoted by John Baillie in D. M. Baillie, *The Theology of the Sacrament* (New York: Charles Scribner's Sons, 1957) p. 35.

23. Corinthians 15:10.

24. D. M. Baillie, *God Was in Christ* (London: Faber and Faber; and New York: Charles Scribner's Sons, 1948), p. 114.

> at all, so far as there is any good in them, does not the same or a similar paradox, taken at the perfect and absolute pitch, appear as the mystery of the Incarnation?[25]

In other words the union of divine and human action, which occurs whenever God's grace works effectively in a man's or a woman's life, operated to an absolute extent in the life of Jesus.

Now Baillie's suggestion—which has its roots in the thought of St. Augustine, and earlier in Origen, and in Theodore of Mopsuestia and others of the later Antiochene school—does have the advantage that it offers some degree of understanding of what it means to say that the life of Jesus was a fully divine as well as a fully human event. But of course, in making the idea of incarnation thus to some extent intelligible, Baillie discards the traditional Chalcedonian language of Jesus having two natures, one human and the other divine, and of his being in his divine nature of one substance with the Father. That was a way of expressing it which made sense within the philosophical world of the early Christian centuries but which has now become little more than a mysterious formula which is obediently repeated but no longer bears any intrinsic meaningfulness. Thus the kind of reinterpretation that Baillie offers should be seen as an attempt to bring the doctrine of the Incarnation to life in the modern mind, giving it meaning as a truth which connects with our human experience and which is at least to some extent intelligible in contemporary terms. For, whilst few people today (outside the ranks of rather traditional professional theologians) use the concept of 'substance', or find the idea of a person with two natures other than grotesque, all Christians have some experience and appreciation of the reality of divine grace operating in human life. Further, they can connect this reality with the extraordinary events of the New Testament.

The other recent Protestant theologian to whose work I should like to refer is the Anglican Geoffrey Lampe, who was Regius Professor of Divinity at Cambridge University until his death in 1980. I shall be referring in particular to his last book, *God as Spirit*. Lampe uses as his clue or 'model' for the understanding of Christ the activity within human life of the Holy Spirit, the Spirit of God. And 'the Spirit of God', he says, 'is to be understood, not as referring to a divine hypostasis distinct from God the Father and God the Son or Word, but as indicating God himself as active towards and in his human creation'.[26] Again, 'The Spirit of God is God disclosing himself as Spirit, that is to say, God creating and giving life to the spirit of man, inspiring him, renewing him, and making him whole.'[27] The principal activity in relation to humanity of God as Spirit is inspiration; and accordingly the Christology which Lampe presents is 'a Christology of inspiration'.[28] For

> the concept of the inspiration and indwelling of man by God as Spirit is particularly helpful in enabling us to speak of God's continuing creative relationship towards human persons and of his active presence in Jesus as the central and focal point within this relationship.[29]

Again, 'The use of this concept enables us to say that God indwelt and motivated the human spirit of Jesus in such a way that in him, uniquely, the relationship for which man is intended by his Creator was fully realized. . . .'[30]

Accordingly Lampe does not accept the traditional model of 'the incarnation of a pre-existent divine being, the Logos who is God the Son'.[31] For that model is bound up with the two complementary notions of the primal fall of humanity from righteousness to sin, and then God's intervention by coming to earth in the person

25. Ibid., pp. 117–18.

26. Geoffrey Lampe, *God as Spirit* (Oxford: Clarendon Press, 1977) p. 11.

27. Ibid., p. 61.

28. Ibid., p. 96.

29. Ibid., p. 34.

30. Ibid., p. 11.

31. Ibid., p. 14.

of Jesus of Nazareth to redeem mankind by the sacrifice of his own life upon the cross. Instead, Lampe prefers to follow the early Greek-speaking Fathers of the Church, such as Irenaeus, in thinking of a continuous on-going divine creation of humankind:

> Irenaeus speaks of the making of man according to God's image and likeness as a continuous creation. . . . Man gradually progresses until he attains the perfection of created humanity, which consists in likeness to the perfection of uncreated deity. . . . Man, according to Irenaeus, is first moulded by God's hands, then he receives the infusion of the soul, the life-principle, and finally through Christ he is given the life-giving Spirit that makes him God's son.[32]

Thus, 'the Spirit transforms man into that which he was not; yet this transformation is continuous with creation; it is the completion of creation'.[33] On this view, the Spirit of God has always been active within the human spirit, inspiring men and women to open themselves freely to the divine presence and to respond in their lives to the divine purpose. This continuous creative activity of God as Spirit means that 'God has always been incarnate in his human creatures, forming their spirits from within and revealing himself in and through them.'[34] We must accordingly 'speak of this continuum as a single creative and saving activity of God the Spirit towards, and within, the spirit of man, and of his presence in the person of Jesus as a particular moment within that continuous creativity'.[35] For 'a union of personal deity with human personality can only be a perfected form of inspiration.'[36]

I suggest that in relation to the question of religious pluralism the momentous consequence of this kind of reinterpretation of the doctrine of the Incarnation is that it no longer necessarily involves the claim to the unique superiority of Christianity which the more traditional understanding involved. For if one says, with the older Christian formulations, that the divine substance was present on earth once and once only, namely in Jesus Christ, it follows as a corollary that the Christian religion, and no other, was founded by God in person; and it certainly seems in turn to follow from this that God must want all human beings to accept Christianity as the religion which God has created for them. From this starting-point, all other religious traditions have to be regarded as in various ways preliminary or defective or inferior—which is of course the way in which the Church has in fact usually regarded them in the past. But if, with Baillie, we see in the life of Christ a supreme instance of that fusion of divine grace and creaturely freedom that occurs in all authentic human response and obedience to God, then the situation changes. For we are no longer speaking of an intersection of the divine and the human which only occurs in one unique case, but of an intersection which occurs, in many different ways and degrees, in all human openness and response to the divine initiative. There is now no difficulty in principle in acknowledging that the paradox of grace was also exemplified in other messengers of God or indeed, more broadly, in other human beings who are markedly Reality-centred rather than self-centred.

Of course Christians who feel impelled to claim superiority for their own tradition can still find a way to do so. For they can claim that the paradox of grace, which occurs whenever a human being freely responds to God, was more fully exemplified in the life of Christ than in any other life. This indeed appears to have been Baillie's own view. But it is important to note that, whilst this is still a claim to an unique superiority, yet the epistemological nature of the claim has changed. It is no longer an *a priori* dogma but now is, or ought to be, a historical judgement, subject to all the difficulties and uncertainties of such judgements. Lampe also, given his understanding of God's action in Christ as the supreme instance of divine inspiration, is

32. Ibid., p. 18.
33. Ibid.
34. Ibid., p. 23.
35. Ibid., p. 100.
36. Ibid., p. 12.

still able to make an unique claim for this particular moment of divine activity. For 'this moment is', he says, 'the fulfilment of all the divine activity which preceded it, and . . . it determines the mode in which God the Spirit is experienced in all subsequent history'.[37] 'The evidence', he continues, 'that this claim is justified is the actual fact that Christians find in Christ their source of inspiration, they are attracted by him to reorient their lives towards faith in God and love towards their neighbours, and they see in him the pattern of this attitude of sonship and brotherhood.'[38] However, that for which Lampe claims this unique significance is not the historical Jesus himself, in isolation, about whom our information is often fragmentary and uncertain, but the 'Christ-event' as a whole. 'The Christ-event . . . for which we claim so central a place in the history of the divine self-disclosure to man includes all human thought inspired by God which has Jesus as its primary reference-point.'[39] In other words, the uniquely central inspiration-event is virtually Christianity itself as a historical tradition focused upon the person of Jesus Christ. Thus Lampe says that,

> If a saying in the Gospels, such as, for instance, one of the Beatitudes, touches the conscience and quickens the imagination of the reader, it does not matter greatly whether it was originally spoken by Jesus himself or by some unknown Christian prophet who shared 'the mind of Christ'. It is in either case a word of God communicated through a human mind. It is an utterance of man inspired by God the Spirit.[40]

Thus it is not vitally important whether the famous words of Christ in the Gospels were actually spoken by the Jesus of history:

> We value them because we find truth in them and gain inspiration from them, and we acknowledge Jesus to be uniquely significant because he is either their author or else the originator of the impulse which evoked them from the minds of others—from people whose debt to him was so great that they composed them in his name, as his own.[41]

Here again, as in the case of Donald Baillie's 'paradox of grace' theory, we see a separating in principle of Christology from the theology of religions. That is to say, the unique superiority of the Christian revelation no longer follows as a logical corollary from either Baillie's or Lampe's Christology. To see Jesus as exemplifying in a special degree what Baillie calls the paradox of grace, and what Lampe calls the inspiration of God the Spirit, is thus far to leave open the further question as to how this particular exemplification stands in relation to other exemplifications, such as those that lie at the basis of some of the other great world religions. Baillie believes that the realisation of the paradox of grace (or of divine inspiration) in the life of Jesus was unique because total and absolute. But the point that I want to stress is that this belief is no longer, in the light of either Baillie's or Lampe's Christology, a necessary inference from the nature of God's action in Jesus, but must instead be a judgement based upon historical evidence. And the main problematic question that arises, for any Christian who is familiar with the modern scholarly study of the New Testament, is whether we have a sufficiently complete knowledge of the historical Jesus to be able to affirm that his entire life was a perfect exemplification of the paradox of grace or of divine inspiration.

We saw that in Lampe's thought there is a shift from the historical Jesus to the Christian movement as a whole as the locus of the uniquely 'central and focal' revelatory event. But if we do not have enough historical information to attribute absolute religious value to the historical Jesus, we have, I should think, too much historical information to be able to make such a judgement about Christianity as an historical

37. Ibid., p. 100.
38. Ibid.
39. Ibid., p. 106.
40. Ibid.
41. Ibid., p. 107.

phenomenon. To Lampe it was self-evident that Christianity is the central and decisive strand of human history. But, clearly, this is not self-evident to those whose spiritual life has been developed in a different religious environment and whose relationship to the Divine has been shaped by a different spirituality. At this point Lampe is left witnessing to an unargued presupposition.

It is thus an important feature of these modern Christologies that, without necessarily intending this, they can make it possible for Christians to think without basic inconsistency in terms of religious pluralism. And my plea is that we should have an integrated faith in which our Christology and our theology of religions cohere with one another.

William James

CONCLUSIONS

A brief biography of James appears on page 338.

Let us agree, then, that Religion, occupying herself with personal destinies and keeping thus in contact with the only absolute realities which we know, must necessarily play an eternal part in human history. The next thing to decide is what she reveals about those destinies, or whether indeed she reveals anything distinct enough to be considered a general message to mankind. We have done as you see, with our preliminaries, and our final summing up can now begin.

I am well aware that after all the palpitating documents which I have quoted, and all the perspectives of emotion-inspiring institution and belief that my previous lectures have opened, the dry analysis to which I now advance may appear to many of you like an anticlimax, a tapering-off and flattening out of the subject, instead of a crescendo of interest and result. I said awhile ago that the religious attitude of Protestants appears poverty-stricken to the Catholic imagination. Still more poverty-stricken, I fear, may my final summing up of the subject appear at first to some of you. On which account I pray you now to bear this point in mind, that in the present part of it I am expressly trying to reduce religion to its lowest admissible terms, to that minimum, free from individualistic excrescences, which all religions contain as their nucleus, and on which it may be hoped that all religious persons agree. That established, we should have a result which might be small, but would at least be solid; and on it and round it the ruddier additional beliefs on which the different individuals make their venture might be grafted, and flourish as richly as you please. I shall add my own over-belief (which will be, I confess, of a somewhat pallid kind, as befits a critical philosopher), and you will, I hope, also add your over-beliefs, and we shall soon be in the varied world of concrete religious constructions once more. For the moment, let me dryly pursue the analytic part of the task.

Both thought and feeling are determinants of conduct, and the same conduct may be de-

From William James, The Varieties of Religious Experience, Lecture 20. First published in 1902.

termined either by feeling or by thought. When we survey the whole field of religion, we find a great variety in the thoughts that have prevailed there; but the feelings on the one hand and the conduct on the other are almost always the same, for Stoic, Christian, and Buddhist saints are practically indistinguishable in their lives. The theories which Religion generates, being thus variable, are secondary; and if you wish to grasp her essence, you must look to the feelings and the conduct as being the more constant elements. It is between these two elements that the short circuit exists on which she carries on her principal business, while the ideas and symbols and other institutions form loop-lines which may be perfections and improvements, and may even some day all be united into one harmonious system, but which are not to be regarded as organs with an indispensable function, necessary at all times for religious life to go on. This seems to me the first conclusion which we are entitled to draw from the phenomena we have passed in review.

The next step is to characterize the feelings. To what psychological order do they belong?

The resultant outcome of them is in any case what Kant calls a 'sthenic' affection, an excitement of the cheerful, expansive, 'dynamogenic' order which, like any tonic, freshens our vital powers. In almost every lecture, but especially in the lectures on Conversion and on Saintliness, we have seen how this emotion overcomes temperamental melancholy and imparts endurance to the Subject, or a zest, or a meaning, or an enchantment and glory to the common objects of life.[1] The name of 'faith-state,' by which Professor Leuba designates it, is a good one.[2] It is a biological as well as a psychological condition, and Tolstoy is absolutely accurate in classing faith among the forces *by which men live.*[3] The total absence of it, anhedonia,[4] means collapse.

The faith-state may hold a very minimum of intellectual content. We saw examples of this in those sudden raptures of the divine presence, or in such mystical seizures as Dr. Bucke described.[5] It may be a mere vague enthusiasm, half spiritual, half vital, a courage, and a feeling that great and wondrous things are in the air.[6]

When, however, a positive intellectual content is associated with a faith-state, it gets invincibly stamped in upon belief,[7] and this explains the passionate loyalty of religious persons everywhere to the minutest details of their so widely differing creeds. Taking creeds and faith-state together, as forming 'religions,' and treating these as purely subjective phenomena, without regard to the question of their 'truth," we are obliged, on account of their extraordinary

1. Compare, for instance, pages 166, 178, 181, 183, 199 to 204, 218 to 220 [1902 edition].

2. American Journal of Psychology, vii. 345.

3. Above, p. 153 [1902 edition].

4. Above, p. 124 [1902 edition].

5. Above, p. 136.

6. Example: Henry Perreyve writes to Gratry: "I do not know how to deal with the happiness which you aroused in me this morning. It overwhelms me; I want to *do* something, yet I can do nothing and am fit for nothing. . . . I would fain do *great things.*" Again, after an inspiring interview, he writes: "I went homewards, intoxicated with joy, hope, and strength. I wanted to feed upon my happiness in solitude, far from all men. It was late; but, unheeding that, I took a mountain path and went on like a madman, looking at the heavens, regardless of earth. Suddenly an instinct made me draw hastily back—I was on the very edge of a precipice, one step more and I must have fallen. I took fright and gave up my nocturnal promenade." A. Gratry: Henry Perreyve, London, 1872, pp. 92, 89.

This primacy, in the faith-state, of vague expansive impulse over direction is well expressed in Walt Whitman's lines (Leaves of Grass, 1872, p. 190):—

"O to confront night, storms, hunger, ridicule, accidents, rebuffs, as the trees and animals do. . . .
Dear Camerado! I confess I have urged you onward with me, and still urge you, without the least idea what is our destination,
Or whether we shall be victorious, or utterly quell'd and defeated."

This readiness for great things, and this sense that the world by its importance, wonderfulness, etc., is apt for their production, would seem to be the undifferentiated germ of all the higher faiths. Trust in our own dreams of ambition, or in our country's expansive destinies, and faith in the providence of God, all have their source in that onrush of our sanguine impulses, and in that sense of the exceedingness of the possible over the real.

7. Compare Leuba: Loc. cit., pp. 346–349.

influence upon action and endurance, to class them amongst the most important biological functions of mankind. Their stimulant and anaesthetic effect is so great that Professor Leuba, in a recent article,[8] goes so far as to say that so long as men can *use* their God, they care very little who he is, or even whether he is at all. "The truth of the matter can be put," says Leuba, "in this way: *God is not known, he is not understood; he is used*—sometimes as meat-purveyor, sometimes as moral support, sometimes as friend, sometimes as an object of love. If he proves himself useful, the religious consciousness asks for no more than that. Does God really exist? How does he exist? What is he? are so many irrelevant questions. Not God, but life, more life, a larger, richer, more satisfying life is, in the last analysis, the end of religion. The love of life, at any and every level of development, is the religious impulse."[9]

At this purely subjective rating, therefore, Religion must be considered vindicated in a certain way from the attacks of her critics. It would seem that she cannot be a mere anachronism and survival, but must exert a permanent function, whether she be with or without intellectual content, and whether, if she have any, it be true or false.

We must next pass beyond the point of view of merely subjective utility, and make inquiry into the intellectual content itself.

First, is there, under all the discrepancies of the creeds, a common nucleus to which they bear their testimony unanimously?

8. The Contents of Religious Consciousness, in The Monist, xi. 536, July 1901.

9. Loc. cit., pp. 571, 572, abridged. See, also, this writer's extraordinarily true criticism of the notion that religion primarily seeks to solve the intellectual mystery of the world. Compare what W. BENDER says (in his Wesen der Religion, Bonn, 1888, pp. 85, 88): "Not the question about God, and not the inquiry into the origin and purpose of the world is religion, but the question about Man. All religious views of life are anthropocentric." "Religion is that activity of the human impulse towards self-preservation by means of which Man seeks to carry his essential vital purposes through against the adverse pressure of the world by raising himself freely towards the world's ordering and governing powers when the limits of his own strength are reached." The whole book is little more than a development of these words.

And second, ought we to consider the testimony true?

I will take up the first question first, and answer it immediately in the affirmative. The warring gods and formulas of the various religions do indeed cancel each other, but there is a certain uniform deliverance in which religions all appear to meet. It consists of two parts:—

1. An uneasiness; and
2. Its solution.

1. The uneasiness, reduced to its simplest terms, is a sense that there is *something wrong about us* as we naturally stand.
2. The solution is a sense that *we are saved from the wrongness* by making proper connection with the higher powers.

In those more developed minds which alone we are studying, the wrongness takes a moral character, and the salvation takes a mystical tinge. I think we shall keep well within the limits of what is common to all such minds if we formulate the essence of their religious experience in terms like these:—

The individual, so far as he suffers from his wrongness and criticises it, is to that extent consciously beyond it, and in at least possible touch with something higher, if anything higher exist. Along with the wrong part there is thus a better part of him, even though it may be but a most helpless germ. With which part he should identify his real being is by no means obvious at this stage; but when stage 2 (the stage of solution or salvation) arrives,[10] the man identifies his real being with the germinal higher part of himself; and does so in the following way. *He becomes conscious that this higher part is coterminous and continuous with a* MORE *of the same quality, which is operative in the universe outside of him, and which he can keep in working touch with, and in a fashion get on board of and save*

10. Remember that for some men it arrives suddenly, for others gradually, whilst others again practically enjoy it all their life.

himself when all his lower being has gone to pieces in the wreck.

It seems to me that all the phenomena are accurately describable in these very simple general terms.[11] They allow for the divided self and the struggle; they involve the change of personal centre and the surrender of the lower self; they express the appearance of exteriority of the helping power and yet account for our sense of union with it;[12] and they fully justify our feelings of security and joy. There is probably no autobiographic document, among all those which I have quoted, to which the description will not well apply. One need only add such specific details as will adapt it to various theologies and various personal temperaments, and one will then have the various experiences reconstructed in their individual forms.

So far, however, as this analysis goes, the experiences are only psychological phenomena. They possess, it is true, enormous biological worth. Spiritual strength really increases in the subject when he has them, a new life opens for him, and they seem to him a place of conflux where the forces of two universes meet; and yet this may be nothing but his subjective way of feeling things, a mood of his own fancy, in spite of the effects produced. I now turn to my second question: What is the objective 'truth' of their content?[13]

The part of the content concerning which the question of truth most pertinently arises is that 'MORE of the same quality' with which our own higher self appears in the experience to come into harmonious working relation. Is such a 'more' merely our own notion, or does it really exist? If so, in what shape does it exist? Does it act, as well as exist? And in what form should we conceive of that 'union' with it of which religious geniuses are so convinced?

It is in answering these questions that the various theologies perform their theoretic work, and that their divergencies most come to light. They all agree that the 'more' really exists; though some of them hold it to exist in the shape of a personal god or gods, while others are satisfied to conceive it as a stream of ideal tendency embedded in the eternal structure of the world. They all agree, moreover, that it acts as well as exists, and that something really is effected for the better when you throw your life into its hands. It is when they treat of the experience of 'union' with it that their speculative differences appear most clearly. Over this point pantheism and theism, nature and second birth, works and grace and karma, immortality and reincarnation, rationalism and mysticism, carry on inveterate disputes.

At the end of my lecture on Philosophy I held out the notion that an impartial science of religions might sift out from the midst of their discrepancies a common body of doctrine which she might also formulate in terms to which physical science need not object. This, I said, she might adopt as her own reconciling hypothesis, and recommend it for general belief. I also said that in my last lecture I should have to try my own hand at framing such an hypothesis.

The time has now come for this attempt. Who says 'hypothesis' renounces the ambition to be coercive in his arguments. The most I can do is, accordingly, to offer something that may fit the facts so easily that your scientific logic will find no plausible pretext for vetoing your impulse to welcome it as true.

The 'more,' as we called it, and the meaning of our 'union' with it, form the nucleus of our inquiry. Into what definite description can these words be translated, and for what definite facts do they stand? It would never do for us to place ourselves offhand at the position of a particular

11. The practical difficulties are: 1, to 'realize the reality' of one's higher part; 2, to identify one's self with it exclusively; and 3, to identify it with all the rest of ideal being.

12. "When mystical activity is at its height, we find consciousness possessed by the sense of a being at once *excessive* and *identical* with the self: great enough to be God; interior enough to be *me*. The 'objectivity' of it ought in that case to be called *excessivity*, rather, or exceedingness." RÉCÉJAC: Essai sur les fondements de la conscience mystique, 1897, p. 46.

13. The word 'truth' is here taken to mean something additional to bare value for life, although the natural propensity of man is to believe that whatever has great value for life is thereby certified as true.

theology, the Christian theology, for example, and proceed immediately to define the 'more' as Jehovah, and the 'union' as his imputation to us of the righteousness of Christ. That would be unfair to other religions, and, from our present standpoint at least, would be an over-belief.

We must begin by using less particularized terms; and, since one of the duties of the science of religions is to keep religion in connection with the rest of science, we shall do well to seek first of all a way of describing the 'more,' which psychologists may also recognize as real. The *subconscious self* is nowadays a well-accredited psychological entity; and I believe that in it we have exactly the mediating term required. Apart from all religious considerations, there is actually and literally more life in our total soul than we are at any time aware of. The exploration of the transmarginal field has hardly yet been seriously undertaken, but what Mr. Myers said in 1892 in his essay on the Subliminal Consciousness[14] is as true as when it was first written: "Each of us is in reality an abiding psychical entity far more extensive than he knows—an individuality which can never express itself completely through any corporeal manifestation. The Self manifests through the organism; but there is always some part of the Self unmanifested; and always, as it seems, some power of organic expression in abeyance or reserve."[15] Much of the content of this larger background against which our conscious being stands out in relief is insignificant. Imperfect memories, silly jingles, inhibitive timidities, 'dissolutive' phenomena of various sorts, as Myers calls them, enter into it for a large part. But in it many of the performances of genius seem also to have their origin; and in our study of conversion, of mystical experiences, and of prayer, we have seen how striking a part invasions from this region play in the religious life.

Let me then propose, as an hypothesis, that whatever it may be on its *farther* side, the 'more' with which in religious experience we feel ourselves connected is on its *hither* side the subconscious continuation of our conscious life. Starting thus with a recognized psychological fact as our basis, we seem to preserve a contact with 'science' which the ordinary theologian lacks. At the same time the theologian's contention that the religious man is moved by an external power is vindicated, for it is one of the peculiarities of invasions from the subconscious region to take on objective appearances, and to suggest to the Subject an external control. In the religious life the control is felt as 'higher'; but since on our hypothesis it is primarily the higher faculties of our own hidden mind which are controlling, the sense of union with the power beyond us is a sense of something, not merely apparently, but literally true.

This doorway into the subject seems to me the best one for a science of religions, for it mediates between a number of different points of view. Yet it is only a doorway, and difficulties present themselves as soon as we step through it, and ask how far our transmarginal consciousness carries us if we follow it on its remoter side. Here the over-beliefs begin: here mysticism and the conversion-rapture and Vedantism and transcendental idealism bring in their monistic interpretations[16] and tell us that the finite self rejoins the absolute self, for it was always one

14. Proceedings of the Society for Psychical Research, vol. vii. p. 305. For a full statement of Mr. Myer's views, I may refer to his posthumous work, 'Human Personality in the Light of Recent Research,' which is already announced by Messrs. Longmans, Green & Co. as being in press. Mr. Myers for the first time proposed as a general psychological problem the exploration of the subliminal region of consciousness throughout its whole extent, and made the first methodological steps in its topography by treating as a natural series a mass of subliminal facts hitherto considered only as curious isolated facts, and subjecting them to a systematized nomenclature. How important this exploration will prove, future work upon the path which Myers has opened can alone show. Compare my paper: 'Frederic Myers's Services to Psychology,' in the said Proceedings, part xlii., May, 1901.

15. Compare the inventory given above on pp. 365–366, and also what is said of the subconscious self on pp. 188–190, 193–195 [1902 edition].

16. Compare above, pp. 147ff.

with God and identical with the soul of the world.[17] Here the prophets of all the different religions come with their visions, voices, raptures, and other openings, supposed by each to authenticate his own peculiar faith.

Those of us who are not personally favored with such specific revelations must stand outside of them altogether and, for the present at least, decide that, since they corroborate incompatible theological doctrines, they neutralize one another and leave no fixed result. If we follow any one of them, or if we follow philosophical theory and embrace monistic pantheism on non-mystical grounds, we do so in the exercise of our individual freedom, and build out our religion in the way most congruous with our personal susceptibilities. Among these susceptibilities intellectual ones play a decisive part. Although the religious question is primarily a question of life, of living or not living in the higher union which opens itself to us as a gift, yet the spiritual excitement in which the gift appears a real one will often fail to be aroused in an individual until certain particular intellectual beliefs or ideas which, as we say, come home to him, are touched.[18] These ideas will thus be essential to that individual's religion; —which is as much as to say that over-beliefs in various directions are absolutely indispensable, and that we should treat them with tenderness and tolerance so long as they are not intolerant themselves. As I have elsewhere written, the most interesting and valuable things about a man are usually his over-beliefs.

Disregarding the over-beliefs, and confining ourselves to what is common and generic, we have in *the fact that the conscious person is continuous with a wider self through which saving experiences come,*[19] a positive content of religious experience which, it seems to me, *is literally and objectively true as far as it goes.* If I now proceed to state my own hypothesis about the farther limits of this extension of our personality, I shall be offering my own over-belief—though I know it will appear a sorry under-belief to some of you—for which I can only bespeak the same indulgence which in a converse case I should accord to yours.

The further limits of our being plunge, it seems to me, into an altogether other dimension of existence from the sensible and merely 'understandable' world. Name it the mystical region, or the supernatural region, whichever you

17. One more expression of this belief, to increase the reader's familiarity with the notion of it:—

"If this room is full of darkness for thousands of years, and you come in and begin to weep and wail, 'Oh the darkness,' will the darkness vanish? Bring the light in, strike a match, and light comes in a moment. So what good will it do you to think all your lives, 'Oh, I have done evil, I have made many mistakes'? It requires no ghost to tell us that. Bring in the light, and the evil goes in a moment. Strengthen the real nature, build up yourselves, the effulgent, the resplendent, the ever pure, call that up in everyone whom you see. I wish that every one of us had come to such a state that even when we see the vilest of human beings we can see the God within, and instead of condemning, say, 'Rise, thou effulgent One, rise thou who art always pure, rise thou birthless and deathless, rise almighty, and manifest your nature.' . . . This is the highest prayer that Advaita teaches. This is the one prayer: remembering our nature." . . . "Why does man go out to look for a God? . . . It is your own heart beating, and you did not know, you were mistaking it for something external. He, nearest of the near, my own self, the reality of my own life, my body and my soul.—I am Thee and Thou art Me. That is your own nature. Assert it, manifest it. Not to become pure, you are pure already. You are not to be perfect, you are that already. Every good thought which you think or act upon is simply tearing the veil, as it were, and the purity, the Infinity, the God behind, manifests itself—the eternal Subject of everything, the eternal Witness in this universe, your own Self. Knowledge is, as it were, a lower step, a degradation. We are It already: how to know It?" SWAMI VIVE-KANANDA: Addresses, No. XII., Practical Vedanta, part iv. pp. 172, 174. London, 1897; and Lectures, The Real and the Apparent Man, p. 24, abridged.

18. For instance, here is a case where a person exposed from her birth to Christian ideas had to wait till they came to her clad in spiritistic formulas before the saving experience set in:—

"For myself I can say that spiritualism has saved me. It was revealed to me at a critical moment of my life, and without it I don't know what I should have done. It has taught me to detach myself from worldly things and to place my hope in things to come. Through it I have learned to see in all men, even in those most criminal, even in those from whom I have most suffered, undeveloped brothers to whom I owed assistance, love, and forgiveness. I have learned that I must lose my temper over nothing, despise no one, and pray for all. Most of all I have learned to pray! And although I have still much to learn in this domain, prayer ever brings me more strength, consolation, and comfort. I feel more than ever that I have only made a few steps on the long road of progress; but I look at its length without dismay, for I have confidence that the day will come when all my efforts shall be rewarded. So Spiritualism has a great place in my life, indeed it holds the first place there." Flournoy Collection.

19. "The influence of the Holy Spirit, exquisitely call the Comforter, is a matter of actual experience, as solid a reality as that of electromagnetism." W. C. BROWNELL, Scribner's Magazine, vol. xxx. p. 112.

choose. So far as our ideal impulses originate in this region (and most of them do originate in it, for we find them possessing us in a way for which we cannot articulately account), we belong to it in a more intimate sense than that in which we belong to the visible world, for we belong in the most intimate sense wherever our ideals belong. Yet the unseen region in question is not merely ideal, for it produces effects in this world. When we commune with it, work is actually done upon our finite personality, for we are turned into new men, and consequences in the way of conduct follow in the natural world upon our regenerative change.[20] But that which produces effects within another reality must be termed a reality itself, so I feel as if we had no philosophic excuse for calling the unseen or mystical world unreal.

God is the natural appellation, for us Christians at least, for the supreme reality, so I will call this higher part of the universe by the name of God.[21] We and God have business with each other; and in opening ourselves to his influence our deepest destiny is fulfilled. The universe, at those parts of it which our personal being constitutes, takes a turn genuinely for the worse or for the better in proportion as each one of us fulfills or evades God's demands. As far as this goes I probably have you with me, for I only translate into schematic language what I may call the instinctive belief of mankind: God is real since he produces real effects.

The real effects in question, so far as I have as yet admitted them, are exerted on the personal centres of energy of the various subjects, but the spontaneous faith of most of the subjects is that they embrace a wider sphere than this. Most religious men believe (or 'know,' if they be mystical) that not only they themselves, but the whole universe of beings to whom the God is present, are secure in his parental hands. There is a sense, a dimension, they are sure, in which we are *all* saved, in spite of the gates of hell and all adverse terrestrial appearances. God's existence is the guarantee of an ideal order that shall be permanently preserved. This world may indeed, as science assures us, some day burn up or freeze; but if it is part of his order, the old ideals are sure to be brought elsewhere to fruition, so that where God is, tragedy is only provisional and partial, and shipwreck and dissolution are not the absolutely final things. Only when this farther step of faith concerning God is taken, and remote objective consequences are predicted, does religion, as it seems to me, get wholly free from the first immediate subjective experience, and bring a *real hypothesis* into play. A good hypothesis in science must have other properties than those of the phenomenon it is immediately invoked to explain, otherwise it is not prolific enough. God, meaning only what enters into the religious man's experience of union, falls short of being an hypothesis of this more useful order. He needs to enter into wider cosmic relations in order to justify the subject's absolute confidence and peace.

That the God with whom, starting from the hither side of our own extra-marginal self, we come at its remoter margin into commerce should be the absolute world-ruler, is of course a very considerable over-belief. Over-belief as it is, though, it is an article of almost every one's religion. Most of us pretend in some way to prop

20. That the transaction of opening ourselves, otherwise called prayer, is a perfectly definite one for certain persons, appears abundantly in the preceding lectures. I append another concrete example to reinforce the impression on the reader's mind:—

"Man can learn to transcend these limitations [of finite thought] and draw power and wisdom at will. . . . The divine presence is known through experience. The turning to a higher plane is a distinct act of consciousness. It is not a vague, twilight or semi-conscious experience. It is not an ecstasy; it is not a trance. It is not superconsciousness in the Vedantic sense. It is not due to self-hypnotization. It is a perfectly calm, sane, sound, rational, common-sense shifting of consciousness from the phenomena of sense-perception to the phenomena of seership, from the thought of self to a distinctively higher realm. . . . For example, if the lower self be nervous, anxious, tense, one can in a few moments compel it to be calm. This is not done by a word simply. Again I say, it is not hypnotism. It is by the exercise of power. One feels the spirit of peace as definitely as heat is perceived on a hot summer day. The power can be as surely used as the sun's rays can be focused and made to do work, to set fire to wood." The Higher Law, vol. iv. pp. 4, 6, Boston, August, 1901.

21. Transcendentalists are fond of the term 'Over-soul,' but as a rule they use it in an intellectualist sense, as meaning only a medium of communion. 'God' is a causal agent as well as a medium of communion, and that is the aspect which I wish to emphasize.

it up upon our philosophy, but the philosophy itself is really propped upon this faith. What is this but to say that Religion, in her fullest exercise of function, is not a mere illumination of facts already elsewhere given, not a mere passion, like love, which views things in a rosier light. It is indeed that, as we have seen abundantly. But it is something more, namely, a postulator of new *facts* as well. The world interpreted religiously is not the materialistic world over again, with an altered expression; it must have, over and above the altered expression, *a natural constitution* different at some point from that which a materialistic world would have. It must be such that different events can be expected in it, different conduct must be required.

This thoroughly 'pragmatic' view of religion has usually been taken as a matter of course by common men. They have interpolated divine miracles into the field of nature, they have built a heaven out beyond the grave. It is only transcendentalist metaphysicians who think that, without adding any concrete details to Nature, or subtracting any, but by simply calling it the expression of absolute spirit, you make it more divine just as it stands. I believe the pragmatic way of taking religion to be the deeper way. It gives it body as well as soul, it makes it claim, as everything real must claim, some characteristic realm of fact as its very own. What the more characteristically divine facts are, apart from the actual inflow of energy in the faith-state and the prayer-state, I know not. But the over-belief on which I am ready to make my personal venture is that they exist. The whole drift of my education goes to persuade me that the world of our present consciousness is only one out of many worlds of consciousness that exist, and that those other worlds must contain experiences which have a meaning for our life also; and that although in the main their experiences and those of this world keep discrete, yet the two become continuous at certain points, and higher energies filter in. By being faithful in my poor measure to this over-belief, I seem to myself to keep more sane and true. I *can,* of course,

"Many Paths to the Same Summit"

Ramakrishna

God has made different religions to suit different aspirants, times, and countries. All doctrines are only so many paths: but a path is by no means God Himself. Indeed, one can reach God if one follows any of the paths with wholehearted devotion. One may eat a cake with icing either straight or sidewise. It will taste sweet either way.

As one and the same material, water, is called by different names by different peoples, one calling it water, another eau, a third aqua, and another pani, so the one Everlasting-Intelligent-Bliss is invoked by some as God, by some as Allah, by some as Jehovah, and by others as Brahman.

As one can ascend to the top of a house by means of a ladder or a bamboo or a staircase or a rope, so diverse are the ways and means to approach God, and every religion in the world shows one of these ways.

As the young wife in a family shows her love and respect to her father-in-law, mother-in-law, and every other member of the family, and at the same time loves her husband more than these; similarly, being firm in thy devotion to the deity of thy own choice, do not despise other deities, but honour them all.

Bow down and worship where others kneel, for where so many have been paying the tribute of adoration the kind Lord must manifest himself, for he is all mercy.

The devotee who has seen God in one aspect only, knows him in that aspect alone. But he who has seen him in manifold aspects is alone in a position to say, 'All these forms are of one God and God is multiform.' He is formless and with form, and many are his forms which no one knows.

put myself into the sectarian scientist's attitude, and imagine vividly that the world of sensations and of scientific laws and objects may be all. But whenever I do this, I hear that inward monitor of which W. K. Clifford once wrote, whispering the word 'bosh!' Humbug is humbug, even though it bear the scientific name, and the total expression of human experience, as I view it objectively, invincibly urges me beyond the narrow 'scientific' bounds. Assuredly, the real world is of a different temperament,—more intricately built than physical science allows. So my objective and my subjective conscience both hold me to the over-belief which I express. Who knows whether the faithfulness of individuals here below to their own poor over-beliefs may not actually help God in turn to be more effectively faithful to his own greater tasks?

POSTSCRIPT

In writing my concluding lecture I had to aim so much at simplification that I fear that my general philosophic position received so scant a statement as hardly to be intelligible to some of my readers. I therefore add this epilogue, which must also be so brief as possibly to remedy but little the defect. In a later work I may be enabled to state my position more amply and consequently more clearly.

Originality cannot be expected in a field like this, where all the attitudes and tempers that are possible have been exhibited in literature long ago, and where any new writer can immediately be classed under a familiar head. If one should make a division of all thinkers into naturalists and supernaturalists, I should undoubtedly have to go, along with most philosophers, into the supernaturalist branch. But there is a crasser and a more refined supernaturalism, and it is to the refined division that most philosophers at the present day belong. If not regular transcendental idealists, they at least obey the Kantian direction enough to bar out ideal entities from interfering causally in the course of phenomenal events. Refined supernaturalism is universalistic supernaturalism; for the 'cras-

The Saviour is the messenger of God. He is like the viceroy of a mighty monarch. As when there is some disturbance in a far-off province, the king sends his viceroy to quell it, so wherever there is a decline of religion in any part of the world, God sends his Saviour there. It is one and the same Saviour that, having plunged into the ocean of life, rises up in one place and is known as Krishna (the leading Hindu incarnation of God), and diving down again rises in another place and is known as Christ.

Every man should follow his own religion. A Christian should follow Christianity, a Mohammedan should follow Mohammedanism, and so on. For the Hindus, the ancient path, the path of the Aryan sages, is the best.

People partition off their lands by means of boundaries, but no one can partition off the all-embracing sky overhead. The indivisible sky surrounds all and includes all. So common man in ignorance says, 'My religion is the only one, my religion is the best.' But when his heart is illumined by true knowledge, he knows that above all these wars of sects and sectarians presides the one indivisible, eternal, all-knowing bliss.

As a mother, in nursing her sick children, gives rice and curry to one, and sago arrowroot to another, and bread and butter to a third, so the Lord has laid out different paths for different men suitable to their natures.

Dispute not. As you rest firmly on your own faith and opinion, allow others also the equal liberty to stand by their own faiths and opinions. By mere disputation you will never succeed in convincing another of his error. When the grace of God descends on him, each one will understand his own mistakes. . . .

ser' variety 'piecemeal' supernaturalism would perhaps be the better name. It went with that older theology which to-day is supposed to reign only among uneducated people, or to be found among the few belated professors of the dualisms which Kant is thought to have displaced. It admits miracles and providential leadings, and finds no intellectual difficulty in mixing the ideal and the real worlds together by interpolating influences from the ideal region among the forces that causally determine the real world's details. In this the refined supernaturalists think that it muddles disparate dimensions of existence. For them the world of the ideal has no efficient causality, and never bursts into the world of phenomena at particular points. The ideal world, for them, is not a world of facts, but only of the meaning of facts; it is a point of view for judging facts. It appertains to a different '-ology,' and inhabits a different dimension of being altogether from that in which existential propositions obtain. It cannot get down upon the flat level of experience and interpolate itself piecemeal between distinct portions of nature, as those who believe, for example, in divine aid coming in response to prayer are bound to think it must.

Notwithstanding my own inability to accept either popular Christianity or scholastic theism, I suppose that my belief that in communion with the Ideal new force comes into the world, and new departures are made here below, subjects me to being classed among the supernaturalists of the piecemeal or crasser type. Universalistic supernaturalism surrenders, it seems to me, too easily to naturalism. It takes the facts of physical science at their face-value, and leaves the laws of life just as naturalism finds them, with no hope of remedy, in case their fruits are bad. It confines itself to sentiments about life as a whole, sentiments which may be admiring and adoring, but which need not be so, as the existence of systematic pessimism proves. In this universalistic way of taking the ideal world, the essence of practical religion seems to me to evaporate. Both instinctively and for logical reasons, I find it hard to believe that principles can exist which make no difference in facts.[22] But all facts are particular facts, and the whole interest of the question of God's existence seems to me to lie in the consequence for particulars which that existence may be expected to entail. That no concrete particular of experience should alter its complexion in consequence of a God being there seems to me an incredible proposition, and yet

22. Transcendental idealism, of course, insists that its ideal world makes *this* difference, that facts *exist*. We owe it to the Absolute that we have a world of fact at all. 'A world' of fact!—that exactly is the trouble. An entire world is the smallest unit with which the Absolute can work, whereas to our finite minds work for the better ought to be done within this world, setting in at single points. Our difficulties and our ideals are all piecemeal affairs, but the Absolute can do no piecework for us; so that all the interests which our poor souls compass raise their heads too late. We should have spoken earlier, prayed for another world absolutely, before this world was born. It is strange, I have heard a friend say, to see this blind corner into which Christian thought has worked itself at last, with its God who can raise no particular weight whatever, who can help us with no private burden, and who is on the side of our enemies as much as he is on our own. Odd evolution from the God of David's psalms!

"Truth or Repose"

Ralph Waldo Emerson

God offers to every mind its choice between truth and repose. Take which you please—you can never have both. Between these, as a pendulum, man oscillates. He in whom the love of repose predominates will accept the first creed, the first philosophy, the first political party he meets—most likely his father's. He gets rest, commodity and reputation; but he shuts the door of truth. He in whom the love of truth predominates will keep himself aloof from all moorings, and afloat. He will abstain from dogmatism, and recognize all the opposite negations between which, as walls, his being is swung. He submits to the inconvenience of suspense and imperfect opinion, but he is a candidate for truth, as the other is not, and respects the highest law of his being.

it is the thesis to which (implicitly at any rate) refined supernaturalism seems to cling. It is only with experience *en bloc,* it says, that the Absolute maintains relations. It condescends to no transactions of detail.

I am ignorant of Buddhism and speak under correction, and merely in order the better to describe my general point of view; but as I apprehend the Buddhistic doctrine of Karma, I agree in principle with that. All supernaturalists admit that facts are under the judgment of higher law; but for Buddhism as I interpret it, and for religion generally so far as it remains unweakened by transcendentalistic metaphysics, the word 'judgment' here means no such bare academic verdict or platonic appreciation as it means in Vedantic or modern absolutist systems; it carries, on the contrary, *execution* with it, is *in rebus* as well as *post rem,* and operates 'causally' as partial factor in the total fact. The universe becomes a gnosticism[23] pure and simple on any other terms. But this view that judgment and execution go together is that of the crasser supernaturalist way of thinking, so the present volume must on the whole be classed with the other expressions of that creed.

I state the matter thus bluntly, because the current of thought in academic circles runs against me, and I feel like a man who must set his back against an open door quickly if he does not wish to see it closed and locked. In spite of its being so shocking to the reigning intellectual tastes, I believe that a candid consideration of piecemeal supernaturalism and a complete discussion of all its metaphysical bearings will show it to be the hypothesis by which the largest number of legitimate requirements are met. That of course would be a program for other books than this; what I now say sufficiently indicates to the philosophic reader the place where I belong.

If asked just where the differences in fact which are due to God's existence come in, I should have to say that in general I have no hypothesis to offer beyond what the phenomenon of 'prayerful communion,' especially when certain kinds of incursion from the subconscious region take part in it, immediately suggests. The appearance is that in this phenomenon something ideal, which in one sense is part of ourselves and in another sense is not ourselves, actually exerts an influence, raises our centre of personal energy, and produces regenerative effects unattainable in other ways. If, then, there be a wider world of being than that of our everyday consciousness, if in it there be forces whose effects on us are intermittent, if one facilitating condition of the effects be the openness of the 'subliminal' door, we have the elements of a theory to which the phenomena of religious life lend plausibility. I am so impressed by the importance of these phenomena that I adopt the hypothesis which they so naturally suggest. At these places at least, I say, it would seem as though transmundane energies, God, if you will, produced immediate effects within the natural world to which the rest of our experience belongs.

The difference in natural 'fact' which most of us would assign as the first difference which the existence of a God ought to make would, I imagine, be personal immortality. Religion, in fact, for the great majority of our own race *means* immortality, and nothing else. God is the producer of immortality; and whoever has doubts of immortality is written down as an atheist without farther trial. I have said nothing in my lectures about immortality or the belief therein, for to me it seems a secondary point. If our ideals are only cared for in 'eternity,' I do not see why we might not be willing to resign their care to other hands than ours. Yet I sympathize with the urgent impulse to be present ourselves, and in the conflict of impulses, both of them so vague yet both of them noble, I know not how to decide. It seems to me that it is eminently a case for facts to testify. Facts, I think, are yet lacking to prove 'spirit-return,' though I have the highest respect for the patient labors of Messrs. Myers, Hodgson, and Hyslop, and am somewhat impressed by their favorable conclusions. I consequently leave the matter open, with this brief

23. See my Will to Believe and other Essays in Popular Philosophy, 1897, p. 165.

word to save the reader from a possible perplexity as to why immortality got no mention in the body of this book.

The ideal power with which we feel ourselves in connection, the 'God' of ordinary men, is, both by ordinary men and by philosophers, endowed with certain of those metaphysical attributes which in the lecture on philosophy I treated with such disrespect. He is assumed as a matter of course to be 'one and only' and to be 'infinite'; and the notion of many finite gods is one which hardly any one thinks it worth while to consider, and still less to uphold. Nevertheless, in the interests of intellectual clearness, I feel bound to say that religious experience, as we have studied it, cannot be cited as unequivocally supporting the infinitist belief. The only thing that it unequivocally testifies to is that we can experience union with *something* larger than ourselves and in that union find our greatest peace. Philosophy, with its passion for unity, and mysticism with its monodeistic bent, both 'pass to the limit' and identify the something with a unique God who is the all-inclusive soul of the world. Popular opinion, respectful to their authority, follows the example which they set.

Meanwhile the practical needs and experiences of religion seem to me sufficiently met by the belief that beyond each man and in a fashion continuous with him there exists a larger power which is friendly to him and to his ideals. All that the facts require is that the power should be both other and larger than our conscious selves. Anything larger will do, if only it be large enough to trust for the next step. It need not be infinite, it need not be solitary. It might conceivably even be only a larger and more godlike self, of which the present self would then be but the mutilated expression, and the universe might conceivably be a collection of such selves, of different degrees of inclusiveness, with no absolute unity realized in it at all.[24] Thus would a sort of polytheism return upon us—a polytheism which I do not on this occasion defend, for my only aim at present is to keep the testimony of religious experience clearly within the proper bounds. (Compare p. 115 above [1902 edition].)

Upholders of the monistic view will say to such a polytheism (which, by the way, has always been the real religion of common people, and is so still to-day) that unless there be one all-inclusive God, our guarantee of security is left imperfect. In the Absolute, and in the Absolute only, *all* is saved. If there be different gods, each caring for his part, some portion of some of us might not be covered with divine protection, and our religious consolation would thus fail to be complete. It goes back to what was said on pages 115–116 [1902 edition], about the possibility of there being portions of the universe that may irretrievably be lost. Common sense is less sweeping in its demands than philosophy or mysticism have been wont to be, and can suffer the notion of this world being partly saved and partly lost. The ordinary moralistic state of mind makes the salvation of the world conditional upon the success with which each unit does its part. Partial and conditional salvation is in fact a most familiar notion when taken in the abstract, the only difficulty being to determine the details. Some men are even disinterested enough to be willing to be in the unsaved remnant as far as their persons go, if only they can be persuaded that their cause will prevail—all of us are willing, whenever our activity-excitement rises sufficiently high. I think, in fact, that a final philosophy of religion will have to consider the pluralistic hypothesis more seriously than it has hitherto been willing to consider it. For practical life at any rate, the *chance* of salvation is enough. No fact in human nature is more characteristic than its willingness to live on a chance. The existence of the chance makes the difference, as Edmund Gurney says, between a life of which the keynote is resignation and a life of which the keynote is hope.[25] . . .

24. Such a notion is suggested in my Ingersoll Lecture on Human Immortality, Boston and London, 1899.

25. Tertium Quid, 1887, p. 99. See also pp. 148, 149.

INDEX